Why We Remember

"*A people without history is like wind on the buffalo grass.*"

—*Lakota/Dakota proverb*

"*One of the ways of helping to destroy a people is to tell them they don't have a history, that they have no roots.*"

—*Archbishop Desmond Tutu*

"*We are tomorrow's past.*"

—*Mary Webb*

"*Those who cannot remember the past are condemned to fulfill it.*"

—*George Santayana*

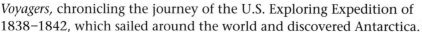

About the Author

Dr. Herman J. Viola, curator emeritus with the
Smithsonian Institution, is a distinguished historian,
author, and curator. Dr. Viola received his Ph.D. in
American history from Indiana University. He founded
the scholarly journal *Prologue* at the National Archives.
Dr. Viola also served as director of the National An-
thropological Archives at the Smithsonian Institution.
There he organized two major historical exhibitions:
Seeds of Change, highlighting the cultural and biotic
exchange after the Columbus voyages, and *Magnificent
Voyagers,* chronicling the journey of the U.S. Exploring Expedition of
1838–1842, which sailed around the world and discovered Antarctica.

A nationally recognized authority on American Indians, the history of the
American West, and the Civil War, Dr. Viola is the author of many historical
works for both adults and young readers.

Books written or edited by Herman J. Viola

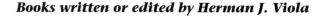

Thomas L. McKenney: Architect of America's Early Indian Policy

The Indian Legacy of Charles Bird King

Diplomats in Buckskins

The National Archives of the United States

*Magnificent Voyagers: The U.S. Exploring Expedition,
1838–1842*

Exploring the West

*After Columbus: The Smithsonian's Chronicle of the Indians of
North America Since 1492*

Seeds of Change: A Quincentennial Commemoration

Ben Nighthorse Campbell: An American Warrior

The Memoirs of Charles Henry Veil

For young readers

Andrew Jackson

Giuseppe Garibaldi

Sitting Bull

After Columbus: The Horse's Return to America

Osceola

Addison-Wesley

Why We Remember

United States History

Herman J. Viola

Contributing Authors
Helen Wheatley
Diane Hart

*To Dav,
a great teacher!*

*Herm J Viola
11-21-95*

▲ **Addison-Wesley Publishing Company**

Menlo Park, California • Reading, Massachusetts • New York • Don Mills, Ontario
Wokingham, England • Amsterdam • Bonn • Paris • Milan • Madrid • Sydney
Singapore • Tokyo • Seoul • Taipei • Mexico City • San Juan

Contributing Authors

Dr. Helen Wheatley, Assistant Professor of History at Seattle University, specializes in United States, environmental, and world history. A former Fulbright fellow, she is active in promoting history education through the World History Association.

Diane Hart is a writer and consultant specializing in history and social studies. A former teacher and Woodrow Wilson fellow, she has written a number of textbooks for middle school students.

Reviewers and Consultants

Dr. Pedro Castillo
Associate Professor of History and American Studies and Co-Director, Chicano/Latino Research Center, University of California, Santa Cruz

Dr. David Barry Gaspar
Professor of History, Duke University, Durham, North Carolina

Dr. Joseph E. Harris
Professor of History, Howard University, Washington, D.C.

LaDonna Harris
President, Americans for Indian Opportunity, Bernalillo, New Mexico

Tedd Levy
Teacher, Nathan Hale Middle School, Norwalk, Connecticut

Dr. Glenn Linden
Associate Professor of History and Education, Southern Methodist University, Dallas, Texas

Charlene Pike
Teacher, L'Ance Creuse Middle School South, Harrison Township, Michigan; past president, National Middle School Association

Esther Taira
Teacher Advisor, Division of Instruction, Los Angeles Unified School District, Los Angeles, California

Dr. Ralph E. Weber
Professor of History and Chair, Department of History, Marquette University, Milwaukee, Wisconsin

Acknowledgments

Susan P. Viola, literature consultant, is librarian at The Langley School in McLean, Virginia. She received her M.S.L.S. from The Catholic University of America.

Dr. Viola wishes to acknowledge **Jan Shelton Danis** for her research and editorial assistance and historians **Felix C. Lowe,** Smithsonian Institution, for drafting Chapter 25; **Roger A. Bruns,** National Archives and Records Administration, for drafting Chapter 26; and **Dr. George C. Chalou,** National Archives and Records Administration, for drafting Chapters 28 and 29. **Ronald E. Grim** of the Library of Congress Geography and Map Division and **Howard W. Wehman** of the National Archives helped with preparation of the Scholar's Tool Kits on pages 85 and 173, respectively.

Acknowledgments of permission to reprint copyrighted materials appear on page R116.

ISBN 0-201-84303-X

2 3 4 5 6 7 8 9 10 - VH - 00 99 98 97

Table of Contents

Getting to Know This Textbook

This book tells the story of our country from its beginnings to the present. To help you learn—and remember—this important history, the book has many special features. These features are explained on this page and the pages that follow.

Keys to History Time Line

As you glance through this text, you will see that each chapter begins with a two-page time line that shows the time period covered in the chapter.

Each time line entry is a **Key to History**—an important event, person, or idea from the period. The key symbol highlights these keys to the past.

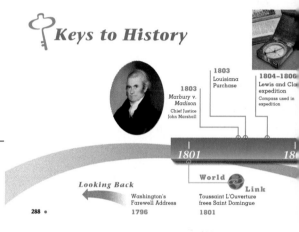

Keys to History

1803
Marbury v. Madison
Chief Justice John Marshall

1803
Louisiana Purchase

1804–1806
Lewis and Clark expedition
Compass used in expedition

1801

18

288

Looking Back
Washington's Farewell Address
1796

World
Link
Toussaint L'Ouverture frees Saint Domingue
1801

History Mystery

Historians sometimes think of history as a series of mysteries to be unraveled. The magnifying glass symbol at the start of each chapter points out a **History Mystery** feature. Read the feature and look for clues in the chapter to help you unravel the mystery.

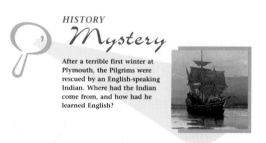

HISTORY
Mystery

After a terrible first winter at Plymouth, the Pilgrims were rescued by an English-speaking Indian. Where had the Indian come from, and how had he learned English?

Citizenship Skills

Americans study our country's past to be better citizens today. In the Chapter Survey at end of each chapter, you will see a star symbol. It points out an activity in which you can practice **Citizenship Skills** by applying information you learned in the chapter.

Scholar's Tool Kit

How Do We Know?

How do we know what we know about history? Where does our knowledge of history come from? In this book you will learn about ten different "tools" that historians use to uncover information about the past. Each tool is featured in a Scholar's Tool Kit, which comes before a new unit. You can recognize the tool kits by their notebook design.

Beginning the Story with

Most students find that stories about people are the most interesting part of history. Each chapter in this book begins with the story of a person or group of people. Some of the people are famous; some are not. Most of the stories tell something about the people when they were near your age. All the people in the stories are representative of those who lived during the time period. Remembering their stories will help you remember the significance of that period in history.

Beginning the Story with

Jaime Escalante

On May 19, 1982, 18 high-school seniors filed into Room 411 of Garfield High School in a mostly poor and Hispanic area of east Los Angeles. Many had had trouble sleeping the night before. Some had broken down and cried with nervousness as they prepared to take a grueling college examination in calculus. Jaime Escalante (HI-mee es-kuh-LAHN-tay), their calculus teacher, paced nervously in a nearby classroom. After three hours, his students finally emerged from Room 411, tired but happy. On seeing their teacher, one student exclaimed, "Kimo! That was a piece of cake."

Escalante's students passed the exam with flying colors. Their joy turned to dismay, however, when 14 of the 18 were accused of cheating because their answers to one question looked suspiciously similar. Escalante was outraged at the accusation. He had known that his drill-like approach to teaching would result in similar student responses to questions. "I stand behind my kids," he said. "I believe in my students."

The Move to California

Growing up in La Paz, Bolivia, Jaime had no idea that he would become a teacher. When he reached his teen years, however, he found that he had a talent for math and science. He decided to become a physics teacher. Soon Jaime earned enough to support his wife and small son.

In 1963 Jaime and his wife left Bolivia for the United States, where they hoped to find more opportunities for their son. Upon arrival in Los Angeles, the Escalantes received a rude shock. Jaime's edu-

Link to Art

Throughout our history, artists have expressed themselves in works that give us a sense of what life in America was like. Their drawings, paintings, sculpture, architecture, and other creations reflect America as they knew it, from important events to broad themes to images of daily life. The Link to Art feature found in each chapter provides us with a window on the past.

World Link

This book is primarily about United States history. Yet the history of our nation has always been linked to happenings in other parts of the world. In each chapter you will learn more about these global links.

Link to the Present

Have you ever asked, "What does history have to do with my life?" As you read each chapter, you will find a Link to the Present that provides one example of how the past has influenced life today.

Point of View

Today's news reports often feature people expressing conflicting points of view. In the past, too, people had different opinions on the issues of the day. Furthermore, historians often disagree about how to interpret past events. In each chapter's Point of View feature, you will read about different perspectives on a historical issue.

Point of View

Lexington: Who fired the first shot?

side claimed that the other fired first. Lexington. Thirty-four minutemen a statement swearing that

lst our backs were turned on the ops, we were fired on by them, and a nber of our men were instantly killed wounded. Not a gun was fired by any son in our company on the regulars, our knowledge, before they fired on and they continued firing until we d all made our escape.

tish Lieutenant William Sutherland things differently:

eard Major Pitcairn's voice call out oldiers, don't fire, keep your ranks, rm and surround them.' Instantly me of the villains who got over the edge fired at us which our men for he first time returned. . . . It is very nlikely that our men should have fired [first], otherwise they [might] have hurt heir own officers who galloped in amongst this armed mob.

Which side did fire that first fateful shot? cause eyewitnesses disagree, we can never ow for sure. What does seem clear is at neither side wanted the blame.

rom Concord to Boston

Once in Concord, the British troops found nly two or three small cannons. After a rief battle with minutemen at Concord's orth Bridge, the frustrated redcoats headed ack to Boston. The march was a nightmare. British officer reported "heavy fire from all sides, from walls, fences, houses, trees,

barns." A soldier noted that "even women had firelocks [guns]."

By the time the British reached Boston, 74 had been killed and 200 wounded. American losses totaled 49 killed and 41 wounded. Riders raced through the colonies shouting the news, "The war has begun!" A Philadelphia woman wrote to a British officer she knew in Boston:

All ranks of men amongst us are in arms. Nothing is heard now in our streets but the trumpet and drum; and the universal cry is 'Americans, to arms!'

The Second Continental Congress

The fighting had broken out shortly before the Second Continental Congress was to meet in Philadelphia. When the delegates

Link to the Present

The information superhighway "The British are coming!" "The war has begun!" It took three weeks for riders to reach South Carolina with news of Lexington and Concord. Today people can learn about a distant event within moments. We take television for granted, just as we do telephones and computers.

The so-called information superhighway—with its use of computer, phone, and television technology—promises new sources of instant communication. We will be sending and receiving an ever greater variety and amount of information—in a fraction of the time it took Paul Revere to saddle his horse.

1775–1783 Chapter 8 ● **207**

Hands-On HISTORY

History is not just a subject for you to read. It is also something you can "do." The activities described in each Hands-On History feature will give you a chance to re-create or interact with some aspect of our nation's past. In addition to the Hands-On Histories listed here, you will also find them at the beginning of each unit and in the "Beginning the Story with . . ." feature at the start of each chapter.

To get at the causes of poverty, Kennedy proposed more federal aid to improve schools and city housing. He also asked for laws providing health insurance for the aged. Congress refused to act. As you will read in Section 3, Congress also refused to pass a bill to enforce African Americans' **civil rights**—the rights guaranteed to all Americans by the Constitution.

Kennedy's Assassination

Looking ahead to a second term, Kennedy hoped to have more success with his programs to fight poverty and protect civil rights. He never got the chance.

In Dallas, Texas, on November 22, 1963, Kennedy and his wife, Jacqueline, were riding in an open car past cheering crowds when rifle shots rang out. The President slumped forward. Struck in the neck and the head, he died quickly.

That day Dallas police arrested a young man named Lee Harvey Oswald and charged him with the President's assassination. Two days later, while police were moving him to another jail, Oswald himself was shot dead by a man named Jack Ruby.

In 1964 an investigation by the Warren Commission, headed by Chief Justice Earl Warren, concluded that Oswald had acted alone. Still, many people were sure that the assassination was part of a group that had planned the assassination. Although the evidence was examined again in the 1970s, the motive for the murder remains a mystery.

Hands-On HISTORY

Collecting memories of Kennedy's assassination A woman who was a teenager when John F. Kennedy was assassinated remembers it this way: "I was in English class when the public address system suddenly came on, but it was not the principal talking. It was a radio broadcast, a very confused one. It took us a few minutes to realize what was being said—that President Kennedy had been shot. My teacher started crying. I felt frozen, numb."

This frame from a home movie shows Kennedy being struck by the first bullet.

Activity Interview an adult who remembers the assassination of President Kennedy.

1. Ask the person for permission to do the interview and to share the results with your class.

2. Before the interview, write a list of questions. Plan to ask for personal recollections of the assassination.

3. Conduct the interview. Tape it or make detailed notes. If the person says something you want to hear more about, ask follow-up questions.

4. Report on the interview. Play the tape or quote the questions and answers. Include your observations about the person's reactions.

Skill Lab

In science classes, you participate in labs where you practice skills used in scientific study. In this book, the Skill Lab in each chapter gives you a chance to learn and apply skills used by historians. The labs will help you develop skills in acquiring information, thinking critically, and using information. You can use these skills in everyday problem solving and decision making as well as in your study of history.

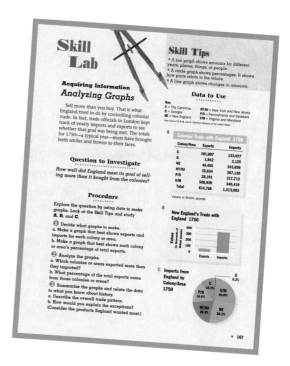

Acquiring Information

Thinking Critically

Using Information

Geography Lab

You cannot fully understand history without also understanding geography. When you think of geography you may think of maps, but geography is much more than reading maps. The Geography Lab in each chapter has readings and pictures as well as maps to help you learn how geography influenced history—and how history influenced geography.

Alternative Assessment

As you study history, you and your teacher will want to know how much you are learning. Your teacher will probably give you paper-and-pencil tests to assess your knowledge and skills. In the Chapter Survey, you will also have the opportunity to demonstrate what you have learned through an alternative assessment activity. To receive a good evaluation of your work, you will need to be sure to meet the criteria provided.

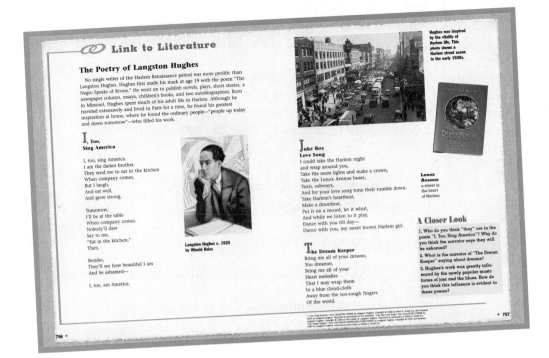

Link to Literature

Just as artists give us visual pictures of the past, writers of literature give us word pictures of the past. Sometimes works of literature are based on true events, but often they are fiction. In each unit, you will read a short segment of a work of literature that will help you better understand the time period. Perhaps the segment will make you want to read the whole book from which it was taken.

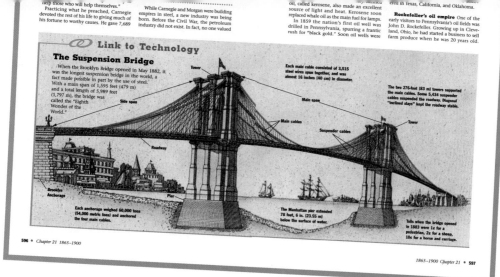

help those who will help themselves."

Practicing what he preached, Carnegie devoted the rest of his life to giving much of his fortune to worthy causes. He gave 7,689

While Carnegie and Morgan were building empires in steel, a new industry was being born. Before the Civil War, the petroleum industry did not exist. In fact, no one valued

oil, called kerosene, also made an excellent source of light and heat. Kerosene soon replaced whale oil as the main fuel for lamps.

In 1859 the nation's first oil well was drilled in Pennsylvania, spurring a frantic rush for "black gold." Soon oil wells were

ered in Texas, California, and Oklahoma.

Rockefeller's oil empire One of the early visitors to Pennsylvania's oil fields was John D. Rockefeller. Growing up in Cleveland, Ohio, he had started a business to sell farm produce when he was 20 years old.

Link to Technology

The Suspension Bridge

When the Brooklyn Bridge opened in May 1882, it was the longest suspension bridge in the world, a fact made possible in part by the use of steel. With a main span of 1,595 feet (479 m) and a total length of 5,989 feet (1,797 m), the bridge was called the "Eighth Wonder of the World."

Tower

Side span

Main span

Each main cable consisted of 3,515 steel wires spun together, and was almost 16 inches (40 cm) in diameter.

The two 276-foot (83 m) towers supported the main cables. Some 5,434 suspender cables suspended the roadway. Diagonal "inclined stays" kept the roadway stable.

Main cables

Suspender cables

Tower

Roadway

Brooklyn Anchorage

Pier

Each anchorage weighed 60,000 tons (54,000 metric tons) and anchored the four main cables.

The Manhattan pier extended 78 feet, 6 in. (23.55 m) below the surface of water.

Tolls when the bridge opened in 1883 were 1¢ for a pedestrian, 2¢ for a sheep, 10¢ for a horse and carriage.

Link to Technology

Some of the most dramatic changes in our nation have resulted from technological inventions. In each unit you will learn about one advance in technology, illustrated by diagrams or cutaway drawings.

Unit Survey

Making Connections

1. What caused conflicts between the colonies? What forces and events drove the colonies to work together? Did those forces and events have a lasting effect on the conflicts between the colonies? Explain.
2. In 1818 John Adams said, "The Revolution was effected [achieved] before the war commenced [began]. The Revolution was in the minds and hearts of the people." What do you think Adams

meant? Who might have disagreed with him and why?
3. "From the beginning of the French and Indian War through ratification of the Constitution, many Americans resisted the creation of a strong central government." Support that statement with three specific examples from the unit.

Linking History, Language Arts, and Music

Creating a Patriotic Song

First, then, throw aside your topknots of pride,
Wear none but your own country linen,
Of Economy boast, let your pride be the most,
To show clothes of your own make and spinning.

Those are the lyrics to part of a song that the Daughters of Liberty sang during the boycott of British goods. Throughout the revolutionary period, Americans wrote and sang songs to protest British rule, to rally their spirits, and to honor the memory of important events. Imagine yourself as part of a colonial songwriting team. You and your partner want to create a song that supports the Patriot cause.

Project Steps

Work with a partner to complete the following steps.
1 Plan to write a song (a) to protest a British action against the colonies, (b) to rally the Continental Army's spirits when things look grim during the war, or (c) to

honor the memory of a major event of the period. Choose the specific topic or event for your song.
2 Decide what to do about a tune for your song. You may write the tune yourself or use a tune from either an existing modern tune or a historical one like "Yankee Doodle."
3 Write the lyrics for the song. Keep the specific purpose of the song in mind; also remember that you are writing for the Patriots. Make sure the lyrics and the tune work together.
4 Teach the song to your classmates. Hand out copies of the song, or write it on the board or on a transparency for display. You might first sing the song or play a tape of yourselves singing it.

Thinking It Over Songs can have strong effects on our emotions. What qualities set a powerful song apart from a song that fails to move us? How might the Patriots have felt when they heard your song? How might the Loyalists have felt?

256 •

Interdisciplinary Projects

Although this is a history book, you will discover that much of the information you learn relates to other subjects, such as science, math, and music. In each Unit Survey, you will find an interdisciplinary project that links history to one or more of these other subjects.

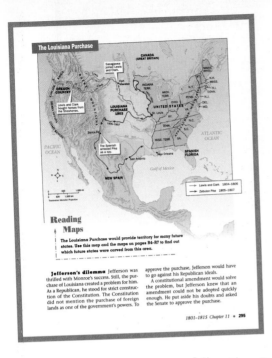

Maps

Maps are the constant companions of historians. Maps are also tools you will use in everyday life. For many centuries maps were drawn by hand. Recently, however, map makers have begun to make maps with computers.

Most of the maps in this book have been created especially for this book using computers. Computers make it possible to include all the latest geographic information and reflect the most precise detailing possible. They also enable map makers to include color and explanations that are difficult to achieve with hand-drawn maps.

Workmen and officials celebrate the railroad they said "unites the two great oceans of the world."

y 10, 1869, The Union he Central oint, Utah. (1,747 km)).

Leland Stanford, president of the Central Pacific, marked the occasion by driving a gold spike that linked the two sets of tracks. As Stanford's hammer hit the spike, a telegraph wire connected to it relayed the news of the event to Americans across the nation.

Maps

Environmental Protection

Reading Maps

Judging from the examples shown on the map, what are some different kinds of environmental problems that Americans have tried to solve in recent years?

Chapter 31 1974–Present

Charts, Graphs, and Diagrams

Some information is easier to undersand when it is presented in charts, graphs, and diagrams rather than in words. Throughout this book you will find these kinds of graphics. Like the maps in the text, these features are computer-generated and represent the latest techniques in data presentation.

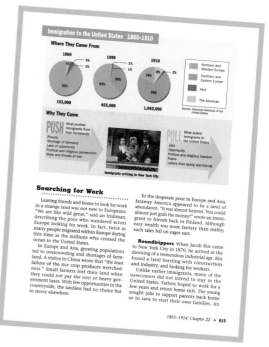

Epilogue

Into the Future

The Epilogue consists of an activity in which you and your classmates predict, based on the past and present, what the future holds for our nation and for you.

Constitution Handbook

In this text you will read about many important documents in our country's history. No document is as important for you to understand, though, as the United States Constitution. The Constitution Handbook includes the complete text of the Constitution as well as information that can help you better understand it and appreciate its importance in your life today.

Prologue
The Land

" Wilderness is the raw material out of which man has hammered . . . civilization."

Aldo Leopold

The land is the stage upon which human history unfolds. It provides people with the basic necessities of life—food, clothing, and shelter. Beyond that, the varied landscape captures our imagination and inspires us. Before there were people in the Americas, there was the land—a vast wilderness of forests, grasslands, mountains, valleys, plains, deserts, and swamps.

As the first peoples came into the Americas thousands of years ago, they learned to use the land's gifts. The land not only affected how they lived day to day, but also how they thought about their place in nature. "The earth is our mother," wrote an Abnaki Indian a century ago. "She nourishes us. That which we put into the ground she returns to us."

Over the centuries Americans have altered the land. They have carved out farms and ranches. They have constructed dams and mines. They have built towns of brick and timber and cities of concrete and steel, linking them with steel railroads, asphalt highways, and invisible electronic networks. Even though most Americans today live in towns and cities, they still depend on the land for resources, recreation, and inspiration. To understand the story of the United States and its people, we need to start by looking at the land.

The American Landscape

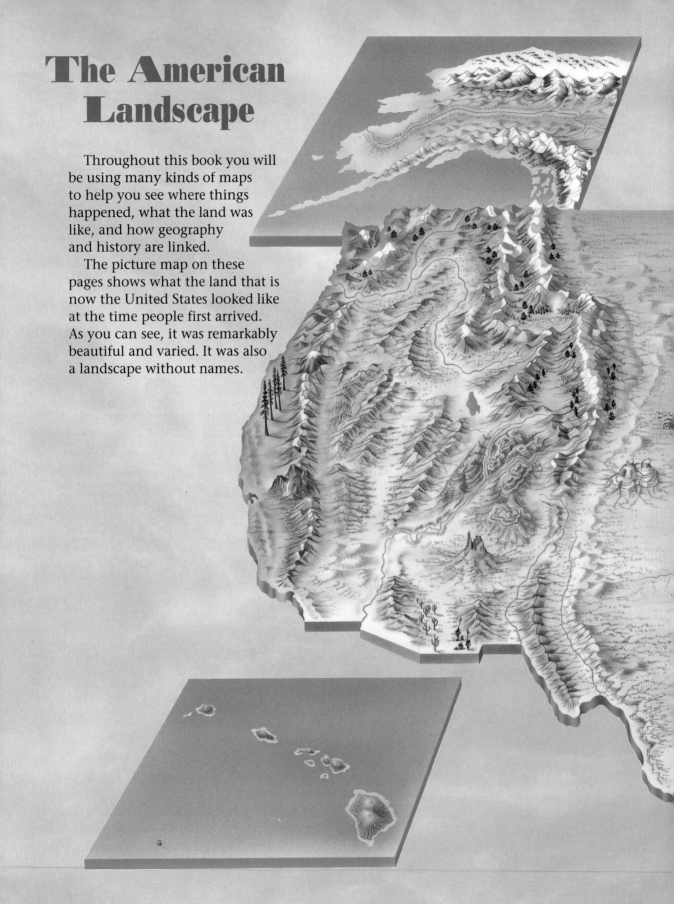

Throughout this book you will be using many kinds of maps to help you see where things happened, what the land was like, and how geography and history are linked.

The picture map on these pages shows what the land that is now the United States looked like at the time people first arrived. As you can see, it was remarkably beautiful and varied. It was also a landscape without names.

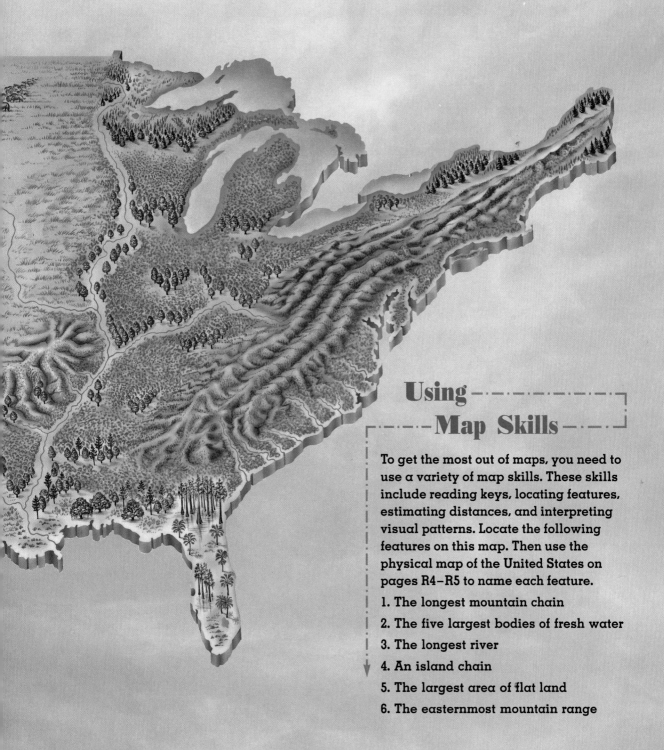

Using Map Skills

To get the most out of maps, you need to use a variety of map skills. These skills include reading keys, locating features, estimating distances, and interpreting visual patterns. Locate the following features on this map. Then use the physical map of the United States on pages R4–R5 to name each feature.

1. The longest mountain chain
2. The five largest bodies of fresh water
3. The longest river
4. An island chain
5. The largest area of flat land
6. The easternmost mountain range

Geographic Regions

Geographers divide the United States into regions in order to study geographic patterns. They describe a region as an area with some feature or features that set it apart from other areas.

A region may be defined by natural features, such as climate or types of vegetation. A region can also be defined by human features, such as cultural heritage or main industry. The regions shown on this map are geographic regions, defined according to the physical characteristics of the land.

Rocky Mountains

Western Plateaus

Pacific Mountains and Valleys

Basins and Ranges

Western Plateaus

Great Plains

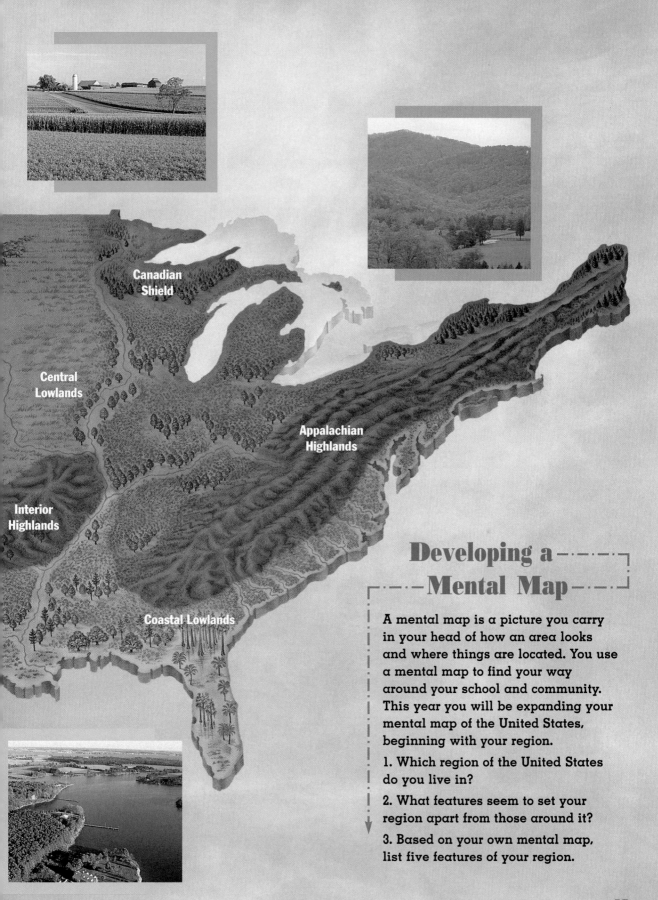

Canadian
Shield

Central
Lowlands

Appalachian
Highlands

Interior
Highlands

Coastal Lowlands

Developing a Mental Map

A mental map is a picture you carry in your head of how an area looks and where things are located. You use a mental map to find your way around your school and community. This year you will be expanding your mental map of the United States, beginning with your region.

1. Which region of the United States do you live in?

2. What features seem to set your region apart from those around it?

3. Based on your own mental map, list five features of your region.

Geography and History

Geography and history are closely linked. The land is the geographic setting for the human drama we call history. It provides the raw materials out of which humans shape their cultures and civilizations. The way people use these materials changes over time as different players set foot on the stage of history.

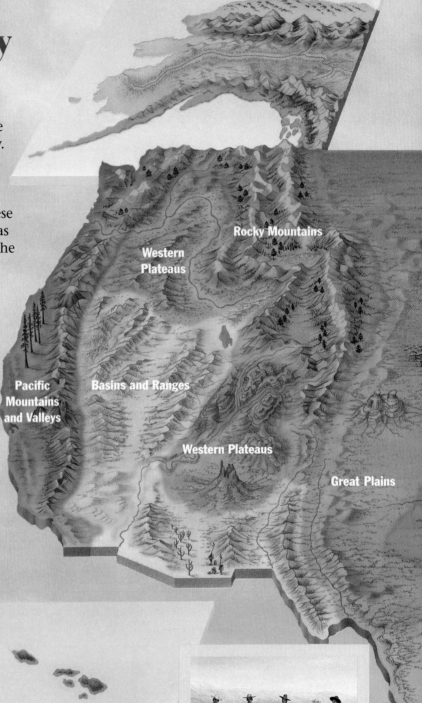

Rocky Mountains

Western Plateaus

Pacific Mountains and Valleys

Basins and Ranges

Western Plateaus

Great Plains

Gold mining in California

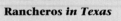

Rancheros in Texas

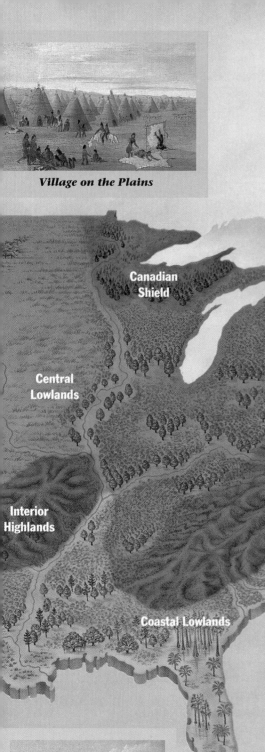

Village on the Plains

Steel mills in Pennsylvania

Canadian Shield

Central Lowlands

Appalachian Highlands

Interior Highlands

Coastal Lowlands

Shipbuilding on the Delaware

Cotton in Mississippi

Link to History

As you read about people and events, try linking the *who* and the *what* to the *where*. Ask yourself why peoples settled where they did. How did where people settled help shape their way of life? In turn, what effect did those ways of life have on the land? Put yourself into one of the pictures on these pages.

1. Who are you and what are you doing?

2. Where are you? How does being in that place influence your activities?

3. Are your activities changing the place? If so, how?

(Top) Dr. Viola in his home office, and (bottom) seeking out clues to history in the Congressional Cemetery.

A Note from the Author . . .

Introducing Scholar's Tool Kits

Did you ever wonder how historians are able to write about the past? It is not a secret. Anyone who has a curious mind, likes to solve mysteries, and knows how to use the "tools" of historical scholarship can "do" history.

Historians build knowledge much like carpenters build houses, only their tools are unlike anything a carpenter would use. A scholar's tools are ancient bones, pots, jewelry, and sculpture. They are drawings, maps, lithographs, and photographs. They are stories and remembrances passed down from person to person. They are letters, diaries, and newspapers. They are, in fact, anything that helps unlock the mysteries of history.

A scholar's tools, you will see, are easy to learn about and fascinating to use. The ten Scholar's Tool Kits in this book each tell about how one tool is used, and give you a chance to try out "doing" history.

As you read the stories and information in this or any history book, think about the tools the historian who wrote the book used to learn about the past. What questions are still unanswered? What tools would you use to answer them? You will soon see that you, too, can use the tools of history to re-create the past.

Sincerely,

Herman J. Viola

Herman J. Viola

How Do We Know?

You can see the archaeologists' camp in this photo of the Ozette site.

Archaeology

The rain had been falling for days—far more heavily than usual. Nearby creeks overflowed. The ground, with its tangle of trees, shrubs, and vines, was soaked. In the little seaside village of Ozette, the people stayed home, carving, weaving, and repairing tools for fishing and whale hunts.

The mudslide came suddenly. The water-soaked soil on the hill behind the houses gave way, and tons of dirt, rocks, trees, and brush poured into the village. Mud and debris flowed over eight houses, sealing up all their contents. There the houses stayed, buried and undisturbed, for almost 500 years.

Using Science to Unlock the Past

The mudslide was a disaster for the people of Ozette, a Makah Indian village in what is now the state of Washington. To historians and to today's Makahs, though, the site is a priceless treasure. Because the early Makahs left no written records, historians knew little about how they lived—until scientists unearthed the buried village. There they found hundreds of clues to how the Makah people had lived in the past.

Anthropologists are scientists who study human beings and how they live in groups. Anthropologists who search for clues to how human beings lived in the past are called **archaeologists**. Among the clues that archaeologists study are **artifacts**—objects made by human work—as well as remains of bones and teeth. Archaeologists also look for larger pieces of evidence, such as ruins of buildings.

1

Archaeologist Richard Daugherty and Makah crew member Meri Flinn carefully open a fragile basket. Even the contents of the carrying basket—rolls of cedar bark—were preserved by the mud.

Critical Thinking

1. Peoples along the Northwest Coast relied heavily on the sea for survival. As an archaeologist, what evidence would you look for at Ozette to show that the Makahs relied on the sea? Why?

Dating artifacts To help figure out the age of their findings, archaeologists use many methods. The most common method of dating the remains of ancient plants, animals, and human beings is **radiocarbon dating**. This technique is based on the fact that all living things absorb radiocarbon from the atmosphere. This radiocarbon decays at a steady rate, even after the plant or animal dies. By measuring the amount of radiocarbon remaining in an item, scientists can figure out its age.

Searching for Clues

When the Makah Tribal Council asked archaeologist Richard D. Daugherty to study Ozette, he eagerly agreed. Daugherty put together a team of scientists aided by students, some of whom were Makah Indians. First the team took photographs and made a map. Then they began the long, delicate process of excavating—uncovering—the site inch by inch.

Critical Thinking

2. Some tribes were involved in trade up and down the Northwest Coast. What would you look for as evidence of extensive trading? Why?

Because the artifacts were so fragile, the excavators used a fine spray of water rather than metal tools. Team members made a record of everything they found and carefully protected the artifacts.

This wooden owl club was likely used in ceremonies.

In all, the archaeologists found more than 55,000 artifacts at Ozette—timbers and benches from houses, nets, cedar bark baskets, sleeping mats, cradles, tools used for woodworking, carved cedar boxes, wooden dishes, and paddles. These items were beautifully preserved by the mud.

By using radiocarbon dating and other dating techniques, the scientists learned that the mudslide at Ozette took place between 300 and 500 years ago—perhaps about the same time that the explorer Christopher Columbus reached the Americas.

Telling the Story of an Ancient People

Using the findings at Ozette as well as the knowledge of Makah tribal elders, archaeologists have pieced together a picture of the lives of the early Makah people. For example, we know that the sea was all-important to the Makah way of life. Houses faced the beach, where canoes could be landed. Tools included devices used to hunt whales and seals, to fish for halibut and salmon, and to collect clams, crabs, and other shellfish. Evidence also showed that the Makahs relied on the forests nearby for cedar to build houses and make tools and ceremonial objects. Three looms and the folded remains of a blanket woven of dog hair, cattail fluff, feathers, and cedar bark show that early Makahs were weavers.

Archaeologists' discoveries at Ozette changed some old theories and raised new questions about the lives of early coast Indian people. They also gave today's Makahs fresh insight into their own past.

? **Critical Thinking**

3. Is there an archaeological site in or near your community? If so, describe the site. What do the archaeologists hope to learn? What kind of artifacts have they found?

Scholar at Work

Imagine that your classroom has been buried in a mudslide. It is now 500 years in the future, and archaeologists have discovered the burial and excavated it.

Make an excavation map of the site (your classroom) by making a string grid across the room. List the artifacts that an archaeologist would find within each grid square. What hypotheses might these scientists make about the date of the slide and about the people who "inhabited" this site?

Unit 1

Chapters

1. The First Americans

2. Africa, Asia, and Europe in the 1400s

3. Voyages of Exploration

Hands-On → *HISTORY*

Activity

People tell stories in many ways—with spoken words and written words, in song, dance, puppetry, and pantomime, to name a few. Pictures also tell stories. The pictures you see here were made on red sandstone walls just above a narrow ledge in Canyon de Chelly. They tell the story of the arrival of a group of Spaniards accompanied by an Indian. Suppose that you want to pass the story down to younger people. Choose a different method of storytelling and retell the story as you see it.

Navajo mural, Canyon de Chelly, Arizona

Three Worlds Meet

Chapter 1

The First Americans

Keys to History

by 20,000 B.C.
Earliest
inhabitants
spread across
North America

7000 B.C.
Agriculture
begins in the
Americas

A.D. 300–900
Mayan
civilization
flourishes
Statue of Mayan
ballgame player

20,000 B.C. 9000 B.C. 7000 B.C. A.D. 300

Looking Back

World **Link**

Pleistocene
Epoch begins
2,000,000 B.C.

Earliest known
agriculture
9000 B.C.

HISTORY *Mystery*

This photo shows an aerial view of a mound created by Indians thousands of years ago. It measures a quarter mile (390 m) long and five feet (1.5 m) tall. Why do you think people built the mound? Read the chapter to learn more about such mounds.

600
Mound Builders establish the city of Cahokia
Figure from the ruins of Cahokia

1000s
Anasazis build cliff dwellings
Stone "apartments" at Mesa Verde

1300s
Aztecs establish their capital, Tenochtitlán
Turquoise and shell mosaic mask

1400s
Inca Empire dominates the Pacific Coast of South America
Alligator made of solid gold

A.D. *1000*

A.D. *1500*

Looking Ahead

Europeans arrive in the Americas
A.D. **1492**

The Stone Seekers

The hair on the back of the young man's neck prickled. He could hear them out there, just beyond the light of the dying campfire. The dim shapes looming in the darkness were dire wolves, great shaggy beasts that sometimes hunted humans. The young man looked across the fire at the old man, his leader on this long journey away from the People. The old man nodded. At this signal, both grabbed burning sticks from the fire and charged at the wolves. The beasts scattered. Even so, it would be a nervous night for the stone seekers.

The Long Journey

The two men had been walking for days—as many as the fingers of three hands. They had left the People to journey north to the place of the multi-colored stone. The stone at this distant quarry was the best—better than any

Archaeologist Dennis Stanford, a leader in research on the earliest Americans, demonstrates how the stone seekers might have made flaked stone points. The points below date to around 11,500 years ago and show the beauty and workmanship of such tools.

the People could find near their hunting grounds. The old man explained why. The rock there was striped with the colors of the earth—red, yellow, black, and white. The stone was extremely smooth. Spear points made from this stone would have the sharpest, most deadly edge.

The young man was pleased to have been chosen for the journey. He had already proven himself as a hunter. Now he was recognized as a man by the People, though he was only 15 and not yet married.

At the age of 35, the old man's hunting days were nearly over. Good hunters needed more strength and agility than he seemed to have now. No one, however, could equal his skill in making sharp stone points for spears. A hunter armed with such a spear could bring down a woolly mammoth or long-horned bison. A few of the old man's points were so perfect they were never used for hunting. Instead, they were brought out during ceremonies when the People prayed for—or celebrated—a successful hunt.

During the long journey, the young hunter listened carefully to the old man's stories about the landmarks on their route. They had already crossed the wide river and were nearing the red bluffs. In a few more days they would reach the quarry where they would find the special stones. The young man knew that the stories would help him remember the way to the quarry in future years. To the old man's tales he would add his own story of their frightening encounter with the dire wolves near the hidden spring.

The Special Stones

Once the two men arrived at the quarry, the hard work began. With great care they broke off large chunks of stone with just the right grain and no flaws. A careless slip of a tool could shatter a stone into a dozen useless pieces. They filled their leather sacks with as many stones as they could carry. Then, bending under their heavy burdens, they began retracing their route back to the People. Luckily, the old stone seeker said to himself, the young man was strong.

On the return journey, the young stone seeker thought of the months ahead. Now that he was a man, he would join the other men hunting. After a good hunt, the People would celebrate by feasting on the meat. Between hunts, he would work with the other men to make and repair their stone-tipped tools and weapons. They would replace broken points with new ones chipped out of the precious stones he himself had carved out of the distant quarry.

Hands-On HISTORY

Activity

The points made by the stone seekers were precious to them—precious enough for them to walk hundreds of miles to select just the right stones. Write a description for a future historian of an object in your life that you value both for its usefulness and its beauty. Tell how you use the object and why you consider it beautiful. How did you acquire the object? Finally, tell what you expect to do with the object ultimately—will you save the item, discard it, or pass it along to someone else? Be prepared to bring the object to class.

1. First Peoples in the Americas

Reading Guide

New Terms **migration, glaciers, nomads, culture**

Section Focus **The beginnings of human history in the Americas**

1. How did humans come to live in the Americas?
2. How did agriculture change the way of life of early Americans?

The stone seekers in the story are imaginary. However, the beautiful points really exist, and the quarry has been found in Wyoming. America's ancient hunters who used stone tools are called *Paleo-Indians*, meaning "ancient Indians." Little is known about these people, but what we do know is that their ancestors migrated from Asia. A **migration** is a movement of people from one region to another. Over the course of thousands of years, Paleo-Indians spread throughout North and South America.

Beringia

The arrival of human beings in the Americas took place during the last ice age, when a third of the earth was locked in ice two miles (3.2 km) thick in some places. It was a time when nature's bulldozers, vast slow-moving masses of ice called **glaciers,** transformed huge areas of the earth's surface as they gouged and crushed everything in their path.

So much water turned into ice that it lowered the water level of the oceans. The lowered waters exposed a bridge of land as much as 1,000 miles (1,600 km) wide linking the continents of Asia and North America. Geologists call this land bridge Beringia (bayr-IN-jee-uh). Across Beringia came bison,

musk oxen, elephants, caribou, and other large animals. Behind them followed small groups of hunters who depended on these animals for their very existence.

Link to the Present

***Indian* as a term** Europeans of the 1400s used the term *Indies* to refer to India, China, Japan, and the other Asian lands. When Christopher Columbus landed in the Bahamas in 1492, he was certain he had reached the Indies. He called the native people he met *Indians*.

Although Columbus was wrong about where he had landed, the name *Indian* stuck. Today, many descendants of America's earliest people prefer *Indian* over terms like *Amer-Indian* or even *Native American*. However, the first preference for most is to be called by the name of their tribe or nation, such as Arapaho, Cherokee, Mandan, or Zuni. In most Indian languages, the tribal name means "the people."

ARCTIC OCEAN

Bluefish Caves
(12,000–25,000
years old)

ATLANTIC
OCEAN

PACIFIC
OCEAN

Folsom
(10,000
years old)

Clovis (10,000–
12,000 years old)

Meadowcroft
(25,000? years old)

Pedra Furada
(30,000–50,000?
years old)

N
W — E
S

Monte Verde
(33,000? years old)

→ Possible migration route

⌒ Present-day coastline

• Early American site

☐ Ice sheet

▨ Beringia

0   1,000   2,000 mi
0 1,000 2,000 km
Miller Projection

Reading Maps

1. How do you know that the map shows the earth at a time when the climate was different than it is today?

2. Would migrating Paleo-Indians know when they had reached a new continent? Explain.

Although scholars disagree about when these hunters first arrived, by 20,000 B.C. descendants of the hunters had spread across North America. They eventually spread throughout South America as well. These small groups of people lived as **nomads,** people with no permanent home who move in search of food. To survive, the hardy nomads hunted animals and birds and gathered nuts, berries, and edible plants. They used fire for cooking and comfort, and wore clothes made of animal skins and furs.

Folsom and Clovis People

Paleo-Indian families used a variety of tools, such as stone knives, hammers, and scrapers, and bone needles. Today their best-known tools are their stone points, like the ones made by the stone seeker.

The person who discovered the first of these points was a cowboy named George McJunkin. In 1926, while looking for stray cattle near Folsom, New Mexico, McJunkin noticed the sun-bleached bones of a large animal peeping through the dirt. The bones proved to be those of a type of buffalo or bison that roamed the earth 10,000 years ago. With the bones archaeologists found several stone points.

The discovery of the points with the bones excited scientists and historians. It was the first proof that humans had lived in the Americas at the same time as ice-age mammals. In 1932 a similar discovery near Clovis, New Mexico, thrilled archaeologists. Since then, the points—referred to as Clovis points—have been found all over North America and even in parts of South America.

The land bridge disappears About 10,000 years ago, the earth began to warm. Glaciers melted, oceans rose, and the land bridge disappeared beneath the Bering Strait. All that remains of the land bridge today are a few islands in a channel 50 miles (80 km) wide between Alaska and Russia.

Point of View

When did the first settlers migrate to America?

Archaeologists and anthropologists who first studied Clovis points believed that Clovis people were the first Americans and that they came about 11,500 years ago. Yet recent research dates the migration anywhere from 20,000 to even 50,000 years ago.

While firm evidence of pre-Clovis people exists, certain finds have stirred debate. For example, in Pedra Furada, Brazil, French archaeologist Niéde Guidon has found artifacts she says are at least 30,000 and perhaps 50,000 years old. Some archaeologists question these dates.

One problem is proving that stone "tools" are in fact human-made and not formed by nature. As for burned remains, archaeologist David Meltzer raises this question: "How do you know it was a piece of charcoal touched by human hands and not just a piece of burned tree?" Guidon responds, "If they had been left by forest fires, carbon deposits would have been found scattered across a wide area." Instead, the charcoal is often ringed by stones, a sign that these were fires made by humans.

If humans got to South America even by 13,000 years ago, they would have had to cross Beringia many thousands of years before. At that time ice sheets would have blocked the path south. Archaeologists are still looking for explanations. Guidon's own answer is controversial. She thinks that the immigrants might have come to South America in boats from Asia.

Archaeologists who study the first Americans continue to dig and search, to study and disagree. As archaeologist Dennis Stanford of the Smithsonian Institution puts it, "This is a hot area of research. Man's origin in the New World [the Americas] is one of the major unanswered questions of archaeology."

Beginnings of Agriculture

Soon after the land bridge disappeared, ice-age mammals in the Americas began to die off. Climate change might have been the cause, or perhaps over-hunting by the Paleo-Indians.

Whatever the reason, people began to seek other ways to survive. Plants and fish

Archaeologist Tom Dillehay's team works at Monte Verde, Chile, a site that made scientists question the Clovis theory. Unusual natural conditions preserved not only stone and bone artifacts, but also organic materials such as mastodon meat, potatoes, and even seaweed from the Pacific coast. Radio-carbon dating shows these materials to be 12,500 years old.

The spread of agriculture How did the practice of agriculture spread throughout the world? Did the first farmers teach their neighbors, who then taught *their* neighbors? Or did people in different places get the same idea at about the same time? The answer is: both.

The earliest farming took place about 9000 B.C. in the Middle East and spread outward from there. The first farmers in northern Africa, southern Europe, and India all got the idea from their neighbors in the Middle East.

In eastern Asia, agriculture started about 7500 B.C., with farmers planting rice and millet. Agriculture in the Americas started about 7000 B.C., in what is now Mexico. Historians can find no evidence that the first farmers in eastern Asia or in the Americas had any contact—either direct or indirect—with Middle Eastern farmers. Instead, they seem to have developed agriculture on their own, and at about the same time.

with wild maize (corn) in order to grow larger cobs. At the same time, groups living in what is now the eastern United States began to grow beans and squashes.

Agriculture brings change The development of agriculture was a major turning point in history. Once people began to grow their own food, they settled down in one place to tend their fields. In good crop years these farming villages could produce extra food and store it for the future. People were healthier and lived longer, and populations began to grow.

Farming changed the way of life—also known as **culture**—of these communities. Culture includes people's arts, beliefs, inventions, traditions, and language. With a good supply of food, not everyone had to farm. People with special skills or talents could become weavers or potters or healers. Individuals' special roles and jobs became a part of the culture of the community.

In addition, the goods people made and the extra food farmers grew could be sold to people outside the community. Trade began, and villages grew into larger towns and then into cities. As you will see, city life paved the way for even greater changes.

replaced meat at the center of their diet. As a result, smooth rocks for crushing nuts and grinding wild grains replaced spear points in their tool kits. People learned to weave baskets from plant fibers and to make clay pots for storing seeds, flour, and berries.

Over time, people learned that certain plants grew better and faster than others, so they devoted more attention to those plants. In this way agriculture got its start. As long ago as 7000 B.C., people in what is today central Mexico began to experiment

1. Section Review

1. Define **migration, glaciers, nomads, and culture.**

2. How did people come to live in the Americas?

3. What evidence pointed scientists to the dates of early humans in America?

4. Critical Thinking The culture of a group of people is said to include ideas, customs, skills, and arts. Choose one of these aspects of culture and explain how it might have changed with the shift from nomadic life to farming life.

2. Early Civilizations

Reading Guide

New Terms civilization, tribute

Section Focus The advanced civilizations that arose in Mesoamerica and South America

1. What civilizations arose in the Americas after the development of agriculture?
2. How do we know about ways of life of early American civilizations?
3. What were some major achievements of early civilizations in the Americas?

As agriculture flourished and populations grew, cities became centers of government and religious life. Some people became officials or priests. Others studied science and developed systems of writing. Artists and craftspeople created a variety of products.

With the development of cities came the beginnings of civilization. A **civilization** is a society in which a high level of art, technology, and government exists. Over the centuries several civilizations rose and fell in the Americas. The largest civilizations arose in what is now Peru, and in *Mesoamerica*, a term archaeologists use for the part of Mexico and Central America that had civilizations before A.D. 1500.

The Olmecs

A people called the Olmecs created the earliest great civilization in Mesoamerica. It flourished between 1200 B.C. and 600 B.C. along the Gulf Coast in what are now the Mexican states of Veracruz and Tabasco. In this rainy, swampy lowland, people can grow corn and other crops year-round. Olmec civilization is now known as the "mother culture" of Mesoamerica because later societies built on Olmec ideas.

Religion and art Much of what we know about the Olmecs comes from discoveries at places where they held religious ceremonies. Huge statues and beautiful carvings show that the Olmecs worshiped many gods, including a jaguar god and gods of rain, fire, corn, and fertility. These gods were important in all later Mesoamerican religion and art.

The Olmecs had a highly organized society that was ruled by priests. Their elaborate religious centers featured large earthen mounds topped with temples, broad plazas,

Colossal Olmec heads are thought to be either individual portraits of Olmec rulers or stylized portraits of Olmec gods. In addition to huge carvings, Olmec artists crafted lovely small figurines as well, often using prized green stones such as jade.

and carved altars. For such monuments, the Olmecs dragged stone over long distances. At one site colossal heads, carved from black stone called basalt, weigh as much as 20 tons. Amazingly, Olmecs dragged the basalt through miles of dense jungle to the site. We know that the Olmecs carried on trade because their pottery and sculpture have been found at sites throughout Mesoamerica.

This Mayan mural, from a temple wall in the city of Chichén Itzá, shows village life. What can you infer about Mayan daily life from the scene?

Science Olmec scientists invented a calendar based on their study of the movement of the earth in relation to the sun, moon, and planets. They used a system of bars and dots to record dates of astronomical and historical events. Archaeologists say that this system was an early form of writing.

We know very little about how and why Olmec civilization disappeared. After the decline of the Olmec "mother culture," though, several other city centers rose to power in Mesoamerica.

Teotihuacán

The largest and most influential city center was Teotihuacán (TAY-ō-TEE-wah-KAHN). Located in the Valley of Mexico—where Mexico City is today—Teotihuacán drew people from small farms. At its peak in A.D. 500 it had a population of 200,000, making it the sixth largest city in the world at that time. Not only was Teotihuacán big, it also was powerful, dominating its neighbors through trade and warfare.

Teotihuacán's orderly city plan took over 500 years to carry out. The city covered over 8 square miles (21 square km) and was orga-

nized around a religious center. Visitors to Mexico City today can still visit Teotihuacán's Pyramid of the Sun, an awesome structure of stone and dirt.

Around the middle of the 600s, fire destroyed Teotihuacán. Was the fire caused by rebellion against a hated ruler or by invasion? Historians still debate the answer.

The Mayas

After the decline of Teotihuacán, power in Mesoamerica shifted south to the energetic Mayan city-states. Located in tropical lowlands of present-day Yucatán, Guatemala, Belize, and Honduras, Mayan civilization flourished from A.D. 300 to 900.

Many historians believe the Mayas created the most advanced early civilization in the Americas. Like the Olmecs, the Mayas built hundreds of religious centers, such as Palenque (pah-LENG-kay), Uxmal (ooz-MAHL), Tikal (tee-KAHL), and Copán (kō-PAHN). Dramatic temples crowned stepped pyramids. Intricate carvings covered palaces and monuments.

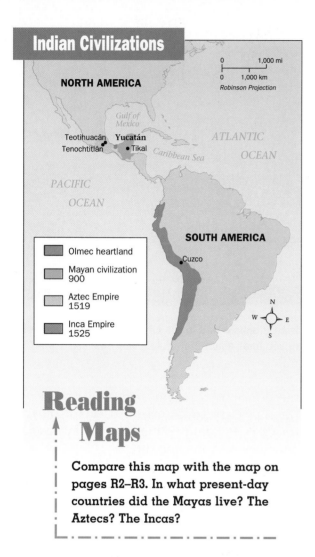

Indian Civilizations

NORTH AMERICA

Gulf of Mexico

Teotihuacán
Tenochtitlán • Tikal Yucatán

ATLANTIC OCEAN

Caribbean Sea

PACIFIC OCEAN

SOUTH AMERICA

Cuzco

0   1,000 mi
0   1,000 km
Robinson Projection

- ▮ Olmec heartland
- ▮ Mayan civilization 900
- ▮ Aztec Empire 1519
- ▮ Inca Empire 1525

N W E S

Reading Maps

Compare this map with the map on pages R2–R3. In what present-day countries did the Mayas live? The Aztecs? The Incas?

torians think that the Mayas wore out their soil for farming, leading to a food shortage.

The collapse of Mayan civilization may be a mystery, but the Mayan people themselves have survived. About 700,000 Mayas live in the Mexican state of Chiapas. Nearly 5 million more live on the Yucatán Peninsula and in Central America. Most of them live in villages and tend small farms. They speak the Mayan language and some still use the ancient calendar.

The Aztecs

To the north of the fading Mayan empire, the powerful Aztec empire began to rise. In the 1100s or 1200s the Aztecs migrated into the Valley of Mexico. By 1345 they had set up their island capital of Tenochtitlán (teh-NŌCH-tee-TLAHN) in marshy Lake Texcoco (tes-KŌ-kō). In the following century, the Aztecs' strong army and well-organized government enabled them to extend their power throughout central Mexico.

The Aztec army was bent on gaining land and collecting **tribute**—forced payment—from conquered peoples. Aztecs collected

Every ceremonial center had an observatory, and the Mayas excelled at mathematics and astronomy. They understood the concept of zero and had a symbol for it long before the rest of the world. Their calendar was far more accurate than those used in Europe hundreds of years later. In addition, the Mayas developed a written language.

A mysterious collapse Like Teotihuacán, the Mayan civilization collapsed suddenly and mysteriously. Perhaps enemies invaded or the city-states fought among themselves. A drought or overpopulation might have damaged the environment, making it hard for people to survive. Some his-

The Aztec writing system used pictures and symbols to represent ideas and sounds. This page from an Aztec book shows men playing a game. The curved symbols by two of the men represent speech.

tribute in the form of gold, cotton, turquoise, feathers, incense, and food. Tribute also included human beings for sacrifice to the Aztec sun god. The Aztecs believed that unless the sun god was fed hearts and blood, the world would come to an end. At one especially bloody four-day celebration, 20,000 prisoners had their hearts cut out.

The Aztecs were very successful at agriculture. Farmers grew crops on irrigated hillside terraces around Lake Texcoco. They also cultivated vegetables and flowers in *chinampas* (chee-NAHM-pahs), farm plots built by digging ditches in the lakeshore to channel the water and then piling up the fertile mud into raised beds.

Aztec trade, like Aztec agriculture, showed careful organization and government direction. Merchants traveled through the empire and beyond to Central America and north into the present-day United States. They brought a great variety of goods to Tenochtitlán. Orderly markets displayed meat, vegetables, cloth, rope, pottery, precious metals, jade, feathers, and animal skins.

The Incas

Far to the south, the Inca empire rivaled the Aztecs in size and power. Beginning in the early 1400s, the Incas dominated much of the Pacific Coast of South America. Their capital was the city of Cuzco (KOOS-kō), located high in the Andes Mountains. The supreme ruler, the Sapa Inca, had total control of his subjects. Priests and nobles helped him rule his empire.

The well-organized Incas could communicate over a vast area. They built a road system

Hands-On *HISTORY*

Re-creating a temple treasure Ordinary activities sometimes lead to extraordinary discoveries. In Mexico City in 1978, a worker digging a trench came upon the buried ruins of el Templo Mayor—the "Great Temple" of the Aztecs.

As archaeologists uncovered the temple, they found thousands of items the Aztecs had buried as offerings to their gods. These included turtle shells, snake skins, jaguar skeletons, crocodile heads—and the remains of sacrificed humans. There were wonderful treasures too: gemstones, jewelry, masks, musical instruments, knives, pottery, statues of gods, and carvings of animals. Some items were made by Aztec artists. Others were antiques from previous civilizations like the Olmecs. Most came from peoples the Aztecs had conquered.

El Templo Mayor model

Activity Suppose you wanted to bury a "treasure chest" containing items of special value to you. Make a list of what you would put in the chest. Include at least one item from each of these four categories: artworks, antiques or heirlooms, items with political or religious meaning, and special everyday objects. Explain each of your choices.

The Incas built the city of Machu Picchu in the Andes on a narrow ridge some 8,000 feet (2,400 m) above sea level. This small Inca town was not only considered a strategic site on the edge of the empire but also a sacred place in Inca myths. Here you can see the intricate stone structures and terraced ledges used for farming on steep mountainsides.

that stretched 2,500 miles (4,000 km) from present-day Ecuador to central Chile. Swift runners carried messages. Because the Incas did not have a written language, runners memorized the messages. They also carried *quipu* (KEE-poo), cords tied with knotted strings of different colors. The colors and knots were a code for complex information such as financial accounts.

Inca technology The Incas are known for their monumental architecture, much of which still stands. Although they did not have iron tools, the wheel, or large animals, they built temples, palaces, and forts from huge stone blocks. The force of gravity, not cement, holds the stones together, their fit so snug that a knife cannot slip between them. During earthquakes, the blocks slide but do not tumble apart.

The Incas also made great advances in agriculture and medicine. Inca engineers built a system of terraces for farmers to grow potatoes and other crops on steep mountainsides. Inca doctors performed brain surgery, opening the skulls of patients even without metal instruments.

By the late 1400s the Incas were at the height of their power. They had created a vast, well-organized empire with extensive trade and great riches. As you will read, in the 1500s both the Aztecs and Incas fell prey to a new enemy: conquerors from far-away Spain. Hungry for riches, these ruthless conquerors were to shatter the last great civilizations of Mesoamerica and Peru.

 2. Section Review

1. Define **civilization** and **tribute**.
2. Choose two civilizations and explain how we know that religion was an important part of the society of each.
3. Give two examples of how farmers adapted to their environments in early civilizations.
4. List two accomplishments for each of these civilizations: Olmecs, Mayas, Aztecs, and Incas.
5. Critical Thinking Explain how a civilization differs from a culture. Give examples to support your answer.

3. Ancient Cultures in North America

Reading Guide

New Term irrigation

Section Focus Ancient cultures that rose and fell in North America

1. What ways of life developed among the ancient societies of the Southwest?
2. What were some characteristics of ancient Indian societies of the Eastern Woodlands?

At the same time that mighty civilizations were developing in Mesoamerica and Peru, complex cultures existed north of Mexico. Archaeologists have found evidence of several early farming cultures in the lands that became the United States.

Desert Farmers

Thousands of years after the Paleo-Indians of the Southwest made their famous spear points, three desert societies lived in the same lands. The Mogollons, the Hohokams, and the Anasazis settled into permanent villages and towns to grow corn, beans, squash, cotton, and tobacco.

Mogollons The name Mogollon (MUG-ee-YŌN) means "mountain people." It refers to the mountains of New Mexico and Arizona where these people once lived.

By around 100 B.C. the Mogollons were growing corn and beans in their desert environment by building dams and terraces on hillsides to make use of the small amount of rain. This system of **irrigation**—supplying land with water by use of dams, ditches, and channels—was very important because it provided a steady source of food.

The Mogollons crafted many kinds of objects for religious and personal use, such as tobacco pipes, masks, and stone and shell beads. However, they are best known for their pottery painted with striking red-on-white and black-on-white designs.

Hohokams The Hohokams (hō-HŌ-kahmz) lived mostly in the Sonoran Desert to the west of the Mogollon people. They are noted for their elaborate irrigation system.

The Mogollons often placed pots in graves along with the dead. They punched holes in the bottom of the pots, perhaps to "kill" the pots or release the spirits of the painted figures (here a frog and a turkey).

They built hundreds of miles of canals criss-crossing their desert homeland.

The Hohokams traded widely with people in Mesoamerica, and their artifacts show strong Mexican influences. They used mirrors made in Mesoamerica, kept tropical birds as pets, and imported rubber balls to play a Mesoamerican game. Their craftsmen imitated Mesoamerican jewelry styles.

No one knows for sure why the Hohokams disappeared. Perhaps their irrigation system let salt into the soil, killing their crops. Perhaps they were overcome by a drought in the Southwest in the 1200s.

Some scholars believe that the Hohokams, weakened by food shortages and attacks, scattered to small villages, surviving to become ancestors of today's Pima (PEE-muh) and Papago (PAH-puh-GŌ) Indians of Arizona. Indeed, the name Hohokam comes from a Pima word meaning "many things used up" or "the vanished ones."

Anasazis The Anasazis (AH-nuh-SAH-zeez) lived in the high desert country of the Colorado Plateau of northern Arizona and New Mexico. By about A.D. 700 they had found ways to grow corn, squash, and beans in their dry environment. At first they lived in pit houses like the Mogollons. Later they built large apartment-like communities made of stone, wood, and sun-dried mud called *adobe* (uh-DŌ-bee).

After about A.D. 1000, the Anasazis began building their villages in high canyon walls as protection from their enemies. For this reason the Anasazis are sometimes referred to as cliff dwellers. Some Anasazi structures had as many as 200 rooms and 20 *kivas* (KEE-vuhz)—round underground rooms

Anasazis built this dwelling, called Cliff Palace, under a protective overhang in what is today Mesa Verde National Park in Colorado. Builders began at the back, and as the apartments grew out and up, the dark first rooms became storage areas. On top of the underground kivas were courtyards. You can see the round kivas, now roofless, in this aerial view.

Link to Art

Emergence of the Clowns (1988) Today Pueblo peoples continue the Anasazi tradition of artworks in clay. Sculptor Roxanne Swentzell (b. 1962) lives in Santa Clara, a Tewa pueblo in northern New Mexico. This sculpture shows clowns called *koshares,* who act out the Tewa story of where humans came from. Swentzell says these koshares "came out of the earth first and brought the rest of the people to the surface." The sculpture's message? "Remember where you came from." **Discuss** What emotions do the koshares show? Why do you think they are experiencing these feelings?

used by the men of the community for religious ceremonies.

The Anasazis began leaving their cliff dwellings in the late 1200s to establish new communities in the Rio Grande Valley. The reason they moved may have been a drought or attacks by warlike Indians such as the Apaches (uh-PACH-eez) and Navajos (NAV-uh-hōz). Some historians believe that the Indians the Spanish later met in Arizona and New Mexico were descendants of the Anasazis. The Spanish called these Indians the Pueblo (PWEB-lō) Indians. *Pueblo* is the Spanish word for "town."

The Mound Builders

In the eastern part of what is now the United States, archaeologists have found rich evidence of ancient cultures inside thousands of earthen mounds. These mounds still exist in a vast region stretching from Kansas in the west to the Appalachian Mountains in the east, and from the Great Lakes in the north to the Gulf of Mexico in the south.

Scholars call the Indians who created these mounds the Mound Builders. The best-known Mound Builder cultures are the Adena (1000 B.C.–A.D. 200), the Hopewell (300 B.C.–A.D. 700), and the Mississippian (A.D. 700–1500).

Many of the huge earthen mounds mark the graves of dead leaders, but some were used for religious ceremonies. Some mounds look like mythological or real creatures, such as the gigantic 1,300-foot (390 m) Great Serpent Mound near present-day Cincinnati, Ohio. (See photo on page 7.)

Adenas The Adenas lived in the woodlands of Ohio, Kentucky, Indiana, Pennsylvania, and West Virginia. They got most of their food from hunting and gathering in their rich environment. In fact, even though they did very little farming, they could still settle down in one place without using up the food resources around them.

In their burial mounds the Adenas included grave goods—items buried with the dead—that tell archaeologists about their lives. For example, stone pipes show that the Adena smoked tobacco, which they grew. Beads made of seashells and bracelets made of copper from Michigan show that the Adenas carried on trade. The fact that some graves held more luxurious goods than others is a sign that certain people had a higher rank in society than others.

This cross section of a burial mound in Louisiana was painted in the mid-1800s. Several Mound Builder burial sites were excavated in the early to mid-1800s, though modern research has shed more light on these cultures. This painting shows the different levels in the burial site.

Hopewells Hopewell culture gradually replaced the Adena after about 300 B.C. This culture had many of the same elements as Adena culture, but on a grander scale. The architecture of Hopewell mounds is more elaborate and their art is more refined.

With a larger population, the Hopewells were more dependent on farming than the Adenas. They also had a greater trading network. Rich burial sites contained obsidian from the Black Hills and the Rockies, mica from the Appalachians, and even alligator skulls from Florida and grizzly bear teeth from the far west.

Over time, the Hopewell culture spread over a vast area. From its core in the Ohio and Illinois River valleys, it stretched out across much of the present-day midwestern and eastern United States.

What became of the Hopewell culture? As with many Mesoamerican and Southwest cultures, historians have a variety of theories about why it vanished. The reason might have been climate changes or invasion, but no one knows for sure. Whatever the reason, another culture soon came to dominate the area: the Mississippian.

Mississippians The Mississippian people lived in the fertile valleys of the Ohio and Mississippi River basins. They grew corn, beans, squash, and pumpkins in the rich soil there. They also fished, gathered wild plants, and hunted deer, raccoons, and wild turkeys for meat. This way of life, a combination of agriculture and hunting-gathering, supported their large population.

Most Mississippian people lived in villages and on farms clustered around central towns, where religious and government leaders lived. Some of these towns grew quite large. For example, Cahokia (kuh-HŌ-kee-uh), in present-day Illinois, was the largest Indian town in what is now the United States. Established in A.D. 600, Cahokia had at least 10,000 inhabitants at its peak between 1050 and 1250. Its "downtown" covered five square miles (13 square km).

Farmers came to towns like Cahokia to trade, to take part in religious ceremonies, and for protection in times of war. In turn, leaders probably required the farmers to pay taxes in the form of crops or labor to build and maintain the massive mounds.

Like the Adenas and the Hopewells, the Mississippians built mounds. However, Mississippian mounds were even more massive, with temples and leaders' houses on top. The center of Cahokia had nearly 100 temple and burial mounds arranged around central plazas.

Grave goods from the mounds show that the Mississippians had an extensive network of trade. Scholars believe that the Mississippian people even had contact with Mesoamericans, either through trade or migration. They point to the similarities in their temples and villages, art styles, religious symbols, and farming practices.

By the time Europeans arrived in the early 1500s, Mississippian population had dropped off dramatically, leaving only a shadow of the culture's former splendor. Perhaps diseases had spread through their crowded towns, which lacked good sanitation. Later tribes in the region—the Cherokees, Creeks, Seminoles, Choctaws, and Chickasaws—are believed to be descendants of the Mississippians.

3. Section Review

1. Define **irrigation.**
2. How did the desert farmers adapt to their environment?
3. What common characteristics did Mound Builder cultures share?
4. Critical Thinking Why do you think it is hard for archaeologists to find out why an ancient society collapsed?

Geography Lab

Sheep herding on the Colorado Plateau

The Colorado Plateau

The Anasazis made their home in the region we call the Colorado Plateau. What was their environment like?

A **plateau** is a large expanse of high, flat land. The Colorado Plateau covers nearly 150,000 square miles (390,000 square km) and stretches over parts of four western states.

Although the plateau is mostly flat, wind and water have carved deep canyons and oddly beautiful rock formations into its surface. In 1869 Major John Wesley Powell surveyed the plateau's most famous canyon—the Grand Canyon—and found it to be more than a mile deep in places.

Look at the photograph of Mesa Verde on page 20 and at the illustrations and the words of Powell, below, to help you picture the Colorado Plateau region.

Yucca, a dry-region plant

Basket of yucca fibers

John Wesley Powell's Report

"Wherever we look there is but a wilderness of rocks—deep gorges where the rivers are lost below cliffs and towers and pinnacles, and ten thousand strangely carved forms in every direction, and beyond them mountains blending with the clouds."

Developing a Mental Map

Use the maps on pages P4–P5, R4–R5, and R6–R7 to help answer the questions.

1. The Colorado Plateau covers parts of which states?

2. Compare the area of the Colorado Plateau with the area of your state.

3. How high is the plateau?

4. What do the photographs tell you about the climate? Explain.

5. What features of the landscape did John Wesley Powell describe? List at least four.

6. **Hands-On Geography** Imagine that you and your family are camping on the Colorado Plateau. Write a letter to a friend describing the trip. What do you see? What does the air feel like? Will you be glad or sorry to leave? Why?

4. North America in the 1400s

Reading Guide

New Term **diversity**

Section Focus **Indian societies of North America at the time Europeans arrived**

1. What factors determined where North American Indians lived?
2. How did different Indian groups adapt to their environments?

The first Europeans to reach the Americas met members of only a few Indian groups. These Europeans had no idea that they had reached two enormous continents. Nor did they know the numbers and **diversity**—variety—of people who lived in North and South America. For on these two continents lived as many as a thousand different Indian groups—descendants of the hunters who migrated across the land bridge from Asia thousands of years earlier.

Population Distribution

Even today our knowledge of the peoples of North America around 1500 is incomplete. Certain facts about the population are clear, however. Fewer Indians lived in what is today Canada and the United States (around 2 million people) than in Mexico, Central America, and South America (around 40 million people).

We also know that the food available in a certain area helped determine the population size. In North America, more people lived along the coast, with its steady supply of seafood, than lived inland. More lived on the Pacific coast, where the climate was mild and food abundant, than on the Atlantic coast. More lived in the south than in the north, where harsh winters limited farming and other food supplies.

Where Indians lived by farming, their population was much larger than in nonfarming areas. As you have seen, farming made it possible for people to settle down and for their population to grow. One exception to this pattern was in the Northwest Coast area, where seafood was so abundant that Indians there had plenty to eat without farming.

Language and Ways of Life

In language and ways of life, the peoples of North America were as different from each other as the peoples of Europe. It is misleading, therefore, to speak about *the* American Indian. Indians were not—and are not—one people with a single culture.

For example, in 1492, the year Europeans first arrived in the Americas, the peoples of North America spoke nearly 550 different languages. Even tribes who lived near each other sometimes had to use sign language in order to communicate. Today, North American Indians still use about 200 of these languages.

From region to region across North America, Indian groups had very different ways of life. Some lived in wooden houses, while others made houses of animal skins. Some dug out wooden boats. Others built boats of bark or animal hides. Some wore copper armbands; others tattooed their faces. In some groups men did the weaving; in others women were the weavers. Some Indian tribes honored their warriors. Others considered war a terrible thing and violence a form of insanity.

Tribes that lived near each other and shared a similar way of life are said to have shared the same culture. The region in which they lived is known as a *culture area*.

North American Culture Areas

The map on page 29 shows the locations of major culture areas at the time Europeans reached the Americas. Refer to the map as you read about North American cultures.

Arctic and Subarctic The Arctic area was home to the Aleuts (AHL-ee-oots) and the Inuits (IN-oo-wits). Few in number, they lived in a vast and harsh land, some of it covered with ice all year long. The weather was too cold for farming, so people survived on fish, shellfish, birds, and marine mammals such as whales, seals, and walrus.

Arctic peoples lived in small family groups. Many were nomads, traveling to follow food. They had no organized governments, but lived by general rules. The most important rule was that everyone cooperate to survive. Their arts included music, storytelling, and ivory carving.

South of the Arctic region lay the dense forests of the Subarctic. With a climate too cold for farming, Subarctic peoples such as the Crees, Chipewyans (CHIP-uh-WĪ-uhns),

∞ Link to Technology

The Birchbark Canoe

The birchbark canoe originated among the Indians of the Great Lakes region, who used the canoes to glide along shallow rivers and creeks. When they needed to cross land, they simply lifted the lightweight canoes and carried them to the next waterway. The canoes were also easy to repair using materials from the forest—tree bark, spruce gum, and roots. When Europeans arrived in the region they quickly adopted this technology, allowing them to travel deep into the continent of North America.

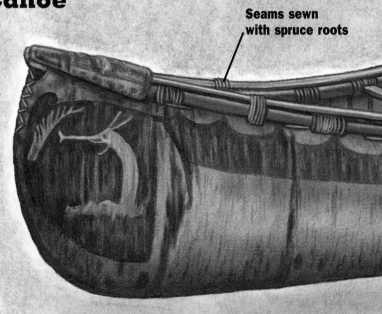

Seams sewn with spruce roots

and Kaskas relied on animals and plants of the forest for food. Most migrated to follow the caribou, and also hunted moose, bear, and smaller animals. They used bones and hides of animals to make sleds and snowshoes. They glided along the rivers and lakes in birchbark canoes.

Northwest Coast In the region of the Pacific Northwest, warm ocean currents swirled along the coast, creating a mild, moist climate. Deer and bears roamed forests rich with roots and berries. Rivers swarmed with salmon. With so much food available, people here were able to live in large, permanent settlements even though they were not farmers.

In this rich land, the Tlingits (TLING-gits), Kwakiutls (KWAH-kee-OOT-uhls), Chinooks (chi-NOOKS), Coos, and other tribes developed complex cultures. Skilled at carpentry, they built large wood-planked houses from the region's giant trees. They carved *totems*, large posts displaying the animal spirits of their clan. They also hollowed out 60-foot (18-m) canoes to travel to other seaside villages for trade and to follow schools of halibut and cod far out to sea.

These Pacific people enjoyed a life of wealth and comfort. One of their most interesting customs was the *potlatch*, meaning "to give away." A potlatch was a celebration of abundance at which the hosts showered their guests with gifts of food, woven cloth and baskets, canoes, and furs. A family's rank and status were judged by how much wealth it could give away.

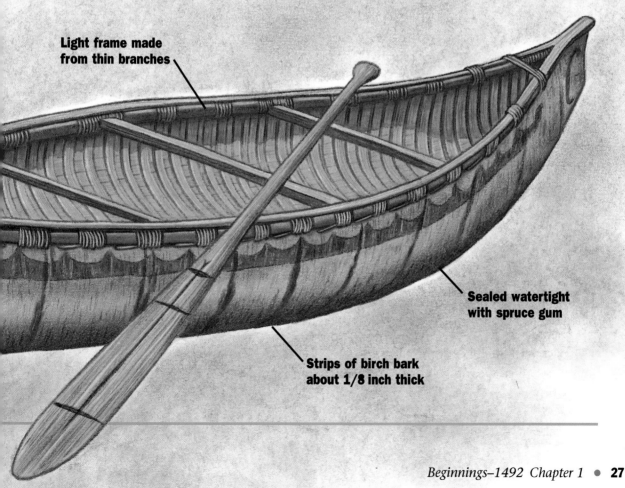

Light frame made from thin branches

Sealed watertight with spruce gum

Strips of birch bark about 1/8 inch thick

Far West The Far West included three culture areas: California, Plateau, and Great Basin. The Great Basin and parts of the Plateau area are mountainous and dry, which made farming difficult and life hard. The people of the Great Basin—the Paiutes (PĪ-yoots), Shoshones (shō-SHŌ-neez), and Utes (YOOTS)—traveled in small groups to find food. They gathered acorns, seeds, and roots, and caught fish, insects, and rodents.

In California, with its warm summers and mild winters, life was not so hard. Food was abundant. People there ate small game, fish, and berries. Oak trees grew nearly everywhere, and acorns were a main source of food for the Hupas, Pomos, Chumashes, and other semi-nomadic tribes.

Indians of the Far West are known for weaving some of the world's finest baskets. The baskets, used as tools and containers, are both beautiful and practical. Some were so watertight Indians used them to cook stew.

Plains Indians of the Plains culture area relied mainly on the buffalo (bison), for survival. In these dry grasslands, buffalo gave the Plains Indians meat for food, skins for blankets and cone-shaped shelters called *tepees*, and horn and bone for tools.

Following the great herds meant a nomadic way of life for tribes such as the Kiowas (KĪ-ō-wahz) and Comanches (kuh-MAN-cheez). Along the Missouri River the Mandans and Hidatsas (hi-DAH-tsuhz) settled in earth lodges and raised crops. Still, they hunted buffalo every spring after planting and every autumn after harvest.

Plains Indians hunted buffalo on foot, for there were no horses in the Americas at that time. Their clever hunting methods included stampeding buffalo over cliffs and trapping them in ice at winter waterholes. There the hunters could kill the beasts with spears and arrows. Women and children did the butchering.

Once Plains tribes such as the Sioux, Cheyenne, and Comanche obtained horses, which came to America after Columbus, they became mighty enemies of the Europeans who later invaded their homeland.

Eastern Woodlands The many Indian groups in the large Eastern Woodlands region lived on the rich resources of the forests and coasts. They gathered wild plants and mollusks and hunted bears and deer as well as small animals such as rabbits, squirrels, birds, and turtles.

Still, farming provided the staples of the Eastern Indians' diet—corn, beans, and squash. Men cleared trees to make fields, probably using fire. Women planted, tended, and harvested the crops. If nutrients in the soil got used up after 10 or 20 years, the group would move its village a few miles and clear new fields. They built their houses from thin saplings, covering the frame with bark, animal hides, or mats made of plant fibers.

Eastern villages were often surrounded by tall fences to keep out wild animals and human enemies. War was fairly common, especially among the Iroquoian (IR-uh-KWOY-uhn) and Algonquian (al-GAHN-kee-uhn) groups in the Northeast. Algonquians such as the Narragansetts, Algonkins, Massachusets, and Delawares, and Iroquoians such as the Mohawks, Eries, Iroquois, and Hurons were among the first Indians to meet European explorers and settlers.

Southwest Indians of the dry Southwest culture area adapted to the environment much as the earlier Anasazis had. All the groups in the area did some farming, although certain groups also moved to follow animals they hunted.

Pueblo Indians such as the Hopis (HŌ-peez) and Zunis (ZOO-neez) had stable towns that lasted for hundreds of years. While the Pueblo Indians themselves were

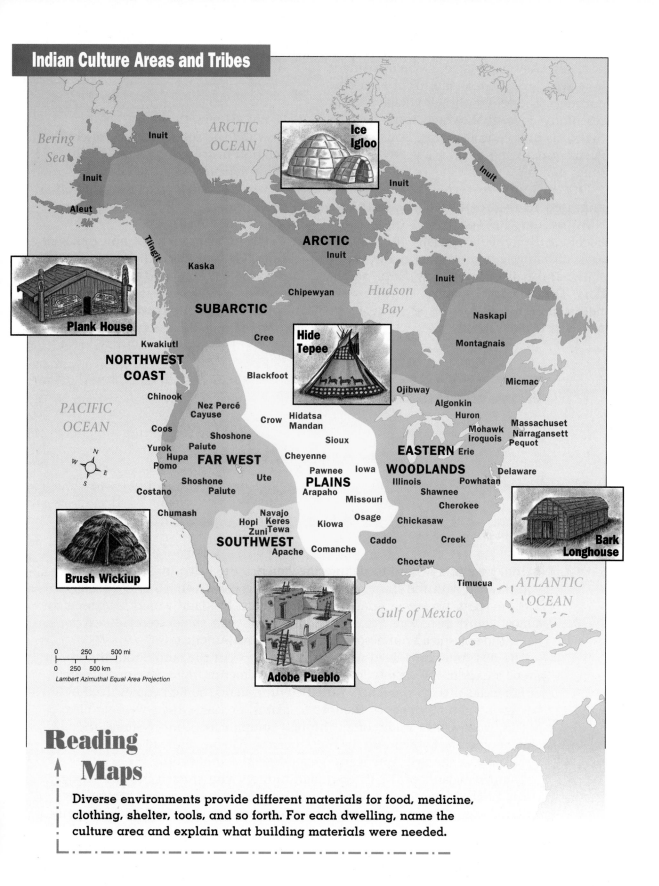

Indian Culture Areas and Tribes

Ice Igloo

Plank House

Hide Tepee

Brush Wickiup

Bark Longhouse

Adobe Pueblo

Bering Sea

ARCTIC OCEAN

Inuit
Inuit
Aleut
Tlingit
Kaska
Chipewyan

ARCTIC
Inuit

Hudson Bay

Inuit
Inuit

Naskapi
Montagnais
Micmac

SUBARCTIC
Cree

Kwakiutl
NORTHWEST COAST
Chinook
Coos
Yurok
Hupa
Pomo
Costano
Chumash

Blackfoot
Nez Percé
Cayuse
Crow
Shoshone
Paiute
FAR WEST
Shoshone
Ute
Paiute

Hidatsa
Mandan
Sioux
Cheyenne
Pawnee
Iowa
PLAINS
Arapaho
Missouri
Kiowa
Osage
Comanche
Caddo

Ojibway
Algonkin
Huron
Mohawk
Iroquois
Erie
Delaware
Powhatan
Illinois
Shawnee
Cherokee
Chickasaw
Creek
Choctaw
Timucua

EASTERN WOODLANDS

Massachuset
Narragansett
Pequot

PACIFIC OCEAN

Navajo
Hopi
Keres
Zuni
Tewa
SOUTHWEST
Apache

ATLANTIC OCEAN

Gulf of Mexico

N W E S

0   250   500 mi
0 250 500 km
Lambert Azimuthal Equal Area Projection

Reading Maps

Diverse environments provide different materials for food, medicine, clothing, shelter, tools, and so forth. For each dwelling, name the culture area and explain what building materials were needed.

peaceful, they built large adobe apartment houses to give them shelter from attack by outsiders. The center of their village life was ceremony and ritual, which took place in the kivas and central plazas. Today, some Pueblo groups still practice a yearly cycle of ritual drama.

Other Southwestern Indian groups migrated to the region. While both the Navajos and the Apaches at first raided Pueblo settlements, eventually the Navajos took up farming and adapted many crafts, skills, and beliefs from their Hopi neighbors. The nomadic Apaches continued to raid neighboring groups and came to be feared as fierce warriors.

4. Section Review

1. Define **diversity.**
2. How did the supply of food affect the population distribution of Indians in North America?
3. In what ways did the way of life of different Indian groups reflect the region in which they lived?
4. Critical Thinking At one archaeological site bits of pottery, the foundation of a large stone building, and traces of an irrigation canal have been found. Would you hypothesize that the people who lived here were nomadic or settled? Explain.

Why We Remember

The First Americans

Today we find it hard to picture the America the Paleo-Indians knew. Had you traveled with the stone seekers, you would have seen no paved roads, no cars, no signs, no power lines, no tall buildings. The land would have seemed almost empty of people. Yet over thousands of years the descendants of the Paleo-Indians spread out across North and South America.

The first Americans lived well on the resources of the land. From the frozen Arctic shores to the steamy lowlands of Mesoamerica, they developed ways of life well-suited to the land's varied environments. Some peoples lived by harvesting natural riches of the forests, plains, or seas. Others were farmers. Making good use of water, often through complex irrigation systems, they grew food crops known only in the Americas. As you will read, these foods were some of the first Americans' greatest gifts to the world.

The descendants of the Paleo-Indian hunters who crossed the land bridge created rich cultures and splendid civilizations. Many of these cultures have endured over thousands of years. We remember the first Americans not only because they shaped the history of the Americas for countless centuries, but also because their cultures still help define what it means to be an American.

Skill Lab

Skill Tips

Keep in mind:

• Begin and end both of your parallel time lines with the same dates.

• Divide the time lines into equal units of time. (But see the next skill tip.)

• If the time lines cover a very long period of time, use jagged lines to show that a particular time span has been left out.

Acquiring Information
Time Lines

One group built dwellings of stone and clay along the sides of cliffs. Another created a city—complete with markets, temples, and an emperor's palace—on an island in the middle of a lake. Only a thousand miles and a few hundred years separated the Anasazis and the Aztecs. Yet their cultures, like others throughout the Americas, differed greatly.

Question to Investigate

How did some early American cultures differ in their development?

Procedure

One way to compare developments in different cultures is by using **time lines.** A time line is a chart that shows when, and in what order, events occurred in the past. Two or more time lines that cover the same time span but different sets of events are called **parallel time lines.**

❶ With **B** as a model, make two parallel time lines. Refer to **A, B,** and **C** for events.

❷ Look for similarities and differences. Write three summary statements, such as "__ was made in South America before it was made in North America."

❸ For each summary statement, write down two questions that it raises in your mind. For example, "Did people in __ learn about __ from people in __?"

❹ For each question you wrote, tell what else you would need to know in order to answer it. Explain why you cannot answer it just from the information on the time line.

Data to Use

A Make a list of the events and their dates given in the chapter time line and throughout Chapter 1.

B

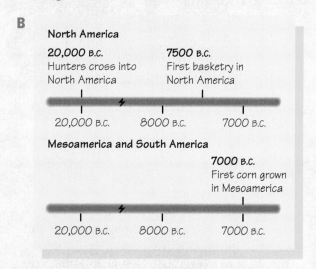

North America

20,000 B.C.
Hunters cross into North America

7500 B.C.
First basketry in North America

20,000 B.C.   8000 B.C.   7000 B.C.

Mesoamerica and South America

7000 B.C.
First corn grown in Mesoamerica

20,000 B.C.   8000 B.C.   7000 B.C.

C Additional Events and Dates

3150 B.C. First pottery in South America

2000 First pottery in North America

2000 First potatoes grown in South America

1500 First metalwork in South America

A.D. 750 Pueblos built in North America

800 First use of bow and arrow in North America

1000 First use of bow and arrow in Mesoamerica

Chapter Survey

Reviewing Vocabulary

Define the following terms.
1. migration
2. glaciers
3. nomads
4. culture
5. civilization
6. tribute
7. irrigation
8. diversity

Reviewing Main Ideas

1. Why did the ancestors of the Paleo-Indians travel across Beringia?
2. How did farming make each of the following possible? (a) larger populations (b) people specializing in one kind of work (c) development of trade
3. Tell one way historians know that some early groups carried on trade with other groups. Give an example of such trade.
4. Describe one achievement of Meso-american civilizations in each of the following areas. (a) science (b) agriculture (c) architecture. Identify the civilization in each case.
5. How did the Mogollons and the Hohokams get the most benefit from the small amount of water available to them?
6. How were the cultures of the Adenas, Hopewells, and Mississippians similar? How were they different?
7. For each of the following groups, explain how the environment affected the way the group obtained food. (a) Inuits (b) Chinooks (c) Shoshones (d) Comanches (e) Iroquois

Thinking Critically

1. Analysis Why is it so difficult to know for sure when people first came to live in the Americas? What different scientists might need to work together to help determine human origins in the Americas?
2. Analysis List three differences between most North American cultures and those of Mesoamerica and Peru around 1500. Why do you think the differences developed?
3. Why We Remember: Synthesis The "Why We Remember" on page 30 explains why we study the lives of the first Americans. State one reason in your own words and give three supporting examples from the text or your own observations.

Applying Skills

Creating time lines Use what you learned on page 31 and work with your family to create parallel time lines. Show (1) major events in the United States and (2) important events in your family during a certain time period, such as the last fifty years. Does there seem to be a relationship between major events and events in your family? If so, describe the relationship. If not, tell why you think there is no obvious relationship.

History Mystery

The Great Serpent Mound The reasons for building the Great Serpent Mound shown on page 7 and the meaning of the design remain a mystery. While some mounds were burial sites, no burial remains have been found within this mound. The age of the mound is also unknown, though scholars believe it to be Adena. Why do you think people who could not view the mound from the air created the structure?

Writing in Your History Journal

1. Keys to History (a) The time line on pages 6–7 has seven Keys to History. In your journal, list each key and describe why it is important to know about. (b) Look back over the chapter and find other important places,

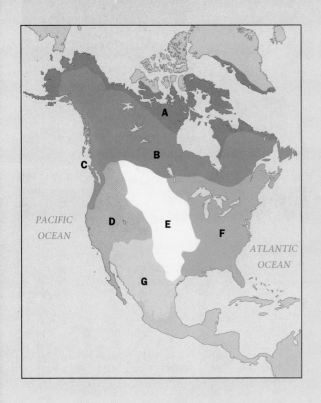

PACIFIC OCEAN

ATLANTIC OCEAN

A

B

C

D

E

F

G

Reviewing Geography

1. For each letter on the map, write the name of the culture area and the name of one tribe that lived in that culture area around 1500.

2. Geographic Thinking Natural settings affect the way people live. For example, people who live in the Arctic dress differently from people who live in deserts. However, people also affect their natural settings. Identify two examples of changes that Indians made in their natural settings. Tell who the Indian groups were and why they made the changes. Then give two examples of how people have changed the natural setting where you live.

groups, or ideas. Add them to the list in your journal, along with why you think they are important to remember.

2. The Stone Seekers The story on pages 8 and 9 gives one explanation of how the spear points from an ancient quarry in Wyoming might have ended up in New Mexico—over 200 miles (320 km) away. In your journal, write your own short story explaining how the stone might have traveled such a long distance.

3. Citizenship Suppose a person finds an ancient artifact or bone in his or her backyard. Does the person have the right to keep it? Should the person turn it over to a museum, the government, or some other authority? Does it make a difference if the person finds the item on public property, such as at a park, or on his or her own property? Write your responses in your journal, and explain why you feel as you do.

Alternative Assessment

Preparing a museum exhibit Imagine that your class is the staff of a history museum planning a new wing called "The First Americans." With a group of other staff members, prepare an exhibit on one of the cultures or civilizations described in the chapter. Your exhibit might include artifacts, drawings, models, and audiotapes, as well as written material like labels and captions. Start with the information in the chapter and do additional research as needed to make the culture or civilization come alive for museum visitors.

Your exhibit will be evaluated on whether:
• it shows such aspects of the culture or civilization as daily life, interaction with the environment, and achievements
• it provides information that is accurate
• it presents the information in clear, inviting ways

Chapter 2

Africa, Asia, and Europe in the 1400s

Keys to History

476
Fall of the Roman Empire
Bronze statue of Roman soldier

1095
Crusades begin
Battle between Christians and Muslims

400   *1000*

Looking Back

Land bridge disappears
8000 B.C.

World **Link**

Polynesians arrive in Hawaii
A.D. 400

HISTORY *Mystery*

In the early 1400s China had the world's greatest sailing fleet, commanded by Admiral Zheng He. By the early 1500s few Chinese ships sailed the seas. What happened to the Chinese navy? (In Chapter 2 you will learn more about this History Mystery.)

Photo from Louise Levathes' *When China Ruled the Seas* (1994)

1271
Marco Polo travels to China

1324
Mansa Musa's journey from Mali to Mecca

1419
Prince Henry's ships start to explore West African coast

1460s
Songhai is the most powerful trading empire in West Africa

1250

1460

Looking Ahead

Vasco da Gama sails around Africa to India
1498

● **35**

Beginning the Story with

Prince Henry the Navigator

On March 4, 1394, Queen Philippa of Portugal gave birth to her third son, Prince Henry. At the time Henry was born, Europeans had little contact with Asia and Africa. They were completely isolated from North and South America. No one in Europe even suspected that these continents existed.

As Queen Philippa held her son, she could not have dreamed that he would grow up to help lead Europe out of its isolation. She might have found a clue to Henry's future, though, in his horoscope. It predicted that her son was "bound to attempt the discovery of things which were hidden from other men and secret."

The Young Conqueror

Prince Henry grew up to be a serious, deeply religious young man. He had no interest in politics. Instead, he spent his time learning about military matters and studying mathematics and astronomy. Henry was also very curious about the world beyond Europe. He read everything he could find about distant lands, trying to sort out fact from legend.

As a young man, Henry helped his father, King John I, plan a raid on the North African trading town of Ceuta (SYOOT-ah). Located on the Strait of Gibraltar, which connects the Mediterranean Sea and the Atlantic Ocean, Ceuta was a natural meeting point for African, Arab, and European traders. Both father and son agreed that Ceuta would be a rich prize indeed. As they laid their plans, Henry pleaded, "When God pleases that we arrive at Ceuta, let me be among the first to embark."

King John granted his son's wish. In 1415 Prince Henry led the way when Portuguese troops stormed and captured Ceuta. The young conqueror was amazed by the wealth that he found there. He saw houses and shops filled with Oriental rugs, gold and silver coins, precious jewels, and sacks of cinnamon, pepper, and other spices.

The gold, Henry learned, came from West Africa. Many of the other goods came from "the Indies," as Europeans called the Asian lands of India and China and the islands off the Asian mainland. After seeing Ceuta, Henry began to dream of the wealth that would pour into Portugal if only it could trade directly with these distant lands.

The prince knew that all land routes to Africa and Asia were controlled by Arab traders, so he looked to the sea. If Portuguese traders could reach Africa and Asia by sea, they could bypass the Arabs completely.

The flags on this Portuguese map, made in 1502, show Portugal's successful efforts to find a sea route to Africa and explore its coasts.

The Navigator

Back home in Portugal, Prince Henry turned to making his dream a reality. Around 1419 he began by sending ships out to explore the west coast of Africa and establish trade for gold. The prince never joined these voyages, but because he set their course, he was nicknamed "the Navigator."

The greatest challenge facing Prince Henry was fear of the unknown. Most European sailors were deathly afraid of sailing far from familiar waters. In their minds, the Atlantic Ocean was a mysterious "Green Sea of Darkness."

Henry ignored such fears. As his ships prepared to leave for Africa, he advised his captains to record everything they saw. When the ships returned, Henry listened carefully to his captains' reports and then gave new orders. "Go back," he always said. "Go back, and go still farther."

The voyages begun by Henry would eventually lead European explorers to the Americas. However, Henry did not act alone. People and events in Africa, Asia, and the rest of Europe set the stage for his voyages. This chapter gives you a picture of those peoples and events, bringing the story up to the mid-1400s.

Hands-On HISTORY

Activity

The sailors sent out by Prince Henry had heard many tales about the "Green Sea of Darkness." There were stories of giant sea snakes that fed on ships, whirlpools strong enough to sink ships, and winds fierce enough to push ships to the ends of the earth. Imagine that you are a sailor on one of Henry's ships as it enters unexplored waters. Write a diary entry describing your greatest fear.

1. Trading Empires of Africa

Reading Guide

Section Focus Africa's links with the world in the 1400s

1. What trade links existed between Africa, the Middle East, and Asia?
2. What supported the wealthy empires of Ghana, Mali, and Songhai?
3. What ways of life did most West Africans share?

In the mid-1430s two of Prince Henry's sea captains sailing south along the coast of West Africa found footprints of men and camels in the sand. Hearing the news, Henry quickly ordered the captains to

"go as far as you can, and try to bring news of these people. . . . To me it would be no small thing to have some man to tell me of this land!"

As you will read in Section 3, much of Europe had been isolated from the rest of the world for hundreds of years. Thus, the continent of Africa was a land of mystery to Henry, as to most Europeans.

In fact, in the 1400s Africa was home to flourishing cultures and civilizations that had long been linked by trade to the Middle East, India, and China. Now, African peoples and African goods were to play an important role in arousing European interest in the resources of the rest of the world.

A Long History of Trade

Africans have a long history of trade, going back as far as 3100 B.C., when the great civilization of Egypt arose. Archaeologists have learned much about this trade from records, artifacts, and scenes of daily life painted on walls.

Egyptian traders sailed throughout the eastern Mediterranean Sea and the Red Sea to bring home cedar logs, silver, and horses. Following land routes south from Egypt, they found ivory, spices, copper, and cattle. For these goods, Egyptians traded gold, wheat, and papyrus, a kind of paper made from reed plants.

South of Egypt rose another ancient civilization called Kush that was a trading power by 250 B.C. The Kushites traded not only in Africa but also in Arabia, India, and China. They also learned how to use iron to make tools and weapons. Archaeologists have found heaps of ironworking waste in their capital city, Meroë. It was a great ironworking center and a crossroads for trade.

East African Trade

About A.D. 1000, trade centers began to appear in eastern Africa. The most powerful was Zimbabwe (zim-BAH-bway), which became the center of a flourishing empire in the 1400s.

Zimbabwe traders took gold, ivory, and precious stones to east coast seaports. From there, Arab and Indian ships carried the goods to Asia. The ships returned with porcelain (china), spices, cloth, and jewels from China and India.

This trade brought prosperity to East African seaports. Kilwa, the chief trading center, was one of the most beautiful cities in the world. Houses were built of stone and coral, and gardens flourished everywhere.

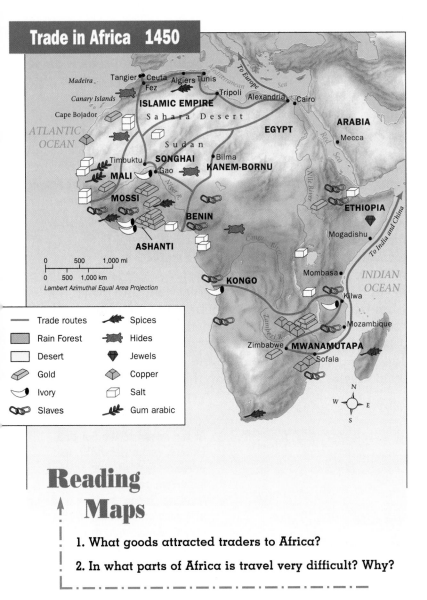

Trade in Africa 1450

Madeira
Tangier • Ceuta • Algiers Tunis
Fez • Tripoli
Canary Islands • Alexandria • Cairo
ISLAMIC EMPIRE
Cape Bojador
S a h a r a   D e s e r t
ATLANTIC OCEAN
ARABIA
EGYPT
• Mecca
S u d a n
Timbuktu SONGHAI • Bilma
• Gao KANEM-BORNU
MALI
Niger R.
MOSSI
BENIN
ETHIOPIA
Congo River
ASHANTI
Mogadishu •
To India and China
KONGO
Mombasa •
INDIAN OCEAN
Kilwa •
Zambezi R.
• Mozambique
Zimbabwe • MWANAMUTAPA
• Sofala

0   500   1,000 mi
0   500 1,000 km
Lambert Azimuthal Equal Area Projection

— Trade routes
▨ Rain Forest
▢ Desert
▱ Gold
◡ Ivory
∞ Slaves
✦ Spices
⊷ Hides
◆ Jewels
◇ Copper
▢ Salt
✿ Gum arabic

N W E S

Reading Maps

1. What goods attracted traders to Africa?

2. In what parts of Africa is travel very difficult? Why?

Western Trading Empires

Trading empires also appeared in the Sudan, a broad belt of open country sandwiched between the Sahara Desert and the rain forests of West Africa. The most powerful were the empires of Ghana, Mali, and Songhai.

The wealth of these empires came from the gold and salt trade. Parts of West Africa had huge deposits of gold but were desperate for salt. Yet to the north, in the Sahara, salt was so common that people used blocks of it to build houses.

North African caravans crossed the Sahara Desert, carrying salt as well as sugar, grain, and cloth. Merchants traded these goods in the Sudan for gold, ivory, spices, and other products from West Africa. By taxing the trade, rulers in the Sudan became rich.

Ghana Ghana, which took control of this trade in the 400s, became the first great empire of West Africa. The Spanish-Arab geographer al-Bakri wrote of King Tenkamenin of Ghana:

❝He sits in a pavilion around which stand ten horses with gold embroidered trappings. Behind the king stand ten pages holding shields and gold-mounted swords. . . . The door of the pavilion is guarded by dogs . . . who wear collars of gold.❞

The spread of Islam Followers of a new religion called Islam joined caravans from North Africa. Islam began in Arabia in the early 600s with the Prophet Muhammad. By the mid-700s his followers, called Muslims, had conquered the Middle East, parts of Asia, North Africa, and Spain. Throughout this vast Islamic Empire, people of different cultures converted to the new faith.

Muslim traders brought their faith across the Sahara. Soon African ruling families and merchants were converting to Islam.

Through Muslim traders, West African gold spread throughout the Islamic Empire and to Europe, which was running out of precious metals. Soon much of the gold used to make European and Islamic coins came from West Africa.

Mali and Songhai In the mid-1200s a new kingdom called Mali took control of the gold and salt trade. Its rulers adopted Islam and spread the faith to many people.

Mali's greatest emperor was Mansa Musa (MAHN-sah MOO-sah), a devout Muslim. Under his rule, Timbuktu, the capital, became a center of learning for students and scholars from across the Muslim world.

In 1324 Mansa Musa made a spectacular journey to Mecca, a holy city of Islam. With him he took 60,000 men, including 500 slaves. Each slave carried a bar of gold weigh-ing about four pounds. News of the trip spread even to Europe. Europeans were so impressed with Mansa Musa's wealth that they pictured him on a map of Africa.

By the mid-1400s, when Prince Henry's ships were sailing along the West African coast, Songhai (SONG-hī) had replaced Mali as the largest and most powerful trading empire in West Africa. Within 50 years, it would control the gold and salt trade in a region larger than all of western Europe.

The Slave Trade

Along with gold, salt, and ivory, slaves were of value in trading centers like Songhai. Most African kingdoms, like those in ancient civilizations the world over, had long used slaves to do some of the labor. Prisoners of war, criminals, and people who could not

At the height of the Songhai Empire, Jenne (jeh-NAY), in present-day Mali, was an important center of trade and learning. Today, bustling trade still goes on in Jenne. In this recent photograph, people gather at a weekly market to buy and sell local products as well as products from other countries.

pay their debts were often sold into slavery. While visiting a West African city, an Arab traveler known as Leo Africanus wrote:

"There is a place where they sell countless . . . slaves on market days. A fifteen-year-old girl is worth about six ducats and a young man nearly as much; little children and aged slaves are worth about half that sum."

Around the 1100s the slave trade began to grow. More and more Muslim traders were coming into Africa, buying enslaved Africans, and selling them throughout the Islamic Empire.

Later the Portuguese and other Europeans would also find profit in the slave trade. As you will read in Chapter 6, millions of West Africans were to be taken across the Atlantic and sold as slaves. These peoples would play a vital part in creating and enriching new cultures in the Americas.

West African Life

When Prince Henry's mariners finally reached West Africa, they met a bewildering mixture of peoples and languages. Despite the differences, however, West Africans had much in common.

Most West Africans made their living by farming. Farmland was so valued that it belonged to the village, not to individuals. As a local chief explained, the land in his village belonged to "a vast family, of which many are dead, few are living, and countless members are unborn." As members of a village "family," West Africans put social harmony and the needs of the community above personal concerns.

Religion Although some West Africans had converted to Islam by the time the Portuguese arrived, most still followed their traditional religions. They believed that the world had been created by a single High God. Beneath this deity stood lesser gods who controlled daily life. These were the gods West Africans prayed to for rain, a good harvest, or a cure from disease.

West Africans believed that the dead become spirits. They treated the spirits of the dead with great respect. In return, they hoped the spirits would bless the living.

The arts Most West African art had a religious purpose. Sculptors created carved masks representing the gods. When people wore these masks at religious ceremonies, it was believed that the power of the gods flowed through them.

Dance was also an important part of West African ceremonies. People danced to the complex music of drums, which wove together many rhythms at once. They heard each rhythm as a distinct pattern and then chose one to follow with their feet.

Storytelling was another important art. West Africans used stories to teach the young about their religion and history. Many tales featured the trickster, a character who used cunning to outwit others, even the High God.

West Africans valued poetry and the art of public speaking. They recited poems to honor the gods and praise great deeds. They chanted work poems, or songs, to make hard jobs easier. Good speakers were greatly admired for their ability to inspire, teach, and entertain with well-chosen words.

Roots of African American Culture

The West Africans who were brought to the Americas as slaves were forced to give up much of their way of life. Elements of their culture, however, survived and even thrived on this side of the Atlantic.

Three court musicians play the drums in the court of the Oba, or king, of Benin.

The mother of the king of Benin had a great responsibility— she taught the king's heir how to rule.

These statues show messengers who traveled to Benin from the nearby city of Ife (EE-feh).

Link to Art

Benin bronze Bronze heads made in the kingdom of Benin (beh-NEEN) in West Africa are among the finest statues ever made. In the 1400s Benin sculptors produced these statues for their kings by lost-wax casting. In this difficult process, molds were shaped from soft wax, coated with damp clay, and heated. The heat hardened the clay mold and melted out—or "lost"—the wax. Molten bronze, poured into the mold, hardened to form the statues. **Discuss** Suggest some reasons why kings might have wanted the statues. What do the statues tell us about civilization in Benin?

African religious beliefs, for example, are still followed in many parts of the Americas. African rhythms can be heard in styles of American music ranging from Dixieland jazz to Delta blues and from rock and roll to reggae. Many of our most inspiring public speakers—leaders such as Martin Luther King, Jr., Marian Wright Edelman, and Jesse Jackson—have drawn on a tradition that places great value on the power of the spoken word.

1. Section Review

1. What did East Africans and Asians trade?
2. How did trade create the empires of Ghana, Mali, and Songhai?
3. Critical Thinking A West African chief said the land in his village belonged to "a vast family, of which many are dead, few are living, and countless members are unborn." What do you think he meant?

Skill Lab

Acquiring Information
Reading History

Skill Tips

Reading history is a two-step process:
- First read to answer *who*, *what*, and *where* questions.
- Then read with imagination to answer *why* and *how* questions, putting yourself in the place of people of the past.
- Be sure your imagination is grounded in reality.

"These [Muslims] have many horses, which they trade and take to the land of the Blacks, exchanging them with the rulers for slaves. Ten or fifteen slaves are usually given for one of these horses, according to their quality."

So wrote one of the first Portuguese travelers in West Africa in the 1400s. The Europeans soon greatly expanded the slave trade in Africa, but slavery itself was common there long before their arrival.

Question to Investigate

Why did Africans practice slavery?

Procedure

Often the most interesting questions in history are not *what, who,* and *where* but rather *why* and *how*. Why did people of the past act, believe, or think as they did? How did they live? Such questions are hard to answer because we cannot simply ask the people involved. Instead we have to use our imaginations as we read. To explore the Question to Investigate, read sources **A** and **B**.

1 Look first for factual information.
a. Who were the slaves? In what places did slavery exist?
b. What kept slavery growing?

2 Reread the sources with imagination to explore *why* and *how* questions.
a. Imagine you were an African ruler who allowed slavery. Write a paragraph explaining your views on the slave trade.
b. Imagine you were a Muslim slave trader. Write a paragraph describing why you bought slaves.

Sources to Use

A Reread "The Slave Trade" on page 40.

B "At Benin [people objected to] the enslavement of the natives of the country—of men and women, that is, who were within the protection of the Oba of Benin, a monarch whose power derived from God. By custom and by moral law, [they said,] slaves ought to be men and women captured from neighboring peoples. They ought to be 'outsiders,' 'unbelievers.' This rule was often broken."

From Basil Davidson, *Black Mother: The Years of the African Slave Trade* (Little, Brown, 1961)

3 Historians sometimes combine factual information with interpretations. Good historians let the reader know when they are imagining. Answer the Question to Investigate by combining facts and imagination.

4 Think about the benefits and risks in reading history imaginatively.
a. Describe one benefit.
b. Describe one risk.

2. The Wealth of Asia

Reading Guide

New Term navigation

Section Focus **Asia's links with the world in the 1400s**

1. How did trade goods travel across Asia and from Asia to Africa and Europe?
2. What Asian ideas and inventions had a great impact on the world?
3. What enabled China to be the most powerful country in the world in the 1400s?

One of the books that inspired Prince Henry's interest in exploration was written by an Italian traveler named Marco Polo. In 1271 the 17-year-old Polo had crossed Asia to China with his father and uncle. They returned 24 years later with a fortune in jewels.

Polo's book about their adventures, *Description of the World*, is filled with amazing stories. In one he describes a day at the court of the Great Khan, China's ruler:

"On this day the Great Khan receives gifts of more than 100,000 white horses, of great beauty and price. And on this day also there is a procession of his elephants, fully 5,000 in number. . . . Each one bears on its back two strong-boxes . . . filled with the Khan's plate [dishes of silver or gold].**"**

Europeans, who knew almost nothing about the civilizations of Asia, found such tales hard to believe. Still, the hope of finding lands rich in gold, silver, jewels, fine cloth, and spices drew them eastward like a magnet.

This picture shows Italian merchants trading bolts of cloth for products of Asia. It was an illustration in Marco Polo's book *Description of the World.* Completed in 1298, the book awakened European interest in Asia.

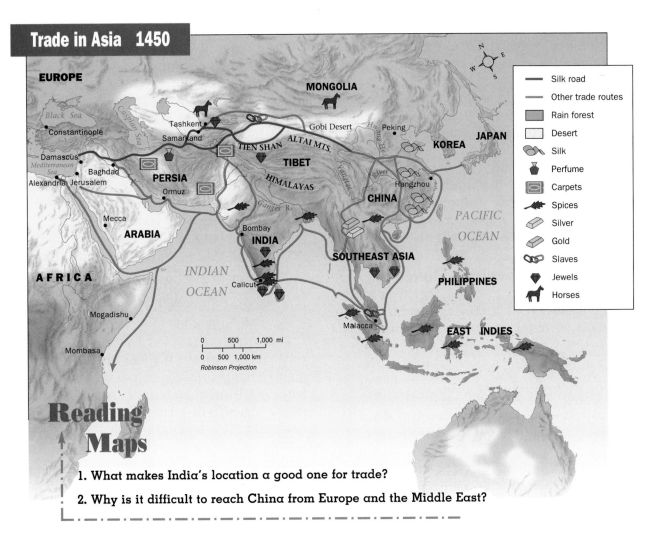

Trade in Asia 1450

Silk road	
Other trade routes	
Rain forest	
Desert	
Silk	
Perfume	
Carpets	
Spices	
Silver	
Gold	
Slaves	
Jewels	
Horses	

EUROPE

Black Sea
Constantinople

MONGOLIA

Gobi Desert   Peking

Tashkent   ALTAI MTS.   KOREA   JAPAN

Samarkand   TIEN SHAN

Damascus   TIBET

Baghdad   HIMALAYAS   Hangzhou

Alexandria Jerusalem   PERSIA

Ormuz   CHINA

Ganges R.   PACIFIC OCEAN

Mecca

ARABIA   Bombay

INDIA

AFRICA   INDIAN OCEAN   Calicut

SOUTHEAST ASIA

PHILIPPINES

Mogadishu

Malacca   EAST INDIES

Mombasa

0   500   1,000 mi
0   500   1,000 km
Robinson Projection

Reading Maps

1. **What makes India's location a good one for trade?**

2. **Why is it difficult to reach China from Europe and the Middle East?**

Trade in India

When the Polos were traveling in Asia, they had no idea of the history that lay behind the shimmering cities and bustling trade that they saw. As early as 2500 B.C., people in cities in India had well-planned roads and water systems with drains and sewers. At about a hundred sites, archaeologists have uncovered the ruins of these large ancient cities.

Archaeologists have also found evidence of widespread trade. Soapstone seals from India, which traders used to identify property or sign contracts, have been found in the ruins of Middle Eastern cities.

Hinduism and Buddhism Around 1500 B.C., people called Aryans invaded northern India. The Aryans dominated India for the next 2,000 years, spreading their language, customs, and religious ideas. Out of those ideas came two of the world's major religions. The first, Hinduism, became the major religion of India and remains so today. The second, Buddhism, spread across China, Korea, Japan, and Southeast Asia.

India in the 1400s By the 1400s Muslim armies had conquered much of India. Under Muslim rule, trade continued to flourish. Foreign merchants came to India to buy silk and cotton cloth, spices, jewels, perfumes, sugar, and rice. Their ships carried the wealth of India to eastern Africa and the Middle East.

Through trade, people discovered Indian ideas and inventions unknown to their own cultures. Often they adapted these to their own way of life. Indian mathematicians developed the decimal number system we use today, and it passed on to Arabs and then Europeans. Indian fairy tales, too, spread to Arabia and Europe. "Cinderella," for example, was originally an Indian story.

China, a Great Power

Northeast of India lay the largest and most powerful country in the world at that time—China. As early as 221 B.C., a strong ruler had unified China. Later rulers added to the empire until it covered a large part of the continent of Asia. Highways, canals, and a postal system linked it together.

Expanding trade As the Chinese empire expanded, so did its trade. China established trade links with India, Korea, Japan, the Middle East, and Africa.

Some Chinese trade goods began to reach Europe by about A.D. 100. Silk, bronze goods, pottery, and spices flowed west from China, as well as India, along a route known as the Silk Road. On the shores of the Mediterranean, Romans paid for these goods with glass, dyes, and gold.

Few traders traveled the entire 4,000 miles (6,400 km) of the Silk Road. Instead, goods changed hands at points along the way. A Chinese merchant, for example, might sell silk to a trader in central Asia, who sold it to a Persian dealer, who then sold it to a Roman merchant. With each exchange, the price went up.

As trade expanded, China's trade centers grew into cities. By the 1200s Hangzhou (HAN-JOW) was the world's largest city. Chinese cities had public carriages, street drains, coal for heat, and paper money—none of which were known to Europeans at that time.

New technology China also had a higher level of technology than any other civilization. Around 1050 the Chinese invented printing with movable type—some 400 years before this technology was developed in Europe.

Gunpowder was also a Chinese invention, used in fireworks as well as weapons. By the 1300s the Chinese had a cannon they could use on land and on their many warships at sea.

The Chinese made great advances in **navigation**—the science of getting ships

Silk was one of China's most prized items of trade. Here women unwind the delicate strands from silk-worm cocoons and form them into a long thread of raw silk.

As a result of Zheng He's voyages, foreign ambassadors came to China to pay tribute to the emperor. Ambassadors from Malindi on the coast of East Africa brought this giraffe.

from place to place. They invented the magnetic compass, which made it possible for ships to sail out of sight of land and still find their way home. This technology spread to Arab sailors, who passed it on to Europeans. The compass made it possible for European explorers to sail to the Americas and back.

The Chinese also developed a new kind of sailing ship called a junk. The largest junks had four decks and four to six masts, and could carry 500 sailors. Below deck were watertight compartments—not seen in European ships until much later—that helped keep the ship afloat.

By the 1300s Chinese junks were sailing trade routes that stretched from Japan to East Africa. These ships were not only reliable but also comfortable. Writing of his voyage on a four-decked junk, an Arab traveler described "cabins and saloons for merchants, . . . and garden herbs, vegetables, and ginger [growing] in wooden tubs."

The Voyages of Zheng He

In the early 1400s, when Prince Henry's sea captains were creeping down the West African coast, Chinese junks were sailing throughout the Indian Ocean. The great admiral Zheng He (JUNG HUH) assembled a fleet of more than 300 ships, with a total crew of 28,000 men, to visit other countries. The ships were part of the greatest navy in the world at that time.

Like later European voyagers, Zheng He's goal was to increase his country's wealth

World Link

Polynesian navigators More than 2,000 years before Zheng He's voyages, a seafaring people called Polynesians were sailing the Pacific. About A.D. 400 they reached the islands that today make up the state of Hawaii.

Polynesian navigators did not have maps or instruments. Instead, they used their knowledge of the sun, stars, winds, and ocean currents. They passed this knowledge from generation to generation in the form of chants.

For their journeys, the Polynesians built huge canoes with sails made of woven leaves. The canoes carried not only people but also plants and livestock—everything the Polynesians needed to survive in their new island homes.

and power by expanding trade. Between 1405 and 1433, he sailed to places as far away as India, Arabia, East Africa, and perhaps even Australia.

Zheng He fought pirates and unfriendly rulers to make China a major power in the Indian Ocean. He traded China's prized silks and porcelains for ivory, precious stones, spices, and medicines. He also brought back firsthand knowledge of distant lands.

Then, suddenly, the voyages stopped. After 1433 China began withdrawing its navy from the open seas. "Warships, no longer sent out to sea on patrols, were anchored in ports where they rotted from neglect," wrote the historian Lo Jung-pang. In 1525 the government ordered all ocean-going ships to be destroyed and the merchants who sailed them to be arrested.

Point of View

Why did the Chinese voyages stop?

Why did China withdraw from the seas? Louise Levathes, author of *When China Ruled the Seas,* sees part of the answer in a power struggle at court. Some officials favored China's foreign trade. They had gained wealth and power from it. Other officials believed that China did not need foreign trade. If they could stop the trade, they could also curb their rivals' power.

According to historian Levathes, the anti-trade officials created

❝a series of government restrictions limiting boat size and civilian participation in overseas trade. If court officials could not control . . . trade activities, at least they could impede [hinder] them.❞

Historian Paul Kennedy sees the threat of invasion as a reason for ending the voyages.

❝The northern frontiers of the empire were again under some pressure from the Mongols [enemies of the Chinese]. . . . Under such circumstances, a large navy was an expensive luxury.❞

What if Zheng He had continued his voyages? According to Kennedy, his ships "might well have been able to sail around Africa and 'discover' Portugal several decades before Henry the Navigator's voyages began earnestly to push south [along the West African coast]."

Asian Roots in America

It was not until the mid-1800s that Chinese began crossing the Pacific to seek new opportunities in the Kingdom of Hawaii and the United States. In the next 150 years, people from China as well as Japan, Korea, the Philippines, India, and elsewhere in Asia came to America.

Over the years, Asian immigrants have played vital roles in building the nation's railroads, working its mines, introducing new crops and farming methods, and expanding science and technology. The diverse cultures they have brought with them have also enriched American life.

2. Section Review

1. Define **navigation.**
2. What early trade links existed between Europe and Asia?
3. Give at least two examples of Asian ideas or inventions that spread to other parts of the world.
4. Critical Thinking How might the United States be different today if Chinese explorers had reached the Americas in the mid-1400s?

3. Europe Looks Outward

Reading Guide

New Terms **feudalism, colony**

Section Focus **Europeans' interest in new trade routes to Africa and Asia**

1. What happened in Europe after the fall of the Roman Empire?
2. How did the Crusades change life in Europe?
3. Why did Portugal take the lead in exploration?

As the Chinese withdrew from the seas in the 1400s, trade between Asia, Africa, and the Middle East was left mostly to Arab merchants. It would not be long, though, before Europeans—like Prince Henry—began to look for ways to bite off a piece of this rich trade.

Europeans, however, were in no position to challenge the Arabs for control of their trade routes. In the 1400s Europe was still relatively weak, emerging from centuries of hard times, unrest, and isolation.

Europe's Beginnings

Like Africa, Asia, and the Americas, Europe had seen the rise and fall of civilizations. The most powerful of these—the Roman Empire—ruled most of Europe, the Middle East, and northern Africa from 27 B.C. to A.D. 476.

The Romans not only unified this entire area under one rule but also brought peace to its many different peoples. Trade moved along a system of new roads linking all parts of the empire. Roman laws applied to all people.

Fall of the Roman Empire The Roman Empire collapsed in the 400s when invaders captured its towns and cities. Europe then split into many small, warring kingdoms. Law and order ended. Trade declined and almost disappeared. Cities everywhere shrank to towns, and towns gave way to fields.

Only manors—large estates owned by wealthy lords—survived. The lands of a manor were worked by peasants called serfs. The serfs were not free to leave the service of their lords. For their part, lords had to protect their serfs from attacks by bandits and foreign invaders.

In the 900s new invaders appeared. The most feared of all were sea raiders from

This stained-glass window shows a serf planting grain seeds by hand. The entire family took part in the production of food.

The appeal of spices Why were spices a driving force in European voyages of exploration? Spices did not just make food delicious. In the days before refrigeration, spices helped keep food from spoiling—and disguised the taste once spoilage occurred. They were also used as medicines.

In time, spices native to Asia came to be grown in other places, including the West Indies and South America. Today you can find the spices Europeans once prized in every grocery store.

Scandinavia called Vikings or Northmen. The Vikings looted and burned towns and killed or sold as slaves any people they captured. Across western Europe, frightened people prayed, "From the fury of the Northmen, Good Lord, deliver us!"

Feudalism A new system of government arose as people turned to their lords for protection against invaders. This system, known as **feudalism,** was based on agreements between a lord and his vassals. A lord might be a king or a wealthy landowner. A vassal was someone who promised to serve a lord in exchange for a grant of land.

The most important service vassals owed their lords was to fight for them. Under the feudal system, a lord could quickly pull together an army of his vassals to ward off Viking raiders or other enemies.

Life became more settled under feudalism. Serfs cleared forests to make more farmland and produce more crops. The growing food supply could feed more people. Between 1050 and 1300, Europe's population tripled. Trade expanded. Villages grew into towns, and towns into cities.

At the same time, feudalism divided Europe into thousands of small territories, each ruled by its own lord. When not fighting invaders, these lords often fought among themselves.

Europe Rises Out of Feudalism

The Christian religion was the one unifying force in European life. Christianity had begun in Palestine during the Roman Empire. This faith was based on the ideas of a Jewish teacher named Jesus. Christianity spread rapidly, and by feudal times the Roman Catholic Church had become the center of religious life in western Europe.

Europe's Christians called Palestine the Holy Land because it was there that Jesus had lived and died. For centuries, devout Christians had traveled to Palestine to visit holy shrines. Then in 1070 the Seljuk Turks, who were Muslims, took control of Palestine and closed it to Christian travelers.

The Crusades Pope Urban II, the head of the Catholic Church, was outraged by the Turks' actions. In 1095 he called on Europe's lords to stop fighting among themselves and unite to free the Holy Land from the Turks.

Thousands answered the pope's call. They sewed the symbol of their faith—the Christian cross—on their clothes and called themselves crusaders, from the Latin word *crux,* which means "cross." The crusaders marched off to war under the battle cry "God wills it."

For two centuries, armies of crusaders battled the Turks for Palestine. In the end, the Europeans failed in their mission.

New trade In Palestine, however, the crusaders were introduced to a new world of exotic goods from Asia—sugar, melons, lemons, fine silk and cotton cloth, perfumes,

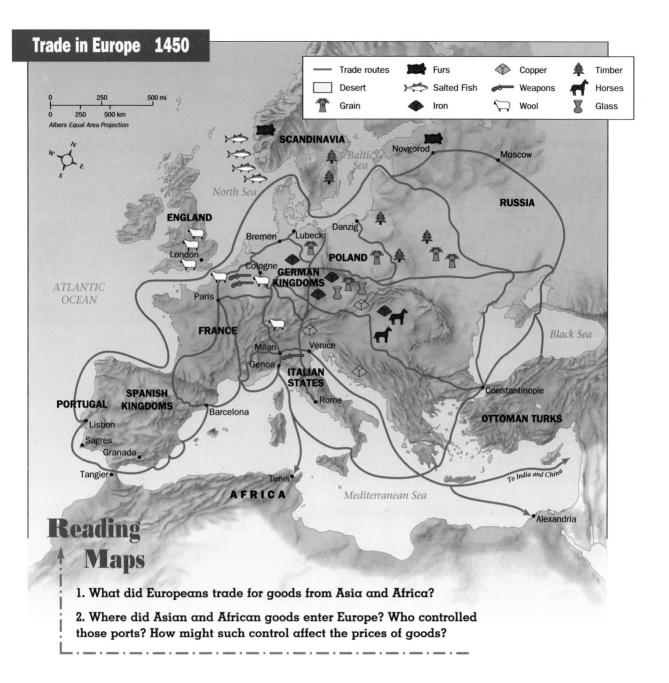

Trade in Europe 1450

Legend:
- —— Trade routes
- Desert
- Grain
- Furs
- Salted Fish
- Iron
- Copper
- Weapons
- Wool
- Timber
- Horses
- Glass

0   250   500 mi
0   250   500 km
Albers Equal Area Projection

SCANDINAVIA
Novgorod
Moscow
Baltic Sea
North Sea
RUSSIA
ENGLAND
Bremen
Lubeck
Danzig
London
Cologne
POLAND
GERMAN KINGDOMS
ATLANTIC OCEAN
Paris
FRANCE
Milan
Venice
Black Sea
Genoa
ITALIAN STATES
Rome
Constantinople
PORTUGAL
SPANISH KINGDOMS
Barcelona
OTTOMAN TURKS
Lisbon
Sagres
Granada
Tangier
Tunis
To India and China
AFRICA
Mediterranean Sea
Alexandria

Reading Maps

1. What did Europeans trade for goods from Asia and Africa?

2. Where did Asian and African goods enter Europe? Who controlled those ports? How might such control affect the prices of goods?

and spices. Europeans could not get enough of these wonderful new luxuries.

A brisk trade sprang up between Europe and the Middle East. Arab merchants sold spices, perfumes, and other goods to Italian traders from Venice and Genoa. The Italians then resold the goods at high prices to merchants in other parts of Europe.

Western European merchants resented the high prices. Some dreamed of cutting their costs by trading directly with Africa and Asia. Since Arabs controlled existing trade routes, the only hope was to find a new sea route to those distant lands. Such an undertaking, however, would need the support of a strong and ambitious ruler.

Hands-On *HISTORY*

A printing shop in the 1500s

The rise of nations Under feudalism, Europe's rulers were no stronger than the lords they were supposed to rule. The Crusades, however, helped to break down feudalism. While many lords were fighting in Palestine, kings took advantage of their absence to increase their power.

Gradually, a few kings were able to unify large areas under their rule, creating nations. By the early 1400s there were three nations in western Europe: England, France, and Portugal.

The rulers of these new nations envied the wealth that poured into Venice and Genoa. They saw that they could increase their wealth and power by expanding trade. Like the merchants, they wanted to find a water route to the trade of Asia and the gold of Africa.

The Renaissance Interest in finding other routes to Asia and Africa occurred at a time when Europeans were more and more curious about the world around them. They wanted to explore nature, the arts, ancient cultures, and distant lands. These new attitudes were part of the Renaissance—the rebirth—that Europeans experienced between the 1300s and the 1500s.

Portugal Leads the Way

The Renaissance, the rise of nations, merchants' dreams of new trade and sources of gold—all these forces set the stage for an era of exploration. Only leadership and know-how were missing.

Prince Henry supplied both. He had great curiosity about the world and was determined to succeed. A deeply religious man, he hoped not only to expand Portuguese power but also to spread Christianity to new lands.

Of the three nations in Europe, only Portugal was in a position to begin seeking new sea routes. France and England were locked in a war that would last until the mid-1400s. Portugal was at peace. The Portuguese were also a seafaring people.

A center for exploration Henry set up a center for exploration at Sagres (SAH-greesh) in southern Portugal. He brought mathematicians, geographers, and sea captains to this center to teach his crews everything they knew about navigation and maps. It was here that the Portuguese prince earned the name Henry the Navigator.

At Sagres, sailors learned how to use the magnetic compass—which Arab seamen had brought to Europe from China—to find their direction at sea. They also learned how to use an instrument called the astrolabe to determine their precise latitude, which means distance from the equator.

Henry's shipbuilders developed a new kind of European ship called the caravel. The caravel carried two kinds of sails—one square, one triangular—so that it could sail into the wind as well as with the wind. The new ship gave Henry's crews confidence to venture far from Portugal, knowing that they could turn around and come home no matter which way the wind blew.

Exploring the African coast Henry's first target was West Africa and its gold trade. To reach that goal, his ships would have to sail south, past Cape Bojador (BAHJ-uh-DOR). Time and again they turned back before rounding the cape, stopped by the widespread belief that

❝beyond this cape there is no race of men . . . and the sea [is] so shallow . . . while the currents are so terrible that no ship having once passed the cape, will ever be able to return.❞

In 1434 a ship finally rounded the cape and wiped away "the shadow of fear." From then on, Henry's explorers sailed farther and farther southward.

Along the way the Portuguese discovered the island of Madeira off the African coast. After seeing samples of the soil, Prince

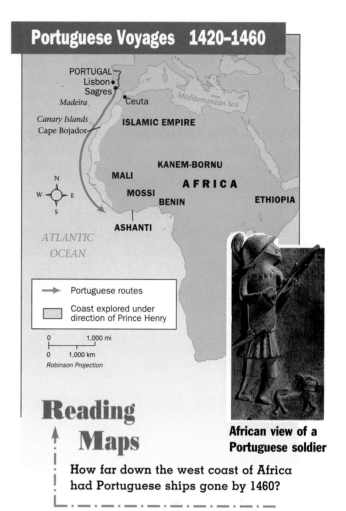

Portuguese Voyages 1420–1460

Map labels: PORTUGAL, Lisbon, Sagres, Madeira, Ceuta, Canary Islands, Cape Bojador, Mediterranean Sea, ISLAMIC EMPIRE, KANEM-BORNU, MALI, AFRICA, MOSSI, BENIN, ETHIOPIA, ASHANTI, ATLANTIC OCEAN

→ Portuguese routes

Coast explored under direction of Prince Henry

0   1,000 mi
0   1,000 km
Robinson Projection

Reading Maps

How far down the west coast of Africa had Portuguese ships gone by 1460?

African view of a Portuguese soldier

Henry established a colony on the sunny island to grow sugar cane. A **colony** is a settlement made by a group of people in a distant place that remains under the control of their home country.

West African trade In the 1440s Henry's ship captains made contact with African and Arab merchants and found a resource as valuable as gold: people to do work. In 1444 Henry's explorers brought 200 Africans home to sell as slaves.

Henry also sent enslaved Africans to his colony on Madeira to work in the cane fields. As European demand for sugar grew, so did the demand for slaves. The slave trade proved so profitable that in 1448

Henry had a trading post built on an island off the West African coast. This was the first European trading post established overseas.

The Portuguese relied on the help of African princes who had slave-dealers bring enslaved men, women, and children to the coast. There, they were traded to the Portuguese in exchange for cloth, beads, metal goods, and firearms.

The impact of Prince Henry When Henry died in 1460, his ships had not yet reached the southern tip of Africa. Nor had they found their way to Asia. The prince, however, had opened the way for such voyages. In time, others would take over where he left off and find a sea route to the wealth of Asia.

In the process, European explorers would bump into another great source of wealth—the Americas. Thousands of Europeans would stream across the Atlantic, bringing their cultures to these lands, one of which became the United States.

3. Section Review

1. Define **feudalism** and **colony.**
2. What united Europe after the fall of Rome? What divided it?
3. What effect did the Crusades have on trade? On the rise of nations?
4. Critical Thinking How did Prince Henry show the spirit of the Renaissance?

Why We Remember

Africa, Asia, and Europe in the 1400s

In the 1400s Africa and Asia had the resources and the trade they needed and wanted. They were not reaching out for more. In fact, China turned inward, withdrawing from exploration and trade.

Europe, however, was looking outward. Several forces pushed Europeans toward exploration. One was the appetite for gold and the luxuries introduced by the crusaders. Another was the curiosity sparked by the Renaissance. A third was that new European nations saw trade as a way to gain greater wealth and power.

Prince Henry was no explorer himself, but he did something more important. He helped conquer the greatest difficulty facing Europeans—fear of the unknown. Under his direction, the Portuguese went where no Europeans had gone before, and began replacing ancient fears with facts. The voyages inspired by Henry would eventually lead European explorers to the Americas. There the story of what would become the United States begins.

Geography Lab

Comparing Historical and Modern Maps

Claudius Ptolemy (TAHL-uh-mee) was a great geographer who lived in Egypt around A.D. 150. Ptolemy did not have computers or satellites, as mapmakers do today. He relied on the word of travelers and his own calculations. Then he used his imagination to fill in the gaps.

Europeans were still using Ptolemy's maps in the mid-1400s. The diagram below compares the outline of Ptolemy's map (right) with a modern map to help you see what Europeans in the mid-1400s thought the world was like.

Using Map Skills

1. Is the earth's surface mostly land or mostly water? What did Europeans in the mid-1400s think?

2. Which continent does Ptolemy's map show most accurately? Least accurately? Does that surprise you? Why or why not?

3. Imagine this map on a globe. If you were using such a globe, what would you say was the best route from Europe to China? Why?

4. **Hands-On Geography** Draw a map of a part of your community that you travel through often. Use memory and your imagination, not another map. When you are through, meet with four or five other students to review maps. What places could someone find by using your map? Where might they get lost?

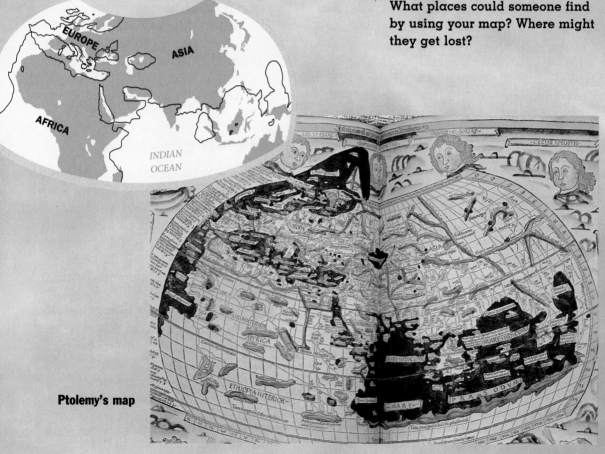

Ptolemy's map

Chapter Survey

Reviewing Vocabulary

Define the following terms.
1. navigation
2. feudalism
3. colony

Reviewing Main Ideas

1. What goods were the basis of trade between West African trading empires and North Africa?
2. Name three beliefs or ways of life that most West Africans shared.
3. Describe two ways that Asian goods reached other continents.
4. (a) What Chinese invention helped make European voyages of exploration in the 1400s possible? (b) How did Europeans obtain this invention?
5. How did feudalism change the way that people lived in Europe?
6. (a) How did the Crusades help to increase trade between Europe and the Middle East? (b) Were western European merchants satisfied with the trade? Explain why or why not.
7. Why was Portugal the only European nation to begin seeking new sea routes in the early 1400s?

Thinking Critically

1. **Synthesis** How might the history of Africa, Asia, or Europe have been changed if the Islamic Empire had *not* existed? Support your answer with examples from the text.
2. **Evaluation** In the late 1400s a government official in China described the expeditions of Zheng He as a waste of money—and of sailors' lives. "Although he [Zheng He] returned with wonderful, precious things, what benefit was it to the state? This was merely . . . bad government." Do you agree with the official's opinion? Explain.
3. **Why We Remember: Analysis** What forces pushed Europeans toward exploration in the 1400s? Which force do you think was the most important? Give supporting examples from the text.

Applying Skills

Reading history Review the information about how the Crusades began. Then use what you learned on page 43 to write an answer to this question: Why did so many Europeans fight for so long to try to capture the land of Palestine from the Seljuk Turks?

History Mystery

The Chinese navy Answer the History Mystery on page 35. How would you go about learning more about the decision of the Chinese government to get rid of the navy? How might China's history have been changed if the navy had continued to exist?

Writing in Your History Journal

1. **Keys to History** (a) The time line on pages 34–35 has six Keys to History. In your journal, list each key and describe why it is important to know about. (b) If you could have been present at one event on the time line, which would you choose, and why? Write your response in your journal.
2. **Prince Henry the Navigator** Prince Henry sent ships out to explore the west coast of Africa and advised his captains to report everything they saw. In your journal, write a dialogue between Prince Henry and one of his captains who has just returned from a voyage.

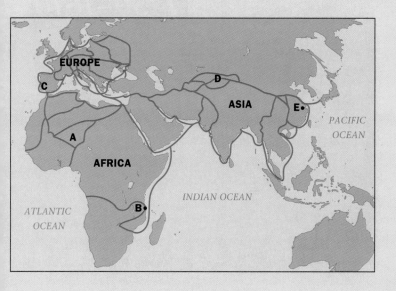

Reviewing Geography

1. For each letter on the map, write the name of a city, a trade route, a trading empire, or a nation.

2. Geographic Thinking People move from place to place for many different reasons. Sometimes people want to move; other times, they are forced to.

List at least three reasons why people moved in the 1400s. Then list at least three reasons why people move today. How are the causes of movement in the past and the present similar? How are they different?

3. Citizenship In their daily lives, most West Africans put social harmony and the needs of the village above personal concerns. In addition, farmland belonged to the village, not to individuals. What advantages might this way of life have? What disadvantages? Write your responses in your journal.

Alternative Assessment

Teaching a class at Sagres Imagine that you are going to teach a class at Prince Henry's center for exploration at Sagres. The topic is the economy of Africa, Asia, or Europe. The prince wants you to provide explorers with as much information as possible about trade and technology. Explorers will also need to know about people's ways of life.

❶ Choose the continent you want to discuss—Africa, Asia, or Europe.

❷ Prepare an outline of what you plan to teach and make a list of the materials you need, including visual aids. For example, you may want to use a large, illustrated map of the continent.

❸ Start with the information in the chapter and do additional research as needed to provide enough background.

❹ When your planning is complete, teach the class.

Your work will be evaluated on the following criteria:
• you provide adequate information to present a picture of the continent
• you provide information that is accurate
• you present the information in clear, interesting ways

Chapter 3

Voyages of Exploration

Keys to History

SANTA MARIA
NAO CAPITANEADA POR CRISTOBAL COLON EN EL DESCUBRIMIENTO DE AMERICA 1492. AL NAUFRAGAR, SE SE CONSTRUYE CON SUS RESTOS EL FUERTE NAVIDAD EN LA ISLA LA ESPAÑOLA, PRIMER ASENTAMIEN DE ESPAÑOLES EN EL NUEVO MUNDO

1492
Christopher Columbus reaches the Americas
Columbus's flagship

1492
Columbian Exchange begins
Columbus took chilies back to Europe

1450	1475

Looking Back

Aztecs build Tenochtitlán
1345

World **Link**
Ferdinand and Isabella expel Jews from Spain
1492

HISTORY
Mystery

Areas of land and bodies of water are often named for explorers. It was from the voyages of Christopher Columbus that Europeans first learned of the American continents. Why are these areas of land not called North and South Columbia?

1497
Search for the Northwest Passage begins
Arctic iceberg

1507
"America" is first used on a map

1519–1522
Magellan's expedition circles the globe

1607–1611
Henry Hudson explores for England and the Netherlands

1500   1525   1550   1600

Looking Ahead

The Dutch buy Manhattan Island
1626

● **59**

Beginning the Story with

Christopher Columbus

August 13, 1476. For an Italian sailor named Christopher Columbus, it was a day of disaster—a day when he looked death in the face and said, "Not yet." The 25-year-old Columbus was a member of the crew aboard a trading snip sailing from Genoa, Italy, to England. On that August morning, French pirates attacked the ship off the coast of Portugal. The battle raged all day amid smoke and flames. As night fell, the battered trading vessel sank to the bottom of the sea.

Columbus would have sunk as well, had he not grabbed a long wooden oar to keep himself afloat. All through the night, he forced his tired legs to kick, rest, then kick again. Miraculously, he managed to reach the shore of Portugal, some 6 miles (10 km) away. Local people took him in and cared for him. As soon as he was well enough to travel, Columbus made his way to Lisbon, the capital of Portugal.

The Weaver's Son

Up until he arrived in Lisbon, there was nothing about Columbus that seemed to mark him for greatness. He was born in the bustling seaport of Genoa about 1451. His father, Domenico Colombo, was a weaver of wool. His mother, Susanna, came from a family of weavers. In those days a weaver's son could only dream of going to school. Instead, Columbus worked at the looms with his father.

Yet the restless boy gazed longingly at the hardworking trading ships that lined Genoa's busy docks, and at the age of 14 Columbus took to the sea. For the next few years, he divided his time between trading voyages and helping his father on shore.

In Lisbon, however, Columbus's life changed forever. In 1476 Portugal was the European center of seagoing exploration and trade. Merchant ships crowded the harbor. People swarmed in and out of trading and banking houses. Christopher's younger brother Bartholomew was already in Lisbon, making detailed maps of coastlines called *charts*. Chart makers were often the first to hear the reports of voyages to foreign shores.

Working with Bartholomew, Christopher learned chart making. He also learned to speak Portuguese and taught himself to read and write both Latin and Spanish. He read every geography and travel book he could lay his hands on. One of his favorites was Marco Polo's *Description of the World*. After the excitement of Lisbon, Columbus could never return to Genoa and his father's looms.

In 1992—500 years after Columbus set sail for the Americas—Spanish authorities built this replica of his flagship, the *Santa María*.

The Merchant Seaman

In 1477, undaunted by his narrow escape from death, Columbus left chart making to go to sea once more. Trading ships took him as far north as Iceland and as far south as the Portuguese posts in West Africa. At every port he listened to stories, studied maps, and collected information. Gradually he became an expert navigator, ship's officer, and finally captain.

Columbus became convinced that ships could reach the Indies most easily by sailing westward across the Atlantic. Although most educated people of his day knew that the world was round, few believed a ship could survive such a voyage. The distance simply seemed too great. Sailors feared that far out at sea there would be no breezes to power their sailing ships. Helpless in the still air, they would perish from thirst or starvation.

Such fears did not stop Columbus. In his travels he had heard tales of boiling seas near the equator, but he had crossed the equator and seen for himself that the seas did not boil. Surely the fear that there were no breezes in the middle of the ocean would also turn out to be untrue. All he needed was a chance to show that his ideas about a route to Asia were right. Given that chance, he would find wealth beyond dreams. Given that chance, he would change the world.

Hands-On HISTORY

Activity

Imagine that you are Columbus applying for a job as commander of a fleet of ships. The fleet will be going on a voyage of exploration into unknown seas. As Columbus, list the experiences you would put on your job application to convince the owner of the ships that you are qualified for command.

1. The Quest for Trade Routes by Sea

Reading Guide

New Terms expedition, cape, finance

Section Focus How Europe's search for trade routes led to new and surprising knowledge

1. What is known about the people who reached the Americas before Columbus?
2. What did Dias and da Gama add to Europe's store of knowledge?
3. What did Columbus achieve, and what did he think he had achieved?

If you had been in school 50 years ago and your teacher had asked, "Who discovered America?" you would probably have answered, "Columbus!" But was Columbus really the first? In Chapter 1 you read that Paleo-Indians crossed Beringia to the Americas thousands of years earlier. There are also many theories about non-Indian visitors to the Americas before Columbus.

For example, an Irish monk named Brendan who lived during the 500s told of a voyage to a "land of promise." His descriptions fit parts of North America. Polynesians, too, may have visited the Americas. Some scholars believe that statues on Easter Island off the coast of Chile were made long ago by voyagers from Polynesia.

Other scholars suggest that Egyptians, Romans, Africans, or Asians may have reached the Americas long ago. So far, however, no firm evidence has been found for any visitors except the Vikings—the seagoing people of Scandinavia that you read about in Chapter 2.

The Vikings

In 1963 archaeologists found the remains of one Viking settlement at L'Anse aux Meadows, in Newfoundland. The discovery suggests that old Norse sagas—stories of heroic deeds—are indeed true.

One saga tells of Thorfinn Karlsefni, who sailed about A.D. 1010 with 250 men and women and a herd of livestock. The group settled in a place they named Vinland, or Land of the Vine. Scholars believe that L'Anse aux Meadows could be Vinland.

People the settlers called Skraelings (SKRAY-lings) came to trade skins and furs for swords and axes. The Vikings offered milk and red cloth instead. When a Skraeling tried to steal a weapon, the Vikings killed him. A fierce fight followed. The settlers decided to abandon the new land "since there would always be fear and strife . . . there on account of those who already inhabited it."

New Trade Routes

If other Europeans ever heard the Vinland saga, they thought it was just a story. Four hundred years later, they still had no idea that two great continents lay across the ocean to the west. As you read in Chapter 2, Portuguese sailors navigated by hugging the coast instead of sailing the open sea. By 1484 their ships had reached more than halfway down Africa's west coast, and they were carrying on a brisk trade in pepper, ivory, gold, and slaves.

Meanwhile, King John II sent Portuguese ships further and further down the African coast. The Portuguese were drawn on by their desire to find a new route to the Indies.

Dias In 1487 Bartolomeu Dias [DEE-us] set out on an **expedition**—a journey organized for a definite purpose. King John II of Portugal had ordered him to find the tip of Africa. Dias had sailed for thousands of miles along the coast when a violent storm arose, driving his ships far out to sea. The sailors were certain they would all die.

When the storm passed, the crew discovered that they had been blown around the **cape**—a piece of land sticking into the sea—at the southern tip of Africa. Dias named it the Cape of Storms. He wanted to sail on, but his frightened crew forced him to turn back.

When the king heard Dias's report, he felt that the wealth of the Indies was within his reach. Overjoyed, he gave a new name to the Cape of Storms. He called it the Cape of Good Hope, by which it is still known.

Columbus In 1484, before the Dias expedition, Columbus had told King John of his own plan to reach the Indies by sailing westward. He fully expected the king to **finance**—which means to supply money for—his voyage.

The king's advisors thought that Columbus's estimates of the size of the earth and its oceans were wrong. In fact, Columbus had miscalculated. He believed that Japan was about 3,000 nautical miles (5,556 km) from Portugal. Actually, it is more than 10,000 miles (18,519 km). The king turned Columbus down.

Today, re-creations of Viking longhouses stand at L'Anse aux Meadows in northern Newfoundland. Archaeologists began to study the site in the 1960s. They discovered traces of dwellings, remains of fire pits, and bits of worked iron. They also found a Norse-style weight used to spin yarn and a piece of bone.

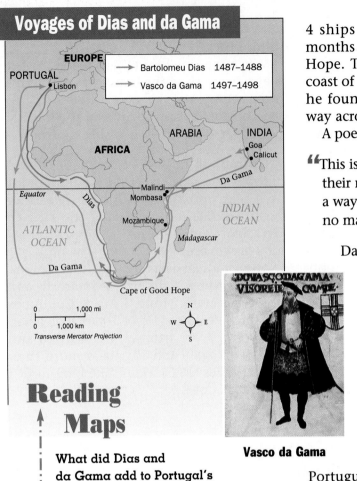

Voyages of Dias and da Gama

EUROPE
PORTUGAL
• Lisbon

→ Bartolomeu Dias   1487–1488
→ Vasco da Gama   1497–1498

ARABIA   INDIA
AFRICA   • Goa
                       • Calicut

Equator   Malindi
                 Mombasa
                            Da Gama
        Dias

ATLANTIC   Mozambique   INDIAN
OCEAN   OCEAN

              Madagascar

Da Gama

              Cape of Good Hope

0   1,000 mi
0   1,000 km
Transverse Mercator Projection

N
W ⊕ E
S

Reading Maps

What did Dias and da Gama add to Portugal's knowledge of Africa?

Vasco da Gama

4 ships and a crew of 170. In only four months da Gama rounded the Cape of Good Hope. Then he made his way up the east coast of Africa, stopping now and then until he found an Arab guide to show him the way across the Indian Ocean.

A poet later described da Gama's triumph:

"This is the story of heroes who, leaving their native Portugal behind them, opened a way to Ceylon and further, across seas no man had ever sailed before."

Da Gama's fleet reached India in May 1498. He filled his ships with silks, pepper, cinnamon, and other goods. By the time he got back to Lisbon in September 1499, however, he had lost half of his fleet and most of his crew, including his brother.

The rewards were great, though. The king named him Admiral of the Sea of India and gave him an income for life. Dazzled by the promise of enormous wealth, Portuguese merchants rushed to follow in da Gama's tracks, and Portugal became the center of a thriving Asia trade.

Columbus did not give up easily. The success of Dias, however, dashed his hopes of finding support in Portugal. Why would the king risk money on his plan for an Atlantic crossing when Portuguese ships were sure to reach the Indies by sailing around Africa?

The Portuguese Reach Asia

Indeed, a tough and strong-willed sea captain, Vasco da Gama, did complete the all-water route from Portugal to Asia. He sailed from Lisbon on July 8, 1497, with

Admiral of the Ocean Sea

Meanwhile, Columbus, having failed in Portugal, moved on to Spain. There he tried to persuade King Ferdinand and Queen Isabella to support him. The king and queen did not say yes, but they did not say no, either. Columbus had to wait.

One reason for the delay was that Spain was at war. Ferdinand and Isabella were fighting to unify Spain as a strong, Catholic nation. In 1492, they succeeded in driving out Spain's Muslims and forcing its Jews to convert to Christianity or flee. Then the royal couple turned their attention to Columbus's plan.

Perhaps their recent victory filled the king and queen with pride. Perhaps they hoped for a sea route to rival the Portuguese route to the Indies. Whatever the reason, they agreed to sponsor Columbus. It was the wisest investment they ever made.

The king and queen gave Columbus two caravels—the *Niña* and the *Pinta*—and a cargo ship, the *Santa María*. On August 3, 1492, the little fleet left Spain, first sailing south to the Canary Islands, then west into the open sea. As they left the Canaries, Columbus wrote:

"This day we completely lost sight of land, and many men sighed and wept for fear they would not see it again for a long time. I comforted them with great promises of land and riches.**"**

Reaching the Americas As the days passed, the crew grew rebellious. Columbus soothed their fears by lying to them. He said they had gone a shorter distance each day than they really had. He did not want them to know they were so far from home. Fortunately, on October 12, 1492, they spotted land—a low island in what today is the Bahamas, in the Caribbean Sea.

Relieved to have found land at last, Columbus had himself rowed to shore. The landing party gave a prayer of thanks, then solemnly planted Spanish banners and a cross. In those days, Europeans thought that a Christian nation had a right to take over any land not ruled by a Christian. So, despite the fact that the island was inhabited, Columbus claimed it for Spain and Christianity and named it San Salvador, which means "Holy Savior."

Although San Salvador did not look at all like the Indies, Columbus was certain that he had reached Asia. He called the Taino (Tī-nō) people who lived there *Indios*— Indians. He wrote in his diary:

"All those that I saw were young people, for none did I see of more than thirty years of age. They are all very well-formed. . . . They believe very firmly that I, with these ships and crew, came from the sky, and in such opinion they received me at every place where I landed, after they lost their terror.**"**

A short time later, the *Santa María* ran aground. With the *Niña* and the *Pinta* Columbus sailed back to Spain to report that he had reached Asia. He took with him several natives whom he had captured, as well as curiosities such as parrots, strange plants, and gold trinkets.

Columbus was greeted as a hero. Crowds cheered him wherever he went, and Ferdinand and Isabella rewarded him with the title Admiral of the Ocean Sea.

World Link

Expulsion of Jews from Spain In 1492 Ferdinand and Isabella ordered Spanish Jews to convert to Christianity or leave the country. That order started a chain of events that led to an early Jewish community in what is now the United States.

Many Spanish Jews resettled in Portugal. To please Ferdinand and Isabella, Portugal also ordered Jews to convert or leave. This time many Jews went to the Netherlands, and eventually some moved on to a Dutch settlement in Brazil. When that settlement fell to the Portuguese in 1654, a small group of Spanish-Portuguese Jews found their way to another Dutch settlement in what is now New York State.

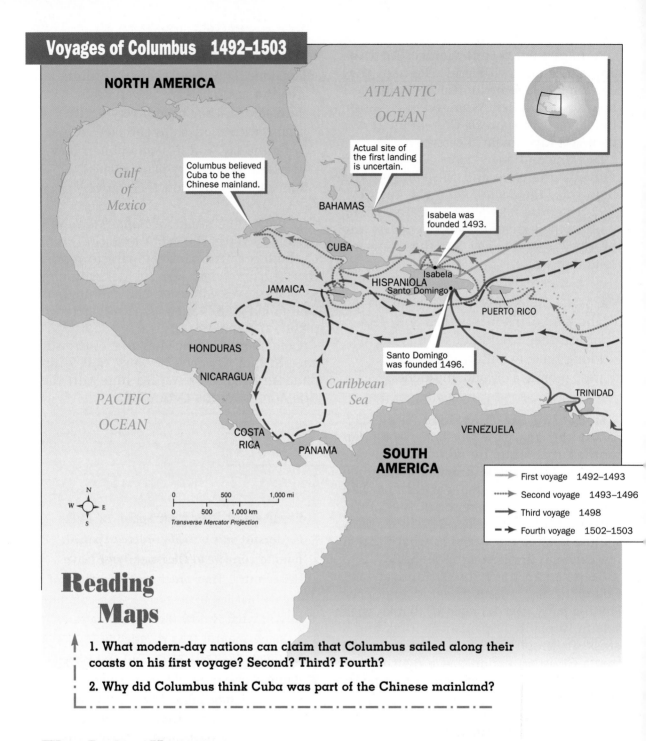

Voyages of Columbus 1492–1503

NORTH AMERICA

ATLANTIC OCEAN

Gulf of Mexico

Columbus believed Cuba to be the Chinese mainland.

Actual site of the first landing is uncertain.

BAHAMAS

Isabela was founded 1493.

CUBA

JAMAICA

Isabela
HISPANIOLA
Santo Domingo

PUERTO RICO

HONDURAS

Santo Domingo was founded 1496.

NICARAGUA

Caribbean Sea

PACIFIC OCEAN

TRINIDAD

COSTA RICA

PANAMA

VENEZUELA

SOUTH AMERICA

0   500   1,000 mi
0   500   1,000 km
Transverse Mercator Projection

N W E S

→ First voyage 1492–1493
····· Second voyage 1493–1496
→ Third voyage 1498
--→ Fourth voyage 1502–1503

Reading Maps

1. What modern-day nations can claim that Columbus sailed along their coasts on his first voyage? Second? Third? Fourth?

2. Why did Columbus think Cuba was part of the Chinese mainland?

The Later Voyages

The king and queen were eager to profit from the discoveries of their new admiral. They asked Columbus to establish a colony in the faraway land he had claimed for Spain.

Columbus sailed west again in September 1493. This time, instead of 3 small vessels, he commanded a proud fleet of 17 ships crowded with carpenters, farmers, soldiers, and missionaries. The missionaries hoped to win over the native people to the Catholic faith.

In his diary Columbus wrote about the beaches of San Salvador. He also described jewelry like the gold nose ring worn by this Cuna woman today.

The ships carried everything Columbus thought the colony would need. Columbus chose a site for Spain's first permanent colony, Isabela, on a large island that came to be called Hispaniola (HIS-puhn-YŌ-luh). Isabela was too near a swamp, however, and had little fresh water. When Columbus left Hispaniola, he gave his brother Bartholomew instructions to establish a new settlement—Santo Domingo.

Altogether, Columbus made four trips to the Americas. On his final visit in 1502 he sailed along the Central American coast. He named the area Costa Rica, meaning "Rich Coast," which showed that his hope for wealth in these lands was still alive.

Columbus returned from his voyage a discouraged man. He had proved to be a failure as governor of Hispaniola. In Spain, jealous people worked to deprive him of the honors and income Isabella and Ferdinand had promised. Until his death on May 19, 1506, however, Columbus held to the belief that he had reached the Indies.

A Land "We May Call America"

Although Columbus may have gone to his grave believing he had reached Asia, his rivals knew otherwise. One was Amerigo Vespucci (AH-meh-REE-gō ves-POOT-chee), an Italian trader. He searched nearly the full length of the South American coast, looking for a way to India. He wrote that a "new world" lay between Europe and Asia.

In 1507 German geographer Martin Waldseemüller (VAHLT-zay-MYOOL-er) published a new map. It featured a previously unknown land which, he wrote, "since Amerigo found it, we may call . . . America." Other map makers followed. Thus lands of the Western Hemisphere were named after Vespucci instead of Columbus.

However, the foothold Columbus established in the Caribbean would expand into a vast empire. By 1600, Spain would control much of North and South America, and would be one of the world's richest nations. Spain owed much of this wealth and power to the vision and determination of the Admiral of the Ocean Sea.

1. Section Review

1. Define **expedition, cape,** and **finance.**
2. What evidence suggests that the Vikings reached North America?
3. How did the route that Dias and da Gama established help Portugal?
4. Why did Ferdinand and Isabella sponsor Columbus?
5. What areas did Columbus explore on his four expeditions?
6. Critical Thinking What qualities do you think people like Dias, da Gama, and Columbus must have had to lead their crews on such risky voyages?

2. Seeds of Change

Reading Guide

New Terms infectious diseases, plantation, legacy

Section Focus The worldwide exchange of plants, animals, diseases, and people begun by Columbus

1. Why did infectious diseases have such a terrible effect on American Indians?
2. How did the exchange of food plants benefit Europeans?
3. How did the transfer of animals change the lives of some American Indians?

Is popcorn one of your favorite snacks? French fries, peanut butter, chocolate, cola? All of these treats come from plants that were first raised by American Indian farmers. Not one was known outside of the Americas before the voyages of Columbus. Now they are known around the world.

The voyages of Columbus marked the beginning of a great biological and human exchange between the Eastern and Western Hemispheres. As Columbus sailed back and forth to the Americas, he carried the beginnings, or "seeds," of great changes that would affect the whole world.

Among these seeds of change were diseases, plants, and animals. Scholars call this transfer the Columbian Exchange. According to historian Alfred Crosby, the Columbian Exchange "was the most important event in human history since the end of the Ice Age."

Disease, Accidental Seed of Change

Disease was the first of the seeds of change to make itself felt in the Americas. On Columbus's first voyage, some of the Taino Indians he met caught a lung disease from his crew. Many died because they had no immunity—natural protection.

Before Columbus, the Indians had few **infectious diseases**—illnesses passed from one person to another. Thousands of years earlier their ancestors had passed through the ice and snow of Siberia and Alaska on their long trek into the Americas. The cold had killed the germs of many serious illnesses. For centuries, Indians were free of smallpox, cholera, measles, and even influenza, which is also known as the flu.

On the other hand, infectious diseases were common in the Eastern Hemisphere. For example, a disease called bubonic plague or the Black Death swept into Europe from Asia in the mid-1300s. One out of every three Europeans died.

Rapid spread of disease Columbus, and the Europeans and Africans who came after him, unknowingly carried diseases to which the Indians had no immunity. These infectious diseases spread rapidly, passing from Indian to Indian.

Wherever people met to trade, there was a chance that they were passing on diseases as well as trade goods. Racing ahead of explorers and settlers, the invisible killers often destroyed whole populations of Native Americans. Sometimes, when Europeans and Africans reached an area for the first time, they found that the Indians who once lived there had all died.

In despair, one Mayan Indian described a smallpox epidemic among his people:

"Great was the stench of the dead. After our fathers and grandfathers succumbed [died], half of the people fled to the fields. The dogs and vultures devoured [ate] the bodies. . . . Your grandfathers died. . . . So it was that we became orphans, oh, my sons! So we became when we were young. . . . We were born to die!"

By the end of the 1700s, there were fewer than half—perhaps only one-tenth—as many native people in the Americas as there had been before Columbus's voyages. Disease was the main cause of this terrible destruction.

The Exchange of Plants

While the people of North and South America were dying of new diseases, foods from the Americas were causing population growth in the Eastern Hemisphere. Corn and potatoes—which grow in many climates—and other American crops greatly improved the food supply. As a result, the population of Europe and Asia increased. Africa's population grew, too, though not until the 1800s.

Hands-On *HISTORY*

Simulating the spread of smallpox Epidemics of infectious diseases have changed the course of history. For centuries, smallpox epidemics swept the Eastern Hemisphere. The germ spread easily, and there was no treatment. As many as 70 percent of the infected people died. Survivors were usually permanently scarred, and some were blinded.

The last known case of smallpox occurred in 1977. Today, smallpox exists only in a few scientific laboratories. Although scientists did not find a cure, vaccination wiped out the disease. Unfortunately, vaccination came too late for hundreds of millions of people.

Activity To see how epidemics can affect populations, estimate how quickly smallpox could spread in your school.

① Suppose that on Day 1 a single student with smallpox infects one other student. On Day 2, each of those two students infects one other student, for a total of four infected students. It goes on this way through Day 3, Day 4, and so on. How many days would it take for every student in your class to be infected?

② Then calculate how long it would take for every student in your school to be infected.

③ Show your results in a graph or an illustration.

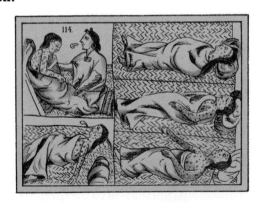

Smallpox victims, from an old Aztec book

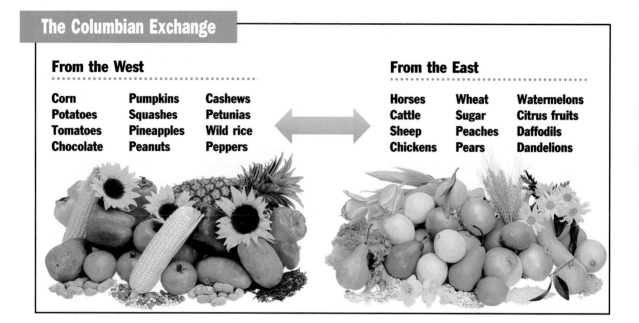

The Columbian Exchange

From the West

Corn	Pumpkins	Cashews
Potatoes	Squashes	Petunias
Tomatoes	Pineapples	Wild rice
Chocolate	Peanuts	Peppers

From the East

Horses	Wheat	Watermelons
Cattle	Sugar	Citrus fruits
Sheep	Peaches	Daffodils
Chickens	Pears	Dandelions

Corn and potatoes Columbus was probably the first to take corn to Europe. He wrote in his diary that he had learned of "a sort of grain [the Taino] called *maiz*." In Europe today corn is known as *maize*.

Corn spread quickly into Europe, Africa, and Asia. Although northern Europeans did not eat much corn themselves, they fed it to their livestock. As a result, they had larger and healthier livestock to provide their meat and milk.

Potatoes came from high in the Andes in South America. Even today, people of the Andes grow many varieties of potatoes—large and small, white, yellow, red, blue, pink, and purple.

At first some Europeans feared that potatoes would cause disease or even death. Gradually, they realized that potatoes were easy to grow and provided more food per acre than other crops. With potatoes helping to ease hunger in northern Europe, the population of Europe grew.

Other American plants Other plants from the Americas also helped improve diets in the Eastern Hemisphere. Nigerians learned to grow sweet potatoes and corn, Italians added tomato sauce to pasta, Hungarians put paprika in goulash, Eastern European Jews enjoyed potato pancakes, and Chinese added chilies and peanuts to stir-fried vegetables.

Sugar The exchange of plants went both ways. On his second voyage, Columbus brought plants such as wheat, grapes, and sugar cane for his settlers on Hispaniola. Of these plants, sugar cane was to have the greatest impact on human history.

Hoping to earn great profits from growing sugar cane, the settlers created plantations. A **plantation** is a large estate where a single crop is grown for profit. Plantation crops require a large labor force.

The Spanish began clearing Caribbean islands of their trees to plant sugar cane. At first they forced Indians to work the plantations. As the Indians were wiped out by European diseases, the Spanish looked to Africa for workers. They were following the example of the Portuguese, who made captive Africans work plantations on Madeira and the Canary Islands.

The Slave Trade

Suddenly there was a great need for labor and much money to be made in the slave trade. Arab and African traders raided villages, capturing men, women, and children to sell to Europeans as slaves.

Point of View

How did the slave trade affect Africa?

Traders, ship captains, and plantation owners saw the slave trade as a way to profit. King Nzinga Mbemba (ehn-ZING-ah ehm-BEM-bah) of the Kongo had a different view. In 1526 he wrote a letter calling on King John III of Portugal to end the trade.

"Sir, Your Highness should know how our Kingdom is being lost in so many ways. . . . We cannot reckon how great the damage is, since merchants are taking every day our natives. . . . Our country is being completely depopulated, and Your Highness should not agree with this or accept it. . . . It is our will that in these Kingdoms there should not be any trade of slaves."

There is no record of King John's reply, but the enslavement of Africans went on. In the process, African societies were destroyed as millions of their people were sent to the Americas.

The Transfer of Animals

Little good came to Native Americans from the Columbian Exchange. The main exception was animals. Before Columbus, Indians had only a few useful domestic animals: dogs, ducks, turkeys, guinea pigs, and llamas. Imagine what a difference cattle, sheep, pigs, goats, and horses made in their diet, clothing, and transportation.

Of all the animals that Columbus brought to America, the Indians were most interested in horses. At first the strange creatures terrified the Indians. They called horses "sky dogs," believing they were monsters or messengers of the gods.

Because horses were an advantage in hunting and war, the Spanish tried to keep them out of Indian hands. However, many Indian tribes quickly learned to value the beauty and strength of the horse. Especially on the grasslands of North and South America, Indians made the horse an important part of their lives.

The Exchange Continues

Columbus's voyages began a huge exchange of plants, animals, and diseases between the Eastern and Western Hemispheres. They also set off a movement of peoples—Europeans, Africans, and Asians. In fact, the story of the Americas since Columbus's time is often the story of people on the move. This movement of people and of the other seeds of change continues. The Columbian Exchange is the true **legacy**—something handed down from past generations—of Christopher Columbus.

2. Section Review

1. Define **infectious diseases, plantation,** and **legacy.**
2. Why did European diseases have such a severe effect on Native Americans?
3. How did American food plants affect the population of Europe? Explain.
4. How did the spread of sugar lead to a great movement of people?
5. Critical Thinking List two examples of the following statement: The movement of people and of the other seeds of change continues today.

Geography Lab

The Horse Comes to North America

The horses that the Spanish introduced into the Americas greatly changed how some Indians lived. Some of the horses got loose, and soon herds of wild horses were roaming the grasslands of North America. Indians rounded up wild horses. They also captured horses from the Spanish invaders. For Indians who acquired the horse, life was never the same again. Use the map and pictures to draw conclusions about how the horse changed their lives.

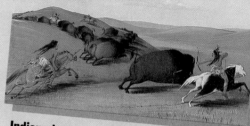

Indians hunting with bows and lances

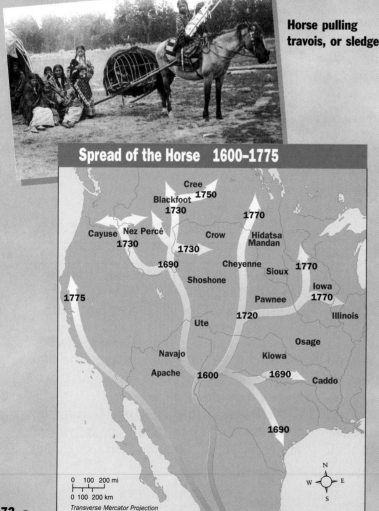

Horse pulling travois, or sledge

Spread of the Horse 1600–1775

Cree 1750
Blackfoot 1730
1770
Cayuse 1730
Nez Percé 1730
Crow 1730
Hidatsa Mandan
1690
Cheyenne
Sioux
Shoshone
Iowa 1770
1775
Pawnee 1770
1720
Illinois
Ute
Osage
Navajo
Kiowa
Apache 1600
1690
Caddo
1690

0 100 200 mi
0 100 200 km
Transverse Mercator Projection

Link to History

1. (a) Into what geographic regions did the horse spread? To answer, refer to the map on pages P4–P5. (b) List 5 tribes that adopted the horse. (c) The Spanish first brought horses into Mexico in 1519. How long did it take horses to spread to the northernmost point on this map?

2. When some tribes acquired the horse, they gave up farming and began to move from place to place. Using the pictures as evidence, what reasons can you think of for this change?

3. **Hands-On Geography** Plains Indians often decorated buffalo hides with picture histories of tribal life. Included were tribal "firsts," such as the first time a member of the tribe saw a horse. Draw a picture to show how a Plains Indian artist might have depicted his or her first sighting of a horse.

3. The Race for Discovery

Reading Guide

New Term strait

Section Focus **Europe's search for a way around or through the Americas**

1. What did Balboa and Magellan add to Europeans' knowledge of the world?
2. What were the results of the search for the Northwest Passage?
3. Why did European interest begin to shift from Asia to the Americas?

Spain and Portugal were the first to seek sea routes to Asia. Other nations, however, were determined to share the Asia trade, too. Before long, England, the Netherlands, and France were also racing to find routes.

Treaty of Tordesillas

At first, Portugal's King John II claimed the islands Columbus had found. After all, he said, they were near other Portuguese islands. To settle the dispute, Spain and Portugal agreed to the Treaty of Tordesillas (TORD-uh-SEE-yuhs) in 1494.

The treaty fixed an imaginary Line of Demarcation through the Atlantic from the North to the South Pole. Spain could claim lands west of the line. Portugal could claim lands to the east. The line guaranteed Portugal its ocean route around Africa.

The line brought Portugal good luck in 1500, when Pedro Álvares Cabral set sail from Lisbon intending to follow da Gama's route. He swung so far out into the Atlantic, however, that he landed on the coast of Brazil. He claimed the land for Portugal.

Balboa

Meanwhile, Europeans were still trying to reach the Indies by sailing west. They searched for a way around the Americas.

Little did they realize what a great ocean lay between the Americas and Asia.

The first European to see that ocean's eastern shores was Vasco Núñez de Balboa. He was seeking his fortune in Panama in 1513 when he heard Indians tell of a vast sea. With a large force of Spaniards and Indians, Balboa struggled over snake-infested marshlands, steaming rain forests, and steep mountains until he reached the sea.

Balboa called it the South Sea because he thought it lay to the south of Panama. We call it the Pacific Ocean. He plunged in and claimed the sea and all its coasts and bays for Spain. He never profited from his discovery, however. Rivals accused him of betraying the king, and he was beheaded.

Magellan

Balboa saw the Pacific, but Ferdinand Magellan was the first European to try to cross this vast ocean. No one knew what an ordeal that would be.

Magellan, a Portuguese sea captain, had made several voyages around Africa to India and the Spice Islands in present-day Indonesia. Like Columbus, he thought the world was smaller than it is. Convinced that he could find a short route to the Indies by sailing west, Magellan persuaded Charles I, the new king of Spain, to finance the trip.

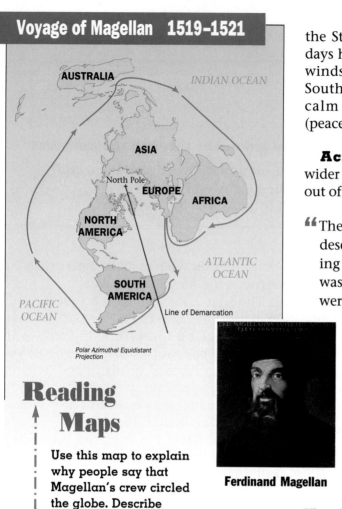

Voyage of Magellan 1519–1521

AUSTRALIA

INDIAN OCEAN

ASIA

North Pole

EUROPE

AFRICA

NORTH
AMERICA

ATLANTIC
OCEAN

PACIFIC
OCEAN

SOUTH
AMERICA

Line of Demarcation

Polar Azimuthal Equidistant
Projection

Ferdinand Magellan

Reading Maps

Use this map to explain why people say that Magellan's crew circled the globe. Describe their route.

The Strait of Magellan Magellan crossed the Atlantic in 1519 with 5 ships and a crew of 280 and began to look for a way around South America. That winter bad luck began to plague him. One ship wrecked. He had to stop a mutiny. Then he learned that his suppliers had given him only a third of the supplies he had paid for.

Nevertheless, in spring Magellan went on. As he reached the tip of South America, some of his crew deserted, taking one ship.

With three ships Magellan headed into a **strait**—a narrow waterway connecting larger bodies of water. This twisting 350-mile-long (563-km) passage is now called the Strait of Magellan in his honor. For 38 days he battled rough currents and howling winds. When he finally reached Balboa's South Sea, Magellan was so struck by its calm that he renamed it the Pacific (peaceful) Ocean.

Across the Pacific The Pacific was wider than Magellan imagined. His men ran out of food. One sailor described their ordeal:

"The biscuit we were eating no longer deserved the name of bread. It was nothing but dust and worm. The water . . . was putrid [rotten] and offensive. We were even so far reduced to eat pieces of leather, sawdust, and even mice that sold for half a ducat [a silver coin] apiece."

In spite of hardships, Magellan reached the Philippines in March 1521. There, after surviving the dreadful voyage, he was killed in a war between islanders.

Two ships sailed on. One sprang a leak and sank. The other, the *Victoria*, picked up a cargo of cloves in the Spice Islands. Then the Portuguese captured half its crew when it stopped for supplies.

For the 18 survivors, the terrible voyage finally ended on September 6, 1522, when they reached Spain at last. The first Europeans to circle the globe, they had proved that Columbus was right. Ships could reach Asia from Europe by sailing west, but the way was long and difficult.

The Northwest Passage

Columbus and Magellan had sailed under the Spanish flag. In other countries, too, people dreamed of Asia's treasures. Soon English, French, and Dutch ships were crossing the Atlantic. Spain's rivals hoped to find a northern route, or Northwest Passage, through the Americas. They looked to the north because Spanish warships patrolled the waters off South America.

English Exploration

The first to take up the challenge was John Cabot, an Italian living in England. In 1497 he reached Newfoundland with one small ship. Like Columbus, Cabot believed he had reached Asia.

The next year Cabot returned to the Americas with five ships full of trade goods. One turned back. The others were never heard from again. Cabot lost his life, but his voyages gave England a basis for claiming land in North America.

Meanwhile, a debate raged over the best route to Asia. Several ships tried to sail

Link to Art

Inuit man and woman with child (about 1577) Martin Frobisher captured an Inuit family near Hudson Bay and brought them to London, where they died within a month. John White made this drawing of the Inuits aboard Frobisher's ship. **Discuss** Exploring parties often included an artist. What were the benefits of having someone along who could draw? Today, would an exploring party take an artist along? Explain your answer.

northeast around Norway and Russia. Some men froze to death. Others turned back, discouraged by everlasting wind and ice.

Frobisher In 1576 English explorers again took up the quest. Martin Frobisher made three voyages looking for a Northwest Passage. One of his seamen marveled at the icebergs they saw:

"Of what great bigness and depth some islands of ice be here, . . . islands more than half a mile [around].**"**

At one point Frobisher found stones that he thought sparkled with gold. Actually, it was iron pyrite, or "fool's gold." He also thought he found a passage, but it was the body of water today called Frobisher Bay, in northern Canada. Frobisher took tons of worthless rocks back to England, but he also took back valuable information about sailing the icy Arctic waters.

Hudson Despite their failures, the English stubbornly continued the search for the Northwest Passage. Three times they sent an eager sea captain, Henry Hudson, "to discover a Passage by the North Pole to Japan and China." Blocked by fields of ice on his first voyage in 1607, he tried again the following year but met the same result.

Again in 1610, Hudson worked for the English. His ship, the *Discovery*, sailed into a huge body of water he felt sure was the Pacific. Then winter fell, and the waters turned to ice, imprisoning the ship.

The ice broke in the spring, and Hudson was eager to move on. When he refused to stop for fresh food, the crew mutinied. They cast Hudson, his son John, and some of the crew adrift to die amid chunks of ice in the bay now called Hudson Bay. A few mutineers lived to tell the tale, but they were never punished. What they knew was too valuable to future explorers.

Dutch Exploration

In 1609—the year before his final voyage—Hudson had sailed under the Dutch flag. Dutch merchants wanted a share of the Indies trade, so they hired Hudson to find the Northwest Passage. Instead, Hudson found the river that is now named for him—the Hudson River, in present-day New York. Although it proved to be another dead end, Hudson's third voyage gave the Netherlands a claim in North America.

French Exploration

France was too involved with European affairs to seek a route to Asia at first. Then King Francis I, who desperately needed money, heard about Magellan's profitable load of cloves. He thought about the opportunities he might be missing. The king decided to join the search for a way to the wealth of Asia.

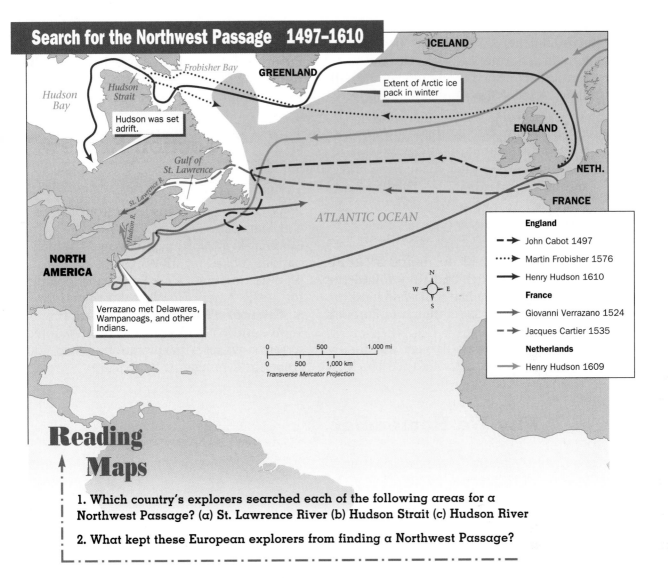

Search for the Northwest Passage 1497–1610

ICELAND

Frobisher Bay

GREENLAND

Hudson Bay

Hudson Strait

Hudson was set adrift.

Extent of Arctic ice pack in winter

ENGLAND

NETH.

Gulf of St. Lawrence

St. Lawrence R.

Hudson R.

FRANCE

ATLANTIC OCEAN

NORTH AMERICA

Verrazano met Delawares, Wampanoags, and other Indians.

N
W — E
S

England
- ⇢→ John Cabot 1497
- ·····▶ Martin Frobisher 1576
- ─→ Henry Hudson 1610

France
- ─→ Giovanni Verrazano 1524
- - -→ Jacques Cartier 1535

Netherlands
- ─→ Henry Hudson 1609

0   500   1,000 mi
0   500   1,000 km
Transverse Mercator Projection

Reading Maps

1. Which country's explorers searched each of the following areas for a Northwest Passage? (a) St. Lawrence River (b) Hudson Strait (c) Hudson River

2. What kept these European explorers from finding a Northwest Passage?

Verrazano In 1524 King Francis sent Giovanni Verrazano (vehr-rah-TSAH-nō), an Italian navigator, "to discover new lands" and find the passage to Asia. Verrazano landed on the coast of present-day North Carolina where, he boasted, "there appeared to us a new land never before seen by anyone, ancient or modern."

Verrazano sailed as far north as Newfoundland, landing at several places along the way. He wrote the earliest account of the east coast of North America, but he did not find the Northwest Passage.

Cartier Jacques Cartier followed Verrazano to North America. Cartier's three trips between 1534 and 1541 laid the basis for French claims. He, too, failed to find a passage to Asia, but he did explore the Gulf of St. Lawrence.

The king had told Cartier "to discover certain islands and lands where it is said a great quantity of gold and other precious things are to be found." Thus, when Cartier heard Indian tales of a land rich in gold and silver, he ventured far up the St. Lawrence River looking for it. He found no precious metals, but he did settle the first French colony in the Americas, near Quebec.

Cartier established friendly relations with Indians. A sailor described one meeting:

> " We . . . made signs to them that we wished them no harm and sent two men on shore to offer them some knives and other iron goods. . . . They sent on shore part of their people with some of their furs; and the two parties traded. "

Europeans still had not found a Northwest Passage. Neither had they found the gold and spices they had looked so hard for. However, they had added much to Europe's geographic knowledge.

In fact, a Northwest Passage was finally discovered in 1906, although ice blocks it most of the year. Long before, however, Europeans had begun to realize that the timber, furs, and fish of North America were worth as much to them as the spices of Asia.

3. Section Review

1. Define **strait**.

2. What did Europeans learn from Balboa and Magellan?

3. What is a "Northwest Passage"? Which nations looked for it? Why?

4. What resources were Europeans looking for in the Americas? What did they find?

5. Critical Thinking If this were the 1500s, and your 15-year-old cousin wanted to join a voyage of exploration, would you argue for it or against it? Explain.

Why We Remember

Voyages of Exploration

Christopher Columbus expected to be remembered as the man who opened a westward route to Asia. Instead, he died in 1506 a nearly forgotten man. No important people came to his funeral. No one put up a statue in his honor. No one wrote the story of his life until 300 years later.

At the time of his death, Europeans were still puzzled by what Columbus had found. For centuries they had believed that the earth consisted of Europe, Asia, and Africa. Only gradually did they realize that Columbus had explored lands entirely new to them.

Today we can look back and see that Columbus did more than alter European views of the world. He began a chain of events that completely reshaped the Americas. Disease drastically reduced the Indian population of the Americas. Meanwhile, peoples from Europe and Africa, and then from all parts of the globe, streamed in. Out of this blending of the world's peoples have come new cultures and new nations, including our own.

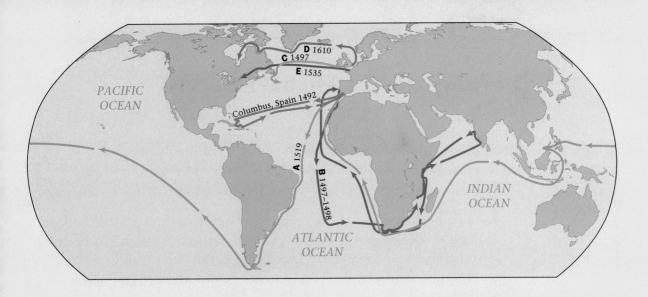

Reviewing Geography

1. For each lettered route on the map, write the name of the explorer and the country for which he was sailing.

2. Geographic Thinking In 1492, German geographer Martin Behaim made the first globe. It showed the earth as Europeans imagined it when Columbus first set sail. What oceans and continents were on that globe? List three vital new pieces of information map makers had to consider when they revised the globe 75 years later.

think Columbus Day should be remembered? In your journal write a letter to the editor of a newspaper in your state answering that question. Give your reasons.

Alternative Assessment

Holding a debate People generally agree that the "discovery" of the Americas by Columbus had both positive and negative results. With three other students, plan a debate on the issue: "Columbus: Hero or Villain?" Consider the question of whether the positive results of Columbus's voyages outweighed the negative, or vice versa.

1 Divide your group into two opposing teams with two people on each team.

2 In preparing your team's arguments, consider what you have read in this chapter, and then do additional research as needed. Be sure to think about the effects of Columbus's discovery on people and events of today, as well as the effects on people and events of the 1400s and 1500s.

3 When you have finished preparing your arguments, hold the debate.

Your work will be evaluated on the following criteria:
• you present your arguments clearly
• you back up your arguments with facts
• your arguments are logical
• you base your arguments on reasons, not on emotions

Morning Girl by Michael Dorris

The novel *Morning Girl* describes the life of Arawak Indians living on a Caribbean Island in the late 1400s. Author Michael Dorris, a Modoc Indian, tells the story through the eyes of 12-year-old Morning Girl and her younger brother, Star Boy. The following passage is narrated by Morning Girl.

Dawn made a glare on the ocean, so I splashed through the shallow surf and dived without looking. . . . Then, far in the distance, I heard an unfamiliar and frightening sound. It was like the panting of some giant animal, a steady, slow rhythm, dangerous and hungry. And it was coming closer.

I forgot I was still beneath the surface until I needed air. But when I broke into the sunlight, the water sparkling all around me, the noise turned out to be nothing! Only a canoe! The breathing was the dip of many paddles! It was only *people* coming to visit, and since I could see they hadn't painted themselves to appear fierce, they must be friendly or lost.

I swam closer to get a better look and had to stop myself from laughing. The strangers had wrapped every part of their bodies with colorful leaves and cotton. Some had decorated their faces with fur and wore shiny rocks on their heads. Compared to us, they were very round. . . . But really, to laugh at guests, no matter how odd, would be impolite, especially since I was the first to meet them. If I was foolish, they would think they had arrived at a foolish place. . . .

I kicked toward the canoe and called out the simplest thing. "Hello!"

One of the people heard me, and he was so startled that he stood up, made his eyes small, as fearful as I had been a moment earlier. Then he spotted me, and I waved like I've seen adults do when visitors arrive, my fingers spread to show that my hand was empty.

The man stared at me as though he'd never seen a girl before, then shouted something to his relatives. They all stopped paddling and looked in my direction.

"Hello," I tried again. "Welcome to home. My name is Morning Girl. My mother is She Wins the Race. My father is Speaks to Birds. My brother is Star Boy. We will feed you and introduce you to everyone."

All the fat people in the canoe began pointing at me and talking at once. In their excitement they almost

Arawak wooden carving

Caribbean Island settlement today

turned themselves over, and I allowed my body to sink beneath the waves for a moment in order to hide my smile. One must always treat guests with respect, . . . even when they are as brainless as gulls.

When I came up they were still watching, the way babies do: wide eyed and with their mouths uncovered. They had much to learn about how to behave.

"Bring your canoe to the beach," I shouted. . . . "I will go to the village and bring back Mother and Father for you to talk to."

Finally one of them spoke to me, but I couldn't understand anything he said. Maybe he was talking Carib or some other impossible language. But I was sure that we would find ways to get along together. It never took that much time, and acting out your thoughts with your hands could be funny. You had to guess at everything and you made mistakes, but by midday I was certain we could all be seated in a circle, eating steamed fish and giving each other presents. It would be a special day, a memorable day, a day full and new.

I was close enough to shore now for my feet to touch bottom, and quickly I made my way to dry land. . . .

"Leave your canoe right here," I suggested in my most pleasant voice. "It will not wash away, because the tide is going out. I'll be back soon with the right people."

The strangers were drifting in the surf, arguing among themselves, not even paying attention to me any longer. They seemed worried, very confused, very unsure what to do next. It was clear they hadn't traveled much before.

I hurried up the path to our house. . . . As I dodged through the trees, I hoped I hadn't done anything to make the visitors leave before I got back, before we learned their names. If they were gone, Star Boy would claim that they were just a story, just my last dream before daylight. But I didn't think that was true. I knew they were real.

Carib: A language spoken by one group of Indian people who lived on islands in the Caribbean Sea.

A Closer Look

1. How does Morning Girl describe the strangers in the boat?

2. How do you think the strangers would have described themselves?

3. What do you learn about Arawak customs for treating guests?

From *Morning Girl* by Michael Dorris. Copyright © 1992 by Michael Dorris. Reprinted by permission of Hyperion Books for Children.

Unit Survey

Making Connections

Review

1. Suppose that you know nothing about history beyond what you have read in this unit. Considering what you have learned, what would you predict for the peoples of North America after Europeans arrived? Why?

2. Modern life in the United States has roots in Africa, Asia, and Europe as well as in the Americas. Give two examples of each of these influences.

3. Agree or disagree with this statement: If Columbus had not come upon the Americas, some other European would have. Give evidence for your position.

Linking History, Health, and Art

Project

Healthy Foods from Around the World

A trip to the grocery store would be very different if the Columbian Exchange had never happened. Where do the foods you eat come from? How can you build a healthy diet with foods from around the world?

Project Steps

Work alone or with a partner.

❶ Study the Food Guide Pyramid.

❷ Plan a day's meals and snacks to fit with the pyramid. Keep in mind:

• Plan for variety in each food group.
• Limit fats, oils, and sweets.
• Include some foods you have never tried. For ideas, check cookbooks or magazines.
• Include combination foods, listing main ingredients. For example, pizza: wheat crust, tomato sauce, cheese, sausage.

❸ Do research to find out what continents your foods originally came from. Start with a dictionary and an encyclopedia, then move on to books about food.

❹ Create a poster showing your food plan and origins of the various foods.

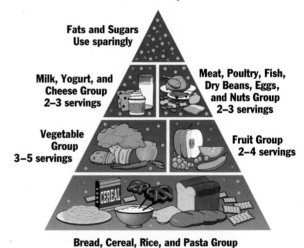

Food Guide Pyramid

Fats and Sugars
Use sparingly

Milk, Yogurt, and Cheese Group
2–3 servings

Meat, Poultry, Fish, Dry Beans, Eggs, and Nuts Group
2–3 servings

Vegetable Group
3–5 servings

Fruit Group
2–4 servings

Bread, Cereal, Rice, and Pasta Group
6–11 servings

Source: U.S. Department of Agriculture, U.S. Department of Health and Human Services

❺ Share your poster with classmates. Make a class list of continents represented.

Thinking It Over How difficult would it be to plan a healthy, varied diet if you could use only foods native to the Americas? What evidence do you see that new foods are still being brought to our country?

How Do We Know?

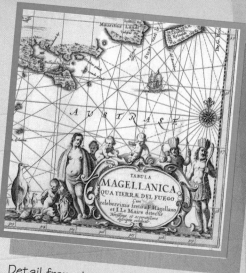

Detail from Jansson's Magellanica map

Scholar's Tool Kit

Maps

Imagine that you are an explorer sailing from Europe in the 1500s or 1600s. You sail through waters that no European has charted. You lay eyes on lands that no European has seen before. How do you describe these places? What do you call them?

European explorers often faced these questions as they gathered information about new places. Map makers, seeking to draw what the explorers described, also faced the naming question. What did they do? They gave lands and waters names. Many of the names explorers and map makers gave are the ones we use today. Others have changed. By examining early maps, historians can trace the history of place names. That is one reason why maps are an important tool of history.

A Map Maker's Dilemma

The map shown on the next page was published in the Netherlands around 1709. That was about 200 years after Magellan's historic voyage around the world, which you read about in Chapter 3. The map shows the region at the tip of South America known today as Tierra del Fuego. When Magellan found a water route through its maze of islands, he called the sea on the western side the "Pacific" because it seemed so peaceful. Seven years earlier, though, explorer Vasco Núñez de Balboa had seen the same ocean and named it "Mar del Sur," meaning "South Sea."

Jan Jansson, the famous Dutch map maker, was obviously aware of the two names for the same body of water. He recorded both names

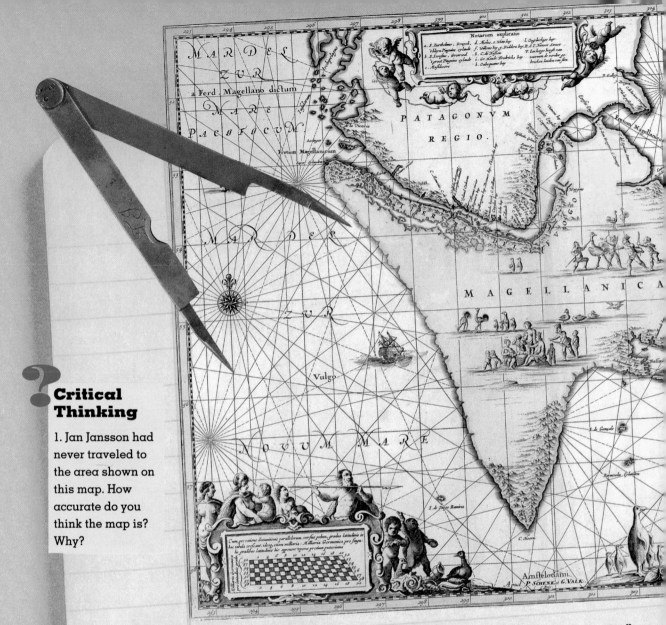

Critical Thinking

1. Jan Jansson had never traveled to the area shown on this map. How accurate do you think the map is? Why?

Critical Thinking

2. What patterns do you notice in the areas that are labeled and not labeled on the map? How do you explain these patterns?

on this map. In the upper left-hand corner is printed "Mar Dee Zur"—Dutch for "South Sea." Below it are the Latin words "a Ferd. Magellano dictum Mare Pacifico," meaning "Pacific Ocean as named by Ferdinand Magellan." Over time, though, Pacific Ocean became the accepted name.

What's in a Name?

Although Magellan himself was killed in the Philippine Islands and his record of the voyage was lost, one of the survivors kept a diary. He was Antonio Pigafetta, an Italian who went on the expedition as a tourist and not as a crewman or officer. In his diary Pigafetta not only described the various places Magellan visited, but also recorded the

names Magellan gave to those places. According to Pigafetta, Magellan named the strait at the tip of South America "Channel of All Saints." Over the years the strait received other names, but eventually became known as the Strait of Magellan.

While going through the strait, Magellan named the land on either side. The land to the north he named "Patagonia," because the people who lived there supposedly had big feet. The land to the south he named "Tierra del Fuego," or Land of Fire, because the people there lit bonfires at night. The name Patagonia stuck, but map makers labeled the southern land Magellanica in honor of Magellan, as shown on this map. Eventually, however, Tierra del Fuego became the permanent name.

Like many early maps, this one shows fanciful people and creatures as decoration. At least one creature shown here is based on fact: the penguin. Pigafetta described penguins in his diary. Interestingly, a species of penguin native to this region is named Magellanica in Magellan's honor.

Contrary to what you might think, the naming process is not over. Thanks to today's technology, explorers are at work on new frontiers, finding unnamed geographical features. These new frontiers are outer space and the ocean floor. As in the age of sail, features of these new frontiers are often named in honor of those who explore them.

? Critical Thinking

3. How has your community changed in recent years? See if you can find an old map of your area at the local library. How have names and places changed over time?

Scholar at Work

Create a map of your route from home to school. Rename certain features to honor yourself and your friends who follow the same route. Add decorative pictures to make your map more interesting. Then give your map to a classmate who does not use your route to see if he or she can follow it.

Unit 2

Chapters

Hands-On → *HISTORY*

Activity

Assume that it is 1720 and you live on a farm like the New York farm in this painting. Imagine growing up here before electricity, cars, and cameras were invented. You keep a scrapbook of souvenirs of places, people, and events that are especially important to you. Think of at least ten items for your scrapbook.

Van Bergen Overmantel (detail) attributed to John Heaten, 1732–1733

Newcomers in the Americas

Chapter 4

The Conquest of the Americas

Keys to History

1513
Ponce de León explores Florida

1519
Cortés begins the conquest of Mexico
Spanish helmet

1540
Las Casas argues for Indian rights before the king

1500

1550

Looking Back

Columbus reaches the Americas
1492

HISTORY
Mystery

A huge Aztec army beat back the first Spanish attack on Tenochtitlán—a city of hundreds of thousands of people. When fewer than 600 Spanish launched a second attack, however, the city fell, and with it, the empire. How did so few conquer so many?

1565

Founding of
St. Augustine

Fort in St. Augustine

1588
Defeat of
the Spanish
Armada

1608
Champlain
founds Quebec

1682
La Salle explores
the Mississippi

Detail from *La Salle Erecting
a Cross and Taking Possession
of the Land* by George Catlin

1600   **1650**   **1700**

World Link

Drake and the Cimarrons
steal Spanish gold

1573

Looking Ahead

France gives up its lands
in North America

1763

Beginning the Story with

Bartolomé de Las Casas

Have you ever heard someone speak words so powerful, so heavy with truth, that, try as you might, you can neither ignore nor forget them? On December 11, 1511, Bartolomé de Las Casas heard such words spoken by a priest on the Caribbean island of Hispaniola. For three years he tried to push the priest's words out of his mind. Finally, though, they would change his life completely.

The Soldier-Priest

As a teenager in Seville, Spain, Bartolomé de Las Casas had seen the Indians Columbus brought from America. At the time, he thought little about these strangers from a distant shore. He went to a university, and, after completing his studies, sailed to America with dreams of making a fortune.

Las Casas served as a soldier in the Spanish conquest of the Caribbean islands. Like other Spanish soldiers, he received a large piece of land as a reward. He also received a certain number of captive Indians to till the soil and dig for ore on his new land. Las Casas had the Indians mine for gold on his estate. Their labor soon made him a wealthy man. In 1510, when he was 36, Las Casas became a Catholic priest. Still, he continued his money making.

Then, on that December day in 1511, Las Casas heard a priest named Antonio de Montesinos preach against the enslavement of Indians. The priest looked out at his well-fed flock of Spanish colonists and asked:

"Tell me, by what right or justice do you hold these Indians in such a cruel and horrible servitude? On what authority have you waged such detestable [horrible] wars against these people who dwelt so quietly and peacefully in their own land? . . . Why do you keep them so oppressed [crushed] and exhausted, without giving them enough to eat or curing them of the sicknesses they incur [get] from the excessive labor you give them? . . . Are you not bound to love them as you love yourselves? Don't you understand this? Don't you feel this?**"**

Montesinos's words troubled Las Casas so much that he wrote them down in his diary. Still, he refused to give up his land or the labor of the Indians, arguing that he was fair to the native people who worked his land. The next year, Las Casas helped to conquer Cuba, for which he was awarded more land and more Indian labor. For a time, the stinging questions raised by Montesinos faded from his mind.

Protector of the Indians

Las Casas stayed in Cuba as a village priest. In 1514, while preparing a sermon, he came across a passage in the Bible that brought Montesinos's words back to him. By this time, Las Casas knew, more than nine-tenths of the Indians on Hispaniola had died of disease and ill-treatment. The native peoples of Cuba, he feared, were about to suffer a similar fate.

"Don't you understand this?" Las Casas remembered Montesinos asking. "Don't you feel this?" Yes, yes, he answered at last.

At that moment Las Casas suddenly saw that everything done to the Indians thus far was unjust. He knew that he would spend the rest of his life trying to right those wrongs.

Las Casas immediately gave up his lands and Indian workers. He began writing fiery protests against the mistreatment of native peoples. In 1516 he made the first of several trips to Spain to appeal for help in his cause. Spanish officials gave him the title "Protector of the Indians." In Spain and in Spanish America, his arguments set off a stormy debate over treatment of Indians. That bitter battle lasted for more than two centuries.

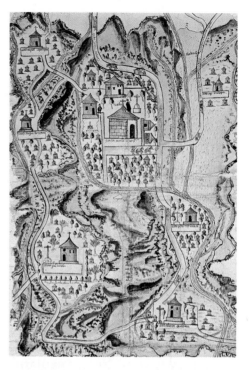

While priests like Las Casas spoke out against Spanish abuse of Indians, they also toiled to convert them. In Indian villages priests often replaced local temples with Christian churches.

Hands-On
HISTORY

Activity

Imagine you are Las Casas on your way back to Spain in 1516. Your goal is to persuade government officials to find ways to protect the native peoples of America from mistreatment by Spanish colonists. Decide what facts, figures, and arguments you might use to get their attention. Then outline a short speech using those arguments.

1. Spain Carves Out an American Empire

Reading Guide

New Term **conquistadors**

Section Focus **How Spain conquered mighty Indian civilizations and gained great wealth and a vast empire**

1. How did the Spanish conquer Mexico and Peru?
2. What did the Spanish gain from the conquest of Mexico and Peru?
3. How did expeditions into lands north of Mexico benefit Spain?

Twenty-five years after Columbus's first voyage, Spain had settlements on many Caribbean islands. Next, Spaniards eagerly looked to the mainland. They had three goals: to win converts to Christianity, to gain gold for their king and themselves, and to bring glory to Spain. Holding to those goals, they carved out an empire in the Americas.

In this Indian drawing, Malinche translates for Cortés. The curled symbols represent speech.

The Conquest of Mexico

The men who shaped Spain's empire are known as **conquistadors** (kahn-KEES-tuh-dorz), which means "conquerors." The first to earn great fame as a conquistador was Hernán Cortés, conqueror of Mexico.

Conquistadors hoped to gain wealth. They compared themselves to knights, but many put wealth above all other values. Cortés himself said, "My men and I suffer from a disease that only gold can cure!"

In fact, dreams of gold brought Cortés to Hispaniola as a young man of 19. Seven years later, like Las Casas, Cortés joined in the Spanish conquest of Cuba. For his services the government rewarded him with land, Indian workers, and a job as secretary to the governor of the Caribbean islands.

When Cortés heard rumors of a fabulous civilization in central Mexico, he saw his chance for riches. He got permission from the governor to organize an expedition.

Cortés's expedition Cortés was lucky as well as ambitious. When he reached the Mexican coast in 1519, he learned that many Indians there feared the powerful Aztecs of central Mexico. These enemies of the Aztecs, Cortés saw, could help him.

As a sign of goodwill, a village chief gave Cortés an enslaved woman named Malinche (mah-LEEN-chay). She spoke Nahuatl (NAH-WAHT-l), which is the Aztec language, and other Indian languages. The Spaniards renamed her Doña Marina (DŌN-yah mah-REE-nah). She learned Spanish quickly and became Cortés's most trusted guide.

The march to Tenochtitlán When Cortés was ready to march inland, he told his men to destroy their ships. Cortés told them that they could "look for help from no one except from God, and would have to rely on their own good swords and stout hearts." They could not turn back.

Hearing about Cortés, some Aztecs thought he might be the god Quetzalcoatl (ket-SAHL-kō-AHT-l). According to tradition, Quetzalcoatl had set out to sea long ago on a raft of serpents, promising to return one day from the east. The Aztec emperor, Moctezuma (MAHK-tuh-ZOO-muh), feared that Quetzalcoatl might be returning now to claim his kingdom.

Hoping to keep Quetzalcoatl away, Moctezuma sent messengers to Cortés with gifts of gold and silver. The gifts did not have the effect Moctezuma hoped for. They made the Spaniards even more eager to reach the capital of the Aztec empire, Tenochtitlán. An Indian described the scene:

"When they were given these presents, the Spaniards burst into smiles; their eyes shone with pleasure. . . . They picked up the gold and fingered it like monkeys. . . . They hungered like pigs for that gold.**"**

The Spaniards' route took them through Tlaxcala (TLAHS-KAHL-uh), where icy winds blew off the mountains. The route was fortunate, though. The Tlaxcalans, enemies of the Aztecs, joined Cortés.

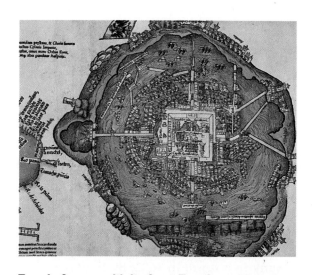

Temple Square, with its Great Temple—*el Templo Mayor*—is at the center of this old Spanish map of Tenochtitlán. Six causeways, which are roadways raised above the water, lead to the island city.

When the Spaniards saw Tenochtitlán at last, they were astonished. Houses, towers, and temples sparkled in the sun. "Some of our soldiers asked whether the things that we saw were not a dream," wrote one.

Moctezuma The emperor welcomed the Spaniards as guests. The Spaniards soon took Moctezuma prisoner, however, planning to control the empire through him. They made him send gifts to the Spanish king. The Spaniards also stumbled onto Moctezuma's hidden treasure. So great was the store of gold, silver, and jewels that it took three days to remove it.

Meanwhile, Cortés tried to convert Moctezuma to the Christian faith. Cortés warned the priests of Tenochtitlán's *Templo Mayor*, "I shall be happy to fight for my God against your gods." Then he smashed the religious figures in the temple.

The Aztecs rebelled, stoning Moctezuma to death for failing to rid them of the Spaniards. Aztecs and Spaniards clashed in a terrible battle that cost the lives of thousands. Finally, the Spanish army fled Tenochtitlán and took refuge in Tlaxcala.

Fall of the Aztecs In Tlaxcala Cortés reorganized his army. Then he turned toward Tenochtitlán, this time with 600 Spanish soldiers and thousands of Tlaxcalans. Cortés's army took the towns around Tenochtitlán one by one, cutting off Aztec supply lines. Then they attacked the city.

Although the Aztecs far outnumbered them, the Spanish had several advantages. They had guns and iron swords, while the Aztecs had lances and arrows tipped with stone. Spanish horses amazed the Aztecs, who had never faced such strange creatures in battle. In addition, thousands of Indians who were eager to destroy the Aztecs fought side by side with the Spanish.

Most important of all, the Spanish had a silent and deadly helper, smallpox. It killed many thousands of Aztecs, even while they were fighting to save their city. Wrote Bernal Díaz del Castillo (DEE-ahs del kahs-TEE-yō), who served with Cortés:

"The streets, the squares, the houses and the courts . . . were covered with dead bodies. We could not step without treading on them, and the stench [smell] was intolerable."

On August 13, 1521, after a fierce struggle, Tenochtitlán fell. The Aztec empire ended that day. In a well-known poem, "Broken Spears," one Aztec mourned his loss:

"Broken spears lie in the roads;
We have torn our hair in our grief.
The houses are roofless now. . . .
And the walls are splattered with gore. . . .
We have pounded our hands in despair
Against the adobe walls
For . . . our city is lost and dead."

The Conquest of Peru

Far to the south of Mexico lay the Inca empire of Peru. It, too, was destroyed by a conquistador with the help of smallpox.

Rumors of wealth lured Francisco Pizarro (pih-ZAR-ō) and his small army to Peru. Smallpox had arrived before him, killing thousands of Incas. Thousands more had died in Incan wars. When Pizarro arrived in 1532, the wars were over, and Atahualpa (AH-tuh-WAHL-puh) was ruler.

Pizarro had a plan to conquer Peru. He invited Atahualpa to a meeting, then kidnapped him. Pizarro said he would free Atahualpa for a room filled once with gold and twice again with silver. To save their ruler, many Incas gave up their gold and silver. Pizarro was not to be trusted, though. Once he had the treasure, he had Atahualpa killed, then quickly subdued the empire.

Tales of treasure soon drew more Spaniards to Peru. From there, expeditions went out to Ecuador, Colombia, and Chile. The land of the Incas became a stepping-stone to the rest of South America.

Hands-On HISTORY

Planning a modern-day entrada Explorers tried to be prepared. They took foods like grain and beans, along with livestock and poultry for future slaughter. They carried items to trade with the native peoples, as well as armor, guns, and swords in case the people proved to be unfriendly. For practical reasons, they packed shovels, hoes, and pans. For symbolic reasons, they carried flags, banners, and crosses.

Activity Imagine yourself as the leader of a modern-day entrada. You plan to take 50 people into a remote area to build 10 vacation cabins. There is a paved road for the first 50 miles, but you do not know what lies beyond. Your sponsors have asked you to list the items you need for 6 months and to explain why you need them. Answer this request in a letter. Keep these tips in mind:

- If you use vehicles, they will need fuel. If you use animals, they will need food and water.

- You will be far from stores and hospitals.

- You may have to deal with a variety of weather conditions and geographic features.

Explorers unloading supplies

Wealth of the Indies The treasures of the great Indian civilizations aroused envy in everyone who heard about them. In the long run, however, it was the gold and silver mines of Mexico and South America that created the greatest wealth.

The Spanish forced Indians to dig gold and silver ore. They produced so much that it was sent to Spain in large fleets of ships. These treasure fleets made tempting targets for pirates and for private ships paid for by Spain's jealous rivals, England and France.

Into the Borderlands

In Mexico and Peru, conquistadors had found riches beyond their wildest dreams. Hoping for more, the Spanish soon began to send *entradas*—armed expeditions—northward into lands that are now northern Mexico and the southern United States. This area was known as the borderlands.

Ponce de León Juan Ponce de León (PAHN-suh day lay-ŌN) made the first entrada north. He had come to the Americas with Columbus and stayed to conquer Puerto Rico. Ponce de León heard of an island with much gold and a spring that gave eternal youth to anyone who drank its waters. In March 1513 he reached a land he named Florida, but Indians drove him out. He did not find gold or a "Fountain of Youth."

Cabeza de Vaca More dramatic is the story of Álvar Núñez Cabeza de Vaca (kah-BAY-sah day VAH-kah). He was an officer on an entrada led by Pánfilo de Narváez (nahr-VAH-ays). They reached Florida in 1528 and marched inland.

When Indians drove Narváez and his men back to the coast, they could not find their ships, so they set out to sea in hastily built rafts. Many of the Spaniards, including Narváez, soon drowned or died of hunger and thirst.

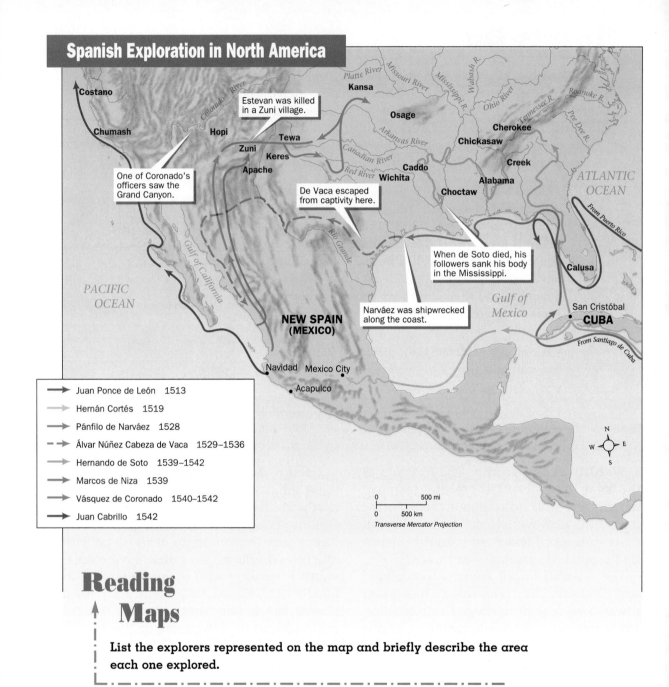

Spanish Exploration in North America

Costano

Chumash

Hopi

Estevan was killed in a Zuni village.

Tewa

Zuni

Keres

Apache

One of Coronado's officers saw the Grand Canyon.

De Vaca escaped from captivity here.

Kansa

Osage

Cherokee

Chickasaw

Creek

Caddo

Wichita

Alabama

Choctaw

ATLANTIC OCEAN

When de Soto died, his followers sank his body in the Mississippi.

Calusa

PACIFIC OCEAN

Gulf of California

Rio Grande

NEW SPAIN (MEXICO)

Narváez was shipwrecked along the coast.

Gulf of Mexico

San Cristóbal

CUBA

From Santiago de Cuba

Navidad   Mexico City

Acapulco

Platte River   Missouri River   Mississippi R.   Wabash R.   Ohio River   Tennessee R.   Roanoke R.

Colorado River   Arkansas River   Canadian River   Red River   Pee Dee R.

From Puerto Rico

→ Juan Ponce de León   1513

→ Hernán Cortés   1519

→ Pánfilo de Narváez   1528

- → Álvar Núñez Cabeza de Vaca   1529–1536

→ Hernando de Soto   1539–1542

→ Marcos de Niza   1539

→ Vásquez de Coronado   1540–1542

→ Juan Cabrillo   1542

0   500 mi
0   500 km
Transverse Mercator Projection

N W E S

Reading Maps

List the explorers represented on the map and briefly describe the area each one explored.

Cabeza de Vaca washed up on the Texas coast, where Indians enslaved him for six years. Finally he escaped and set out for Mexico City. Along the way he joined three other castaways from the Narváez expedition—two Spaniards and an African named Estevan (eh-STAY-bahn). The wanderers arrived safely in Mexico City in April 1536.

Cabeza de Vaca had not seen treasures during his years of wandering in the borderlands, but he had heard stories about "towns of great population and great houses." His stories set off rumors of Seven Cities of Gold supposedly to be found somewhere to the north, and the rumors spurred on other explorers.

De Soto Hernando de Soto, governor of Cuba, heard the rumors of Seven Cities. He had been with Pizarro in Peru, where he filled his purse with Inca gold. Vowing to find more treasure, he left his wife, Doña Ysabel (DŌ-nyah IZ-uh-BEL), to govern Cuba and sailed for Florida.

De Soto landed in Florida in 1539 with hundreds of soldiers, herds of pigs and horses, and packs of fierce dogs. For four years he searched the southeastern part of the present-day United States, chasing rumors of gold and looting Indian villages.

De Soto found a few pearls but no gold. Sick and depressed, he died near the Mississippi River in May 1542. After that, his troops wanted only to get to safety. The survivors—300 men and a woman—made it to Mexico in the fall of 1543.

Coronado The Mexican viceroy, or governor, had also heard Cabeza de Vaca's stories. In 1539 he sent Marcos de Niza into what is now New Mexico and Arizona to find the cities. Cabeza de Vaca's companion Estevan went along. As Estevan entered one Zuni pueblo—a village of flat-roofed stone or adobe buildings—the Indians killed him.

Watching from a distance, de Niza thought the adobe shimmering in the sun was gold. He rushed back to Mexico with the news that he had found one of the cities of gold.

In 1540 the viceroy sent Francisco Vásquez de Coronado, with de Niza as guide, to conquer the city. Coronado found only an adobe village. "Such were the curses that some hurled at [de Niza]," wrote one Spaniard, "that I pray God may protect him from them." Enraged, Coronado sent de Niza home.

Coronado's expedition stayed at the pueblo that winter, forcing the Indians to share their food. When the Indians rebelled, Coronado burned 13 villages. The Pueblo Indians would not forget the Spaniards.

Some of Coronado's men traveled as far north as present-day Kansas, but they found no golden cities. Discouraged, they returned to Mexico. Although they found no treasure, they did bring back knowledge of the land and its people. They had seen pueblos, prairies, bison, the Colorado River, the Rio Grande, and the Grand Canyon.

Cabrillo In 1542 Juan Rodríguez Cabrillo (kah-BREE-yō) led one more entrada in search of gold. His two tiny ships sailed from Mexico's Pacific shore northward as far as what is now southern Oregon. Although Cabrillo died during the voyage, his expedition explored 1,200 miles (1,931 km) of coastline and claimed it for Spain.

Spain's American Empire

Within just 50 years of Columbus's first voyage, Spain had become the richest, most powerful nation in Europe. It possessed a huge empire in the Americas, and its treasure ships brought great wealth home to Spain.

Although conquistadors did not find cities of gold and silver north of Mexico, the entradas into the borderlands expanded Spain's empire. Spain could now claim an area larger than all of Europe.

1. Section Review

1. Define **conquistadors**.

2. Give an example of how each of Spain's three goals in the Americas was carried out.

3. Why were the Spaniards able to defeat the Aztecs? The Incas?

4. What part of North America did each of these people explore: Ponce de León, Cabeza de Vaca, de Soto, Coronado?

5. Critical Thinking Spaniards in the 1500s took pride in the boldness of the conquistadors. At the same time some were disturbed by the conquistadors' treatment of the Indians. Give reasons for each view.

Geography Lab

Merchants, from an Aztec book

Reading a Terrain Map

Since ancient times, travelers have tried to find ways to show others where they went, how they got there, and what the **terrain**— all the physical features of an area of land— was like. People have thought of several different solutions to this problem.

The Aztec picture record on this page is one attempt to show a route and the land it went through. In the picture, Aztec traders are going out from Tenochtitlán into the surrounding countryside. The modern map of Cortés's route is another example. Compare the Aztec record and the modern map to help you understand maps that show terrain.

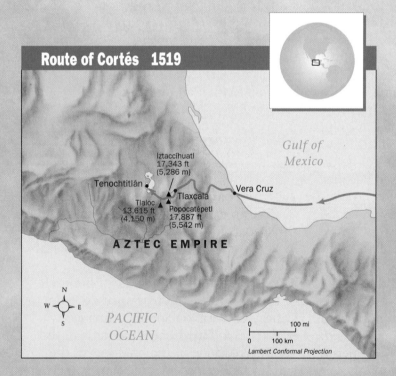

Route of Cortés   1519

Iztaccíhuatl
17,343 ft
(5,286 m)

Tenochtitlán

Tlaxcala

Vera Cruz

Tlaloc
13,615 ft
(4,150 m)

Popocatépetl
17,887 ft
(5,542 m)

AZTEC EMPIRE

Gulf of Mexico

PACIFIC OCEAN

N W E S

0   100 mi
0   100 km

Lambert Conformal Projection

Using Map Skills

1. Why is it helpful to know the terrain of land you plan to travel through?

2. What does the Aztec picture record tell you about terrain near Tenochtitlán? How?

3. How does the map of Cortés's invasion route support the picture record?

4. Why did Cortés avoid the places marked on the map with triangles? How do you suppose he managed to avoid them?

5. **Hands-On Geography** Suppose you are going on a bicycle trip from Chicago to San Francisco. You want to follow the most direct route, while avoiding as many mountains as you can. Use the maps on pages R4–R5 and R6–R7 to help you plan your route. Draw your route on an outline map of the United States. Explain why the route is a good one to take.

2. Spanish America

Reading Guide

New Term **mercantilism**

Section Focus **How a distinctive culture arose in Spanish America**

1. How did Spain govern its colonies?
2. How did Spaniards treat Native Americans?
3. Why did Spain establish settlements in the borderlands?

By 1530 the time of the conquistadors was passing. Soldiers who had come to the Americas to conquer stayed to run plantations, ranches, and mines. Settlers arrived, and new missionaries came to bring the Catholic faith to the Indians.

To rule his American empire, in 1535 Spain's King Charles I divided it into two parts—Peru and New Spain. He appointed a viceroy to govern each part. They were to create a society like the one they had left behind in Spain.

The Church

In Spain the king was the head of the Catholic Church as well as the government. King Charles saw it as his duty to establish the Church in the Americas and convert Indians to Christianity.

To teach Indians Christianity, as well as Spanish crafts and farming methods, missionaries gathered them into villages called missions. Some Indians adopted Christianity quickly. In 1524 one missionary wrote:

"When the [missionaries] travel, the Indians come out to the roads with their children in their arms, and with their sick on their backs, . . . demanding to be baptized.**"**

Indians, however, did not want Christianity forced on them. Although missionaries often meant well, their work uprooted Indian cultures. Some Indians kept their old beliefs. Others practiced the two religions side by side.

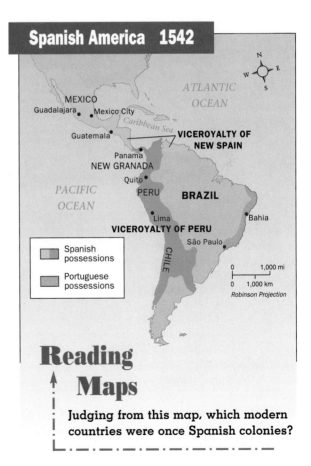

Spanish America 1542

MEXICO
Guadalajara • Mexico City
ATLANTIC OCEAN
Guatemala •
Caribbean Sea
VICEROYALTY OF NEW SPAIN
Panama •
NEW GRANADA
Quito •
PACIFIC OCEAN
PERU
BRAZIL
Lima •
• Bahia
VICEROYALTY OF PERU
São Paulo •
CHILE

☐ Spanish possessions
☐ Portuguese possessions

0   1,000 mi
0   1,000 km
Robinson Projection

Reading Maps

Judging from this map, which modern countries were once Spanish colonies?

As missionaries spread out, soldiers were sent to protect them and any settlers who went with them. Thus forts, called *presidios,* grew up alongside many missions.

The Laws of the Indies

The viceroys carried out orders that the king's advisors—the Council of the Indies—sent from Spain. These orders were signed *Yo el Rey,* which means "I, the King." The council organized its rules into a code called the Laws of the Indies.

The Laws of the Indies applied Spanish thinking to colonial society. For example, each city in the colonies was to be laid out like a city in Spain, with a public square, a church, a jail, and "arcades for tradesmen."

The child in this painting has a Spanish father and an Indian mother. By 1800 about a third of the people of Spanish America and Brazil had a mixed heritage.

Social classes Society in Spain was divided into social classes, from the king down to peasant farmers, with African slaves at the bottom. Following that pattern, the Laws divided the people of the colonies into social classes, too.

At the top were *peninsulares* (PEH-nihn-soo-LAHR-ays)—people born in Spain. They held the highest church and government positions. Next in importance were *creoles,* born in the Americas to Spanish parents. They might have wealth and education, but never the influence of peninsulares.

Many Spaniards who came to the colonies married Indian women. Their children, part Spanish and part Indian, belonged to the third class, called *mestizos*. They could not own land but worked on farms and ranches and at crafts in the cities.

By law, Indians and Africans were included in Spanish society. However, they were in the lowest classes and had the fewest rights and opportunities.

Throughout the colonies, Spaniards, Indians, and Africans intermarried. As a result, an entirely new group of people arose—people known today as *Latinos.*

Increasing Spain's Wealth

Charles and the kings who came after him applied a new economic idea called **mercantilism** to Spain's empire. According to this idea, a nation became strong by filling its treasury with gold and silver. It could add to its wealth by owning gold and silver mines or by selling more to other countries than it bought from them.

Colonies played an important part in Spain's mercantilism. On the one hand, they sent gold and silver to Spain. On the other hand, colonists bought manufactured goods from the home country. Strict rules forced colonists to trade only with Spanish merchants.

✍ Link to Art

Church of Santa Clara, Tunja, Colombia This church ceiling is a blend of Spanish and Indian ideas. Spanish priests had Indians build churches like the ones in Spain. Indian artisans carved and painted the walls and ceilings, following Spanish examples. However, they were also inspired by their own traditions of colorful, complex patterns. The sun symbol is both Indian and European. Many Indians worshipped the sun as the creator of their people. In Europe the sun symbolized knowledge, as well as heaven. **Discuss** To create this ceiling, what native skills do you think Indians used?

Encomiendas Although the colonies existed for the good of Spain, the king thought it was Spain's duty to care for the Indians. The two ideas clashed in the *encomienda* (ehn-kō-mee-EHN-dah) system.

Under this system the king gave favored Spaniards a right to the labor of a certain number of Indians. For example, the king gave Cortés the services of 100,000 Indians in a 25,000-square-mile (64,750-square-km) area. Some Spaniards thought of the Indians as similar to the serfs who labored for European landowners.

Point of View

How should Spaniards treat Indians?

A person who received an encomienda was supposed to protect the Indians and teach them Christianity. In practice, however, many colonists treated Indians as slaves.

Antonio de Montesinos was the first to speak out against this treatment of Indians, and his words moved Bartolomé de Las Casas. Las Casas, in turn, inspired others to take up the cause, but he also set off a hot debate.

One Spanish scholar, Juan Ginés de Sepúlveda, reasoned that it was natural for some people to be slaves. Didn't Indians deserve harsh treatment, he asked, because they had been guilty of such sins as human sacrifice and idol worship? He argued:

"How can we doubt that these people—so uncivilized, so barbaric, contaminated with so many impieties and obscenities [sins and immoral acts]—have been justly conquered by such an excellent, pious, and most just king? . . . [The Spanish] can destroy barbarism and educate [Indians] to a more humane and virtuous life. And if the [Indians] reject such rule, it can be imposed upon them by force of arms."

In 1540 Las Casas returned to Spain to put his case before the king. He used sarcasm to point out that Spaniards were failing in their duty to protect and educate Indians.

"The Spaniards entered . . . like wolves, tigers, and lions which had been starving for many days, and since forty years they have done nothing else . . . than outrage, slay, afflict, torment, and destroy. In this way have they cared for [Indian] lives—and for their souls."

Stirred by Las Casas, King Charles I reformed the encomienda system in 1542. However, many colonists protested the reforms and ignored the limits on their rights to Indian labor.

Settling the Borderlands

At first, Spain did little to encourage settlement of the areas explored by Cabeza de Vaca, de Soto, and Coronado. When rival nations began to show an interest, however, the king changed his mind. News of French or English threats encouraged him to send soldiers, settlers, and missionaries to protect the borderlands.

Foreign threats One threat to Spain's empire came from France. In 1564, a party of French Protestants built Fort Caroline in Florida. When 13 of the settlers used the colony's only boat to raid Spanish ships, the king of Spain quickly sent a cold-hearted soldier, Don Pedro Menéndez de Avilés, to drive the French out.

Nearby in Florida, Menéndez founded the colony of St. Augustine in 1565. It was too far from Spain's other settlements to prosper, but Spain held on to it for almost 300 years. St. Augustine is the oldest permanent European settlement in the United States.

Francis Drake Another threat came from the English pirate, Francis Drake. Drake sailed around the tip of South America into the Pacific, where he captured a treasure ship off the coast of Peru. He then sailed up the California coast, returning home across the Pacific in 1580. It was only the second voyage around the world.

The Spanish were convinced that Drake had found the fabled Northwest Passage from the Atlantic to the Pacific. Did this mean that England could easily attack New Spain on both the east and west coasts?

New Mexico and Arizona In 1598 Juan de Oñate (ō-NYAH-tay) led 400 settlers, including slaves and missionaries, into the area they called New Mexico. About 40,000 Indians already lived there in some 60 pueblos along the Rio Grande. At first the Pueblo people gave Oñate shelter and let the missionaries baptize converts.

In 1609 a new leader, Pedro de Peralta, laid out the city of Santa Fe, following the Laws of the Indies. By the time English Pilgrims landed at Plymouth Rock, the New Mexico colony was well established.

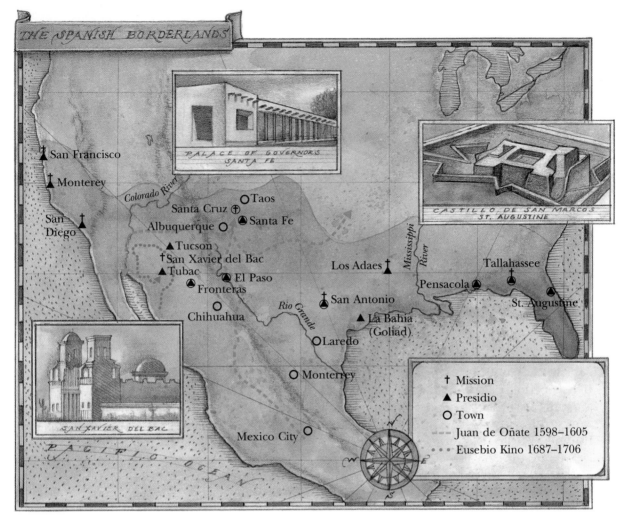

THE SPANISH BORDERLANDS

San Francisco
Monterey
Colorado River
San Diego
Santa Cruz ⊕
Taos ○
Albuquerque ○
Santa Fe ▲
Tucson ▲
†San Xavier del Bac
Tubac ▲
El Paso ⬤
Fronteras
Chihuahua ○
Rio Grande
Los Adaes ▲
San Antonio †
La Bahia ▲
(Goliad)
Laredo ○
Monterrey ○
Mexico City ○
Mississippi River
Pensacola ⬤
Tallahassee †
St. Augustine ⬤

PALACE OF GOVERNORS
SANTA FE

CASTILLO DE SAN MARCOS
ST. AUGUSTINE

SAN XAVIER DEL BAC

PACIFIC OCEAN

† Mission
▲ Presidio
○ Town
— Juan de Oñate 1598–1605
⋯ Eusebio Kino 1687–1706

Reading Maps

Compare this map with the map of the United States today on pages R6–R7.
In which states would you expect to find evidence of Spanish influence?

Unfortunately, here, as in other parts of the Americas, kindness was repaid with cruelty. The Spaniards forced Pueblo Indians to labor for them, to pay tribute, and to practice the Catholic religion. In 1680, a Tewa Indian named Popé (pō-PAY) planned a revolt. On August 10—at the same hour of the day—Tewas, Keres, Hopis, Zunis, and other tribes rose up and drove the Spanish out. Twelve years passed before the Spanish returned.

Meanwhile, in 1687 a missionary and explorer, Eusebio Kino (ay-oo-ZA-byō KEE-nō), built a chain of missions in present-day Arizona. A few hundred settlers and miners trickled in after Kino, but the Spanish population of Arizona remained small.

Texas Rumors of a French settlement sent Spanish soldiers hurrying to Texas in 1689. They found that a tiny French colony had failed. However, the Spanish leader,

Between 1672 and 1687 unknown numbers of Indian laborers cut limestone blocks, hauled them, and fitted them together to make the walls of Castillo de San Marcos. This Spanish fort could shelter as many as 1,500 people. More than once its massive walls have resisted cannon fire, and the old fort still stands in St. Augustine, Florida.

Alonso de León, gave a glowing report of native people called Tejas (TAY-hahs), from an Indian word for friends: "Certainly it is a pity that people so rational should have no one to teach them [Christianity]."

Missionaries hastened to Texas, but the Tejas ordered them out. In 1718, Spanish soldiers, settlers, and priests returned and established the mission and presidio of San Antonio—again to warn the French.

California The last part of North America that Spain colonized was California. In the mid-1700s the Spanish heard about Russian fur hunters in Alaska. They worried that the Russians would move south.

Gaspar de Portolá (POR-tō-LAH), a soldier, and Junípero Serra, a missionary, led a band of Spaniards to San Diego Bay in 1769. There they built the first of a chain of 21 missions and 4 presidios that would one day link San Diego and San Francisco. As for the Russians, they did plant a settlement in California, but not until 1812.

The arc of settlements The Spanish population of the borderlands grew slowly. By the middle of the 1700s, though, Spain had scattered missions, presidios, and towns in a great arc across what is now the southern United States. The people who made their way into the region brought Spanish ways: skills in arts and architecture, the Spanish language, the Catholic religion, and ranching and mining techniques.

Today, many Americans can trace their ancestry to these settlers. In addition, the influence of Spanish culture is easy to see in buildings, place names, and ways of life in what were once New Spain's borderlands.

2. Section Review

1. Define **mercantilism**.
2. Explain the following statement and give two examples: Spanish America was closely controlled by the king of Spain.
3. Why did Spain establish missions and settlements in each of the following places: Florida, New Mexico, Texas, California?
4. Critical Thinking Compare the hopes of the Spanish kings for the encomienda system with the settlers' expectations.

Skill Lab

Skill Tips

Ask yourself:
- At first glance, what does the painting show?
- Does it try to create a mood (for example: cheerful, gloomy, calm, violent)?
- What details create that mood?
- What do the details and the mood tell me about the artist's purpose?

Acquiring Information
Analyzing a Painting

The painting below is more than 400 years old and shows a scene from Spanish America in the 1500s. For centuries artists have used paintings to express their feelings about people, places, and events. Paintings can be a valuable source of information about history. Often the ones in museums or books have captions. However, try to draw your own conclusions rather than relying on captions.

Question to Investigate

What was the relationship between the Spanish and the Indians in the 1500s?

Procedure

To use a painting as a source of information, you must ask both "what" and "why" questions. Analyze this painting to determine its basic features as you explore the Question to Investigate.

Source to Use

① Determine *what* information the painting provides about Spanish America.
a. Identify the main image, if any.
b. Identify the smaller details.

② Think about possible reasons *why* the artist made the painting.
a. Did the artist try to create a certain mood? Explain your answer.
b. Was the artist trying to get the viewer to think or feel a certain way about Spanish America? Explain.

③ Based on the painting alone, how would you answer the Question to Investigate?

④ Evaluate how useful the painting is as a source of information.
a. In light of what you have read in the chapter, how accurate do you think this painting is? Explain.
b. What other kinds of information might you look for in order to check the accuracy of this painting?

3. Challenges to Spain

Reading Guide

New Terms persecution, league

Section Focus **The American colonies of Spain's European rivals**

1. How did Europe's Protestant Reformation affect the Americas?
2. In what ways did New France differ from New Spain?
3. In what ways did New Netherland differ from New Spain?
4. Why did England's early colonies fail?

During the 1500s, Spain ruled the world's largest empire. Europeans said, "When Spain moves, the world trembles." Two forces were at work, however, to change Spain's position. One force for change was that rival nations began to establish their own colonies. The other was religious rivalry.

Catholics and Protestants

For centuries the Catholic Church was the only Christian church in western Europe. Then in 1517 Martin Luther, a German monk, spoke out against what he saw as false teachings and acts within the Church. Other people, including John Calvin in Switzerland, began to protest, too. Because they were protesting, they were called Protestants, and the movement they started was called the Protestant Reformation.

Protestants and Catholics struggled for power in the name of God. Spain, France, Belgium, and most of Germany remained Catholic. Switzerland, the Netherlands, England, and the Scandinavian countries became Protestant. Catholics in Protestant countries and Protestants in Catholic countries were often victims of **persecution.** That means they were attacked, thrown in prison, tortured, or killed for their beliefs.

Europe's religious conflicts affected the Americas in two ways. First, rival nations saw colonies as a chance to spread their religion. Second, people who suffered persecution saw colonies as a means of escape.

New France

Hoping to find wealth to rival Spain's and to convert Indians to Christianity, the French explored nearly two-thirds of North America. They did not find gold or a passage to Asia. Instead, their treasure was mink, beaver, and other furs prized in Europe for fashionable clothing.

Canada French fishermen had been catching cod near Newfoundland since the early 1500s. They often stopped along shore to trade cloth, knives, and kettles for furs offered by Indians. To expand this trade, in 1608 a young French geographer, Samuel de Champlain, built a trading post atop cliffs along the St. Lawrence River. He called the place by its Indian name, *Quebec*. For the next 150 years Quebec was a base for French traders, trappers, soldiers, and missionaries.

Adventurous French trappers and traders, called *coureurs de bois* (koo-rer duh BWAH) hacked through thick woodlands, and boatmen called *voyageurs* (vwah-yah-ZHERZ)

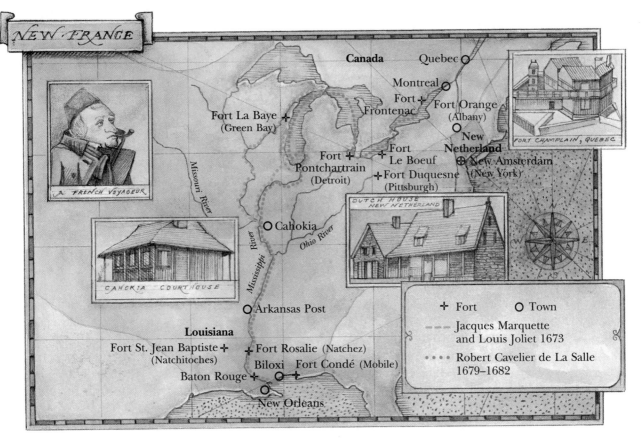

NEW·FRANCE

Canada
Quebec ○
Montreal ○
Fort ✛
Frontenac ✛ Fort Orange
(Albany)
Fort La Baye ✛
(Green Bay)
○ New
Netherland
Fort ✛ Fort ✛
Pontchartrain Le Boeuf ⊕ New Amsterdam
(Detroit) ✛ Fort Duquesne (New York)
(Pittsburgh)

Missouri River

A FRENCH VOYAGEUR

DUTCH HOUSE
NEW NETHERLAND

○ Cahokia
Ohio River

Mississippi River

CAHOKIA COURTHOUSE

○ Arkansas Post

FORT CHAMPLAIN, QUEBEC

Louisiana
Fort St. Jean Baptiste ✛
(Natchitoches)
✛ Fort Rosalie (Natchez)
Biloxi Fort Condé (Mobile)
Baton Rouge ✛ ○ ✛
○ New Orleans

✛ Fort   ○ Town
--- Jacques Marquette
and Louis Joliet 1673
•••• Robert Cavelier de La Salle
1679–1682

Reading Maps

↑ Compare this map with the map on page 105. In what areas do you think French
and Spanish interests were most likely to conflict? Explain your reasons.

paddled along winding streams. Robed missionaries went, too, preaching to Indians. By the 1660s these woodsmen and priests had tramped all around the Great Lakes.

New France grew slowly, however. One reason was that farmers were discouraged by Canada's harsh climate and short growing season.

Another reason was that the king barred the people most willing to come—French Protestants, called *Huguenots* (HYOO-guh-NAHTS). Catholics, permitted in the colony, had little reason to leave France. So New France was left largely to those who chose to roam its forests and sail its rich coastal waters rather than settle down.

The fur trade Because the French were more interested in furs than land, they did not set out to conquer the Indians as the Spanish had done. Instead, the French and Indians became business partners.

Champlain made trade agreements with the tribes near Quebec, especially the Hurons. Huron traders took yearly trips into the forest north of the St. Lawrence. There they traded Huron farm products to other tribes for furs.

Back in Quebec, or in nearby Montreal, they exchanged the furs for European goods, which they used to buy more furs, and so on. To the south the Iroquois made similar agreements with Dutch and English traders.

The French government tried to force its colonists in America to farm the land. The fur trade was so profitable, however, that by 1680 one out of every three men in New France was a trapper.

Louisiana Seeking new trading partners, the French ventured farther inland along the rivers and lakes of North America. Jacques Marquette (zhahk mar-KET), a missionary who had been working near Lake Michigan, heard about a great river to the west. He and Louis Joliet (LOO-ee JŌ-lee-ET), a coureur de bois, set out to find it. In 1673 they paddled a canoe 700 miles (1,127 km) south on the Mississippi River and then made their way back again.

Word of Marquette and Joliet's journey reached Robert Cavelier de La Salle, who was building forts and trading posts in the Great Lakes area. La Salle followed Marquette and Joliet's route, but he went all the way to the Gulf of Mexico. On April 9, 1682, he planted a French flag at the mouth of the river and claimed the Mississippi Valley for France. He named it Louisiana for King Louis XIV.

To keep other Europeans out, the French built a chain of forts and posts along the St. Lawrence and down the Mississippi. The cities of Montreal, Green Bay, Chicago, Detroit, St. Louis, Natchez, and New Orleans all began as French forts or posts.

New Netherland

Another American city, New York, owes its start to the Dutch. During the 1600s tiny Netherlands was a major trading nation. Its merchants formed the Dutch West India Company to carry out trade. Based on Henry Hudson's voyage for the Netherlands, they claimed lands along the Hudson River.

Dutch traders flocked to the area. Soon Dutch settlers formed the colony of New

The Iroquois League The Hurons were glad to have French help against the Iroquois. For years the Hurons and the Iroquois tribes—Mohawks, Oneidas, Onondagas, Cayugas, and Senecas—had fought each other. The Iroquois tribes had also feuded among themselves.

In about 1570 two men—Deganawida and Hiawatha—had a vision of what they called a "Great Peace." They convinced the Iroquois tribes to form a **league,** which is a group with a common purpose. The Iroquois League, or League of the Five Nations, ended the feuding between the tribes. It also made them stronger against their enemies.

The rivalry between the Iroquois and the Hurons grew, spurred on by competition for furs. When the Iroquois killed off the fur-bearing animals in their territory, they moved onto Huron lands. In 1649 they attacked the Hurons and scattered them into the forests. Then the Iroquois defeated one tribe after another until they had destroyed nearly all the tribes that traded with the French.

Netherland. Its largest community, New Amsterdam, was on an island at the mouth of the Hudson. The company wanted good relations with Indians, so it gave Governor Peter Minuit the following instructions:

> "In case there should be any Indians living on the . . . island, . . . they must not be expelled with violence or threats but be persuaded with kind words . . . or should be given something."

Obeying his orders, in 1626 Minuit bought the island from the Manhattan Indians for trade goods worth about $24. Manhattan Island is the heart of New York City today.

To encourage settlement, the company gave land to wealthy landlords called *patroons*, who were to bring in settlers. The Dutch accepted people of different religions. Among New Netherland's first settlers were Protestants fleeing persecution in Belgium.

New Sweden New Netherland soon felt competition from Sweden, which established a trading company in 1637. The next year the company hired the former Dutch governor, Peter Minuit, to lead 50 Swedish, Finnish, and Dutch settlers to the banks of the Delaware River near present-day Wilmington. The Delaware Indians were eager to trade, and the colony prospered.

The people of New Netherland looked on their neighbors in New Sweden as intruders. In 1655 a new Dutch governor, the fiery, one-legged Peter Stuyvesant, led an attack on New Sweden. Minuit's settlers gave in, and New Sweden became part of New Netherland.

English America

England mostly ignored the Americas until 1558, when Elizabeth became queen. Determined to make England powerful, she united her Protestant subjects in a fierce rivalry against Catholic Spain.

A group of English sea captains, called the Sea Dogs, had been raiding Spanish ports and ships. When the boldest Sea Dog of all, Francis Drake, seized a treasure ship—as you read in Section 2—and sailed home across the Pacific with millions of dollars worth of gold, the queen was delighted. On board his ship, the *Golden Hind*, she made him a knight.

The Spanish Armada Philip II of Spain, the son of King Charles, was furious. He demanded that Elizabeth punish Drake. When she refused, Philip assembled a mighty armada—fleet of warships—and in July 1588 sent it to crush England. One English observer described the Armada:

> "the Spanish fleet with lofty turrets like castles, [in a formation] like a half-moon, the wings thereof spreading out about the length of seven miles, . . . and the ocean groaning under the weight of them."

World Link

Cimarrons Thousands of Cimarrons—Africans who had escaped slavery on Spanish plantations—lived in the dense brush and rain forests of Spanish America. In 1573 a group of Cimarrons helped Francis Drake raid a mule train carrying treasure from Peru to Panama. According to one of Drake's men, the Cimarrons were glad to join in "to revenge the wrongs . . . the Spanish nation had done to them." Later, Africans who fled enslavement on English plantations to live in the forests of North America were called Maroons, after the Cimarrons.

This portrait of Queen Elizabeth I celebrates the defeat of the Spanish Armada. Her hand rests atop the globe, a sign of English power. In one picture on the wall behind her, wind fills the sails of the English fleet. In the other, a storm dashes the Armada against the rocks. The war between Spain and England dragged on, however, ending officially in 1604, a year after Elizabeth's death.

Cannonballs flew as the Armada and the English fleet, led by Drake, blasted away in the waters between England and France. On the night of August 7 the English filled eight ships with gunpowder, set them afire, and launched them toward the Armada. Expecting explosions, the Armada scattered northward. Then on August 13, a mighty storm arose. It battered what remained of the Spanish fleet. Fewer than half the ships ever returned to Spain.

The defeat of the Armada marked a turning point in history. Spain had been the greatest power in Europe for nearly a century. Now, Spain declined. In the future England would control the seas and create an empire that stretched around the globe.

England's first attempts At first England's path to empire was rocky. Sir Humphrey Gilbert tried to plant a colony in Newfoundland in 1583, but he and his colonists lost their lives in a storm at sea.

Gilbert's brother, Sir Walter Raleigh, chose a site further south, on Roanoke Island off the coast of present-day North Carolina. He named his colony Virginia in honor of

Elizabeth, who was called the Virgin Queen. Unfortunately, the settlers were more interested in gold than crops. Sir Francis Drake rescued the hungry survivors in 1586.

The next year Raleigh tried again, sending settlers under the command of John White. White returned to England for supplies, leaving behind 117 settlers, including his daughter and her family.

White could not get back to Roanoke until 1590. When he arrived, all he found was an empty fort, a few tattered books, and pieces of rusty armor. On a doorpost were carved the letters C R O A T O A N. White guessed that the colonists had taken refuge with friendly Indians on nearby Croatan Island, but he never found them.

Future colonies Although the earliest English colonies failed, there were lessons to be learned from the effort. Gilbert and Raleigh had put up their own money. Now others could see that keeping a colony going might be too big an undertaking for any one man and his wallet.

People in England, however, kept dreaming of colonies in the Americas. In an

English play written in 1605, a sea captain described the Americas of his dreams:

"Gold is more plentiful there than copper is with us. Why, Man, all their dripping pans are pure gold, and all the chains . . . are massive gold. For rubies and diamonds, they gather them by the seashore to hang on their children's coats."

Richard Hakluyt, a minister, had another dream. English colonies, he wrote, "may stay [stop] the Spanish king . . . from flowing over all the face of . . . America."

3. Section Review

1. Define **persecution** and **league**.
2. Explain two ways the Reformation spurred colony-building in the Americas.
3. Why was New France so sparsely settled?
4. What was the chief interest of the Netherlands in North America?
5. Give two reasons why England's first colonies failed.
6. Critical Thinking Compare the relationship between Indians and the French with the relationship between Indians and the Spanish.

Why We Remember

The Conquest of the Americas

Bartolomé de Las Casas returned to Spain at the age of 72. He spent his remaining 20 years writing. He filled one work, *A Very Brief Report of the Destruction of the Indies*, with sickening descriptions of cruel treatment of Indians. Las Casas may have exaggerated the number of Indians who perished as a result of the conquest. Still, no one could deny that for many native peoples, the arrival of Europeans was a disaster beyond measure. That fact alone would be reason enough to remember the conquest of the Americas.

There are other reasons why we remember this period, however. It was a time of great adventures and extraordinary accomplishments. Even today, the stories of men like Cortés, Pizarro, Cabeza de Vaca, Drake, and Champlain have the power to surprise, amaze, astonish, and appall us.

Perhaps most important, we remember the period as a time of endings and beginnings. While the old civilizations of the Americas were being destroyed, new ones were being born. From these painful beginnings would come the new peoples and nations of North and South America.

Chapter Survey

Reviewing Vocabulary

Define the following terms.
1. conquistadors   3. persecution
2. mercantilism   4. league

Reviewing Main Ideas

1. What advantages enabled the Spanish to conquer the Aztecs?
2. What did the Spanish find in Mexico and South America that produced the greatest wealth for them?
3. In what ways were the Spanish entradas into lands north of Mexico both a failure and a success?
4. What did the Spanish missionaries want to accomplish? Describe three effects their actions had on Indians.
5. Explain the following statement: Without meaning to, Spain's rivals encouraged Spain to settle the borderlands. Give two supporting examples.
6. What kinds of relationships did the French and the Dutch establish with Indians? Why?
7. What lesson did the English learn from the failures of their first American colonies?

Thinking Critically

1. Analysis Reread the statements by Antonio de Montesinos, Juan Ginés de Sepúlveda, and Bartolomé de Las Casas. Based on those statements, list the basic beliefs of each man. Could Montesinos or Las Casas have persuaded Sepúlveda to change his mind? Why or why not?
2. Synthesis Imagine that you are one of Queen Elizabeth's advisors and are on a trip to Spain. Write a letter to the queen telling her what you see in Spain and why it makes you think that England should rush to establish colonies in North America.

3. Why We Remember: Application

Imagine a television series called *A Very Brief Report on the Creation of the Americas*. Each program will feature one present-day country. The program will be divided into three parts: (1) the old ways of life, (2) people who made a difference, (3) the new way of life. Choose one country. List two or three topics you would include in each part of a program about that country.

Applying Skills

Analyzing a Painting Read the Section Focus and Reading Guide questions on page 120. Choose a painting in that section to analyze. Answer numbers 1–3 without looking at the caption. Then read the caption and answer number 4. Keep in mind what you learned in the Skill Lab on page 107.
1. Identify the main image in the painting, if any. Identify as many smaller details as you can.
2. Describe the painting's mood. How does the artist create that mood?
3. Summarize the story that the painting tells. What do you think was the artist's purpose?
4. What similarities and differences do you find between what you have written and what the caption says?

History Mystery

Analyzing forces of destruction Answer the History Mystery on page 91. In what ways could a widespread epidemic affect a large city today? How might such an event disrupt peoples' lives? How might it affect peoples' states of mind? How would people react?

ATLANTIC
OCEAN

PACIFIC
OCEAN

Reviewing Geography

1. The letters on the map represent European possessions in the Americas in 1650. Write the name of each possession.

2. Geographic Thinking Many places in the United States have Spanish or French names. List five or more places with Spanish names and five or more with French names. Use the maps on pages R4–R5 and R6–R7, an atlas, or a dictionary for help, if you need it. What patterns, if any, do you see in the locations of the names? What other evidence of Spanish or French influence might you expect to find in a place with a Spanish or French name?

Writing in Your History Journal

1. Keys to History (a) The time line on pages 90–91 has seven Keys to History. In your journal, describe why each one is important. (b) Choose one of the events on the time line, and imagine yourself as a news reporter on the scene. Write a list of 10 facts you plan to include in your news story.

2. Bartolomé de Las Casas As Las Casas, write a diary entry expressing your thoughts at the moment you decided to give up using the forced labor of Indian workers on your land.

3. Citizenship You have read that King Charles of Spain reformed the encomienda system to limit the colonists' rights to Indian labor. Without knowing the details of his reforms, why do you suppose the colonists paid so little attention to them? Write your response in your journal.

Alternative Assessment

Recalling a life With classmates, prepare slips of paper each with the name of one person from the chapter on it, for example, Cortés, Moctezuma, Cabeza de Vaca, de Soto, Popé, and Queen Elizabeth. Put the slips in a bag and take turns drawing out one name apiece.

Imagine that you are the person whose name you have drawn. Prepare a presentation that answers these questions: What did you do with your life? Why? How did you serve your people? What are you proud of? How do you answer your critics? The presentation may include acting out, speech, and visual aids.

Your work will be evaluated on the following criteria:
• you present the person's life accurately
• you present the person's point of view
• you make the person seem real

Chapter 5

1600–1750

Planting English Colonies

Sections

Beginning the Story with Pocahontas

1. **The First English Colonies**
2. **Puritan Colonies in New England**
3. **Later English Colonies**

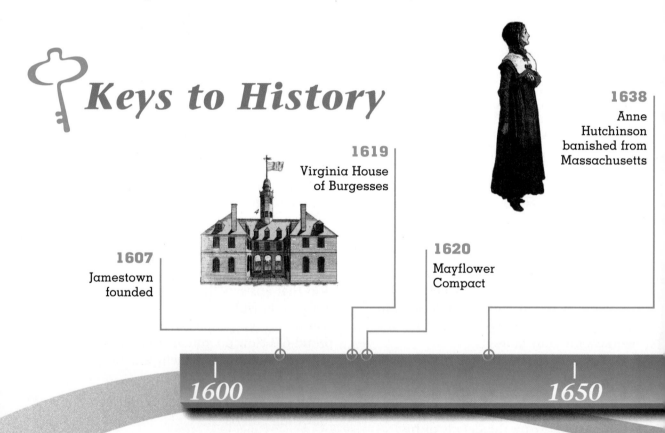

Keys to History

1638 Anne Hutchinson banished from Massachusetts

1619 Virginia House of Burgesses

1620 Mayflower Compact

1607 Jamestown founded

1600

1650

Looking Back

"Lost Colony" of Roanoke

1590

HISTORY
Mystery

After a terrible first winter at Plymouth, the Pilgrims were rescued by an English-speaking Indian. Where had the Indian come from, and how had he learned English?

1675

King Philip's War

Chief Metacomet, known as King Philip

1681

Penn plans "holy experiment" in Pennsylvania

Plate showing German settlers

1732

Georgia, the last English colony

James Oglethorpe, founder of Georgia

1700

1750

World Link

Huguenots flee France
1685

Looking Ahead

Spain gives up Florida
1819

● **117**

Beginning the Story with

Pocahontas

For two bitterly cold weeks Captain John Smith had been led from one Indian town to another. In late December 1607, the English captive was finally brought to the village of Powhatan, the powerful chief of the Indians in Virginia. As Smith entered Powhatan's longhouse, he was greeted by a shout—a salute to him as a chief of the recently arrived English colonists.

In the dim light of the longhouse, Smith saw rows of men and women "with their heads and shoulders painted red." He also saw Powhatan, a tall, impressive man draped in a fur robe. He did not notice a 12-year-old girl standing in the shadows. Her name was Pocahontas. Smith would soon owe her his life.

Helping the English Strangers

Pocahontas listened as her father, Powhatan, and his council debated the stranger's fate. Then she heard the decision: The white chief must die.

Warriors grabbed Smith, pushed his head down on a stone, and raised their clubs to strike him dead. At that instant Pocahontas darted forward and begged her father to have mercy. Smith later wrote that she "got [my] head in her arms, and laid her own upon [mine] to save [me] from death." A few days later, Smith was safely back in the English settlement of Jamestown.

To save Smith, Pocahontas had followed a custom of her people and adopted him as her brother. She may have rescued Smith out of curiosity, or perhaps she acted out of sympathy. Smith himself wrote that her "compassionate, pitiful heart . . . gave me much cause to respect her."

Adopting Smith was, for Pocahontas, a serious commitment. That winter the settlers would have starved had she not helped them. "Every once in four or five days, Pocahontas with her attendants brought . . . provision [food]," wrote Smith. "She, next under God, was . . . the instrument to preserve this colony from death, famine, and utter confusion."

From Pocahontas to Rebecca

Smith returned to England in 1609. After that, relations between Indians and the colonists began to grow tense. Fearing war, the English kidnapped Pocahontas in 1613 and held her hostage in Jamestown to prevent an attack on the settlement.

Unlike her friends and relatives who mistrusted the English, Pocahontas was fascinated by the strangers from across the sea. She took advantage of her time in Jamestown to learn the language and customs of the colonists. The settlers were especially pleased by her interest in their religion. They believed it their duty to bring the Christian faith to American Indians.

At least one colonist found the Indian hostage equally fascinating. That summer John Rolfe fell in love with Pocahontas. In a letter to the colony's governor, Thomas Dale, Rolfe asked for permission to marry her. He said he was making this request

This detail from a map of Virginia prepared by John Smith shows Powhatan and his council deciding Smith's fate.

❝for the good of this plantation [Jamestown], for the honor of our country, for the glory of God, . . . and for the converting to the true knowledge of God and Jesus Christ [of] an unbelieving creature, namely Pocahontas, to whom my hearty and best thoughts are, and have [for] a long time been, so entangled.❞

How did Pocahontas feel about this marriage? She may have fallen in love with Rolfe. Certainly she impressed him with "her great appearance of love to me." She may also have hoped that their marriage would bring peace between the colonists and her people. It was probably for that reason that both Governor Dale and Powhatan approved the match.

Pocahontas completed her instruction in the Christian religion and was baptized as Rebecca. Within a year she and Rolfe were wed. For the next few years, colonists and Indians lived together without conflict, protected by Rebecca and John Rolfe's "married peace."

Hands-On HISTORY

Activity

In his *Generall Historie of Virginia*, John Smith wrote about his rescue by Pocahontas, but we have no account of this event from her point of view. Write the story of her decision to save the white chief as you think she might have told it.

1. The First English Colonies

Reading Guide

New Terms **invest, joint-stock company, exports, indentured servants, representatives, legislature, royal colony**

Section Focus **England's colonies in Virginia and Plymouth**

1. Why did the English want to establish colonies in America?
2. How did Virginia change between 1607 and 1624?
3. What goal did Plymouth colonists have, and how did they reach it?

The dramatic story of Pocahontas, the young Indian woman who saved John Smith and married John Rolfe, took place in Virginia, the first permanent English colony in North America. Between 1607 and 1732, England was to start 13 colonies along the Atlantic coast.

What caused this great interest in colonies? Why did the English government encourage it? The answers to these questions are found in two great changes that were taking place in England. One change was economic, the other was religious.

An Economic Revolution

The changes in England's economy have been called an economic revolution. As a result of the revolution, some people gained great wealth, while others were plunged into poverty. To both the wealthy and the poor, colonies in America offered opportunity and hope.

Strange as it may seem, the revolution began with sheep. In the 1500s the demand for woolen cloth in Europe suddenly soared. To meet the demand, English landowners enclosed their farms, fencing off large areas as grazing lands for sheep. Manufacturers, in turn, spun and wove the wool into cloth, which merchants sold throughout Europe.

This trade brought great wealth to landowners, wool manufacturers, and merchants. Many of them began looking for ways to invest their new wealth. To **invest** means to use your money to help a business get started or grow, with the hope that you will earn a profit. As you will see, colonies began to look like a good investment.

The uprooted While the wool trade brought wealth to some, it caused great hardship for countless English families. For generations, farmers had rented small plots from large landowners. When landowners enclosed their fields to raise sheep, these farmers lost their farms—and their jobs.

Uprooted men, women, and children drifted from countryside to town to city, looking for work. Many were reduced to begging or stealing to survive. Is it any wonder that many of these desperate people would risk the long voyage to North America in the hope of a fresh start in colonies?

English leaders, too, saw colonies as a way to solve the problem of the growing numbers of the poor. Worried by the "swarms of idle persons," one observer noted:

"If we seek not some ways for their foreign employment, we must provide shortly more prisons and corrections for their bad conditions.**"**

This idea of sending "idle persons" to colonies fit well with the government's policy of mercantilism. England wanted to sell more to other countries than it bought. In colonies, England's poor could produce raw materials, such as lumber, that England would otherwise have to buy from foreign nations. At the same time, the colonists would buy England's manufactured goods, thus adding to the nation's wealth.

Religious Conflict

Meanwhile, conflict over religion was causing others in England to think of starting colonies. In the mid-1500s England had broken away from the Roman Catholic Church and established the Church of England. By law, all English people had to worship in this new Protestant church.

Not everyone accepted the Church of England, though. On the one hand, many English Catholics wanted to keep their old religion. Some English Protestants, on the other hand, thought the Church of England was too much like the Catholic Church. These people were called Puritans because they believed in simpler, "purer" forms of worship.

The government of England tried to force both Catholics and Puritans to accept the Church of England. According to William Bradford, who later became governor of Plymouth Colony,

"Some [Puritans] were taken and clapped up in prison, others had their houses . . . watched night and day, and hardly escaped."

Both Catholics and Protestants began to think of colonies in North America as a place where they might practice their religion without interference. Thus, conflict over religion, as well as new wealth and desperate poverty, pushed England into an era of colonization.

Despite the ban on the Roman Catholic Church, many English Catholics practiced their faith in secret. Angered by anti-Catholic laws, this group of men plotted against government leaders in 1605.

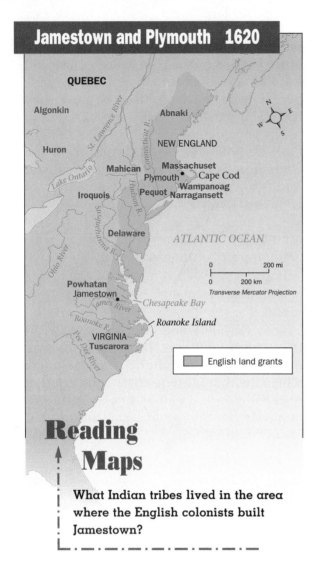

Jamestown and Plymouth 1620

QUEBEC

Algonkin

Abnaki

Huron

NEW ENGLAND

Mahican
Massachuset
Plymouth • Cape Cod
Iroquois
Pequot
Wampanoag
Narragansett

Delaware

ATLANTIC OCEAN

0   200 mi
0   200 km
Transverse Mercator Projection

Powhatan
Jamestown
James River — Chesapeake Bay

Roanoke R. — Roanoke Island

VIRGINIA
Tuscarora

English land grants

Reading
Maps

What Indian tribes lived in the area where the English colonists built Jamestown?

Virginia, the First Colony

Merchants founded the first permanent English colony in Virginia. They hoped to find precious metals and other raw materials that England needed.

Establishing a colony was expensive and risky. Thus, the merchants organized the Virginia Company of London. It was a **joint-stock company**—a business that raised money by selling shares, called stock, to investors. The profits were to be divided among the investors according to the number of shares each had.

In a document called a charter, the king, James I, granted the Virginia Company the right to "plant," or establish, colonies in Virginia. Investors eagerly bought stock. As a result, the company was able to buy the ships and supplies it needed to launch a colony.

Building Jamestown In the spring of 1607, 105 men and boys sailed up a broad river in Chesapeake Bay. They named the river the James and their settlement Jamestown in honor of their king.

From the first, Jamestown was in trouble. Ignoring orders from the Virginia Company, the leaders located their settlement on low, swampy ground. The only drinking water was salty, and the area swarmed with mosquitoes. Disease spread rapidly.

Then, instead of planting crops, the colonists rushed off to search for gold. As Captain John Smith later wrote:

"There was no talk, no hope, no work, but dig gold, wash gold, refine gold, load gold.**"**

Too late did they learn that their gold was really fool's gold.

Hard times During the first 7 months in Jamestown, 73 colonists died of hunger and disease. The rest owed their lives to the inspired leadership of John Smith and to the friendship of Pocahontas.

After Smith took control of the colony in 1608, he forced the settlers to plant crops. He declared, "He that will not work, shall not eat." More supplies also arrived from England. So did more colonists.

A year later, Smith was burned in a gunpowder explosion and returned to England. Without him, the colony fell into disorder. As supplies ran out, people ate rats to stay alive. The winter of 1609–1610 became known as the "starving time." When spring came, only 60 of 500 colonists were still alive.

Changes in Virginia

Hope for survival of the colony came from tobacco, an American "weed" that had become very popular in Europe. The soil of Virginia was ideal for growing tobacco, and in 1612 John Rolfe, husband of Pocahontas, developed a method of drying it for shipment to England.

Tobacco exports soared. **Exports** are goods sent out of one country to sell in another. The Virginia Company was pleased by the new tobacco trade. However, life in Jamestown was very hard, and few English people wanted to live there.

To stir up interest in Virginia, in 1616 the company brought Pocahontas and John Rolfe to England. Everywhere Pocahontas went, she caused a sensation. Merchants, church leaders, and even the king and queen were eager to meet her.

To attract more settlers, the Virginia Company also made several important changes in the colony. First, in 1618 the company gave colonists the right to own land. Until then, the company had owned all land in Virginia. Now people who paid their own way to the colony were granted 50 acres. They received another 50 acres for each new settler they brought with them.

Indentured servants To encourage settlers who could not afford to pay their own way to Virginia, the company allowed

No one knows what Jamestown looked like in 1607 because some of the site has been washed away by the James River. This artist's view shows how the colonists might have built a protective wall around their tents and huts.

them to come as **indentured servants.** That is, they signed a contract called an indenture, agreeing to work four to seven years without pay for the person who paid their passage. At the end of the period, indentured servants were free. Usually they received some new clothes and perhaps money or tools to help them start supporting themselves.

It was as indentured servants that many of England's uprooted farmers came to the colonies. They were willing to set out for a new land in the hope that at the end of the contract they could find work or buy a plot of land to farm.

In 1619 the company sent 90 young women to Virginia. It hoped that settlers who married and started families would make Virginia their permanent home. Many of the women married at once. Each husband paid the cost of his wife's transportation in tobacco. The women who did not marry became indentured servants.

The House of Burgesses The year 1619 also marked the first step toward self-government in Virginia. Until then the Virginia Company had appointed the governor and his council of advisors.

Now the company allowed adult male landowners to elect **representatives**—people who are chosen to speak and act in government for their fellow citizens. This system was more like the one in England. There citizens had a voice in their government through representatives they elected to a legislature called Parliament. A **legislature** is a group of people chosen to make laws.

In Virginia the representatives, called *burgesses*, were to meet as an assembly called the House of Burgesses. The assembly, along with the governor's council, became the colony's legislature. It gave the English colonists a degree of self-government that was unheard of at that time in the Spanish and French colonies in America.

Conflict Between Colonists and Indians

Tobacco gave settlers a valuable product to sell, and new tobacco farms spread along the James River. Soon planters were expanding into the lands of neighboring Indian tribes. Conflict erupted as Indians tried to protect their lands and families.

In March 1622 Indian warriors attacked the colony, killing 347 settlers. One of them was John Rolfe, whose marriage to Pocahontas had given hope of peace between Indians and colonists. Pocahontas herself had died of smallpox in England.

The colonists struck back with such thoroughness that they broke the power of the

This photograph of Plymouth today gives a sense of the harshness of the Pilgrims' first winter in New England. In 4 months, 44 people died.

Virginia tribes. In one example of revenge, described by colonist Robert Bennett, 200 Indians were killed at a peace conference because the wine they drank "was sent of purpose . . . to poison them."

A royal colony The warfare left much of Jamestown in ruins and the Virginia Company in serious difficulties. In 1624 only 1,200 colonists remained, and the investors had lost nearly $5 million.

As a result, King James I took away the Virginia Company's charter. He made Virginia a **royal colony,** which means that the king appointed the governor and the council of advisors. James tried to do away with the House of Burgesses, but the Virginians insisted on having a voice in government. Like the struggling colony, the House of Burgesses clung to life.

Plymouth Colony

The colony of Virginia had been started by investors and adventurers looking for profits and gold. The people who planted the next English colony were seeking something far different—the right to worship as they wished. They became known as Pilgrims because they made their journey for religious reasons.

Earlier in this section you read about conflict between Catholics and Puritans and the Church of England. Most Puritans stayed within the church and tried to change it. The Pilgrims, however, were Puritans who decided to set up a separate church. Because they were breaking English law, they were persecuted.

A small group of Pilgrims fled to the Netherlands. There they could worship as they wished, but they feared their children would grow up more Dutch than English.

As a result, a number of Pilgrims decided to establish their own community in North America. King James gave them permission to settle north of Jamestown as long as they did not stir up trouble.

In September 1620 about 100 voyagers set out from Plymouth, England, in a leaky, overcrowded boat named the *Mayflower*. One-third of them were Pilgrims. The others were non-Pilgrim "strangers," who planned to settle in Virginia.

The Mayflower Compact After a stormy 66-day voyage, the *Mayflower* reached the American coast at Cape Cod, in the region the English called New England. The ship had been blown far north of Virginia, where the Pilgrims had permission to settle. The laws in their charter applied only to Virginia, so the group decided they must organize their own government.

Pilgrim leaders drafted an agreement known as the Mayflower Compact, which 41 Pilgrims and "strangers" signed on board the *Mayflower*. In the compact, the signers agreed to make laws "for the general good of the colony, unto which we promise all due . . . obedience." Dated November 21, 1620, the Mayflower Compact helped establish the American tradition that government rests on the consent of the governed.

Help from Squanto The early history of Plymouth Colony is one of suffering. The site was barren. Half of the colonists sickened and died during the first year.

Like the settlers in Jamestown, who relied on Pocahontas, the Pilgrims owed their survival to an Indian. His name was Squanto, and he was a Wampanoag (WAHM-puh-NŌ-ahg) who had been to England and could speak English.

Squanto's story was not as unusual as you might think. Since the 1500s, English fish-ermen and Indians had been trading along the Atlantic coast. Some captains kidnapped the Indians to sell as slaves. Squanto was captured in 1614 and sold in Spain.

Squanto escaped to England, where he lived for several years before being sent to Newfoundland. Unhappy there, Squanto returned to England and found a ship headed for Cape Cod. When he arrived at last, in 1619, he discovered that disease had wiped out his entire village.

To the Pilgrims, Squanto must have seemed like a gift from God. He not only taught the colonists about farming but helped them establish friendly relations with neighboring tribes. Sadly, Squanto died from a disease brought to America by the people he did so much to help.

The Pilgrims' contributions Despite Squanto's help, Plymouth Colony never prospered. In 1691 it was taken over by the nearby colony of Massachusetts.

Plymouth, however, remains important in our nation's history. The Pilgrims believed that people have the right to create their own laws and to worship as they wish. Such ideas are among the building blocks of the government we have today.

1. Section Review

1. Define **invest, joint-stock company, exports, indentured servants, representatives, legislature,** and **royal colony.**
2. How did the movement to enclose farmland affect English hopes for colonies?
3. Describe two important changes in Virginia in 1618 and 1619. How did the changes help the colony?
4. Critical Thinking How were the Puritans and the Pilgrims similar? How were they different?

Geography Lab

The Coastal Lowlands

The explorer Giovanni Verrazano once called the Coastal Lowlands "spacious land, . . . with many beautiful fields and plains, full of the largest forests." The English later planted colonies in this fertile region that stretches from Massachusetts to Texas. The lowlands are watered by many rivers that plunge from higher ground to the north and west. The place where the higher ground drops abruptly to the plains below is known as the **Fall Line**. Use John Smith's description and the illustrations on this page to gather information about the Coastal Lowlands.

Chesapeake Bay, Maryland

John Smith on Virginia

"The land—white hilly sands, . . . and all along the shores great plenty of pines and firs. . . . Here are mountains, hills, plains, valleys, rivers, brooks, all running most pleasantly into a fair bay. . . . The more southward, the farther off from the bay are those mountains, from which fall certain brooks which [become] navigable rivers. . . . The [vegetation] of the earth in most places doth . . . prove the nature of the soil to be lusty and very rich."

Baltimore, Maryland, 1752

Developing a Mental Map

Refer to the map of regions on pages P4–P5, as well as the maps on pages R4–R5 and R6–R7 to help you answer the questions.

1. What states lie within the Coastal Lowlands?

2. Estimate the width of the lowlands.

3. What two large plains do the Coastal Lowlands include?

4. What parts of Smith's description of Virginia also apply to the places pictured on this page?

5. **Hands-On Geography** Baltimore, Maryland, is just one city that was built where a river crosses the Fall Line. Imagine that you are one of Baltimore's founders. Write a letter to a newspaper in England bragging about Baltimore's location.

2. Puritan Colonies in New England

Reading Guide

New Term **bicameral**

Section Focus **The colonies established by the English Puritans**

1. What dream did the Puritans have, and how did they make it real?
2. Why were new colonies established in New England?
3. What caused conflict between Puritans and American Indians?

"Follow the counsel of Micah: to do justly, to love mercy, to walk humbly with our God. For this end, we must . . . rejoice together, mourn together, labor and suffer together, always having before our eyes . . . our common work."

So said Puritan leader John Winthrop to his followers in a sermon in 1630. On board a ship sailing to North America, Winthrop urged them to build the Christian community God wanted for his people. Such a community, Winthrop promised, would be "like a city upon a hill"—an example for all people to follow.

Massachusetts

In England, many Puritans were prosperous landowners and merchants. They had gained power in England's Parliament and were using it to try to purify the Church of England.

Faced with this threat, King Charles I set out to destroy the Puritans. He had Puritan leaders jailed, and some were even tortured. Winthrop and a group of leading Puritans decided that their only hope was to leave England and establish a colony based on Puritan ideas in America.

In 1629 a group of Puritans formed a joint-stock company, which they called the Massachusetts Bay Company. The king gave them a charter to settle on land north of Plymouth. Unlike other charters, this one did not require company stockholders to meet in England. As a result, the Puritans were able to move the company to Massachusetts and to set up the kind of colony they wanted.

Self-government was vital to the leaders of the Massachusetts Bay Company because they had a clear goal. They planned to create a community where Puritans would live together according to the true law of God as they understood it.

The Great Migration The Puritans wanted their "city upon a hill" to be an economic success as well as a model Christian community. They came well-prepared for life in a new land, bringing plenty of food, tools, livestock, and supplies. As a result, there was no "starving time," as in Jamestown, or winter of horror, as in Plymouth.

Every year ships brought new supplies and colonists. Between 1630 and 1640, in what was called the Great Migration, some 20,000 people arrived in Boston, the capital city of Massachusetts.

By no means were all of the new arrivals Puritans. Driven by hard times in England and hopes for a better life in America, non-Puritans also came to Massachusetts.

Representative government At first, all decisions were made by 12 stock-holders of the company acting as a legislature called the General Court. They also elected the governor and his assistants. Winthrop became the first governor and served a total of 16 years.

Faced with a few leaders making all the rules, other colonists demanded a voice in government. In 1631 government leaders allowed all male members of Puritan churches to attend the General Court.

As the population grew, the General Court became too large. In 1634 church members in each town began electing deputies to represent them in the General Court. Ten years later, the General Court became a **bicameral**, or two-house, legislature, with the governor's assistants sitting in one "house" and the deputies in the other.

Dissent Leads to Expansion

Religion was closely tied to government in Massachusetts. All colonists, Puritan or not, were bound by law to live by Puritan rules. Winthrop and other colony leaders would not permit dissent.

Except for places like the Connecticut Valley, soil in New England was thin. Lured by the promise of good farmland, these followers of the Reverend Thomas Hooker traveled to Connecticut, driving their cattle before them.

Thus, it was not long before conflicts began. Puritans who questioned beliefs or rules were punished or driven out. Others chose to leave. In the next 50 years, 3 new colonies were formed in New England, out of range of Massachusetts control.

Rhode Island

Roger Williams was the first to break away. Williams had arrived in Massachusetts in 1631. Although he was a Puritan minister, he soon accused leaders of not following the teachings of the Bible. Then he opposed the law that everyone must go to religious services. Finally, he questioned the colonists' right to take Indian lands without paying for them.

Williams's views so angered Puritan leaders that in 1635 the General Court ordered him sent back to England. Governor Winthrop, however, worried that Williams would be arrested in England. Warned by Winthrop, Williams fled with a few of his followers. The group spent the winter with nearby Narragansett (NAYR-uh-GAN-sit) Indians.

The next year Williams bought land from the Narragansetts and established the settlement of Providence. Under his leadership, Providence and several neighboring towns formed a colony called Rhode Island. They received a charter from the king in 1644.

In his new home, Williams rejected the idea of close ties between church and government. He promised that no colonist would be punished "for any differences in opinion in matters of religion."

Point of View

Are there limits to liberty?

People of all faiths came to Rhode Island for religious freedom. Soon, however, some began to argue that they should also be free from obeying the colony's laws. Roger Williams disagreed. In a letter written in 1655, he said that colonists could worship as they wished, but they had to obey the laws. To make his point, he used the example of passengers and a commander on a ship at sea.

"There goes many a ship to sea with many hundred souls in one ship. . . . Papists [Catholics] and Protestants, Jews and Turks [Muslims] may be embarked in one ship. . . .

All the liberty of conscience that ever I pleaded for turns upon these two hinges—[1] that none of the Papists, Protestants, Jews, or Turks be forced to come to the ship's prayers or worship, [2] nor compelled [kept] from their own particular prayers or worship, if they practice any. . . .

[However,] I never denied that . . . the commander of this ship ought to command the ship's course, yea, and also command that justice [and] peace . . . be kept and practiced, both among the seamen and all the passengers."

As Americans, we treasure our liberty, but what would it be like to live without any laws?

Anne Hutchinson Like Roger Williams, Anne Hutchinson also clashed with Puritan leaders in Massachusetts. The wife of a wealthy merchant and the mother of 11 children, she arrived in Boston in 1634. Strong-willed and brilliant, she attracted followers who came to weekly meetings in her home to discuss religion.

Hutchinson got in trouble when she questioned church teachings and said that God spoke to people directly instead of through church officials. Puritan leaders thought Hutchinson's views were dangerous to the colony, and they ordered her to stand trial. In the spring of 1638 the General Court banished her "as being a woman not fit for our society."

Hutchinson and her family fled to Rhode Island and later to New Netherland. In 1643 she and five of her children were killed by Indians. Governor Winthrop had taken pity on Roger Williams, but he could not forgive Anne Hutchinson. Her death, he wrote in his journal, was "a special manifestation [sign] of divine [God's] justice."

Connecticut

As early as 1633, Puritans seeking good farmland and fur trade opportunities had begun to move into the region that is today the state of Connecticut. The region also attracted the Reverend Thomas Hooker, who had disagreed with Puritan leaders about religious issues.

In 1636 Hooker led three church congregations into the Connecticut River valley, where they established farms and towns. A year later the residents organized the colony of Connecticut. For 25 years, it remained an independent colony without a charter from the king.

In 1639 representatives from the towns drew up a plan of government called the Fundamental Orders of Connecticut. Hooker's belief in government based on the will of the people became part of the Fundamental Orders. Although the plan set up a government like that of Massachusetts, the right to vote was not limited to church members.

New Hampshire and Maine

In their search for good farmland, colonists from Massachusetts also moved north, almost to the border of New France. In the region that is now New Hampshire and Maine, they built settlements and farmed and fished.

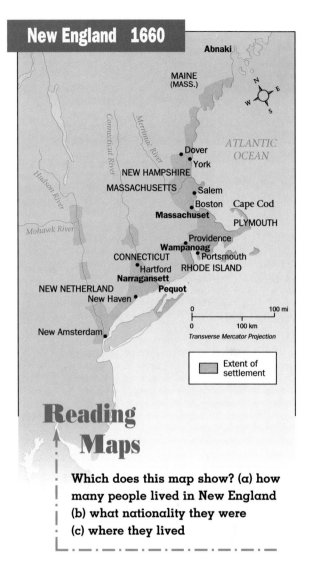

New England 1660

Reading Maps

Which does this map show? (a) how many people lived in New England (b) what nationality they were (c) where they lived

Massachusetts claimed that both of these areas were a part of its territory. In 1679, however, the king established a separate colony called New Hampshire. Maine would remain a part of Massachusetts until 1820.

Puritans and Indians Clash

Lured by what seemed to be unlimited empty land, the Puritans had quickly spread throughout New England. Of course, the land was not really empty. American Indians had lived and farmed and hunted there for thousands of years.

As a child, Metacomet watched the Puritans take over Indian lands and force his people to obey English laws. After he became chief, he led New England tribes in resisting the English colonists.

lacked clear evidence that the Pequots were involved, they set fire to the Pequots' main village. Out of 500 Indians in the village, "not over eight escaped out of our hands," boasted one colonist.

King Philip's War The longest, bloodiest war between Indians and colonists in New England broke out in 1675. This time the spark was Plymouth Colony's trial and hanging of three Wampanoags for the murder of a Christian Indian. In response, Wampanoag chief Metacomet, who was called King Philip by the English, organized the New England tribes to drive out the English colonists.

The conflict, known as King Philip's War, spread from Massachusetts to Maine. By the time peace was agreed on in 1678, some 600 colonists had been killed. Half the English towns suffered damage, and 12 were completely destroyed.

The power of the New England tribes was also destroyed, however. Colonists killed about 3,000 Indians, including Metacomet. They sold his wife and child and hundreds of other Indians into slavery in the West Indies. Never again would the tribes pose a serious threat to New England.

Although Indians like Squanto had been of vital help to them at first, most Puritans thought of Indians as savages. By contrast, they saw themselves as chosen by God. Thus they felt no guilt about taking Indian lands. In fact, when the Puritans learned that disease had killed thousands of Indians not long before their arrival, they saw it as a sign of God's helping hand.

With two groups—the Indians and the colonists—both claiming their right to the land, conflict was bound to occur. In 1637 colonists blamed the murder of two English traders on the Pequot (PEE-kwaht) Indians of Connecticut. Although the colonists

2. Section Review

1. Define **bicameral.**
2. John Winthrop hoped Massachusetts would be "like a city upon a hill." What did he mean?
3. Give two reasons why people settled in Rhode Island and Connecticut.
4. What were the causes and effects of conflict between the Indians and the Puritans?
5. **Critical Thinking** The Puritans came to America with a mission. Do you think Americans today have a mission? If so, what do you think it is?

3. Later English Colonies

Reading Guide

New Term **proprietary colonies**

Section Focus **The founding of new English colonies in North America**

1. How did the hopes and plans of founders shape the colonies they started?
2. How did the English compete with the Spanish and Dutch in America?

Certain names are always connected with the founding of the English colonies. John Smith and Pocahontas saved Virginia. John Winthrop led the Puritans to Massachusetts. Roger Williams started Rhode Island.

In the 1630s wealthy "royal favorites" began to start colonies on land given them by the king. These were called **proprietary colonies** because the owners, known as proprietors, organized the colonies, controlled the land, and appointed governors.

The motives of the proprietors varied. Some sought wealth. Others wanted to help the persecuted or the poor. As a result, the proprietary colonies lured a wide variety of people from England and Europe who were looking for a fresh start in life.

Maryland

Maryland was the first successful proprietary colony. It was planned by George Calvert, Lord Baltimore, as a refuge for Catholics who, like Puritans, were being persecuted in England.

King Charles I granted land north of Virginia to his friend Calvert and named it "Marilande" for his queen, Henrietta Maria. Calvert died before the charter was issued in 1632, so the colony went to his son Cecilius.

Two years later the first colonists arrived in Maryland. From the start, Calvert allowed both Catholics and Protestants to follow their religions. Soon people from both groups were moving to Maryland, where they grew tobacco and corn.

As proprietor, Calvert had complete power to govern the colony. However, the charter required that he heed the advice of landowners. Thus, in 1635 Calvert allowed residents to elect an assembly to make laws.

Religious toleration Many settlers in Maryland were wealthy Catholics. Many more, though, were Protestant workers and indentured servants. Calvert feared the Protestants would try to prevent the Catholics from following their religion.

At Calvert's request, the Maryland assembly passed the Toleration Act of 1649. According to the act, the government would tolerate, or respect, the beliefs of both Catholics and Protestants. The act did not tolerate non-Christian religions, such as Judaism. Yet considering the strict rules in England and Massachusetts, this was a step toward greater religious freedom.

Two Carolinas

In 1663 King Charles II granted the land between Virginia and Spanish Florida to a group of eight noblemen. He hoped that having English colonists in the area would keep the Spanish from advancing any farther into North America.

Huguenots flee France

Huguenots flee France In 1685 the French government banned the Protestant religion. Huguenots (Protestants) were ordered to educate their children in the Catholic faith, and they were not allowed to leave the country.

In spite of these laws, more than 50,000 Huguenot families fled France. Many of them settled in South Carolina, New York, and Massachusetts.

Many Huguenots were merchants and skilled craftspeople. Their loss was a blow to the industry and trade of France—and a great boon to the English colonies.

From the start, Carolina, the "land of Charles," was a divided colony. Independent farmers from Virginia moved into the northern part. Ignoring the Carolina proprietors' claim to the land, they settled down to raise tobacco, corn, and livestock.

Carolina's proprietors were more interested in the southern part of the colony, where they built the port city of Charles Town (now Charleston). Settlers came from England's West Indies islands, which had been captured from Spain. However, the proprietors had a terrible time finding ways to make the colony prosper.

Planters tried to raise crops that could not be grown in England, such as olives, grapes, and sugar cane. None did well. The colonists had better luck with cattle and hogs as well as "naval stores" for ships—tar, pitch, and turpentine, made from pine sap.

The most money was to be made from the Indian slave trade, however. Carolina traders bought Indians who had been taken prisoner in wars between local tribes. Then they shipped the captives to the West Indies to be sold as slaves. This trade caused more warfare between tribes as well as conflict between colonists and Indians.

Finally, in the 1690s Carolina found a crop well-suited to its soil and climate—rice. English planters knew nothing about growing rice, however. They depended on the knowledge and labor of enslaved Africans brought into Carolina from rice-growing areas in West Africa. By the early 1700s "Carolina gold," as rice was called, had ensured the prosperity of the colony.

The colony divides Conflict between the proprietors and the colonists led to the division of Carolina. Colonists complained that the proprietors ignored their right of self-government and failed to protect them from Spanish and Indian attacks.

In 1719 angry colonists in the southern part of the colony rebelled, and the king made South Carolina a separate royal colony. Ten years later, North Carolina also became a royal colony.

Fall of New Netherland

While Carolina was being built to stop the Spanish in the south, the English were getting rid of another competitor farther north. King Charles II thought the Dutch colonists of New Netherland had no right to settle on what he believed was English territory. The Dutch also were competing with English merchants for colonial trade.

In 1664 Charles decided to capture the Dutch colony. In August four British warships sailed into New Amsterdam's harbor. The British sent Governor Peter Stuyvesant a note demanding surrender. Stuyvesant tore up the note and called on the people of the town to fight.

They refused. They hated the harsh Stuyvesant. If anyone complained of his

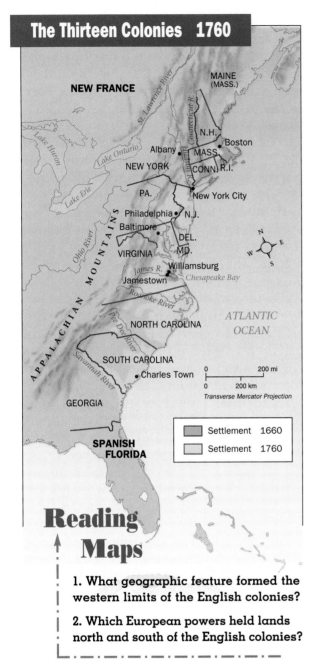

The Thirteen Colonies 1760

NEW FRANCE

MAINE (MASS.)

N.H.

Albany • MASS. • Boston

NEW YORK

CONN. R.I.

PA.

New York City

Philadelphia • N.J.

Baltimore •

DEL.

VIRGINIA MD.

James R. Williamsburg

Jamestown • Chesapeake Bay

NORTH CAROLINA

ATLANTIC OCEAN

SOUTH CAROLINA

• Charles Town

GEORGIA

SPANISH FLORIDA

0   200 mi

0   200 km

Transverse Mercator Projection

Settlement 1660

Settlement 1760

Reading Maps

1. What geographic feature formed the western limits of the English colonies?

2. Which European powers held lands north and south of the English colonies?

rule, he had warned, "I will make him a foot shorter, and send the pieces to Holland [the Netherlands], and let him appeal that way."

Forced to give in, Stuyvesant surrendered without a shot. Charles II noted with pleasure the capture of New Amsterdam and its new name: "A very good town, but we have got the better of it, and 'tis now called New York." By fall, England had conquered the rest of the Dutch colony.

New Jersey and New York

Charles gave New Netherland to his brother, James, Duke of York. In time, four proprietary colonies were carved out of the former Dutch colony—New Jersey, New York, Pennsylvania, and Delaware.

Soon after the conquest, James gave his lands between the Hudson and Delaware Rivers to his friends Lord John Berkeley and Sir George Carteret. They named the territory New Jersey for Carteret's home, the island of Jersey in the English Channel.

Lured by rich farmland, some Dutch, Swedes, and Finns had already settled in New Jersey. Soon Puritans began to arrive, searching for better land or greater religious freedom than New England offered.

Eager to bring in more colonists, the proprietors leased land at fair rents and permitted a representative assembly. The colony grew quickly, but conflict erupted between the colonists and the proprietors. In 1702 New Jersey became a royal colony.

New York James kept the northern part of New Netherland, which he renamed New York. Already New York City was on its way to becoming a major trading center that attracted people from many parts of the world. Most of the settlers were Dutch, but many English, Swedes, French, Portuguese, and Africans lived there as well.

The former Dutch residents praised James's fairness. He let them keep their land and practice their own religion.

English settlers, however, complained that James treated New York like a conquered country. They demanded the right to elect a legislature. James refused, arguing that it would destroy "the peace of the government." In fact, New York did not get its first elected assembly until 1683.

Pennsylvania

William Penn, who started the colony of Pennsylvania, was a very different sort of proprietor. Penn was destined to be rich and powerful. He was the son of a wealthy admiral and friendly with the future King Charles II and James, Duke of York.

In the mid-1660s Penn joined a new religion, the Religious Society of Friends. Members were called Quakers because they "quaked" before God.

Quaker beliefs upset religious and government leaders in England. Quakers treated everyone as equals. They saw no need for ministers and refused to pay taxes to the Church of England. They did not believe in war and refused to serve as soldiers.

As a result, Quakers were persecuted in England and also in Massachusetts. Penn himself was jailed for eight months in the Tower of London for writing a pamphlet that praised the Quaker faith.

Penn dreamed of finding a haven for Quakers in America, and his connections with the king made it come true. In 1681 he received a grant from Charles II for territory north of Maryland. He called it Pennsylvania—"Penn's Woods." Penn's father had loaned Charles money, which the king had not repaid. By repaying the debt with American land, Charles also helped his old friend.

Penn's "holy experiment" Penn viewed Pennsylvania as a "holy experiment," where Quakers and others would "shape their own laws." His Frame of Government for the colony called for a legislature to be elected by all adult men who owned property or paid taxes. The plan also allowed settlers to practice any religion based on a belief in God.

Penn also believed in dealing fairly with his Indian neighbors, the Delawares. He learned their language and bought land from them at fair prices. Pennsylvanians and Delawares lived in peace for many years.

Settlers from many countries in Europe flocked to Pennsylvania, and the population soared. Soon the colony's major town was well underway. Penn called the town Philadelphia, the Greek word for "brotherly love."

Delaware To give his colony an outlet to the sea, in 1682 Penn obtained the land called Delaware from the Duke of York. By 1704 people in Delaware had their own assembly but shared a governor with Pennsylvania. Delaware did not become a separate colony until 1776.

Hands-On HISTORY

Advertising the colonies Imagine that you work for an advertising company. You are to come up with an ad to lure settlers to one of the 13 English colonies.

Activity

❶ After reading the chapter, choose a colony and the type of ad you will create, such as a brochure, poster, or jingle.

❷ Decide what makes your colony special. Why should people in the 1700s move there? To answer that question, review the information in the chapter and do research if necessary.

❸ Create the ad and present it to your classmates. Are they ready to sail to North America?

1609 ad for Virginia

Link to Art

The Peaceable Kingdom (1835) Edward Hicks, an artist and Quaker preacher, painted historical and religious scenes. In the foreground of this painting, he shows animals that are enemies on earth living in peace with children in God's kingdom. In the background, William Penn and the Delaware Indians sign a treaty. **Discuss** What do you think is the message of the painting?

Georgia

The founder of Georgia, the last of England's 13 colonies, had a dream. As a young man, James Oglethorpe had been shocked when a friend died in prison. The friend's only crime was being too poor to pay his debts. Knowing that thousands of poor men and women in England faced the same fate, Oglethorpe decided to help them get a fresh start in America.

In 1732 Oglethorpe and a group of wealthy friends got a charter from King George II to found a colony between South Carolina and Spanish Florida. The king named it Georgia after himself.

From the start, Oglethorpe had two goals. One was to provide land where debtors could become independent farmers. The other was to serve the king by stopping the Spanish in Florida from moving north.

Oglethorpe succeeded in holding off the Spanish. He built forts and brought in English troops to protect the colony. He also had the good luck to gain the friendship of Mary Musgrove, whose mother was a Creek Indian and whose father was English. Mary Musgrove helped maintain good relations between the powerful Creeks and the English in their struggles against the Spanish.

Less successful were Oglethorpe's plans for debtors. He wanted Georgia to be a community of small farms, so he limited the size of land holdings and banned slavery. To control the colony's development, he refused to allow a representative assembly.

Under these conditions, few settlers, debtors or not, wanted to come to Georgia. The ones who did come demanded changes or moved to other colonies. As a result, Oglethorpe's rules were given up, and in 1752 Georgia became a royal colony. Only then did Georgia begin to prosper.

3. Section Review

1. Define **proprietary colonies.**
2. Compare the reasons for establishing Maryland, Pennsylvania, and Carolina.
3. Why did England take over New Netherland, and what were the results?
4. Critical Thinking Did James Oglethorpe's plans help or hurt the colony of Georgia? Explain your answer.

Why We Remember

Planting English Colonies

If you visit Washington, D.C., and the Capitol building where Congress meets, take a moment to stand in the rotunda under the great dome. There you will see a mural showing the history of the United States. One of the earliest scenes shows Pocahontas being baptized in Jamestown.

At that moment, Powhatan's daughter could not have known what her efforts to help the English in Jamestown would lead to. In little more than a century, her people would be almost wiped out, and the number of colonies would soar. By the time Georgia was founded in 1732, the English had planted a string of 13 colonies stretching from Canada to Florida along the Atlantic coast.

Today we remember the planting of English colonies because it was, in part, from those seeds that the United States would later grow. The men and women who first came to England's colonies brought with them the religious, political, and economic ideas that would help shape the early history of the United States.

Skill Lab

Skill Tips

- Arrange the information so it is logical and easy to follow.
- Make the title and the row and column headings accurate and clear.
- Look across rows and down columns for similarities, differences, increases, or decreases.

Acquiring Information
Analyzing Statistical Tables

Between 1680 and 1750 the total colonial population grew rapidly—from a mere 150,000 to almost 1,200,000. As the total population grew, some colonies went through bigger changes than others.

Question to Investigate

Between 1680 and 1750 which colonies were growing fastest?

Procedure

Exploring changes in population involves analyzing statistics—facts in the form of numbers. A **statistical table** is an orderly arrangement of such numbers in rows and columns. To answer the question, you will be creating and analyzing your own table.

1 Arrange the data in columns and rows. Use **A** and **B** to create a statistical table titled "Population by Colony: 1680 and 1750."

2 Compare the data by reading across the rows.
a. Compare each colony's populations in 1680 and 1750. How many went up? Down?
b. Compare each colony's percentages in 1680 and 1750. How many went up? Down?

3 Compare the data by reading down the columns.
a. Which two colonies had the largest populations in 1680? In 1750?
b. Look at the differences in percentages—first for 1680 and then for 1750. In which year was there a greater variety? Explain.

4 Summarize the data. Based on the data in your table, answer the Question to Investigate.

Data to Use

A

Population by Colony 1680			
Colony	Population	Percentage of Total	Rank
Connecticut	17,246	11.4%	4
Delaware	1,005	0.7%	11
Maryland	17,904	11.8%	3
Massachusetts	46,152	30.5%	1
New Hampshire	2,047	1.3%	9
New Jersey	3,400	2.2%	8
New York	9,830	6.5%	5
North Carolina	5,430	3.6%	6
Pennsylvania	680	0.4%	12
Rhode Island	3,017	2.0%	7
South Carolina	1,200	0.8%	10
Virginia	43,596	28.8%	2

B In 1750 New Hampshire's population was 27,505, or 2.3% of the total population. Figures for other colonies: Massachusetts, 188,000 (16.1%); Rhode Island, 33,226 (2.8%); Connecticut, 111,280 (9.5%); New York, 76,696 (6.6%); New Jersey, 71,393 (6.1%); Pennsylvania, 119,666 (10.2%); Delaware, 28,704 (2.5%); Maryland, 141,073 (12.1%); Virginia, 231,033 (19.7%); North Carolina, 72,984 (6.2%); South Carolina, 64,000 (5.5%); and Georgia, 5,200 (0.4%). Georgia became a colony in 1732.

Source: *Historical Statistics of the United States*

Chapter Survey

Reviewing Vocabulary

Define the following terms.
1. invest
2. joint-stock company
3. exports
4. indentured servants
5. representatives
6. legislature
7. royal colony
8. bicameral
9. proprietary colonies

Reviewing Main Ideas

1. Why did starting colonies make sense to the English government?
2. Describe two changes the Virginia Company made to help its colony survive after the "starving time."
3. How did the people who started Plymouth Colony differ from those who started Virginia Colony?
4. What led to the founding of each of the following colonies? (a) Massachusetts (b) Rhode Island (c) Connecticut
5. What was the main reason for conflict between Puritans and Indians? Describe the situation after King Philip's War.
6. Which colonies resulted from England's competition with Spain? With the Netherlands? Explain why.
7. What general goal did the founders of Maryland, Pennsylvania, and Georgia have in common? How successful was each colony in achieving that goal?

Thinking Critically

1. Synthesis What qualities did the Jamestown colonists probably have in order to leave home and settle in a land unknown to them? Explain why you chose particular qualities.
2. Application Respect for the beliefs of non-Protestants led to greater religious freedom in the colonies. How did individual colonies contribute to this change?

3. Why We Remember: Analysis How were relations between colonists and Indians different in the English, Spanish, and French colonies?

Applying Skills

Analyzing statistical tables How does the population distribution of the 13 colonies in 1750 compare with the distribution among those states today?
1. Create a statistical table titled "Populations of Selected States in 1995." For each state, show the population, the percentage of the total population of those 13 states, and the rank. You can get population figures from the table on pages R19–R23.
2. Analyze your table. Which states have the largest percentages? What similarities and differences can you find between the data in this table and the table you made for the Skill Lab?

History Mystery

Help from an Indian Answer the History Mystery on page 117. How would you go about learning more about Squanto's life in America and Europe? How might the history of Plymouth Colony have been different if the Pilgrims had not met Squanto?

Writing in Your History Journal

1. Keys to History (a) The time line on pages 116–117 has seven Keys to History. In your journal, list each key and describe why it is important to know about. (b) In your journal, make a chart with two columns. Label one column "Causes," and the other "Effects." Choose an event on the time line and describe the causes and the effects of that event.

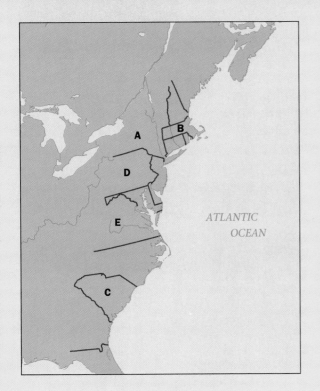

ATLANTIC
OCEAN

1. For each letter on the map, write the name of the colony.

2. Geographic Thinking In 1699 colonists moved the capital of Virginia from Jamestown to Williamsburg, a town that had been settled in 1633. Williamsburg is about 7 miles (11 km) from Jamestown, on a high ridge between the James and York Rivers. What might be some advantages of Williamsburg's location over that of Jamestown? What might be some disadvantages?

2. Pocahontas Write the following headings in your journal: "Jamestown Colonist," "Virginia Indian." Under each heading, list at least three words that such a person might have used to describe Pocahontas. Add a third heading, your name, and list three words that you would use to describe Pocahontas. Then write a paragraph explaining any differences in these views of Pocahontas.

3. Thinking Historically How might relations between the Indians and the Puritans have been different if the Puritans had followed William Penn's beliefs and practices? Write your responses in your journal.

Alternative Assessment

Citizenship: Planning a colony
Imagine that the English king has given your class a charter to start a proprietary colony in North America. How will you organize it?

❶ With a group of three or four other proprietors, prepare a plan for the colony. Start with the information in the chapter and do additional research as needed to decide the goals of the colony and how you expect to achieve them.

❷ As you make your plan, consider these questions: What will you do to attract settlers to the colony? How will you avoid the problems that the Jamestown and Plymouth colonists had? How will you make the colony prosper? How will you govern the colony?

Your plan will be evaluated on the following criteria:
• it presents the information in clear, interesting ways
• it provides information that is realistic for the colonial period
• it provides information that takes into account the successes and failures of other colonies

Chapter **6**

Life in the English Colonies

Sections

Beginning the Story with Benjamin Franklin

1. **Different Ways of Life**
2. **Diversity in the Colonies**
3. **Colonial Government**

Keys to History

1619
First Africans brought to Jamestown
Notice of sale of slaves

1636
First college in the English colonies
Embroidery of Harvard College

| 1600 | 1650 |

Looking Back

Founding of St. Augustine
1565

HISTORY Mystery

The banjo was unknown in England and Europe, yet it was a well-known musical instrument in the English colonies. Where did the banjo come from?

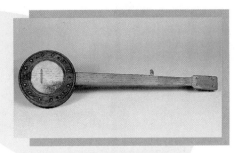

1730s
Great Awakening begins
Preacher George Whitefield

1732
Ben Franklin publishes *Poor Richard's Almanac*
Picture in almanac

1735
Trial of Peter Zenger
Zenger's newspaper

1676
Bacon's Rebellion

1700

1750

World Link

War between England and France
1689

Looking Ahead

Colonists protest against the Stamp Act
1765

Beginning the Story with

Benjamin Franklin

On a Sunday morning in 1723, a 17-year-old stepped off a boat onto Philadelphia's Market Street wharf. His pockets bulged with extra socks and shirts. He was tired, dirty, hungry—and nearly broke.

The young man walked until he found a bakery. He later recalled trying to buy "biscuits such as we had in Boston." The baker did not make biscuits. "I asked for a three-penny loaf, and was told they had none such." His stomach growling, he finally asked the baker for "three-penny worth of any sort."

> **"**He gave me, accordingly, three great puffy rolls. I was surprised at the quantity, but took it, and, having no room in my pockets, walked off with a roll under each arm, and eating the other. Thus I went up Market Street as far as Fourth Street, passing by the door of Mr. Read, my future wife's father, when she, standing at the door, saw me and thought I made, as I certainly did, a most awkward, ridiculous appearance.**"**

The embarrassed young man followed a crowd of "clean dressed people" into a Quaker meetinghouse and promptly fell asleep.

The Runaway from Boston

The sleeping teenager with crumbs on his shirt was a runaway apprentice named Benjamin Franklin. At the age of 12, Franklin had been apprenticed to his brother James, who owned a printing shop in Boston. Apprentices, like indentured servants, were bound by contracts to work for their masters for a fixed number of years. Ben's contract was for nine years. During this period, the apprentice was expected to work long hours for no pay. In exchange for his brother's labor, James promised to teach Ben the printing trade.

Like many masters, James felt free to beat his apprentice when displeased with his work. Ben came to resent his brother and "the blows his passion too often urged him to bestow upon me." After five years of such treatment, Ben decided to run away.

A sympathetic sea captain smuggled Franklin to New York City. He walked and then took another boat to Philadelphia. There, Franklin quickly found work as a printer's assistant. In a few years he was able to open his own printing shop.

Business Success

To succeed, Franklin had to print something people would buy. His first big seller was a newspaper called the *Pennsylvania Gazette*. Late in 1732 the *Gazette* carried an advertisement for a new almanac written by "Richard Saunders" and printed by B. Franklin. In fact, the author and printer were one and the same, a secret kept by Franklin for many years.

The Philadelphia that Ben Franklin knew lives on today in Elfreth's Alley. The brick houses were built in the early 1700s. The streetlamps are based on a design by Franklin.

Like other almanacs, *Poor Richard's Almanac* contained a calendar of the coming year along with weather predictions and planting times for crops. Between these topics, Franklin inserted wise and witty sayings. Here are three examples:

❝Work as if you were to live 100 years, pray as if you were to die tomorrow.
When the well's dry, we know the worth of water.
Three may keep a secret, if two of them are dead.❞

Poor Richard's Almanac quickly became the most popular book in the English colonies after the Bible. It made Franklin a wealthy man.

Benjamin Franklin went on to become a well-known scientist and inventor, a colonial leader, and a diplomat. It was said that only in the English colonies of North America could a penniless runaway become a success simply through talent and hard work.

Hands-On *HISTORY*

Activity

Imagine that you are Poor Richard. Create a calendar of the coming week, including information about class and school events. Then write a saying for each day of the week. Keep your sayings short and to the point.

1. Different Ways of Life

Reading Guide

New Terms **subsistence farming, literacy, imports, Tidewater, cash crops**

Section Focus **The different ways of life in the English colonies**

1. How did colonists use the land and resources they found in North America?
2. What patterns of settlement did they create in different regions?
3. How did settlement patterns affect towns and schooling?

When Ben Franklin sat down to write *Poor Richard's Almanac*, he had a clear picture of his readers in mind. Most were farming folk who did **subsistence farming.** That means they raised just enough to subsist—to survive—on, with perhaps a little surplus to sell or trade.

Even so, visitors traveling through the colonies were struck by how different life was from region to region. The way the colonists lived depended in part on the land and the resources they found. In some cases it also depended on where the colonists came from and the ideas they brought with them about the kinds of societies they hoped to build.

The New England Colonies

The colonists who settled in New England found a "rocky, barren, bushy, wild-woody" land. During the last ice age, glaciers scraped across New England's hilly land, carrying off most of the soil. They dumped the rich earth into the sea, where it mounded into great banks. Ocean plants thrived on these undersea banks, as did millions of fish.

Making a living The soil the glaciers left behind is thin and rocky. The region also has only five months of warm weather between killing frosts. In that short growing season, it was hard for colonial farmers to raise much of a surplus to sell.

Given the poor land and harsh climate, many settlers chose to make their living from the sea and the forests. Fishing grounds were rich in cod, mackerel, and halibut. New Englanders dried and salted fish and sold them to other colonies, the English West Indies, and to Europe.

From the forests came lumber for building fishing boats and merchant ships. Soon every port town had a shipyard as well as ropemakers, sailmakers, and blacksmiths. In time, New England ships carried Virginia tobacco, Carolina rice, and other colonial products to England. There the ships were loaded with manufactured goods to be sold in the colonies.

Settling in towns Unlike colonists in other regions, New Englanders settled in close-knit towns. The geography of the region encouraged this pattern of settlement. It was natural for colonists to cluster around good fishing harbors or pockets of fertile farmland.

Puritan religious beliefs also supported this settlement pattern. The Puritans hoped to build a model Christian community. In this community, people would live, work, and worship together. Each person would "watch over his neighbor's soul as his own."

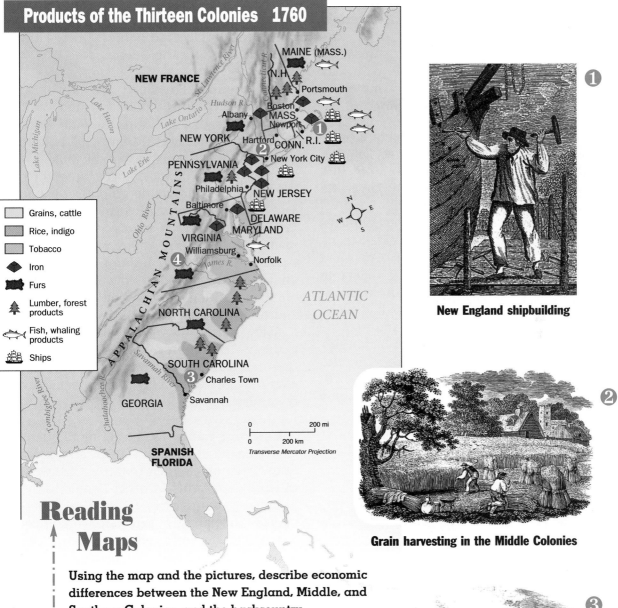

Products of the Thirteen Colonies 1760

NEW FRANCE

MAINE (MASS.)
N.H.
Portsmouth
Boston
MASS
Albany
Newport
NEW YORK
Hartford
CONN. R.I.
New York City
PENNSYLVANIA
Philadelphia
NEW JERSEY
Baltimore
DELAWARE
MARYLAND
VIRGINIA
Williamsburg
Norfolk
NORTH CAROLINA
SOUTH CAROLINA
Charles Town
GEORGIA
Savannah

SPANISH
FLORIDA

ATLANTIC
OCEAN

St. Lawrence River
Lake Huron
Lake Michigan
Lake Ontario
Lake Erie
Hudson R.
Connecticut R.
Ohio River
James R.
Savannah River
Chattahoochee R.
Tombigbee R.
APPALACHIAN MOUNTAINS

Legend:
- Grains, cattle
- Rice, indigo
- Tobacco
- Iron
- Furs
- Lumber, forest products
- Fish, whaling products
- Ships

0   200 mi
0 200 km
Transverse Mercator Projection

N W E S

❶

New England shipbuilding

❷

Grain harvesting in the Middle Colonies

Reading Maps

Using the map and the pictures, describe economic differences between the New England, Middle, and Southern Colonies, and the backcountry.

❹

Subsistence farming in the backcountry

❸

Southern rice growing

Town life centered around the meeting-house where Puritans gathered to worship. They built their homes close by, so that no one lived too far away to come to Sunday meetings. Just as important, no one could escape a neighbor's "holy watching."

Family life Daily life centered around the family, which was usually large. Families with 8 or 9 children were common. Ben Franklin's family was unusually large—he was the youngest of 17 children.

There was plenty of work for every member of the family to do. Crops had to be planted, cared for, and harvested. Cows had to be milked, and livestock fed. Vegetable gardens and orchards had to be tended. Butter, bread, cheese, and cider had to be made, as did clothing, candles, and soap.

By the age of 8, most children had begun working. Boys joined their fathers in the fields or in the family business. At age 10, Franklin was cutting wicks and filling molds in his father's candle-making shop.

Girls helped their mothers with household, barnyard, and garden tasks. In addition, wives and daughters helped with the harvesting, delivered babies, nursed the sick, and cared for the elderly.

Education The Puritans, as well as most other colonists, placed a high value on **literacy**—the ability to read and write. They wanted their children to be able to read God's word directly from the Bible.

To encourage literacy, Massachusetts led the colonies in providing schools. A law in 1647 required every town of 50 or more families to hire an instructor to teach reading and writing. Young children were taught by women at home in what were known as dame schools. Older boys attended grammar schools provided by larger towns and run by male schoolmasters.

A few young men went on to Harvard College near Boston. The Puritans had founded Harvard in 1636, only six years after they arrived, mainly to prepare men to be ministers.

Leaving home By the age of 12, many New England children were sent away from home to complete their training. Girls went to work as servants in other families. Boys became apprentices to farmers or tradespeople. An apprentice agreed to work under a skilled master for a certain period of time in order to learn a trade and perhaps reading and writing.

During these years, young people learned the skills they would need to succeed on their own. Those who were not apprenticed or working as servants lived and worked at home until they married.

After young people married, they often left their hometowns in search of better land and opportunities. As they moved, they took with them the pattern of settling in towns rather than on scattered farms. Throughout New England today, there are towns that trace their history back to Puritan founders.

Over time, small schools, paid for by local taxes, spread across New England. A single teacher would teach students, from 3-year-olds to teenagers, in a one-room schoolhouse.

The Middle Colonies

From the beginning of the colonial period, the Middle Colonies attracted a great variety of settlers. Some were drawn to the area by the promise of good land. Others came for the freedom to worship as they wished in Pennsylvania.

As a result, the population of the Middle Colonies grew rapidly. Between 1680 and 1750, the number of colonists in Pennsylvania alone increased from 680 to more than 119,000.

The land The smaller Middle Colonies, New Jersey and Delaware, lay on the flat Atlantic Coastal Plain. The two larger colonies, Pennsylvania and New York, stretched from the coastal plain up to hill country known as the Piedmont. Beyond the Piedmont lay the Appalachian Mountains.

Rivers both great and small flow eastward out of the Appalachians to the Atlantic Ocean. At the eastern edge of the Piedmont, the land drops sharply. Here rivers tumble in waterfalls and rapids to the coastal plain below. For this reason, the eastern edge of the Piedmont is known as the Fall Line.

Making a living Both the coastal plain and the Piedmont offered settlers deep, rich soil. William Penn told the truth when he advertised Pennsylvania as "a good and fruitful land, in some places . . . like to our best vales [valleys] in England."

So good was the soil that the region was soon exporting wheat, barley, oats, and livestock to the Southern Colonies and the West Indies. Most farmers in the Middle Colonies spread out across the land rather than following the New England pattern of settling in towns.

Some colonists used the rapidly falling water along the Fall Line to provide power to mills, ironworks, and other kinds of workshops. Visitors to the region found skilled workers making hardware, clocks, watches, locks, guns, glass, stoneware, nails, paper, rope, and cloth.

Trade in the Middle Colonies kept port towns bustling. The hub of Pennsylvania's commerce was Philadelphia. By the mid-1700s it was the largest city in the colonies. New York City, the other great center of business in the Middle Colonies, was the second largest.

Into both cities poured crops and livestock for shipment to other regions or abroad. From England came imports—books, paintings, clothing, and furniture. **Imports** are products brought in from another country to be sold. New ideas came, too. When the fork became the latest fashion for dining, wealthy city people quickly learned how to use it.

Education Like the Puritans, the Quakers wanted their children to be able to read the Bible. So did members of many other religious groups that settled in the Middle Colonies. Just how children were to be educated was left up to each family or group to decide. Some religious groups, such as the Quakers, built schools for their children. Other children were taught at home.

The Southern Colonies

The Southern Colonies covered a large area with a great variety of climates and soils. By 1750 they also had the most colonists. Life here was very different from New England and the Middle Colonies.

The land Seen from the ocean, the Southern Colonies appeared to have no solid shoreline. From Maryland to Georgia, the Atlantic Coastal Plain is laced with rivers, bays, swamps, and estuaries. The water level of all these waterways moves up and down with the daily rise and fall of the tide. For this reason, colonists called this low, wet area the **Tidewater.**

The Tidewater is well-suited for growing crops on a large scale. The soil is fertile, and rainfall is plentiful. Best of all, the growing season lasts up to eight months.

This area was not, however, a healthy place for people in colonial times. The wetlands bred a deadly combination of mosquitoes and disease. As temperatures rose each summer, so did the death rate.

As a result, life expectancy in the Southern Colonies was lower than in New England and the Middle Colonies. In one county in Virginia, nearly one-fourth of the children had lost both parents by the age of 13.

Making a living Most of the settlers in the Southern Colonies did subsistence farming. They raised grain and vegetables on small farms. A few had the help of indentured servants, but most relied on the family to work the farm.

The kind of farming for which the Southern Colonies became famous, though, was the plantation, where a single crop was grown for profit. Crops that are raised to be sold for a profit are called **cash crops.**

The tobacco of Virginia, Maryland, and North Carolina became the most profitable cash crop of the English colonies. After the 1690s, rice became an important cash crop in South Carolina and Georgia. Later, in the 1740s, 17-year-old Eliza Lucas of South Carolina produced the first successful crop of indigo, a plant used to make blue dye. It, too, became a cash crop.

Plantation life To succeed, a plantation owner needed a large tract of good land and a large work force. As you will read in the next section, finding enough workers was one of the planters' biggest problems.

Link to Technology

A Colonial Sawmill

Colonial Americans relied heavily on water power to fuel industry. A mill placed at the bottom of a waterfall used the force of the falling water. Sawmills were especially common because wood was plentiful and colonists used lumber to build homes and ships and to make millions of barrels for trade and industry. Lumber was also a major colonial export.

① The water wheel, turned by a waterfall or stream, provided the power to operate the mill.

② The water wheel powered the mechanism that moved the logs through the mill.

③ Gears attached to the water wheel moved the saw blade up and down to cut the logs as they moved past.

④ The cut lumber—100 board feet an hour—fell into the stream at the end of the mill, to be gathered later.

Hands-On HISTORY

Writing rules of conduct Learning good manners was an important part of a child's education in the Southern Colonies. As a boy, George Washington copied down a list of 110 "rules of civility and decent behavior in company and conversation." Here are a few examples.

"1st Every action done in company ought to be with some sign of respect to those that are present. . . .

37th In speaking to men of quality do not lean nor look them full in the face, nor approach too near them. . . .

46th Take all admonitions [advice] thankfully. . . .

110th Labor to keep alive . . . that little spark of celestial [heavenly] fire called conscience."

Activity
If Washington were alive now, what rules of conduct would he need to learn? Write three of your own "rules of decent behavior in company and conversation" to guide him.

The Rapalje children, 1768

By the early 1700s, plantations had spread out along most Tidewater rivers. Oceangoing ships moved up and down the rivers, picking up crops and dropping off goods made in England and in other colonies. Access was so easy that few towns grew into centers of trade.

The distance between neighbors meant that plantations had to be self-sufficient—able to take care of their own needs. Like a New England town, a large plantation had its own blacksmith, miller, weaver, and butcher. People met in their homes rather than in meetinghouses.

As for education, some wealthy planters hired indentured servants or tutors from northern colleges to teach their children at home. Others provided funds for private schools. Still others sent their children to schools in England. Almost everyone else did without schooling.

The Backcountry

To the west of the Tidewater, the land slopes upward onto the Piedmont and the foothills of the Appalachians. This region of low, rolling hills stretches from Pennsylvania south to Georgia. Settlers called it the backcountry.

The land The backcountry was a hilly, densely wooded region. Its forests teemed with fish and wildlife, making it a prized Indian hunting ground. Tucked among the hills were fertile hollows and valleys with good soil.

To settlers from Scotland and Ireland the backcountry offered just what they had crossed the Atlantic to find—a kind of freedom that they called "elbowroom." For decades the Scots and Irish had lived under the rule of English landlords and soldiers.

them it at once vexet him: he in a loud voice
Said look in here in this place pointing with his finger

luck   John

Old mrs. Flansman Killing a Hog and a beef.
for mr. Dr. John Rouse in 1802 her general practice.

At hog killing time in the fall, settlers joked that "all the hog was used but the squeal." The meat from four large hogs, salted in barrels, could keep a family fed through winter. Settlers made the fat into lard to use for cooking. They used the intestines to make sausage skins and long hair from the tail to sew buckskin clothing.

Far off in the backcountry, they were at last beyond the reach of both.

Daily life Backcountry settlers lived rough, simple lives. Families were large and close-knit. Home was usually a log cabin set in a small clearing. Wives and daughters raised small crops of corn and vegetables while husbands and sons hunted and fished. Schools were few and far between, so children were taught what they needed to know at home.

Most backcountry settlements were far from the colonial assemblies that governed them. When trouble arose between Indians and settlers who were taking their lands for farms, the settlers often felt that their government failed to protect them.

Tension boiled over in Virginia in 1676. There, a planter named Nathaniel Bacon led a group of 300 neighbors in attacking local Indian villages. Then, to show their anger at the colonial government, they burned Jamestown.

Bacon's Rebellion, as it was called, ended when Bacon died of an illness. However, relations between colonial governments and backcountry settlers would continue to be strained.

1. Section Review

1. Define **subsistence farming, literacy, imports, Tidewater,** and **cash crops.**

2. What resources were most important to the colonists' success in New England? In the Southern Colonies?

3. What attracted settlers to the Middle Colonies? To the backcountry?

4. What conditions led to the growth of colonial towns? What conditions hurt their growth?

5. Critical Thinking In which region would you have most wanted to live? Give reasons to support your answer.

2. Diversity in the Colonies

Reading Guide

New Terms **prejudice, revival, racism**

Section Focus **How the great variety of people shaped life in the colonies**

1. What prejudices did settlers bring to the colonies?
2. Why did conflicts arise between colonists and American Indians?
3. What caused the enslavement of Africans to become part of colonial life?

On his first journey from Boston to Philadelphia in 1723, Ben Franklin must have been struck by the mix of people he met. Unlike mostly Puritan New England, Pennsylvania boasted many nationalities and religions. A Maryland doctor who made a tour of the colony in the 1740s wrote of dining at a tavern with

❝Scots, English, Dutch, Germans, and Irish; there were Roman Catholics, Churchmen, Presbyterians, Quakers, Newlightmen, Methodists, Seventh Day men, Moravians, Anabaptists, and one Jew.❞

Differences Among European Americans

The first settlers in the colonies were mostly English. After the 1680s, a growing number came from other parts of Europe. Each group brought with it old patterns of prejudice against people of other nationalities. A **prejudice** is a bad opinion of people based only on such factors as their religion, nationality, or appearance.

English colonists, for example, often looked down on settlers from France and other parts of Europe. Such people, with their diverse languages and customs, seemed strange to the English.

In Pennsylvania, prejudice was especially strong against settlers from a part of Germany called the Palatine. The Palatines continued to speak German and stayed apart from their English neighbors. By the 1760s Germans made up one-third of the population of Pennsylvania. A worried Ben Franklin asked:

❝Why should Pennsylvania, founded by the English, become a colony of aliens [foreigners], who will shortly become so numerous as to Germanize us?❞

In time, such prejudice softened. As people began working together to build new lives, the importance of national backgrounds faded.

Religious prejudice Religious prejudice was slower to fade. Although most colonists were Protestants, they belonged to many different sects, with different beliefs. Most sects were intolerant of people who did not share their beliefs.

When Quakers came to Virginia, for example, laws were passed to try to drive them out. Prejudice against Roman Catholics was even stronger, even in Maryland, which had been founded as a haven for Catholics. By the early 1700s, Protestants in the Maryland legislature had put limits on Catholics' freedom to worship.

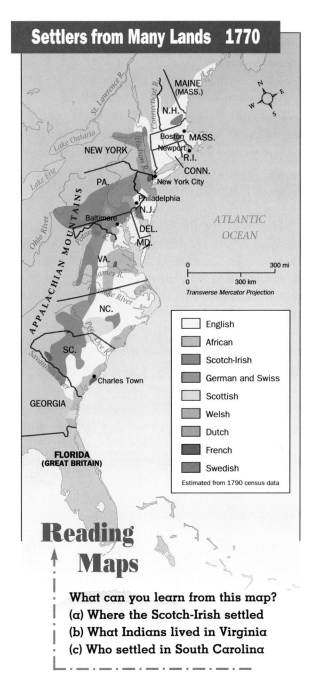

MAINE
(MASS.)
N.H.
Boston MASS.
Newport
R.I.
CONN.
New York City
Philadelphia
N.J.
Baltimore
DEL.
MD.
VA.
NC.
SC.
Charles Town
GEORGIA
FLORIDA
(GREAT BRITAIN)
NEW YORK
PA.
St. Lawrence R.
Lake Ontario
Lake Erie
Ohio River
Connecticut R.
Hudson R.
Potomac R.
James R.
Roanoke River
Pee Dee R.
Savannah R.
APPALACHIAN MOUNTAINS
ATLANTIC
OCEAN

0   300 mi
0   300 km
Transverse Mercator Projection

- English
- African
- Scotch-Irish
- German and Swiss
- Scottish
- Welsh
- Dutch
- French
- Swedish

Estimated from 1790 census data

Reading Maps

What can you learn from this map?
(a) Where the Scotch-Irish settled
(b) What Indians lived in Virginia
(c) Who settled in South Carolina

Jews suffered as well. Nowhere in the colonies did Jews have the right to vote or hold office. Still, they were allowed to worship and work in peace. As a result, in the mid-1700s the 1,000 or so Jews in the English colonies were probably the freest Jews on earth.

The Great Awakening

In the early years, religion played a very important part in the lives of most colonists. As time went by, however, faith faded and church membership declined. "The forms of religion were kept up," a Puritan said, but the "power of godliness" was missing. Another colonist wrote that "religion lay a-dying."

A revival of faith In the 1730s and 1740s, a **revival**—a renewed interest in religion—swept the colonies. The colonists called this renewal of faith the Great Awakening.

The flames of revival were fanned by preachers who traveled from town to town holding outdoor meetings. At these gatherings they delivered fiery "awakening sermons," urging listeners to renew their commitment to Christian faith.

The most famous preacher of the Great Awakening was an Englishman named George Whitefield. Wherever he spoke, he drew huge crowds. One day in Boston he preached to 20,000 people. His message made women tremble and men weep.

Results of the Awakening Revivals touched the hearts and souls of countless colonists. In Philadelphia, Franklin wrote:

"From being thoughtless or indifferent about religion, it seemed as if all the world were growing religious, so that one could not walk through the town in an evening without hearing psalms sung in different families of every street."

The Great Awakening divided religious groups everywhere. New England was hit especially hard as church members chose sides. Some clung to old churches and teachings. Others were attracted to the revivalist message that all souls were equal before God, and all people could have a personal experience of faith.

The split between these groups led to new prejudices. At the same time, the Great Awakening showed the need for religious toleration if the colonists were to live together in peace.

Colonists and Indians in Conflict

Although some patterns of prejudice were fading, others were growing stronger. These prejudices arose from **racism**—the belief that one race of people is superior to another. The first people to suffer from racism in the English colonies were American Indians.

Early meetings Most early meetings between colonists and Indians were friendly. In Chapter 5 you read that Pocahontas and Squanto saved the first English settlers from starving. Sadly, such early friendships did not last.

Racism colored the colonists' attitude toward Indians. Sure that the English way of life was best, they at first tried to turn native peoples into English Protestants like themselves. The Indians, though, had no interest in giving up their own cultures. They were happy to trade with the colonists, but not to live like them.

Point of View

How should children be educated?

An incident in 1744 shows the different views of colonists and Indians. It took place at a meeting between Virginia officials and Iroquois leaders. As a gesture of goodwill, the officials offered to send some Iroquois youths to college and to "bring them up in the best manner."

The Iroquois thanked the officials but said no. They had already sent some of their sons to the colonists' college. When the teenagers came home,

"they were bad runners, ignorant of every means of living in the woods, unable to bear either cold or hunger, knew neither how to build a cabin [or] take a deer, . . . [and] they were totally good for nothing.**"**

The Iroquois then offered to educate the colonists' sons, promising to "instruct them in all we know, and to make men of them." This offer was also refused.

Both Indians and colonists preferred their own ways of life. Would it be possible for them to live together in peace?

Who Owns the Land?

The greatest source of misunderstanding was over land. Indians did not believe that land belonged to people. Instead, people belonged to the land where they farmed, hunted, fished, and gathered foods. The idea of buying and selling land was as strange to them as that of buying and selling the wind or the sky.

The colonists saw land as private property. In their view, the best use of the land was for farms and settlements. They thought it was wasteful to leave some land wild, as Indians often did. Thus they did not hesitate to take over land that Indians had been using for generations. Land, wrote Governor John Winthrop of Massachusetts, should belong "to any that could and would improve it."

To fight or flee As the colonies grew, settlers cleared and plowed more and more land, and forests disappeared. So did the animals that Indian hunters needed to feed their families. In 1642 Miantonomo, a Narragansett chief, complained:

American Indians, such as these fishermen and the women making maple syrup, believed in taking from nature just enough to live on. Colonists, though, saw such resources as profitable trade goods.

"Our fathers had plenty of deer, . . . fish and fowl. But these English have gotten our land. . . . Their cows and horses eat the grass, and their hogs spoil our clam banks, and we shall all be starved."

Hunger, combined with European diseases, wiped out many tribes. The rest faced a terrible choice. Should they fight the invaders or flee their ancient homelands?

Endless conflict You have read that some tribes did stand and fight, only to be destroyed. Others fled to what they hoped would be safety in the backcountry. They were not safe for long.

As colonists moved into the backcountry, new conflicts arose. Indians saw settlers as greedy invaders who stole their land and burned their villages. Settlers saw Indians as dangerous, ready to attack at any moment.

Such attitudes were to exist wherever Indians and settlers confronted each other.

African Americans

The second group to suffer from racism in the English colonies were Africans. The first Africans were brought to Virginia in 1619. Historians think that at least some of them worked as indentured servants and were later freed. A few bought land and white and black servants of their own.

By the late 1600s, however, southern planters were in need of workers. Fewer English people were coming to the colonies as indentured servants. To solve the problem, planters adopted a system that had long been used on Caribbean sugar plantations—slavery. Under this system, workers belonged to their owners for life. So did their children.

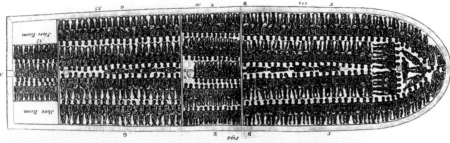

Enslaved Africans going to America were crammed so closely together in slave ships that they could barely move. After the voyage came the terror of sale. Olaudah Equiano, a victim of the slave trade, described his experiences in a book.

The Atlantic Slave Trade

When Tidewater planters began buying enslaved Africans in large numbers, the Atlantic slave trade was already a big business. Every year American and European captains sailed to West Africa. There they traded cloth, rum, and guns for Africans captured by slavers. They carried their human cargoes back across the Atlantic for sale in the Americas as slaves.

For the captured Africans, the horrors of that voyage, known as the "Middle Passage," were beyond imagining. Packed into ships, many died of disease or despair and were thrown overboard. The sharks that followed slave ships seldom went hungry. Olaudah Equiano, who was born in 1745 in present-day Nigeria, made that voyage at about the age of 10. Later he wrote:

"The closeness of the place, . . . added to the number in the ship, which was so crowded that each had scarcely room to turn himself, almost suffocated us. . . . The shrieks of the women, and the groans of the dying, rendered the whole a scene of horror."

Terrified, Equiano refused to eat anything, hoping "for the last friend, Death, to relieve me." However, he was among those who survived.

Even with the high death rate, the slave trade was very profitable. Many colonial merchants earned fortunes by trading in human beings. Between the 1500s and the 1800s, at least 10 million Africans were sent into slavery in North and South America. Some historians claim the real figure was closer to 20 million.

"Slave Young, Slave Long"

By the early 1700s, enslaved Africans could be found in every English colony. In the New England and Middle Colonies, though, farmers did not have plantations, which required large work forces. Thus there were never many slaves living in the northern colonies.

The slave population grew rapidly in the Southern Colonies, however. Planters in Maryland, Virginia, and North Carolina bought thousands of Africans to work their tobacco fields. South Carolina rice planters were eager to have slaves from rice-growing regions of Africa. They also used slaves to raise indigo and cattle.

Slaves faced a lifetime of unrewarded toil. Most worked as field hands, raising the cash crops that allowed their owners to live well. Others worked at skilled trades or as household servants. They began working by age 6 and continued until they died. As one old enslaved African put it, "Slave young, slave long."

A New African American Culture

On their arrival in the English colonies, some Africans rebelled by refusing to work or trying to run away. Escape in an unknown land was very difficult, though, and rebellion was severely punished.

As a result, most Africans learned to survive as best they could. They came from many different cultures, with different languages and traditions. Under the most difficult of conditions they began to create a new African American culture.

This new culture preserved much that slaves had brought with them from Africa. Their music and dances pulsed with African rhythms. Musical instruments like the banjo were African, too. African designs showed up in their weavings, wood carvings, pottery, and quilts.

African legends and stories survived, as well. Children still heard the tale of how the lion got its roar. Br'er Rabbit, the wily hero of many slave tales, was based on the African trickster Shulo the Hare.

Planters with large estates often hired overseers to supervise the work of slaves. The overseer in this picture probably got fired for doing more relaxing than overseeing. As one planter complained, "The overseer there is but a chattering fellow, promises much but does little." By the mid-1700s some large plantations no longer used overseers.

Link to the Present

Gullah "If unna kyant behave unna self, I'll tek yu straight home." Can you figure out what that sentence means? It is in a language called Gullah. Developed by enslaved Africans 300 years ago, Gullah is still spoken in parts of the southeastern United States.

Enslaved Africans came from a variety of cultures, each with its own language. Brought together on plantations, they needed to communicate with both the planters and one another. In South Carolina and Georgia, especially on the Sea Islands off the coast, slaves combined African languages and English to create Gullah.

Gullah is still a living language. In 1994 the American Bible Society published part of the New Testament in Gullah. The Gullah name for the Book of Luke is "De Good Nyews Bout Jedus Christ Wa Luke Write."

In time, most slaves adopted the Christian faith. They were drawn by its message that all people are equal in the sight of God and its promise of a better life to come after death. Here, too, African Americans blended elements of African religions with the new faith.

Free but Not Equal

Free African Americans—who had been given their freedom or who had escaped—lived throughout the colonies. Most worked as laborers or household servants. A few prospered. Benjamin Banneker, a mathe-

matician, was the son of a freed slave. He became famous for his almanacs.

Free African Americans did not have the same rights or opportunities as other colonists did, though. Few whites were willing to accept blacks as their equals.

Why did whites think blacks were less than equal? Colonist John Woolman, a Quaker, blamed the system of slavery itself. When whites heard blacks called "slaves" and saw them doing only the hardest, dirtiest work, he wrote,

" [it] tends gradually to fix a notion in the mind that they [African Americans] are a sort of people below us in nature.**"**

Woolman spoke out against slavery. Still, the racist thinking of most white colonists continues to haunt America today.

2. Section Review

1. Define **prejudice, revival,** and **racism.**
2. What old prejudices did settlers bring with them to the English colonies?
3. What was the greatest source of conflict between colonists and American Indians? Explain why.
4. Critical Thinking What conditions enabled slavery to become so firmly rooted in the Southern Colonies?

Geography Lab

The Atlantic Slave Trade

Enslaved Africans were the key laborers on plantations in North and South America. The exact number will never be known, but at least 10 million Africans were sent into slavery in the Americas. Use the map and the table to determine some lasting effects of this huge forced movement of peoples.

The Way People Describe Themselves 1990s				
	White	Black	*Mixed	Other
United States	80%	12%		8%
Haiti		95%	5%	
Jamaica		75%	13%	12%
Brazil	53%	11%	34%	3%
Nicaragua	10%	9%	77%	4%
Venezuela	20%	9%	69%	2%

*Different mixtures of black, white, and Indian ancestors

Source: Encyclopædia Britannica

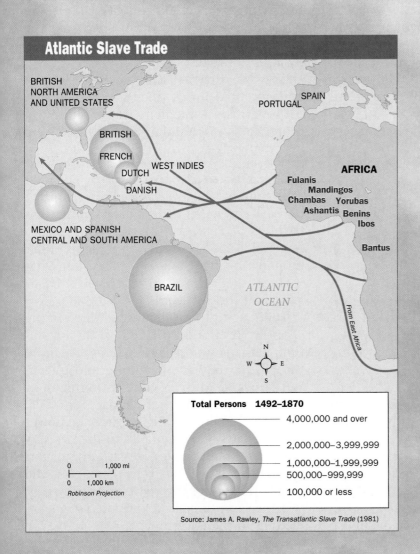

Atlantic Slave Trade

BRITISH NORTH AMERICA AND UNITED STATES

BRITISH

FRENCH

DUTCH

DANISH

WEST INDIES

MEXICO AND SPANISH CENTRAL AND SOUTH AMERICA

BRAZIL

PORTUGAL

SPAIN

AFRICA

Fulanis
Mandingos
Chambas   Yorubas
Ashantis   Benins
Ibos

Bantus

From East Africa

ATLANTIC OCEAN

N W E S

0   1,000 mi
0   1,000 km
Robinson Projection

Total Persons   1492–1870
- 4,000,000 and over
- 2,000,000–3,999,999
- 1,000,000–1,999,999
- 500,000–999,999
- 100,000 or less

Source: James A. Rawley, *The Transatlantic Slave Trade* (1981)

Link to History

1. From what parts of Africa were African laborers sent?

2. What countries took part in the Atlantic slave trade?

3. Where in the Western Hemisphere were the largest number of Africans sent? The smallest number?

4. On the map on pages R2–R3 locate the nations listed in the table. How do you explain the differences in the makeup of the population in the different nations?

5. **Hands-On Geography** Imagine that you are writing a book on African traditions in one country in the Western Hemisphere. List six cultural characteristics you might study to find evidence of links to Africa. Cultural characteristics include ideas, customs, skills, and arts. For example, you might compare foods eaten in the country you chose with the traditional dishes of Africa.

3. Colonial Government

Reading Guide

New Terms tyranny, militia, libel

Section Focus How the colonists learned to govern themselves

1. What rights and freedoms did the colonists value?
2. How did colonial governments work?
3. How did Great Britain try to control colonial affairs?

At the age of 42, Ben Franklin retired from business. For a time, he threw himself into the study of a new form of energy called electricity. This research brought him fame at home and in Europe.

In 1753 Franklin was appointed postmaster general for the colonies. The growth of the colonies had been truly astonishing. In 1650 there had been barely 50,000 colonists, most of them living in Massachusetts and Virginia. By 1750 there were more than a million colonists spread from Maine to Georgia.

In his new job Franklin traveled throughout the colonies, looking for ways to improve postal service. Along the way he met people of every background. Despite their differences, he found that most colonists had something in common: a deep attachment to their basic rights and freedoms.

A Love of Liberty

English colonists' love of liberty was rooted in their past. The English had a long history of struggling to protect their rights from the **tyranny**—the harsh use of power—of rulers.

The Magna Carta The first victory in that struggle came in 1215 when English nobles forced King John to sign the Magna Carta, or Great Charter. This agreement said that a monarch could not tax the people without consulting them. It also gave people accused of crimes the right to a trial by a jury of their peers, or equals.

This was the first time an English ruler had accepted limits on his or her power. Although the agreement was intended to protect only nobles, the rights it listed were eventually given to all English people.

The Declaration of Rights The next milestone in the struggle was the founding of Parliament in 1265. Parliament was formed of representatives from across England. They met regularly to advise their monarch on new laws and taxes. But what if their ruler refused to take their advice? Who had the last word?

That question was finally answered in the Glorious Revolution of 1688. In the revolution, Parliament forced King James II off the throne. In 1689 the new king and queen, William and Mary, signed an agreement called the Declaration of Rights.

The Declaration of Rights gave the power to make laws and levy taxes to the people's elected representatives in Parliament and no one else. It also listed the rights of all the people, including the right to trial by jury and the right to make a petition, or written request, to the government.

The Right of Self-Government

One of the freedoms the colonists valued most was the right of self-government. In no other country on earth, not even in Great Britain,* did ordinary people have as much freedom to run their own affairs as did the colonists.

By the 1750s every colony had its own elected assembly. Like Parliament, each assembly had the power to pass laws and levy taxes. The assemblies also decided how tax money should be spent.

Colonists were also used to governing their local communities. New Englanders, for example, held town meetings to discuss such issues as how much to pay the schoolmaster or how to organize a **militia**—citizens trained to fight in an emergency. After everyone had a chance to speak, they took a vote to settle the issue.

Assemblies and governors

Besides an assembly, most colonies had governors appointed by the crown. The governor was responsible for seeing that the colony followed English laws. He had to approve any act passed by the assembly before it could become law. In theory, this meant the governor had a great deal of power.

In practice, however, assemblies found ways to get around governors. One way was to refuse to vote a salary for a governor who did not cooperate. Another way was to refuse to vote money for something a governor wanted. Franklin called this practice the "purchase of good laws." To the governors, it felt more like blackmail.

Soldiers burned Peter Zenger's newspaper that criticized the New York governor. The trial of Zenger led to one of the earliest calls for freedom of the press.

Peter Zenger and a Free Press

Many colonial governors were hardworking and honest. Some, however, were lazy or corrupt. Today we expect our free press to tell us if officials are dishonest. In colonial times, however, freedom of the

---

*In 1707 the Kingdom of England and Wales united with the Kingdom of Scotland under one government, called Great Britain. Colonists, however, continued to speak of "England."

War between England and France

In the late 1600s a great struggle was shaping up between England and France for power in Europe as well as in North America. Between 1689 and 1748, three bitter wars engulfed Europe. People in North America were unable to stay out of them. To help pay for the wars, England needed more revenue than ever before from its American colonies.

In 1754 another war would break out. In the end it would determine which nation would win the competition for power in Europe and North America.

press did not exist in England or in the English colonies. Under English law, criticizing an official in print was dangerous.

A New York printer named Peter Zenger learned this lesson when he was thrown into jail in 1734 and held for ten months. Zenger had printed articles in his newspaper, the *Weekly Journal*, accusing New York's governor of taking bribes. He was charged with **libel**—printing statements that damage a person's good name.

When his trial began in 1735, Zenger's cause seemed hopeless. The judges had been handpicked by the governor. They chose a young, inexperienced lawyer to defend Zenger. As the defense began, however, a white-haired gentleman limped forward to address the court on Zenger's behalf. He was Andrew Hamilton, probably the ablest lawyer in the colonies.

A call for freedom of the press
Hamilton admitted that Zenger had printed the statements criticizing the governor. If those statements were false, they would indeed be libel. But the statements were true, he argued, and the truth could never be called libel. The real issue, Hamilton told the jury, was not libel, but rather the freedom to print the truth. He concluded:

"The question before the court . . . is not of small or private concern. It is not the cause of a poor printer, nor of New York alone. . . . It may in its consequence affect every free person that lives under a British government. . . . It is the best cause. It is the cause of liberty, . . . the liberty both of exposing and opposing arbitrary power [abuse of power] by speaking and writing truth.**"**

The jury took just ten minutes to decide that Zenger was not guilty.

Although the verdict freed Zenger, it did not change English law, and therefore it did not guarantee freedom of the press in the English colonies. However, the Zenger case did inspire other colonists to continue the fight for freedom of the press and to criticize officials who abused their power.

The Navigation Acts

The one area of life that colonists did not control was trade. Beginning in 1660, Parliament passed a series of laws known as the Navigation Acts. The purpose of these acts was to control trade with the colonies in three ways.

First, all trade goods coming to and from the colonies had to be carried in English or colonial ships. This law was good for both English and colonial shipowners.

Second, the Navigation Acts listed colonial products that could be sold only in England. The list included tobacco, sugar, forest products, and furs. This control ensured the British a steady flow of colonial

This detail from a 1739 sketch shows the importance of Charles Town (now Charleston), South Carolina, as a center of trade. It also was the port of entry for more than 40 percent of the enslaved Africans brought directly to the colonies.

products at low prices. It hurt the colonists, however. They could not sell their goods in other countries, even if the prices were higher there.

Third, any goods coming to the colonies from countries other than England had to pass through England. There they were taxed and loaded onto English or colonial ships. This law, too, helped English merchants but hurt colonists. The taxes made the foreign goods more expensive for colonists to buy than similar English goods.

For nearly 100 years, colonists accepted these trade controls with little complaint. For one thing, the laws were not often enforced. When they were, merchants got around them by smuggling goods in and out of the colonies.

Britain Prepares to Crack Down

In the 1750s, however, British leaders began paying closer attention to their American colonies. Britain still saw the colonies in terms of mercantilism. The colonies were to make the home country richer by trading only with it, and they were to obey the rules laid down by Parliament.

Instead, colonists were ignoring the Navigation Acts. To make matters worse, colonial assemblies were gaining power at the expense of their governors and acting too independently.

In a humorous verse, Benjamin Franklin compared Great Britain to a mother who insists on treating her grown children (the colonists) like babies:

> **"**We have an old mother that
>   peevish is grown;
> She snubs us like children that
>   scarce walk alone;
> She forgets we're grown up and
>   have sense of our own.**"**

Britain, however, had other ideas. The time had come, it decided, to crack down on the colonies.

3. Section Review

1. Define **tyranny, militia,** and **libel.**

2. What were the sources of the rights and freedoms that were important to the colonists?

3. In what ways were colonial assemblies like Parliament?

4. What was the purpose of the Navigation Acts?

5. Critical Thinking Should the press be free to print anything about anyone, as long as it prints the truth? Why or why not?

Why We Remember

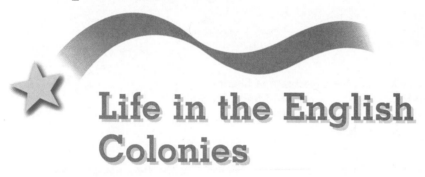

Life in the English Colonies

By 1750 the English colonies were home to more than a million people. With the exception of a few individuals like Ben Franklin, most of them are long forgotten. Their legacy, however, is still very much alive.

The colonists came from a world where most people were desperately poor and would remain so. In that world, wealth and power belonged to the privileged few. Also, people looked, talked, and thought like their neighbors. Differences in language, religion, or ways of life could lead to war.

On the east coast of North America, the colonists created a different world. Here a penniless runaway could become a success through talent and hard work. Ordinary people had a greater voice in running their governments. People were freer to work, worship, and raise their children as they thought best. In this world most people found it better to tolerate differences than to fight over them. This was the world that they passed on to the future.

The colonists left another, more painful legacy as well: a pattern of racism toward people of color. This legacy led to the destruction of countless native peoples and the enslavement of millions of Africans. This legacy of prejudice is also part of our world today.

Skill Lab

Acquiring Information
Analyzing Graphs

Sell more than you buy. That is what England tried to do by controlling colonial trade. In fact, trade officials in London kept track of yearly imports and exports to see whether that goal was being met. The totals for 1750—a typical year—must have brought both smiles and frowns to their faces.

Question to Investigate

How well did England meet its goal of selling more than it bought from the colonies?

Procedure

Explore the question by using data to make graphs. Look at the Skill Tips and study **A**, **B**, and **C**.

1 Decide what graphs to make.
a. Make a graph that best shows exports and imports for each colony or area.
b. Make a graph that best shows each colony or area's percentage of total exports.

2 Analyze the graphs.
a. Which colonies or areas exported more than they imported?
b. What percentage of the total exports came from those colonies or areas?

3 Summarize the graphs and relate the data to what you know about history.
a. Describe the overall trade pattern.
b. How would you explain the exceptions? (Consider the products England wanted most.)

Skill Tips

- A bar graph shows amounts for different years, places, things, or people.
- A circle graph shows percentages. It shows how parts relate to the whole.
- A line graph shows changes in amounts.

Data to Use

Key:
C = The Carolinas
G = Georgia
NE = New England
NY/NJ = New York and New Jersey
P/D = Pennsylvania and Delaware
V/M = Virginia and Maryland

Data Source for **A, B,** and **C**: *Historical Statistics of the United States*

A

Colonial Trade with England 1750		
Colony/Area	Exports	Imports
C	191,607	133,037
G	1,942	2,125
NE	48,455	343,659
NY/NJ	35,634	267,130
P/D	28,191	217,713
V/M	508,939	349,419
Total	814,768	1,313,083

Values in British pounds

B

New England's Trade with England 1750

Values (in thousands of British pounds): 0, 100, 200, 300, 400

Exports   Imports

C Imports from England by Colony/Area 1750

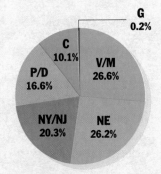

G 0.2%
C 10.1%
V/M 26.6%
P/D 16.6%
NY/NJ 20.3%
NE 26.2%

Chapter Survey

Reviewing Vocabulary

Define the following terms.
1. subsistence farming
2. literacy
3. imports
4. Tidewater
5. cash crops
6. prejudice
7. revival
8. racism
9. tyranny
10. militia
11. libel

Reviewing Main Ideas

1. Describe one way that people made a living in each of the following regions. (a) New England (b) the Middle Colonies (c) the Southern Colonies

2. In which region were children *most* likely to attend school? Why? In which region were children *least* likely to attend school? Why?

3. (a) What religious prejudices did most colonists have? (b) How did the Great Awakening affect religious prejudice?

4. How did colonists' attitudes about land contrast with those of Indians?

5. (a) Why did the use of indentured servants give way to the practice of buying slaves in the Southern Colonies? (b) Why were there fewer slaves in New England and the Middle Colonies?

6. How did colonists take part in governing themselves?

7. How were the Navigation Acts designed to control colonial trade? Why did the colonists accept the acts for so long?

Thinking Critically

1. Application Imagine that you found a letter written by a colonist. Part of the letter reads: "Of mills, brick kilns [ovens for baking bricks], and tile ovens, we have the necessary number. Our surplus of grain and cattle we trade to Barbados [a West Indies island] for rum, syrup, sugar, and salt." In what region do you think the colonist lived? Why?

2. Evaluation Explain why you agree or disagree with the following statement: If there had been no racism in the English colonies, colonists and American Indians would have lived in peace, and slavery would not have existed.

3. Why We Remember: Analysis A historian wrote: "In a number of ways what Americans would be for generations to come was settled in the course of those first hundred years [of English settlement]." Give three examples from the text that support this view.

Applying Skills

Analyzing graphs In the Skill Lab on page 167 you made graphs using import and export data that English trade officials collected more than 200 years ago. How much do you depend on imports? For example, how much of your clothing is imported (made in other countries)?

1. Count the items of clothing you own. Look at the labels and list the countries where the items were made.

2. Tally the number of items from each country.

3. Use your data to make a graph to answer the question: "Where does most of my clothing come from?"

4. Analyze your graph and summarize what it shows.

History Mystery

The banjo Answer the History Mystery on page 143. How would you go about learning how the banjo has changed since the 1600s? How would you find out what kinds of modern music use the banjo?

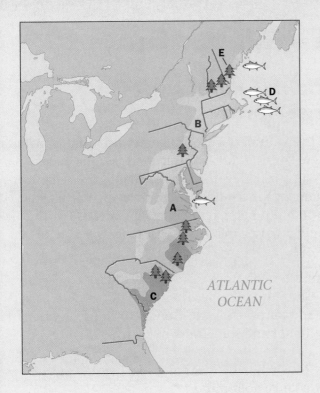

ATLANTIC
OCEAN

Reviewing Geography

1. For each letter on the map, write the colonial product or products.

2. Geographic Thinking One colonist wrote that the people of the New England, Middle, and Southern Colonies were "as different as their climates." How did geography influence ways of life in the regions? Do you think differences in climate are as important to people today as they were in colonial times? Explain your answer.

Writing in Your History Journal

1. Keys to History (a) The time line on pages 142–143 has six Keys to History. In your journal, list each key and describe why it is important to know about it. (b) Imagine that you are a colonist. Choose one of the events on the time line and write a letter to a friend or a relative describing the event and your reactions to it.

2. Benjamin Franklin English colonists boasted that North America offered plenty of opportunities for hard-working people to rise to success. Do you think Ben Franklin would have agreed with this view? In your journal, explain why or why not.

3. Citizenship Most people in the English colonies loved liberty and cherished the right of self-government. Do you think that Americans today share the colonists' values? Why or why not? Write your responses in your journal.

Alternative Assessment

Creating a mural With your classmates, create a mural called "Life in the English Colonies: A Story of Diversity." The mural should have three sections: the New England Colonies, the Middle Colonies, and the Southern Colonies.

1 As a class, decide on the height and width of the whole mural. Then discuss how you will show the diversity of people in the colonies as well as the diverse ways of life.

2 Divide into three groups to illustrate the sections of the mural. You may want to do additional research before you begin.

Your mural will be evaluated on the following criteria:
• it portrays the diverse people and ways of life in the English colonies
• it provides information that is accurate
• it presents the information in clear, inviting ways

Link to Literature

The Witch of Blackbird Pond
by Elizabeth George Speare

At age 16, Kit Tyler comes to live with her Uncle Matthew and Aunt Rachel in a Puritan town in colonial New England. Kit makes friends with a Quaker widow named Hannah Tupper—an isolated woman the Puritans view with suspicion. When three children die of a mysterious fever, townspeople blame Hannah, saying she must be a witch. Kit helps Hannah escape before a mob burns her hut. One morning some townspeople pay a visit to Kit's home.

deacon:
a leader in the church

constable:
policeman

contempt:
scorn

summat:
something

There were four callers, one a deacon from the church, the constable of the town, and Goodman Cruff and his wife. They were not excited this morning. They looked hard and purposeful, and Goodwife Cruff's eyes glittered toward Kit with contempt and something else she could not interpret.

"I know you don't hold with witchcraft," the constable began, "but we've summat to say as may change your mind."

"You arrested your witch?" asked Matthew with impatience.

"Not that. The town's rid of that one for good."

Matthew stared at him in alarm. "What have you done?"

"Not what you fear. We didn't lay hands on the old woman. She slipped through our trap somehow."

"And we know how!" hissed Goodwife Cruff. Kit felt a wave of fear that left her sick and dizzy.

The deacon glanced at Goodwife Cruff uneasily. "I don't quite go along with them," he said. "But I got to admit the thing looks mighty queer. We've combed the whole town this morning, ever since dawn. There's not a trace of her. Don't see how she could have got far."

"We know right enough. They'll never find her!" broke in Goodwife Cruff. "No use trying to shush me, Adam Cruff. You tell them what we saw."

Her husband cleared his throat. "I didn't rightly see it myself," he apologized. "But there's some as saw that big yeller cat of hers come arunnin' out of the house. Couple of fellers took a shot at it. But the ones as got a good look claims it had a great fat mouse in its mouth, and it never let go, even when the bullets came after it."

His wife drew a hissing breath. *"That mouse was Hannah Tupper!"* 'Tis not the first time she's changed herself into a creature. They say when the moon is full—"

"Now hold on a minute, Matthew," cautioned the constable at Matthew's scornful gesture, "you can't

hornbook

Trial of a suspected witch in Puritan New England

gainsay it. There's things happen we better not look at too close. The woman's gone, and I say good riddance."

"She's gone straight back to Satan!" pronounced Goodwife Cruff, *"but she's left another to do her work!"*

Kit could have laughed out loud, but a look at Goodwife Cruff sobered her. The woman's eyes were fastened on her face with a cunning triumph.

gainsay: deny, speak against

"They found summat when they searched her place. Better take a look at this, Matthew." The constable drew something shining from his pocket. It was the little silver hornbook.

"What is it?" asked Matthew.

"Looks like a sort of hornbook."

"Who ever saw a hornbook like that?" demanded Goodman Cruff. "'Tis the devil's own writing."

"Has the Lord's Prayer on it," the constable reminded him. "Look at the letters on the handle, Matthew."

Matthew took the thing in his hands reluctantly and turned it over.

"Ask *her* where it came from," jibed Goodwife Cruff, unable to keep silent.

There was a harsh gasp from Rachel. Matthew lifted his eyes from the hornbook to his niece's white face. "Can this be yours, Katherine?" he asked.

Kit's lips were stiff. "Yes sir," she answered faintly. . . .

"I don't understand this, Katherine. I forbade you—you understood it perfectly—to go to that woman's house."

"I know. But Hannah needed me, and I needed her. She wasn't a witch, Uncle Matthew. If you could have only known her—"

Matthew looked back at the constable. "I am chagrined," he said with dignity, "that I have not controlled my own household. But the girl is young and ignorant. I hold myself to blame for my laxness."

"Take no blame to yourself, Matthew." The constable rose to his feet. "I'm sorry, what with your daughter sick and all, but we've got to lock this girl up."

hornbook: a page with the alphabet, numbers, etc., mounted on a board and protected by a thin, clear sheet of horn

chagrined: embarrassed

laxness: carelessness

A Closer Look

1. What is Matthew's attitude toward the witch hunt?

2. How does the author characterize Goodwife Cruff? Give examples.

3. Do you think the constable and the deacon believe Kit is a witch? Explain.

Unit Survey

Making Connections

Review

1. What reasons did Europeans have for establishing colonies in the Americas?

2. Describe the diversity of peoples living in North America (including what is now Mexico) in 1700.

3. Compare the Spanish colonies with the English colonies in terms of government, religion, and economy.

Linking History, Math, and Art

Project

Reconstructing the Jamestown Fort

As eager as they were to search for gold, the founders of Jamestown still built a wooden fort during their first month in Virginia. Historians have known this for a long time; what they have *not* known is exactly what the fort looked like—or where it was located. Prompted by the 400th anniversary of Jamestown's founding, archaeologists have renewed their efforts to find the fort. While they dig, try your hand at reconstructing the fort.

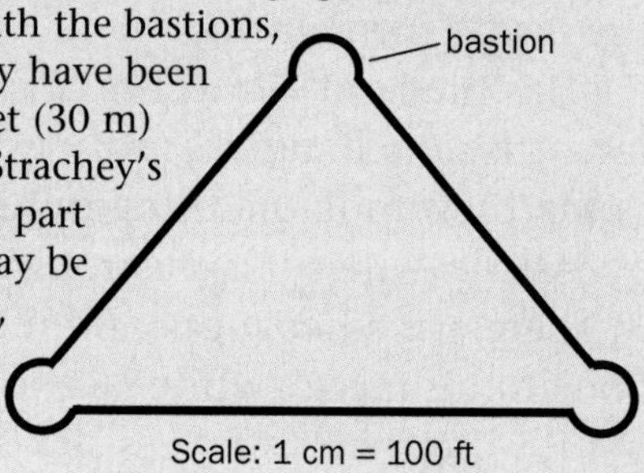

Project Steps

Work with a group.

❶ Study the information in the box, refer to the sample diagram shown here, and look at the picture on page 123.

❷ Find out more about what the fort and settlement may have looked like. In addition to library books, check recent newspaper and magazine articles for new information on Jamestown.

❸ Plan a model of the Jamestown fort.
• Calculate the approximate length of each side of the fort.
• Decide what scale you will use.
• Based on your research, decide what buildings and other items to include inside

One colonist, William Strachey, wrote that the fort was triangular, 300 by 300 by 420 feet (90 by 90 by 126 m) and close to the James River. Because the river now covers at least 100 yards (90 m) of what was shoreline, historians assume the fort is underwater. But some archaeologists think Strachey's numbers did not include the half-moon-shaped bastion at each corner of the fort, where large guns were mounted. With the bastions, each side may have been about 100 feet (30 m) longer than Strachey's figures. Thus, part of the fort may be underground, not underwater.

bastion

Scale: 1 cm = 100 ft

the fort and what size to make them. It may help to sketch as you plan.

❹ Gather your materials and begin construction. To identify buildings and other items, either make labels and attach them to the model, or make and label a drawing of the finished fort as viewed from above.

Thinking It Over Historians today must continually adjust their thinking in light of new discoveries. Do you think historians 400 years from now will have to do the same as they study our lives? Explain.

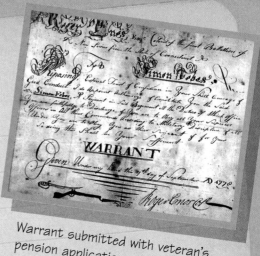

Warrant submitted with veteran's pension application

How Do We Know?

Scholar's Tool Kit
Public Records

As the year 1776 drew to a close, the American Revolution seemed on the brink of collapse. General George Washington confided to his cousin, "Our only dependence now is upon the speedy enlistment of a new army."

One of those who answered Washington's appeal for help was Andrew Allard. Leaving behind his young wife Zerviah and an infant son, Private Allard marched with his militia unit to join Washington in New York.

Learning About the Life of a Soldier

In writing the history of the American Revolution, scholars have a difficult time learning about the lives of ordinary people like Andrew Allard. Most Americans at the time could neither read nor write. As a result, the majority of these early Americans have been lost to history.

One place that historians look for information about Americans from times past is in the National Archives in Washington, D.C. The Archives is responsible for saving public records. These records include tax, court, and census records, military service and pension files, legal documents, treaties, and correspondence. If it were not for these records we would not know the Allard story.

After the American Revolution, Congress passed several acts giving free land and pensions to war veterans and their widows and children. When applying for pensions, veterans often sent Congress diaries,

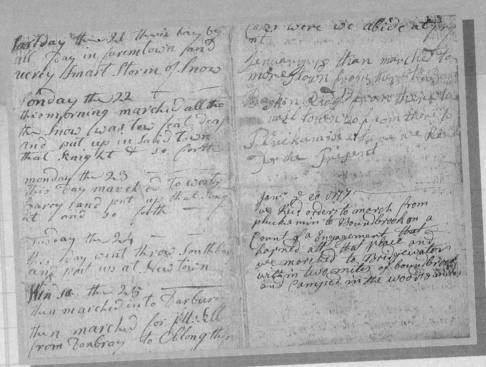

These pages from Allard's journal tell about events in December 1776 and January 1777. What could historians learn from his account?

? Critical Thinking

1. The National Archives keeps only 2 to 3 percent of the documents the government generates. How do you suppose the Archives decides what to keep?

? Critical Thinking

2. Millions of ordinary citizens visit the Archives each year to research their family history or satisfy their curiosity about historic events. Suppose you were to spend an afternoon at the Archives. What subject or event would you want to research? Why?

letters, and other documents to prove that they had served in the Continental Army. These items then became a part of the public records at the National Archives.

Among the 80,000 Revolutionary War Pension Application Files is one from Private Allard's widow Zerviah. In 1844 the 88-year-old woman asked Congress for a pension based on her husband's service in the Continental Army. Fortunately for us, Andrew Allard was one of the few colonial soldiers who could write. With her application Zerviah submitted six tattered pages from his diary, a letter he wrote her, and a letter from one of his fellow soldiers.

Telling the Story

The public records in the Allard pension application file tell a touching story—one that puts a human face on the war. "Desember 16 1776 This morning i lef my Hom in Order to march for Newyork," Andrew wrote in his diary. Five days later he recorded a "verey Smart Storm of Snow" that covered the ground "tow feat deap."

From Bound Creek, Connecticut, 390 miles (624 km) from home, Private Allard sent Zerviah a letter in the winter of 1777. Although in good health, he had had a narrow escape from the British.

"I went out a scout one day this week a Long with Lt. Willson and a Eleven more and wee all had A Chans to Come a Cross the Lite hors [British cavalry]. I being a littel Distanc from the Rest of our men had Like to have ben taken by them but thru the Goodness of God I Got to Rest of our party and wee made a stand and wee keep them Back til . . . they Retreated. . . . I Remain Your Loving Andrew Allard."

That was the last time Zerviah heard from her husband. By September 1777 Private Allard was dead—killed not by enemy bullets, but by an illness called "camp distemper."

Zerviah learned of her husband's death from Elias Green, one of Andrew's fellow soldiers. Green informed her of the "vary heavy Peas of news" in a letter written from Blandford, Massachusetts on August 25, 1777. "No Pains was wanting in takeing cair of him," Green assured her. "He had a good feather bed to Lay on, but all means was to no afect." Green sent Zerviah Andrew's diary "for his sun thit he might have it to Remember him by."

Because Zerviah applied for a pension, we now know of one soldier's small but honorable contribution to the cause of American liberty. Private Allard was not a war hero, but he served his country at a time when victory seemed impossible and when many other soldiers chose to defect or desert. Without his diary and letters, and without the National Archives files, we would never have known Private Allard's story.

Scholar at Work

For historians, the National Archives is like a giant family collection of memories. Every family acquires and saves documents that it may later need. Work with your family to list the kinds of documents your family saves. From these records, what story could a historian tell about your family?

Unit 3

Chapters

Hands-On *HISTORY*

Activity

In this painting a group of trusted and important citizens are shown meeting to make a decision that will affect all Americans. The event took place in 1776. If you were to photograph a similar event today, how would your picture differ from this painting? For example, this picture shows men wearing ruffled shirts and breeches and writing with quill pens. In a present-day photograph how might people be dressed? How might they be taking notes? Describe your photograph, explaining the differences you would expect to see.

The Declaration of Independence, 4 July 1776 (detail) by John Trumbull, 1786–1794

A New Nation Begins

Chapter **7**

The Years of Conflict

Keys to History

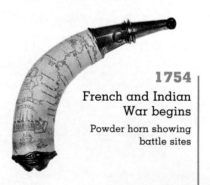

1754
French and Indian War begins
Powder horn showing battle sites

1765
Stamp Act
Teapot protesting the Stamp Act

1754   1763

Looking Back

World Link

Zenger freedom of press trial

1735

France surrenders most claims in India to Britain

1763

HISTORY *Mystery*

This skull and crossbones cartoon was a protest against stamps like the one shown next to it. Why would the colonists consider a small stamp dangerous enough to label it with a skull and crossbones?

1767

Sam Adams emerges as protest leader

1770

Boston Massacre

Coffin sketches with initials of some victims

1773

Boston Tea Party

British engraving made in 1789

1774

First Continental Congress

1769

1774

Looking Ahead

Battles of Lexington and Concord

1775

Beginning the Story with

George Washington

By the time he was 22, George Washington was a commander of militia fighting French soldiers in the backcountry. How did this young man who grew up on a Virginia plantation end up leading soldiers at such a young age? For Washington, it was the result of ambition.

At the age of 15 George Washington knew what he wanted in life—to be rich and respected. His problem was that he had no land. His older brother Lawrence had inherited the family plantation when their father died. First, George learned to be a surveyor. That career was a dead end, though. He would be working for the rich, not joining their ranks. There had to be a better way to reach his goals.

An Officer and a Gentleman

That better way, Washington decided, was to become an officer in the British army. As an officer and a gentleman, he would command respect and receive a handsome salary. The only problem was that most British officers believed that colonists made poor soldiers. Still, Washington had his mind set on a military career. The first step was to get some experience. In 1752, at age 20, he was made a major in the Virginia militia.

The following year, the young major got a chance to prove himself. A volunteer was needed to lead a small expedition north into French territory. Virginia's governor was alarmed by rumors that French soldiers based near Lake Erie were about to move south into the Ohio Valley, an area claimed by Virginia. If the rumors were true, the French had to be warned to stay out or risk war. Major Washington eagerly stepped forward to carry the message.

After two months of hard travel across 1,000 miles (1,600 km) of rugged land in the dead of winter, Washington reached Fort Le Boeuf [leh BUFF] near Lake Erie. The French officers of the fort invited him to dine with them. He later wrote in his journal, "The wine, as they dosed themselves pretty plentifully with it, soon banished restraint. They told me that it was their absolute design to take possession of the Ohio." The French made no effort to hide the fleet of more than 200 canoes that would carry them into the Ohio Valley when spring came.

Washington rushed back to Virginia with the news. As a reward for completing the dangerous mission, the governor promoted him to lieutenant colonel in the militia.

Washington's first military mission, in the winter of 1753, was nearly his last. He almost froze to death crossing an ice-clogged river.

"I Heard the Bullets Whistle"

In the spring of 1754, Washington led a small militia force to the Ohio Valley. They were to protect Virginians building a fort where the Allegheny (al-uh-GAY-nee) and Monongahela (muh-NAHN-guh-HEE-luh) Rivers meet to form the Ohio River. He arrived too late. The French had already chased the Virginians away and built a fort named Fort Duquesne (doo-KAYN).

In Washington's eyes the French had committed an act of war. At that point he made one of the few mistakes of his military career. He attacked a small French force camped nearby, even though France and Britain were not at war. It was an easy victory. "I heard the bullets whistle," he wrote in a letter home, "and, believe me, there is something charming in the sound."

The French sent a large force to punish the Virginians. Washington and his men quickly built a fort that he called Fort Necessity. In the first day of fighting, the French killed a third of Washington's soldiers. Realizing that it was hopeless to hold out, Washington decided to surrender.

The French allowed the young officer and his men to return home, where Washington was welcomed as a hero. He had stood up to the French against great odds. To British army leaders, however, his surrender was more proof that colonials were not officer material.

Hands-On → *HISTORY*

Activity

You read what Washington wrote home after his victory over the French. Write another letter home from Washington after his surrender of Fort Necessity. Describe the feelings he might have had about his own future in the military and about the ability of the colonial militia.

1. The French and Indian War

Reading Guide

New Terms allies, blockade, cede

Section Focus Why the British fought and defeated the French

1. Why were Indians involved in the conflict between the French and British?
2. Why did the colonies reject a plan for their common defense?
3. How did Britain win the French and Indian War, and what did it gain?

The battle George Washington fought at Fort Necessity in 1754 was only one of many in a long-running conflict over control of western lands and the fur trade. Since the 1600s French fur trappers and their Indian **allies**—helpers in times of trouble—had clashed with English settlers.

In 1756 the conflict became part of a wider war between France and Britain—the fourth time they had fought in less than a century. Each of the previous three wars had left little change in North America. However, this war—known in the colonies as the French and Indian War—would make Britain the main power on the continent.

Conflict in the Backcountry

Describing the conflict in North America as the "British" fighting the "French and Indians" paints too simple a picture. Only colonies that claimed western lands were eager to fight the French. Meanwhile, the colonies competed with one another in trying to settle the backcountry and expand the fur trade. Whenever the militia from one colony helped another to fight the French, it was out of self-interest.

Referring to the "French and Indians" is also misleading because not all the Indian tribes were allies of the French. The French usually had better relations with Indians because the French wanted to trade, not take land. By favoring some tribes over others, however, they made enemies, including the powerful Iroquois League.

The Indians of each tribe looked to their own needs in deciding whether to side with the French, with the British, or with neither. Playing one side against the other, they considered what goods they could get at what price, how much respect they were given, and who seemed more powerful.

For their part, the French and British constantly competed for Indian allies. They needed Indian friends to trade with and to protect them from attacks by other Indians. Most importantly, Indian allies could help them when they fought each other.

The Albany Plan

In 1754, as the French built fort after fort in the Great Lakes region, the Iroquois began having second thoughts about being allies with the British. Britain ordered colonies from Virginia northward to send delegates to meet with the Iroquois leaders in Albany, New York. Despite attempts to convince them to help if war broke out, the Iroquois decided not to take sides.

After the Iroquois leaders left the meeting, Benjamin Franklin proposed a plan for all of the colonies to unite in defending

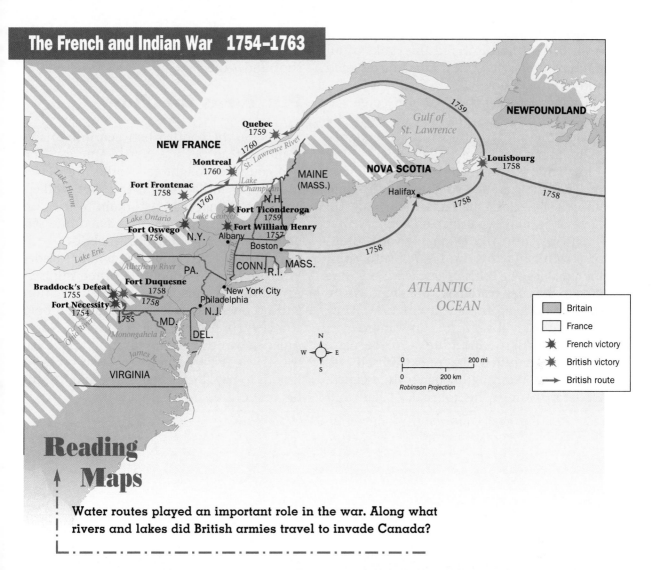

The French and Indian War 1754–1763

Reading Maps

Water routes played an important role in the war. Along what rivers and lakes did British armies travel to invade Canada?

themselves. His plan called for the colonial legislatures to send representatives to a council led by a governor appointed by the king. The council would act for all the colonies in making Indian treaties, raising an army, and building forts. To pay its expenses, it would have the power to collect taxes.

When the plan was sent to the legislatures, though, not a single one approved it. They believed that only representatives elected by the people should decide on taxes. So ended the Albany Plan, the first attempt to unite all the colonies. Clearly they were not yet willing to cooperate with one another.

Braddock's Defeat

After the failure of the Albany Plan and Washington's defeat at Fort Necessity, Virginia's governor asked Britain for help. In 1755 Britain sent 1,400 soldiers under General Edward Braddock to try to drive the French from the Ohio Valley. Virginia and nearby colonies were asked to pay for the troops' supplies and to provide militia for a march on Fort Duquesne.

As the militiamen were being organized, one officer was noticeably absent—George Washington. When he returned from Fort Necessity, Washington learned that orders from Britain had lowered the ranks of all militia officers. His pride injured, he resigned and returned home.

George's brother had died, so George was now running the plantation. Still, he missed the military. He wrote to Braddock to ask about a position. When offered only a low rank, he declined. Instead, he joined the general's staff as a volunteer. If he could impress Braddock, perhaps there was still hope of becoming a British officer.

The march to Fort Duquesne was a disaster. Ambushed by the French and their Indian allies, the British panicked. They were used to the open battlefields of Europe, where they could keep the enemy in view. They were not ready for hit-and-run warfare.

Two-thirds of Braddock's force were killed or wounded. Braddock himself was killed, and Washington narrowly escaped. He later wrote in his journal, "I had four Bullets through my Coat and two horses shot under me."

Pitt Turns the Tide

In 1756 the conflict between Britain and France spread beyond North America. The two countries fought each other for power in Europe, India, Africa, the West Indies, and on the high seas. As Britain focused on the fighting in Europe, it suffered one setback after another in North America.

The tide turned when the brilliant leader William Pitt was appointed prime minister in 1757. Boasting "I can save this nation and no one else can," Pitt launched a bold strategy. He decided that victory in North America was the key to winning the global war. He got Parliament to raise taxes in Britain to pay for a larger army, and he sent his best officers to North America.

The British won a decisive victory at Quebec in 1759. A British artist showed the landing and the battle taking place at the same time.

Pitt ordered a blockade of New France. A **blockade** is the shutting off of a place by ships or troops to prevent supplies from reaching it. In 1758 the British captured Louisbourg, giving them control of the Gulf of St. Lawrence. (See map on page 183.)

The blockade strangled French supply lines, leading most of France's Indian allies to make peace with the British. Lacking supplies and help from the Indians, the French abandoned Fort Duquesne, burning it to the ground. The British later built their own fort there, naming it Fort Pitt. The site today is Pittsburgh. Other victories followed rapidly, as British forces captured one French fort after another.

The British attack Quebec The British delivered their crushing blow at Quebec in 1759. Quebec guarded the St. Lawrence River, the gateway to supplying French forts in the interior. Under the cover of darkness, General James Wolfe led his troops up the cliffs and onto the Plains of Abraham outside the city. They were ready when the French awoke.

The British won the fierce battle that followed, in which both Wolfe and his brave opponent, General Louis Joseph de Montcalm (mōn-KALM), lost their lives. A year later the fall of Montreal marked the end of French power in North America.

Britain Triumphs

The war dragged on for several years. Finally, in 1763, Britain and France signed the Treaty of Paris, ending the global conflict that became known in Europe as the Seven Years' War.

The previous year France had agreed to **cede**—give up—Louisiana to Spain. In the Treaty of Paris, France now ceded Canada to Britain. French forces left North America, and France surrendered to Britain almost all her claims in India. The door had opened to

World Link

The British in India The Treaty of Paris in 1763 sealed Britain's triumph over France—not only in North America but also in India. France gave up most of its claims there, opening the door to almost 200 years of British control.

The British saw India as a glittering prize, with its rich trade in spices, silks, and jewels. After the American colonies broke away, India was the "jewel in the crown" of Britain's empire. Not until 1947 was it granted independence.

a vast British empire upon which, it would be said, "the sun never set."

The sun had set, though, on Washington's hope for a place of honor within that empire. After Fort Duquesne fell in 1758, he again asked to be made a British officer and was turned down. He decided to turn his back on the military. He took pride, however, in having protected what he called his "country," Virginia. He would return to his plantation there.

1. Section Review

1. Define **allies, blockade,** and **cede.**
2. What role did the Indians play in the conflict between the French and British?
3. What was the purpose of the Albany Plan and why was it rejected?
4. What were the main causes and effects of the British victory in the war?
5. Critical Thinking If the French had won, do you think they would have taken control of the 13 colonies? Explain.

2. Growing Pains

Reading Guide

New Terms **proclamation, customs duties, revenue, writs of assistance, repeal, boycott**

Section Focus **Why the colonists began to resent British rule**

1. Why did Britain and the colonists come into conflict over western lands?
2. Why and how did the colonists protest the Stamp Act?
3. What were the effects of the Townshend Acts?

For Britain and the 13 colonies, the joy over winning the French and Indian War was short-lived. The mother country soon came into increasing conflict with her "children," as both Britain and the colonies began to feel growing pains.

For Britain the growing pains were the burdens of organizing a larger empire. How would it govern the vast territory that had been New France? How would it pay the increased cost of defending its empire? To meet these challenges, Parliament decided to take tighter control over the colonies and get more money from them.

For a long time the colonies had felt the growing pains of challenging the mother country's authority. British trade laws were rarely enforced. Colonial merchants often defied these laws by smuggling goods into the colonies. Meanwhile, colonial legislatures could usually get royal governors to cooperate with them by threatening not to pay their salaries.

Before the war, the colonies had been used to governing themselves. Now, in trying to control a wider empire, Parliament would pass laws that clashed with the colonists' desire to preserve their tradition of self-government. As the conflict worsened, many colonists would come to believe that they had more in common with one another than with Britain.

Problems in the West

Two main problems faced Britain as it tried to govern the large area that had been New France. One was how to deal with the Indian tribes who lived there. The other was whether to allow settlers to move west, turning Indian hunting grounds into farms.

Pontiac's Rebellion Britain's victory had stunned France's Indian allies. Their fears for the future deepened when they found the British to be stingy, greedy, and eager for revenge. The French had given the Indians many presents and allowed them to buy goods on credit. Not so the British, whose Indian policy was now being set by harsh officials like Lord Jeffrey Amherst.

Amherst declared that the former French allies "must be punished but not bribed." He refused to give them any gunpowder, although they depended on guns for hunting. If they starved, all the better, he believed. He even suggested sending "the Small Pox among those dissatisfied tribes."

The fear and frustration of the Great Lakes tribes erupted in 1763, in Pontiac's Rebellion. Pontiac, an Ottawa chief who was a great religious and political leader, gathered neighboring tribes to attack British forts. By July 1763 only Detroit, Fort Pitt, and Fort Niagara remained in British hands.

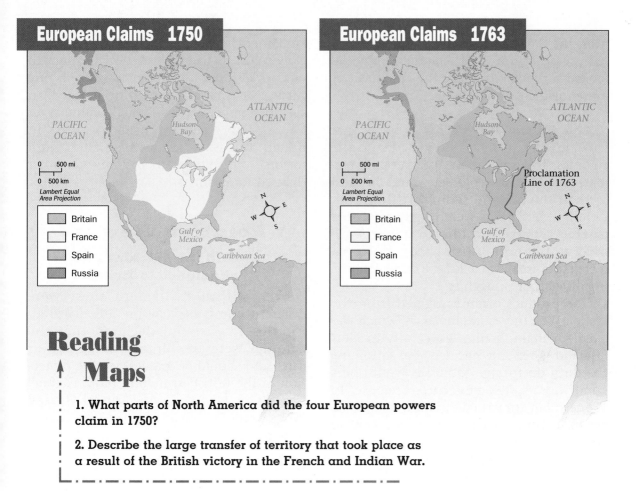

European Claims 1750

PACIFIC OCEAN

ATLANTIC OCEAN

Hudson Bay

Gulf of Mexico

Caribbean Sea

0 500 mi
0 500 km
Lambert Equal Area Projection

- Britain
- France
- Spain
- Russia

European Claims 1763

PACIFIC OCEAN

ATLANTIC OCEAN

Hudson Bay

Proclamation Line of 1763

Gulf of Mexico

Caribbean Sea

0 500 mi
0 500 km
Lambert Equal Area Projection

- Britain
- France
- Spain
- Russia

Reading Maps

1. What parts of North America did the four European powers claim in 1750?

2. Describe the large transfer of territory that took place as a result of the British victory in the French and Indian War.

Without their usual help from the French, the tribes could not fight for long. They finally signed peace treaties with the British. The Indians had made Amherst pay dearly, though. They had captured or killed nearly 2,000 Englishmen.

The Proclamation of 1763 Parliament had to face the question of how to prevent further conflict with the Indians. It came up with an answer in the Proclamation of 1763. This **proclamation**—which means an official announcement—said that colonists could not settle west of the Appalachians. Settlers already living there were ordered to leave. In addition, the British government would take control of the fur trade.

The law was meant to buy time until Britain could sign treaties with the Indians. Land buyers, fur traders, and settlers, however, saw things differently. Now that the French were defeated and Pontiac's Rebellion had ended, they were eager to push westward. Most ignored the proclamation.

Parliament Taxes the Colonies

To enforce the Proclamation of 1763 and protect the colonists from the Indians, Britain declared that it needed an army of 10,000 soldiers in North America. But who should pay to support them? Taxpayers in Britain were already burdened with the debt from the French and Indian War. The new British prime minister, George Grenville, looked for a way to make the colonies pay more for their own defense.

The Sugar Act Grenville knew that Parliament had never directly taxed the colonies. The Navigation Acts had only regulated trade so the colonies would do most of their buying and selling with Britain. Colonial merchants were to pay **customs duties**—charges on foreign imports—in order to sell non-British goods. However, merchants usually avoided the duties by bribing officials or smuggling.

One product often smuggled from the French West Indies was molasses, which was used for making rum, especially in New England. Grenville decided that enforcing the duty on foreign molasses would be a good way to raise **revenue**—income. In 1764 Parliament passed the Sugar Act, which cut in half the duty on foreign molasses to encourage merchants to pay it. However, the law also gave officials new powers to crack down on smuggling.

Under the Sugar Act, customs officials could enter any building at any time, using general search warrants called **writs of assistance.** Colonists accused of smuggling would face a panel of British judges instead of a jury of their peers. Also, they would be considered guilty unless proven innocent. Many colonists saw these searches and the denial of a jury trial as threats to their rights as Englishmen.

Meanwhile, Parliament's effort to get revenue went against the colonists' belief that they could only be taxed by their own legislatures. Protests against "taxation without representation," however, came mainly from New England merchants, who were most affected by the Sugar Act.

The Stamp Act To get even more revenue to pay for the colonies' defense,

Parliament passed the Stamp Act in 1765. Now colonists had to buy special stamps to put on legal documents, dice, and playing cards. Newspapers had to be printed on special stamped paper. Though stamp taxes had already been imposed for years in Britain, this was Parliament's first attempt to force the colonies to pay any tax other than customs duties.

Point of View

Did the colonies owe obedience to Britain?

Even within Parliament there were different points of view on this question. Charles Townshend declared that the colonies were "children planted by our care" and should be grateful for the protection of the British army and navy. Colonel Isaac Barré, who had served under General Wolfe in the French and Indian War, angrily responded,

"They planted by your care? No! Your oppressions planted them in America. They fled from your tyranny to a then uncultivated and unhospitable country. . . . And believe me, remember I this day told you so, that same spirit of freedom . . . will accompany them still.**"**

Britain would soon feel the effects of that spirit of freedom in the colonies.

Protesting the Stamp Act
● ●

Unlike the Sugar Act, the Stamp Act affected people of every colony and social class, including leaders such as lawyers, newspaper publishers, and ministers. Protestors argued that only representatives they elected should be able to tax them. Such men lived near them and understood their needs, unlike Parliament, which met thousands of miles across the sea. The protestors insisted that Parliament was taking their money against their will.

Concern was so widespread that nine colonies sent delegates to a meeting in New York called the Stamp Act Congress. The delegates saw the need for the colonies to put aside rivalries over land claims and trade in order to meet the common threat. Said Christopher Gadsden of South Carolina, "There ought to be no New Englanders, no New Yorkers known on the continent, but all of us Americans."

The delegates declared that British citizens could not be taxed without representation and that Parliament did not represent the colonies. They sent a petition to Parliament asking it to **repeal**—do away with—the Stamp Act and the Sugar Act.

Many colonists took matters into their own hands. Calling themselves Sons and Daughters of Liberty, they decided to **boycott**—refuse to buy—British goods. Daughters of Liberty agreed to wear homespun wool dresses rather than buy imported British cloth. Such pledges, known as nonimportation agreements, were common throughout the colonies.

Some protests turned ugly. Tax collectors complained about "Sons of Violence" who tried to pressure them by breaking windows in their houses and even threatening their lives. Boston tax collector Andrew Oliver got a grim warning when an effigy—a dummy—of him was hanged and burned. A crowd in Connecticut even started to bury a tax collector alive. Only after hearing dirt being shoveled onto the coffin lid did he agree to resign.

Britain tried to tax the colonists by requiring them to buy special stamps for all legal documents and for newspapers. Tax collectors were appointed to sell the stamps, but most colonists refused to buy them. In one form of protest, they burned stamped papers.

Repeal of the Stamp Act

Within a few short months the protests had stopped efforts to collect the stamp tax. A shocked Parliament met in 1766 to debate whether to repeal the Stamp Act. Some members argued that giving in would encourage colonists to defy Parliament. Others worried that ordering the army to enforce the Stamp Act would lead to rebellion.

Grenville insisted that Parliament had a right to impose any laws, not just those regulating trade. "Great Britain protects America; America is bound to yield obedience," he declared. "If not, tell me when the Americans were emancipated [made free]?" William Pitt angrily replied, "I desire to know when they were made slaves."

Meanwhile, British merchants had been hurt by the boycotts and begged for repeal of the Stamp Act. After a fierce debate Parliament finally voted to do so. The Sugar Act, though, remained in effect.

To save face, Parliament passed an act declaring it could make laws for the colonies "in all cases whatsoever." Colonists paid little attention to this Declaratory Act. Parliament could claim any right it wanted, as long as it did not try to act on its claim. In the meantime, colonists celebrated the repeal of the Stamp Act by ringing church bells and setting off fireworks.

The Townshend Acts

Parliament continued to struggle with the debt problem. Soon it looked again to the colonies for revenue. In 1767 Charles Townshend, now in charge of the British treasury, came up with a new plan.

Townshend knew that many colonial leaders had recognized Parliament's right to regulate trade. Therefore, he convinced Parliament to pass the Townshend Acts. These laws imposed duties on popular goods that could only be imported from Britain: paint, lead, glass, paper, and tea.

The colonists saw the Townshend duties for exactly what they were—taxes in disguise. Even worse, some of the revenue

Link to the Present

Boycotts Would you be willing to give up eating grapes or lettuce? In the 1960s and 1970s, the United Farm Workers union, led by Cesar Chavez, urged shoppers not to buy those products. They hoped a boycott would force grape and lettuce growers to pay them better wages and provide better working conditions.

The idea behind a boycott is simple—if you make your opponents lose enough money, they will do what you want. The challenge is to get enough people to go along with the boycott. In the case of the farm workers, each boycott took more than four years before being declared a success.

Cesar Chavez

WILLIAM JACKSON,
an IMPORTER; at the
BRAZEN HEAD,
North Side of the TOWN-HOUSE,
and Opposite the Town-Pump, in
Corn-hill, BOSTON.

It is desired that the Sons and
Daughters of LIBERTY,
would not buy any one thing of
him, for in so doing they will bring
Disgrace upon themselves, and their
Posterity, for ever and ever, AMEN.

Colonial boycott notice

went to pay salaries of the royal governors, who had up until then been paid by the colonial legislatures. Now the governors would be more likely to support Parliament than to speak up for the colonies.

Colonial Leaders of Protest

Several protest leaders emerged in 1767 to alert colonists that their self-government was threatened. Most notable was Samuel Adams of Boston, a master at inflaming people with symbols and words.

On one day Adams might be seen staging a rally to hang a tax collector in effigy from a "liberty pole." On another he would be writing an essay criticizing the governor, who once complained that "every dip of his pen stung like a horned snake." Adams had a motto, "Take a stand at the start," and he never let up.

More cautious but equally passionate about the colonists' rights was Sam's cousin John Adams, a lawyer. Like Samuel Adams, John had come to believe that Parliament did not represent the colonies and therefore had no right to pass any laws binding them, not even on matters of trade.

Perhaps the best speaker among the protest leaders was Patrick Henry, a member of the Virginia House of Burgesses. A back-country lawyer with a silver tongue, he could move listeners to tears. He would later become famous for declaring, "Give me liberty or give me death."

Colonial legislatures joined in the rising protest. The Massachusetts legislature urged other colonies to boycott British goods. The New York legislature refused to house British troops as required by a law called the Quartering Act. Parliament dismissed both legislatures and sent troops to Boston.

Such actions seemed to confirm what leaders like Sam Adams were warning—that Britain intended to end the colonists' tradition of self-government. George Washington, who had joined in the boycott, wrote:

❝At a time when our lordly Masters in Great Britain will be satisfied with nothing less than the [loss] of American freedom, it seems highly necessary that something should be done to . . . maintain the liberty which we had derived from our ancestors. . . . Yet arms [war] should be the last resource.❞

The Boston Massacre

Tensions in the colonies rose with each passing day, and protests turned violent. On March 5, 1770, an angry crowd taunted nine British soldiers guarding the Boston customs building. The crowd threw whatever they could get their hands on—sticks, snowballs, oyster shells, and ice chunks.

The frightened soldiers opened fire, killing five and wounding several more. The first to die was Crispus Attucks, a former slave who had become a sailor and one of the Sons of Liberty. The British commander and soldiers were charged with murder.

John Adams thought that the crowd had provoked the soldiers, and he successfully defended them in court. Sam Adams saw the shooting as a chance to whip up anti-British feeling. He called it "the Boston Massacre." Paul Revere, a local silversmith, made an engraving showing soldiers firing on unarmed citizens. Prints of the picture were sent throughout the colonies.

The Colonists Cool Off

On the very day of the Boston Massacre, Parliament met to discuss the effects of the Townshend Acts. King George III urged restraint, not wanting to drive the colonies to revolt. Parliament agreed and repealed the duties except the one on tea, which provided the most income.

Parliament assumed that the colonists were so fond of tea that they would be willing to pay the duty. Keeping the tea duty was also its way of saying it had the right to impose laws. The Sugar Act also remained.

Most colonists were satisfied just to get rid of the other Townshend duties. Despite Sam Adams' warning that every calm day "strengthens our opponent and weakens us," the protests died down. For his part, John Adams was lying low. "I shall certainly

Paul Revere

John Adams

Samuel Adams

become more retired and cautious," he wrote in his diary. "I shall certainly mind my own farm and my own office."

Two years passed without serious incident, but Sam Adams was on the alert. He was certain that Parliament would make another mistake, and when it did he would be ready. "Where there is a spark of patriotic fire," he wrote, "we will enkindle [light] it."

2. Section Review

1. Define **proclamation, customs duties, revenue, writs of assistance, repeal,** and **boycott.**
2. What was the purpose of the Proclamation of 1763, and how did colonists react?
3. Explain the uproar over the Stamp Act.
4. Why did the colonists oppose the Townshend Acts?
5. Critical Thinking Do you think that violent protests were necessary to get the Stamp Act repealed? Explain.

Skill Lab

Thinking Critically

Primary and Secondary Sources

Was the Boston Massacre a killing of helpless, unresisting colonists? At the trial of British Captain Thomas Preston and his soldiers, some witnesses said that the colonists provoked the shooting. Others disagreed.

Question to Investigate

Who was to blame for the Boston Massacre?

Procedure

To explore the question, you will look at some primary and secondary sources. A **primary source** is an artifact or record from someone who experienced the event described. A **secondary source** is made by someone who did not experience the event described. Secondary sources, such as this textbook, are based on primary sources. Read the sources and do the following.

❶ Identify whether each source is primary or secondary. Explain how you can tell.

❷ Identify the information each source gives.
a. What people and actions does each one describe?
b. From what types of primary sources do you think the secondary sources got their information? Explain.

❸ Compare the information.
a. What do the sources have in common?
b. Do they agree with each other? Explain.
c. Do you think the Question to Investigate can ever be answered for certain? Explain.

Skill Tips

• Some examples of primary sources are autobiographies, records of oral interviews, diaries, letters, photos, films, and artifacts like tools or weapons.
• Some examples of secondary sources are biographies, history books, and encyclopedias.
• Paintings, political cartoons, and newspaper articles can be either primary or secondary sources.

Sources to Use

A "One of these people [Crispus Attucks], a stout man with a long cordwood stick, threw himself in, and made a blow at [struck] the officer. I saw the officer try to ward off the stroke. The stout man then turned around and struck the soldier's gun. He knocked his gun away and struck him over the head. This stout man cried, 'Kill the dogs. Knock them over.' This was the general cry. The people then crowded in."

From the trial testimony of Andrew, an enslaved African American

B "The prosecution attacked vigorously, parading witness after witness to the stand; . . . all of them agreed that the Captain gave the order to fire—and, equally important, that there was no provocation for it beyond name-calling and a few snowballs."

From "The Boston Massacre," by Thomas J. Fleming, *American Heritage,* December 1966

C "I asked him then . . . whether he thought they fired in self-defense or on purpose to destroy the people. He said he really thought they did fire to defend themselves; that he did not blame the man, whoever he was, who shot him."

From the testimony of Dr. John Jeffries, who treated a wounded colonist who later died

D Reread the description of the Boston Massacre on page 192.

3. The Road to Revolution

Reading Guide

New Term monopoly

Section Focus What led Britain and the colonies to the brink of war

1. Why were Committees of Correspondence formed?
2. Why and how did the colonists unite to protest the Tea Act?
3. What were the purpose and results of the First Continental Congress?

Although it repealed most of the Townshend Acts in 1770, Parliament still insisted it had complete power over the colonies. Also, warships patrolling the Atlantic coast were a reminder that Britain was willing to use force.

Committees of Correspondence

In June 1772 the calm was shattered after the *Gaspee*, a British schooner chasing smugglers, ran aground in Rhode Island. That night colonists removed the crew and burned the boat to the waterline. Rumors spread that if any of the colonists were caught they would be sent to Britain for trial, denying their right to a trial by a jury of their peers.

Four days later, Massachusetts Governor Thomas Hutchinson announced that Parliament would now pay his salary. This news reopened a simmering issue. Did Parliament or the colonial legislatures control the governors? Hutchinson had also written to friends in London suggesting that colonists' liberties should be limited for the good of the empire. When the public learned of these letters, there was an outcry of protest.

Samuel Adams made good use of these events. To him, all such British actions were part of a plot to deny the colonists their rights as Englishmen. In November 1772 he began organizing groups of letter writers known as "Committees of Correspondence" to spread news from town to town about British threats to those rights. The more outrageous the story, the better Adams liked it. Within two years all the colonies were linked by Committees of Correspondence.

Still, Sam Adams had not found an issue powerful enough to rally all the colonies around. "I wish we could arouse the continent," he wrote to a friend.

The Tea Act

In 1773 Adams got the issue he wanted when Parliament passed the Tea Act. This law gave the British East India Company a **monopoly**—complete control—of sales of British tea in the colonies. Colonial merchants thought this would put many of them out of business. They also suspected that British monopolies on other products would soon follow.

Parliament had not intended the Tea Act to be a slap in the face to the colonists. It was passed to help another part of the empire. The British East India Company was responsible for governing India, but was heavily in debt. The Tea Act would help it get back on its feet. The colonists objected that Parliament had no right to finance other parts of its colonial empire by running their merchants out of business.

Committees of Correspondence urged colonists to boycott East India tea. A group of 51 women in Edenton, North Carolina, for instance, agreed not to drink British tea or wear clothing from Britain until the Tea Act was repealed. The boycott was so effective that most of the company's ships returned to Britain without unloading their cargoes.

The Boston Tea Party

Massachusetts Governor Hutchinson challenged the boycott. He declared that the company ships in Boston harbor would not leave until their cargo was unloaded. The Sons of Liberty decided to do the unloading, but not in the way the governor had in mind.

Disguised as Indians, they boarded three East India Company ships on the evening of December 16, 1773. As hundreds of Bostonians cheered from the docks, the "Indians" chopped open 342 chests of tea and tossed them into the sea.

In Britain and in the colonies, most people saw the Boston Tea Party as a point of no return. John Adams declared, "This Destruction of the Tea is so bold, so daring, so firm, intrepid and inflexible, and it must have so important Consequences." King George III declared, "The Colonies must either submit [give in] or triumph."

The "Intolerable Acts"

To punish Massachusetts, Parliament passed a series of laws in 1774 called the Coercive Acts. The navy would blockade Boston harbor until the ruined tea was paid

Members of the Sons of Liberty protested the Tea Act by dumping chests of tea into Boston harbor to make "salt water tea."

Hands-On *HISTORY*

Tax collector being tarred and feathered

Activity

1. Make a list titled "Colonial Protests." Give specific examples, such as "refusing to buy British tea."

2. Make a list titled "Protests Today." Give specific examples.

3. Sort the examples into general types, such as "boycotts" or "destroying property." Identify each type as violent or nonviolent.

4. Arrange the examples in a table with four columns labeled "Type of Protest," "Violent or Nonviolent?," "Colonial Examples," and "Modern Examples."

5. Write a paragraph summarizing similarities and differences between protests then and now.

---

for. Also, a military governor would rule Massachusetts. British officials charged with crimes would be tried outside the colony. Colonists would have to house and feed British troops. Angry colonists called these laws the "Intolerable Acts."

By punishing Massachusetts, Parliament hoped to make the other colonies afraid to challenge British authority. Instead, the Coercive Acts had the opposite effect. Even though many colonists believed that destroying the tea was going too far, they saw the British reaction as a greater threat. When Boston's port was closed, merchants across America closed shops in sympathy, flags flew at half-mast, and other colonies sent donations of food and money.

Meanwhile, Parliament also passed the Quebec Act to provide government for the French people of Quebec. Quebec would be ruled by a governor with no elected legislature. Its boundaries would expand to include much of the territory between the 13 colonies and the Mississippi River. Many colonists saw the Quebec Act as a threat to the future of their self-government.

The First Continental Congress

When Virginia's legislature proposed a day of fasting and prayer for the people of Boston, the governor dissolved the legislature. The legislators then met at a nearby inn and drew up a resolution declaring that the blockade of Boston was an attack on all the colonies. They called for a Continental Congress to meet "to consult upon the present unhappy state of the colonies."

In September 1774 delegates from all of the colonies except Georgia met in Philadelphia as the First Continental Congress. Their goal was to look for a peaceful way to resolve their conflict with Britain.

Patrick Henry urged the delegates to look beyond their own colonies and consider the interests of all. "Virginians, Pennsylvanians, New Yorkers, and New Englanders are no more," he declared. "I am not a Virginian but an American."

Politically, the Congress was split about equally into three groups: conservatives, moderates, and radicals. The conservatives opposed anything that might lead to a break with Britain. George Washington was among the moderates, who believed that Parliament had a right to regulate trade but not tax the colonies.

The radicals included John Adams and Sam Adams. They argued that Parliament had no right to impose laws on the colonies.

Steps Toward the American Revolution 1763–1774

British Law	What It Did	Colonial Reaction
Proclamation of 1763	Prohibited settlement west of the Appalachians	Protests, defiance
Sugar Act (1764)	Lowered duties on molasses, but first time duties used to collect revenue; denied jury trial to accused smugglers	Protests, petitions
Stamp Act (1765)	Required all written materials to be printed on stamped paper; first direct tax to get revenue (repealed in 1766)	Stamp Act Congress, petitions, boycotts, demonstrations
Declaratory Act (1766)	Declared Parliament's right to impose any laws on colonies	Little notice because of Stamp Act repeal
Townshend Acts (1767)	Taxed tea, lead, glass, paint, and paper; governors to be paid by Parliament (most repealed in 1770)	Boycotts, riots, demonstrations
Tea Act (1773)	Required that only East India Company may import and sell tea	Boycotts, Boston Tea Party
Coercive Acts (1774) ("Intolerable Acts")	Closed Boston port until destroyed tea paid for; suspended town meetings; appointed military governor of Massachusetts; permitted trials of government officials to be in England	Other colonies sent food and money to Massachusetts; call for Continental Congress

Source: Oxford Book of Reference on English History

In spite of their differences, the delegates all opposed the Coercive Acts. They approved a Declaration of Rights and Grievances, which condemned the Coercive Acts and affirmed the rights to life, liberty, and property. The declaration denied Parliament's right to tax the colonies.

The Congress recommended that every county, town, and city form committees to enforce a boycott on British goods. The overall attitude was a willingness to resist with force only if all else failed. The delegates agreed to meet again the following May if Britain did not change its policies.

War Clouds

Towns formed committees to enforce the boycott. Violators faced punishments ranging from having their names published in newspapers to being tarred and feathered.

Some colonists, though, were alarmed by such actions. One conservative accused the committees of "knocking out any Man's Brains that dares presume to speak his Mind freely about the present Contest."

In case the boycott did not work, the colonists rushed to organize militias. The colonies stood on the brink of war.

3. Section Review

1. Define **monopoly.**
2. What was the purpose of the Committees of Correspondence?
3. Why did the Tea Act anger the colonists?
4. What actions did the First Continental Congress take and why?
5. Critical Thinking Why might Parliament have thought that the Boston Tea Party was the most dangerous protest yet?

Why We Remember

The Years of Conflict

When George Washington was a boy growing up in Virginia, he often spoke of Britain as "home." So did most colonists. During the years of conflict, as Britain tried to tighten its control over the colonies, such feelings of loyalty began to change to resentment. Many colonists feared that the rights and liberties they had come to value were suddenly at risk.

Washington and his fellow colonists faced a clear choice. It would have been easier not to take action. That was not the choice of many brave colonists. Rich and poor, humble and proud, these Americans stood up to every attack on their freedoms. They fought back at first with boycotts and demonstrations. When peaceful measures failed, many were prepared to take up arms and fight for their rights. We live in a free country today because Washington and thousands like him refused to accept tyranny.

Geography Lab

Colonial Communication

Surrounded by "howling wilderness," as one settler called it, the earliest colonists traveled little. When they did, they floated down rivers or picked their way along Indian footpaths. In time, some paths became horse trails, and horse trails became roads. The British government improved some roads and built others so that post riders—mail carriers on horseback—could get through.

Still, travel was difficult. So how were colonists able to share the news and the ideas that eventually brought them closer together?

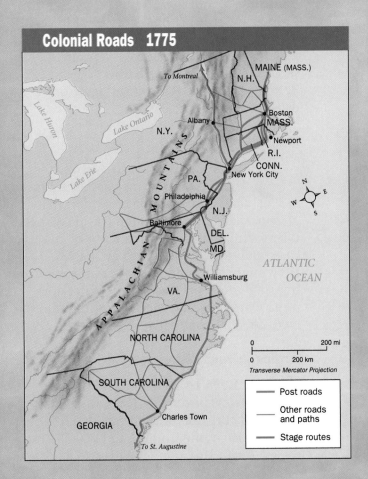

Colonial Roads 1775

To Montreal · Lake Huron · Lake Ontario · Lake Erie · MAINE (MASS.) · N.H. · Albany · N.Y. · Boston · MASS. · Newport · R.I. · CONN. · New York City · PA. · Philadelphia · N.J. · Baltimore · DEL. · MD. · APPALACHIAN MOUNTAINS · Williamsburg · ATLANTIC OCEAN · VA. · NORTH CAROLINA · SOUTH CAROLINA · GEORGIA · Charles Town · To St. Augustine

0   200 mi
0   200 km
Transverse Mercator Projection

— Post roads
— Other roads and paths
— Stage routes

Postal Milestones

1692 Royal colonial post opens. Boston–Philadelphia mail: 1 week.

1720 New York–Philadelphia mail: 3 days.

1753 Parliament appoints Benjamin Franklin postmaster. New York–Philadelphia mail: 1½ days.

1756 New York–Philadelphia by stagecoach: 3 or more days.

1758 Colonial post begins to carry newspapers.

1764 New York–Philadelphia mail: 1 day.

1771 New York–Philadelphia by stagecoach: 2 days.

1775 Continental Congress authorizes a postal service. Royal post closes.

1775 There are twice as many colonial newspapers as in 1755.

Link to History

1. Imagine that it is 1775. Someone says, "How can the colonists organize a rebellion? They can barely communicate with each other!" What is your answer?

2. Agree or disagree: Without meaning to, the British helped colonial unity. Explain.

3. **Hands-On Geography** The year is 1771. Your stagecoach line just bought new coaches to deliver passengers and packages. Prepare an advertisement to attract customers. Include information about improved routes and schedules.

Chapter Survey

Reviewing Vocabulary

Define the following terms.

1. allies
2. blockade
3. cede
4. proclamation
5. customs duties
6. revenue
7. writs of assistance
8. repeal
9. boycott
10. monopoly

Reviewing Main Ideas

1. What role did the Iroquois play in the conflict between the French and the British in North America?
2. Explain how William Pitt's actions helped lead to Britain's victory in the French and Indian War.
3. Why did Britain order the colonists to stay east of the Appalachian Mountains in the Proclamation of 1763? How did the colonists respond?
4. Describe each of the following with regard to the Stamp Act: (a) its purpose (b) what it required colonists to do (c) what argument colonists made against it
5. Why did the colonists oppose the idea of paying the duties required by the Townshend Acts?
6. What two incidents led to the formation of Committees of Correspondence?
7. Explain how each event led to the next: (a) Tea Act (b) Boston Tea Party (c) Coercive Acts (d) First Continental Congress

Thinking Critically

1. **Analysis** The First Continental Congress succeeded where the Albany Congress failed. Explain how and why.
2. **Synthesis** Imagine that the year is 2024. Everyone in the United Colonies of America is getting ready to celebrate the 250th anniversary of the Declaration of Loyalty to the British Empire. Describe the events that led to that declaration in 1774.

How did Britain and the colonies avoid the split that had threatened them?
3. **Why We Remember: Analysis** Why do you think some colonists protested against the British policies but other colonists did not?

Applying Skills

Primary and secondary sources The Boston Massacre is one of the many examples of a conflict that each side blamed the other for starting. Find an example of such a conflict today. It might be an event described in a newspaper or magazine article, or a conflict between two people or groups that you know. Then do the following:

1. Identify at least three sources of information about the conflict.
2. Tell whether each source is a primary or secondary source. Explain how you can tell.
3. Tell what ways the sources agree or disagree.

History Mystery

The "fatal" stamp Answer the History Mystery on page 179. The skull and crossbones cartoon that appears next to the stamp was published by a Philadelphia newspaper to blame the stamp for "killing" the newspaper. How might the stamps hurt a newspaper? Imagine yourself as a colonist. What are some ways in which the stamps might have affected your daily life?

Writing in Your History Journal

1. Keys to History (a) The time line on pages 178–179 has six Keys to History. In your journal, describe why each one is important. (b) Discuss the events in this chapter with two adults.

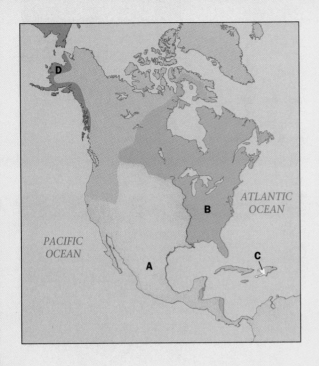

PACIFIC OCEAN

ATLANTIC OCEAN

Reviewing Geography

1. For each colored area marked with a letter on the map, write the letter and the name of the European country that claimed the area.

2. Geographic Thinking About 3,000 miles (4,800 km) of ocean separate London and Boston. Historians often point to this separation as a major influence on the conflict between Britain and its American colonies. What evidence do you find in the chapter to support this idea? Do you think that physical separation between government and the people must always lead to conflict? Explain your answer.

What other events do the three of you think should be on the time line? Write those events and their dates in your journal, and tell why you think each event should be added.

2. George Washington Imagine that you are a British officer in 1754. You have received a report of Washington's actions against the French in the Ohio Valley. In your journal, write your thoughts about whether he deserves to be made an officer in the British army. Give reasons to support your opinion.

3. Citizenship Imagine that you are a colonist living in 1774. Do you support the conservatives, the moderates, or the radicals? Why? Write your responses in your journal.

Alternative Assessment

Citizenship: Role-playing the Continental Congress With two other students, role-play a discussion at the First Continental Congress. One member will play the role of a conservative, another a moderate, and the third a radical.

❶ Meet as a group to decide what role each member will play.

❷ Each member will review the chapter and do other research as needed to become familiar with his or her role.

❸ Meet again as a group to plan the role play to include the following: (a) each member presents a position and summarizes reasons for it; (b) each of the other members responds to that position; and (c) the group decides on a course of action.

❹ Do the role play.

Your work will be evaluated on the following criteria:
• you reenact the events of the Congress accurately
• your group presents its position and arguments clearly
• you stay "in character" as a delegate

Chapter 8

The War of Independence

Sections

Beginning the Story with Joseph Martin

Keys to History

1776
Common Sense published

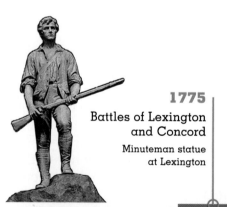

1775
Battles of Lexington and Concord
Minuteman statue at Lexington

1776
Declaration of Independence

1775

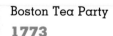

World Link

Looking Back

Boston Tea Party
1773

Spanish priests build Mission San Francisco
1776

HISTORY
Mystery

General Washington's best spies in Philadelphia informed him that the British wanted their laundry returned immediately, "finished or unfinished." Why did Washington care about the British soldiers' laundry?

1777–1778
Winter at Valley Forge
General Lafayette and General Washington at Valley Forge

1781
British surrender at Yorktown

1783
Treaty of Paris recognizes American independence

1779

1783

Looking Ahead

Constitutional Convention
1787

Beginning the Story with

Joseph Martin

In 1830 an aging farmer in the village of Prospect, Maine, picked up his pen and began to write. His name was Joseph Martin. He was not a writer by trade or training. Still, Martin had a story he wanted to tell. The events he began to write about had taken place more than half a century earlier. Yet they were as fresh in his mind as if they had happened only yesterday.

Martin thought back to his childhood. "I lived with my parents until I was upwards of seven years old," he began. When his father lost his job, Joseph was sent to live with his grandparents on their Connecticut farm. Martin grew up hearing about the quarrels between the colonies and Britain:

Joseph Martin did not arrive in New York soon enough to see the king's statue being toppled. The lead was made into musket balls so the king's troops might have "melted majesty" fired at them.

"I remember the stir in the country occasioned by the Stamp Act, but I was so young that I did not understand the meaning of it. I likewise remember the disturbances that followed the repeal of the Stamp Act, until the destruction of the tea at Boston and elsewhere. I was then thirteen or fourteen years old and began to understand something of the works going on."

This recruiting poster shows how to fire a musket. Recruits were offered an annual wage of $60 and an opportunity for "honorable service."

On a spring day in 1775, Martin was plowing when "all of a sudden the bells fell to ringing and three guns were repeatedly fired in succession down in the village." Martin knew at once that "something more than the sound of a carriage wheel was in the wind." That something was the outbreak of fighting between the colonies and Britain.

"I was now what I had long wished to be"

In Martin's village, young men were enlisting in the militia. Each man who signed up was paid a one-dollar bonus. At 15, Martin was too young to enlist. "O, thought I, if I were but old enough to put myself forward, I would be the possessor of one dollar." He would also be out from under his grandparents' supervision.

A year later, recruiters were back in Martin's village. They were looking for volunteers to go to New York, where the British were rumored to have a force of 15,000 troops. "I did not care if there had been fifteen times fifteen thousand," wrote Martin. "I never spent a thought about numbers; the Americans were invincible [unbeatable] in my opinion."

The Connecticut teenager traded his plow for a musket and set off for New York City. "I was now what I had long wished to be," he wrote, "a soldier." For Joseph Martin, the adventure of a lifetime had begun. He would witness not only one of the darkest moments of the war—the winter at Valley Forge—but also the victory at Yorktown that led to peace. As you read this chapter, put yourself in his place. Imagine how he and other soldiers might have gone from near-despair to triumph.

Hands-On ▸ *HISTORY*

Activity

What would have convinced you to join Joseph Martin in 1776? Patriotism? Love of liberty? Bonus money? Thirst for adventure? Design your own recruiting poster aimed at persuading colonists your age to take up arms against Britain.

1. The War Begins

Reading Guide

New Term **minutemen**

Section Focus **How the conflict with Britain led to war**

1. What triggered the outbreak of fighting?
2. How did the Second Continental Congress respond to the crisis?
3. Why did British troops finally leave Boston in 1776?

The conflict that turned Joseph Martin into a soldier began in Massachusetts. For months after the passage of the Intolerable Acts, the militia drilled and marched throughout New England. These volunteers called themselves **minutemen** because they were ready to fight at a minute's notice.

The governor of Massachusetts, General Thomas Gage, believed that the minutemen were preparing for war. When Gage's spies reported that guns and powder were being stored in the village of Concord, he decided to act. Gage ordered 700 British soldiers to march the 20 miles (32 km) from Boston to Concord and seize the colonists' weapons.

First Shots at Lexington

The colonists also had spies. When Gage's troops slipped out of Boston late on April 18, 1775, they were closely watched. Paul Revere and William Dawes then galloped through the countryside, spreading the word that the British were coming.

In the misty light of dawn, about 70 minutemen gathered nervously in front of the tavern in Lexington, a village on the road to Concord. Their leader, Captain John Parker, ordered, "Stand your ground. Don't fire unless fired upon! But if they mean to have a war, let it begin here."

As the British approached, the minutemen headed for cover behind a stone wall. Suddenly a shot rang out. The redcoats rushed forward, firing wildly. When the guns fell silent, eight minutemen lay dead or wounded. The British gave three cheers for victory and marched on to Concord.

In their march from Concord to Boston, the British looted and burned houses. A cartoon shows them as greedy wolves.

Lexington: Who fired the first shot?

Each side claimed that the other fired first at Lexington. Thirty-four minutemen signed a statement swearing that

"Whilst our backs were turned on the troops, we were fired on by them, and a number of our men were instantly killed or wounded. Not a gun was fired by any person in our company on the regulars, to our knowledge, before they fired on us, and they continued firing until we had all made our escape.**"**

British Lieutenant William Sutherland saw things differently:

"I heard Major Pitcairn's voice call out 'Soldiers, don't fire, keep your ranks, form and surround them.' Instantly some of the villains who got over the hedge fired at us which our men for the first time returned. . . . It is very unlikely that our men should have fired [first], otherwise they [might] have hurt their own officers who galloped in amongst this armed mob.**"**

Which side did fire that first fateful shot? Because eyewitnesses disagree, we can never know for sure. What does seem clear is that neither side wanted the blame.

From Concord to Boston

Once in Concord, the British troops found only two or three small cannons. After a brief battle with minutemen at Concord's North Bridge, the frustrated redcoats headed back to Boston. The march was a nightmare. A British officer reported "heavy fire from all sides, from walls, fences, houses, trees,

barns." A soldier noted that "even women had firelocks [guns]."

By the time the British reached Boston, 74 had been killed and 200 wounded. American losses totaled 49 killed and 41 wounded. Riders raced through the colonies shouting the news, "The war has begun!" A Philadelphia woman wrote to a British officer she knew in Boston:

"All ranks of men amongst us are in arms. Nothing is heard now in our streets but the trumpet and drum; and the universal cry is 'Americans, to arms!'**"**

The Second Continental Congress

The fighting had broken out shortly before the Second Continental Congress was to meet in Philadelphia. When the delegates

Link to the Present

The information superhighway "The British are coming!" "The war has begun!" It took three weeks for riders to reach South Carolina with news of Lexington and Concord. Today people can learn about a distant event within moments. We take television for granted, just as we do telephones and computers.

The so-called information superhighway—with its use of computer, phone, and television technology—promises new sources of instant communication. We will be sending and receiving an ever greater variety and amount of information—in a fraction of the time it took Paul Revere to saddle his horse.

gathered as planned on May 10, 1775, they faced a situation far worse than they had expected. The hope that boycotts would bring a peaceful solution was gone. Now war seemed certain.

Congress had to decide who should command the New England militiamen camped around Boston. John Adams proposed creating a Continental Army with troops from all the colonies.

To lead the new army, Adams nominated a gentleman who would command the respect "of all America and unite . . . the colonies better than any other person." That gentleman was Colonel George Washington of Virginia. On June 15 Washington was unanimously elected commander in chief of the army.

The Battle of Bunker Hill

The militiamen did not wait for orders. On the night of June 16, about 1,000 of them slipped onto the Charlestown Peninsula near Boston to take control of Bunker Hill and nearby Breed's Hill. They built a fort on top of Breed's Hill to allow them to rain cannon fire on the British.

Governor Gage and his officers decided to end this threat at once. The following afternoon about 2,200 scarlet-coated British soldiers formed long rows at the base of Breed's Hill. When General William Howe gave the order to attack, the men moved slowly but steadily up the slope. "Our troops advanced with great confidence," wrote a British officer, "expecting an easy victory."

Sweating under 100 pounds of gear and hot wool uniforms, the British regroup for another attack in the Battle of Bunker Hill.

In their hilltop fort, the Americans swallowed their fear, determined to obey the order, "Don't fire until you see the whites of their eyes." Only when the redcoats were within 15 to 20 paces did trigger fingers tighten. The red lines were shattered by what one British officer described as "a continued sheet of fire."

The stunned redcoats fell back, regrouped, and within a half-hour attacked once more. Again the Americans stopped the advance with gunfire. The British troops fled down the hill, stumbling over fallen comrades. Howe ordered yet a third attack. This time his troops took the hill, but only because the Americans ran out of gunpowder and were forced to throw stones.

The British losses that day were staggering. More than 1,000 British troops had been killed or wounded, compared with about 400 Americans. Describing what became known as the Battle of Bunker Hill, British General Henry Clinton called it "a dear bought victory" and added that "another such would have ruined us." The battle, which proved to be the bloodiest of the war, had shown that colonists could fight and that British soldiers could be stopped.

The Invasion of Canada

While the militia clashed with British troops in Massachusetts, Congress made plans to invade Canada. If Britain lost Canada as a base to attack the colonies, it would talk peace, or so Congress hoped.

Early in 1775, soon after Lexington and Concord, troops led by Benedict Arnold and Ethan Allen captured Fort Ticonderoga, which controlled a key route into Canada. In the fall, 300 troops under Richard Montgomery attacked Montreal. The city fell without a fight, but ahead lay the fortress city of Quebec. Near Quebec, Montgomery's force was joined by 600 troops led by Arnold.

The Americans had hoped that Canadians would join their struggle. Most Canadians, however, were satisfied under British government. To them, the Americans looked like invaders.

Without Canadian help, the Americans were too weak to storm Quebec. Instead they attacked at night during a howling blizzard, hoping to catch defenders off guard. The attack was a disaster. Montgomery and about 100 of his men were killed. Arnold was wounded but escaped to Fort Ticonderoga with the survivors.

Victory in Boston

A week after Bunker Hill, Washington arrived in Boston to take command. He brought order to the ragtag group of undisciplined soldiers, but the army lacked experience. Washington dared not attack without artillery—large guns—to bombard the British. He sent men to bring cannons from Fort Ticonderoga. They loaded 59 cannons onto huge sleds and dragged them 300 miles (480 km) to Boston.

On March 4, 1776, the British awoke to an astonishing sight. The ridges overlooking the city bristled with cannons. Rather than risk another Bunker Hill, the British abandoned Boston. Many Americans hoped that the war was over. In fact, it had just begun.

1. Section Review

1. Define **minutemen.**
2. Why did the war begin?
3. What were two important decisions that the Second Continental Congress made?
4. Why did the British leave Boston?
5. **Critical Thinking** Why can Bunker Hill be called both a defeat and a victory for the colonists?

Skill Lab

Skill Tips
- Statements of fact usually relate to "what," "when," "where," and "who" questions.
- Opinions usually relate to questions like: "Was it right or wrong?" "Was it good or bad?" "How important was it?"

Thinking Critically
Statements of Fact and Opinions

"They are raw, undisciplined, cowardly men." So sneered a British leader who saw the minutemen as no match for the redcoats. Along the road from Concord to Boston on April 19, 1775, the two sides showed signs of how they would match up.

Question to Investigate

What was the outcome of the clashes along the road from Concord to Boston?

Procedure

Descriptions of historical events often mix statements of fact with opinions. A **statement of fact** is a word, phrase, or sentence that can be either proved or disproved. An **opinion** expresses a feeling or thought that cannot be proved or disproved. Keep this difference in mind as you read sources **A** to **E**.

❶ Identify the statements of fact and opinions.
a. List examples in a table with columns labeled "Source," "Statements of Fact," and "Opinions."
b. Pick one of the statements of fact and explain how it might be proved or disproved.
c. Pick one of the opinions and explain why it cannot be proved or disproved.

❷ Analyze differences in the statements of fact.
a. List the differences.
b. How would you explain the differences?
c. Do the differences seem important? Explain.

❸ Analyze the opinions.
a. Pick two opinions from the two primary sources.
b. For each of these opinions, explain why you think the person thought this way.

❹ Do you think the Question to Investigate has one "right" answer? Explain.

Sources to Use

A "From Concord to Boston," on page 207.

B "Casualties had been remarkably light. . . . The Americans' marksmanship had been atrocious [very bad]; of upward of some 75,000 rounds fired by the rebels only 274 hit home."

From Richard Snow, *American Heritage*, April 1974

C "The total casualties on both sides were not large: the British lost 73 killed, 174 wounded, and 26 missing; the Americans, 49 killed and 39 wounded."

From John M. Blum et al., *The National Experience* (Harcourt, 1968)

D "A great number of the houses on the road were plundered . . . several were burned . . . old men peaceably in their houses were shot dead, and such scenes exhibited as would disgrace . . . the most uncivilized nation."

From a letter by Joseph Warren of the Massachusetts Assembly to the people of Britain, April 26, 1775

E "They would never engage us properly." "They did not make one gallant attempt . . . but kept under cover."

British soldiers' comments about the minutemen

2. The Issue of Independence

Reading Guide

New Terms **Patriots, Loyalists, mercenaries**

Section Focus **The debate and challenges of seeking independence**

1. What reasons did the Second Continental Congress give for declaring independence?
2. How did declaring independence divide Americans?
3. What were the strengths and weaknesses of each side in the war?

In spite of the fighting in Massachusetts and Canada, few colonists actually wanted independence from Britain. Most were still loyal British subjects. They just wanted Parliament to recognize their rights and give up its hateful policies.

The Olive Branch Petition

Many Americans pinned their hopes for peace on King George III. Once the king understood their position, they told themselves, he would convince Parliament to change its policies.

In the summer of 1775, Congress sent a petition—a written request—to George III, swearing loyalty and begging him to help end the quarrel. John Adams called this petition an "olive branch" because olive tree branches are an old symbol of peace.

The king refused to even read the Olive Branch Petition. The Battle of Bunker Hill had been the last straw. Declaring that the colonies were now in a state of rebellion, he called on Parliament to prepare for war.

Common Sense

With the rejection of the Olive Branch Petition, the colonies faced a difficult deci-sion. They could surrender and hope that the British would show mercy. On the other hand, they could choose to fight for inde-pendence. Were the colonies ready to take such a bold step?

It was Thomas Paine, recently arrived from England, who took the horror out of the idea of separation. Early in 1776 Paine published a pamphlet titled *Common Sense*. In it he argued passionately that Americans had nothing to gain and much to lose from remaining tied to Britain:

"Everything that is right and reasonable pleads for separation. The blood of the slain, the weeping voice of nature cries, 'TIS TIME TO PART.**"**

Paine's words electrified the colonies. Within a few months readers had snapped up more than 100,000 copies of *Common Sense*. Paine pointed out that independence would give Americans the freedom to set up their own government and trade with whomever they pleased. They could shape their own future.

Suddenly the idea of independence began to seem sensible rather than unthinkable. "I find *Common Sense* is working a powerful change in the minds of many men," observed Washington.

The Declaration of Independence

In the spring of 1776, Congress appointed a committee to prepare a declaration of independence. The task of writing it went to 23-year-old Thomas Jefferson, who said little but could speak brilliantly with his pen.

Jefferson's job was to explain to the world why the colonies should separate from Britain. His argument was simple but revolutionary. It began with the statement that all people have certain natural rights:

"We hold these truths to be self-evident, that all men are created equal, that they are endowed by their Creator with certain unalienable rights, that among these are life, liberty, and the pursuit of happiness.**"**

People create governments, argued Jefferson, "to secure these rights." If a government fails to do so, "it is the right of the people to alter or abolish it." That is just what the Americans intended to do.

Jefferson went on to list the wrongdoings of King George III. The king had not, he wrote, allowed laws "necessary for the public good." He had taxed Americans "without our consent." Now he was "waging war against us." For these and other reasons, declared Jefferson, "these united colonies are, and of right ought to be, free and independent states."

By July 2, the declaration was ready for Congress to debate. Most delegates liked what they saw, except for a passage on slavery. Jefferson had charged the king with violating the "sacred rights of life and liberty . . . of a distant people [by] carrying them into slavery."

Almost no one in Congress supported this charge. Southern delegates worried that it might lead to demands that the slaves be freed. Even delegates who opposed slavery felt that blaming the king for slavery was unfair. The passage was struck out.

On July 4, 1776, Congress approved the final version. In doing so they promised to support the cause of independence with "our lives, our fortunes, and our sacred honor." John Hancock, president of Congress, signed the document with a flourish.

By approving the Declaration, the delegates showed great bravery. If the new "free and independent states" failed to win the war, these leaders could be hanged for

Hands-On HISTORY

Promoting the Declaration of Independence exhibit The original Declaration of Independence is preserved in a glass and bronze case at the National Archives in Washington, D.C. The case is filled with helium to protect the fragile, faded document from the air. The shatterproof glass is tinted to protect it from the light. Each night the case is lowered into a reinforced vault beneath the floor.

Activity Create an announcement to encourage people to visit the exhibit. You can make a script for a TV or radio commercial, a layout for a magazine or newspaper ad, or a poster. "Sell" the exhibit to your viewer or listener by telling how the document and its ideals relate to our lives today.

Declaration of Independence exhibit

treason. Benjamin Franklin joked that "we must all hang together, or most assuredly we shall all hang separately."

Patriots and Loyalists

Not everyone in the colonies supported the Declaration. Only about a third of Americans called themselves **Patriots**—strong supporters of independence. Another third were **Loyalists**—colonists who did not want independence. They saw themselves as law-abiding people, faithful to king and country. The last third did not want to risk their lives or their property by taking sides in the struggle.

Disagreements over independence pitted neighbor against neighbor, friend against friend. One of John Adams's closest friends was a Loyalist. Ending that friendship, wrote Adams, was "the sharpest thorn on which I ever set my foot." Even families were divided. Franklin's son William was a Loyalist, much to his father's distress.

African Americans and the war
For African Americans, the Declaration of Independence raised hard questions. If "all men are created equal," how could there be slaves? Would independence mean that African Americans who were slaves would be freed? Should African Americans join the Patriots in the hope that a society based on equal rights would end slavery?

Many African Americans did join the Patriot cause. Black minutemen fought at Lexington and Concord. When the British stormed up Breed's Hill, they were fired on by black as well as white Patriots.

When Washington first took command, however, he did not let African Americans join the army. He feared it would encourage slaves to leave their owners. The British, on the other hand, promised to free any slaves of Patriots if they escaped. Thousands of slaves answered the call.

Patriot spy James Armistead received this letter of praise from General Lafayette for his reports on British troop movements in Virginia.

A shortage of white volunteers soon forced Washington to enlist black soldiers. Some 5,000 African Americans fought on the Patriot side.

Indians and the war The conflict divided not only white Americans and black Americans but also Indians. Most Indians remained neutral or sided with the British, who they hoped would defend them against land-hungry colonists. However, some helped the Patriots.

Within the Iroquois Confederacy, most of the Senecas, Cayugas, Onondagas, and Mohawks sided with the British, but most of the Oneidas and Tuscaroras helped the Patriots. The war divided many Indian families as well. One Oneida warrior, for instance, was captured by his brother, a British supporter, who then handed him over to the Senecas to be killed.

In the end, the war would bring neither Indians nor African Americans the rewards they sought. Even those Indians who sided with the Patriots would soon find their lands taken by settlers. Meanwhile, thousands of the slaves who had joined the Continental Army were returned to their masters after the war.

British Strengths and Weaknesses

In preparing for war, Britain was confident of its strength. It had a well-trained army that would soon be joined by 30,000 **mercenaries**—soldiers who fight for money. These mercenaries were called Hessians because most of them came from Hesse–Cassel, a part of Germany.

Surely the redcoats and Hessians would crush the Continental Army. Meanwhile, the mighty British navy would rule the sea, landing troops and supplies anywhere along the coast.

Still, the British faced huge problems. One was the distance between Britain and America. Sending troops and supplies across 3,000 miles (4,800 km) of ocean was slow and costly. A second problem was that the colonists were fighting a defensive war to protect their own land. The British could not stamp out the rebellion by simply capturing a few cities. They would have to break the Patriots' will to fight.

American Weaknesses and Strengths

The Patriots had their own weaknesses. One was lack of money. Having refused to give Congress the power to tax, the 13 newly independent states squabbled over

This fortified house at Johnstown, New York, was a site of frequent meetings between British troops and their Indian allies.

how much each should pay for the war effort. As a result, the army was constantly short of weapons, clothing, and food.

The army also lacked experienced soldiers. Frustrated by low pay and eager to return to their farms and workshops, many enlisted for only six months or a year. Just when they were learning to be soldiers, they picked up their muskets and went home.

The army did slowly improve in discipline, skills, and confidence, largely because of great leadership. George Washington inspired the respect of his soldiers. Their faith in him held the army together. Patriot leadership also shone on the seas. Though the Continental Navy had just a few ships, daring captains like John Paul Jones scored stunning victories.

What most kept the Patriot cause alive, though, was the dedication of ordinary people who gave their lives and property to gain independence. These people were the soldiers, like Joseph Martin, who kept re-enlisting. They were the seamen on the privateers—privately owned ships that attacked enemy ships and ports. They were the Patriots at home. Haym Salomon, for instance, gave his fortune to Congress to help pay for the war effort.

Women and the war Women helped the war effort by keeping farms and workshops going and working as camp cooks and nurses. An artillery officer's wife named Mary Ludwig Hays often carried water to thirsty troops during battles. This act of courage and kindness earned her the nickname "Molly Pitcher." A few women, like Deborah Sampson, even dressed as men and joined the army.

The Patriots' strength was not in numbers but in the dedication and leadership of those who remained faithful through the darkest days of the war. Without them the struggle would soon have been lost.

Many Patriot women knew how to use muskets to defend their homes. Deborah Sampson (above) enlisted in the army disguised as a man.

2. Section Review

1. Define **Patriots, Loyalists,** and **mercenaries.**

2. According to the Declaration of Independence, why was it necessary to break away from Britain?

3. Why did the idea of independence divide Americans?

4. Name two British strengths and two weaknesses. Name two American strengths and two weaknesses.

5. Critical Thinking Explain what you think the Declaration's rights to "life, liberty, and the pursuit of happiness" mean to Americans today.

3. The War in the North

Reading Guide

New Term profiteers

Section Focus How the Continental Army survived the darkest days of the war

1. What was the British plan for winning the war?
2. Why was the Battle of Saratoga a turning point in the war?

After the British fled Boston in March 1776, Washington knew that they would try to take New York City. A victory there would give them an excellent harbor and a good location for launching attacks on Boston and Philadelphia.

Washington rushed the Continental Army to New York, where Joseph Martin joined their ranks. Hoping to "snuff a little gunpowder," he had enlisted two days after the signing of the Declaration.

The British Capture New York

By the time Joseph Martin joined the army, it had swelled to about 23,000 soldiers. Even so, the Americans were outnumbered by the 32,000 British and Hessian troops camped on nearby Staten Island. When the two forces met in late summer, the British drove Martin and his fellow Patriots out of New York and chased them across New Jersey. As the weather turned cold and hopes faded, soldiers deserted.

When Washington reached safety in Pennsylvania that fall, he had only 3,000 soldiers. Most of these soldiers had agreed to fight just until the end of December. Unless more troops could be found soon, Washington wrote, "I think the game will be pretty well up."

Victory in New Jersey

On December 23, 1776, Washington gathered what was left of his troops to listen to a reading from Thomas Paine's new pamphlet, *The Crisis:*

"These are the times that try men's souls: The summer soldier and the sunshine patriot will, in this crisis, shrink from the service of their country; but he that stands it NOW, deserves the love and thanks of man and woman. Tyranny, like hell, is not easily conquered; yet . . . the harder the conflict, the more glorious the triumph."

The words inspired the war-weary soldiers. Still, Washington desperately needed a victory to bolster the spirits of the tiny army. He revealed a bold plan to attack Hessian troops camped for the winter in Trenton, New Jersey.

On the night of December 25, while the Hessians celebrated Christmas in cozy Trenton houses, Washington's army was leaving Pennsylvania and crossing the ice-choked Delaware River in small boats. From their landing point in New Jersey, the troops marched silently toward Trenton. A violent snowstorm chilled them to the bone, and ice cut through their flimsy footwear. When

 Link to Art

Washington Crossing the Delaware (1851) This painting, by the German-born American artist Emanuel Leutze, caused a sensation when first shown in New York City. Newspapers reported that "crowds throng to see it." One paper called it "the most majestic, and most effective painting ever exhibited in America." **Discuss** Why do you think this painting was so popular? Why do you think an art critic in 1851 said that it "should be viewed and studied by every American"?

dawn broke, the Americans' route could be traced by a trail of bloody footprints.

The Hessians were caught completely by surprise and quickly surrendered. Not one American was killed in the attack. Usually Washington kept his feelings under tight control, but not now. "This is a glorious day for our country!" he cried.

So it was. As news of the victory at Trenton spread, thousands of volunteers joined the Continental Army. The Patriots' cause was still alive.

Britain's Victory Plan

In early 1777 the British General John Burgoyne came up with what seemed a sure-fire plan to end the war. He would lead an army south from Canada into New York to capture the upper Hudson River Valley. Lieutenant Colonel Barry St. Leger would lead a flanking army from the west. At the same time General Howe would lead troops upriver from New York City to conquer the lower Hudson River Valley.

World **Link**

Spanish settlers in California While Britain fought to keep its colonies, on the other side of the continent Spain continued to claim more land. Father Junípero Serra had been sent north from New Spain with an expedition of priests and soldiers to occupy California.

Reaching San Diego Bay in 1769, Serra used Indians to build Mission San Diego. In 1776 Mission San Francisco was founded. By 1823 Serra and other priests had founded 21 missions in California.

The three armies were to meet at Albany. By controlling the valley, the British could choke off the flow of men and supplies from New England. Officials in London had approved Burgoyne's plan. They had also given Howe permission to attack Philadelphia. They expected him to defeat the Patriot forces quickly and be ready in time to help Burgoyne.

Burgoyne began his invasion of New York in late June. He left Canada with 8,000 troops and several hundred Indian warriors. (See the map on page 220.) On reaching Lake Champlain, he loaded his army onto boats and sailed south to Fort Ticonderoga. The fort fell without a fight on July 6, 1777.

Burgoyne's mistake Burgoyne could have sailed south on Lake George to the upper Hudson River. Instead, he made a fateful decision to take a shortcut across 23 miles (32 km) of rugged, roadless land.

On a map it looked like a short walk, but Burgoyne had more than 600 wagons with him. Thirty held his personal baggage. (Even on a march "Gentleman Johnny" ate off silver plates.) His troops spent weeks hacking a road through tangled forests and soggy swamps. By the time they staggered out, the Americans were ready.

The Battle of Saratoga

Burgoyne fought his way to Saratoga on the Hudson River. There his battered army was caught in a trap. Militiamen directed by Polish engineer Thaddeus Kosciusko (kosh-CHOOSH-kah) had built well-fortified defenses above the river.

Burgoyne looked for help, but in vain. Howe was busy playing hide-and-seek with Washington's forces around Philadelphia. St. Leger had been forced to turn back after attacking Fort Stanwix. Without help from either the west or south, Burgoyne admitted defeat on October 17, 1777.

Historians have called the victory at Saratoga a turning point. Up to this point, the American cause had looked hopeless. Even Britain's traditional enemies, France and Spain, had refused to get involved. Now, however, the Americans did not look like losers. They had taken on one of the finest fighting forces in the world and had won.

Early in 1778 the United States and France signed a treaty of alliance. France sent money and soldiers. French warships began attacking British ships in American waters. The following year Spain entered the war against Britain. The American cause no longer looked hopeless.

Winter at Valley Forge

The war was far from won, however. While Burgoyne was going down to defeat in New York, Howe had taken Philadelphia. During the fall Washington tried but failed to recapture the city. When the weather turned cold, he moved his army to winter quarters at Valley Forge, Pennsylvania.

These cabins were built in Valley Forge National Historical Park to recall the Continental Army's bitter "Winter of Despair" in 1777–1778. During that winter, about one quarter of the 10,000 soldiers there died from cold, starvation, and smallpox.

That winter at Valley Forge was memorable for its misery. For Thanksgiving, wrote Joseph Martin, the troops received "half a gill [four tablespoons] of rice and a tablespoon of vinegar." He added:

❝The army was now not only starved but naked. The greatest part were not only shirtless and barefoot, but destitute of [lacking] all other clothing, especially blankets. Hungry, barefoot, and clothed in rags, many soldiers deserted.❞

Men went hungry because local farmers preferred selling food to the British, who paid in gold coin, not the paper money issued by Congress. The men were half-naked because merchants in Boston had raised their prices for uniforms and blankets.

Wherever General Washington turned in his search for supplies, he met wartime **profiteers**—people who demanded unfair profits for their goods. It made his blood boil. "No punishment," he wrote, "is too great for the man who can build his greatness upon his country's ruin."

Help from von Steuben Despite its misery, the army survived. Washington put Baron Friedrich von Steuben in charge of training. Newly arrived from the German region of Prussia, von Steuben knew little English, but his ear-splitting curses helped take the men's minds off their growling stomachs. Martin described the Prussian's training as "continual drill."

Von Steuben's methods worked wonders. "The army grows stronger every day," wrote one officer. "There is a spirit of discipline among the troops that is better than numbers." Meanwhile, an unbreakable bond had grown between Washington and the soldiers who survived that winter.

Spring brought new life and hope to the troops at Valley Forge. The army had endured. The Patriots had won new allies. Now could they drive the British off American soil? That was the question that Washington still had to answer.

3. Section Review

1. Define **profiteers**.
2. How did the British plan to win the war?
3. Why was the Battle of Saratoga important?
4. **Critical Thinking** Von Steuben noted that American soldiers often questioned orders. What might explain this attitude?

Geography Lab

The Patriot army retreats across New Jersey, December 1776.

Reading a War Map

In July 1776 a great fleet carrying the largest army the British had ever sent overseas—32,000 troops—sailed into New York harbor. The map and painting on this page provide information about what happened over the next year and a half of fighting. What can you learn about the American War of Independence from the map? In what way does the painting expand upon the story that the map tells?

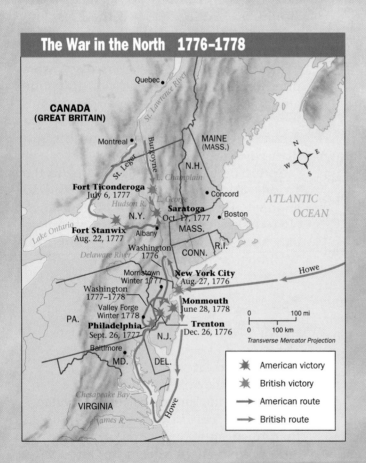

The War in the North   1776–1778

Quebec

CANADA
(GREAT BRITAIN)

St. Lawrence River

Montreal

Burgoyne

St. Leger

MAINE
(MASS.)

N.H.

L. Champlain

Fort Ticonderoga
July 6, 1777

Hudson R.

L. George

Concord

Boston

Saratoga
Oct. 17, 1777

N.Y.

*ATLANTIC
OCEAN*

Lake Ontario

Fort Stanwix
Aug. 22, 1777

Albany

MASS.

Washington
1776

Delaware River

CONN.

R.I.

Morristown
Winter 1777

New York City
Aug. 27, 1776

Howe

Washington
1777–1778

Valley Forge
Winter 1778

Monmouth
June 28, 1778

PA.

Philadelphia
Sept. 26, 1777

Trenton
Dec. 26, 1776

Baltimore

N.J.

MD.

DEL.

0   100 mi

0   100 km

Transverse Mercator Projection

Chesapeake Bay

VIRGINIA

James R.

Howe

✸ American victory
✴ British victory
→ American route
→ British route

Using Map Skills

Study the map. Then use the map and the painting to understand events of 1776 and 1777.

1. What do the bold lines on the map represent? The arrows? The splashes of color?

2. Which side won the earliest battle shown on the map?

3. If you wanted to follow Washington's exact route from New York to Trenton today by car, could you do it using this map? Why or why not?

4. Compare the map and the picture. What do you learn about the American War of Independence from each?

5. **Hands-On Geography**
You are an aide to General Washington. The Continental Congress wants a report on the events of 1777. Washington asks you to prepare a short summary of troop movements and important battles. Prepare a presentation for Congress, including any visual aids you think will help.

4. The End of the War

Reading Guide

New Term **guerrillas**

Section Focus **How Americans won their war of independence**

1. How was the war fought in the southern states and across the Appalachians?
2. How did the Americans finally defeat the British?
3. What did the new United States gain from the treaty ending the war?

In the spring of 1778, Washington received a message from his best spies in Philadelphia, the washerwomen. Their British customers had suddenly ordered all laundry to be returned at once, "finished or unfinished."

To Washington, this news could mean only one thing. The British were about to abandon Philadelphia. General Henry Clinton, who had replaced Howe, had heard that the French fleet was heading for North America. He decided to move his troops back to defend New York City. Now it would be Washington's turn to chase an army across New Jersey.

The Battle of Monmouth

Washington caught up with the British near the town of Monmouth and attacked. His second-in-command, General Charles Lee, took charge of leading the assault on the enemy's rear guard. Lee started forward with no real battle plan. When British reinforcements arrived, he ordered a retreat. Joseph Martin reported what happened next:

"In a few minutes the Commander-in-Chief . . . crossed the road just where we were sitting. I heard him ask our officers, 'by whose order the troops were retreating,' and being answered, 'by General Lee's.' He said something, but . . . he was too far off for me to hear it distinctly. Those that were nearer to him said that his words were 'd—n him.' Whether he did thus express himself or not I do not know. It was certainly very unlike him, but he seemed at the instant to be in a great passion."

Washington angrily charged forward to halt the retreat. By the end of the day, it was the British who were pulling back. That night the British slipped back into New York City. Washington camped his troops near the city and wrote in his journal:

"It is not a little pleasing . . . that after two years maneuvering . . . both armies are brought back to the very point they set out from."

The Patriots had held their own against the British, which was a victory in itself.

The War Moves South

Having failed in the northern states, the British moved the war south. In 1780 Clinton led a force that took Charles Town, the major southern port. This was the worst defeat suffered by the Patriots in the war. Clinton returned to New York, leaving General Charles Cornwallis in control of South Carolina.

The Patriot cause was kept alive by guerrilla fighters like Francis Marion, the famous "Swamp Fox." **Guerrillas** are soldiers who are not part of the regular army and who make hit-and-run attacks. Marion's guerrillas repeatedly attacked the British, then faded like ghosts into the tidewater swamps.

In 1780 Washington sent his best commander, General Nathanael Greene, south to slow the British advance. To avoid losing his small army in large battles, Greene led the British on an exhausting chase through the backcountry. Greene summed up his strategy in these words: "We fight, get beat, rise, and fight again."

The strategy worked. In 1781 General Cornwallis announced that he was "quite tired of marching about the country." He decided to move his army north to a sleepy tobacco port in Virginia called Yorktown.

Victory in the West

Small Patriot forces also made their mark fighting the British in the west. In 1777 a young Virginian named George Rogers Clark headed west across the Appalachian Mountains. Clark's mission was as large as his ambition. He planned to drive the British out of the Ohio River Valley and the Great Lakes region.

Clark could find only 200 backcountry Patriots to join his mission impossible. Still he pressed on, writing to a friend that "great things have been effected by a few men well conducted [led]." Clark and his small force did do great things. Sailing down the Ohio River on flatboats, they captured one British fort after another. By 1779 the Americans had seized control of the Ohio River Valley.

Francis Marion, known as the "Swamp Fox," led his band of guerrillas on daring raids in the Carolinas. They terrorized Loyalist militia and kept the British busy protecting supply lines.

The War in the South and West 1778–1781

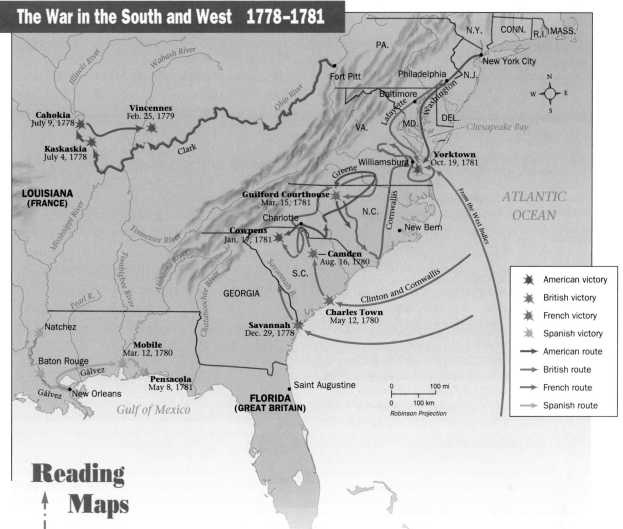

Reading Maps

1. Describe the British army's route from Charles Town to Yorktown.

2. Use the map to explain how the Americans and French trapped Cornwallis.

Help from Spain Clark was helped during his campaign by Bernardo de Gálvez, the governor of Spanish Louisiana. Gálvez sent Clark gunpowder and supplies from his base in New Orleans.

When Spain finally declared war on Britain in 1779, Gálvez could do more than send aid. He quickly pulled together a force of soldiers from Spain, Mexico, and the Caribbean. With his troops Gálvez drove the British from their forts along the Mississippi River.

In 1781 Gálvez organized a much larger army and attacked a British base in Pensacola, Florida. There he trapped 2,500 British soldiers, troops who would no longer be able to come to the aid of Cornwallis in Virginia.

Between them, Clark and Gálvez had broken Britain's hold on the vast region between the 13 states and the Mississippi River. When the time came to talk peace, their success meant that this area would become part of the United States, not Canada.

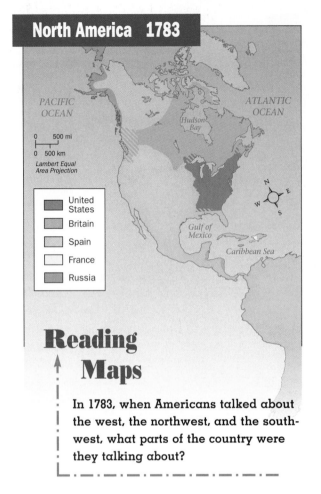

North America 1783

PACIFIC
OCEAN

ATLANTIC
OCEAN

Hudson
Bay

0   500 mi

0   500 km

Lambert Equal
Area Projection

Gulf of
Mexico

Caribbean Sea

- United States
- Britain
- Spain
- France
- Russia

Reading Maps

In 1783, when Americans talked about the west, the northwest, and the southwest, what parts of the country were they talking about?

Victory at Yorktown

By the summer of 1781, Cornwallis was comfortably settled on the shores of the Chesapeake Bay. He knew that as long as the Royal Navy controlled the seas, British ships could keep his army supplied. He could always get his soldiers out by sea, though he was sure that would not be necessary.

Cornwallis would not have felt so confident if he had known what France was up to. Since entering the war in 1778, the French had sent 5,000 soldiers to America. In 1781, they decided to send 3,000 more in 28 warships.

Washington decided it was time to lay a trap. American and French troops under the Marquis de Lafayette and Baron von Steuben moved south from New York to Virginia. There they surrounded Yorktown by land. Meanwhile, French warships brought Washington's troops south from Baltimore, arriving just in time to seal off the entrance to Chesapeake Bay. Cornwallis was now cut off from the British fleet.

The trap was sprung on October 7, 1781. Joseph Martin was watching when a rising flag signaled the American and French artillery to open fire on Yorktown. He wrote:

"About noon the much-wished-for signal went up. I confess I felt a secret pride swell in my heart when I saw the "star-spangled banner" waving majestically in the very faces of our . . . adversaries [enemies]. . . . A simultaneous discharge of all the guns followed.**"**

The pounding of exploding cannonballs and rockets went on for days, Martin wrote, until "most of the guns in the enemy's works were silenced." On October 19, 1781, Cornwallis surrendered.

The next morning, 8,000 British troops left Yorktown to lay down their arms. They marched slowly to the tune of "The World Turned Upside Down." Martin wrote that "it was a noble sight to us, and the more so, as it seemed to promise a speedy conclusion to the contest."

The Treaty of Paris

That promise came true. As a result of the American victory at Yorktown, Britain began peace talks with its former colonies. Early in 1783, the United States and Britain signed a peace treaty in Paris.

In the Treaty of Paris, Britain recognized the United States as an independent nation. It also agreed to cede to the new nation all lands between the Atlantic Coast and the Mississippi River, from Florida to Canada.

The United States, in turn, agreed to return property taken from Loyalists during the war. It also promised to allow British merchants to collect debts owed to them by Americans. Eight years had passed since Joseph Martin heard the bells that marked the beginning of war. Now the War of Independence was finally over.

Not all Americans were pleased with the peace terms. Despite promises of fair treatment, more than 27,000 Loyalists, both white and black, gave up their homes to resettle in Canada. They feared for their lives if they stayed, and for good reason. During the war Loyalists had often been badly treated by their neighbors.

Still, for most Americans, the end of the war was a time for rejoicing. They had won the freedom to shape their own future.

Looking ahead, George Washington was awed by the responsibility that came with that freedom. "With our fate," he wrote at war's end, "will the destiny of unborn millions be involved."

4. Section Review

1. Define **guerrillas**.

2. How could General Greene lose his battles but still "win" his struggle against the British?

3. How did the American victory at Saratoga make Yorktown possible?

4. Critical Thinking What effect did the victories of Clark and Gálvez have on British peace terms in the Treaty of Paris?

Why We Remember

The War of Independence

Joseph Martin died in 1850 at the age of 90. His tombstone bears the words "A Soldier of the Revolution." Today we still remember Martin and his fellow soldiers for their heroism and sacrifice. They risked everything, even life itself, to fight for freedom. For their service, they got little but thanks. "I never received any pay worth the name while I belonged to the army," recalled Martin.

We remember their War of Independence because it gave birth to the United States of America as a free nation. It also won for the new nation vast lands into which its people would soon expand.

The war left other results as well. For Indians who had sided with Britain, the result would soon prove tragic. Without British protection, they would not be able to stop settlers from moving into their homelands. For African Americans, the effects of the war were mixed. Some had won their freedom fighting for independence. Many others, though, remained slaves.

Even so, Americans today remember the War of Independence as a glorious beginning. A new nation had been born based on new ideas.

Chapter Survey

Reviewing Vocabulary

Define the following terms.
1. minutemen   4. mercenaries
2. Patriots   5. profiteers
3. Loyalists   6. guerrillas

Reviewing Main Ideas

1. Why were British soldiers from Boston sent to Concord in April 1775? What happened as a result?
2. According to the Declaration of Independence, why do people create governments? When do people have the right to alter or abolish their government?
3. What did the Patriots lack at the beginning of the war? What were the strengths of the Patriots?
4. What did General Burgoyne's plan for winning the war involve? Why did the plan fail?
5. How did the victory at Saratoga help the American cause?
6. How was Britain's hold on the region between the 13 states and the Mississippi River broken?
7. Describe the trap that led to the British surrender at Yorktown.

Thinking Critically

1. Synthesis How did the Second Continental Congress show that it wanted peace but was ready for war in the summer of 1775?
2. Evaluation Agree or disagree with this statement: "If the Americans had fought the War of Independence by themselves, they would have lost." Explain why you think as you do.
3. Why We Remember: Synthesis Create an imaginary conversation between Joseph Martin and a friend who tries to convince him not to enlist.

Applying Skills

Statements of fact and opinions Read an editorial in a newspaper or magazine about the effects of a recent battle somewhere in the world.
1. Make a chart with the headings "Statements of Fact" and "Opinions."
2. Under the headings, write down the examples of each fact and opinion that you find in the editorial.
3. Exchange charts with a partner. Do you agree with each other's choices for each column? If you cannot agree on the choices, explain why.

History Mystery

British uniforms Answer the History Mystery on page 203. Now imagine yourself as a Patriot living in a city occupied by the British. What considerations would you have to weigh in deciding whether to spy on the British? As a spy, how might you gather information about the British?

Writing in Your History Journal

1. Keys to History (a) The time line on pages 202–203 has six Keys to History. In your journal, describe why each one is important to know about. (b) Choose any two events on the time line. Write an explanation of how the two events are related.
2. Joseph Martin An epitaph is a short statement in memory of a person who has died. It is usually put on the person's gravestone. In the past, epitaphs often began with the words "Here lies [person's name], who . . ." and went on to tell why the person would be mourned and remembered. In your journal, write an epitaph for Joseph Martin.

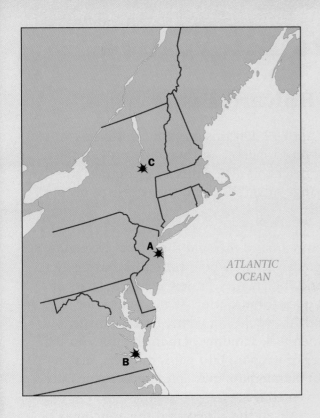

ATLANTIC
OCEAN

Reviewing Geography

1. The letters on the map represent three major battles in the War of Independence. Write the name of each.

2. Geographic Thinking In Europe in the 1700s, battles were fought face to face in open fields, with soldiers moving forward and firing in tight, orderly groups. American warfare turned out to be quite different. How did the Americans make successful use of their environment to win the War of Independence? Why do you suppose the British and Hessian soldiers did not do the same?

3. Citizenship George Washington accepted the position of commander in chief of the Continental Army on the condition that he receive no salary. He asked only for reimbursement for his expenses. Why do you suppose that he refused to accept any pay? Write your response in your journal.

Alternative Assessment

Acting out opposing roles With a partner, prepare and present a play consisting of conversations between a Patriot and a Loyalist during the War of Independence.

❶ Choose the two characters that you will role play. They can be men or women, members of the same family or neighbors, northerners or southerners, white or black or Indian.

❷ Pick four scenes, in chronological order. For example, Scene 1 might occur after Lexington and Concord, Scene 2 after the Declaration of Independence, Scene 3 after Saratoga, and Scene 4 after Yorktown.

❸ Create conversations for each scene. Be sure they include descriptions of events as well as opinions of the events and the people involved in them.

Your work will be evaluated on the following criteria:
• you describe the four historical events accurately
• you describe the events in the correct chronological order
• you describe experiences and express opinions that real Patriots and Loyalists might have held
• you hold your audience's interest with a lively presentation

April Morning by Howard Fast

The year is 1775. The day is April 19. On this misty morning 15-year-old Adam Cooper finds himself holding a musket and standing on Lexington Green with his father and their neighbors. The British are coming, and the confrontation to follow will change Adam's life and the course of history.

I looked at the men and boys around me, and their faces were gray and drawn and old in the predawn. The whole eastern sky was gray now; we were a part of it; and the gray lay in dew upon the grass of the common. My belly was queasy, but out of fatigue not out of fear; and I told myself that the British would not come. Had we made fools of ourselves? How did the men feel, standing here in the lines on the common, with every manner of weapon, bird guns, muskets, match-locks, rifles, and even an old blunderbuss that Ephraim Drake insisted was the best weapon ever invented. . . .

And then, after all the waiting, all the climax and the anticlimax of the long night, the British came and dawn came. Men who were talking dropped their voices to whispers, and then the whispers stopped, and in the distance, through the morning mist, we heard the beat of the British drums. It began as a rustle. Then it was the sound of a boy running through the reeds of a dry swamp. Then it was my own sound as I ran along a picket fence with a stick, and how did I come to be here, grown, with a gun in my wet hands? Fear began. I felt it prickle on my spine. I felt it like a weight in my belly. I felt it like a sickness around my heart, and its accompaniment was the steady, increasing roll of the redcoat drums. . . .

First, there were three officers on horseback. Then two flag-bearers carrying the British colors. Then a corps of eight drums. Then rank after rank of redcoats, stretching back on the road and into the curtain of mist, and emerging from the mist constantly, so that they appeared to be an endless force and an endless number. . . .

And the redcoats did not quicken their pace or slow it, but marched up the road with the same even pace, up to the edge of the common; and when they were there, one of the officers held up his arm—and

Continental Army musket

the drums stopped and the soldiers stopped. . . .

The three officers sat on their horses, studying us. The morning air was cold and clean and sharp, and I could see their faces and the faces of the redcoat soldiers behind them, the black bands of their knap-sacks, the glitter of their buckles. Their coats were red as fire, but their light trousers were stained and dirty from the march.

Then, one of the officers sang out to them, "Fix bayonets!" and all down the line, the bayonets sparkled in the morning sun, and we heard the ring of metal against metal as they were clamped onto the guns.

Militiaman Amos Doolittle showed his view of what happened on Lexington Green in his 1775 drawing.

One of the officers spurred his horse, and holding it at hard check, cantered onto the common with great style, rode past us and back in a circle to the others. He was smiling, but his smile was a sneer. . . .

Then another British officer—I discovered afterward that he was Major Pitcairn—called out orders: "Columns right!" and then, "By the left flank," and "Drums to the rear!" The drummers stood still and beat their drums, and the redcoats marched past them smartly, wheeling and parading across the common, while the three mounted officers spurred over the grass at a sharp canter, straight across our front and then back, reining in their prancing horses to face us. Meanwhile, the redcoats marched onto the common, the first company wheeling to face us when it was past our front of thirty-three men, the second company repeating the exercise, until they made a wall of red coats across the common, with no more than thirty or forty paces separating us. Even so close, they were unreal; only their guns were real, and their glittering bayonets too—and suddenly, I realized, and I believed that every-one else around me realized, that this was not to be an exercise or a parade or an argument, but something undreamed of and unimagined.

bayonet: a short sword attached to the barrel of a rifle

canter: moderate gallop

A Closer Look

1. What details does the author use to contrast the men and boys on the Green with the British soldiers?

2. How does Adam view himself as he takes part in the confrontation?

3. What does Adam mean when he calls the confrontation "something undreamed of and unimagined"?

Chapter 9

Creating the Constitution

Sections

Keys to History

1776
State constitutions created
An American flag design

1781
Articles of Confederation ratified
The Great Seal of the United States

1776

1781

World

Looking Back

First Continental Congress
1774

Link
American trade with China begins
1784

HISTORY
Mystery

This is part of a piece of furniture known as the "Rising Sun Chair." The chair has been preserved for over 200 years. What has made it famous?

1787
Shays' Rebellion
Daniel Shays

1787
Northwest Ordinance

1787
Constitutional Convention
Inkstand used for signing the Constitution

1788
Constitution ratified
Banner celebrating ratification

1791
Bill of Rights ratified

1786

1791

Looking Ahead

Federalist and Republican parties formed

1792

Beginning the Story with

James Madison

If the young James Madison pictured here were to walk into your classroom today, you would not be impressed. Madison was a small, pale, and sickly boy with a thin, weak voice. He was also painfully shy.

Madison was born in 1751 and was raised on a plantation in Virginia. All his life he was plagued by fevers. He also suffered from seizures in which his entire body would stiffen for several moments. His doctor said these attacks were a form of epilepsy, a disorder of the nervous system. Young James called the seizures his "falling sickness."

The Young Scholar

One thing that was neither small nor sickly about Madison was his mind. By the time he was 11, Madison had read every one of the 85 books in his father's library. When Madison ran out of books to read at home, his father sent him to school in a neighboring county. James was a good student, quickly learning French, Latin, and Greek so that he could read books written in those languages. He also studied history, geography, astronomy, algebra, and geometry.

At the age of 18, Madison entered Princeton College in New Jersey. He threw himself into his studies, working hard enough to finish a three-year course of studies in two years. He also found time to join in student pranks such as setting off firecrackers in a newcomer's bed.

After graduating from Princeton, Madison suffered a mental collapse. It is true that he had been studying hard and getting by on very little sleep. Still, he was suffering from more than exhaustion. Most likely, the young scholar was depressed because he did not know what he wanted to do with his life.

Madison was quite sure that he did not want to be a planter like his father, who depended on slaves to work his land. While at Princeton Madison had come to hate slavery. He had to find another career. But what?

His voice was too weak for him to be a minister. Who would want to listen to him preach? He found the study of law depressingly "coarse and dry." That left running for public office. In a letter to a friend, however, Madison had declared, "I do not meddle in politics."

In this dark mood, Madison became convinced that he was destined to die young. Not that it mattered much to him anyway. In a letter to a friend he said that he was "too dull and infirm [sickly] now to look out for any extraordinary things in this world." He could not have been more wrong.

A North-West Prospect of Nassau Hall (detail) by Reverend Jonathan Fisher, 1807

Madison and about 100 other students studied, dined, and slept in Princeton College's Nassau Hall.

"Meddling in Politics"

It was "meddling in politics" that pulled Madison out of his depression. As the colonies moved toward a showdown with Britain, he was swept up in the struggle. In 1774 the young man joined the local Orange County Committee of Safety to help prepare Virginia for war. Two years later he was elected to represent his county at a state convention. There he voted to throw Virginia's support behind the Declaration of Independence.

In 1780 Virginia sent Madison to Philadelphia as a delegate to the Continental Congress. At 29, he was the youngest member of Congress, and the smallest—"No bigger than a half piece of soap," said one delegate. He was also the shyest. After inviting Madison to a party, one delegate's wife described him as "a gloomy stiff creature . . . with nothing engaging or even bearable about his manners."

During his first six months in Congress, Madison did not so much as open his mouth. When he finally did manage to speak, his voice was so weak that other members had to strain their ears in order to hear him. The delegates to Congress quickly learned, however, that when the young man from Virginia spoke, he was worth listening to. James Madison may not have known it yet, but he had found his career at last.

Hands-On *HISTORY*

Activity

Make a chart of school subjects that compares what Madison studied with what you, your parents, and your grandparents studied. Gather information from your parents and grandparents through interviews, including information about what their United States history courses were like. Use your chart to identify what has changed and what has stayed the same.

1. The Nation's Shaky Start

Reading Guide

New Terms **constitution, republic, bill of rights, confederation, depression**

Section Focus **The problems the new nation faced after independence**

1. What kind of government did the Articles of Confederation create?
2. What problems led to calls for a convention to revise the Articles?

When the War of Independence ended, no one was happier than James Madison. He had doubts, though, about whether the 13 former colonies could create a new nation. During the war they had squabbled over land, trade, and the question of how much power to give the Continental Congress.

New State Governments

After declaring themselves "free and independent states" in 1776, each state had quickly created a **constitution**—a plan of government. In effect, each became a separate **republic,** a government run by elected representatives of the people.

These new states were determined to prevent the tyranny they had accused Britain of imposing. State constitutions gave most of the power to legislatures elected by the people. Officials once appointed by the king—governors and judges—were now elected for a limited term. Most state constitutions included a **bill of rights,** a list of rights and freedoms guaranteed to the people.

Articles of Confederation

As the war raged on, the state governments had seen the need for a central authority to direct the army and deal with foreign nations. Yet the states feared giving Congress too much power. A strong national government might trample the very rights they were fighting for.

In 1777 Congress proposed a plan to create a **confederation**—an alliance of independent states. This plan, called the Articles of Confederation, was finally approved by all of the states in 1781. Under the Articles each state would have one vote in Congress. Major decisions had to be approved by 9 of the 13 states.

The Articles gave Congress the right to raise an army and navy, control foreign affairs, coin money, and set up a postal system. However, Congress was not allowed to regulate trade or to tax. The states were fearful of handing those powers over to a central government.

Both during and after the war, Congress had to beg for money to carry out its policies. All too often, states ignored these humble requests. The result, said Madison, was that Congress was about as effective at uniting the states as "a rope of sand."

Settling Western Lands

Congress did manage to decide how to develop the western lands that Britain ceded to the United States after the war. Even before the War of Independence, pathfinders like Daniel Boone had begun leading small groups of settlers across the

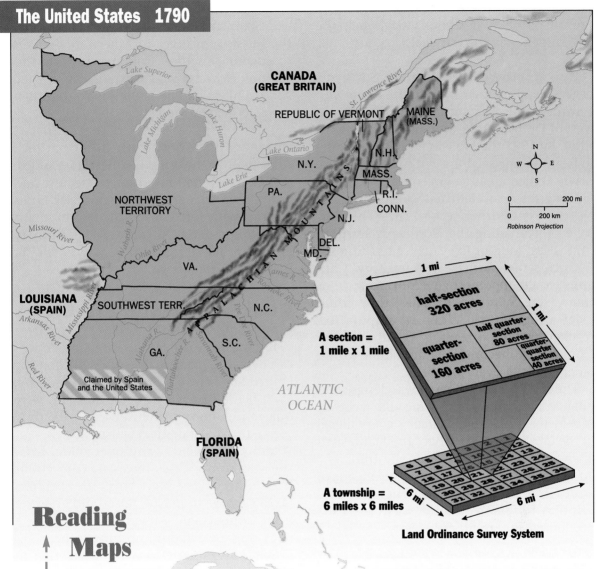

Land Ordinance Survey System

Reading Maps

1. Under the Land Ordinance of 1785, how big was a township section?

2. Which five states were eventually created out of the Northwest Territory? (Refer also to the map on pages R6–R7.)

Appalachians. After the war, this trickle of settlers turned into a flood.

There was no orderly way of dividing up and selling western lands. Settlers simply claimed land they liked. To mark a claim, they might cut their initials into trees along its boundaries. Imagine the confusion that arose. Where did one settler's claim end and another's begin?

To end such confusion, Congress passed the Land Ordinance of 1785. This law divided the western land "purchased of the Indian inhabitants" into areas called townships. Each township was 6 miles (10 km) square, with 36 sections (see map on this page). Four sections were set aside for use by the national government. Income from another section would support public schools. Money from the sale of the other sections would help the government pay the war debt.

The Northwest Ordinance Surveyors began mapping townships in the Northwest Territory—the area north of the Ohio River, west of Pennsylvania, and east of the Mississippi. By 1787 the job was far enough along to begin selling sections, but how would the newly settled areas be governed?

Congress answered that question in the Northwest Ordinance of 1787. This law called for dividing the Northwest Territory into three, four, or five smaller territories.

Once settlers arrived in a territory, Congress would appoint a governor. As soon as there were 5,000 adult males, they could elect a legislature. When its population reached 60,000, a territory could apply to Congress to become a state, equal to the older states in every way.

The Northwest Ordinance was designed to ensure that democracy moved west. It included a bill of rights, made slavery illegal in the territories, stated that "good faith shall always be observed towards the Indians," and declared that "schools and the means of education shall forever be encouraged." Thomas Jefferson saw the western lands becoming "an Empire for Liberty."

Disputes with Britain and Spain

Congress was less successful in dealing with other nations. Britain refused to give up forts in the Northwest Territory, despite promises to do so in the Treaty of Paris. The British argued that Americans had broken the treaty by not paying debts owed to British merchants. Congress had no power either to force the British out or to make Americans live up to the treaty terms.

Spain, meanwhile, challenged American claims to the land between the Ohio River and Spanish Florida. In 1784 Spain closed the Mississippi River to American shippers to discourage settlers from moving into this region. Now settlers west of the rugged Appalachians had no good way to ship their crops to distant markets in the east.

These disputes showed the country's weakness in dealing with other nations. After the war the army had been disbanded, and Congress had no funds to create a new army. The new nation could not back up its protests with force. This sad state of affairs led Congressman Alexander Hamilton to grumble that the government was "fit for neither war nor peace."

Quarrels Among the States

Britain and Spain felt free to ignore American demands because they thought that the United States would not be united for long. Even before the war ended, the states were quarreling among themselves. Peace only seemed to make matters worse.

Many arguments were over trade. After the war some states began taxing goods from other states. New York, for example, taxed cabbage from New Jersey and firewood from Connecticut. Merchants complained, but Congress could do nothing to help.

States also quarreled over boundaries. In one conflict, Maryland and Virginia almost went to war because both claimed the Potomac River where it ran between them. Many Europeans believed such quarrels would tear the United States apart. Then Britain and Spain would be ready to pick up the pieces.

Money Troubles

The not-so-United States also had money troubles. Congress had little gold and silver to make into coins. Faced with a money shortage, the states began printing their own

Link to Technology

Minting a Coin

Today Americans agree on a common form of money—coins and bills made by the United States government. In the years after the War of Independence, though, there was no one system. State governments as well as private individuals printed bills and made coins by a process known as **minting**. The illustrations show a coin minting process used at the time of the War of Independence.

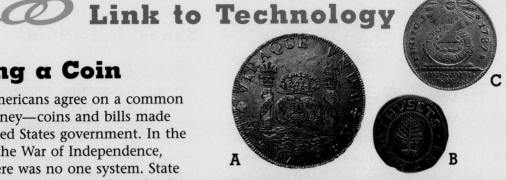

(A) Spanish dollar, or "Piece of Eight," one of the most common coins in colonial America; (B) Pine Tree Shilling, one of the first coins minted in America, introduced in 1652; (C) Fugio Cent, the first official United States coin, introduced in 1787

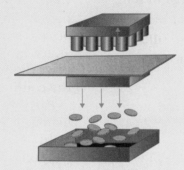

1 The cast metal is rolled several times to even out its thickness.

2 A machine called a blanking press punches out the coin shapes, called *blanks*.

3 The blank is stamped with its design, and a *reeding plate* forms the ridged edge.

A Coin Today

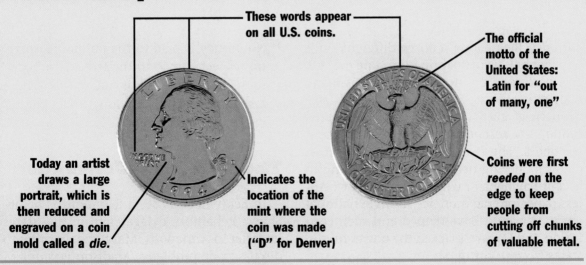

These words appear on all U.S. coins.

The official motto of the United States: Latin for "out of many, one"

Today an artist draws a large portrait, which is then reduced and engraved on a coin mold called a *die.*

Indicates the location of the mint where the coin was made ("D" for Denver)

Coins were first *reeded* on the edge to keep people from cutting off chunks of valuable metal.

The China trade Squabbles over currency and taxes were not the only problems facing American merchants. After Britain banned American trade with the British West Indies in 1783, these merchants had to scramble to find new overseas markets.

One possibility was China. As a first step, some merchants outfitted a ship called the *Empress of China*. It sailed from New York in 1784 with a cargo of rum, furs, and ginseng, a medicinal herb. The ship returned loaded with tea, silk, and porcelain. Gradually China became an important partner in trade.

Foreign ships in a Chinese port

currency. Before long, a dozen different kinds of paper bills were floating from state to state.

Americans came to see the bills as being nearly worthless. Some states passed laws requiring creditors—people who lent money—to accept paper money as payment for debts. The result was the odd sight of creditors fleeing debtors to avoid having to accept payment in what they saw as worthless paper, or "rag money." A single national currency would have helped end such confusion, but Congress lacked the power to stop states from printing money.

Shays' Rebellion

By the mid 1780s the country was in the grip of a **depression,** a long, sharp decline in economic activity. Farmers in western Massachusetts were especially hard hit by falling crop prices. Many did not earn enough to pay their debts and state taxes. Judges ordered them to sell their livestock or land to pay off the debts.

The desperate farmers asked the state legislature to allow them to pay debts with their crops instead of money. When the legislature refused, they took matters into their own hands. Led by Daniel Shays, a hero of Bunker Hill, they protested in front of courthouses, waving their muskets. The angry mobs struck fear into the hearts of even the toughest judges, forcing many of the courts to close.

Early in 1787 Shays and his followers marched on the national arsenal at Springfield. They were planning to seize the weapons stored there. Since Congress had no army to defend the arsenal, Massachusetts had to send the state militia to restore order. The troops crushed the uprising and arrested Shays.

To many Americans, Shays' Rebellion was yet another sign that the nation could not hold together. A worried Madison wrote to a friend that:

❝No money is paid to the public treasury; no respect is paid to the federal authority [Congress]. . . . It is not possible that a government can last long under these circumstances.❞

The Call for a Convention

In September 1786, a few months before Shays' Rebellion, delegates from five states had met in Annapolis, Maryland, in order to discuss trade problems. Madison was one of

When Daniel Shays led his band of angry farmers into Springfield, Massachusetts, in January 1787, they were met by state militia. The troops fired to protect the federal arsenal. As a present-day marker bears witness, by the end of February Shays' Rebellion had been completely crushed.

the leaders at this meeting. The Annapolis Convention ended with a call for a meeting of delegates from all 13 states in Philadelphia in May 1787 to consider "the situation of the United States."

The shock of Shays' Rebellion spurred every state but Rhode Island to agree to send delegates. Congress suspected that the delegates might seek to scrap the current plan of government. Therefore, it declared that the meeting should be "for the sole and express purpose of revising the Articles of Confederation."

Dumping the Articles of Confederation, however, was exactly what Madison had in mind. A year earlier he had written Thomas Jefferson, then the American ambassador to France, asking Jefferson to send him any books that "may throw light on . . . confederacies which have existed." The books arrived by the hundreds.

Madison threw himself into the study of governments, both ancient and modern.

The lesson of the past, he found, was always the same: federations with weak central governments would soon be torn apart by quarrels and disputes. Had Americans learned that lesson well enough? Were they ready to create a stronger government?

1. Section Review

1. Define **constitution, republic, bill of rights, confederation,** and **depression.**
2. How did fear of tyranny affect the creation of the state constitutions and the Articles of Confederation?
3. What were the main weaknesses of the new government under the Articles of Confederation?
4. Critical Thinking Do you think Shays and his followers had a good reason to rebel against the government? Why or why not?

Geography Lab

Midwest corn and dairy farm

The Central Lowlands

Free of British rule, restless Americans sought land and opportunity west of the Appalachians. Many headed for the Northwest Territory, most of which lay in the geographic region now known as the Central Lowlands.

Throughout much of the territory, settlers had to chop down trees to clear land for farms. However, in some places there were meadows, and settlers who traveled to the western edge of the territory found themselves on a vast prairie, surrounded by tall grasses as far as they could see.

James Smith, a Virginian who explored the area in the 1790s, praised the land. What pictures of the Central Lowlands come to mind as you read his statement?

James Smith's Statement

"Bordering on the rivers, the land exceeds description. Suffice it to say that the soil is amazingly rich, . . . as level as a bowling plain, and vastly extensive. . . . [Away from the rivers] the land is still amazingly fertile, covered with a heavy growth of timber, such as white and red oak, hickory, ash, beech, sugar tree [sugar maple], walnut, buckeye, etc. . . . As to mountains, there are properly speaking none; there are, however, high hills from which a beautiful view of the adjoining [neighboring] country presents itself. . . . [W]hite clover and blue-grass grow spontaneously wherever the land is cleared. . . . A country so famous for grass must of course be excellent for all kinds of stock. Here I saw the finest beef and mutton [cattle and sheep] that I ever saw, fed on grass. Hogs also increase and fatten in the woods in a most surprising manner."

Developing a Mental Map

Refer to the map of geographic regions on pages P4–P5 and the maps on pages R4–R5 and R6–R7 to answer the questions.

1. What states lie partly or completely within the Central Lowlands?

2. Most of the Central Lowlands region falls within one elevation range. What is that range?

3. The Central Lowlands are sometimes described as "flat to gently rolling." What evidence of that do you find on this page?

4. One early writer called the Central Lowlands "The Garden of the World." Would James Smith agree? How does the picture on this page support that description?

5. **Hands-On Geography** With a partner, imagine that you are members of a farming family in Maryland in 1788. You are trying to decide whether to move to the Northwest Territory or stay put. Carry on a conversation in which you give arguments for and against the move.

2. The Constitutional Convention

Reading Guide

New Terms **legislative branch, executive branch, judicial branch, ratify**

Section Focus **How the Constitutional Convention drafted a new plan of government**

1. Who attended the Constitutional Convention?
2. How did the new plan of government differ from the Articles of Confederation?
3. What compromises did the delegates reach to produce the constitution?

Philadelphia was already hot and humid when delegates to the convention began drifting into the city. None of them knew it yet, but they would be there all summer.

A Profile of the Delegates

All of the 55 delegates were white males, and almost all were well-educated and wealthy. About a third owned slaves. There were half a dozen planters and almost three dozen lawyers. The convention delegates were the nation's ablest political leaders. Many had been leading Patriots and had helped draw up state constitutions. Thomas Jefferson, who was still in France, called them "an assembly of demi-gods."

James Madison was the best-prepared of the delegates. Despite his weak voice, he would address the convention more than 200 times in the weeks ahead. His influence was so great that later he would be called the Father of the Constitution.

When not speaking, Madison took notes. Sitting near the front of the room so that he would miss nothing, he wrote down almost every word in his own shorthand. At night he rewrote his notes in longhand. Today Madison's notes cover more than 600 printed pages. From this record we know what went on at the convention day by day.

Getting Started

On May 25 the convention began. For the next four months the east room of the Pennsylvania State House would be the center of the delegates' lives. When they arrived each morning, the east room was cool and inviting. By noon it was an oven. Despite the hot weather, the windows had to be locked for secrecy and for protection from insects.

The delegates' first action was to elect George Washington president of the convention. No man was more admired or respected. Washington's presence would keep the convention from flying apart in its worst moments.

Next the delegates agreed on a set of rules. Each could speak twice on a subject, and no one was to whisper, pass notes, or read while others spoke. Each state had one vote, and decisions would be by majority vote of the states present.

The most important rule was secrecy. No one was to say anything to anyone about what went on in their discussions. The delegates wanted to feel free to state their opinions and even change their minds later on. The rule of secrecy was taken very seriously. During that long summer, not a single word about the convention debates appeared in any newspaper.

The Virginia Plan and the New Jersey Plan

By May 29 the stage was set for debate, and the Virginia delegates wasted no time. Thanks largely to Madison's ideas and research, they already had a plan. The Articles of Confederation, they said, were beyond mending and should be scrapped. A national government—one with real authority—should replace the loose alliance of independent states.

Under the Virginia Plan, the government would have three parts, or branches. The first was a bicameral **legislative branch,** which would make the laws. The second was an **executive branch,** which would carry out those laws. The third was a **judicial branch,** a system of courts to interpret the laws.

After two weeks of debate, the delegates agreed on the need for a new national government with three branches. They wanted most of the power to rest with the legislative branch, just as it did in each state. The question of how to elect members of Congress, therefore, was critical. It would rock the convention for more than a month.

The Virginia Plan proposed that members of Congress be directly elected by the voters, rather than by the state legislatures. The number of members representing each state would be based on that state's population. States that had a larger number of people would have more representatives.

Delegates from small states hated the Virginia Plan because they feared that the large states would always be able to outvote them. They came up with a plan of their own, which William Paterson of New Jersey presented on June 15.

Under the New Jersey Plan, Congress would have just one house, and each state would have one vote. Representatives to Congress would be elected by the state legislatures.

Madison argued that the New Jersey Plan would leave too much power in the hands of each state. He said it would do little to cure the problems the nation had faced under the Articles of Confederation. After much debate, the majority agreed and voted to reject the small states' plan.

This illustration captures a Philadelphia street scene around the time of the Constitutional Convention. A church steeple rises on the left.

∞ Link to Art

Signing the Constitution (1940) This famous painting by Howard Chandler
Christy (1873–1952) is on display in the Capitol building, Washington, D.C.
Discuss What impression of the delegates do you get and why? Now
compare this painting with the one on page 217. How are they similar?

The Great Compromise

The debate over representation in
Congress did not end with that vote. It grew
more bitter day by day. Small states insisted
that if they were not given a fair share of
power, they would quit the convention.
When the delegates' tempers seemed to be
at the breaking point, Benjamin Franklin
proposed beginning each day's session with
a prayer asking for wisdom. As the meetings
moved into July, the convention seemed
close to collapse.

A committee led by Roger Sherman tried
to break the deadlock. It proposed that
Congress have a House of Representatives
and a Senate. In the House the number of
members from a state would be based on its
population and elected directly by voters. In
the Senate each state would have two
senators elected by its legislature.

Neither side liked this plan. Madison
opposed it for two weeks but finally agreed
that it was better to compromise than to
fail. Because the plan saved the convention,
it is known as the Great Compromise.

The Three-Fifths Compromise

The delegates still had to decide how many members each state would have in the House. The southern states wanted slaves to count as part of a state's population. Northern delegates objected. Their states had few slaves. Besides, they said, slaves were treated as property, not as citizens.

Still, the northern delegates knew that without southern support a new plan of government could not be approved. They finally agreed to count a slave as three-fifths of a person when determining a state's population. This settlement became known as the Three-Fifths Compromise.

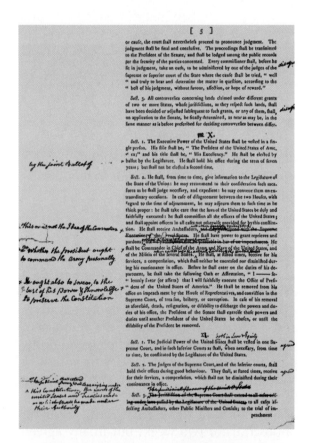

A page of a draft of the Constitution has notes by Virginia's George Mason. He suggested that the President take an oath to obey the Constitution.

Compromises on Trade

Northerners and southerners also disagreed on trade issues. Most northerners wanted Congress to control trade between the states and with other countries. A national trade policy would protect their industries against foreign competition.

Southerners worried that Congress might tax their exports, such as rice and tobacco. Some also feared that the slave trade would be outlawed. In fact, ten states had already passed laws against bringing in Africans to be sold as slaves.

Many delegates, including slave owners like Madison and Washington, were urging a national ban on the slave trade. Delegates from North and South Carolina and Georgia were determined to protect it. One warned that "the true question at present is whether the southern states shall or shall not be parties to the Union."

Again, a compromise saved the convention. The northerners agreed that Congress could not end the slave trade for 20 years, until 1808. Nor could it tax exports. In exchange, the southern delegates agreed that Congress could control most other trade.

Electing the President

During that steamy summer, the delegates struggled over how to choose the President. Could ordinary voters be trusted to make a wise choice? On the other hand, could a President who was elected by Congress feel free to act independently?

After some 60 votes, the delegates agreed to create a special body called the Electoral College. Every four years each state would choose as many electors as it had members in the House and Senate. The electors would vote for a President and Vice-President. If the Electoral College could not reach agreement, the House of Representatives would choose.

From the Articles to the Constitution

Government Under the Articles of Confederation

A loose alliance of independent states

A one-house legislature

No executive or judicial branches

Only states can tax

States may coin money

No regulation of trade between states

Most power held by states

Government Under the Constitution

A national government representing all Americans

A two-house legislature

Executive and judicial branches established

Congress also has power to tax

Only national government may coin money

National government regulates trade between states

Most power held by national government

Signing the Constitution

By summer's end, the hard work was nearly over. A final question, though, remained. Who should **ratify**—approve—the new plan of government—the people or the state legislatures?

The majority of delegates agreed that the Constitution would be ratified by the people. As Madison put it, the people were "the fountain of all power" and therefore should have the final say. Also, the delegates knew that the state legislatures probably would have rejected the new plan because it would weaken their power.

On September 17, 1787, the delegates gathered to sign the final document. Madison recorded Franklin's confident thoughts on the convention's accomplishment:

❝Doct. Franklin, looking towards the President's chair, at the back of which a rising sun happened to be painted . . .

'I have,' said he, 'often in the course of the session . . . looked at that [sun] behind the President without being able to tell whether it was rising or setting: But now, at length, I have the happiness to know that it is a rising and not a setting sun.'❞

The elderly printer saw a new day dawning for the young United States.

2. Section Review

1. Define **legislative branch, executive branch, judicial branch,** and **ratify.**
2. How did the Constitution make the national government stronger?
3. In what sense was the Constitution a "creature of compromise"?
4. Critical Thinking How representative of "the people" was the Constitutional Convention? Explain your conclusion.

3. The Struggle for Ratification

Reading Guide

New Terms **amendments, due process of law**

Section Focus **How the Constitution became the law of the land**

1. Why did many Americans fear and oppose the new Constitution?
2. Why was a bill of rights added to the Constitution in 1791?

In October 1787, Madison wrote to Jefferson that creating the Constitution was "a miracle." Now, it seemed, another miracle would be needed to get it ratified.

Nine states would have to approve the Constitution before it could go into effect. The decision on whether to ratify was to be made by a special convention in each state. Delegates to these conventions were to be elected by the voters. Many of those delegates would be suspicious of a plan for a strong national government.

The Federalists

Supporters of ratification called themselves Federalists. They wanted to assure Americans that the Constitution would create a more effective national government, not an all-powerful one. Madison threw himself into the fight. With the help of Alexander Hamilton and John Jay, he wrote a series of newspaper articles telling how the new plan would work. These articles were later collected and published in book form as *The Federalist.*

The writers explained how the Constitution would unite the quarreling states into a single strong republic. This government would not threaten liberties because its powers were limited. The states would make most decisions affecting people's lives. Also, the writers argued, power would be divided among the three branches of government. Each would keep the other two from abusing their powers.

The Anti-Federalists

The people who opposed ratification were known as Anti-Federalists. The Anti-Federalists did not have an effective strategy for swaying public opinion. At the ratifying conventions, however, they spoke strongly of fears that the national government would have too much power over the states.

Patrick Henry warned that the Constitution "squints toward monarchy" in giving the President command of an army and navy. Anti-Federalists also warned that federal courts would swallow up state courts, and Congress would burden the people with new taxes. They complained that there was no bill of rights. Most of all, they feared that a powerful national government might bring a tyranny as bad as the British rule they had freed themselves from.

The Massachusetts Debate

Despite Anti-Federalist fears, ratification moved along smoothly at first. By early 1788, Delaware, Pennsylvania, New Jersey, Georgia, and Connecticut had all ratified. At the Massachusetts convention, however, memories of Shays' Rebellion were still fresh. Many farmers who had fought alongside Shays were suspicious of a more powerful government.

Point of View

Should the Constitution be ratified?

During the Massachusetts convention, an old farmer named Amos Singletry warned:

❝These lawyers and men of learning, and moneyed men that talk so finely . . . They expect to be the managers of this Constitution, and get all the power and all the money into their own hands. And then they will swallow up us little fellows.❞

Jonathan Smith, another delegate who was also a farmer, disagreed:

❝I have lived in a part of the country where I have known the worth of good government by the want [lack] of it. There was a black cloud [Shays' Rebellion] that rose in the east last winter and spread over the west. . . . When I saw this Constitution, I found that it was a cure for these disorders. . . . I don't think worse of the Constitution because lawyers, and moneyed men, are fond of it. . . . These lawyers, these moneyed men, these men of learning, are all embarked on the same cause with us, and we must swim or sink together.❞

Smith's words, however, did little to calm Anti-Federalist fears.

The Federalists looked to the only person who might tip the balance in their direction. That person was the state's proud governor, John Hancock. He had stayed away, in part because his feet were swollen from an attack of gout. More important, he did not want to commit himself until he saw how the delegates were leaning.

The desperate Federalists promised to support Hancock for Vice-President if the Constitution were ratified. Taking the bait, he had himself carried into the convention, his swollen feet wrapped in bandages. His support and the Federalists' promise to add a bill of rights turned the tide. The vote was close, 187 to 168, but Massachusetts became the sixth state to ratify.

Three days before the ratification vote in New York, the Federalists held a parade in New York City. A float honoring Constitutional Convention delegate Alexander Hamilton led the parade.

Ratification at Last

In June 1788 the Constitution was officially approved when the ninth state, New Hampshire, voted to ratify. The new government would stand little chance of survival, though, without approval by the four remaining states, which had about 40 percent of the total population.

The promise of a bill of rights finally turned the tide. Virginia ratified by the narrow vote of 89 to 79. In New York the margin was 3 votes, 30 to 27.

By late 1788, every state but one had ratified. Rhode Island remained out of the new union until 1790. Meanwhile, elections were held for the first Congress. The Electoral College also met and elected George Washington President and John Adams Vice-President.

The Bill of Rights

In 1789 Representative James Madison urged Congress to fulfill the Federalists' promise to add a bill of rights. He then put forward a list of 12 **amendments,** which are changes to the Constitution.

Under the Constitution, three-fourths of the states must ratify an amendment before it can become law. The states rejected the first two amendments. One would have limited the size of Congress, and the other would have limited when members of Congress could raise their salaries. Both were considered unnecessary. By 1791, the states had approved the other ten, which together form the Bill of Rights.

The Bill of Rights guarantees our most cherished freedoms, such as the freedoms of speech, the press, assembly, and worship. It provides legal rights such as trial by jury. It also prohibits the government from taking away "life, liberty, or property" without **due process of law,** which means following legal steps in a court of law. The full text of the Bill of Rights is on pages R59–R62.

When Madison first proposed the Bill of Rights, some people called them useless "paper barriers" against abuses of power. These protections, though, have proved far stronger than Madison had hoped.

3. Section Review

1. Define **amendments** and **due process of law.**
2. What arguments did Anti-Federalists make against the Constitution?
3. Why did the promise to add a bill of rights help win ratification?
4. Critical Thinking The Federalists saw the debate in Massachusetts as a key test of whether the Constitution would be ratified. Why do you think they felt this way?

Skill Lab

Thinking Critically
Point of View

Skill Tips

Ask yourself:
- What do I know about the person's background (age, culture, social position, beliefs)?
- What does the person seem to think is important or not?
- How might the person's background affect how he or she feels?
- Who might feel differently? Why?

How does the First Amendment apply to students? In 1969 the Supreme Court declared, "It can hardly be argued that either students or teachers shed their constitutional rights to freedom of speech or expression at the schoolhouse gate." But in a 1988 case the Court ruled that schools can censor student publications if an educational purpose is served. People bring a variety of beliefs and values to this continuing debate.

Question to Investigate

How much freedom should writers and editors of student newspapers have?

Procedure

Different people often see and report the same thing differently. Therefore, historians and others who want to understand history must first understand **point of view**—the background or position from which a person observes something. Study the Skill Tips. Then read the sources and answer the following questions.

1 Compare the opinions.
a. Which ones agree with the 1988 Supreme Court decision? Why?
b. Which ones disagree? Why?

2 Ask yourself how personal backgrounds might affect the opinions.
a. Put yourself in the shoes of one of the persons who disagrees with the decision. Why might that person feel this way?
b. Put yourself in the shoes of one of the persons who agrees with the decision. Why might that person feel this way?

3 The Question to Investigate asks for an opinion. What answer do you think each person would give? Explain.

4 Which person do you agree with the most? The least? How do you think your own background affects your opinion?

Sources to Use

A "This [1988 Supreme Court] decision cuts the First Amendment legs off the student press."

Paul McMasters, professional journalist

B "The authority of boards of education would have been threatened if this [1988 Supreme Court] case had been lost."

Francis Huss, school superintendent

C "We are human beings, we have rights— they must not be ignored."

Priscilla Marco, student journalist

D "First Amendment rights and censorship have nothing whatsoever to do with putting out a student newspaper. It's a matter of teaching students to write well and responsibly."

Dr. Howard Hurwitz, school principal

4. An Enduring Framework

Reading Guide

New Terms **federalism, separation of powers, checks and balances**

Section Focus **The ideas that have made the Constitution an enduring framework of government**

1. How has the Constitution been able to meet the needs of changing times?
2. How is power divided between the federal and state governments and among the three branches of the federal government?
3. How does the system of checks and balances work?

You will find the full text of the Constitution on pages R34–R73.

When the Constitutional Convention ended, a woman asked its oldest delegate, "What kind of government have you given us, Dr. Franklin?" Replied Franklin, "A Republic, Madame, if you can keep it." A republic is a government run by representatives elected by the people. It is based on the idea of popular sovereignty—letting the people rule.

Like many Americans, Franklin was not at all sure that such a government could last. Madison hoped it would "still be around when the nation's population neared 200 million." Yet even he had his doubts. In fact, the United States has survived more than 200 years of growth and change. No other nation on earth has had such an enduring framework of government.

Federalism

Powers of National Government	Shared Powers	Powers of State Governments
• Maintain army and navy	• Enforce laws	• Conduct elections
• Declare war	• Establish courts	• Establish schools
• Coin money	• Borrow money	• Regulate businesses within the state
• Regulate trade between states and with foreign nations	• Protect the health and safety of the people	• Establish local governments
• Make all laws necessary for carrying out delegated powers	• Build roads	• Regulate marriages
	• Collect taxes	• Assume other powers not given to the national government or denied to the states

Hands-On → *HISTORY*

Proposing an amendment More than 10,000 ideas for amendments to the Constitution have been proposed. Very few have even made it past Congress. Even when Congress approves an amendment, ratification is far from assured. The failure of the Equal Rights Amendment (ERA) is an example.

Any citizen or group of citizens may propose an amendment. One recent proposal is to allow prayer in public schools. Another is to require the federal government to balance its budget. The test for these and other ideas is whether they can gain widespread support.

Activity Test your idea for an amendment.

① Write the amendment.

② Explain why you think it could be ratified.

③ Read your proposal to 12 people old enough to vote. Ask if each would support it and why.

④ If fewer than 9 supported it, explain how you would reword it to gain more support.

ERA demonstration

A Flexible Plan

The men who framed, or wrote, the Constitution knew that they could not imagine every problem that might arise. Therefore, they made the government flexible enough to adapt to new situations.

One way the Constitution is flexible is that it can be amended. The framers purposely made the amendment process difficult, though, so that people would have to think carefully about making changes. Thousands of proposals for amendments have been brought before Congress, but only 27 have been approved.

The framers also provided flexibility by stating the purposes and powers of the government in broad terms instead of going into detail. For example, the Constitution says that one of the purposes of the government is "to establish justice." Just how to do that is left up to Congress.

Likewise, the Constitution gives Congress the power "to make all laws which shall be necessary and proper" to carry out the purposes of government. This broad power is sometimes called the "elastic clause" because it can be stretched to fit changing needs over time.

While giving the government elbowroom to carry out its duties, the Constitution also limits the government's powers. Woven throughout the document are three main principles that keep the government from becoming too powerful. These principles are federalism, separation of powers, and checks and balances.

A Federal System

The division of power between the states and the national government is known as **federalism.** Madison believed that the national government had to have more power than the states if the nation were to survive. He also knew that most people felt a deep loyalty to their states and would not support a plan that stripped state governments of

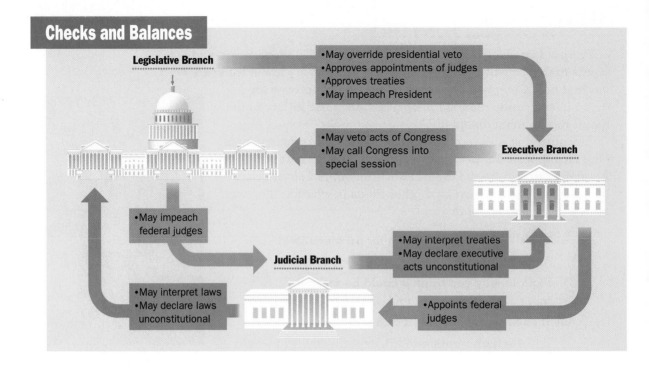

Checks and Balances

Legislative Branch

- May override presidential veto
- Approves appointments of judges
- Approves treaties
- May impeach President

- May veto acts of Congress
- May call Congress into special session

Executive Branch

- May impeach federal judges

Judicial Branch

- May interpret treaties
- May declare executive acts unconstitutional

- May interpret laws
- May declare laws unconstitutional

- Appoints federal judges

---

their power. The solution was to create a federal system that divides power between the state and national levels.

Some powers belong only to the national, or federal, government, such as powers to declare war or coin money. All federal powers are listed in the Constitution. Other powers are shared by the federal and state governments, such as the powers to levy taxes and set up court systems.

Some powers belong to the states alone. Only the states can set up public school systems. Marriage and divorce laws are made by state legislatures, not by Congress. Most criminal laws are state laws. Such laws may differ from state to state, depending on local needs, attitudes, and conditions.

Separation of Powers

The division of government power among legislative, executive, and judicial branches is called **separation of powers.** Only Congress makes the laws, only the executive branch enforces them, and only the courts

have the final say in interpreting them. As a result, no one branch of government can become too powerful.

The principle of separation of powers was first proposed in 1748 by the Baron de Montesquieu, a well-known French philosopher. The idea was familiar to most Americans in 1787 and was already included in several state constitutions.

Montesquieu argued that if the same person or group had all the power to make, enforce, and judge the laws, the result was likely to be tyranny. If these powers were separated, then one branch could act as a brake on the other two if they began to misuse their powers.

Checks and Balances

The system by which each branch of government can check—limit—the power of the other two is called **checks and balances.** The President, for example, can check the lawmaking power of Congress by vetoing—refusing to approve—a law he thinks unwise or unfair. Congress can check the President's veto power by overriding a veto with a two-thirds vote of both houses. The Supreme Court can check both the President and Congress by declaring their actions unconstitutional, that is, in violation of the Constitution.

The system of checks and balances was designed to control government power. As Madison wrote in *The Federalist:*

"If men were angels, no government would be necessary. If angels were to govern men, . . . [no] controls on government would be necessary. . . . You must first enable the government to control the governed; and in the next place, oblige [force] it to control itself."

Because the Constitution has provided a flexible framework for controlling both the people who govern and the people who are being governed, it has served the American people long and well.

4. Section Review

1. Define **federalism, separation of powers,** and **checks and balances.**
2. What makes the Constitution flexible?
3. Why did the framers provide for separation of powers and for checks and balances?
4. Critical Thinking What do you think are some advantages and disadvantages of a federal system?

Why We Remember

Creating the Constitution

Despite his prediction that he would die young, James Madison lived to the ripe old age of 85. During his life, he hid away his notes on the Constitutional Convention. They were not published until after his death in 1836. Only then did Americans learn what a close call the creation of the Constitution had been and how often the convention had been held together by "no more than the strength of a hair."

Today we study and remember the creation of the Constitution for two reasons. First, as citizens we need to understand how our government works. To do this, it helps to know a bit about the hopes, fears, and beliefs of the people who created the framework for the federal government.

Second, we remember the framing of the Constitution because it is a written plan of self-government by the people. For thousands of years, nations had been built by the strong and ruled by force. In 1787 Americans set out to test the idea that a nation could be built on the consent of the people. That their experiment succeeded at all is remarkable. That it succeeded so well is truly amazing.

Chapter Survey

Reviewing Vocabulary

Define the following terms.

1. constitution
2. republic
3. bill of rights
4. confederation
5. depression
6. legislative branch
7. executive branch
8. judicial branch
9. ratify
10. amendments
11. due process of law
12. federalism
13. separation of powers
14. checks and balances

Reviewing Main Ideas

1. What powers did Congress have under the Articles of Confederation? What powers did it lack? List two results of Congress's lack of power.
2. How did the Virginia Plan differ from the Articles of Confederation?
3. Describe one of the compromises that the delegates made at the Constitutional Convention.
4. What did Anti-Federalists fear would happen under the new Constitution?
5. Why did the Federalists promise to add a bill of rights to the Constitution?
6. Describe one way in which the Constitution makes the government flexible enough to adapt to new situations.
7. How did the framers try to ensure that no one branch of the federal government could become too powerful?

Thinking Critically

1. Application Agree or disagree with this statement: Under the Articles of Confederation, the United States was really 13 nations. Support your answer with evidence from the chapter.
2. Synthesis Suppose delegates to the Constitutional Convention had leaked information about their discussions to newspaper writers. What might have happened as a result?
3. Why We Remember: Analysis In what way was the Constitution an experiment? Why do you think this experiment was important?

Applying Skills

Point of view Write about a recent freedom of speech issue or situation that several people you know reacted to or described in different ways. Then, recalling what you learned about point of view in the Skill Lab on page 249, write responses to the following questions:
1. How do these people's points of view, or backgrounds, differ?
2. How might these differences have affected their reactions or descriptions?

History Mystery

The "Rising Sun Chair" Answer the History Mystery on page 231. Why do you think this chair became an important symbol of the Constitutional Convention? Do you think that symbol is as meaningful today as it was to Franklin and others of his time? Explain.

Writing in Your History Journal

1. Keys to History
a. The time line on pages 230–231 has seven Keys to History. In your journal, describe why each one is important to know about.
b. Choose one of the events on the time line. Imagine yourself as someone who was alive when the event occurred. Write a diary entry as that person, describing your reactions to the event.

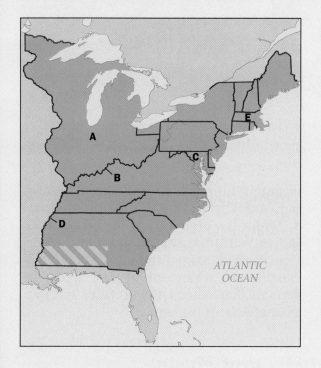

ATLANTIC OCEAN

Reviewing Geography

1. The letters on the map represent a territory, two rivers, and two states. Write the name of each.

2. Geographic Thinking The survey system used in the Northwest Territory was later used in states and territories across the nation. Look at the map on pages R6–R7. Compare the boundaries of states west of the Appalachian Mountains—especially those west of the Mississippi River—with those of eastern states. What main difference do you see, and how do you account for it? Describe the way in which fields, roads, and communities are laid out where you live, and try to account for that.

2. James Madison In your journal, write a brief description of a plot for a movie about Madison titled *The Comeback Kid*. Your plot should begin with Madison's experiences as a young boy and end with his involvement as a delegate to the Constitutional Convention.

3. Citizenship Read the Bill of Rights on pages R59–R62. Which of the rights in the first ten amendments is most important to you? Why? Write your responses in your journal.

Alternative Assessment

Creating a Constitution exhibit With a partner or a small group, create an exhibit about the Constitution for fifth grade students. Your exhibit should tell and show the following:
• what led to the call for a Constitutional Convention
• what happened during the Constitutional Convention

• what the main features of the Constitution are
• how the Constitution affects the lives of Americans today

Your exhibit might include posters, flowcharts, drawings, audiotapes, and pictures and articles you have copied or cut out of newspapers and magazines.

Start with the information that is presented in this chapter and then do additional research as needed. You might interview some relatives, neighbors, and friends about what the Constitution means to them.

Your work will be evaluated on the following criteria:
• it covers a variety of topics related to the Constitution
• it presents accurate information about the Constitution
• it presents the information in ways that are understandable and motivating to younger students

Unit Survey

Making Connections

Review

1. What caused conflicts between the colonies? What forces and events drove the colonies to work together? Did those forces and events have a lasting effect on the conflicts between the colonies? Explain.

2. In 1818 John Adams said, "The Revolution was effected [achieved] before the war commenced [began]. The Revolution was in the minds and hearts of the people." What do you think Adams meant? Who might have disagreed with him and why?

3. "From the beginning of the French and Indian War through ratification of the Constitution, many Americans resisted the creation of a strong central government." Support that statement with three specific examples from the unit.

Linking History, Language Arts, and Music

Project

Creating a Patriotic Song

First, then, throw aside your topknots of pride,
Wear none but your own country linen,
Of Economy boast, let your pride be the most,
To show clothes of your own make and spinning.

Those are the lyrics to part of a song that the Daughters of Liberty sang during the boycott of British goods. Throughout the revolutionary period, Americans wrote and sang songs to protest British rule, to rally their spirits, and to honor the memory of important events. Imagine yourself as part of a colonial songwriting team. You and your partner want to create a song that supports the Patriot cause.

Project Steps

Work with a partner to complete the following steps.

❶ Plan to write a song (a) to protest a British action against the colonies, (b) to rally the Continental Army's spirits when things look grim during the war, or (c) to honor the memory of a major event of the period. Choose the specific topic or event for your song.

❷ Decide what to do about a tune for your song. You may write the tune yourself or use a tune from either an existing modern song or a historical one like "Yankee Doodle."

❸ Write the lyrics for the song. Keep the specific purpose of the song in mind; also remember that you are writing for the Patriots. Make sure the lyrics and the tune work together.

❹ Teach the song to your classmates. Hand out copies of the song, or write it on the board or on a transparency for display. You might first sing the song or play a tape of yourselves singing it.

Thinking It Over Songs can have strong effects on our emotions. What qualities set a powerful song apart from a song that fails to move us? How might the Patriots have felt when they heard your song? How might the Loyalists have felt?

How Do We Know?

Young Omahaw, War Eagle, Little Missouri, and Pawnees, (1821), by Charles Bird King

Scholar's Tool Kit

Pictures

Imagine walking down the dusty, unpaved streets of Washington, D.C., in the early 1800s and coming upon groups of Indians, some in buckskins and some in suits and ties. Indian leaders often visited Washington to meet with government officials. In November 1821 a delegation of Plains Indians—Pawnees, Omahas, Kansas, Otos, and Missouris—arrived. Officials showed them the sights and gave them friendship medals bearing the likeness of President James Monroe.

One official was particularly eager to meet the visitors. He was Thomas McKenney, superintendent of Indian trade, and later the head of the Bureau of Indian Affairs. Because McKenney believed that settlers were destroying the Indians' ways of life, he was trying to preserve information about them. He collected clothing, weapons, samples of medicines, and other objects Indians used.

"Perfect Likenesses"

McKenney also wanted a record of how the Indians looked and dressed. In the days before photography, drawings and paintings were the usual way to record how people looked. So McKenney persuaded the delegates to have their portraits painted. He asked artist Charles Bird King to make "perfect likenesses," showing not only the faces of his subjects, but also their clothing and the way they wore their hair. King made many paintings of the Plains delegation. He sent a portrait home with each delegate and McKenney kept eight to hang in his office. These were the first of many paintings McKenney would collect.

The painting on the left is Charles Bird King's 1828 portrait of Hoowaunneka (Little Elk) of the Winnebago delegation. Henry Inman painted a copy, from which the lithograph on the right was made.

Critical Thinking

1. Compare the portrait with the lithograph. Do you think the lithograph is a "perfect likeness"? Which would you trust more?

Critical Thinking

2. If you were trying to find out about one of the Indians who visited Washington, what kind of information could you gain from a lithograph that you might not gain from a written description?

McKenney thought of the paintings as tools for future historians. He also saw them as a way to get rich. McKenney knew that people all over the world were curious about American Indians. His idea was to publish copies of the paintings in books and sell the books here and in Europe.

Luckily for McKenney, a new printing method called *lithography* had come to the United States from Europe in 1818. Pictures made by this process are called *lithographs*. Lithography was quicker and cheaper than older methods of printing pictures. Now even ordinary people could afford prints of paintings, drawings, and maps.

The German inventor of lithography based the process on the fact that grease and water do not mix. First he drew a picture on a stone with a greasy crayon. Then he spread water on the stone. The water dampened the stone but not the crayon lines. Next he smeared greasy ink on the stone. The ink did not stick to the damp parts of the stone, but it did stick to the crayon. Finally the lithographer pressed heavy paper onto the stone. The picture printed on the paper. Because the printer could use only one color of ink at a time, the print was usually black. Someone would then paint the colors on it by hand.

To make lithographs of Charles Bird King's paintings, McKenney hired another artist, Henry Inman, to copy the paintings. Next, a lithograph artist copied each of Inman's copies onto a stone.

When the 20 volumes of the *History of the Indian Tribes of North America* were published between 1834 and 1844, they included hand-colored lithographs of 120 Indians. McKenney advertised the pictures as "perfect likenesses."

A Lasting Record

Meanwhile, many of the original paintings were sent to the Smithsonian Institution, where, tragically, a fire destroyed most of them in 1865. Whether or not McKenney's lithographs are perfect likenesses, historians are lucky they exist. Inman's copies and McKenney's lithographs are now the only portraits we have of some of the most famous Indians who lived in the early 1800s.

Historians and anthropologists use the lithographs as a valuable source of information. A historian might want to see, for example, which Indians were awarded medals. An anthropologist might compare the clothing worn by members of different tribes.

In the mid-1800s, photography began to take the place of lithography as a way of copying works of art. For example, the pictures of paintings you see in this book are photographs of the paintings. Like lithographs, photographs give us information about people, places, events, and works of art we would not otherwise see. Images captured today in photographs, as well as on film and video-tape, will be data for historians in the future.

? Critical Thinking

3. An artist's point of view affects how he or she portrays a subject. What attitudes did King express? Are King's paintings a reliable source of information?

Scholar at Work

As a class, choose a building, person, or event in your community. Work with a partner to draw a detailed picture of the subject. Then display the class's pictures. With your partner, imagine that you are historians 100 years from now. What questions would you ask yourselves about the pictures? Write a brief report explaining what you might learn. What other sources of information might you check?

Unit 4

Chapters

Hands-On HISTORY

Activity

At the left of this view of New Orleans in 1803, you can see the Mississippi River. Suppose that it is 1803 and you want to start a business. You have just inherited the piece of land in the foreground—the one with the three cows in it. Examine the whole scene for clues to economic opportunities in the city, then decide what business to put on your land. Draw a plan for your business and write a statement explaining why you expect it to be successful.

☆UNDER ☆ MY ☆

A View of New Orleans Taken from the Plantation of Marigny, November, 1803 (detail) by **Boqueto de Woieseri**

The Early Years

Chapter 10

The First Years of the Republic

Sections

Beginning the Story with Abigail Adams

1. **The First Difficult Years**
2. **Conflicts at Home and Abroad**
3. **The Birth of Political Parties**

Keys to History

1789
Washington becomes first President

1789
French Revolution begins

REPUBLICA

Turn out, turn out and save you try from ruin !

From an *Empire*—from a *King*—from the iron grasp of a *British Tory Faction*—and dith of British speculators. The hireling tools and emissaries of his majesty king G changed our city and diffused the poison of principles among us.

DOWN WITH THE TORIES, DOWN THE BRITISH FACTION.

Before they have it in their power to enslave you, and reduce your families to disgrace Republicans want no Tribute-laws—they want no ship-Owner-laws—they want to find —they want no Varick to find it over them—they want no Jones for senator, who foug against the Americans in time of the war—But they want in their places such men as

Jefferson & Clinton,

who fought their Country's Battles in the year '76

1792
First political parties formed

Republican campaign poster

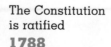

1789

179

Looking Back

The Constitution is ratified

1788

HISTORY
Mystery

One evening at dinner, three people sat down and struck a deal that led to the building of one of the great cities of the world. Who were these people, and what was the deal?

1794
Whiskey Rebellion
Farmers tar and feather a tax collector

1796
Washington's
Farewell Address

1798
Alien and Sedition Acts
Cartoon of battle in Congress

1800
Nation's capital moves to Washington, D.C.
Detail of design for Capitol building

1795

1798

1801

World **Link**

Kingdom of Hawaii is founded
1795

Looking Ahead

The Louisiana Purchase
1803

● **263**

Beginning the Story with

Abigail Adams

When a young lawyer named John Adams first met 15-year-old Abigail Smith in 1759, he was not impressed. He wrote in his diary that Abigail and her sisters were "not fond, not frank, not candid."

The Smith girls would probably have agreed. As daughters of a Puritan minister, they had learned to control their emotions. They could not openly express "joy or grief, love, or any other passion."

Adams did admit that the girls had "wits." Abigail and her sisters had been taught reading and writing along with the "womanly arts" of house-keeping and sewing. The schooling of most New England girls stopped there. Reverend Smith was determined, however, that his daughters would be educated. After learning to read, Abigail began reading the books in her father's library and soon came to share his passion for knowledge.

"Partner of all my joys and sorrows"

Two years later, John Adams met Abigail Smith again. This time he saw her differently. Not only did Abigail appear attractive and gracious, she was also bright, witty, and remarkably well-read. He later wrote in his diary:

❝Tender feelings, sensible, friendly. Not a disagreeable word or action. Prudent, modest, delicate, soft, sensible, obliging, active.❞

They were the words of a man falling in love.

Abigail was equally attracted to John Adams. Why? Certainly not because of his looks. John was a short, lumpy man. And certainly not for his money. John was not rich, and as a colonial lawyer he was unlikely to become so. He did, however, have a brilliant mind and was passionate about books, ideas, and politics. When her mind met his, sparks flew.

Still, Abigail was cautious about giving away her heart. At that time, a wife was expected to obey her husband, not think for herself. Abigail knew that she would die in such a marriage. She longed for someone who would treat her as an equal, as well as love her. "Alas," she wrote, such men were as scarce as "justice, honesty, prudence, and many other virtues."

Abigail found that rare man in John Adams. While he teased Abigail about her "unladylike habit of reading, writing and thinking," he loved her sense of independence. She was very pleased when he asked her to be "the dear partner of all my joys and sorrows." On October 25, 1764, they were married.

Abigail and John Adams spent the first 20 years of their marriage in this house in Quincy (formerly Braintree), Massachusetts. Abigail ran the farm during John's long absences.

Wife and "Widow"

So began a remarkable partnership. The couple spent their first years together on a farm near Boston, where John became a leader in the rebellion against British rule. During this time Abigail gave birth to five children.

In 1774 Massachusetts sent John Adams to the Continental Congress in Philadelphia. Abigail and the children remained on the farm. At first, they expected that John would be away a few weeks. The weeks soon stretched into months. When Congress chose Adams to represent the United States in France during the Revolutionary War, months lengthened into years.

During her years of "widowhood" Abigail raised the children and managed the family's finances. She found that she had a good head for business, ordering glassware and rugs from Europe and selling them to local housewives. Abigail also kept in touch with John's political friends, and knew as much about politics in America as any man.

Abigail and the children finally joined John in France in 1784. They moved to England a year later when John was appointed ambassador to Great Britain. By 1788 the couple was eager to come home. With a constitution soon to be approved, John looked forward to a role in the new government. Abigail had hoped that he was done with politics so that she could return "to our own little farm, feeding my poultry and improving my garden." Retirement, however, would have to wait.

Hands-On → HISTORY

Activity

Drawing from the story above and the chapter to follow, make a time line of Abigail's life. Choose at least five events to place on the time line. Some examples might be when Abigail first meets John, and when she moves to France. Next to the year for each event, write down Abigail's age at the time.

1. The First Difficult Years

Reading Guide

New Terms **inauguration, cabinet, tariffs, bond, speculators, constitutional, strict construction, loose construction**

Section Focus **The challenges of creating a new government for a new nation**

1. How were the new executive and judicial branches organized?
2. How did the new government deal with its financial problems?
3. What issues divided Hamilton and Jefferson?

John and Abigail Adams returned from England before the nation's first election. As expected, Washington was elected President and Adams Vice-President. John headed for New York, the capital, where America's experiment in democracy was to begin.

Launching the New Government

On April 30, 1789, George Washington was sworn in as President. A cheering crowd witnessed his **inauguration,** the ceremony that installs a new President.

Washington did not share the crowd's enthusiasm. In a nation of 13 quarreling states, he knew it would be difficult to turn the Constitution into a real government. Washington's hands shook during his inaugural address as he spoke of the "experiment" entrusted to Americans. With them rested the future of liberty.

A divided Congress Washington had reason to feel uneasy about his new job. He headed a government with no money and a deeply divided Congress.

There were two main groups in Congress. One was eager to build a strong national government that would discourage rebel-lions and invasions and solve the nation's financial problems. Alexander Hamilton led this group, known as the Federalists. Thomas Jefferson guided the second group, the Republicans. They wanted to protect the rights of states by keeping the central government weak.

The title debate John Adams learned how divided Congress was when he asked it to create a title for the President. Adams pointed out that European rulers had titles like "Your Majesty." Many in Congress objected that a President was not a king. The debate fizzled out when Washington made clear that he was content to be known simply as "Mr. President."

Setting Up the Executive Branch

Next, Congress created three executive departments: a State Department to carry on relations with other nations, a Department of War to defend the country, and a Treasury Department to handle the government's money. In addition, an Attorney General would serve as the President's legal advisor and a Postmaster General would run the postal system.

President Washington (far right) is pictured with his first cabinet: Henry Knox, Thomas Jefferson, and Alexander Hamilton (left to right). Today, the President's cabinet has grown to 14 members.

Washington chose Jefferson as his Secretary of State and Hamilton as Secretary of Treasury. He made Henry Knox Secretary of War. At first, Washington met with his department heads alone. Later, he found it useful to meet with them as a group. Together, the executive department heads became known as the President's **cabinet.** The cabinet would advise the President and help carry out the nation's laws.

Organizing the Federal Courts

The Constitution called for Congress to plan a federal court system headed by a Supreme Court. This time, Congress fought over what kind of judicial branch to create. The Federalists, favoring a strong federal government, called for a court system with broad powers. The Republicans, favoring

the powers of the states, preferred no courts other than the Supreme Court.

In 1789 Congress passed the Judiciary Act. It created a national court system with three levels, as shown below. District courts, one in each state, would try cases involving federal laws. Cases from district courts could be appealed to circuit courts and finally to the Supreme Court.

Federalists were pleased with this plan and with Washington's appointment of John Jay as the first Chief Justice of the Supreme Court. Republicans called the new court system "monstrous."

Federal Court System 1789

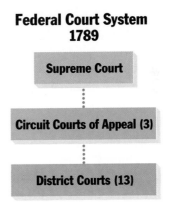

Funding the New Government

The greatest problem facing the new government was money. The treasury had no money to pay government salaries or to begin paying off the nation's debts.

Congress agreed to raise funds through **tariffs,** which are taxes on imports. They could not, however, agree on which imports to tax. Southerners called for a tariff on molasses brought from the West Indies. New Englanders, who imported molasses to make rum, objected to this plan. When someone called for a tariff on slaves, it was the southerners' turn to say no, never!

Pennsylvania proposed a tariff on iron products to protect its iron industry from

Link to Art

The Federal style Architecture is the art of designing and constructing buildings. In the early years of the United States, architects looked to Greece and Rome, the birthplaces of democracy, for inspiration. Elements of this architecture, known as the Federal style, included such Greek forms as columns, gently sloping roofs, and smooth stone walls. Domes, a feature that the Romans loved and perfected, were often used as well. Pictured here is Monticello, the home Jefferson designed for himself in Virginia. Other examples include many of the government buildings in Washington, D.C. **Discuss** What kind of buildings in your area have Federal style features?

competition. Southerners did not want to pay more for imported nails and hinges.

In 1792 Congress finally passed a weak tariff bill. Having watched the endless quarreling, Abigail Adams wrote, "I firmly believe if I live ten years longer, I shall see a division between the northern and southern states." Abigail's fears were not unfounded. A split would indeed take place, but not for another 70 years.

Paying the Nation's Debts

The fight over tariffs was a warm-up for the battle over paying the nation's debts. The federal and state governments had borrowed large sums of money from American citizens and foreign banks to wage the revolution. Now their reputation was on the line. If they did not repay the loans, who would take the new nation seriously?

In 1790 Hamilton presented Congress with a two-part plan for paying off these debts. The first plan dealt with the federal debt, the second with the states' debts.

The federal debt During the war Congress had issued bonds to patriots and foreign banks that lent it money. A **bond** is a piece of paper given in exchange for money. The bond is a promise to repay the loan plus interest by a certain date.

After the war, Congress had no funds to pay off its bonds. People desperate for money sold their bonds to speculators for less than their original value. **Speculators** take a risk on buying something, hoping to make money if the price for it rises.

The speculators were gambling that the government would one day repay its bonds at full value. Hamilton's plan proposed to do just that. Critics said that the plan would reward speculators, which was unfair to patriots who had helped pay for the war for independence.

The states' debts The second part of Hamilton's debt plan called for the federal government to pay off the states' debts. Northern states had large debts and favored the plan. Most southern states opposed it. They had paid their debts. Why should they help states that had not done the same?

Neither side would budge. Finally, a frustrated Hamilton appealed to Jefferson. After listening to Hamilton's concern about the debt, Jefferson agreed to arrange a dinner meeting to discuss the issue.

At dinner Hamilton offered to make a deal with Madison and Jefferson. The men knew that northerners and southerners were at odds over the location of the nation's permanent capital. Hamilton, a northerner, promised to support a southern capital city on the Potomac River if Jefferson and Madison agreed to get southern support for the debt plan.

Both northern and southern states accepted the deal. Hamilton's debt plan became law.

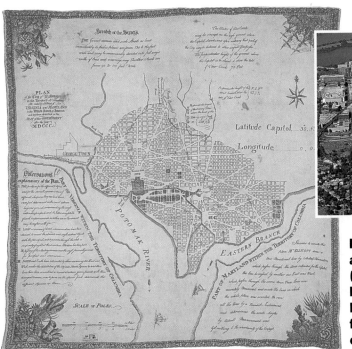

Pierre L'Enfant designed grand boulevards and squares in his plan for Washington, D.C. (left). When L'Enfant left the country with his plans, African American scientist Benjamin Banneker recreated them entirely from memory. Above is a view of the capital today.

Establishing a National Bank

Hamilton next asked Congress to set up a national bank. This bank would keep tax funds safe, issue paper money that people could trust, and make loans. Hamilton's proposal had strong opponents. They raised two questions: Who would benefit from the bank, and was it **constitutional**—permitted by the Constitution?

Hamilton's view Hamilton was a northern city lawyer. He believed that the nation's future was in manufacturing and trade. A national bank would make loans to businesses to build factories and ships. As business expanded, Hamilton argued, the nation would prosper and all would benefit.

Hamilton saw loans to farmers as wasteful. He thought the nation already depended too much on farming.

Jefferson's view Jefferson was a southern planter. He believed that the country's future lay with its honest, free-thinking, independent farmers. A national bank, he argued, would help only bankers and merchants. The government should deposit its money in small local banks that would help the common people, rather than making a few city folk even richer.

Strict versus loose construction Jefferson also believed that a national bank was unconstitutional. He called for **strict construction,** the view that the government has the power to do only what is written in the Constitution. If it is not in the Constitution, he said, then Congress cannot do it. The Constitution means exactly what it says. Any other view would give Congress "a boundless field of power."

Hamilton, in contrast, favored **loose construction,** the view that the federal government has broader powers than those listed in the Constitution. He argued that the "elastic clause" allows the government to do what is needed to carry out its functions. One of the government's duties is to uphold the value of money. A national bank would fulfill that duty.

In the end, Congress voted for the bank. Yet to this day, Americans disagree on how to interpret the Constitution.

The Election of 1792

By 1792 Washington was ready to retire. Endless bickering in Congress had left him weary of political life. He told Madison that he would rather "go to his farm, take his spade in hand and work for his bread, than remain in his present situation."

Because of the growing rift between Hamilton and Jefferson, both men convinced Washington to run for a second term. He was the only leader, they said, who was able to stand above the quarrels and keep the new government from flying apart.

That fall, Washington was re-elected President and Adams Vice-President. Both men knew that the national experiment in government by the people had just begun. Difficult times still lay ahead.

1. Section Review

1. Define the terms **inauguration, cabinet, tariffs, bond, speculators, constitutional, strict construction,** and **loose construction.**
2. Why did some people oppose the title "Your Majesty" for the President?
3. What were the two parts of Hamilton's solution to the debt problem?
4. Critical Thinking Imagine that as a member of Congress you voted against the tariff of 1792. Where might you come from and why did you vote no?

Geography Lab

A Philadelphia street scene in 1790

Reading a Population Density Map

The first United States census began on August 2, 1790. Counting the population was not easy. Most Americans lived in rural areas, where census takers had to walk or ride over poor roads—or no roads at all. In addition, many people did not understand why the government wanted to know about them. Some hid, others refused to answer questions, and a few even attacked the census takers.

This map is based on the first census. It shows **population density**—the average number of people in a certain-sized area. On this map, the colors stand for the average number of people in a square mile.

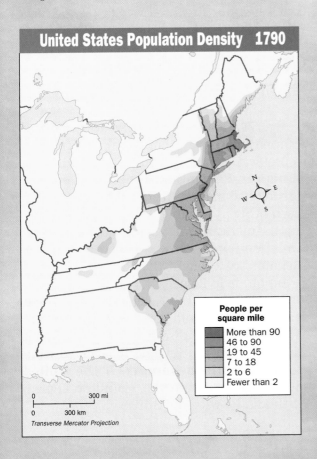

United States Population Density 1790

People per square mile
- More than 90
- 46 to 90
- 19 to 45
- 7 to 18
- 2 to 6
- Fewer than 2

0   300 mi
0   300 km
Transverse Mercator Projection

Using Map Skills

Study the map. Then answer the questions. Refer to the maps on pages R4–R5 and R6–R7, if necessary.

1. What was the range of population densities in Pennsylvania?

2. Starting at the Atlantic Coast and moving inland, describe Virginia in terms of its population density.

3. Find the spots where the population density was 90 and over. What cities are at those spots?

4. How does the map support the claim that the Appalachians slowed down but did not stop Americans moving westward?

5. **Hands-On Geography** Imagine that one morning you wake up somewhere in the United States—200 years ago. Of all the places on the map, where would you want to wake up? To help you decide, with a partner make a chart listing advantages and disadvantages of living in high, medium, and low population density areas in 1790.

2. Conflicts at Home and Abroad

Reading Guide

New Terms **neutral, excise tax, impressed**

Section Focus **Washington's struggles to keep the nation out of war**

1. How did the French Revolution divide Americans?
2. What was the basis of Washington's foreign policy?
3. How did Washington deal with tax rebels and Indian lands beyond the Appalachians?

Weary of political life, Abigail Adams decided to remain in Massachusetts during John's second term as Vice-President. John, missing Abigail, wondered if "some fault unknown has brought upon me such punishments, to be separated both when we were too young and when we are too old." He especially missed her advice as the nation debated the drama unfolding in France.

The French Revolution

In 1789 the people of France had risen up against their king. The leaders of this revolution promised a democracy. Three years later, France became a republic and declared "a war of all peoples against all kings."

At first, these events thrilled many Americans. Jefferson and his followers were inspired to call themselves Republicans because of the French uprising. They saw it as part of a great crusade for democracy and "the liberty of the whole earth" that had begun with the American Revolution.

In time, however, news from France caused Americans to think again. Riots broke out in Paris as the poor turned against the rich. Mobs cheered as the new government chopped off the heads of 17,000 wealthy French men and women. In 1793, during the "Reign of Terror," a radical group

beheaded the king. France, they declared, would never have a king again.

Hamilton and his Federalist followers were horrified by the bloodshed in France. Many of them were wealthy themselves, and they began to wonder if the common people in America had too much power. "Behold France," warned a Federalist, "an open hell . . . in which we see . . . perhaps our own future."

Washington Proclaims Neutrality

By 1793 France was at war with most of Europe and Great Britain. The conflict posed a problem for the United States. During the American Revolution, the Americans and French had made a treaty promising to help each other in wartime. Without French support, Americans might not have won their independence. Now, Jefferson and the Republicans thought the United States had a duty to help France.

Hamilton and the Federalists argued that aiding France would mean war with Britain. That would be a disaster. The government depended on the income it received from tariffs on British imports. If the United States sided with anyone, Hamilton argued, it should be with the British.

Washington listened, but knew the nation was not ready for war. He chose to remain **neutral,** which means not taking either side in a conflict. In April 1793, the President issued a Proclamation of Neutrality. It warned Americans "to avoid all acts" that might help any warring nation.

The Genêt Affair That same month, a minister from the French government arrived in South Carolina. Edmond Genêt [zheh-NAY] liked to be called "Citizen" Genêt to show he was a man of the people.

As he made his way north, Citizen Genêt was greeted by cheering crowds. His popularity quickly went to his head. In his speeches he attacked "Old Washington" and the Proclamation of Neutrality. Genêt urged Americans to join France in war against Britain, and encouraged American seamen to attack British ships.

Jefferson admired France but could not stomach Genêt's actions. Calling the minister "indecent toward the President," Jefferson agreed to ask France to call Genêt home. When the French replaced Genêt, the threat to neutrality faded.

Problems West of the Appalachians

With Genêt replaced, Washington could breathe easier. He had steered the nation away from war. At home, however, he faced two major challenges in the Ohio Valley.

The Whiskey Rebellion In 1791 Congress had put an **excise tax**—a tax on the production or sale of a certain product— on whiskey. Backcountry farmers, from Georgia to Pennsylvania, hated this tax.

Opponents of the French Revolution were beheaded in public. Some Americans were shocked by this brutal turn of events in France.

The only time a President has led troops into battle is when George Washington did so to put down the Whiskey Rebellion.

Whiskey, distilled from grain, was often used to buy goods when cash was scarce. Backcountry farmers protested loudly to Congress against the whiskey tax.

After hearing these protests, Congress lowered the excise tax in 1794. Most farmers began to pay up. In western Pennsylvania, however, tax rebels known as "Whiskey Boys" terrorized farmers who paid the hated tax. Tax collectors in the area were tarred and feathered and burned with hot irons.

Hamilton urged Washington to stamp out the Whiskey Rebellion before it became another Shays' Rebellion. In the summer of 1794, commander in chief Washington led an army of 13,000 soldiers across the mountains. In the face of this force, the rebels vanished into the woods.

To Jefferson and the Republicans, sending an army to arrest a few tax dodgers seemed silly. Hamilton and Washington, however, believed they had done what was needed to make sure that federal law was "the supreme law of the land."

Conflicts over Indian lands At the same time, Washington faced a second problem in the Ohio country. Alarmed by land-hungry settlers, Indian tribes there had formed a loose confederacy to protect their homelands. They declared the Ohio River to be the border between their lands to the north and the United States to the south.

The United States government, however, ignored the boundary. It allowed settlers to cross the Ohio River into Indian lands and cut down the forests for farms. Led by Little Turtle of the Miamis and Blue Jacket of the Shawnees, the Indians raided these settlements, burning houses and fields.

President Washington refused to talk with the Indians. Instead, he sent two armies north of the Ohio River to defend the settlers. In 1791 the Indians crushed the armies in the biggest defeat that Indians ever dealt the United States. More than 900 soldiers were killed or wounded. The Indians felt unbeatable.

Washington gave command of the next army to General "Mad Anthony" Wayne. He was nicknamed "Mad Anthony" because of his reckless conduct in battles. Wayne spent almost two years training his soldiers.

The Battle of Fallen Timbers As the battle neared, the Indians hoped to surprise Wayne's men at a place called Fallen Timbers. Wayne took so long to reach it, however, that many Indians had returned to their villages. The result was an easy victory for Wayne in August 1794.

Kamehameha unifies Hawaii

As the United States struggled through its early years, another new nation was born thousands of miles away. For centuries, local chiefs had controlled different parts of the Hawaiian islands. In 1782 a power struggle broke out between chiefs on the big island of Hawaii. One of the chiefs, a remarkable man named Kamehameha [kah-MAY-hah-MAY-hah], eventually won control of the island. By 1795 he had unified all but two islands into the kingdom of Hawaii.

Little Turtle (above) and other Indian leaders signed the Treaty of Greenville in 1795 after their defeat at the Battle of Fallen Timbers.

Wayne's troops had made deadly use of their bayonets. An Ottawa Indian said:

❝We could not stand against the sharp ends of their guns. . . . Our moccasins trickled blood in the sand, and the water was red in the river.❞

The defeat at Fallen Timbers crushed the spirit of the Indians in the Northwest. They had little choice but to accept the 1795 Treaty of Greenville. With it, they lost much of Ohio and Indiana to the settlers. The Indians were forced to retreat even further into the North American continent.

Conflict with Britain

Many Americans blamed Britain for the troubles in the Ohio Valley. The British had kept their forts there after the American

Jay's Treaty angered most Americans. Here a crowd burns an effigy of John Jay.

ships—or thrown into foul prisons. Americans were outraged by such treatment.

In 1794 Congress urged Washington to find a peaceful way out of the conflict. Just in case, however, Congress also voted to raise an army and build a navy.

Jay's Treaty

Washington sent Chief Justice John Jay to London to persuade the British to stop attacking American ships and sailors. He was also to ask the British to give up their forts in the Northwest.

Jay's Treaty, the result of his trip, was both a success and a failure. The British agreed to give up their forts. They refused, however, to halt attacks against American ships trading with France. Nor would the British stop impressing American seamen. John Adams knew that the treaty would be unpopular. "I am very much afraid of this Treaty!" he wrote to Abigail.

The American response As Adams had feared, Jay's Treaty stirred up a storm of protest. In Boston an angry mob burned a British ship. When Alexander Hamilton spoke in favor of the treaty, New Yorkers pelted him with rocks.

Republican newspapers heaped insults on both Washington and Jay. The papers called the President a "hypocrite," and accused Jay of selling out his country. One paper wrote:

❝John Jay, ah! the arch traitor—
seize him, drown him, hang him,
burn him, flay him alive!❞

Such attacks sickened Abigail Adams. She wrote angrily of the "orators and printers" who had opened the "floodgates of scurrility [nastiness] and abuse upon the President and Mr. Jay." Despite the uproar, the Senate approved Jay's Treaty. For all of its faults, the treaty did keep the United States out of war.

Revolution. Now they were letting Canadian fur traders use them to do business with the Indians. Settlers suspected, though, that the forts were more than trading posts. They accused Britain of supplying the Indians with weapons to resist the settlers.

Troubles at sea Americans had a second reason for being angry with Britain. France and Britain were at war in 1794. American merchants believed that as long as the United States remained neutral in the war, their ships should be free to trade with both nations. Britain and France did not share this view. They attacked American ships heading for each other's ports.

Since Britain had the larger navy, it did more damage, seizing hundreds of American ships. The sailors on these vessels were **impressed**—forced to work on British war-

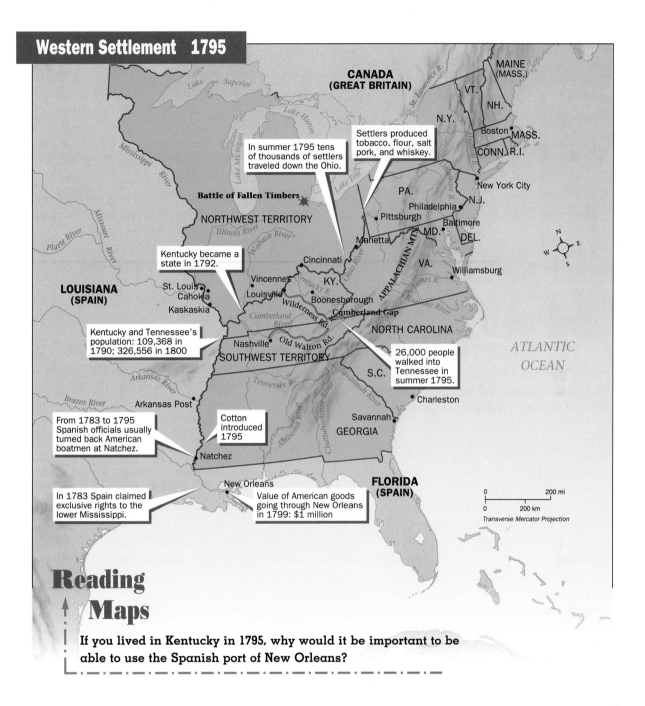

Western Settlement 1795

CANADA (GREAT BRITAIN)

In summer 1795 tens of thousands of settlers traveled down the Ohio.

Settlers produced tobacco, flour, salt pork, and whiskey.

Battle of Fallen Timbers

NORTHWEST TERRITORY

Kentucky became a state in 1792.

Kentucky and Tennessee's population: 109,368 in 1790; 326,556 in 1800

LOUISIANA (SPAIN)

St. Louis
Cahokia
Kaskaskia

Vincennes
Louisville
Boonesborough
Cincinnati

Nashville
SOUTHWEST TERRITORY
Old Walton Rd.
Cumberland Gap

KY.

26,000 people walked into Tennessee in summer 1795.

From 1783 to 1795 Spanish officials usually turned back American boatmen at Natchez.

Cotton introduced 1795

Arkansas Post
Natchez

In 1783 Spain claimed exclusive rights to the lower Mississippi.

New Orleans

Value of American goods going through New Orleans in 1799: $1 million

NORTH CAROLINA

S.C.
Charleston

Savannah
GEORGIA

FLORIDA (SPAIN)

MAINE (MASS.)
VT.
NH.
N.Y.
Boston **MASS.**
CONN. R.I.
New York City
PA.
Philadelphia
Pittsburgh
N.J.
Baltimore
Marietta
MD. DEL.
VA.
Williamsburg

ATLANTIC OCEAN

| 0 | 200 mi |
| 0 | 200 km |

Transverse Mercator Projection

Reading Maps

If you lived in Kentucky in 1795, why would it be important to be able to use the Spanish port of New Orleans?

Pinckney's Treaty

Jay's Treaty served another purpose. It helped Thomas Pinckney make a deal with Spain. Pinckney had gone to Spain to settle boundary disputes and to gain the right of Americans to send goods through New Orleans. Afraid that Jay's Treaty might lead to an alliance between the United States and Britain, Spain cooperated with Pinckney.

Pinckney's Treaty of 1795 was good news to western farmers. It gave Americans use of the Mississippi and the port of New Orleans for shipping goods. Spain also gave up its claim to a large chunk of territory north of Florida. Americans welcomed the new treaty.

Politics sometimes turned violent, such as when Republican Matthew Lyon and Federalist Roger Griswold attacked each other in Congress.

Washington Retires

As Washington's second term came to a close, the President announced that he would not run again. As with his cabinet meetings, Washington set a model for future Presidents to follow. No President would serve more than two terms until President Franklin Roosevelt was elected to third and fourth terms in the 1940s.

The Farewell Address Before leaving office in 1796, Washington prepared an address to his "Friends and Fellow Citizens." He reminded Americans of all that united them, despite their diversity:

❝ With slight shades of difference, you have the same religion, manners, habits, and political principles. You have in a common cause fought and triumphed together.**❞**

Washington then warned of two threats to the nation. The first was the fighting between Federalists and Republicans over such issues as the national bank and foreign alliances. Such conflicts, he said, arise from strong "passions," and could tear the nation apart.

Second, Washington warned Americans not to risk their "peace and prosperity" by getting involved in European power struggles. "It is our true policy," he said, "to steer clear of permanent alliances with any portion of the foreign world."

Washington's Farewell Address is one of the most famous speeches in American history. His advice to avoid foreign alliances guided American foreign policy for nearly 150 years.

Washington's accomplishments The President retired amid cheers from Federalists. Despite some criticism from Republicans, Washington could take pride in what he had accomplished.

The new government was up and running. The nation was on a sound financial footing. Settlers were moving westward so rapidly that two new states had already joined the Union—Kentucky in 1792 and Tennessee in 1796. Most of all, Washington had steered his government safely through difficult, quarrelsome times. He left the nation united and at peace.

2. Section Review

1. Define **neutral, excise tax,** and **impressed.**
2. How did the Federalists view the French Revolution?
3. Describe two ways that Washington tried to steer clear of foreign conflicts.
4. Critical Thinking If you were a western farmer, would you have supported or opposed the Jay and Pinckney treaties? Explain your reasons.

3. The Birth of Political Parties

Reading Guide

New Terms political parties, aliens, sedition, nullify, states' rights

Section Focus The rise of political parties and their impact on American politics

1. What issues and ideas divided the Federalists and Republicans in 1796?
2. What were the Alien and Sedition Acts? Why were they approved? Why were they opposed?
3. What made the election of 1800 a turning point for the country?

When John Adams heard that Washington was planning to retire, he wrote to Abigail that "either we must enter upon ardours [labors] more trying than any ever yet experienced; or retire . . . for life." Abigail replied that were it left to her, "I should immediately say retire."

The Federalists and Republicans did not wait for John and Abigail to decide their future. With Washington's announcement, both groups began organizing for the next presidential election in 1796.

Political Parties Develop

The framers of the Constitution had expected that the most able leader in the nation would be chosen President. They did not imagine the rise of **political parties**—organized groups of people with similar ideas about government. By the early 1790s, however, two political parties were fighting for control of the nation's government. The party with the most votes could control both Congress and the presidency.

The Republicans In 1796 the Republican Party backed Thomas Jefferson for President. Jefferson favored the power of individual states over the federal government in most matters. His message was that the new national government, under the Federalists, had grown too large.

The Republicans also attacked Federalist plans for the economy (see the chart on the next page) as helping the wealthy few rather than the common people. Such talk appealed to farmers and working people, particularly in southern and western states.

The Federalists Unlike the Republicans, the Federalists believed in a strong government that would protect trade and help business. It would also guard against foreign attacks. These ideas appealed to businesspeople and merchants.

Alexander Hamilton, the leader of the Federalists, distrusted the common folk who "are turbulent and changing; they seldom judge or determine [what is] right." He longed to be President, but his economic ideas had made him too many enemies. Instead, the Federalists backed John Adams.

The Election of 1796

When the vote came in, Adams had won the presidency by just three electoral votes. Jefferson came in second, which made him Vice-President. The nation was in a difficult situation. Its top two leaders belonged to different political parties.

The First Political Parties

Federalists	Republicans
Leaders	**Leaders**
Alexander Hamilton	Thomas Jefferson
John Adams	James Madison
Regions	**Regions**
strongest in northern towns and coastal south	strongest in northern farming areas and southern and western backcountry
Hamilton	Jefferson
Beliefs	**Beliefs**
rule by wealthy, educated people	rule by the common people
strong national government	weak national government
loose construction of the Constitution	strict construction of the Constitution
limits on states' rights	protection of states' rights
laws to help businesspeople	laws to help farmers
high tariffs to protect manufacturers in the United States	low tariffs to keep goods cheap for farmers
powerful national bank	no national bank
pro-British	pro-French

At first, President Adams tried to work with Jefferson. Political differences, however, could ruin old friendships. Jefferson himself wrote sadly that "men who have been intimate [close] all their lives cross the streets to avoid meeting, and turn their heads another way."

Unable to work with Jefferson, Adams turned to Abigail for advice. One senator complained that "the President would not dare make a nomination" without his wife's approval. Abigail responded tartly that even "if a woman does not hold the reins of government, I see no reason for her not judging how they are conducted."

Trouble with France

As the war between France and Britain dragged on and on, Adams found it hard to continue a policy of neutrality. French leaders, seeing Jay's Treaty between the United States and Britain as a threat, had increased attacks on American ships.

The XYZ Affair Adams sent three diplomats to France to seek an end to the attacks. Upon arrival, they were met by three secret agents of the French government. The agents—known as Mr. X, Mr. Y, and Mr. Z—demanded a tribute, or bribe, of

$250,000 before any peace talks began. The American delegates refused to pay.

The XYZ Affair enraged Americans. The Federalists, who distrusted France, prepared for war. Their slogan was "Millions for defense, but not one cent for tribute."

The "half war" The United States, too weak to risk all-out war, instead fought an undeclared war, a "half war," by capturing more than 80 French ships. In 1800 Adams again sent envoys to a French government now led by Napoleon Bonaparte. Napoleon agreed to end the 1778 alliance between the United States and France. In exchange, Adams dropped demands that France pay for ships it had seized.

With this agreement Adams lost the support of anti-French Federalists—support he would need to win a second term as President. Even so, Adams believed he had done what was right. He later wrote:

❝I desire no other inscription over
my gravestone than: 'Here lies
John Adams, who took upon himself
the responsibility of the peace with
France in the year 1800.'❞

Alien and Sedition Acts

During the "half war," some Federalists spread wild rumors that French spies were plotting to burn down churches, free slaves, and chop off heads in every town square. Meanwhile, Republican papers criticized the Federalists, describing the President as "bald, blind, crippled, toothless Adams."

Fearful of these harsh attacks, and of rumors about spies, the Federalists passed the Alien and Sedition Acts in 1798. **Aliens** are foreigners who are not yet citizens of the nation in which they live. The Alien Acts gave the President power to jail or deport aliens if they were troublesome or suspected to be spies. The Alien Acts frightened some foreigners into leaving the country.

Sedition is action that might cause people to rebel against the government. The Sedition Act banned writing or speech that stirred up hatred against Congress or the President. Republicans believed that this act was mostly a Federalist attempt to silence them. In fact, several Republican newspaper editors were arrested under this law. A few were convicted and fined.

What role should a President's wife play? Like Abigail Adams (left), Nancy Reagan (middle) and Hillary Clinton (right) have been criticized for advising their husbands.

New Columbia? From the start, the residents of Washington, D.C., have been second-class citizens. They live in a city without a state. This means they have no senators. Their delegate to the House of Representatives can make speeches but cannot vote. As a result, Washingtonians have no voice in making the nation's laws. Furthermore, although they elect a mayor and city council, Congress can overturn any city council decision.

For years Washingtonians have demanded statehood for the District of Columbia. In 1993 the House voted down a bill that would have created the state of New Columbia. Statehood supporters, however, vow to continue their fight.

Point of View

Are there limits to freedom of the press?

Republicans denounced the Sedition Act. They said it violated the First Amendment, which protects freedom of speech and of the press. John Allen, a Federalist congressman, defended the act in a speech to the House. He read an attack on Adams that was full of lies, then asked:

"Because the Constitution guarantees . . . freedom of the press, am I at liberty to falsely call you a murderer, an atheist [a nonbeliever in God]? . . . Freedom of the press was never understood to give the right of publishing falsehood and slanders [lies], nor of inciting [calling for] sedition."

How would you answer Representative Allen? Would you put limits on freedom of the press? Why or why not?

The Virginia and Kentucky Resolutions

The Alien and Sedition Acts created a crisis for the young republic. Jefferson and Madison, fearful of tyranny by the federal government, turned to the states to protect people's freedoms. The two men drew up resolutions—statements—opposing these acts. The Virginia and Kentucky state legislatures approved their resolutions.

Both resolutions charged that the Alien and Sedition Acts were unconstitutional. The Kentucky Resolution also said that if an act of Congress violates the Constitution, states have the right to nullify it. To **nullify** means to declare that a certain law will not be enforced. The idea that states may nullify federal laws became known as the **states' rights** theory.

Abigail Adams wondered how the nation could remain united if states chose to obey some laws of Congress and to nullify others. In the end, no other state adopted the Virginia and Kentucky Resolutions. The states' rights theory, however, would be debated many times in the years ahead.

The New Capital

While controversy raged over the Alien and Sedition Acts, the government moved to its new capital, Washington, D.C. (see plan, page 269). Life was not easy in the unfinished capital. Rain turned its unpaved roads into impassable swamps. When Abigail Adams arrived, she found a few buildings "scattered over a space of ten miles, and trees and stumps in plenty."

One of those buildings was the "President's House." The First Lady described it as

Hands-On HISTORY

Designing political party symbols A donkey and an elephant—almost everyone recognizes them as the symbols of today's Democratic and Republican parties. The Democrats' donkey first appeared in the 1820s. It was later made famous by Thomas Nast, a political cartoonist, who also invented the Republican elephant in an 1874 cartoon.

Imagine that you are a political cartoonist in 1800 and you need to design a symbol for both the Federalist and Republican parties. They should be kept simple, and should not favor any one party.

Democratic donkey

Republican elephant

Activity

1. Review the information about the Federalists and Republicans, especially the chart on page 280.

2. Draw sketches or write descriptions of symbols you might use.

3. When you have decided which two symbols work best, do a final sketch or description of each.

4. Show or describe your symbols to your classmates. Explain why you chose them.

---

a place where "not one room or chamber is finished." She used the East Room for hanging laundry, as it was unfit for anything else. As the 1800 election approached, John and Abigail Adams tried to adjust to life in the new capital.

Election of 1800

In the election of 1800 John Adams ran for a second term. He campaigned on his achievements as President. Many people in his own Federalist party, however, objected to his agreement with France. They were not eager to see him re-elected.

The Republicans backed Jefferson for President and Aaron Burr for Vice-President. Jefferson portrayed himself as the defender of freedom and states' rights. He wanted to shrink the government by getting rid of the army and reducing the navy. He also opposed alliances with any nation.

The campaign was run as much on insults as on issues. Republicans attacked Adams as a tyrant who wanted to turn the presidency into a monarchy so that he could be king, followed by his children as well. Federalists labeled Jefferson an atheist who, if elected, would "destroy religion."

Who is President? When the votes were counted in early 1801, it was clear that Adams had lost. But to whom? To Jefferson or to Burr?

Each elector cast two votes for President. The candidate with the most votes was to become President, the second-place candidate Vice-President. In 1800 each Republican elector cast one vote for Jefferson and one vote for Burr. The result was a tie. In a presidential election, the House of Representatives breaks such a tie.

Although Jefferson was the Republican choice for President, the Federalists wanted to embarrass him. They voted for Burr. For 6 days and 35 ballots the tie continued. At last, Hamilton broke the tie by throwing his support to Jefferson. Of the two candidates, he told his fellow Federalists, Jefferson is "by far not so dangerous a man."

In 1804 the Twelfth Amendment was added to the Constitution to prevent such a tie again. Electors now vote separately for the President and Vice-President.

A peaceful change The 1800 election was a victory for the Republicans and for peaceful change. In most countries at the time, power changed hands through war or revolution. Here, power had passed peacefully from one party to another without bloodshed.

3. Section Review

1. Define **political parties, aliens, sedition, nullify,** and **states' rights.**
2. What areas of the country favored the Federalists? the Republicans? Explain why.
3. What fears motivated the Federalists to pass the Alien and Sedition Acts?
4. **Critical Thinking** Republicans thought the Alien and Sedition Acts were as bad as British rule before the Revolution. Why do you agree or disagree?

Why We Remember

The First Years of the Republic

For John and Abigail Adams the 1800 election was a painful defeat. For all of their married lives, they had put serving their country above their own happiness. Being rejected by the voters hurt. Abigail and John hurried home to their farm in Quincy, Massachusetts, as soon as they could leave the capital. Abigail died in Massachusetts on October 28, 1818.

The republic's early years were filled with conflicts and quarrels. Abigail herself had grown disgusted with the new politics. The "abuse and scandal," she wrote, were "enough to ruin . . . the best people in the world." Still, Americans had learned important lessons. They found that writing a constitution was only the first step; turning that piece of paper into a real government was a huge challenge. Doing so in the face of intense disagreements over what the Constitution meant was an even greater challenge—and remains so today.

Finally, Americans learned that it was far better to fight for their beliefs with political parties and votes than with armies and bullets. Elections like the one in 1800 may seem nasty, but they allow the opposition to be heard and they give Americans clear choices between candidates and ideas. Once voters have made that choice, power can pass peacefully from one group to another.

Skill Lab

Thinking Critically

Cause and Effect

Imagine being arrested for criticizing the President. That is exactly what happened to Representative Matthew Lyon of Vermont in 1798. After Lyon mocked John Adams and attacked his administration's policy toward France, he was fined $1,000 and thrown in jail for violating the Sedition Act.

Question to Investigate

What were some causes and effects of the Sedition Act?

Procedure

A cause is something that brings about an event, which is the effect. An **immediate cause** directly brings about an event. A **long-range cause** takes months or even years to bring about an event. An **immediate effect** occurs right away. A **long-range effect** occurs months or even years later. Read sources **A** to **C** to explore the causes and effects of the Sedition Act.

1 Identify causes and effects.
a. State two causes of the act.
b. State two effects of the act.

2 Distinguish between immediate and long-range causes or effects.
a. State an immediate effect of the act.
b. State a long-range effect of the act.

3 Compare descriptions of causes and effects in the different sources.
a. State one way in which the sources agree.
b. How do **B** and **C** differ on the seriousness of the act's effects?

Skill Tips

• Words like *reason, purpose,* and *design* signal causes. Words like *reaction, result,* and *outcome* signal effects.
• Any event may be both a cause and an effect, and may have more than one cause and one effect.
• Different authors have different opinions about causes and effects.

Sources to Use

A Reread pages 281–282.

B "Many outspoken Jeffersonian [newspaper] editors were indicted [charged] under the Sedition Act, and ten were brought to trial. All of them were convicted, often by packed [biased] juries swayed by prejudiced Federalist judges. . . . This attempt by the Federalists to crush free speech and silence the opposition party, high-handed as it was, undoubtedly made many converts for the Jeffersonians."

From Thomas A. Bailey and David M. Kennedy, *The American Pageant* (Heath, 1991)

C "Every defendant was a Republican, every judge and almost every juror a Federalist. . . . All this was labeled by the Jeffersonians, 'The Federalist Reign of Terror.' Looked at in the perspective of history, it was nothing of the sort. . . . Nobody was drowned, hanged, or tortured, nobody went before a firing squad. A few scurrilous [abusive] journalists were silenced, a few received terms in jail. . . . Nobody was prevented from voting against the Federalists in the next elections, state or national. . . . [In] the congressional elections of 1800, the Republicans obtained emphatic majorities in House and Senate. Thus, in 1801 the Federalists went out of power in every branch of government except the judiciary."

From Samuel Eliot Morison et al., *Growth of the American Republic* (Oxford Univ., 1980)

Chapter Survey

Reviewing Vocabulary

Define the following terms.

1. inauguration
2. cabinet
3. tariffs
4. bond
5. speculators
6. constitutional
7. strict construction
8. loose construction
9. neutral
10. excise tax
11. impressed
12. political parties
13. aliens
14. sedition
15. nullify
16. states' rights

Reviewing Main Ideas

1. Describe the executive and judicial branches as Congress first organized them.
2. What was the greatest problem facing the new government, and how did Congress solve it?
3. Describe how Jefferson and Hamilton differed in their interpretations of the Constitution.
4. How did Washington respond to the war between France and Britain? Why did he respond as he did?
5. What two challenges arose west of the Appalachian Mountains during Washington's presidency? How did Washington deal with them?
6. How did Federalists and Republicans differ in their views on each of the following? (a) strength of the national government (b) states' rights (c) tariffs
7. Explain how each event led to the next. (a) Jay's Treaty (b) XYZ Affair (c) "half war" (d) Alien and Sedition Acts (e) Virginia and Kentucky Resolutions

Thinking Critically

1. Analysis How did Jay's Treaty and Pinckney's Treaty affect the new nation's growth and security?
2. Application Agree or disagree with this statement: Washington's foreign policy was the best one for that period in our history. Explain why you agree or disagree, and support your answer with evidence from the chapter.
3. Why We Remember: Evaluation Jefferson supported the idea of political parties, but Washington feared that they might be more harmful than useful to the nation. Do you agree with Jefferson or Washington? Explain your answer.

Applying Skills

Cause and effect Think of a recent effort to censor something, such as the effort to reduce violence on television. Then do the following:
1. Identify the causes. Explain how they led to that effort to censor.
2. Identify the effects. Explain how they resulted from that effort to censor.
3. Make a flowchart to summarize these causes and effects. As you did in the Skill Lab on page 285, identify which ones are immediate and which are long-range.

History Mystery

The nation's capital Answer the History Mystery on page 263. How would you go about finding out who these people are and what deal they made with each other? What problems were the three people trying to solve? If such a deal had not been struck, what location would you have chosen for the nation's capital and why?

Writing in Your History Journal

1. Keys to History (a) The time line on pages 262–263 has seven Keys to History. In your journal, describe why each one is important to know about. (b) What other events

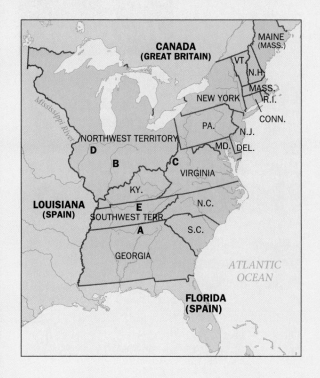

Map labels:
CANADA (GREAT BRITAIN)
MAINE (MASS.)
VT.
N.H.
MASS.
R.I.
NEW YORK
CONN.
PA.
N.J.
MD. DEL.
NORTHWEST TERRITORY
Mississippi River
D
B
C
VIRGINIA
KY.
LOUISIANA (SPAIN)
E
SOUTHWEST TERR.
A
N.C.
S.C.
GEORGIA
ATLANTIC OCEAN
FLORIDA (SPAIN)

Reviewing Geography

1. Each letter on the map represents a river that empties into either the Mississippi or the Ohio. Write the name of each river.

2. Geographic Thinking Look at the maps on pages R4–R5 and R6–R7. From those maps alone, could you guess that the site of the nation's capital was a compromise between northern and southern interests? Explain. What else does the capital site tell you about what was important to people in 1790? If the nation's leaders had known how the United States would eventually expand, might they have chosen a different site? Why or why not?

from the chapter would you add to the time line? Write those events and their dates in your journal and tell why you think each event should be added.

2. Abigail Adams Abigail was attacked, at times, for giving her husband advice about political matters. How do you think she felt about such criticism? In your journal write a conversation Abigail might have had with a close friend about it.

3. Thinking Historically If you had been alive in 1800, which of the two political parties—Federalist or Republican—would you have favored? Why? What ideas do you like in both parties? Write your responses in your journal.

Alternative Assessment

Citizenship: Campaigning for President With several other students, reenact the presidential election campaign of 1800. First, divide into two groups representing the Federalist and Republican parties. Within your group, assign someone to be the candidate: John Adams or Thomas Jefferson. Other group members will be campaign aides.

Think of your class as voters. You want to win their support for your candidate. To do so, you might create campaign posters and cartoons, write news articles supporting the candidate, and write a speech that your candidate can deliver to the voters. Keep an eye on what the other party does in the campaign, and help the voters be aware that your candidate is the better one.

Your work will be evaluated on the following criteria:
• you make a strong effort to get your candidate elected
• your campaign activities and materials reflect the issues facing the parties and candidates in 1800 and their positions
• your campaign activities and materials are appealing and persuasive

Chapter 11

The Jefferson Era

Sections

Keys to History

1803
Marbury v. Madison
Chief Justice John Marshall

1803
Louisiana Purchase

1804–1806
Lewis and Clark expedition
Compass used in expedition

1801   1805

World **Link**

Looking Back

Washington's Farewell Address
1796

Toussaint L'Ouverture frees Saint Domingue
1801

HISTORY *Mystery*

The greatest American victory in the War of 1812 was in a battle that need not have been fought. What was the battle, and why was it unnecessary?

1811
Tecumseh's forces meet Harrison's troops at the Battle of Tippecanoe

1812–1815
War of 1812
An American sailor

1814
Francis Scott Key writes "The Star-Spangled Banner"
Flag that inspired Key

1815
Battle of New Orleans

1810

1815

Looking Ahead

Monroe Doctrine is issued
1823

Beginning the Story with

When the Shawnee chief Tecumseh [tuh-KUM-suh] was born in present-day Ohio in 1768, his people still followed their traditional way of life. They lived in small villages throughout the Ohio Valley. In the summer, while the men hunted, the women planted crops and gathered the gifts of the forest. It was a good life, so good that whites taken prisoner by the Shawnees often preferred to stay with them, even after being "rescued" by other whites.

In the 1770s settlers from the east began crossing the mountains into the Indians' lands. By 1774, some 10,000 settlers lived in Kentucky alone. That same year, Tecumseh's father was killed in a bloody clash between the Shawnees and the settlers. While still a child, Tecumseh also lost two brothers and countless friends and relatives in battles with settlers. Three times he experienced the terror of having his village attacked and burned by white raiders.

As Tecumseh watched the flames devour his home, he saw more than a village being destroyed. The settlers threatened the very existence of the Shawnees and their way of life. Tecumseh's horrifying experiences as a child drove him, as a man, to unite the tribes of the Ohio country into a great coalition against the settlers' advance.

The Young Tecumseh

Tecumseh's Shawnee name was *nila ni tekamthi msi-pessi*, which meant the Man Who Waits, the Crouching Panther, or the Shooting Star. His people had named him well. As the boy grew to manhood, he would be all of these and more. Unable to pronounce the name, settlers called him Tecumseh.

In 1794 Tecumseh fought with the Miami chief Little Turtle against American soldiers at the Battle of Fallen Timbers. Sometime after this defeat,

Shawnees originally farmed and hunted along the Cumberland River in present-day Kentucky. Settlers forced them north of the Ohio River by the end of the 1700s. Even there they would not find security from the flood of settlers.

he befriended a white woman named Rebecca Galloway, the daughter of Ohio farmers. She taught him about Shakespeare, the Bible, and American history. Rebecca would have married Tecumseh if he had agreed to give up the Indian way of life, but he refused. Instead, he devoted the rest of his life to driving the settlers from his homeland.

The "Shooting Star" Unites His People

"Where today are the Narrangansetts, the Mohawks, the Pocanets, and many other once powerful tribes of our people? They have vanished before . . . the white man, as snow before a summer sun." So spoke Tecumseh as he rallied his people. By 1805, Tecumseh the Shooting Star was in constant motion, visiting tribes from the Great Lakes to Florida. At each stop his message was the same: By themselves, America's native peoples could not survive against the white man. They must either stop fighting among themselves and unite against the settlers, or lose everything. To his Creek Indian friends Tecumseh declared:

"Burn their dwellings. Destroy their [live] stock. The red people own the country . . . [make] war now. War forever. War upon the living. War upon the dead. Dig up their corpses [bodies] from the grave. Our country must give no rest to a white man's bones.**"**

Among Indians, Tecumseh inspired hope, pride, and unity of purpose. As his fame spread, even his enemies came to admire him. Tecumseh's message fired the hearts of Indians from Canada to the Gulf of Mexico and cast a long shadow on the events that would lead to the War of 1812.

Hands-On HISTORY

Activity

Imagine that you are a newspaper reporter in the United States today. Going back in time, you visit Tecumseh in his village of Prophetstown for a newspaper interview. Write a short article describing Tecumseh's view of the settlers, and what he wants to do as an Indian leader and why.

1. The New Republican President

Reading Guide

New Term **judicial review**

Section Focus **How Jefferson put his Republican ideas to work as President**

1. How did the Supreme Court establish its power of judicial review?
2. How did President Jefferson double the size of the United States?
3. Who were the first Americans to explore the vast new territory of Louisiana?

In 1801 Thomas Jefferson became the first President to take the oath of office in Washington, D.C. Jefferson's inauguration fit his Republican beliefs that government should be kept small and simple.

Washington and Adams had traveled to their inaugurations in fancy carriages. Jefferson, however, walked from his rooming house to the Capitol building. His simple suit, wrote one reporter, "was, as usual, that of a plain citizen."

In his inaugural address, Jefferson tried to heal the wounds left by the election and offer hope for the future:

"Let us, then, fellow citizens, unite with one heart and one mind. . . . We are all Republicans, we are all Federalists.**"**

Republican Ideas Put to Work

As President, Jefferson tried to live by his words and put Republican ideas about government to work. To keep the government small, he cut the number of federal officials and the size of the army and navy. To protect people's liberties, he let the Alien and Sedition Acts expire. Jefferson also convinced Congress to end the hated excise tax on whiskey.

On the other hand, the new President did not try to undo Federalist economic policies. His government continued to pay off the national debt and allowed the Bank of the United States to function.

At the President's House, Jefferson the Republican ended many of the customs of Presidents Washington and Adams. Guests now shook hands with the President, instead of bowing before him. Formal receptions were replaced with informal dinners at a round table, so that no person appeared superior to anyone else. Jefferson hired a French chef, however, and served fine wines.

A New Role for the Court

With Jefferson's election, Republicans controlled both Congress and the presidency. Thanks to John Adams, however, Federalists dominated the third branch of government, the judicial branch.

During his last weeks in office, Adams had taken several steps to keep the judicial branch in Federalist hands. One was to choose John Marshall to be Chief Justice of the Supreme Court. Although Marshall was a cousin of Thomas Jefferson, and a fellow Virginian, he despised Jefferson's Republican ideas. Marshall's firm will and sharp mind were to make him a worthy opponent for Jefferson's strong personality.

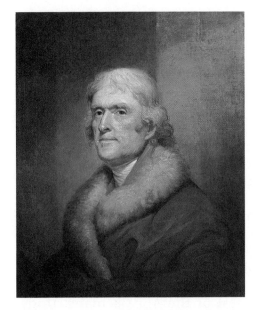

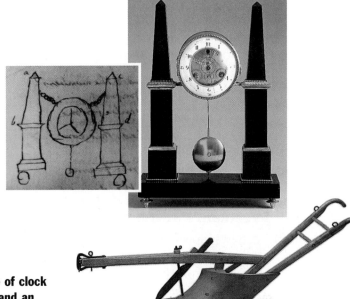

As an inventor, Jefferson designed a new type of clock and plow. He was also a musician, a farmer, and an architect, and he spoke many languages.

Midnight judges Adams had also pushed the Judiciary Act of 1801 through Congress. This act created more positions for judges, which Adams rushed to fill. Indeed, the night before Jefferson's inauguration, Adams stayed up late signing commissions—orders—appointing loyal Federalists to these new judgeships.

Marbury v. Madison Soon after taking office, Jefferson noticed that a stack of commissions for new judges had not been delivered. Without receiving a commission, a person could not act as a judge. Calling the Federalist commissions "an outrage," Jefferson told Secretary of State James Madison not to deliver them.

One man who did not receive his commission was William Marbury. Marbury turned to the Supreme Court for help. The Judiciary Act of 1789 gave the Supreme Court the power to force federal officials to perform their duties. Therefore, Marbury argued, the Court could order Madison to give him his commission.

In 1803 the Supreme Court looked at the case of *Marbury* v. *Madison*. (The v. stands for versus, or against.) The outcome of the case forever changed the relationship of the three branches of government.

In his decision, Chief Justice Marshall agreed that the Judiciary Act of 1789 had given the Supreme Court the power to force federal officials to do their jobs. However, Marshall and the Court ruled that the Judiciary Act of 1789 was unconstitutional because the Constitution did not grant such power to the Court. Therefore, the Supreme Court could not force Madison to give Marbury his commission.

Judicial review John Marshall's decision in *Marbury* v. *Madison* was important because it established the power of judicial review for the Supreme Court. **Judicial review** is the power to decide whether or not an act of Congress is constitutional. Just as the President could veto acts passed by Congress, now the Supreme Court could rule them unconstitutional.

In the decision, Marshall wrote that it was the "duty" of the Court "to say what the law is." This case was a new development in American democracy. It put the Supreme Court on an equal footing with Congress and the President. Instead of power resting with just two branches of the federal government, a third branch now shared federal power.

Point of View

Did the Court attack the President's power?

Republican newspapers saw the ruling in *Marbury* v. *Madison* as an attack on the President's role as the only one who could veto laws. The *Independent Chronicle* wrote:

"The attempt of the Supreme Court . . . to control the Executive . . . seems to be no less than a commencement [beginning] of war between the . . . departments [branches]. The Court must be defeated."

The historian James McGregor Burns, writing in 1982, disagreed. This case, he believed, established a new role for the Supreme Court.

"Republicans had missed the point. The court had not invaded the executive [the President]. . . . What the Chief Justice had done was far more important. Marshall, in voiding an act of Congress signed by the President . . . was creating the great precedent of judicial invalidation [repeal] of congressional action."

The Supreme Court's new power stunned the Republicans. The Federalists, on the other hand, welcomed the Court's decision. Why do you think the two parties reacted so differently?

The Louisiana Purchase

Meanwhile, the United States was growing rapidly. West of the Appalachians, new territories were being organized. Even farther west, across the Mississippi River, lay vast lands little known by Europeans. This immense region, called Louisiana, was first claimed by France. It was given to Spain after the French and Indian War.

In 1800 the French ruler Napoleon Bonaparte bullied Spain into giving Louisiana back to France. Napoleon planned to settle Louisiana with farmers who would raise food for France's Caribbean sugar colonies.

Napoleon's dreams frightened Americans living west of the Appalachians. Under Pinckney's Treaty with Spain, they had freely used the Mississippi River and the port of New Orleans to ship their crops to market. What if Napoleon closed New Orleans to American goods? It would be a disaster for western farmers.

An unexpected bargain In 1803 Jefferson sent James Monroe to France. His mission was to persuade Napoleon to sell New Orleans to the United States.

While Monroe was crossing the Atlantic, Napoleon changed his plans for Louisiana. A few months earlier, enslaved people in the Caribbean colony of Saint Domingue [sahn doh-MING] successfully rebelled against French rule. Having lost his most valuable sugar colony, Napoleon no longer needed to turn Louisiana into a breadbasket for Saint Domingue (later renamed Haiti).

On the brink of war with Great Britain, Napoleon also knew that he did not have a navy to protect French lands in North America. Rather than lose Louisiana to Britain, why not sell it to the Americans? Monroe accepted Napoleon's offer. On April 30, 1803, he signed a treaty with France in which the United States agreed to buy Louisiana for about $15 million.

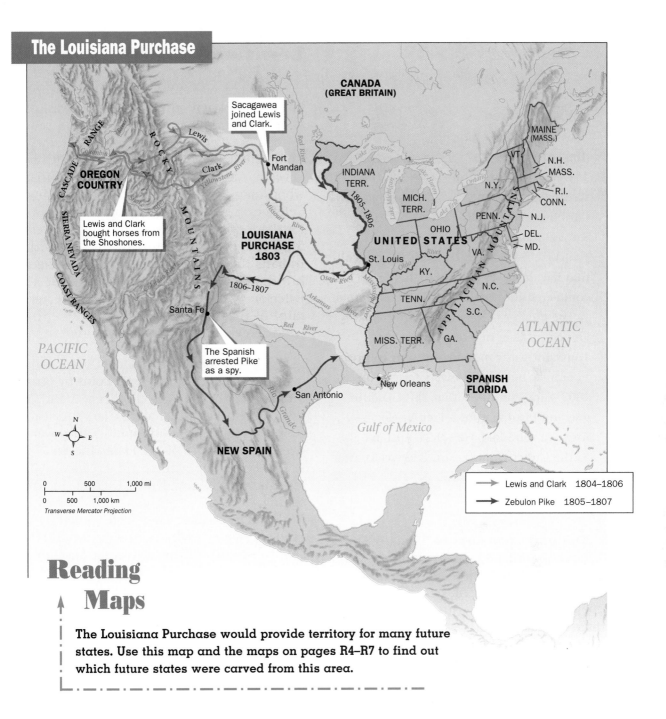

The Louisiana Purchase

CANADA
(GREAT BRITAIN)

Sacagawea joined Lewis and Clark.

Fort Mandan

1805–1806

INDIANA TERR.

MICH. TERR.

OHIO

UNITED STATES

St. Louis

KY.

MAINE (MASS.)

VT

N.H.

MASS.

N.Y.

R.I.

CONN.

PENN.

N.J.

DEL.

MD.

VA.

OREGON COUNTRY

Lewis and Clark bought horses from the Shoshones.

LOUISIANA PURCHASE 1803

1806–1807

Santa Fe

The Spanish arrested Pike as a spy.

Red River

MISS. TERR.

TENN.

N.C.

S.C.

GA.

ATLANTIC OCEAN

PACIFIC OCEAN

San Antonio

New Orleans

SPANISH FLORIDA

NEW SPAIN

Gulf of Mexico

N
W   E
S

0   500   1,000 mi
0   500   1,000 km
Transverse Mercator Projection

Lewis and Clark   1804–1806
Zebulon Pike   1805–1807

Reading Maps

The Louisiana Purchase would provide territory for many future states. Use this map and the maps on pages R4–R7 to find out which future states were carved from this area.

Jefferson's dilemma Jefferson was thrilled with Monroe's success. Still, the purchase of Louisiana created a problem for him. As a Republican, he stood for strict construction of the Constitution. The Constitution did not mention the purchase of foreign lands as one of the government's powers. To approve the purchase, Jefferson would have to go against his Republican ideals.

A constitutional amendment would solve the problem, but Jefferson knew that an amendment could not be adopted quickly enough. He put aside his doubts and asked the Senate to approve the purchase.

World  Link

Haiti breaks free

Toussaint L'Ouverture [too-SAHN loo-vehr-TYOOR] was born into slavery in the French Caribbean colony of Saint Domingue (now Haiti). Self-educated, he led a slave revolt that began in 1791. By 1801 his army had conquered the entire island of Hispaniola.

The next year Napoleon sent 20,000 French soldiers to retake the colony. Toussaint was captured and sent to prison in France, but his followers fought on. By 1803 Napoleon knew that Saint Domingue and his dream of a French North America were lost. He sold Louisiana to the United States just a few weeks after Toussaint died in prison.

The purchase debate To many Americans, the Louisiana Purchase looked like the bargain of the century. The new territory would double the size of the United States at the low price of three cents an acre. Even so, there was opposition.

The size of the new territory bothered people who believed that it would make the United States too large to govern. Others fussed about the cost. "We are to give money of which we have too little," wrote a Boston critic, "for land of which we already have too much."

The Senate finally approved the treaty late in 1803. The Louisiana Purchase doubled the size of the United States, and added 200,000 Native American, French, and Spanish inhabitants.

Lewis and Clark

Louisiana was now American territory, but no one knew just how large it was, or what treasures it contained. To find out, Jefferson asked his 27-year-old secretary, Meriwether Lewis, to lead an expedition. Lewis chose William Clark, an experienced woodsman and soldier, as co-leader.

Jefferson gave Lewis and Clark instructions for the journey. They were to explore rivers for a route to the Pacific, open trade with Indians they met, and, most of all, collect information. "Objects worthy of notice," Jefferson wrote, "will be the soil and face [terrain] of the country, the animals, . . . the winds prevailing at different seasons."

Up the Missouri In May 1804, Lewis and Clark's expedition left St. Louis by boat and headed up the Missouri River. About 30 men joined them, including Clark's African American slave, York. By summer they were deep into the land of the Plains Indians.

The expedition wintered in a Mandan village in what is now North Dakota. In the spring of 1805, they continued up the Missouri in canoes. They were joined by a guide, Toussaint Charbonneau [too-SAHN shar-bah-NOH], and his 17-year-old Shoshone wife, Sacagawea [SAK-uh-juh-WEE-uh]. Sacagawea had been kidnapped as a child and taken far from her mountain homeland. She would serve as an interpreter.

On to the Pacific Late that summer they reached Shoshone country in the foothills of the Rockies. One day, Lewis wrote:

"[Sacagawea began] to dance and show every mark of the most extravagant joy. . . . A woman [Sacagawea's sister] made her way through the crowd toward Sacagawea, and recognizing each other, they embraced with the most tender affection."

Hands-On HISTORY

Designing a peace medal On their journey to the Pacific, Lewis and Clark carried peace medals from President Jefferson to give as offerings of friendship to Indians that they met. President Washington had begun the tradition of giving out medals in the United States, and it continued for 100 years.

President Clinton revived the tradition in 1994 when he invited Indian leaders from across the nation to a meeting at the White House. There he gave Jefferson peace medals to his guests. One side of the medal features an image of Jefferson, whom Clinton admires very much. On the other is a handshake of peace.

Jefferson peace medal

Activity Imagine that you are to explore a region where you will encounter people who are unknown in the United States.

1 Design a medal to give to these people in friendship. What would you put on the front of your medal? On the back?

2 Draw the design on a surface large enough for the entire class to see.

3 When you present your design to the class, explain the images that you chose for the medal.

Sacagawea also recognized the Shoshone chief as her brother, Cameahwait [kah-MAY-eh-wayt]. She persuaded him to guide the expedition across the rugged Rocky Mountains before early snows blocked the passes. They struggled over range after range of mountains, finally reaching the great Columbia River "and the object of all our labors," the Pacific Ocean.

The expedition spent its second winter camped near the ocean, in dismal conditions. Almost constant rain rotted their clothes and spoiled their food. When spring came, they recrossed the Rockies and Great Plains. Arriving in St. Louis on September 23, 1806, Lewis wrote to President Jefferson:

"It is with pleasure that I announce to you the safe arrival of myself and party at twelve o'clock today at this place [St. Louis] with our papers and baggage. In obedience to our orders, we have penetrated the continent of North America to the Pacific Ocean."

Lewis and Clark had done even more than "penetrate the continent." They had exceeded President Jefferson's wildest expectations. Their "papers and baggage" contained a treasure trove of priceless information about the newly purchased lands that would soon beckon Americans westward.

Pike's Expedition

While Lewis and Clark were on their way home in 1806, another expedition set out from St. Louis to explore a different part of the Louisiana Purchase. This one was led by an adventurous army officer and explorer named Zebulon Pike.

Pike and his party pushed west across the Kansas plains along the Osage and Arkansas Rivers. Upon reaching the Colorado Rockies, Pike caught sight of the "Grand Peak," now named Pikes Peak.

As winter closed in, Pike and his men became lost and wandered south into present-day New Mexico. There, Spanish soldiers arrested them as spies and took them deep into Mexico. Pike's party was held captive until the spring of 1807.

Link to Art

Landscape with a Lake (1804) During Jefferson's presidency, American painting entered the Romantic period. Romantic artists celebrated the beauty of nature. Their work reflected feelings of hope and nationalism as Americans expanded into new lands. During his painting career, Washington Allston developed a "love for the wild and marvellous." In this painting, he contrasts the majesty of nature with the tiny human figure. **Discuss** Do you think the artist intended to depict nature as friendly or dangerous? Explain your answer.

On his return home, Pike wrote a popular book about his journey. In it he praised the Spanish settlers in New Mexico for their "heaven-like qualities of hospitality and kindness." Pike also described the sea of grass that covered much of the whole region, calling it a desert. Later, mapmakers would label the Great Plains as desert. For the next half century, settlers would avoid this region.

1. Section Review

1. Define **judicial review.**
2. What reasons did the United States have for purchasing Louisiana?
3. Critical Thinking How might a map of the United States look different today if all Presidents had followed a strict construction of the Constitution?

Geography Lab

The Rocky Mountains

When Lewis and Clark set out on their journey, they did not know how rugged the Rocky Mountain region would be. After struggling across the Bitterroot Range of the Rockies, Clark wrote, "I have been wet and as cold . . . as I ever was in my life." Another member of the party described the Bitterroots as "the most terrible mountains I ever beheld."

Rugged. Terrible. Majestic. These words describe the Rockies. What other words come to your mind as you study this page?

Grand Tetons, Wyoming (above). Mountain goat (left). San Juan Mountains, southern Colorado (below).

Developing a Mental Map

Refer to the maps on pages P4–P5 and R4–R7.

1. Through what states do the Rockies extend? Where is the highest peak? Between what two states does the Bitterroot Range lie?

2. What region lies east of the Rocky Mountains? Looking at the picture on the lower left side, compare the two regions.

3. The Rocky Mountain region is one of the least populated in the United States. It is also a major tourist destination. How do you explain these facts?

4. Hands-On Geography Write a travel plan for a week-long vacation in the Rockies. You may want to do some research. Consider these questions: What season of the year will you go, and why? What parks will you visit? What sights do you expect to see? What activities do you expect to enjoy?

2. Troubles at Sea

Reading Guide

New Term **embargo**

Section Focus **How the United States responded to threats to American trade from other nations**

1. How did the United States deal with pirates from the Barbary States?
2. How did Britain and France treat American ships and sailors?
3. How did Jefferson try to protect American trade? How effective was his policy?

In 1804 Jefferson won re-election for President by overwhelming his opponent, the Federalist Charles Pinckney. Although the election went smoothly, trouble lay ahead. Threats to American trade forced Jefferson, like the nation's first two Presidents, to turn his attention away from home.

The Barbary Pirates Strike

For years, pirates from the four Barbary States of North Africa—Morocco, Algiers, Tunis, and Tripoli—had seized American ships in the Mediterranean Sea. Presidents Washington and Adams had quietly paid tribute money to these states in exchange for protection against pirate raids.

In 1801 the ruler of Tripoli demanded still more tribute money. Jefferson refused to pay up, and the Barbary pirates once again plundered American ships. Jefferson sent the small American navy to the Mediterranean. It was too weak, however, to end the pirate attacks. Only in 1815 did a rebuilt navy join a European fleet to destroy the pirate bases.

Other Threats to Trade

Pirates were not the only threat to American trade. During Jefferson's presidency, France and Britain were almost continuously

at war. In 1803 Jefferson declared the United States neutral, as Washington had done before him. As the war dragged on, however, Jefferson found it more and more difficult to maintain neutrality.

Link to the Present

Sea piracy today The end of the Barbary pirates was not the end of piracy. Today's sea pirates capture booty worth as much as $250 million every year. Pirate attacks can take place almost anywhere, though most occur off the coasts of South and Southeast Asia. Ships in the waters off Singapore are favorite targets.

Some raids involve a few men armed with knives and swords. They board a ship and take whatever cash and valuables they can carry off. Other attacks involve large, well-organized groups. Such pirates might use radar and automatic weapons in their plan to steal a ship's entire cargo—anything from coffee to videocassette recorders. Some pirates have stolen entire ships!

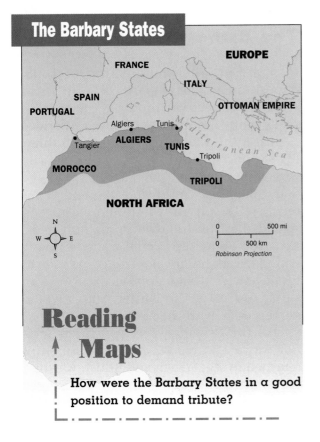

The Barbary States

FRANCE
SPAIN
PORTUGAL
EUROPE
ITALY
OTTOMAN EMPIRE
Algiers
Tunis
Tangier
ALGIERS
TUNIS
Tripoli
MOROCCO
TRIPOLI
Mediterranean Sea
NORTH AFRICA

0   500 mi
0   500 km
Robinson Projection

Reading Maps

How were the Barbary States in a good position to demand tribute?

In 1806 Britain clamped a blockade around French-controlled ports in Europe. Napoleon struck back, ordering a blockade of Britain. Both nations seized American ships heading for the other's ports.

Worse yet, British sea captains began searching ships along the American coast, looking for deserters—sailors who leave ship without permission. Any sailor who appeared to be English could be impressed, even if he was an American citizen. Jefferson complained that "England has become a den of pirates and France has become a den of thieves."

The *Chesapeake–Leopard* Affair

Britain's policy of impressment angered Americans. Their anger turned to rage with the *Chesapeake–Leopard* affair.

In 1807 the *Leopard,* a British warship, stopped the *Chesapeake,* an American naval ship, off the Virginia coast. Captain James Barron of the *Chesapeake* invited a British officer aboard to exchange mail. Once on board, the officer declared that he would search the ship for deserters. "Sir!" Barron replied hotly, "This is a national vessel of the United States." No one, he declared, would search his ship.

In reply, the *Leopard* opened fire on the *Chesapeake,* killing or wounding 21 American sailors. When the *Chesapeake* surrendered, the British found only one deserter aboard. They promptly hanged him.

Jefferson's Embargo

As the battered *Chesapeake* limped into port, Americans came down with a severe case of war fever. Not since the battle at Lexington during the War for Independence, had Jefferson seen the people so ready for war. The British had, he wrote, "given us cause for war

In 1803 a young naval officer, Stephen Decatur (lower right), led an attack against the Barbary pirates of Tripoli.

This cartoon opposing the embargo shows the turtle Ograbme ("embargo" backwards) snapping at an American trying to trade with Britain.

The Embargo Fails

In the presidential election of 1808, opposition to the embargo was an issue. Thomas Jefferson, looking forward to shaking off "the shackles of power," decided against a third term as President. He threw his support behind James Madison, who won easily.

In 1809, just days before the end of his term, Jefferson ended the embargo and signed the Non-Intercourse, or non-trade, Act. Now Americans could trade with any nation except Britain and France. As soon as those powers would stop seizing American ships and men, the United States would reopen trade with them.

Like the embargo, the Non-Intercourse Act was a failure. When American ships returned to sea, French and British warships seized them once again. In 1810 a frustrated Congress tried a new policy. Americans could trade with both France and Britain until one of the powers stopped seizing American ships. The United States would then cut off trade with the other.

When this policy also failed, a growing number of Americans saw war as unavoidable. The question was: War with France or war with Britain?

before. . . . But now they have touched a chord which vibrates in every heart."

Still, Jefferson dreaded going to war. Knowing his navy was weak, he proposed an **embargo**—a complete halt in trade—with other nations. Under the Embargo Act of 1807, no ships could leave American ports and no foreign ships could enter them. Jefferson hoped that the embargo would prove so painful to France and Britain that they would stop attacking American ships.

Instead, Americans suffered more from the embargo than Europeans did. Thousands of sailors lost their jobs. Only soup kitchens set up in port cities kept them from starving. Merchants, meanwhile, watched helplessly as their ships rotted away at deserted docks.

As the embargo continued, many seamen survived by smuggling goods into the country. New Englanders opposed the "Dambargo," and even talked of forming their own nation. Jefferson snapped back:

"New England commerce has kept us in hot water from the commencement [beginning] of our government, and is now engaging us in war."

2. Section Review

1. Define **embargo**.
2. What did the Barbary States want from the United States? How did Jefferson respond to their demand?
3. What happened to the *Chesapeake* that so outraged Americans?
4. Critical Thinking Briefly explain Jefferson's policy toward Britain and France. Describe a different way that the United States might have responded. What might the results have been?

3. The War of 1812

Reading Guide

New Term **nationalism**

Section Focus **How the United States fought its second war with Britain**

1. Why did the United States declare war against Britain in 1812?
2. What was the impact of the war on the Indians of the Ohio country?
3. What was the final effect of the war on the United States?

Two events pushed the United States toward war with Britain. First, in 1810 Napoleon declared that France would end its attacks on American ships. Without waiting to see if France would keep its promise, President Madison cut off trade with Britain. However the British continued to seize American ships. Madison began to think that war was the only way to make Britain respect American rights.

Tecumseh and the Prophet

Even before President Madison stopped trade with Britain, developments in the Indiana Territory had increased tensions with Britain. There, Tecumseh was moving forward with his dream of an Indian confederacy that would stop the spread of settlers. Tecumseh's brother played an important role in pursuing this dream.

As a young man, the brother had been a loud, drunken troublemaker. Then, one day in the spring of 1805, he fell into a deep sleep. Upon awakening, he reported that he had died and visited the Great Spirit in paradise. He returned to life with a message from the Great Spirit: Indians must reject the ways of white people if they wanted to enter paradise after death.

The Shawnees called Tecumseh's brother Tenskwatawa [ten-SKWAH-tah-wah], or

"Open Door." In their eyes, he had opened the door to paradise. To others, he was known as the Prophet.

Together, Tecumseh and the Prophet were a powerful team. They spoke of Indian unity, urged tribes not to surrender any more land, and warned them against drinking alcohol. Wherever the two went, Indians listened.

Prophetstown Followers of Tecumseh and the Prophet built Prophetstown, their capital, on the Tippecanoe River in the present-day state of Indiana. As Prophetstown and the Indian alliance grew, so did the worries of settlers.

William Henry Harrison, the governor of the Indiana Territory, had warned that Tecumseh was "one of those uncommon

The Prophet urged Indians to follow their traditional way of life and avoid contact with settlers. Only then, he claimed, would they have the will to stop the settlers.

Indian forces and United States soldiers battled in the forests near the Tippecanoe River. In 1811 President Madison had ordered Governor Harrison to strike at the Indians living in the area.

geniuses [who] . . . produce revolutions." President Jefferson had dreaded a conflict with the Indians. He urged Harrison to avoid war. "Our system is to live in perpetual [lasting] peace with the Indians," he declared.

The Battle of Tippecanoe

Governor Harrison continued to watch the growth of Prophetstown with alarm. In the fall of 1811, while Tecumseh was away visiting southern tribes, Harrison marched more than 1,000 soldiers to Prophetstown. His plan was to attack the Indians living there with "bayonets and buckshot," and then burn the village.

The Shawnee Prophet made plans of his own. He promised the outnumbered Indians that his magic would make the white soldiers powerless. As a cold rain began to fall just before sunrise on November 7, the Indians made a surprise charge into Harrison's army camp on the Tippecanoe River. When they failed to gain an easy victory, though, they lost hope and deserted Prophetstown.

Harrison could hardly believe his luck, since the Indians had lost no more lives than had his army. He burned Prophetstown down to the ground.

Harrison's victory did not prevent the outbreak of an Indian war. Instead, it scattered Tecumseh's followers, who took revenge on isolated settlements across the Indiana Territory. Settlers fled the area.

Westerners blamed the British for their troubles. Harrison agreed. In the ashes of Prophetstown he had found British-made weapons. Harrison wrote that "the Indians on this frontier have been completely armed and equipped from the British [in Canada]." To make the area safe for settlers, the British must be forced out of Canada.

War Is Declared

By 1812 war fever was rising among southern and western Republicans. They were so eager for battle that Federalists called them "War Hawks." The War Hawks disliked the British for their mistreatment of American sailors and for supporting Indian resistance to settlers in the Indiana Territory. Southern War Hawks hoped to seize Florida from Britain's ally, Spain.

Surprisingly, support for war was weakest in New England, which had suffered most from attacks on ships. The embargo had taught New England merchants that some trade with Britain was better than none.

In June 1812 the War Hawks persuaded Congress to declare war on Britain. That same month Britain agreed to stop attacking American ships. The news did not reach

Washington, D.C., for weeks, however. By then, it was too late. The United States and Britain were at war.

The Invasion of Canada

The United States was not prepared for war. The army had only 7,000 untested soldiers, the navy only 16 ships. Nor were Americans united behind the war. Northern Federalists opposed it. In the election of 1812, Madison won a second term only by carrying the southern and western states.

The War Hawks, however, were confident that conquering Canada was "a mere matter of marching." Half a million Canadians would be no match for 8 million Americans. Besides, they said, Canadians would welcome Americans as liberators.

Rather than welcoming the Americans, however, Canadians united to push back the invaders. Tecumseh's followers joined the Canadians in this effort. Americans tried to invade Canada three times in 1812. Each attempt ended in failure.

Oliver Perry's victory The following year, Americans scored two victories in the Northwest. The first occurred on the Great Lakes, where Captain Oliver Perry had assembled a makeshift fleet of ten vessels. He then requested of his commander:

When the British nearly destroyed Oliver Perry's ship, his men rowed him to another, from which he continued the battle.

"Give me men, sir, and I will gain both for you and myself honor and glory on this lake [Erie], or perish in the attempt."

In September 1813, Perry's navy destroyed a British fleet on Lake Erie. In what is now a famous phrase, Perry reported: "We have met the enemy, and they are ours!" Perry soon controlled the Great Lakes and sent the British into retreat.

Tecumseh dies Perry's success on the Great Lakes encouraged William Henry Harrison to invade Canada with 4,500 soldiers. On October 5, 1813, they met a combined British and Indian force at the Thames [temz] River north of Lake Erie.

The Battle of the Thames ended in a victory for the United States. However, it was a disaster for the Indians of the region. Tecumseh was killed, and with him died the dream of a united Indian people. A few weeks later, the Indians of the Ohio country signed a peace treaty with Harrison.

Farther south, Indians suffered another defeat. In March 1814 American troops and Cherokees led by General Andrew Jackson crushed a Creek force at Horseshoe Bend in present-day Alabama. The Creeks were forced to give up large parts of Georgia and Alabama. The Indians' struggle to save their land and way of life seemed hopeless.

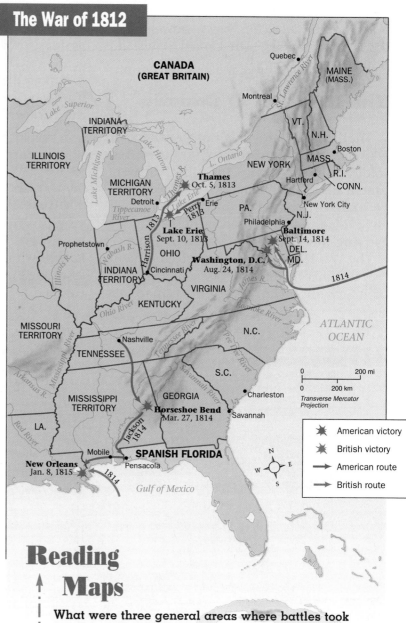

The War of 1812

CANADA (GREAT BRITAIN)

Quebec

MAINE (MASS.)

Montreal

VT.

N.H.

Boston

INDIANA TERRITORY

ILLINOIS TERRITORY

Lake Superior

Lake Michigan

Lake Huron

L. Ontario

NEW YORK

MASS.

R.I.

Hartford

CONN.

MICHIGAN TERRITORY

Detroit

Thames Oct. 5, 1813

Erie

New York City

Perry 1813

PA.

N.J.

Philadelphia

Baltimore Sept. 14, 1814

Tippecanoe River

Lake Erie Sept. 10, 1813

Prophetstown

Wabash R.

OHIO

DEL.

MD.

Illinois R.

INDIANA TERRITORY

Cincinnati

Washington, D.C. Aug. 24, 1814

1814

MISSOURI TERRITORY

Ohio River

KENTUCKY

VIRGINIA

Roanoke River

ATLANTIC OCEAN

Nashville

N.C.

TENNESSEE

Tennessee River

S.C.

Arkansas R.

Mississippi River

MISSISSIPPI TERRITORY

GEORGIA

Savannah River

Charleston

0   200 mi
0   200 km
Transverse Mercator Projection

LA.

Red River

Horseshoe Bend Mar. 27, 1814

Savannah

Jackson 1814

New Orleans Jan. 8, 1815

Mobile

SPANISH FLORIDA

Pensacola

1814

Gulf of Mexico

N

W   E

S

★ American victory

✹ British victory

→ American route

→ British route

Reading Maps

What were three general areas where battles took place during the War of 1812? Give the outcome of one battle in each area.

Britain Strikes Back

In August 1814, the British decided to bring the war to American soil by marching on Washington, D.C. When they reached the nation's capital, they set it on fire. Washington burned as the President and the United States government fled to Virginia. The British then enjoyed a splendid dinner at the President's House. After finishing their meal, they set fire to the house as well.

"The Star-Spangled Banner" Next, the British attacked nearby Baltimore, a vital port city on Chesapeake Bay. Fort McHenry guarded the entrance to Baltimore's harbor. On September 13, 1814, British warships bombed the fort all day and night. Exploding rockets cast a red glare over the harbor.

Through the night, Francis Scott Key, an American lawyer, watched the bombardment from a ship in the harbor. As dawn broke, he was thrilled to see a tattered American flag still waving above the fort. Key captured his feelings in a poem called the "The Defense of Fort McHenry." Later set to music as "The Star-Spangled Banner," it was adopted as the national anthem in 1931.

The Hartford Convention

Despite Britain's failure to take Baltimore, American hopes seemed dim in late 1814. Britain was sending more troops to North America. The federal government had no money, and the capital was burned to the ground. A visitor found President Madison looking "miserable." Congressman Daniel Webster predicted that "if peace does not come this winter, the government will die of its own weakness."

In December, New England Federalists met in Hartford, Connecticut, to discuss their opposition to President Madison and the war with the British. The Federalists proposed seven amendments to the Constitution that would give New England a stronger voice in Congress.

When delegates from the Hartford Convention arrived in Washington, though, no one paid attention to them. Instead,

people were celebrating the Battle of New Orleans and the Treaty of Ghent.

The Battle of New Orleans

While Federalists were meeting in Hartford, 5,300 experienced British troops had been preparing to attack a fortified New Orleans. The city was defended by General Andrew Jackson and a "backwoods rabble" of untrained troops, free African Americans, Indians, and a few pirates.

Some people objected to Jackson's decision to arm the 200 free African Americans—it might encourage slaves to revolt. Nonsense, replied Jackson, "the free men of color would make excellent soldiers." He insisted they be treated the same as his other troops.

On January 8, 1815, the British launched a grand assault against Jackson's army. The Americans greeted them with a storm of gunfire. The battle turned into a slaughter. At least 2,000 British were killed or wounded, while only 8 Americans died. After just half an hour, the British surrendered. One soldier described the battleground as "a sea of blood."

When news of this stunning victory reached Washington, D.C., Andrew Jackson became a national hero. The gloom that had hung over the nation for the previous few months lifted.

A New Feeling of Pride

Soon the nation received even more good news. A peace treaty had been signed two weeks before Jackson's troops defeated the British at New Orleans. Thus, the Battle of New Orleans had been unnecessary.

The Treaty of Ghent ended the war, but it did not deal with British seizure of American ships. John Quincy Adams, the American negotiator, said the agreement "settled nothing." Still, Americans were pleased to have peace, even without victory.

Peace brought with it a new spirit of **nationalism**—a strong feeling of pride in one's country. Americans were proud that their young nation had stood up against the most powerful nation in the world. Never again would Great Britain threaten the United States.

"The people," wrote Treasury Secretary Albert Gallatin, "are more American. They feel and act more as a nation." For many, this new feeling of national pride was victory enough.

3. Section Review

1. Define **nationalism.**
2. Why did the War Hawks want war with Great Britain?
3. What effect did the war in Canada have on Tecumseh's dream for the Indians?
4. **Critical Thinking** The War of 1812 involved the Americans, British, and American Indians. Who do you think lost the most? Who gained the most? Explain.

Why We Remember

The Jefferson Era

Between 1801 and 1817, the United States was led by two founders of the Republican Party, Thomas Jefferson and James Madison. For many people in the United States, the Jefferson era was a time of growth and national pride. For Indians, however, it was a time first of hope and then of defeat.

During this time, Jefferson and the Republicans tried to put their political ideas into practice. The task was not easy. They believed in strict construction of the Constitution, but they put that belief aside to buy Louisiana. They supported states' rights, yet they paid little attention to the needs of the New England states during the embargo and the War of 1812.

Looking back on this era, historians describe it as an exciting time of expansion and exploration. The Louisiana Purchase doubled the size of the young nation. Lewis and Clark, as well as Pike, began exploration of that vast region. At the same time, a flood of settlers poured into the Ohio and Mississippi Valleys.

Indians remember the Jefferson era differently. Settlers were an unwelcome threat to their homeland and way of life. In response to this danger, Tecumseh became a great Indian leader and his brother, Tenskwatawa, a prophet. For a time they brought hope to many Indians that they could live as they had always done. With the defeat at Tippecanoe and the death of Tecumseh, that hope gave way to despair. In the future, although Indians in other regions would resist expansion by settlers, no leader would again try to unite Indians from Canada to Florida.

Skill Lab

Skill Tips

To detect bias, look for:
- "loaded"—emotionally charged—words
- exaggerations
- opinions stated as if they were obvious truths
- focus on only one side of an issue
- what the person does *not* say

Thinking Critically
Detecting Bias

Americans were shocked when the British burned Washington, D.C., in 1814. Never before or since has an enemy invaded our nation's capital. As you might expect, American and British observers at the time viewed the event quite differently.

Question to Investigate

How did different people react to the burning of the nation's capital?

Procedure

To explore the question, read sources **A** and **B**. Look for evidence of **bias,** a one-sided or slanted view. Bias is related to point of view (see page 249). A person's general background can lead to a one-sided view on a topic. Study the Skill Tips and then do the following.

1 Identify clues to bias in the sources.
a. List words and phrases from source **A** that reflect bias.
b. List words and phrases from source **B** that reflect bias.

2 Describe the bias of each writer.
a. Describe the bias in source **A.**
b. Describe the bias in source **B.**

3 Consider how point of view might contribute to the bias of each writer.
a. Why do you think **A** refers to the President's "house," while **B** calls it a "palace"?
b. Why do you think the Capitol building and the President's House might mean so much to the writer of source **A**?

4 Tell what else you might do to answer the Question to Investigate.

Sources to Use

A "Those beautiful pillars in [the] Representatives' Hall were cracked and broken. The roof, that noble dome, lay in ashes.

In the President's House, not an inch but its cracked and blackened walls remained. That scene, when I last visited it, was so splendid! It was crowded with the great, the ambitious, and patriotic heroes. Now it was nothing but ashes.

Was it these ashes, now crushed underfoot, which once had the power to inflate pride? . . . Who would have thought that this mass, so magnificent, should in the space of a few hours be thus destroyed?"

From a letter by Margaret Bayard Smith, a resident of Washington, D.C.

B "You can conceive nothing finer than the sight. . . . The sky was brilliantly illumined by the different [fires]; and a dark red light was thrown upon the road, sufficient to permit each man to view his comrade's face. . . . Of the senate-house, the President's palace, the barracks, the dockyard, &c. [etc.] nothing could be seen, except heaps of smoking ruins; and even the bridge, a noble structure upwards of a mile in length, was almost wholly demolished."

From an account by George R. Glieg, a British officer who took part in the invasion

Chapter Survey

Reviewing Vocabulary

Define the following terms.
1. judicial review   3. nationalism
2. embargo

Reviewing Main Ideas

1. What is judicial review? In what case did the Supreme Court establish its power of judicial review?
2. Why did Napoleon want to sell Louisiana? Why did Jefferson want to buy it?
3. What was the main goal of the Lewis and Clark expedition? How did the expedition meet Jefferson's expectations?
4. What happened to American ships when they tried to sail to British or French ports in 1806 and 1807? Why did the British search American ships along the American coast?
5. Explain the purpose of the Embargo Act, and why it was not effective.
6. Why did the United States go to war with Britain rather than with France?
7. How did the War of 1812 affect each of the following? (a) Indians' hopes for their future (b) white Americans' feelings toward their country

Thinking Critically

1. **Analysis** How did *Marbury* v. *Madison* strengthen the constitutional principle of checks and balances?
2. **Evaluation** Choose at least three events during Jefferson's presidency. Do you see these events as failures or successes for Jefferson? Explain.
3. **Why We Remember: Analysis** Explain the following statement: The Jefferson era was a time of new opportunities for settlers, and lost opportunities for the Ohio Valley Indians. Give examples for both groups of people.

Applying Skills

Detecting bias The accounts you read on page 309 showed two different ways of looking at the burning of Washington, D.C. Think of a recent news event involving a conflict between nations or people. Find at least two articles that describe the event and that contain evidence of bias.
1. List the clues to bias that you found in each article.
2. Summarize each writer's bias.
3. Explain how each writer's background might contribute to his or her bias.

History Mystery

The unnecessary battle Answer the History Mystery on page 289. How could you find out how news traveled at that time? How might such news travel today? What role did poor communications play at the beginning of the war?

Writing in Your History Journal

1. **Keys to History** (a) The time line on pages 288–289 has seven Keys to History. In your journal, describe why each is important to know. (b) Choose three other events or people in the chapter that you would like to add to the time line and explain why.
2. **Tecumseh** The Prophet led the Indians into battle at Tippecanoe River. Tecumseh himself was not there. In your journal write what Tecumseh's thoughts might have been when he received the news about the battle.
3. **Citizenship** Imagine that you are Thomas Jefferson in the year 1808. Write a letter to James Madison explaining why you have decided

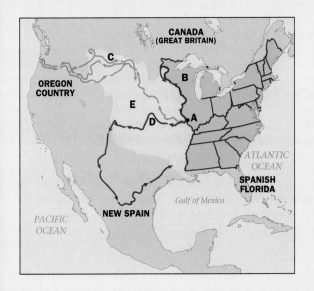

Reviewing Geography

1. The letters on the map represent two territories, two expeditions, and the starting place of the expeditions. Write the name of each.

2. Geographic Thinking Before the Louisiana Purchase, Jefferson wrote to a friend, "There is on the globe a single spot, the possessor of which is our natural and habitual enemy. It is New Orleans." Study the map on page 277. Why was New Orleans vital as a port? What alternatives would western farmers have had if Napoleon had closed New Orleans or if the British had taken it in the War of 1812? How adequate would those alternatives have been? What do Jefferson's words tell you about the importance of the West in the early 1800s?

not to run for President again and why you think he should run.

Alternative Assessment

Creating a front page It is June 1812, and Congress has just declared war on Britain. With several classmates, create the front page for tomorrow's edition of the newspaper.

First, decide where the paper is published: the North, South, or West. Then make a plan for the front page by following these guidelines:

• Every item on the page should relate to the declaration of war.

• There should be one major article plus sidebars. Sidebars are shorter articles that further explain some part of the information in the main article and are printed alongside it. One sidebar might be "Events

That Led to Declaration of War." Another might be "Local Reaction to the War."

• Your publisher wants you to include an editorial stating the publisher's opinion of the declaration of war.

When your planning is complete, write the articles and headlines and prepare some illustrations that will make the front page more interesting. For illustrations, include at least one picture, one cartoon, and one map. Lay out the front page on a large sheet of paper or poster board. Put it on the bulletin board so others can read it.

Your front page will be evaluated on the following criteria:

• it provides in-depth information about the causes of the War of 1812

• it reflects regional attitudes of the time

• it is snappy, creative, and grabs the attention of readers

The Journals of Lewis and Clark

As explorers, part of Lewis and Clark's job was to keep a record of their journey. Whenever they had a spare moment—usually at night by the campfire—the tired explorers opened their leather-bound notebooks, took out their quill pens and bottle of ink, and wrote down what they saw and did that day. When reading these passages, remember that Lewis and Clark were soldiers, not scholars. Their spelling, punctuation, and use of words look strange to us today. Still, their diaries are treasures of history.

Lewis

ferocity:
fierceness

mantle:
cape

plunder:
to rob by force

Saturday April 13th 1805. We found a number of carcases of the Buffaloe lying along shore, which had been drowned by falling through the ice in winter. We saw also many tracks of the white bear of enormous size, along the river shore and about the carcases of the Buffaloe, on which I presume they feed. We have not as yet seen one of these anamals, tho' their tracks are so abundant and recent. The men as well as ourselves are anxious to meet with some of these bear. The Indians [tell] of the strength and ferocity of this animal, which they never dare to attack but in parties of six eight or ten persons; and are even then frequently defeated with the loss of one or more of thier party.

Sunday August 11th 1805. I was overjoyed at the sight of this stranger [a Shoshone Indian]. . . . I mad[e] him the signal of friendship known to the Indians of the Rocky mountains and those of the Missouri, which is by holding the mantle or robe in your hands at two corners then th[r]owing [it] up in the air higher than the head bringing it to the earth as if in the act of spreading it, thus repeating three times. . . . He did not remain untill I got nearer than about 100 paces when he suddonly turned his ho[r]se about, gave him the whip leaped the creek and disapeared in the willow brush in an instant and with him vanished all my hopes of obtaining horses for the preasent.

Tuesday August 20th 1805. I can discover that these people are by no means friendly to the Spaniards. Their complaint is, that the Spaniards will not let them have fire arms and amunition. . . . Their bloodthirsty neighbours to the east of them, being in possession of fire arms, hunt them up and murder them without rispect to sex or age and plunder them of their horses on all occasions. They told me that to avoid their

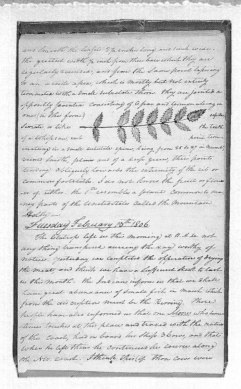

This page from William Clark's journal shows his detailed description of an evergreen shrub.

enemies . . . they were obliged to remain in the interior of these mountains . . . sometimes living for weeks without meat and only a little fish roots and berries. But this, added Câmeahwait, with his ferce eyes and lank jaws grown meager for the want of food, would not be the case if we had guns. We could then live in the country of buffaloe and eat as our enimies do and not be compelled to hide ourselves in these mountains and live on roots and berries as the bear do.

meager: thin

compelled: forced

Clark

Wednesday [Sunday] Septr. 15th 1805. Several horses sliped and roled down steep hills which hurt them verry much. The one which carried my desk & small trunk turned over & roled down a mountain for 40 yards & lodged against a tree, broke the desk the horse escaped and appeared but little hurt. When we arrived at the top, we could find no water and concluded to camp and make use of the snow we found on the top to make our supe.

Wed 17th Sept 1806. At 11 A.M. we met a Captin McClellin assending in a large boat. This gentleman was somewhat astonished to see us return and appeared rejoiced to meet us. We found him a man of information and from whome we received a partial account of the political state of our country. We were makeing enquires and exchangeing answers untill near midnight. This gentleman informed us that we had been long since given [up] by the people of the U S generaly and almost forgotton. The president of the U. States had yet hopes of us.

A Closer Look

1. What were some of the challenges and dangers Lewis and Clark faced?

2. What seems to be the attitude of the explorers toward the new things they are seeing? What words give you these clues?

3. What did the explorers learn about what some Indians thought of the Spanish? Why might this be useful to Americans?

From *Original Journals of the Lewis and Clark Expedition, 1804–1806*, edited by Reuben Gold Thwaites. New York: Arno Press, 1969.

Chapter *12*

The Confident Years

Keys to History

1790
Samuel Slater builds the first spinning mill

1793
Eli Whitney's cotton gin

1790

1800

Looking Back

Slavery banned in Northwest Territory
1787

HISTORY
Mystery

In 1830 hundreds of Americans gathered to watch a race between two trains. Why did the train that lost the race turn out to be the real winner?

1807
First voyage of the *Clermont*

1817–1825
Era of Good Feelings

1820
Missouri Compromise
Congress permits expansion of slavery

1823
Monroe Doctrine
President James Monroe

1825
Opening of the Erie Canal

1810

1820

1830

World Link

Looking Ahead

Russia claims much of Pacific Northwest
1821

Strike by Lowell millworkers
1836

● **315**

Beginning the Story with

The Mill Girls

When the mill girls, as they were called, felt overworked, underpaid, or just plain homesick, they sang:

"Oh, isn't it a pity that such a pretty girl as I
Should be sent to the factory to pine away and die?**"**

Going to work in the cotton mills of New England was hardly a death sentence, though. Most young women worked for only three or four years before returning home or leaving to get married.

The Lure of Millwork

The opportunity for women to become millworkers came about when a group of businessmen called the Boston Associates opened the first of many cotton mills in Massachusetts in 1815. They offered to pay New England farm girls up to three dollars a week. This pay was six times what a woman working as a teacher or a servant might make. The Boston Associates knew, though, that men would demand twice as much money for the same jobs.

To convince farm families to let their daughters live and work away from home, the mill owners built boarding houses and assured nervous parents that their daughters would live under the watchful eyes of "respectable women." They also promised to make "every provision for religious worship."

"Another Pay Day"

Most young women found working in the mills both an adventure and a trial. Few had ever been away from home before. Many liked the independence of living in a boarding house—even with six boarders in a room, sleeping three

In mills owned by the Boston Associates, raw cotton was spun into thread. Then the thread was woven into cloth on power looms. This picture shows mill girls operating the machines that wound the thread onto huge bobbins, or spools, for weaving.

to a bed. One girl wrote home bragging, "I don't even have my bed to make. Quite a lady, to be sure."

Compared to farm chores, millwork was not hard. The hours, however, were long. Harriet Farley described her workday:

> "We go in at five o'clock; at seven we come out to breakfast; at half-past seven we return to our work, and stay until half-past twelve. At one . . . we return to our work, and stay until seven at night. Then the evening is all our own."

Millwork also offered young women a chance to exchange the isolation of farm life for city life. During their evenings, many mill girls in Lowell, Massachusetts, took classes, went to concerts, and read books from the library. Some even wrote and published their own magazine, the *Lowell Offering.*

Then as now, though, the best day was payday. Being paid for their work was a new experience for most young women. So was having money of their own. A New Hampshire mill girl wrote to her sister:

> "Since I have wrote you, another pay day has come around. I earned 14 dollars and a half, nine and a half dollars beside my board [payment for a room and meals]. . . . I like it well as ever and Sarah don't I feel independent of everyone! The thought that I am living on no one is a happy one indeed to me."

The mill girls were not the only Americans to face new experiences in the years after the War of 1812. New technology and the growth of industry were changing the way Americans lived.

Hands-On HISTORY

Activity

Imagine that you are a 15-year-old living on a New England farm in 1817. You and your parents have seen an ad seeking young women to work in a cotton mill. Create a dialogue between you and your parents about whether you should take a job as a millworker.

1. A Revolution in Industry

Reading Guide

New Terms **Industrial Revolution, mass production, protective tariff**

Section Focus **New technology that began to change the way Americans lived**

1. How did the Industrial Revolution change the way goods were produced?
2. Why was the invention of the cotton gin important to southern farmers?
3. How did the federal government help American business grow?

Few of the young women who first went to work in the cotton mills knew it, but their work was helping bring to reality the dreams of three enterprising men. The first was a mechanic with an amazing memory. The second was a tinkerer who loved inventing things. The third was a merchant blessed with both brains and money. These three men were creating a revolution in industry in the United States.

Slater's Spinning Mill

The mechanic—Samuel Slater—came to the United States from England in 1789. At that time, almost all of the goods Americans needed were made by hand, either at home or in small workshops.

This way of producing goods had existed in England, too, until the mid-1700s. Then English mechanics invented the spinning

The Blackstone River supplied the power for Samuel Slater's first spinning mill. Slater hired families, including children as young as 8, to turn cotton into thread. Weavers working at home wove the thread into cloth.

Two machines were vital in cotton production. Cotton gins, like these in the picture, removed the seeds. Then huge presses packed the ginned cotton into bales for easier transport to market.

jenny, a machine that could spin wool or cotton fiber into thread. The new machine was powered by water turning a water wheel. For this reason, spinning mills, or factories, were built beside fast-flowing rivers.

The spinning jenny began a revolution in the way goods were produced. This shift of production from hand tools to machines and from homes to factories is known as the **Industrial Revolution.**

The first American mill The British wanted to keep the spinning jenny their secret. They would not allow drawings of the machines, or people who used the machines, to leave the country.

Samuel Slater got around this restriction by memorizing every detail of a spinning jenny. Then he sailed to the United States disguised as a farm worker. Once there, Slater teamed up with merchant Moses Brown to turn his memories into machines. In 1790 they built the nation's first spinning mill at Pawtucket, Rhode Island. The Industrial Revolution in the United States had begun.

Whitney's Cotton Gin

By 1815 Slater had helped to build 20 spinning mills. As the number of mills multiplied, so did the demand for cotton. Finding enough cotton could have been a problem had it not been for a Massachusetts inventor named Eli Whitney.

In 1792 Whitney traveled to Georgia. At that time, southerners were facing hard times. Prices for their cash crops—tobacco, rice, and indigo—were so low that it hardly paid to plant them. As they planted less, their demand for slave labor declined. It seemed that slavery might soon die out.

While visiting a plantation, Whitney saw slaves picking seeds out of raw cotton. It was such slow work, planters said, that they could not make a profit growing cotton. As Whitney later recalled:

❝All agreed that if a machine could be invented that would clean the cotton with expedition [speed], it would be a great thing . . . to the country.❞

In 1793 Whitney invented just such a machine. His cotton engine, known as a "gin," cleaned 50 times as much cotton in a day as a worker could by hand. Planters now had what they wanted most—a profitable cash crop.

The cotton kingdom Cotton production soared, and with it a renewed demand for slaves to do the work. Soon ambitious southerners were moving westward, looking for new land to plant in cotton. They took their slaves west with them or bought slaves from traders. Instead of dying out, slavery became an important part of what became known as the "cotton kingdom."

Lowell's Cotton Mill

In 1810 a Boston merchant named Francis Cabot Lowell went to England for a vacation. There he took a close look at a new English invention, the power loom. This machine wove thread into cloth much faster than any hand weaver could.

Lowell returned to Boston with the loom's design in his head. In 1815 he and his partners, the Boston Associates, opened a cotton mill on the Merrimack River in Waltham, Massachusetts. It was the first American mill that did both spinning and weaving under one roof. As one observer said, the mill

"took your bale of cotton in at one end and gave out yards of cloth at the other, after goodness knows what digestive process."

Lowell needed more than new technology to succeed. He also needed a steady supply of workers. He solved this problem by hiring young women from the New England countryside. Many were happy to become mill girls, trading unpaid farm work for a job with real wages.

Lowell died in 1817, but the success of his mill convinced the Boston Associates to expand. Soon they opened a second and larger cotton mill in a new town they called Lowell. By 1855 there were 52 cotton mills on the Merrimack River, all patterned after the cotton mill that Francis Cabot Lowell had opened in 1815.

Mass Production

The cotton gin was not the only contribution Eli Whitney made to the Industrial Revolution. He was also a pioneer in **mass production**—using machines to make large quantities of goods faster and cheaper than they could be made by hand.

In 1798 Whitney opened a factory to make muskets for the United States Army. Before that time, muskets had been made by skilled gunsmiths who painstakingly shaped and fitted together the parts. Whitney's machines turned out interchangeable parts. For example, every trigger was exactly the same and could be used in any musket.

In his factory each worker had just one or two simple tasks to do. Thus Whitney could hire less-skilled workers who could produce muskets faster and at lower cost. Workers could take little pride in such jobs, though. The work was boring and required little training or skill.

Whitney's methods were widely copied by other businesses. Slowly but surely, crafting products by hand at home gave way to mass production in factories. In time, factories would produce everything from clocks and clothing to shoes and shovels.

The city of Lowell, Massachusetts, grew up around the water-driven cotton mills on the Merrimack River. Today the mills have been restored in a part of the city that the United States government has made into a national historic park.

The American System

Pleased with the rise of new industries, President Madison called on Congress to help American business grow and compete in the world. In response, Representatives Henry Clay and John C. Calhoun shaped a package of bills they called the American System. There was something in the package, they promised, to meet the needs of every section of the country.

A new national bank The first part of the American System was the creation of a new national bank. The charter for the first bank had ended in 1811 and was not renewed. In 1816 Congress set up a new Bank of the United States with a 20-year charter. This part of the package appealed mostly to northern businesspeople, who wanted bank loans for building industries and merchant ships.

A protective tariff The second part of the American System was a **protective tariff**—a tax placed on imported goods. The tariff would protect American manufacturers. By making imported goods more expensive, it would encourage people to buy American-made goods.

Southerners, who had little manufacturing to protect, opposed the tariff. Still, after a heated debate, Congress passed the nation's first protective tariff in 1816.

Internal improvements The American System also included a bill to fund an improved transportation system—called "internal improvements." In introducing this bill, Calhoun called on Congress to unite the growing nation. "Let us bind the republic together," he said, "with a perfect system of roads and canals."

Congress passed the internal improvements bill, but President Madison vetoed it. He felt the Constitution needed to be amended to give Congress the power to act in this area. Even without federal funds, though, the United States was beginning a transportation revolution.

1. Section Review

1. Define **Industrial Revolution, mass production,** and **protective tariff.**
2. Compare the way that goods were made before and after the Industrial Revolution.
3. What did Congress do to encourage Americans to buy American-made goods?
4. Critical Thinking What was the relationship between the cotton gin and the cotton kingdom?

2. New Forms of Transportation

Reading Guide

Section Focus **New transportation that linked the nation together**

1. How did new roads and riverboats improve transportation?
2. What triggered canal building in the 1820s?
3. How did the railroad era in the United States begin?

For many mill girls, the adventure of leaving home to go to work began with the journey to Lowell, Massachusetts. If they made the trip by sled in winter, snow made bumpy roads fairly smooth. Winter travelers, however, faced the risk of being stranded midway through their journey by a sudden thaw.

Those who traveled in warmer seasons faced other hazards. In dry weather, the roads were dusty and deeply rutted. Girls traveling to Lowell by stagecoach arrived shaken and covered with grime. When it rained, they were lucky to arrive at all. Wet weather turned unpaved roads into swamps in which a horse could sink up to its belly.

The National Road

In fact, in the early 1800s good roads were hard to find anywhere in the United States. The few that existed were usually turnpikes—roads built by private companies that charged travelers a fee known as a toll.

In 1806 Congress had voted funds to build a road across the Appalachian Mountains. The purpose of this highway was to tie the new western states to the rest of the country. By 1818 the National Road stretched from Baltimore to the town of Wheeling on the Ohio River.

Compared with most roads, the National Road was a joy to travel. It was paved with layers of crushed rock and gravel. Stone bridges spanned streams along its route. It

was still dotted with tree stumps, but according to one report they had been "rounded and trimmed so as to present no serious obstacles to carriages." So many people used the National Road that one traveler observed:

"Old America seems to be breaking up and moving westward. We are seldom out of sight, as we travel on this grand track, towards the Ohio, of family groups before and behind us."

As popular as the National Road was, though, Madison's veto of internal improvements (see page 321) meant that there would be no other roads like it for some time.

Rivers and Steamboats

Since colonial times, Americans had used their rivers as highways. Traveling by water was faster and cheaper than by land, at least when floating downstream. Moving upstream against a swift current was another matter.

River travel was revolutionized by an inventor named Robert Fulton. In 1807 Fulton connected a steam engine to two huge paddle wheels mounted on a raft. He named his new steam-powered riverboat the *Clermont*. Onlookers called it "Fulton's Folly."

Fulton tested his odd-looking "furnace on a raft" on the Hudson River. When he fired up the engine, it showered him with sparks and soot. Then, to almost everyone's

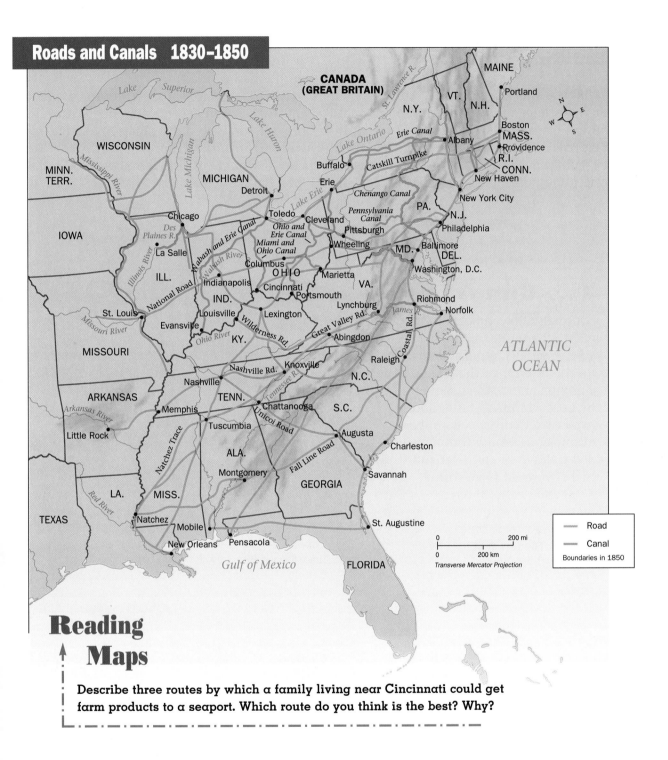

Roads and Canals 1830–1850

CANADA (GREAT BRITAIN)

MAINE

• Portland

VT. N.H.

N.Y.

Boston
• MASS.
Albany • • Providence
R.I.
CONN.
New Haven

Erie Canal

Catskill Turnpike

Buffalo

Erie

New York City

Chenango Canal

PA. N.J.

Pennsylvania Canal

Philadelphia

Pittsburgh

MD. Baltimore
DEL.

Wheeling

Washington, D.C.

Ohio and Erie Canal

Miami and Ohio Canal

Cleveland

Toledo

Detroit

Columbus

OHIO

Marietta

VA.

Indianapolis

Cincinnati

Portsmouth

Lynchburg

Richmond

Norfolk

James R.

IND.

Louisville

Lexington

Great Valley Rd.

Abingdon

Wilderness Rd.

KY.

Evansville

Ohio River

Coastal Rd.

ATLANTIC OCEAN

Chicago

La Salle

ILL.

National Road

Wabash and Erie Canal

Wabash River

Des Plaines R.

Illinois River

IOWA

Mississippi River

WISCONSIN

Lake Michigan

Lake Huron

Lake Superior

Lake Ontario

Lake Erie

St. Lawrence R.

MINN. TERR.

MICHIGAN

Missouri River

MISSOURI

St. Louis

Nashville Rd.

Knoxville

Raleigh

N.C.

Memphis

Nashville

TENN.

Chattanooga

S.C.

ARKANSAS

Arkansas River

Little Rock

Natchez Trace

Tuscumbia

Unicoi Road

Augusta

Charleston

ALA.

Montgomery

Fall Line Road

GEORGIA

Savannah

Tennessee R.

LA.

MISS.

Natchez

Red River

Mobile

New Orleans

Pensacola

St. Augustine

Gulf of Mexico

FLORIDA

0   200 mi
0   200 km
Transverse Mercator Projection

—— Road
—— Canal
Boundaries in 1850

Reading Maps

Describe three routes by which a family living near Cincinnati could get farm products to a seaport. Which route do you think is the best? Why?

amazement, the *Clermont* began to move. Before long, it was chugging up the Hudson at almost 5 miles (8 km) per hour.

Fulton wrote of that momentous day, "I overtook many boats and passed them as if they had been at anchor. The power of the steamboat is now fully proved." By the 1820s smoke-belching steamboats were hauling passengers and freight up and down eastern and western rivers and across the Great Lakes.

Building Canals

"Rivers are ungovernable things," Ben Franklin once wrote. "Canals are quiet and always manageable." Canals had two advantages over rivers and roads. First, they could be built where rivers did not run. Second, one mule pulling a canal boat could haul as much freight as 50 horses or mules could on the best of roads.

In 1817 the New York governor, DeWitt Clinton, convinced his state legislature to provide funds to dig a canal 40 feet (12 m) wide to link the Hudson River and Lake Erie. It would cut through about 360 miles (580 km) of wilderness.

∞ Link to Technology

The Canal Lock

Canals allowed boats to move through what otherwise would have been impassable waterfalls, rapids, or shallows, opening up the interior of the United States to shipping and trading. Sending freight by boat was much faster and less expensive than by wagon. For example, to send a ton of freight 360 miles (580 km) overland in 1825 would have cost $100 and taken 20 days. By canal, the same load would have cost only $10, and taken just 8 days.

Upstream water level

Upstream gates closed

Securing pos

Valves open

Upstream gates closed

Downstream gates open

Downstream water level

When finished in 1825, the Erie Canal created an all-water route from New York City to the Great Lakes. For the first time farmers in the Old Northwest had a good way to ship their crops to eastern cities.

The Erie Canal was an instant success. It cut the cost and time of hauling freight from Lake Erie to New York City. It also pro-vided an inexpensive way for people to move into present-day Michigan. Canal traffic was so heavy that "Clinton's Big Ditch" paid for itself in just nine years.

The success of the Erie Canal spurred other canal projects. Within a few years all kinds of goods were moving from town to town on a growing network of canals.

How a Boat Moves Upstream Through a Lock

1 The water in the lock is lowered to the downstream level by draining water from the downstream end. The boat enters the lock.

2 Once the gates are closed behind the boat, the boat is fastened to securing posts and valves open on the upstream end. The water level in the lock rises to the upstream level.

3 The upstream gates are opened, and the boat passes out of the lock.

The process is reversed for a boat traveling downstream.

In this sketch, excited passengers cheer the moment when *Tom Thumb* overtook and passed the horse-drawn car. Although the steam engine did not win, it showed the potential of steam power over horse power.

Travel on Rails

It turned out, however, that the future of transportation lay not on water but on rails. Like canals, rails could go where rivers did not run. Laying rails was far cheaper than digging canals, though, and rails did not freeze up in wintertime.

The first railroads used horses to pull a train of wagons on rails over short distances. Then in 1827 a group of Baltimore business leaders decided to build a much longer railroad across the Appalachians to the Ohio Valley. They hoped a railroad would bring western business to Baltimore.

The owners of the Baltimore and Ohio Railroad planned to use horses to pull the trains over the mountains. Mechanic Peter Cooper, however, had a better idea.

Tom Thumb In 1830 Cooper mounted a small steam engine on a wagon to create an "iron horse." The engine, called *Tom Thumb*, reached the amazing speed of 18 miles (29 km) an hour, three times the top speed of a horse-drawn train.

Local stagecoach companies did not want to compete with steam engines. They organized a race to prove that a horse could outrun any "teakettle on a truck."

Hundreds of onlookers gathered outside Baltimore to watch the race. The horse got off to a faster start. *Tom Thumb* gained speed slowly, but soon, according to one witness, "the race was neck and neck, nose and nose—then the engine passed the horse." Sudenly, the engine began to wheeze, and the horse galloped to victory.

Still, Cooper was the real winner that day. He had proved that steam engines could move faster than horses and haul heavier loads. Within months of *Tom Thumb*'s defeat, steam railroad companies had begun laying track in several states. The railroad era in the United States had begun.

 ## 2. Section Review

1. Why did the invention of the steamboat increase river travel?

2. What made the Erie Canal so useful to western farmers?

3. Critical Thinking Many people predicted that railroads would be the fastest and least expensive way to move goods throughout the nation. Give three facts they could have used to support that prediction.

Geography Lab

Steamboats and Westward Expansion

In September 1811 the steamboat *New Orleans* set out from Pittsburgh with a crew of 12 and 3 passengers—Nicholas Roosevelt, his wife, and the family dog. They steamed down the Ohio River and then the Mississippi. The boat survived rapids, an earthquake, and an Indian attack before reaching New Orleans in January 1812. It was the first steamboat on western waters.

Other steamboats followed, bringing people west. In 1835 a St. Louis newspaper reported, "Every steamboat that arrives at our wharves is crowded with passengers. . . . Many of these remain with us."

Steamboats in the West

Year	Number of boats
1817	17
1820	69
1830	187
1840	536
1850	740
1860	735

Source: Louis C. Hunter, *Steamboats on the Western Rivers*

Population 1810–1860

Year	St. Louis	New Orleans
1810	—*	17,242
1820	—*	27,176
1830	4,977	46,082
1840	16,469	102,193
1850	77,860	116,375
1860	160,773	168,675

*No figures available before 1830

Source: John L. Andriot, *Population Abstract of the United States*

Herman Melville's Trip on the Mississippi

Herman Melville wrote this description of his fellow steamboat passengers: "[There were] natives of all sorts, and foreigners; men of business and men of pleasure; parlor men and backwoodsmen; farm-hunters and fame-hunters, heiress-hunters, gold-hunters, buffalo-hunters. . . . Fine ladies in slippers, and moccasined [Indian women]; northern speculators and eastern philosophers; English, Irish, German, Scotch, Danes; Santa Fe traders in striped blankets . . . [and] Mississippi cotton planters; Quakers in full drab, . . . slaves . . . and young Spanish creoles."

Link to History

Use the quotations and tables to draw conclusions about how steamboat travel affected westward expansion.

1. Name three types of people who were traveling west with Melville. Speculate about where they were headed, and why.

2. How did St. Louis and New Orleans change between 1810 and 1860? What is the connection between that change and the change in steamboats?

3. Write a sentence summarizing how steamboats affected westward expansion.

4. **Hands-On Geography** Imagine that you are a Boston newspaper reporter in 1830. You have just completed a steamboat trip from New Orleans to St. Louis. Write a short article describing what you have seen.

3. A Bold Foreign Policy

Reading Guide

New Term **immigration**

Section Focus **The new directions in foreign policy set by James Monroe and John Quincy Adams**

1. How did the United States improve its relations with Great Britain?
2. How did Florida become part of the United States?
3. What was the purpose of the Monroe Doctrine?

The tradition of Republican Presidents from Virginia continued in 1816 with the election of James Monroe. Compared with Jefferson and Madison, Monroe was not a great leader or thinker, but he was admired for his long service to the party. Fortunately, he was wise enough to appoint the best people he could find to his cabinet.

Monroe's most brilliant choice was John Quincy Adams to be Secretary of State. The son of John and Abigail Adams, John Quincy had served as the nation's ambassador to four European countries. He had also helped to negotiate the peace treaty ending the War of 1812. As Secretary of State, Adams shaped a bold foreign policy that would guide the United States in world affairs for the century to come.

Agreement with Britain

The first goal of Adams's foreign policy was to make a lasting peace with Britain. Adams knew that the Treaty of Ghent had not settled the disputes that led to the War of 1812 (see page 307). He was determined to build a new relationship with Britain based on cooperation, not conflict.

Adams improved relations with Britain by settling old boundary issues. In a treaty known as the Convention of 1818, the border between Canada and the Louisiana Purchase was fixed at the 49th parallel (see the map on page 330). The United States and Britain also agreed to share Oregon Country in the Pacific Northwest.

Canadian suspicions Despite this agreement, Canadians remained suspicious of the United States. In 1775 and again in 1812, Americans had invaded Canada. No treaty could ease Canadians' deep distrust of their southern neighbor.

After the War of 1812, the British government encouraged immigration to Canada. **Immigration** is the movement of people from one country to make their home in another. Settlers poured into Canada from England, Scotland, and Ireland.

Immigrants from the United States were not so welcome. Americans moving to certain areas in Canada could not buy land until they had lived there for seven years. Still, some Americans did settle in Canada, especially African Americans fleeing slavery and prejudice in the United States.

Takeover of Florida

The second goal of Adams's policy was to acquire the Spanish colony of Florida. Over the years, Spain's hold on Florida had grown weak. When farmers in Georgia complained

The War of Independence Since the time of the Mayas, Mexican artists have been creating murals, or wall paintings, to tell the history of their people. The scene at right is part of a huge mural in the National Museum of History in Mexico City. Painted by Juan O'Gorman in 1960 and 1961, the mural tells the story of the Mexican War of Independence. In this detail Father Miguel Hidalgo (center) calls for revolt against Spanish rule.

Discuss What words would you use to describe the people in the mural? Based on this scene, why do you think murals are called "the people's art"?

about raids by Seminole Indians and escaped slaves who lived with the Seminoles in Florida, Spain could do little to halt the attacks. In 1818 Monroe called on Andrew Jackson—the hero of the Battle of New Orleans—to stop the raids.

General Jackson marched 3,000 troops into Florida to track down the raiders. Once there, he pursued the Seminoles, destroyed their villages, and executed two chiefs. He also went beyond his orders and seized two Spanish military posts. Spain protested and demanded that Jackson be punished for disobeying orders.

Adams-Onís Treaty Instead, Adams sent Spain this message: Get control of Florida or get out. Spain, faced with problems in its Latin American colonies, decided to get out. In the 1819 Adams-Onís Treaty, Spain ceded Florida to the United States and gave up its claim on Oregon Country.

New Latin American Nations

Meanwhile, revolution was sweeping Latin America. Colonists from Mexico to Argentina fought to throw off Spanish rule. Spain wanted Adams to promise not to recognize the independence of its rebelling colonies. Adams refused to make that promise.

Mexico wins independence In Mexico the drive for independence was inspired by a priest named Miguel Hidalgo (mee-GEL ee-DAHL-gō). In 1810 the priest cried out to his people, "My children, when will you recover lands stolen from your ancestors 300 years ago by the hated Spaniards?"

Hidalgo was put to death by the Spanish, but his speech touched off a revolution that lasted ten long years. In 1821 Mexico won its independence. Three years later, it became a republic with an elected president.

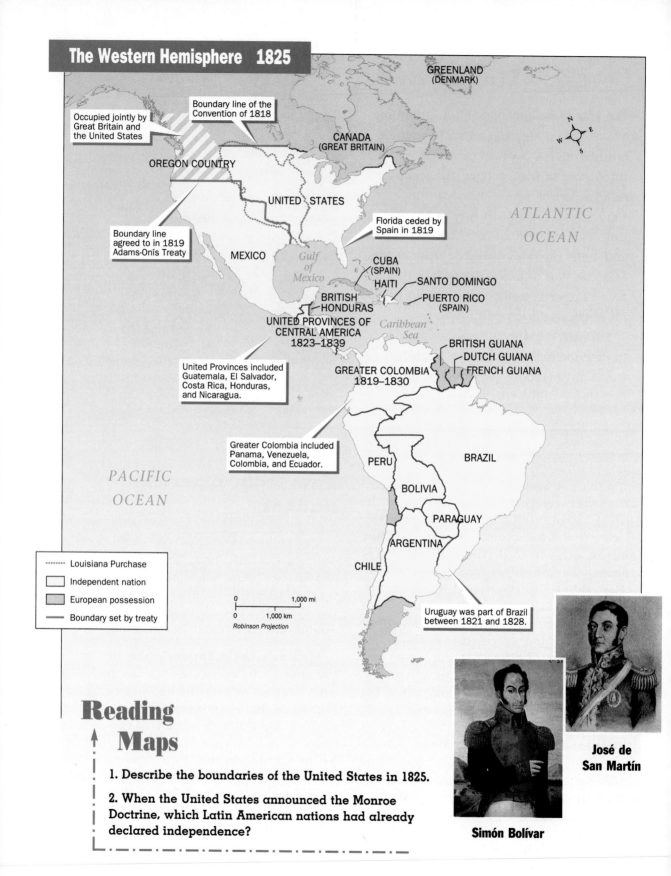

The Western Hemisphere 1825

GREENLAND (DENMARK)

Boundary line of the Convention of 1818

Occupied jointly by Great Britain and the United States

OREGON COUNTRY

CANADA (GREAT BRITAIN)

UNITED STATES

Boundary line agreed to in 1819 Adams-Onís Treaty

Florida ceded by Spain in 1819

ATLANTIC OCEAN

MEXICO

Gulf of Mexico

CUBA (SPAIN)

HAITI   SANTO DOMINGO

PUERTO RICO (SPAIN)

BRITISH HONDURAS

UNITED PROVINCES OF CENTRAL AMERICA 1823–1839

Caribbean Sea

United Provinces included Guatemala, El Salvador, Costa Rica, Honduras, and Nicaragua.

GREATER COLOMBIA 1819–1830

BRITISH GUIANA
DUTCH GUIANA
FRENCH GUIANA

Greater Colombia included Panama, Venezuela, Colombia, and Ecuador.

PERU

BRAZIL

BOLIVIA

PARAGUAY

ARGENTINA

CHILE

PACIFIC OCEAN

Uruguay was part of Brazil between 1821 and 1828.

- ········· Louisiana Purchase
- ☐ Independent nation
- ☐ European possession
- — Boundary set by treaty

| 0 | 1,000 mi |
| 0 | 1,000 km |

Robinson Projection

José de San Martín

Simón Bolívar

Reading Maps

1. Describe the boundaries of the United States in 1825.

2. When the United States announced the Monroe Doctrine, which Latin American nations had already declared independence?

World Link

Russia claims much of Pacific Northwest

Startling news reached Secretary of State John Quincy Adams in 1821. Russia had claimed a stretch of the Pacific Northwest from the Bering Strait south to Oregon Country—land already claimed by both the United States and Britain.

Since 1741 a colony of Russians in Alaska had been trading with the Indians for furs. In 1812 they moved south into Spanish California, where they established a trading post called Fort Ross, north of San Francisco.

Angered by Russia's new claim, Adams warned that "the American continents are no longer subjects for *any* new European colonial establishments." In 1824 Russia canceled its claim on Oregon Country.

Independence for South America

Two great leaders freed South America from Spanish rule. In 1810 General Simón Bolívar (see-MŌN bō-LEE-vahr), a Venezuelan, launched a revolution in northern South America. By 1819 Bolívar had liberated Venezuela, Colombia, Panama, Ecuador, and part of Peru.

An Argentine general, José de San Martín (hō-SAY day SAHN-mahr-TEEN), led the struggle for independence in southern South America. After freeing Argentina, Uruguay, and Paraguay, San Martín drove Spain out of Chile.

The liberation of South America from Spanish rule was completed in 1824. That year Bolívar's forces defeated a Spanish army in Peru, and the last Spanish troops left South America.

The Monroe Doctrine

Both the United States and Great Britain supported the Latin American revolutions. The monarchs of Europe did not. They were alarmed by the spread of democracy. Some, especially the rulers of France and Russia, began to talk of helping Spain recover its lost colonies.

In 1823 Britain asked the United States to join it in sending a message to Spain, France, and Russia. The message would warn them to leave Latin America alone. Adams, however, argued that the United States should speak for itself. President Monroe agreed. He asked Adams to draft an American statement on the subject.

In 1823 President Monroe issued that statement, which became known as the Monroe Doctrine. The Americas, he said, were closed to "future colonization by any European powers." He warned Europe not to interfere with the new nations of Latin America "for the purpose of oppressing them, or controlling . . . their destiny." In return, he promised, the United States would stay out of Europe's affairs.

Most people in the United States liked Monroe's message that the Americas were for Americans. In the years ahead, the Monroe Doctrine would remain a pillar of the nation's foreign policy.

3. Section Review

1. Define **immigration**.
2. What agreement did the United States and Britain make about Oregon Country?
3. How did the United States solve the problems between Georgia and the Spanish colony of Florida?
4. **Critical Thinking** How did events in Latin America and in Europe lead to the Monroe Doctrine?

4. Strains on National Unity

Reading Guide

New Terms **financial panic, sectionalism**

Section Focus **The events that tested Americans' spirit of unity after the War of 1812**

1. Why was there an "era of good feelings" after the War of 1812?
2. What led to the Panic of 1819?
3. How did the issue of statehood for Missouri threaten national unity?

At his first inauguration in 1817, President Monroe spoke not as a Republican or a Virginian. He spoke as an American filled with pride in his country, saying:

"If we look to the history of other nations, we find no example of a growth so rapid, so gigantic, of a people so prosperous and happy. . . . How near our government has approached to perfection."

The Era of Good Feelings

After taking office, the Republican Monroe toured New England, the stronghold of the Federalist Party. Even there, however, Americans had turned away from the Federalists for failing to support the War of 1812. Wherever Monroe went, he was greeted by thousands of people lining the streets to cheer him. One newspaper reported:

"The visit of the President seems to have wholly allayed [calmed] the storms of party. People now meet in the same room who, a short while since, would scarcely pass along the same street."

So many New Englanders turned out to greet Monroe that a Boston newspaper reported the beginning of "the era of good feelings."

These good feelings were to assure Monroe of easy re-election in 1820. By then, however, new problems were arising to threaten national unity.

The Panic of 1819

The good feelings were sorely tested when the nation was hit by a financial panic in 1819. A **financial panic** is widespread fear caused by a sudden downturn in prices or change in property values.

After the War of 1812, prices for American farm products in Europe had risen sharply. Happy farmers rushed out to buy more land on which to plant cash crops. As a result, land prices soared.

State banks fueled the boom by loaning money to almost anyone who needed cash to buy land. The Bank of the United States, too, loaned large sums to land buyers. For a time, everyone seemed to be making money in land deals.

Boom to bust The boom went bust in 1819 when crop prices overseas dropped like a stone. Cotton, which had soared to 33¢ a pound, fell to 14¢. Suddenly, many farmers could not pay their debts. They risked being sent to debtors' prisons, where they would remain until friends or relatives paid the debts.

In the Monroe era—as today—Congress often met in the evening. This painting shows a debate that took place in the Capitol, newly rebuilt after being burned in the War of 1812. Pawnee chief Petalesharro, a visitor to Washington, watches from an upper gallery.

In the next three years, the panic spread from farms to towns and cities. Many shops and factories failed, and thousands of workers lost their jobs. Citizens of a hard-hit Pennsylvania town sent a petition to Congress asking for help. They reported:

"The larger part of the people . . . can hardly obtain the very necessaries [essentials] of life. . . . Debts are unpaid, creditors dissatisfied, and the jails full of honest but unfortunate persons whose wives and children have thereby become a burden on the township.**"**

The Bank of the United States made a bad situation worse by taking over the property of borrowers who could not pay their debts. Thousands of people lost their farms, homes, and businesses to the bank. As a result, wrote one observer, "the bank was saved and the people were ruined."

The Expansion of Slavery

An even heavier blow to the Era of Good Feelings fell when controversy over slavery flared up in Congress. The issue was whether to permit slavery to expand into the new states that were being formed out of the Louisiana Purchase.

The Northwest Ordinance of 1787 had set out the steps for forming new states (see page 236). It had also banned slavery in the Northwest Territory. Thus, the new states of Ohio, Indiana, and Illinois were "free states"—states where slavery was not permitted. New states south of the Northwest Territory—Kentucky, Tennessee, Louisiana, Mississippi, and Alabama—allowed slavery.

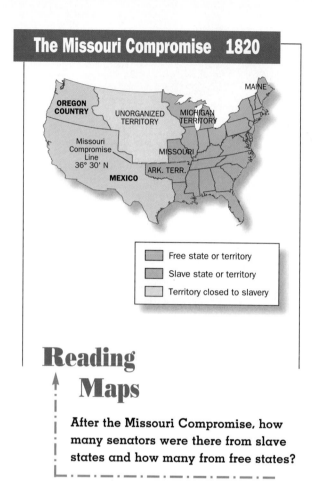

The Missouri Compromise 1820

Legend:
- Free state or territory
- Slave state or territory
- Territory closed to slavery

Map labels: OREGON COUNTRY, UNORGANIZED TERRITORY, MICHIGAN TERRITORY, MAINE, Missouri Compromise Line 36° 30' N, MISSOURI, ARK. TERR., MEXICO

Reading Maps

After the Missouri Compromise, how many senators were there from slave states and how many from free states?

Early in 1819 Missouri Territory—part of the Louisiana Purchase—asked to join the Union as a "slave state." By then, every state north of Delaware had taken action to end slavery. Part of Missouri lay as far north as many of these free states.

The Tallmadge Amendment Northerners in Congress wanted to keep slavery from spreading. Many thought slavery was wrong. In addition, they feared that representatives from new slave states would increase the power of the southern states in the House and the Senate. Senator Rufus King of New York put the matter bluntly:

"If slavery be permitted in Missouri, . . . what hope can be entertained [kept] that it will ever be prohibited in any of the new states that will be formed in the immense region west of the Mississippi?"

Thus, when the bill to make Missouri a state came before Congress in February 1819, northerners reacted quickly. Representative James Tallmadge of New York introduced an amendment to the bill that called for an end to slavery in Missouri.

Southerners in Congress greeted the Tallmadge Amendment with a roar of protest. What constitutional power, they asked, did Congress have to decide whether a state should be slave or free? That choice belonged to the people of each state. Besides, if Congress were allowed to meddle with slavery in Missouri, might it not try to abolish slavery elsewhere?

The Tallmadge Amendment was approved by the House of Representatives. There the North, with its greater population, had a majority. In the Senate, however, the North and the South had the same number of votes, and southerners blocked the amendment. Congress was deadlocked and would remain so for more than a year.

The growth of sectionalism As the debate over expanding slavery raged on, it became increasingly bitter. The good feelings and sense of national unity that had come out of the War of 1812 soon gave way to sectionalism. **Sectionalism** is devotion to the interests of one's own section over those of the nation as a whole.

The Missouri Compromise

Sectional differences on the Missouri question ran so deep in Congress that they worried Henry Clay, the Speaker of the House. "The words *civil war* and *disunion* are uttered almost without emotion," Clay reported. Under his guidance, Congress reached a compromise in March 1820.

Hands-On → HISTORY

Making compromises Henry Clay's "mode of speaking is very forcible. He fixes the attention by his earnest and emphatic [strong] tones and gestures." So said a member of the House of Representatives in 1820. Clay's success in settling disputes in Congress earned him the name the Great Compromiser.

Henry Clay

→ Activity

① Try being a Great Compromiser. Choose a problem or dispute at the school, local, state, or national level that you think needs settling.

② Find out as much as you can about the problem. Interview family members, friends, or neighbors. Read newspaper or magazine articles and listen to television or radio broadcasts.

③ Write a description of the problem, the solutions proposed, and a compromise that all sides might agree to accept. Keep in mind that in a compromise each side gives up part of what it wants.

④ Describe the compromise to your classmates. Will it work? What do they think?

The Missouri Compromise allowed Missouri into the Union as a slave state. At the same time, Maine, which had recently asked to join the Union, entered as a free state. In this way the balance between slave and free states in the Senate was preserved at 12 states each.

The compromise also drew a line across the Louisiana Purchase at latitude 36° 30'. North of that line, slavery was forever banned, except in Missouri. South of that line, slavery was permitted.

Although it passed, the compromise pleased few people. In the North, members of Congress who had voted for it were accused of selling out. In the South, the new ban on slavery was deeply resented.

The compromise especially alarmed former President Thomas Jefferson. He wrote to a friend that "this momentous question, like a firebell in the night, awakened and filled me with terror."

Point of View

Was the Missouri Compromise good for the nation?

Secretary of State John Quincy Adams had very mixed feelings about the Missouri Compromise. Adams hated slavery. In his eyes it was "the great and foul stain" on the United States. Even so, he decided not to speak out against Clay's compromise and advised President Monroe to approve it.

Although Adams wanted to abolish slavery, he believed that the Constitution did not give that power to the federal government. "The abolition of slavery where it is already established," he wrote, "must be left entirely to the people of the state itself." The compromise seemed to be the best that could be passed under the circumstances.

In the privacy of his diary, however, Adams revealed his inner conflict over the wisdom of remaining silent:

"I have favored this Missouri Compromise . . . from extreme unwillingness to put the Union at hazard [risk]. But perhaps it would have been a wiser as well as a bolder course to have persisted in the [no-slavery] restriction upon Missouri. . . . If the Union must be dissolved, slavery is precisely the question upon which it ought to break."

The conflict over slavery had been settled for now, but Adams feared that sectionalism would continue to strain national unity. In fact, the debate over slavery in Missouri was just the beginning of a struggle that was to lead to a tragic civil war.

4. Section Review

1. Define **financial panic** and **sectionalism**.
2. What led to an "era of good feelings" after the War of 1812?
3. Who was hardest hit by the Panic of 1819 and why?
4. When Congress approved the Missouri Compromise in 1820, what problem did it solve? What problem did the Missouri Compromise cause?
5. Critical Thinking Do you think that the growth of sectionalism in 1819 could have been avoided? Give evidence from the text to support your answer.

Why We Remember

The Confident Years

The Missouri Compromise put the slavery question aside, at least for a time. With that issue behind them, most Americans quickly regained their sense of confidence in the nation's future. Everywhere they saw signs of progress and growth.

Despite the setbacks of the Panic of 1819, the nation's economy was soon growing again. Southern cotton production rose every year. In the Old Northwest, forests gave way to a landscape of farms. In the Northeast, mills and factories sprouted beside every river, and young women left farms to become mill girls. New forms of transportation carried goods made in those factories to more Americans every year.

During these confident years, President Monroe issued the nation's first bold statement of foreign policy. The Monroe Doctrine asserted that the United States would not accept European interference in American affairs—not in North America, Central America, or South America. By its very boldness, the doctrine told the world that the United States was becoming a strong, confident nation.

Skill Lab

Thinking Critically
Generalizations

Columbian Exchange. Half War. Industrial Revolution. Labels like these have been used to describe time periods or events of the past. An accurate label can be a helpful tool when we try to understand the past. An inaccurate label, however, can lead to misunderstandings about history.

Question to Investigate

Is the label *Era of Good Feelings* a good description of James Monroe's presidency?

Procedure

A label like *Era of Good Feelings* is an example of a **generalization,** a broad statement that is meant to sum up the specific characteristics of something. A generalization can be a phrase or a sentence. To determine how accurate a generalization is, you need to check how well it is supported by specific examples. Explore the Question to Investigate by doing the following.

❶ Identify who or what the generalization is about.
a. Write a sentence explaining what the generalization *Era of Good Feelings* means.
b. What time period does it refer to? Who was feeling good about what?

❷ Evaluate the generalization.
a. List examples from sources **A** and **B** that support the generalization.
b. List examples from sources **A** and **B** that are exceptions to the generalization.
c. In your mind, weigh the examples against the exceptions and answer the Question to Investigate.

❸ Write your own generalization about Monroe's presidency. Explain why you think it is accurate.

Sources to Use

A Reread Section 4 (pages 332–336).

B "Although Monroe's personal popularity during his first term had brought glowing references to his administration as an 'era of good feelings,' his second term was a time of quite bad feelings. True, the President was still well liked, and party politics had virtually disappeared—almost everyone professed [claimed] to be a Republican. But sectionalism was on the increase. And with everybody in the same party, factional disputes [disagreements within the party] began to break out."

From Margaret L. Coit et al.,
The Growing Years
(Time Inc.: 1963)

Exceptions:

1.
2.

Examples:

1.
2.
3.

Chapter Survey

Reviewing Vocabulary

Define the following terms.
1. Industrial Revolution 4. immigration
2. mass production 5. financial panic
3. protective tariff 6. sectionalism

Reviewing Main Ideas

1. Describe how Samuel Slater, Eli Whitney, and Francis Cabot Lowell contributed to the Industrial Revolution.
2. (a) What was the goal of the American System? (b) Which parts of the system were put into practice?
3. What were the advantages of using (a) rivers instead of roads? (b) canals instead of rivers? (c) railroads instead of canals?
4. How did Secretary of State Adams achieve his goals of lasting peace with Britain and the takeover of the Spanish colony of Florida?
5. (a) What was the purpose of the Monroe Doctrine? (b) What events led President Monroe to issue the doctrine?
6. How did the Bank of the United States help to make the Panic of 1819 worse?
7. (a) What were the main provisions of the Missouri Compromise? (b) Were northerners and southerners satisfied with the compromise? Explain.

Thinking Critically

1. Evaluation Southern farmers believed that the invention of a machine to clean cotton quickly would be a "great thing . . . to the country." Do you think that the invention of the cotton gin was a "great thing"? Explain why or why not.
2. Analysis What impression of the United States might Europeans get as a result of the Monroe Doctrine? As a result of the Missouri Compromise?

3. Why We Remember: Analysis The period around 1815 has been called one of the major turning points in the history of the United States. What major economic changes were taking place at this time? How did these changes affect Americans?

Applying Skills

Generalizations Think about your school experiences over the years and focus on a period of time that stands out in your mind.
1. Write a generalization about that period. It can be a phrase such as "Fifth Grade: The Time of Troubles," or a sentence such as "Seventh grade was an easy year."
2. List at least two examples that support your generalization.
3. List any exceptions to your generalization.
4. Explain why your generalization is accurate. Note how the supporting examples outweigh any exceptions.

History Mystery

The train race Answer the History Mystery on page 315. Not all Americans welcomed the railroads. One critic said, "The railroad . . . is the Devil's own invention, compounded of fire, smoke, soot, and dirt, spreading its infernal poison throughout the fair countryside." What would you say in reply to this criticism? What advantages did railroads have?

Writing in Your History Journal

1. Keys to History (a) The time line on pages 314–315 has seven Keys to History. In your journal, describe why each one is important to know about. (b) Imagine that you are a foreign visitor traveling in the United

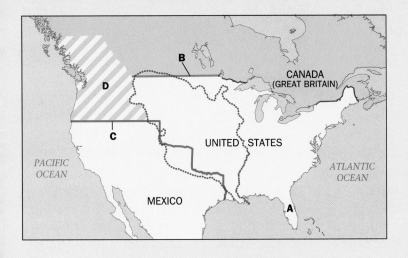

Reviewing Geography

1. For each letter on the map, explain how a dispute over land or a boundary was settled.

2. Geographic Thinking In the early 1800s Americans viewed the environment as "a challenge requiring action." Give three examples of how Americans faced that challenge and changed the environment to meet their needs. Then give two examples of how Americans had to adapt to the environment.

States in 1830. Which events on the time line would you be most interested in and why? Write your response in your journal.

2. The Mill Girls Would you have preferred to work in a New England mill or on the family farm? In your journal, explain your reasons. Consider such issues as pay, living and working conditions, and personal freedom.

3. Citizenship The Missouri Compromise filled Thomas Jefferson with terror. John Quincy Adams thought it was "a title page to a great tragic volume." What did both leaders fear? Should northerners have continued to oppose the compromise? Why? Write your responses in your journal.

Alternative Assessment

Writing about current events With a partner, carry on a correspondence about three events between 1816 and 1830.

❶ You and your partner each choose a person you want to be—a cotton planter in Georgia, a mill owner in Rhode Island, a farmer in Indiana, or a riverboat captain on the Hudson River or Mississippi River.

❷ In a letter to your partner, describe your reaction to one of the following events: creation of the new Bank of the United States, passage of the first protective tariff, the Panic of 1819, the Missouri Compromise, the Monroe Doctrine, the opening of the Erie Canal. Your partner reads and replies to your letter, describing his or her reaction to the event.

❸ Next, your partner chooses one of the events above and writes to you about it, and you reply.

❹ Decide which partner will write a letter about the third event, and which will reply.

Your work will be evaluated on the following criteria:
• you describe historical events accurately
• the ideas you express are reasonable
• your letters are imaginative and interesting

Unit Survey

Making Connections

1. Compare the way Presidents Washington, Jefferson, Madison, and Monroe handled relations with Britain.

2. Physically, the United States was very different in 1830 than it had been only 40 years before. Describe three differences.

3. Support the following: Conflict between the North and the South over the Missouri question was not new; its roots went back at least as far as Washington's presidency.

Linking History, Technology, and Art

Inventing a New Gadget

"Build a better mousetrap and the world will beat a path to your door." That old saying reflects the hopes and dreams of inventors throughout time.

The ideas of inventors like Eli Whitney, Robert Fulton, and Peter Cooper have changed the lives of people and nations. Other ideas never get off the ground. Protective goggles for chickens and a parachute cap to wear when jumping from a burning building are two examples. Yet the inventors were serious about wanting to improve people's—not to mention chickens'—lives. What invention can you come up with to make life better?

Project Steps

Work on your own or with a partner.

❶ Decide what task you would like to do faster or more easily. It might be anything from combing the cat to watering the plants or taking out the trash. How could a new invention help you do it?

❷ Design the invention. What materials will it be made of? How will they be put together? How will it work? Make sketches and jot down descriptions as you plan.

❸ Make a scale drawing or model. In a model, you can substitute materials if necessary. For example, you can use aluminum foil for steel.

❹ Write an explanation to go with your drawing or model. Include why you think your invention is useful.

❺ Share your invention with your classmates. Do they agree that it is an idea whose time has come?

Thinking It Over Many inventions that eventually changed history were scorned as crazy at first. Why do you suppose that happened? Do you think it still happens today? What qualities does an invention of lasting value have?

How Do We Know?

Dr. Theresa Singleton of the Smithsonian Institution

Scholar's Tool Kit
Oral History

How do historians know about the lives of African Americans on southern plantations before the Civil War? Since most were slaves and not allowed to read or write, they left few written records. Yet historians working today have been able to piece together much of this history. An important tool in their research is **oral history**—historical data in the form of personal recollections or stories passed on by word of mouth.

Theresa Singleton, an anthropologist and archaeologist, uses oral history to gather information about this period. "I want to know how these African Americans spent their daily lives," she says. "How did they build their homes? How did they prepare their food? How did they craft their household equipment and personal possessions?" Most of all, she says, she wants to know how their African heritage lived on.

Using the Tools of History

How does Dr. Singleton use oral history now, nearly 150 years after slaves in the South were freed? After slavery was abolished, scholars and other interested people interviewed former slaves to learn as much as they could about life under slavery. These stories were written down, and some were published as slave narratives. Even though the stories are now in written form, we refer to them as oral history because they are in the words of the people who told them. Dr. Singleton studies these stories to learn how African Americans spent their daily lives.

Dr. Singleton also uses a second tool of history—archaeology—to give her a more complete picture. Her team excavates areas where slaves once lived. They find pieces of pottery, broken glass, food bones, and tools in the ground where houses once stood. This evidence can confirm and add to what Dr. Singleton learns from oral history.

What Scholars Have Learned

By studying oral history and archaeological evidence, Dr. Singleton and her colleagues have learned a great deal about African American life. "Despite the oppressive and inhuman conditions of slavery," she declares, "enslaved Africans and their descendants were able to nurture and sustain a few aspects of their African heritage."

For example, broken pieces of pottery found at sites of slave quarters seem to show a connection to African traditions. "The use of this pottery," says Singleton, "suggests that enslaved African Americans prepared their food to suit their own tastes according to African cuisines. Slaves liked to eat gumbos and pilafs, which they prepared in a single pot. These tasty dishes are today popular meals in the South and represent a legacy of African-introduced cooking practices."

Also commonly found are colored glass beads, especially blue ones. Oral history helped Dr. Singleton understand. In the words of former slave Mollie Dawson, "Most all the young girls had what we called a charm string. They was a lot prettier than these strings we buys at the store now. This charm string was supposed to bring good luck to the owner of it."

Especially rich sources of information are the root cellars, or storage pits, that slaves sometimes dug under the floors of their houses. Archaeologists have found tools, locks, nails, buttons, glass, pottery, and discarded food bones in these pits.

The pits were intended for storage, but they were also excellent places to hide things. Slaves hid tools, food, guns, and other things they took from their owners or were forbidden to own. The practice of hiding food is confirmed by oral history. Said former slave Charles

? Critical Thinking

1. Why is oral history an especially useful tool in studying what life was like for slaves? For what other areas of research would oral history be valuable?

? Critical Thinking

2. What questions about the source might you ask yourself when listening to or reading an oral history?

At least five of the women in this 1862 photograph are wearing beaded necklaces like the ones Mollie Dawson described.

? Critical Thinking

3. Dr. Singleton uses both oral history and archaeology in her research. What other tools of history might a scholar use to piece together the story of what slave life was like? How might those tools be useful?

Grandy, "I got so hungry I stole chickens off the roost. . . . We would cook the chicken at night, eat him, and burn the feathers. We always had a trap in the floor to hide these chickens in."

Scholars like Dr. Singleton are learning many things about slave life not known from written sources. "For example, the frequency with which lead pencils, slates, eye glasses, and gun parts turn up at archaeological sites," she says, "suggests that more slaves had access to fire-arms and possessed literacy [reading] and number skills than previously thought from the study of written records alone."

As the study of oral history and archaeological sites continues, scholars like Dr. Singleton are likely to continue to shed new light on African American history. Their findings will become a part of the history that a new generation of scholars will study.

Scholar at Work

Collecting oral history is something you can do now. Ask a member of your family to tell you a true story about his or her life. You may use a tape recorder or take notes to capture the details of this oral history. Be prepared to tell the story to your class. What might the story tell someone in the future about what life was like at the time?

Unit 5

Chapters

Hands-On *HISTORY*

Activity

The people in this painting have left their homes east of the Mississippi River to try their luck in the West. Imagine that one of them—a friend or relative—wants you to go along. Make a storyboard or cartoon strip of 6 to 10 panels illustrating your discussion with that person. Write the dialogue in the panels. Be sure to include your reasons for going or not going.

Westward the Course of Empire Takes Its Way (detail)
by Emanuel Gottlieb Leutze, 1861

Expansion and Reform

Chapter 13

The Age of Jackson

Keys to History

1824 John Quincy Adams elected President by House of Representatives

Image of Adams on Indian peace medal

1828 Andrew Jackson elected President

Wooden statue of Andrew Jackson

1828 Tariff of Abominations

1824

1828

World Link

Looking Back

Battle of New Orleans
1815

Panama Congress
1826

HISTORY
Mystery

In 1838 many residents of homes like this were forced to leave their communities. Who were these people, and why were they driven away?

1830

Webster-Hayne debates

Daniel Webster (left) and Robert Hayne

1830

Indian Removal Act

1838

The Trail of Tears

Detail of *The Endless Trail* by Jerome Tiger

1840

"Tippecanoe and Tyler, too!"

An election campaign souvenir: a miniature log cabin

1832   *1836*   *1840*

Looking Ahead

Republican Party formed
1854

Beginning the Story with

Andrew Jackson

Have you ever taken a close look at the portrait on a $20 bill? It is the long, thin face of Andrew Jackson, our seventh President. He looks every bit a President, very calm and dignified. Now look again, especially at the eyes. They were his most striking feature. When Jackson felt strongly about something, his eyes blazed. At such moments he could inspire love, respect, and even terror.

A Rough Childhood

The man behind those eyes was born to poor Scotch-Irish parents in the Carolina backcountry. Jackson never knew his father, who died before the boy was born. His mother dreamed of her son becoming a minister. Jackson, however, was not cut out for the church. He loved sports more than schoolwork. There was also something reckless about him. Jackson would pick a fight at the drop of a hat and, as a friend said, "he'd drop the hat himself."

Jackson's childhood was cut short by the War of Independence. At the age of 13 he joined the local militia and was captured by British troops. One day an officer ordered Jackson to clean the officer's boots. "Sir," the boy replied with stubborn pride, "I am a prisoner of war and demand to be treated as such." The outraged officer responded with a slash of his sword, gashing Jackson's head and cutting his hand to the bone. Jackson carried those scars, and a hatred of the British, to his grave.

Worse was yet to come. The British released Jackson just as a smallpox epidemic hit the Carolinas. The boy barely survived the disease. "When it left me I was a skeleton," he remembered, "not quite six feet tall and a little over six inches thick." His mother was not so lucky. "When tidings of her death reached me," Jackson recalled, "I at first could not believe it. When I finally realized the truth, I felt utterly alone."

After joining the militia at the age of 13 during the War of Independence, Jackson was captured by the British. When he refused to polish a British officer's boots, the officer slashed him with a sword.

Backcountry Lawyer

With peace came fresh opportunities for young Americans with ambition. Jackson decided to become a lawyer, even though he had few qualifications. He disliked reading and had never mastered spelling. His speech and writing often showed poor grammar, though he could at times be persuasive.

At the age of 20, Jackson moved to Salisbury, North Carolina, to work in a law office. He soon made a reputation as "the most roaring, rollicking, game-cocking, horse-racing, card-playing, mischievous fellow" to hit that town. The wonder is that he learned any law at all.

A year later, Jackson crossed the Appalachians to practice law in Nashville, Tennessee. In 1788, Nashville was just a tiny cluster of rough log cabins and tents overlooking the Cumberland River. Still, there was plenty of business for a backcountry lawyer. Jackson built a thriving practice, earning enough money to buy land and slaves and to set himself up as a planter.

"Old Hickory"

Jackson wore a number of hats before he became President. He served as a United States senator and as a judge on the Tennessee Supreme Court. It was as a military hero, though, that he won the hearts of Americans everywhere. He led a crushing defeat of the Creek Indians in Alabama. He followed that triumph with his surprising victory over the British in the Battle of New Orleans during the War of 1812. Then he drove the Spanish from Florida.

By 1820 Jackson was the most famous man in the United States and the nation's first real hero since George Washington. He seemed so tough—like hickorywood—that his soldiers called him "Old Hickory." It was the perfect nickname.

Hands-On HISTORY

Activity

Imagine yourself as one of Jackson's supporters in his campaign to become a United States senator. Opponents are saying that Jackson is not worthy to be a senator because he is not well educated. Write an editorial arguing that his background and personal characteristics qualify him to serve his nation in the Senate.

1. The New Spirit of Democracy

Reading Guide

New Terms **caucus, suffrage, mudslinging**

Section Focus **How Andrew Jackson became President**

1. How did the Democratic Party get its start?
2. Why did many Americans cheer the election of 1828 as a victory for democracy?

George Washington, a war hero, had made an outstanding President. Andrew Jackson's friends thought he would do equally well, and they encouraged him to run.

In many ways, though, Jackson did not fit the mold. All of the previous Presidents had been polished, well-educated men who had been born into wealthy families. Although Jackson was now a successful plantation owner, he was a rough-cut, self-made man from the ranks of the "common people"—small farmers and tradespeople.

The Election of 1824

The election of 1824 marked a turning point in American politics. Traditionally, a political party chose a single candidate at a **caucus,** a private meeting of party leaders. As the election approached, a caucus nominated William Crawford of Georgia to be the Republican candidate. However, sectionalism was now dividing the party. Other Republican candidates from other sections of the country challenged Crawford.

One leading rival was John Quincy Adams, who had strong support from the manufacturing and shipping interests of the Northeast. Jackson of Tennessee and Henry Clay of Kentucky were the two other main candidates. Both looked to western farmers for support. Crawford, meanwhile, appealed to the plantation owners of the South.

When the election was over, no one was a clear winner. Jackson had more popular and electoral votes, but he did not have a majority in the Electoral College. In such situations, the House of Representatives must choose from among the three leading candidates. Clay had come in fourth, so he was out of the running. He urged his backers in the House to support Adams. As a result, Adams became President.

As President, Adams named Clay to be his Secretary of State. The arrangement made sense because Clay and Adams both supported the American System and a strong national government. Jackson's followers, though, accused Adams and Clay of making "a corrupt bargain." They promised to get revenge in the next election.

The Adams Presidency

In fact, Adams was an honest, patriotic leader. He had a grand vision for the nation. The national government would support economic growth by building roads and canals while also promoting "the elegant arts, the advancement of literature, and the progress of the sciences."

The President's hope for a stronger, more active national government, however, was out of step with the growing sectionalism of the times. Southerners feared that his proposals would have a high price tag, to be paid

John Quincy Adams, a man of patriotism and firm principles, believed in a strong national government.

21, even if they did not own property. Pressured by reformers in eastern cities, most other states followed the West's lead.

Many decades would pass before women, Indians, and most African Americans were granted the right to vote. Still, democracy was on the march.

The method of electing the President had become more democratic, too. By 1828, presidential electors in all but two states were chosen directly by the voters rather than by the state legislatures.

Van Buren saw that the time was ripe for a new party. He and other Jackson backers adopted the name Democratic Party and called themselves Jacksonian Democrats. Their candidate, they claimed, would speak for "the people"—average Americans, rather than the wealthy and privileged.

by higher tariffs. They also suspected that a stronger government might try to do away with slavery.

Meanwhile, Adams offended westerners by supporting the Bank of the United States. Many westerners had lost farms and homes to the Bank during the Panic of 1819 (see page 332).

The President's policy of trying to protect Indian lands was unpopular with both southerners and westerners. When he wanted to send troops to protect the lands of the Creek Indians in Georgia, for instance, Congress refused to support him. It was clear that he would face an uphill campaign for re-election in 1828.

A New Democratic Party

Right after Jackson lost in 1824, his supporters began looking ahead to the election of 1828. Their campaign was masterminded by Martin Van Buren, a stout, red-haired Senator from New York who was nicknamed the "Red Fox" and the "Little Magician."

Van Buren was well aware that there would be thousands of new voters casting ballots in 1828, and most would be common people. In the West, the newly admitted states had granted **suffrage**—the right to vote—to most white men over the age of

World Link

The Panama Congress John Quincy Adams had a vision of a United States powerful enough to stand up to the nations of Europe. Simón Bolívar—"the Liberator" of South America—had a similar goal for Latin America.

As a first step toward a stronger Latin America, Bolívar called for a congress of Latin American nations to take place in Panama City in 1826. Against his wishes, the United States was also invited. Adams, however, feared being drawn into an agreement to protect Latin America. He need not have worried, for only four nations sent delegates. The congress did set the stage, though, for later cooperation among Latin American nations to achieve common goals.

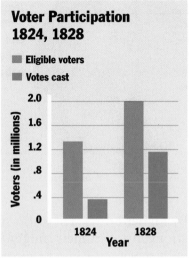

Voter Participation 1824, 1828

- Eligible voters
- Votes cast

Source: *Historical Statistics of the United States*

Artist George Caleb Bingham often painted scenes that expressed the spirit of expanding democracy. In *Stump Speaking*, a candidate addresses a crowd of voters in the countryside. Behind him sits a rival taking notes.

Meanwhile, Adams and his followers had chosen a new name for their party. They now called themselves National Republicans to reflect their belief in a strong national government.

The Election of 1828

As the election of 1828 approached, Democrats and National Republicans both hoped for support from every section of the country. Therefore, they avoided taking stands on sectional issues like slavery. They focused instead on the personal backgrounds of Adams and Jackson.

Republicans sneered that Jackson was crude and uneducated. Jackson himself admitted he was a poor speller, joking that he could not respect someone who spelled a word only one way. Republicans also tried to label him as a gambler and a brawler. They even called him a murderer because he had fought a number of duels.

Democrats portrayed Adams as out of touch with the common people. Adams himself admitted, "I am a man of reserved, cold, and forbidding manners." Even an admirer of Adams said that he was "hard as a piece of granite and cold as a lump of ice."

The election marked the beginning of modern politics with all its hoopla. Democrats organized huge parades, rallies, and barbecues, where neighbors gathered to cheer for "Old Hickory." Afterward supporters went home waving hickory sticks and chanting campaign slogans like, "Adams can write, but Jackson can fight."

With both sides avoiding the issues, the contest was marked by **mudslinging**—wild charges and lies about the candidates. Democrats falsely charged Adams with using taxpayers' money to buy gambling tables for the White House. Republicans unfairly accused Jackson of knowingly marrying his wife Rachel before the divorce from her first husband became final.

When the mudslinging was over, Jackson had won a solid victory: 647,000 votes for him and 508,000 for Adams. The electoral vote was 178 to 83. Jackson and his vice-presidential running mate, John C. Calhoun of South Carolina, carried all sections of the country except New England.

The election of 1828 has often been viewed as a western and southern victory because much of Jackson's support came from those sections of the country. "Old Hickory" could not have won, though, without the votes of many eastern factory workers and other daily wage earners.

With the increase in the number of eligible voters, more than twice as many ballots were cast in 1828 as in 1824. Ordinary people across the country had voted, and Jackson was their choice. More than anything, it was a victory for control of government by the common people—an idea that became known as Jacksonian Democracy.

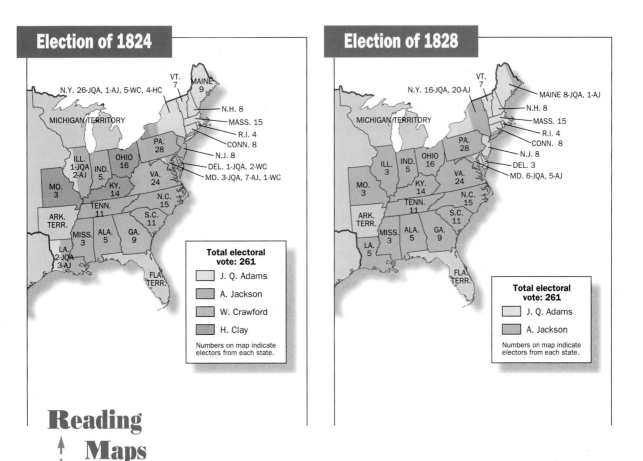

Reading Maps

1. **Count the number of electoral votes for each candidate in 1824. By how many votes did Jackson miss getting a majority?**

2. **Summarize the differences between the two elections in each of the following areas. (a) the number of political parties (b) number of candidates (c) how easy it is to tell who won the most electoral votes, and why**

Hands-On HISTORY

Planning an inauguration The celebration that followed Andrew Jackson's inauguration was anything but well planned. It did send a message to the nation, though. By making "common people" guests at the White House, Jackson was signaling that he would use his power to open up opportunities for average Americans.

A crowd at the White House after Jackson's inauguration

Activity Since Jackson's time, inaugural celebrations have been carefully planned to reflect the President's beliefs and goals for the nation. Imagine that you have been elected President and are planning your celebration.

1. State your two or three main goals for the nation.

2. For each goal, make a list of events—such as parades, parties, and concerts. Explain how each one represents your goal.

3. Make a schedule, with times and places.

Jackson's Inauguration

On Inauguration Day, thousands filled the streets of Washington to welcome their hero. Senator Daniel Webster commented:

"I never saw such a crowd here before. People have come five hundred miles to see General Jackson, and they really seem to think that the country has been rescued from some dreadful danger."

Jackson gave a dignified inaugural address. What followed has become an Inauguration Day legend. Jackson was "nearly pressed to death" by admirers crowding into the White House to wish him well. He had to sneak out a back door and hide in a nearby hotel.

Meanwhile, the rowdy guests smashed crystal and china and ruined rugs with their muddy boots. Only after waiters moved the food and drink outside did people leave—some by climbing out the windows.

One witness described the scene as "the reign of King Mob." Socialite Margaret Bayard Smith wrote:

"Ladies fainted, men were seen with bloody noses, and such a scene of confusion took place as is impossible to describe. . . . But it was the People's day, and the People's President, and the People would rule."

 1. Section Review

1. Define **caucus, suffrage,** and **mudslinging.**
2. Who organized the Democratic Party and why?
3. What was Jacksonian Democracy?
4. Critical Thinking What dangers do you think wealthy Americans saw in the idea of "letting the people rule"?

Geography Lab

From Forest to Farm

Once, much of eastern North America was densely forested. Because early settlers found no European-style farms and towns, they thought of the land as empty. They plunged into the forest, axes in hand, to create farms. Historian David Lowenthal describes the settlers' attitude toward land: "Empty, it must be filled; unfinished, it must be completed; wild, it must be tamed."

These pictures, made around 1850, show changes in a farm in western New York over a period of years.

A

B

C

Link to History

1. According to Lowenthal, what did settlers hope to do?

2. Describe the changes in this New York farm the way the family who owned the farm might have described them.

3. What might someone who had been a trapper in the northeastern woodlands since about 1800 have said about the changes, and why?

4. Imagine that you are looking at a picture showing this same New York area today. List three changes you would probably find between picture **C** and that area today.

5. **Hands-On Geography** People often disagree about how to use land. Write two different captions for this set of scenes as if the captions were written by different people with opposing views on clearing land.

2. Jackson Takes Charge

Reading Guide

New Terms **spoils system, secede, sovereignty**

Section Focus **Jackson's response to a threat to the Union**

1. Why did the issue of nullification arise again?
2. What steps did Jackson take to preserve the Union?

Jackson handled the presidency as he handled everything else in life—he took firm control. Unlike earlier Presidents, he rarely met with his cabinet. He was more likely to seek advice from trusted friends, who were said to meet in the White House kitchen. The so-called "Kitchen Cabinet" actually had little influence. Final decisions were Jackson's alone.

As defender of the common people, Jackson set out to change the national government. It was too powerful, he said, and favored the rich. He vowed that he would reduce it "to that simple machine which the Constitution created."

The Spoils System

One practice Jackson considered unfair was giving government workers lifetime jobs. He said they should be forced to "go back to making a living as other people do." When a new President replaced workers with new appointees, he argued, it made democracy stronger by giving more people a chance to serve.

Critics replied that workers should be chosen for their ability rather than for their loyalty to the President's political party. They called the practice of rewarding political supporters with jobs the **spoils system.** The term came from the saying "to the victor belong the spoils [prizes]."

Jackson's enemies exaggerated the number of Republicans he replaced. Of 10,000 workers, only about 900 lost their jobs. Jackson did replace more workers than any previous President, however, starting a trend that later Presidents were glad to follow.

Still, Jackson put patriotism above party loyalty. One worker who had been replaced confronted him and said:

❝Sir, I have been removed as postmaster from Albany but there is something I wish to show you. I want you to see my wounds, sir, received while defending my country from the British . . . and my thanks is removal from my office, the only position I have to sustain me in my old age.❞

"Button your jacket," Jackson replied. "You are still postmaster."

A "Tariff of Abominations"

Jackson's patriotism and leadership were soon challenged by an issue that threatened to break up the Union. The crisis had begun when Congress passed the Tariff of 1828.

New England manufacturers welcomed the tariff. Now they could raise prices and still outsell imported products. However, southern planters resented having to pay more for manufactured goods.

In South Carolina, state leaders demanded that the government reduce the Tariff of 1828, which they called the "Tariff of Abominations." If not, they threatened that their state would **secede**—break away from the United States.

Into the conflict stepped Vice-President John C. Calhoun. He realized that his chance to be President would be destroyed if his home state seceded. Looking for a solution, he argued that a state could nullify, or reject, a federal law it considered unconstitutional. Nullification had been proposed before (see page 282). This time, however, the idea seemed to strike at the heart of the union.

This cartoon protests that the Tariff of 1828 placed a burden on southern planters in order to help northern manufacturers get rich.

Point of View

Can a state disobey the federal government?

In 1830 two of the most gifted speakers in the Senate—Robert Hayne of South Carolina and Daniel Webster of Massachusetts—debated this question.

Hayne argued that the states had created the Constitution and therefore still had **sovereignty**—the power to control their affairs. Any state legislature, he said, could nullify a federal law to protect its citizens' liberties. Hayne declared:

"The very life of our system is the independence of the states. I am opposed, therefore, in any shape, to all unnecessary extension of the power or the influence . . . of the Union over the states."

Webster responded that the national government gets its authority directly from the people, not the state legislatures:

"It is the people's Constitution, the people's government, made for the people, made by the people, and answerable to the people."

Webster argued that the Constitution allows only the Supreme Court to declare a law unconstitutional. He warned that if each state could reject federal laws, the nation would be torn apart. He closed with a ringing appeal for "Liberty and Union, now and forever, one and inseparable."

The Nullification Crisis

Everyone was anxious to know whether Jackson would agree that a state could refuse to obey a federal law. The answer came at a dinner on April 13, 1830, honoring Thomas Jefferson's birthday. All the leading Democrats were there.

At the dinner, southerners made a series of toasts to states' rights. Jackson rose, looked directly at Calhoun, and proposed his own toast: "Our Union—it must be preserved." Calhoun skillfully countered with: "The Union, next to our liberty, most dear."

Jackson's toast revealed he was not as strong a supporter of states' rights as southerners had hoped. As a southern planter, though, he understood objections to the tariff. In 1832 he got Congress to lower it.

In a dramatic Senate debate, Daniel Webster attacked the view that a state could nullify, or reject, a federal law. At the far left sits John C. Calhoun, who had proposed the idea of nullification.

South Carolina leaders refused to accept the new, lower tariff. They spoke of preparing for war if the national government tried to collect the tariff by force. Jackson reacted swiftly to their threat, warning that "disunion by armed force is treason." He told one South Carolina congressman:

"They can talk and write resolutions and print threats to their hearts' content. But if one drop of blood be shed there in defiance of the laws of the United States, I will hang the first man of them I can get my hands on to the first tree I can find.**"**

In 1833 Jackson got Congress to pass the "Force Bill," which gave him power to use the army and navy, if needed, to collect the tariff. In public, though, he controlled his temper to avoid adding fuel to the fire.

A combination of events finally ended the nullification crisis. First, no other state threatened to secede. Meanwhile, Jackson urged Congress to pass a compromise tariff. He signed the Force Bill and the tariff on the same day. South Carolina accepted the tariff. Jackson had played a major role in holding the Union together.

 2. Section Review

1. Define **spoils system, secede,** and **sovereignty.**
2. What were some arguments for and against nullification?
3. How did Jackson respond to South Carolina's threat to secede?
4. Critical Thinking Could a civil war have broken out over the tariff? Explain.

3. Jackson's Indian Policy

Reading Guide

Section Focus **The Indian Removal Act and its effects**

1. Why did Jackson support forcing Indians to move off their lands?
2. How did the eastern Indian tribes react to forced removal?

When Andrew Jackson became President, very few Indians—only about 125,000—still lived east of the Mississippi River. Disease, war, and enslavement had greatly reduced their numbers. Meanwhile, the nation's population had grown to nearly 13 million. Indian lands east of the Mississippi were more and more in demand.

Ever since the Louisiana Purchase in 1803, the federal government had been encouraging Indians to sell their lands and move west of the Mississippi. As President, one of Jackson's major goals was to speed up this removal of the Indians.

The Roots of Jackson's Policy

Jackson's goal was shaped by his earlier experiences fighting against the Creeks and Seminoles. He respected his opponents, who called him "Big Knife." When he became President, however, the wars over Indian lands east of the Mississippi had mostly ended. Jackson believed that the settlers now had a right to those lands.

As a politician, Jackson saw that removing Indians from their homelands would open up opportunities for many southern and western farmers and small businessmen—the people who had voted for him. He would make sure that nothing stood in their way—neither the Indians nor the federal government.

At the same time, though, Jackson argued that removing the Indians was the best way to protect them. In letters to the tribes, he warned that if they stayed in their homelands they would be destroyed by settlers:

"Where you now are, you and my white children are too near to each other to live in harmony and peace. Your game is gone, and many of your people will not work and till the earth. . . . The land beyond the Mississippi belongs to the President and no one else, and he will give it to you forever."

This offer, however, did not appeal to most of the eastern Indians. They wanted to remain in their homelands.

Indians in the Southeast

The majority of eastern Indians were members of five southeastern tribes—the Cherokees, Creeks, Chickasaws, Choctaws, and Seminoles. Hoping to be allowed to keep their lands, many had taken up farming and adapted to white culture. Some even had large plantations and owned slaves.

Many learned to read and write English. A Cherokee named Sequoyah [sih-KWOY-uh] also invented a system for writing the Cherokee language. The Cherokees had their own newspaper and a constitution modeled after the United States Constitution.

The people whom white settlers called "the Five Civilized Tribes" would have been content to live peacefully with their neighbors, but that was not to be. Planters wanted the tribes' rich lands because cotton farming had exhausted the soil on their own plantations. They demanded that the federal government remove the Indians.

Planters in Georgia, which was home to the Cherokees and the Creeks, pointed to an agreement made with the federal government back in 1802. Georgia had given up its claim to a large area of western land. In return, the federal government had agreed to remove the Indians as soon as treaties could be negotiated.

By 1828, the federal government still had not acted, so Georgia declared that Cherokee lands belonged to the state. The Cherokees, faced with losing their lands, appealed to the federal government for protection.

Jackson Versus the Court

In his annual message before the Congress in December 1829, Jackson declared his support for Georgia. He said that a state had a right to control lands within its borders, and that Indians living there must obey the state's laws. His view was shared by most members of Congress.

Reformers in New England, church groups, and especially missionaries who lived with the Cherokees all protested that the Cherokees had a right to keep their land. When Congress and the President ignored their protests, the Cherokees and their allies appealed to the Supreme Court.

The Court, under Chief Justice John Marshall, ruled that the Cherokees should be able to keep their lands because of an early treaty with the federal government. Such a treaty with an Indian tribe, the Court declared, was an agreement between two nations and therefore could not be overruled by a state.

The Court's decision proved to be a hollow victory. Georgia officials ignored it, and Jackson refused to enforce it. He thought that treating Indian tribes as nations was senseless. Also, he believed that his oath as President bound him to obey the Constitution as *he*, not the Court, interpreted it. He is reported to have said, "Well, John Marshall has made his decision, now let him enforce it."

The Indian Removal Act

In May 1830, at Jackson's urging, Congress passed the Indian Removal Act. The act allowed the President to make treaties with eastern tribes to exchange their lands for land west of the Mississippi.

The removal treaties were supposed to be voluntary. In fact, though, federal agents got tribal leaders to sign the treaties by misleading them. Indians were also threatened by armed settlers who had already begun to occupy their lands.

The government agreed to pay the Indians for any property they left behind. It promised to protect them in their new lands and give them food and clothing for one year. Despite these promises, the removals rarely went smoothly. They turned out to be poorly planned and caused much suffering.

Indian Resistance

Indian removal is a tragic chapter in American history. Most of the tribes accepted their fate with little or no resistance. They signed the treaties, packed belongings, and moved to the barren lands set aside across the Mississippi. A few tribes, though, strongly resisted removal.

The Black Hawk War Black Hawk, a leader of the Sauk and Fox Indians of the Wisconsin Territory, challenged a removal treaty. When the government forced most of the Sauk and Fox across the Mississippi to Iowa Territory in 1831, Black Hawk refused to stay in Iowa. Instead, he returned the next year to tribal lands in Illinois, even though settlers now lived there.

Tempers flared and shots were fired. The result is known as the Black Hawk War, although it was more like a massacre. Most of Black Hawk's followers were killed as they tried to escape by crossing the Mississippi. He was captured and sent to prison.

The Trail of Tears Most Cherokees refused to leave their homes. In 1838, two years after Jackson left the presidency, the Georgia militia was ordered to force them out. Soldiers brutally rounded up 17,000 Cherokees and marched them to Indian Territory, which is today Oklahoma.

As many as 4,000 Cherokees died along the way. The tribe remembers this terrible journey as "The Trail Where They Cried." History books call it "The Trail of Tears." Many years later, a Georgia soldier who participated in the dreadful removal of the Cherokees said:

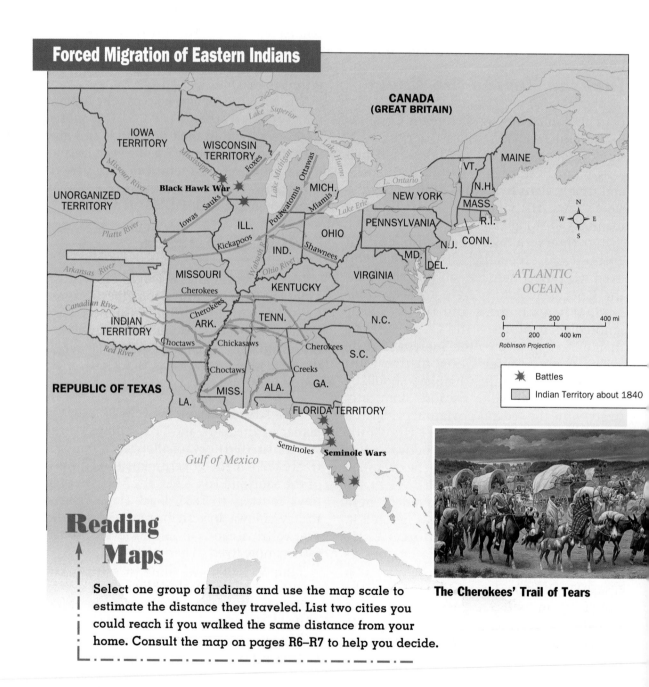

Forced Migration of Eastern Indians

The Cherokees' Trail of Tears

Reading Maps

Select one group of Indians and use the map scale to estimate the distance they traveled. List two cities you could reach if you walked the same distance from your home. Consult the map on pages R6–R7 to help you decide.

"I fought through the Civil War and have seen men shot to pieces and slaughtered by the thousands, but the Cherokee removal was the cruelest work I ever knew."

The Seminole War The Indians who fought most strongly against removal were the Seminoles of Florida. They were helped by former African American slaves who had escaped from plantations in Georgia and Alabama.

Beginning in 1835 the Seminoles and their allies waged fierce guerrilla campaigns against the United States Army. The Seminole chief, Osceola [os-ee-Ō-lah], was captured in 1837 while flying a flag of truce, but the Seminoles fought on. The long struggle that is known as the Seminole War did not end until 1842. It was the most costly Indian war that the United States ever fought.

A number of Seminoles eventually were sent to Indian Territory. However, many hid in the Florida swamps and never surrendered. Their descendants remain in Florida to this day.

Seminole chief Osceola died in prison only a few days after George Catlin finished painting this portrait in 1837.

Link to the Present

The Cherokee Nation Exhausted, sick, and starving, the last Cherokees staggered into Indian Territory in early 1839. In their suffering and sorrow, it would have been easy to give up. Instead, they rebuilt their lives by starting schools, farms, ranches, and mines.

Events that led to Oklahoma statehood in 1907, however, almost destroyed the Cherokees. The federal government took away much of their land and officially dissolved their nation. Forced to depend on the federal government for financial support, many Cherokees lived in poverty and despair.

The 1970s brought renewed hope, as Congress gave Indian nations the authority to govern themselves. Under the leadership of strong chiefs like Wilma Mankiller, the Cherokees built roads and water systems, set up health-care clinics, and organized job-training programs. As they did after the Trail of Tears, the Cherokees have rebuilt their nation as well as their faith in themselves.

3. Section Review

1. Why did Jackson support efforts to remove the eastern Indian tribes from their homelands?

2. What were different ways in which eastern tribes responded to the government's policy of removal?

3. Critical Thinking How do you think Jackson should be judged for his Indian policy? Explain.

4. "The Bank War" and Its Effects

Reading Guide

Section Focus **The causes and effects of Jackson's "war" with the Bank of the United States**

1. Why was Jackson an enemy of the Bank of the United States?
2. What led to the forming of the Whig Party?
3. Why did the Democrats lose the election of 1840?

Jackson took his strongest stand as defender of the common people in fighting a "war" with the Bank of the United States. The Bank was a private corporation chartered by Congress in 1816. The national government owned one-fifth of the stock and kept all of its deposits there.

In Jackson's eyes, the Bank was a "monster"—a monopoly created to make "rich men . . . richer by act of Congress." To him, the main villain was the Bank's wealthy president, Nicholas Biddle.

The Power of the Bank

Biddle was one of the most powerful men in the country. He owned much of the Bank's stock, appointed its officials, set interest rates, and decided who got loans. He saw it as his duty to make sure the Bank's currency was "good as gold." Therefore, he insisted on keeping a reserve of 50 percent—50¢ worth of gold and silver coins for every paper dollar the bank loaned out.

State banks loaned money more freely, usually keeping only a 25 percent reserve. In western territories, most independent "wildcat banks" kept no reserve. In short, paper money issued by the Bank of the United States was the most dependable. Sometimes Biddle tried to force small banks to be more cautious by refusing to accept their paper money at branches of the Bank.

Poor southerners and westerners who needed to borrow money to buy land hated Biddle's policy toward small banks. Jackson shared their bitterness. He believed the Bank was trying to keep wealth in the hands of a few and deny opportunity to the many. Jackson made no secret of the fact that when the Bank's charter came up for renewal in 1836, he would oppose it.

Clay Forces the Issue

Biddle was not worried—he had powerful friends. Among them was Henry Clay, who planned to run for President in 1832. Clay made the Bank a major issue in his campaign. He asked Biddle to apply for early renewal of the charter. Clay figured that if Jackson signed the bill, he would offend voters in the South and West. If he vetoed it, he would offend the Northeast.

The plan worked to a point. In the summer of 1832, Congress agreed to recharter the Bank. When the bill came to him, Jackson lay sick in bed in the White House. He told his close friend Martin Van Buren that the bill was a personal attack. "The Bank, Mr. Van Buren, is trying to kill me," he said, "but I will kill it."

True to his word, Jackson vetoed the Bank bill. He explained that the Bank gave unjust advantages to the wealthy at the expense of "humble members of society—the farmers, mechanics, and laborers." His arguments were so effective that friends of the Bank in Congress were unable to override the veto.

Clay was wrong about the effect of the veto on the 1832 election. Voters cared less about the Bank than he and Biddle had thought. Jackson easily won re-election, crushing Clay by a margin of 219 to 49 electoral votes. Van Buren became the new Vice-President.

Jackson was not content simply to let the Bank die a natural death. Instead of waiting until the Bank's charter expired in 1836, he moved to destroy it immediately. "I have it chained," Jackson gloated. "Now the monster must perish."

He ordered the government to take all federal money out of the Bank and put it in state banks. His enemies called them his "pet banks," charging that the state banks selected for holding federal money were those run by loyal Democrats.

The Rise of the Whig Party

One result of the "bank war" was the rise of a new political party. The National Republicans, the party of John Quincy Adams and Henry Clay, joined forces with many states' rights supporters, bankers, and Democrats unhappy with Jackson. They formed the Whig Party.

This cartoon shows Andrew Jackson in the middle of a nightmare. He drags Henry Clay behind him as he attacks the "monster" Bank of the United States.

The Whigs took their name from the Whig Party in England, which stood for limiting the king's powers. They said the United States now had its own tyrant. They mockingly called President Jackson "King Andrew the First."

The election of 1836 The Whigs agreed on only one thing—their hatred of Jackson and his policies. Otherwise the party was very disorganized and lacked a statement of political beliefs. In the election of 1836, the Whigs were not strong enough to defeat the Democratic candidate, Van Buren.

Van Buren had won after promising to follow in Jackson's footsteps. In fact, many people saw his election as Old Hickory's third presidential victory. Voters had shown they still loved Jackson by electing his handpicked successor.

The Panic of 1837

Two months after Van Buren took office, the country slipped into the worst economic depression it had ever known—the Panic of 1837. Van Buren was blamed for it, but in fact Jackson's economic policies were part of the cause.

During the last years of Jackson's presidency, state banks had been freely lending paper money to people who made quick profits by buying and selling public lands. Jackson had worried that land prices would rise too quickly. In 1836 he had ordered that only gold or silver coins, known as specie, could be used to buy public lands.

The order, called the Specie Circular, slowed land sales but also weakened the banks. Panicked customers brought their paper money into banks, demanding gold and silver coins in return. If the President did not trust paper money, they thought, why should they?

Meanwhile, a financial crisis in Britain led British bankers to demand that American banks repay their loans. The British also stopped buying cotton, so cotton and land prices tumbled. Many banks failed and unemployment rose. The depression continued throughout Van Buren's term.

"Tippecanoe and Tyler, Too!"

As the election of 1840 approached, the Whigs smelled victory. They were confident that voters would blame "Martin Van Ruin" for the depression. They picked a candidate—William Henry Harrison of Ohio—who would appeal to common people in every section of the country. To attract southern votes, they nominated John Tyler of Virginia for Vice-President.

Like Jackson, Harrison had been a general who became famous as a military hero. He was the victor at the Battle of Tippecanoe in 1811. Also, like Jackson, he had risen from poverty to wealth by his own effort.

Instead of taking a stand on issues, each party criticized the other's candidate. One Democrat poked fun at the 68-year-old Harrison's age, saying he should just sit in a log cabin and drink cider the rest of his days. The joke backfired, as Whigs contrasted their "log cabin" candidate with the rich-looking Martin Van Buren. Calling Harrison a true representative of the common people, they said Van Buren's table was set with the finest golden plates.

In what became known as the "log cabin campaign," Whigs held huge rallies to entertain voters. They shouted "Tippecanoe and Tyler, Too!" and sang songs from the *Log Cabin Songbook*. Calling Harrison "Old Tip" and Van Buren "Matt," one song declared:

"Old Tip, he wears a homespun shirt,
    He has no ruffled shirt, wirt, wirt.
But Matt, he has the golden plate,
    And he's a little squirt, wirt, wirt.**"**

In their 1840 campaign, the Whigs distributed many items—songsheets, pamphlets, handkerchiefs, and even hairbrushes—promoting William Henry Harrison as the "log cabin candidate."

The campaign was filled with monkey business that has never since been equaled. Whigs rolled huge balls covered with campaign slogans from town to town and state to state. As the supporters of "Tip and Ty" pushed the balls, they sang:

"Tippecanoe and Tyler, too.
    And with them we'll beat little
Van, Van, Van.
    Oh! Van is a used-up man."

The Democrats were amazed. One veteran of the 1828 campaign moaned, "We have taught them to conquer us!" The Whigs gained control of Congress, and Harrison defeated Van Buren by an electoral vote of 234 to 60. The popular vote was much closer. Harrison won by 150,000 votes out of the 2.4 million cast.

Harrison had little opportunity to enjoy his victory, though. He caught a severe cold on Inauguration Day and died of pneumonia a month later.

"His Accidency"

John Tyler was now President. For the first time, a Vice-President had reached the highest office because of a President's death. Some people began referring to Tyler as "His Accidency."

The Whigs planned an ambitious program and expected Tyler to approve it. They wanted to set up another Bank of the United States and to spend more federal money on canals and roads. They were also in favor of a higher tariff.

Tyler, who was a strong believer in states' rights, would have none of this. Although he had left the Democratic Party because of Jackson's stand on nullification, at heart he was still a Democrat. He opposed his new party on almost every issue. He vetoed bills in support of a national bank, tariffs, and internal improvements.

As a result, angry Whig leaders kicked Tyler out of the party. They refused to nominate him for re-election in 1844.

Jackson watched these events with keen interest. Politics was one of the few pleasures left to the old warrior, now in ill health at the Hermitage, his estate near Nashville. When Harrison won the election of 1840, Jackson had said he hoped to live long enough to see another Democrat as President. In a way, his wish came true with Tyler.

When Tyler recommended that Congress add Texas to the Union, Jackson was overjoyed. A strong nationalist to the end, he exclaimed: "All is safe at last!"

4. Section Review

1. Why did Andrew Jackson oppose the Bank of the United States?
2. Why was the Whig Party formed?
3. Why did the Democrats lose the election of 1840?
4. Critical Thinking Why do you think that serious issues received little attention in the political campaigns leading up to the election of 1840?

Why We Remember

The Age of Jackson

When Old Hickory died in the spring of 1845 at the age of 78, the nation went into mourning. All across the country there were solemn services marking the passing of a remarkable leader.

The Age of Jackson was over, but Jackson's legacy lived on. One of his gifts to the future was the Democratic Party. It is our oldest political party.

Jackson changed American politics forever. In the past, politics had been for the wealthy and powerful. Jackson and his Democrats brought common folk into politics for the first time by making campaigns more exciting.

Jackson also changed the role of the President. Until he took office, most Presidents had seen their duty as running the executive branch and carrying out the will of Congress. Jackson, however, believed the President's job was to represent the will of the people in national affairs. He was the first President to veto acts of Congress that, in his view, did not do what the people wanted done. He would not be the last.

Finally, Jackson gave new meaning to the American Dream. Presidents before him had all been well born and well educated. Jackson was neither. When a woman who knew him as a young man heard he was running for President, she exclaimed:

❝What! Jackson up for President? JACKSON? ANDREW Jackson? The Jackson that used to live in Salisbury? . . . Well, if Andrew Jackson can be President, anybody can!❞

Skill Lab

Skill Tips

Some clues to stereotypes:
- exaggerated statements or pictures
- overly negative or overly positive statements or pictures
- generalizations that are too broad (often containing words like *all*, *every*, or *none*)

Thinking Critically
Recognizing Stereotypes

In the presidential campaign of 1828, Democrats sneered that John Quincy Adams was an aristocrat like his father, John Adams. "King John the Second," they called him. Little did Jackson's supporters dream that Jackson himself would be labeled "King Andrew" during his presidency.

Question to Investigate

Was it fair of Andrew Jackson's critics to accuse him of acting like a king?

Procedure

"King Andrew" is an example of a **stereotype**—an oversimplified image of a person, group, or idea. Stereotypes can be expressed in statements or pictures. They can be negative or positive. Either way, you need to recognize them in order to judge people and events fairly. Study the political cartoon, which appeared during Jackson's second term.

1 Identify the stereotype.
a. List features of the cartoon that fit clues in the Skill Tips.
b. Explain whether the stereotype is positive or negative.

2 Identify who might have created the stereotype and why.
a. Did the cartoonist support or oppose Jackson? Explain.
b. Why do you think the cartoon was created? Explain, using details from the cartoon.

3 Evaluate how well the stereotype fits.
a. List examples of Jackson's actions under two headings: *Kinglike* and *Not Kinglike*.
b. Answer the Question to Investigate.

Source to Use

BORN TO COMMAND.

OF VETO MEMORY.

HAD I BEEN CONSULTED.

KING ANDREW THE FIRST.

Reviewing Vocabulary

Define the following terms.
1. caucus
2. suffrage
3. mudslinging
4. spoils system
5. secede
6. sovereignty

Reviewing Main Ideas

1. How did the candidates and campaigns during the election of 1828 differ from those during the election of 1824?

2. What events led to the nullification crisis of 1832?

3. How did Jackson respond to South Carolina's actions and why?

4. Explain why Jackson favored the removal of eastern Indians from their homelands.

5. Describe how each of the following tribes resisted removal and what happened as a result. (a) Sauk and Fox (b) Seminoles (c) Cherokees

6. Why did Jackson see the Bank as a threat to common people?

7. What were the political and economic effects of Jackson's "war" with the Bank?

Thinking Critically

1. Application Mudslinging occurs today, just as it did in the elections of Jackson's time. Give two examples from recent political campaigns. Why do you think mudslinging has been so common? How do you think it affects our democracy?

2. Analysis Find evidence from the chapter to support the following statement: Andrew Jackson can be called a bundle of contradictions.

3. Why We Remember: Evaluation How did Jackson give new meaning to the American Dream? Do you think his election was good for the future of American democracy? Explain.

Applying Skills

Recognizing stereotypes Recalling what you learned about stereotypes on page 369, find a recent political cartoon that presents a stereotype of a government official or candidate. Then write responses to these questions:

1. Describe the stereotype. Explain whether it is positive or negative.

2. Why do you think the cartoonist created the stereotype?

3. Based on what you know about the official or candidate, how well do you think the stereotype fits? Explain.

History Mystery

A Georgia plantation Answer the History Mystery on page 347. The two-story brick mansion shown in the photo was built in 1804 and is now a state historic site. The owner of this mansion had 800 acres of farmland, 42 cabins, 6 barns, a mill, a trading post, and more than 1,000 peach trees. Recall why this person and others like him decided to live in houses like this and to farm the land. Considering their reasons, why do you think they might have been surprised and angry at being told they had to leave?

Writing in Your History Journal

1. Keys to History (a) The time line on pages 346–347 has seven Keys to History. In your journal, describe why each one is important to know about. (b) Decide on a category of additional events for the time line, such as *Economic Events* or *Events Related to Indian Removal*. Write the appropriate events and their dates in your journal, along with why you think the events should be added.

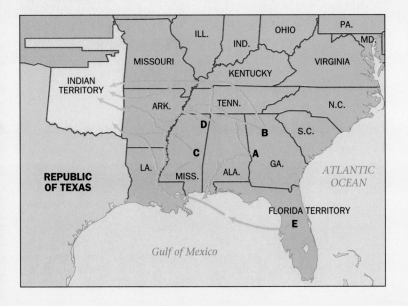

Map labels: ILL., OHIO, PA., MD., IND., MISSOURI, VIRGINIA, KENTUCKY, INDIAN TERRITORY, ARK., TENN., N.C., D, B, S.C., C, A, GA., LA., MISS., ALA., REPUBLIC OF TEXAS, ATLANTIC OCEAN, FLORIDA TERRITORY, E, Gulf of Mexico

Reviewing Geography

1. Each letter on the map represents one of the tribes forced to move west of the Mississippi in the early 1800s. Write each letter and the name of the tribe.

2. Geographic Thinking In Jackson's time people thought of the United States as having three distinct sections, or regions. What were those three sections? Where were they? How did they differ? Do people today think of the United States as having those same three sections? Explain.

2. Andrew Jackson Imagine that you went to grade school with Andrew Jackson. Would you vote for him as the classmate "Most Likely to Succeed" or the one "Least Likely to Succeed"? Explain in your journal. If necessary, review the information on page 348.

3. Citizenship Imagine two modern presidential candidates, one with a personality and views like John Quincy Adams and another with a personality and views like Andrew Jackson. Which candidate do you think would be more likely to be elected President today? Why? Write your response in your journal.

Alternative Assessment

Journal writing Imagine that you lived during "The Age of Jackson" and were writing journal notes on events and issues of your day.

❶ Decide what kind of person you are: your gender, the section of the country where you live, your type of job, and your social background.

❷ Write one or more journal entries on each of the following topics, describing the topics and also your thoughts and reactions to them.
• The election of 1828
• The Webster-Hayne debates
• Jackson's Indian policy
• The "bank war"
• The election of 1840

Your work will be evaluated on the following criteria
• you are careful to base your descriptions on historical facts
• your reactions to the topics reflect the likely viewpoint of the type of person you represent
• your journal entries are interesting and creative

Chapter 14

The Westward Movement

Keys to History

1821
William Becknell blazes the Santa Fe Trail
American merchants sight Santa Fe

1823
First fur trappers' rendezvous
Painting of a mountain man

1820

1830

Looking Back

Lewis and Clark Expedition
1804–1806

For many years the words "Great American Desert" appeared on maps of North America. Yet this desert does not actually exist. What part of the United States was once known as the "Great American Desert," and why?

1835–1836

"Remember the Alamo" becomes Texas rallying cry

Stamp honoring the battle of the Alamo

1836

Whitmans lead first families on the Oregon Trail

Monument to women pioneers

1846–1848

War with Mexico

Treaty of Guadalupe Hidalgo, ending the war

1849

Height of California gold rush

1840

1850

World Link

Wars between Britain and China

1839–1860

Looking Ahead

First transcontinental railroad completed

1869

Beginning the Story with

John and Jessie Frémont

When John C. Frémont (FREE-mont)—a dashing, charming, and intensely ambitious army officer—first visited the Washington home of Missouri Senator Thomas Hart Benton, the two men found they shared a passionate interest in expanding the nation westward. As much as the senator and his wife liked Frémont, however, neither had thought of him as a husband for their 16-year-old daughter Jessie.

At age 27, Frémont seemed too old for Jessie. His family background was also questionable. Frémont's mother had left her husband to live with a penniless French artist. Frémont had managed to get a good education, but he had been expelled from college his senior year for cutting classes. He just was not what they had in mind for a son-in-law.

Their daughter Jessie—a talented, bold, headstrong young woman—had different ideas. When Jessie looked at John Frémont, she saw her future. John and Jessie were married in a secret ceremony in 1841, when Jessie was just 17. A month later, her parents gave their blessing.

Exploring the West

Soon after the wedding, Frémont took charge of an army expedition to survey a route from the Mississippi River to the Rocky Mountains. With him went a German map maker named Charles Preuss, a fur trapper and guide named Kit Carson, and Jessie's 12-year-old brother Randolph. Senator Benton sent his son to prove that western travel was safe even for children.

Traveling west across the plains, Frémont and Preuss made detailed observations of landscapes, plants, and animals. With this information they would later produce the most accurate maps yet made of the region. As the expedition neared the Rocky Mountains, someone warned Frémont that the Cheyennes and Sioux would attack anyone who crossed into their hunting grounds. Frémont responded with his own warning:

"We are few, and you are many, and may kill us all. . . . Do you think that our great chief [the President] will let his soldiers die and forget to cover their graves? Before the snows melt again, his warriors will sweep away your villages."

The Indians let the expedition pass unharmed. When Frémont finally reached the crest of the Rockies, he climbed the tallest peak he could find and unfurled an American flag. When he returned home weeks later, he draped this same flag over Jessie, who lay in bed resting after the birth of their first child. "This flag was raised over the highest peak of the Rocky Mountains," he announced dramatically. "I have brought it to you."

This scene from one of Frémont's reports shows members of his party in the Sierra Nevada. They are stamping out a spot in the snow to make a campsite.

The Pathfinder

Frémont also brought Jessie his expedition notes, which she helped turn into an official report. In fact, although John's name was on the report, Jessie actually wrote much of it. "The horseback life, the sleep in the open air," she later explained, "had unfitted Mr. Frémont for the indoor work of writing." Luckily for him, his wife had a way with words. Thanks to her skillful pen, the report became a bestseller.

During the next few years Frémont led more expeditions west. After each journey, Jessie helped him write books that excited readers in the East about the beauty and bounty of the West. Frémont's widely read books helped to inspire a great westward migration. They also served as guides for would-be settlers, providing them with information about routes, campsites, rivers, wildlife, and weather. Little wonder that Frémont became known to his adoring public as "The Pathfinder."

Hands-On → *HISTORY*

Activity

Imagine that the Frémonts have hired you to paint a portrait of each of them. They have decided what to wear. Now you must think of special objects—for example, a pen or a map—to put in each portrait to help viewers understand John and Jessie Frémont. For each portrait list three such objects and suggest an appropriate background. Then make sketches for the portraits.

1. Trappers and Traders Blaze the Way

Reading Guide

New Term expansionists

Section Focus Events that drew Americans' attention to the West

1. What was Manifest Destiny?
2. How did the activities of mountain men and Santa Fe traders create enthusiasm for the Far West?

In the early 1800s, when an American talked about "the West," he or she probably meant the Old Northwest or the Old Southwest. These were the lands between the Appalachians and the Mississippi River.

Already, however, a few American explorers and adventurers were moving beyond the Mississippi, into the Louisiana Territory and farther. Better transportation—especially the steamboat—encouraged some. Hard times pushed others west in search of fresh opportunities.

When these Americans talked about "the West," they meant the land just west of the Mississippi River. The land that lay far across the continent from the Atlantic Coast became known as "the Far West."

Gradually many different kinds of people drifted into the West—Americans, Germans, French, and others. They were trappers, farmers, adventurers, and people who simply wanted to get away from everyone else. Some were heroes and some were villains. In the West they met the Indians and the Mexicans who already lived there.

The story of the West is a story of possibilities and of danger. Most of all, it is the story of the meeting of many different peoples. From this meeting, new ways of life would emerge.

Manifest Destiny

John C. Frémont, his wife Jessie, and her father, Thomas Hart Benton, were eager **expansionists**—people who believe that their country's prosperity depends on enlarging its territory. They dreamed of a United States with borders stretching from coast to coast. Jessie called it "a grand plan."

In 1845 John O'Sullivan, the editor of a New York newspaper, gave the grand plan a name. He called it Manifest Destiny. In an editorial he declared that God had given the United States a "manifest destiny to overspread the continent."

Manifest means obvious, or clear. Destiny means fate. Supporters of Manifest Destiny believed that God had blessed their country. It was clear to them that Americans had the right, even the duty, to expand their way of life and their government westward until the United States reached across the continent to the Pacific Ocean.

Some people argued that by expanding the nation to the Pacific Coast, Americans could fulfill the dreams of Christopher Columbus. According to these expansionists, the United States would become the route to Asia that Europeans had searched for for so long. Thomas Hart Benton urged:

> **"**Let us vindicate [set right] the glory of Columbus by realizing his divine idea of arriving in the east [Asia] by going to the west.**"**

Of course, most of the land west of the United States in the 1840s belonged to Mexico. The rest was part of Oregon Country, which the United States shared with England. The claims of other nations did not stop the dreams of expansionists, though. Neither did the fact that many Indians already occupied the land.

Mountain Men

American enthusiasm for the Far West began with the stories of Lewis and Clark and the trappers and traders who followed them. When Lewis and Clark returned from the Far West in 1806, they reported mountain streams teeming with beaver. At the time, velvety beaver fur was popular for top hats worn by gentlemen of fashion. It was also used to trim cloaks, boots, and dresses.

The year after Lewis and Clark's return, Manuel Lisa, a Spanish American trader from St. Louis, ventured up the Missouri River to the Yellowstone River. Where the Little Bighorn River meets the Yellowstone, he built Fort Manuel. From there he sent trappers into the Rocky Mountains.

Other fur companies followed Lisa. These companies hired restless young men willing to risk their lives in the western mountains for an annual salary of $200. The trappers were known as mountain men.

Mountain men worked alone or in small groups. Their lives were often lonely, usually dangerous, and always hard. Many of them earned colorful reputations. For example,

Manuel Lisa

Jim Beckwourth

This picture of two mountain men at work looks quite peaceful. In fact, trapping was dangerous. Some hazards that trappers might face were drowning, bad falls, gunshots, rattlesnakes, bears, and infections.

Hugh Glass lived to tell about his hand-to-paw fight with a grizzly bear. Jim Beckwourth, son of a Virginia slave, became a chief of the Crow Indians.

In fact, many trappers owed their mountaineering skills and knowledge of trails to Indians. Often they lived and worked side by side with Indians and married Indian women. American writer Washington Irving once observed:

❝You cannot pay a free trapper a greater compliment than to persuade him you have mistaken him for an Indian.❞

The rendezvous Each summer between 1823 and 1837, trappers met at a prearranged spot for a large gathering known as the rendezvous (RAHN-day-voo). Indian traders and trappers were welcomed, too. Here they met supply wagons sent from St. Louis by the fur companies.

The rendezvous was a grand fair where trappers sold furs and bought necessities and luxuries for the next year, such as ammunition, traps, axes, sugar, and coffee. It was also a time for games, gossip, and gambling. By the end of a rendezvous, more than one mountain man found he had gambled away all the money he had earned from his furs that year.

Western guides The time when mountain men roamed the West was short. By 1840 the beaver were almost extinct from over-hunting, and beaver hats had gone out of style.

By then, though, the mountain men had learned much about the landscape of the West. Like Kit Carson, Frémont's guide, other mountain men took jobs as guides and interpreters. Government exploration parties and settlers heading west depended on mountain men to show them the way.

∞ Link to Art

The Trapper's Bride (1850) The wedding in this painting took place in 1837. That was the year William Stewart, a Scottish adventurer, invited artist Alfred Jacob Miller to the Rockies. During the summer rendezvous of hundreds of trappers and thousands of Shoshones, Crows, Nez Percés, and other Indians, Miller sketched the people around him.

Back home in New Orleans, he used his sketches as models for paintings that showed friendly relations between trappers and Indians. **Discuss** How does the painting indicate that mountain men and Indians saw each other as equals?

Santa Fe Traders

Santa Fe traders also played a big part in drawing people west. In 1800 Santa Fe was a distant outpost of the Spanish empire. Mexico City, the capital of Mexico, lay more than 1,500 miles (2,413 km) to the south over difficult mountain roads. Santa Fe had almost 4,000 citizens and a rich supply of silver and furs, but lacked manufactured goods such as cloth, cooking utensils, and tools.

As early as 1804 an enterprising merchant from Illinois went to Santa Fe hoping to open up trade. Suspecting the merchant of spying, Spanish authorities arrested him. The situation changed dramatically, however, when Mexico won its independence from Spain in 1821 (see page 329). After that, Mexico opened its northern borders to foreign traders.

In that same year William Becknell, a Missouri trader, reached Santa Fe with a train of pack mules loaded with goods. He made such a large profit that he returned the following year with wagons.

Becknell became known as the Father of the Santa Fe Trail. The route he blazed stretched across nearly 800 miles (1,287 km) of wide prairies and scorching deserts between Independence, Missouri, and Santa Fe. Other traders rushed to use the new route. One outfit went to Santa Fe with merchandise worth $35,000 and returned with silver and furs worth $190,000.

The stories of the Santa Fe traders—like those of the mountain men—encouraged Americans to think about moving west, even beyond the boundaries of the United States. The traders proved that wagon trains were a practical and safe means of crossing the plains. They also brought back word that the borders of Mexico were weakly guarded. They led immigrants to believe that they could move into Texas, New Mexico, and California with little risk.

1. Section Review

1. Define **expansionists**.
2. For Americans, how did the meaning of the expression "the West" change between 1800 and 1820?
3. What was one argument in favor of Manifest Destiny?
4. How did the mountain men and the Santa Fe traders each make it easier for Americans to think about moving west?
5. Critical Thinking Write three questions that you would ask a mountain man in 1840 if you were thinking about moving from an eastern city to an area west of the Rockies.

2. The Republic of Texas

Reading Guide

New Term **annex**

Section Focus **How Texas became an independent nation**

1. Why did Americans want to settle in Texas, and why did Mexico let them?
2. Why did Mexico ban American immigration to Texas in 1830?
3. What caused the United States to reject Texas annexation in 1836?

Trappers and traders were not the only Americans interested in Mexican land. Southern farmers began to hear of Texas, an ideal place to grow cotton. However, Texas belonged to the King of Spain, and he had ruled it off limits for Americans.

Austin's Dream

In 1820 Missouri banker Moses Austin went to San Antonio, capital of Spanish Texas, and asked authorities to grant him land in Texas. He planned to sell it to American settlers at a profit. Spanish authorities approved. In return, he promised to bring in 300 families who would swear loyalty to Spain. They would defend the area against illegal American immigrants.

In 1821, as Austin prepared to launch his community, he fell gravely ill. On his deathbed he asked his son Stephen to carry on his dream. Although Stephen had hoped to become a lawyer, he felt he could not say no. He appealed to Spanish authorities, who gave him permission to carry on in his father's place. Later, Stephen recalled:

"I bid an everlasting farewell to my native country, and adopted this [Mexico], and in so doing I determined to fulfill rigidly all the duties and obligations of a Mexican citizen.**"**

Approval from Mexico

Stephen Austin brought the first group of settlers to land lying between the Brazos and Colorado Rivers in 1821. He named the area San Felipe de Austin. Thus began what would become the state of Texas.

Soon Austin learned that Mexico had won its independence. Would the new government allow the Americans to stay? Austin set out on the 1,200-mile (1,931-km) journey to Mexico City to talk to officials.

Austin ended up staying in Mexico City for more than a year. He learned to speak Spanish. Then he quietly presented his case. He promised to fill the land with respectable people who would defend it against Apaches, Comanches, and American bandits and horse thieves.

In April 1823 the Mexican authorities approved the colony, with certain conditions. Every settler had to become a Mexican citizen and abide by Mexican laws. Every settler also had to promise to become a Roman Catholic. Austin agreed.

Settling Texas

Austin's colony prospered. By 1830 it had as many as 20,000 people. Some were from other parts of Mexico, but most were Americans. They included hundreds of farmers from the South looking for good cotton land. The population also included African Americans, both free and enslaved.

Pleased by the success of Austin's colony, Mexico granted land to other Americans. The new settlers, however, did not always become Roman Catholics and abide by Mexican laws, as they had promised.

The rapid growth of American settlements alarmed Mexican authorities. In 1828 a Mexican general reported that Americans in Texas outnumbered Mexicans ten to one. "Either the government occupies Texas now," he wrote, "or it is lost forever."

In 1830, fearful that the settlers might seize Texas, the Mexican government banned American immigration. The government also outlawed the slave trade, put customs duties on goods from the United States, and sent troops to enforce the new laws.

The Quarrel with Mexico

Texans did not like the government's actions. They especially resented it when Mexico combined Texas with another state, Coahuila (KŌ-uh-WEE-luh), and moved its capital to a city 500 miles (805 km) away. To make matters worse, Texas got only one seat in the Coahuila-Texas legislature.

In 1833 Texans learned that an army officer named Antonio López de Santa Anna had taken over Mexico's government. They signed petitions asking the new government to change the immigration law. They also asked that Texas be made a separate Mexican state so they could run their own affairs.

Stephen Austin carried the petitions to Mexico City. There he got the government to lift the immigration ban. He also heard that Santa Anna could not be trusted. Worried,

San Antonio was already a century old in the 1830s when Americans began to quarrel with Mexico. Across the main plaza you can see the clock above the old town hall, the center of power in Spanish Texas.

Austin wrote a letter urging Texans to form their own government. "The fate of Texas depends upon itself," he wrote.

When Santa Anna's officials found out about the letter, they thought Austin was plotting to tear Texas away from Mexico. They had Austin arrested and held in prison in Mexico City for nearly two years.

The Texas Revolution

In 1835 Santa Anna took total control of the Mexican government. Wherever Mexicans rebelled, Santa Anna ordered the army to put them down. Texans learned that Santa Anna was sending troops to Texas.

In November Texans held a convention in San Felipe. At first, they could not agree on whether they were loyal Mexicans fighting for statehood or rebels fighting for independence. In any case, they chose an ex-governor of Tennessee, Sam Houston, to command their volunteer army. Houston was a powerful leader.

Meanwhile, Texas volunteers in San Antonio surrounded the Alamo, a former mission occupied by a small Mexican army.

The Texans let the Mexican troops go when they promised not to fight Texans again.

The Alamo Then word came that Santa Anna's army was marching on San Antonio. One of the American volunteers, Jim Bowie, declared that saving Texas meant saving San Antonio first. He wrote:

"[Commander] Neill and myself have come to the solemn resolution that we will rather die in these ditches than give it [San Antonio] up to the enemy."

Americans, together with Mexicans who opposed Santa Anna, gathered at the Alamo. On February 23 Santa Anna demanded unconditional surrender. Two days later Captain Juan Seguin slipped out of the Alamo with a desperate plea from Lieutenant Colonel William Travis:

"It will be impossible for us to keep them out much longer. If they overpower us, we fall a sacrifice at the shrine of our country. . . . Give me help, oh my Country!"

The Alamo was first a mission, then a fort. Today the Lone Star flag flies over the restored building in memory of those who fought for Texas independence.

No help came. On March 6 Santa Anna's troops captured the Alamo, killing its more than 180 defenders. Among the dead was Davy Crockett, a former congressman from Tennessee. A few women and children survived the terrible ordeal.

Santa Anna ordered 18-year-old Susannah Dickerson, an Alamo survivor whose husband had just been slain, to ride out and spread word of the Texans' defeat. He hoped that news of the bloodshed at the Alamo would stop further rebellion. Instead, "Remember the Alamo!" became a rallying cry that inspired Texans to fight on.

Point of View

Why did Texans declare their independence?

In 1836, in a town called Washington-on-the-Brazos, Texans wrote a declaration of independence. In their view, they were not declaring war on Mexico, but on Santa Anna's government.

"Now, the good people of Texas . . . do solemnly declare:

1st. That they have taken up arms in defense of their Rights and Liberties, . . . and in defense of the . . . Constitution of Mexico.

2nd. That Texas is no longer, morally or civilly, bound by the compact of Union; yet . . . they [Texans] offer their support and assistance to such of the Mexicans . . . as will take up arms against their military despotism [Santa Anna's tyranny].

3rd. That they do not acknowledge that the present authorities of [Mexico] have the right to govern . . . Texas.

4th. That they will not cease to carry on war against the . . . authorities whilst their troops are within . . . Texas.

5th. That they hold it be their right . . . to establish an independent Government; but they will continue faithful to the Mexican Government so long as that nation is governed by the Constitution."

Santa Anna viewed the rebellion differently. In a speech to Mexican troops, he claimed that American settlers had planned all along to fill Texas with Americans and then take it away from Mexico:

"Forgetting what they owe to the supreme government of the nation which so generously admitted them to its bosom, gave them fertile lands to cultivate, and allowed them all the means to live in comfort and abundance—they have risen . . . , under the pretense of sustaining a system [supporting the old government] which an immense majority of Mexicans have asked to have changed, thus concealing their criminal purpose of dismembering [tearing apart] the . . . Republic [Mexico]."

It was too late for either side to listen to the other, however. The day the Texans finished writing their Declaration of Independence was the same day Travis wrote his plea for help. By the time the delegates received the message, Travis and the others were dead.

Independence

Santa Anna's troops marched across Texas, burning towns as they went. After his victory at Goliad, Santa Anna ordered all prisoners shot. The Texas rallying cry became, "Remember the Alamo! Remember Goliad!"

Sam Houston had a clever idea. He let everyone think that he and his troops were retreating. Santa Anna followed Houston

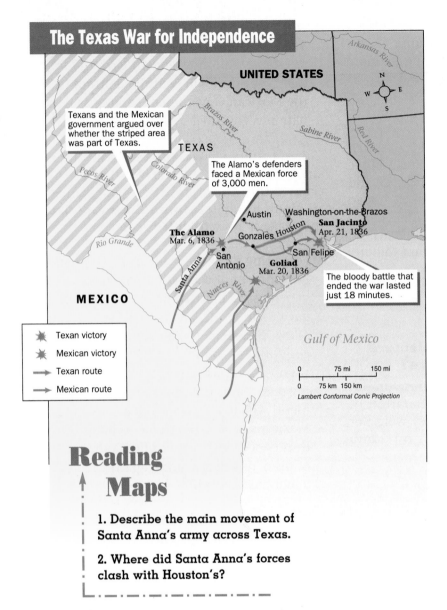

The Texas War for Independence

Texans and the Mexican government argued over whether the striped area was part of Texas.

UNITED STATES

The Alamo's defenders faced a Mexican force of 3,000 men.

TEXAS

The Alamo
Mar. 6, 1836

Austin

Washington-on-the-Brazos

San Jacinto
Apr. 21, 1836

Gonzales

Houston

San Felipe

San Antonio

Goliad
Mar. 20, 1836

The bloody battle that ended the war lasted just 18 minutes.

MEXICO

Gulf of Mexico

0	75 mi	150 mi
0	75 km	150 km

Lambert Conformal Conic Projection

★ Texan victory

✦ Mexican victory

→ Texan route

→ Mexican route

Reading Maps

1. Describe the main movement of Santa Anna's army across Texas.

2. Where did Santa Anna's forces clash with Houston's?

Lone Star Republic

Meanwhile, Texans ratified a constitution and elected Sam Houston President. Because most Texans had come from the South, their constitution made slavery legal. Texans expected the United States to recognize Texas as an independent nation, then **annex** it, which means to take territory and add it on to a country.

Southerners welcomed the idea of annexation. It would mean another slave state in the Union. Northerners opposed it for the same reason. Many people on both sides feared that annexation would lead to war with Mexico. As a result, Congress recognized Texas as a nation but did not annex it.

Texas—also known as the Lone Star Republic because of the single star on its flag—was independent for nearly ten years. In that time the Texas question remained a controversial issue in United States politics.

deep into Texas. On April 21, 1836, Houston's forces turned suddenly and trapped Santa Anna's troops at the San Jacinto River. To gain his freedom, Santa Anna ordered all his armies to leave Texas immediately. The Texans released him several months later.

The Mexican Congress was furious with Santa Anna. They refused to recognize that Texans had won. Other urgent problems, however, kept them from sending a new army to retake Texas.

2. Section Review

1. Define **annex.**

2. Explain why Americans settled in Texas.

3. Why did Mexico encourage Americans at first, then ban American immigration?

4. Why did the United States government decide against annexing Texas in 1836?

5. Critical Thinking Choose three events and explain how each one helped lead to Texas's independence.

3. Trails West

Reading Guide

Section Focus **How Americans began to settle the Far West**

1. What drew American settlers to California and Oregon?
2. What was life like on the Oregon Trail?
3. Why did the Mormons go west?
4. What did Indians and Mexicans think of the rush of settlers?

While Texans were fighting for independence, other Americans were looking for lands to settle even farther west. They eagerly listened to the stories told by explorers, trappers, and traders.

Early reports had been discouraging. In the 1820s Major Stephen Long had explored the plains from the Mississippi River to the Rockies. Because he saw few trees and very little water, he made the mistake of thinking that the plains could never become good farmland. He called a large area that is now part of Kansas and Colorado the "Great American Desert."

More appealing were the stories that trappers and traders told of the Far West. Although California and Oregon Country were not part of the United States, by the 1830s Americans were eyeing them with great interest.

Huge cattle ranches sprawled across Mexican California. Cowboys called *vaqueros*—like those racing down this dusty road—were expert riders.

California

As you read in Chapter 1, California was home to many Indian tribes. The first Europeans to arrive were the Spanish. Between 1769 and 1823 Spanish missionaries established a chain of 21 missions along the California coast from San Diego to Sonoma, north of San Francisco.

When Mexico became independent, California was part of the new nation. Communication was slow, though, between the faraway government in Mexico City and the small population of *Californios,* the descendants of the Spanish settlers. Over time, Californios began to think of themselves as separate from Mexico.

The first Americans to reach California came by sea. In the 1820s they sailed along the coast buying cow hides to be used for making shoes and animal fat for candles.

The California Trail

In 1833 fur trader Benjamin Bonneville hired mountain man Joseph Reddeford Walker to find a practical overland route to California. With 40 men Joe Walker left the Green River in the Rocky Mountains, crossed the Great Basin, and climbed to the crest of the Sierra Nevada. Walker's route into California became known as the California Trail.

Californians greeted Walker and his party warmly. Mexican cattle ranchers entertained Walker's party with barbecues and displays of roping and riding.

Like Texas, California was sparsely settled. Mexican authorities in California offered Walker land if he would bring in reliable settlers. Walker turned down the offer, but six of his men stayed in California.

Back in the United States, Walker told about the rich soil, warm sun, and good times to be found in California. One of his men, Zenas Leonard, expressed the same eagerness as other expansionists:

" Our government . . . should assert her claim by taking possession of the whole territory as soon as possible—for we have good reason to suppose that the territory west of the mountain [Rockies] will some day be equally as important to [the] nation as that on the east. "

The Oregon Trail

The California Trail branched off from an earlier route that fur traders and trappers had made by following Indian trails west. Later known as the Oregon Trail, that route stretched from Independence, Missouri, west across 2,000 miles (3,219 km) of prairies, mountains, and deserts.

The Oregon Trail ended in Oregon Country. (See the map on page 387.) In 1818 the United States and England had agreed to occupy the region jointly. At that time, the only British and American citizens in the area were a few fur traders.

Then Christian missionaries became interested in Oregon. In 1836 Marcus and Narcissa Whitman started west on the Oregon Trail with Eliza and Henry Spalding. Marcus had already scouted the trail. Now, the Whitmans wanted to prove that women—indeed, entire families with their wagons—could travel to Oregon.

The Whitmans' main goal was to convert the Cayuse Indians to Christianity, so they built a mission in eastern Oregon. They are best remembered, though, because their glowing reports of Oregon's climate and soil attracted settlers by the thousands.

What started as a trickle became a flood. By 1840 only 13 people had followed the Whitmans to Oregon. In spring 1843 almost 1,000 people left Missouri and headed west.

Frémont's surveys In 1842, to encourage even more Americans to go west, the United States government sent John C. Frémont to survey the Oregon Trail. Frémont

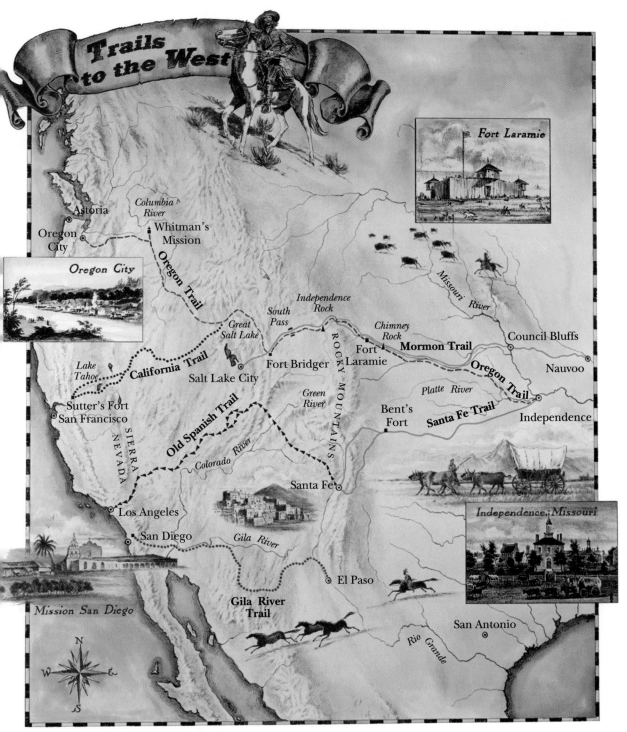

Trails to the West

Fort Laramie

Oregon City

Astoria
Oregon City
Columbia River
Whitman's Mission
Oregon Trail
South Pass
Independence Rock
Chimney Rock
Mormon Trail
Council Bluffs
Missouri River
Great Salt Lake
Fort Bridger
Fort Laramie
Oregon Trail
Nauvoo
California Trail
Lake Tahoe
Salt Lake City
Green River
Platte River
Bent's Fort
Santa Fe Trail
Independence
Sutter's Fort
San Francisco
Old Spanish Trail
Colorado River
ROCKY MOUNTAINS
SIERRA NEVADA
Los Angeles
San Diego
Gila River
Santa Fe
Independence, Missouri
Mission San Diego
Gila River Trail
El Paso
San Antonio
Rio Grande

N
W E
S

Reading Maps

Select one trail. Describe landforms you would expect to meet as you traveled westward on that trail. Refer to the map on pages R4–R5 for additional information.

Hands-On HISTORY

Activity

1. With a partner, imagine you are on the Oregon Trail in 1850. Your possessions include a rifle, ammunition, bedding, hatchet, flour, iron stove, tin dishes, clothing, washbowl, dried beef, hoe, coffee, violin, plow, shovel, clock, china dishes, chest of drawers, coffeepot, and rocking chair. Write each item on an index card or slip of paper.

2. In addition, on each of six cards write a hazard you might meet on the trail. For example: "You come to the flooded Platte River. Lighten your load before crossing."

3. Take turns: One person draws a hazard card and reads it aloud. The other person chooses two items to throw out.

4. When you have finished, look at the items that remain. Compare your results with those of other teams. What team made the best choices? Explain.

followed up the first survey with two other trips, one of them with Joe Walker as guide.

The government published the reports Frémont wrote with his wife, Jessie, and a detailed map of the trail. The map showed river crossings, pastures, and hazards. It was printed in seven large sections that could be read easily, even in bouncing wagons.

Life on the Trail

Thanks in part to Frémont's work, hopeful immigrants gathered in Independence, Missouri, each spring, bound for Oregon and California. They organized into wagon trains—lines of wagons traveling together. Each train chose a captain—often a former mountain man—who was expected to know the route and make key decisions.

Life on the trail quickly fell into a routine. Everyone had to be up and about before

sunrise. Women and girls prepared breakfast. Men and boys yoked the oxen. As the sun rose, the wagon train got under way. By evening on a good day, the train might have traveled 15 miles (24 km).

Timing was vital, however. Wagon trains had to leave Independence by May to get across the mountains before winter. Travelers caught in the Rockies or Sierra Nevada when snow fell faced disaster. In 1846 a group of 87 people bound for California—the Donner party—was trapped by early winter storms in the Sierra. Only 45 of them survived starvation and the freezing snows.

Snow was just one danger. Wagons broke down, and horses and oxen died. Travelers also faced snakebites, stampedes, raging rivers, and grassland fires. They killed each other in robberies and arguments.

Still, most deaths were caused by disease, especially cholera. In 1852 Ezra Meeker met

11 wagons returning east, all driven by women. Cholera had killed every man in the wagon train. That same year a woman pioneer noted in her diary that she had seen 21 freshly dug graves in 18 miles.

The mighty highway In spite of danger and death, the Oregon Trail became a mighty highway, in some places a mile wide where wagons moved along side by side. Because so many horses, oxen, and other livestock traveled with the trains, simply finding grass to feed the animals was a major chore. Pierre de Smet, a Catholic missionary, described the situation in 1851:

"This noble highway . . . is as smooth as a barn floor swept by the winds, and not a blade of grass can shoot up on it on account of continued passing."

The lead wagons of one train were sometimes only a few yards behind the last wagons of the train in front of them. Imagine what it must have been like to be part of a procession such as the one James Wilkins described in his diary on June 13, 1850:

"[I] find many companies continually in sight. In fact it is one continued stream. As far as we can see, both in front and near the horizon is dotted with white wagon covers of emigrants, like a string of beads."

Four days after Wilkins wrote these words, 6,034 people passed Fort Laramie, Wyoming, an all-time record for one day on the Oregon Trail. Between 1840 and 1860 more than 250,000 people trooped over the trail. In some places their wagon wheels carved deep ruts in the earth that can still be seen today.

The Mormons

Oregon and California were not the only destinations of the overland trails. Members of the Church of Jesus Christ of Latter-day Saints, more commonly known as Mormons, made their way to Utah.

Joseph Smith founded the church in New York in the 1820s. However, some of the Mormons' neighbors thought their beliefs were dangerously different. For example,

In this painting, westward-bound pioneers are seeking the advice of an experienced mountain man. The earliest immigrants knew little about the geography of the land that lay ahead of them after they left Missouri. Often all they knew was that they were heading for the setting sun.

Mormons at first shared all property, and some Mormons believed that a man could have more than one wife.

Smith and his followers moved several times to find a place where they could practice their religion in peace. They founded Nauvoo, Illinois, to be a model Mormon community. Instead, in 1844 mobs angered by Mormon beliefs killed Joseph Smith and threatened other Mormons.

After Smith's death, Brigham Young became head of the church. He and other leaders studied Frémont's report on the West, then chose an isolated valley near the Great Salt Lake to be the Mormons' next home.

Making the desert bloom Moving large numbers of people from Illinois to Utah was a challenge. Some Mormons came from even farther away—Germany, England, and Scandinavia. Following a route that paralleled the Oregon Trail, the first 148 settlers arrived at Salt Lake in July 1847. Within ten years their number had swelled to more than 20,000.

After a year of near-starvation, the colony started to prosper. Thanks to hard work and a well-planned irrigation system, green fields sprouted out of the arid landscape.

Indians in the Far West

What about the people who already occupied the Far West? Spaniards and their Mexican descendants had been there for more than 100 years. Indians had lived in

In the 1850s these Mormon converts from Europe walked 1,300 miles (2,092 km) from Iowa to Utah, pulling their belongings in hand carts.

Sarah Winnemucca spoke five languages, including Spanish and English. She became a valued interpreter, scout, and teacher, and spoke out for the rights of the Paiute people.

the region for many centuries. What did they make of the newcomers?

Some Indians were alarmed. Sarah Winnemucca, a member of the Paiute tribe, described what happened when the first wagon train came into Nevada in the late 1840s.

❝What a fright we all got one morning to hear that white people were coming. Our mothers buried me and my cousin. They placed sage bushes over our faces to keep the sun from burning them and there we were left all day. They told us if we heard any noises not to cry out, for if we did the white people would surely kill us and eat us.❞

Still, many Indians found it in their interest to trade with settlers. In addition, some Indians earned money by helping wagon trains. For example, members of the Kansa tribe ferried wagons across the Platte River for a fee.

However, misunderstandings occurred, and conflicts broke out. The Whitmans' mission and school among the Cayuse Indians was the site of the first major violence between Indians and American settlers in the Far West.

The Cayuses had welcomed the mission at first. Then Cayuse children caught measles

from a white visitor. The disease spread, killing half the tribe. The grieving survivors attacked the mission, killing the Whitmans and ten others. In return, settlers attacked Indians, even some who had had nothing to do with the raid. Indians and settlers in the West began to distrust one another.

Americans in California

By the end of 1845 roughly 800 Americans had settled among the 7,500 Mexicans and 72,000 Indians in California. At first, Mexican Californians welcomed the Americans.

However, when John C. Frémont's third expedition reached California in 1845, his party of 60 or so well-armed men worried the Mexican authorities. Having heard how Texas had slipped from Mexico's grasp, they ordered Frémont to leave California.

The next year some Californios met to discuss how to make the area strong and prosperous. One suggested an alliance with the leading naval power, Britain. Another favored France. Then voices spoke up for joining the United States. "With the United States," said one, "California will grow strong and flourish." Meanwhile, the idea that California's future lay with the United States was growing among American expansionists, too.

3. Section Review

1. How did Americans first became interested in settling in California? In Oregon?
2. Describe three dangerous situations that could arise on the Oregon Trail.
3. Why did the Mormons settle in Utah?
4. Critical Thinking Imagine that you were a *Californio* at the 1846 meeting about California's future. What is one argument you might have heard against joining the United States?

Skill Lab

Thinking Critically
Determining Credibility

"[He] is one of the most extraordinary men of the present era. His fame . . . is far surpassed by . . . personal traits of courage, coolness, fidelity [loyalty], kindness, honor, and friendship." So ran one biography of Kit Carson, whose widely reported adventures made him a larger-than-life hero.

Question to Investigate

Was Kit Carson a brave man or a coward?

Procedure

Read these two accounts of an event that occurred during one of John Frémont's expeditions, when Carson and another man chased Indians who had stolen horses. To get at the truth, try to determine the **credibility,** or believability, of each source.

1 Consider how the writer got the information.
a. How did Frémont and Preuss probably learn of the encounter with the Indians?
b. What effect might the source of information have on the accuracy of their accounts?

2 Consider the writer's point of view and purpose.
a. Recall what you know about Frémont. How might his point of view and purpose affect his accuracy?
b. Preuss was a foreign visitor who kept a diary. How might these factors affect his accuracy?

3 Compare the sources.
a. List similarities and differences in the accounts.
b. Suggest where you might find more information in order to answer the Question to Investigate.

Skill Tips

When you read a source, ask yourself:
- How did the writer get his or her information?
- What else do I know about the writer, such as point of view and purpose for writing?
- Is there any reason to think the writer might exaggerate, leave out important facts, or otherwise fail to tell the truth?
- What other sources might I compare with this one?

Sources to Use

A "[Kit Carson and Alex Godey] . . . proceeded quietly and had got within thirty or forty yards of their object, when a movement among the horses discovered them to the Indians; giving the war shout, they [Carson and Godey] instantly charged into the camp, regardless of the number [of Indians] which the four lodges would imply. The Indians received them with a flight of arrows . . . ; our men fired their rifles upon a steady aim and rushed in. Two Indians were stretched on the ground, fatally pierced with bullets. . . ."

From *Report of the Exploring Expedition to the Rocky Mountains* by John C. Frémont (University Microfilms, 1966)

B "Yesterday we stopped here to give Godey and Kit a chance to pursue the horsethieves. . . . Are these whites not much worse than the Indians? . . . These two heroes . . . shot the Indians [by] creeping up on them from behind. . . . The Indians are braver in a similar situation. Before they shoot, they raise a yelling war whoop. Kit and Alex sneaked, like cats, as close as possible. Kit shot an Indian in the back."

From *Exploring with Frémont* by Charles Preuss (University of Oklahoma Press, 1958). Preuss was the German map maker who accompanied Frémont.

4. Manifest Destiny Triumphs

Reading Guide

Section Focus **Final steps to achieving Manifest Destiny**

1. Why did the United States go to war with Mexico?
2. What were President Polk's goals in the war?
3. What is the Treaty of Guadalupe Hidalgo?
4. How did the discovery of gold change California?

In the mid-1840s Americans were scattered throughout the Far West and in Texas. As more and more Americans made the West their home, the idea grew that the area should belong to the United States.

By 1844 Manifest Destiny was becoming a powerful force in American politics. One delegate to a New Jersey political convention pledged, "We will give him [any young American] Oregon for his summer shade and the region of Texas as his winter pasture."

Annexing Texas and Oregon

The Democrats' candidate for President in 1844 was James K. Polk of Tennessee. Polk was a strong believer in Manifest Destiny.

President John Tyler, a Whig, also supported the idea of Manifest Destiny and planned to annex Texas if he won re-election. However, the majority of Whigs were strongly antislavery and opposed admitting

This painting became famous in the 1800s because it expressed the feelings of many Americans about Manifest Destiny. In it the spirit of Manifest Destiny is leading settlers west, stringing telegraph wires as she goes. How does the artist show his biases about American settlement of the West?

Texas as a slave state. Rather than nominate Tyler for a second term, the Whigs chose Henry Clay as their candidate.

Polk's victory in the election showed that the voters were in an expansionist mood. Congress quickly annexed Texas, which became a state in December 1845.

"Fifty-four Forty or Fight!" Once in office, Polk turned his attention to Oregon. In the past the United States had offered to divide Oregon Country with Britain at the 49th parallel of latitude.

Britain had refused. Now, however, Polk and the Democrats were demanding all of Oregon—54° 40′ north latitude. They rallied behind the slogan, "Fifty-four Forty or Fight!"

In 1846 the British said they were ready to divide Oregon at the 49th parallel. They also pledged to stay out of disputes between the United States and Mexico. Polk put the question to the Senate, which accepted the 49th parallel as the Oregon boundary.

War with Mexico

Meanwhile, Mexican officials were enraged over the annexation of Texas. They became even angrier when the United States claimed the Rio Grande as its boundary with Mexico. Mexicans placed the Texas boundary at the Nueces River, north of the Rio Grande.

Hostilities begin In late April 1846, Mexican troops fired at an American patrol along the Rio Grande, killing or wounding 16 soldiers. Mexico claimed that the patrol was in its territory. Polk, however, charged:

❝ Mexico has passed the boundary of the United States, has invaded our territory and shed American blood upon the American soil. **❞**

He asked Congress to declare war.

Some Americans were against the war. For example, Abraham Lincoln, then a congressman from Illinois, believed the American soldiers had actually been on Mexican soil. An American colonel in Texas privately agreed. He wrote in his diary:

❝ It looks as if the government sent a small force on purpose to bring on a war, so as to have a pretext [excuse] for taking California and as much of this country as it chooses. . . . My heart is not in this business. **❞**

Congress voted, however, eagerly for war: 40 votes to 2 in the Senate and 173 to 14 in the House. On May 12, 1846, the United States declared war on Mexico.

The first campaign Polk's first goal was to drive the Mexicans away from the Rio Grande. General Zachary Taylor led troops into northern Mexico and captured the fort at Monterrey in September.

In February 1847 General Santa Anna attacked Taylor at Buena Vista in a mountain pass near Monterrey. For two days more than 15,000 Mexicans tried to dislodge a smaller American army from the rocky heights. Instead, Taylor forced Santa Anna to retreat, which ended the fighting in northern Mexico.

New Mexico Polk's second goal was to occupy New Mexico and California. New Mexicans had mixed feelings about the United States. Like Texans, they were a long way from Mexico City. Their closest trade ties were north, along the Santa Fe Trail. In August 1846 General Stephen Watts Kearny captured Santa Fe without a shot. Although some New Mexicans opposed him over the next few months, Kearny kept control.

California John C. Frémont was in California when war broke out. Without authority, he encouraged Americans, as well

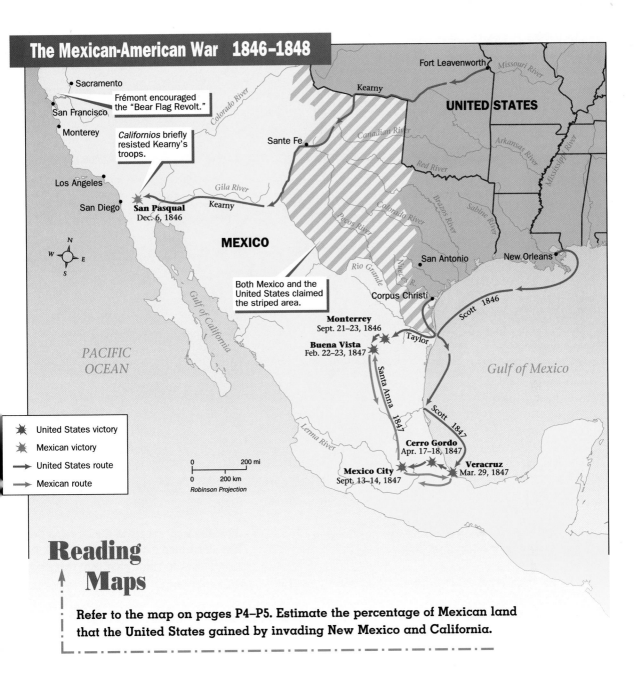

The Mexican-American War 1846–1848

- Sacramento
- San Francisco
- Monterey
- Los Angeles
- San Diego

Frémont encouraged the "Bear Flag Revolt."

Californios briefly resisted Kearny's troops.

San Pasqual
Dec. 6, 1846

Kearny

Gila River

MEXICO

Sante Fe

Fort Leavenworth

Missouri River

Kearny

UNITED STATES

Canadian River

Red River

Arkansas River

Mississippi River

Colorado River

Pecos River

Both Mexico and the United States claimed the striped area.

San Antonio

New Orleans

Brazos River

Sabine River

Monterrey
Sept. 21–23, 1846

Buena Vista
Feb. 22–23, 1847

Rio Grande

Nueces R.

Corpus Christi

Scott 1846

Taylor

Gulf of Mexico

PACIFIC OCEAN

Gulf of California

Santa Anna 1847

Scott 1847

Lerma River

Cerro Gordo
Apr. 17–18, 1847

Mexico City
Sept. 13–14, 1847

Veracruz
Mar. 29, 1847

N W E S

Legend:
- ✳ United States victory
- ✳ Mexican victory
- → United States route
- → Mexican route

0 — 200 mi
0 — 200 km
Robinson Projection

Reading Maps

Refer to the map on pages P4–P5. Estimate the percentage of Mexican land that the United States gained by invading New Mexico and California.

as some Mexican citizens, to declare independence and establish the Bear Flag Republic.

United States naval vessels arrived in San Francisco and Monterey Bays in July. Bear Flaggers joined the naval forces led by Admiral Robert Stockton, and by August they took Santa Barbara, Los Angeles, and San Diego. While Kearny was in Santa Fe, Americans were gaining control in California.

Like the people of New Mexico, Californians were divided. Some resisted. Others quietly agreed to American rule because they thought it would make California more prosperous.

Kearny arrived in December. Due to a mix-up over their orders, he and Stockton had a dispute over who had the highest authority in California. Frémont sided with Stockton.

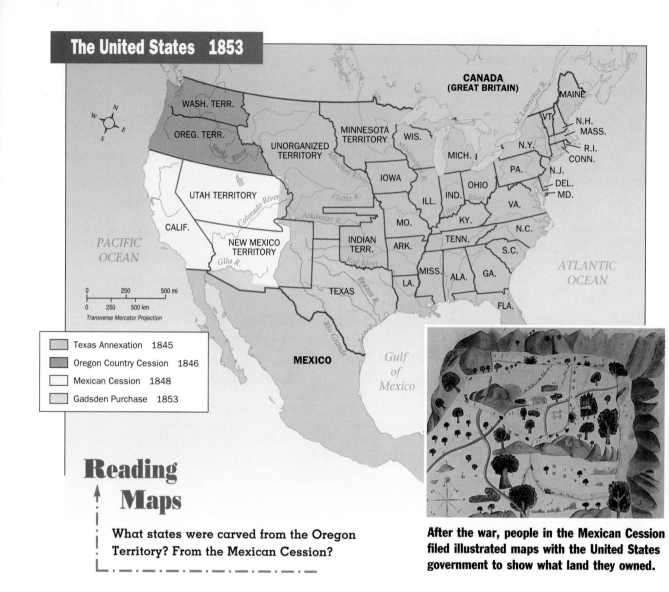

The United States 1853

WASH. TERR.

OREG. TERR.

CANADA
(GREAT BRITAIN)

MAINE

VT.

N.H.

MASS.

R.I.

CONN.

N.Y.

PA.

N.J.

DEL.

MD.

MINNESOTA
TERRITORY

WIS.

MICH.

UNORGANIZED
TERRITORY

IOWA

OHIO

IND.

ILL.

VA.

UTAH TERRITORY

CALIF.

NEW MEXICO
TERRITORY

MO.

KY.

N.C.

INDIAN
TERR.

ARK.

TENN.

S.C.

PACIFIC
OCEAN

Gila R.

Colorado River

Arkansas R.

Red River

MISS.

ALA.

GA.

LA.

TEXAS

Brazos R.

FLA.

ATLANTIC
OCEAN

Snake River

Missouri River

Platte R.

Mississippi R.

Ohio River

St. Lawrence R.

MEXICO

Rio Grande

Gulf
of
Mexico

0   250   500 mi
0   250   500 km
Transverse Mercator Projection

- Texas Annexation   1845
- Oregon Country Cession   1846
- Mexican Cession   1848
- Gadsden Purchase   1853

Reading Maps

What states were carved from the Oregon Territory? From the Mexican Cession?

After the war, people in the Mexican Cession filed illustrated maps with the United States government to show what land they owned.

Even after Kearny won out, Frémont defied him. Kearny had Frémont arrested. A military court convicted Frémont of disobedience and conduct unbecoming an officer. Frémont's military career was over. Still, in the eyes of many, he remained a hero.

The final campaign Polk's final goal was Mexico's surrender. General Winfield Scott landed at Veracruz, where Cortés had landed centuries before. At nearby Cerro Gordo, Scott won a decisive victory. Like Cortés, Scott marched toward Mexico City, which he captured in September 1847.

The Treaty of Guadalupe Hidalgo

The Treaty of Guadalupe Hidalgo, signed in February 1848, marked the final triumph of Manifest Destiny. Mexico had to give up more than 500,000 square miles (1,295,000 square km). In return for this land, known as the Mexican Cession, the United States paid $15 million.

Almost 70,000 Mexicans lived in the Mexican Cession. These people became Americans overnight. Although the treaty guaranteed them citizenship and property rights, some Mexican Americans lost their land. Many, feeling like foreigners in their own homeland, emigrated to Mexico.

Most Mexican Americans remained, hoping to carve out a future in the United States. Today, Mexican traditions of religion, language, and architecture flourish in Mexican Cession lands—now the American Southwest.

The Gadsden Purchase In 1853 the United States acquired still more land from Mexico. James Gadsden, the United States Minister to Mexico, negotiated the $10 million purchase of a strip of land south of the Mexican Cession. The United States wanted to build a railroad, and this land was the only part of the West that was relatively flat.

California Gold Rush

As part of Mexico, California had had a tiny population. With the discovery of gold however, the world rushed in.

Gold was first discovered on land belonging to John Sutter. A Swiss by birth, Sutter

"Golden Mountain" The Chinese who came to California to find a fortune in gold called the land *Gam Saan*—"The Golden Mountain." Many Chinese were fleeing hard times. Between 1839 and 1860 China lost two wars to Britain. Meanwhile, a bloody civil war was raging in China. Economic conditions were harsh, too, and overcrowded farmlands made poverty worse.

Most of the Chinese who came were men. Hoping to return with bags of gold, they left their families behind. Like other miners, however, few Chinese actually struck it rich. About half returned to China. When the gold rush was over, however, thousands found other work and made California their home.

Word of the California gold rush was greeted in China with great excitement. Young men dreamed of possibilities, not only of being gold miners like the men in this photo, but also farmers and merchants. Often they borrowed money for the trip at high interest rates to be paid back from profits they expected to make in America. Between 1850 and 1900 more than 300,000 Chinese came to the United States.

had come to California in 1839 and built a trading post where Sacramento is today. On January 24, 1848, one of his workers scooped up a handful of sand from the American River. In it were flakes of gold.

The news spread like wildfire. American, French, Hawaiian, Australian, Irish, German, Chinese, Italian, and Mexican prospectors rushed to California. African Americans came, too. Some were slaves, but most were free. By 1852 California had the wealthiest black population of any state.

Among the luckiest of Californians were the Frémonts. They had bought a ranch in California. To their delight, they found gold on their land and became multimillionaires.

In 1849, at the height of the rush, as many as 80,000 gold-seeking "forty-niners" poured in. Although few made fortunes, many stayed to farm or start businesses. A year later, California became the 31st state.

4. Section Review

1. Explain how the idea of Manifest Destiny contributed to war with Mexico.
2. Summarize Polk's goals in the war.
3. What did the United States gain from the Treaty of Guadalupe Hidalgo?
4. Critical Thinking List the main points in an argument between two California neighbors in 1846. One wants California to remain part of Mexico. The other favors an American takeover.

Why We Remember

The Westward Movement

When John Frémont and Thomas Hart Benton first met, the idea of the United States reaching to the Pacific seemed a dream. By 1850, that dream had become a reality. Looking back on her husband's role in the settlement of the West, Jessie Frémont wrote, "From the ashes of his campfires have sprung cities."

Between 1845 and 1850 the nation grew in area by about a third. It also became more diverse. The new territories were home to Indians, Mexicans, and a sprinkling of Europeans and Americans. Once gold was discovered in California, treasure seekers from around the world added to the mix of peoples.

As a result, Americans' view of their place in the world began to change. They had long thought of the United States as part of the European world. They had looked to Europe for ideas, technology, and trade. Now the nation shared borders with Latin America and looked across the Pacific toward Asia. For many Americans today, ties with Latin America and Asia are as important as ties with Europe. This change has been, perhaps, the most unexpected result of America's reach westward.

Geography Lab

Basins and Ranges

In the mid-1800s Americans were beginning to travel across the Basin and Range region. Susan Magoffin set out from Missouri with her husband, a Santa Fe trader, in 1847. In New Mexico they trekked through a basin called *Jornada del Muerto,* Spanish for "Dead Man's Journey." In 1849 Delos Ashley crossed Nevada by way of the Humboldt Sink. A sink is a low place where a river flows into a lake. What mental picture of the Basins and Ranges do their travel diaries give you?

Amargosa Valley, Nevada

Developing a Mental Map

Refer to the maps on pages P4–P5, R4–R5, and R6–R7.

1. What mountains border the Basin and Range region?

2. The region includes what states? What major cities?

3. On what points do Ashley and Magoffin agree? In what ways does the photograph confirm their diaries?

4. **Hands-On Geography** As a traveler to the West in 1850, write a letter to someone in the East. Describe the difficulties you faced crossing the Basin and Range region.

Delos Ashley's Diary

Tues., July 17. Very warm—sand roads. Toilsome as hell.

Wednes., July 18. Sand!!! Hot!!! Grass parched & dry.

Thurs., July 19. Camped 10 P.M. No grass (wheugh!!!).

Fri., July 20. 10 o'clock. Hot!!! No halt at noon. Camped 6 o'clock P.M. Grass 3 miles. Spring at slough [a low, muddy area].

Sat., July 21. Stayed at slough.

Sun., July 22. From slough to [Humboldt] Sink (Oh, barrenness).

Susan Magoffin's Diary

Monday 1st. . . . We are almost at the mouth of the Jornada (the long journey without water) have been traveling slowly the roads being exceedingly heavy, with two or three severe hills; . . . all the teams [were] doubled and were then just able to get over.

Friday 5th. . . . The wind blew high all the evening and the dust considerable. . . . "The dead man's lake," "Laguna del muerto" is some six ms. from where we are camped on the road. Travelers generally stop here and send off their animals to water at this spring quite a long distance too, but tis quite necessary as we shall not find water again till we strike the River [Rio Grande] forty miles ahead.

Monday 8th. . . . Camped on a high bluff about two miles from the water, and sent the stock down to it. . . . I have been bold enough to climb up and down these beautiful and rugged cliffs both yesterday and today, but I shall be more careful hereafter, as it is really dangerous.

Chapter Survey

Reviewing Vocabulary

Define the following terms.
1. expansionists
2. annex

Reviewing Main Ideas

1. Describe the role each person played in westward expansion. (a) John C. Frémont (b) Jessie Frémont (c) John O'Sullivan (d) Manuel Lisa (e) William Becknell
2. (a) Why were many southern farmers eager to move to the Mexican state of Texas? (b) Why was Mexico agreeable to American settlement at first? (c) Why did Mexico finally ban American immigration?
3. Texas was once part of a Mexican state. Explain the disagreements that led to its becoming an independent republic.
4. (a) Why were easterners attracted to Oregon and California in the mid-1840s? (b) What was it about Utah that attracted Mormons in the same period?
5. How did the reactions of Indians and Mexicans to American settlers in the Far West change over time?
6. (a) Why was the Mexican government angry at the United States in early 1846? (b) What event triggered war between the two countries?
7. Two events of early 1848 changed the West in major ways. What were those events, and what impact did each have?

Thinking Critically

1. Application Support the following statement with three examples from the chapter: There were as many reasons for going west as there were people who did so.
2. Analysis Only about half a century separated the Texas Revolution from the American Revolution. What evidence is there that Texans of 1836 viewed their situation as similar to the colonists' in 1776? How did the two situations differ?
3. Why We Remember: Synthesis Imagine a parent who was born in 1805 and a son or daughter who was born in 1833. Each one turned 20 years old in what year? How would each one have described the size of the United States, its boundaries, and its place in the world in those years?

Applying Skills

Credibility In their writings, John Frémont and Charles Preuss presented conflicted portrayals of Kit Carson. Likewise, modern-day writers offer different portrayals of people in the news.
1. Look through newspapers or magazines to find an article that describes a news maker in very positive or very negative terms. Write a short summary of the article.
2. Recalling what you learned about determining credibility on page 392, write a paragraph that tells:
• whether you think the article is a credible source
• why you think as you do
• how you might find information to support your opinion

History Mystery

Great American Desert Answer the History Mystery on page 373. What is a desert? Why would simply calling an area "desert" discourage people from settling there?

Writing in Your History Journal

1. Keys to History (a) The time line on pages 372–373 has six Keys to History. In your journal, explain why it is important to know about

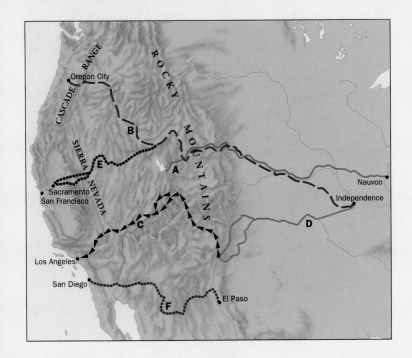

1. Each letter on the map represents a trail to the West. Name each trail.

2. Geographic Thinking Some people have compared the huge westward migration that began in the 1840s with the migration to the English colonies in America during the 1600s and 1700s. How were the two migrations similar?

each one. (b) If you could have been at one event on the time line, which would you choose, and why? Write your response in your journal.

2. John and Jessie Frémont Imagine that it is 1842, and the federal government has hired you to encourage people to move to the Far West. In your journal, write an ad focusing on one present-day state in the Far West. Keep in mind how successful Jessie Frémont's writing was, and make your ad descriptive and appealing.

3. Citizenship Many different people had an influence on the government's policy of Manifest Destiny. Imagine that you are able to go back in time and affect the course of history. Would you try to influence the government to halt or to carry out Manifest Destiny? Explain your reasons.

Alternative Assessment

Planning a western Today, movie westerns are quite different from the ones your parents and grandparents saw. Today's moviemakers usually try to portray events and people more realistically.

Imagine that you are a movie director. With a partner, write a plan for a short western film. Include a summary of the plot, a descriptive list of characters, brief descriptions for each of the movie's six scenes, and a script for one of the scenes.

Keep these guidelines in mind:
• Characters must be from at least two groups in this chapter, for example, American settlers, Indian trappers, Mexican ranchers, Chinese miners.
• At least one character must be a real person you read about in this chapter.
• The story must include at least one event you read about in this chapter.

Your plan will be evaluated on the following criteria:
• it describes the movie thoroughly
• it shows knowledge of historical people and events and of different points of view
• it is imaginative

Chapter **15**

Americans at Mid-Century

Keys to History

1831
Nat Turner's Revolt
Painting of execution of Nat Turner

1831
McCormick reaper invented

1835–1836
Workers protest wages and hours in 140 strikes

1830

Looking Back

Whitney invents cotton gin

1793

HISTORY *Mystery*

From New England ponds came a product much in demand in the Caribbean, India, and other tropical lands. What was that product and why was it popular?

1840s

Clipper ships speed overseas trade

1844

Samuel F. B. Morse demonstrates the telegraph

Early telegraph key

1846

Elias Howe invents sewing machine

1849

Know-Nothing Party formed

Know-Nothing election poster

1840

1850

World Link

The Great Famine in Ireland
1845

Looking Ahead

Uncle Tom's Cabin is published
1852

● **403**

Beginning the Story with

Although he was barely 16, Frederick Augustus Washington Bailey was headed for trouble. To begin with, he had learned to read. Even more troubling, Frederick had organized a Sunday school to teach children how to read the Bible. What was so wrong? Frederick was in trouble because he was a slave, and slaves were not allowed to learn to read nor to meet with other slaves. Slave owners feared that such activities would lead slaves to escape or organize rebellions.

Indeed, Frederick's owner decided his slave's independent spirit had to be broken. In 1834 he sent Frederick to a professional slave breaker named Edward Covey.

"Broken in Body, Soul, and Spirit"

Covey was an expert at turning strong-minded African Americans into obedient slaves. His method, Frederick soon learned, consisted of equal parts of violence, fear, and overwork.

Frederick had not been on Covey's farm for a week before he received his first flogging. The lash left his body covered with bloody welts. After that he was beaten so often that "aching bones and a sore back were my constant companions."

Covey's ability to instill fear in slaves was as effective as the lash. They never knew when Covey was watching them. Frederick recalled:

"He had the faculty of making us feel that he was always present. . . . I was prepared to expect him at any moment. . . . He would creep and crawl in ditches and gullies; hide behind stumps and bushes, and practice so much the cunning of the serpent, that Bill Smith [another slave] and I—between ourselves—never called him by any other name than 'the snake.'"

Breakup of families was a constant threat to enslaved African Americans. Frederick Douglass's mother was hired out to another planter, and he saw her only four or five times. Slaves sold at auctions like the one in this picture were often separated from family members and friends forever.

The last part of Covey's method, Frederick wrote, was to work his slaves beyond endurance:

"It was never too hot or too cold; it could never rain, blow, hail, or snow too hard for us to work in the field. . . . The longest days were too short for him, and the shortest nights too long for him. I was somewhat unmanageable when I first went there, but a few months of this discipline tamed me. . . . I was broken in body, soul, and spirit."

"The Turning Point in My Life"

Frederick finally "reached the point at which I was *not afraid to die*." The next time Covey started to beat him, the young man threw his abuser to the ground. Master and slave fought for two hours before Covey gave up. For Frederick, this battle was "the turning point in my life as a slave." He wrote of that moment:

"I felt as I never felt before. . . . My long-crushed spirit rose, cowardice departed, bold defiance took its place; and I now resolved that, however long I might remain a slave in form, the day had passed when I could be a slave in fact. I did not hesitate to let it be known of me, that the white man who expected to succeed in whipping, must also succeed in killing me."

In 1838 Frederick Augustus Washington Bailey escaped from slavery and became a free man in fact, as well as in spirit. He settled in Massachusetts where he took the name by which we know him today: Frederick Douglass.

Hands-On → *HISTORY*

Activity

Imagine that you are writing the script for a movie about the young Frederick Douglass. Based on the story above, create a list of scenes to show on film. Give a brief description of the importance of each scene.

1. Life in the North and the South

Reading Guide

Section Focus **Differences between the economies of the North and the South in the mid-1800s**

1. What were the major economic activities in the Northeast?
2. How did the Old Northwest become the nation's breadbasket?
3. How did cotton growing shape life in the South?

When Frederick Douglass first escaped to the North in 1838, he thought the people there must be very poor. After all, none of them owned slaves. "Regarding slavery as the basis of wealth," he later wrote, "I fancied that no people could become very wealthy without slavery."

It was a natural mistake for someone raised in the South. There, owning slaves was a sign of wealth. In the free states of the North, however, wealth was measured in different terms. These differences shaped how people worked and lived in the mid-1800s.

The Industrial Northeast

Frederick Douglass realized his mistake soon after settling in the port town of New Bedford, Massachusetts. There he was surprised to find

❝the very laboring population of New Bedford living in better houses, more elegantly furnished . . . than a majority of the slaveholders on the Eastern Shore of Maryland.❞

How, he wondered, could such people live so well?

Whaling On his first visit to the waterfront, Douglass began to unravel the mystery of New Bedford's wealth. There he saw "full-rigged ships of finest model, ready to start on whaling voyages."

New Englanders had long made a good living from fishing. By the mid-1800s whaling had also become a profitable business for enterprising seamen. Whale oil was in demand because it burned cleanly in lamps. Other parts of whales were used to manufacture everything from buggy whips to women's corsets.

Whalers sailed the world's oceans on voyages lasting three or four years. They often stopped in the Hawaiian Islands for supplies and repairs. By 1850 Honolulu was a major whaling port.

Trade Douglass saw that trade, too, was a source of wealth in the Northeast. New Bedford's docks were lined "by large granite-fronted warehouses, crowded with the good things of this world."

By the mid-1800s American merchant ships were trading around the world, even in such distant lands as Russia, India, and China. New commerce developed after 1854. In that year Commodore Matthew Perry opened American trade with Japan.

One of the most successful trade items was ice. Blocks of ice cut from frozen New England ponds in winter were packed in sawdust and shipped to customers in the Caribbean and India. In those hot lands, ice was an almost unknown luxury. By the 1850s ice

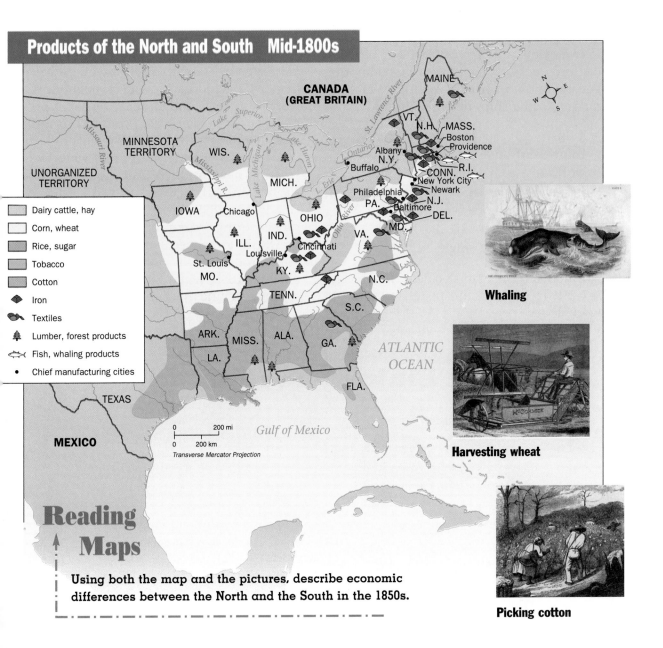

Products of the North and South   Mid-1800s

CANADA
(GREAT BRITAIN)

MAINE

MINNESOTA
TERRITORY

WIS.

MICH.

VT.

N.H.   MASS.
Boston
Providence
Albany
N.Y.   CONN.   R.I.
Buffalo
New York City
Newark
N.J.
DEL.
MD.

UNORGANIZED
TERRITORY

IOWA   Chicago

OHIO

Philadelphia
PA.
Baltimore

ILL.   IND.
Louisville   Cincinnati
St. Louis
MO.   KY.

VA.

N.C.

TENN.

ARK.

MISS.   ALA.

S.C.

GA.

ATLANTIC
OCEAN

LA.

FLA.

TEXAS

0   200 mi
0   200 km
Transverse Mercator Projection

Gulf of Mexico

MEXICO

Legend

- Dairy cattle, hay
- Corn, wheat
- Rice, sugar
- Tobacco
- Cotton
- Iron
- Textiles
- Lumber, forest products
- Fish, whaling products
- Chief manufacturing cities

Whaling

Harvesting wheat

Picking cotton

Reading Maps

Using both the map and the pictures, describe economic
differences between the North and the South in the 1850s.

was the nation's second leading export after
cotton in the number of tons shipped.

Clipper ships American cargoes fairly
flew to their destinations on the clipper
ships developed in the 1840s. Long and
narrow, with huge sails, these ships were
built "to go at a good clip." They set speed
records between ports in the United States,
Europe, and Asia. For example, in 1849 the
clipper *Sea Witch* sailed from Hong Kong to

New York in 74 days—a journey that previously had taken 6 months.

By the 1850s American clipper ships had
taken over much of the China trade. During
the California gold rush, clippers carried
freight and passengers from New York to
San Francisco in record time.

Within two decades, however, the day of
the clipper ship was almost over. New ships
powered by steam could carry more cargo
and did not have to depend on the wind.

Industry and invention On the New Bedford docks, Douglass discovered another key to the Northeast's wealth. Watching men unload a ship, he observed

“industry without bustle. . . . Everything went on as smoothly as the works of a well-adjusted machine. . . . In a southern port, twenty or thirty hands would have been employed to do what five or six did here, with the aid of a single ox.”

Northerners, Douglass decided, were always inventing smarter and faster ways to get work done.

By the mid-1800s the production methods pioneered by Francis Lowell and Eli Whitney in New England had spread throughout the Northeast. More and more of the goods people used every day were produced in mills and factories by workers using machines.

At the same time, inventors were busy creating new products and industries. The rubber industry was built on Charles Goodyear's 1839 discovery of how to make rubber strong. Dozens of new products, from fire hoses to rubber bands, were the result. Mass production of clothing became possible after 1846, when Elias Howe invented a sewing machine that could make 250 stitches a minute.

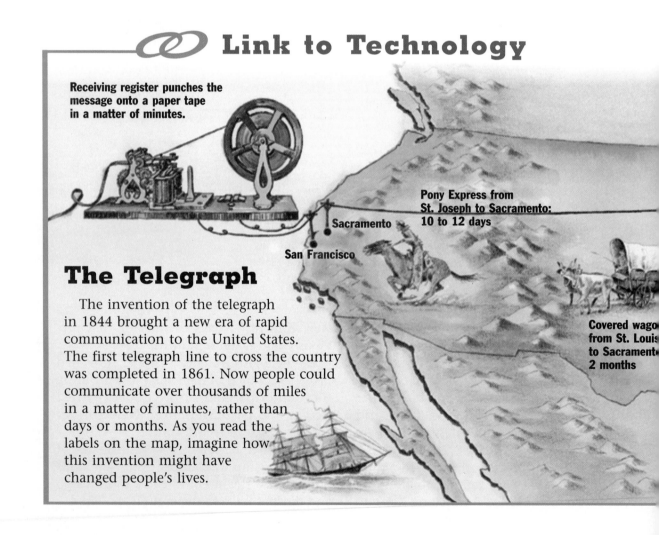

Link to Technology

Receiving register punches the message onto a paper tape in a matter of minutes.

Sacramento

San Francisco

Pony Express from St. Joseph to Sacramento: 10 to 12 days

Covered wago from St. Louis to Sacramento 2 months

The Telegraph

The invention of the telegraph in 1844 brought a new era of rapid communication to the United States. The first telegraph line to cross the country was completed in 1861. Now people could communicate over thousands of miles in a matter of minutes, rather than days or months. As you read the labels on the map, imagine how this invention might have changed people's lives.

The invention of the telegraph by Samuel F. B. Morse gave birth to a new communications industry. Before Morse successfully demonstrated the telegraph in 1844, messages could travel only as fast as the fastest horse or ship. Four years later telegraph wires were speeding messages to people and businesses in almost every state east of the Mississippi.

Cities grow up around industry

This burst of industry and invention greatly increased the number of factories. Factories, in turn, attracted workers, many of whom came from farms. Factory owners also found a source of low-cost labor in the immigrants entering the United States in search of opportunity.

As a result, cities began to grow up around industry in the Northeast. For example, in the 1820s Lowell, Massachusetts, was a small farming village. Two decades later it had become an industrial city of 30,000 people built around busy textile mills.

With all of this enterprise and industry, life moved at a fast pace in the Northeast. There were always people on the go, sailing to distant ports, starting new businesses, and inventing new products. In their restless activity, northerners were pioneering a new pattern of life—a pattern set by the clock, the factory bell, and the rhythms of machines.

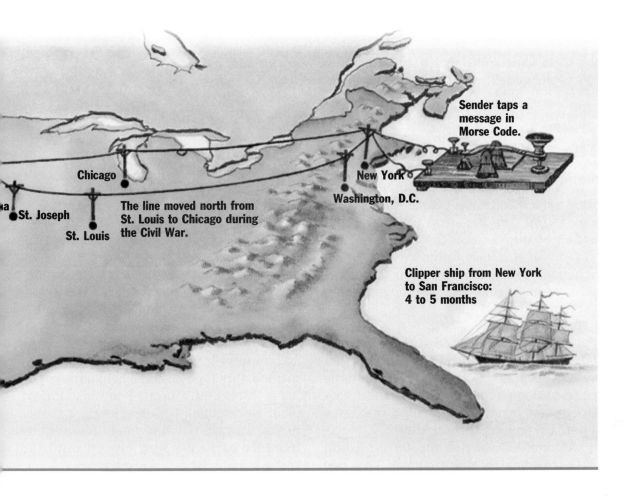

Sender taps a message in Morse Code.

Chicago

St. Joseph

St. Louis

The line moved north from St. Louis to Chicago during the Civil War.

New York

Washington, D.C.

Clipper ship from New York to San Francisco: 4 to 5 months

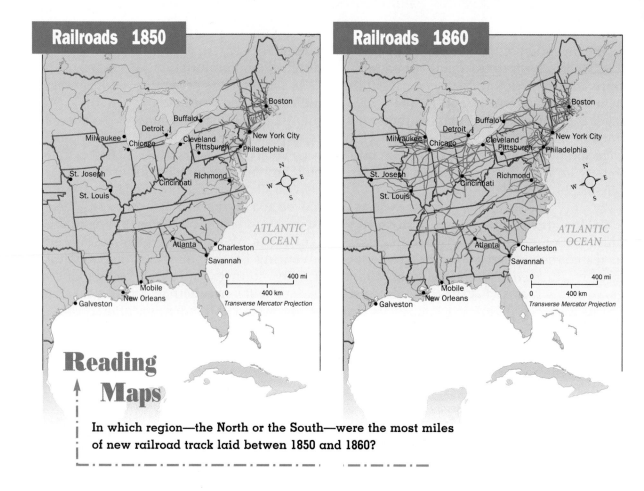

Railroads 1850

Railroads 1860

Reading Maps

In which region—the North or the South—were the most miles of new railroad track laid betwen 1850 and 1860?

The Agricultural Midwest

In the Midwest, as the Old Northwest came to be called, most people still followed a pattern of life based on the rising and setting of the sun and the rhythm of the seasons. Farmers there cultivated some of the richest soil on earth. The grain and cattle raised on that fertile ground brought wealth to the region.

The McCormick reaper The farmers who settled in the Midwest used tools that had changed little in centuries. Then, in the mid-1800s a Virginia farmer named Cyrus McCormick invented a machine that revolutionized farming there.

McCormick knew that the harvest season was a cruel time for wheat farmers. They had only a few days to bring in their crop before the ripe grain fell to the ground. To get the job done in time, they hired crews of reapers to cut the grain by hand.

McCormick spent years developing a machine that would do the back-breaking work of the harvest crew. He was assisted by Joe Anderson, one of the McCormick family's slaves. The result in 1831 was a horse-drawn harvesting machine that cut as much grain in a day as three workers.

McCormick continued to test his machine and improve it. Finally, in 1842 he began to manufacture the reaper. To help farmers pay for it, McCormick created the installment plan. Under this plan, he allowed a farmer to make a cash down payment followed by monthly payments with interest until the cost was paid off.

Looking for more customers, McCormick built a reaper factory in Chicago, Illinois. In 1848 he sold 500 reapers. By 1850 he had sold 4,000 more. A new age of mechanized farming had begun.

Transportation links Chicago, home of McCormick's reaper factory, was one of many new cities in the Midwest. Some, such as Cincinnati and St. Louis, grew up beside the Ohio and Mississippi Rivers. Other cities, like Chicago and Detroit, sprouted on the shores of the Great Lakes.

Transportation was the key to the growth of these cities. Crops flowed into them for shipment to northeastern cities. The boats and trains that carried crops east returned to the Midwest bringing factory goods. They also brought new settlers. By 1850 half of all Americans lived west of the Appalachians.

At mid-century railroads were just beginning to compete with riverboats and canals in the Midwest. Ten years later, the region was crisscrossed by rail lines. Railroads bound the Northeast and the Midwest so closely together that southerners viewed the two regions as one—the North.

The Cotton-Growing South

By mid-century the South was a vast cotton-growing region. As you read in Chapter 12, the invention of the cotton gin in 1793 turned cotton into the South's most important cash crop. Cotton planters put their money into land and slaves. By 1850 they had pushed the cotton kingdom west beyond the Mississippi, into Texas.

As more land was planted in cotton, production skyrocketed. By 1850 southerners were producing more than 2 million bales a year. They exported about 75 percent of it, mainly to Britain, making cotton the nation's leading export. The remaining 25 percent went to New England mills. No wonder white southerners boasted that "cotton is king."

Chicago became a center of both water and railroad transportation. A visitor in 1855 observed that Chicago "fairly smokes and roars with business."

This 1840 painting shows wealthy southern planters and their families gathering for the excitement of horse racing at the Oakland Race Course in Louisville, Kentucky. Families like these, though relatively few in number, were the political and social leaders of the South.

The spread of slavery The growth of the cotton kingdom caused a great demand for slave labor. Congress banned the Atlantic slave trade in 1808, so no new slaves could legally be brought into the country. Instead, slave traders traveled throughout the south-eastern states buying up slaves to sell in the new southwestern cotton lands.

The demand for slave labor caused prices to soar so high that only wealthy planters could continue to buy slaves. In 1850 there were about 347,000 slaveholding families in the South. Only one-third of those families owned more than ten slaves.

About three-fourths of white southerners owned no slaves at all. Many of these people lived on small farms, grew their own food, and tended a few acres of cotton or tobacco as cash crops. Eager to "move up" in society, ambitious small farmers saved to buy land and slaves of their own.

Aware of the money to be made from cotton, southerners continued to put their money in land and slaves rather than in factories and railroads. As a result, the South remained the less industrialized section of the country. Compared to the North, the South had relatively few factories, canals, or railroads. Hinton Helper, a South Carolina writer, complained:

❝We are compelled to go to the North for almost every article . . . from matches, shoe-pegs, and paintings to cotton mills, steamships, and statuary.❞

Still, most southern planters showed little interest in the technology that was changing life in the North.

1. Section Review

1. Describe at least two important economic activities in the Northeast.
2. What enabled people in the Midwest to be productive farmers?
3. Why was more and more land in the South planted in cotton after 1793?
4. Critical Thinking If machinery to cultivate and pick cotton had been developed in the mid-1800s, what effects might it have had on the southern economy and way of life?

Geography Lab

Reading Climate Maps

"King Cotton" came to rule over the South largely because of the climate there. What kind of climate do you think is best for growing cotton—warm or cool, wet or dry? One way to find out is to look at climate maps.

You may have seen weather maps on TV or in the newspaper. Climate maps are similar. The lines on such maps, called **isolines,** mark off areas that are the same in some way. For example, the area between two isolines on a map that shows **precipitation**—moisture from rain and snow—will receive a similar amount of precipitation.

Cotton field, Mississippi

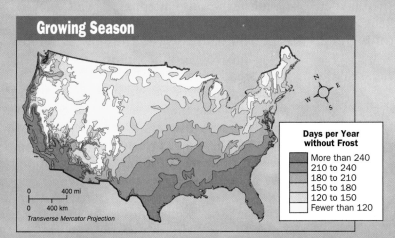

Growing Season

Days per Year without Frost

- More than 240
- 210 to 240
- 180 to 210
- 150 to 180
- 120 to 150
- Fewer than 120

0 — 400 mi
0 — 400 km
Transverse Mercator Projection

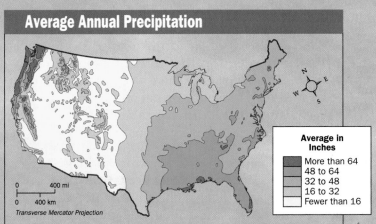

Average Annual Precipitation

Average in Inches

- More than 64
- 48 to 64
- 32 to 48
- 16 to 32
- Fewer than 16

0 — 400 mi
0 — 400 km
Transverse Mercator Projection

Using Map Skills

Refer to the maps on pages 407 and R6–R7 to answer the questions.

1. Name 4 states with areas that receive at least 64 inches of precipitation each year. What 5 states have areas that receive 16 inches or less each year?

2. Name 6 states that have growing seasons longer than 240 days. What 6 states have growing seasons shorter than 120 days each year?

3. What is the least amount of moisture and the minimum growing season needed for an area to be part of the "Cotton Kingdom"? Refer to the maps on this page and on page 407.

4. **Hands-On Geography** Imagine that you can move to any state in the United States. What state would you choose and how would the climate, including the precipitation, influence your decision?

2. African American Life

Reading Guide

New Terms **slave codes, discrimination**

Section Focus **African American life in the South and the North**

1. What were the living conditions of enslaved African Americans?
2. How did African Americans resist slavery?
3. What problems did free African Americans face?

One day in 1841, at a meeting of the Massachusetts Antislavery Society, Frederick Douglass was asked to tell his experiences as a slave. Having never spoken in public before, Douglass was so nervous he "trembled in every limb."

Still, he gave such a moving speech that he was named a lecturer for the society. In the next 14 years he traveled throughout the North speaking against slavery. He became one of the greatest public speakers in American history.

Life Under Slavery

In 1850 there were more than 3 million enslaved African Americans in the United States. By law they were property, not human beings. They could be bought and sold, and even passed down in wills. Slaves had none of the rights that free people often took for granted. As Douglass told his listeners:

"In law, the slave has no wife,
no children, no country, no home.
He can own nothing, possess nothing,
acquire nothing."

Living conditions Seven out of eight enslaved African Americans worked on plantations. Most were field hands who toiled from dawn to dark tending cotton, tobacco,

rice, or sugar cane. Even after dark there was still water to carry, wood to split, pigs to feed, and corn to shuck.

Not all enslaved African Americans worked in the fields. Some were skilled carpenters, blacksmiths, or mechanics. Others worked in the master's house as cooks, butlers, maids, or nursemaids. In addition to their regular work, some also served the slave community as preachers, nurses, or midwives.

On small plantations, owners personally directed the work or even worked in the fields alongside their slaves. On large plantations, many owners hired overseers to supervise the work. Overseers were paid to "care for nothing but to make a large crop." They often drove slaves mercilessly.

Many owners viewed their slaves as they did their land, something to be used hard and "worn out, not improved." They spent as little money as possible on the care of their work force.

Enslaved African Americans often lived crowded together in small wooden cabins. The owner gave them weekly rations of corn-meal and pork or bacon. Slaves improved their diets with vegetables when they were allowed to have gardens. A few times a year they received a new set of rough clothes.

The importance of families Under these difficult conditions, enslaved African Americans did their best to create families

Link to Art

Harriet Powers's Bible quilt After finishing evening chores, enslaved African American women often worked late into the night making quilts. Using techniques from West Africa, they created quilts that told stories with bold shapes and bright colors. This picture shows part of a quilt made by Harriet Powers, who was born into slavery in Georgia in 1837. Stitched in the early 1880s, the quilt shows Bible stories. **Discuss** Compare this quilt with the quilt on page 149. How are they similar? How are they different?

and care for each other. Despite the threat of separation, they married, often using African ceremonies, and raised children.

Slaves struggled to keep their families together and to reunite separated family members. After Samuel Johnston gained his freedom in 1811, he worked for five years to earn enough money to buy his wife and children. In 1815 the Virginia legislature refused to free his children. For the next 22 years, Johnston tried without success to bring his family together.

Resistance to Slavery

Although they had no rights, enslaved African Americans had plenty of will and wits. Harriet Jacobs used hers when she escaped in 1835. She hid in an attic for seven years before she could make her way north. Later she wrote:

"My master had power and law on his side; I had a determined will. There is might [power] in each."

Hands-On HISTORY

Analyzing how you use space Many enslaved African Americans spent what little free time they had in the yards outside their cabins. There they cooked, raised vegetables for themselves, and gathered to socialize. Such patterns of using yards and gardens, some of which may have begun in Africa, are still found in the rural South.

Activity

1 Whether it is a garden, a yard, a porch, or a balcony, many people have some private or semiprivate space outside the home. What space do you have?

2 Study the photograph, and the diagram based on it, on the right. Then make a diagram of your space. Add a key.

3 Write a paragraph describing where the space is and how you use it.

4 Share your diagram and description with classmates.

Key:
- Cook pot
- Open fire
- Rain barrel
- Vegetable garden
- Shade tree
- Swept area

An African American yard in North Carolina, 1914

Throughout the South, enslaved African Americans resisted slavery by striking back, escaping, and organizing revolts.

Striking back Slaves became experts at secretly striking back at their masters. Field hands "accidentally" broke their tools or destroyed crops. House servants "liberated" food from the master's kitchen.

Slaves also pretended to be stupid, clumsy, sick, or insane to avoid work. "The only weapon of self-defense I could use successfully," recalled an enslaved African American named Henry Bibb, "was that of deception."

Striking back could turn deadly. So many slaves set fire to their masters' homes that the American Fire Insurance Company refused to insure property in the South.

Escaping to freedom Many slaves resisted slavery by escaping to freedom. The risks of escaping, though, were enormous. Most slaves knew little about the world beyond their plantation. Once missed, they were hunted by "slave catchers." If caught, escapees were severely punished. As Frederick Douglass planned his escape, he was filled with doubts:

❝I was making a leap in the dark. . . . It was like going to war without weapons—ten chances of defeat to one of victory.❞

Despite the dangers, thousands of slaves took the risk. Every year about 1,000 slaves fled to the North, Canada, or Mexico. Some walked to freedom, following the North Star by night. Some escaped by boat or train, using forged identity cards and clever disguises. A few slaves had themselves shipped north in boxes and coffins.

Slave revolts For slaves who stayed home, resistance sometimes took the form of open revolt. As early as 1739, slaves killed more than 20 whites in the Stono Uprising in South Carolina.

Fear of revolts haunted white southerners. A visitor noted:

"I have known times here when not a single planter had a calm night's rest. They never lie down to sleep without . . . loaded pistols at their sides."

One of the bloodiest revolts erupted in Virginia in 1831. Nat Turner, a slave and a preacher, rose up to "slay my enemies with their own weapons." Before the two-day reign of terror ended, Turner and his followers had killed nearly 60 white men, women, and children.

Stricter slave codes Nat Turner's revolt chilled white southerners. In response, southern states passed stricter **slave codes**—laws that tightened owners' control over slaves. The new codes barred slaves from leaving their plantations without permission. They could not meet in large groups without a white person present. It was now illegal to teach a slave to read.

State after state passed new laws making it more difficult for slaves to gain freedom. They also passed laws that limited the rights of free African Americans.

Free African Americans

Of the more than 3.5 million African Americans living in the United States at mid-century, nearly 500,000 were free. Some had gained freedom when northern states banned slavery. Others escaped or were freed by southern owners. Still others, who were allowed to earn money, bought their own freedom.

Link to the Present

Buxton reunions Some escaped slaves settled in new African American communities in the North. One such community was Buxton in Ontario, Canada.

Buxton grew out of the dream of William King, an Irish-born minister who wanted to help African American refugees settle in Canada. In 1849 King organized a joint-stock company to buy land near Lake Erie and sell plots to African Americans. By 1861 the thriving town had 2,000 residents.

Although many Buxton residents returned to the United States to fight in the Civil War, descendants of some of the original settlers still live there. Each year they have a reunion during the Labor Day weekend. People come from as far away as Louisiana and California to honor freedom-loving African Americans who built a successful community in Canada.

About half of the free African Americans lived in the South, half in the North. Most of them worked as laborers, craftspeople, household servants, seamstresses, or washerwomen. A few started their own businesses and some became quite wealthy.

No matter where they lived, free African Americans suffered from **discrimination**—the unfair treatment of a group of people compared with another group. Because of discrimination, free black Americans did not have the same rights and opportunities as white Americans.

In the South White southerners saw free African Americans as a dangerous influence.

Mary and John Jones of Chicago were both born free. They helped escaped slaves reach freedom in Canada. John Jones also led the fight against Illinois laws that banned free African Americans from voting or testifying in court.

"The superior condition of the free persons of color," complained a group of slave owners, "excites discontent among our slaves."

As a result, free African Americans in the South were not allowed to own guns or watchdogs. Nor could they travel freely. They were severely punished for even the most minor crimes. Such harsh treatment led Douglass to declare that "no colored man is really free in a slaveholding state."

In the North Even in the North, equality was little more than a dream for African Americans. A white New Yorker named Gerrit Smith observed in the 1840s:

❝Even the noblest black is denied that which is free to the vilest [worst] white. The omnibus, the [railroad] car, the ballot-box, the jury box, the halls of legislation, the army, the public lands, the school, the church, the lecture room, the [restaurant] table are all . . . denied to him.❞

Frederick Douglass learned about northern racism when he tried to join the Elm Street Church in New Bedford:

❝I was not allowed a seat in the body of the house . . . on account of my color. . . .

I tried all the other churches in New Bedford with the same result.❞

Faced with discrimination, free African Americans turned to their own communities for hope and pride. As early as the 1780s, they began forming their own Christian churches, which became centers of African American life in northern cities.

Meanwhile, free African Americans worked to gain rights for themselves and for those still enslaved. They sent petitions to Congress and state legislatures demanding equal treatment. They raised money to help escaped slaves and planned boycotts of slave-made goods. Through their efforts, they exerted a steady pressure for change.

 2. **Section Review**

1. Define the terms **slave codes** and **discrimination.**

2. How did close family ties help slaves deal with the harshness of slavery?

3. Give two examples of ways that slaves resisted their owners' control.

4. Critical Thinking Compare the life of free African Americans in the North and the South. What was different? The same?

3. Workers and Immigrants

Reading Guide

New Terms trade union, strike, nativism, nativists

Section Focus The struggle of workers and immigrants to make better lives for themselves

1. How did work change as the nation became more industrialized?
2. Why did workers form trade unions?
3. What problems did immigrants face in the mid-1800s?

After escaping to freedom in 1838, Frederick Douglass worked at a number of jobs. As he later recalled, he "sawed wood—dug cellars—shoveled coal—swept chimneys—helped to load and unload vessels—worked in Ricketson's candle works—in Richmond's brass foundry and elsewhere."

As a wage earner, Douglass worried about whether he could support himself and his family. It was a problem faced by a growing number of workers in the North.

The New Wage Earners

Since colonial times, the United States had been a good land for wage earners, especially those with skills, such as printers or carpenters. Skilled workers were well paid because there were so few of them. Most worked for wages only until they had saved enough to buy farms or start businesses.

By the early 1800s, however, working for wages began to be a way of life for many people, not a temporary condition. There were now plenty of skilled workers, too, so wages began to drop.

Also, in the new mills and factories, jobs once done by skilled workers were taken over by unskilled workers running machines. These new wage earners—many of the women and children—were paid far less than the skilled workers they replaced.

Forming Trade Unions

Faced with falling wages, skilled workers began to form trade unions. A **trade union** is a group of people who try to improve wages and working conditions in their trade, or craft. By 1810 most of the nation's larger cities had unions of printers, shoemakers, carpenters, and painters.

Philadelphia's union of shoemakers called the first organized strike in 1799 to protest pay cuts. In a **strike,** employees refuse to work, hoping to force their employer to meet their demands. After ten weeks, however, hunger drove the striking shoemakers back to work at the lower wages.

Other efforts by the early trade unions to protect workers' wages were more successful. However, in the hard times following the Panic of 1819 (see pages 332–333), thousands of workers lost both their jobs and their faith in unions.

Protesting wages and hours The economy improved in the 1830s, but wages and hours did not. As a result, labor organizations revived. In 1835 and 1836 alone, workers organized 140 strikes to protest wage cuts and longer work hours. "Ten hours . . . is as much as an employer ought to receive, or require, for a day's work," angry workers declared.

Many of the strikes took place in factories and mills. By the 1830s millworkers were forced to labor up to 13 hours a day, 6 days a week. In 1836 more than 1,500 women workers in Lowell walked out to protest pay cuts. Eleven-year-old Harriet Hanson was one of the strikers. She later recalled:

"When the girls in my room stood irresolute, uncertain what to do . . . I, who began to think they would not go out, after all their talk, became impatient, and started on ahead. . . . As I looked back at that long line that followed me, I was more proud than I have ever been since.**"**

The strike failed. Within a month, the strikers had run out of money. Some strag-gled back to work. The leaders of the strike, including Harriet, were fired.

In fact, going on strike was a risky business at that time. Strikes were illegal—and so were unions. Workers involved in them could be fined and arrested. It was not until the 1842 court decision in *Commonwealth* v. *Hunt* that unions and strikes were declared legal.

Newcomers to America

By the 1840s many mill and factory workers were being replaced by immigrants. In the 50 years between 1776 and 1825, only 1 million immigrants had entered the country. In the 10 years between 1845 and 1854, close to 3 million newcomers arrived.

The majority of these immigrants came from northern Europe, mainly Ireland,

On the overcrowded ships that brought them to America, Irish immigrants suffered from hunger and disease. As many as 20 percent of them died during the trip.

Germany, England, Scotland, and Scandinavia. Some moved to the Midwest in search of farmland. More settled in the Northeast where they found work in factories or building canals and railroads.

The arrival of so many newcomers in a short time caused fear and resentment among many native-born Americans. For one thing, the immigrants were willing to accept low wages for factory and construction jobs. When employers then lowered wages for everyone, angry American-born workers blamed the immigrants.

Differences in culture also raised suspicions among native-born Americans. Most of them were descended from English Protestants. They feared the effect that people with different languages, traditions, and religions would have on what they saw as the American way of life.

Nativism The belief that immigrants threaten traditional American culture and institutions is called **nativism.** People who hold that belief are known as **nativists.**

Nativists were especially hostile to Roman Catholic immigrants—mostly Irish and German. In eastern cities, bloody anti-Catholic riots broke out.

The Know-Nothings Hoping to keep immigrants from gaining political power, nativists formed secret societies and promised never to vote for an immigrant or Catholic. In 1849 one society, the Order of the Star-Spangled Banner, became a political party. It was nicknamed the "Know-Nothing Party" because its members answered any questions about the party by saying, "I know nothing."

The Know-Nothings supported only white, Protestant, native-born candidates. The appeal of their nativist message was felt in elections in 1854 and 1855. Voters from Massachusetts to California sent more than 75 Know-Nothings to Congress.

World Link

The Great Famine in Ireland Chances are, you have never thought of the potato as a powerful force in history. Yet potatoes—or the lack of them—set off a huge wave of Irish immigration to the United States in the mid-1800s.

Almost as soon as the potato reached Europe from South America in the 1500s, Europeans became dependent on it. The potato was both nutritious and easy to grow. In Ireland, people grew almost nothing else.

Then, beginning in 1845, a plant disease called a blight destroyed Ireland's potato crop. Famine set in. Before the blight ended, a million Irish people had died of starvation or disease. Another million had fled to the United States.

Point of View

Who is a true American?

In 1854 the Know-Nothings visited Abraham Lincoln, an Illinois lawyer, and offered to support him if he ran for the Senate. Lincoln declined their offer. In a letter to a friend, he revealed his reason:

❝As a nation, we began by declaring *'all men are created equal.'* We now practically read it 'all men are created equal, *except Negroes.'* When the Know-Nothings get control, it will read 'all men are created equal, except Negroes, *and foreigners, and Catholics.'* ❞

In Lincoln's view, it was wrong to discriminate against people simply because they had been born elsewhere or were Catholics. He told the Know-Nothings that the Indians are the true native Americans. "We pushed them from their homes, and now turn upon others not fortunate enough to come over as early as our forefathers."

As Lincoln hoped, the Know-Nothing Party soon faded away, but nativism has continued to appeal to some Americans. When the economy slows down and jobs are scarce, immigrants are often accused of taking jobs away from native-born workers. They are also viewed with suspicion and even hostility depending on their race, their religion, and the country from which they come.

3. Section Review

1. Define the terms **trade union, strike, nativism,** and **nativists.**
2. How did working for wages change in the early 1800s?
3. What were the goals of the trade unions of the 1830s? Why was it dangerous to be a union member at that time?
4. What fears led some Americans to become nativists?
5. Critical Thinking Compare attitudes in the North toward immigrants and free African Americans. How were attitudes similar? How were they different?

Why We Remember

Americans at Mid-Century

In 1855 Frederick Douglass wrote a book about his life titled *My Bondage and My Freedom.* In it he described the misery of slavery in the South and the injustices of racism in the North. Still, he wrote, despite "the ten thousand discouragements" facing African Americans, "progress is yet possible."

The belief that we can make life better by our own efforts was widely shared by mid-century Americans. It led people to start new businesses. It encouraged inventors to create new technologies. It sent farmers and planters west to clear new land. It inspired enslaved African Americans to seek freedom and workers to organize for decent wages. And it lured immigrants from lands where progress seemed a dim hope.

Even as Douglass was writing those words, however, a gap was widening between the North and the South. While the North saw progress in terms of industry and transportation, the South committed itself ever more firmly to the system of plantations based on slavery. Increasingly, the economic interests of the two sections were coming into conflict. Increasingly, too, opposition to slavery was driving a wedge between them. The progress on which Douglass pinned his hopes would have to contend with the realities of sectional conflict.

Skill Lab

Skill Tips

- A claim may be stated directly, or it may be implied—suggested. Read carefully.
- General types of evidence that might support a claim include statistics, names, dates, events, and descriptions.
- To evaluate how well the evidence supports a claim, ask yourself: Is the evidence specific? Is it clear? Is there enough of it? What else would I ask the writer if I could?

Thinking Critically
Identifying Evidence

Not all wage earners of the early and middle 1800s worked in large mills or factories. Many, especially women, worked at home or in small workshops. In 1828 Matthew Carey, a businessman, called attention to the hardships of their lives:

"I have known a lady to expend 100 dollars on a party; pay 30 or 40 dollars for a bonnet, and 50 for a shawl; and yet make a hard bargain with a seamstress or washerwoman, who had to work at her needle or at the washing tub for 13 or 14 hours a day to make a bare livelihood for herself and a numerous family of small children."

Question to Investigate

Were women who worked at home or in workshops in the 1800s treated fairly?

Procedure

Explore the Question to Investigate by reading the letter on this page. It was written by a seamstress. Like many descriptions of historical situations and events, the letter includes a claim and supporting evidence. A **claim** is something that someone says is true. **Evidence** is information—facts, not opinions—given to support the claim. Read the source and do the following.

1 Identify the claim being made. Decide what the letter writer is trying to prove, and state that claim in a sentence.

2 Identify the evidence that supports the claim. List specific facts that the letter writer uses to support her claim.

3 Evaluate the evidence.
a. Answer the questions in the last point under Skill Tips.
b. How would the letter writer answer the Question to Investigate? How would you? Explain.

Source to Use

"Only think of a poor woman, confined to her seat fifteen hours out of twenty-four to make a pair of . . . pantaloons, for which she receives only twenty-five cents. And indeed, many of them [seamstresses] are not able to make a pair in much less than two days. . . .

Only think of twelve and a half cents for making a shirt, that takes a woman a whole day, if she attends to any other work in her family. . . . How shall she clothe her poor children, or even feed them at this rate? Yet there are many poor women of my acquaintance that are placed in the disheartening [discouraging] situation I have mentioned; and many of them are widows, with a number of children. And the tailors scold us when we bring . . . the work, and some of them say the work is done ill [poorly], and then take out half the price, or give us nothing if they [choose] . . . and God help us, we have to submit to the injustice."

From a seamstress's letter that appeared in *Mechanics Free Press,* December 18, 1830

Chapter Survey

Reviewing Vocabulary

Define the following terms.
1. slave codes   4. strike
2. discrimination   5. nativism
3. trade union   6. nativists

Reviewing Main Ideas

1. (a) How did economic activities in the Northeast and Midwest differ? (b) What tied these two regions together?
2. (a) Describe the economy of the South. (b) Who owned slaves? Who did not?
3. How did most slave owners try to get the greatest benefit from their slaves?
4. Describe three ways that enslaved African Americans resisted slavery.
5. (a) Why did Frederick Douglass say that "no colored man is really free in a slave-holding state"? (b) What problems did free African Americans face in the North?
6. Why did some factory workers in the North go on strike in the 1830s?
7. Why were some native-born Americans suspicious of the immigrants who came to the United States in the mid-1800s?

Thinking Critically

1. **Analysis** The economy of the North in the mid-1800s can be described as a diversified, or varied, economy. Why do you think this description is accurate? What label would you use to describe the economy of the South? Why?
2. **Synthesis** Predict how economic differences between the North and the South might contribute to conflict between the two regions.
3. **Why We Remember: Application** Frederick Douglass believed that "if there is no struggle there is no progress." Give three supporting examples from the text or your own observations.

Applying Skills

Identifying evidence In the Skill Lab on page 423 you investigated claims of unfair working conditions by a seamstress more than 150 years ago.
1. Find a recent claim of unfair working conditions. It may involve someone you know or a situation you have read about.
2. Identify the claim being made.
3. Identify the evidence that supports the claim.
4. Explain how the evidence supports the claim. Note if the evidence is specific and clear and if there is enough of it. What else would you ask if you could?

History Mystery

A popular product Answer the History Mystery on page 403. What invention would destroy demand for this product? Explain.

Writing in Your History Journal

1. **Keys to History** (a) The time line on pages 402–403 has seven Keys to History. In your journal, describe why each one is important to know about. (b) Imagine that you are going to teach fifth-grade students about the events on the time line. Choose one event. In your journal, state what you would say about the causes and effects of the event to help younger students understand it.
2. **Frederick Douglass** It is 1841. Yesterday, you attended the meeting of the Massachusetts Antislavery Society where Frederick Douglass first spoke about his life as a slave. In your journal, write a letter to Douglass giving your personal reactions to at least two specific comments he made. You can get ideas about what he might have said from the quotations in the text.

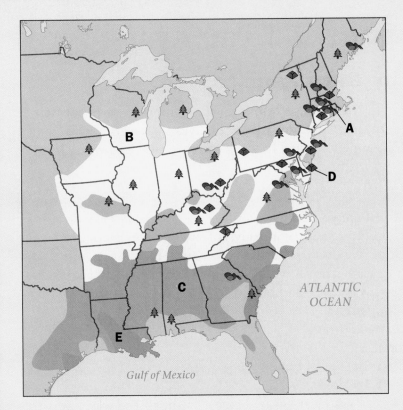

ATLANTIC
OCEAN

Gulf of Mexico

Reviewing Geography

1. For each letter on the map, write the name of the product or products identified.

2. Geographic Thinking Your library probably has books that rate the states according to how desirable they are to live in. Imagine that you are writing a guide to the states in 1850. Choose one state and review information in the text, including the maps and the Geography Lab.

Write a brief description of the climate and economic opportunities that might make this state one of the best places to live.

3. Citizenship In the early 1860s Charlotte L. Brown, a free African American, boarded a streetcar in San Francisco, in the free state of California. As she later wrote, the conductor informed her that "colored persons were not allowed to ride" and ordered her to get out. Charlotte refused, telling the conductor that she "had a right to ride, it was a public conveyance [vehicle]." Finally, he forced her out of the car. What would you have done in this situation? Why? Write your thoughts in your journal.

Alternative Assessment

Planning a time capsule Imagine that you live in 1850 in the North or the South. The people of your town have decided to bury a time capsule in the town square.

They want to help future generations understand their past. The capsule will contain items that reflect the events, issues, and people of the years 1830 to 1850. You are on the committee to collect items for the time capsule.

With the other committee members, make a list of 15 items to include in the capsule. The items can be objects, documents, or pictures. Write a description of each item and explain why it was chosen to represent life in the mid-1800s.

Your work will be evaluated on the following criteria:
• the items you choose are appropriate for the time period and region
• the items you choose reflect major aspects of life in the mid-1800s
• you explain clearly how each item relates to the time period and region

Nightjohn by Gary Paulsen

Gary Paulsen's novel, *Nightjohn,* is told from the point of view of Sarny, a 12-year-old slave. On the plantation where she lives she meets a man named John. One night, John quietly begins to teach Sarny to read and write. In the following scene, Sarny's mammy catches John teaching Sarny the letter *B*.

"What in the *hell* are you doing? Don't you know what they do to her if they find her trying to read? We already got one girl tore to pieces by the whip and the dogs. We don't need two. . . . Child, they'll cut your thumbs off if you learn to read. They'll whip you until your back looks knitted— until it looks like his back." She pointed to John, big old finger. "Is that how you got whipped?"

He shook his head. "I ran."

"And got caught."

"Not the first time."

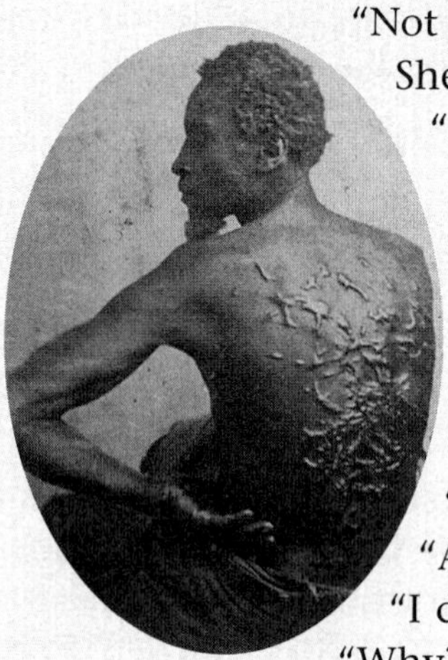

She waited. I waited.

"First time I got clean away. I went north, all the way. I was free."

I'd never heard such a thing. We couldn't even talk about being free. And here was a man said he had been free by running north. I thought, How can that be?

"You ran and got away?" mammy asked.

"I did."

"You ran until you were clean away?"

"I did."

"And you came *back?*"

"I did."

"Why?"

He sighed and it sounded like his voice, like his laugh. Low and way off thunder. It made me think he was going to promise something, the way thunder promises rain. "For this."

"What you mean—this?"

"To teach reading."

It's never quiet in the quarters. During the day the young ones run and scrabble and fight or cry and they's always a gaggle of them. At night everybody be sleeping. But not quiet. Alice, she's quiet. But they's some of them to cry. New workers who are just old enough to be working in the fields cry sometimes in their sleep. They hurt and their hands bleed and pain them from new blisters that break and break again. Old workers cry because they're old and getting to the end and have old pain. Same pain,

quarters: lodging place for slaves

young and old. Some snore. Others just breathe loud.

It's a long building and dark except for the light coming in the door and the small windows, but it's never quiet. Not even at night.

Now it seemed quiet. Mammy she looked down at John. Didn't say nothing for a long time. Just looked.

I had to think to hear the breathing, night sounds.

Slave quarters were often large buildings that housed several families.

Finally mammy talks. Her voice is soft. "You came back to teach reading?"

John nodded. "That's half of it."

"What's the other half?"

"Writing." He smiled. "Course, I wasn't going to get caught. I had in mind moving, moving around. Teaching a little here, a little there. Going to do hidey-schools. But I got slow and they got fast and some crackers caught me in the woods. They were hunting bear, but the dogs came on me instead and I took to a tree and they got me."

Another long quiet. Way off, down by the river, I heard the sound of a nightbird. Singing for day. Soon the sun would come.

"Why does it matter?" Mammy leaned against the wall. She had one hand on the logs, one on her cheek. Tired. "Why do that to these young ones? To Sarny here. If they learn to read—"

"And write."

"And write, it's just grief for them. Longtime grief. They find what they don't have, can't have. It ain't good to know that. It eats at you then—to know it and not have it."

"They have to be able to write," John said. Voice pushing. He stood and reached out one hand with long fingers and touched mammy on the forehead. It was almost like he be kissing her with his fingers. Soft. Touch like black cotton in the dark. "They have to read and write. We all have to read and write so we can write about this—what they doing to us. It has to be written."

Mammy she turned and went back to her mat on the floor. Moving quiet, not looking back. She settled next to the young ones and John he turned to me and he say:

"Next is *C*."

hidey-schools: secret schools

crackers: scornful term for poor whites

A Closer Look

1. What is mammy's reaction to Sarny learning to read? Why?

2. What does the author's description of the quarters tell you about the lives of those who live there?

3. How does mammy's attitude change as she and John talk? Why do you think this change occurs?

From *Nightjohn* by Gary Paulsen. Copyright © 1993 by Gary Paulsen. Used by permission of Delacorte Press, a division of Bantam Doubleday Publishing Group, Inc.

Chapter 16

Religion and Reform

Sections

Beginning the Story with Sojourner Truth

1. **Revival and Reform**
2. **Movements to End Slavery**
3. **Working for Women's Rights**
4. **American Voices**

⚷ *Keys to History*

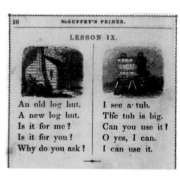

Early 1800s
Second Great Awakening sweeps the nation
Carving of a revival preacher

1830s
Horace Mann urges spread of public schools
McGuffey reader, an early schoolbook

1820

1830

Looking Back

Slave trade banned in the United States

1808

Dr. Blackwell graduated at the top of the class of 1849 from the medical school of Geneva College. Yet years earlier this brilliant student had been turned down by nearly a dozen schools. Why was Blackwell rejected?

1833
American Anti-Slavery Society established
William Lloyd Garrison

1848
Seneca Falls Convention on women's rights

1850s
Harriet Tubman makes heroic journeys as part of the Underground Railroad

1845
Frederick Douglass publishes *Narrative of the Life of Frederick Douglass*

1840

1850

World Link

Britain abolishes slavery
1833

Looking Ahead

13th Amendment ends slavery
1865

● **429**

Beginning the Story with

Sojourner Truth

Sojourner Truth had heard enough. She had come to this church in Akron, Ohio, to discuss the rights of women. And what had she heard instead? One minister after another explaining why women were too weak in mind and body to do much of anything except raise children.

Her patience worn out, she rose from her seat to reply. The idea of an African American woman, especially a former slave, making a public speech shocked some members of the audience. "No! No!" they shouted. "Don't let her speak!"

"Ain't I a Woman?"

Quite unafraid, the tall woman walked to the pulpit and began to speak. "The poor men seem to be all in confusion," she began with a laugh.

> **"**The man over there says women need to be helped into carriages and lifted over ditches and over puddles, and have the best places everywhere. Nobody helps me into carriages or over puddles, or gives me the best place—and ain't I a woman? Look at my arm! I have plowed and planted and gathered into barns, and no man could head [outdo] me—and ain't I a woman? I could work as much and eat as much as a man—when I could get it—and bear the lash as well! And ain't I a woman? I have borne thirteen children, and seen most of 'em sold into slavery, and when I cried out with my mother's grief, none but Jesus heard me—and ain't I a woman?**"**

As usual, Sojourner Truth had gone straight to the heart of the matter and spoken the truth. At the same time, she had charmed her listeners. "This unlearned African woman has a magnetic power over an audience [that is] perfectly astounding," observed an admirer. As Sojourner Truth put it, "I cannot read a book, but I can read people."

"I'll Keep You Scratching"

Sojourner Truth's legal name was Isabella ("Belle") Van Wagener. She was born in New York around 1797. Growing up in slavery, she had seen all of her 12 brothers and sisters sold by her master, a wealthy Dutch landowner. She herself was sold twice before the age of 14. One of her owners boasted that Belle was "better to me than a *man*—for she will do a good family's washing in the night, and be ready in the morning to go into the field where she will do as much raking and binding as my best hands."

In a time with no television or radio, public speaking on issues was a common way to raise public awareness and support.

New York ended slavery for adults in 1827. By that time Belle had borne several children. On gaining her freedom, she learned that her youngest son Peter was still enslaved, despite his master's promise to free him. Belle took the daring step of suing for his freedom in a state court. She won. Then, taking her two youngest children, she moved to New York City and began a new life.

Belle was a strongly spiritual person who felt very close to God. She composed hymns and memorized much of the Bible. In 1843, at nearly the age of 50, Belle came to believe that God was calling her to be a traveling minister. She changed her name to Sojourner Truth and began traveling through the northern states. She preached in churches, at open-air gatherings called camp meetings, and on city streets, telling all who would listen about God's goodness and the brotherhood of all his children.

As a speaker, Sojourner Truth was absolutely fearless. Her confidence rested in her belief that God was with her and that she was doing the Lord's work. She became active in the antislavery and women's rights movements and was a popular speaker for these causes. Her faith, as well as a ready wit, helped protect her from hecklers and their insults. In one debate a lawyer dismissed her, saying, "Old woman, do you suppose people care what you say? Why, I don't care any more for your talk than I do for the bite of a flea."

"Maybe not," Truth replied with a laugh. "But Lord willing, I'll keep you scratching."

Hands-On HISTORY

Activity

Like Sojourner Truth, some public speakers today talk of "reading people." For example, politicians try to read an audience to judge whether they have support. On the left side of a sheet of paper, list three or more clues a speaker might look for in reading people. On the right, suggest what messages the clues might give the speaker. Be prepared to demonstrate the clues and their meanings.

1. Revival and Reform

Reading Guide

New Terms **social reform, temperance, utopias**

Section Focus **The religious revivals and reform movements that swept the nation**

1. What was the Second Great Awakening?
2. What movements for social reform arose in the first half of the 1800s?
3. How did utopias show a longing for a better society?

Religious faith was the main influence on Sojourner Truth's life. Nothing mattered more than doing the things God called her to do—fighting for justice and building harmony among people. Her religious motives were typical of people of her time who sought to make society better. The early 1800s was a period of religious revivals known as the Second Great Awakening.

The Second Great Awakening

The rapid spread of the Second Great Awakening caused church membership to boom. The message of the revival was the message of evangelical Christianity—that people should turn from evil, or repent, and receive God's love and forgiveness. For people new to the Christian faith, this experience was known as conversion. The message was a democratic one: conversion was equally open to everyone.

Camp meetings One way that revival spread was through camp meetings—large outdoor gatherings that lasted several days. Families traveled for miles to attend. People slept in tents, wagons, or shelters made of tree branches and ate meals together in the open air. Often Baptist, Methodist, and Presbyterian ministers sang and preached in different parts of the camp at the same time.

The largest of all camp meetings took place at Cane Ridge, Kentucky, in August 1801. It lasted six days and attracted more than 10,000 excited people. The shouting and singing could be heard for miles. James Finley, a famous preacher, claimed:

❝The noise was like the roar of Niagara [Falls]. The vast sea of human beings seemed to be agitated as if by a storm. I counted seven ministers all preaching at once, some on stumps, others in wagons.**❞**

Circuit riders The revival message was welcomed in the West. To reach people in these sparsely populated areas, traveling ministers called circuit riders rode horseback over regular routes known as circuits. They preached sermons and tended to the spiritual needs of people too isolated and too poor to support a full-time minister.

The person credited with pioneering the circuit rider ministry was the Methodist bishop Francis Asbury. He was a circuit rider for 45 years. Because of the zeal of Asbury and his fellow preachers, the Methodists had the largest following of any Protestant church in America by the 1840s.

Preachers at camp meetings felt that God's message was for everyone. They urged their listeners to turn away from bad habits, and many people did change. "Drunkards, profane swearers, liars, quarrelsome persons, etc., are remarkably reformed," reported one preacher.

African American churches The Methodists had a separate branch for African American members. It began in 1787 when church officials in Philadelphia told three free African Americans they could not sit with white members. Insulted, Richard Allen and Absalom Jones organized their own church, the Mother Bethel African Methodist Episcopal (AME) Church. AME churches are still active today.

In addition to the AME Church, which continued to spread, African Americans formed other churches in the North. African Americans could not form churches in the South until after the Civil War because laws prevented them from assembling.

When Isabella Van Wagener moved to New York City in 1829, she joined the AME Church. She was active in the church for 15 years before setting off on her traveling ministry as Sojourner Truth.

Revivals and Reform

A major outcome of the Second Great Awakening was a new spirit of **social reform**—the effort to make society better and more fair for everyone. People who converted to evangelical Christianity felt moved to improve their personal lives and also to help others. Such men and women believed that they could and should work to correct the evils in society.

Religious revivals, combined with the democratic spirit of the Age of Jackson, produced in Americans a deeper belief in equality. Caught up in religious and democratic fervor, many Americans believed that it would be simple to lift the curtains of ignorance by improving public education throughout the nation. They also turned their energies toward freeing those who were physically or mentally enslaved.

Before the early 1800s, most teachers were men. As reformers pushed for schools to train women teachers, more women took up teaching. This Winslow Homer painting shows a one-room country school.

Improving Public Education

The drive to improve public education was probably the most successful social reform effort before the Civil War. The ideal of public education for all children fit with the ideals of Jacksonian democracy—equality and the importance of the common person. Educating all citizens would make them better able to take part in democratic government. Christian reformers also valued education. They wanted every American to be able to read the Bible.

Except in New England, most Americans in the early 1800s saw education as the responsibility of parents. School attendance was not required. In the South and the Middle Atlantic regions, most schools were run either by religious groups or by schoolmasters paid directly by parents. The few public schools that existed were thought of as being for poor children and were seen as inferior to private schools.

Education reformers faced two major problems. They had to convince public officials and voters that public schools—supported by tax dollars—were important. They also had to ensure that the schools were open to all children equally.

Horace Mann In the 1830s Horace Mann led the effort to provide education for all children. Known as the "Father of American Public Schools," Mann believed that only educated citizens could make a democracy work. He urged that school be required for all children. He also pushed for special schools to train teachers.

Mann's reports on education won him wide respect. Some of his views stirred argument, though. For example, Mann opposed whipping and other physical punishment in school. Critics called him unpatriotic and impractical. They believed that children were

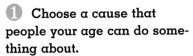

Hands-On HISTORY

Speaking to persuade Speech can be a powerful tool. Reformers like Sojourner Truth knew that power. A good speech, well delivered, can move an audience to laughter or tears, persuade them to change their beliefs or to join a cause, and leave them with words and ideas they never forget.

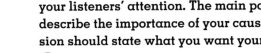**Activity** Remember the qualities Sojourner Truth had as you write and deliver a speech. Your goal is to persuade your classmates to join you in working for a cause.

① Choose a cause that people your age can do something about.

② Decide what action you will ask the audience to take. This is the main point of your speech.

③ Do any research needed to make your speech more interesting and persuasive.

④ Write your speech. The introduction should catch your listeners' attention. The main part should describe the importance of your cause. The conclusion should state what you want your listeners to do.

⑤ Rehearse your speech in front of a family member or friend. Ask for ideas to improve the content and delivery.

Martin Luther King, Jr., an outstanding speaker

Help for the Disabled

Dedicated reformers also sought to improve opportunities for disabled persons. Scores of inspired men and women devoted their lives to helping the deaf, the blind, and the mentally ill.

Schools for the deaf and the blind In 1817 Thomas Hopkins Gallaudet opened a school in Connecticut for the education of deaf students. Gallaudet's success in teaching his students to read and write, to read lips, and to communicate by hand signs brought him worldwide fame. Soon similar schools were set up elsewhere.

Samuel Gridley Howe of Massachusetts achieved similar success with blind students. At the famous Perkins Institution, Howe taught his students to read using braille—an alphabet

naturally bad and only stern handling could make them useful citizens.

Thanks to reformers' efforts, the American public school system began to grow. State funds for education doubled, the quality of public schools improved, and the school year was extended to a minimum of six months. Three schools opened to train teachers.

By the 1860s, public high schools were still rare, but the number of elementary schools had greatly increased. Most northern states offered elementary education for all white children. Free black children attended separate—and inferior—schools.

of raised codes. He also taught them skills that would help them get jobs and lead independent lives.

The mentally ill No reformer accomplished more than Dorothea Lynde Dix, who worked with the mentally ill. A deeply religious Boston school teacher, Dix found her life's calling after teaching a Sunday school class for women at a jail. What she saw shocked her. Locked up in small, dark, unheated cells at the rear of the prison were several mentally ill women who had not committed any crime.

The environmental movement

"Rarely has a movement in so short a time gained such popular support, had such legislative and regulatory impact, produced so many active organizations, or become so embedded in a culture."

The author of those words was describing today's environmental movement. With roots in the 1800s, the movement itself began in the 1960s. In 1970 the government set up the Environmental Protection Agency, and activists held the first Earth Day.

Today, hundreds of groups work to preserve nature, conserve resources, and reduce pollution. They hold demonstrations and bring lawsuits against polluters. They also work to get government to pass laws protecting the environment.

Millions of individuals also do their part. They recycle, reduce their use of resources, and choose products that do minimum damage to the environment. Still, much work remains to be done. Americans will continue to strive for a cleaner, healthier planet.

The sight spurred Dix to make a two-year study of all of the jails and poorhouses in Massachusetts. Dix saw the same inhumane conditions wherever she went. In 1843 she presented her report before the state legislature:

"I tell what I have seen. . . . Insane persons confined . . . in cages, closets, cellars, stalls, pens! Chained, naked, beaten with rods, and lashed into obedience."

After getting Massachusetts to set up a hospital for the mentally ill, Dix took her cause nationwide. By 1860, as many as 15 states and Canada had separate hospitals for the mentally ill. Few reformers could claim such immediate and widespread success.

Prison Reform

Dorothea Dix was also a leader in prison reform. Prisons in her day were poorly organized. Most had large rooms with all the prisoners, including women and children, kept together. Some of these prisoners had committed violent crimes, while others were guilty only of being in debt.

Thanks to Dix and others, new prisons separated men and women and gave prisoners useful work to do. Reformers pushed for special schools for juvenile criminals and "houses of correction" for people who had committed minor crimes. These measures separated youths and petty criminals from the influence of hardened criminals.

In addition to improving conditions in prisons, reformers worked to end cruel punishment. They fought against the use of flogging, branding, and mutilation. As a result, many states outlawed such punishments.

Prison reformers won a major victory in getting rid of prisons for people whose only crime was not being able to pay their debts. As many as half of the people in these jails in the early 1800s owed less than $50. Some owed only a few pennies. How could people ever pay off even these small debts if they were in prison? By the mid-1830s debtor prisons were a thing of the past.

Dorothea Dix

Temperance Movement

Many reformers blamed crime, poverty, and even mental illness on drunkenness. The use and abuse of alcohol was common in the early 1800s. People drank at weddings, funerals, political rallies, and even on the job. As more and more people experienced religious revival, alcohol abuse became a major concern of reform-minded preachers and church members. They began to speak out against "Demon Rum."

At first the enemies of alcohol called for **temperance**—moderation in drinking habits. Their crusade became known as the temperance movement. During the 1830s some crusaders began to demand that people not drink at all. They pushed for laws banning the sale of alcohol. The first state to pass such a law was Maine in 1846. Although a dozen other states passed similar laws, many Americans protested, and most states later repealed the bans.

Utopias

As reformers sought to create the perfect society, some people decided to form groups to achieve their goal in small communities. The communities they formed were known as **utopias,** meaning perfect societies. More than a hundred utopias sprang up between 1800 and 1900.

The Shakers Some utopias were religious communities of people who wanted to live out their faith among others with the same beliefs. You read about the Mormons in Chapter 14. Another religious community was the United Society of Believers, better known as the Shakers.

Founded by "Mother Ann" Lee, the Shakers believed in the equality of all people. They worshiped together and expressed their religious feelings in song and dance. The

Temperance crusaders published pamphlets to warn against the effects of drinking. These drawings show the change in a family from the parents' first drink to their complete ruin as violent alcoholics.

name "Shaker" came from one form of worship dance.

The Shakers were well organized, generous, and hard working. They shared all their possessions in common. At the society's peak in the 1840s, it had about 6,000 members. It then went into a slow and steady decline, in part because its members were not allowed to marry and thus had no children to carry on the community. A handful of believers kept the faith until well into the 1900s.

Oneida Another community based on religious ideas was the Oneida Community organized by John Noyes in 1848. Its main goal was perfection in every activity. Members believed in release from illness and sin through faith in God. Since Noyes considered marriage between one man and one woman to be "selfish love," he invented a

Noted for their simple way of life, the Shakers made a style of furniture still admired today. The drawing above shows a form of Shaker worship dance.

system in which all members of the community were married to each other.

Although Oneida thrived economically, its marriage practices caused public protest. In 1879 the community reorganized as a business company. The Oneida company still makes manufactured goods and is known for its silverware.

New Harmony and Brook Farm
Other utopian communities were based on nonreligious ideals. In 1825 Robert Owen, who owned mills in Scotland, founded New Harmony in Indiana. Owen's ideal was a community with good working conditions, in which members shared all property.

For a short time, New Harmony appeared to be a brilliant success. However, most of the people who came there wanted more individual freedom. The community split up after only three years.

The members of Brook Farm, founded in 1841 near Boston, included some of America's most brilliant thinkers, such as Ralph Waldo Emerson, John Greenleaf Whittier, and Nathaniel Hawthorne. Members shared possessions, divided work equally, and set aside time for social and literary activities. "Our . . . aim is nothing less than Heaven on Earth," one member declared.

Brook Farm survived for a time because of an excellent school that attracted paying students from outside the community. Yet the community had more thinkers than workers, and after a few years it could not make enough money to stay afloat. In 1847 the farm had to be sold to pay bills.

1. Section Review

1. Define **social reform, temperance, and utopias.**
2. How did the Second Great Awakening spur the impulse toward reform?
3. Choose two reform movements and explain how they showed reformers' urges to create a more fair society.
4. Critical Thinking Imagine that you are starting a utopian community. What ideals would be important to you? How would you organize your community to meet your goals?

Geography Lab

The First Big City Park

How could America's crowded cities be made more livable? One answer, Frederick Law Olmsted believed, was to bring nature into the city. Olmsted designed the nation's first large urban park—Central Park in New York City. The park looked so natural that visitors could not believe it was deliberately planned.

Use the quotations and picture to understand Olmsted's reasons for the park.

Central Park around 1865

Statements by Frederick Law Olmsted

"It is a scientific fact that the occasional contemplation [observation] of natural scenes . . . is favorable to the health and vigor of men and especially to the health and vigor of their intellect."

"My notion is that whatever grounds a great city may need for other public purposes, for parades, for athletic sports, for fireworks, for museums of art or science, it also needs a large ground scientifically and artistically prepared to provide such a poetic and tranquilizing [calming] influence on its people as comes through a pleasant contemplation of natural scenery."

"[Central Park has] a distinctly harmonizing and refining influence . . . favorable to courtesy, self-control, and temperance."

Link to History

1. What did Olmsted think were the benefits of observing nature?

2. How did Central Park reflect Olmsted's ideas?

3. Today, Central Park includes an open-air theater, a zoo, an art museum, playgrounds, and facilities for baseball, tennis, volleyball, handball, and miniature golf. What might Olmsted think of modern-day Central Park?

4. **Hands-On Geography** Develop a proposal for improving a park in your community. Include "before" and "after" drawings or maps to show the park as it is now and as it would look after your ideas were put into practice.

439

2. Movements to End Slavery

Reading Guide

New Terms emancipation, abolition

Section Focus How the movement to end slavery gained strength in the early 1800s

1. How did free African Americans work to end slavery?
2. What effects did revivals and reform movements have on antislavery efforts?
3. Who objected to abolition and why?

Sojourner Truth's best-known reform work was her effort to end slavery. Indeed, in the great swell of reform movements of the early to mid-1800s, the antislavery movement came to overshadow all others. How could people even dream of a perfect world, many reformers asked, when millions in America were enslaved?

Early Efforts

Some opposition to slavery had existed since the first Africans arrived in the early 1600s. The steady pressure for change by African Americans, combined with Quaker calls for **emancipation**—freeing of slaves—made slow progress. By 1804 the seven states from Pennsylvania north had promised to free their slaves.

Free African Americans in the North worked hard against slavery in the South. They organized antislavery societies and mutual-aid associations to help each other and to shelter, clothe, and feed African Americans who escaped slavery.

African Americans also took political action. In 1800 James Forten, a wealthy Philadelphia businessman, presented a petition to Congress calling for emancipation. Out of 86 congressmen, only 1 sided with Forten's cause. Still, for the rest of his life Forten worked to end slavery.

Colonization

One idea popular with early supporters of emancipation was to settle freed slaves in Africa. In 1815 Paul Cuffe, a wealthy free African American, transported 38 volunteers to West Africa. There, he believed, freed slaves would have more opportunity than in the United States, where racism was strong. Cuffe intended to send groups each year, but he died before finishing his plans.

Liberia The American Colonization Society, founded in 1817, urged slaveowners to free their slaves and send them to Africa. It obtained land in West Africa and named it Liberia, from the Latin word for freedom. The Society had support from southerners who feared that if freed slaves stayed in the South, they might stir up rebellion.

Volunteers began moving to Liberia in 1821, but the colonization plan never took root. Most African Americans saw the United States as their home, not Africa. Also, the few who did go faced poverty and disease in the new colony. No more than 15,000 people moved to Liberia before the Civil War.

Northerners soon saw that colonization would not work. James Forten crusaded against colonization. He believed that slaves should be freed and educated to take their place as equals in American society.

James Forten and his granddaughter Charlotte worked for African American rights.

Reformers Join the Cause

In the 1820s a strong antislavery movement began. Revival leaders called on Christians to denounce slavery as evil. The democratic spirit of the time caused people to see that slavery did not fit the American values of liberty and equality. People called for **abolition**—putting an end to slavery.

Antislavery newspapers began to pop up in the North and the Midwest. Benjamin Lundy began *Genius of Universal Emancipation* in Ohio in 1821. In 1827 Samuel Cornish and John Russwurm started *Freedom's Journal,* the first African American newspaper. Such papers increased the number of people calling for abolition.

Revivalist ministers also won people to the cause. One of the most influential was Theodore Dwight Weld, a student at Lane Theological Seminary in Cincinnati. He was so fired up with antislavery fever that the school forced him to leave. Weld and his followers moved to Oberlin College, which became a center of the antislavery movement.

The American Anti-Slavery Society

While some abolitionists believed that slavery should be ended gradually, by the 1830s others had grown impatient. These abolitionists now demanded that slavery be abolished everywhere immediately.

William Lloyd Garrison Perhaps the most famous white abolitionist was William Lloyd Garrison of Boston. Garrison had worked on Lundy's newspaper but considered him too timid. On New Year's Day, 1831, Garrison began publishing his own paper, *The Liberator.* In fiery language he demanded an immediate end to slavery:

"I am in earnest—I will not equivocate [be vague]—I will not excuse—I will not retreat a single inch—AND I WILL BE HEARD.**"**

Britain abolishes slavery Petitions to abolish slavery were so heavy that the men carrying them into Parliament staggered under the weight. British antislavery activists were demanding immediate abolition throughout the British Empire.

They got part of what they wanted in the Emancipation Act of 1833. Slavery in British colonies such as Jamaica was abolished—but not right away. Only slaves under age 6 gained immediate freedom. The rest had to stay with their owners as unpaid apprentices for several years.

In the United States, news of Britain's action fueled the flame of the abolitionist movement. While William Lloyd Garrison was disgusted by how gradual the British act was, abolitionists in general took hope in their cause.

In 1833 Garrison, along with two wealthy New York silk merchants, Arthur and Lewis Tappan, formed the American Anti-Slavery Society. Soon the society grew to 200,000 members, black and white, male and female.

In time, the society would split apart. Some members thought the only hope of ending slavery was to do it gradually, not all at once. Some feared that letting women and African Americans give speeches and play leadership roles would turn many Americans against the antislavery cause.

The Grimké sisters Among the women who played important roles in the American Anti-Slavery Society were Sarah and Angelina Grimké. Daughters of a wealthy South Carolina slaveholder, the Grimké sisters had turned against slavery after becoming Quakers.

The sisters moved north to work for abolition. They began publishing antislavery pamphlets and making speeches, at first in homes and then in public. In 1838 Angelina appeared before the Massachusetts legislature to present an antislavery petition signed by 20,000 women.

African American Leaders

African American leaders welcomed the formation of the American Anti-Slavery Society. They thought it would help them spread the message about the evils of slavery. James Forten cheered *The Liberator* and said that Garrison's work had "roused up a spirit in our young people."

Meanwhile, African Americans continued their own long fight for abolition. From lecturing to writing to political action, African Americans worked tirelessly for the cause.

Frederick Douglass The best-known African American abolitionist was Frederick Douglass, whom you read about in Chapter 15. In addition to being a brilliant lecturer, Douglass was an effective writer. In 1845 he published an autobiography, *Narrative of the Life of Frederick Douglass*, which became popular reading among abolitionists.

Douglass wrote for *The Liberator*, but in 1847 he started his own paper, *North Star*. He made it clear that African Americans must lead the fight against slavery:

❝No one else can fight [the battle] for us. . . . Our relations to the [white] Anti-Slavery movement must be and are changed. Instead of depending upon it we must lead it.❞

Sojourner Truth No less effective as an abolitionist was Sojourner Truth. She may have lacked the education of Douglass, but she made up for it with her humor and clever comments. When they spoke at the same events, she would often poke fun at Douglass, and he once grumbled that she "seemed to feel it her duty to trip me up in my speeches."

On her travels through the North and West, Truth drew large crowds wherever she spoke. In 1850 a fellow abolitionist wrote the story of her life, *Narrative of Sojourner Truth,* and Truth supported herself by selling copies of the book at antislavery gatherings.

The use of force Some African Americans called for force as the only way to throw off slavery. In 1829 David Walker published a pamphlet titled *Appeal to the Colored Citizens of the World.* He urged slaves to fight for their freedom. His message terrified southerners, who offered rewards for his arrest or death. In 1830 Walker was found dead near his Boston shop.

Henry Highland Garnet, a newspaper editor, also urged slaves to resist, using force if necessary. In an 1843 speech, Garnet compared slave resistance to the American Revolution:

"Let it no longer be a debatable question, whether it is better to choose LIBERTY or DEATH! Let your motto be RESISTANCE! RESISTANCE! RESISTANCE!— No oppressed people have ever secured their liberty without resistance."

Underground Railroad

Perhaps the most dramatic part of the antislavery movement was the Underground Railroad. This "railroad" had nothing to do with trains. It was a secret network of people who would shelter and feed escaping slaves along their way to freedom. Thousands of African Americans used this network.

"Conductors," many of them former slaves, risked their freedom and their lives to help slaves escape. One of the most famous conductors was Harriet Tubman, who had escaped alone as a young woman. Tubman guided more than 300 slaves north to freedom. In her 19 trips into the South, she never lost a "passenger."

In northern states free blacks and sympathetic whites directed escaping slaves to secret hiding places in homes or barns. These "stations" of the Underground Railroad were places to sleep and get food and clothes before continuing. Chased by dogs and slave catchers, escaping slaves would

"I appear before the immense assembly this evening as a thief and a robber. I stole this head, these limbs, this body from my master, and ran off with them."

Frederick Douglass, from a speech to an antislavery audience in 1842

Leading abolitionists of the time were black and white, male and female, as shown in this rare daguerreotype. Frederick Douglass is seated at the right end of the table.

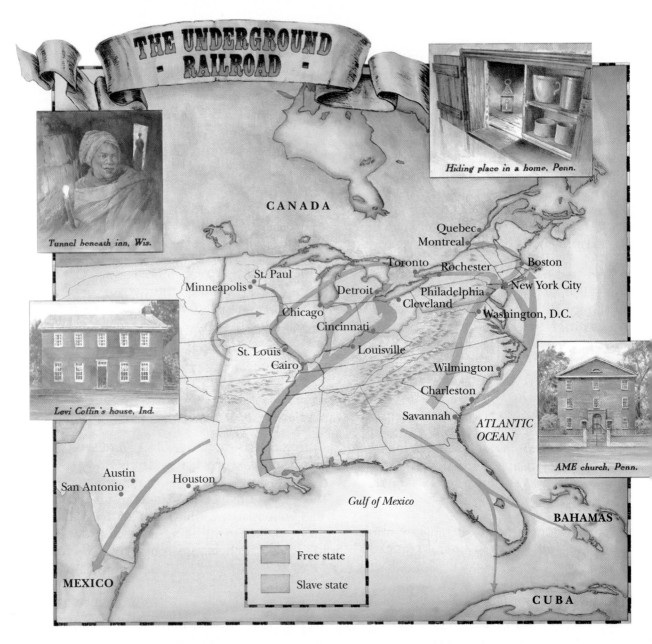

THE UNDERGROUND RAILROAD

Hiding place in a home, Penn.

Tunnel beneath inn, Wis.

CANADA

Quebec
Montreal
Toronto
Rochester
Boston
St. Paul
Minneapolis
Detroit
Philadelphia
New York City
Cleveland
Chicago
Washington, D.C.
Cincinnati
St. Louis
Louisville
Cairo
Wilmington
Charleston
Savannah
ATLANTIC
OCEAN

Levi Coffin's house, Ind.

AME church, Penn.

Austin
San Antonio
Houston

Gulf of Mexico

BAHAMAS

MEXICO

Free state
Slave state

CUBA

Reading Maps

Judging by the map, where did African Americans who were escaping slavery hope to find freedom?

often sleep by day and travel by night, following the North Star.

No one knows the actual number of slaves who used the Underground Railroad because everything about it was kept secret. Some historians estimate that as many as 100,000 African Americans used it to escape from the South.

This 1837 anti-abolitionist riot took place the night Elijah Lovejoy was killed. With five bullets in his body, Lovejoy died defending his press.

Opposition to Abolitionism

The determined efforts of abolitionists, both black and white, alarmed and even enraged some whites. In 1835 a mob destroyed Garrison's press and dragged him through the streets of Boston. Two years later a mob in Illinois killed Elijah Lovejoy, another antislavery newspaper editor.

Anti-abolitionists had several reasons for opposing an end to slavery. Obviously slaveholders—and even some southerners who did not have slaves—objected to abolition. They saw it as a threat to their way of life.

In the North, some of the violence was planned by businessmen, merchants, and bankers. They depended on southern agriculture—worked by slaves—for the raw materials their businesses needed. At the same time, northern factory workers feared that they would lose their jobs to freed slaves.

The "gag rule" In Congress, opponents of abolition became alarmed as the antislavery movement gained strength. Abolitionists were flooding Congress with petitions to outlaw slavery and the slave trade in Washington, D.C. In 1836 southern congressmen managed to pass a "gag rule" barring debate on antislavery petitions in the House of Representatives.

Former President John Quincy Adams was a representative at the time. He was not an abolitionist, but he was furious about the gag rule. To him, it violated the Bill of Rights guarantee of freedom of speech and the right of petition. It took Adams eight years, but in 1844 he finally convinced the House to repeal the obnoxious gag rule.

In spite of opposition, the abolition movement grew stronger and its message more urgent. You will see in the next chapter that the issue of slavery became linked to westward expansion, as Americans argued over whether to allow slavery in new territories and states. Even people who wanted to ignore the issue would no longer be able to, as the conflict over slavery widened the split between North and South.

2. Section Review

1. Define **emancipation** and **abolition.**
2. Choose three of the following and explain how each fought slavery: James Forten, Paul Cuffe, Samuel Cornish and John Russwurm, Frederick Douglass, Sojourner Truth, David Walker, Henry Highland Garnet, Harriet Tubman.
3. What reasons did people have for opposing abolition?
4. Critical Thinking What reasons did reformers have for opposing slavery? Why do you think slavery became the foremost issue in the United States during this time?

Skill Lab

Skill Tips

A historian is interpreting the past when he or she:

- makes claims about people or events
- gives opinions about whether something or someone was important, right, or good
- stresses one side of an issue

Thinking Critically
Historical Interpretations

"An agreement with hell" is what abolitionist William Lloyd Garrison called the Constitution because it allowed slavery. Garrison once burned a copy of it in protest. Such words and actions led most white southerners—and many white northerners—to call him extreme. Even some who shared Garrison's hatred of slavery thought he was hurting their cause.

Question to Investigate

Did William Lloyd Garrison do the antislavery movement more harm than good?

Procedure

Historians disagree about Garrison's effect on the antislavery movement. Writing about history involves interpreting the past. In a **historical interpretation,** a historian offers an opinion about an event or person. This opinion is usually supported both by statements of fact and by other opinions. The source on this page is one historian's interpretation of Garrison's role.

1 Identify the interpretation.
a. State the historian's opinion.
b. How do you think this historian would answer the Question to Investigate? Explain.

2 Identify how the interpretation is supported.
a. List the statements of fact.
b. List the opinions.

3 Evaluate how *well* the interpretation is supported.
a. State two questions you would ask this historian about his view of Garrison.
b. Has this historian persuaded you that his interpretation makes sense? Explain.
c. What is some information you would need in order to further explore the Question to Investigate?

Source to Use

"Garrison had accomplishments of crucial importance to his credit. He had led the fight to make slavery a moral rather than a political issue. . . . The issue of slavery could no longer be postponed or dismissed as a Southern problem. Historians who have been . . . critical of Garrison for his fanaticism and rigidity have missed the point. The first voice to speak out . . . against a social injustice that the rest of society has come to take largely for granted *must* speak violently. . . . He has to shatter carefully constructed defenses, penetrate ears tuned out to his message. . . . Shock and trauma are his necessary and inevitable [unavoidable] weapons. . . .

An ally of Garrison's and a frequent critic [of him], Lydia Maria Child, made one of the best evaluations of the abolitionist leader when she called him a 'remarkably pure-minded man, whose only fault is that he cannot be moderate on a subject which it is exceedingly difficult for an honest mind to examine with calmness.'"

From Page Smith, *The Nation Comes of Age,* Vol. 4 (McGraw-Hill, 1981)

3. Working for Women's Rights

Reading Guide

Section Focus **The struggle for women's rights in the early 1800s**

1. How did the antislavery movement spur women to seek their rights?
2. What progress did women make in education and the professions?
3. Who were some important women active in the women's rights movement, and what did they accomplish?

The antislavery movement marked the first time that American women had played a major political role. As they fought to free slaves, however, women saw more clearly their own lack of freedom. Angelina Grimké pointed out:

❝We cannot push abolitionism forward with all our might until we take up the stumbling block out of the road. . . . What then can woman do for the slave, when she herself is under the feet of man and shamed into silence?❞

Women in the Early 1800s

The Grimkés' belief that men and women were equal was rare at that time. At the start of the 1800s, American women—especially married women—were second-class citizens with few rights. A wife's property and any money she earned belonged to her husband. Some state laws allowed husbands to beat their wives "with a reasonable instrument." No woman in America could vote, sit on a jury, or hold public office.

Before the 1830s no college or university in the United States accepted female students. Men commonly believed that the effort to learn subjects like mathematics and science would cause women to suffer nervous breakdowns. The few girls who advanced beyond elementary school attended girls' schools that prepared them to be good wives and mothers.

Progress in Education

One of the first areas that women sought to reform was education. Of the many women who crusaded for better schooling for young women, two of the most famous were Emma Hart Willard and Mary Lyon.

Women struggled for the right to an education. This daguerreotype was taken in about 1850 in a Boston school for girls.

A woman's outfit typical of the 1850s included a whale-boned bodice, tight corset, and several petticoats. In 1851 Amelia Bloomer shocked the public with her comfortable short skirt and full "pants," which people called bloomers.

When Elizabeth Cady Stanton's embarrassed son asked her not to come to his school in bloomers, she replied:

"Now suppose you and I were taking a long walk in the fields and I had on three long petticoats. Then suppose a bull should take after us. Why, you, with your arms and legs free, could run like a shot, but I, alas! should fall. . . . Then you in your agony, when you saw the bull gaining on me, would say, 'Oh! how I wish mother could use her legs as I can!' Now why do you wish me to wear what is uncomfortable, inconvenient, and many times dangerous?"

In 1819 Willard urged the Pennsylvania state legislature to support a program to train women to be teachers. The legislature said no, but that did not stop Willard. In 1821 she opened the first high school for girls, Troy Female Seminary, in Troy, New York. The school taught girls such traditionally "male" subjects as mathematics, history, geography, and physics.

Mary Lyon dreamed of starting a college for women. In 1837 she opened Mount Holyoke Female Seminary with 80 students, aged 17 and older. Instruction at Mount Holyoke was equal to that at men's colleges. Still, it was not until 1888—40 years after Lyon died—that the school was officially recognized as a college.

In 1833 Oberlin College became the first men's college to admit women. The Ohio college made two reforms at one time by opening its doors to both women and African Americans in 1833.

Women in Professions

Women who wanted to enter professions had a hard time breaking through the education barriers. Yet as doors began to open to them, women sought training in medicine, law, the ministry, journalism, and education.

One determined woman was Elizabeth Blackwell, the first woman to earn a medical diploma in the United States. When she applied to medical school, the administrators expected her to fail. Instead, she graduated first in her class in 1849. She went on to start a nursing school and a hospital for women and children in New York City.

Women also sought training in the ministry. Revivals had already given them leadership roles in churches. Elizabeth Blackwell's sister-in-law, Antoinette Brown Blackwell, was the first woman to study at Oberlin's theological school and became the first ordained woman minister.

Women Organize

The successes of women in education and the professions were milestones, but many doors were still closed to them. Reform-minded women realized that only with an organized movement for women's rights could they make real progress.

Elizabeth Cady Stanton

The question of women's rights surfaced in a dramatic way at the 1840 World Anti-Slavery Convention in London. Eight American women journeyed across the Atlantic, only to be told they could not take part because they were women. They had to sit behind a curtain, hidden from view. William Lloyd Garrison, one abolitionist who supported women's rights, sat with them in silent protest.

Shocked by their experience in London, Elizabeth Cady Stanton and Lucretia Mott decided to take matters into their own hands. Stanton and Mott realized that as long as the law did not protect women's rights, they could never achieve their goals as reformers. The two women agreed to organize the first-ever convention on women's rights.

The Seneca Falls Convention Mott, Stanton, and 3 other women called the convention for July 1848 in Seneca Falls, New York. Some 300 people, including 40 men, showed up.

To attract attention to their cause, Stanton drafted a "Declaration of Sentiments" cleverly based on the Declaration of Independence. She changed "all men are created equal" to "all men *and women* are created equal" and substituted the word "man" for "King George." Of 18 grievances in the Declaration, the last one summed up the general feeling about man's treatment of woman:

“He has endeavored, in every way that he could, to destroy her confidence in her own powers, to lessen her self-respect, and to make her willing to lead a dependent and abject [degraded] life.”

The attendees spent two days discussing the Declaration and its resolutions. They debated and voted for resolutions demanding equality in property rights, education, work, and church activities.

When Lucretia Mott spoke out against slavery, she was often the target of angry mobs.

Stanton asked that women be given the full rights of citizens—including the right to vote. The idea of woman suffrage was so radical at the time that even Lucretia Mott warned Stanton, "Why, Lizzie, [you] will make us ridiculous! We must go slowly." Still, with the help of Frederick Douglass, who attended the convention, the resolution on the vote passed by a slim margin.

Most historians view the convention as the beginning of the women's movement in the United States. At the time, however, newspapers and magazines scorned and ridiculed the convention, causing a number of women to withdraw their support. The issue of suffrage raised a storm of protest, and many of those who had signed the Declaration of Sentiments later asked to have their names removed.

Campaigning for Rights

Despite the ridicule, Stanton and other women leaders pressed forward. In 1851 the movement gained an important new member in Susan B. Anthony. Already active in the temperance and antislavery efforts, she took on women's rights, making woman suffrage her most important goal.

Anthony and Stanton formed a close team. Stanton was a strong writer and Anthony a gifted organizer and campaigner. Stanton would write fiery speeches that Anthony would travel to deliver in town after town. As Henry Stanton remarked to his wife, "You stir up Susan and she stirs up the world."

The Susan B. Anthony dollar, minted from 1979 to 1981, was the first United States coin to picture a woman (other than a symbolic type).

Another campaigner for women's rights was Lucy Stone. In 1847 Stone became the first Massachusetts woman to earn a college degree. When she married Henry Blackwell (Elizabeth Blackwell's brother), she became the first American woman to keep her maiden name. Women who did so later became known as "Lucy Stoners."

An excellent speaker, Stone had been a lecturer for the American Anti-Slavery Society before she began speaking out for women's rights. She stood up to heckling and even rioting crowds, often at great risk. She refused to pay taxes, since without the vote "women suffer taxation, and yet have no representation."

As you read earlier, Sojourner Truth began by speaking out about her religious beliefs and slavery, and ended up speaking out for women's rights as well. She delivered her famous "Ain't I a Woman?" speech at a women's convention in 1851. She also took up the cause of woman suffrage, and Elizabeth Cady Stanton and others often asked her to speak at suffrage gatherings.

Women's rights were slow in coming, and the female crusaders lost many battles. They did succeed in convincing some states to allow married women to own property and to grant women the right to keep their own wages. The demand for suffrage, however, made little progress during this period.

Point of View

What did women think about the vote?

The women and men at Seneca Falls were some of the most forward looking of their time when it came to the issue of women's rights. Still, the resolution on the vote roused heated debate even among these reformers.

Some women feared that the issue of the vote—because it was so outrageous to most people—would keep them from winning

In 1860 women shoe-makers marched for fair pay. Today, women continue to demand equal opportunities.

other rights. Others believed that women had enough say in government by use of petitions. As one woman said:

❝Women do not need the ballot to accomplish their ends. If they are really in earnest they can secure whatever they are willing to work for in the way of . . . legislation [through petition].❞

Another common view of a woman's role was that she should influence government by influencing her sons who would vote. A woman who opposed suffrage wrote:

❝Patriotism for a woman does not begin at the ballot box. It begins when she takes pains to instruct her young son

concerning the dignity and sacredness of the ballot. . . . Women who [train] the voters will eventually hold more power than if voting themselves.❞

Yet in the minds of Elizabeth Cady Stanton and Susan B. Anthony, women would only have equality when they had the vote. Referring to the Constitution, Anthony said:

❝It is downright mockery to talk to women of their enjoyment of the 'blessings of liberty' while they are denied the only means of securing them provided by this democratic-republican government—the ballot.❞

Neither Stanton nor Anthony would live to see the day when all women in the United States would have the ballot. Yet what they started would be fulfilled some 70 years later in the Nineteenth Amendment to the Constitution.

⭐ 3. Section Review

1. Why did women involved in the anti-slavery movement also become interested in women's rights?

2. What educational opportunities were open to women at the start of the 1800s? What actions did women take to overcome their lack of opportunity?

3. Imagine that you are a woman in the mid-1800s. Choose three of the following and write a journal entry telling how each inspires you: Emma Hart Willard, Mary Lyon, Elizabeth Blackwell, Antoinette Brown Blackwell, Elizabeth Cady Stanton, Lucy Stone, Sojourner Truth.

4. Critical Thinking The Seneca Falls Convention passed a number of resolutions on women's rights. Why do you think suffrage seemed so different from other rights?

4. American Voices

Reading Guide

Section Focus **The flowering of American literature and art**

1. Who were some of the great American writers of the period?
2. How did these writers express American subjects and themes?
3. What was the Hudson River School and what made its style American?

The early to mid-1800s saw a flowering of intellectual and creative life in the United States. While earlier American writers and painters had looked to Europe for examples and inspiration, a new generation of creative voices celebrated being uniquely American.

American Stories

American writers began to break free of European traditions in the stories they told. They focused instead on subjects and themes of American life.

Irving and Cooper Two of the earliest writers to focus on American subjects were Washington Irving and James Fenimore Cooper. Irving wrote the humorous short stories "Rip Van Winkle" and "The Legend of Sleepy Hollow." In "Rip Van Winkle" (1820) Irving explored the theme of progress in the tale of a man who falls asleep for 20 years and wakes to find his world changed.

Cooper wrote tales of the American back-country during colonial times, idealizing relations between whites and Indians. His hero was Natty Bumppo, a frontiersman featured in such classics as *The Last of the Mohicans* (1826) and *The Deerslayer* (1841).

Hawthorne and Melville Later story-tellers included novelists Nathaniel Hawthorne and Herman Melville. Hawthorne lived in Salem, Massachusetts, the center of famous witchcraft trials. He often set his works in 1600s Puritan New England. His two best-known works, *The Scarlet Letter* (1850) and *The House of the Seven Gables* (1851), focus on the themes of sin and human frailty.

Melville drew on his experiences at sea and living on South Pacific islands for the material in his novels. No one has outdone the realistic depiction of whaling in *Moby-Dick* (1851), considered Melville's greatest work. The spine-tingling adventure tells of an obsessed sea captain who destroys himself and his crew in pursuit of a white whale. Captain Ahab remains one of the most memorable characters in American fiction.

African American narrative This period also saw publication of works in the African American narrative tradition. Such works as Frederick Douglass's *Narrative of the Life of Frederick Douglass* (1845), the *Narrative of Sojourner Truth* (1850), and Harriet Jacobs's *Incidents in the Life of a Slave Girl* (1861) became immensely popular.

American Poetry

American poetry also flourished during these years. American poets, diverse in their styles, reached new heights of literary genius.

Henry Wadsworth Longfellow Perhaps the most popular poet of the time was Henry Wadsworth Longfellow. Many of his

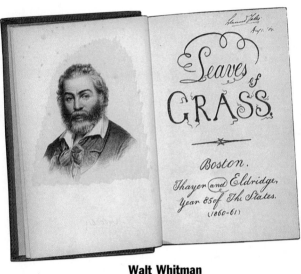

Walt Whitman

Herman Melville

Emily Dickinson

Nathaniel Hawthorne

poems celebrate events in American history. Even today people recognize the opening lines from his poem, "Paul Revere's Ride" (1863): "Listen, my children, and you shall hear / of the midnight ride of Paul Revere. . . ."

Longfellow wrote with a reformer's spirit. He opposed slavery and in 1842 published *Poems on Slavery* voicing his views. In *The Song of Hiawatha* (1855), he sought to show the humanity of Indians, often viewed as savages by white Americans of the time.

Walt Whitman Another reform-minded poet was Walt Whitman. Whitman loved democracy and once wrote that "the United States themselves are essentially the greatest poem." He wrote about common people, and often would ride on ferries and stagecoaches just to talk with ordinary Americans. He began to write his masterpiece, *Leaves of Grass*, in 1848, and continued to add to it for the rest of his life.

Edgar Allan Poe Poet, short-story writer, and critic Edgar Allan Poe did not share Whitman's optimism. He believed

that people could not improve society by their efforts. His works often explore the dark side of human nature. Though called the father of mystery and detective fiction, Poe is best known for his tales of terror and his poems, such as "The Raven."

Emily Dickinson Today considered one of the greatest American poets, Emily Dickinson was unknown in her own time. The shy and reclusive Dickinson once asked in a poem, "I'm nobody! Who are you? / Are you—Nobody too?" Only 7 of the 1,775 poems Dickinson composed were published during her lifetime, and some of those were published anonymously.

Transcendentalists

Many writers of the time were influenced by a philosophy called transcendentalism. Transcendentalists believed that people find truth within themselves, not just through experience and observation. Simply put, they believed they could "transcend," or rise

✪ Link to Art

Landscape with Rainbow (1859) While American literature was blossoming, so was American art. The Hudson River School, a group of artists named for the area that first inspired them, wanted Americans to develop a deeper appreciation of the vast American wilderness. The painting above is by Robert S. Duncanson, an African American painter of the Hudson River School. **Discuss** From the painting, how do you think the artist views the relationship between man and nature?

above, the limits of the human mind. They emphasized self-reliance and individuality.

Transcendentalists met frequently as a discussion group in Concord, Massachusetts, beginning in 1836. The leading American transcendentalists included Ralph Waldo Emerson, Henry David Thoreau, Bronson Alcott, and Margaret Fuller. Many were committed to reform movements of the time. Transcendentalists also formed the utopian Brook Farm, which you read about earlier.

Ralph Waldo Emerson The leader of the American transcendentalists was Ralph Waldo Emerson, an essayist, poet, and public speaker. He urged people to discover strength within themselves rather than borrow ideas from others.

In tune with the democratic ideals of the time, Emerson believed in the equality of all people. Though he rejected organized religion, he shared with revivalists the belief that all people should work to improve themselves.

Henry David Thoreau Among those Emerson touched was Henry David Thoreau. Thoreau, also a gifted writer and poet, shared Emerson's zeal for reform. He opposed slavery and participated in the Underground Railroad. He valued individualism, especially in deciding right and wrong. He wrote:

"If a man does not keep pace with his companion perhaps it is because he hears a different drummer. Let him step to the music he hears."

Thoreau took the message of self-reliance to an extreme. He built a cabin at Walden on Emerson's property and then described his attempt at simple living in his most famous work, *Walden* (1854).

4. Section Review

1. Name three American writers of the period and give some characteristics of their work.
2. What were some of the main beliefs of the transcendentalists? How did these beliefs affect their lives?
3. Critical Thinking In what ways did the works of American writers and painters of the early to mid-1800s express a uniquely American style?

Why We Remember

Religion and Reform

"I have been 40 years a slave and 40 years free," remarked Sojourner Truth late in life, "and would be here 40 years more to have equal rights for all."

Looking back, Truth could see what reformers had accomplished. Armed with strong religious faith and democratic ideals, they had attacked a number of social problems. Reformers had made progress in improving public education, prisons, and the treatment of the mentally ill. Abolitionists had shined a spotlight on the issue of slavery. Women had begun to speak up for their rights. Still, in Sojourner Truth's eyes, there was much more to be done.

What Sojourner Truth and other reformers could not see was that they had done more than improve society in their time. They had helped shape the American ideal that ordinary people should work to help others.

That belief has endured. Americans today are among the most generous people on earth when it comes to giving their time and money to good causes. Some causes, such as improving the environment or ending world hunger, might surprise Sojourner Truth and her fellow reformers. What would not surprise them is that so many Americans still care about improving their communities, helping the less fortunate, and fighting for equality for all.

Chapter Survey

Reviewing Vocabulary

Define the following terms.
1. social reform
2. temperance
3. utopias
4. emancipation
5. abolition

Reviewing Main Ideas

1. How did the message of the Second Great Awakening spread?
2. Describe the progress made by one of the following reform movements: public education, help for the disabled, prison reform, or temperance.
3. Name four people who fought against slavery, and tell what each person did for the antislavery cause.
4. What were two economic reasons behind opposition to abolitionism in the North?
5. (a) In what ways were women's rights limited in the early 1800s? (b) What progress had been made by the middle 1800s? (c) What goal would not be achieved for many years?
6. Name three people who worked to expand women's rights and opportunities, and tell what each person did for the cause.
7. Describe how each writer focused on American subjects or themes: (a) James Fenimore Cooper (b) Nathaniel Hawthorne (c) Henry Wadsworth Longfellow (d) Walt Whitman

Thinking Critically

1. Application How well does the quote by Henry David Thoreau on page 455 describe the reformers of the early and mid-1800s? Support your answer with examples from the chapter.
2. Synthesis Choose a reformer from the chapter and imagine that he or she could observe life in our country today. What might his or her reaction be? Why?

3. Why We Remember: Analysis What two basic beliefs drove reformers in the 1800s? How do they compare with the beliefs that drive modern-day Americans to work for improvements? Give examples.

Applying Skills

Historical interpretations Outspoken, controversial figures like William Lloyd Garrison are part of our past—and our present. Think of such a person in the news today. Write descriptions of the person that reflect two different ways the person might be viewed by historians of the future. Make sure your descriptions include:
• an interpretation
• support for the interpretation, in the form of facts and opinions

History Mystery

Medicine in the 1800s Answer the History Mystery on page 429. Elizabeth Blackwell had been turned down by every medical school in Philadelphia and New York City, as well as by Harvard, Yale, and Bowdoin. After she entered Geneva College she learned that she was only admitted there because administrators and students thought her application was a prank by a rival school. Why do you think they expected her to fail?

Writing in Your History Journal

1. Keys to History (a) The time line on pages 428–429 has six Keys to History. In your journal, describe why each one is important. (b) Choose a key event and imagine yourself as a television reporter assigned to cover it. In your journal, write what you will say about the event on tonight's broadcast.

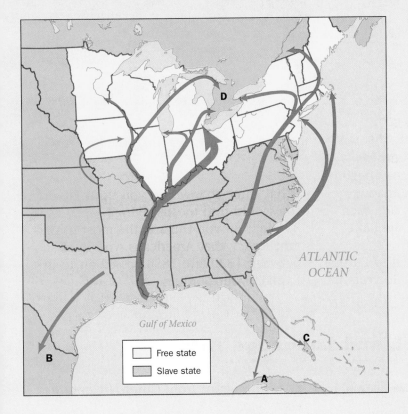

Gulf of Mexico

ATLANTIC
OCEAN

Free state
Slave state

Reviewing Geography

1. The letters on the map represent foreign places to which slaves escaped. Write the name of each.

2. Geographic Thinking The people who traveled the Underground Railroad used natural features like caves and forests to hide and travel safely. Use this map and the one on pages R6–R7 to write about natural features and the railroad routes. Consider, for example, why no route went from Louisiana to Cuba, or why the route from Georgia did not branch into Indiana or Ohio.

2. Sojourner Truth In your journal, reflect on how Sojourner Truth was representative of the people of her time. You might want to think about each section of this chapter and how Sojourner Truth fits in.

3. Citizenship As in many reform movements, supporters of abolition and women's rights held a range of views, from conservative to radical. Does a wide range of views benefit or hurt a reform movement? Why? Write your response in your journal.

Alternative Assessment

Working for reform Work with a group. Imagine that your group has been hired by the leaders of one of the reform movements of the 1800s. Your task is to develop a campaign to advance the reformers' cause.

① Choose the reform movement.

② Brainstorm a list of campaign tactics. For example, your list might include hanging posters in public places, giving speeches, and submitting petitions to Congress.

③ For each tactic, name the result you hope to achieve, such as changing the law or swaying public opinion.

④ When you have finished your list, choose two tactics and share them with the class in a concrete way. For example, you might make and display posters and write a petition to hand out for signatures.

Your work will be evaluated on the following criteria:
• you make a strong effort for the cause
• you accurately reflect the beliefs and goals of reformers of the period
• your campaign activities and materials are appealing and persuasive

Unit Survey

Making Connections

Review

1. Compare and contrast the journeys made along the Trail of Tears, the Oregon Trail, and the Underground Railroad. Consider such factors as who made each journey, why they did so, and the hardships they encountered.
2. Suppose an American traveled to Europe in 1820 and did not return for 30 years.

What three changes do you think he or she would find most striking?
3. What do you think is the most important legacy that Americans who lived between 1820 and 1850 passed on to us? Explain your opinion.

Linking History, Art, and Language Arts

Project

Writing and Illustrating Historical Fiction

Have you heard the term *historical fiction*? These stories are called *fiction* because they contain some imaginary features, such as characters, events, or dialogue. They are called *historical* because they portray life as it was in the past and may include real people and places as well as imaginary ones. Try your hand at creating a piece of historical fiction.

Project Steps

Work on your own to write and illustrate your story.

❶ Choose an interesting main character. The character can be real or imaginary, male or female, and of any age—as long as he or she lived in America between 1820 and 1850. Look through the unit to get ideas. Here are a few possibilities:
• a Seminole in hiding in Florida
• the young woman forced to spread the news of the defeat at the Alamo
• the employee of John Sutter who discovered gold
• a slave escaping to freedom

• an immigrant from China, Ireland, or elsewhere
• a teenager on a farm that is a station of the Underground Railroad

❷ Decide who your other characters will be, where and when the story will take place, and what the story's plot will be.

❸ Gather background information. You may want to look through some nonfiction books for realistic historical details to include.

❹ Write the story. Do a first draft to get your thoughts on paper quickly. Then read and revise as many times as necessary to add interest, improve sentence and paragraph flow, and correct any errors in grammar, punctuation, or spelling. Keep your story under 3,500 words.

❺ Draw a cover for your story.

❻ Share your story with classmates by reading it aloud or passing it around.

Thinking It Over How do you think historical fiction compares with nonfiction as a way to learn about history? Explain your opinion.

How Do We Know?

Charles Henry Veil

Scholar's Tool Kit
Memoirs

The Battle of Gettysburg, fought in July 1863, was one of the bloodiest battles of the American Civil War. Few battles in history caused more casualties. As many as 51,000 Confederate and Union soldiers failed to answer roll call after the three days of fighting.

A Crucial Moment

At a crucial moment early in the battle, Confederate forces were rushing through a cornfield to capture a key hill. Scrambling up the other side was a Union regiment. From atop his horse at the crest of the hill, Major General John Fulton Reynolds of the Union army watched as the two forces swept toward each other. With him were staff officers and his 21-year-old orderly, Private Charles Henry Veil.

As the Union infantry crested the hill, Confederate musket fire knocked down the first line of soldiers. Those behind them stopped and fell back in confusion. Anxious to prevent a terrible defeat, General Reynolds turned in his saddle and tried to rally the Union men.

"Forward!" he shouted. "Forward men! Drive these fellows out of there! Forward! For God's sake, forward!"

At that moment Reynolds slumped over and fell from his horse. A Confederate sharpshooter more than 200 yards (180 m) away had just made the shot of a lifetime. General Reynolds was the highest-ranking officer of the Union army killed during the Civil War.

Sketch of the death of Union General John Reynolds near Gettysburg

? Critical Thinking

1. Why do you think historians care about knowing the accurate story of the Battle of Gettysburg?

That story is certain. What happened afterwards is not so certain. What we know is based largely on the testimony of Private Veil.

Veil Tells His Story

For Veil, the death of General Reynolds was such an important episode that he told and retold the story many times. He also described the event at length in his memoirs, which he wrote some 30 years later. **Memoirs** are a person's written remembrances of the events of his or her life.

Memoirs are key historical documents, but sometimes they pose dilemmas for historians. This was true in Veil's case. In a letter to a friend dated April 7, 1864—only months after the event—Veil wrote:

"When the General fell, the only persons who were with him was Captain Mitchell & Baird and myself. When he fell we sprang from our horses. . . . We were under the impression that he was only stunned, this was all done at a glance. I caught the Gen[era]l under the arms while each of the Capt[ain]s took hold of his legs, and we commenced to carry him out of the woods. . . ."

? Critical Thinking

2. When reading someone's memoirs, what information would you like to have about the person? Why?

Yet in his memoirs, written some 30 years after the event, Veil claimed that he was the only witness at the critical moment when General Reynolds was killed. Here is how Veil told the story then:

"General Reynolds fell upon his face, his arms outstretched toward the enemy. I at once sprang from my horse and ran to his side, gave one glance at his body and seeing no wound or blood, turned his body upon its back. . . . My next impression was to save him from falling into the hands of the enemy. Not having any assistance, not

460 •

one of our men being near, I picked him up by taking hold under his arms and commenced pulling him backward toward our line. As I did so, the Confederates yelled 'Drop him! Drop him!' But I kept on backing off as fast as I could and finally got over the brow of the rise, where I found some men and where we were out of range of the enemy's fire."

How Do Historians Know?

As time passed, Veil obviously enlarged his role in the event. He made himself more of a hero than he really was, failing to mention those who helped him take the body off the battlefield.

Certainly, Veil had no need to add to the facts. His role in saving the general's body from the enemy was widely known, and he was well rewarded—even by President Lincoln himself. The change in Veil's story could have been deliberate, or he could simply have forgotten. As people age, their memories sometimes fade or they have "selective memory"—remembering only the facts they want to remember.

Accounts of an event are more likely to be accurate when written closer in time to the event. In Veil's case, he gave a more believable account in his April 1864 letter. Because memories can be unreliable, scholars seek evidence from several sources in addition to memoirs. They go over all the descriptions of the event to figure out the facts. In this way, a scholar is like a detective. New discoveries of memoirs and other sources continue to affect the story we call history.

?
Critical Thinking

3. Veil's memoirs are now published in book form. If you read the memoirs, how might you go about checking the accuracy of his accounts?

Scholar at Work

Anyone can write memoirs. Think of an important event that happened in your life. Write your memory of the event, telling the story with as many details as possible.

When your memoir is finished, share it with someone else—a parent, brother, sister, or friend—who was also a part of the event. Ask the person to point out any difference in his or her recollections. Working together, try to construct the most accurate story you can.

Unit 6

Chapters

Hands-On HISTORY

Activity

In the 1860s there was no radio, television, or Internet. People got their news mainly from newspapers. Imagine that it is 1862 and you are a journalist for a daily paper. You have just arrived at the Battle of Shiloh, in Tennessee, where both sides in the Civil War are suffering heavy losses. Send a telegram to your editor describing the sights and sounds of the battlefield.

Battle of Shiloh—April 6th, 1862 (detail) published by the McCormick Harvesting Machine Co., Chicago, 1885

Civil War and Reconstruction

Chapter 17

The Gathering Storm

Sections

Beginning the Story with Abraham Lincoln

1. **Efforts to Save the Union**
2. **The Failure of Compromise**
3. **On the Brink of War**

Keys to History

1850
Compromise of 1850
Abolitionist poster

1852
Harriet Beecher Stowe publishes *Uncle Tom's Cabin*

1854
Republican Party is formed

1850

1854

Looking Back

Missouri Compromise
1820

HISTORY

Mystery

In 1855 fewer than 3,000 voters lived in this territory. However, more than 6,000 people voted there in the March election that year. What was the territory, and how could so many people turn out on election day?

1857
Dred Scott decision

1859
John Brown leads raid on Harpers Ferry

1861
Confederate forces seize Fort Sumter—Civil War begins
Confederate flag

1854–1856
"Bleeding Kansas"

1857

1861

World Link

Russian serfs are freed by Czar Alexander II
1861

Looking Ahead

Civil War ends
1865

465

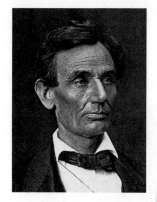

Beginning the Story with

Abraham Lincoln

More than a century ago, the great Russian writer Leo Tolstoy visited his country's wild Caucasus Mountains. There, in the south of Russia, he met the chief of a mountain tribe. After listening to Tolstoy for a time, the chief said to him:

❝But you have not told us a syllable about the greatest general and greatest ruler of the world. We want to know something about him. He was a hero. He spoke with a voice of thunder, he laughed at the sunrise and his deeds were strong as the rock. . . . He was so great that he even forgave the crimes of his greatest enemies. . . . His name was Lincoln and the country in which he lived is called America. . . . Tell us of that man.❞

The Frontier Scholar

Perhaps no one at birth seemed so unlikely a candidate for greatness as Abraham Lincoln. He was born in Kentucky in 1809. His parents, Nancy and Thomas Lincoln, were frontier farmers who lived in a crudely built log cabin and barely knew how to read or write. Searching for a better life, Thomas moved his young family to Indiana, where Abe's mother died when Abe was just 9. The family later moved to Illinois. Bad luck and poverty, however, seemed to follow Thomas Lincoln wherever he went.

Living on the frontier, young Abe had very little education. All in all, he figured that his schooling "did not amount to a year." It was enough, however, to excite a craving for knowledge. Abe read everything he could lay his hands on. "My best friend," he said, "is the man who'll get me a book I ain't read." A cousin recalled, "Abe made books tell him more than they told other people."

"The Rail Splitter"

By the age of 17, Abe Lincoln had grown into a lanky giant well over 6 feet tall. He was amazingly strong and could handle an ax as well as any man. His skill at splitting logs into fence rails would earn him the nickname "The Rail Splitter." Still, Abe disliked physical labor:

“My father taught me work, but not to love it. I never did like to work, and I don't deny it. I'd rather read, tell stories, crack jokes, talk, laugh—anything but work.”

Lincoln tried a number of jobs, from running a store to surveying. As a shopkeeper, he earned a reputation for honesty that stuck with him for life. Stories were told of "Honest Abe" walking 6 miles to return a few cents to a woman who was over-charged for her goods. He finally found his career in the law, where he was paid for doing what he most loved—talking to people. Concerned more with gaining justice for his clients than with making money, Abe charged fees that fellow lawyers thought were laughably low.

As a young man, Abe Lincoln lived an active life. He split logs for fence rails, worked on a river flatboat on two trips to New Orleans, and fought in the Black Hawk War.

Lincoln's concern for justice was matched by his sense of humor, as revealed in the following story. One day, Lincoln said, he and a judge were talking about trading horses. They finally agreed to make a trade at nine o'clock the next morning. Neither man was to see the other's horse before that hour. The following morning the judge arrived leading a pathetic-looking creature not much bigger than a dog. A few minutes later, Lincoln appeared carrying a wooden sawhorse. Looking at the judge's puny horse, Lincoln said, "Well, Judge, this is the first time I ever got the worst of a horse trade."

During the stormy 1850s, Lincoln's sense of justice drew him into politics. At moments of frustration and even failure, his sense of humor saved him from despair. "I laugh," he once said, "because if I didn't I would weep." As Honest Abe became a national leader, he would need all the joy and comfort that laughter could bring.

Hands-On → *HISTORY*

Activity

Abe Lincoln loved to tell stories about his life in a down-to-earth way, spiced with humor. Think about some gift you received or something that happened to you that was funny or embarrassing. It could involve your family, perhaps, or a sports event. Then write or tell the story. Remember that you may be President someday and may use this story to help people get to know you.

1. Efforts to Save the Union

Reading Guide

New Term popular sovereignty

Section Focus Conflict over slavery revives as the United States expands westward

1. How did southerners and northerners differ over the issue of slavery in the territories?
2. What events led to the Compromise of 1850?
3. How did the Compromise of 1850 deal with the issue of slavery?

Abraham Lincoln entered politics during a time of increasing tension between the North and the South. The tension centered around the question of slavery. As the antislavery cause in the North grew in strength, proslavery southerners responded with equal force.

Attempts by the North and South to reach a middle ground did not solve the basic question: Do some people have the right to enslave others? A compromise would ease tensions only until a new crisis arose. In the 1850s the debate over slavery also brought into the open disagreements over states' rights—the idea that states can overrule federal laws—and secession.

Moderates and Radicals

In both North and South, people were divided over slavery. Northern moderates accepted slavery where it existed, but did not want it introduced into new states and territories. Northern radicals demanded an end to slavery everywhere in the United States.

Before the 1830s southern moderates viewed slavery as a necessary evil that would gradually give way to freedom for enslaved people. Southern radicals, however, insisted on the right to extend slavery into all new territories.

Slavery in the West

The slavery controversy came to center stage during the war with Mexico. In 1846 Congressman David Wilmot, a radical northerner, proposed that slavery be prohibited in all territory acquired from Mexico. Southern radicals fought back by demanding that slavery be permitted in all new territories.

To settle the conflict, some moderates from both regions suggested extending the Missouri Compromise line to the Pacific. Other moderates proposed giving voters in each territory **popular sovereignty**—the right to decide for themselves whether to allow slavery. To many people, popular sovereignty seemed the best way to end the debate over slavery in the territories.

The debate did not end, however. Although Wilmot's proposal was defeated in Congress, it exposed hostile feelings between the regions that continued to boil.

Balance of power An ongoing cause of tension was the balance of power in the Senate. As long as there were the same number of free states and slave states, neither North nor South could win a vote on laws related to slavery.

In 1848 slave and free states were, in fact, equal in number. However, Minnesota and

Oregon, where residents opposed slavery, had applied for statehood. To avoid upsetting the balance of power, Congress put off admitting them to the Union.

The Election of 1848

During the 1848 presidential campaign both Democrats and Whigs avoided the topic of slavery. The Democrats chose a northern moderate, Senator Lewis Cass, as their candidate. The Whigs turned to General Zachary Taylor, a hero of the War with Mexico.

Angry that the two major parties were ignoring the slavery issue, antislavery forces formed the Free Soil Party. With former President Martin Van Buren as their candi-

date, the Free Soilers won enough northern votes away from the Democrats to throw the election to Taylor and the Whigs. The Free Soilers' success showed that the conflict over slavery in the territories was not over.

California and Popular Sovereignty

In 1849 the issue of slavery demanded fresh attention when California voters adopted a constitution banning slavery in their territory. President Taylor, who favored popular sovereignty, supported their decision and called for California statehood. People in present-day New Mexico and Utah also wanted their areas to become free states.

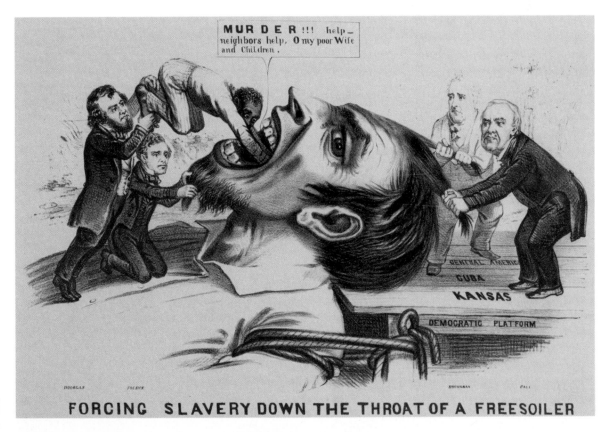

MURDER !!! help—neighbors help, O my poor Wife and Children.

FORCING SLAVERY DOWN THE THROAT OF A FREESOILER

As this cartoon shows, Free Soilers feared that popular sovereignty would force the slave system down their throats.

Taylor's action launched one of the greatest debates in the Senate's history. This time, the argument went beyond the issue of slavery. It called into question the very future of the United States.

The Compromise of 1850

Two generations met on the Senate floor to debate the issue of slavery in the territories. Henry Clay, Daniel Webster, and John C. Calhoun represented the older generation. Among those who would lead the Senate in the future were Jefferson Davis, Stephen A. Douglas, and William H. Seward.

Clay Henry Clay, with a reputation for settling disagreements, led the Senate session. The "Great Compromiser" had pre-vented a showdown between the North and South in 1820 when he pushed through the Missouri Compromise. Many senators hoped that he could do it again.

Now 73 years old and in ill health, Clay fashioned a plan for dealing with the two main issues: slavery in the West and the return of escaped slaves. He called for admitting California as a free state, but not restricting slavery in the other territories gained from Mexico. He also proposed a more aggressive fugitive slave law.

Calhoun John C. Calhoun, a southerner, rejected Clay's plan. It would not guarantee the right to slavery in the territories, he claimed. He also demanded an even tougher fugitive slave law. Treat the South fairly, he warned the Senate, or the South would secede.

In his final role as the Great Compromiser, Henry Clay (center) tried to persuade the Senate to vote for the Compromise of 1850.

Henry Clay

John C. Calhoun

COMPROMISE OF 1850

Provisions favoring proslavery forces

• New Mexico and Utah to become territories. The slavery question to be decided by popular sovereignty.
• The new Fugitive Slave Law to require the return of escaped slaves, even slaves who had reached the North.
• Slavery still legal in Washington, D.C.

Provisions favoring antislavery forces

• California to be admitted to the Union as a free state.
• The slave trade to be abolished in Washington, D.C.

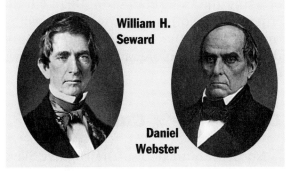

William H. Seward

Daniel Webster

Weakened by throat cancer, Calhoun had another Senator read his speech:

"How can the Union be saved? She [the South] has no compromise to offer. If you are unwilling [to meet our demands] we should part in peace."

Webster Daniel Webster, a northern moderate, pleaded for the nation's unity:

"I wish to speak today, not as a Massachusetts man, nor as a northern man, but as an American. I speak today for the preservation of the Union."

Webster's plea fell on deaf ears as northern radicals took on southern radicals. William H. Seward saw compromise over slavery as "radically wrong." Representative Horace Mann believed that the world would view the United States "with disgust" for allowing slavery.

Agreement at last Events took a sudden twist when President Taylor—a staunch opponent of compromise—fell ill from cholera and died on July 9, 1850. The new President, Millard Fillmore, came out firmly for Clay's compromise. By this time Congress knew that voters in both the North and the South favored compromise. As a result, it passed the Compromise of 1850 (see chart to the left and map on page 474).

With the passage of the Compromise of 1850, President Fillmore claimed that the nation had found "the final settlement" that would end the arguments over slavery. In fact the nation did settle into a prosperous peace for the next few years. However, Fillmore had spoken too quickly. The crisis over slavery was far from ended.

 1. Section Review

1. Define **popular sovereignty**.
2. Explain the positions of northern radicals and moderates on the issue of slavery.
3. What problem did President Taylor confront and how did he handle it?
4. **Critical Thinking** As a southern radical, how would you have voted on each measure in the 1850 Compromise and why?

2. The Failure of Compromise

Reading Guide

New Terms transcontinental railroad, platform

Section Focus Events in the 1850s continue to divide the North and South

1. How did the Fugitive Slave Law and *Uncle Tom's Cabin* affect the slavery debate?
2. How did the Kansas-Nebraska Act increase tensions between the North and the South?
3. Why did the new Republican Party form and what was its impact at the time?

The Compromise of 1850 brought only temporary relief to the nation. Americans were still deeply divided over slavery and states' rights, and it was not long before conflicts broke out again.

Three events shattered the calm. They were the enforcement of the new Fugitive Slave Law, the publication of the antislavery novel *Uncle Tom's Cabin,* and a violent struggle over slavery in Kansas. This time, efforts at compromise would fail.

The Fugitive Slave Law

Most northerners despised the Fugitive Slave Law of 1850. The law denied escaped slaves the right to have a jury trial and to testify in court on their own behalf. Anyone who helped a slave escape could be fined $1,000 and jailed for six months. Slave catchers received $10 for every African American they kidnapped in the North and brought to a slave owner in the South.

Before the new law, slavery had existed far from where most northerners lived. Now they had a firsthand look, as slave hunters came north, seeking escaped slaves. Almost 200 African Americans, even some free blacks who were not escaped slaves, were captured and sent to the South.

Northerners reacted against the kidnappings to the point of violence. A Pennsylvania mob killed a kidnapper. Frederick Douglass, himself an escaped slave, declared that "the only way to make the Fugitive Slave Law a dead letter [law] is to make half a dozen dead kidnappers."

The Fugitive Slave Law drove a deeper wedge between the North and the South. Southerners were outraged at northern resistance to it. They accused the North of breaking the Compromise of 1850. Northerners, on the other hand, were shocked by the cruelty of the law. It caused many of them to become more radical in their views of slavery.

Uncle Tom's Cabin

Northern outrage over the Fugitive Slave Law was mild, though, compared to the storm that arose when Harriet Beecher Stowe published *Uncle Tom's Cabin* in 1852. In this dramatic tale a religious and loyal old slave named Uncle Tom is beaten to death by orders of Simon Legree, one of the most hated villains in American literature.

Have you ever read a book that changed your way of thinking? Stowe's goal was to write such a book. By depicting the brutality of slave life on a plantation, she wanted to awaken Americans to the evil in their midst.

Stowe succeeded beyond her wildest dreams. Within a year the book was a best-seller, outsold only by the Bible. As a play it shocked audiences around the world. People who read or saw *Uncle Tom's Cabin* could no longer close their eyes to slavery.

Many southerners, however, claimed that the story was full of lies. They feared that it would strengthen the influence of anti-slavery radicals in the North.

The Election of 1852

In the election of 1852, the Democrats nominated Franklin Pierce, who had promised to enforce the Compromise of 1850—including the Fugitive Slave Law. The Whig candidate, General Winfield Scott, took no stand on the compromise.

Pierce won almost every state. His landslide victory proved that despite the angry feelings caused by the Fugitive Slave Law and *Uncle Tom's Cabin,* most Americans still clung to the hope that the issue of slavery had been settled.

The Kansas-Nebraska Act

As it turned out, the 1852 election marked only a brief pause in the sectional conflict over slavery. The struggle started again when Senator Stephen Douglas of Illinois introduced a bill to be known as the Kansas-Nebraska Act.

A new railroad Douglas proposed that the nation build a **transcontinental railroad**—a rail line across the continent, linking east and west. He wanted it to begin at Chicago, in his home state of Illinois, and run to California. This transcontinental railroad would only succeed, Douglas thought, if the land west of the Mississippi was organized into territories.

Meanwhile, railroad boosters in the South wanted a southern route to California and the Pacific. They advised that their route would have several advantages. It would be much easier to lay tracks across the flat terrain of this route. In addition, the land needed for such a rail line—the Gadsden Purchase—had already been obtained from Mexico in 1853 (see map on page 396).

The cruelty and terror of slave life is captured by this poster for *Uncle Tom's Cabin.* Harriet Beecher Stowe (above) mistakenly feared that her future bestseller would be a failure.

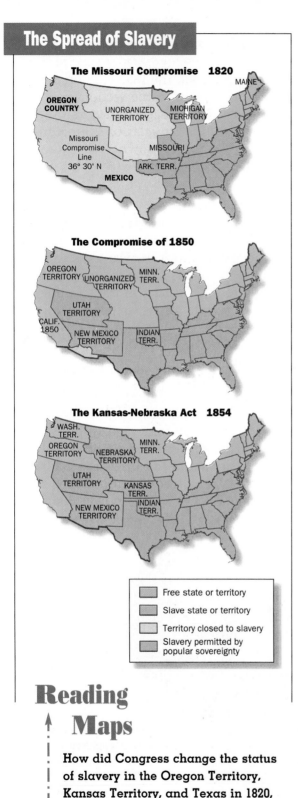

The Spread of Slavery

The Missouri Compromise 1820

OREGON COUNTRY
UNORGANIZED TERRITORY
MICHIGAN TERRITORY
MAINE
Missouri Compromise Line 36° 30' N
MISSOURI
ARK. TERR.
MEXICO

The Compromise of 1850

OREGON TERRITORY
UNORGANIZED TERRITORY
MINN. TERR.
UTAH TERRITORY
CALIF. 1850
NEW MEXICO TERRITORY
INDIAN TERR.

The Kansas-Nebraska Act 1854

WASH. TERR.
OREGON TERRITORY
NEBRASKA TERRITORY
MINN. TERR.
UTAH TERRITORY
KANSAS TERR.
NEW MEXICO TERRITORY
INDIAN TERR.

- Free state or territory
- Slave state or territory
- Territory closed to slavery
- Slavery permitted by popular sovereignty

Reading
↑ Maps

How did Congress change the status of slavery in the Oregon Territory, Kansas Territory, and Texas in 1820, 1850, and 1854?

Kansas and Nebraska To win southern support for his northern route, Douglas called for popular sovereignty in lands to be organized as the Kansas and Nebraska territories (see map on this page).

Southerners supported the popular sovereignty idea because it allowed for the possibility of additional slave states. Northerners, however, were angry that the Kansas-Nebraska Act would overturn the Missouri Compromise of 1820, which barred slavery from that area.

What had begun as a proposal for a transcontinental railroad quickly turned into another crisis over slavery in the territories. Northern objections to Douglas's bill were loud and hostile. Still, with the support of southern congressmen and President Franklin Pierce, a Democrat, the Kansas-Nebraska bill became law in May 1854.

"Bleeding Kansas"

Douglas thought that the tempers that had flared during the Kansas-Nebraska debate would soon cool. Instead, the fight moved beyond the Senate floor to Kansas itself. The question of slavery there was to be decided by whichever side had the most voters. Senator William H. Seward of New York laid down the challenge:

"Gentlemen of the Slave States, we will engage in competition for the virgin soil of Kansas, and God give victory to the side which is . . . right.**"**

Antislavery settlers from the North raced to Kansas. They were met by proslavery settlers from the South, particularly from Missouri. Each group hoped to gain control of the territory in the upcoming election.

Two Kansas governments On election day in March 1855, nearly 5,000 Missouri residents crossed into Kansas. Their illegal votes gave the victory to proslavery candidates. The new legislature quickly passed laws protecting slavery in Kansas.

Outraged antislavery settlers in Kansas refused to accept the proslavery legislature. They elected their own legislature and set up their own government.

John Brown in Kansas With sides now sharply drawn, Kansas became a dress rehearsal for the Civil War. In May 1856 a proslavery army of "Border Ruffians" from Missouri marched into the antislavery town of Lawrence and set it on fire.

The "sack of Lawrence" inspired an abolitionist named John Brown to seek revenge. Lean, strong, and "straight . . . as a mountain pine," Brown led four of his sons and several others to a proslavery settlement. There they murdered five men by splitting open their heads with swords. In retaliation, proslavery forces killed one of Brown's sons. Brown did not back down. He vowed:

"I have only a short time to live [and] only one death to die, and I will die fighting for this cause.**"**

These brutal deaths touched off a year-long war in Kansas. Two hundred lives were lost and many homes were burned before federal troops finally restored order to "Bleeding Kansas" in late 1856.

Violence in the Senate The violence in Kansas spilled over into the halls of Congress. In a speech in May of 1856, Charles Sumner, an abolitionist senator from Massachusetts, attacked slaveholders for the "crime [committed] against Kansas."

Three days later, Representative Preston Brooks of South Carolina broke his cane over Sumner's head while Sumner was seated at his desk. Brooks was furious that Sumner had insulted Brooks's uncle in the speech. Sumner, severely injured, did not return to the Senate for more than two years.

Hands-On HISTORY

Creating an advertisement for Kansas Has your family ever used a travel agent? Present-day travel agencies help people arrange vacation trips. In the 1850s, agencies in the North served another purpose: to help antislavery settlers move to the Kansas Territory so that it would become a free state.

Activity Imagine you are an agent working for a northern antislavery organization in 1854. Create an advertisement encouraging people to move to Kansas.

❶ Design and write a full-page advertisement that appeals to your readers' feelings about slavery, and to their dislike for the opposing side. You will also want to highlight the attraction of Kansas itself: good soil and plenty of open land.

❷ What illustrations might you use?

❸ Share your finished ad with your classmates. Do they find it persuasive? Why or why not?

Poster promoting Kansas

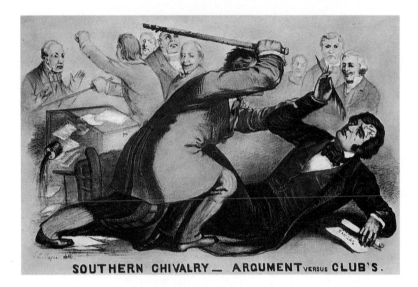

SOUTHERN CHIVALRY — ARGUMENT VERSUS CLUB'S.

Senator Sumner was praised by fellow New Englanders for his speech attacking slaveholders. Preston Brooks, a southern member of Congress, detested the speech, however. He is shown here beating Sumner on the Senate floor.

A New Republican Party

Meanwhile, northerners who opposed the spread of slavery had grown impatient with the Democratic and Whig parties. They wanted a party that would commit itself to antislavery issues. In 1854 such a party was formed. It was named the Republican Party, after the party founded by Jefferson.

The Republican Party **platform**—a statement of a political party's beliefs—took stands against the Kansas-Nebraska Act and the Fugitive Slave Law. Running on that platform, Republican candidates swept the 1854 elections in the North, especially in the Midwest. Soon, northern Whigs and Democrats were joining the new party, adding to its strength. As a result, the Democrats' main base of power shifted to the South.

The Election of 1856 The Republicans first attempted to gain the presidency in 1856. They selected John C. Frémont, western explorer and opponent of slavery, as their candidate. He campaigned with the slogan, "Free Soil, Free Speech, and Frémont." Abraham Lincoln, who had joined the Republicans, narrowly missed being nominated for Vice-President.

The Democrats were expected to nominate Stephen A. Douglas. However, they knew that the Kansas-Nebraska Act had made him unpopular with northern voters. Instead, the Democrats chose James Buchanan. He had been serving overseas as minister to England, and thus he had not taken a stand in the Kansas-Nebraska debate.

Although Frémont took 11 of the 16 free states, Buchanan won the election by carrying the southern states and 5 of the free states. As people became more alarmed that the nation might break apart, it remained to be seen if President Buchanan could hold the country together.

2. Section Review

1. Define **transcontinental railroad** and **platform.**
2. Why did southerners support the Kansas-Nebraska Act?
3. Why was the Republican Party founded?
4. **Critical Thinking** As a northerner, which would have affected your feelings about slavery more: the Fugitive Slave Law or *Uncle Tom's Cabin*? Explain why.

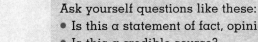

Skill Lab

Using Information
Asking Historical Questions

Its promoters called it "The Greatest Book of the Age." It ranked second only to the Bible as a bestseller. *Uncle Tom's Cabin* awakened northerners to the cruelties of slavery—and enraged proslavery southerners. In essays, speeches, and even poems, southerners defended slavery as being good for both master and slave.

Question to Investigate
•••••••••••••••••••••••••••••••

How were slaves treated?

Procedure
•••••••••••

Imagine that you are a historian studying how slaves were treated. As you read the following sources, direct your research by asking historical questions.

1 Write a sentence stating your goal.

2 Identify the information.
a. Read sources **A** through **C** carefully.
b. Make a column for each source. List what each source says about the treatment of slaves.

3 Identify questions to ask.
a. Read the Skill Tips for examples.
b. List three questions about each source.

4 Decide how to get the answers.
a. Write the answers you know.
b. Name three ways you might get more information.

Is this source believable?

Skill Tips

Ask yourself questions like these:
- Is this a statement of fact, opinion, or fiction?
- Is this a credible source?
- How might the author's background affect what he or she wrote?
- Are the claims supported by enough evidence?
- Are there signs of bias, overgeneralizations, or stereotypes?

Sources to Use
•••••••••••••••••••

A Reread Frederick Douglass's statements on pages 404–405.

B "The negro slaves of the South are the happiest and, in some sense, the freest people in the world. . . . The women do little hard work, and are protected from the despotism [cruelty] of their husbands by their masters. The negro men and stout boys work, on the average, in good weather, not more than nine hours a day."

From an 1857 essay by the Virginia lawyer George Fitzhugh

C "'And now,' said Legree, 'come here, you Tom. . . . take this yer gal and flog her; ye've seen enough on't to know how.'

'I beg Mas'r's pardon,' said Tom, '. . . It's what I an't used to—never did— and can't do, no way possible.'

'Ye'll larn a pretty smart chance of things ye never did know before I've done with ye!' said Legree, taking up a cowhide and striking Tom a heavy blow across the cheek, and following up the infliction by a shower of blows. 'There!' he said, 'now will ye tell me ye can't do it?'

'Yes Mas'r,' said Tom, putting up his hand to wipe the blood that trickled down his face. 'I'm willin' to work night and day, and work while there's breath in me; but this yer thing I can't feel it right to do; and Mas'r, I *never* shall do it—*never!*'"

From Harriet Beecher Stowe's 1852 novel, *Uncle Tom's Cabin*

3. On the Brink of War

Reading Guide

Section Focus **The causes of the final break between North and South**

1. How did Dred Scott and the Lincoln-Douglas debates keep the slavery issue alive?
2. How did John Brown's raid and the 1860 election doom hopes for compromise?
3. What was the South's response to Abraham Lincoln's election?

The 1856 election had avoided an all-out fight over the slavery question. However, whether it bubbled below the surface or exploded into open debate, slavery was an issue that would not go away.

James Buchanan had been President only two days when yet another crisis rocked the nation. On March 7, 1857, the Supreme Court announced its decision in the case of *Dred Scott* v. *Sandford.*

Dred Scott Decision

Dred Scott had been the slave of a Missouri surgeon, who had taken him to Illinois and the Wisconsin Territory. They lived there for several years before returning to Missouri. In 1846 Scott claimed in court that the years he had lived on free northern soil had made him a free man. The jury ruled in his favor, but the Missouri Supreme Court overruled the decision.

Soon after the Court ruled that Dred Scott must remain a slave, Scott finally gained his freedom from a new owner. He died just a year later.

Scott took his case to the United States Supreme Court. In *Dred Scott* v. *Sandford,* the Court ruled against Scott by a vote of 7 to 2. In the first place, the justices said, Scott did not have a right to a trial. African Americans—enslaved or free—were not citizens, and thus could not bring suits in federal court.

The Court also ruled that the Missouri Compromise was unconstitutional, and slavery could not be banned in any territory. Slaves were property, they reasoned, and the Fifth Amendment guaranteed the right to property. Slaveowners had the right to take slaves into any territory. Living in a free territory had not made Scott a free man.

Southern radicals praised the decision. Now all territories were open to slavery. Northerners were shocked. They accused the South of plotting with the Supreme Court and the new President to expand slavery. Buchanan had, in fact, encouraged the justices to rule in the South's favor. Instead of putting to rest the question of slavery in the territories, the Dred Scott decision only added fuel to the fire.

Lincoln-Douglas Campaign

Unhappy with the President's support of proslavery interests, Republicans wanted to "overthrow" the Democrats. In 1858 Abraham Lincoln agreed to help. He would run against Democrat Stephen A. Douglas, who was seeking re-election to the Senate from Illinois.

Stephen A. Douglas Douglas felt up to the challenge. He was a short, sturdy man, whom admirers called the "Little Giant." Douglas had a strong, deep voice and a brilliant mind. Although his support for the Kansas-Nebraska Act had damaged his reputation in the North, he still hoped to become President in 1860.

Abraham Lincoln Illinois Republicans believed that Lincoln, a small-town lawyer in Springfield, had the best chance of defeating Stephen Douglas. Lincoln opposed the expansion of slavery into new territories, but he was not known as a northern radical. He had been a powerful speaker at the 1856 Republican convention. Douglas himself remarked:

"I shall have my hands full. He [Lincoln] is the strong man of his party . . . the best speaker . . . in the West."

Still, the tall, gangly Lincoln seemed awkward beside the polished Douglas. Lincoln had a quick wit, but his voice sometimes squeaked and he used pronunciations like "git" for "get" and "thar" for "there."

Lincoln-Douglas Debates

Lincoln's strategy was to follow Douglas on the campaign trail. Douglas would arrive in a town in his private railroad car. He brought along a brass cannon to announce his arrival and to draw a large crowd. Riding as an ordinary passenger on the same train, Lincoln would address the crowd after Douglas had finished his speech.

Douglas supporters made fun of Lincoln, saying he could not attract crowds of his own. Lincoln responded by challenging Douglas to a series of debates.

Douglas accepted the challenge. He thought such debates would draw national attention

Lincoln and Douglas tried to win votes in their 1858 debates. Presidential candidates Bill Clinton, George Bush, and Ross Perot continued the tradition in their 1992 debates.

and boost his chances to become President. The two men met seven times in seven different Illinois towns.

In the debates, Lincoln appealed to antislavery voters by attacking Douglas's stand on slavery. Douglas did not care, Lincoln claimed, "whether slavery was voted down or voted up."

The Freeport Doctrine In the town of Freeport, Lincoln challenged Douglas to declare his position on slavery in the territories now that the Dred Scott decision had made it legal. Douglas was in a tight spot. His answer came to be called the Freeport Doctrine.

In the Freeport Doctrine, Douglas admitted that it was now legal for an owner to bring a slave into any territory. However, he said, a legislature could refuse to pass laws protecting slavery in their territory. Without such laws, slavery could not be enforced.

The result of the debates The seven debates were the highlight of a hard-fought campaign. Lincoln and Douglas spoke to crowds almost daily for four months. In the days before microphones, public speakers had to shout to be heard. By election day Douglas's throat was so sore he could barely talk.

Although Douglas narrowly defeated Lincoln, the election had broader results. The Freeport Doctrine turned many southern Democrats against Douglas, and would hurt his chances of becoming President in 1860. Lincoln, on the other hand, emerged as a national figure. His skill at challenging Douglas put the presidency within his reach.

Raid at Harpers Ferry

An event that terrified the South occurred on October 16, 1859. John Brown, the abolitionist from Kansas, appeared at Harpers Ferry, Virginia. With 21 followers he seized a federal arsenal there. He planned to give the guns to escaped slaves who in turn were to ignite a slave revolt across the South.

The plan had no hope of success. Brown never freed any slaves. Colonel Robert E. Lee led a force of marines who captured Brown and killed ten of his men, including two of his sons. Virginia authorities quickly convicted Brown of treason and of trying to start a rebellion. He was hanged six weeks later.

John Brown met his death with a dignity that made him a hero and "a new saint" for the antislavery cause. Brown also struck fear through the South. Would there be such raids in the future? Southerners were now convinced that the North would stop at nothing to destroy slavery.

Link to Art

John Brown Going to His Hanging (1942) Most artists go to art school to develop their talent at painting. African American artist Horace Pippin did not. Instead, he taught himself. Pippin (1888–1946) painted many subjects, including landscapes, people, and historical scenes. In this painting, John Brown rides his coffin to the gallows. **Discuss** What is the mood in this scene? How does the artist use color and shapes to express the mood?

The Election of 1860

The presidential election of 1860 drove a final wedge between North and South. The Democratic Party split. Northern Democrats nominated Stephen A. Douglas and came out for popular sovereignty in the territories. Southern Democrats picked John C. Breckinridge, who supported slavery in all territories.

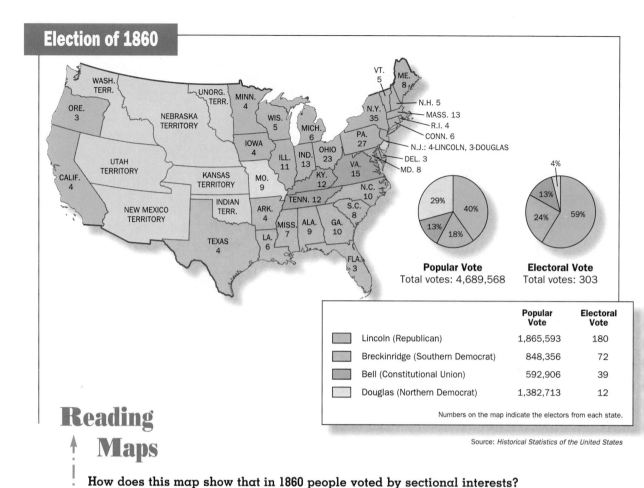

Election of 1860

		Popular Vote	Electoral Vote
	Lincoln (Republican)	1,865,593	180
	Breckinridge (Southern Democrat)	848,356	72
	Bell (Constitutional Union)	592,906	39
	Douglas (Northern Democrat)	1,382,713	12

Numbers on the map indicate the electors from each state.

Source: *Historical Statistics of the United States*

Popular Vote
Total votes: 4,689,568

Electoral Vote
Total votes: 303

Reading
Maps

How does this map show that in 1860 people voted by sectional interests?

In a Chicago meeting hall packed with his supporters, Lincoln won the Republican nomination. The party did not call for the abolition of slavery. Rather, with Lincoln, it viewed slavery as "an evil not to be extended, but to be tolerated."

A fourth candidate, John Bell of Tennessee, was nominated by the Constitutional Union Party. This new party avoided the issue of slavery and supported the Union.

Lincoln's victory Although he won only 40 percent of the popular vote, Lincoln received a majority of the electoral votes. Thanks to the split in the Democratic Party, Abraham Lincoln was elected as the first Republican President.

The South Secedes

As Lincoln had predicted in 1858, "a house divided against itself cannot stand." Within weeks of his election, South Carolina left the Union. Alabama, Mississippi, Georgia, Florida, Louisiana, and Texas soon followed. Together they formed the Confederate States of America, with Jefferson Davis as their President.

Point of View

Is secession ever justifiable?

Many northerners agreed with Lincoln that "no state . . . can lawfully get out of the Union." Most southerners, however, believed that secession was justified. The Declaration of Independence, they pointed out, stated that people have the right to throw off an unjust government. Edmund Ruffin, a Virginia planter, declared:

> **“**Slaveholding states . . . [must proclaim] another declaration of independence [from the United States]. We, the children of those [founding] fathers . . . have submitted to oppression and wrong incalculably [far] greater than ever England inflicted.**”**

Can a state ever legally secede from the nation? Under what conditions?

The Northern Response

At first few northerners took secession seriously. Some thought the South simply needed time to cool off. Others urged compromise again. Some abolitionists were happy to see the South go its separate way. Buchanan, still President in the months before Lincoln took office, hoped that Congress would reach a compromise. He did nothing, however, to help achieve one.

Lincoln’s inaugural address Before his inauguration, Lincoln avoided making any statements. When he took office on March 4, 1861, though, he made his positions clear. He believed he had no legal right to interfere with slavery “in the States where it exists.” However, he expressed his determination to hold the Union together:

> **“**The Union of these States is perpetual. . . . No state . . . can lawfully get out of the Union. . . . I therefore consider that . . . the Union is unbroken.**”**

Lincoln would oppose all attempts at secession, but believed that there was no need for “bloodshed or violence.” He concluded with the plea: “We are not enemies but friends. We must not be enemies.”

The Outbreak of War

Southern radicals ignored Lincoln’s plea. While the new President organized his government, Confederate leaders prepared for war. The first test came at Fort Sumter, in the harbor at Charleston, South Carolina.

Fort Sumter Fort Sumter—a federal fort—was running short of supplies. Trying to avoid armed conflict, Lincoln announced that while he would be sending food to the fort, he would send no soldiers.

World Link

Freedom for Russian serfs In 1861 the slavery issue in the United States was coming to a crisis. In that same year 22 million Russian serfs gained their freedom with the stroke of a pen when Czar Alexander II signed the Emancipation Act.

Serfs were peasants who farmed pieces of land owned by lords. They gave part of their crop to the lord for rent and did many jobs for the lord as well. Unlike slaves in the United States, who had been forcibly brought from Africa, serfs were Russians like their lords. Like the slaves, though, they worked hard, lived in poverty, and were not allowed to move.

Under the Emancipation Act, Russian serfs could buy land, but few could find the money to pay for it. Most former serfs remained poor and discontented.

Fort Sumter guarded one of the South's most important seaports. Thus, Confederate President Davis decided that the fort must not remain in Union hands. Confederate forces demanded that Major Robert Anderson, the commander of Fort Sumter, surrender immediately. Anderson refused.

Early in the morning of April 12, 1861, Confederate cannons opened fire. The fort withstood an intense artillery attack for over 30 hours. Anderson finally surrendered on April 13, 1861. He ordered a 50-gun salute to the United States flag as the Confederate army took the fort. The Civil War had begun.

3. Section Review

1. Why did the Supreme Court deny Dred Scott his freedom?

2. What were Lincoln's two strategies in challenging Douglas for the Senate? Did they work?

3. Why was John Brown a hero to the abolitionist cause?

4. Critical Thinking As a southerner, would you still have voted for secession if you had first heard Lincoln's inaugural address? Why or why not?

Why We Remember

The Gathering Storm

When Abraham Lincoln learned that he had been elected President in 1860, he said to reporters, "Well, boys, your troubles are over. Mine have just begun." As the dark clouds of secession rolled across the South, it became clear how serious those troubles would be. The survival of the United States, and the fate of 4 million enslaved people, rested in Lincoln's hands.

The stormy 1850s were a turning point for the nation. Again and again Congress tried to find a lasting compromise on slavery in the territories. Yet each compromise created new problems. Lincoln understood why. Slavery was not only a political problem, it was also a deeply moral issue. As he wrote in a letter to a friend, "If slavery is not wrong, nothing is wrong."

American democracy is based on the ideal that "all men are created equal." After his election, Lincoln declared his unshakeable belief in that ideal:

"That sentiment [ideal of equality] in the Declaration of Independence . . . gave liberty not only to the people of this country, but hope to all the world. . . . I would rather be assassinated on this spot than surrender it.**"**

As the gathering storm broke over Fort Sumter, the nation would finally decide whether or not to live and die by that simple but powerful ideal.

Geography Lab

The southern Appalachian Mountains

The Appalachian Mountains

In the isolated valleys that twist and turn through the Appalachian Mountains, the issues that divided the North and South seemed far away. Most people who lived in the hollows and thick forests of the southern Appalachians—less rugged than the Rockies—did not own slaves. Farmers there did not want to secede from the Union. The photograph and readings that follow will help you form an image of the region.

From James Paulding's Letters

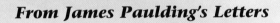

"[W]e first caught a view of the distant undulating [wavy-looking] mountain, whose fading blue outline could hardly be distinguished from the blue sky. Between us and the mountain was spread a wide landscape—shade softening into shade . . . as blended the whole into a . . . harmony. Over all was spread that rich purple hue [color]."

From a Novel by William Simms

"Let the traveler . . . look down upon the scene below. Around us, the hills gather in groups on every side. . . . The axe has not yet deprived them of a single tree, and they rise up, covered with the honored growth of a thousand summers. . . . The leaves cover the rugged limbs which sustain them, with so much ease and grace, as if for the first time they were so green and glossy. . . . The wild flowers begin to flaunt [show off] their blue and crimson draperies [curtains] about us. . . . In the winding hollows of these hills, beginning at our feet, you see the first signs of as lovely a little hamlet [village] as ever promised peace to the weary and the discontent."

From *Charlemont* by William Simms

Developing a Mental Map

Refer to pages R4–R5 and R6–R7.

1. In what states do the Appalachian Mountains lie?

2. What are the highest peaks in the Appalachians and the Rocky Mountains? How do they compare?

3. How does the photograph of the Appalachians resemble the descriptions by Paulding and Simms?

4. **Hands-On Geography** Imagine that you have just completed a hike along the Appalachian Trail—a 2,000-mile footpath from Maine to Georgia. To show your friends and family what it was like to be in the Appalachians, create a diary with pictures. Write a list of topics, and a list of types of photographs, to include in the diary. You may need to look at some additional books before you begin.

Chapter Survey

Reviewing Vocabulary

Define the following terms.
1. popular sovereignty
2. transcontinental railroad
3. platform

Reviewing Main Ideas

1. What did the various groups of radicals and moderates want to do about slavery in territory acquired from Mexico?
2. What were the terms of the Compromise of 1850, and why did Congress pass it?
3. How did the Fugitive Slave Law increase the sectional conflict between the North and the South?
4. Describe how each event led to the next. (a) Kansas-Nebraska Act (b) settlers' race to Kansas (c) sack of Lawrence (d) "Bleeding Kansas"
5. (a) What was the focus of the Republican Party platform? (b) What happened to the Democratic and Whig parties as the Republicans gained support in the 1850s?
6. How did the Supreme Court's decision in *Dred Scott* v. *Sandford* affect the issue of slavery in the territories?
7. (a) How did Abraham Lincoln become a national figure? (b) Why did he win the election of 1860? (c) What was the South's immediate response to the election?

Thinking Critically

1. **Evaluation** Did the Compromise of 1850 favor the North, the South, or neither? Explain your answer.
2. **Application** Abolitionists attacked the Supreme Court for basing its Dred Scott decision on the Fifth Amendment in the Bill of Rights. Why would they be furious about such reasoning?

3. Why We Remember: Synthesis
Could the conflict between North and South have been resolved peacefully after Lincoln's election? If yes, describe a solution that might have worked. If no, explain why war was unavoidable.

Applying Skills

Asking historical questions Slavery is rare in today's world, but other violations of human rights—such as torture of prisoners—still occur. Imagine that you are a reporter. You are to interview someone who claims to have witnessed a human rights violation in another country. Write a list of five questions to ask the person. For each question, write a sentence that tells why you would ask it. Keep in mind what you learned on page 477.

History Mystery

Kansas elections Answer the history mystery on page 465. How would you find out why more people voted in the election than lived in the territory? Why did so many people vote in the election and how might you have prevented them from voting?

Writing in Your History Journal

1. Keys to History (a) The time line on pages 464–465 has seven Keys to History. In your journal, describe why each one is important to know about.
(b) Choose one of the events on the time line. Write a paragraph in your journal that describes how the course of history might have been different if that event had not taken place.
2. Abraham Lincoln Imagine that you are Leo Tolstoy trying to reply to the

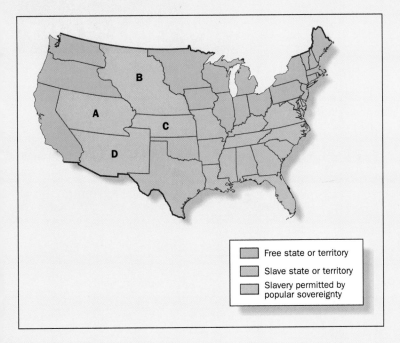

Free state or territory

Slave state or territory

Slavery permitted by popular sovereignty

Reviewing Geography

1. Each letter on the map represents a territory as it existed after the Kansas-Nebraska Act. Write the name of each.

2. Geographic Thinking Look at the map on page 474. President Fillmore believed that the 1850 Compromise ended arguments over slavery in the territories. What territory did he ignore in his conclusion? Why was a decision not reached on the question of slavery there? How might this area be organized in a way that would appeal to both South and North?

mountain chief's request for information about Abraham Lincoln (see page 466). In your journal, write down three things about Lincoln that you believe are most important for the chief to know. Include a specific example from Lincoln's life to support each point.

3. Thinking Historically A terrorist uses violence to advance a political cause. Would you call John Brown a terrorist or a hero? Explain why. How would you compare him with terrorists today? Write your response in your journal.

Alternative Assessment

Citizenship: Covering the 1860 election on TV If television had existed in 1860, what might coverage of the presidential election have been like? With several classmates, act out an election-night broadcast as a television network might do.

In your broadcast:

❶ Give a live report from the campaign headquarters of the candidates.

❷ Interview two voters, one from the South and one from the North. Ask them who they think will win and what the result could mean for the nation.

❸ After each live report and interview, give an election update on how many votes each candidate is receiving.

❹ Include an election map, pictures, or some other visuals in your broadcast.

Your broadcast will be evaluated on the following criteria:
• it clearly presents the issues, the candidates, and the results of the 1860 election
• it resembles a television news show
• it is interesting to your audience

Chapter 18

The Civil War

Keys to History

1862
September
Battle of Antietam

1862
March
Monitor vs. Merrimac

1861
July
First Battle of Bull Run

1861

1862

World **Link**

Looking Back

Lincoln elected
President
1860

Britain stays neutral
in Civil War
1861–1865

HISTORY *Mystery*

Although Lyons Wakeman enlisted in the Union army, family members kept this fact secret and hid the letters they received. Who was Lyons Wakeman, and what knowledge was the family hiding?

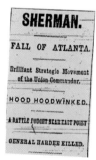

1863
January

Lincoln issues Emancipation Proclamation

Forever Free, statue of mother and children

1863
July

Battles of Gettysburg and Vicksburg

First day of Battle of Gettysburg

1864
September

Sherman's forces seize Atlanta

1865
April

Lee surrenders to Grant at Appomattox Court House

1863

1864

1865

Looking Ahead

14th Amendment guarantees equality
1868

Beginning the Story with

Clara Barton

On September 17, 1862, Confederate and Union troops clashed in a fierce battle along Antietam (an-TEET-uhm) Creek in western Maryland. As the bullets whizzed past and the cannon balls crashed, a lone woman appeared on the battlefield. Her face darkened by gun smoke, she moved from one wounded soldier to another. To some she gave a little food and water. To others she applied bandages. Once she dug a bullet out of flesh with her pocketknife.

All through that long day the bodies piled up. At times the woman had to stop and wring the blood from her skirt to keep moving. She was so close to the raging battle that as she bent over one man a bullet clipped her sleeve and killed him. Later, after darkness fell and the pitiful cries of the wounded replaced the din of combat, she continued to help the injured and dying.

The woman helping wounded soldiers on that day of death was Clara Barton. Later generations would remember her as the founder of the American Red Cross. To the Union troops at the Battle of Antietam, she was simply "the lady" or, as a grateful army doctor put it, "the angel of the battlefield."

"I Remember Nothing But Fear"

As a young child, this fearless angel of mercy had been anything but bold. Born on Christmas Day in 1821 in Massachusetts, the youngest of five children, Clara never felt comfortable with herself. She thought she was too short and too fat. She preferred studying "boys' subjects," such as mathematics and science, to such "womanly" tasks as cooking and sewing.

Clara was also painfully shy. To help overcome her self-doubts, her parents encouraged her to excel at sports and horseback riding. Doing exciting things helped Clara hide her inner fears. So did helping others. Their praise made her feel better about herself. Nonetheless, looking back on her childhood, Clara said, "I remember nothing but fear."

Clara Barton wanted to "go to the rescue of the men who fell." She treated them right on the battlefield rather than in hospitals behind the lines. This picture shows wounded Union soldiers in a field near Fredericksburg, Virginia.

"Between the Bullet and the Battlefield"

Clara Barton's self-doubts followed her into adulthood. She did not, however, let them keep her from standing up for herself. Once she quit a teaching job because the school board hired a man to do the same work at a higher salary. "I may sometimes be willing to teach for nothing," she declared, "but if paid at all, I shall never do a man's work for less than a man's pay."

Clara also stood her ground when she took a job as a clerk in the United States Patent Office in 1854. As one of the first women hired by the federal government, she was resented by the male clerks. They called her names, blew cigar smoke in her face, and spit tobacco juice at her feet. Their insults, she told a friend, made "about as much impression upon me as a sling shot would upon the hide of a shark."

It was as a volunteer nurse in the Civil War that Clara completely overcame her childhood fears. When the war began, neither side was prepared to care for wounded soldiers. Countless men died for lack of medical treatment. This waste of lives infuriated Clara, and she began to collect medical supplies to care for the wounded herself. In spite of the disapproval of Union officers, she followed the army into battle after battle. Her place, she said, was "anywhere between the bullet and the battlefield."

Clara's courage in battle amazed all who knew her, and perhaps even herself. In the face of death and suffering, her old fears faded away. "I may be compelled to face danger," she once told an audience, "but never *fear* it. While our soldiers can stand and *fight,* I can stand and feed and nurse them."

Hands-On HISTORY

Activity

War correspondents traveled with the Union and Confederate armies to gather news for their papers. Imagine that you are a war correspondent with the Union army. Write a report of an interview with Clara Barton after the Battle of Antietam. Include at least three questions and her answers.

1. Preparing for War

Reading Guide

New Terms **habeas corpus, martial law**

Section Focus **The resources of the Union and the Confederacy**

1. Which slave states did not join the Confederacy?
2. Why did volunteers rush to join the Union and Confederate armies?
3. What advantages did each side have as the war began?

The Confederate attack on Fort Sumter on April 12, 1861, plunged the nation into civil war. In Washington, D.C., Clara Barton witnessed the confusion and fear. Rumors spread wildly. The city was torn between supporters of the Union and of the Confederacy. In the Patent Office, where Clara worked, some people openly supported the Confederate cause.

Clara was a staunch Republican. In this crisis, she looked to President Lincoln to take action against "those who have dared to raise the hand of rebellion." Lincoln responded quickly and firmly. On April 15 he called for 75,000 volunteers for 90 days to put down the rebellion in the 7 Confederate states.

Taking Sides in the War

Lincoln's action had a powerful effect on the eight slave states of the Upper South. These "Border States" had not yet decided whether to join the Confederacy or stay in the Union. After Lincoln's call for volunteers, Virginia, Arkansas, North Carolina, and Tennessee seceded from the Union. Richmond, Virginia, became the capital of the Confederacy.

People in the mountainous western part of Virginia, however, remained loyal to the Union. They broke away to form the new state of West Virginia, which joined the Union in 1863.

Slave states in the Union Of the other four Border States, Delaware voted unanimously to stay in the Union. Maryland, Kentucky, and Missouri, though, were deeply divided. Lincoln knew he had to keep Maryland in the Union because the state surrounded Washington, D.C., on three sides.

When a pro-Confederate mob attacked Union soldiers traveling through Maryland on their way to Washington, Lincoln sent troops to keep order. He had pro-Confederate leaders arrested. Then he used his constitutional power to suspend the right of **habeas corpus,** which protects people from being held in prison unlawfully. Maryland stayed in the Union.

At first, Kentucky tried to stay neutral. However, when fighting broke out between pro-Confederate and pro-Union groups, Kentucky sided with the Union.

In Missouri, Union and Confederate supporters fought each other fiercely. Lincoln kept Missouri in the Union by putting the state under martial law. **Martial law** is rule by the army instead of by the usual government officials.

The war brought special anguish to people in the Border States. Brothers, cousins, and even fathers and sons fought on different sides. Clifton Prentiss of Maryland fought for

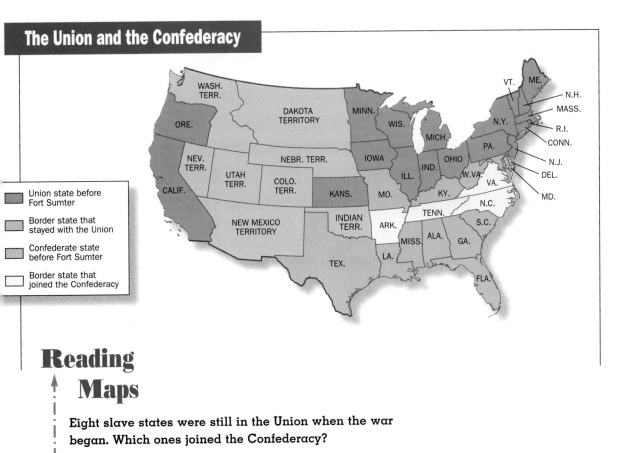

Reading Maps

Eight slave states were still in the Union when the war began. Which ones joined the Confederacy?

the Union while his brother, William, was in the Confederate army. In 1865 the two brothers finally met again on their deathbeds in a hospital in Washington, D.C.

Far West states and territories Most of the states and territories of the Far West were loyal to the Union from the beginning. Early in the war, however, Union and Confederate forces struggled for control of the huge New Mexico Territory.

Texas, a Confederate state, feared a Union invasion from New Mexico, so it sent troops into the territory in 1861. They defeated the main Union forces and captured Tucson, Albuquerque, and Santa Fe.

Their victory was short-lived, though. In March 1862 Union volunteers from Colorado and New Mexico smashed a Confederate force at Glorieta Pass. The Confederates retreated to Texas, their hopes of conquering the Southwest shattered.

The Confederates had more success winning the support of the Cherokees, Creeks, Choctaws, Chickasaws, and Seminoles. Now living in Indian Territory, these southern tribes had been resettled in the West under the Indian removal policy of President Andrew Jackson (see pages 359–363). Many owned slaves and leaned strongly to the South's cause.

All five tribes signed alliances with the Confederacy. In return for their support, they received the right to send delegates to the Confederate Congress. About 15,000 Indian soldiers fought in the Confederate army.

At least 3,000 Indians fought for the North, including 135 Oneida volunteers from Wisconsin. Ely S. Parker, a New York Seneca, served as Ulysses S. Grant's military secretary.

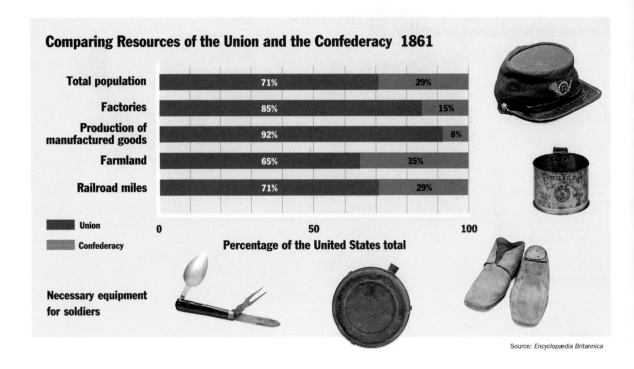

Comparing Resources of the Union and the Confederacy 1861

	Union	Confederacy
Total population	71%	29%
Factories	85%	15%
Production of manufactured goods	92%	8%
Farmland	65%	35%
Railroad miles	71%	29%

Union
Confederacy

0   50   100
Percentage of the United States total

Necessary equipment for soldiers

Source: *Encyclopædia Britannica*

Resources for Waging War

In the spring of 1861 most people expected a short war. Northerners felt sure they would defeat the South in a few battles. Southerners were equally optimistic. An Alabamian predicted peace by 1862 because "we are going to kill the last Yankee [northerner] before that time. . . . I think I can whip 25 myself." In fact, each side had advantages it was counting on to bring it victory.

Economic strengths Northerners were confident of their greater economic strength. The Union had almost twice as much farmland as the Confederacy and would be better able to feed its armies as well as the people at home.

The graph above shows that 85 percent of the nation's factories were in the North. These factories produced almost all of the nation's manufactured goods, including guns, cloth, boots, and shoes.

The Union also had 71 percent of the nation's railroad lines, which would be essen-tial for moving troops and supplies. The Union had a navy, too, and nearly all the nation's shipbuilding took place in the North. The Confederacy had few shipyards and no navy.

Finally, the Union had more than twice as many people as the Confederacy. This greater population made little difference at first, when the two armies were fairly equal in size. Later, however, having twice as many men available to fight would turn out to be a great advantage to the Union.

Military strengths In one area the Confederacy clearly had the edge at the start of the war—it had the nation's best military leaders. One of them was Robert E. Lee of Virginia, who had graduated from the United States Military Academy at West Point and served in the Mexican-American War. During that war, Lee had been described by General Winfield Scott as "the very best soldier that I ever saw in the field."

Lee had opposed secession. When Virginia joined the Confederacy, however, everything changed. "I must side either with or against my section," he told a friend. With a heavy heart, Lee declined President Lincoln's offer of command of the Union army. "I cannot raise my hand against my birthplace, my home, my children," he explained.

Raising Armies

Expecting a short, glorious war, volunteers rushed to enlist. Southerners, who were called Johnny Rebs (for rebels), were determined to defend their homes, their loved ones, and the South's way of life from an invading Union army. One southerner wrote, "Our men *must* prevail [win] in combat, or lose their property, country, freedom, everything."

Northerners, called Billy Yanks or Yankees, fought to preserve the Union. Ted Upson of Indiana joined the army when he was barely 16. He told his father: "This Union your ancestors and mine helped to make must be saved from destruction."

Interest in having an adventure or earning a paycheck also led young men to join the army. Benjamin F. Chase joined the 5th Volunteer Infantry of New Hampshire to see the country and help his parents, who had 11 children to support. "i don't buy eny of the foolish stuff," he assured his parents when sending money home. "You may think i do but i certain don't."

Like many recruits in 1861, Chase was delighted with his new experiences and confident of a brief war. "What a good ride we shall have going south," he boasted in one of his first letters home. Even after three months in uniform, he was still enthusiastic. On January 8, 1862, he wrote:

❝All of the boys in our tent are very well indeed and enjoying their health first rate. i hant been a mite home sick sense we ben out hear and have not ben a mite sick ether. Mother don't worrough a bout me a mite for i think we shall be home before long.❞

Like many recruits, these soldiers posed for portraits before marching off to war: (left) Johnny Clem, 11-year-old Union drummer, 22d Michigan Regiment; (center) unidentified Union soldier from New York; (right) Confederate Private Edwin Jennison, 2d Louisiana Cavalry.

Link to Art

Sounding Reveille (1865) Almost every family North and South had someone in uniform. People at home were desperate for news of their loved ones. "Special artists" helped satisfy that demand. Hired by illustrated newspapers, special artists went to battlefields and camps to sketch what they saw. The most gifted of these artists was Winslow Homer, who worked for *Harper's Weekly* newspaper. In this painting of a Union camp by Homer, a bugler and two drummers sound reveille, a signal to wake the soldiers each morning. **Discuss** In what ways does this painting show the everyday life of soldiers?

Although the Union and the Confederacy had rules banning boys from enlisting, many managed to join. Historians estimate that between 10 and 20 percent of all soldiers— 250,000 to 420,000—were 16 years old or younger. John Mather Sloan of the 9th Texas was only 13 when he lost a leg in battle. He claimed his only regret was that "I shall not soon be able to get at the enemy."

Women soldiers Hundreds of women, too, fought for the cause. Their exact number will never be known, for they had to change their names and disguise themselves as men. Rosetta Wakeman, who joined the 153d Regiment New York State Volunteers, called herself "Lyons Wakeman" and wore men's clothing. Some women even wore fake mustaches or charcoal "whiskers."

Many of the women who enlisted were patriotic or adventurous. Some joined to be with husbands, boyfriends, or brothers. At the Battle of Antietam, Clara Barton tended a soldier, shot in the neck, whose real name turned out to be Mary Galloway. Later she helped to reunite Mary and her wounded boyfriend. After the war, Mary and her husband named their first daughter Clara, after Clara Barton.

Point of View

Should the Union have refused to enlist African Americans?

From the moment the war began, free African Americans flocked to recruiting centers in the North. During the first two years of war, though, the Union refused to enlist African Americans.

Lincoln's reasons for the ban were political. He feared that the slave states still in the Union would view the enlistment of black soldiers as a threat to slavery. Using African American soldiers, he argued, might drive the Border States, especially Kentucky, out of the Union and into the Confederacy. He wrote to a friend:

❝I think to lose Kentucky is nearly the same as to lose the whole game. [With] Kentucky gone, we cannot hold Missouri, nor, as I think, Maryland. These [states] all against us, and the job on our hands is too large for us. We would as well consent to separation at once, including the surrender of this capital.❞

Many white northerners thought that African Americans had no right to fight in the war. When a group of African Americans asked to form a regiment, Governor David Todd of Ohio refused, saying:

❝Do you know that this is a white man's government; that the white men are able to defend and protect it; and that to enlist a Negro soldier would be to drive every white man out of the service?❞

Frederick Douglass was outraged by such racist talk. He urged the government to focus on the goal of winning the war. He said:

❝Why does the government reject the Negro? Is he not a man? Can he not wield a sword, fire a gun, march and countermarch, and obey orders like any other? . . . Men in earnest don't fight with one hand, when they might fight with two, and a man drowning would not refuse to be saved even by a colored hand.❞

At the start of the war, most northerners were too confident of victory to listen to Douglass's advice. Only later, as the war turned long and bloody, would the Union decide to fight with two hands instead of one.

1. Section Review

1. Define the terms **habeas corpus** and **martial law.**

2. Why did Maryland, Kentucky, and Missouri decide to stay in the Union during the Civil War?

3. Give at least three reasons why volunteers rushed to join the Union and the Confederate armies.

4. Critical Thinking A Confederate said, "The longer we have them [northerners] to fight, the more difficult they will be to defeat." What do you think the Confederate meant? Explain why you agree or disagree with this view.

2. The First Two Years of War

Reading Guide

New Term casualties

Section Focus The failure of either army to win a victory that would end the war

1. What were the Union and Confederate strategies for winning the war?
2. Why did these strategies fail to end the war quickly?

From the first, many people in both the Union and the Confederacy believed that the war would be a short one. No one, in 1861, could imagine that it would drag on for four long, bloody years.

Strategies for Victory

In Washington and Richmond, Presidents Lincoln and Davis planned their strategies. Davis's goal was to defend the Confederacy against invasion. "All we ask," he declared, "is to be left alone."

To achieve their goal, the Confederates would just push back invading Union forces. They hoped to make the war so costly that the North would give up. In this struggle, the Confederates expected help from Britain and other nations that needed the South's cotton.

Lincoln's goal was to bring the Confederate states back into the Union. His first strategy was to prevent supplies from reaching the Confederacy. He took the first step on April 19, 1861, when he ordered a naval blockade of southern seaports (see map, page 501). In a second step a year later, he ordered Union troops to take control of the Mississippi River.

Lincoln's second strategy was to capture Richmond, the Confederate capital, which was only 100 miles (160 km) from Washington. There had not been time to train an army, but northerners were anxious to end the war quickly. "On to Richmond!" they urged, and Lincoln agreed.

First Battle of Bull Run

Lincoln sent General Irvin McDowell with 30,000 soldiers into northern Virginia. Their orders were to crush the Confederate forces at the town of Manassas and then move on to Richmond.

At Manassas, McDowell found General Pierre G. T. Beauregard and a Confederate force of 21,000 in the hills above Bull Run,* a small stream. Certain of a Union victory, congressmen, reporters, and curious Washingtonians drove the 26 miles (42 km) to enjoy a picnic and watch the battle.

On the morning of July 21, 1861, the Union troops attacked, and the Confederate line began to crumble. Thomas J. Jackson and his brigade of Virginians, however, stood firm. "There is Jackson, standing like a stone wall! Rally around the Virginians!" yelled a Confederate officer.

The bravery of Stonewall Jackson—as he was called from then on—stopped the Union advance. Now the Confederates rushed forward. The Union soldiers retreated in panic. Some even stole horses and carriages from the onlookers.

*Union forces usually named a battle for the natural feature nearest the fighting, such as a stream or hill. The Confederates named the battle for a nearby town. Thus, the Battle of Bull Run was known in the South as the Battle of Manassas.

In 1864 a Union fleet led by Admiral David G. Farragut, shown in the ship's rigging, captured the Confederate port at Mobile Bay, Alabama.

The First Battle of Bull Run shocked northerners into realizing that the war would not be quickly won. Lincoln immediately called for a million volunteers to serve in the army for three years. At the same time, the easy victory gave southerners a false sense of confidence. Maybe, they thought, 1 rebel could whip 25 Yankees after all.

The War at Sea

President Lincoln had more success with his strategy of blockading southern seaports. The blockade crippled the South's ability to trade its cotton in Europe for the supplies needed to support its war effort.

In a desperate attempt to break the blockade of Norfolk, Virginia, the Confederates developed an "ironclad" warship. They covered a wooden steamship—the *Merrimac*—with iron plates and attached a large iron beak to its prow to ram and sink the ships blockading Norfolk's harbor.

Renamed the *Virginia*, the ironclad sank two Union ships and ran another aground. However, the Union, too, had built an ironclad, the *Monitor*. On March 9, 1862, the two ships battled for hours, with neither able to claim victory. The battle dashed Confederate hopes of breaking the Norfolk Harbor blockade.

Confederate sea raiders In an effort to hurt northern sea trade, the Confederacy had several warships built in England. These ships, including the *Florida* and the *Alabama*, destroyed 250 northern merchant ships. However, the loss had little effect on the Union's ability to wage the war.

The Fight for the Mississippi

President Lincoln gave the task of gaining control of the Mississippi River to General Ulysses S. Grant. Grant was one of many officers who had left the army after the Mexican-American War. He quickly rejoined with the outbreak of the Civil War.

Grant proved to be an able leader. In February 1862 he captured Fort Henry and Fort Donelson. These two Confederate posts guarded the upper approaches to the Mississippi River at the Tennessee border. Grant showed his fierce determination to win by refusing to discuss terms for the Confederate surrender at Donelson. After that, U. S. Grant was sometimes known as "Unconditional Surrender" Grant.

The Battle of Shiloh With the surrender of Donelson, Confederate troops retreated south. Grant and his army followed. On April 6 the Confederates surprised them near a church named Shiloh. By the end of the day, Grant's forces were close to defeat.

Some Union officers advised retreat. "Retreat? No!" Grant replied. "I propose to attack at daylight and whip them." The next day, Grant did just that, driving the Confederates farther south.

The Battle of Shiloh gave the Union control of much of Kentucky and Tennessee. Now Union forces advanced to Memphis, Tennessee, taking the city in early June.

Farragut Meanwhile, Captain David G. Farragut led a fleet up the Mississippi River. On April 29, 1862, New Orleans surrendered. Baton Rouge, Louisiana, fell a few weeks later.

The next target was the well-defended town of Vicksburg, which was vital to Union success. Lincoln declared, "Vicksburg is the key. The war can never be brought to a close until the key is in our pocket."

Farragut was unable to take Vicksburg, and the Union's Mississippi strategy stalled. It was to be more than a year before Grant could finally capture that important Confederate stronghold.

Campaign to Seize Richmond

In the East, Lincoln now renewed the effort to capture Richmond. To command the new Army of the Potomac he chose General George B. McClellan.

McClellan took months training his raw recruits. At last, in March 1862 he landed 100,000 men on the Virginia Peninsula and advanced slowly toward Richmond. Confederate troops under General Joseph E. Johnston were waiting. They stopped the Union army at the Battle of Seven Pines on May 31 and June 1.

At this point, Robert E. Lee took over command of the Army of Northern Virginia from the wounded Johnston. In late June Lee launched a series of attacks against the Union army that drove them off the peninsula (see map, page 501).

Second Battle of Bull Run Before the Union forces could regroup, Lee surprised them on August 29 in a second battle at Bull Run. **Casualties**—soldiers killed, wounded, captured, or missing—were enormous. Clara Barton was horrified by the casualties. "The men were brot down from the [battle]field and laid on the ground beside the train . . . 'till they covered acres," she wrote. One Union soldier later recalled:

❝Long rows of wounded men were lying around. . . . The surgeons were cutting off arms, feet, hands, limbs of all kinds. As an arm or leg was cut off, it was thrown out an open window. It was an awful sight.**❞**

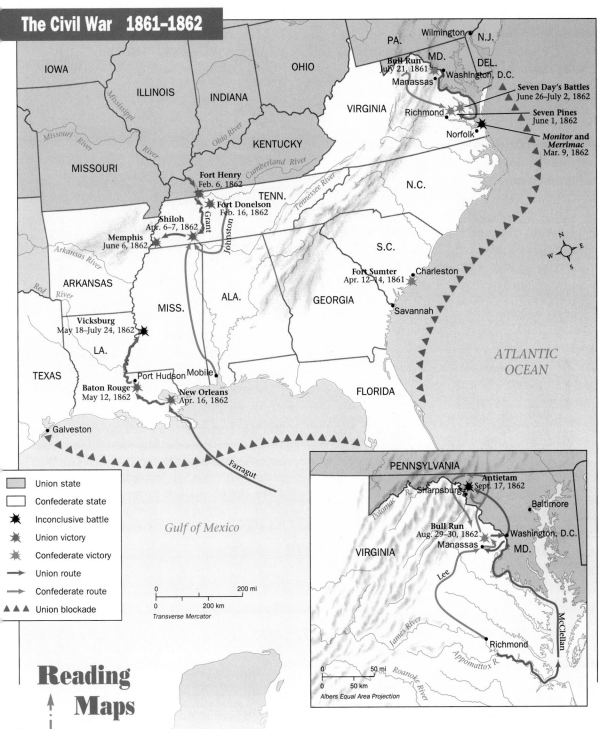

The Civil War 1861–1862

IOWA

ILLINOIS

INDIANA

OHIO

PA.

Wilmington · N.J.

Bull Run
July 21, 1861

MD.

DEL.

Washington, D.C.

Manassas

VIRGINIA

Seven Day's Battles
June 26–July 2, 1862

Richmond

Seven Pines
June 1, 1862

Norfolk

Monitor and
Merrimac
Mar. 9, 1862

MISSOURI

KENTUCKY

Fort Henry
Feb. 6, 1862

N.C.

Fort Donelson
Feb. 16, 1862

Shiloh
Apr. 6–7, 1862

Memphis
June 6, 1862

S.C.

Fort Sumter
Apr. 12–14, 1861

Charleston

ARKANSAS

MISS.

ALA.

GEORGIA

Savannah

Vicksburg
May 18–July 24, 1862

ATLANTIC
OCEAN

LA.

Port Hudson · Mobile

TEXAS

Baton Rouge
May 12, 1862

New Orleans
Apr. 16, 1862

FLORIDA

Galveston

Farragut

Grant

Johnston

Union state
Confederate state
Inconclusive battle
Union victory
Confederate victory
Union route
Confederate route
Union blockade

Gulf of Mexico

0   200 mi
0   200 km
Transverse Mercator

PENNSYLVANIA

Antietam
Sept. 17, 1862

Sharpsburg

Baltimore

Bull Run
Aug. 29–30, 1862

Washington, D.C.

Manassas

MD.

VIRGINIA

Lee

McClellan

James River

Richmond

Appomattox R.

0   50 mi
0   50 km
Albers Equal Area Projection

Roanoke River

Potomac

Reading Maps

1. What Confederate states would be cut off from the rest of the Confederacy if the Union controlled the entire Mississippi River?

2. What Confederate victories forced McClellan to retreat from Richmond? What route did Confederate forces under Lee take to invade the Union?

Link to Technology

The Camera

A major development in technology around the time of the Civil War greatly changed the way we view past events. This development was the camera. While photographic technology had existed for many years, the early 1860s marked the beginning of the wide use of such technology. For the first time, even people far from the front lines could glimpse the grisly scenes of war. As a scholar's tool, photographs provide historians an important window to history—both the history of major events and of ordinary people.

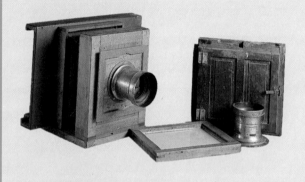

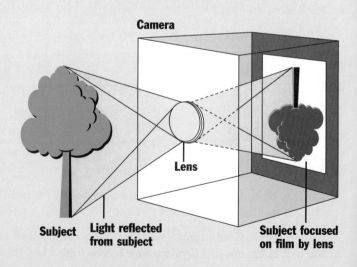

Civil War photographers would rush to the battle scene, set up cameras, then develop the photos on the spot. Perhaps the most famous Civil War photographer was Mathew Brady, who is pictured above with his portable darkroom. The top picture shows the type of photo that made Brady famous. His 1860 camera is pictured at left.

1 A shutter opens quickly, allowing light reflected from the subject to pass through the lens and expose the film.

2 The film is coated with light-sensitive silver crystals. When the reflected light touches them, they turn dark. This process is called *exposure.*

3 Where the subject is dark, it reflects very little light. Where it is bright, it reflects more light. The exposure makes a reverse image, or *negative,* on the film.

4 When the film is developed, the image becomes fixed, and a positive image can be printed—the photograph.

Camera

Lens

Subject

Light reflected from subject

Subject focused on film by lens

Antietam was the first Civil War battlefield to be photographed before the dead had been buried. Arriving soon after the battle ended, photographer Alexander Gardner took this photo of Confederate dead. Photographs like this captured the horror of war for Americans.

The Battle of Antietam

With the Union forces in chaos, Lee boldly crossed into Maryland in September 1862. He hoped a successful invasion of the North would encourage Britain and France to give aid to the Confederacy.

With a little luck, Lee's gamble might have worked. However, a copy of his orders fell into Union hands, and McClellan learned the exact position of Lee's forces.

On September 17 the two armies clashed at Antietam Creek. It was to be the bloodiest day of the war, but neither side could claim victory. Lee slipped back into Virginia. McClellan, ignoring Lincoln's orders, did not pursue him.

Close to 5,000 soldiers died at Antietam, and 18,500 were wounded. One soldier who survived was Benjamin Chase. His letter home was filled with sadness and fear for the future:

"i was so lucky to get out of it alive. i thought to myself if thear mothers could only see . . . [their dead sons] they would be crasy."

Chase prayed for the "happy day" when he could talk to his mother again. "When will that day come?" he wondered. "i cant tell that, . . . perhaps never."

The Battle of Antietam was a turning point in the war. The battle ended Lee's invasion of the North, destroyed a third of his army, and shattered Confederate hopes of getting aid from abroad.

As 1862 drew to a close, neither side held a clear advantage over the other. Lee's failure at Antietam, however, gave President Lincoln the chance to take a bold step that would change the course of the war.

2. Section Review

1. Define **casualties**.
2. What was the basic goal of the Confederacy? The Union?
3. What brought Union advances to a standstill in 1862?
4. **Critical Thinking** How might the outcome of the war have been different if Lee had won a decisive victory at the Battle of Antietam?

3. The War Effort at Home

Reading Guide

New Terms draft, income tax

Section Focus The Civil War's effect on northerners and southerners at home

1. What was the effect of the Emancipation Proclamation?
2. How did women contribute to the war effort?
3. What challenges did Lincoln and Davis face as wartime leaders?

From the start of the Civil War, President Lincoln had resisted pleas to abolish slavery. Although Lincoln personally hated slavery, the purpose of the war, he said, "*is* to save the Union, and is *not* either to save or to destroy slavery."

As hopes for peace dimmed, however, Lincoln changed his mind. He came to see that emancipation—freeing all slaves—was "essential to the preservation of the Union."

Moving Toward Emancipation

Several factors led Lincoln to favor emancipation. One was that it made sense from a military point of view. The Confederacy was using enslaved African Americans to build fortifications, haul supplies, and grow crops. If Lincoln freed the slaves, the Confederates would lose a vital source of labor—and the Union would gain one.

In fact, since the war began, thousands of enslaved African Americans had sought freedom by fleeing to join Union forces invading the South. Union commanders paid the escaped slaves to work as cooks, carpenters, guides, and drivers. Some commanders also accepted escaped African Americans as soldiers, forming regiments in South Carolina and Louisiana.

A second reason for emancipation was to keep European nations from helping the Confederacy. Slavery had long been abolished in Europe. Lincoln believed that emancipation would win public support for the Union in those countries.

A third factor in Lincoln's decision was pressure from abolitionists. More and more people were coming to believe that it was time to settle the slavery issue once and for all. "This rebellion has its source . . . in slavery," a Republican told the House of Representatives. Defeating the South would be useless "if slavery shall be spared to canker [infect] the heart of the nation anew."

The Emancipation Proclamation

By the summer of 1862, Lincoln's emancipation plan was ready. The President decided not to announce it, though, until Union forces had won a victory. He did not want it to seem like an act of desperation.

When the Union army turned back Lee's troops at Antietam, Lincoln saw his chance. On September 22, 1862, he issued a warning to the Confederate states: Unless they returned to the Union by January 1, 1863, he would free their slaves. The Confederacy ignored the warning.

True to his word, on January 1, 1863, Lincoln signed the Emancipation Proclamation. It stated that all slaves in the Confederate states "are, and henceforward shall be, free." Slaves in areas loyal to the United States or under Union control were not affected. Lincoln had no constitutional power to act against slavery there.

The Emancipation Proclamation changed the war into a struggle for freedom as well as for the Union. It turned the Union army into a liberating army wherever it went in the South. It won European approval for the Union cause. It was also a giant step toward abolishing all slavery. Lincoln believed that it was the "one thing that will make people remember I ever lived."

African American Troops

After the Emancipation Proclamation, African Americans could join the Union army as soldiers. About 186,000 African Americans, most of them former slaves, enlisted to fight for the Union and for their own freedom. Another 30,000 joined the navy, which had been accepting black sailors since 1861.

Even though they were risking their lives, African American soldiers were discriminated against. They were assigned to all-black regiments commanded by white officers. Most were given more than their share of digging trenches and building fortifications and bridges.

This picture shows the 54th Massachusetts Infantry leading an assault on Fort Wagner, South Carolina. Although the attack failed, the 54th fought courageously, suffering almost 50 percent casualties.

⚭ Link to the Present

The American Red Cross A hurricane pounds a Florida town. Floods destroy homes and farms in Iowa. An earthquake tumbles buildings in California. Wherever disaster strikes, the American Red Cross is there to help the victims.

While in Switzerland in 1869, Clara Barton learned of the International Committee of the Red Cross, a group of volunteers who aided wounded soldiers. Impressed by its work, she founded the American branch of the Red Cross in 1881.

Barton soon expanded Red Cross activities to include disaster relief. Today the Red Cross also collects and distributes blood and teaches first aid. Most workers are volunteers, and programs are funded by private—not government—contributions.

At first, African American troops were paid as laborers, not soldiers, and all received the same pay no matter what their rank. To protest such unequal treatment, many soldiers refused to accept any pay at all. In a letter to President Lincoln, Corporal James Henry Gooding of the 54th Massachusetts Infantry asked:

❝The main question is, are we soldiers, or are we laborers? . . . We have done a soldier's duty. Why can't we have a soldier's pay?❞

In 1864 Congress finally granted black soldiers equal pay, including all back pay.

Some northerners doubted that African Americans would make good soldiers. Such doubts were quickly put to rest in battle.

For example, in a suicidal attack on Fort Wagner, South Carolina, in 1863, the 54th Massachusetts Infantry lost its commander, most of its officers, and almost half of its troops. Although terribly wounded, Sergeant William Carney carried the regiment's flags to safety. He was the first of 20 African American soldiers to win the Congressional Medal of Honor.

New Challenges for Women

Until the Civil War, women had few choices of jobs outside the home other than teacher, factory worker, or house servant. With thousands of men fighting in the war, though, women took over family farms and businesses. They also had the chance to tackle jobs usually closed to them.

Women worked in mints making coins and in offices copying documents, as Clara Barton did in the Patent Office. Women also worked in arsenals making ammunition. This was a dangerous business. After 21 women were killed in an explosion in Washington, D.C., President Lincoln led the funeral procession to Congressional Cemetery. There the victims, mostly Irish immigrants, were buried in a common grave.

Setting up hospitals When the war began, there were almost no large military hospitals. Medical officers scrambled to convert barns, tobacco warehouses, schools, and even large boats into hospitals.

Conditions in most hospitals were terrible. They lacked ways to treat water and sewage to prevent the spread of disease. In fact, twice as many soldiers died of disease as of combat wounds. Mary Boykin Chesnut described her visit to a hospital in Richmond:

❝I can never again shut out of view the sights I saw of human misery. . . . Long rows of ill men on cots. Ill of typhoid fever, of every human ailment.❞

Women played many roles in the war. Women workers prepared cartridges for Union guns at the arsenal in Watertown, Massachusetts. Alice Buckner of Virginia tried—without success—to smuggle medicine in her petticoat to the Confederates. Captain Sally Tompkins founded one of the best small hospitals for soldiers in the South.

Many women took wounded soldiers into their homes. Sally L. Tompkins set up a hospital in a Richmond house where she treated more than 1,300 patients. Jefferson Davis rewarded her services by appointing her a captain of cavalry.

Nursing the wounded Many noted women reformers threw themselves into the effort to nurse the wounded. Dorothea Dix, who had reformed mental hospitals, worked with Dr. Elizabeth Blackwell to set up a training program for female nurses. Dix's rules were so strict that she became known as "Dragon Dix."

Clara Barton felt "cramped" in hospitals. She preferred being on the battlefield. There she treated wounded soldiers, some of whom had gone for days without food or water.

Harriet Tubman also helped tend the wounded, working with Clara Barton in the Sea Islands off the coast of South Carolina.

Sojourner Truth worked in Union hospitals and in camps for escaped slaves. She also recruited black soldiers for the Union army. Two were her sons.

Opposition at Home

Not everyone was as patriotic and eager to serve as the brave women working in the arsenals and hospitals of the Union and the Confederacy. As the war dragged on and hopes for a quick victory faded, Presidents Davis and Lincoln both faced growing opposition at home.

States' rights A serious problem for Davis was lack of cooperation by the states in the Confederacy. Holding fast to the idea of states' rights, they resisted paying taxes and cooperating on military matters. At one point, Georgia even threatened to secede from the Confederacy.

Britain stays neutral in Civil War

"No power dares . . . to make war on cotton. Cotton is king." So said Senator James Hammond of South Carolina in 1859. When the Civil War broke out, southern leaders expected British support. They thought Britain would want to protect the supply of cotton flowing to its textile mills.

What went wrong? Between 1860 and 1862, bad weather ruined Europe's grain crops while Union farmers were having record harvests. Britain needed northern grain more than southern cotton.

Meanwhile, in 1861 British mills had a surplus of cotton. By the time it ran out, they had found new sources of cotton in India and Egypt. Thus, Britain could afford to stay neutral in the Civil War.

Copperheads For his part, Lincoln led a Union that was far from united. Many northern Democrats were more interested in restoring peace than in saving the Union or ending slavery. Republicans called these Democrats "Copperheads," after the poisonous snake.

The draft The hottest issue faced by both the Union and the Confederacy was the **draft**—a system that requires men to serve in the military. At first both armies had more than enough volunteers. As casualties mounted, though, enlistments dropped.

In 1862 the Confederacy passed the first draft law in United States history. With a few exceptions, all white men aged 18 to 35 could be called for military service for 3 years. A draftee could avoid serving by paying for a substitute to take his place. Anyone who owned 20 slaves or more was excused from the draft. Angry southerners protested that it was "a rich man's war and a poor man's fight."

Soon the Union had to resort to the draft as well. Its draft act applied to all men aged 20 to 45. As in the South, a draftee could pay for a substitute. The Union's draft act was passed only 2 months after the Emancipation Proclamation. Copperheads accused the government of forcing white workers to fight to free the slaves, who would then compete for their jobs after the war.

When the first draft was held in July 1863, riots broke out. The worst was in New York City. There a mob, mostly Irish Americans, went on a 4-day rampage, burning draft offices and lynching African Americans. At least 105 people were killed.

Years of war aged President Lincoln, as this 1865 portrait shows, but he never doubted his war aims.

Economic Strains of the War

The war placed a great strain on the economies of both sides. To pay for the Union war effort, Congress passed the nation's first **income tax**—a tax on money people earn from work or investments. The Union also raised millions of dollars through the sale of war bonds. People who bought bonds were, in effect, lending money to the government.

Unable to raise enough money to pay their bills, both governments printed money. Union notes were called "greenbacks" because of their color. Since paper money was not backed by gold or silver, it lost value during the war. Between 1862 and 1865, the value of a one-dollar Union note dropped to half that amount in gold. A similar Confederate note was worth about two cents.

Getting supplies The Union economy was up to the challenge of supplying both troops and people at home during the war. Aided by the McCormick reaper, farmers produced large crops of wheat and corn. Labor-saving machines enabled factories to keep soldiers well clothed and armed.

The Confederacy, however, suffered increasingly from shortages. Its economy, based largely on cotton and with few industries, was ill-suited to supporting a war effort.

Early in the war, southerners had made a serious mistake. They stopped shipping cotton abroad, hoping to force Britain to aid the Confederacy. The plan backfired. As you have seen, Britain did not help the South—and the South lost an important source of income.

Meanwhile the Union blockade made it increasingly difficult for the Confederacy to import supplies. After southern victories, desperate Confederate soldiers stripped dead and wounded Union soldiers of their weapons, shoes, and even uniforms.

President Davis had the heavy responsibility of organizing a new nation and guiding it in war.

The Union's naval blockade was working. It was strangling the southern economy and, with it, the Confederate war effort. As a Confederate officer later admitted, the blockade "shut the Confederacy out from the world, deprived it of supplies, [and] weakened its military and naval strength."

3. Section Review

1. Define **draft** and **income tax.**
2. Why did Lincoln wait to issue the Emancipation Proclamation?
3. Describe at least two contributions made by women to the war effort.
4. Critical Thinking How might public opposition in the Union and the Confederacy have weakened the war effort?

Skill Lab

Using Information

Making a Hypothesis

"All persons held as slaves within any [rebellious] state . . . shall be . . . forever free." With those words, Abraham Lincoln ensured his place in history as the "Great Emancipator." Historians have long disagreed, however, about Lincoln's reasons—and timing—for the Emancipation Proclamation.

Question to Investigate

Why did President Lincoln issue the Emancipation Proclamation?

Procedure

Any answer to that question is a **hypothesis—** a theory to explain the event. Part of a historian's job is to develop hypotheses for events and situations. Then each hypothesis must be tested against available information.

1 Gather information.
a. Read sources **A**, **B**, and **C**.
b. As you read, take notes on possible reasons for the proclamation.

2 Develop several hypotheses.
a. Write the hypotheses suggested by source **A**.
b. Write two more hypotheses that sources **B** and **C** suggest to you.

3 Test each hypothesis.
a. From what you know, does each hypothesis give an adequate explanation for why Lincoln issued the proclamation? Is one hypothesis more valid? Explain.
b. What can you do to test how reasonable each hypothesis is?

Skill Tips

Keep in mind:
● To qualify as a hypothesis, a theory must be able to be tested.
● There may be more than one reasonable hypothesis to explain an event.
● Even the best hypothesis may need to be tested again if new information is available.

Sources to Use

A Reread pages 504–505.

B "Thousands of jubilant [joyful] slaves, learning of the proclamation, flocked to the invading Union armies, stripping already rundown plantations of their work force. . . . The North now had much the stronger moral cause. In addition to preserving the Union, it had committed itself to freeing the slaves."

From Thomas A. Bailey and David M. Kennedy, *The American Pageant* (D.C. Heath: 1991)

C "Three developments caused Lincoln to change his mind [and to abolish slavery]. First, the bloody fighting made many northerners want to hurt the South as much as possible. Abolishing slavery would help do that. Second, slavery helped the southern war effort. Slaves helped to build military fortifications, and they produced food. Third, slavery was a crucial issue on the Union's diplomatic front with Britain. Britain's leaders would not support a war whose aim was to keep the United States together. However, British public opinion would back a war against slavery. . . . The Emancipation Proclamation also encouraged the recruitment of black soldiers into the Union army. . . . All told, nearly 300,000 blacks served in the Union army."

From Winthrop D. Jordan et al., *The Americans* (McDougal, Littell: 1991)

4. From War to Peace

Reading Guide

New Term **total war**

Section Focus **Union victories that finally ended the war**

1. Why were the Battles of Gettysburg and Vicksburg turning points in the war?
2. What was Grant's strategy for winning the war?
3. What events led to Lee's surrender at Appomattox?

The year 1862 ended in despair for the Union. The war effort in Virginia and on the Mississippi had stalled. Many northerners began to speak openly about letting the Confederacy have its independence. President Lincoln kept his sights on his goal—to win the war. He knew, however, that he needed a general he could count on to "fight battles and win victories."

Two Confederate Victories

After the Battle of Antietam, Lincoln fired General McClellan for refusing to attack Lee's retreating army. He gave command to General Ambrose E. Burnside. In December 1862 Lee soundly defeated Burnside's forces at Fredericksburg, Virginia. Benjamin Chase died that day. He was only 18 years old.

Next Lincoln turned to General Joseph Hooker. Lee stopped Hooker, too—at Chancellorsville, Virginia, in May 1863. Lee's victory was clouded, however, by the death of Stonewall Jackson. "I know not how to replace him," confessed Lee.

After Chancellorsville, Lee decided to invade the Union again. He thought that another victory, this time on northern soil, would prove to northerners and Europeans that the Confederacy could win the war. His invasion might also draw Union troops away from Vicksburg on the Mississippi.

The Battle of Gettysburg

In June 1863 Lee led his confident troops across Maryland and into Pennsylvania. On July 1 Confederate soldiers met Union soldiers in the little town of Gettysburg. General George C. Meade, the new commander of the Army of the Potomac, had been following Lee's forces. He rushed his army to Gettysburg and forced Lee to take a stand.

Courtesy of the R. W. Norton Art Gallery, Shreveport, Louisiana

The greatest loss to the South at Chancellorsville was the death of Stonewall Jackson, Lee's "right arm." Jackson was accidentally shot by his own men.

On the first day of the Battle of Gettysburg, Confederate troops attacked Union lines. Union forces, though, had more troops, greater firepower, and a strong defensive position on high ground.

For two days Union and Confederate forces fought furiously. Finally, on July 3, Lee risked everything on an infantry charge led by General George E. Pickett. About 15,000 Confederates hurled themselves at the center of the Union line on Cemetery Ridge. Pickett's Charge was a disaster. Half of his men were struck by Union fire as they rushed uphill. More fell in hand-to-hand combat when they reached the ridge.

The Battle of Gettysburg was a turning point in the war. On July 4 Lee, who had lost a third of his army, retreated to Virginia. From this point on, he would be fighting a defensive war on southern soil.

The Gettysburg Address The casualties at Gettysburg were staggering—23,000 for the Union and 28,000 for the Confederates. The bloodshed was so appalling that a national cemetery was created for the soldiers who died there. At the dedication ceremony on November 19, 1863, President Lincoln delivered a brief speech.

The Gettysburg Address is one of the most eloquent statements of American democracy. In it Lincoln vowed:

“We here highly resolve that these dead shall not have died in vain; that this nation, under God, shall have a new birth of freedom; and that government of the people, by the people, for the people shall not perish from the earth.”

Victory on the Mississippi

The Union victory at Gettysburg was quickly followed by good news from the Mississippi. After failing to storm the hilltop stronghold of Vicksburg, General Grant had surrounded it while Union gunboats bombarded it. The starving citizens held out for

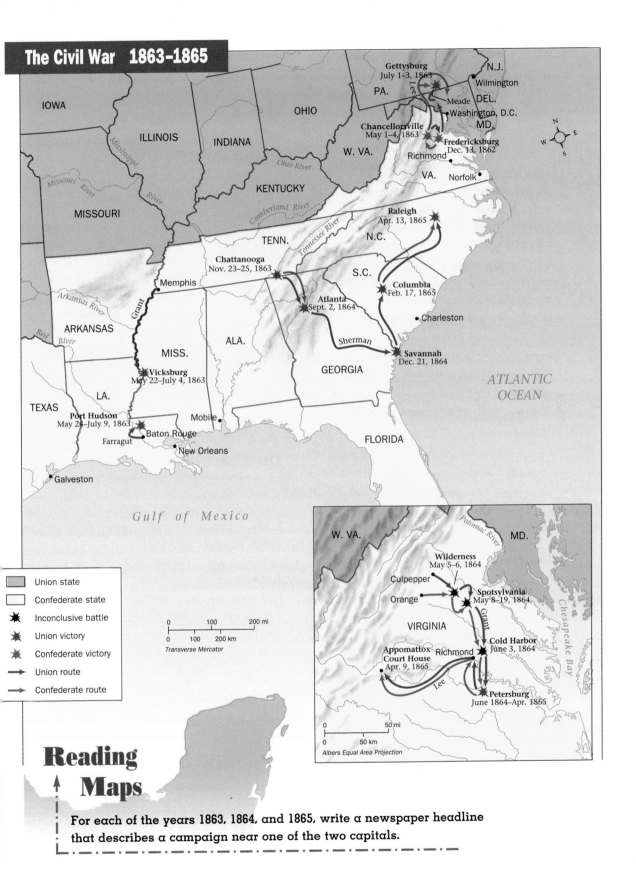

The Civil War   1863–1865

IOWA

ILLINOIS

INDIANA

OHIO

MISSOURI

KENTUCKY

W. VA.

PA.

N.J.

Wilmington

DEL.

MD.

Gettysburg
July 1–3, 1863

Meade

Washington, D.C.

Chancellorsville
May 1–4, 1863

Fredericksburg
Dec. 13, 1862

Richmond

VA.

Norfolk

Raleigh
Apr. 13, 1865

N.C.

TENN.

Chattanooga
Nov. 23–25, 1863

Memphis

S.C.

Columbia
Feb. 17, 1865

Atlanta
Sept. 2, 1864

Charleston

ARKANSAS

ALA.

MISS.

GEORGIA

Savannah
Dec. 21, 1864

Vicksburg
May 22–July 4, 1863

LA.

TEXAS

Port Hudson
May 24–July 9, 1863

Mobile

Baton Rouge

Farragut

New Orleans

FLORIDA

ATLANTIC
OCEAN

Galveston

Gulf of Mexico

Mississippi River

Missouri River

Ohio River

Cumberland River

Tennessee River

Arkansas River

Red River

Grant

Sherman

Lee

Legend

▭	Union state
▭	Confederate state
✹	Inconclusive battle
✹	Union victory
✹	Confederate victory
→	Union route
→	Confederate route

0   100   200 mi

0   100   200 km

Transverse Mercator

Inset map

W. VA.

MD.

Potomac River

Wilderness
May 5–6, 1864

Culpepper

Orange

Spotsylvania
May 8–19, 1864

VIRGINIA

Grant

Cold Harbor
June 3, 1864

**Appomattox
Court House**
Apr. 9, 1865

Richmond

Lee

Chesapeake Bay

Petersburg
June 1864–Apr. 1865

0   50 mi

0   50 km

Albers Equal Area Projection

Reading
Maps

For each of the years 1863, 1864, and 1865, write a newspaper headline
that describes a campaign near one of the two capitals.

Hands-On HISTORY

Commemorating the Civil War Since the guns fell silent more than 130 years ago, Americans have continued to remember the Civil War. In paintings, monuments, and books, as well as in movies and television dramas, we have commemorated the people and events of that dramatic period in the nation's history.

Activity You may never write a book or create a television drama about the Civil War, but you can plan a way to commemorate it.

1. Decide what part of the war to commemorate. It might be an event, a person or group of people, or a theme, such as life at home.

2. Decide what form to create—for example, a plaque, monument, play, pageant, or story.

3. Put your plan on paper. For example, draw a picture of a statue or write a program for a pageant. Share it with your classmates.

War monument

"The art of war is simple enough. Find out where your enemy is. Get at him as soon as you can. Strike at him as hard as you can and as often as you can, and keep moving on."

Grant believed in **total war**—war against armies and also against a people's resources and will to fight.

Now Grant mapped out a strategy to end the war. He would lead the Army of the Potomac against Lee and capture Richmond. Meanwhile, he ordered General William Tecumseh Sherman to invade Georgia and take Atlanta.

almost seven weeks, living in caves and eating rats, cats, dogs, and mules.

Vicksburg finally surrendered on July 4, 1863—another turning point in the war. Port Hudson, the last Confederate stronghold on the Mississippi, gave up five days later. Union forces now controlled the entire river. Lincoln was thrilled. "Grant is my man," he exclaimed, "and I am his for the rest of the war."

President Lincoln named Grant commander of all western forces. Grant responded by capturing Chattanooga, a key railroad center in Tennessee, in November 1863.

Total War

At last, Lincoln had found a general who could win battles. In March 1864 he gave Grant command of all Union forces.

The new commander had a common-sense way of looking at war. He wrote:

The battle for Richmond On May 4, 1864, Grant invaded northern Virginia with 120,000 troops. They clashed with Lee's army of 61,000 in the Wilderness, a dense forest. In 2 days of fighting, Grant's troops suffered 18,000 casualties. Instead of turning back, though, Grant pressed on toward Richmond.

The two armies next met at Spotsylvania Court House. Again Grant suffered heavy losses but would not retreat. "I propose to fight it out along this line if it takes all summer," he said. The two armies clashed at Cold Harbor, again with high casualties.

In a month, Grant's army had lost 50,000 soldiers, compared with about 30,000 Confederate losses. The greater population of the North meant that Grant could get more troops. Lee, however, could not replace his losses. By the time the Confederate Congress decided to use African American troops in March 1865, it would be too late to make a difference.

Lee moved on to defend Petersburg, an important rail center 20 miles (32 km) from Richmond. If Petersburg fell, the Confederates could not hold Richmond.

The capture of Atlanta Meanwhile, Sherman moved toward Atlanta. The Confederates made Union forces pay for every advance, but by mid-July of 1864 Sherman had surrounded Atlanta.

The Confederates hoped to hold out until the Union's presidential election. They thought that war-weary northerners would reject Lincoln and elect General George McClellan, who called for an end to the war. However, on September 2, 1864, Atlanta fell. News of Sherman's victory raised spirits in the North and ensured Lincoln's reelection.

Sherman now put into effect Grant's idea of total war. To break the South's will to continue fighting, his troops burned Atlanta. Then they marched almost unopposed across Georgia. Along the way they torched barns and houses and destroyed railroad tracks, crops, and livestock.

In December Sherman reached the sea at Savannah. Then, leaving destruction in his wake, he marched north through South Carolina and into North Carolina. From there he drove on toward Richmond.

Lee Surrenders

For nine months Grant's forces battered Lee's defenses at Petersburg, the gateway to Richmond. They finally broke through on April 1, 1865. Two days later, Union troops marched into Richmond.

Lee fled with 30,000 soldiers. Grant followed. At this point, other Union forces

This painting commemorates the end of the Civil War. General Lee (left) signs the agreement surrendering his army to General Grant (right).

cut off Lee's escape route. Outnumbered and surrounded, Lee decided that further fighting would be useless.

On April 9, 1865, Lee surrendered at Appomattox Court House. Grant gave generous terms. Lee's troops could go home if they promised to fight no more. All soldiers could keep their own horses. Grant also provided food for Lee's starving soldiers. In the next few days, all Confederate forces followed Lee's lead. The last general to surrender was Stand Watie of the Cherokee Nation. On May 10, Jefferson Davis was captured.

Costs of war The bloodiest war in the history of the nation had finally ended. The Union had been saved, but at the horrifying cost of more than 620,000 Union and Confederate dead.

Almost every family on both sides had lost a friend or loved one. Benjamin Chase's mother never overcame the shock of his death. Daniel and Rebecca Hite of Virginia had watched five sons go off to war. Only two came home. Clara Barton set up a "missing persons" office to help thousands of families searching for missing relatives.

For President Lincoln, the end of the war was the happiest day of his life. "Thank God I have lived to see this," he said. "I have been dreaming a horrid nightmare for four years, and now the nightmare is over."

4. Section Review

1. Define **total war.**

2. Why were the Battles of Gettysburg and Vicksburg turning points in the war?

3. What Union advantage helped Grant defeat Lee in 1865?

4. Critical Thinking Do you think Sherman should have used total war in Georgia and the Carolinas? Give reasons for your answer.

Why We Remember

The Civil War

The Civil War, wrote the *New York Times* after the guns fell silent, "leaves us a different people forever." Nowhere was this truth easier to see than in the longstanding issue of slavery. The Union's victory in the war destroyed the system of slavery and paved the way to freedom for 4 million African Americans. Many of them had helped win that freedom on the battlefield. To Clara Barton, each one was a "soldier of freedom."

The Civil War also changed how Americans viewed their country. Before the war, most Americans thought of the United States as a loose union of separate states. When talking of their country, they said, "The United States *are.*" Afterward, people in both the North and the South saw the country as a single nation and began to say, "The United States *is.*"

Geography Lab

Reading a Grid Map

Each year close to 1.5 million people visit the Gettysburg National Military Park in Pennsylvania. There they can trace the events of the battle by car or on foot.

The map shows the site of the Battle of Gettysburg. As with road maps, this map has a grid of intersecting lines. Note that the spaces between horizontal lines are labeled with letters, while the spaces between vertical lines are labeled with numbers. Thus, the squares in the grid can be referred to as A-1, A-2, and so on. The labeled grid makes it easy to find sites and describe their location on the map.

Gettysburg National Cemetery, Pennsylvania

Using Map Skills

1. Confederates approached Gettysburg on a road that passes through grid locations A-1, A-2, and B-2. What is the name of the road?

2. A Union line curled around what two hills in C-3 and C-4?

3. Confederate troops lined Seminary Ridge. From there Pickett's men charged Union troops atop Cemetery Ridge. To keep their sense of direction, they focused on a clump of trees. Give its grid location.

4. President Lincoln delivered his address where Soldier's Monument is today. Give its grid location.

5. **Hands-On Geography**
Use the map to plan a tour of the Gettysburg battle site. Begin at the Visitor's Center and end at McPherson's Barn, with five stops in between. Imagine a path through the park. Write instructions for the tour, using grid locations and compass directions to describe the route and the stopping points along it.

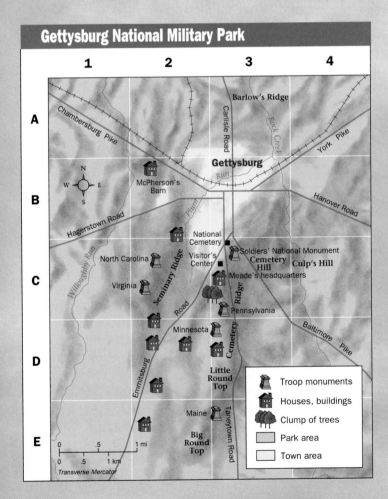

Gettysburg National Military Park

Troop monuments
Houses, buildings
Clump of trees
Park area
Town area

1 mi
1 km
Transverse Mercator

Chapter Survey

Reviewing Vocabulary

Define the following terms.
1. habeas corpus
2. martial law
3. casualties
4. draft
5. income tax
6. total war

Reviewing Main Ideas

1. When the Civil War began, which side had the advantage in the following areas? (a) farmland (b) factories (c) military leadership (d) population (e) transportation
2. How did President Davis plan to win the war? How did President Lincoln?
3. By the end of 1862, how successful had Lincoln been in achieving his war goal? Give supporting examples.
4. (a) What were the provisions of the Emancipation Proclamation? (b) How did the proclamation affect the war?
5. What were two problems faced at home by President Lincoln? By President Davis?
6. Describe two events that took place in the first week of July 1863 that changed the course of the war.
7. What led Lee to surrender his Army of Northern Virginia in April 1865?

Thinking Critically

1. Analysis The Battle of Saratoga was a turning point in the American War of Independence. The Battle of Antietam was a turning point in the Civil War. Compare the results of the two battles.
2. Synthesis Why do you think Grant's terms of surrender at Appomattox were so generous? If you had been in his place, what terms would you have offered? Why?
3. Why We Remember: Analysis In the Gettysburg Address, President Lincoln vowed that "this nation, under God, shall have a new birth of freedom." What do you think he meant?

Applying Skills

Making a hypothesis When Lincoln issued the Emancipation Proclamation, he was using a power of the presidency. A presidential proclamation—also called an executive order—does not require any action by Congress.

Look in newspapers and magazines to find a recent example of an executive order. Then use what you learned on page 510 to do the following:
1. Create three hypotheses to explain why the President issued the executive order.
2. Test each hypothesis against the information available to you.
3. List your hypotheses and tell which of them best explains the President's action. If you cannot choose one, explain why not. What might you do next?

History Mystery

An army recruit Answer the History Mystery on page 489. Where might you find information about Lyons Wakeman's experiences? Where would you look for evidence that Wakeman was, in fact, a soldier?

Writing in Your History Journal

1. Keys to History (a) The time line on pages 488–489 has seven Keys to History. In your journal, list each key and describe why it is important to know about. (b) Imagine that you are a reporter or "special artist" covering the Civil War. If you could cover only one event on the time line, which one would you choose? In your journal, explain the reasons for your decision.
2. Clara Barton During the Civil War, thousands of women felt the same urge to help as Clara Barton had. Imagine that

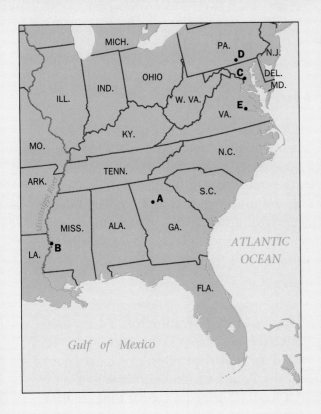

Gulf of Mexico

Reviewing Geography

1. For each letter on the map, write the name of a town or city that was important during the Civil War.

2. Geographic Thinking One of the major Union strategies was to capture Richmond, which was only 100 miles (160 km) from Washington, D.C. As a result, many battles took place on Virginia soil.

The Confederate capital was originally at Montgomery, Alabama (see the map on pages R6–R7). Imagine that Montgomery had remained the Confederate capital. How do you think Union strategy might have changed? How might it have remained the same?

you are living then. Choose a role for yourself—man or woman, old or young. Describe what you would like to do to help in the war effort.

3. Citizenship Today, the growth of cities is threatening the sites of many famous Civil War battlefields, including Gettysburg and Petersburg. Imagine that you own property on the site of Gettysburg. A developer has offered to buy your land and plans to build a factory. In your journal, write your thoughts about the offer.

Alternative Assessment

Writing a play Divided loyalties, especially in the Border States, led brothers, cousins, and fathers and sons to fight on different sides in the Civil War. With several classmates, write a one-act play about the reunion of a divided family after the war.

❶ Decide who the family members are, where they live, what they did before the war, and what role they played on which side in the war.

❷ As part of the play, have each person describe an event in which he or she took part. It might be a battle, an aspect of the war effort at home, or Lee's surrender. Use the information in the text and do additional research as needed to provide background.

❸ When your play is complete, present it to the class.

Your work will be evaluated on the following criteria:
• you describe historical events and attitudes accurately
• you include both Union and Confederate views in the dialogue
• you present the characters and action in believable ways

Bull Run by Paul Fleischman

Bull Run, the first battle of the Civil War, took place 26 miles (42 km) outside of Washington, D.C. In his novel, *Bull Run,* author Paul Fleischman creates "eyewitnesses" who tell a vivid story of the battle—a doctor, an enslaved woman, a photographer, two soldiers, and Edmund Upwing, an African American carriage driver. In the following passage, Upwing tells of driving two congressmen and their wives to watch the Union army crush the Rebels. Like the scores of other picnickers who come to watch the "fun," Upwing's passengers experience the shock of their lives.

Morning

nags:
worn-out
horses

daft:
foolish

'Twas dark as Hell's cellar when we left for Washington. I'd thought they would sleep, but they chattered like sparrows. I caught a good deal of it, as usual. Cabmen dull witted as their nags? Don't be daft! They know more of Washington than the President. Though whenever a question is put to me, I ignore it until it's asked a fourth time, that my passengers mightn't suspect I have ears.

There were plenty of other spectators heading south. The shooting commenced as we neared Centreville. We passed through the village and found a fine grassy spot on a hill overlooking Bull Run. Every last horse and buggy for hire in Washington seemed to be there. Linen tablecloths were spread out and people of quality spread out upon 'em. My passengers were in a merry mood—all but one of the men who let out that McDowell had been given command for no better reason than that he'd come from Ohio, whose governor had Lincoln's ear and had

feigned:
pretended

whispered "McDowell" in it constantly. 'Tis a fact. I feigned deafness, but took the precaution of noting our fastest route of retreat.

Afternoon

teamsters:
wagon drivers
who hauled
goods

The shout went 'round, "The Rebels are upon us!" The words struck the picnickers like a storm, sent them shrieking into their coaches, and sent every coach bolting toward the road. My riders commanded that I put on all speed. Every driver heard the same demand. The road was narrow and choked with coaches. This mass of wheels and whips blocked the soldiers, who seemed even more eager than we to be gone. They were furious with us. How their teamsters swore! Those on foot rushed around us like an April torrent. They were bloody, dusty, and wild-eyed as wolves. "The Black Horse Cavalry is coming!" one bellowed. The air rang with rumors of hidden batteries, heartless horsemen, rivers

This sketch of the chaos as Union forces fled Bull Run appeared in a British newspaper, the *Illustrated London News.* Illustrated newspapers sent out "special artists" to cover events of the war.

red with blood, and visions worthy of the Book of Revelation. One frantic soldier cut a horse free from a wagon's team and took off bareback. Another fugitive tried to unseat me. I drove him off with my whip. 'Tis a fact. Then there came a terrific boom. Women screamed. A Rebel shell had fallen on the road. The caravan halted. The way was blocked by a tangle of overturned wagons. The soldiers scattered or froze in fear. Men fled their buggies. A second shell struck. Then a young officer galloped up, leaped down, and dragged the vehicles away. His courage was acclaimed. We jerked forward afresh. My sharp ear learned that the man's name was Custer. All predicted that he was destined for great deeds.

Book of Revelation: the last book of the Bible, which tells about the end of the world

Night

Rain came on during the night. It soaked the men, turned the roads to muck, and added more misery to the retreat. It was past midnight when we reached Washington. . . . How my passengers railed against the soldiers! And their know-nothing officers, and the profiteers, and the press, and the generals, and the President. I learned later that week that Jeff Davis and Beauregard were pulled to pieces the same way for not pressing on toward Washington. A few days after the battle, Lincoln sent McDowell packing. This raised spirits some, but not everyone's. I heard that Horace Greeley himself, the most powerful editor in the land—who'd first told Lincoln to let the South secede, then insisted that Richmond be taken—now had sent Lincoln a letter stating that the Rebels couldn't be beaten! The winds blew fickle about the President, but he had his feet on the ground. I'm proud to say he ignored the letter.

fickle: changeable in loyalty

A Closer Look

1. How does the author's portrayal of Upwing and his passengers help paint a picture of the scene?

2. Do you think Upwing shares his passengers' expectation that the Union will win quickly? Explain.

3. How does Upwing view public opinion about the war?

Chapter 19

Reconstruction

Sections

Beginning the Story with Susie King Taylor

1. **Rebuilding the Union**
2. **The South Under Reconstruction**
3. **The Legacy of Reconstruction**

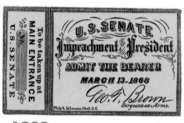

Keys to History

1868

President Johnson's impeachment and trial

Admission ticket for the President's trial

1865

President Lincoln is assassinated

1868

14th Amendment guarantees equality under the law for all

1865   1870   1875

Looking Back

Civil War begins
1861

HISTORY
Mystery

More than 130,000 African Americans could vote in Louisiana in 1896. Four years later Louisiana had only 5,000 African American voters. What happened to all the other voters?

1877
Reconstruction ends
Federal troops leave the South

1880s
Jim Crow laws
An African American being evicted from a train car

1896
Plessy v. *Ferguson*

1905
W. E. B. Du Bois helps launch the Niagara Movement

1880   1895   1900   1905

World **Link**
European powers divide up Africa
1884–1885

Looking Ahead
World War I begins
1914

● **523**

Beginning the Story with

Susie King Taylor

Susie King Taylor wrote about her fellow African Americans during the Civil War, "Oh, how those people prayed for freedom!" Indeed, for the 4 million enslaved people in the United States, the meaning of the war was bound up in that one precious word—freedom. It was dangerous, though, to speak that word aloud. Susie, who was 13 years old and living in Savannah, Georgia, when the war began, remembered when her grandmother went to a church meeting one night. The people gathered at this meeting fervently sang an old hymn that spoke of their longing for freedom. "Yes," they said, "we shall all be free when the Lord shall appear."

At that moment the police burst in and arrested the churchgoers, accusing them of plotting to escape from slavery. The police claimed that when the slaves sang about being free "when the Lord shall appear," they really meant that they would be set free when the Yankees appeared. Although it was the last such meeting that Susie's grandmother attended, she never forgot that night. Susie, too, did not forget her grandmother's story. From that time forward she dreamed of meeting the Yankees herself.

Freedom on the Sea Islands

Susie's chance came in 1862 when Union ships bombarded Fort Pulaski at the entrance to Savannah's harbor. After Union troops captured the fort, General David Hunter promised freedom to all slaves in the area who could escape and reach the Union-controlled Sea Islands off the Georgia coast. Susie later wrote:

❝Two days after the taking of Fort Pulaski, my uncle took his family of seven and myself to St. Catherine Island. We landed under the protection of the Union fleet, and remained there two weeks. . . . At last, to my unbounded joy, I saw the 'Yankee.'❞

On the Sea Islands, Susie met an escaped slave named Edward King. They fell in love and were soon married. Edward King enlisted with other former slaves to form the Union army's first African American regiment, the 33rd U.S. Colored Troops. Susie King joined her new husband, serving as a nurse and laundress in the regiment. Having learned how to read and write as a child, Susie was also in great demand as a teacher. She later wrote of her war years:

African Americans, freed from slavery, are shown here in front of their log cabin after the Civil War. Susie King Taylor lived in a similar home along the coast of Georgia.

"I taught a great many of the comrades in Company E to read and write, when they were off duty. Nearly all were anxious to learn. . . . I gave my services willingly . . . without receiving a dollar."

"Every prospect before you is full of hope"

After the war ended, Commander C. T. Trowbridge disbanded the African American regiment to which Susie's husband belonged. In the commander's final message to the troops, he asked them

"to harbor no feelings of hatred toward your former masters. . . . The church, the school-house, and the right forever to be free are now secured to you, and every prospect [chance for success] before you is full of hope and encouragement. The nation guarantees you full protection and justice."

Susie and Edward King returned to Savannah full of hope. "A new life was before us now," Susie wrote, "all the old life left behind." Still, they could not help but wonder what that new life would hold. Most of all, they wondered how white southerners would now treat their former slaves.

For decades, most white southerners claimed that blacks were an inferior people. With slavery swept away, would whites change their often racist views? Or would the end of slavery be just the first stage of a long struggle for equality?

Hands-On HISTORY

Activity

In the story above, you have read several quotes from Susie King Taylor's own detailed account of her life. Imagine that you are Susie and that you want to write three more entries in your diary. Choose three events in Susie's life from the story you just read and from the chapter to follow. Write what Susie might have felt and thought at these three different moments in her life.

1. Rebuilding the Union

Reading Guide

New Terms **freedmen, Reconstruction, black codes, impeach**

Section Focus **The President and Congress differ over the reconstruction of the South**

1. What challenges did white and black southerners face after the Civil War?
2. What effect did President Johnson's Reconstruction plan have on southerners?
3. Why did Congress fight Johnson for control of Reconstruction policy?

Susie and Edward King were not the only people thinking about the future as the war ended. The entire nation longed for peace. But what kind of peace? A peace that would punish the South for starting the war, or one that would help rebuild the southern states? In his second inaugural address in 1865, President Lincoln spoke of a healing peace:

❝With malice [ill will] toward none, with charity for all, with firmness in the right as God gives us to see the right, let us . . . bind up the nation's wounds . . . [and] do all which may achieve and cherish a just and lasting peace.❞

Lincoln Is Assassinated

The country would never know how Lincoln might have achieved such a "just and lasting peace." On April 14, 1865, only days after the war ended, the President was shot while watching a play at Ford's Theater in Washington, D.C. When Lincoln died the following morning, Andrew Johnson was sworn in as the new President.

Lincoln had been assassinated by John Wilkes Booth, an actor and southerner who sought revenge against Lincoln and the North. Soldiers tracked Booth to a barn in Virginia where he was fatally shot.

The North reacted with sorrow to Lincoln's death. Never before had so many people "shed tears for the death of one they had never seen," wrote poet James Russell Lowell. However, sorrow soon turned to rage. Northerners blamed the South both for the war and for Lincoln's death. From across the North came the cry: "The South must be punished!"

The Defeated South

Northerners did not realize how much the South had already suffered. In addition to the staggering loss of human life, the southern economy had been destroyed. Wherever armies had marched, they had left behind smoking cities, ruined farms, and deserted plantations.

Confederate money was now worthless. Planters, without slaves, did not know how to go on. "There is nothing else I know anything about," said one, "except managing a plantation." With their society shattered, many white southerners found it hard to see a future for themselves.

The Freedmen

Black southerners, on the other hand, were overjoyed by the arrival of peace. For these former slaves, now called **freedmen** (a term that applied to both women and men), peace meant freedom.

The Emancipation Proclamation had abolished slavery in the Confederate states. In 1865 the Thirteenth Amendment freed slaves everywhere in the nation. Until the last day of their lives, freedmen would remember that precious moment when the "freedom sun shone out." Houston Holloway recalled that when he was freed:

> "I felt like a bird out of a cage. Amen. Amen. Amen. I could hardly ask to feel any better than I did that day."

The dilemma of freedom Freedom appeared to open up a new world for former slaves. In the past, a husband and wife could be sold to different owners, never to see each other again. Freedom now meant that marriage could last "until death do us part."

It also meant that African Americans could be paid for their work and could choose how to spend their money.

Freedmen now had the freedom to move, but to where? Some took to the road in a painful search for family members sold away during slavery. Others moved to towns and cities. Susie and Edward King went to Savannah after the war. There they joined a community of freedmen struggling to build new lives.

Wherever they lived, though, most freedmen faced huge problems. Few knew much about the world beyond the plantation. Frederick Douglass described the freedman's desperate situation:

> "He had neither money, property, nor friends. . . . He was turned loose, naked, hungry, and destitute [poor] to the open sky."

After the Civil War, the streets and buildings of Richmond, Virginia, lay in ruins. Many southern cities suffered similar destruction.

It did not take long for the 4 million freedmen to realize that their freedom was very limited. Most were unable to read or write, and had no land or money. Some were even driven from the only home they knew. One angry planter told his former slaves as he pushed them off his land, "The Yankee freed you. Now let the Yankee feed you."

The Freedmen's Bureau

Shortly before the war ended, Congress established the Freedmen's Bureau. This government agency was to give food and medical care to both blacks and whites in the South. Above all else, however, newly freed slaves wanted land and an education. The Bureau tried to provide both.

Schools and land The Freedmen's Bureau worked with educated former slaves and northern churches and charities to open up more than 4,300 schools in the South. Susie King, for example, ran a school for black children in Savannah. The educator and author Booker T. Washington later described the hunger for learning as "a whole race trying to go to school."

Freedmen were also desperate to get land of their own to farm. Congressman Thaddeus Stevens proposed breaking up the South's plantations and giving every freedman "forty acres and a mule." He argued:

The federal government helped African Americans build thousands of schools like this one in the years following the Civil War. Before the war, it had been illegal to teach slaves how to read.

"We have turned . . . loose 4 million slaves without a . . . cent in their pockets. . . . This Congress is bound to provide for them until they can take care of themselves."

Congress, however, refused to take plantations from their owners. Doing so, most congressmen believed, would violate the Constitution's protection of property. As a result, few black southerners were able to obtain land.

Johnson's Plan for the South

After Lincoln's assassination, the task of **Reconstruction**—bringing Confederate states back into the Union—fell to President Johnson. A former Democrat from Tennessee, he favored an easy and smooth return to the Union for the southern states.

In May 1865 Johnson announced his Reconstruction plan. Each southern state could rejoin the Union once it had:

- written a new state constitution
- elected a new government
- repealed its act of secession
- canceled its war debts
- ratified the Thirteenth Amendment, which outlawed slavery in the United States (see page 527)

Republicans in Congress asked the new President to add one more requirement to his list. They wanted freedmen to be guaranteed the right to vote. Johnson ignored their request. "White men alone," he said, "must manage the South."

The First Effort at Reconstruction

By the fall of 1865, every southern state had rejoined the Union under President Johnson's plan. Not surprisingly, leaders of

Link to the Present

Juneteenth On June 19, 1865, the Civil War had been over for more than two months. The Emancipation Proclamation had been law for more than two years. But until Union soldiers landed in Galveston on that day, slaves in Texas had no idea they were free. Their owners had not told them.

Juneteenth is the name given to the day when the last slaves discovered they were free. From Houston to San Francisco, people now celebrate Juneteenth with parades, concerts, and barbecues. It is a way to look back on the struggle and remember that slavery did not end overnight.

the new state governments were often the same men who had held power in the South before the Civil War.

The black codes Once in office, these leaders did their best to bring back the way of life of the old South. They passed laws called **black codes** that set limits on the rights and opportunities of African Americans. Black codes also helped planters find workers to replace their freed slaves. An African American without a job could be arrested and sent to work for a planter.

In fact, the codes barred African Americans from any jobs but farm work and unskilled labor. As a result, Susie King's husband, Edward, could not continue to work as a carpenter after the war. The only job he could find was unloading boats in Savannah's harbor.

The black codes did give certain rights to freedmen: the right to marry, own property, work for wages, and sue in court. Other basic rights, such as serving on juries and owning weapons, were denied in most southern states. No southern states allowed freedmen the right to vote.

Black codes also barred black children from attending the new public schools in the South. According to a Louisiana lawmaker, it made no sense to use public money to educate "any but the superior race of man—the white race."

Johnson vs. Congress

As 1865 came to a close, President Johnson announced that Reconstruction was over. The former Confederate states were once again part of the Union.

Northerners and black southerners were stunned. What Johnson called Reconstruction, critics said, was "no reconstruction at all." They were outraged that the same southern men who had led the nation into its bloodiest war were now back in power. Worse yet, they feared that the black codes in the South would bring back the horrors of slavery in all but name.

Representative Thaddeus Stevens (left) and Senator Charles Sumner (right) introduced many bills in Congress meant to protect the rights of African Americans.

Radical Republicans A group of Republicans in Congress, called Radicals, demanded that the southern states meet stricter requirements for coming back into the Union. In contrast to Johnson's plan, they insisted on full and equal rights for freedmen—a revolutionary idea in both the North and the South in 1865.

Early in 1866 the Radical Republicans, led by Representative Thaddeus Stevens of Pennsylvania and Senator Charles Sumner of Massachusetts, pushed two bills through Congress. One bill extended the life of the Freedmen's Bureau and gave it power to build more schools. A second bill, the Civil Rights Act, declared that freedmen were full citizens with the same rights as white citizens. Johnson vetoed both bills.

The Radical Republicans fought back. They persuaded Congress to act against the President's wishes. For the first time in the nation's history, a two-thirds majority in Congress voted to override a President's vetoes. Both the Freedmen's Bureau Act and the Civil Rights Act became law.

The Fourteenth Amendment Worried that the Supreme Court might overturn the Civil Rights Act, Republicans put the protections of the act into a Fourteenth Amendment. The proposed amendment gave all people born in the United States, including African Americans, the right to "equal protection of the laws." No state could deprive a citizen of "life, liberty, or property without due process of law."

Johnson opposed the amendment. In 1866 congressional elections were to be held. Johnson took his case to the people by touring northern cities and urging voters to elect Democrats. Wherever he spoke, however, he ended up in shouting matches with hecklers. The tour was a disaster. Republicans won control of both houses of Congress. They, not the President, now controlled Reconstruction.

This sketch shows an African American election judge and voters in Washington, D.C., in 1867.

Radical Reconstruction

In 1867 the Radical Republicans passed their own Reconstruction Act. State governments in the South were declared illegal. The region, except Tennessee, was divided into five districts under the control of the army.

To rejoin the Union, each state would have to do the following:

- adopt a constitution guaranteeing all male citizens, black and white, the right to vote
- elect a new government
- ratify the Fourteenth Amendment

No white southerners who had served as Confederate soldiers or officials could vote on the new state constitutions.

Radical Republicans had hoped for more. They wanted to divide up plantations into small farms for black and white southerners and build enough schools for every child in the South. However, these ideas were rejected by the full Congress.

To keep Johnson from stopping the new Reconstruction plan, Congress passed two laws to reduce his power. The Command of the Army Act limited the President's power over the army. The Tenure of Office Act barred Johnson from firing certain federal officials, including those who supported Congress instead of him, without Senate approval.

The Impeachment of Johnson

President Johnson believed both laws were unconstitutional. In February 1868 he fired Secretary of War Edwin Stanton. The House promptly voted to **impeach**—to accuse of wrongdoing and bring to trial—the President. It charged him with violating the Tenure of Office Act.

The President's lawyers argued that the Tenure of Office Act was unconstitutional. His only "crime," they said, had been to disagree with Congress. A two-thirds vote by the Senate was needed to remove him from office. Seven Republicans joined the Senate's Democrats in voting "not guilty." The President escaped removal from office by just one vote. He finished his term, but his power was broken.

1. Section Review

1. Define **freedmen, Reconstruction, black codes,** and **impeach.**

2. How did the Freedmen's Bureau try to help former slaves start a new life?

3. Why did Congress overturn President Johnson's Reconstruction plan?

4. Critical Thinking As an African American, explain why you might have been disappointed by President Johnson's Reconstruction plan.

2. The South Under Reconstruction

Reading Guide

New Terms scalawags, carpetbaggers, corruption

Section Focus **Radical Reconstruction in the South and why it ended**

1. Who were the new voters in the South and how did Congress protect them?
2. What did the southern Reconstruction governments accomplish?
3. How was the Democratic Party able to regain control of the South?

Radical Republicans had clear goals for Reconstruction in the South. With the slave system now dead, they believed they had a rare opportunity to shape "a more perfect Union." They wanted to build a new society based on the equality of all citizens.

The key to equality, Radical Republicans argued, was the right to vote. African Americans could use the ballot to protect their rights. Therefore, ensuring voting rights was central to the Republicans' bold new Reconstruction plan.

The South's New Voters

Under the Reconstruction Act, the army returned to the South in 1867. Its first job was to register voters. Three groups of men registered to vote: African Americans, white southerners who could swear that they had opposed the war, and northerners now living in the South. The law barred from voting anyone who had fought against, or otherwise been disloyal to, the Union.

Freedmen African Americans made up the largest group of new voters. Most joined the Republicans, whom they saw as their protectors. As with new white voters in Andrew Jackson's time, many blacks had no experience in politics. Yet they knew what they wanted. An Alabama convention of freedmen declared:

"We claim exactly the same rights . . . as are enjoyed by white men—we ask for nothing more and will be content with nothing less."

"Scalawags" The army also registered a sizable group of white southerners who swore they had not supported the Confederacy. Some were small farmers who lived in the pro-Union hill areas and had never voted before. Others were southern businessmen who lived in the towns.

A large number of the new white voters joined the Republicans, too. They saw the southern Democrats as the party of wealthy planters, while the Republicans were the party of opportunity and equality.

The South's planters were shocked that they had lost control of the political system. To them, white southerners who joined the party of Lincoln and emancipation were traitors to the South. They scorned such people, calling them **"scalawags,"** or scoundrels.

"Carpetbaggers" The last group of new voters were northerners who had moved south after the war. Some were teachers, ministers, or Freedmen's Bureau agents. Others

Hands-On HISTORY

Getting out the vote Did you know that voter turnout in the United States today is much lower than in most democracies? Only about half of all possible voters actually vote. Those who fail to vote may think their votes do not matter. However, voting does matter. For example, African Americans, voting for the first time, helped President Grant win the 1868 election.

Activity Create a presentation that will persuade people in your community to vote.

1. First, choose the best way to convince people in your area to vote. You might make posters and brochures to display at a mall, or produce a commercial for radio or television.

2. Next, plan your presentation. If you have a registration table, make an attention-getting sign and a brochure explaining why voting counts. If you do a radio or television commercial, write one or make an audio or video tape of one.

3. Show your sign and brochure to the class. If you have a commercial, act it out or play it on audio or video tape for the class.

Young people work to get out the vote.

were businessmen or former Union soldiers looking for new opportunities. Most of them also registered as Republicans.

Yankee-hating southerners called these newcomers **"carpetbaggers,"** after a type of travel handbag. They saw carpetbaggers, often unfairly, as fortune hunters who had come south "to fatten on our misfortunes."

Grant Elected President

The army registered about 635,000 white voters and 735,000 black voters across the South in time for the 1868 election. That year the Republicans nominated Union war hero Ulysses S. Grant. He supported the Republicans' Reconstruction experiment.

The Democrats chose Horatio Seymour, the former governor of New York, as their candidate. Seymour wanted to return power in the South to its traditional leaders—white Democrats.

Grant won the election with the help of an estimated 500,000 African Americans who cast their first votes for the Republican candidate. The Republican Party learned a valuable lesson from the 1868 election—African Americans could contribute heavily to its election victories.

The Fifteenth Amendment Shortly after Grant's election, Congress passed the Fifteenth Amendment guaranteeing former slaves the right to vote. It states that a citizen's right to vote "shall not be denied . . . on account of race, color, or previous condition of servitude." At the time, the right of women to vote was not advanced.

Radical Republicans supported the amendment for two reasons. First, they wanted to make sure that African Americans would retain their right to vote even if the Democrats someday regained power in the South.

Second, many northern states at the time still barred African Americans from voting.

Reconstruction Begins and Ends

State	Readmitted to the Union	Reconstruction government falls
Tennessee	1866	1869
Alabama	1868	1874
Arkansas	1868	1874
Florida	1868	1877
Louisiana	1868	1877
North Carolina	1868	1870
South Carolina	1868	1877
Georgia	1870	1871
Mississippi	1870	1875
Texas	1870	1873
Virginia	1870	1870

Radical Republicans wanted voting rights granted to all men throughout the country. "We will have no peace," wrote one, "until this right is made national."

The Reconstruction Governments

Meanwhile, southern Reconstruction was under way. The first task was to rebuild state governments. Delegates were elected to constitutional conventions in each state. Many were African Americans—mostly educated men such as preachers and teachers.

New constitutions The conventions wrote the most forward-looking state constitutions in the nation. These constitutions outlawed racial discrimination and guaranteed the right to vote to every adult male, regardless of race. They also called for public schools that would be, according to Georgia's constitution, "forever free to all the children of the state."

With the new constitutions ratified, elections were held to fill state offices. To no one's surprise, but to the disgust of the South's traditional leaders, a majority of those elected were Republicans. The new southern legislatures quickly passed the Fourteenth and Fifteenth Amendments.

By 1870 all the former Confederate states had met the requirements of Congress for coming back into the Union. Reconstruction seemed complete, and federal troops withdrew from the South.

African American office-holders The South's new Reconstruction governments included a number of African American officials. In South Carolina, blacks made up a majority of the legislature for two years, and Jonathan J. Wright served for six years on the state supreme court.

Sixteen African Americans served in Congress as well. Of these, 14 men served as representatives in the House, while Mississippi sent Hiram R. Revels and Blanche K. Bruce to the Senate. The conduct of these new legislators impressed Maine's Representative James G. Blaine, who observed:

❝The colored men who took their seats in both the Senate and House . . . [were] earnest, ambitious men, whose public conduct . . . would be honorable to any race.❞

Most whites in the South detested the Reconstruction governments. They resented having had these governments "forced" on them by the much-hated Yankees. Even more they resented seeing former slaves holding public office and talking about equality.

Despite such resentment, Reconstruction governments set to work rebuilding roads and bridges and expanding the South's railroads. They built badly needed schools, as well as hospitals, orphanages, and prisons. Of course, such projects were expensive. To pay for them, the states had to raise taxes.

Pictured above are the seven African Americans who served in Congress in 1872. Twenty years later there was only one African American member of Congress.

Return to "White Man's Rule"

To win support and return their states to "white man's rule," Democrats blamed Republicans for the higher taxes. They also accused them of **corruption**—using public office for illegal purposes. While some officials did line their pockets with tax money, most were honest and capable. Still, as taxes increased, so did resentment of white and black Republican officeholders.

White terrorism Certain whites were willing to use any means necessary to stop blacks from voting and thus return the South to its traditional leaders. They formed secret organizations, such as the White League and the Ku Klux Klan, to terrorize African Americans. The White League declared that "this should be a white man's government, [and] as far as our efforts go, it shall be."

Wearing long, hooded robes, Ku Klux Klan members spread terror by night. They thundered across the countryside on horse-back, warning both black and white Republicans not to vote.

The Klan burned down the homes of Republicans who ignored their threats. African Americans were often beaten and murdered. To combat Klan terrorism Congress passed the Enforcement Acts in 1870 and 1871. These laws directed President Grant to send federal troops back into the most violent areas to protect black voters. Witnesses, however, feared the Klan's revenge and refused to testify. Few terrorists were convicted.

Democrats back in power In 1872 the Amnesty Act forgave former Confederates and gave them back the right to vote. By then, white Republicans were returning to the Democratic Party. The Democrats began to win elections in state after state.

By 1876 Democrats had regained control of all but three southern states. Republicans clung to power in South Carolina, Louisiana, and Florida, but only with the help of federal troops.

Klan members disguised themselves with hoods and robes. These men posed in a professional photography studio in 1868.

The End of Reconstruction

While white terrorism was increasing and Republican power weakening in the South, the North was losing interest in the task of Reconstruction. The Civil War had been over for a decade. It was time, many northerners argued, to "let the South alone."

The disputed 1876 election In 1876 Americans went to the polls to vote for a new President. The Democrats had nominated Governor Samuel J. Tilden of New York. Rutherford B. Hayes from Ohio headed the Republican ticket. Hayes knew that most voters were tired of thinking about Reconstruction, the Klan, and "the everlasting Negro question." In his campaign he had said little about these issues.

When the election returns came in, Hayes was 20 electoral votes short of victory, but 20 electoral votes from 4 states remained in dispute. The Republican-controlled Congress awarded all the disputed electoral votes to Hayes. The Democrats cried foul and threatened to block his inauguration. As Inauguration Day drew near, the nation was without a new President.

The Compromise of 1877 At the last moment, the two parties worked out a compromise. The Democrats agreed to accept Hayes as President. In return, Hayes agreed to give the southern states the right to control their own affairs.

True to his word, President Hayes removed all federal troops from the South. With the army gone, Democrats quickly gained control of the last three southern states. "This is a white man's country," boasted Senator Ben Tillman of South Carolina, "and white men must govern it."

While white southerners cheered the end of Reconstruction, African Americans feared what the future might hold. Henry Adams, a Louisiana freedman, observed sadly:

"The whole South—every state in the South . . . has got into the hands of the very men that held us as slaves.**"**

2. Section Review

1. Define **scalawags, carpetbaggers,** and **corruption.**
2. Under the Republican Reconstruction plan, who could vote in the South and who could not?
3. How did white southern Democrats regain control of state government?
4. Critical Thinking Describe at least two more actions that the government or citizens might have taken to stop the rise of the Klan in the South.

Skill Lab

Using Information
Making Decisions

If President Lincoln had not been assassinated on April 14, 1865, he might have gone down in history as "the Great Reconstructor" as well as "the Great Emancipator." Instead, the question of how to rebuild the Confederate states was left to a new President and to a Congress opposed to that new President's ideas.

Question to Investigate

What was the best way to rebuild the South?

Procedure

Although historical events may seem inevitable to us, many have resulted from deliberate decisions that people have made. Imagine that you are a member of Congress after the Civil War. You must decide whether to support the President's Reconstruction plan or one offered by the Radical Republicans.

1 Identify the problem and your goal.
a. State the problem to be solved.
b. State your goal—what you hope to achieve.

2 Identify the options.
a. Read source **A**.
b. Summarize the two plans.

3 Evaluate each option.
a. Read sources **B** and **C**.
b. List the possible good and bad results of each plan.

4 Choose one option and explain why you chose it.

- When making decisions people often have several options, some better than others. However, there is almost never a perfect solution.
- People base decisions partly on the available facts and partly on their biases, or slanted views.

Sources to Use

A Reread the two plans on pages 529–531.

B "Let us go down to Louisiana. . . . We find the Negro downtrodden. Men are imprisoned for speaking their opinions about Negro suffrage. The worst features of the slave laws are revived. The Rebels . . . are rapidly pushing their state back to the terror and gloom of the [pre-Civil War] period. They know full well that if we [northerners] leave the Negro in their hands . . . they will have little trouble in perpetuating [continuing] a system more degrading than slavery."

From Horace Greeley, *New York Daily Tribune*, November 15, 1865

C "I think if the whole regulation of Negroes, or freedmen, were left to the people of the communities in which they live, it will be administered for the best interest of the negroes as well as of the whites. I think there is a kindly feeling [by white southerners] towards the freedmen. . . . I think there is a willingness to give them every right except the right of suffrage. . . . They will eventually be endowed with that right. It is only a question of time; but it will be necessary to prepare for it by slow and regular means, as the white race was prepared. . . . It would be disastrous to give the right of suffrage now."

By James D. B. De Bow, editor of the New Orleans-based *De Bow's Review* from 1846 to 1867

Option 1
+

Option 2
+

–

3. The Legacy of Reconstruction

Reading Guide

New Terms **tenant farmers, sharecropping, poll tax, grandfather clause, segregation, Jim Crow laws**

Section Focus **The return to power of southern Democrats and its impact on the lives of black southerners**

1. Why did the South remain mostly rural and poor after Reconstruction?
2. What happened to the rights and conditions of black southerners after Reconstruction?
3. In what ways did African Americans respond to segregation and violence?

As Reconstruction ended, southern leaders vowed to build a "New South" that would hum with industry. Under the slogan "Bring the cotton mills to the cotton," they expanded the region's textile industries by nine times between 1880 and 1900. Meanwhile, Birmingham, Alabama, became a major iron-making center.

In 1886 Georgia newspaper editor Henry Grady bragged:

“ We [the South] have . . . put business above politics. We have challenged your spinners in Massachusetts and your iron-makers in Pennsylvania. ”

Despite Grady's boasts, industry in the South did not develop as he had hoped. In the decades following the war, the North would emerge as an industrial giant. Most southerners—both black and white—would remain trapped, however, in a region that was mostly rural and poor.

Life in the "New South"

The South was still staggering from the effects of the Civil War when Reconstruction ended. The average income of southern-

ers was just 40 percent that of northerners. Many whites had lost everything in the conflict—homes, farms, and businesses. Rebuilding crushed lives would be slow work.

Freedmen under freedom For most freedmen, poverty was the unwelcome companion of freedom. They began their new lives, as Frederick Douglass noted, "empty-handed, without money . . . without a foot of land on which to stand."

For Susie King, the struggle to survive was made more difficult by her husband Edward's death. Unable to support herself and her baby on the tiny salary of a teacher, she was forced to find other work. Despite her education, the only job she could get was as a household servant.

Other freedmen also supported themselves as best they could on the pitiful wages they earned. Virginia tobacco workers reported:

“ It is impossible to feed ourselves and family—starvation is certain unless a change is brought about. ”

Tenant farming Once-wealthy planters also faced hard times. With little cash to pay workers, planters had to divide their land into small plots, which they rented to tenant farmers. **Tenant farmers** pay rent for the use of land on which they grow crops. Rather than pay cash, some tenant farmers paid a part—or share—of their crop as rent. This system is known as **sharecropping.**

To landless southerners—both black and white—tenant farming looked promising at first. They hoped to save enough money to buy the land. First, though, they had to borrow money to buy seeds and tools.

Had crop prices been high after the war, these farmers might have been able to repay their loans. Instead, prices fell. By 1900 two-thirds of southern farmers found themselves buried in debts and trapped in the tenant-farming, sharecropping system.

Education in the "New South"

During Reconstruction, many African Americans pinned their hopes for a better future on education. Reconstruction governments responded by opening thousands of public schools in the South.

However, when white southern Democrats regained control of their states, they cut spending on education. "Free schools are not a necessity," explained the governor of Virginia, "they are a luxury . . . to be paid for, like any other luxury, by the people who wish their benefits."

Many southern schools closed down for lack of funds. Others charged fees. By the 1880s, less than 60 percent of white children and 49 percent of black children still attended school in the "New South."

Reversing Reconstruction

Free public education was not the only Reconstruction program that the new southern leaders ended. They also found ways to rob African Americans of what remained of their political power. Freedmen still voted in the South, but white election officials refused to count their votes. A black voter in Georgia observed:

> **"**We are in a majority here, but . . . there's a hole gets in the bottom of the boxes some way and lets out our votes.**"**

New voting laws Still not satisfied, southern whites passed laws in the 1890s that made it even harder for African Americans

Sharecroppers who could not read relied on the landowner to keep records of how much money they owed. Even when harvests were good, they were often told that they owed more to the landowner than they had the year before.

to vote. All citizens now had to pay a **poll tax**—a fee for voting. The tax was set high to make voting, like schooling, a luxury that very few black southerners could afford.

Some southern states also made potential voters pass a literacy test to prove that they could read. A person who failed the test could not vote.

Lawmakers claimed that these laws did not violate the right to vote, since they applied to white voters, too. Whites, though, were protected by a **grandfather clause** in the laws after 1898. This clause said that voting laws did not apply to a man whose father or grandfather could have voted before January 1, 1867. Before that day, of course, only whites had been able to vote.

African Americans appealed to the Supreme Court in 1898 to protect their right to vote under the Fifteenth Amendment. To their shock, the Court ruled against them. The Court accepted the argument that the voting laws were constitutional because they applied equally to blacks and whites.

Jim Crow Laws

During Reconstruction most southern state governments had outlawed **segregation**—the forced separation of races in public places. Once back in power, however, white southern Democrats began to pass segregation laws that whites called **Jim Crow laws.** Whites used the term Jim Crow

African Americans in Congress

1876

■ Senator
■ Representative

1896

Reading Maps

Compare the number of African Americans in the House of Representatives in 1876 and 1896. Explain the difference.

Link to Art

Aspects of Negro Life: From Slavery through Reconstruction (1934)

In Aaron Douglas's striking mural, the story unfolds from right to left. On the right side the Emancipation Proclamation is read in 1863. In response to the news, an enslaved man has broken his chains. The center section pays tribute to black leaders in the South from 1867 to 1876. On the left side black figures fall and the sky darkens as the Ku Klux Klan terrorizes black people after the 1870s. **Discuss** What symbols does Douglas use in "telling" the story? How does he use light and color to enhance the story?

to refer to blacks in an insulting way. In the 1880s one state after another drew a "color line" between blacks and whites.

Point of View

Were Jim Crow laws to be taken seriously?

Most whites in the South welcomed Jim Crow laws. The brave editor of the *News and Courier* in Charleston, South Carolina, was an exception. To convince his readers that segregation was unjust, he tried poking fun at Jim Crow laws. He wrote an article drawing what he thought was an extreme picture of where Jim Crow laws might lead:

"If there must be Jim Crow cars on railroads, there should be Jim Crow cars on the street railways . . . on all passenger boats. . . . Jim Crow waiting saloons [rooms]. . . . Jim Crow eating houses. . . . Jim Crow sections of the jury box, and a . . . Jim Crow Bible for colored witnesses to kiss."

What seemed absurd to the editor was not so ridiculous to other white southerners, and it turned out to be a tragedy for African Americans. In the years to come, nearly all of the editor's ideas actually became law as segregation tightened its grip on the South.

Europeans divide up Africa In 1884

European nations were racing frantically to acquire more colonies. That year the European powers met in Berlin, Germany, to carve up Africa. Soon the continent was under European control. Only Ethiopia and Liberia escaped colonization.

Ethiopia remained an independent kingdom after it defeated an invading Italian army in 1896. Liberia, founded as a home for freed American slaves in 1821, had been a republic since 1847. Whenever Europeans threatened to take over Liberia, the United States would speak up and the Europeans would back down.

Plessy v. Ferguson

Many Americans believed that Jim Crow laws violated the Fourteenth Amendment's guarantee of "equal protection of the laws." When Homer Plessy was arrested for riding in a "whites-only" railroad car in Louisiana, he appealed his case to the Supreme Court.

In 1896 the Supreme Court handed down its decision in *Plessy* v. *Ferguson*. It ruled that segregation laws did not violate the Fourteenth Amendment. Facilities for both races could be separate as long as they were roughly equal.

Only one justice, John Marshall Harlan, disagreed. "Our Constitution is color blind," he wrote. He also warned that Jim Crow laws were deeply destructive. "What can more certainly arouse race hate," he asked, than these laws?

The Supreme Court's support for segregation in *Plessy* v. *Ferguson* led to a flood of new Jim Crow laws. Despite the "separate but equal" rule, though, schools and parks for whites were always better than those set aside for blacks.

The color line drawn between black and white southerners was to remain firmly in place for decades. In fact, segregation was the law of the South until 1954, when the Supreme Court finally ruled in *Brown* v. *Board of Education* that racial segregation is unconstitutional.

Responses to Segregation

As the noose of segregation tightened in the South, African Americans responded in a variety of ways. Some bravely disobeyed segregation laws. Others left the South for new homes in the North and West. Still others looked for ways to work together to improve opportunities and protect the rights of African Americans.

Open disobedience Some African Americans refused to obey Jim Crow laws. To do so, however, was dangerous. Almost 3,000 black southerners were lynched—killed by mobs—between 1892 and 1903. Most were lynched because they refused to accept segregation and "white rule."

Jim Crow laws kept blacks and whites separated for many years. This photo of a public fountain was taken in 1950 in North Carolina.

Migration Rather than put up with segregation and violence, many thousands of African Americans left the South. Some moved to the North. Susie King, for example, moved to Boston with her son. There she met and married her second husband, Russell Taylor.

Some freedmen headed west. Benjamin "Pap" Singleton organized the "Exodus of 1879"—a migration of black southerners to Kansas. Within two years close to 40,000 African Americans had moved to Kansas. Life on the plains had its hardships, but as one "Exoduster" put it, "We had rather suffer and be free."

In 1878 a group of 200 freedmen decided that "the colored man had no home in America." They chartered a ship and sailed to Liberia, a West African nation founded by freed American slaves in the 1820s. Still, few African Americans chose to leave the United States. "We are not Africans now," wrote one, "but colored Americans, and are entitled to American citizenship."

Self-help The majority of black southerners remained in the South where they had the support of their families, churches, and a close-knit community. Believing that their best hope lay in education, they built many schools and colleges. By 1900 more than 1.5 million African American children were attending school. In the South's 29 black colleges, students were preparing to become teachers, lawyers, and doctors.

Two approaches to change No African American believed more strongly in the power of education and self-help than

A teacher and his students work in a laboratory at the Tuskegee Institute in 1903. The college continues to serve African Americans, with over 3,000 students enrolled today.

the educator Booker T. Washington. In 1881 he founded the Tuskegee Institute in Alabama to teach practical skills such as farming and carpentry. Washington urged his students to worry less about the injustice of segregation and racial violence, and more about getting education and jobs.

Other African Americans disagreed. They were led by another outspoken black educator, William E. B. Du Bois [doo-BOYS] of Atlanta University. Unlike the more cautious Washington, Du Bois urged blacks to stand up against discrimination and demand equality. Black southerners needed leaders who would demand equal opportunities, Du Bois argued, or many jobs would remain out of their reach.

In 1905 Du Bois met with other African American reformers to form a national organization called the Niagara Movement. Five years later, this movement gave birth to the National Association for the Advancement of Colored People (NAACP).

The Failure of Reconstruction

Du Bois could not know how long and difficult the struggle would be. In the decades that followed Reconstruction, white southerners had erected cruel barriers of segregation to strip African Americans of their rights and opportunities.

During the same period, most white southerners, too, had failed to prosper. Only many years later would opportunity and equality finally come to the South.

3. Section Review

1. Define **tenant farmers, sharecropping, poll tax, grandfather clause, segregation,** and **Jim Crow laws.**
2. Explain how the right to vote was denied to black southerners.
3. How did Booker T. Washington's ideas for bettering African American lives differ from those of William E. B. Du Bois?
4. Critical Thinking As a black southerner, how would you have responded to Jim Crow laws, and why?

Why We Remember

Reconstruction

In 1898 Susie King Taylor returned to the South after many years in Boston. On that journey she rode in Jim Crow railroad cars, and heard stories about African Americans being beaten and murdered. "Each morning you can hear of some Negro being lynched," a porter told her. "We have no rights here." Taylor was outraged. "Was the [Civil] war in vain?" she asked. "Has it brought freedom, in the full sense of the word, or has it not made our condition hopeless?"

Looking back at Reconstruction, it is easy to understand and even share Taylor's bitterness. After the Civil War, the world had seemed full of hope to Taylor and her fellow freedmen. With support from the Republican Congress until 1876, the South's Reconstruction governments had built schools and granted voting rights to help make African Americans full and equal citizens.

Still, racism proved stronger than Congress's laws. The chance to breathe new life into the nation's ideals of freedom and equality was lost. These ideals were not, however, forgotten. The belief that all people deserve the same opportunities and rights was kept alive by black families, churches, and schools. Even in the worst moments, Taylor believed that some day blacks and whites would live as equal citizens in America. "I know I shall not live to see the day," she wrote, "but it will come." This faith that the nation could overcome racism and live up to its ideals would be Reconstruction's most hopeful legacy.

Geography Lab

The Civil War and Southern Agriculture

Visitors to the South at the end of the Civil War described it as "almost a desert." The farmland was a ruin of burned buildings, trampled crops, and dead livestock. Use the photo and the tables to understand some of the war's effects on southern agriculture.

Union troops dig into the hillside of a plantation.

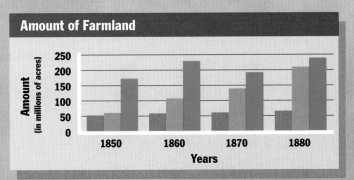

Amount of Farmland

Amount (in millions of acres)

250
200
150
100
50
0

1850   1860   1870   1880

Years

Source: *Historical Statistics of the United States*

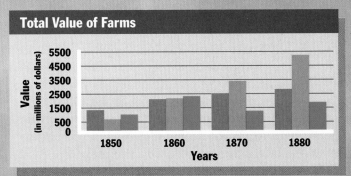

Total Value of Farms

Value (in millions of dollars)

5500
4500
3500
2500
1500
500
0

1850   1860   1870   1880

Years

Source: *Historical Statistics of the United States*

Link to History

1. How did farm values change between 1850 and 1880 in the Northeast and North Central regions?

2. How did the value and amount of farmland in the South change between 1860 and 1870? Give at least three reasons for the change.

3. From 1850 to 1880 which region had the largest increase in the amount of farmland?

4. **Hands-On Geography** Imagine that you and your family must turn the land shown in the photo back into productive farmland. You have very little cash. Create a three-step plan to restore your farmland. Explain the plan and the reasons that you chose this plan.

Chapter Survey

Reviewing Vocabulary

Define the following terms.
1. freedmen
2. Reconstruction
3. black codes
4. impeach
5. scalawags
6. carpetbaggers
7. corruption
8. tenant farmers
9. sharecropping
10. poll tax
11. grandfather clause
12. segregation
13. Jim Crow laws

Reviewing Main Ideas

1. What was life like for freedmen immediately after the Civil War?
2. (a) Why did the Radical Republicans want to take control of Reconstruction? (b) How did they get that control?
3. (a) Who were the South's new voters and officeholders? (b) What did the Reconstruction governments accomplish?
4. Describe the events that led to the return of "white man's rule" in the South.
5. Why did southern farmers turn to sharecropping, and what were the results?
6. What were three ways that southern Democrats reversed the gains that African Americans made during Reconstruction?
7. How did African Americans respond to their treatment after Reconstruction?

Thinking Critically

1. **Analysis** Most white southerners resented Reconstruction, while many white northerners gave up on it. Why did the two groups take these positions?
2. **Evaluation** If you had been an African American in the South in the late 1800s, how might you have responded to the rising tide of segregation? Why?
3. **Why We Remember: Synthesis** Susie King Taylor once asked, "Was the [Civil] war in vain?" How would you have responded at the time, and today?

Applying Skills

Making decisions The specific problems that people face today are different from those faced by people in the United States after the Civil War. However, the basic need to solve problems by making decisions has never changed. Think about a problem you need to solve in your own life. It does not have to be a big problem, but its solution should require careful thought. Use what you learned on page 537 to decide on the best solution to the problem. Then write the following:
• a description of the problem
• steps you took in making the decision
• why you made the decision you did

History Mystery

Voting in the South Answer the History Mystery on page 523. How might such a decline in voting by African Americans after 1896 have been prevented?

Writing in Your History Journal

1. **Keys to History** (a) The time line on pages 522–523 has seven Keys to History. In your journal, describe why each one is important to know about. (b) What three events from the chapter would you add to the time line? Write those events and their dates in your journal, and tell why you think each event should be added.
2. **Susie King Taylor** People often "vote with their feet" rather than stay in a difficult or dangerous situation. In your journal, describe the times when Taylor did this. Then write responses to the following questions: What do her choices tell you about Taylor as a person? Did she make the right choice in each case? Why or why not?

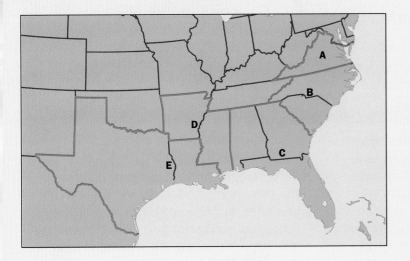

1. Each letter on the map represents one of five military districts in which former Confederate states, except Tennessee, were divided. After each letter, write the name of the state or states in the district.

2. Geographic Thinking In looking back at Chapters 17 and 19, what factors determined the organization and use of farmland in the South before and after the Civil War? Give at least three reasons why these changes occurred.

3. Thinking Historically Reread the editor's opinions in the Point of View on page 541 and review the Supreme Court's decision in *Plessy* v. *Ferguson* on page 542. In your journal, write down the thoughts and ideas that you would want to express to the editor and to all southerners about Jim Crow laws and the Court's decision.

Alternative Assessment

Citizenship: Improving on Reconstruction Imagine that a few days from now, you will travel back through time to the Washington, D.C., of 1867. There, you will present to the members of Congress a "new and improved" Reconstruction plan. The purpose of your plan is to answer the critics of Johnson's 1865 plan while preventing the problems that you have learned will result if the Radical Republicans have their way.

Work with a partner to develop the Reconstruction plan and present it to Congress (your classmates).

In your presentation:

❶ Explain what roles former Confederate soldiers, officials, and supporters will play.

❷ Tell what rights freedmen will gain.

❸ Explain how those rights will be protected under your plan.

❹ Describe what will be done to improve the lives of all southerners.

❺ Tell what the federal government will do to make your Reconstruction a success.

❻ Include the costs of your Reconstruction and how they will be paid.

Your presentation will be evaluated on the following criteria:
• it shows a knowledge of Reconstruction
• it offers creative yet practical solutions to the challenges of the historical period
• it is clear and convincing

Unit Survey

Making Connections

1. From 1850 to 1876, the nation struggled over the issues of slavery, secession, and Reconstruction. Could these issues have been solved in any other way than they were? Use examples to explain your answer.
2. What similarities do you suppose Southerners saw between secession and the American Revolution? What differences might Northerners have seen?

3. Although the Constitution balances the powers of the legislative and executive branches, at different times one or the other has been stronger. Which branch was stronger during the 1850s? During the Civil War? During Reconstruction? Why do you think these shifts occurred?

Linking History, Geography, and Art

Your State in the Civil War

Did armies clash on the soil of your state between 1861 and 1865? Or was your state less directly involved in the war that split our nation? Even if your state was not yet a state, it was somehow affected by the Civil War. Find out how. Present what you learn in a pictorial map.

Project Steps

Work with a group.

❶ Choose one or two topics on which to focus. Here are some possibilities:
• battles that were fought in your state
• production of food, weapons, or other supplies in your state
• military or political leaders who came from your state
• citizens of your state who went to war
• contributions to the war effort by various organizations in your state
• effects of fighting, blockades, etc.

❷ Gather information about your topics. Start with this book. Then check your school or local library or the local historical society. Some students' families might

have information—even photographs, letters, or other items to copy.

❸ Draw a large map of your state as it existed during the Civil War. Draw the map to scale, and include cities, land and water features, and any war-related features, such as battle sites or supply routes. Display the map on the bulletin board.

❹ Prepare pictorial or descriptive items and arrange them around the state map. Here are some possibilities:
• graphs
• drawings, paintings, or photographs
• letters or diary entries
• newspaper or magazine headlines, articles, or political cartoons
• descriptions of the events or the effects of the war
   If an item relates to a specific place, use pushpins and yarn to connect the item to the correct spot on the map.

Thinking It Over How would you explain the fascination that the Civil War has for modern-day Americans? What aspect of the war do you find most interesting? Why?

How Do We Know?

Metal detectors played a crucial role in researching the true story of the Battle of the Little Bighorn.

Scholar's Tool Kit
Technology

One of the most dramatic incidents in American history is commonly known as Custer's Last Stand. On June 25, 1876, the U.S. Cavalry battled Sioux and Cheyenne warriors on the banks of the Little Bighorn River. For more than a century scholars have tried to understand how the warriors could destroy the elite 7th Cavalry led by the famous Civil War general, George Armstrong Custer. Recently, researchers using state-of-the-art metal detectors at the battle site have made discoveries that shed new light on the events of that fateful June day.

Custer's Last Stand?

Because none of the troopers with Custer survived the battle, the only witnesses were the victorious Indians. They reported that the attacking soldiers caught them by surprise. After some initial confusion, angry warriors urged by Sitting Bull, Crazy Horse, Two Moons, and Lame White Man rushed toward the soldiers to defend their families. The battlefield became a nightmare of dust, smoke, gunshots, and war cries. Arrows and bullets began to rain down on the soldiers, who had paused in their attack to look for a place to cross the river. Frightened cavalry horses started to break free from the soldiers holding them.

Perhaps surprised by the bold Indian counterattack, the soldiers with Custer failed to put up much of a defense. Instead, many pan-icked and ran away. According to Iron Hawk, a Sioux warrior, "Custer's

Red Horse, an eyewitness, made several drawings of the battle. What do you learn about his view of what happened?

? Critical Thinking

1. Why did the American public refuse to believe Indian accounts? Why do you think opinions of the battle have changed over time?

men in the beginning shot straight, but later they shot like drunken men, firing into the ground, into the air, wildly in every way."

Neither the U.S. Army nor the American public was willing to accept Indian accounts of the battle. They preferred to believe that Sitting Bull had lured the soldiers into a trap. The doomed battalion had fought bravely to the end, with Custer and a handful of troopers making a heroic last stand. This story, it turns out, is largely a myth, but it remained unchallenged for over 100 years.

Using Technology to Study the Battle Site

The evidence that revealed the truth about the battle came from scientific analysis of the battlefield. In 1983 a fire burned away the brush covering the Little Bighorn battlefield. It enabled military historians to use modern technology to find an explanation for the Custer disaster. These scholars studied the battlefield like police officers investigating the scene of a murder.

The scholars' primary research tool was the metal detector, which they used to scan a major portion of the battlefield. They found approximately 1,700 metal artifacts, mostly iron arrowheads, empty shell casings made of brass, and lead bullets.

The bullets and shell casings were taken to a laboratory for examination. With the aid of powerful microscopes, scientists studied and photographed the firing-pin marks and other scratches on the empty cartridge cases. They also examined the grooves on the lead bullets caused by the gun barrels. As a result, the scientists could identify the weapons the soldiers and Indians used, as well as where on the

? Critical Thinking

2. Archaeologists, anthropologists, medical examiners, lab technicians, computer scientists, and historians all took part in the investigation. Explain the role that each might have played.

battlefield the weapons were used. For instance, when an Indian or soldier fired his gun, he usually ejected the shell casing, reloaded, and then moved to another position and fired again. At each spot, the rifleman left behind an empty shell casing identified through the scratches caused by the ejecting mechanism.

? Critical Thinking

3. The battle site is located in what used to be called Custer Battlefield National Monument. Why do you think the name was changed to Little Bighorn National Monument in 1991?

Telling the Story of the Battle

The arrowheads, shell casings, and bullets were carefully plotted on a detailed grid of the battlefield. Researchers could then see certain clusters of artifacts. These clusters told a surprising story about the course of the battle.

One surprise was that the Indians were better armed than anyone had suspected. Many had repeating rifles, while the soldiers had only single-shot carbines. Another surprise was that Custer's men did relatively little shooting. Evidence indicates that the troopers with Custer at first maintained good order. Then the troop formations rapidly fell apart, as some troopers evidently panicked and fled. Scholars now believe that superior Indian fire power and the breakdown of troop unity both contributed to the disaster.

Scholars also believe that the first Indian accounts of the battle were reliable. The archaeological evidence contradicts none of the early Indian testimony. By itself each shell casing, bullet, or arrowhead found on the battlefield was relatively unimportant. As a group, they unlocked the mystery that has surrounded the Battle of the Little Bighorn.

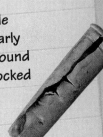

Scholar at Work

Conflicting stories are always a problem for historians. Today, technology such as tape recorders and video cameras can aid in gathering data for interpretation. Choose an incident at your school or in the community that has caused controversy. Work with a group to videotape interviews with at least three witnesses. Review the tapes and write a history of the event based on your interpretation of the accounts.

Unit 7

Chapters

Hands-On   *HISTORY*

Activity

This illustrated map of a bustling city in 1900 provides a bird's-eye view of its railroads, houses, churches, and factories. Imagine that you are looking down at the town in which you live from a similar viewpoint—perhaps a hill, a tall building, or an airplane. From such a viewpoint, draw a map that shows major buildings, roads, airports, bodies of water, and other features of your town that would be of interest to visitors. How might a map drawn in 1900 differ from your map?

*Panoramic View,
City of Cincinnati, U.S.A., 1900
by J. L. Trout*

New Horizons

Chapter *20*

The Changing West

Keys to History

1867
First cattle drive over the Chisholm Trail

1869
First transcontinental railroad completed at Promontory Point

1862
Congress passes the Homestead Act
Steel plow

1860

Looking Back

The Trail of Tears
1838

World  Link

New Zealand Maoris found Pai Marire movement
1864

HISTORY *Mystery*

In the eastern half of the United States, 160 acres of farmland was plenty to support a family. Farmers with 160 acres on the plains found it hard to survive. Why?

1890
Massacre at
Wounded Knee

1876
The Battle of the Little Bighorn
Sioux quiver with bow and arrows

1887
Congress passes
the Dawes Act

1895
Only about
1,000 buffalo
left in North
America

1880

1900

Looking Ahead

Panama Canal opens
1914

● **555**

Beginning the Story with

Quanah Parker

When Cynthia Ann Parker was a little girl living in Texas in 1836, a Comanche raiding party swooped down on the Parker ranch and carried her off. The Comanches raised Cynthia Ann, calling her Naudah, and in time she forgot her former life. She married a Comanche warrior and had three children. One of them she named Quanah.

When Quanah was still a young boy, Texas Rangers attacked his village and recaptured his mother. Although Cynthia Ann wanted to return to her Comanche family, she was forced to stay with her white relatives in Texas. Several years later she died, some say of a broken heart.

A Comanche Chief

Quanah grew up to become a famous warrior and a chief of his tribe. Although he fought to keep his people free, the Comanches were eventually forced to move onto a reservation in Oklahoma.

Indians looked up to Quanah because he learned how to deal with white people. Speaking of Quanah's wisdom a Comanche man said, "He has things, as it were, written on his tongue. What he learns from the government he writes on his tongue, and we learn from him." Another Comanche said of Quanah, "He is just like light. You strike a match in a dark room and there is light. That is the way with Quanah. Wherever he is there is light."

Although Quanah valued many of the ways of white people, he remained true to Comanche culture. He wore his hair in braids. He also kept several wives, even though the government wanted him to have only one. "You pick out the one who should be my only wife," he challenged when government officials pressed the issue. "I have had children by all my wives. I love them equally and I love my children and care for them equally."

Quanah earned the respect of the government officials. One official said:

Quanah Parker stands with his wife Tonarcy on the porch of their Oklahoma ranch house.

"If ever nature stamped a man with the seal of headship, she did it in this case. Quanah would have been a leader and a governor in any circle where fate might have cast him. It is in his blood."

Although Quanah had fought to keep settlers off the Comanche reservation, the white people of Texas and Oklahoma respected him, too. They admired his honesty and pride. They saw that he had adapted to changes in the West, yet he always spoke up for his people.

Texas ranchers were especially grateful to Quanah because he allowed them to pasture their livestock on the rich grass of the Comanche reservation. The arrangement gave the Comanches a much-needed income. In appreciation the ranchers built Quanah a large ranch house on the reservation. There he welcomed Indian and white visitors alike.

A Man of Two Worlds

Quanah's name comes from the Comanche word *kwaina*, which means fragrant. As an adult and after his tribe moved onto the reservation, he added Parker to his name in honor of the mother he had lost. Thereafter, he was known as Quanah Parker, a man of two peoples, a man of two worlds.

Quanah never forgot his mother. He asked to visit her grave in Texas, but her family kept him away. At last, however, the Parker family allowed him to move Cynthia Ann's remains to his home in Oklahoma. There she was reburied in a graveside service conducted by Baptists and Mennonites.

Quanah gave a brief speech of thanks to the many Comanche and white friends who had come to witness the ceremony. He spoke first in Comanche and then in English. Quanah told the hushed crowd that his mother loved Indians so well, she did not want to go back to her white folks. That was all right, he said, because "we are all the same people anyway."

Hands-On HISTORY

Activity

Quanah was the last Comanche chief to surrender to life on a reservation. He became the most successful of Indian chiefs at negotiating with the whites for favorable conditions for his people. As he gave up the skills of the warrior, what new skills do you think Quanah had to develop? List or describe three such skills and explain how each might have been useful to Quanah.

1. Mining and Railroads

Reading Guide

New Term extermination

Section Focus How mining and railroads disrupted the lives of Plains Indians

1. How did life for Plains Indians change after 1850?
2. How did mining affect the West?
3. What role did the transcontinental railroad play in developing the West?

To the early pioneers, like the mountain men you read about in Chapter 14, the homeland of Quanah Parker and the Plains Indians was little more than endless miles of grass, rattlesnakes, and buffalo. They were content to leave this "desert" to the nomadic Indian tribes who spent their lives on horseback, following the movement of the buffalo.

In the second half of the 1800s, these attitudes changed. Miners swept through the plains looking for valuable minerals. Next came railroad lines, connecting mining towns in the West to cities in the East and Midwest. Settlers soon followed.

Suddenly the "Great American Desert" became more than just a wasteland to be crossed on the way to the Far West. It was a place of opportunity for settlers. This was a problem for the Plains Indians who already lived there. Their way of life clashed with the settlers' hunger for land, and before long conflicts between the two groups broke out.

John Mix Stanley was traveling with an army survey party when he saw this herd of bison. Such large herds had vanished by the 1880s.

Buffalo on the Plains

Before the settlers came, the Great Plains supported some 30 different Indian tribes. The region was also home to millions of bison, usually called "buffalo."

These large, shaggy creatures were the lifeblood of the Plains Indians. They provided the Indians with food, shelter, tools, ornaments, and even toys. When Plains Indians died they expected to go to a land teeming with buffalo. Some said the broad trail of stars across the sky that we call the Milky Way was dust raised by the hoofs of buffalo herds in the spirit world.

The Fort Laramie Treaty

In the 1850s miners swarmed across the Great Plains on their way to the countless river valleys and mountains of the West. As they went they trespassed on Plains Indian land, trampling the buffalo range and killing the animals for food and sometimes just for sport. The Indians resented the miners and their disrespect for the Indian way of life. They began to wage war.

In an attempt to reduce conflict and protect the travelers, the government decided to strike a bargain with the Indians. In 1851 government officials met with between 8,000 and 12,000 Indians from 8 tribes at Fort Laramie, in what is now Wyoming. There the officials convinced the Indian representatives to sign the Treaty of Fort Laramie.

The treaty gave the government the right to build more roads and forts on the plains. It also defined geographical boundaries within which the Indian tribes could hunt. The government agreed to make yearly payments to the Indians, and promised the tribes that they could live and hunt on this land forever. As you will read, Fort Laramie was the first of many treaties that the United States government made with the Plains Indians—but did not honor.

Government officials and Indian leaders met at Fort Laramie in 1851 and again in 1868, above, to try to bring peace to the plains.

Western Mines

In the 1860s miners continued to cross the plains in full force, desperately hunting for gold. No spot was too hot, too dry, too cold, or too wet to discourage people hoping to strike it rich. Miners swarmed through the Rockies, the Sierra Nevada, and the Black Hills. They braved the scorching sands of Arizona and New Mexico as well as the frosty waters of Alaska.

The Comstock Lode One of the biggest finds was in Nevada in 1859. A group of miners had found a little gold on a hillside, but were frustrated by dark blue sand and a gummy soil that slowed their work. When they had the soil tested, the men got the shock of their lives. The soil was almost pure silver. The gold and silver ore in the deposit was worth $3,200 to $4,800 a ton.

The find was called the Comstock Lode for Henry Comstock, a prospector who bragged that he had discovered it all. Comstock's claims were only a small part of one of the richest mineral fields ever found in the West. Comstock sold one claim for only $11,000 and another for two mules. Eventually, the Comstock Lode made others very wealthy. It produced more than $300 million in gold and silver.

Comstock's story was not unusual. Individual prospectors—people who search for gold and silver and other precious ores—rarely got rich. It took expensive machinery and skilled mining engineers to extract the valuable minerals that lay like gigantic spider webs within the mountains of the West. The people who made the great mining fortunes were investors in large companies that bought the rights to the mines from the prospectors who discovered them.

Boomtowns

Despite the odds against striking it rich, hordes of hopeful prospectors rushed to each new site. Within days, mining camps would spring up in areas that had been mostly barren and desolate land. The camps were little more than tents and shacks built in a matter of days. They were known as "boom and bust" towns, because when the gold or silver was gone they disappeared as quickly as they had appeared.

The cycle of boom and bust repeated itself over and over. In 1857 newspaperman J. Ross Browne described the creation of Gila City in present-day Arizona:

❝Enterprising men hurried to the spot with barrels of whiskey and billiards tables, . . . ready-made clothing, and fancy wares. Traders crowded in with wagons of pork and beans. Gamblers came with cards and Monte [gambling] tables. There was everything in Gila City within a few months but a church and a jail.❞

Seven years later Gila City was a ghost town. All that remained, Browne wrote, were "three chimneys and a coyote."

Although most prospectors got little more than calluses on their hands for their efforts, they did leave behind a legacy of colorful place names such as Ground Hog's Glory, Miller's Defeat, Bogus Thunder, Poverty, and Deadman's Bar. A few of these boomtowns, such as Denver and Reno, survived the cycle and grew into cities.

Justice in the mining camps Keeping order in the mining camps was a challenge. Gold strikes meant quick money, which attracted gamblers, thieves, and outlaws. Crime and fighting were common. Many towns had no jails, so the options for punishment were often banishment, whipping, or death. One young man in California wrote a letter describing his fate:

❝Dear Friend:
I take this opportunity of writing these few lines to you hoping to find you in good health me and Charley is sentenced to be hung today at 5 o'clock for a robbery good by give my best to Frank and Sam and Church.
John Bucroft❞

Placerville, California, held so many hangings it was called "Hangtown." In Montana, citizens hanged a sheriff when they learned he was the leader of an outlaw gang. They also hanged 24 members of the gang.

The Transcontinental Railroad

As more and more Americans settled in the West, they needed fast and reliable transportation to carry people and supplies back and forth. In 1862 President Lincoln signed the Pacific Railway Bill. It called for a

In 1860—two years after prospectors discovered gold in the area—Denver's population was 4,500. A railroad line completed in 1870 helped the town grow as a supply center for nearby mines. Today, Denver is the chief commercial city of the Rocky Mountain area.

transcontinental railroad linking the Atlantic and Pacific coasts. Trains on this line could cross the country in just one week instead of taking a whole month, as stagecoaches had.

The transcontinental railroad was to be built by the Union Pacific and the Central Pacific railroad companies. To help the companies pay for the huge project, the government donated the land for the tracks and gave the companies sections of free land in return for every mile of track they laid. The government also loaned the companies money at low interest rates.

The Union Pacific began building westward from Omaha, Nebraska. The Central Pacific started in Sacramento, California. The two companies raced to see which could lay the most track—and earn the most free land from the government.

Building the railroad Building the transcontinental railroad was dangerous, backbreaking, and low-paying work. The two crews laid from 2 to 5 miles (3 to 8 km) of track each day, and it took them 6 years to finish the project.

Most of the workers were immigrants to the United States, eager for work. The Union Pacific employed as many as 10,000 laborers from Ireland. They had to fight off numerous attacks by Plains Indians who resented the workers for trespassing. They also had to cut through the Rocky Mountains.

The Central Pacific hired about 10,000 men as well, most of whom were Chinese. They learned about the project through pamphlets the company handed out in China. Central Pacific workers dynamited tunnels through solid rock. They marked their progress in inches a day as they laid track across the snowcapped Sierra Nevada. One winter they shoveled a path through drifts of snow 50 feet (15 meters) deep to lay track on the frozen ground.

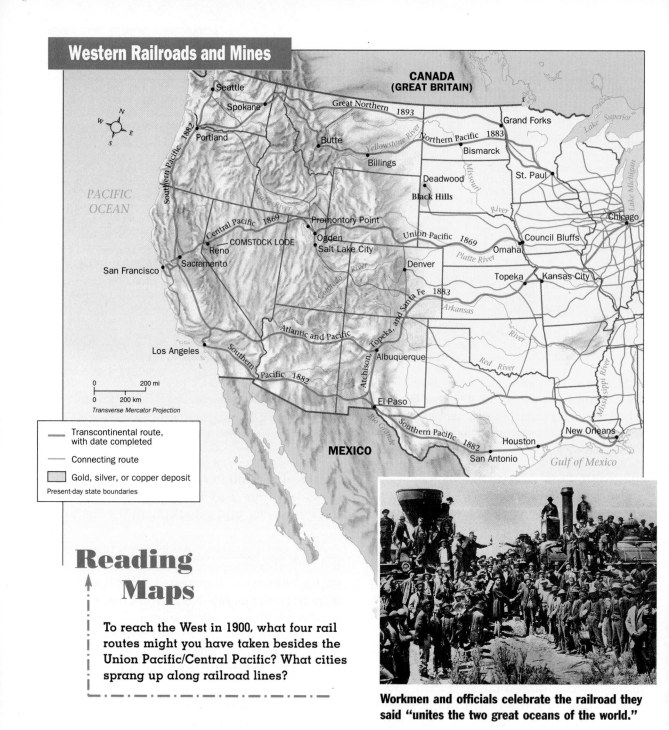

Western Railroads and Mines

CANADA
(GREAT BRITAIN)

Seattle
Spokane
Great Northern 1893
Grand Forks
Southern Pacific 1882
Portland
Butte
Northern Pacific 1883
Bismarck
Yellowstone River
Billings
St. Paul
PACIFIC
OCEAN
Deadwood
Missouri River
Lake Superior
Black Hills
Lake Michigan
Snake River
Promontory Point
Chicago
Central Pacific 1869
Ogden
Union Pacific 1869
Council Bluffs
COMSTOCK LODE
Salt Lake City
Reno
Omaha
San Francisco
Sacramento
Denver
Platte River
Colorado River
Topeka
Kansas City
Atchison, Topeka, and Santa Fe 1883
Arkansas River
Atlantic and Pacific
Los Angeles
Southern
Albuquerque
Red River
Pacific 1882
El Paso
Mississippi River
Rio Grande
Southern Pacific 1882
New Orleans
MEXICO
Houston
Gulf of Mexico
San Antonio

0   200 mi
0   200 km
Transverse Mercator Projection

— Transcontinental route,
with date completed

— Connecting route

▭ Gold, silver, or copper deposit

Present-day state boundaries

Reading Maps

To reach the West in 1900, what four rail
routes might you have taken besides the
Union Pacific/Central Pacific? What cities
sprang up along railroad lines?

**Workmen and officials celebrate the railroad they
said "unites the two great oceans of the world."**

Promontory Point On May 10, 1869,
the job was finally finished. The Union
Pacific engine No. 119 met the Central
Pacific's Jupiter at Promontory Point, Utah.
Union Pacific had laid 1,086 miles (1,747 km)
to Central Pacific's 689 (1,109 km).

Leland Stanford, president of the Central
Pacific, marked the occasion by driving a
gold spike that linked the two sets of tracks.
As Stanford's hammer hit the spike, a telegraph wire connected to it relayed the news
of the event to Americans across the nation.

Settlers on the plains Railroad lines transformed the country. They offered easy, inexpensive transportation to a new life and new opportunities. Thousands of settlers took advantage of these opportunities, moving their families from crowded eastern cities to the great empty spaces of the Great Plains. Settlements and towns quickly sprang up along the tracks.

The End of the Buffalo

The Plains Indians depended on the buffalo. Yet as miners, railroad workers, and settlers traveled across the Great Plains, they slaughtered millions of the animals.

Railroad companies hired hunters to shoot buffalo to feed their workers. William F. Cody earned his nickname, "Buffalo Bill," by slaughtering 4,000 buffalo in 8 months. Sometimes passengers on the trains would shoot buffalo from the windows just for amusement, leaving the remains to rot.

By 1895 the buffalo faced **extermination**—total destruction. Where once there had been 50 million buffalo in North America, only about a thousand were left. The extermination of the buffalo was disastrous for the Plains Indians. A Lakota Sioux warrior said of the white hunters:

❝ Our living was their sport, and if you look at it one way, they might as well have been killing us as the buffalo. ❞

The Plains Indians could not stop the government, which had parceled out more than 150 billion acres of land to the railroad companies, nor the settlers, who were building homes on the plains. Government officials and settlers often ignored the Fort Laramie Treaty and other agreements. As a result, Indian tribes lost much of their land. As you will read, the conflict led to decades of warfare on the plains.

⬯⬯ Link to the Present

Buffalo make a comeback Thanks to the efforts of early conservationists, the buffalo were not completely wiped out. Today about 200,000 live on public lands and private ranches. Ranchers have discovered that buffalo are hardy and easy to raise. Consumers have discovered that buffalo meat tastes good and has less fat and cholesterol than some other meats.

To modern-day Lakotas and other Plains Indians, the buffalo is sacred, as it was to their ancestors. Members of the InterTribal Bison Cooperative raise buffalo for ceremonial purposes as well as for food and income.

The cooperative, which represents more than 30 tribes in 15 states, is also working to save the buffalo at Yellowstone National Park. The herd is threatened with slaughter because nearby ranchers fear it will spread disease to cattle, though there have been no proven cases.

1. Section Review

1. Define **extermination.**
2. What problems did Plains Indians face in the 1870s?
3. Why did so few miners strike it rich? Who did become rich from mining?
4. How did the transcontinental railroad change the way people thought about moving west?
5. Critical Thinking Imagine that you lived in a boomtown in the 1860s. What are some ways, besides mining for gold, that you could make a living?

2. War for the Plains

Reading Guide

New Term **reservations**

Section Focus **How the Plains Indians tried to hold onto their land**

1. What events threatened the survival of the Plains Indians?
2. Why did people keep trespassing on Indian land and how did Indians react?
3. What were the government's policies toward Plains Indians?

In 1874 Quanah Parker and 700 Indian warriors attacked a group of hunters camped in a deserted Texas trading post called Adobe Walls. The hunters had been killing buffalo by the thousands for their hides, which they sold for leather.

The hunters had such superior weapons that they won the fight easily. Quanah Parker was wounded in the shoulder, and his horse was killed. This battle was just one of many conflicts that raged across the plains for the next two decades. Sometimes called the Indian Wars, they pitted Plains Indians, fighting for their land, against the United States Army, sent to make the plains safe for travelers and settlers.

The Sand Creek Massacre

The extermination of the buffalo was one thing that destroyed the way of life of the Plains Indians. Miners passing through the plains was another. In 1859 miners found gold near Pikes Peak in Colorado. By the end of that year, 100,000 miners were trespassing on land promised to the Cheyenne and Arapaho Indians in the Fort Laramie Treaty eight years before.

The government tried to negotiate a new treaty, but the Indians were filled with resentment over the broken treaty. They refused to sell their land. Parties of Cheyennes and Arapahos attacked wagon trains, stagecoaches, and mining camps.

Hoping to restore order, the governor of the Colorado Territory put together a military force. In November 1864 Colonel John Chivington led his soldiers in a surprise attack on a peaceful Cheyenne village camped at Sand Creek. Chief Black Kettle waved an American flag and then a white flag of truce, but Chivington attacked.

General Nelson A. Miles later called the Sand Creek Massacre the "foulest and most unjustifiable crime in the annals [history] of America." More than 200 Cheyenne men, women, and children were brutally slaughtered. Word of the massacre spread among the Indians, stiffening their determination to resist the oncoming settlers.

Reservations

Wars raged across the Great Plains throughout the 1860s. Indians continued to raid white settlements and wagon trains, and settlers continued to ignore boundaries and pass through areas set aside for Indians.

In 1867 Congress decided that the best way to end the fighting was to separate Indians and settlers. To do this the federal government would create **reservations**—areas of land set aside for Indian nations—and force Indians to move onto them.

Link to Art

Apache Sunrise Ceremony (1890s) With vegetable dyes on doeskin, Naiche, son of Chief Cochise, preserved the memory of an Apache Sunrise Ceremony. At this coming-of-age celebration, people give thanks that young girls have reached womanhood safely. In the painting seven girls dance, each wrapped in a blanket with the older woman who is her guardian. Dancers on the far side of the fire represent spirits from a nearby mountain. **Discuss** What other times in peoples' lives are important enough to mark with special events, documents, or pictures?

The reservation system forced Plains Indians to change their way of life. Instead of living as nomads and hunting buffalo, they had to settle on specific pieces of land and raise crops. Many people expected the Indians to give up their old ways and learn the customs of the settlers. Beginning in 1867 a number of tribes, doomed without buffalo to hunt, signed treaties and tried to adapt to life on reservations.

Red Cloud's War

In 1863 gold was discovered in Montana, and miners poured in. Most took the Bozeman Trail, which branched off of the Oregon Trail. It led to the mines by cutting through the homeland of the Teton Sioux Indians. Angry Teton Sioux warriors attacked mining parties as they trespassed on Sioux land. To guard the Bozeman Trail, the government built three forts.

Red Cloud, a capable and strong-willed chief, was determined to protect the Teton Sioux homeland at all costs. He, as well as Crazy Horse, led his warriors in repeated attacks on travelers along the trail. After months of conflict and the death of 80 soldiers, the federal government finally agreed to abandon the forts. In 1868, as soldiers left the forts, Red Cloud signed a peace agreement—the Second Treaty of Fort Laramie.

Although Red Cloud's War was a victory for the Plains Indians, the treaty he signed established a reservation for northern Plains Indians that covered much of present-day Montana, Wyoming, and the Dakotas—the Great Sioux Reserve. Red Cloud hated to move his people onto a reservation, but he was satisfied that he had accomplished the goal of saving his people's homeland for all time.

The Battle of the Little Bighorn

The peace brought by the Second Treaty of Fort Laramie was short-lived. When prospectors found gold in the Black Hills in 1874, hundreds of miners flocked to the site even though it was on Sioux and Cheyenne hunting grounds. Angry warriors attacked mining camps, so the government ordered all the Sioux and Cheyenne bands onto reservations. When leaders of the several Indian bands refused, the government sent the United States Army against them.

Custer's Last Stand

The result of this poorly thought-out campaign was the Battle of the Little

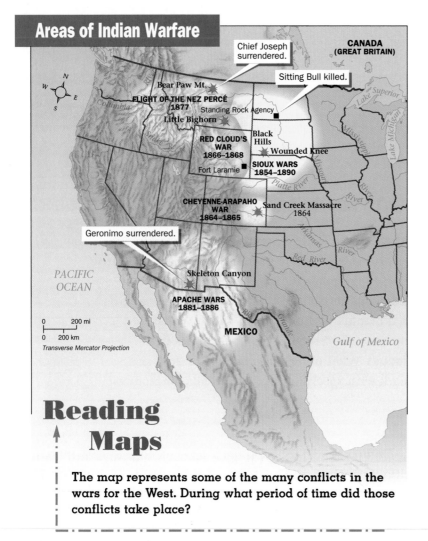

Areas of Indian Warfare

Chief Joseph surrendered.

CANADA (GREAT BRITAIN)

Sitting Bull killed.

Bear Paw Mt.

FLIGHT OF THE NEZ PERCÉ 1877

Standing Rock Agency

Little Bighorn

Black Hills

RED CLOUD'S WAR 1866–1868

Wounded Knee

Fort Laramie

SIOUX WARS 1854–1890

Geronimo surrendered.

CHEYENNE-ARAPAHO WAR 1864–1865

Sand Creek Massacre 1864

PACIFIC OCEAN

Skeleton Canyon

APACHE WARS 1881–1886

MEXICO

Gulf of Mexico

0   200 mi
0   200 km
Transverse Mercator Projection

Reading Maps

The map represents some of the many conflicts in the wars for the West. During what period of time did those conflicts take place?

Bighorn, on June 25, 1876. Along the banks of the Little Bighorn River, in present-day Montana, Sioux and Cheyenne warriors led by Sitting Bull, Crazy Horse, Two Moons, and Lame White Man destroyed the 7th Cavalry commanded by Lieutenant Colonel George Armstrong Custer.

The Battle of the Little Bighorn is the most famous battle of the Indian Wars. It was a great victory for the Indians—but it was their last. Before another year had passed, most of the Sioux and Cheyennes had been defeated in battle or had moved onto reservations. Crazy Horse was captured and murdered, while Sitting Bull escaped to Canada with a handful of followers.

Chief Joseph's Retreat

The next year the Nez Percé Indians of Oregon, Washington, and Idaho found themselves under increasing pressure from settlers who wanted their land. Although most of the Nez Percés eventually signed a treaty and moved to a reservation, some refused to do so. A group of young Nez Percés, resentful at being forced off their land, attacked and killed four settlers.

The Nez Percés' Chief Joseph, though, wanted to avoid war. Joseph, with White Bird and Looking Glass, led some 800 men, women, and children in an amazing retreat. For three and a half months and almost 2,000 miles (3,218 km) they traveled the Lolo Trail over the Bitterroot Range— the route Lewis and Clark had taken 75 years earlier to reach the

Chief Joseph

Pacific. The Nez Percés hoped to reach Canada to join Sitting Bull.

Throughout their ordeal the Nez Percés behaved with honor, paying for supplies and doing little harm to settlers. They might have made it all the way had they not stopped to rest some 40 miles from the border. It was there that federal troops caught up with them. About 300 of the Nez Percés managed to escape into Canada. On a bitterly cold October day, the rest, including Chief Joseph, surrendered. He told the soldiers:

❝I am tired of fighting. My heart is sick and sad. From where the sun now stands, I will fight no more forever.❞

The Nez Percés who surrendered were sent to Oklahoma. A few years later they were allowed to join their relatives on the Nez Percé reservation in Idaho.

Geronimo's Maneuvers

By 1881 most Indians were living on reservations. An exception was a small group of Apaches who were determined to hold onto their freedom. Led by Geronimo, the band roamed the mountains of Arizona and New Mexico, as well as northern Mexico. Although government soldiers tracked this group closely, it took them five years to capture the Indians.

By 1886 Geronimo's group had declined from 150 to a few dozen men, women, and children. These Apaches had successfully evaded 5,000 United States troops and 3,000 Mexican soldiers.

End of the Indian Wars When Geronimo's group finally surrendered in 1886, a generation of Indian wars ended. The group moved onto a reservation. Geronimo himself was imprisoned for two years and lived out the rest of his life in exile in Florida and Oklahoma, never to return to his homeland.

The plight of the Maoris After New Zealand became a British colony in 1840, the native Maoris (MAH-ō-reez) found themselves in a position much like that of the Plains Indians. Pressured by land-hungry settlers, they fought back against the British.

A movement similar to the Ghost Dance arose. Called Pai Marire, which means "Good and Peaceful Religion," the movement was founded in 1864 by Te Ua Haumene. Inspired by a vision of the angel Gabriel, Te Ua Haumene convinced his followers that they would be protected against British bullets by shouting in battle "Pai Marire, hau, hau!" For this reason, followers of Pai Marire came to be called Hauhau. Despite the bravery of Hauhau warriors, the Maoris were defeated in 1872 and lost most of their land to the British.

The Ghost Dance Religion

More than two decades of fighting and bloodshed had left the Plains Indians defeated and depressed. Most were living in poverty on barren and isolated reservations where they were forced to accept a way of life they neither understood nor wanted.

Looking for a miracle to help them improve their situation, in the late 1880s many Indians turned to a new religion that swept across the West. The religion was founded by a Paiute named Wovoka. He had a vision of a deliverer coming to rescue the Indians and give them back their lands.

Believers in this new religion wore shirts and dresses of white cotton or buckskin. They danced, chanted, and prayed for dead friends and relatives to come back to life and the buffalo to return to the plains. Settlers named the new religion the Ghost Dance because of its emphasis on the living reuniting with the dead.

The Death of Sitting Bull

Sitting Bull, who returned from Canada in 1881, became a believer in the Ghost Dance religion. Afraid that he might try to lead other believers to war, the government tried to talk Sitting Bull into banning the religion. When the chief refused, the government decided to arrest him.

In December 1890, 43 Indian policemen surrounded Sitting Bull's cabin at Standing Rock Reservation in North Dakota and told him he was under arrest. At first Sitting Bull agreed to go with them, but when he got outside he changed his mind, shouting, "I will not go." In the scuffle that followed he was killed, along with seven of his followers and six policemen.

The massacre at Wounded Knee Alarmed by the death of their chief, Sitting Bull's followers fled. Some disappeared into the Badlands of South Dakota, an area of deep gullies and steep hills. There they joined other believers in the Ghost Dance religion led by Chief Big Foot.

It was bitterly cold, and Big Foot's group decided to go to the Pine Ridge Reservation. Near Wounded Knee Creek they met troops of the Seventh Cavalry.

On December 29, 1890, the cavalrymen decided to disarm the Indians. When someone discharged a rifle, nervous soldiers fired into the group. Many Indians ran for cover. In the bloody struggle that followed at least 150 Indian men, women, and children and 25 soldiers lost their lives.

Sitting Bull, above, hoped that the Ghost Dance religion would bring about a just and beautiful new world. Believers made special clothing for Ghost Dance ceremonies, such as the Arapaho dress, left, and Sioux shirt, right. Some Sioux made their shirts of muslin flour sacks.

Reformers

Even before the massacre at Wounded Knee the public was waking up to the tragic situation of Native Americans. Reservations were becoming more crowded and living conditions were growing worse.

Furthermore, the government kept breaking promises to provide Indians with food, supplies, and money. Eventually, dedicated people, both Indian and white, began to protest and call for reforms.

One reformer was Helen Hunt Jackson. In 1879 she heard speeches by Standing Bear, a Ponca chief, and Susette La Flesche, an Omaha. Horrified by their accounts of mistreatment of Indians, Jackson decided to devote herself to their cause.

In 1881 she published *A Century of Dishonor*. In it she documented the many broken promises made to Indians. Her most famous book, *Ramona*, was a fictional account of Indians treated unfairly by settlers. *Ramona* stirred public sympathy for the plight of Indians much as Harriet Beecher Stowe's *Uncle Tom's Cabin* had caused anger at the cruelty of slavery.

Another influential reformer, Sarah Winnemucca, was the daughter of a Paiute chief from Nevada. While living with a trader's family, Sarah learned to read and write English. She spent her life speaking out to audiences in the East for the Paiutes' right to their land.

The Dawes Act

Some reformers believed that the only way to help the Plains Indians was to convince them to adapt to American culture. Congress responded to this idea by passing the Dawes Act in 1887. The goal of the act was to end tribal ownership of lands and give plots of land to individual Indian families to farm.

Members of Congress had different reasons for supporting the Dawes Act. Some felt that they were doing the right thing for Indians. Like the reformers, these politicians wanted to "Americanize" Indians by dealing with them as individuals, rather than as tribes. Carl Schurz, the Secretary of the Interior, agreed that

> "[land ownership would] inspire the Indians with a feeling of assurance as to the permanency of their ownership of the lands they occupy and cultivate. . . . It will be the most effective measure to place the Indians and white men upon an equal footing as to the protection and restraints of law common to both."

Other members of Congress who voted for the act had no interest in supporting the rights of Indians. They wanted to isolate Indians on out-of-the-way plots of land. They realized that this solution was cheaper and safer than fighting Indians for the good farmland. One government official explained it this way:

> "[Giving Indians plots of land would not] cause any considerable annoyance to the whites. . . . [The pieces of land] consist, for the most part, of ground unfitted for cultivation, but suited to the peculiar habits of the Indians."

Reformers rejoiced over the passage of the Dawes Act. However, in the long run the act failed to benefit Indians.

Failure of the Dawes Act Although Plains Indian families were assigned plots of land, few of them wanted to farm. Farming was not part of their tradition.

To make matters worse, the land they were given was often the poorest farmland on the plains. Unable to raise enough food to live on, Indians were forced to rely on weekly food rations from the government.

Because they had never officially owned land as individuals before, Indians did not understand how much money it was worth to the advancing settlers. Some settlers took advantage of this lack of knowledge and talked Indians into selling their land for a fraction of its value. In 1887 Indians owned 138 million acres of land. By 1934 they owned only close to 49 million acres.

Changes on the Great Plains

With Indians confined to reservations, buffalo nearly extinct, and railroads reaching westward across the continent, the Great Plains was a different place by 1880 than it had been 20 years earlier. As you will read, over the next few decades cattle ranchers and farmers moved onto the plains, and with them came new ways of life.

2. Section Review

1. Define **reservations.**
2. Give two examples of situations that threatened the Plains Indians' way of life in the last half of the 1800s.
3. Explain why Congress established the reservation system.
4. What was the Dawes Act? Did it help Indians?
5. Critical Thinking If you were a reformer in the 1880s, how would you try to help the Plains Indians?

Geography Lab

Pine Ridge Reservation, South Dakota, shown in 1890, was once part of the Great Sioux Reserve.

A Map that Shows Change

The Second Treaty of Fort Laramie established a huge reservation as a permanent home for the Sioux. Before long, though, miners, railroaders, and farmers were demanding parts of the Great Sioux Reserve.

Senator Henry Dawes of Massachusetts introduced a bill that would let the government take pieces of the reservation, paying the Sioux for their land. Reformers thought the Sioux Bill offered the best terms the Sioux were likely to get. They pressured the tribe into accepting the bill.

Dakota Reservations 1875 and 1900

Missouri River
Little Missouri River
Red River
Sheyenne River
Cannonball River
Cedar Creek
Grand River
Moreau River
Missouri River
Belle Fourche River
GREAT SIOUX RESERVATION
Big Sioux River
Vermillion River
James River
Black Hills
White River
Cheyenne River

Legend:
- Indian reservations 1875
- Indian reservations 1900
- Present-day state boundaries

0   50   100 mi
0 50 100 km
Lambert Conformal Conic Projection

Using Map Skills

1. What are the colored areas? What do the heavy lines stand for? What change does the map show?

2. Describe what happened to the Great Sioux Reserve over time. Include information about the Black Hills, which the Sioux hold sacred.

3. How does the photograph add to what you can learn from the map?

4. **Hands-On Geography** Find out how the boundaries of your community have changed in the past century. Then make a map of your community 100 years ago and today.

3. Cattle and Farming

Reading Guide

New Terms open range, homesteaders, prairie, sod

Section Focus How the Great Plains region was settled by ranchers and farmers

1. Why did cattle ranching rise and then collapse on the plains?
2. What attracted farmers to the Great Plains?
3. Who were the homesteaders and what challenges did they face?

For settlers in the 1860s and 1870s, the Great Plains was a place of both opportunity and hardship. Some people fared better than others. Still, everyone who tried life on the plains faced new challenges.

The Cattle Industry

While Indians were being forced onto reservations, enterprising cattle ranchers were bringing herds of longhorn cattle onto the plains. Longhorn cattle got their name because of the wide span of their horns—up to 7 feet (2 m) across. They were hardy descendants of the cattle the Spaniards brought to America in the early 1700s.

Originally from Texas and other parts of the Southwest, the cattle ranchers were attracted by the **open range**—thousands of miles of unfenced grassland. Longhorns thrived on this lush grass. Ranchers would claim cattle as their own by putting special marks, called brands, onto their hides with hot branding irons. Then they would let the animals roam free on the open range.

The market for beef, however, was not in the sparsely populated Great Plains, but in the crowded cities to the east. Cows worth $3 or $4 a head in Texas brought as much as $50 in Chicago, New York, or Philadelphia. The problem was getting them there.

Cow Towns

Railroads provided the solution. In 1867 Joseph G. McCoy established the first cow town—Abilene, Kansas—a sleepy cluster of log huts along the Kansas Pacific Railroad. That summer McCoy built stockyards, pens, loading chutes, and a hotel.

That year, 35,000 longhorns were herded to Abilene and shipped east. Four years later Abilene shipped 700,000. From 1867 to 1887 some 5.5 million head of cattle were herded north to Abilene and other cow towns, such as Wichita and Dodge City, that grew up along the tracks.

The Long Drive

Herding cattle across the plains to the cow towns was known as the "long drive." It was a two-month adventure for a dozen or so cowboys with herds of about 3,000.

On the long drive cowboys herded the cattle along trails known to have grass and water. The best-known trail—the Chisholm Trail—was named for Jesse Chisholm, a part-Cherokee trader. With no fences or barriers, the cowboys could let the herds graze wherever they wanted along the way.

Comanche lands Of course most of the range land was, in fact, private property.

The federal government had given much of it to various Indian tribes for their reservations. For example, the Comanches, whose chief was now Quanah Parker, were blessed with especially fertile grazing land.

In June 1876 ranchers drove several herds across the Comanche reservation in Oklahoma. Parker quickly realized the value of the land. He began charging the ranchers a dollar per head to let their cattle cross. With the money the tribe bought their own cattle.

Later Quanah Parker leased land to the ranchers, which allowed their cattle to graze on the reservation. These agreements provided cash for Comanche families and encouraged ranchers to hire Indians to tend the herds.

The Cowboy

In people's imaginations, the cowboy is one of the most romantic characters in American history. In reality, the cowboy led a difficult, lonely, and dangerous life. Longhorn cattle were ornery and touchy. A clap of thunder or a gunshot could send thousands off in a mad rush called a stampede.

The life of the cowboy revolved around the long drive. After two or three months on the trail, cowboys arrived in the cow towns eager to let off steam by drinking, gambling, and fighting. Many towns had a cemetery known as "boot hill," for men who had "died with their boots on."

Cowboy life appealed to men from many different backgrounds. In fact, nearly one in three cowboys was either African American or of Mexican or Spanish ancestry.

One African American cowboy named Jack Spicer, of the Loomis-Ostrander ranch in Texas, was a noted broncobuster. His job was to train young horses to be ridden. When the owner of the ranch asked him how he learned to ride so well, Jack replied:

"When I was a boy my old master made me ride pitching [bucking] horses. When I was thrown off he used to give me a licking and make me get back on the horse until I rode him. That's the way I learned to stay on.**"**

Spanish origins The American cowboy owes his clothes, gear, and some of his vocabulary to the Spanish and Mexican vaqueros. The cowboy's hat, lasso, and chaps (SHAPS)— leather leggings that protect his legs from thorns—were first used by vaqueros. Many cowboy terms are English versions of Spanish words, such as chaps from *chaparreras* and stampede from *estampida*.

Cowboys rode specially trained ponies for cutting out—or separating— a single cow from the rest of the herd.

Collapse of the Cattle Industry

No one could have predicted the huge impact the cattle industry had on the plains. By the mid-1880s, millions of cattle grazed freely on the plains. The very success of the open-range cattle industry, however, was what finally led to its collapse.

The main problem was the number of cattle. As the number increased, cattle prices fell. Still, ranchers bred more, hoping prices would rise. Soon there were too many cattle for the amount of open range.

The next problem was the weather. The winter of 1885–1886 was cold and blustery. Many cattle froze to death. The summer that followed was hot and dry, burning away much of the grass. Longhorns had trouble finding enough food to survive.

By the fall of 1886, ranchers could see that the herds were in trouble. Steers that had been worth $30 a head the year before were now lucky to bring $10.

Those who sold their cattle—even at low prices—were wise. The next winter was worse. When spring arrived a ghastly sight awaited ranchers. Cattle had died by the thousands. Those animals that survived were little more than walking skeletons.

Sheepherders Even before the cattle industry collapsed, sheepherders had begun to compete for the open range. For years cattle and sheep ranchers fought bitter wars—with guns and in the courts—over rights to water and land. In time, though, attitudes softened. Sheep, it turned out, were easier to raise and more profitable than long-horns. Some cattle ranchers even decided to raise sheep.

In 1886 *Harper's Weekly,* a popular news magazine, showed the effects of the terrible blizzards that had swept across the plains that winter. The next winter was just as bitterly cold. Hundreds of thousands of cattle died. The two terrible winters changed cattle ranching. Ranchers began to keep smaller herds and raise hay as feed for winter instead of letting the cattle graze on the open range.

The collapse of the cattle industry meant many lost dreams and fortunes. Ranchers who survived the crash reduced their herds and fenced their pastures. Many cowboys took more stable but less exciting jobs on the new ranches.

Homesteaders

As the cattle industry was shrinking, a new industry—farming—was growing on the plains. In the East, cheap farmland was in short supply. To help farmers acquire land in the West, in 1862 Congress passed the Homestead Act.

Under the act a person could claim 160 acres of free land for a small registration fee. If they built a house and worked the land for at least five years, it became theirs. Between 1862 and 1900 some 500,000 **homesteaders**—people who took advantage of the Homestead Act—moved to the Great Plains, where they claimed 80 million acres of land.

Challenges of homesteading Homesteaders faced many challenges when they tried to turn grasslands into farmlands. One challenge was having too little land.

The Homestead Act did not take into account the difference between farming in the East, where rainfall was plentiful, and farming on the **prairie**—the eastern part of the plains where the grasses grow tall. A family could support itself on 160 acres in the East. On the dry prairie a greater number of acres were needed.

The dry climate created another problem. In summer, lightning could start fires in the dry prairie grasses as readily as a careless match. Raging prairie fires could outrun horses. The fires left everything in their paths in charred and smoking ruins.

Winter brought its own terrors. Perhaps worst were the blizzards with their winds, sleet, and snow. Farmers strung ropes

A Kansas woman collects buffalo chips to use for fuel. With little wood available, settlers burned dried hay, corncobs, and sunflower stalks, too.

between buildings to keep from getting lost walking from their houses to their barns.

Homesteaders also had to contend with the locust, a large grasshopper that thrived on the plains. Huge clouds of locusts would darken the sky and eat everything edible in their path, even laundry on the line.

Sod houses Building shelter on the treeless plains was another challenge. Lumber from the East was expensive. Instead, homesteaders built with chunks of **sod**—the mat of roots and earth beneath the prairie grasses.

Sod houses could be snug in winter and cool in summer, but they leaked terribly. Emma Brown, a Kansas homesteader, described one heavy rainstorm:

“When nearly everything in the house was soaked and the fuel gone, I went to a neighbor's . . . dugout. But before morning there was six inches of water in it so we had to make another move.”

Hands-On HISTORY

Sod house in the Dakotas, about 1885

Designing a sod house "Soddies," as sod houses were called, could be built in a week for the cost of a little lumber, a few windowpanes, door and window hardware, and nails. A typical soddy was one story high, with a rectangular floor plan and inside dimensions of about 16 feet by 20 feet (5 m × 6 m), though many soddies were smaller than that. The sod walls usually were 2 to 4 feet thick.

Activity Imagine you are part of a family preparing to build a soddy on the Great Plains. Make a scale drawing (1/2 inch = 1 foot) of the floor plan. Include a door, at least two windows, and furniture. Keep the following in mind:

1 Your family has three adults and three children, one of whom is an infant.

2 You can divide your soddy into rooms, but interior walls take up precious space.

3 You own a wood-burning stove for cooking and heating, though you will have to burn corncobs and dried manure because so little wood is available.

4 You will be fetching water from an outside well.

5 All your possessions, except for tools that can go in the barn, must fit in the soddy.

Solving the Problems

Most homesteaders were used to the moist climates of the East. Defeated by the problems of farming on the dry and treeless plains, many gave up in despair. Gradually, however, using new techniques and inventions, those who stayed adapted to their difficult new environment.

Dry farming Over much of the Great Plains, less than 20 inches (50 cm) of rain falls each year, usually not enough for wheat and other grains. Farmers put the wind to work by using windmills to pump water from underground streams.

A Nebraskan named Hardy W. Campbell found that if he plowed deeply, he reached moist soil. The moisture would rise through the plowed soil to the plants' roots. To keep the moisture from rising to the surface and evaporating, he packed the topsoil firmly.

Campbell experimented with this technique on grains that require little water. His method, called dry farming, let plains farmers raise crops even in times of drought.

Farming inventions Plains farmers also benefited from new inventions. In 1838 John Deere of Illinois had developed the steel plow. In 1868 James Oliver patented a plow modified to cut through plains sod. Oliver's plow made it easier for "sodbusters," as plains farmers were called, to plow the plains.

In 1874 Joseph Glidden patented barbed wire. It was advertised as "light as air, stronger than whiskey, and cheaper than dirt." Farmers across the plains fenced off their land to protect it from grazing cattle.

In 1879 John Appleby introduced the twine binder, a reaper that gathered and tied bundles of wheat automatically. An acre of wheat that took 60 hours to reap by hand could be harvested and bundled in 3 hours by machine.

Windmills, dry farming, and the new inventions made huge farms possible. Some of the largest were more than 30,000 acres.

Opportunities on the Plains

Homesteading was a hard, often lonely life. Still, it offered opportunities not available in the East.

Women homesteaders On homesteads women did everything men did. They ran machinery, hitched horses, and handled guns. Living far from towns they had to be teachers, nurses, cooks, laundresses, and seamstresses. For many women, homesteading was an opportunity to prove themselves equal to men even though they might not have had as much physical strength. As Harriet Strong of Wyoming announced:

❝It takes brains, not brawn, to make farms pay. We need more women farmers!❞

Under the Homestead Act a woman could apply for her own land grant. By 1890, a quarter of a million women ran farms and ranches. By 1910, 10 percent of all homesteaders were women. Elinore Pruitt Stewart, who filed for a homestead in Wyoming in 1909, shared her feelings in a letter to a friend:

❝I realize that temperament has much to do with success in any undertaking, and persons afraid of coyotes and work and loneliness had better let ranching alone. At the same time, any woman who can stand her own company, can see the beauty of the sunset, loves growing things, and is willing to put as much time at careful labor as she does over a washtub, will certainly succeed.❞

Exodusters Former slaves also found opportunities on the plains. They called themselves "Exodusters," for the Bible's book of Exodus, which tells the story of Jews leaving Egypt for the Promised Land of Israel.

Within a few years African Americans had established homesteads and towns in Kansas. They called one community Nicodemus, the name of the first slave in the United States to buy his freedom.

In 1878 Nicodemus boasted 700 residents, two hotels, a barber shop, several general

The Shores family poses in front of their sod house near Westerville, Nebraska, in 1887.

stores, a wagon shop, a drug store, a bank, a blacksmith shop, and a lumber dealer. It had a baseball team, a literary society, and two newspapers.

The West in 1900

An eagle flying over the West in 1900 would have seen a vastly different landscape than it would have only a quarter-century earlier. The Great Plains was no longer a vast sea of grass dotted with Indian camps and herds of buffalo. Instead, the region was criss-crossed by railroad tracks and barbed-wire fences, scattered with towns, ranches, and farms. The Indians, now on reservations, had been replaced by millions of settlers.

The Great American Desert was no more. In its place was the "Breadbasket of America," a rich agricultural area.

3. Section Review

1. Define **open range, homesteaders, prairie,** and **sod.**
2. What problems did ranchers face on the plains? What problems did farmers face?
3. How did the United States government encourage farmers to move to the plains?
4. Critical Thinking Homesteaders faced many challenges. If you had chosen the life of a homesteader, what might your reasons have been?

Why We Remember

The Changing West

Quanah Parker was a witness to the changes that reshaped the West. During his life he made a remarkable transition from Comanche warrior to cattle rancher and leader of his people. By the time he died in 1911, Quanah had ridden in trains and automobiles and visited the President. For him, as for countless Americans today, the West was a land of opportunity.

We remember other changes, too. Vast herds of buffalo were reduced to an endangered species—showing how fragile nature can be. Some people also saw that plowing the plains could damage the soil. Quanah Parker warned:

❝ We love the white man, but we fear your success. This [was] pretty country you took away from us, but see how dry it is now. It is good only for red ants, coyotes, and cattlemen.**❞**

Finally, it was in the West that many Indians died trying to preserve their way of life. The survivors lived with the bitterness of defeat. Still, Nez Percés, Comanches, Sioux, and others endured. In doing so, they preserved a valuable cultural heritage, not only for themselves, but for all Americans.

Skill Lab

Acquiring Information
Analyzing a Photograph

Skill Tips
Keep in mind:
- Most photographs show things as they really are, or were. There is little or no exaggeration, as there often is in a painting.
- The captions that accompany some photographs can be helpful. Usually, though, you need to go beyond the caption to draw reasonable conclusions.

Western towns sprang up with incredible speed. In one day, Guthrie, Oklahoma, changed from a tiny railroad stop to a city of more than 10,000 people. How did it happen? Bowing to pressure from would-be homesteaders, the U.S. government declared that on April 22, 1889, almost 2 million acres of Indian Territory (present-day Oklahoma) would be open for settlement. At noon, the Oklahoma Land Rush began as thousands raced to stake claims in Guthrie and elsewhere.

Question to Investigate

What needs did people in the new western towns have?

Procedure

Like paintings, photographs can be valuable sources of information about people and events of the past. Analyze this photograph to explore the Question to Investigate.

1 Identify the main subject of the photograph.
a. Identify where and when the photograph was taken. Does the photograph itself provide any clues? Explain.
b. Identify in general what the photograph shows.

2 Identify details in the photograph.
a. What will the sign at the far right be used for?
b. What service is the long sign at the far left advertising?
c. Which signs do not advertise services?

3 Draw conclusions based on the photograph.
a. Name four needs that people had in western towns. For each one, explain how you can tell from the photograph.
b. Why do you think people in western towns had these needs?

Source to Use

Shop in Guthrie, Oklahoma, 1889

Chapter Survey

Reviewing Vocabulary

Define the following terms.

1. extermination
2. reservations
3. open range
4. homesteaders
5. prairie
6. sod

Reviewing Main Ideas

1. Why did the government present the Treaty of Fort Laramie to the Plains Indians in 1851?
2. In general, who made fortunes in mining? Who did not? Why?
3. Name one positive effect and one negative effect of the building of transcontinental railroads.
4. List three ways that the Plains Indians reacted to pressure from trespassers and the government.
5. Why did people who believed in doing the right thing for Indians support the Dawes Act?
6. What led to the collapse of the cattle industry?
7. Give two examples of how homesteaders met the challenges of living and farming in a dry, treeless environment.

Thinking Critically

1. **Analysis** How did technology change the West? Include at least three examples in your answer.
2. **Synthesis** Is there something that the Plains Indians could have done to successfully resist the pressures exerted by settlers and the United States government? If so, what? If not, why not?
3. **Why We Remember: Evaluation** If you were going to write an article emphasizing positive changes that reshaped the West after 1865, what topics would you include? In an article on negative changes, what topics would you include?

Applying Skills

Analyzing photographs Bring in several photographs from home, preferably a mix of posed portraits and casual shots. Exchange photographs with a classmate. Imagine that you are a historian 100 years from now, studying the photographs as historical records. Write a paragraph describing the conclusions about life in the past that you draw from the photographs. Keep in mind what you learned in the Skill Lab on page 579.

History Mystery

The arid Great Plains Answer the History Mystery on page 555. As you travel westward from 100° of longitude, the climate becomes drier. Average yearly rainfall ranges from between 40 and 50 inches (100–125 cm) near the Mississippi to less than 10 inches (25 cm) between the Rockies and the Sierra. Why might some people prefer a rainy climate and others prefer a dry one?

Writing in Your History Journal

1. Keys to History (a) The time line on pages 554–555 has seven Keys to History. In your journal, describe why each one is important to know about. (b) If you could travel back in time and prevent one of the events on the time line, which would you choose? Why? Write about it in your journal.

2. Quanah Parker Imagine that you have just heard Quanah Parker speak at his mother's burial service. A stranger standing next to you criticizes Parker for accepting both the white and the Indian worlds. "He ought to choose one and stick to it," the stranger says. In your journal, write your reaction.

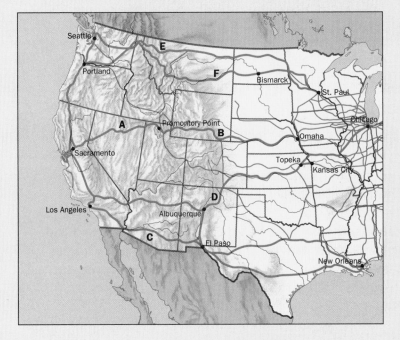

1. Each letter on the map represents a western railroad. Name each railroad.

2. Geographic Thinking Some boomtowns went on to become big cities. Looking at the map on page 562, what reasons can you give for the growth of Denver and Reno? Why do you suppose Deadwood never did become a large city? Think about other cities you have been in or heard about. What kinds of locations or other physical characteristics help a small town become—and remain—a large city?

3. Citizenship Some people have the idea that, until recently, the United States government played only a minor role in the country's economic and social development. After reading this chapter, do you agree or disagree with that idea? Why? Write your responses in your journal.

Alternative Assessment

Portraying success and defeat One historian has said, "The West is the place where everybody was supposed to escape failure, but it didn't happen that way." With classmates, create a bulletin-board display that portrays both the successes and the defeats that people experienced in the West.

❶ Divide into two groups, one to portray the successes and one to portray the defeats in the settlement of the West.

❷ With the rest of your group, decide who and what you will portray. Think of events you have read about—for example, Indians, railroad workers and owners, prospectors, ranchers, and homesteaders. Also think of places, such as ranches, farms, mining sites, boomtowns, ghost towns, and so on.

❸ Gather materials for your display. These might include drawings or other artwork, interesting quotes, maps, charts, and so on. You may want to do research in sources besides the text.

❹ Assemble the display. Give it a title.

Your display will be evaluated on the following criteria:
• it shows understanding of the positive or negative aspects of the changing West
• it provides accurate information
• it presents the information in clear, attractive, inviting ways

Dragon's Gate
by Laurence Yep

In the novel *Dragon's Gate*, author Laurence Yep tells the story of Otter, a 15-year-old boy who travels from China to California to join his father and uncle at work on the transcontinental railroad. Otter finds the two men in the Sierra Nevada, where the Chinese crew is laboring to build tunnels through the solid rock of the mountains. Shocked and angered by the miserable conditions, the barbaric treatment of the workers, and the danger of the work itself, Otter asks his friend Sean to find out whether the "western"—white—crews work under similar conditions. In the following scene, he discusses a letter from Sean with other members of the Chinese crew.

It was a surprise to learn what the western crews earned. Each westerner earned thirty-five dollars a month while we earned only thirty; and the railroad paid for their food as well while we had to pay out of our own pockets. Moreover, it was official company policy that no one should work in the tunnels for more than eight western hours at a time—a policy that was applied to westerners but not T'ang crews.

T'ang crews: a reference to the Chinese railroad workers

When I read it to the crew, Dandy did some figuring. "When you deduct the charges for food, we make a third as much."

Honker was waiting patiently on his bunk for his turn to wash. Though it was hot now, he wore his scarf against the dust. "It kind of sticks like a bone in your throat, doesn't it?" he asked. By now, I could understand even his scarf-muffled words. "I mean, we do all the dirty work."

Cape Horn: name given to a part of the Sierra Nevada that was especially treacherous for the railroad workers

Curly glanced at me and then said, "And all the dangerous jobs. Like when they want to stop an avalanche."

"When we were at Cape Horn," a wispy little voice said, "Kilroy didn't even try to ask his western crews." The voice sounded raspy, as if it had not been used in a long time. We all turned to see; it was Shaky. His head nodded up and down constantly as he spoke the only words I had ever heard from him. "He came to my crew. We were all

Kilroy: an overseer of the railroad workers

Railroad worker, Sierra Nevada

Railroad construction in the Sierra Nevada involved tunneling through solid rock and building trestles like the one shown here.

young and fresh off the boat. What did we know?" He looked around the cabin. "We wound up dangling over a cliff in a basket, swaying on a rope while we hammered away with a chisel, with only the basket bottoms between us and a fall into forever. And sometimes after we packed the holes and lit the fuses, the fuses were too short or the crew took too long to haul us up. We were lucky if there was enough to bury. Even when the rest of my crew was dead, he kept ordering me to go over. Remember. Someone please remember."

We stared in astonishment as Shaky lapsed into his usual silence; but he was lost now in his own terrifying memories, and the nodding of his head changed into a gentle rocking of his whole torso.

With a sigh, Bright Star started to strip. "The westerners' history books will write about what a big hero Kilroy was."

"And us?" Dandy asked. As the headman, Bright Star got to wash first. When he rose from the bucket, his face was scarlet from the hot water. "They're their history books. And the T'ang historians won't care a thread what happens in this barbaric land."

A Closer Look

1. What does Otter learn from the letter he receives? What effect does the information have on the men?

2. Why do you think Shaky says "Remember. Someone please remember"? How does his plea affect the others?

3. Why do you think Bright Star refers to America as "this barbaric land"?

Chapter *21*

The Rise of Industry and Big Business

Keys to History

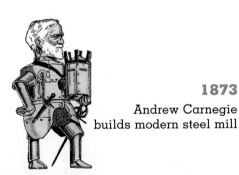

1873
Andrew Carnegie builds modern steel mill

1873
Cornelius Vanderbilt extends railroad empire to Chicago

1865

1875

Looking Back

Tom Thumb, successful railroad steam engine
1830

World **Link**

Japan becomes an industrial nation
1868–1900

Some people called her "Mother." Others said she was "the most dangerous woman in America." Who was she? What did she do to earn such different reputations?

1882
John D. Rockefeller forms Standard Oil Trust

1886
American Federation of Labor founded

1887
Interstate Commerce Act

1892
Homestead Strike

1894
Pullman Strike

1885

1900

Looking Ahead

Wagner Act guarantees workers the right to join unions

1935

Beginning the Story with

Andrew Carnegie

Although he missed his home in Scotland, 17-year-old Andrew Carnegie knew his future lay in the United States. In a letter to his uncle, he wrote:

" Although I sometimes think I would like to be back in Dunfermline, working at the loom, it's very likely I would have been a poor weaver all my days, but here, I can surely do something better than that. If I don't it will be my own fault, for anyone can get along in this country. **"**

Andrew certainly got along. While many immigrants in the United States struck it rich, few enjoyed Carnegie's success. Born the son of a poor weaver, Andrew grew up to be one of the richest men in the world.

Becoming a "Bread Winner"

Life in Scotland had been difficult for Andrew's family. His father, William, toiled endless hours over a hand loom in their little cottage. His mother, Margaret, repaired shoes. Together they barely eked out a living. Then came power looms, which put cottage weavers like William out of work. Rather than face a life of poverty, Margaret insisted the family emigrate to the United States, where her two sisters already lived. The Carnegies arrived in 1848 and settled near Pittsburgh.

Andrew, now 13, found a job in a textile mill as a "bobbin boy." He worked 12 hours a day, 6 days a week for $1.20 per week. "I have made millions since," he later said, "but none of these gave me so much happiness as my first week's earnings. I was now a helper of the family, a bread winner."

After a year of millwork, Andrew found a job as a messenger for a telegraph office. There he earned $2.50 a week, delivering telegrams to customers. To Andrew, the job seemed like heaven, "with newspapers, pens, pencils, and sunshine about me."

When not delivering telegrams, Andrew learned the language of the telegraph. Messages came into the office in the form of dots and dashes punched into narrow strips of paper. The dots and dashes represented letters of the alphabet translated into Morse code.

Most telegraph operators would then "read" the strips of paper to translate the coded message back into words. Not Andrew. He trained himself to decode the dots and dashes by listening to the sound they made as the message clicked over the telegraph key. Astonished customers stood around the telegraph office just to watch him take messages.

A Teenage Capitalist

One of the people most impressed by Carnegie's skill was Thomas A. Scott, superintendent of the Pennsylvania Railroad. Scott hired Andrew as his personal assistant. The teenager's primary job was to send telegraph orders to trains moving between Philadelphia and Pittsburgh.

One day Scott asked Carnegie if he could find $500 to invest. Without knowing where the money would come from, Andrew replied, "Yes, sir; I think I can." Scott said, "Very well, get it; a man has died who owns ten shares in the Adams Express Company which I want you to buy."

Andrew turned to his mother for help. Determined "to give our boy a start," she raised the $500 by borrowing on the family's home. Carnegie was now the proud owner of ten shares of Adams Express stock, which paid a monthly dividend (part of the company's profits). When he showed his first check for $5 to his friends, they were astonished. They had never received money except from work. Carnegie later recalled:

Andrew Carnegie became the greatest American steelmaker by using new technology to produce inexpensive, durable steel.

❝How money could make money . . . led to much speculation upon the part of the young fellows; and I was for the first time hailed as a 'capitalist.'❞

Carnegie quickly learned how to use his money to make money. He built this first investment into a fortune.

Hands-On

▸ *HISTORY*

Activity

In the early 1850s Andrew Carnegie invested $500 in Adams Express stock. If you wanted to make a similar investment today, you would need to raise $9,000. Write a plan describing how you would raise the money and what investments you would make.

1. Railroads Spur Industrial Growth

Reading Guide

New Terms **rebates, consolidation, regulate, free enterprise, interstate commerce**

Section Focus **How railroads spurred industrial growth in the nation**

1. What were the causes and effects of the rapid expansion of railroads?
2. How did railroad companies limit competition and increase profits?
3. What led to the passage of the Interstate Commerce Act?

Andrew Carnegie's rise from bobbin boy to businessman took place during a time of rapid industrial growth in the United States. The forces behind this change can be traced to the Industrial Revolution that began in the early 1800s (see pages 318–320). By 1860, machines, mass production, the factory system, and railroads had all made their appearance.

Reasons for Growth

After the Civil War, enterprising individuals like Andrew Carnegie brought these elements of industry together on a larger scale than Americans had ever seen before. Machines took over much of the nation's work. Factories, rather than small workshops, now produced most of the nation's manufactured goods.

Abundant natural resources A wealth of natural resources made such growth possible. The nation's many rivers carried freight and served as sources of power. Forests supplied wood for railroad ties and bridges. Coal deposits provided fuel for steam engines and the furnaces of the iron industry. Ample supplies of iron ore kept steel mills booming.

Fuels made from oil became widely used for light, heat, and power.

Statistics tell the story of the United States' coming of age as an industrial nation. Between 1865 and 1900, the number of factories increased from 140,000 to 510,000. The number of people who worked in factories and mills swelled from 1.3 million to 5.1 million. The value of manufactured goods leaped from $2 billion to over $18 billion. By 1900 the United States had become the world's leading industrial nation.

Railroads expand The driving force behind the industrial growth of the United States was the booming railroad industry. In 1865 the nation had about 30,000 miles (48,000 km) of track. By 1900, 200,000 miles (320,000 km) of track covered the nation like a giant spider web. It was the biggest railroad system in the world.

While some railroaders were laying track in the West, others were building lines in the East and the Midwest. The South repaired lines wrecked during the Civil War and added seven times as many miles of track. When a railroad reached Harrison, Arkansas, people welcomed it with booming cannons. The local newspaper declared, "Harrison Is a Railroad Town at Last."

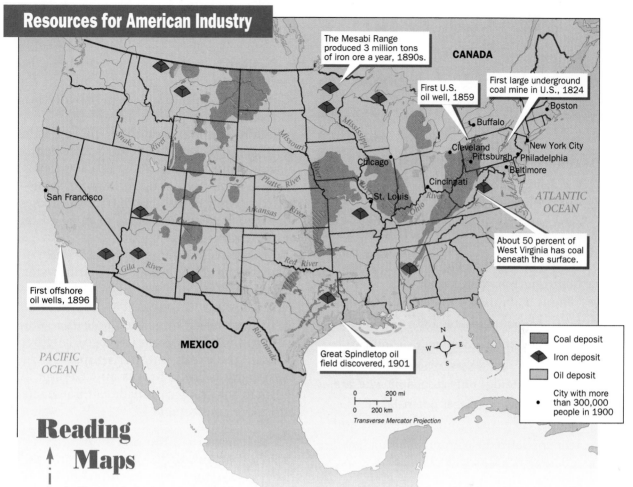

The Mesabi Range produced 3 million tons of iron ore a year, 1890s.

CANADA

First U.S. oil well, 1859

First large underground coal mine in U.S., 1824

Boston

Buffalo

Cleveland

New York City

Pittsburgh Philadelphia

Baltimore

ATLANTIC OCEAN

Chicago

Cincinnati

St. Louis

About 50 percent of West Virginia has coal beneath the surface.

San Francisco

First offshore oil wells, 1896

MEXICO

Great Spindletop oil field discovered, 1901

PACIFIC OCEAN

Coal deposit

Iron deposit

Oil deposit

City with more than 300,000 people in 1900

0   200 mi

0   200 km

Transverse Mercator Projection

Reading Maps

1. For each resource, name the areas of the United States where major deposits are found.

2. What characteristics besides being close to resources contribute to making a city an industrial center?

Railroads Link the Nation

As railroad lines crisscrossed the United States, they created a national market for the nation's raw materials and manufactured goods. Railroads carried coal from the mines of West Virginia, Kentucky, and Pennsylvania to factories in Chicago, Cleveland, Buffalo, and Pittsburgh. "Minnesota flour and Iowa lard," a historian wrote, "went into pies baked in Ohio-made ovens by Vermont matrons."

With so many new customers, manufacturers could increase production. They opened new and bigger factories, bought better machines, and hired more workers.

Mail-order businesses Now that merchants could ship goods to locations across the country, shopping by mail began. In 1872 Aaron Montgomery Ward, a young salesman, had an idea for giving farmers a greater selection of goods than they could find in local stores. That year he sent out a

one-page list of items for sale. By 1874 his single sheet had grown to a 72-page catalog.

Ward soon had a competitor, Sears, Roebuck and Company. The Sears catalog, called "the Great Wish Book," came to include more than 1,000 pages of items, from children's shoes to tractors.

Madame C. J. Walker created a national market for her hair-care products both by sending them through the mail and by hiring young women to sell them door to door. Starting her company in the early 1900s with $1.50, she was the first African American woman in the nation to become a millionaire.

Improving railroad service With hundreds of companies building and running railroads, it was difficult to create an efficient rail system. For example, railroaders in the North used a narrower gauge, or distance between rails, than was used in the South. As a result, trains could not travel on all tracks.

Finally, the major railroads chose a standard gauge. Railroads in the South had to narrow almost 13,000 miles (20,800 km) of track. In one day—Sunday, May 30, 1886—frantic crews using crowbars and sledgehammers pushed thousands of miles of rail closer together.

Other developments also improved railroad service. The railway telegraph system developed by Granville T. Woods helped prevent collisions. Gustavus F. Swift and Philip D. Armour used refrigerated railcars to ship western beef safely from Chicago slaughterhouses to eastern butcher shops. George Westinghouse's air brakes and George M. Pullman's sleeping cars made rail travel safer and more comfortable.

Railroads and the environment The rapid expansion of the railroads came at a heavy cost to the environment. Lumber companies cut down whole forests for wood to make railroad ties and build bridges. Lumber was also used to build homes and furnish pulp for making paper. In 1901 one observer mourned the loss of forests in Georgia:

" In 1864 when I first went over the railroad from Savannah to Thomasville there was an almost unbroken forest of magnificent pines . . . but now one may go over that same route and scarcely see a [saleable] pine. From most of the visible land the timber is entirely gone. **"**

Most Americans, though, were excited by the opportunities offered by expanding railroads and other industries. Furthermore, it was hard to believe that our vast natural resources would ever run out.

(Right) Switchmen and signalmen run train traffic through a railroad yard in 1886. (Above) Dispatchers today control train traffic from huge video maps at computer centers.

Railroad Competition

The railroad boom led to cutthroat competition. In the late 1870s, for example, there were 20 competing routes betweeen St. Louis and Atlanta.

Railroad companies that served the same area tried to drive one another out of business. Rate wars, in which competing railroads tried to charge less than their rivals, were common. The railroad that won a rate war then raised its rates to make up for lost revenue. Shippers had no choice but to pay the new rate.

Railroad companies also made secret deals with large shippers. They offered **rebates,** or refunds, of part of the shipping costs. In return, the shipper promised to use only that railroad.

Limiting competition To protect themselves from rate wars and rebate agreements, competing railroads sometimes combined to form "pools." The companies in a pool agreed to share freight business and fix prices at high levels. Pools did not always work, though. Members often broke agreements to make quick profits.

Another way to curb competition was by **consolidation.** In this method several companies were combined into one large company.

Cornelius Vanderbilt became a master at railroad consolidation. In the 1860s he began buying small railroad lines in New York. When the New York Central Railroad refused his offer, Vanderbilt stopped service between his lines and the Central. The loss of freight and passenger business forced the Central's directors to sell to Vanderbilt.

By 1873 Vanderbilt owned railroad lines that extended as far west as Chicago. Before his consolidation, passengers traveling from New York to Chicago had to change trains 17 times during a 50-hour trip. On Vanderbilt's lines, travel time was less than 24 hours.

A consolidated railroad could be run more efficiently and cheaply. With no competition, however, there was no reason to offer lower fares and shipping rates.

Regulating the Railroads

The main victims of cutthroat competition were the customers. Especially hard hit were

After some fierce competition, a small number of companies gained control of the railroads, sometimes by unfair means. This cartoon shows the "railroad barons" carving up the United States and even seeking to expand into Europe. The cartoon is entitled, "Let them have it all, and be done with it!"

small farmers and small business owners, who did not get rebates. To farmers, wrote novelist Frank Norris, the railroad was

❝the [sea monster] with tentacles of steel clutching into the soil, . . . the Master, the Colossus, the Octopus.❞

Faced with unfair shipping rates, they demanded that government **regulate**—make rules for—the railroads.

Up to this time, most Americans believed that government should not interfere with **free enterprise,** the economic system in which businesses are free to compete without government rules. Many people saw free enterprise as the reason for the nation's economic progress. Now, though, some Americans began to complain that free enterprise did not always serve the common good.

In the 1870s several midwestern states passed laws to halt unfair railroad practices. However, in 1886 the Supeme Court ruled that a state could not regulate the rates of railroads that crossed state lines. Only Congress had the power to regulate **interstate commerce**—business between states.

The Interstate Commerce Act The Court's decision led Congress to pass the Interstate Commerce Act in 1887. This act declared that all railroad rates must be "reasonable and just." It also set up the Interstate Commerce Commission (ICC) to investigate charges of unfair railroad practices. Railroads that refused to stop such practices could be taken to court by the ICC.

Although the courts usually sided with the railroads against the ICC, an important step had been taken. Congress had established a commission to regulate an industry. In the future such commissions would be created to oversee other industries.

1. Section Review

1. Define **rebates, consolidation, regulate, free enterprise,** and **interstate commerce.**
2. How did railroads change in the late 1800s? What effects did the changes have?
3. Describe two ways railroad companies tried to force competitors out of business.
4. Critical Thinking If you were in a debate about government regulation of railroad rates, what is one argument you would use for it? Against it?

Geography Lab

The Canadian Shield

Glaciers once ground across the rocky landscape of the Canadian Shield, leaving thousands of lakes behind. One of Minnesota's early governors, William R. Marshall, described the area as a "forest region of rocks, swamps, and marshes . . . accessible only by travel through the woods on foot, or by canoe on the rivers."

Much of the iron ore that fed the Industrial Revolution came from the Canadian Shield. In 1890 Leonidas Merritt and his brothers discovered huge deposits of iron ore there, in the Mesabi Range. The Merritts turned to business leader John D. Rockefeller to finance their mining operations. Rockefeller soon owned it all, though he leased most of the mines to Andrew Carnegie. Study the photos on this page to learn more about the Canadian Shield.

Lake Superior shoreline, Minnesota

Developing a Mental Map

Use the maps on pages P4–P5, R4–R8, and R11 to help answer the questions.

1. The Canadian Shield covers parts of which states? In what state is the Mesabi Range?

2. We often think of rocky regions as being mountainous. Is that the case in the Canadian Shield? Explain.

3. What characteristics of the Canadian Shield do the photographs portray?

4. The Canadian Shield is a popular vacation destination. Does that surprise you? Explain.

5. **Hands-On Geography** Imagine that it is 1892 and you have just arrived at the Mesabi Range to work in the mines. Write a diary entry describing your impressions of your new surroundings.

Open pit mine in the Mesabi Range

2. The Growth of Big Business

Reading Guide

New Terms capital, corporation, stockholders, dividends, trust

Section Focus Why new ways to organize businesses developed

1. Why did businesspeople organize corporations in the late 1800s?
2. What new way did business leaders find to combine businesses?
3. Why and how did government try to regulate big business?

The booming railroad industry spurred growth throughout the American economy. The railroads' demand for coal, iron, and wood boosted the mining and timber industries. Steel mills expanded, as did factories producing rails, ties, and cars.

As industries in the United States grew, farsighted business leaders found new ways to organize and control them. In the process, some became very rich.

Carnegie and Steel

Andrew Carnegie pioneered many of the changes in American business. He followed a simple formula for success: "Adopt every improvement, have the best machinery, and know the most" about your business. That formula made Carnegie into what admirers called a "captain of industry."

Carnegie's first venture was building iron bridges. From a friend, he had learned that wooden bridges would have to be replaced. The sparks from steam engines set them on fire and the trains were too heavy for wooden trestles. In 1865 Carnegie and four partners formed the Keystone Bridge Company.

The Bessemer process Carnegie knew that steel was better than iron for large construction projects because it was stronger and more flexible. However, making iron into steel was expensive.

In 1872 Carnegie went to Britain to see a process invented by Henry Bessemer. It greatly reduced the cost of making steel. Upon his return, Carnegie announced, "The day of iron has passed. Steel is king!"

A year later, Carnegie and several partners chose Pittsburgh, Pennsylvania, as the site for a steel mill that used the Bessemer process. Now steel could be used for rails, locomotives, railroad cars, and bridges.

Carnegie's steel empire Between the 1870s and 1890s, steel production in the nation rose rapidly. Competition for customers was fierce. Carnegie was determined to win out by selling a better product at a lower cost than other companies. He hired scientists to improve his steel and the best managers he could find to produce it.

Carnegie also set out to control every step in the steelmaking process. He did not want to pay outsiders for work his own company could do at a lower cost. By the 1890s Carnegie's company was mining all the ore it needed from its own iron mines. His own ships and railroad transported the ore to his Pittsburgh mill.

Carnegie was also gaining control of the steel industry through consolidation. In the 1870s and 1880s he bought out several rival companies. In 1892 he combined them to form the giant Carnegie Steel Company. It produced 25 percent of the nation's steel.

Corporations

To build and operate big businesses, owners like Andrew Carnegie needed large amounts of **capital**—money used to produce goods. To get it, they formed corporations. A **corporation** is a type of business that raises money by selling shares of stock to investors. The investors, who are known as **stockholders,** then own part of the business. They elect the board of directors that runs the business.

If a corporation is profitable, its stockholders earn **dividends,** or part of the profits. At the same time, they are protected if the corporation goes bankrupt. They lose only the amount they invested.

Morgan and Banking

To manage the huge sums of money obtained from investors, corporations came to rely on investment bankers. The bankers sold stock, arranged loans, and gave advice on how to run profitable businesses.

In the late 1800s the most powerful investment banker in the United States was J. Pierpont Morgan. Believing that cutthroat competition was wasteful, he bought failing railroads and consolidated them.

Next Morgan decided to merge his railroads with steel companies into a single large corporation. Only Andrew Carnegie stood in his way. Instead of challenging Carnegie, the wily Morgan offered to buy him out. The idea appealed to Carnegie, who was now 66 years old. He sent Morgan a scrap of paper with his price on it: $480 million. Morgan agreed on the spot.

In 1901 Morgan formed the United States Steel Corporation. The largest corporation in the world at the time, it made three-fifths of the nation's steel.

The "Gospel of Wealth"

The sale of his company made Carnegie one of the richest people in the world, with a fortune of $500 million. He already knew what he was going to do with it.

Hands-On *HISTORY*

Choosing worthy causes "Pity the poor millionaire, for the way of the philanthropist is hard." So wrote an exhausted Andrew Carnegie after more than a decade of philanthropy—donating money to worthy causes. Carnegie gave away more than $300 million, mostly to causes that he listed in the following order of worthiness.

1. universities
2. free libraries
3. hospitals
4. parks
5. concert and meeting halls
6. swimming baths [pools]
7. churches

Carnegie with libraries

Activity Imagine that you have a fortune to give away. Choose seven causes to which you will make donations. List the causes in order of importance to you. Share the list with your classmates, giving reasons for your choices.

In an 1889 article called "The Gospel of Wealth," Carnegie had pointed out the wide gap between the mass of Americans struggling to make a living and business leaders who had gained great wealth. Such wealth, he argued, carried with it the social responsibility to "help those who will help themselves."

Practicing what he preached, Carnegie devoted the rest of his life to giving much of his fortune to worthy causes. He gave 7,689 organs to churches, built more than 1,900 libraries for towns throughout the United States, and supported colleges.

Rockefeller and Oil

While Carnegie and Morgan were building empires in steel, a new industry was being born. Before the Civil War, the petroleum industry did not exist. In fact, no one valued

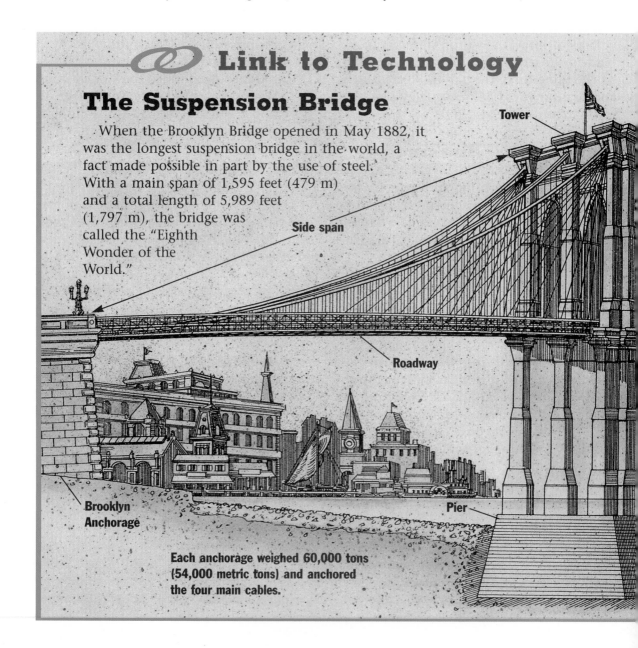

Link to Technology

The Suspension Bridge

When the Brooklyn Bridge opened in May 1882, it was the longest suspension bridge in the world, a fact made possible in part by the use of steel. With a main span of 1,595 feet (479 m) and a total length of 5,989 feet (1,797 m), the bridge was called the "Eighth Wonder of the World."

Tower

Side span

Roadway

Brooklyn Anchorage

Pier

Each anchorage weighed 60,000 tons (54,000 metric tons) and anchored the four main cables.

petroleum, often called oil, except to grease wagon axles or to take as medicine.

Then in 1855 a scientist reported that oil was a good lubricant for machinery. Refined oil, called kerosene, also made an excellent source of light and heat. Kerosene soon replaced whale oil as the main fuel for lamps.

In 1859 the nation's first oil well was drilled in Pennsylvania, spurring a frantic rush for "black gold." Soon oil wells were pumping in Kentucky, Ohio, Illinois, Indiana, and West Virginia. By the early 1900s huge new oil fields had been discovered in Texas, California, and Oklahoma.

Rockefeller's oil empire One of the early visitors to Pennsylvania's oil fields was John D. Rockefeller. Growing up in Cleveland, Ohio, he had started a business to sell farm produce when he was 20 years old.

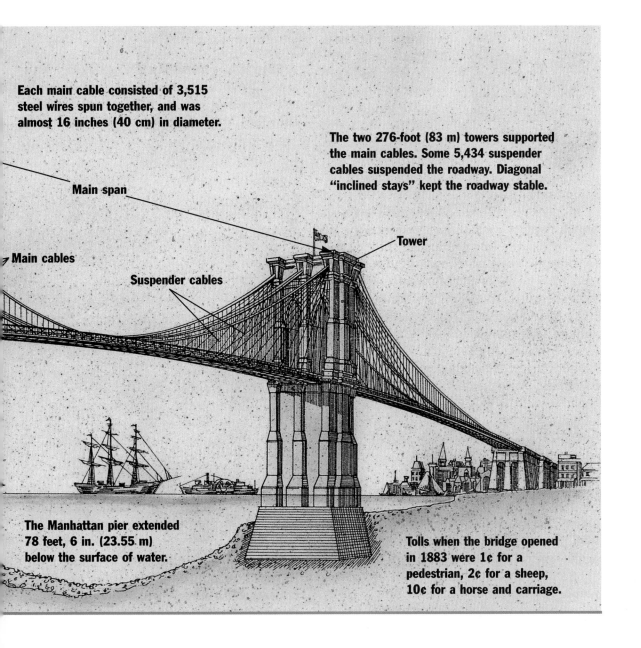

Each main cable consisted of 3,515 steel wires spun together, and was almost 16 inches (40 cm) in diameter.

The two 276-foot (83 m) towers supported the main cables. Some 5,434 suspender cables suspended the roadway. Diagonal "inclined stays" kept the roadway stable.

Main span

Tower

Main cables

Suspender cables

The Manhattan pier extended 78 feet, 6 in. (23.55 m) below the surface of water.

Tolls when the bridge opened in 1883 were 1¢ for a pedestrian, 2¢ for a sheep, 10¢ for a horse and carriage.

Instead of fighting in the Civil War, he paid for a substitute and expanded his business.

In 1862 Rockefeller established an oil-refining business in Cleveland. Eight years later he reorganized the business as a corporation, Standard Oil of Ohio.

John D. Rockefeller

Faced with intense competition and falling prices, Rockefeller set out to gain control of the oil-refining industry. He made deals with railroads to give rebates to Standard Oil. He could then lower his prices and force rival refineries out of business. In a depression that began in 1873, he bought the bankrupt companies.

To keep costs down, Rockefeller also set out to control each step of production. He bought pipelines and ships for moving oil. He built his own warehouses and made his own barrels. He even counted the drops of solder required to seal oil containers.

By 1880 Standard Oil controlled 90 percent or more of the nation's refining and almost all oil transportation. That made it a monopoly—a single business with the power to control prices in the market.

Organizing Trusts

To manage his empire better, in 1882 Rockefeller combined all the corporations he controlled into the Standard Oil Trust. A **trust** was a new form of business combination in which a board of trustees, or managers, controlled the member corporations.

Stockholders of Standard Oil's member corporations still owned their stock. However, the board of the Standard Oil Trust, headed by Rockefeller, managed the corporations. In return, stockholders received "trust certificates" that paid dividends from Standard's profits.

The Standard Oil Trust ensured that the oil industry would operate more efficiently than it had in the past. The danger was that, as a monopoly, it had the power to set high prices for oil and oil products. The free-enterprise system depended on competition to keep prices fair. By getting rid of competition, Standard seemed to threaten the free-enterprise system itself.

The Sherman Antitrust Act Meanwhile, other business leaders saw the advantages of the Standard Oil Trust. Soon they had formed trusts in other industries,

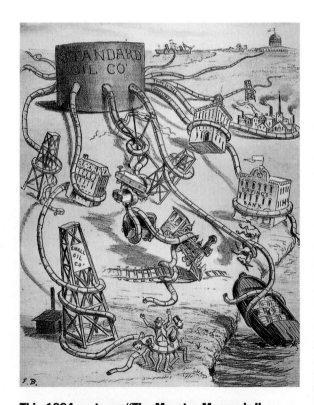

This 1884 cartoon, "The Monster Monopoly," attacked John D. Rockefeller's Standard Oil Company, which almost completely controlled the oil industry in the United States.

including sugar, meatpacking, leather, copper, and farm machinery. The growth of monopoly power alarmed many Americans. They demanded reasonable prices and the chance for smaller businesses to compete in any market.

In response to public pressure, Congress passed the Sherman Antitrust Act in 1890. The act declared that

"every contract, combination in the form of trust or otherwise, or conspiracy in restraint of trade . . . is hereby declared to be illegal.**"**

However, the Sherman Act proved difficult to enforce because it did not define what a trust or a monopoly was. In fact, the act was not enforced until the early 1900s, when the courts finally broke up two trusts for using unfair business practices. One was the Standard Oil Trust.

Captains of Industry or Robber Barons?

As companies grew, so did the wealth of their owners. There had been very few millionaires in the United States before the Civil War. By the 1890s, however, there were more than 4,000 of them. Most of them were entrepreneurs—people who start businesses—who had made their fortunes by driving their competitors out of business, sometimes by unfair methods. Critics called them "robber barons."

At the same time, many people could not help but admire what entrepreneurs like Carnegie, Morgan, and Rockefeller had accomplished. By seeing opportunities and forming large business combinations, these captains of industry had made the steel and oil industries grow and prosper. In so doing they had helped the United States become the leading industrial nation in the world.

World Link

Japan becomes an industrial nation Half a world away from booming American factories, Japan's leaders were creating another industrial giant. Their efforts were spearheaded by Emperor Meiji (MAY-jee), who was only 15 years old when he came to the throne in 1867. A year later he announced his plan to make Japan an industrial nation.

To achieve his goal, Emperor Meiji looked outward. "Knowledge shall be sought throughout the world," the emperor declared. He sent groups of Japanese to Europe and the United States to study modern industrial technology. During the late 1800s, Japan built railroads, telegraph lines, shipyards, seagoing vessels, and factories.

2. Section Review

1. Define **capital, corporation, stockholders, dividends,** and **trust.**
2. Name two forms of business organization that developed in the late 1800s and describe how they operated.
3. How did Andrew Carnegie and John D. Rockefeller deal with fierce competition?
4. Why did Congress pass the Sherman Antitrust Act? Explain why the act was not successful.
5. Critical Thinking Captains of industry argued that consolidated companies were more efficient than many small, competing companies. As the owner of a small business, how would you have responded?

Skill Lab

Skill Tips

- Use present tense for statements in flowchart boxes.
- Use as few words as possible.
- Any step may be both a cause (with one or more effects) and an effect (with one or more causes).

Acquiring Information
Analyzing a Flowchart

In 1865 dozens of companies were building oil wells and refineries. Within 15 years, though, Standard Oil had gobbled up most of them, gaining almost complete control over the industry. The oil industry is a dramatic example of the fact that few businesses could survive the fierce competition of the late 1800s.

Question to Investigate

Why did many businesses rise and fall in the late 1800s?

Procedure

One way to explore the Question to Investigate is by creating a **flowchart**—a diagram that uses words and arrows to show steps in a process. A box indicates an individual step. Arrows connect the steps in order. By showing at a glance how one step leads to another, a flowchart is useful for showing cause–effect relationships.

1 Identify the cause–effect relationships.
a. Read source **A**.
b. State each cause–effect relationship in a few words.

2 Arrange the causes and effects into a flowchart.
a. Study **B** as a model and copy it to begin your flowchart.
b. Add arrows and statements in boxes to show the causes and effects described in **A**. Refer to the Skill Tips.

3 Analyze the flowchart in order to answer the Question to Investigate.

Sources to Use

A "Briefly, then, machinery reduced production costs and expansion opened new markets. Profits rose. New entrepreneurs were attracted into the field, competed vigorously with each other, produced a surplus and, under the necessities of business warfare, slashed prices. Profits fell. There was then a general mortality [death] among marginal firms—those that could not push their costs of production down beneath new low prices. Finally, the assets of the deceased [dead] organizations were taken over by a reduced number of survivors. Competition had yielded concentration as one of its fruits."

From Bernard Weisberger et al., *The Life History of the United States*, Vol. 7 (Time-Life Books, 1974).

B

Machinery reduces production costs.   Expansion opens new markets.

Profits rise.

3. Workers Struggle for a Better Life

Reading Guide

New Terms collective bargaining, arbitration, injunction, socialism

Section Focus How American workers responded to changes brought about by industrialization

1. What conditions led workers to organize unions after the Civil War?
2. What methods did workers use to try to improve their wages and working conditions?
3. How successful were workers in achieving their goals?

In 1874 a brakeman applied for a job at a railroad yard. The yardmaster asked,

"'When will you be ready to go to work?' 'Right away,' I said.
The yardmaster looked at his watch. 'Well, you had better get your dinner first. There's no use of your getting killed on an empty stomach.'**"**

That afternoon a co-worker was crushed to death between two cars.

Changes in the Workplace

Such accidents occurred frequently on the railroads—and in other industries as well. It seemed as if the safety and well-being of workers were of little or no concern to the captains of industry.

In fact, the rapid industrial growth in the late 1800s greatly changed the relations between employers and their workers. Gone were the days when most goods were produced in small shops where owners knew their workers and took an interest in their welfare. Instead, as Andrew Carnegie wrote, "all [communication] between them is at an end . . . and often there is friction between the employer and the employed."

Gone, too, were the days when skilled workers were in demand. In many factories now, workers endlessly repeated one or two tasks that called for little skill or training. They could be replaced as easily as the parts in their machines.

To make matters worse, there were plenty of workers available. Immigrants and people from rural areas streamed into the cities, eager to take any job at any wage. With many workers to choose from, business owners could pay very low wages.

Working Families

Indeed, wages were so low that the average man could not earn enough to support his family. Wives and children, too, had to get jobs. Employers were glad to hire them at lower wages than men.

In 1900 as many as 2 million children went to work instead of to school. They sold newspapers and shined shoes. They worked in mills, factories, and mines. At the Triangle Shirtwaist Company, Pauline Newman remembered:

In many industries, wages were so low that two working parents could not support a family. Children, too, were sent to work. Here men and boys work in a mine and in a glass factory. Women (top) labor in a "sweatshop" in the garment industry. A family (left) works at home making artificial flowers.

"We were young, eight, nine, ten years old. . . . The hours were from 7:30 in the morning to 6:30 at night when it wasn't busy. When the [busy] season was on we worked until 9 o'clock. No overtime pay, not even supper money. . . . My wages were $1.50 for a seven-day week.**"**

Many women worked in the garment industry, making clothes in factories or in crowded rooms called "sweatshops." Their pay was based on the number of pieces they produced. In 1885 a New York City seamstress received $1.50 for a dozen pairs of trousers, 15¢ for a vest, and 90¢ for a dozen pairs of gloves.

The Growth of Labor Organizations

Compared to the manager of a large mill or factory, an individual worker had little power. Desperate workers began to realize that they could improve wages and working conditions only if they organized into groups to fight for common goals.

As you read in Chapter 15, working people in the United States had begun forming unions in the early 1800s. The rapid rise of industry after the Civil War led to another upsurge in union organizing.

As before, employers tried to kill the union movement. They offered jobs to workers who promised never to join unions. They fired union members and put them on "blacklists," ensuring that other businesses would not hire them. Despite this opposition, many brave workers did join labor organizations.

The Knights of Labor One of the most important new unions was the Knights of Labor, which was founded in 1869. Unlike earlier unions, the Knights accepted any worker, skilled or unskilled, male or female, of any race.

Growth was slow until Terence V. Powderly, a machinist recently elected mayor of Scranton, Pennsylvania, became the leader of the Knights in 1879. An idealist, Powderly attracted members by calling for an eight-hour workday, equal pay for equal work by men and women, and an end to child labor.

One of the most successful organizers for the Knights—and other unions—was a seamstress named Mary Harris Jones. From the 1870s through the 1920s, she traveled around the country urging workers to join unions. Most of her work was with coal miners, but she also helped metal and railroad workers and women garment workers, and led protests against child labor. She later said,

❝My life work has been to stir up the oppressed to a point of getting off their knees and demanding that which I believe is rightfully theirs.❞

Grateful miners called Mary Harris Jones "Mother" Jones. Mine owners, however, regarded her as "the most dangerous woman in America."

The Great Railroad Strike

As unions gained strength, they were able to organize strikes to force employers to make changes. In 1877 workers on the Baltimore and Ohio Railroad went on strike to protest pay cuts. Railroad workers across the country joined them, setting off the first nationwide strike.

Bloody battles broke out when state and federal troops were called in to put down the strike. By the time the workers gave up, more than 100 had been killed.

The Great Railroad Strike failed, but between 1884 and 1886 the Knights held a series of successful strikes against wage cuts. Their victories attracted new members to the union. By 1886 the Knights had more than 700,000 members.

The Haymarket Bombing

Then, at the height of their success, a violent incident dealt a fatal blow to the Knights of Labor. On May 3, 1886, striking workers in Chicago clashed with police. Several strikers were killed.

A mass meeting to protest the killings was held the next evening in Haymarket Square. As the meeting was ending, the police arrived. Suddenly a bomb exploded. The police responded by opening fire. Altogether eight policemen and seven or eight people in the crowd were killed. About a hundred were wounded.

Although no evidence linked the Knights to the bombing, the Haymarket affair turned public opinion against them. From 1886 on, membership in the Knights dropped rapidly.

The American Federation of Labor

As the Knights declined, a new national union was gaining strength. In 1886 representatives of many trade unions formed the American Federation of Labor (AFL). The AFL admitted only skilled workers, and most of its member unions barred women, African Americans, and immigrants.

The guiding spirit of the AFL was its president, Samuel Gompers. Born in London of Dutch-Jewish parents, Gompers came to the United States in 1863, when he was 13. At the age of 14, he became a member of the Cigarmakers' International Union. There he quickly showed his talent as a writer, speaker, and labor organizer.

Under Gompers, the AFL grew rapidly. By 1900 it claimed a million members. As head of the AFL, Gompers focused on practical issues. He fought for higher wages, shorter hours, and better working conditions.

Gompers believed that the best way to obtain these goals was through **collective bargaining**—the process by which the representatives of a union and a business discuss and reach agreement about wages and working conditions. However, if collective bargaining failed, Gompers did not hesitate to call a strike.

Samuel Gompers

Point of View

Should unions use the strike?

The question of whether to use the strike divided organized labor. Terence Powderly of the Knights of Labor believed that "strikes are a failure." He preferred **arbitration**—using a third party to settle a dispute. One of the Knights' major goals, Powderly wrote, was to

> "[substitute] arbitration for strikes, whenever and wherever employers and employees are willing to meet on [equal] grounds."

AFL leader Samuel Gompers was more enthusiastic about strikes. He saw them as a useful tool to achieve goals if all else failed. He also believed workers have the right to strike. In a letter in 1894, he wrote:

> "What shall workers do? Sit idly by and see the vast resources of nature and the human mind be used and monopolized for the benefit of the . . . few? No. The laborers must learn to think and [strike, so that] . . . their rights to life can be secured."

In the years to come, the question of whether to strike would be on the minds of workers, employers, and the public as strikes wracked the nation.

The Homestead Strike

Several violent strikes shook the labor movement in the 1890s. One of the worst involved Andrew Carnegie.

In 1892 the Carnegie steel plant at Homestead, Pennsylvania, cut wages. The Amalgamated Association of Iron and Steel Workers, one of the most powerful trade unions in the country, called a strike.

In this illustration from *Harper's Weekly*, armed guards surrender to striking workers at the Carnegie steel plant in Homestead, Pennsylvania. Soon after, the state militia drove the strikers out of the plant, and strikebreakers began work.

No one acted more upset at the turn of events than Carnegie. "The works [mill] are not worth a drop of human blood," he wrote. "I wish they had sunk." In fact, though, he had supported Frick throughout the strike.

The Pullman Strike

In 1894 an even more violent clash between unions and employers erupted in Pullman, Illinois, just outside of Chicago. The Pullman Palace Car Company required its workers to live in this company-owned town, where they had to pay more for rent and food than in nearby towns. Pullman workers bitterly joked,

❝We are born in a Pullman house, fed from the Pullman shop, taught in the Pullman school, catechized in the Pullman church, and when we die, we shall be buried in the Pullman cemetery and go to the Pullman hell.❞

When a depression hit the nation in 1893, the company cut workers' wages but refused to lower the rents in Pullman. In May 1894 desperate workers went on strike, demanding higher wages or lower rents.

Henry Clay Frick, the Homestead manager, decided to break the union. He locked the workers out of the plant and hired 300 armed guards to protect the strikebreakers—outside workers to replace those on strike—he planned to hire.

When the guards arrived on July 6, 1892, thousands of angry men and women were waiting for them. A battle broke out. Four guards and ten strikers were killed.

The strike dragged on until November. By then, strikebreakers had reopened the mill and the union was dead. Forty years would pass before a successful union was organized in the steel industry.

The Ironworkers' Noontime (1880) Vulgar. Crude. Shocking. These were some of the reactions to Thomas Anshutz's painting of ironworkers. Unlike most painters in the late 1800s, Anshutz did not paint portraits of the rich or murals of idealized landscapes. Instead, he was interested in realistic scenes of day-to-day life. **Discuss** Why might Anshutz have chosen to paint industrial workers? What does the artist want you to think about the workers and their lives?

The American Railway Union

Many Pullman workers belonged to the American Railway Union (ARU), founded by Eugene V. Debs. When the Pullman workers struck, 150,000 ARU members nationwide supported them. They derailed railroad cars and blocked tracks. Soon the 24 railroad lines leading out of Chicago stood idle.

The federal government then entered the conflict. In July 1894 a federal court issued an **injunction**—a court order—based on the Sherman Antitrust Act. The court charged the union with interfering with interstate commerce because the trains could no longer deliver mail. The injunction ordered the strikers back to work.

When they refused, federal troops were sent to Chicago. Days of rioting followed, with 34 lives lost. After Debs and other union leaders were sent to prison, both the strike and the ARU collapsed.

During his six months in jail, Debs learned about **socialism,** the belief that government, rather than individuals, should own a nation's major industries. He became the leader of the Socialist Party of America, founded in 1901.

Most workers, though, did not want to destroy the nation's system of free enterprise. Instead, they wanted to make it fairer. Indeed, union membership continued to grow. More and more workers had learned the lesson in the Knights of Labor motto, "An injury to one is the concern of all."

3. Section Review

1. Define **collective bargaining, arbitration, injunction,** and **socialism.**
2. Describe two ways that industrial growth affected the conditions of workers.
3. Critical Thinking If you had been a union member in the late 1800s, would you have agreed to go on strike? Why or why not?

Why We Remember

The Rise of Industry and Big Business

One day a friend asked Andrew Carnegie how he was doing. "I'm rich, I'm rich," he replied. In his spectacular rise from rags to riches, Carnegie and the other pioneers of big business reshaped the American dream.

Ever since colonial times, the United States had been a place where dreams of freedom, cheap land, and a decent reward for hard work came true. Never before, however, had a few business leaders amassed such great wealth. The hope of getting rich became part of the American dream—and still inspires ambitious entrepreneurs today.

The Carnegies, Morgans, and Rockefellers are not the only reasons for remembering the rise of industry and big business, however. Their great business empires could not have been built without the brains and brawn of millions of laboring men, women, and children.

Toiling under conditions most of us would find intolerable, these workers built the nation's industries. Many of them also organized to demand what Americans had always dreamed of—a decent reward for hard work. In doing so, they kept the American dream alive for all us.

Chapter Survey

Reviewing Vocabulary

Define the following terms.

1. rebates
2. consolidation
3. regulate
4. free enterprise
5. interstate commerce
6. capital
7. corporation
8. stockholders
9. dividends
10. trust
11. collective bargaining
12. arbitration
13. injunction
14. socialism

Reviewing Main Ideas

1. Why did shopping by mail become practical in the late 1800s?
2. Who was helped by the consolidation of railroads, and how? Who was hurt, and how?
3. How did Andrew Carnegie, J. Pierpont Morgan, and John D. Rockefeller view competition? Explain.
4. What was the major flaw in the Sherman Antitrust Act?
5. Describe industrial working conditions in the late 1800s.
6. Give at least two examples of how labor unions tried to improve wages and working conditions.
7. What was the outcome of each of the following events? (a) Haymarket bombing (b) Homestead strike (c) Pullman strike

Thinking Critically

1. **Analysis** What arguments might captains of industry have used to keep the wages of workers low?
2. **Evaluation** Terence Powderly of the Knights of Labor believed that strikes were not a good way for workers to achieve their goals. Do you agree or disagree? Give evidence from the chapter to support your answer.

3. Why We Remember: Application

Imagine that you are a teenager in the late 1800s. Who are your role models: entrepreneurs like Carnegie and Rockefeller, union leaders like Gompers and Debs, or factory workers like your parents? Explain.

Applying Skills

Making a flowchart Find a newspaper or magazine article about a recent business event, such as a merger (consolidation) or a sharp rise or fall in the value of a company's stock. Make a flowchart to show the causes and effects described in the article. Keep in mind what you learned in the Skill Lab on page 600.

History Mystery

"The most dangerous woman in America" Answer the History Mystery on page 585. A writer said of Mary Harris Jones: "With one speech she often threw a whole community on strike and she could keep the strikers loyal month after month on empty stomachs and behind prison bars." How does this description help to explain her reputation among mine owners?

Writing in Your History Journal

1. **Keys to History** (a) The time line on pages 584–585 has seven Keys to History. In your journal, list each key and describe why it is important to know about. (b) Choose one of the events on the time line. Imagine you were an ordinary American when the event occurred. Write a diary entry as that person, describing your reactions to the event.
2. **Andrew Carnegie** An obituary is a notice of a person's death that appears in a

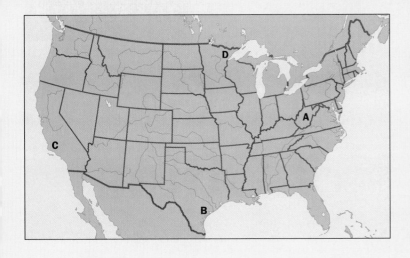

1. For each letter on the map, write the major mineral resource—iron, coal, or petroleum—found in the area.

2. Geographic Thinking How did the environment in the United States make rapid industrial growth possible? How did rapid industrial growth, in turn, affect the environment? Support your answers with evidence from the text as well as your own observations.

newspaper. Many obituaries give a short account of the person's life and achievements. Imagine that you are the obituary editor at a major newspaper in 1919, when Andrew Carnegie died. In your journal, write the obituary that will appear in the newspaper.

3. Citizenship Did the government "do the right thing" in regulating business in the late 1800s? Do you think that the government should have done more? Should the government have done less? Write your thoughts in your journal.

Alternative Assessment

Participating in a round table

Imagine that you live in 1895, and a round table (conference) sponsored by a group of concerned citizens is about to take place. The topic for discussion is "Big Business: Fair or Unfair." With five classmates, participate in the round table.

❶ Meet as a group to assign roles: Andrew Carnegie, J. Pierpont Morgan, John D. Rockefeller, a person who owns a small business, a farmer, and a factory worker.

❷ Develop a plan for the round table. For example, you might begin by having each participant briefly answer the question, giving examples from the chapter. Then you might take turns reacting to one another's answers.

❸ Act out the round table for the class.

Your work will be evaluated on the following criteria:

• you cover a wide variety of issues, including consolidation in railroads and other industries, the growth of trusts, government regulation, working conditions, the growth of labor organizations, and conflict between workers and employers

• you present your positions clearly

• you stay "in character" in your roles

Chapter 22

The Growth of Cities

Sections

🔑 *Keys to History*

1884–1885
First metal-frame skyscraper is built
Home Insurance building in Chicago

1879
Edison invents electric lightbulb

1882
Chinese Exclusion Act

1865

1875

1885

Looking Back

Great Famine drives Irish immigrants to United States
1845

World 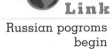 **Link**

Russian pogroms begin
1881

HISTORY *Mystery*

Although she never actually swam across the ocean, the "Atlantic swimmer" well deserved her title. Who was she and how did she earn her nickname?

1907
Peak year for immigration
Ellis Island

1911
Triangle Shirtwaist factory fire in New York City

1888
Electric streetcar system built in Richmond, Virginia
Restored streetcar in Seattle

1906
San Francisco earthquake and fire

1895

1905

1915

Looking Ahead

Congress sets first quotas on immigration
1921

Beginning the Story with

Jacob Riis

It was a wet and windy October night in New York City. A hungry young immigrant from Denmark named Jacob Riis (rees) sat along the banks of the river, gazing into its dark waters. Winter would soon be coming and he had no money, no home, no job, not even a winter coat to wear. Numb with cold and filled with an aching loneliness, how could he go on? No one would know or care if he threw himself into the river to end his misery, he told himself.

Suddenly, another shivering body pressed close to his. A little dog that had been following Jacob for days had found him again. As Jacob reached down to pet it, the dog climbed into his lap and licked his face. "The love of the faithful little beast thawed the icicles in my heart," he later wrote. Jacob picked up the dog and walked back into the city to seek shelter for the night.

The only place he could find was a lodging room at the police station. Jacob was caught trying to smuggle the dog in under his jacket, and the police forced him to leave it outside. There the dog shivered through the night alone.

During the night, a man stole a gold locket that Jacob kept hidden beneath his shirt. The locket was given to him by Elisabeth—the girl back home in Denmark whom he loved and hoped someday to marry. Even with an ocean between them, Elisabeth's face still haunted his dreams.

In the morning, tearful and angry, Jacob told the police sergeant that he had been robbed. When the sergeant did not believe that a poor man like Jacob Riis could have owned something as valuable as a gold locket, Jacob yelled at him. Following the sergeant's order, a guard kicked Jacob down the steps and out into the city street. The furious Jacob was then marched out of the neighborhood and forced onto the first ferry leaving New York City.

Seeking to show the terrible living conditions of immigrants in the late 1800s, Riis photographed this courtyard at 22 Baxter Street in New York City. In such tenements "piles of garbage [were] fairly alive with diseased odors, [with] numbers of children filling every nook."

Homeless in a New World

The year was 1870 and Jacob Augustus Riis was one of hundreds of thousands of European immigrants pouring into the United States each year. Unable to find work as a carpenter in his hometown in Denmark, Jacob had left for the United States at the age of 21.

When he arrived, Jacob discovered that many other young men were also seeking work. He took whatever jobs he could find, from picking vegetables to hauling bricks. He wandered the streets, moving from job to job.

Sometimes Jacob had money to buy a meal. At other times he rummaged through garbage cans for food.

Jacob lived in the worst neighborhoods of New York City. He stayed in cheap lodging houses, where at best he could rent a tiny bedroom with a cot, and at worst sleep on a musty mattress along with a dozen or more other lodgers.

Jacob Riis Becomes a Reporter

Not long after that terrible night at the police station, though, Jacob's luck began to change. A friend told him about a reporting job on a New York City newspaper. To his amazement, he got the position.

As a reporter, Jacob Riis covered the daily dramas of the city, from terrible fires to everyday life in the slums. His stories were known for their accuracy and compassion—rare qualities in the newspaper business at the time. Even with his success, Riis never forgot how difficult life had been for him, and how difficult it continued to be for millions of others.

Hands-On → *HISTORY*

Activity

Jacob Riis wrote stories about people living in a strange new land. As a television reporter, you have been sent back in time to explore the lives of immigrants in Jacob Riis's time. What scenes would you show in your television special? What four questions might you ask to help immigrants describe their lives to your audience?

1. Land of Promise

Reading Guide

New Terms anti-Semitism, ethnic neighborhoods, assimilate

Section Focus The great new wave of immigrants to the United States

1. Who were the new immigrants after the Civil War and why did they come?
2. What experiences did immigrants have in making their way to the United States and after they arrived?
3. How did native-born Americans respond to the new arrivals?

To a 13-year-old boy, departing for the United States from his homeland of Macedonia, it appeared as if

"the whole world had discovered America at the same time . . . and was in a hurry to get there.**"**

Everyone, it seemed, had "America fever." After the Civil War the number of Europeans crossing the Atlantic—and Asians crossing the Pacific—skyrocketed. Millions of people were now on the move. Who were these new immigrants? How did they differ from earlier newcomers? What forces pushed them from their homes and attracted them to the United States?

The New Wave of Immigrants

To the poor farmers of Europe and Asia, America meant jobs and freedom. Between 1870 and 1920 nearly 27 million people arrived. They were seeking new lives—or at least the opportunity to make and save money to take back to their homelands.

European immigrants Europeans made up 21 of the 24 million people who came to the United States between 1880 and

1920. This wave of Europeans, though, differed from earlier ones. Before, most had come from northern Europe—Britain, Ireland, Germany, and Scandinavia. Now many came from southern and eastern Europe.

Italians, Poles, and eastern European Jews made up some of the larger groups of the new immigrants. Nearly 5 million Italians came during this time, and 3 million Jews. Greeks, Serbs, Czechs, and Slovaks also joined the migration. In cities throughout the nation, a chorus of languages—including Polish, Italian, and Yiddish—filled the air. Jewish synagogues and Catholic and Eastern Orthodox churches sprang up.

These immigrants differed from earlier ones in another important way. Few had money to buy land and start farms. Instead, most settled in cities and took whatever jobs they could find.

Asian immigrants The new wave of immigrants also included Asians. In 1849, 325 Chinese joined the California gold rush. They were followed by more than 300,000 Chinese who crossed the Pacific in the next 50 years. Japanese began migrating to the United States in the 1870s. Almost 400,000 had made their way here by the 1920s. Koreans and Filipinos also arrived from Asia, while Armenians, Lebanese, and Syrians came from the Middle East.

Where They Came From

1860

4%
4%
1%
92%

153,000

1890

1%
1%
35%
63%

455,000

1910

9%
2%
19%
70%

1,042,000

Northern and Western Europe

Southern and Eastern Europe

Asia

The Americas

Source: *Historical Statistics of the United States*

Why They Came

PUSH What pushed immigrants from their homelands

Poverty
Shortage of farmland
Lack of opportunity
Political and religious persecution
Wars and threats of war

PULL What pulled immigrants to the United States

Jobs
Opportunity
Political and religious freedom
Peace
Letters from family and friends

Immigrants arriving in New York City

Searching for Work

Leaving friends and home to look for work in a strange land was not new to Europeans. "We are like wild geese," said an Irishman, describing the poor who wandered across Europe looking for work. In fact, twice as many people migrated within Europe during this time as the millions who crossed the ocean to the United States.

In Europe and Asia, growing populations led to overcrowding and shortages of farmland. A visitor to China wrote that "the least failure of the rice crop produces wretchedness." Small farmers lost their land when they could not pay the rent or heavy government taxes. With few opportunities in the countryside, the landless had no choice but to move elsewhere.

To the desperate poor in Europe and Asia, faraway America appeared to be a land of abundance. "It was almost heaven. You could almost just grab the money!" wrote an immigrant to friends back in Finland. Although easy wealth was more fantasy than reality, such tales fell on eager ears.

Roundtrippers When Jacob Riis came to New York City in 1870, he arrived at the dawning of a tremendous industrial age. Riis found a land bursting with construction and industry, and looking for workers.

Unlike earlier immigrants, many of the newcomers did not intend to stay in the United States. Fathers hoped to work for a few years and return home rich. The young sought jobs to support parents back home or to save to start their own families. An

Russian pogroms begin "I feel that every cobblestone in Russia is filled with Jewish blood," mourned a Jew who fled to the United States during the organized attacks on Jews that began in Russia in 1881. These attacks—called pogroms (po-GRAHMS)—were touched off by rumors that Jews were involved in the assassination of Czar Alexander II.

In fact, the rumors were false. The czar had been killed by revolutionaries. Fearing that revolution would spread, the government tried to convince discontented Russians that Jews were to blame for their problems. It whipped up anti-Jewish feelings in Russia, then looked the other way when mob violence against Jews took place.

The pogroms ended in 1884. Then in 1903 a second wave began, driving hundreds of thousands of Jews to escape to the United States.

Irishwoman known as "the Atlantic swimmer" made six round trips by ship between Ireland and the United States.

Longing for Freedom

While many immigrants were seeking work, others were longing for freedom. Harsh laws and religious persecution pushed them from their homelands.

For centuries **anti-Semitism**—hatred and persecution of Jews—had simmered in Europe. In the 1880s treatment of Jews turned cruel and violent. Laws forced Jews to live in certain areas and barred them from owning land. They suffered from mass killings and destruction of their homes.

Jews were not alone in their suffering. Throughout Europe religious persecution, tyranny, wars, and threats of war drove people from their lands.

Dreams of America satisfied other yearnings for freedom, too. Many young people wanted to begin new lives. They believed that by moving to the United States they could "escape from the priest's eye and from the parent's eye."

The Journey

Compared to the days of sailing ships, the journey was easier for these immigrants. They traveled by rail from their homes in Europe and Asia to ports where they boarded steamships. Steamships shortened the Atlantic voyage from 7 weeks to 12 days.

Eager to fill their ships, steamship companies paid agents up to $8 for each person they brought aboard. Thousands of agents combed China and Europe for passengers, sometimes emptying entire villages of their populations. Agents provided clothing for the trip and loaned passengers money for tickets—to be repaid once they found work.

Steerage Still, the voyage could be a nightmare. Few immigrants could afford private rooms. Instead, they crammed together in steerage—large compartments below deck, just in front of the rudder that steered the ship. Jacob Riis traveled in steerage, enduring the cramped, dirty quarters, rotten meat, and foul drinking water.

Given the hardships of the voyage, it is easy to understand the excitement immigrants felt as they arrived at their destination. Riis recalled:

❝As I looked over the rail at the miles of ferryboats and pleasure craft on the

Hands-On → *HISTORY*

Two immigrant boys in 1896

Discussing a move to America One immigrant wrote to his brother back in Poland, "[I]f you want to come to America, then come. You could . . . earn some money so that you could pull yourself out from under that misery and be a man." Watching their younger son eagerly read the letter, his parents may have wished they had hidden it from him.

Activity Create and act out a conversation that might have taken place between members of a poor family in Europe in 1890. The children, ages 13 and 16, want to move to the United States. Their parents oppose the idea.

1 Working with three classmates, write a script for the conversation. How might the teens persuade their parents to let them go? For example, how might they compare conditions in Poland to those in the United States? What objections might the parents raise?

2 When finished writing, assign roles and rehearse until you have memorized the script.

3 Present the conversation—"live" or on videotape—to the class.

river, my hopes rose high that somewhere in this teeming hive there would be a place for me. **"**

Making a New Life

Many immigrants first stepped onto American soil at one of two entry stations—Ellis Island in New York or Angel Island in San Francisco. Inspectors checked their identification documents and their health.

A person with tuberculosis or other contagious disease could be refused entry. Officials who could not pronounce foreign names gave immigrants new, more simple spellings of their names, whether they wanted them or not.

Once admitted to the United States, the newcomers faced the challenge of finding work and a place to live. Jacob Riis had difficulty at first, even though he spoke some English and was a carpenter. Luckily, a Danish diplomat helped him get a job.

Ethnic neighborhoods Like Riis, immigrants often relied on people from their homelands to help them get started. They clustered in **ethnic neighborhoods**—areas where people shared the same languages and culture. There they found familiar foods, newspapers in their native languages, and help from earlier arrivals.

For example, Jewish immigrants settled in large numbers on New York City's Lower East Side and worked in the garment industry. Chicago's meatpacking industry attracted Polish immigrants. In western cities, Chinese established neighborhoods called Chinatowns. Japanese who worked in Hawaii's sugar cane fields opened Japanese-language schools and built Buddhist temples.

Immigrants transformed American cities. In 1890 nearly 80 percent of New Yorkers were foreign-born or children of the foreign-born. By 1900 they made up over 30 percent of the populations of Chicago, Cleveland, Minneapolis, and San Francisco.

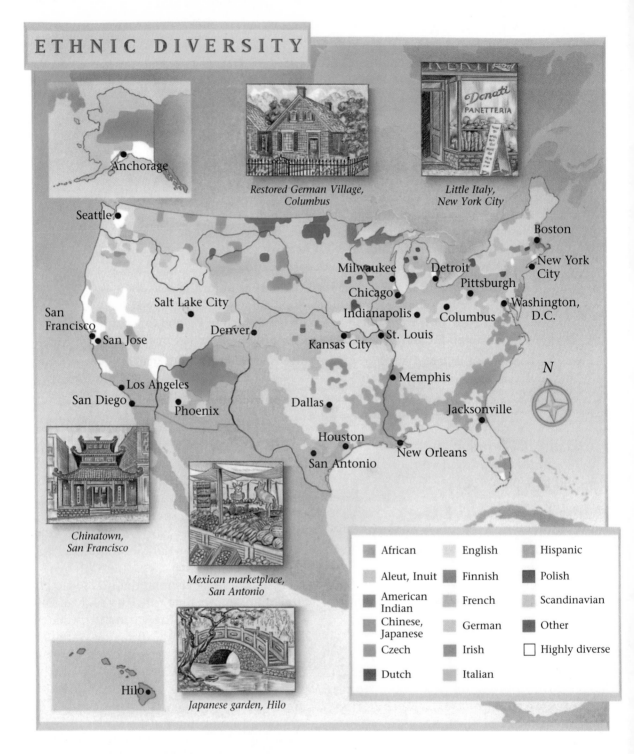

ETHNIC DIVERSITY

Restored German Village, Columbus

Little Italy, New York City

Anchorage

Seattle

Boston

New York City

Milwaukee   Detroit

Chicago   Pittsburgh

Salt Lake City   Indianapolis   Washington, D.C.

San Francisco   Columbus

Denver   St. Louis

San Jose   Kansas City

Los Angeles   Memphis

San Diego   Dallas   Jacksonville

Phoenix

Houston   New Orleans

San Antonio

N

Chinatown, San Francisco

Mexican marketplace, San Antonio

■ African	□ English	■ Hispanic
□ Aleut, Inuit	■ Finnish	■ Polish
■ American Indian	■ French	□ Scandinavian
■ Chinese, Japanese	□ German	■ Other
■ Czech	■ Irish	□ Highly diverse
■ Dutch	■ Italian	

Hilo

Japanese garden, Hilo

Reading Maps

Ancestors of Americans came from what continents? What groups settled in your area? (Not every group is shown on the map.)

Some cities became identified with certain nationalities. Milwaukee was known as a largely German city, Minneapolis a Scandinavian city, and Boston an Irish and Italian one. The South, with fewer cities and jobs, did not attract many immigrants.

Hardships and fears Bright dreams brought immigrants across the ocean. The reality they found was often far different. They crowded into tiny apartments, often with several other families, and worked long hours to earn barely enough to live on.

Meanwhile, they saw their children beginning to speak English and adopt American customs. Some parents encouraged their children to **assimilate,** which means to be absorbed into the main cultural group. Others, especially roundtrippers who planned to return to their homelands, feared losing their children to the new land.

The Nativist Reaction

The question of assimilating immigrants into American society worried many native-born Americans, too. Overwhelmed by the huge numbers of newcomers, they felt threatened by the different languages and religions. Sometimes they found themselves competing with immigrants for jobs and opportunities. The result was friction and a rebirth of nativism—hatred of immigrants (see Chapter 15).

Irish looking for work were faced with signs that read "No Irish need apply." Jews, barred from renting in many neighborhoods, realized that anti-Semitism existed in the United States, too. Urged by nativists, Congress placed restrictions on immigration. For example, workers whose passage across the ocean was paid by American companies could not enter the country.

Lee Wai She and her children lived in Hawaii, where the labor of many Chinese Americans helped make sugar "king."

The Statue of Liberty, which has become a symbol of freedom and hope to immigrants, was given to the United States by the people of France in 1884.

A Lamp Beside the Golden Door

In 1883, amid the nativist outcry, a poet lifted her voice with a different message for the immigrants struggling to make a life in the United States. In a poem now inscribed at the base of the Statue of Liberty, Emma Lazarus painted a picture of the United States as a beacon of freedom and a land of hope:

> **"**Give me your tired, your poor,
> Your huddled masses yearning
> to breathe free,
> The wretched refuse of your
> teeming shore.
> Send these, the homeless, tempest-
> tossed to me:
> I lift my lamp beside the
> golden door!**"**

The Chinese Exclusion Act Nativists were most successful in their attacks on Asians. Nativists in California accused the Chinese of working for lower wages. They pushed for laws that unfairly taxed Chinese immigrants and kept the children of Chinese from attending public schools. In 1882 they persuaded Congress to pass the Chinese Exclusion Act, which banned Chinese laborers from coming to the United States.

With Chinese workers unable to enter the country, California farmers and businesses hired Japanese to work in the fields, on the railroads, and in canneries. In 1907 and 1908, under nativist pressure, the United States negotiated the Gentlemen's Agreement with Japan by which Japan agreed to limit immigration to the United States.

Nativists in California and other states were not satisfied. They soon passed laws that banned Japanese Americans from owning or even renting farmland.

Whether they came and then returned home, or came and made the United States their home, millions of people responded to that promise. One immigrant, Emmanuel Goldenberg, expressed the feeling of many who stayed to start new lives: "At Ellis Island I was born again."

1. Section Review

1. Define **anti-Semitism, ethnic neighborhoods,** and **assimilate.**

2. Describe two ways in which immigrants after the Civil War differed from earlier immigrants to the United States.

3. What factors pushed and pulled people from their homelands to the United States?

4. Critical Thinking As an immigrant from Asia, why might you have been confused by the various reactions of Americans to your arrival?

Geography Lab

A West Side Chicago Neighborhood, 1895

In 1893 Agnes Sinclair Holbrook, a worker at Hull House (page 626), studied the ethnic mix of a Chicago neighborhood made up mainly of immigrants. She used the results of a house-to-house survey to create a map like the one on this page. The colors reflect the percentages of people of various ethnic backgrounds living in each building, not the actual number of people. English-speaking residents were usually the children of immigrants who spoke another language.

Link to History

1. What group made up the largest percentage of the households on each street?

2. On the map, what evidence can you find that Germans had lived in the neighborhood for several decades while Italians had begun coming very recently?

3. **Hands-On Geography** Imagine that you live with your parents in this neighborhood in 1895. Write a letter to a friend in the old country. Describe your neighbors and the sights, sounds, and scents of your surroundings.

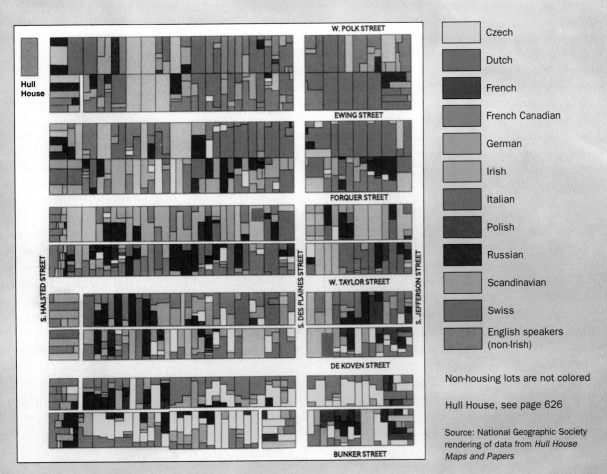

W. POLK STREET
Hull House
EWING STREET
FORQUER STREET
S. HALSTED STREET
S. DES PLAINES STREET
W. TAYLOR STREET
S. JEFFERSON STREET
DE KOVEN STREET
BUNKER STREET

Czech
Dutch
French
French Canadian
German
Irish
Italian
Polish
Russian
Scandinavian
Swiss
English speakers (non-Irish)

Non-housing lots are not colored

Hull House, see page 626

Source: National Geographic Society rendering of data from *Hull House Maps and Papers*

2. The Rise of American Cities

Reading Guide

New Terms urbanization, tenements, political machine, settlement house

Section Focus The effects of immigration and industry on American cities

1. Why did cities grow so quickly in the decades following the Civil War?
2. What problems did growing cities face, and how did political leaders respond?
3. How did reformers and immigrants try to solve the problems of cities?

As a boy in Denmark, Jacob Riis had listened carefully to stories of the American West told by a man who had dug for gold there. With those stories filling his head, Riis arrived in New York City in 1870. He half expected to meet cowboys and see buffalo charging through the streets. Instead, he found a city "quite as civilized as Copenhagen," with paved streets, electric lights, and tall buildings.

The Growth of Cities

Riis had landed in New York at a time when the industrial age was transforming the United States from a nation of farmers to a nation of city dwellers. Cities with good transportation links to the outside world—large harbors, railroads, and steamships—grew into industrial centers. Their factories attracted immigrants as well as American migrants from farms and small towns.

The nation was undergoing **urbanization**—the movement of people into cities. In 1860 only one-fifth of Americans lived in cities with more than 2,500 people. By the dawn of the twentieth century, almost one-half of Americans were city dwellers.

From coast to coast, cities now dotted the American landscape. In 1900 three cities had over 1 million people—New York, Chicago, and Philadelphia—and 35 others had more than 100,000 residents.

Outward and Upward

American cities before the Civil War were "walking cities"—compact and easily crossed on foot or in horse-drawn carriages. Now, as urbanization put pressure on cities to expand, new technologies made it possible for them to grow outward and upward.

Streetcars In 1890 the main form of public transportation was the horse-drawn streetcar. Tons of horse manure clogged the streets and filled the air with foul smells. Also, crowded streetcars cruelly strained the horses. In New York City alone, 15,000 horses died each year on the streets.

The solution was found in the electric streetcar or trolley, which was powered by an overhead electric wire. In 1888 Frank J. Sprague built a 12-mile (19-km) streetcar line for Richmond, Virginia. Three years later, 50 cities had electric streetcars.

Streetcar tracks radiated outward like spokes from the downtown hub. With an easy way to get to work, middle-class people—businesspeople and highly skilled workers—moved to quieter neighborhoods beyond the busy city core.

Skyscrapers Cities not only expanded outward. They grew upward, too, thanks to improved materials and to electricity. Buildings with walls framed in steel or iron were

City	1860	1910	Percentage increase
New York City	1,175,000	4,770,000	306%
Chicago	109,000	2,185,000	1886%
Cleveland	43,000	560,000	1202%
Detroit	46,000	465,000	911%
Los Angeles	4,400	319,000	7173%

Source: John L. Andriot, *Population Abstract of the United States*

In 1909 streetcars, wagons, and people jammed the streets of Chicago—a city bursting with new construction and industry.

strong enough to reach higher than the old limits of four or five stories. Electric lights and elevators made it possible for people to live and work in the new "skyscrapers" sprouting up in cities across the country.

Problems in Cities

These new modes of transportation and construction encouraged urbanization. With urbanization, though, came new problems.

Tenements One serious problem was overcrowding. Cities were filling with immigrants and newcomers from American farms and small towns. Too poor to rent their own apartments, they crammed together into **tenements**—apartment houses where large families shared one or two rooms, often without heat or water.

The tenement areas of American cities were among the most densely populated places in the world. An observer in 1888 described tenements as

"great prison-like structures of brick, with narrow doors and windows, cramped passages and steep rickety stairs. . . . In case of fire they would be perfect death-traps.**"**

Fire In fact, fire was a major threat in the cities. In 1871 the great Chicago fire

Chicago Style After the Chicago fire the city embarked on a massive rebuilding effort. Architects were needed, and Louis Sullivan became one of the finest. Sullivan rejected the old style of dark, thick-walled skyscrapers. He wanted them to be pieces of art. He designed thinner walls to make them more graceful, with larger windows to let in more light. Then Sullivan adorned the walls with elaborate decoration. Like a sculptor, he shaped buildings "into new forms of use and beauty." Sullivan's style, shown here in the Guaranty building in Buffalo, New York, came to be called the Chicago Style. **Discuss** What building in your area would you redesign to make more beautiful? What shapes, colors, or construction materials might you use?

destroyed the heart of that city. When San Francisco was shaken by its 1906 earthquake, the fires that followed did more damage than the quake itself. Thousands of buildings burned to the ground.

Fire was a constant danger to factory workers. The most famous factory fire broke out in 1911 in the ten-story Triangle Shirtwaist factory in New York City. Many of the 146 workers who died in that tragedy were young immigrant women. They could not escape because exits were locked and stairways were too narrow. Frances Perkins, a social worker, described the tragedy:

❝We saw the smoke pouring out of the building. We got there just as they started to jump. . . . They came down in twos and threes, jumping together in a kind of desperate hope.❞

Sanitation In the overcrowded cities, sanitation was also a problem. Water systems were unable to supply enough water to swelling city populations. Ill-planned sewers emptied waste into rivers and harbors.

Jacob Riis feared that raw sewage was getting into New York City's drinking-water supply. With a notebook and camera, he set out to document the source of the city's water. Riis found sewage from nearby cities pouring into the rivers. Garbage piled up on riverbanks as well as on city streets. It was not surprising, then, that city dwellers were plagued by diseases such as typhus, tuberculosis, dysentery, and cholera.

Seeking Solutions

The explosive growth of cities made it hard for city governments to keep up with demands for services such as fire protection and sanitation. As problems mounted, elected officials struggled to solve them.

Shocked by disasters like the Triangle Shirtwaist fire, cities passed new laws and building codes. They hired and trained firefighters to replace volunteer firemen. They required building owners to install fire extinguishers and to improve fire escapes. Builders also began to use brick, concrete, and steel instead of wood.

Meanwhile, journalists like Jacob Riis were having an effect. Riis's reports helped push cities to install safer water and sewage-disposal systems.

Machine Politics

To force city officials and landlords to address their problems, citizens had to take action. However, it was hard for the poor—especially immigrants who spoke little English and did not understand the American political system—to make their needs known. Seeing an opportunity, local politicians stepped in.

Many cities were divided into small districts called wards. Voters in a ward elected an alderman to represent them on the city council. The person who ran the Democratic or Republican Party in the ward was called the ward boss.

If a tenement was without heat, if garbage went uncollected, or if a street needed to be paved, people turned to the alderman and the ward boss for help. In exchange for votes at election time, ward bosses tried to give people what they needed.

The organization of a political party that granted favors in return for votes was called a **political machine.** In the cities, political machines worked hard to help solve the problems of the poor in their districts. That was how they gained power—and kept it.

Corruption Political machines, however, were also corrupt. Bosses bought votes and gave city jobs to their supporters, whether they were qualified or not. If a streetcar company wanted to run a trolley in a certain ward, it would bribe the ward boss to let it do so. Tenement owners could keep fire inspectors out of their buildings by paying off the political machine.

Point of View

Were political machines helpful or harmful?

In spite of their corruption, political machines had their defenders. The journalist Frederick Howe reported approvingly that ward bosses

❝were kindly, tolerant; good companions. Their system was human and simple, something any one could understand. It took graft [bribes] . . . and gave help to neighbors when sick or in need.❞

Others condemned the system. Senator Carl Schurz worked tirelessly to wipe out machine politics. He claimed that

❝it attracts to . . . politics the worst elements of our population. . . . The people of some of our great municipalities [cities] are crying out that they have been scandalously misgoverned and robbed and oppressed [by political machines].❞

Political machines continued to dominate the politics of many cities well into the twentieth century. However, reformers and journalists did their best to expose and destroy them.

Early Reformers

Some citizens were shocked by corrupt political machines. They claimed that officials were more interested in taking bribes than in protecting health and safety. Cleaning up cities, they realized, required cleaning up politics as well. (You will read more about political reform in Chapter 23.) Meanwhile, many private citizens—well-educated and middle class—felt it their duty to help the suffering poor.

Women reformers Women played a leading role in these efforts. They formed associations such as the Women's Municipal League to pressure local leaders to build schools and provide other services. Some women worked as teachers and nurses in city neighborhoods. Others became social workers, collecting information on living conditions and working to promote the well-being of poor city dwellers.

Settlement houses On Mulberry Street in New York City, an organization called the King's Daughters helped improve a neighborhood by planting trees and flowers. Realizing that people needed more serious help, they opened a **settlement house**—a community center providing services to the poor.

During the 1880s and 1890s, settlement houses sprang up everywhere. One of the best known was Hull House on Chicago's West Side. Started in 1889 by Jane Addams and Ellen Starr, it provided everything from English-language classes to hot meals. Settlement houses were also places for the poor to meet and discuss problems.

Help for children Settlement houses took a special interest in children. Streets were filled with children—orphans as well as those left to look after themselves while their parents struggled to earn a living. Unable to get into overcrowded schools, some joined gangs. Many toiled in sweatshops to help their families. As many as 350,000 homeless children were put on "orphan trains" and sent to live with families outside the big cities.

Settlement houses ran day nurseries for the children of working parents. Reformers pressed cities to make public schools available to all, and to build playgrounds to provide places for children to play and breathe fresh air.

Religious groups The plight of the poor was of concern to religious groups, too. In the 1880s the Salvation Army began providing the poor with food and shelter. The Young Men's and Women's Christian Associations (YMCA and YWCA) set up clubs and activities for youth. In 1891 James Naismith nailed a peach basket to a wall in a YMCA gymnasium and invented basketball.

Many Protestants worked in settlement houses because they accepted an idea known as the Social Gospel—the belief that the teachings of Jesus require Christians to help the poor. Catholic churches became community centers for immigrants from Catholic regions such as Italy, Poland, and Bohemia.

Self-help Immigrants themselves organized to deal with the hardships of city life. The Hebrew Immigrant Aid Society helped Jewish newcomers. Chinese formed family and neighborhood associations. Immigrants published newspapers in their native languages and joined unions to fight for better wages and working conditions. When they became citizens, they joined political parties in order to have a voice in improving their lives.

2. Section Review

1. Define **urbanization, tenements, political machine,** and **settlement house.**
2. Describe three problems that cities faced.
3. Critical Thinking If you had been an early reformer, what city problem would you have tried to solve first? Why?

3. Cities and a New Way of Life

Reading Guide

New Terms **leisure, vaudeville**

Section Focus **New ways of living that developed in American cities**

1. How did American cities change to become more exciting places to live?
2. What new inventions and products changed daily life for city dwellers?
3. How did people spend their leisure time in the cities?

As you have seen, American cities changed dramatically in the late 1800s—and not simply in size and shape. The American way of life itself was changing. Indeed, cities offered more than jobs for the poor from far and near. They became centers of new ideas, activities, and expectations.

The Excitement of City Life

When people left the countryside for the city, they found a whole new world there. This world included a downtown center with its tall buildings, theaters, stores, and busy streets. Looking back, the author Hamlin Garland described the effect of Chicago's bright lights and bustle on newcomers like him and his brother:

"Everything interested us. The business section so sordid [dirty] to others was grandly terrifying to us. . . . Nothing was commonplace; nothing was ugly to us."

So many people, in fact, flocked downtown that the streets were choked by traffic. To decrease congestion, Boston, Philadelphia, and other cities built underground tunnels—called subways—for their streetcars. Wealthier families, meanwhile, often preferred the quiet, tree-shaded avenues of suburbs, where homes and apartment houses lined streetcar routes.

City Planning

Amid the bustle and excitement of city life, a new idea was taking root. People began to realize that beauty and open space were vital to the well-being of city people.

Until now, cities had grown without plan. Builders threw up tenements and homes as fast as possible. The more families they squeezed onto a lot, the more profits landlords made. They did not provide open spaces where people could escape from the bustle of the streets and breathe fresh air.

Frederick Law Olmstead was convinced of the importance of open spaces to city dwellers. In 1858 he designed Central Park as a green refuge in the middle of New York City. He went on to draw up plans for city parks, elegant boulevards, and entire suburbs from Seattle to Atlanta.

The urban planner Daniel Burnham had even grander plans. He dreamed of making American cities as attractive as London and Paris and the other great capitals of Europe. He would do so by proposing magnificent public buildings, parks, and tree-lined waterfronts. Cleveland, San Francisco, and other cities hired Burnham to lay out plans for them.

Inventions

Meanwhile, new inventions were bringing great changes to the lives of city dwellers. The energy that powered most of these inventions was electricity.

Thomas Edison The genius behind many of the new inventions was Thomas A. Edison. One of his early triumphs was the first phonograph, or record player, in 1877. Edison's big breakthrough, however, came in 1879 when he invented the first practical lightbulb. Then he developed light switches, fuse boxes, and underground electric cables. Edison made electricity an inexpensive source of light for city people.

By 1900 Americans were using over 25 million lightbulbs. Dubbed by admirers the "Wizard of Menlo Park"—the site of his laboratory in New Jersey—Edison dismissed such labels. He credited his achievements, such as the storage battery and the motion picture camera, to hard work, not wizardry. "Genius," he declared, "is one percent inspiration and ninety-nine percent perspiration."

The Bell telephone Equally important in changing daily life was the telephone. Although not the first to believe that electricity might transmit the human voice, Alexander Graham Bell was the first to invent a workable telephone. Investors, slow to provide money for Bell's invention, could not imagine people preferring verbal messages to written ones. By 1890, however, every major city had a telephone system.

Housework Made Easier

New technologies and products also made housework easier. People who had coal and oil stoves no longer had to chop wood for fuel. City dwellers who installed plumbing could replace chamber pots and hand-filled washtubs with toilets and running water.

Housewives could now buy factory-canned fruits and vegetables instead of depending on foods they preserved in jars at home. Thanks to refrigerated railroad cars and steamships, the well-to-do could enjoy oranges from California, fresh meat from Illinois, and bananas from the West Indies.

Meanwhile, clothing—once made at home—was now produced more cheaply in factories. Soiled clothing could be sent to a laundry instead of washed by hand.

Department and chain stores Even shopping was made easier. Instead of going to different stores for each item, shoppers went to department stores, where they could find everything from clothing to furniture in

Alexander Graham Bell invented the telephone in 1876. The first long-distance service began in 1887 when telephone lines were connected between New York City and Philadelphia. Cellular telephones (inset) are now used without any telephone lines.

one place. In the 1890s Macy's store in New York employed 3,000 workers—as many as Carnegie's biggest steel plant.

Shoppers looking for bargains could find them in chain stores—stores owned by one company, with branches in many towns and cities. Chains such as Woolworth's and J. C. Penney could buy items in great quantities and thus offer them at low prices.

The New Leisure

Changes in housework and shopping meant that middle-class families—and poorer families, too—spent less time on daily chores. For the first time in history, ordinary people as well as the rich had a significant amount of **leisure**—free time. As leisure increased, city dwellers began to seek new and different ways to enjoy life.

Newspapers and pulp fiction Reading was one favorite form of entertainment. New ways to make paper, set type, and produce illustrations lowered the cost of newspaper and book production, while the spread of public schools increased literacy. Publishers rushed to satisfy the appetites of the reading public.

By 1900 immigrant communities supported over 1,000 foreign-language newspapers. Daily papers in English thrived, too. Joseph Pulitzer's newspapers appealed to readers with cartoons and sports pages as well as news articles. Reporters like Jacob Riis competed to get the "scoop" on scandals.

Writers followed formulas to churn out detective novels and magazine stories. Such stories became known as "pulp fiction" because they were printed on cheap paper made of wood pulp. They were also called "dime novels" because they cost so little.

Literature Other readers turned to more serious literature. Samuel Clemens, who used the name Mark Twain, wrote of small-town life along the Mississippi River. His humorous portrayal of characters such as Huck Finn and Tom Sawyer made his stories bestsellers.

Twain and other writers of the time were called Realists because they wrote about real life, even if it meant criticizing American society. Stephen Crane's novel *The Red Badge of Courage* evoked the horrors of the Civil War, while Theodore Dreiser described the tragic fates of people who tried to rise out of the working class.

Amusement parks and circuses In search of entertainment, people thronged to

P. T. Barnum's circus traveled across the country by train. Its colorful posters attracted crowds to its shows at every stop.

amusement parks, fairs, and circuses. One young woman, visiting New York's Coney Island with a friend, described it as a "wonderful and beautiful place" with exciting rides and amusements. She recalled:

"When we had been on the razzle-dazzle, the chute and the loop-the-loop . . . I asked her how she liked it. She said: 'It is just like what I see when I dream of heaven.'**"**

P. T. Barnum opened a museum that specialized in exhibits such as the "Feejee Mermaid," with the body of a fish and the head of a monkey. The museum was so successful that Barnum took it on the road as part of his circus, "The Greatest Show on Earth."

One of the most popular forms of entertainment was **vaudeville**—a stage show that combined songs, dance, opera, and comedy. Vaudeville grew in popularity because people could watch it while they talked and socialized.

Baseball and bicycles Beginning in the big cities, baseball soon became a favorite sport. In 1876 teams in eight cities formed baseball's National League. To encourage family attendance, the league banned Sunday games, beer, and gambling.

Prohibitions on beer and Sunday games turned off some fans. A rival organization, the American League, loosened the rules. Together, the two leagues appealed to a broad spectrum of fans and turned baseball into "the national pastime."

By the 1890s women, too, had begun to play sports, including basketball, baseball, and tennis. When turned down by men's athletic clubs, women established their own.

Meanwhile, a craze for bicycling swept the nation. Riders were attracted by the new "safety bicycle," which now had air-filled tires instead of solid ones. Millions of adults and children took to the streets with this new form of recreation.

Dance halls Young people with leisure and a little extra money liked to gather at dance halls. At first, members of the same sex danced with one another, for the custom of dating was almost unknown. Gradually, however, customs changed, and boys began to "treat" girls to a night at the dance hall.

The Blossoming of Culture

Working people, who had rarely had leisure time before, loved the entertainment of dance halls, amusement parks, and sports events. At the same time, people with more wealth and education increasingly turned to "high culture" for entertainment. In cities across the country, bankers and industrialists gave money to establish art museums, symphonies, and opera companies.

The first museums were private and run for profit. Soon, however, universities and cities opened museums devoted to painting, sculpture, and other fine arts. These museums were supported by rich Americans who scoured the collections of Europe, buying masterpieces and hurrying home to show off their treasures.

Meanwhile, American artists began to make their marks on the art world. Thomas Eakins, Mary Cassatt, and Maurice Prendergast painted scenes of Americans at work and

play, while Frederic Remington and Charles Russell portrayed the drama and life of American Indians and cowboys in the West.

In vaudeville, opera singers performed alongside juggling acts. Now, however, business leaders built opera houses and concert halls where performances of classical music could be enjoyed without interruption.

The intent was to educate the public to appreciate art and classical music. The effect, however, was to isolate the rich from the poor. A night at the symphony or opera became an occasion to display one's wealth and status by dressing in fine clothes and jewels. Working people could not afford to buy tickets—nor did they feel at home in

In this 1901 painting, Maurice Prendergast showed well-to-do Americans enjoying a day in New York City's Central Park. How did their lives compare to the lives of the immigrants shown on page 613?

the elegant halls, where talking, laughter, and baskets of food were frowned upon.

Poverty Amid Plenty

Reformers took some pride in city improvements. Better transportation and building codes made life safer. Parks and entertainment provided pleasure for even the poorest families.

Still, much work remained to be done. For many reformers the luxuries and displays of wealth by the rich seemed a waste of money that could be better spent on meeting the needs of the poor. Jacob Riis worried that "the gap between the classes . . . is widening day by day." How could cities cope with the surging tide of eager but penniless newcomers? Said Riis:

❝I know of but one bridge that will carry us over safe—a bridge founded upon justice and built of human hearts.**❞**

As a new century dawned, reformers would take on the challenge of bridging the gap between the rich and the poor.

3. Section Review

1. Define **leisure** and **vaudeville.**
2. What were the goals of city planners and how were they accomplished?
3. What developments gave people more leisure? Give at least three examples.
4. Critical Thinking Why do you think wealthy Americans began to collect art and support concert halls and opera companies?

Why We Remember

The Growth of Cities

Some 25 years after that terrible night in the police station, Jacob Riis showed his friend Theodore Roosevelt around New York City's neighborhoods. Arriving at the police station where he had spent the night so long ago, Riis pointed to a man asleep on a plank. "I was like this once," he told Roosevelt. At that moment, it seemed as though nothing had changed. However, the nation had undergone enormous change. In 1870 the United States was still largely rural. Forty years later, it was a nation of cities. As a reporter, Riis knew the dark side of cities. He also knew their attractions—beautiful parks, splendid museums, and tall buildings that people still enjoy today.

Riis also witnessed another great change. Before 1865 most immigrants had come from northern Europe. By 1900 most arrived from eastern and southern Europe and from Asia. Never had the nation been more diverse—or faced more decisions about how to absorb so many peoples and cultures. Jacob Riis, as a reporter and photographer, helped to bring greater knowledge and understanding to the decisions that Americans made.

Skill Lab

Skill Tips

- Line graphs show changes at a glance, while circle graphs show percentages.
- On a line graph, the vertical axis indicates frequency or amount, while the horizontal axis indicates categories, such as years.

Acquiring Information

Creating Appropriate Graphs

Between 1860 and 1910 the increase in city populations was staggering. Los Angeles, for example, grew from 4,400 to 319,000 people. Meanwhile, Chicago's population soared from 109,000 to more than 2 million. New York grew from 1 million to nearly 5 million.

Question to Investigate

In what ways did population distribution change in the late 1800s and early 1900s?

Procedure

Create three appropriate graphs for exploring the question. Review the Skill Tips here and the Skill Lab on page 167.

1 Decide on the best type of graph to make for each purpose.

a. Decide how to compare urban population percentages in 1860 and 1910.

b. Decide how to show which population—urban or rural—increased faster between 1860 and 1910.

c. Decide how to show the change in percentages of rural and urban populations between 1860 and 1910.

2 Make the three graphs.

a. Use the statistics in **A**.

b. Refer to **B** and **C** as models.

3 Analyze your graphs in order to write an answer to the Question to Investigate.

Sources to Use

A

U.S. Urban and Rural Populations

Year	Urban Population	Urban % of Total Population	Rural Population	Rural % of Total Population
1830	1,127	9	11,739	91
1840	1,845	11	15,224	89
1850	3,544	15	19,648	85
1860	6,217	20	25,227	80
1870	9,902	26	28,656	74
1880	14,130	28	36,026	72
1890	22,106	35	40,841	65
1900	30,160	40	45,835	60
1910	41,999	46	49,973	54

Population in thousands (rounded)
Source: *Historical Statistics of the United States*

B

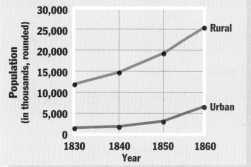

U.S. Urban and Rural Populations 1830–1860

C

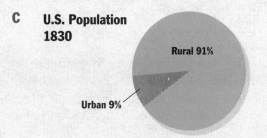

U.S. Population 1830

Rural 91%

Urban 9%

Chapter Survey

Reviewing Vocabulary

Define the following terms.
1. anti-Semitism
2. ethnic neighborhoods
3. assimilate
4. urbanization
5. tenements
6. political machine
7. settlement house
8. leisure
9. vaudeville

Reviewing Main Ideas

1. What were two main reasons for immigration to the United States after 1865?
2. Compare immigrants' expectations of life in the United States with their experiences once they arrived.
3. How did nativists respond to the new immigrants from Europe and Asia?
4. Why did American cities grow after 1865 and what role did new technologies play in helping them to grow?
5. How did political machines respond to city problems?
6. Describe four ways in which early reformers tried to improve city life.
7. (a) Why did people have significant amounts of leisure time in the late 1800s? (b) Give three examples of how city people made use of their newfound leisure.

Thinking Critically

1. Evaluation Given the terrible conditions that many immigrants encountered, why do you think that so many of them decided to remain in the United States?
2. Synthesis Thousands of homeless city children were put on "orphan trains," which took them to new lives in small towns and on farms. Give arguments for and against the idea.
3. Why We Remember: Synthesis If you had been responsible for developing the nation's immigration policy during the period covered in the chapter, what would

your policy have been? Would you recommend following the same policy today, or a different one? Explain.

Applying Skills

Creating appropriate graphs You want to show the following in graph form:
• the change in population of your state's largest city since 1890
• the percentages of people in that city today who belong to various ethnic groups
   Keeping in mind what you learned in the Skill Lab on page 633, decide what kind of graph would be most appropriate for each purpose. Find the information you need in the library. Make the graphs and write a paragraph that summarizes what your graphs show.

History Mystery

Crisscrossing the Atlantic Answer the History Mystery on page 611. How might you find more information about the "Atlantic swimmer"? Why do you think most immigrants did not cross the ocean as many times as she did?

Writing in Your History Journal

1. Keys to History (a) The time line on pages 610–611 has seven Keys to History. In your journal, describe why each one is important to know about. (b) Imagine that, like Jacob Riis, you are a reporter at that time. What two events from the chapter would you add to the time line? Write the events and their dates in your journal. Tell why you think each should be added.
2. Jacob Riis Imagine that you are Jacob Riis. Look at the photographs in the chapter. Choose four of them and write

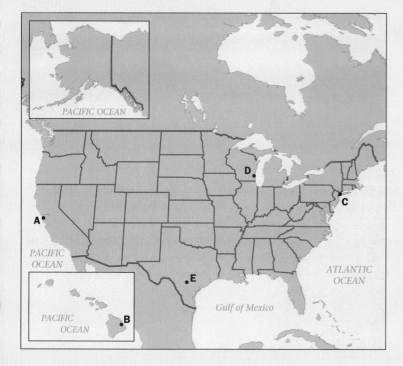

Reviewing Geography

1. For each letter on the map, write the name of the city and of an immigrant group with which it became identified.

2. Geographic Thinking Suppose you visited a modern-day city neighborhood that had been home to one or more immigrant groups in the late 1800s. Would you expect the ethnic groups now living in the neighborhood to be the same as they were back then, or different? If different, why? Even if the new ethnic groups were quite different, what reminders of earlier groups might you find?

new captions that you think Riis might have written. The captions should each be at least two sentences in length, though they may be longer if you wish.

3. Citizenship Think of a problem that modern-day cities face. Is it different from or similar to a problem faced by cities in the late 1800s and early 1900s? What should today's citizens do to try to solve the problem? Write your responses in your journal.

Alternative Assessment

Planning a city guide Today, people who plan to visit or move to a large city can find a variety of helpful guides on bookstore shelves. Imagine that you have been hired to create a newcomers' guide to an imaginary city of the late 1800s.

With a partner, plan the guide. Write a detailed outline of topics and a descriptive list of illustrations, such as maps and photographs. Write a six-paragraph introduction to the city and create an illustration to accompany your introduction.

Keep the following in mind:

❶ The city is New Metropolis, a Midwest industrial and transportation center.

❷ Rural Americans and two groups of immigrants (you choose which two) have flooded into the city in recent years.

❸ New Metropolis has the same kinds of problems and attractions as do cities like New York, Chicago, and San Francisco.

Your work will be evaluated on the following criteria:
• your materials reflect a broad, realistic view of city life at the time
• you arrange topics logically
• you write in appealing, easy-to-understand language

Unit Survey

Making Connections

Review

1. The expansion of the railroads in the middle and late 1800s had a huge impact on the economy, the environment, and people's lives. Describe four specific effects of the railroads.

2. Compare and contrast the lives of a homesteader on the Great Plains and a factory worker in a big city like Chicago in the late 1800s.

3. Some historians would describe the period covered in this unit as an era of great progress in the United States. Others say it was just the opposite, and would call it a dark time in our history. What is your opinion? Support your answer with specific examples from the unit.

Linking History, Economics, and Math

Project

Starting Your Own Business

Many entrepreneurs of the late 1800s—like many entrepreneurs today—plunged into the world of business as teenagers. You may never be as successful as Rockefeller or other captains of industry, but you can make money by starting a business. The best part is, you will be the boss!

Project Steps

Work on your own.

❶ Decide the type of business to start.
• Consider your interests and talents. For example, do you like to cook, make crafts, create computer designs, use a video camera, do yard work, or take care of pets?
• Also consider this business motto: "Find a need and fill it." What need in your school, neighborhood, or community could you help fill?
• Get your family's approval.

❷ Write a business plan, in which you do the following:
• describe your product or service
• list equipment and supplies you need
• identify your target customers
• identify your competitors
• list your marketing methods
• calculate what your expenses will be
• tell how you will get start-up money
• estimate what your income will be
• describe how you will keep records

You might consult library books, local businesspeople, and the Chamber of Commerce, which can also help you find out about legal requirements, if any.

❸ Share your business plan with the class. Ask for ideas for improving it.

❹ Begin carrying out your business plan. As you run the business, keep a journal in which you describe what actions you take and what results occur. After a trial period (perhaps two months) share the journal with the class.

Thinking It Over Consider the qualities that entrepreneurs of the late 1800s had. Which of those qualities do you think are still important for entrepreneurs? Do you think you possess those qualities? Explain.

How Do We Know?

Lewis Hine photographed this young coal miner at work in West Virginia.

Scholar's Tool Kit

Photographs

In 1900 as many as 2 million children under the age of 16 went to work instead of school. Thousands of children only 12 or younger worked in mills and factories at night. Some as young as 3 picked cotton. How do we know the sad stories of these child laborers? In part we know about their lives through the photographs of reformer Lewis Hine.

A Zealous Reformer

Lewis Hine was one of the most zealous opponents of child labor. As a schoolteacher in New York, Hine became concerned about the abuse of child workers. He became an investigative reporter, using his camera to document children at work. "Seeing is believing," Hine would say.

Hine quit teaching and joined the staff of the National Child Labor Committee. "I felt that I was merely changing my educational activities from the classroom to the world." He hoped his photographs would stir the hearts and consciences of concerned citizens, and help bring about reform.

A shy, slender man, Hine risked his life for the cause of social justice. Factory and mill owners wanted to keep wages low and saw Hine as a threat to their profits. To get his pictures, Hine sometimes had to resort to trickery. He would pretend to be a fire inspector or an insurance salesman. Sometimes he claimed he was

Critical Thinking

1. Hine left his job to work full time as a reformer. If you were to devote your life to a cause, which cause would you choose? Why?

One mill owner observed that children made good workers because their hands were small enough to reach into the machinery. Unfortunately those small hands sometimes got caught in the machines. (Above) Boys changing bobbins; (right) girl picking cotton.

taking pictures of machinery and needed children in the shots to give his photographs the proper scale. When unable to get inside mills and factories, he would wait outside and take pictures of children entering and leaving.

Employers had tricks of their own. When inspectors like Hine came to her shirt factory, one girl recalled, "we children [had to] climb into the big boxes the finished shirts were stored in. Then some shirts were piled on top of us, and when the inspectors came—no children."

Critical Thinking

2. Hine called his pictures "photo stories." What stories do the photos here tell?

Recording History

Hine was a careful researcher. He kept accurate records and documented each photograph. He even secretly recorded the height of children by having them stand next to him. He could measure their height because he knew the height from the floor to each button on his vest. "All along," he said, "I had to be double-sure that my photo data was 100 percent pure—no retouching or fakery of any kind."

Hine crisscrossed the country in his crusade. He traveled as many as 50,000 miles (80,000 km) a year by train and automobile. Even he was shocked at what he learned. One in 4 millworkers was a child between the ages of 10 and 15. Children under 10 were not counted as employees.

Hine's pictures of little boys and girls laboring in mines, sweatshops, and cotton fields exposed a shocking side of life hidden from most Americans. His photographs were so striking and effective they helped change child labor laws. After seeing his photographs, one reporter wrote:

"There has been no more convincing proof of the absolute necessity of child labor laws . . . than these pictures showing the suffering, the degradation, the immoral influence, the utter lack of anything that is wholesome in the lives of these poor little wage earners. They speak more eloquently than any work—and depict a state of affairs which is terrible in its reality— and terrible to encounter, terrible to admit that such things exist in civilized communities."

The photographs Hine took as an investigative reporter are now important historical records. Hine documented a part of history that was hidden to many Americans. Today many of these photographs are in the National Archives in Washington, D.C. There they form part of an immense collection of government photographs open for research to all Americans.

? Critical Thinking

3. What made Hine's photographs a reliable source of information? Are photographs always a reliable source of information? Why or why not?

Scholar at Work

Lewis Hine knew that "seeing is believing." As an investigative reporter he used his camera to show the public evidence of child labor. With a group, think of a problem in your school or community and become investigative reporters yourselves. Use a camera to document the problem. Then arrange your photos for a magazine article and write captions explaining the problem. Present your findings to the class.

Unit 8

Chapters

Hands-On → *HISTORY*

Activity

At the right you see part of the Great White Fleet of 16 gleaming white battleships the President sent around the world in 1907 to demonstrate American power. Some Americans feared that this show of force would anger people in other countries, but instead they greeted the fleet with parties and parades. Plan a cover for a Brazilian, Australian, or Japanese magazine featuring the fleet's visit. Include plans for an illustration and titles for three magazine articles about the fleet.

The Fleet Entering the Golden Gate, May 6, 1908 (detail)
by Henry Reuterdahl, about 1908

Questions of Power

Chapter 23

An Era of Reform

Keys to History

1872
Corruption exposed in Grant's administration

1874
Granger movement at its height

1883
Pendleton Civil Service Act

1870

1880

World **Link**

Looking Back

Andrew Jackson defends the spoils system

1829

Wheat production soars in Australia

1880s–1890s

HISTORY
Mystery

As Vice-President, Chester A. Arthur opposed civil-service reform. After he became President in 1881, he supported it. What caused President Arthur to change his mind?

1901

Roosevelt becomes President on assassination of McKinley

Republican campaign poster, 1900

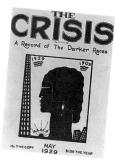

1909

NAACP founded

NAACP magazine

1892

Populist Party organized

Cartoon of Populist, or People's, Party

1906

Publication of *The Jungle*

1913

16th Amendment approves federal income tax

1890

1900

1910

Looking Ahead

19th Amendment gives women the right to vote

1920

● **643**

Beginning the Story with

Jane Addams

It was just a moment in a young girl's life. Jane Addams was 6 years old. Her father, a businessman in Cedarville, Illinois, had taken her to visit one of his mills. There she caught her first sight of poverty. She asked her father why people lived in such "horrid little houses." Jane's father patiently explained that people lived in such conditions out of necessity, not by choice.

Jane reflected on this interesting information. She decided that when she grew up, she was going to have a large house right in the middle of horrid little houses like these. All the children who had no place to play at home, she said, "could come and play in my yard."

An "Ugly, Pigeon-Toed Little Girl"

The moment passed. At the time, Jane later confessed, she was far more worried about feeling like an "ugly, pigeon-toed little girl, whose crooked back obliged her to walk with her head very much upon one side."

Jane, whose mother died when Jane was just 2 years old, loved and admired her "Pa," a free-thinker who hated injustice. Jane would later write of her father that "he was the uncompromising enemy of wrong doing."

John Addams encouraged his daughter to read, think, and be true to her own beliefs. He also taught her compassion. One Sunday morning when it was time to go to church, Jane appeared in a new coat that she was eager to show off to her friends. Her father told her how pretty it looked on her, but suggested she not wear it to Sunday school. It might, he said, make the other children feel unhappy because they could not afford anything so nice.

Jane asked her father why other children did not have new coats like hers. Again he explained that some families did not have enough money to buy all the things they might want. Jane was not satisfied with this reply. "Then what can be done about it?" she asked. John Addams had no good reply. Jane would spend a lifetime trying to find an answer.

Jane Addams and other reformers took a special interest in children's welfare. This rooftop nursery provided day care for children of working parents.

Finding "Life's Purpose"

Jane grew up, went to college, and graduated with her "life's purpose" clearly fixed in her mind. She was going to become a doctor and live with the poor. Then real life stepped in to shatter her dreams. In 1881, shortly before Jane turned 21, her beloved father died. His death was "the greatest sorrow that can ever come to me," Jane wrote to her school friend Ellen Starr.

While still in mourning, Jane entered medical school. She tried to throw herself into her studies, but she disliked her classes and felt she was a failure. After seven months, she collapsed and dropped out of school.

For the next few years Jane battled health problems as well as bouts of depression. If she was not to be a doctor, then just what was she to do with her life? The only careers thought suitable for educated young women in the late 1800s were marriage and teaching. Neither of these appealed to her.

Then it came to her—the long-ago idea of having a big house among all the horrid little houses and being a friend to the people who lived in them.

While wandering through a tenement area of Chicago, Jane found her house, a mansion built by Charles Hull. On September 14, 1889, Hull House opened its doors to the public. Just as Jane had imagined, among her first visitors were children who needed someplace to play. In its first year of operation, Hull House would welcome 50,000 visitors. Jane Addams had found her life's work.

Hands-On → *HISTORY*

Activity

Imagine that you are writing a biography of Jane Addams. Based on the story above, create a list of turning points—points at which significant change occurred in her life. Write a brief description of the importance of each turning point.

1. National Politics and Reform

Reading Guide

New Term civil service

Section Focus **Why political reform became a national issue in the late 1800s**

1. How did party competition affect politics after the Civil War?
2. Why did government corruption increase during Grant's presidency?
3. How did Congress try to reform the spoils system?

In 1905 Jane Addams became a member of the Chicago Board of Education. To her surprise, she found corruption in the schools. Politicians, she wrote,

"received a rake-off in the contract for every new building or coal supply or the adoption of school books.**"**

Since the Civil War, such corruption had reached into every level of government.

The Grant Years

After the Civil War and the bitter struggle over Reconstruction (see Chapter 19), Americans were tired of conflict. In the presidential election of 1868, they elected General Ulysses S. Grant, whose campaign slogan was "Let us have peace."

Grant seemed an ideal leader to unite the nation. Bearded, muscular, and overly fond of cigars, he was admired as the Civil War general who had faced down Confederate General Robert E. Lee. He was also known for his generous terms of surrender to the Confederate armies.

A gentle, modest man, Grant brought a quiet dignity to the White House. During the Civil War, he had disliked the fancy trappings of high military rank. As President he refused to take advantage of his position. When he received a $20 speeding ticket for driving his carriage too fast, he paid it.

Yet Grant was not able to impose his standards on other members of the Republican Party. Despite his promise of peace, Grant's presidency was plagued by political conflicts, corruption, and scandal.

Party Competition

In the years after the Civil War, Republicans and Democrats struggled fiercely for power. As the North and the South gingerly knit themselves together again, the parties took advantage of the passionate memories that remained.

Republicans were quick to remind voters that theirs was the party of Abraham Lincoln. They gained the loyalty of African American voters as well as their traditional northern supporters.

Democrats accused the Republicans of "waving the bloody shirt"—stirring up wartime feelings to appeal to voters even when the issues had nothing to do with the Civil War. Yet Democrats, too, appealed to wartime passions. In the South, where white resentment of Radical Reconstruction still rankled, most whites belonged to the Democratic Party. For years the party would be able to count on the votes of the "Solid South."

The nation as a whole was almost evenly divided between the Democrats and Republicans. Presidential elections were often very close. There were divisions within the parties, too. Thus neither party dared to take too strong a stand on issues for fear of scaring away voters.

Corruption in Government

Corruption tarnished Grant's presidency. Although honest himself, Grant appointed a number of people who used their offices to enrich themselves. The Secretary of War, for example, accepted bribes for contracts to run Indian trading posts in Oklahoma. Whiskey companies owned by government officials bribed Grant's personal secretary to help them avoid paying taxes.

Later Grant apologized for giving appointments to the wrong people. In his last annual message to Congress, he wrote:

❝It was my . . . misfortune to be called to the office of Chief Executive without any previous political training. . . . Errors of judgment must have occurred.❞

Despite Grant's own honesty, political corruption became known as "Grantism."

The Crédit Mobilier scandal The biggest scandal of Grant's presidency involved the Crédit Mobilier (cray-DEE mō-BEEL-YAY) construction company. In the 1860s the federal government had offered special payments to encourage the building of the Union Pacific Railroad. Crédit Mobilier, which built the railroad, exaggerated the construction costs and received much higher payments than it deserved.

The company then bribed members of Congress and even the Vice-President to try to prevent an investigation. Finally, in 1872, the *New York Sun* newspaper exposed Crédit Mobilier as the "king of frauds," leading Congress to investigate.

The spoils system Other levels of the federal government were also guilty of corruption. Since the 1820s, Presidents had used the spoils system to reward political supporters with government jobs (see page 356). After the Civil War, the sharp competition between Democrats and Republicans encouraged the growth of the spoils system.

In this 1872 cartoon, politicians and businessmen beg President Grant for government jobs and work contracts. In his 1868 election campaign, Grant had called for *peace* between northerners and southerners. However, office and contract seekers seemed more interested in getting a *piece* of "government cake."

Officeholders in each party gave government jobs, as well as work contracts, to their supporters. Unfortunately, loyal party members often had no training for their work. Even worse, many were dishonest.

The Gilded Age Novelists Mark Twain and Charles Dudley Warner thought that the golden wealth of the nation masked corruption and greed. They described the years after the Civil War as the Gilded Age.

Civil-Service Reform

The widespread greed and corruption in government enraged many Americans. In the presidential election of 1876, voters chose Rutherford B. Hayes, the respected Republican governor of Ohio. Hayes proposed a system of tests to determine who was best qualified for jobs in the **civil service**—the body of government workers who are hired rather than elected. Congress ignored the proposal, however.

In the presidential election of 1880 the Republicans again captured the presidency. This time, though, the party was split in two. One side sought reform of the civil service, while the other opposed it. The new President, James A. Garfield of Ohio, represented the reformers. Vice-President Chester A. Arthur supported the spoils system.

In July 1881, four months after taking office, President Garfield was shot to death. The assassin was seeking revenge because he had not been given a government job.

Dismayed by the tragedy, Chester Arthur, now President, changed his opinion. He threw his support behind efforts to reform the spoils system.

Hands-On HISTORY

Interviewing a civil-service worker More Americans work for the federal government than for any other employer. In order to get their jobs, most of those 2 million civilian (nonmilitary) employees had to take a civil-service test or other form of evaluation to show that they were qualified for the job.

Activity To find out what it is like to work for the government, rather than for a private business, interview a federal government worker in your community. For example, you might talk to a postal worker or someone who works for the Social Security Administration. Ask questions about the following topics:

National Park Service rangers are federal employees.

• hiring and promotion procedures

• job requirements and responsibilities

• vacations and other benefits

• restrictions, such as limits on collective bargaining

Share what you learn with the rest of the class.

In the 1884 campaign, Republicans and Democrats took few stands on issues. Instead, each party criticized the other's candidate. For the first time a woman, lawyer Belva Lockwood, ran for President. Even if women cannot vote, she argued, "there is no law against their being voted for."

In 1883 Congress passed the Pendleton Civil Service Act. It set up a commission to prepare tests for civil-service jobs. New workers would be chosen from among those with the highest scores. Once hired, they could not be fired for political reasons.

At first, the Civil Service Act applied to only about 10 percent of all government jobs. Over the years, however, Presidents expanded the civil service to cover most government jobs.

The election of 1884 Even with the passage of the Civil Service Act, corruption continued to be an issue. In the presidential election of 1884, Democrat Grover Cleveland, the governor of New York, campaigned for "clean government." His supporters attacked the Republican candidate, James G. Blaine of Maine, for taking bribes when he served in Congress. They chanted: "Blaine, Blaine, James G. Blaine, the continental liar from the state of Maine!"

In a close, bitterly fought election, Cleveland defeated Blaine. Cleveland was the first Democrat to be elected President since the Civil War.

Cleveland came into office committed to civil-service reform. However, after so many years of Republican rule, job-hungry Democrats poured into the nation's capital. "The Washington hotels are crowded," one journalist wrote, "and office seekers are as thick as shells on the beach."

Caught between civil-service reformers and party supporters, Cleveland tried to please both. He rewarded thousands of Democratic Party members with government jobs. At the same time, though, he almost doubled the number of federal jobs covered by civil-service laws.

1. Section Review

1. Define **civil service.**

2. Why did the two political parties avoid taking stands on issues after the Civil War?

3. Why did corruption in the federal government grow during Grant's presidency?

4. How did civil-service reform change the way that workers in the federal government were hired?

5. Critical Thinking How do you think Grant should be judged for the increase of corruption during his presidency? Give evidence to support your answer.

Skill Lab

Acquiring Information

Interpreting a Political Cartoon

Bribery. Corruption. Scandal. Dishonest politicians of the late 1800s provided cartoonists with plenty of material. Angered by the power of biting political cartoons, one corrupt politician complained, "I don't care what they write about me. But those pictures—people understand them!"

Question to Investigate

What were some signs of political corruption in the late 1800s?

Procedure

To explore the question, you will interpret a political cartoon by Edward Kemble.

❶ Identify the cartoon's main subject.
a. Where are the birds perched?
b. What kind of birds are they?
c. What do the birds symbolize?

❷ Identify details in the cartoon.
a. What do you notice about the size of the birds' stomachs?
b. What do you notice about the word *Senate*?
c. What other details involving money do you notice?

❸ Draw conclusions about the point the cartoonist is making.
a. Summarize the cartoon's message about trusts and the Senate.

b. Tell what feelings you think the cartoonist has about his subject. For example, does he find it funny?

c. How do you think this cartoonist would answer the Question to Investigate?

Source to Use

2. Farmers Take Action

Reading Guide

Section Focus **How American farmers responded to changes brought about by industrialization**

1. What problems did farmers face in the late 1800s?
2. What actions did farmers take to improve their economic conditions?
3. How successful were farmers in achieving their goals?

As politicians squabbled over power and business and industry expanded, the nation's farmers were suffering. Frustrated and angry that political leaders were paying little attention to their concerns, they organized to demand help from government. Mary Elizabeth Lease, a leader of the movement, sounded a warning:

"The people are [cornered], let the blood-hounds of money who have dogged us thus far beware.**"**

Farmers' Troubles

As cities grew after the Civil War, so did the farms that fed their hungry people. Between 1860 and 1910, the number of farms tripled. Farmers bought new machines that allowed them to plant more acres and harvest bigger crops. They concentrated on raising cash crops—such as corn, wheat, cotton, and rice—to supply growing markets at home and overseas.

Falling farm prices The expansion of farms did not guarantee prosperity for farmers, however. In fact, farm prices began to fall because farmers were growing more than the American market demanded.

American farmers tried to sell their surplus crops abroad, but other countries were also flooding the world's markets with their crops. In the early 1880s farmers received 80¢ a bushel for their wheat. By 1890 they were lucky to get 71¢.

Although prices were falling, the costs of doing business were not. Farmers paid high interest rates on loans for machinery and land. They paid high prices to merchants for handling and storing their crops. They paid

World Link

Wheat from "Down Under" American wheat farmers of the 1890s faced stiff competition from a place that many had never heard of. The place was Australia, a British colony.

To help farmers, Australia set up experimental farms and agricultural colleges in the 1880s and 1890s. There, improved varieties of wheat were developed and methods of preventing diseases were put into practice. Farmers also began using a superphosphate fertilizer.

The result was greatly increased yields and booming wheat exports. Half a world away, American farmers felt the pinch.

Farmers formed cooperatives to try to lower business costs. In this photo men, women, and children work together on the apple harvest.

high railroad rates to get their crops to market. The editor of a farmers' newspaper angrily declared:

"There are three great crops raised in Nebraska. One is a crop of corn, one a crop of freight rates, and one a crop of interest. One is produced by farmers who by sweat and toil farm the land. The other two are produced by men who sit in their offices and behind their bank counters and farm the farmers."

High or low tariffs? To raise farm prices, farmers sought to increase foreign demand for American crops. They reasoned that if people in the United States bought more foreign goods, then foreigners would have more dollars to spend on American farm products.

To encourage Americans to buy more foreign goods, farmers asked Congress to reduce

tariffs. The Democrats supported the farmers' demands. The Republicans, on the other hand, wanted to keep tariffs high in order to protect American industry from foreign competition.

Republicans won the argument in 1888, when their candidate, Benjamin Harrison, was elected President. Farmers would have to find another solution to their problems.

Grangers and Farmers' Alliances

In 1867 Oliver Kelley, a clerk in the United States Department of Agriculture, had an idea. If the government would not help farmers, he thought, farmers must help themselves. Kelley organized a society called the Patrons of Husbandry. He traveled throughout the nation seeking members. By 1874, nearly 1 million people had joined.

Members called their new society the Grange, based on an old English word for farm buildings. Grangers formed cooperatives to market their products themselves instead of having to pay middlemen. There were cooperative creameries, warehouses, and banks. Grangers also experimented with making their own farm equipment.

A depression in the 1870s caused many Grange cooperatives to fail. Disheartened, many farmers left the Grange.

Rise of Farmers' Alliances As the Grange declined, farmers organized local, state, and then regional Farmers' Alliances to demand help from government. By the late 1880s there were the Northern Farmers' Alliance and the Southern Farmers' Alliance. African Americans formed the Colored Farmers' National Alliance in the South.

In 1890 the Farmers' Alliances plunged into politics. A leader in Kansas was the fiery Mary Elizabeth Lease, known as "the Kansas Pythoness." She traveled tirelessly

Mary Elizabeth Lease was such an effective speaker, one journalist reported, that "she set the crowd hooting or hurrahing at her will."

across the state, whipping up support in more than 160 speeches.

In the elections of 1890, Alliance candidates swept into power across the South and in several midwestern states. More than 50 Alliance candidates were elected to Congress.

The Populist Party

Encouraged by their success, in 1892 the Farmers' Alliances met in Omaha, Nebraska, and formed their own political party. They called it the Populist, or People's, Party.

In the presidential campaign of 1892, the Populist Party proposed a series of reforms. They wanted the government to own and run the railroads "in the interest of the people." They called for a graduated income tax to tax higher incomes more heavily than lower incomes. To win workers' support, they called for an eight-hour workday.

The Populists also thought that people had a right to participate more directly in politics. They proposed that senators be elected by the people, not by state legislatures. They also believed that citizens should be able to vote to approve or disapprove of laws and to propose new ones.

The Populist message appealed to farmers. Their message was not as popular with other groups, though. Business people disliked the demand for a government takeover of railroads. Immigrants resented the call for restricting immigration and limiting land ownership to American citizens.

The election of 1892 In the 1892 election Grover Cleveland received 5.5 million votes, defeating both President Benjamin Harrison and the Populist candidate, James B. Weaver of Iowa. Although Weaver made a strong showing, with 1 million votes, Cleveland ignored the Populists' ideas. He did not believe that government should take a more active role in the nation's economy.

The Panic of 1893

Soon after Cleveland regained the White House, the Panic of 1893 pushed the nation into a depression that threatened to bring the economy to a wrenching halt. Thousands of businesses failed. Unemployment soared. In Chicago, Jane Addams recalled:

❝When the first cold weather came, the police stations and the very corridors of the city hall were crowded by men who could afford no other lodging.❞

By 1894, nearly 3 million workers had been thrown out of work. Debt drove farmers off their land.

Silver or gold? Democrats, Republicans, and Populists all agreed that to end the depression, the nation's money system must be reformed. They disagreed passionately, however, about how to do it.

Populist farmers wanted the government to make more money available. Then they could pay their debts and buy more land and

Link to the Present

The Wizard of Oz

"We're off to see the Wizard!" Whether they have seen the movie or read the book, most American children love *The Wizard of Oz* as much today as

when L. Frank Baum wrote it in 1900.

Few realize, though, that the story is an allegory. Beneath the fantasy of Dorothy in the land of the Munchkins, Baum was writing about the problems of farmers and industrial workers.

To Baum, the Scarecrow stood for farmers and the Tin Woodsman for workers. With Dorothy, who stands for ordinary people, and the loud but powerless Cowardly Lion (William Jennings Bryan), they follow the yellow brick road (the gold standard) to the Emerald City, or Washington, D.C.

Like Coxey's Army, they hope that the Wizard—the President—will solve their problems. When they get there, though, they discover that the Wizard is a fraud who can give them no help at all.

machinery. They urged the government to buy and turn into money all the silver now being mined in the West. This group was called "silverites."

Most business leaders feared American money would lose its value if there was too much of it available. They believed money should be based on the value of gold. President Cleveland and many members of Congress, both Democrats and Republicans, agreed. They were called "goldbugs."

As political leaders wrestled with the money question, the depression grew worse. Millions of people fell into deeper distress. Thousands of unemployed men rode the rails from town to town, searching for work.

"Coxey's Army" Jacob Coxey, a farmer in Ohio, decided that something had to be done to help the jobless. In 1894 he organized an "army" of unemployed workers to march to Washington, D.C. He hoped to persuade Congress to put the unemployed to work building roads. Thousands of jobless men from as far away as California responded to his call.

Despite bad weather and other hardships, Coxey and about 1,000 marchers reached the capital. Looking for an excuse to arrest Coxey, police charged him with walking on the grass on his way to make a speech at the Capitol steps. Coxey's army melted away, but the seed of an idea had been planted. The next century would see many marches on Washington, D.C., to protest injustice.

The Election of 1896

When it came time for the presidential election of 1896, the Democrats were in trouble. They were deeply divided over the silver issue. They could not nominate President Cleveland, for he was widely blamed for the depression that still gripped the nation. Could they agree upon a candidate to oppose the Republican, Governor William McKinley of Ohio?

At their convention in Chicago, the Democrats found their leader when William Jennings Bryan, a congressman from Nebraska, stepped up to deliver a speech. Taking a stand for farmers, Bryan electrified his audience as he thundered:

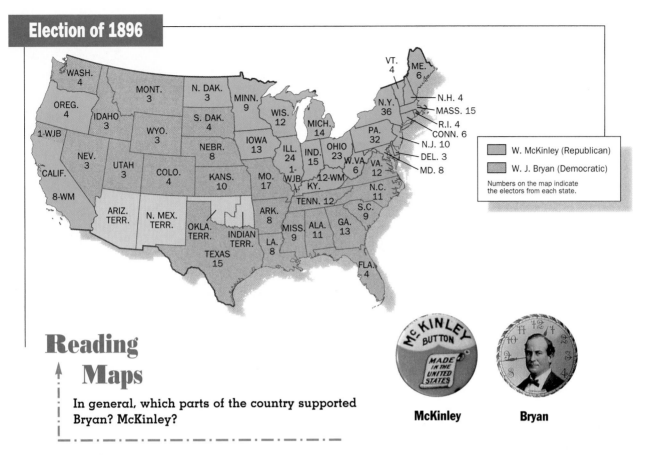

McKinley · W. McKinley (Republican)

W. J. Bryan (Democratic)

Numbers on the map indicate the electors from each state.

Reading Maps

In general, which parts of the country supported Bryan? McKinley?

McKinley   **Bryan**

"Burn down your cities and leave our farms, and your cities will spring up again as if by magic. But destroy our farms and the grass will grow in the streets of every city in the country."

To the goldbugs in his audience, Bryan, a silverite, proclaimed: "You shall not crucify mankind upon a cross of gold."

The crowd went wild. Shouting, "Amen!" the convention delegates gave Bryan the nomination. He also won the support of the Populist Party.

Bryan vs. McKinley Rarely had Americans faced such a sharp contrast between candidates. Bryan was for silver. McKinley was for gold. Bryan stormed across the country giving dozens of speeches a day. McKinley campaigned from his front porch.

More people voted in the 1896 election than ever before. The majority, from the more populated industrial states, voted for McKinley.

The election of 1896 spelled the decline of the Populists, but it did not mean defeat for their ideas. Their demand for "equal rights to all, special privileges to none" was soon taken up by a new group of reformers.

2. Section Review

1. Describe three problems that farmers faced in the late 1800s.
2. Why did the Populist Party develop, and what were its goals?
3. Critical Thinking If you had lost your job in the depression that began in 1893, would you have joined Coxey's Army? Give reasons for your answer.

Geography Lab

The Great Plains

Many of the farmers who were the backbone of the Populist Party lived in the Great Plains region. Wheat covers much of the region, while cattle and sheep graze in the drier areas. The climate of the plains varies, with years of abundant moisture followed by years of drought.

The year 1886 began a decade of especially hot, dry summers. Crops failed and farm families left the land in droves. One wagon heading east carried a sign that read "In God we trusted, in Kansas we busted." Other farmers refused to give up. Author Willa Cather expressed the feelings of those who still found satisfaction in life on the Great Plains. Use her description and the photograph to add to your knowledge of the Great Plains region.

Ripened wheat, Nebraska

Willa Cather's Description

"We were talking about what it is like to spend one's childhood in little towns like these, buried in wheat and corn, under stimulating extremes of climate; burning summers when the world lies green and billowy beneath a brilliant sky, when one is fairly stifled in vegetation, in the color and smell of strong weeds and heavy harvests; blustery winters with little snow, when the whole country is stripped bare and gray as sheet-iron. We agreed that no one who had not grown up in a little prairie town could know anything about it."

Developing a Mental Map

Use the maps on pages P4–P5, R4–R7, and R11 to help answer the questions.

1. Through which states do the Great Plains extend? Does any state lie wholly within the Great Plains?

2. Estimate the area of the Great Plains.

3. If you were driving from east to west over the Great Plains, what would you notice about the elevation?

4. What conclusion about the soil of the Great Plains do you draw from the photograph? What evidence do you find on this page to support the idea that the soil of the Great Plains is extremely fertile?

5. **Hands-On Geography** Imagine that it is 1892, and you are a farmer on the Great Plains. Your relatives in Chicago want you to leave your farm and move to the city. Write a letter to them, giving your answer and explaining your decision.

3. Progressives Battle for Reform

Reading Guide

New Terms **direct primary, initiative, recall, referendum, suffragists**

Section Focus **Progressive efforts to reform city and state governments**

1. How did Progressives build support for reform?
2. What problems existed in city and state governments and how did Progressives try to solve them?
3. How did African American leaders work to influence public affairs?

Jane Addams was shocked by the neighborhood in Chicago in which Hull House was situated. She wrote:

"The streets are inexpressibly dirty, . . . the street lighting bad, [and] the paving miserable. . . . Hundreds of houses are unconnected with the street sewer. . . . Many houses have no water supply save the faucet in the backyards."

Finding that neighborhoods of poor people throughout the city lacked the public services required by law, she set out to force city officials to take action.

Like Jane Addams, people all across the United States were trying to correct injustices. In the early 1900s, their reform efforts blossomed into the Progressive movement.

Progressive Goals

Progressives tackled many problems. They tried to end government corruption and the monopoly power of big business. They fought to improve the conditions of factory workers and to end child labor. They looked for ways to end alcoholism. They struggled to gain woman suffrage.

Whatever their particular interests, Progressives were united in a desire to bring order and fairness to the chaos of a rapidly growing nation. They also believed that people's lives could be improved by putting the public good above self-interest.

The muckrakers Newspapers and magazines helped to make Americans aware of the problems that worried the Progressives. As early as the 1870s, reporter Jacob Riis had described the horrors of New York City slums in his newspaper articles.

In 1902 and 1903 *McClure's Magazine* caused a sensation with a series of articles on John D. Rockefeller's Standard Oil Company. The articles, written by Ida Tarbell, revealed the cutthroat practices that Standard Oil used. "Mr. Rockefeller," Tarbell concluded, "has systematically played with loaded dice."

That same year, Lincoln Steffens uncovered a network of political corruption in St. Louis. Other reporters investigated unsafe factory conditions, especially for working children. David Graham Phillips exposed senators who took thousands of dollars from industrial interests.

Journalists who dug out the dirty secrets of American life earned the name "muckrakers." They bore the title proudly.

Sounding the alarm was just the first step, though. To reform the system, Progressives needed political power.

City Government

Cities presented the first real challenge to Progressives. As you read in Chapter 22, most of the nation's major cities were controlled by corrupt political machines.

Jane Addams knew machine politics well. She lived in Chicago's Nineteenth Ward. Garbage collectors in the ward saw their jobs as a reward for political loyalty, not as an important service. To get the garbage off the streets, Addams herself took on the job of garbage inspector.

The Tweed Ring One of the most corrupt political machines in the nation was run by "Boss" William Marcy Tweed. Between 1869 and 1871, members of the Tweed Ring stole more than $75 million from New York City. They made millions more by accepting bribes from private contractors.

The Tweed Ring controlled the mayor, the city council, the district attorney, and municipal judges. Tweed's power reached to the state legislature and even to the governor.

In 1871 muckraking articles in *Harper's Weekly* exposed the corrupt practices of the Tweed Ring. Boss Tweed was arrested and sent to jail, and the ring broke up.

Reforming the cities Gradually, in one city after another, groups of reformers organized to end corruption. Often the groups united behind a candidate who promised to fight the city's political machine. Between 1889 and 1901, reform mayors were elected in Detroit, Toledo, San Francisco, Cleveland, and New York City.

Reformers also experimented with new forms of city government. After a hurricane destroyed Galveston, Texas, in 1900, citizens set up a commission form of government to rebuild the city. Instead of a mayor and council, voters elected a group of commissioners. Each commissioner took charge of a single department, such as sanitation or finance, and hired experts to run it.

Even more popular was the city-manager form of government. It was first established in Staunton, Virginia, in 1908. There, voters elected a city council to pass laws. The council then hired a city manager—an expert in urban government—to take care of day-to-day city business.

This scene of garbage on a New York City street could have been found in any of the nation's overcrowded cities. Trash, ashes from stoves, and horse manure piled up on streets and in empty lots. It was not surprising that city dwellers were plagued by the stench as well as by diseases.

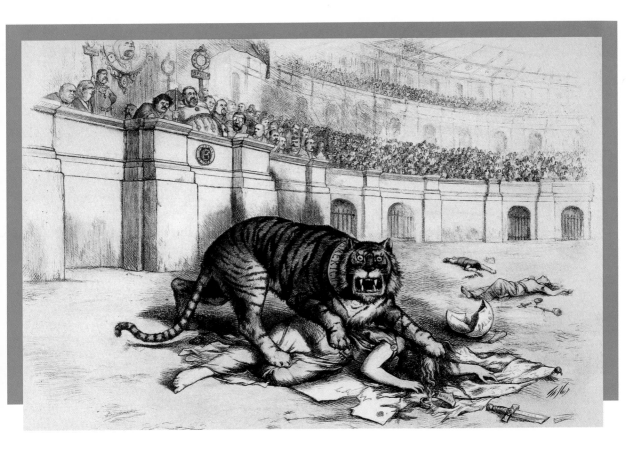

Link to Art

Thomas Nast As chief cartoonist for *Harper's Weekly* from 1862 to 1886, Thomas Nast used his skills as an artist to carry the message of reform to the magazine's readers. At a time when newspapers and magazines were Americans' main source of information, Nast made the cartoon an important political force. This 1871 cartoon was one of a series that helped bring about the downfall of Boss Tweed. **Discuss** In this cartoon, what does Nast want you to think about the power of the Tweed Ring? How does he accomplish his goal?

State Government

Unfortunately, corrupt state governments often blocked the Progressives' reforms in the cities. In many states, the governor and the legislature were in the hands of a political machine controlled by the major state industry, such as the railroads in California and the lumber industry in Wisconsin.

Robert La Follette In trying to reform state governments, Democratic and Republican Progressives often worked together. They found a champion in Robert M. La Follette of Wisconsin. Twice defeated by the state's political machine, "Fighting Bob" finally won election as governor in 1900.

La Follette hired experts to help solve the state's problems. They advised him on

Direct Democracy Reforms

Reform	Effect
Direct election of senators (17th Amendment)	The voters of each state, instead of the legislature, elect their senators.
Direct primary	An election, open to all party members, is held to choose the party's candidates for office.
Initiative	Citizens who want a law that the legislature will not pass can petition to put it on the ballot.
Recall	An elected official can be removed from office by a vote of the people before the end of his or her term.
Referendum	Citizens who do not like a law that was passed by the legislature can petition to put it on the ballot.
Secret ballot	Voters receive an official ballot and vote in a private booth.

reforming the civil service, regulating railroads, and conserving natural resources.

Direct democracy To break the power of Wisconsin's political machine and make the legislature more responsive to the voters, La Follette urged reforms. For example, Wisconsin adopted the **direct primary**—an election, open to all members of a party, to choose candidates to run for office. No longer would party bosses choose candidates behind closed doors.

Encouraged by La Follette's success, Progressives throughout the nation pushed for reforms that forced legislatures to share power with ordinary citizens. By 1916, more than half the states had adopted at least one of the reforms described in the table above.

Laws to Protect Workers

Once they had elected their candidates to governorships and state legislatures, Progressives worked toward their goal of improving people's lives. High on their list was the health and safety of factory workers.

In 1892 Florence Kelley, who worked at Hull House, visited garment factories and sweatshops, collecting evidence on the danger of long hours and unsafe machinery. As a result of her investigations, Illinois passed laws banning child labor and limiting the hours of factory work for women. As the state's first chief factory inspector, Kelley later enforced the laws.

In 1902 Maryland passed the first workers' compensation law to provide income for workers injured on the job. Oregon set limits on the hours women could work. Soon other states passed similar laws.

Temperance Movement

Some Progressives, disturbed by poverty and crime, placed the blame on liquor. They joined the temperance movement, which since the 1830s had been calling attention to the evil effects of alcohol.

In 1873 women in Ohio began to hold prayer meetings at saloons. A year later they formed the Women's Christian Temperance Union (WCTU). It became the largest women's organization in the world, with hundreds of thousands of members.

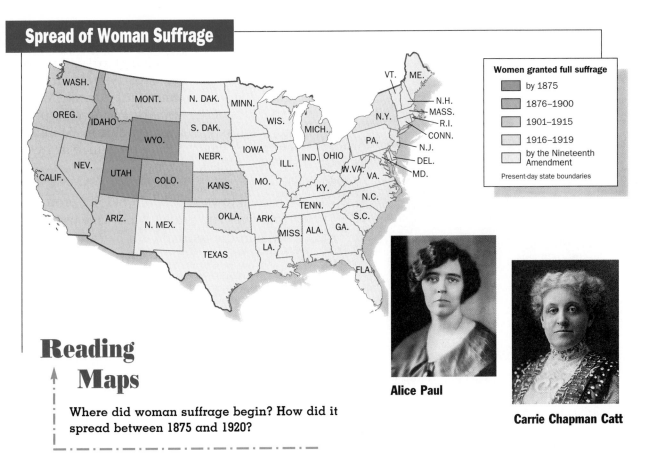

Spread of Woman Suffrage

Women granted full suffrage
- by 1875
- 1876–1900
- 1901–1915
- 1916–1919
- by the Nineteenth Amendment

Present-day state boundaries

Alice Paul

Carrie Chapman Catt

Reading Maps

↑ **Where did woman suffrage begin? How did it spread between 1875 and 1920?**

Frances Willard led the WCTU. She traveled tirelessly throughout the country, calling for laws to control the sale of liquor. By 1914, one-fourth of the states had banned the sale of alcoholic beverages.

Woman Suffrage

Like Frances Willard, many Progressives were **suffragists**—people who supported the right of women to vote. If women could vote, suffragists argued, they could help to elect reform candidates.

The battle for woman suffrage had been going on since the Seneca Falls Declaration of 1848 (see pages 449–450). Still, by 1915, only 11 states had granted full voting rights to women.

Progressives like Jane Addams brought new energy to the suffrage movement. In 1916 a spirited young woman named Alice Paul formed the National Woman's Party to demand that Congress pass a constitutional amendment giving women the vote. She led parades and even picketed the White House.

Meanwhile, Carrie Chapman Catt led the National American Woman Suffrage Association in a campaign to flood Congress with petitions. Suffragists took to the streets, urging people to sign their petitions.

Finally in 1919 Congress approved the Nineteenth Amendment, granting equal suffrage to women. The next challenge was to win ratification by at least 36 of the 48 states.

In August 1920 the 36th state, Tennessee, considered the suffrage amendment. The state senate quickly passed it, but the house was deadlocked for ten days.

Finally, the house ratified the amendment by a margin of only two votes. One of

The anti-lynching crusade that Ida Wells-Barnett began grew to include protest marches and legal action by the NAACP.

those votes was cast by Representative Harry Burn. His district opposed ratification, but Burn had taken the advice of his mother, who wrote to her son, "Don't forget to be a good boy and help Mrs. Catt."

African Americans Seek Equality

Many African American women had supported woman suffrage as part of their larger struggle for equality. Mary Church Terrell, president of the National Association of Colored Women, was a favorite speaker at suffrage conventions.

Few Progressives, however, took an interest in the issues that most concerned black Americans. It was up to African Americans themselves to raise their voices against the injustices of segregation and the violence of lynching they faced in both the South and the North.

Crusade against lynching Between 1892 and 1903, nearly 3,000 African Americans were lynched, mostly by southern mobs. Ida Wells-Barnett, the African American editor of the *Memphis Free Speech*, spoke out fearlessly against lynchings. When a white mob lynched three black men in 1892, she urged black citizens to

❝leave a town which will neither protect our lives and property, nor give us a fair trial in the courts.❞

Taking her advice, 2,000 African Americans moved out of Memphis.

An angry mob wrecked Wells-Barnett's presses and threatened her life. She simply moved north and continued her crusade by writing and speaking against lynching.

The NAACP In 1909 black leaders, including W. E. B. Du Bois, Ida Wells-Barnett, and Mary Church Terrell, formed the NAACP to fight for racial justice (see page 543). A number of white Progressives joined them in their efforts. One who did was Jane Addams.

The NAACP won several legal battles, and membership grew rapidly. Although it failed to get Congress to pass an anti-lynching law, the NAACP became an important voice for the rights of black Americans.

 3. Section Review

1. Define **direct primary, initiative, recall, referendum,** and **suffragists.**
2. What was the relationship between muckrakers and the Progressive movement?
3. What are two ways that Progressives brought about change in city government?
4. **Critical Thinking** What similarities can you find between the issues and methods of white and black reformers? What differences?

4. Progressive Presidents

Reading Guide

New Term conservation

Section Focus **The reforms that the federal government carried out under Progressive Presidents**

1. How did President Roosevelt increase the power of the federal government?
2. In what ways did President Taft follow Roosevelt's policies?
3. How did President Wilson extend Progressive reform?

Theodore Roosevelt, the reform governor of New York, had a decision to make. President William McKinley, who was running for re-election in 1900, had asked him to be the vice-presidential candidate. Vice-Presidents had little to do, though. "I could not *do* anything," Roosevelt worried, "and yet I would be seeing continually things I would like to do." Very reluctantly, he accepted.

McKinley and Roosevelt won the election. Then, on September 6, 1901, only six months into his new term, McKinley was killed by a man later judged to be insane. Theodore Roosevelt became President. The nation now had a reform-minded leader.

Trustbusting

Like most Republicans, Roosevelt believed that big business was good for the United States. Unlike them, he realized that big business often ignored the needs of the public. Therefore, he argued, it was government's reponsibility to regulate business—especially trusts. He declared:

"We do not want to destroy corporations, but we do wish to make them [serve] the public good.**"**

The Northern Securities case Regulating railroads was high on Roosevelt's list.

When Congress refused to pass new laws to control the railroads' monopoly power over shipping rates, the President took action.

First, he had the Attorney General gather evidence that the Northern Securities Company, a railroad trust, was using unfair business practices. Then in 1902 the federal government sued the Northern Securities Company for violating the Sherman Antitrust Act of 1890.

The business world was amazed. It was like "a thunderbolt out of a clear sky," reported the *New York Tribune*. Roosevelt's career as a "trustbuster" had begun. During his presidency the government filed suit against dozens of trusts. In two major victories, it broke up the Northern Securities Company and John D. Rockefeller's oil trust.

The Coal Strike

President Roosevelt's actions reflected his belief that the government should play an important role in the economic affairs of the nation. He had the opportunity to expand that role when a coal strike threatened the nation's fuel supply. In the spring of 1902, 150,000 coal miners in Pennsylvania went on strike for higher wages and an eight-hour workday.

The representative of the mine owners, George Baer, refused to negotiate with the

As coal became scarce during the 1902 strike, the price soared. This photo shows poor New Yorkers lined up to buy coal by the bag.

United Mine Workers (UMW), led by John Mitchell. The strike continued, and the nation began to run out of coal.

President Roosevelt invited both sides to the White House, but even there, mine owners refused to talk to UMW leaders. Roosevelt, furious at Baer's attitude, later said:

"If it wasn't for the high office I hold, I would have taken him by the seat of the breeches and the nape of his neck and chucked him out of that window.**"**

Roosevelt threatened to send troops to take over the mines. Alarmed, the mine owners agreed to government arbitration. The result was a wage increase and shorter workday for the miners.

For the first time the federal government had stepped in, not to break up a strike, but to bring about a peaceful settlement. Later Roosevelt said he had simply been trying to be fair—giving both miners and owners "a square deal."

Point of View

How should labor disputes be resolved?

Efforts to resolve the 1902 coal strike showed the wide gap between business and labor. The mine owners refused to accept unions as legal organizations. At the hearings on the coal strike, George Baer declared:

"We do not admit the right of an organization [a union] to . . . interfere with our management.**"**

UMW lawyer Clarence Darrow asserted that miners had the right to organize. Unless they had a union, the miners would have to

"come to [the owners] with their hat in their hand, each one in a position to be [fired] . . . if they raise their voice.**"**

In the years to come, unions would continue to grow. More and more, business and organized labor would sit down together to work out their differences.

The Square Deal

In the election of 1904, Roosevelt campaigned for "a square deal all around." Americans liked what they heard and elected him President by a large margin. A happy Roosevelt told his wife, "I am no longer a political accident." Meanwhile, Progressives like "Fighting Bob" La Follette were being elected to Congress. There they offered Roosevelt support for further reforms.

Curbing railroad rates Roosevelt continued to strengthen the power of the federal government by persuading Congress to pass new regulatory laws. To curb high railroad rates, he supported the Hepburn Act. Passed by Congress in 1906, it gave the Interstate Commerce Commission (ICC) the power to set the maximum rates that railroads could charge.

Regulating food and drugs For years reformers had urged Congress to pass food-inspection laws. Then in 1906 the muckraker Upton Sinclair published *The Jungle*. Sinclair's novel described the filthy conditions in the Chicago meatpacking industry. To kill rats, Sinclair wrote,

❝the packers would put poisoned bread out for them, they would die, and then rats, bread, and meat, would go into the hoppers together.❞

Horrified by *The Jungle*, Roosevelt demanded action. In 1906 Congress passed the Meat Inspection Act, setting sanitary standards for meatpacking and requiring federal inspection of meats sold in interstate commerce.

That year Congress also passed the Pure Food and Drug Act. This law required manufacturers to list the ingredients they used and to tell the truth about what medicines could do.

Conservation

President Roosevelt was also committed to **conservation**—protecting natural resources and using them wisely. He worried that the nation was using its natural resources at too rapid a rate. He asked the nation's leaders to think about

❝what will happen when our forests are gone, when the coal, the iron, the oil, and the gas are exhausted.❞

With the help of his friend Gifford Pinchot (PIN-shō), the chief of the United States Forest Service, Roosevelt set out to protect the nation's remaining forests. During his presidency he turned 150 million acres of government-owned timberlands into forest reserves, where logging was regulated.

John Muir (right), shown here with President Roosevelt at Yosemite National Park, rallied support for preserving the nation's wilderness areas.

Roosevelt achieved other victories as well. At the urging of naturalist John Muir, he created national parks to preserve some areas of wilderness in their natural states.

From Roosevelt to Taft

Roosevelt yearned to do battle for more reforms, but he had promised to serve only two terms. In 1908 he asked his Secretary of War, William Howard Taft of Ohio, to be the Republican candidate for President. Roosevelt's great popularity with the voters helped Taft win the election.

Calm and easygoing, President Taft was a very different man from Roosevelt. "I don't like politics," Taft wrote. "I don't like the limelight." Instead, he preferred to work quietly, behind the scenes.

Taft carried on Roosevelt's policies, urging Congress to pass new regulatory laws. In 1910 Congress passed the Mann-Elkins Act, which gave the ICC the power to regulate telephone and telegraph companies. Taft also used the Sherman Act even more vigorously against trusts than Roosevelt had.

During Taft's presidency, Congress approved the Sixteenth Amendment, which was ratified by the states in 1913. Originally called for by the Populists, it gave Congress the power to enact a federal income tax. Also ratified in 1913, the Seventeenth Amendment called for direct election of senators by the voters instead of by state legislatures.

Still, some of Taft's actions enraged Progressives. He supported high protective tariffs, forcing Americans to pay more for imported goods. He also fired Gifford Pinchot for disloyalty.

Wilson and Reform

By the presidential election of 1912, the Republicans were badly split. When the party nominated Taft for a second term, the Progressives walked out. They formed the new Progressive Party and nominated Roosevelt, who declared he was "fit as a bull moose . . . and ready for the fight." The party became known as the "Bull Moose" Party.

Roosevelt won more votes than Taft, but neither could defeat the Democratic candidate, Woodrow Wilson. As a native of the South and the reform governor of New Jersey, Wilson had wide appeal.

Lower tariffs Soon after taking office, Wilson proposed reforms long called for by Populists and Democratic Progressives. His first goal was to reduce tariffs. At his urging, Congress passed the Underwood Tariff in 1913. It lowered tariff rates for the first time since the Civil War.

The Federal Reserve System Next, Wilson set out to reform the nation's banking and currency system. Problems with the system had helped cause the Panic of 1893 (page 653) and another in 1907.

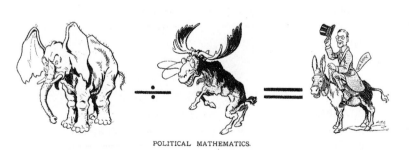

POLITICAL MATHEMATICS.

Before the election of 1912, a cartoonist predicted the results of the split in the Republican Party caused by Roosevelt's Bull Moose Party.

In 1913 Congress passed the Federal Reserve Act, which created the Federal Reserve System. New government banks took control of the nation's currency by issuing Federal Reserve notes. These bills make up nearly all the paper money issued in the United States today.

Antitrust laws When it came to breaking up the power of trusts, Wilson took even stronger action than had Roosevelt or Taft. In 1914 Wilson pushed Congress to create the Federal Trade Commission, which had power to control unfair trade practices. Congress also armed the President with the Clayton Antitrust Act of 1914, which allowed him to enforce antitrust rules against more companies than any President before him.

At the end of his first term, Wilson could say with pride: "We have . . . come very near to carrying out the platform of the Progressive Party as well as our own, for we also are Progressives."

4. Section Review

1. Define **conservation.**
2. In what ways did Taft follow Roosevelt's policies?
3. Give two examples of how Wilson extended Progressive reform.
4. Critical Thinking What benefits do you see in the government trying to intervene in strikes? What dangers?

Why We Remember

An Era of Reform

Today we look back on the Gilded Age and the Progessive Era as a time of corrupt politicians and earnest reformers. It was more than that, though. In many ways it was a testing time for democracy.

For much of this period after the Civil War, it seemed to many Americans that democracy was not working well. The two major political parties ignored the most important issues of the day. At the same time, business interests and political machines wielded far more power than ordinary voters at every level of government. Jane Addams found corruption not only in Chicago's city hall, but also in city schools.

Instead of giving up on democratic government, Americans set to work to fix what was wrong. Sometimes their efforts ended in disappointment and sometimes in success. Most important, the people made their voices heard, and government began to respond. Looking back on this era, Jane Addams wrote, "At moments we believed that we were witnessing a new pioneering of the human spirit." It was that spirit that kept democracy alive through discouraging times.

Chapter Survey

Reviewing Vocabulary

Define the following terms.
1. civil service
2. direct primary
3. initiative
4. recall
5. referendum
6. suffragists
7. conservation

Reviewing Main Ideas

1. Why was civil-service reform an important issue in the Gilded Age?
2. How did falling farm prices contribute to farmers' troubles?
3. Trace the development of the Populist Party from its birth in 1892 through the presidential election of 1896.
4. (a) What new forms of city government did Progressives introduce? (b) What was the overall effect of Progressive reforms in state government?
5. What achievements could Progressives point to in each of the following areas?
(a) protection of workers (b) temperance (c) woman suffrage
6. Give three examples of how President Roosevelt increased the power of the federal government.
7. How did President Wilson help to achieve Progressive goals?

Thinking Critically

1. Analysis Support the following statement with three examples from the chapter: Populist ideas triumphed even though the Populist Party declined.
2. Evaluation W. E. B. Du Bois said that the African American battle for equality was "not for ourselves alone but for all true Americans." What do you think he meant? Do you agree? Why or why not?
3. Why We Remember: Application Progressives like Jane Addams and Robert La Follette had faith that the American people would always do what was right. Was that faith justified, or not? Support your answer with evidence from the chapter and your own observations.

Applying Skills

Interpreting a political cartoon Find a political cartoon about a person or a current issue in government. Keeping in mind what you learned on page 650, identify the main subject and details of the cartoon. Then write the following:
• a brief summary of the cartoon's message
• a statement of how you think the cartoonist feels about the subject

History Mystery

President Arthur changes his mind Answer the History Mystery on page 643. Chester Arthur had been appointed collector of import duties for the Port of New York in 1871. In this position he used the spoils system to reward Republican Party workers with government jobs. In 1878 Arthur was removed by President Hayes for violating an executive order banning federal officials from taking part in political party activities. Why do you think such a ban was a good idea?

Writing in Your History Journal

1. Keys to History (a) The time line on pages 642–643 has eight Keys to History. In your journal, describe why each is important to know about. (b) Choose a key event and imagine yourself as a newspaper reporter assigned to cover it. In your journal, write an article about the event, including its causes and possible effects.

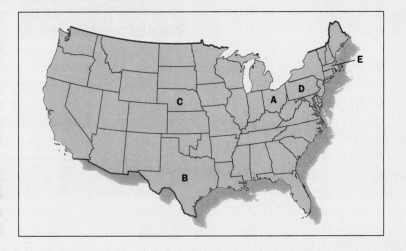

Reviewing Geography

1. For each letter on the map, name the state, tell whether its electoral votes in 1896 went to William McKinley or William Jennings Bryan, and explain why.

2. Geographic Thinking
The first 12 national parks were all located in the West. How might you explain this fact? Do you think these areas could have remained wilderness without government action? Explain, using evidence from the chapter and your own observations.

2. Jane Addams In your journal, reflect on how Jane Addams was representative of the Progressives.

3. Citizenship Some people criticized the muckrakers for writing about nothing but problems in American life. In a 1906 speech, President Roosevelt argued that the people "with the muck-rakes are often [necessary] to the well-being of society, but only if they know when to stop raking the muck." Do you think this criticism was valid? Do modern-day muckrakers help or harm the nation? Write your response in your journal.

Alternative Assessment

Creating public-service announcements If you listen to the radio, you probably have heard announcements that inform listeners about a problem, offer a solution, and call on the public to take part in solving the problem. Work with three classmates to create four public-service announcements that reformers in the late 1800s and early 1900s might have used to gain support.

❶ Choose four areas of reform discussed in the chapter.

❷ Brainstorm ideas for a script for a one-minute public-service announcement for each reform.

❸ Write first drafts of the four announcements, evaluate the drafts, and then produce final scripts.

❹ Take turns presenting the public-service announcements to the class. Your presentations can be "live," or you can make an audiotape and play it for the class.

Your announcements will be evaluated on the following criteria:
• they accurately describe the concerns and goals of reformers of the time period
• they offer specific ways that the public can help, based on the reformers' methods
• they are clear, striking, and persuasive

Chapter 24

Overseas Expansion

Sections

Keys to History

1900
Open Door policy in China declared

1898
Spanish-American War

1867
Alaska Purchase
Russian copy of purchase treaty

1898
Hawaii annexed

1865

1895

World **Link**

Looking Back

Commodore Perry opens trade with Japan
1854

Olympic Games revived
1896

HISTORY
Mystery

In 1898 the United States went to war to help Cuba gain its independence. Why, then, did the first battle of that war take place on the other side of the world?

1907
Great White Fleet
tours the world

1914
Panama Canal opens

1916
Wilson sends troops
into Mexico

1905

1915

Looking Ahead

The United States enters
World War I
1917

● **671**

Beginning the Story with

Theodore Roosevelt

Theodore Roosevelt is often described as the first modern President. When he was born, in 1858, the United States was a nation of 33 states. When he died, in 1919, there were 48 states stretching from sea to sea. The nation and its 26th President came of age together.

When Roosevelt was a child, it seemed doubtful he would come of age at all. Born to a wealthy family in New York City, "Teedy"—as his parents called him—suffered terribly from asthma attacks. Some attacks were so severe that his father would bundle up his wheezing son and ride around the streets of New York in an open carriage, hoping the brisk air would help the boy breathe more easily.

"You Must *Make* Your Body"

Due to his poor health, Teedy never went to school but was instead tutored at home. He was a bright boy who loved studying nature. At the age of 9 he wrote a book about insects. When his mother asked the maid to throw out some dead mice he was preserving in her icebox, Teedy cried, "Oh, no! The loss to science! The loss to science!"

One day his father sat him down for a serious talk. "Teedy," he said, "you have the mind, but you have not the body. Without the help of the body, the mind cannot go as far as it should. You must *make* your body." Teedy took this advice to heart. At his grandfather's country estate he learned to ride horseback and became an expert rifle shot. He also began a vigorous exercise program that included boxing and wrestling. Because of poor eyesight he often took a licking in the boxing ring, but he never quit. He eventually lost the sight in his left eye as the result of a boxing match.

An Unlikely Cowboy

As a young man Roosevelt fell in love, married his sweetheart, and was beginning a career in politics when tragedy struck. His young wife died suddenly. In his grief Roosevelt decided to start life anew in the West, becoming a cattle rancher in Dakota Territory.

The New Yorker made an unlikely cowboy. His neighbors called him "four-eyes" because of his glasses. They laughed at his squeaky voice and strange way of speaking. No rancher they knew exclaimed "By Godfrey!" or ordered ranch hands to "Hasten forward quickly there!" Yet the Dakotans admired this eastern tenderfoot for being honest and hard-working.

As the Republican candidate for Vice-President in 1900, Theodore Roosevelt was already a famous public figure—more popular in the eyes of many Americans than President William McKinley.

President "Teddy"

Perhaps haunted by memories of boyhood weakness, Roosevelt still exercised constantly after he became President. He did so much presidential business while hiking, riding horses, or playing tennis that the Congressmen who shared these sports with him were called the "tennis cabinet."

Many a White House visitor fell prey to Roosevelt's enthusiasm for exercise. One day the French ambassador arrived in formal clothes, expecting to go for a dignified "walk" with the President. Instead, he was taken on a rigorous cross-country hike. When Roosevelt asked the hikers to take off their clothes to keep them dry while wading a deep creek, the ambassador insisted on continuing to wear his fancy gloves. The British ambassador, a veteran of similar adventures, once warned a colleague, "You must always remember that the President is about six years old."

Americans, however, loved their energetic leader. They called him "Teddy" and embraced him as warmly as the stuffed animal named for him, the "teddy bear." He was, most felt, the right leader for a new century in which the United States would flex its muscles as a world power.

Hands-On HISTORY

Activity

Imagine that you are Theodore Roosevelt and have just become President. You have been asked to speak to a group of 12- and 13-year-olds about setting and reaching goals. Prepare a short speech to give them, using your experiences as examples.

1. The Roots of Overseas Expansion

Reading Guide

New Term **imperialism**

Section Focus **Why the United States became interested in overseas expansion**

1. Why and how did the United States increase its influence in the Pacific?
2. What were arguments for and against an overseas empire?
3. Why did the United States almost go to war with Britain?

By 1850 the United States stretched from the Atlantic to the Pacific. For most Americans, the Manifest Destiny "to overspread the continent" had been fulfilled.

Some expansionists, though, wanted more. They believed that the country should look beyond its coasts—particularly westward across the Pacific Ocean. Future prosperity, they argued, would come from strengthening trade with Asia.

Opening Trade with Japan

By the mid-1800s American ships were already crisscrossing the Pacific. American merchants were competing with Europeans in the China trade. They also wanted to trade with Japan, which had kept itself almost completely shut off from the outside world since the 1600s. The United States government decided to try to convince Japan to open its ports.

Four warships led by Commodore Matthew Perry arrived in Japan in 1853. The Japanese were impressed by Perry's modern, steam-powered vessels and by his gifts, which included various machines. The following year they agreed to allow limited trade with American merchants.

Britain, Russia, France, and the Netherlands pressured Japan into similar agreements. Recognizing its weakness, Japan quickly began to change itself from a farming society into an industrialized nation. It also built up a modern army and navy, the first Asian country to do so.

The Purchase of Alaska

In 1867 Secretary of State William H. Seward took another step to increase American power in the Pacific. He convinced Congress to buy Alaska from Russia for $7.2 million, or 2¢ an acre.

Many Americans ridiculed the deal as "Seward's Folly," saying that "Seward's Icebox" would never be worth what it cost. Seward, however, saw potential in Alaska's resources of fur, timber, and fish.

Also, Alaska included the Aleutians, a string of islands stretching halfway across the Pacific. These islands could serve as supply bases where American ships could take on food for their crews and coal to fuel their steam engines. For the same reason, Seward persuaded Congress to annex the tiny Midway Islands, located in the central Pacific between Hawaii and Japan.

Interest in Hawaii

Seward and other expansionists were especially interested in annexing Hawaii. As one newspaper editorial declared, "It will give us command of the Pacific."

Since the early 1800s Hawaii had been a favored port for American whaling and merchant ships. In their wake came missionaries eager to convert the native Hawaiians to Christianity. By mid-century the islands were home to a thriving community of Americans—mainly descendants of the missionaries, many of whom had become wealthy sugar planters.

In 1887 the planters forced Hawaii's King Kalakaua (kah-LAH-KAH-oo-ah) to give them control of the Hawaiian legislature. When Kalakaua died in 1891, his sister Liliuokalani (lih-LEE-OO-Ō-kah-LAH-nee) inherited the throne. Strong-willed, proud, and fiercely independent, "Queen Lil" rallied her people to oppose foreign rule. Her slogan was "Hawaii for the Hawaiians."

Fearful of losing their plantations, the American planters overthrew Queen Lil in 1893. They set up their own government and quickly sent a treaty of annexation to the United States Senate. They hoped to discourage any movement by native Hawaiians to restore Queen Lil to the throne. Becoming part of the United States would increase the planters' profits because Hawaiian sugar would no longer be taxed as an import.

Before the Senate could act, though, President Grover Cleveland withdrew the treaty. He was convinced that the planters had behaved dishonorably. Declaring that Queen Lil should be restored to power, he opposed efforts to annex Hawaii.

An American Empire?

Events in Hawaii sparked the first widespread public debate among Americans about **imperialism**—the policy of taking control of governments and resources of other countries in order to build an empire. Britain, Germany, and France were already racing to grab up colonies in Africa and the Middle East. Should the United States, too, extend its power to people and lands beyond its borders?

Arguments for expansion Expansionists offered a variety of reasons to justify imperialism. Appealing to national pride, they declared that the United States needed to take its place among the world powers. European nations were already gobbling up chunks of real estate around the world. If the United States did not annex the Hawaiian Islands, they argued, some other nation would surely do so.

Queen Liliuokalani of Hawaii tried to free the islands from the control of American sugar planters.

Some expansionists spoke of a duty to bring democracy and Christianity to "uncivilized" peoples. The clergyman Josiah Strong declared that white Americans represented "the largest liberty, the purest Christianity, the highest civilization."

Expansionists also argued that American factories and farms produced more than could be sold at home. They needed overseas markets. Island bases in the Pacific and Caribbean would help American merchants increase trade with China and Latin America.

Arguments against expansion
Critics argued that imperialism violated the nation's democratic beliefs. The United States, they declared, had no right to impose its rule on other peoples.

Some critics also argued that expansion would hurt the economy. They feared that people from American colonies would take jobs away from American workers. An empire would be expensive, too, because it would need a larger army and navy to protect it.

Point of View

Should the United States have an empire?

One leading expansionist was Senator Henry Cabot Lodge of Massachusetts. In 1892 he declared:

"The great nations are rapidly absorbing for their future expansion and their present defense all the waste places of the earth. It is a movement which makes for civilization and the advancement of the race. As one of the great nations of the world, the United States must not fall out of the line of march."

Like other expansionists, Lodge believed that the nation had a new Manifest Destiny to be a world power.

Building a Stronger Navy

If Lodge had called the United States "one of the great nations" just a few years earlier, his boast would have seemed ridiculous. As late as 1880, its navy ranked only 12th in the world. After the Civil War, most of its ships had been scrapped or left to rot. Congress, seeing no need for a large navy in peacetime, had spent little on new ships.

In 1890, though, expansionists convinced Congress to approve funds for a modern fleet of steel battleships. By 1900 the United States had the world's third largest navy, behind only Britain and Germany.

Credit for this turnabout belongs largely to Navy Captain Alfred T. Mahan. His 1890

This 1881 American cartoon criticizes the weak United States Navy for having too many officers and an outdated fleet of old wooden ships.

Olympic Games While European nations competed to build overseas empires, another kind of competition was being revived. Forgotten for almost 1,500 years, the Olympic Games were held in Athens, Greece, in 1896.

The first Olympic competition—a footrace—took place in Olympia, Greece, in 776 B.C. In time, other events were added. Every four years all wars were halted while the athletes competed. Roman rulers ended the games in A.D. 394. An earthquake later destroyed the stadium in Olympia.

Centuries passed. Then in 1875 archaeologists found the long-buried ruins. Fascinated by the finds, a French educator, Baron Pierre de Coubertin (koo-bayr-TAN), saw an opportunity to promote peace through international athletic competition. As a result of his efforts, the Olympics were reborn.

book *The Influence of Sea Power Upon History* argued that a nation's strength depends on a large battle-ready navy and many merchant ships, served by bases around the globe. He pointed to Britain as an example of success through sea power.

Mahan urged quick action to stake claims in the Pacific before Britain and Germany got all the bases. As an example, he pointed to a near-battle in 1889 between American and German warships over the Samoan Islands. The United States finally agreed to share control of Samoa with Britain and Germany. Mahan warned that the navy must be ready for such "dangerous germs of quarrel."

Defending the Monroe Doctrine

Expansionists also feared that quarrels would arise over Latin America if European nations tried to test the Monroe Doctrine. This doctrine, issued in 1823, had warned Europe against interfering in Latin American affairs. (See page 331.)

In 1895 such a test seemed likely to occur when a boundary dispute erupted between the British colony of Guiana and the nation of Venezuela. When the United States warned Britain not to use force against Venezuela, tempers flared on both sides of the Atlantic. Excited by the idea of taking part in a war, Theodore Roosevelt wrote, "Let the fight come if it must. . . . This country needs a war."

In the end, Britain backed down, and the dispute was settled peacefully. Still, many Americans hailed it as a victory for the Monroe Doctrine. Meanwhile, expansionists saw the beginnings of a more active foreign policy. Mahan wrote approvingly:

❝It indicates the awakening of our countrymen to the fact that we must come out of our isolation . . . and take our share in the turmoil of the world.❞

1. Section Review

1. Define **imperialism.**
2. What were early steps toward American expansion in the Pacific?
3. What were reasons for and against overseas expansion?
4. How did the United States defend the Monroe Doctrine?
5. Critical Thinking How were some of the arguments in favor of imperialism similar to reasons given to justify taking Indian lands?

Geography Lab

Understanding a Map's Point of View

Did you know that every map, like every person, has a point of view? A map's point of view is the place at or near the center of the map. It reflects the background and interests of the map maker and the people who will use the map. Because we are Americans and our nation has origins in Europe, most world and hemisphere maps that we use have North America, Europe, or the linking Atlantic Ocean at their center. The world map on pages R2–R3 is a good example.

The map on this page has a different point of view—one that reflects the interests of the expansionists you have been reading about. Perhaps Senator Albert J. Beveridge of Indiana was picturing a map like this one when he stated, "The Pacific is our Ocean."

The View from the Pacific

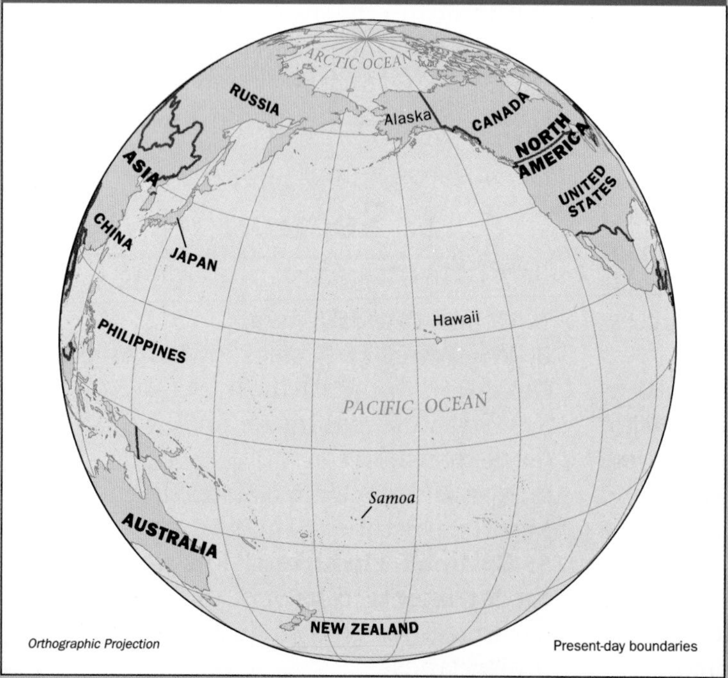

Orthographic Projection

Present-day boundaries

Using Map Skills

1. Look at the map on pages R2–R3. List six countries not in North America that the United States would be most likely to trade with. List six it would be least likely to trade with. Explain.

2. Look at the map on this page. Does your view of likely trading partners change? Explain.

3. What country might Americans see as their chief rival for trade with China and Japan? Why?

4. Suppose someone ridiculed Senator Lodge by saying, "Those islands are mere dots! Why bother?" How might Lodge use this map to defend his position?

5. Hands-On Geography Draw a world map centered on a country (not the United States) from which one of your ancestors came. Put it next to the map on pages R2–R3. Write a summary of the different views of the world that the two maps provide.

2. The Spanish-American War

Reading Guide

New Term **protectorate**

Section Focus **The causes and effects of the war with Spain**

1. Why did the United States go to war with Spain?
2. What were the results of the war?
3. How did the United States govern its new empire?

In looking toward Latin America, expansionists had long hoped to end Spain's rule over Cuba and Puerto Rico. These island colonies—along with Guam (gwahm) and the Philippines in the Pacific—were the remains of Spain's once-mighty empire.

Expansionists argued that taking over Cuba and Puerto Rico would help the United States control trade in the Caribbean. In 1895 a Cuban revolt against Spain provided an opportunity for the United States to expand its influence in the region.

Tensions over Cuba

Since the 1850s several Cuban patriots operating from American soil had tried to organize rebellions against Spain. Although the Spaniards brutally suppressed these revolts, they could not crush the Cubans' desire for independence. In 1895 the Cubans rebelled again, under the leadership of José Martí (mahr-TEE). Spain responded by sending an army under General Valeriano Weyler.

Although Martí was soon killed, the revolution spread rapidly. To choke off support for the rebels, Weyler ordered all Cubans into camps. Any Cuban found outside the camps would be executed.

Disease and starvation quickly turned the camps into death camps. As many as 200,000 Cubans lost their lives. Weyler's plan had worked, though. By the end of 1896, the rebels were in retreat and the revolution seemed lost.

The yellow press Newspaper accounts of events in Cuba aroused tremendous sympathy in the United States. Calls to help the rebels were widespread. American newspapers fed these feelings, as stories of Spanish cruelty appeared daily. The more horrible the story—true or not—the more newspapers were sold. Soon most Americans knew about "Butcher Weyler."

Two rival big-city newspapers—William Randolph Hearst's *New York Journal* and Joseph Pulitzer's *New York World*—fed the hysteria. More interested in selling papers than in providing unbiased news, they competed to find and print the most sensational stories and pictures.

Exaggerated news stories that were meant to appeal to emotion became known as "yellow journalism." The name came from a popular cartoon character in the *Journal* and the *World* called "The Yellow Kid."

Theodore Roosevelt was delighted as public anger over Cuba swelled into calls for war. In a private letter he wrote:

“Until we definitely turn Spain out of the island (and if I had my way that would be done tomorrow) we will always be menaced by trouble there.”

Hands-On HISTORY

Writing yellow journalism The practice of writing exaggerated, emotional news stories did not end with the Spanish-American War. The headlines in the papers you see at supermarket checkout lines today are proof that yellow journalism is still alive and well.

Activity Try your hand at writing a piece of yellow journalism.

1. Look in a daily newspaper for an article about an event or person. Choose an article that seems straightforward and factual.

2. Rewrite the article to turn it into a piece of yellow journalism. To do so, exaggerate some of the information and add emotionally charged words.

3. Exchange articles with a classmate. Then identify the differences between the two versions. Conclude by discussing what might happen if regular daily newspapers adopted the style of yellow journalism.

New York Journal **headline two days after the *Maine* explosion**

President Cleveland, however, feared that a war would open the door to American imperialism. Responding to his critics in Congress, he said:

"There will be no war with Spain over Cuba while I am President. . . . It would be an outrage."

"Remember the *Maine!*" When William McKinley became President in 1897, it appeared that he, too, would try to avoid a war. Roosevelt, who had been named Assistant Secretary of the Navy, expressed his disgust in a private letter. The President, he wrote, had "no more backbone than a chocolate éclair."

Hopes for a peaceful solution received a sudden blow on February 15, 1898. An explosion destroyed the battleship U.S.S. *Maine* in Havana harbor. The ship had been sent to protect Americans in Cuba. Some 260 American sailors died in the blast.

Although the cause of the explosion remains a matter of debate to this day, popular opinion at the time blamed Spain. "Remember the *Maine*!" became the watchword for war supporters in and out of government. Roosevelt called it "an act of dirty treachery on the part of the Spaniards." As the yellow press fanned the flames, Hearst told one of his artists, "You furnish the pictures. I'll furnish the war."

The United States declares war If President McKinley had been made of sterner stuff, he would have stood firm against those who were calling for the United States to fight Spain. Instead, he bowed to the pressure and asked Congress to declare war. On April 20 Congress passed a resolution declaring the independence of Cuba and demanding the withdrawal of all Spanish forces from the island.

To calm the fears of anti-expansionists, Congress passed the Teller Amendment declaring that the United States would not annex Cuba. Two days later McKinley ordered a naval blockade of Cuba. Roosevelt and Hearst had their war.

The War in the Philippines

The United States began the war with a spectacular victory—not in Cuba, but halfway around the world in the Philippines. Expansionists already had their eyes on those islands as a possible prize of winning a war with Spain.

In fact, just ten days after the *Maine* explosion, Roosevelt had taken steps to prepare for war. The Secretary of the Navy made the mistake of leaving his office for a few hours, allowing Roosevelt to be in charge. Without consulting anyone, Roosevelt gave orders readying the navy for a possible conflict. He sent a telegraph message to Commodore George Dewey of the Asian Fleet:

"Order the squadron . . . to Hong Kong. Keep full of coal. In the event [of a] declaration of war [with] Spain, your duty will be to see that the Spanish squadron does not leave the Asiatic Coast, and then [to conduct] offensive operations in Philippine Islands.**"**

The battleship *Maine* mysteriously exploded in Cuba's Havana harbor on February 15, 1898. This illustration was designed to stir up public support for declaring war on Spain.

The shocked Secretary of the Navy wrote in his diary, "Roosevelt has come very near causing more of an explosion than happened to the *Maine*." However, he let the order to Dewey stand.

At dawn on May 1, Commodore Dewey surprised the Spanish fleet anchored in Manila Bay in the Philippines. The American battleships sank all ten Spanish ships without the loss of a single American sailor. In one blow, the United States had crushed Spanish naval power in the Pacific.

With word of Dewey's dramatic victory, the army scrambled to organize a force to fight Spanish soldiers in the Philippines. As war fever swept the nation, the Senate finally voted to annex Hawaii, responding to the argument that the American army and navy needed the islands as a halfway station to the Philippines.

The War in the Caribbean

The Spanish fleet in Cuba, meanwhile, made the mistake of sailing into Santiago harbor. There a stronger American fleet blockaded it. The path was clear for sending in American troops. On June 22 they landed on Cuba's southern coast.

Unlike the navy, the army was woefully unprepared. The thousands of volunteers who rushed to join the war lacked guns, tents, and blankets. Soldiers received heavy woolen uniforms completely inappropriate for the tropics. Their food, leftover canned rations from the Civil War, was disgusting and sometimes even poisonous.

The army camps lacked proper sanitary facilities, and soon the troops suffered from plague and yellow fever. All told, 5,462 Americans lost their lives. Of those deaths, only 379 were the result of combat.

"Rough Riders," "Smoked Yankees"

Among the volunteers who landed in Cuba in June was Theodore Roosevelt. He had quit the Navy Department to become second in command of a volunteer regiment nicknamed the "Rough Riders."

"Rough" was a good name for them because they came from all walks of life—from wealthy socialites to cowhands, Indians, and even a few outlaws. As things turned out, though, few were "riders." A mix-up sent most of their horses elsewhere, so they had to walk into battle.

The key battles in Cuba were the assaults on the hills overlooking the city of Santiago. The main American force attacked San Juan Hill on July 1, 1898.

Meanwhile, the Rough Riders and two regiments of black soldiers, whom the admiring Spaniards called "Smoked Yankees," charged bravely up nearby Kettle Hill. Calling it a "bully fight," Roosevelt claimed that he "would rather have led that charge than served three terms in the U.S. Senate."

In one of the key battles in Cuba, American troops braved heavy fire to seize the Spanish fort on San Juan Hill above the city of Santiago. The soldiers are wearing their thick woolen uniforms in the sweltering heat.

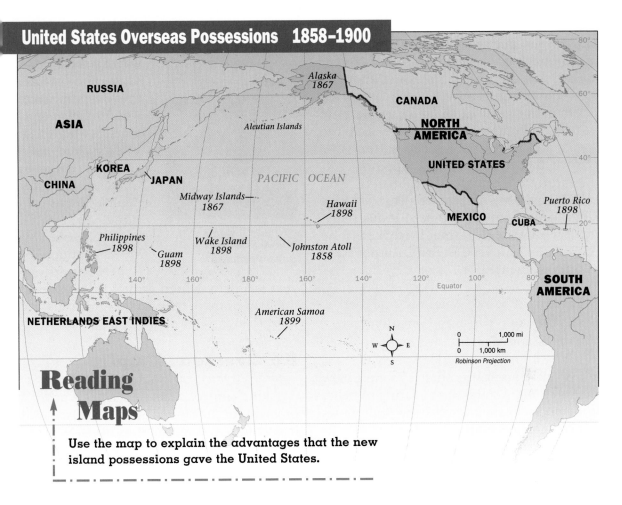

United States Overseas Possessions 1858–1900

Alaska 1867

RUSSIA

CANADA

ASIA

Aleutian Islands

NORTH AMERICA

UNITED STATES

KOREA

JAPAN

PACIFIC OCEAN

CHINA

Midway Islands— 1867

Hawaii 1898

Puerto Rico 1898

MEXICO

CUBA

Philippines —1898

Wake Island 1898

Johnston Atoll 1858

Guam 1898

Equator

SOUTH AMERICA

140° 160° 180° 160° 140° 120° 100° 80°

NETHERLANDS EAST INDIES

American Samoa 1899

0 1,000 mi
0 1,000 km
Robinson Projection

Reading Maps

Use the map to explain the advantages that the new island possessions gave the United States.

With American troops above the city and American ships blocking the harbor, the Spanish ships tried desperately to escape. On the morning of July 3 they went down in a blaze of glory. All were sunk or run aground. Nearly 1,800 Spanish sailors were captured; 474 were killed or wounded. Only one American sailor was killed and two wounded. The stunning victory gave Americans much to celebrate the next day, the Fourth of July.

The Peace Settlement

The Spanish troops in Santiago surrendered on July 17. After American forces landed on neighboring Puerto Rico a week later, Spain began negotiating for peace. A truce was finally signed on August 12, only four months after the war began. The next day American troops, aided by Filipino rebels under Emilio Aguinaldo (ah-gee-NAHL-dō), captured the Philippine capital of Manila.

By the terms of the peace treaty, signed December 10, 1898, Spain gave up Cuba, and the United States took control of Puerto Rico, Guam, and the Philippines. For Spain, the war marked the end of the great empire that Columbus had launched 400 years earlier. For the United States, the victory in what one diplomat called "a splendid little war" marked the arrival of a new world power.

Debate on the Philippines

Before the treaty could become law, though, it had to be ratified by the Senate. Many senators were troubled by its terms.

The war had been fought for the stated purpose of freeing a colony from Spain. Now it looked as if the United States was about to grab colonies of its own.

When the treaty came up for a vote early in 1899, it prompted bitter debate within the Senate and by the public. The hottest issue was whether to annex the Philippines.

Leading opponents of expansion, who called themselves anti-imperialists, included labor leader Samuel Gompers, industrialist Andrew Carnegie, social worker Jane Addams, and Grover Cleveland. Author Mark Twain commented:

"There must be two Americas, one that sets the captive free, and one that takes a once-captive's new freedom away.**"**

Many anti-imperialists shared Twain's view that the United States was violating its belief in democracy. They wanted the Philippines to become independent.

Expansionists countered that the Filipinos were "unfit" to govern themselves, and that if the islands were left alone another country might seize them. They also appealed to national pride. Where once the American flag goes up, they insisted, it must never come down.

The treaty was finally ratified on February 6, 1899, by a vote of more than two to one. The Senate split, however, on a proposal by anti-imperialists to give the Philippines immediate independence. It took a tie-breaking vote of the Vice-President to defeat the proposal. It was, admitted Senator Lodge, the "hardest fight I have ever known."

The Filipino uprising Little did Lodge suspect that the real fight had just begun. The Filipino people were angry at the idea of replacing one foreign ruler with another. Filipino leader Emilio Aguinaldo immediately launched a spirited campaign to rid his homeland of the Americans.

Filipino rebel leader Emilio Aguinaldo

In the resulting war of ambush, massacre, and torture, the American forces were sometimes as brutal as the Spanish soldiers had been against rebels in Cuba. Even after Aguinaldo was captured in March of 1901, his followers continued to fight. The three-year struggle, which ended in 1902, cost the lives of more than 4,000 Americans and more than 20,000 Filipinos.

An Overseas Empire

Taking control of its new empire posed a problem for the United States. The islands it had acquired were useful as overseas bases. However, what would be the status of the native peoples there? If they were given independence, the United States would no longer control the islands. Making them colonial subjects would be un-American. Should they be made American citizens?

In 1901 the Supreme Court declared that new territories could be considered either incorporated or unincorporated. People in incorporated territories would be American citizens. Also, such territories could eventually become states. People in unincorporated territories would not be granted citizenship but might eventually be given independence. The Court left it up to Congress to decide the status of each new territory.

The Philippines To control the Philippines, the United States set up a civil, or nonmilitary, government under an American commission headed by a governor, William Howard Taft. However, it promised the Filipinos independence in the future.

Puerto Rico: The 51st state? To be or not to be a state—that is a question for the Caribbean island of Puerto Rico. In 1993 Puerto Ricans narrowly voted against statehood, but the debate continues.

Some Puerto Ricans strongly favor complete independence from the United States. However, most are satisfied to remain a commonwealth. They think it is "the best of both worlds." They get some benefits that states enjoy, such as economic aid and military protection. At the same time, the island keeps its cultural identity separate from the United States. Meanwhile, Puerto Rican leaders continue to negotiate with Congress to change the definition of commonwealth in ways that will help the island.

In 1902 Congress made the islands an unincorporated territory and allowed Filipinos to elect the lower house in the legislature. Taft's commission served as a senate. In 1916 Congress replaced the commission with a Filipino senate but kept an American governor. The Philippines did not receive independence until July 4, 1946.

Puerto Rico The United States did not promise independence to Puerto Rico. It did, however, gradually give Puerto Ricans a greater voice in their government. In 1917 Congress granted Puerto Ricans citizenship. It gave them control over both houses of the legislature but kept an American governor. In 1952 Puerto Rico became a commonwealth of the United States, subject to federal laws but without the rights that a state has to be represented in Congress.

Cuba The Teller Amendment had pledged that the United States would not annex Cuba. Still, American leaders did not want to give Cuba independence until the island had recovered from the war. Under an American military government, troops distributed food, built roads and schools, and improved sanitation.

Crucial to Cuba's future success was finding a cure for yellow fever. Thanks to the efforts of army doctors led by Walter Reed and William Gorgas (GOR-guhs), the disease was traced to a species of mosquito. Once the carrier was discovered, it was possible to bring the terrible plague under control.

By 1901 the Cubans had adopted a constitution and declared themselves ready for self-government. To guard against another foreign power taking over Cuba, Congress added the Platt Amendment to Cuba's constitution, making Cuba a protectorate of the United States. A **protectorate** is a nation protected and controlled by another nation. Reluctantly, the Cubans agreed.

The Platt Amendment gave the United States the right to intervene militarily to maintain order. American forces did so four times before the amendment was finally repealed in 1934. As a result of a treaty signed in 1903, the United States still has a naval base at Guantánamo Bay.

2. Section Review

1. Define **protectorate.**
2. Why did war break out between the United States and Spain?
3. How did the United States benefit from the Spanish-American War?
4. Did people in former Spanish colonies become American citizens? Explain.
5. Critical Thinking Should the United States have given immediate independence to the former Spanish colonies? Explain.

Skill Lab

Thinking Critically
Comparing Points of View

Upon returning from a tour of the war-torn Philippines, Senator Albert J. Beveridge of Indiana made a name for himself by arguing in favor of annexation. His ideas were opposed by some Americans and, most importantly, by Filipino rebel leader Emilio Aguinaldo.

Question to Investigate

Did the United States have the right to rule the Philippines?

Procedure

Read **A** and **B**. Then do the following.

1 Summarize the speakers' statements.
a. What main points does Beveridge make?
b. What main points does Aguinaldo make?
c. How would each speaker answer the Question to Investigate?

2 Identify the bias of each speaker.
a. Does Beveridge think Americans are superior to Filipinos? Explain.
b. What effects of annexation does Beveridge focus on? What effects does he seem to ignore?
c. Does Aguinaldo think Americans are as fair and honest as he is? Explain.
d. What possible effects of a fight for independence does Aguinaldo focus on? What does he seem to ignore?

3 Consider how point of view can cause bias.
a. Imagine that you are Senator Beveridge. What has led you to feel the way you do?
b. Imagine that you are Emilio Aguinaldo. What has led you to feel the way you do?

Sources to Use

A "The Philippines are ours forever. . . . And just beyond the Philippines are China's illimitable markets. We will not retreat from either. We will not repudiate [reject] our duty in the archipelago [group of islands]. We will not abandon our opportunity in the Orient.

We will not renounce our part in the mission of our race, trustee [supervisor], under God, of the civilization of the world. And we will move forward to our work . . . with gratitude for a task worthy of our strength, and thanksgiving to Almighty God that He has marked us as His chosen people. . . ."

From a speech by United States Senator Albert J. Beveridge, January 9, 1900

B "By my proclamation of yesterday I have published the outbreak of hostilities between the Philippine forces and the American forces of occupation in Manila, unjustly and unexpectedly provoked by the latter. . . . I have tried to avoid, as far as it has been possible for me to do so, armed conflict. . . .

But all my efforts have been useless against the measureless pride of the American Government and of its representatives in these islands, who have treated me as a rebel because I defend the sacred interests of my country and do not make myself an instrument of their dastardly intentions."

From a speech by Filipino leader Emilio Aguinaldo, February 5, 1899

3. A New Role in the World

Reading Guide

New Terms spheres of influence, diplomacy

Section Focus How the United States took a more active role in Asia and Latin America

1. How did the United States try to prevent rivals from gaining power in Asia?
2. How and why did the United States build a canal through Panama?
3. In what ways did the United States intervene in Latin America?

As a result of annexing Hawaii and winning the war with Spain, the United States had firm footholds in the Pacific and the Caribbean. Americans now saw themselves as having a new, more important role in the world. The nation was ready to flex its muscles and take steps to protect and expand its overseas interests.

The Open Door Policy

The United States soon saw a threat to its trade with China. In 1899 the European powers and Japan were rushing to carve China into **spheres of influence**—areas in which each country claimed exclusive rights to trade and invest. The Philippines had given American merchants a base at China's doorstep. Now it seemed that the door might be slammed in their faces.

In 1899 Secretary of State John Hay sent letters to each of the great powers asking them to agree that China's ports would remain open to all nations. Although none made a definite commitment, the next year Hay boldly declared that this "Open Door policy" was in effect.

Meanwhile, many Chinese resented foreign control of their trade. Chinese patriots known as "Righteous and Harmonious Fists" (or "Boxers") called for the destruction of all "foreign devils." The Boxers stormed the capital city of Peking (now called Beijing), killing more than 300 foreigners.

The foreign powers used the Boxer Rebellion as an excuse to invade China and extend their spheres of influence. To make sure that the United States had a hand in settling the

An American cartoon in 1900 shows Uncle Sam opening China to free trade with all nations. Figures representing Britain (left) and Russia look on.

Honolulu Academy of Arts

Link to Art

The Letter (Mary Cassatt, 1891), ***Okita Carrying a Teacup*** (Kitagawa Utamaro, about 1790) The growing trade with Japan introduced many Americans to Japanese art. Impressionist painters such as Mary Cassatt experimented with Japanese styles. Instead of showing depth, the Japanese divided pictures into large flat surfaces. They showed glimpses of everyday life, using silhouettes and decorative patterns. **Discuss** Compare the two paintings. How does Cassatt's painting reflect Japanese influence?

crisis, President McKinley sent troops to help crush the rebellion. Meanwhile, Hay convinced the other powers not to take over Chinese territory and to maintain an "open door" for trade.

Tensions with Japan

As you read in Chapter 23, McKinley's assassination in 1901 made Theodore Roose-velt President. Only 42 years old, Roosevelt was the youngest person to have held the office—and he intended to thoroughly enjoy using his powers as President. He said to his friend Senator Henry Cabot Lodge:

❝It is a dreadful thing to come into the Presidency this way, but it would be a far worse thing to be morbid [gloomy] about it.**❞**

As President, Roosevelt took firm control of **diplomacy**—conducting relations with other nations. He believed that the United States needed to take a strong role to protect its investments and trade. In looking toward Asia, for instance, he wanted to make sure that no other country became powerful enough to control trade there.

In 1905 Roosevelt stepped in to help end a war between Russia and Japan. For more than a year, they had been locked in a bloody conflict over Korea and the Chinese province of Manchuria. Japan won all the battles but was running low on money, and Russia refused to quit. Roosevelt invited both nations to a peace conference in Portsmouth, New Hampshire.

In the Treaty of Portsmouth, Russia recognized Japan's control of Korea, and both nations agreed to withdraw from Manchuria. For his effective diplomacy in ending the Russo-Japanese War, Roosevelt received the 1906 Nobel Peace Prize. Many Japanese, however, resented Roosevelt because he had not supported Japan's demand for large cash payments from Russia.

Tensions with Japan were increased by racist attitudes in the United States. Japanese especially resented a decision by the San Francisco School Board in 1906 to segregate Asian students. In 1907 Roosevelt arranged a "Gentlemen's Agreement" with Japan. In return for Roosevelt getting the school board to give up its plans to segregate Asian students, Japan promised to limit immigration to the United States.

The Great White Fleet Roosevelt, meanwhile, worried about Japan's rising spirit of imperialism. He decided to make a show of naval strength by sending 16 gleaming white warships on a round-the-world tour in 1907.

The tour was a grand success. At every port cheering crowds met "the Great White Fleet." Japan gave the fleet its warmest welcome, as children waved American flags and sang "The Star-Spangled Banner." For the time being, tensions between the two nations eased, and they promised to respect each other's overseas possessions.

The Panama Canal

Meanwhile, Roosevelt had taken steps to fulfill a dream in the Caribbean—building a canal linking the Atlantic and Pacific oceans. Such a canal would greatly reduce the time and cost of trade with Asia. Also, warships could travel more quickly between the oceans to defend the nation's new islands.

During the Spanish-American War, the battleship *Oregon* had to steam 12,000 miles (19,312 km) from San Francisco, around the tip of South America, arriving in Cuba just in time for the battle of Santiago Bay. The trip took 68 days. A canal would have shortened the distance to 4,000 miles (6,437 km).

A canal across Central America was not a new idea. In fact, a French company had begun building one in Panama, then a part of Colombia. When the company went bankrupt, the United States bought its construction equipment.

Then, in 1903, John Hay negotiated a treaty with Colombia for a strip of land across Panama. At the last minute the Colombian Senate rejected an offer of $10 million and $250,000 in annual rent, asking instead for $25 million. This demand threw Roosevelt into a rage.

Meanwhile, Panamanians who were angry at Colombia's rejection of the treaty prepared to rebel against Colombia. They were sure the United States would help them.

On November 2, 1903, the American gunboat *U.S.S. Nashville* arrived in Panama. The next day the rebels struck. When Colombian troops arrived by sea to try to stop the revolt, the *Nashville* turned them back. The United States quickly signed a canal treaty with the new Republic of Panama.

Theodore Roosevelt visited the Panama Canal construction site in 1906, taking time to try out a steam shovel. He was the first President to travel outside the United States while in office. Above, a ship enters one of the canal locks.

No one was more pleased than President Roosevelt. Although critics accused him of encouraging the revolt, he felt no shame or guilt. Indeed, he later boasted, "I took the Canal Zone."

Building the canal Although Roosevelt was anxious to "make the dirt fly," construction proceeded at a snail's pace. First, it was necessary to rid the area of mosquitoes carrying malaria and yellow fever. This task fell to William Gorgas, who had helped eliminate yellow fever in Cuba. Gorgas's workers drained the swamps and ponds where the mosquitoes laid their eggs.

Then a team of army engineers led by George Goethals (GŌ-thuhlz) tackled the immense task of carving a channel through 40 miles (64 km) of solid rock and tropical rain forest. Some 45,000 workers labored on the "big ditch" for seven years. Its completion in 1914 was hailed as a monumental achievement.

"Big Stick Diplomacy"

In conducting diplomacy, Roosevelt followed the advice of an African proverb: "Speak softly and carry a big stick: you will go far." He believed that the threat of military force was the most effective way to deal with other countries.

Roosevelt had waved the "big stick" to stop Colombia from crushing the revolt in Panama. He continued to wave it to warn European nations not to intervene in Latin America.

Many Latin American nations were badly governed and owed huge debts to European investors. Roosevelt feared that European powers might use military force to collect these debts. He warned them that such interference would violate the Monroe Doctrine (see page 331). He then went a step further to argue that the United States had a right to intervene in the affairs of Latin American nations if necessary:

> **"** If we intend to say 'Hands off' to the powers of Europe, sooner or later we must keep order ourselves. **"**

This policy became known as the "Roosevelt Corollary" to the Monroe Doctrine.

The Roosevelt Corollary was first applied in the Dominican Republic in 1905. To settle a financial crisis there, Roosevelt sent officials to take over customshouses and pay off foreign debts. This intervention, and others that followed, caused bitter resentment among Latin Americans.

Taft's "Dollar Diplomacy"

William Howard Taft, who followed Roosevelt as President in 1909, tried a different way to reduce European influence in Latin America. He encouraged United States businesses to invest there as owners of mines, plantations, railroads, and banks.

THE BIG STICK IN THE CARIBBEAN SEA

A 1904 American cartoon shows Roosevelt using military force—the "big stick"—to intervene in Latin American countries.

Taft's "dollar diplomacy" also angered Latin Americans, who resented American control of their industries and banks. When protests erupted in Nicaragua, Taft fell back on Roosevelt's policy and sent in the marines. They remained until 1933, making Nicaragua a United States protectorate.

Wilson's "Moral Diplomacy"

President Woodrow Wilson, who took office in 1913, rejected both Roosevelt's and Taft's policies. He considered big stick diplomacy too aggressive and thought dollar diplomacy mainly served the interests of big business. Wilson offered a new approach to relations with Latin American nations—"moral diplomacy." He declared, "We must prove ourselves their friends and champions upon terms of equality and honor."

In fact, however, Wilson was unable to rely only on a policy based on moral principle. To protect American business interests he, too, ended up sending troops—to Cuba, the Dominican Republic, and Haiti. "The marines have landed" became a common newspaper headline. By the end of Wilson's presidency, Latin America would be dotted with United States protectorates.

Wilson's intervention in Mexico The greatest failure of Wilson's moral diplomacy was in Mexico. In the Mexican Revolution of 1911, Francisco Madero (frahn-SEES-kō mah-DE-rō) overthrew the dictator Porfirio Díaz (pōr-FEE-ryō DEE-ahs). However, Victoriano Huerta (VEEK-tō-RYAH-nō WAYR-tah), an ally of the

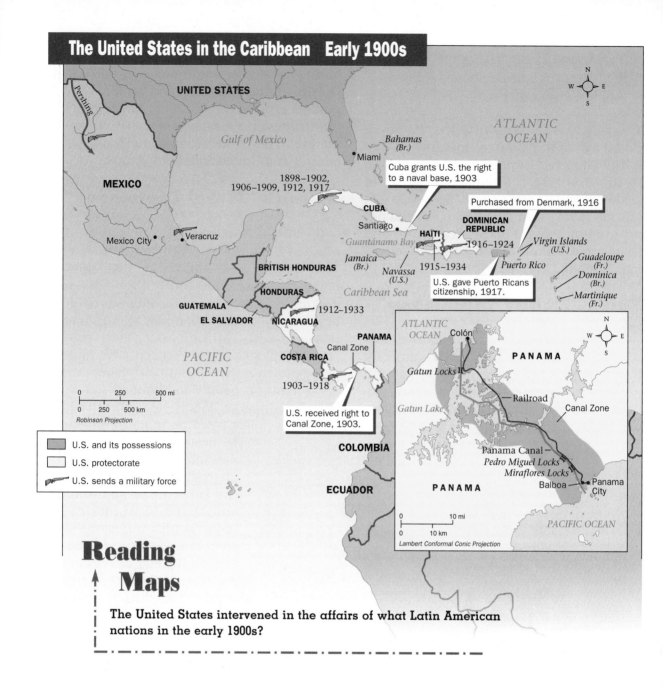

The United States in the Caribbean   Early 1900s

UNITED STATES

Gulf of Mexico

ATLANTIC OCEAN

Bahamas (Br.)

Miami

Cuba grants U.S. the right to a naval base, 1903

1898–1902, 1906–1909, 1912, 1917

MEXICO

Purchased from Denmark, 1916

CUBA

Mexico City

Veracruz

Santiago

HAITI

DOMINICAN REPUBLIC

1916–1924

Virgin Islands (U.S.)

Guantánamo Bay

Jamaica (Br.)

BRITISH HONDURAS

Navassa (U.S.)

1915–1934

Puerto Rico

Guadeloupe (Fr.)

Dominica (Br.)

HONDURAS

Caribbean Sea

U.S. gave Puerto Ricans citizenship, 1917.

Martinique (Fr.)

GUATEMALA

EL SALVADOR

NICARAGUA

1912–1933

PANAMA

PACIFIC OCEAN

COSTA RICA

Canal Zone

ATLANTIC OCEAN

Colón

PANAMA

Gatun Locks

1903–1918

Gatun Lake

Railroad

Canal Zone

0   250   500 mi
0   250   500 km
Robinson Projection

U.S. received right to Canal Zone, 1903.

COLOMBIA

Panama Canal
Pedro Miguel Locks
Miraflores Locks
Balboa

Panama City

U.S. and its possessions

U.S. protectorate

U.S. sends a military force

ECUADOR

PANAMA

PACIFIC OCEAN

0   10 mi
0   10 km
Lambert Conformal Conic Projection

Pershing

Reading Maps

The United States intervened in the affairs of what Latin American nations in the early 1900s?

---

rich landowners, seized power in 1913 and executed Madero.

To escape the fighting, hundreds of thousands of Mexicans emigrated to the United States. There most of them found work in industry and as farm laborers.

Declaring that he would not accept "government by murder," Wilson supported Huerta's rival, Venustiano Carranza (ve-noos-tee-AH-nō kah-RAN-sah). In 1914 Wilson sent marines to Veracruz to prevent a German ship from delivering supplies to Huerta. The marines captured the port after a stiff fight that cost the lives of 19 Americans and 126 Mexicans.

The invasion was a serious blunder. All of Mexico—even Huerta's enemies—united in denouncing it. War with Mexico was averted only when Argentina, Brazil, and Chile offered to mediate.

Carranza soon forced Huerta from power with the help of Francisco "Pancho" Villa (VEE-yah). When Villa then turned against Carranza, Wilson supported Carranza. Villa retaliated by raiding the town of Columbus, New Mexico, killing American citizens.

With Carranza's permission, Wilson sent an army in 1916 under General John J. Pershing to get Villa "dead or alive." When the troops were deep into Mexico, Carranza changed his mind and ordered an end to the search. Tensions between the two nations eased when Wilson withdrew the troops in 1917.

3. Section Review

1. Define **spheres of influence** and **diplomacy.**
2. How did the United States try to limit the power of its rivals in Asia?
3. How did the United States get permission to build a canal across Panama?
4. How were the policies of Roosevelt, Taft, and Wilson toward Latin America similar? How were they different?
5. Critical Thinking Do you think the United States was right to intervene in Latin America? Why or why not?

Why We Remember

Overseas Expansion

As a candidate for Vice-President in 1900, Theodore Roosevelt addressed the Republican National Convention with these words:

> **"**We stand on the threshold of a new century big with the fate of mighty nations. It rests with us now to decide whether in the opening years of that century, we shall march forward to fresh triumphs or whether at the outset we shall cripple ourselves for the contest. Is America a weakling to shrink from the work of the great world powers? No. The young giant of the West stands on a continent and clasps the crest of an ocean in either hand. Our nation, glorious in youth and strength, looks into the future with eager eyes and rejoices as a strong [athlete] to run a race.**"**

We remember the years of overseas expansion because they mark a shift toward active involvement in the affairs of other nations. Under Roosevelt's influence, the United States began to act like one of "the great world powers."

Now, as we enter the twenty-first century, Roosevelt's words still have meaning for Americans. In the uncertain times ahead, will the United States "shrink from the work of the great world powers"? In this age of global communications and trade, just what should that work be?

Chapter Survey

Reviewing Vocabulary

Define the following terms.
1. imperialism
2. protectorate
3. spheres of influence
4. diplomacy

Reviewing Main Ideas

1. How did the United States increase its influence in the Pacific during the middle and late 1800s?
2. Summarize the arguments for and against the idea of an American empire.
3. Describe the events that led up to the Spanish-American War.
4. How did the outcome of the war affect both Spain and the United States?
5. Describe the relationship between the United States and each of the following during the first 20 years after the war. (a) the Philippines (b) Puerto Rico (c) Cuba
6. (a) What policy did the United States pursue in China, and why? (b) Why did tensions arise between the United States and Japan? How did President Roosevelt try to ease those tensions?
7. Why did the United States become increasingly involved in the affairs of Latin American nations?

Thinking Critically

1. **Analysis** What role did racism play in American expansion overseas?
2. **Evaluation** Do you think the Spanish-American War was indeed a "splendid little war"? Explain.
3. **Why We Remember: Evaluation** Reread the quotation from Theodore Roosevelt on page 693. What kinds of attitudes and actions do you think Roosevelt would regard as signs of a "weakling" nation? Do you agree with his view? Explain.

Applying Skills

Comparing points of view Look through newspapers or magazines to find expressions of two points of view about a foreign policy issue. Keeping in mind what you learned on page 686, write three paragraphs in which you do the following:
1. Summarize the two writers' statements.
2. Identify the bias, if any, in each statement and tell how the writer's point of view might have contributed to it.
3. State your own opinion on the issue. Then identify your own bias, if any, and explain what has led you to feel the way you do.

History Mystery

The first battle Answer the History Mystery on page 671. What effect did this victory have on the American public?

Writing in Your History Journal

1. **Keys to History** (a) The time line on pages 670–671 has seven Keys to History. In your journal, describe why each one is important to know about. (b) If you could go back in time, which one of the events on the time line would you most like to observe, take part in, or try to prevent? Why? Write about it in your journal.
2. **Theodore Roosevelt** Mount Rushmore in South Dakota is a memorial to four Presidents: George Washington, Thomas Jefferson, Abraham Lincoln, and Theodore Roosevelt. Some people think Roosevelt does not belong. Based on what you have learned about him in this chapter and in Chapter 23, do you agree or disagree? Why? Write your responses in your history journal.

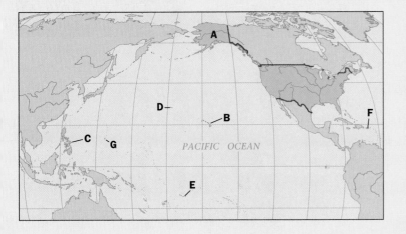

Reviewing Geography

↑ **1.** Each letter on the map represents an American possession. Name each one.

2. Geographic Thinking Nicaragua was the first site favored by most people who dreamed of a canal through Central America. Look at the map on page 692. Where might a Nicaraguan canal have started? What major disadvantage of a Nicaraguan canal site is apparent? If the Panama Canal had not been built when it was, do you think it would be built today? Explain.

3. Thinking Historically Imagine that you are a Hawaiian, a Filipino, a Cuban, or a Puerto Rican during the period of U.S. intervention. Write a letter to the President of the United States in which you describe your feelings about the fact that your homeland is under American control.

Alternative Assessment

Citizenship: Putting expansionism on trial Conduct a "trial" to determine whether American expansionism did more harm or more good for the United States and the world.

❶ Decide on a role for each class member. You will need a judge, a jury of 12, a lawyer for the prosecution (seeking a "Guilty" verdict), a lawyer for the defense (seeking a "Not Guilty" verdict), and the following witnesses:

• Theodore Roosevelt and other American expansionists
• Mark Twain and other American anti-expansionists
• people from the places affected by American expansionism, including Queen Liliuokalani and Emilio Aguinaldo

❷ Have at least one pretrial planning meeting. Plan to have the prosecution present its case first, followed by the defense. Allow time for preparing roles.

❸ Conduct the trial. Then give the jury time to review and discuss the evidence.

Your work will be evaluated on the following criteria:
• you offer evidence that reflects real events and the viewpoints of historical figures
• you present your position and arguments clearly and logically
• you stay "in character"

Chapter 25

World War I

Sections

Beginning the Story with Alvin C. York

Keys to History

1914
Archduke Ferdinand and wife assassinated in Sarajevo

1915
Lusitania sunk by German U-boat

1914

Looking Back

George Washington advises against foreign alliances

1796

HISTORY *Mystery*

Sgt. Alvin C. York received more military awards in World War I than any other American. Twice, however, York had tried to avoid going to war. Why?

1917
United States declares war on Germany

1918
Germany signs armistice

1918
Wilson presents Fourteen Points

1919
Treaty of Versailles signed
Hall of Mirrors, Versailles

1920
Senate refuses to ratify Treaty of Versailles

917

1920

World **Link**
Civil War in Russia
1918–1920

Looking Ahead

The United States enters World War II
1941

Alvin C. York

On the morning of October 8, 1918, American soldiers crouching in their trenches in France looked up to see an incredible sight. Two long lines of German soldiers emerged out of the woods and trudged toward the American lines. Leading this strange cavalcade was an American soldier named Alvin C. York.

"Well, York," his amazed commander said later, "I hear you have captured the whole German army."

"No, sir," York answered, "I have only one hundred and thirty-two." He did not add that he had also captured 35 German machine guns and left 32 Germans dead in the woods—all single-handedly. In recognition of his heroism, York would become the most decorated American soldier of World War I. At the end of his life, however, he credited his remarkable feat to God. "We know there are miracles, don't we?" York would say. "Well, this was one."

The First Miracle

The first miracle in York's life was that he was not in jail or dead when World War I began in 1914. Born in a one-room log cabin in the Cumberland Mountains of Tennessee, York had the restless blood of pioneers, like Daniel Boone and Davy Crockett, flowing through his veins. Even his mother admitted that her tall, lanky, red-haired son was "kind of a wild boy."

Then Alvin C. York fell in love with a churchgoing neighbor named Grace Williams. Through her he found the love of God. As York explained it:

"Miss Gracie said that she wouldn't let me come a-courting until I'd quit my mean drinking, fighting, and card flipping. So you see, I was struck down by the power of love and the Great God Almighty all together.**"**

York changed his wild ways and joined the Church of Christ in Christian Union.

Alvin C. York was one of millions of American soldiers sent to France during World War I. Troops on both sides dug trenches in the frozen ground to protect themselves from enemy fire.

"Thou Shalt Not Kill"

In 1917, at age 30, York received a letter that would change his life. The United States had joined the war in Europe and had sent him a notice to register for the draft. York considered himself as patriotic as any other American. However, he also believed in the Bible's commandment, "Thou shalt not kill." He later admitted, "I just didn't know what to do. I worried and worried. I couldn't think of anything else. My thoughts just wouldn't stay hitched."

On his draft registration form was the question, "Do you claim an exemption from the draft?" He wrote, "Yes. Don't want to fight."

"Blessed Are the Peacemakers"

York tried to be excused from military service because of his religious beliefs. However, because the government did not recognize his church—the Church of Christ in Christian Union—as a traditional pacifist faith, his appeals were denied.

When York learned that he was to be sent to fight on the front lines in France, he again asked to be excused from combat. He explained his religious beliefs to his commanding officer, Major George Edward Buxton. Convinced of York's sincerity, the major granted him a ten-day leave and sent him home to work out his inner conflict.

Back home York talked with his family and pastor. He went into the mountains to pray and think. He reread key passages in the Bible. One gave him special comfort. It said, "Blessed are the peacemakers."

Major Buxton had told York that Americans were going to war in Europe to bring peace to the world. "Was this a goal worth fighting, worth killing, worth dying for?" York asked himself. After much thought, he closed his Bible, looked up at his mother, and said, "I'm a-going."

Hands-On HISTORY

Activity

Imagine that you are Alvin York's friend. It is the year 1917 and Alvin has just received his draft notice. He has written to you for advice. In his letter he explains that he is loyal to his country, yet knows that his religion is against fighting. Draft a response to Alvin telling him what you think he should do and why.

1. The Roots of World War I

Reading Guide

New Term stalemate

Section Focus World War I begins in Europe

1. What incident started World War I and why?
2. How did the nations of Europe choose sides?
3. What weapons and methods were used in the war?
4. How did the United States react to the war?

On June 28, 1914, Alvin York was enjoying life at home in the Tennessee mountains. Little did he—or his fellow Americans—suspect that an incident thousands of miles away was going to rock the world and forever change the direction of his country.

News of the incident reached Americans the next day. The *New York Times* announced the story with bold, front-page headlines:

"Heir to Austria's Throne Is Slain with His Wife by a Bosnian Youth to Avenge Seizure of His Country**"**

Archduke Francis Ferdinand and his wife, Sophie, greet a well-wisher just one hour before their assassination.

The assassination of the Austrian Archduke Ferdinand and his wife, the Duchess of Hohenberg, in Sarajevo, the capital of the Balkan province of Bosnia, caused shock waves to roll through Europe. It caused little concern in the United States, though. Europe and its conflicts felt far removed from life at home.

Wilson's Neutrality Policy

Since the days of George Washington, the United States had tried to avoid involvement in European conflicts. President Woodrow Wilson sought to continue this policy.

On August 4, 1914, Wilson responded to the news of war in Europe by issuing a proclamation of neutrality. He urged Americans to be "impartial [not to take sides] in thought as well as in action." Wilson hoped that the United States could play the role of mediator to help bring peace to Europe.

European Rivalries

In the decades before 1914, Europe had been experiencing a period of industrial growth and prosperity.

As a result, the future looked brighter than it had for a long time.

Even so, European countries distrusted one another. With so many shared boundaries, each wanted to be armed for its own protection. Instead of bringing about the desired security, however, more weapons produced more fear. Feelings of nationalism added urgency to the race to build up arms and supplies.

The powder keg Friction between the nations of Europe was not new. The tiny countries of the Balkan Peninsula, for example, had feuded with one another for centuries over boundary lines. Matters there were so tense that the region was known as "the powder keg of Europe," just waiting to explode.

In truth, all of Europe was a powder keg. For 43 years the French had seethed with anger at Germany for annexing two of its richest provinces—Alsace and Lorraine— after the Franco-Prussian War of 1870–1871. Meanwhile, Italians resented Austrian control of their borderlands.

The powerful empires—Austria-Hungary, Russia, and the Ottoman Empire (including present-day Turkey)—added to the tension with their hunger for land. As you read in Chapter 24, the major powers of Europe had also raced to gobble up large chunks of Africa, Asia, and the Pacific.

The Alliances

Given these frictions, is it any wonder that the nations of Europe sought protection from their neighbors? Their solution was to form military alliances.

In 1871 Otto von Bismarck brought together 50 small, independent cities and states to form the large and powerful nation of Germany. Then "the Iron Chancellor," as Bismarck was known, sought allies to help protect Germany.

In 1882 Germany joined with Italy and Austria-Hungary to form the Triple Alliance. The members of the Alliance agreed to support each other in case of attack.

France, Russia, and Britain viewed the Triple Alliance with alarm. They felt that it upset the fragile balance of power among the nations of Europe. Thus, despite suspicions about one another, in 1907 they formed their own alliance known as the Triple Entente (ahn-TAHNT).

The two alliances maintained Europe's balance of power. They did nothing to defuse the European powder keg, however.

The Balkan Crisis

The powder keg exploded on June 28, 1914, when Archduke Ferdinand was assassinated by a 19-year-old Bosnian student. Austria-Hungary blamed the killing on the Serbian government. In late July it declared war on Serbia. Although none of the major powers wanted war, the very alliances they had made to maintain peace now forced them to take sides.

Russia sent troops to assist its ally, Serbia. Germany responded by declaring war on Russia on August 1 and on France, Russia's ally, two days later. German armies invaded Belgium in order to attack France. England entered the war on August 4 on the side of France and Russia.

Central Powers vs. Allies

Other countries were soon involved in the conflict. Russia's enemy, the Ottoman Empire, and Serbia's enemy Bulgaria sided with Austria-Hungary and Germany. These countries, which formed a large bloc in the center of Europe, became known as the Central Powers.

The forces against them—Britain, France, and Russia—were known as the Allies. Japan

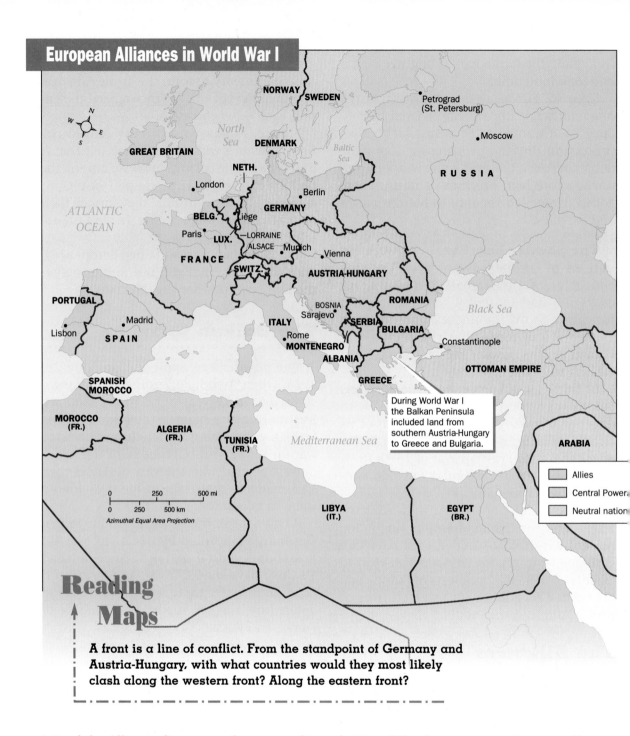

European Alliances in World War I

NORWAY
SWEDEN
• Petrograd (St. Petersburg)
• Moscow

North Sea
DENMARK
Baltic Sea

GREAT BRITAIN

RUSSIA

NETH.
• London
• Berlin
GERMANY

ATLANTIC OCEAN

BELG. • Liège
Paris • LUX.
—LORRAINE
ALSACE • Munich
FRANCE
• Vienna
SWITZ.
AUSTRIA-HUNGARY

PORTUGAL
BOSNIA
• Sarajevo
ROMANIA
Black Sea
ITALY
• Madrid
SERBIA
Lisbon
SPAIN
• Rome
BULGARIA
MONTENEGRO
• Constantinople
ALBANIA
SPANISH MOROCCO
GREECE
OTTOMAN EMPIRE

During World War I the Balkan Peninsula included land from southern Austria-Hungary to Greece and Bulgaria.

MOROCCO (FR.)
ALGERIA (FR.)
TUNISIA (FR.)
Mediterranean Sea
ARABIA

0   250   500 mi
0   250   500 km
Azimuthal Equal Area Projection

LIBYA (IT.)
EGYPT (BR.)

Allies
Central Powers
Neutral nations

Reading Maps

A front is a line of conflict. From the standpoint of Germany and Austria-Hungary, with what countries would they most likely clash along the western front? Along the eastern front?

joined the Allies to discourage German ambitions in the Pacific and Asia. Italy, hoping to gain territory from Austria-Hungary, joined the Allies in 1915. Eventually the Allies included 27 nations.

People on both sides expected a quick and easy victory, but some leaders knew better. "The lamps are going out all over Europe," warned Sir Edward Grey, Britain's foreign minister. "We shall not see them again in our lifetime."

At the time, people called this global conflict the Great War. Today it is known as World War I.

Miracle on the Marne

In August 1914 Germany's plan was to attack first on the western front. It would roll through Belgium to crush France, then turn to the east and defeat Russia.

The plan worked well in the beginning, even though the Germans met unexpectedly stiff resistance from the outgunned and outnumbered Belgian army. The rapid German advance soon had French forces fleeing in disorder toward Paris. Confident of victory, the German commander in chief, Helmuth von Moltke, boasted that the war would be over in six weeks.

On September 6, however, just south of the Marne River and almost in sight of Paris, French and British forces finally overpowered the German troops and forced them to withdraw. The French called the victory "the Miracle on the Marne."

Stalemate on the Western Front

The German defeat on the Marne changed the character of the war. No longer was the conflict one of movement and maneuver. Instead, for three long years the opposing sides were stuck in a **stalemate**—deadlock—on the western front.

Trench warfare Soldiers on both sides of the stalemate dug trenches—long zigzag lines of ditches about 6 feet (1.8 m) deep and 3 feet (0.9 m) wide. Spaces dug into the sides of the trenches protected soldiers from enemy fire and provided room where they could eat and sleep.

Systems of trenches were barricaded with tangles of barbed wire. The stretch of ground between the opposing trenches was called "no man's land."

Hands-On *HISTORY*

Surviving life in a trench Describing the trenches he and fellow British soldiers dug during the war, Frank Richards wrote: "Little did we think when we were digging those trenches that we were digging our future homes for the next four years."

Activity With a group of five classmates, imagine living in a trench 6 feet deep by 3 feet wide by 20 feet long for a week. There is a lull in the fighting, but you must be alert. The enemy is less than 90 feet away, just across "no man's land." In your group of six, brainstorm answers to these questions:

1 If each of you could bring ten items into the trench—besides clothing and weapons—what would they be?

2 What are some activities you could do to pass the time in the trench?

3 What activities would not be a good idea? Why not?

Write down your ideas, and compare them with those of other groups in your class.

American soldiers in a trench

Link to Technology

World War I Planes and Tanks

Both in the air and on the ground, World War I was a different kind of war than had ever been fought before. For the first time planes were adapted to be fighting machines. On the ground the bloody stalemate of trench warfare called for an all-new weapon: the tank.

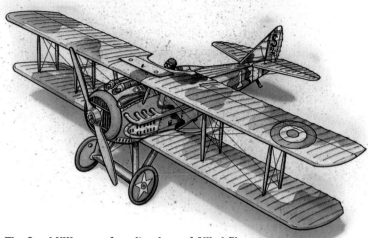

The Spad XIII was a favorite plane of Allied fliers. This fast plane had a top speed of 134 mph (214.4 km/hr) and was very durable. It was armed with two machine guns.

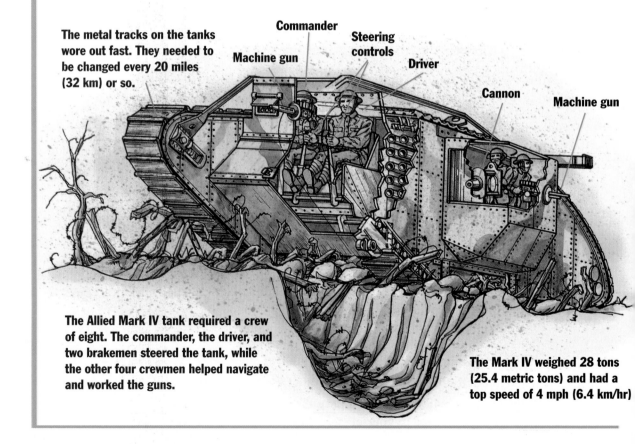

The metal tracks on the tanks wore out fast. They needed to be changed every 20 miles (32 km) or so.

Commander

Steering controls

Machine gun

Driver

Cannon

Machine gun

The Allied Mark IV tank required a crew of eight. The commander, the driver, and two brakemen steered the tank, while the other four crewmen helped navigate and worked the guns.

The Mark IV weighed 28 tons (25.4 metric tons) and had a top speed of 4 mph (6.4 km/hr)

Life in the trenches was horrible. The smell of dead bodies hung in the air. Rats and lice were constant companions. When it rained, soldiers stood and slept in mud. During attacks they had to dodge machine-gun fire. Otherwise, the days were long and tedious. One Allied soldier remembered:

"There was no such thing as cooked food or hot tea at this stage of the War, and rations were very scarce: we were lucky if we got our four biscuits a man daily.

One night there was an enemy attack which we beat off, and the next morning some corpses were to be seen lying just out in front of us. . . . We crawled out the next night and went through their packs, taking anything they had of value from them."

A dense network of trenches stretched for 400 miles (645 km) from Switzerland to the North Sea. Throughout 1915 and 1916 the Allies and Central Powers launched massive attacks against each other. Their gains never amounted to more than a few hundred yards, though, while losses amounted to hundreds of thousands of human casualties.

Modern Warfare

Progress in science and technology before 1914 made modern warfare increasingly destructive. Both sides unleashed new weapons and improved versions of familiar weapons. One new weapon was poison gas. Chlorine and mustard gases floated into the trenches, choking, blinding, and killing soldiers on both sides.

Tanks The British brought automotive technology to the battlefield when they introduced tanks in 1916. These heavily armored cars with tractor treads instead of wheels could travel over rough ground and through barbed wire. Tanks got bogged down in mud, though, and too few were used to make a difference in the outcome of the war.

German U-boats Far more effective and terrifying than tanks were the German submarines known as U-boats. These underwater craft could fire torpedoes into ships, destroying them without warning.

Airplanes To counter the U-boat threat, the Allies made good use of another recent invention—the airplane. Early in the war the Allies used airplanes to guard cargo ships and locate targets for artillery. Later, planes were equipped with machine guns.

The first use of aircraft as bombers was on August 6, 1914. A German zeppelin dropped 13 bombs on the Belgian city of Liège, killing 9 civilians. Now, observed a French writer,

"the conquest of the air was truly complete. Men were going to die in the air as they had for centuries on the ground and on the seas, by killing each other."

For the next three years the war was fought mainly in the trenches. Americans looked on, listening to war reports but supporting Wilson's declaration of neutrality. As casualties continued to grow, however, remaining uninvolved became more and more difficult.

1. Section Review

1. Define **stalemate.**
2. Why, after many years of peace, did war break out in Europe?
3. What effects did developments in science and technology have on the way war was waged during World War I?
4. Critical Thinking Were the countries of Europe wise to form alliances? Why or why not?

2. The United States Enters the War

Reading Guide

New Terms propaganda, pacifists, armistice

Section Focus How the United States helped the Allies win World War I

1. Why did the United States decide to join the Allies?
2. How did the war affect Americans in the armed forces and on the home front?
3. Why did Germany finally admit defeat?

With the war raging in Europe, it became increasingly difficult for Americans not to take sides. Because this is a nation of immigrants, many Americans naturally felt some loyalty to the countries of their ancestors—as well as to the United States. Both the Central Powers and the Allies tried to take advantage of such loyalties as they competed to gain American support.

Propaganda

The Central Powers and the Allies flooded the nation with mail and telegraph messages accusing each other of killing civilians and violating international law. They used a new invention, the radio, to get their message out. The spread of ideas that help one cause and hurt another is called **propaganda.**

The Allies gained the upper hand in the propaganda battle after Britain cut the transatlantic cables linking the Central Powers to the United States, making telegraph communication impossible.

The *Lusitania*

American neutrality was severely shaken when word arrived that a German submarine had torpedoed the British passenger ship *Lusitania* on May 7, 1915. This tragic event took the lives of 1,198 people, including 128 American citizens.

Americans were outraged, and President Wilson lodged a strong protest with the German government. Although the *Lusitania* was in fact carrying arms and explosives to England, Germany apologized, offered to pay damages, and promised not to sink passenger vessels in the future.

Germany would not agree, however, to Wilson's demand that it stop submarine warfare. Using U-boats to cut off military supplies destined for the Allies was the Central Powers' chief chance for victory.

Building Defenses

After the sinking of the *Lusitania*, Wilson realized that the United States could not remain neutral much longer. At his urging, in 1916 Congress passed a series of measures designed to prepare the United States to defend itself from the Central Powers.

The National Defense Act doubled the size of the army, and the Naval Appropriations Bill provided money to build warships. The Council of National Defense was formed to direct and control the supply of the nation's industries and natural resources.

The election of 1916 In his 1916 campaign for re-election, however, Wilson still preached neutrality. Running under the slogan, "He kept us out of war," he narrowly defeated his opponent, Charles Evans Hughes. Once re-elected, Wilson called on both sides to settle for "a peace without victory."

The End of Neutrality

Once again, forces beyond Wilson's control pushed the nation toward war. In January 1917 Germany's foreign minister, Arthur Zimmermann, sent a secret message to Mexico. He promised to help Mexico take back New Mexico, Arizona, and Texas in return for Mexican aid to Germany if the United States entered the war. The British intercepted and decoded the message.

Although Mexico quickly rejected the suggestion, the damage had been done. This violation of the 1823 Monroe Doctrine turned Americans even more against Germany. In March, when German U-boats sank five neutral ships, hopes for continued neutrality gave way to cries for revenge.

The Russian Revolution A final barrier keeping the United States from joining the Allies was lifted in March 1917. That month Russian revolutionaries overthrew their ruler, Czar Nicholas II, and replaced him with a democratic government. For many Americans, Russia was now an acceptable ally.

Declaring war With a heavy heart, President Wilson asked a special session of Congress to declare war on Germany. "The world," he vowed, "must be made safe for democracy." Congress issued the declaration on April 6, 1917.

The American entry into the war was crucial for the Allies. Their will to fight was almost gone. Units of the French army had rebelled, and Britain had lost an entire generation of its young men. The Allies desperately needed American supplies and support.

Americans in the Service

To raise a large army on short notice, Congress passed the Selective Service Act of May 18, 1917. The "draft" required men between the ages of 21 and 30 (later between 18 and 45) to register for military service. By war's end 4 million men were in the army, half of whom served overseas.

Doughboys The official name of the Yankee army was the American Expeditionary Force (AEF), but they were called "doughboys." Some say this name came from the cornmeal cakes they ate, others say it came from their youth and inexperience.

Recruiting posters like this one inspired American men to volunteer for military service.

The doughboys' commander was General Pershing, a hardened career army officer whom you read about in Chapter 24. Pershing worked to ensure that his soldiers were well trained before they saw any combat.

African Americans Some 360,000 African Americans joined the armed forces. African American leaders had encouraged young black men to enlist. They hoped that black patriotism would overcome racist prejudice in American society. As a columnist for the *Washington Bee* declared:

❝I am one of those who believe that the present war will settle forever the colored question in the United States. The black man will be recognized and be treated as a man and a brother.❞

Sadly, a society not yet ready for change dashed such hopes. Although three black regiments received France's highest military honor, the croix de guerre, most black soldiers were assigned to segregated units or to noncombat duty.

Native Americans Indians could not be drafted because they were not yet United States citizens. Even so, an impressive 17,213 Indians volunteered to fight, of whom 6,509 were enlisted. Their percentage was twice the national average. Those who served obtained citizenship.

Indian war heroes included Chauncey Eagle Horn, a Sioux, who was the first decorated soldier from South Dakota. The most brilliant record belongs to Private Joseph Oklahombi, a Choctaw. He received the croix de guerre for scrambling across 210 yards (192 m) of barbed wire, wrestling a machine gun from its crew, and then using it to capture 171 German soldiers.

Women Some 25,000 women contributed to the war effort by working for the armed services. Many served in the army and naval nurse corps or enlisted in the marines. Others were secretaries or telephone operators. Women served as doctors, dentists, decoders, librarians, interpreters, translators, and chauffeurs. They did almost everything except fight.

In response to African American demands that they be permitted to serve as combat troops, two all-black infantry divisions, the 92d and 93d, were formed and sent to France. The soldiers in this 1918 photograph were part of the 92d Division.

Point of View

What would you do if you were drafted?

In 1917 when President Wilson and Congress decided to have a draft, many citizens opposed the war. One group, called the Fellowship of Reconciliation, felt that the United States should not get involved in other countries' wars. They wrote:

"We are patriots who love our country and desire to serve her and those ideals for which she has stood . . . but we cannot believe that participation in war is the true way of service to America.**"**

Other people, like Alvin York, were against the war because their religions opposed fighting for any reason. York explained his decision to join the army by saying:

"I loved and trusted old Uncle Sam and I have always believed he did the right thing. But I . . . didn't want to go and kill. I believed in my Bible. And it distinctly said, 'Thou shalt not kill.' And yet old Uncle Sam wanted me. And he said he wanted me most awful bad.**"**

How would you feel if you were drafted? Can you make a list of three reasons why you would or would not fight?

Financing the War

From the beginning it was clear that the American war effort was going to be costly. To help finance this unexpected expense, in October 1917 Congress passed the War Revenue Act, increasing income taxes.

The government also raised money by selling liberty bonds. Politicians and movie stars gave speeches urging people to buy bonds. Some 21 million Americans bought

As the war took men away from home, women stepped in to take over their jobs. This young woman is filling shells in a munitions factory.

bonds—in effect, loaning money to the government. Through these measures, and by increasing taxes on corporations and on goods such as alcohol and tobacco, the government raised $10.8 billion.

"Use All Left-overs" Four years of war had laid waste to much of Europe. In addition to bullets and bombs, hunger and disease were killing thousands. The Liberty Loan Act of 1917 enabled the government to lend the Allies money to buy food and supplies from the United States.

President Wilson also set up an agency to make sure that there would be enough food for everyone, both at home and overseas. To head the Food Administration he chose Herbert Hoover, an engineer who had led relief efforts in Belgium. The Food Administration raised crop prices to encourage farmers to grow more, and it punished people who hoarded food.

The Rope Dancer Accompanies Herself With Her Shadows

Link to Art

The Rope Dancer Accompanies Herself with Her Shadows (1916)
Starting in 1916, a number of artists reacted to the war by making what they called "works of nonart." This movement was called Dada, a nonsense word that reflected the meaninglessness of the war to these artists. As artists left Europe to escape the war, they brought Dada to the United States. The painting above is by American artist Man Ray. **Discuss** Why do you think this style of art was shocking to Americans in the 1920s?

Hoover preferred voluntary efforts rather than government rules. His slogan, "Use All Left-overs," encouraged people to conserve food. Americans began observing "Wheatless Mondays and Wednesdays" and "Meatless Tuesdays." As a result, three times as much food could be shipped to the Allies.

Labor and the War Effort

The war also placed extraordinary demands on American industry. Almost overnight, factories began producing great quantities of tanks, airplanes, guns, and other war materials.

The dramatic increase in production would not have been possible without the dedication of factory workers. Samuel Gompers and other labor leaders pledged their support, and union members did the rest. During the war, union membership rose from 2.74 million in 1916 to 4.05 million in 1919.

More than 1 million women entered the work force, often taking the jobs of men who had joined the military. They drove trucks, delivered mail, and made ammunition.

The war also brought many more African Americans into the work force. Northern industries sent agents to the South, looking for workers. By 1917, responding to promises of good salaries and fair treatment, as many as half a million black workers had moved north to take factory jobs.

Silencing Opposition and Winning Support

Although most Americans threw themselves into the war effort, a few held back. Some people firmly believed that the nation should stay out of Europe's wars. Others were **pacifists**—people who are against war under any circumstance. Sergeant York was one of 20,000 pacifists to be drafted.

Afraid that opposition would hurt the war effort, Congress passed the Espionage Act in June 1917. The act set strict penalties for anyone who interfered with recruiting soldiers or made statements that might hinder the war effort.

The Sedition Act of May 16, 1918, made it illegal to utter disloyal statements about the Constitution, the government, the flag, or the armed forces. In 1919 the Supreme Court ruled that the government had the right to suspend free speech during wartime.

Winning support While the government was trying to silence opponents, it was also working to drum up support for the war. In May 1917 Wilson appointed newspaper editor George Creel to head the Committee on Public Information. His job was to "sell the war to America."

Creel's efforts had the unpleasant side effect of creating anti-German hysteria in the United States. Schools stopped teaching the German language. The governor of Iowa even banned speaking German on the telephone.

Over There

While the government was busy promoting the war effort in the United States, American troops began sailing for France. By June 1918 more than a million had arrived. As they stormed ashore, many sang the popular World War I song "Over There":

The day after Congress declared war, popular songwriter George M. Cohan wrote "Over There." The patriotic lyrics and catchy tune soon swept across the country.

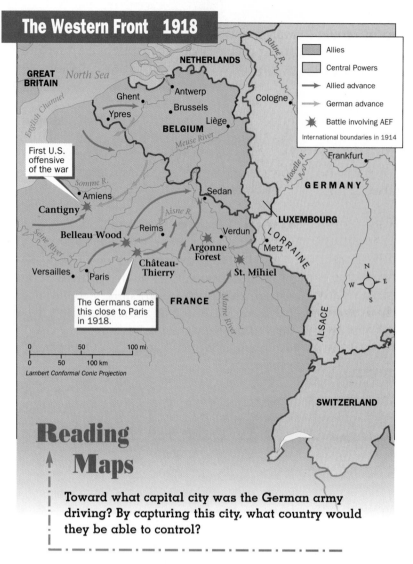

The Western Front 1918

GREAT BRITAIN

North Sea

English Channel

NETHERLANDS

Ghent • • Antwerp
Ypres • • Brussels
Liège
BELGIUM

Meuse River

Cologne •

Rhine R.

Allies
Central Powers
→ Allied advance
→ German advance
✳ Battle involving AEF
International boundaries in 1914

Frankfurt •

Moselle R.

GERMANY

First U.S.
offensive
of the war

Somme R.

• Amiens

Cantigny

Sedan •

LUXEMBOURG

Belleau Wood

Aisne R.

Reims •

Verdun •

Metz •

LORRAINE

Argonne
Forest

Seine River

Château-
Thierry

St. Mihiel •

Versailles •
• Paris

FRANCE

Marne River

The Germans came
this close to Paris
in 1918.

ALSACE

N
W   E
S

0   50   100 mi
0   50   100 km
Lambert Conformal Conic Projection

SWITZERLAND

Reading Maps

Toward what capital city was the German army
driving? By capturing this city, what country would
they be able to control?

"Over there, over there,
 Send the word, send the word over
   there,
 That the Yanks are coming, the Yanks
   are coming,
 The drums rum-tumming ev'rywhere."

The extreme patriotism of the American soldiers puzzled the Germans. After all, many of the doughboys had not even been born in the United States. Indeed, the troops reflected the ethnic makeup of the United States. Their letters home were written in dozens of different languages. Yet, as a

German officer marveled, "These semi-Americans . . . feel themselves to be true-born sons of their country."

Last German Offensive

In the winter of 1917–1918, the Central Powers were gaining an advantage. First they crushed Italian troops on the southern front. Then, in Russia, the short-lived democratic government fell to a wing of the Communist Party called the Bolsheviks, led by Vladimir Lenin. In 1918 the Bolsheviks signed a peace agreement with Germany and pulled out of the war.

With Russia out of the way, Germany could focus on the western front. In the spring of 1918 the Germans launched a massive campaign to capture Paris. By the end of May, German troops were again at the Marne River, only 50 miles (81 km) from Paris. The Allied situation seemed desperate.

Belleau Wood The Americans of the AEF arrived just in time. Frenchmen too old to fight drove thousands of doughboys to the front lines in trucks, taxicabs, and cars. By June 1 American troops had reached Belleau (bel-LŌ) Wood, a square mile of forest between two hills.

For three weeks German and American armies fought each other over this small patch of blood-drenched soil, which had become a symbol far beyond its military importance. The Americans were determined to capture it. The Germans were ordered to hold it at all costs.

On June 25, following an especially heavy day of fighting, United States Marines finally drove the Germans from Belleau Wood. This battle was a turning point for the Allied forces. As one American wrote home, "Folks, we have them on the run."

The AEF on the offensive Belleau Wood was the first Allied victory in which American troops played a part. Now General Pershing, acting under Allied commander Marshal Ferdinand Foch (FŌSH), launched a summer-long offensive campaign. In September half a million doughboys drove the Germans from the town of St. Mihiel (SAHN mee-YEL).

The next target was the Sedan railroad in northern France. For 47 days American forces fought their way through the heavily defended Argonne Forest toward Sedan. It was here that Alvin York made history by capturing 132 Germans.

The Armistice

Although the war ended before Sedan was taken, the doughboys had achieved their objective. "The American troops," Pershing later reported, "had cut the enemy's main line of communications, and nothing but surrender or an armistice could save his army from disaster."

The Central Powers saw that further resistance would be foolish. In November the Ottoman Empire, Bulgaria, and Austria-Hungary signed an **armistice**—a truce.

Finally Germany, its armies in full retreat on every front, admitted defeat. Delegates from Germany traveled to France, where they received the terms of the armistice from General Foch. On the morning of November 11, 1918, later known as Armistice Day, the Germans signed. Later that morning all firing ceased. World War I was over.

Russia's civil war Even as Lenin made peace with Germany, civil war was tearing Russia apart. Lenin's Communist forces, called Reds from the color of their flag, believed that property should be owned by society. Their opponents, the Whites, included landowners and others who stood to lose under communism.

Allied leaders wanted the Whites to win. The Allies were bitter about Russia's withdrawal from the war and desperately wanted Russia to rejoin the fight. Also, they were beginning to view communism as a potential world threat.

In the spring of 1918 Britain, France, and the United States began to send troops to support the Whites. For the most part they pulled out soon after World War I ended. The Reds defeated the Whites in 1920. Communism would hold Russia in its grip for the next 70 years.

2. Section Review

1. Define **propaganda, pacifists,** and **armistice.**
2. Describe three events that led the United States to declare war on Germany.
3. How did the United States raise money and conserve resources for the war?
4. How did American troops help the Allies defeat Germany?
5. Critical Thinking If you had been a member of Congress, would you have voted for the Espionage and Sedition acts? Explain your reasons.

Skill Lab

Skill Tips

Major propaganda techniques include:
- *Card stacking*—presenting only one side or part of a story.
- *Bandwagon*—playing on the desire to be part of a group and the fear of being left out.
- *Transference*—connecting a cause to a respected person, group, or symbol.

Thinking Critically
Analyzing Propaganda

The United States that declared war on Germany was ill-prepared to fight. The government needed everything: money, troops, weapons, supplies—and the support of the American people.

Question to Investigate

How did the United States government try to gain support for the war effort?

Procedure

To explore the Question to Investigate, you will analyze two posters circulated by the government during the war. The posters are examples of propaganda—efforts to promote or oppose a cause by appealing to emotions. Study **A** and **B** and do the following:

❶ Identify the images.
a. Tell who the people are and what is happening in **A**.
b. Do the same for **B**.

❷ Identify the purposes.
a. State the main purpose of **A**.
b. Do the same for **B**.

❸ Identify and evaluate the propaganda techniques used.
a. List the techniques from the Skill Tips used in **A** and **B**.
b. Add your own ideas about the ways **A** and **B** attempt to achieve their purposes.
c. Tell whether you think **A** and **B** were effective in their time, and why or why not.

Sources to Use

A

ONLY THE NAVY CAN STOP THIS

B

3. The Search for Peace

Reading Guide

New Terms self-determination, reparations

Section Focus The struggle over the peace treaty

1. How did the Allies differ in their ideas for a peace treaty?
2. Why did the Senate reject the Treaty of Versailles?
3. How did Wilson try to win support for the Treaty and why did he fail?

When the war began, people thought it would last six weeks. Instead, it lasted more than four years. It was the largest and most costly war the world had ever known. More than 9 million people died, including 116,000 Americans. The financial cost was in the hundreds of billions of dollars.

President Wilson had entered the war reluctantly. Only when it seemed impossible for the United States to remain neutral did he agree to send troops to Europe. His dream was that World War I would serve to restore lasting peace and make the world safe for democracy. Instead, it set the stage for another, even more destructive war that would break out 20 years later.

Wilson's Fourteen Points

Even before the war officially ended, Wilson had developed a plan for a "just and durable peace." On January 8, 1918, he outlined this plan in his famous "Fourteen Points" speech before Congress.

The first five points of Wilson's plan were designed to remove the causes of war. He wanted to guarantee freedom of the seas, remove international tariff barriers, reduce the number of weapons, settle claims for colonies, and end secret treaties.

The next eight points promoted Wilson's belief in **self-determination**—the right of the people of a certain nation to decide how they want to be governed. To ensure self-determination, Wilson wanted to redraw the national boundaries of Europe.

The final point was the one most dear to Wilson's heart. He called for the formation of a League of Nations that would work to protect any nation that was attacked by another. In Wilson's mind, this league was the key to a lasting world peace.

The Paris Peace Conference

To promote his Fourteen Points, Wilson attended the Paris Peace Conference. He was the first American President to go overseas on a diplomatic mission.

Seventy representatives from 27 countries attended the conference, which opened on January 18, 1919. The key decisions, though, were made by the "Big Four": Britain's Prime Minister David Lloyd George, France's Premier Georges Clemenceau [kluh-mahn-SŌ], Italy's Premier Vittorio Orlando, and President Wilson of the United States.

The Allies agreed in principle to Wilson's Fourteen Points, but they brushed aside most of his suggestions as vague and impractical. Clemenceau remarked, "He bores me with his fourteen points. Why, God Almighty has only ten!"

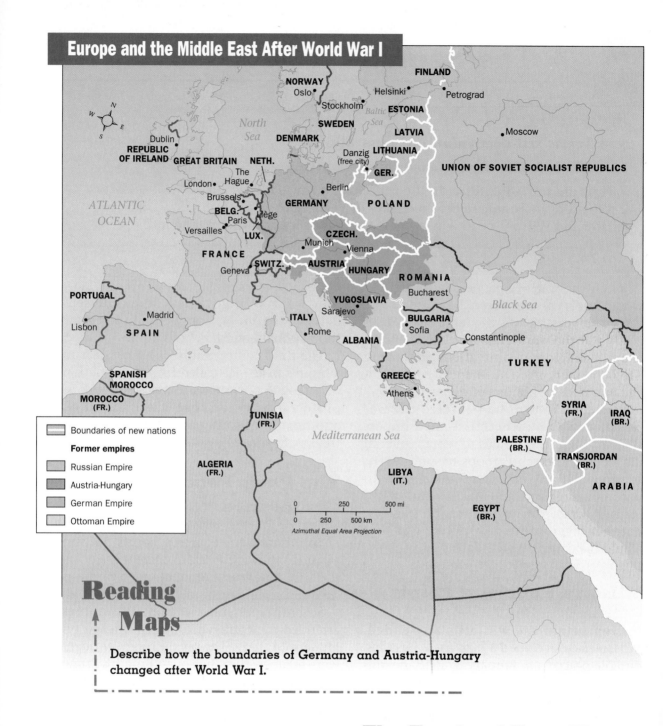

Europe and the Middle East After World War I

Boundaries of new nations

Former empires
- Russian Empire
- Austria-Hungary
- German Empire
- Ottoman Empire

0   250   500 mi
0 250 500 km
Azimuthal Equal Area Projection

Reading Maps

Describe how the boundaries of Germany and Austria-Hungary changed after World War I.

The tone of the peace conference was clear from the start: The victorious Allies had soundly defeated the Central Powers and were determined to punish them, particularly Germany. David Lloyd George had just won re-election in Britain by promising to "Make Germany Pay."

The Treaty of Versailles

After four months of discussion, the delegates at the conference approved a treaty. Many provisions reflected Wilson's goals. The treaty set up a League of Nations and redrew the map of Europe (see map above).

However, Wilson could not prevent the other delegates from including harsh terms designed to punish Germany. The treaty stripped Germany of its armed forces and demanded $33 billion in **reparations**—payments for war damages. Worst of all, in the eyes of Germans, the treaty's "War Guilt Clause," required Germany to admit that it alone was responsible for the war.

German officials resented the terms, but there was little they could do. On June 28, 1919, in the elegant Hall of Mirrors of the Palace of Versailles (ver-SĪ), they signed the treaty. World War I was officially over.

Opposition Even at the time, people realized that the Versailles Treaty was too extreme to establish a lasting peace. Marshal Foch declared, "This is not peace. It is an armistice for twenty years."

Meanwhile, an Austrian army corporal named Adolf Hitler seethed with anger at the terms of the treaty. Twenty years later he was to lead Germany in a war of revenge that became World War II.

When President Wilson returned to the United States to get Senate approval for the treaty, he found that many Americans were unhappy with its terms. The strongest opposition was to the League of Nations.

Senator Henry Cabot Lodge of Massachusetts spoke for those who objected to the treaty. He argued that Article 10, which said that League members would act together against threats to peace, could commit the United States to future wars on foreign soil.

Wilson's defense Refusing to compromise yet realizing that the Senate's opposition would keep the United States out of the League of Nations, Wilson decided to take his ideals straight to the American people. He traveled by train on an 8,000-mile (12,900-km) tour. In just 22 days he delivered 40 speeches in 29 cities. This pace proved too much for the 63-year-old President.

Link to the Present

The United Nations History's largest gathering of leaders took place in New York City in October 1995 to celebrate the 50th anniversary of the United Nations (UN).

The United States is an active member of the UN, which rose from the ashes of the League of Nations in 1945. The UN resembles the League in some ways, but it has been more successful in settling disputes and halting aggression. For example, UN members expelled Iraqi invaders from Kuwait in 1991.

The UN also takes on more humanitarian responsibilities. Agencies like the United Nations International Children's Emergency Fund (UNICEF) and the World Health Organization (WHO) have gone a long way in easing problems like hunger, poverty, and disease.

On September 25, 1919, Wilson gave a speech in Colorado that reflected his heartfelt commitment to the League of Nations:

"There is one thing that the American people always rise to . . . and this is the truth of justice and liberty and of peace. We have accepted that truth, and we are going to be led by it, and it is going to lead us . . . out into pastures of quietness and peace such as the world never dreamed of before.**"**

Soon after he spoke these words, Wilson suffered a stroke that left him partially paralyzed. For the rest of his presidency, Wilson communicated only through his wife, Edith.

Defeat of the Treaty

Twice an amended version of the Versailles Treaty came to a vote in the Senate. Both times Wilson refused to compromise. From his sickbed he instructed Senate Democrats to vote against it.

Wilson in 1919

If President Wilson had been willing to compromise, the Senate might have approved the treaty. Instead, in late November of 1919 the United States concluded a treaty of its own with the Central Powers.

Meanwhile in Geneva, Switzerland, the League of Nations began its peace-keeping efforts. Without American membership, however, it had little hope of success.

3. Section Review

1. Define **self-determination** and **reparations.**
2. What influence did Wilson's Fourteen Points have on the Treaty of Versailles?
3. Why did the United States Senate refuse to ratify the treaty?
4. Critical Thinking Do you think that Wilson should have compromised with the Senate on the Treaty of Versailles? Why or why not?

Why We Remember

World War I

We remember World War I because it marked a sort of "coming of age" for Americans. When the United States declared war in 1917, Americans became involved in their first major overseas conflict. They took this step reluctantly but for the most honorable of reasons. President Wilson stated the nation's purpose in his address to Congress calling for war:

❝The world must be made safe for democracy. Its peace must be founded upon the trusted foundations of political liberty.❞

World War I taught Americans that being peacemakers is never easy, especially when war inflames old hatreds and creates new ones. It also revealed that not everyone shares our reverence for democracy and freedom. There was another lesson as well. World War I reminded us once more that our strength as a nation rests on the willingness of ordinary people like Alvin York to do extraordinary things in defense of our ideals. As the *New York Times* wrote at the time of York's death in 1964, "One likes to think that the United States was built and protected by such . . . simple and pure men."

Geography Lab

The Great Migration

The effort to win the war reshaped our nation in ways that no one could have predicted. For example, people seeking jobs in war-related industries swelled the populations of northern cities. Many job seekers were African Americans from the South. They were recruited by agents from northern companies, who promised free transportation and other benefits as well as good wages.

Thus began a mass migration that would continue for decades. Use the quotations and the data in the table to understand the reasons for this migration and its effects.

Estimated African American Migration to (+) and from (−) Selected States 1910–1920	
Alabama	−70,800
Georgia	−74,700
Illinois	+69,800
Louisiana	−51,200
Michigan	+38,700
Mississippi	−129,600
New York	+63,100
Ohio	+69,400
Pennsylvania	+82,500
South Carolina	−74,500

Source: *Historical Statistics of the United States*

Two Migrants' Stories

"The best wages I could make [in Georgia] was $1.25 or $1.50 a day. I went to work at a dye house at Newark, N.J., at $2.75 a day, with a rent-free room to live in. . . . The company paid my fare North."

"I should have been here [in Chicago] 20 years ago. I just begin to feel like a man. . . . My children are going to the same school with the whites and I don't have to umble [bow] to no one. I have registered—Will vote the next election and there isn't any 'yes sir' and 'no sir'—it's all yes and no and Sam and Bill."

Link to History

1. What reasons for moving to the North do you find in the quotations? What others can you think of?

2. Which state in the table lost the largest number of African Americans? Which state gained the largest number?

3. For each of the following states, tell whether it was likely to have experienced a gain or a loss in African American population between 1910 and 1920: Indiana, New Jersey, North Carolina, Virginia.

4. Name five cities that probably saw their African American populations grow rapidly between 1910 and 1920.

5. **Hands-On Geography** You are a northern company's agent, sent to a southern community in 1917. Make a poster or a brochure to persuade African Americans to apply for jobs at your company.

Chapter Survey

Reviewing Vocabulary

Define the following terms.
1. stalemate
2. propaganda
3. pacifists
4. armistice
5. self-determination
6. reparations

Reviewing Main Ideas

1. How did so many nations get drawn into World War I?
2. Describe the trenches and what life in them was like.
3. What events brought the United States into the war?
4. What were some ways that the United States quickly produced the huge amounts of supplies and weapons needed to fight the war?
5. Why was the Battle of Belleau Wood important?
6. Summarize the terms of the Versailles Treaty.
7. Why did the United States not sign the Versailles Treaty?

Thinking Critically

1. Analysis A total war, as defined in Chapter 18, is a war against armies and also against a people's resources and will to fight. How does World War I fit the definition of total war? Are there any ways it does not fit the definition? Explain your answer.
2. Synthesis Suppose the United States had entered the war two years earlier. How might the course of history have been different? Give three possibilities.
3. Why We Remember: Application What did President Wilson mean when he said, "The world must be made safe for democracy"? Were his Fourteen Points consistent with that statement? Why or why not?

Applying Skills

Analyzing propaganda Find an example of propaganda in a newspaper or magazine, on television or radio, or on a poster or billboard. Keeping in mind what you learned on page 714, write a paragraph describing the following:
• the words and images that make up the piece
• the apparent purpose of the piece
• the propaganda techniques used in the piece
• how effective you think the piece is and why

History Mystery

The choice to fight Answer the History Mystery on page 697. Do you think that Alvin York should have had to serve in the army? Why or why not?

Writing in Your History Journal

1. Keys to History (a) The time line on pages 696–697 has seven Keys to History. In your history journal, list each key and describe why the event is important to know about. (b) Choose any two events on the time line and explain in your journal how the events are related.
2. Alvin York In your journal, write your personal definition of the word *hero*. Then tell whether Alvin C. York fits your definition. Explain your answers.
3. Citizenship In trying to quiet opposition through the Espionage and Sedition acts, did the United States government go too far? How might Americans react to similar acts in a modern war? Explain your responses in your journal.

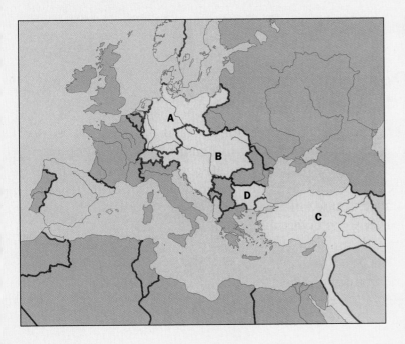

1. Each letter on the map represents one of the Central Powers. Write the name of each.

2. Geographic Thinking
Look at the map on pages R2–R3. How do you think the location of the United States relative to Europe affected the following:
• number of years the United States remained neutral
• impact of the war on Americans once the United States joined the Allies
• attitude of Senate Republicans toward the League of Nations
How might things have been different if the war had been centered in Canada?

Alternative Assessment

Compiling a wartime scrapbook With three classmates, put together a ten-page scrapbook of letters and other mementos that might have been compiled by an American family in World War I.

1 Invent the family. Start by answering these questions:
• What ethnic or racial group do they belong to and where do they live?
• Who serves on the battlefront, and in what ways?
• How do other family members contribute to the war effort?

2 Create materials for the scrapbook, such as articles, journal entries, and letters. Your materials should touch on major events in the chapter, including these:
• assassination of Archduke Ferdinand
• sinking of the *Lusitania*
• America's entry into the war
• the draft
• life on the home front
• trench warfare
• controversy over the Versailles Treaty

3 Assemble the scrapbook.

Your work will be evaluated on the following criteria:
• it realistically portrays how ordinary Americans might have reacted to and been affected by World War I
• it contains materials that are clearly written and full of interesting details
• it shows imagination and creativity

Link to Literature

After the Dancing Days
by Margaret I. Rostkowski

In her novel *After the Dancing Days,* author Margaret I. Rostkowski tells the story of Annie, a 13-year-old girl living in Kansas after World War I. Annie visits a soldiers' hospital where she meets a young veteran, Andrew, who has been badly burned and disfigured by mustard gas. At first repulsed by Andrew's appearance, Annie later befriends him. In the following scene she shares with Andrew some books she has brought.

"What kind do you have today?"

For a moment, I didn't know what he meant. "What?" I finally said.

"Books. What kind of books?" He waved a bandaged hand at my bookbag.

"Oh, maps. I love to look at books of maps. And dream about traveling to all the places I see." My voice died away. I usually didn't talk about my love of maps, and I felt silly doing so now. Especially to this man.

"Let's see them."

"Really? They're just maps."

"I know." He sounded annoyed. "But it's something to do."

I pulled the books out of my bookbag, sliding the cookies and apples down into the bottom, and opened the world atlas.

But he was looking at the other book, *Europe in Pictures.*

"That one." He nudged it with the back of his hand.

I opened the heavy cover and balanced it between us on our knees. A spot of sun reflected off the glossy pages and made it hard to read. I lifted it a bit so the words were in shadow.

"A look at the wonders of Europe in photographs!" I read the subtitle and turned to the table of contents. As I ran my finger down the list of countries, he reached out with one bandaged hand and tapped clumsily on the section titled "France."

"I want . . ." his voice cracked and he swallowed, "to see that."

I paused, my hand covering the page in front of me. "France?" I stared at the page. When he didn't answer, I looked up at him.

I couldn't see his eyes under the shadow of his hat, only the red rippled skin around his nose and mouth. He nodded. So I found the page and opened the book to the section on France. Mounds of grapes lay on a table. A château arched gracefully across a river. People smiled. He motioned for me to turn the page. An ancient city circled with a high

World War I gas mask

World War I ruins, September 1918

wall, a stone church with a steeple pointing into the sky, a palace of white marble.

"I don't remember any of that," he whispered. "Only mud. And burned trees."

I looked at the church and the people standing in the streets of the tiny village on the page before us.

"No people. The church was bombed out. I don't remember . . ."

I couldn't see the happy village. The page glared in the sun.

"There weren't any people. They all left before we got there. And no animals. They'd been eaten. The sergeant said the church was safest. But it'd been bombed. Blown apart. We slept in it anyway, what was left of it. I was afraid to sleep, afraid they'd come back."

He stopped and I slowly closed the book. I tried to imagine the church with the steeple gone.

Then he began again, that slow whisper.

"It had been farmland. When we got there, the barns were gone, fences down. Mud. Mud everywhere. And rats. I can still fell the rats running over my face at night."

I hugged the book to me.

"And then the gas . . ." He stopped and lifted both hands into the air.

I watched him, sick at what I had done with my books.

A Closer Look

1. Describe the two views of France: the one in Annie's book and the one in Andrew's memory.

2. What do we learn about Andrew in this scene? What do we learn about the war?

3. How do you think Annie's interaction with Andrew changes her? Cite examples from the passage to support your view.

From *After the Dancing Days* by Margaret I. Rostkowski. Copyright © 1986 by Margaret I. Rostkowski. Reprinted by permission of HarperCollins Publishers.

Unit Survey

Making Connections

1. How did the role of the federal government in American life change during the era covered in this unit? Support your answer with examples.

2. The State Department handles the United States' relations with other countries. In 1892, a New York newspaper suggested abolishing it because it had so little work to do. Describe five events or situations between 1890 and 1920 that proved the newspaper wrong.

3. Agree or disagree with this statement: "Even while the United States fought to make the world safe for democracy, it failed to live up to its own democratic ideals." Explain your answer.

Linking History, Civics, and Language Arts

Working for Change in Your World

If they could observe American life today, Progressives might view it as a "good news/bad news" situation. The good news is that many of their goals have been accomplished. The bad news is that there are still problems confronting us. There is more good news, though: You can be the kind of citizen who helps solve problems.

Project Steps

Work with a group.

❶ Choose a problem to attack. Brainstorm answers to these questions:
• What problems do you see in your community, state, or country?
• Which of those problems do you care about most deeply?
• Which problem do you think you can do the most to solve?

❷ Begin researching the problem. What caused it? What laws or rules apply to it? Who are the people who could help solve it? The library is a good place to start. You can also get facts through observations and interviews.

❸ Decide exactly what you will try to do about the problem you have chosen. Write a brief statement of your goal. Be specific, concrete, and realistic.

❹ Write an action plan for achieving your goal. Here are some possibilities for activities to include in your plan:
• write letters to business managers and/or government officials
• write and circulate petitions
• make and hang posters
• make speeches at public meetings
• raise money
• organize boycotts
• organize peaceful demonstrations

❺ As you carry out your plan, make periodic progress reports to the class.

Thinking It Over Suppose that all Americans over age 12 spent three hours a week working for the reform of their choice. Could their combined efforts eventually produce a problem-free country? Explain your opinion.

How Do We Know?

Atomic bomb explosion

Scholar's Tool Kit
Classified Records

Have you ever seen a movie about international spies? Then you know that governments around the world keep secret certain information that might affect the safety of their countries. In the United States such information is called "classified" and is labeled according to the degree of secrecy. The main classifications are **Top Secret**, **Secret**, and **Confidential**. The United States began using these classifications in 1917.

Classified records are an important tool for historians. As a result, historians often put pressure on the government to "declassify" documents they think no longer need to be kept secret. Then scholars can study the documents to gain a more complete understanding of that time in history. This was the case with some important World War II documents.

The First Atomic Bomb

During World War II the government classified most of the documents that related to the war effort. Although historians have written many books about World War II, the inability to do research in classified files kept them from giving the complete story of certain key events and incidents. Slowly, over time, files have been declassified, each time enabling scholars to fill in some "blanks" in history.

Among the now-declassified files are ones concerning the development and testing of the first atomic bomb. This top-secret project had the code name "Manhattan Project." Many of its documents were

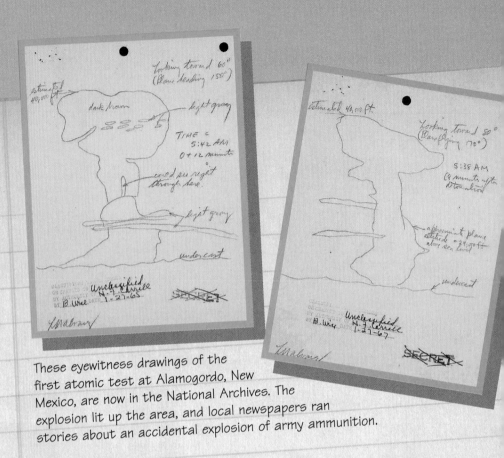

These eyewitness drawings of the first atomic test at Alamogordo, New Mexico, are now in the National Archives. The explosion lit up the area, and local newspapers ran stories about an accidental explosion of army ammunition.

Critical Thinking

1. What types of documents do you think would be most likely to be classified? Why?

Critical Thinking

2. Imagine that you are a spy and that your country does not yet know about the testing of the bomb. What could you learn from these drawings?

declassified in the 1960s, giving scholars a window into this momentous event in history.

The Manhattan Project came about as a result of research by American and European scientists on the element uranium. The scientists discovered in the 1930s that uranium could be an important source of energy. They also suspected that uranium could be used as the basis for a bomb unlike any ever created.

When the brilliant scientist Albert Einstein warned President Franklin Roosevelt of the possibility of "extremely powerful bombs of a new type," Roosevelt knew he had to act. He brought together a group of scientists to organize research on nuclear weapons. This group was already at work when World War II broke out. Then the race was on to produce the first atomic bomb.

The Story in Words and Pictures

The declassified documents from the Manhattan Project files are now in the National Archives. Among them are reports by James B. Conant, a scientist who worked on the bomb. In one report Conant expressed the anxiety Manhattan scientists felt about creating nuclear weapons.

"I suppose everyone concerned with the project would feel greatly relieved and thoroughly delighted if something should develop to prove the impossibility of such an atomic explosion. Civilization would then, indeed, be fortunate—atomic energy for power a reality, for destruction an impossibility."

Conant's hope that atomic energy would have only peaceful uses ended on July 16, 1945. On that day the United States set off the first atomic explosion at a test site in New Mexico. The test was so secret that it was reported as an accident at a military arsenal. The drawings shown on page 726 are by one of the few eyewitnesses, and therefore have been of great interest to historians.

Once-classified information can be very important to scholars who study recent history. That is why scholars continually press the government to declassify records that are still kept from public view. In November 1994, as a part of the commemoration of the 50th anniversary of World War II, President Bill Clinton signed an executive order declassifying almost 21 million pages of documents from the war. The story these documents tell will become a part of the American history that students learn in the future.

? Critical Thinking

3. Why do you think that the process of declassifying documents takes place slowly over time?

Scholar at Work

Imagine that you are a scholar writing the history of World War II, and the Manhattan Project documents (such as the drawings shown on page 726) are still classified. Write a letter to a government official to persuade him or her that the files should be declassified. Explain why the papers are important and why historians should have access to them.

Unit 9

Chapters

Hands-On —————► *HISTORY*

Activity

In the 1930s Dorothea Lange photographed many scenes of rural life. One person said of her subjects, "Contemporary problems are reflected on their faces, a tremendous drama is unfolding before them, and Dorothea Lange is photographing it through them." Write a caption for this photo. Consider these questions: What were these people doing just before Lange took the photo? What is in their boxes? Where are they going? What did the photographer want us to know about them?

One-Man Caravan. Oklahomans on U.S. 99
San Joaquin Valley, California
by Dorothea Lange, 1938

Trials at Home and Abroad

Chapter 26

The Twenties

Sections

Beginning the Story with Zora Neale Hurston

1. **From War to Peace**
2. **The Jazz Age**
3. **The Business Boom**

Keys to History

Ben Shahn: *Bartolomeo Vanzetti and Nicola Sacco* from the Sacco-Vanzetti series of twenty-three paintings (1931–32)

1920
First radio station begins broadcasting

1920
Prohibition begins

1919
Red Scare begins

1919   1921

Looking Back

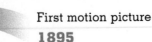

First motion picture
1895

HISTORY *Mystery*

On May 20, 1927, this young American was virtually unknown. Two days later, he was the idol of people throughout the world. Who was he, and why was he so admired?

1925
Scopes trial
Clarence Darrow and
William Jennings Bryan

1927
Lindbergh
completes
transatlantic
flight

1927
First "talking"
motion picture

1924
Immigration
Act of 1924

23   1925   1927   1929

World  **Link**

Hitler tries to seize
power in Bavaria
1923

Looking Ahead

The New Deal begins
1933

Beginning the Story with

Zora Neale Hurston

Zora Neale Hurston's mother used to say that someone put "travel dust" on the doorstep the day that Zora was born. That dust must have been powerful, for during her life Zora journeyed from Eatonville, Florida—where she was born sometime between 1891 and 1903—to Baltimore, New York City, Haiti, California, and back to Florida again. Wherever she traveled, Zora turned her restless mind to studies. She read everything she could, from anthropology to poetry to folktales. Zora's travels and studies inspired her to write seven books and more than 100 short stories, plays, and articles. Zora's special gift, though, was storytelling. Many of her best-loved stories are rooted in her memories of growing up in Eatonville.

Eatonville, Florida

"I was born in a Negro town," Zora Neale Hurston wrote on the first page of her autobiography. "Eatonville is, and was at the time of my birth, a pure Negro town. . . . [It was] the first attempt at organized self-government on the part of Negroes in America." Depending on who was asked in Eatonville, John and Lucy Hurston's seventh child was either sassy or spirited, shameless or bold. Looking back on her childhood years, Zora remembered:

❝Mama exhorted [urged] her children at every opportunity to 'jump at de sun.' We might not land on the sun, but at least we would get off the ground.❞

Zora's favorite place in Eatonville was Joe Clarke's store. Here, neighbors gathered to swap jokes, gossip, and stories. Best of all were the "lying"

Cab Calloway's band entertained jazz lovers in the Cotton Club in New York City's Harlem neighborhood. Hurston made Harlem her home in 1925.

sessions during which people competed to tell the tallest tales. The folktales told on Joe Clarke's porch inspired Zora to create her own stories.

When Zora was 9 death crept into town and took her mother, Lucy Hurston. "Mama died at sundown and changed a world," Zora wrote, "that is, the world that had been built out of her body and heart."

Zora's Wanderings

Zora lost her childhood when she lost her mother. "That hour began my wanderings," she later recalled. Her father remarried. His new wife, wanting nothing to do with stepchildren, sent Zora off to boarding school. When her father stopped paying for her schooling, Zora "was shifted from house to house of relatives and friends and found comfort nowhere."

For years Zora drifted. Money was scarce. She quit school and went to work, finding jobs as a maid or waitress. No matter how hard she worked, Zora never had enough money to return to school. "There is something about poverty that smells like death," she wrote of those dark years.

Zora's wanderings took her north to Baltimore. There, at the age of 26, she enrolled in a night-school class taught by a gifted teacher named Dwight O. W. Holmes. "He made the way clear," Zora wrote in her autobiography. "Something about his face killed the drabness and discouragement in me. I felt that things could be done."

One night, while the class was studying English poets, Zora saw something that would drive her on to college and to a new life in New York City. She saw herself not as a poor waitress, but as a woman who would dare to become a writer. "This was my world [the world of a writer]," she said to herself, "and I shall be in it, and surrounded by it, if it is the last thing I do on God's green dirt-ball."

Hands-On → HISTORY

Activity

Imagine that you are to choose three images that would help illustrate a map of Zora Hurston's life (see page 444 for an example of a map with illustrations). Each image is to represent a different place where Zora lived. Write a description of each of the images that you would like to use, and write a two-sentence caption for each one.

1. From War to Peace

Reading Guide

New Terms communism, anarchism

Section Focus The unrest that gripped the nation after World War I

1. What forms of unrest gripped the United States after the war?
2. What people and ideas were blamed for the nation's troubles?
3. How did Americans respond to the unrest?

Zora began to develop her gift for writing at Howard University just as World War I came to an end. It was a time when Americans were eager to shift their attention away from troubles overseas. They were weary of the storms of war—the death of young people, the stress of raising armies, and the daily news of battle victories and defeats.

Everyone, it seemed, craved rest. The nation retreated from world affairs, however, only to face turmoil at home.

Labor Unrest

During the war, American industry had focused on producing weapons and supplies. With the war over, pent-up demands for goods, and for better wages and working hours, were unleashed.

However, factories that had been producing war materials could not immediately change to making clothing, shoes, cars, and other goods that a peacetime population demanded. Prices for these scarce products rose. Meanwhile, returning soldiers, looking for places to live, drove up the cost of housing. By 1920 prices were twice as high as in 1914.

As rents and prices rose, however, workers' wages remained low. During the war American workers had not gone on strike so as not to hurt the war effort. It was now time, they believed, to push for higher wages and for workdays shorter than 12 hours.

Strikes spread In 1919 union leaders across the nation led workers out on strike. While early strikes succeeded, workers faced growing opposition as the year wore on.

When shipyard workers in Seattle walked off their jobs, other unions in the city showed support by striking, too. Seattle's mayor turned the public against the strikers by falsely claiming that their leaders were radicals—people calling for extreme, often violent, change. The strike failed.

In Pennsylvania and the Midwest, striking steelworkers called for an end to 12-hour workdays and 7-day workweeks. Steel mill owners ignored their demands. They also accused the strikers of being linked with radicals. Whether the accusations were true or not, political leaders and newspapers turned against the workers and sided with business leaders.

After four months the striking steelworkers gave up. This failure dealt a crushing blow to the union movement.

Racial Unrest

The tense mood of the nation was seen in racial violence as well. In 1919 white mobs terrorized black communities from Texas to

Washington, D.C. Black tenant farmers in Arkansas were attacked for attempting to form a union. In Chicago a white mob stoned to death a black swimmer who had strayed into a "white section" of a beach on Lake Michigan. In the violence that followed, 38 people were killed.

Faced with such attacks, and thousands of lynchings since 1890, African Americans launched an anti-lynching campaign. In this campaign, the National Association for the Advancement of Colored People (NAACP) called on Congress to make lynching a federal crime. The Senate, however, refused.

Despite its failure in Congress, the NAACP continued to bring attention to the issue of lynchings. It won several victories in the 1920s, as when a court struck down an Oklahoma law denying blacks the right to vote.

The Red Scare

Alarmed by strikes and race riots, many Americans blamed foreign ideas—especially communism—as the source of the troubles. **Communism** is a system in which property is owned by society as a whole instead of by individuals. People pointed with fear to what was going on in Russia. There, in 1917, radical communists—called Bolsheviks or "Reds"—had taken over the government and seized all private property.

At the end of the war, Communist Parties were gaining support in other parts of Europe. Could the same thing happen in the United States? Rumors spread that unions were influenced by Reds. Old nativist feelings arose, too. Immigrants were accused of bringing dangerous ideas with them. Newspapers called it the "Red Scare."

Striking workers, like these on a Philadelphia street in 1919, often met with violent reactions by the police.

The Palmer raids The Red Scare gained force in April 1919 when the Post Office found bombs in nearly 40 packages addressed to American leaders. In June a bomb exploded at Attorney General A. Mitchell Palmer's home. On Palmer's orders, federal agents carried out raids on the homes and offices of suspected Communists.

The Palmer raids failed to turn up evidence linking these people to the bombs. Most people arrested were neither Communists nor foreigners. Still, over the next year nearly 6,000 people were imprisoned. Many were even deported to Europe.

Although some Americans protested that this treatment—of both citizens and aliens—was unconstitutional, the majority approved it. Support for Palmer's raids died down, however, when Communist revolutions did not break out in Europe and strikes dwindled at home. Still, the Red Scare had done much to encourage anti-immigrant feelings.

The Sacco-Vanzetti case During the heat of the Red Scare, the nation was rocked by news that seemed to prove the danger of immigrants and their ideas. In May 1920 two Italian immigrants, Nicola Sacco and Bartolomeo Vanzetti, were arrested and charged with robbing and murdering a paymaster and a payroll guard in Massachusetts.

The resulting case involved far more than robbery and murder. During the trial, the prosecutors attacked Sacco and Vanzetti for being foreign-born and for believing in **anarchism**—the idea that all forms of government are bad and should be done away with. The judge did nothing to stop the attacks. Although firm evidence linking the two men to the crime was lacking, the judge condemned them to death.

Protests poured in from around the world. The journalist Walter Lippman wrote:

"The Sacco-Vanzetti case . . . is full of doubt. The fairness of the trial raises doubt. The evidence raises doubt. . . . No man, we submit, should be put to death where so much doubt exists."

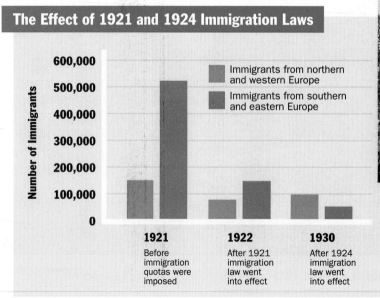

The Effect of 1921 and 1924 Immigration Laws

Legend:
- Immigrants from northern and western Europe
- Immigrants from southern and eastern Europe

Y-axis: Number of Immigrants (0 to 600,000)

1921	1922	1930
Before immigration quotas were imposed	After 1921 immigration law went into effect	After 1924 immigration law went into effect

Source: *Historical Statistics of the United States*

Demand for farmworkers in the fields of Texas and other southwestern states brought thousands of Mexican immigrants to the United States in the 1920s.

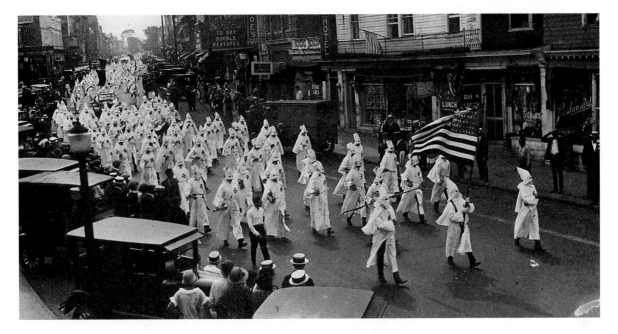

The Ku Klux Klan openly expressed its newfound strength in northern states, as in this Fourth of July parade in Long Branch, New Jersey.

All legal appeals failed, however. In 1927 the two were put to death in the electric chair. For years questions swirled around their trial. Political leaders, though, continued to blame immigrants for postwar troubles. Unrest would end, some argued, only if immigration were stopped.

Anti-Immigration Laws

In fact, efforts to limit immigration had begun early in the decade. In 1921 Congress passed an act limiting the number of immigrants from eastern and southern Europe—the Europeans most anxious to come to the United States.

In 1924 and 1929 Congress imposed even more restrictions on immigrants (see the chart on page 736). Thus, the nation's history of nearly unlimited European immigration came to an end. Meanwhile, most Asian immigration was still banned.

Anti-immigration laws, however, did not apply to people from the Americas. Nearly 500,000 people immigrated from Mexico in the 1920s, and 950,000 from Canada. Most Mexicans migrated to the Southwest, where their labors played a vital role in the growth of farmlands, railroads, and mines.

The Second Ku Klux Klan

As the anti-immigrant mood gripped the nation, an old organization took on new life. Leaders of the Ku Klux Klan, which had terrorized black southerners during Reconstruction, saw a chance to expand the Klan's strength beyond its base in the South.

In 1920 the Klan hired two sales agents to help achieve its goal. In a public campaign boosting "100 percent pure Americanism," they directed hatred against anyone who was not white and Protestant. White-hooded Klansmen and their wives now terrorized Catholics, Jews, Asians, and immigrants as well as African Americans.

By 1925 the Klan had as many as 5 million members. They helped elect five United States

Hitler tries to seize power Bankrupted by war, Germany faced economic chaos in the early 1920s. Industries struggled. Workers could not find jobs. As prices soared, the value of money plunged. Shoppers carried money in wheelbarrows. Housewives burned it for fuel.

Into this turmoil stepped a man named Adolf Hitler. A fiery speaker, he attracted followers by vowing to return Germany to its former greatness. Like leaders of the Ku Klux Klan, Hitler appealed to people who were looking for someone to blame for their problems. He created a private army that terrorized opponents of his Nazi Party.

In 1923 Hitler and his storm troopers tried to seize control of the government of the state of Bavaria. They failed, Hitler went to prison, and the Nazis were outlawed. Hitler was far from finished, though. Released from prison in 1924, he eventually led Germany into another world war (see Chapter 28).

1920. These were the years, too, when President Wilson was urging Americans to support the League of Nations.

As the election of 1920 approached, voters wanted to put war and problems at home behind them. The Republicans nominated a handsome senator from Ohio, Warren G. Harding, who promised a "return to normalcy."

Harding opposed American involvement overseas. He called for pro-business policies such as lower taxes for the wealthy and higher tariffs on imports. As his running mate he chose Governor Calvin Coolidge of Massachusetts. Coolidge was known for his tough treatment of strikers in Boston. Harding easily defeated the Democratic candidate, James M. Cox.

Beginnings of the Boom

Although a recession struck the nation in 1921, by the next year factories were hiring workers to meet the soaring demand for goods. Harding's promise of prosperous times seemed on its way to fulfillment.

President Harding's promise of "normalcy," though, was not to be. Political and labor unrest might be fading, but American society was restless in other ways. For the United States, a period of unsettling social changes was about to unfold.

senators and four state governors—in northern as well as southern states.

However, the Klan's increasing violence began to weaken its appeal. When a Klan leader was convicted of murder in 1925, membership began to drop. By 1930 the Klan had only 50,000 members.

The Election of 1920

Echoes of the Red Scare and anti-immigrant fears continued throughout the 1920s. They were at their height, however, in 1919 and

 1. Section Review

1. Define **communism** and **anarchism**.
2. Why did American workers go on strike after World War I?
3. How did the Ku Klux Klan expand its appeal beyond southern states?
4. Critical Thinking As an immigrant to the United States after World War I, why might you have been worried by events during and after the Red Scare?

2. The Jazz Age

Reading Guide

New Terms suburbs, Prohibition

Section Focus The cultural life of the United States during the 1920s

1. How did African American politics and culture thrive in the 1920s?
2. What great changes took place in American life during the Jazz Age?
3. Why did some Americans resist the social changes of the 1920s?

The 1920s was a dizzying time. The nation was experiencing greater prosperity than ever before. With prosperity came change. People began to create new forms of music and literature. New fashions became the rage. The writer F. Scott Fitzgerald, whose novels and stories captured the spirit of the decade, called it the "Jazz Age." Others called it the "Roaring Twenties."

The 1920s was also a time of conflict. Some Americans, alarmed by rapid changes in values and behavior, struggled to hold on to more familiar ideas and ways of life.

The cafes and art galleries of Paris were magnets for artists and writers rebelling against American tastes and values after World War I.

The Lost Generation

The experience of fighting in Europe had opened up a new world to young Americans. For some, this new world was a troubling one. Many young writers looked back on the war as a monumental waste—a generation of youth killed in a useless war. They were also troubled by the contrast between the horrors of war and the period of prosperity that followed it.

Ezra Pound, an established writer, encouraged younger writers to "despise old forms and the old stuff, to rebel, break away and dare [to be different]." Gertrude Stein, an American poet in Paris, also inspired the young writers. Still, she understood their confusion, writing:

"All of you young people who served in the war, you are the lost generation.**"**

Two of the most successful Lost Generation writers were Ernest Hemingway and F. Scott Fitzgerald. In his novel *The Sun Also Rises*, Hemingway wrote about the lives of the expatriates—

Americans who chose to live abroad. Fitzgerald did the same in *Tender Is the Night*. However, in earlier stories and novels, such as *This Side of Paradise*, he had portrayed the rebellious spirit of postwar youth at home.

Meanwhile, Sinclair Lewis was writing *Babbitt* and *Main Street*. In these novels Lewis criticized, as he saw it, the greed and lack of culture in small towns and small cities.

African Americans in the 1920s

African Americans, too, experienced the hopes and confusions of the postwar world. By 1930 the Great Migration had brought some 2 million black southerners to northern cities looking for factory jobs. There, a vibrant new African American culture took shape. It was to have a strong influence on American art and social life.

Marcus Garvey One aspect of the new culture was based on pride in African traditions. Thousands of African Americans were drawn to the ideas of Marcus Garvey, a Jamaican-born New Yorker. Garvey preached separation from white culture. African Americans, he said, should take pride in their African heritage. Instead of adopting white culture, they should set their own goals and build their own businesses.

Ultimately, Garvey believed, African Americans must go "back to Africa" to become truly free. Only a few of Garvey's followers actually moved to Africa, but his movement gave hope and encouragement to

Marcus Garvey wears his uniform in a 1922 parade.

many more. Although Garvey was jailed for mail fraud in 1925, his movement lasted for many years. Some of his ideas were revived in the 1960s.

Harlem Renaissance Garvey found a fertile field for his movement in the New York City neighborhood called Harlem. It was in Harlem that African American writers, musicians, and artists were finding ways to combine their traditions with the new opportunities of city life.

In fact, Harlem, where the black population more than doubled in the 1920s, gave birth to a flourishing new African American cultural movement. Known as the "Harlem Renaissance," this movement thrived in other American cities as well.

Black writers, in particular, wanted to reflect and strengthen the spirit of their people during the 1920s. Countee Cullen celebrated black culture in his poems. Another poet, Claude McKay, encouraged his African American readers to remain strong in the face of racial violence, for "the struggle is hard and long." James Weldon Johnson, too, hoped "to arouse and deepen the [African American] imagination."

Two writers stood out as central figures in the Harlem Renaissance: Zora Neale Hurston and Langston Hughes. Hurston uncovered the cultural roots of African Americans by exploring songs and tales of African and early American origin. She also published poems and novels. Hughes's poems ranged from powerful protests against racism to joyful celebrations of African American music and dance (see pages 756–757).

In fact, music was central to African American culture. Reaching back to African rhythms and songs, the blues and jazz began in New Orleans and the Mississippi Delta country of northwestern Mississippi.

Black southerners brought jazz north to Kansas City, Chicago, and Harlem. Both white and black music lovers flocked to

Link to Art

Couple in Raccoon Coats (1932) James Van Der Zee grew up in a family of artists and musicians. It came as no surprise, then, that from the day he received his first camera at the age of 14, he pursued the art of photography with passion. In his carefully composed and skillfully lighted portraits and his lively street scenes, Van Der Zee captured the spirit of Harlem in the 1920s and 1930s. **Discuss** What scenes from your life or your neighborhood would you most want to photograph and why?

nightclubs such as Harlem's Cotton Club to hear Joe "King" Oliver, Louis Armstrong, Duke Ellington, and other jazz greats. Armstrong went on to change jazz from primarily band music to a showcase for solo musicians.

The Roaring Twenties

The rhythms of jazz were well suited to the Roaring Twenties, a decade of change. To the journalist Lincoln Steffens, it appeared that "the whole world [was] dancing to American jazz." Indeed, jazz seemed to lead the way in what one fan described as "a blowing off of the lid." Americans were looking for ways to have fun.

Movies and radio Two new sources of entertainment captured the public in the 1920s: movies and radio. All classes of Americans flocked to grand, ornate movie "palaces." At first the films were silent. Then, in 1927 "talking pictures" arrived with *The Jazz Singer*, and the craze was on. By 1930 attendance was 100 million a week—almost one ticket for every American.

Radio turned into entertainment in 1920, when Frank Conrad sent out baseball scores and music to amateur radio operators from a wireless station in his garage. Discovering that he had attracted a national audience, Westinghouse officials set up the first radio station. Later that year, KDKA in Pittsburgh broadcast news of Harding's election. Two years later, more than 500 stations were broadcasting "every night, everywhere."

Heroes of the 1920s Jazz Age Americans were hungry for heroes. From baseball's George Herman "Babe" Ruth, to movie stars like Theda Bara and Rudolph Valentino, Americans made heroes of public figures.

For the first time, sports heroes included women. Babe Didrikson Zaharias competed in almost every sport, from basketball to golf. She eventually set Olympic records in track and field. Gertrude Ederle, meanwhile, broke all records when she swam across the English Channel in 1926.

The greatest hero of all, though, was a shy young pilot from Minnesota. On the drizzly morning of May 20, 1927, Charles A. Lindbergh strapped himself into his plane, *The Spirit of St. Louis*, and headed eastward from New York City. Thirty-four hours and 3,600 miles (5,790 km) later, he was greeted at a Paris airfield by 100,000 wildly cheering admirers waiting in the dark. He was the first person to fly solo across the Atlantic Ocean.

The world was seized by frenzy over the flight of the 25-year-old Lindbergh. Upon his return to the United States, he was given "the greatest welcome any man in history ever received." Soon after, Amelia Earhart became the first woman pilot to fly the Atlantic alone. Such flights boosted the infant airline industry. By 1930, 43 airlines operated in the United States.

New Ways of Living

In 1920, for the first time, a majority of Americans lived in urban rather than rural areas. Of those an increasing number were moving to the **suburbs**—communities on the outskirts of cities. Streetcar lines had first encouraged the growth of suburbs. Now automobiles did so as well.

The automobile age By 1921 automobiles were no longer "carriages of the rich." A family could buy a car for $400, half of what it had cost ten years earlier. Owning a car, advertisements promised, meant that "your freedom is complete." Farmers could enjoy the pleasures of the city, while city dwellers could escape to the country. A love affair blossomed between Americans, their cars, and the freedom of the road.

The lives of women For American women, the 1920s brought other freedoms as well. All women at last had the right to vote. Some women also had more free time as households installed electricity, telephones, and piped water. Electric washing machines, irons, and vacuum cleaners helped ease the tasks of daily life.

More women were working outside the home, too. With wider opportunities—and incomes of their own—young women, particularly, rebelled against old customs. They bobbed—cut short—their hair, threw away

Link to Technology

The Radio

Edwin Armstrong began development of the radio receiver while serving in World War I. By the 1920s he had perfected the technology, and soon millions of Americans had radios. Enthusiastic families crowded around "the magic box" to hear news and entertainment. The technology that Armstrong developed is the same basic design used in almost all radios today. The diagram below shows how radio transmitters and receivers work.

Transmitter

Traffic is heavy!

Sound signal

Amp

Modulator

Combined signal

Amp

Antenna

Radio wave

④

Microphone ①

Carrier signal

Oscillator ②

③

Receiver

Signals from other stations

⑤

Antenna

Amp

Tuner ⑥

Amp

Demodulator

Amp

Speaker

⑦

Traffic is heavy!

Edwin Armstrong displays his "portable" radio.

① At a radio station, a microphone converts sound to a sound signal.

② An oscillator generates a second signal—the carrier signal—set to the frequency of the radio station.

③ A modulator combines the two signals, which are then amplified and sent to the antenna.

④ The movement of the combined signal in the antenna sends the wave into space.

⑤ On the receiver side, waves from many stations create signals in the antenna. The signals are amplified and fed into the tuner.

⑥ The listener chooses a station and the tuner selects that carrier signal.

⑦ The demodulator removes the carrier signal and the speaker broadcasts the sound.

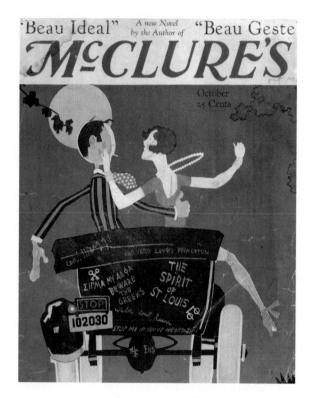

Magazines like *McClure's* spread the new spirit of American youth into even the smallest towns.

their corsets, and went out dancing in short, sleeveless dresses draped with long, beaded necklaces. Journalists called these independent, assertive young women "flappers."

"Flaming Youth" Young Americans created a new world in the 1920s. "The wildest of all generations" found it a thrilling time as they danced to music blaring from phonographs, crowded into movie houses, and took to the road in automobiles. *Flaming Youth*, the title of a 1923 novel, captured the spirit and passion of the time.

There was plenty of silliness, too. College students competed in goldfish-swallowing contests. A man called "Shipwreck" Kelly perched on a flagpole for 23 days, eating and drinking from a bucket raised from below. The idea caught on, and flagpole sitters cropped up everywhere.

In fact, American fads, fashions, music, and movies were spreading beyond the borders of the United States. The 1920s marked the beginning of the worldwide influence of American culture.

Reaction to the Jazz Age
. . . .

Still, many Americans worried that society was changing too quickly. They reacted by trying to enforce old customs and values that they felt were being threatened.

Prohibition Progressives had long promoted **Prohibition**—banning the manufacture, transport, and sale of liquor—as a way to improve people's lives. By 1920 most states had passed some kind of Prohibition laws. In that year ratification of the Eighteenth Amendment made Prohibition law throughout the nation.

From the beginning, though, Prohibition was difficult to enforce. Many people who disagreed with the law willingly broke it. When saloons were closed down, people crowded into illegal clubs called speakeasies. Bootleggers, meanwhile, smuggled liquor into the United States. Criminal empires, run by gangsters like Al Capone, thrived from such activities.

Prohibition clearly was not working. In 1924 alone, $40 million worth of alcohol was smuggled in from Canada and the Caribbean islands. By the end of the decade, many Americans thought that Prohibition had done more harm than good. In 1933 the Twenty-First Amendment repealed it.

Point of View

Was prohibiting the sale of alcohol a good idea?

In 1927 a visitor to the United States, Count von Luckner, described the benefits of Prohibition for American workers:

"The filthy saloons . . . in which the laborer once drank off half of his wages, have disappeared. Now he can instead buy his own car, and ride off for a weekend or a few days with his wife and children in the country or at the sea."

In the same report, however, Count von Luckner continued:

"A large part of the population has become accustomed to disregard and to violate the law without thinking. The worst is, that precisely as a consequence of the law, the taste for alcohol has spread ever more widely among the youth."

The dilemma described by Count von Luckner did not end with the repeal of Prohibition. To this day, Americans debate how best to protect citizens' well-being without interfering with personal freedom.

The Scopes trial Another hot debate arose over ideas put forth by Charles Darwin, an English biologist. Darwin said that all living things, including humans, have gradually developed—or evolved—from simpler forms of life. Many Christians and Jews thought that Darwin's theory of evolution was dangerous because it raised questions about the Bible's story of creation.

In 1925 Tennessee banned teaching about evolution in its schools. To test the new law, town leaders in Dayton, Tennessee, encouraged a teacher named John Scopes to teach evolution in his class. If Scopes went to trial, they thought, it would bring fame and money to Dayton. They were right.

The Scopes trial drew nationwide attention. Reporters, souvenir vendors, and hordes of curiosity seekers descended on Dayton. In this carnival-like setting, William Jennings Bryan, the political leader and powerful speaker, represented those who opposed the

Government agents smashed kegs of beer during the "noble experiment" of Prohibition.

teaching of evolution. Clarence Darrow, a famous lawyer, defended Scopes.

The judge ruled that Scopes was guilty because he had, in fact, broken the Tennessee law. Even so, many believed that Darrow had won because he had made Bryan sound foolish at the trial. The debate over teaching evolution continues to this day.

2. Section Review

1. Define **suburbs** and **Prohibition.**
2. What contributions did African Americans make to American culture and social life in the 1920s?
3. Describe at least three ways in which the lives of women changed in the 1920s.
4. Critical Thinking Could Prohibition have been successful? Explain your answer.

Skill Lab

Thinking Critically
Recognizing Relevant Information

Americans of the 1920s knew that the car was reshaping their lives. Humorist Will Rogers expressed their feelings in this salute to Henry Ford: "It will take a hundred years to tell whether you have helped us or hurt us, but you certainly didn't leave us like you found us."

Question to Investigate

How did cars affect social life in the 1920s?

Procedure

To explore the question, you need **relevant information**—information that applies, relates, or is connected to the particular topic. Study the Skill Tips and do the following.

1 Identify the topic.
a. Use the Question to Investigate to come up with a phrase that names the topic.
b. What does "social life" mean? That is, what relationships or activities does it include? Give four examples of your own.

2 Examine each piece of information in the source to determine whether it is relevant to the topic you are investigating.
a. For each excerpt, **A** to **H**, tell whether it is relevant, partly relevant, or irrelevant to the topic.
b. For each excerpt that is either partly relevant or irrelevant, tell what other topic the information is actually relevant to.

3 Use what you have learned to answer the Question to Investigate.

Sources to Use

Below are excerpts from a report on life in a medium-sized American city: Muncie, Indiana, referred to as "Middletown."

A "At the close of 1923, there were 6,221 passenger cars in the city. . . . Of these 6,221 cars, 41 percent were Fords."

B "'I never feel as close to my family as when we are all together in the car,' said one business class mother."

C "The increase in surfaced roads and in closed cars is rapidly making the car a year-round tool for leisure-time as well as getting-a-living activities."

D "'What on earth *do* you want me to do? Just sit around home all evening!' retorted a popular high school girl of today when her father discouraged her going out motoring for the evening."

E "348 boys and 382 girls in the three upper years of the high school placed 'use of the automobile' fifth and fourth respectively in a list of twelve possible sources of disagreement between them and their parents."

F "A factory can [now] draw from workmen within a radius of forty-five miles."

G "A leading Middletown minister denounced 'automobilitis—the thing those people have who go off motoring on Sunday instead of going to church.'"

H "The automobile has apparently unsettled the habit of careful saving for some families. 'Part of the money we spend on the car would go to the bank, I suppose,' said more than one working class wife."

From Robert S. Lynd and Helen Merrell Lynd, *Middletown* (Harcourt, 1929)

3. The Business Boom

Reading Guide

New Terms assembly line, credit

Section Focus The booming economy of the 1920s

1. How did the policies of Harding and Coolidge favor big business?
2. What new products and methods for selling them fueled the 1920s economy?
3. What signs pointed to troubles ahead for the economy?

As Zora Neale Hurston made her way north from Florida, she dreamed of a new life. She eventually moved to Harlem—the center of African American culture. There she found new opportunities. In fact, opportunity was in the dreams of most people in the 1920s. With President Warren G. Harding, they believed that if American business prospered, there would be opportunity for everyone.

A New Era for Business

As the economy rebounded from its slowdown in 1921, Harding's Secretary of the Treasury, Andrew W. Mellon, went to work. A wealthy banker, Mellon wanted to do everything possible to help business.

To protect American companies and their products, Mellon convinced Congress to raise tariffs on imports. As tariffs forced up prices on foreign goods, production soared at home. Congress also agreed to lower taxes for the wealthiest Americans. Mellon believed that if the rich paid less in taxes, they would use their extra money to build factories and put more people to work.

The economy would grow, too, as factory owners tried new systems for producing goods, invested in machinery, and switched to electric power from steam. Big business carried the nation into a boom—a period of extraordinary growth and prosperity.

Scandals Plague Harding

Harding, meanwhile, had chosen many of his friends from Ohio for jobs in his government. The "Ohio Gang," the public soon learned, had been accepting bribes and stealing money from federal agencies.

Teapot Dome The worst corruption involved Albert Fall, the Secretary of the Interior. He had control over two rich oil fields—one of them at Teapot Dome, Wyoming—that were set aside for the nation's navy. Fall leased the land to private oil companies, which gave him $400,000 in return. Convicted in the Teapot Dome scandal, Fall was the first cabinet member in the nation's history to go to prison.

Harding, depressed by the corruption and scandals, told a friend:

"I have no trouble with my enemies . . . but my friends . . . they're the ones that keep me walking the floor nights!"

To escape from the attention given to his bribe-taking friends, Harding toured the West in 1923. On his way home he suffered a heart attack and died in San Francisco. On a Vermont farm in the early hours of August 3, Vice-President Calvin Coolidge was sworn in as President.

Coolidge Takes Over

After the Harding scandals, Americans appreciated the soft-spoken Calvin Coolidge. Nicknamed "Silent Cal," he ran for election in his own right in 1924. The Democrats nominated John W. Davis. With the nation enjoying prosperity, "Silent Cal" easily won.

The boom continues Calvin Coolidge believed that the main job of government was to support business. "The business of the United States is business," he declared.

Coolidge thought that government should do as little as possible. He appointed department heads who would not enforce government regulations on businesses. He also continued Harding's policy of lowering taxes on businesses and on wealthy Americans.

Between 1923 and 1929 industrial production grew by more than 30 percent. Early on, wages for many Americans went up as well. As wages rose, unions lost power. At the same time more people had more money to buy goods. The faith of Americans in big business reached new heights.

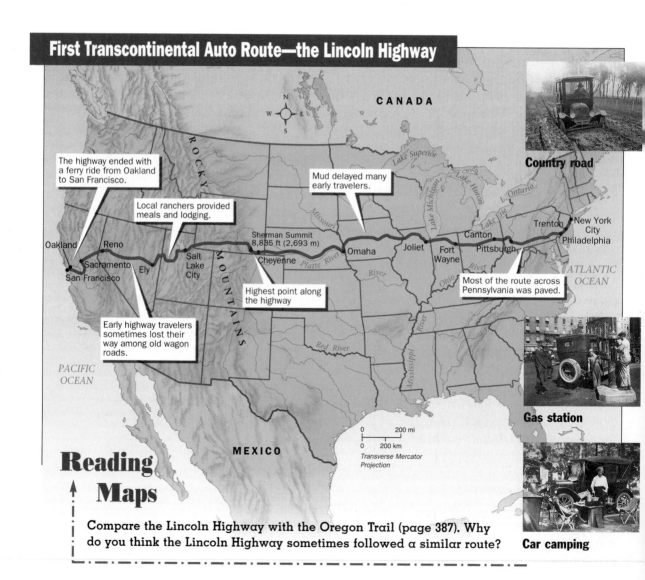

First Transcontinental Auto Route—the Lincoln Highway

CANADA

The highway ended with a ferry ride from Oakland to San Francisco.

Local ranchers provided meals and lodging.

Mud delayed many early travelers.

Country road

Oakland
Reno
Sacramento
San Francisco
Ely
Salt Lake City
Sherman Summit 8,835 ft (2,693 m)
Cheyenne
Platte River
Omaha
Joliet
Fort Wayne
Pittsburgh
Canton
Trenton
New York City
Philadelphia

Highest point along the highway

Most of the route across Pennsylvania was paved.

ATLANTIC OCEAN

Early highway travelers sometimes lost their way among old wagon roads.

PACIFIC OCEAN

Gas station

ROCKY

MOUNTAINS

Missouri

River

Ohio River

Red River

Mississippi River

MEXICO

0   200 mi
0   200 km
Transverse Mercator Projection

Reading Maps

Compare the Lincoln Highway with the Oregon Trail (page 387). Why do you think the Lincoln Highway sometimes followed a similar route?

Car camping

The Automobile Boom

One of the greatest business successes of the 1920s was the automobile industry. Automobiles had been produced since the 1890s, but only the wealthy could afford them.

By the 1920s, however, automobile factories were using a less expensive production method. Developed by Henry Ford in 1913, the **assembly line** is a system in which the product moves from worker to worker, each of whom performs one task.

Demand for automobiles rose dramatically as the price dropped. Reporters were astonished by the throngs that gathered to view new models. When Ford introduced the Model A in 1928, mounted police were called in to control the crowds.

The popularity of automobiles helped fuel the economic boom. Industries essential to auto manufacturing, such as steel, glass, rubber, oil refining, and road construction, experienced rapid growth and created thousands of new jobs. Gas stations and tourist courts (motels)—unknown in horse-and-buggy days—lined the roadsides.

Link to the Present

Beyond the Model T "Of all the noises there is none worse, than a Model T Ford when it's in reverse." Americans were always making jokes about the Model T. They loved the car, though, for its price ($290 in 1924), speed (up to 45 miles/72 km per hour), and endurance. By the mid-1920s, however, many drivers had tired of its bone-rattling ride and lack of frills.

Today's cars have features undreamed of in the 1920s, from speeds of 120 miles an hour to computer-regulated engines. Carmakers also offer extras like air conditioning, sunroofs, and electrically operated windows and locks. Such features, of course, do not come cheap. New car prices range from $10,000 to $30,000 or more—far more than a Model T in 1921.

Workers on a Ford assembly line turned out the famous Model T for a price equal to just three months' pay for an average worker. Ford had hired the production expert Walter Flanders to redesign his factories. More than 1 million automobiles were built in 1916. Just four years later, 8 million came off the line.

New Ways to Sell

Now that American industries were producing more goods than ever before, they needed to sell them. To encourage consumers to buy their products, businesses turned to advertising and the credit system.

Companies bombarded Americans with advertisements on billboards, in newspapers, and on the radio. Ads were used to sell everything from cars to refrigerators. For example an advertisement for Dodge cars boasted:

"America, when she starts, likes to start like a rocket, and here is a car that [does]."

Once they had decided to buy an exciting new product, Americans also had a new way to pay for it. Instead of paying cash, they could buy on **credit**—a system in which a buyer takes home a product and then makes monthly payments until it is paid for.

The credit system allowed many Americans to buy cars and other costly items that they could never have afforded before. Thus, credit buying helped fuel the business boom.

Salespeople proudly display vacuum cleaners, washing machines, and other appliances now manufactured "on a gigantic scale."

Hoover Wins

Republicans took credit for the nation's economic boom. Boasting that their pro-business policies had put "A Chicken in Every Pot, a Car in Every Garage," they promised even better times if Americans put another Republican in the White House.

President Coolidge decided against seeking re-election. The Republican banner passed to Herbert Hoover, a successful businessman. He had gained fame for setting up programs to feed the hungry in Europe after World War I. Hoover, like most Republicans in the 1920s, believed that government should play only a small role in the economy.

Al Smith, four-time governor of New York, became the Democratic candidate and the first Catholic to run for President. In a largely Protestant nation, Smith's Catholic background cost him votes among fearful Protestants. In any case, the voters gave the Republicans credit for the continuing prosperity. Herbert Hoover won by a landslide.

Taking office in March 1929, President Hoover confidently declared:

"We in America are nearer to the final triumph over poverty than ever before in the history of the land."

The Soaring Stock Market

Public confidence that prosperity was here to stay was reflected in an increasing interest in the Stock Market. Before the war, only the wealthiest people could afford to buy stocks and thus share in the wealth created by business corporations. In the 1920s, however,

Hands-On HISTORY

Investing in stocks If you have heard the phrase "playing the market," you might think that buying and selling stocks is a game or a gamble. Most people, however, make careful decisions when choosing a stock to buy.

A stock exchange floor today

Activity Working with a classmate, you are to invest an imaginary sum of $1,000 in a company listed on the New York Stock Exchange.

1. Choose a company in which to invest. Find out what products it makes or services it offers to people. Will there be demand for its products or services in the future?

2. On the day you "invest," find the price of the stock in the stock tables of a newspaper. Under the column labeled "Last," check how much one share will cost you.

3. Each day, look at the stock tables and record the last price of your stock. After one month, has your stock price gone up or down? Compare its value with the stocks of your classmates. Would you "sell" now or wait? Why?

stockbrokers—people who take orders to buy and sell stocks—developed an easy way for ordinary people to invest.

The new system was called "buying on margin." A buyer paid a small sum for shares of stock, with the stockbroker lending the rest of the money. Banks, in turn, loaned money to the stockbrokers. Now that they could buy on margin, people began to buy stocks as easily as they bought cars and refrigerators. By 1928 even bus drivers and elevator operators were "playing the market," expecting to get rich.

The frenzy of investing created a bull market—a period of rising stock prices— that many thought would go on forever. Cautious investors realized that the steady increase in stock prices could be dangerous. Even so, most people agreed with John Raskob, a business leader, who declared:

❝I am firm in my belief that anyone not only *can* be rich, but *ought* to be rich.❞

Signs of Trouble

Blinded by optimism and skyrocketing stock prices, few people could see that the economy was racing toward calamity. A careful observer, however, might have noticed signs warning of trouble.

In fact, a surprising number of Americans did not share in the prosperity. Farms, where 25 percent of Americans still lived, had been in a slump since early in the decade when crop prices had dropped.

Coal miners suffered, too, for oil was replacing coal as a major source of energy. Meanwhile, the textile industry suffered as women's fashions featured shorter dresses with less fabric. Unions, weakened by business and government hostility, had little power to help workers who had been laid off.

Declining demand Even though business profits climbed in the 1920s, business leaders held down workers' wages. This, in turn, led to a decline in demand for cars, homes, and appliances. After 1927, production slowed and more workers lost their jobs.

At the same time, Americans were buying fewer foreign goods. High tariffs had made them expensive. American banks suffered as European nations, unable to sell enough products, failed to pay back the money they had borrowed after World War I.

Failing farms, decreasing demand for goods, and risky bank loans all might have been warning signs that the economy was in trouble. At that time, though, the federal government did not watch such trends or business practices. As the Roaring Twenties drew to a close, few Americans could imagine the devastating events that lay ahead.

3. Section Review

1. Define **assembly line** and **credit**.
2. Describe three developments that helped business to prosper in the 1920s.
3. What factors were signs of economic troubles in the late 1920s?
4. Critical Thinking As an average American at the time, would you have invested in the stock market? Why or why not?

Why We Remember

The Twenties

Some years after the 1920s had become a mere memory, Zora Neale Hurston looked back on her life and wrote that she had "been in Sorrow's kitchen and licked out all the pots. Then I have stood on peaky mountains wrapped in rainbows." Indeed, many Americans spent the 1920s in Sorrow's kitchen. Immigrants lived in fear of Palmer's raids and the Ku Klux Klan. African Americans, weary of racism and the threat of lynch mobs, sought hope in Marcus Garvey's "back to Africa" movement. Farmers lost their farms and their futures, while other workers struggled just to survive.

Many Americans, however, also shared Zora's fond memories of the Jazz Age. Some had enjoyed the new culture created by movies, music, dance, and sports. Others had found expression as writers and musicians, or found new freedom in rebelling against traditional dress and customs. Many had enjoyed a prosperity beyond their wildest dreams. For all these Americans and more, the 1920s was a time wrapped in rainbows. Indeed, it seemed that the nation had never before reached peaks so high as it did in the 1920s. Even President Hoover believed that a "final triumph over poverty" was at hand. Yet as you will see in the next chapter, we also remember the 1920s as the decade that would end in Sorrow's kitchen.

Geography Lab

Filming a western at Lone Pine, California, 1938

Why the Movies Moved to Hollywood

One business that blossomed in the 1920s was the movie industry. The earliest movies were made in New York City and nearby New Jersey, where inventor Thomas Edison had his laboratory. In 1908, Edison's company joined others to form the Motion Picture Patents Company, which held patents on equipment and processes. The company tried to establish a monopoly in movie production, distribution, and exhibition. Independent movie producers fought the Patents Company and each other with lawsuits, spying, and dirty tricks.

Meanwhile, moviemakers discovered Hollywood, a sleepy suburb of Los Angeles. By 1920, 80 percent of the world's movies were made in or near Hollywood. Use the sources on this page to learn why.

Richard V. Spencer, 1911

"Los Angeles and vicinity have acquired their reputation in the production of Western and Indian pictures. Here, of all places, is the ideal location for the production of such films. Here is found the necessary rolling country cut up by foothills, treacherous canyons and lofty mountain ranges in the background."

Fred J. Balshofer

"Los Angeles with its mild climate and sunshine beckoned as an escape both from the winter months of the East as well as the ever-present Patents Company detectives. . . . [Thus,] late in November, 1909, found our little company of players . . . departing for the West Coast."

Link to History

1. Sum up the appeal of the Los Angeles area to moviemakers, according to Richard Spencer.

2. Study the map on pages R6–R7. Why might the Los Angeles area seem like an attractive location to the owners of the New York Motion Picture Company?

3. In what way might Los Angeles's climate be an advantage in making movies? How do the maps on page 413 support that idea?

4. **Hands-On Geography** Many modern movies include scenes shot "on location." Imagine that you work for your state's film office. Write a letter to the head of a Hollywood studio in which you offer reasons why your state would be the ideal location for the studio's next movie.

Chapter Survey

Reviewing Vocabulary

Define the following terms.
1. communism
2. anarchism
3. suburbs
4. Prohibition
5. assembly line
6. credit

Reviewing Main Ideas

1. Explain how economic conditions and racial violence contributed to unrest after World War I.

2. Why were many Americans in an anti-immigrant mood in the 1920s, and what did they do about it?

3. (a) Who belonged to the "Lost Generation"? (b) What was the "Harlem Renaissance"? Name three people who were part of it and describe what they did.

4. Give three examples of how technology changed the everyday lives of Americans in the 1920s.

5. How did some people, worried by social changes occurring during the Jazz Age, try to maintain traditional customs?

6. In what ways did the Harding and Coolidge administrations support business?

7. What role did each of the following play in fueling the economic boom of the 1920s? (a) the automobile (b) advertising (c) credit

Thinking Critically

1. Evaluation Calvin Coolidge believed that "the business of the United States is business." Do you agree, or do you think our nation has other tasks more important than producing goods and services? Explain your answer.

2. Application It is March 1929 and President Hoover is taking office. What groups of Americans probably share his optimism about the future of the nation? What groups may feel more gloomy? Explain.

3. Why We Remember: Synthesis The 1920s has been called the Jazz Age and the Roaring Twenties. Make up your own label for the decade. Explain why you chose it.

Applying Skills

Recognizing relevant information
Much as the automobile did in the 1920s, the computer is reshaping American life today. Look in newspapers or magazines for articles about the impact of computers. Recalling what you learned on page 746, read the articles to find five pieces of information on each of the following questions:
• How are computers affecting workers and businesses?
• How are computers changing communication between people outside of work?
Write answers to the questions based on the information that you find.

History Mystery

A famous flight Answer the History Mystery on page 731. Why did people throughout the world react with such wild enthusiasm to Lindbergh's flight? What consequences do you think it had for travel and future relations between the United States and other nations?

Writing in Your History Journal

1. Keys to History (a) The time line on pages 730–731 has seven Keys to History. In your journal, list each key and describe why it is important to know about. (b) Choose one event on the time line. Imagine that you are a teenager living at the time the event occurred. In your journal, write a letter to a friend giving your reactions to the event.

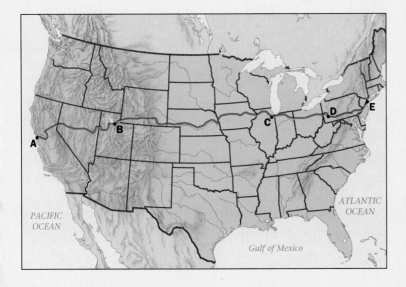

PACIFIC
OCEAN

ATLANTIC
OCEAN

Gulf of Mexico

Reviewing Geography

1. The letters on the map represent cities along the Lincoln Highway. Write the name of each.

2. Geographic Thinking Name one effect that you think the automobile has had on each of the following:
• the natural environment
• the forms that cities, towns, and suburbs take
• people's ideas about the relative locations of places
• regional differences, such as in foods and customs

2. Zora Neale Hurston Sassy, spirited, shameless, bold: people of Eatonville used those words and others to describe young Zora. What other words would you apply to Zora? In your journal, list at least four and explain why you chose them.

3. Citizenship Many years after Prohibition ended, Americans still disagree about whether alcohol, tobacco, and other substances should be legal.
How much should the government regulate or prohibit them? Or should the decision be left entirely to the individual? Why? Write your responses in your journal.

Alternative Assessment

Planning a "decade-in-review" issue

Imagine that you and several classmates are the editors of a weekly magazine. It is July 1929 and you need to begin planning the special end-of-the-decade issue that will be published in December.

❶ Decide how to organize the issue. Although a year-by-year approach is possible, consider having sections of the magazine devoted to topics like entertainment, business, and sports, instead.

❷ Having planned the organization of the issue, think of a snappy title for each section. List the topics that each section will cover. This will be your table of contents.

❸ Create the cover and at least one section of the issue. Write text for the section and decide how you want to illustrate it. Arrange the text and images in a page layout.

Your work will be evaluated on the following criteria:
• it offers an accurate, thorough overview of events and people of the 1920s
• it is organized and written in a clear, logical, and interesting way
• its content and appearance capture the "flavor" of the 1920s

Link to Literature

The Poetry of Langston Hughes

No single writer of the Harlem Renaissance period was more prolific than Langston Hughes. Hughes first made his mark at age 19 with the poem "The Negro Speaks of Rivers." He went on to publish novels, plays, short stories, a newspaper column, essays, children's books, and two autobiographies. Born in Missouri, Hughes spent much of his adult life in Harlem. Although he traveled extensively and lived in Paris for a time, he found his greatest inspiration at home, where he found the ordinary people—"people up today and down tomorrow"—who filled his work.

I, Too, Sing America

I, too, sing America.
I am the darker brother.
They send me to eat in the kitchen
When company comes,
But I laugh,
And eat well,
And grow strong.

Tomorrow,
I'll be at the table
When company comes.
Nobody'll dare
Say to me,
"Eat in the kitchen,"
Then.

Besides,
They'll see how beautiful I am
And be ashamed—

I, too, am America.

**Langston Hughes c. 1925
by Winold Reiss**

Hughes was inspired by the vitality of Harlem life. This photo shows a Harlem street scene in the early 1930s.

Juke Box Love Song

I could take the Harlem night
and wrap around you,
Take the neon lights and make a crown,
Take the Lenox Avenue buses,
Taxis, subways,
And for your love song tone their rumble down.
Take Harlem's heartbeat,
Make a drumbeat,
Put it on a record, let it whirl,
And while we listen to it play,
Dance with you till day—
Dance with you, my sweet brown Harlem girl.

Lenox Avenue a street in the heart of Harlem

The Dream Keeper

Bring me all of your dreams,
You dreamer,
Bring me all of your
Heart melodies
That I may wrap them
In a blue cloud-cloth
Away from the too-rough fingers
Of the world.

A Closer Look

1. Who do you think "they" are in the poem "I, Too, Sing America"? Why do you think the narrator says they will be ashamed?

2. What is the narrator of "The Dream Keeper" saying about dreams?

3. Hughes's work was greatly influenced by the newly popular music forms of jazz and the blues. How do you think this influence is evident in these poems?

Chapter 27

The Depression and New Deal

Keys to History

1934
Indian Reorganization Act

1933
Franklin Roosevelt introduces New Deal bills

The Hundred Days

Tennessee Valley Authority

1929
Stock Market Crash

1929   *1931*   *1933*

Looking Back

World Link

WWI veterans promised a bonus
1924

Brazil's coffee industry begins to collapse
1929

HISTORY
Mystery

In the 1930s thousands of families left their farms on the Great Plains, never to return. What caused this great migration?

1935

Social Security Act

Wagner Act

1935

Works Progress Administration (WPA)

1938

Congress of Industrial Organizations (CIO) founded

35   1937   1939   1941

Looking Ahead

Roosevelt elected to his fourth term

1944

Franklin and Eleanor Roosevelt

On August 10, 1921, Franklin Roosevelt took three of his five children for a sailing lesson in the waters off Campobello Island, New Brunswick. On the way back to their summer house, they spotted a brushfire, dashed ashore, and beat it out with pine branches. Later, Franklin felt a bit shaky. Like his cousin Theodore Roosevelt, his remedy for feeling weak was more exercise. He challenged the children to race him to a pond for a swim before dinner.

Next morning, Franklin's head throbbed. As he walked to the bathroom to shave, his left leg crumpled beneath him. A day later, he could not sit up or stand without help. "I don't know what's the matter," he kept saying. He would soon learn that he had been struck down by polio—one of the most dreaded diseases of his day. He would never walk without help again.

"Will he ever be anything else?"

Until now, Franklin had seemed to be a man who had everything. Born to a wealthy family and gifted with good looks and charm, he had easily won the heart and hand of his distant cousin Eleanor. Those same gifts had served him well when he decided to make politics his career. Wealth and charm had no effect on polio, however. As the disease ran its devastating course, it left Franklin's lower body paralyzed and in pain. A family friend wrote:

> **"**He is only 39—both too old & too young for such a fell [cruel] germ to disable him. He's had a brilliant career as assistant [Secretary] of the Navy under [President] Wilson, & then a few brief weeks of . . . excitement when nominated by the Democrats for the Vice Presidency. Now he is a cripple—will he ever be anything else?**"**

That was a question that tormented Eleanor as she nursed her husband through his illness. She did everything she could to make his life as normal as possible. Still, Eleanor had grave doubts. "Do you really believe that Franklin still has a political future?" she asked Louis Howe, Roosevelt's closest political advisor. "I believe," Howe answered firmly, "that someday, Franklin will be President."

Patience and Persistence

The Roosevelts' lives were changed by Franklin's illness. Eleanor had always been extremely shy and lacking in self-confidence. Now, for her children's sake, she learned to swim, hike, camp, drive a car, and sail a boat. In the process, she became a more adventurous person.

Leaning heavily on the arm of his son James, Franklin Roosevelt, with his wife Eleanor, arrives at the White House after his inauguration as President in 1933.

Eleanor also saw that if Franklin was to have "a political future," she would have to help. "I had never done anything for a political organization before," she recalled, "nor had I ever made a speech in any sizable gathering." When bills began to pile up, she found ways to make money by giving speeches, writing magazine articles, and making guest appearances on the radio.

For the next few years, Franklin spent his energy working to regain his strength and some movement in his legs. His daughter Anna wrote:

"It's a bit traumatic when you're fifteen . . . [to] see your father . . . struggling in heavy steel braces. And you see the sweat pouring down his face, and you hear him saying, 'I must get to the end of driveway today—all the way down the driveway.'"

As difficult as that time was, it was also, wrote Eleanor, "a blessing in disguise." Franklin's struggle, she believed, "gave him strength and courage he had not had before." It also forced him to "learn the greatest of all lessons—infinite patience and never-ending persistence." These hard lessons would serve Franklin Roosevelt well in the years ahead.

Hands-On HISTORY

Activity

Imagine that Franklin Roosevelt is not yet President, and an admirer has written to the Roosevelts asking for advice about how to overcome great personal misfortune. As either Eleanor or Franklin Roosevelt, write a brief reply. In your response, include three general guidelines for facing hard times.

1. The Great Depression

Reading Guide

New Term durable goods

Section Focus The economic disasters that struck the United States in the 1920s and 1930s

1. What caused the Stock Market Crash and the Great Depression?
2. How did the Depression affect people's lives?
3. How did the government respond to the Depression?

Business began to slow in the fall of 1929. The value of stocks drifted down. The decline prompted some people to predict that the economic boom was coming to an end.

Worried investors rushed to sell stocks before the value dropped further. The more stocks they sold, the more the value of the stocks fell. Investors panicked as prices tumbled. To add to the troubles, stockbrokers demanded that people who had bought stocks on margin pay back their loans immediately.

Tuesday, October 29, 1929, was the worst day in Stock Market history. Thousands of frightened investors tried to sell stocks, but there were few buyers. The stocks sold for next to nothing. People who had put all their savings into stocks were ruined.

The Shaky Economy

The Stock Market Crash marked the beginning of the Great Depression, the worst economic crisis in United States history. Economists disagree about whether the Crash caused the Great Depression. Still, most blame basic problems in the economy.

One problem was the gap between the rich and everyone else. In 1929 just 5 percent of Americans earned 33 percent of the nation's personal income. After the Crash, the rich

$100. WILL BUY THIS CAR. MUST HAVE CASH. LOST ALL ON THE STOCK MARKET

This man was lucky. When his stock became worthless, he put his shiny new car up for sale. Shortly after this picture was taken, he sold the car and repaid the money he had borrowed to buy the stocks.

stopped spending, which hurt businesses that depended on them to buy and invest.

Another problem was poor business practices. For example, some large companies bought small companies just to take their profits. There was not enough money left in the small companies to help them through hard times.

A third problem was overproduction. Factories had been making **durable goods**—goods meant to last, like machinery and locomotives—faster than they could be sold. Now factories slowed production and laid off workers. People without jobs had less money to spend in stores, and stores had less money to buy goods from factories. So, more factories had to cut back on production.

Bank failures Banking practices were a problem, too. When customers deposited money, banks kept part of it in cash and invested the rest, sometimes in stocks. As the value of stocks fell, banks lost money.

When depositors saw a bank in trouble, they lost confidence in their own banks and withdrew their money. If a lot of people tried to withdraw money at once—a situation called a "run" on a bank—the bank might not have enough money on hand. Banks that could not pay all their depositors had to close down.

Unemployment

As banks and businesses failed, factory workers and clerks, salespeople and railroad engineers, miners and nurses lost their jobs. At the peak of the Great Depression, one worker out of four was unemployed.

People without work felt fear, shame, and despair. In 1936 a 12-year-old Chicago boy wrote to the Roosevelts:

❝ I want to tell you about my family. My father hasn't worked for 5 months. . . . We haven't paid 4 months rent,

World Link

The coffee crash The Depression struck other nations as well as the United States. Brazil's coffee industry was already troubled by overproduction. Then, during the Depression, the demand for coffee in the United States and other countries dropped. Coffee prices fell from 22¢ a pound in 1929 to 8¢ in 1931. Even so, millions of sacks of coffee sat in Brazilian warehouses. Brazil's government burned and dumped surplus coffee and destroyed some plantations, hoping to raise prices.

A popular American song of the time described Brazil's coffee crash:

❝You can't get cherry soda
'Cause they've got to sell their quota,
And the way things are I guess they
never will,
They've got a zillion tons of coffee
in Brazil!**❞**

The COFFEE SONG (They've Got An Awful Lot Of Coffee In Brazil). Words and Music by Bob Hilliard and Dick Miles. TRO © Copyright 1946 (Renewed) Cromwell Music, Inc., New York, NY. Used by permission.

Everyday the landlord rings the door bell, we don't open the door for him. We are afraid that [we] will be put out, been put out before, and don't want to happen again. . . . My father he staying home. All the time he's crying because he can't find work. I talk him why are you crying daddy, and daddy said why shouldn't I cry when there is nothing in the house. I feel sorry for him. That night I couldn't sleep. The next morning I wrote this letter to you. . . . Please answer right away because we need it. [We] will starve Thank you.**❞**

An encampment of the homeless in Seattle and a soup kitchen in Washington, D.C., were typical of scenes to be found in cities from coast to coast.

Looking for Help

Without work, many people were homeless and hungry. Communities tried to help, but they were not prepared for the numbers of people who needed help. When towns and cities set up soup kitchens, people lined up for blocks.

To get money to aid the poor, cities cut back other services. Some took money from teachers' salaries. Others just closed the schools. Still, local governments could not stop all the suffering.

People help themselves Some people found ways to help themselves and one another. For example, in the countryside people held "penny auctions." When a court ordered a sheriff to auction off farms to pay farmers' debts, friends and neighbors would frighten serious bidders away. Then they would bid just pennies. When the auctions were over, they would "sell" the farms back to their original owners for a few coins.

Some ideas led to trouble, though. Milo Reno believed that farmers were suffering because they grew more than people wanted to buy. If crops were smaller, he said, prices would rise. Reno organized the Farmers Holiday Association in 1932 to urge Iowa farmers to stop growing so much.

Holiday members set up roadblocks to stop other farmers from bringing their hogs and milk to market. Fights broke out. The governor had to call out the National Guard to open the roads.

People on the move Many homeless "rode the rails" looking for work. Too poor to buy tickets, they hopped onto freight trains and hid from railroad detectives. Single women disguised themselves as men to protect themselves.

Some families piled their things onto the family car or truck and took to the highway, looking for work. Many became migrant workers, moving from farm to farm, planting and harvesting crops with the seasons.

"Hoovervilles" Other homeless people huddled together in shacks made of cardboard, wooden boxes, and rusty old cars. They called their shantytowns "Hoovervilles," after President Hoover.

The President had not caused the Depression, but people blamed him. When people covered themselves with newspapers to keep warm, they called them "Hoover blankets." They turned their empty pockets inside out and called them "Hoover flags."

The Bonus Army As unemployment soared in 1932, World War I veterans looked to Washington for help. Congress had promised to pay them $1,000 bonuses in 1945. Instead, Texas Congressman Wright Patman proposed paying the bonuses immediately. When Hoover said the government did not have the money, nearly 20,000 veterans marched on Washington, D.C. Newspapers called them the "Bonus Army."

Hoover refused to meet with the veterans. He ordered General Douglas MacArthur to drive them out of Washington. MacArthur led the cavalry against the veterans' camp and burned it to the ground.

Franklin Roosevelt, who was then governor of New York, told a friend that he had once greatly admired Hoover. Now, he said, "there is nothing inside the man but jelly!"

Hoover Fights the Depression

Seeing that people were losing confidence in him, President Hoover tried to restore faith. "Recovery," he promised, "is just around the corner."

The President called on business and labor to cooperate. He asked business leaders to keep up jobs and wages. He asked labor leaders to stop demanding better wages and hours. To create jobs, he spent federal money on construction. To give people money to spend, he asked Congress to cut taxes.

Hoover hesitated to do more, however. He feared that if the government did too much, it would become too powerful. Worse, people might stop helping themselves.

The 1932 Election

As the 1932 election approached, Republicans nominated Hoover again. Their convention was a gloomy affair, though. They knew the public blamed them for hard times.

The Democrats were optimistic. They nominated Franklin Roosevelt. Warm and enthusiastic, Roosevelt believed that, unlike Hoover, he could inspire public confidence. He told cheering delegates:

❝Republican leaders . . . have failed in national vision, because in disaster they have held out no hope. . . . I pledge you, I pledge myself to a new deal for the American people.❞

Roosevelt said that he had no magic cures for the nation, but he would put the government to work to find solutions. Fifty-seven percent of the voters cast their ballots for Roosevelt and his "New Deal." He won the electoral votes of all but six states. Voters also gave the Democrats a majority in both houses of Congress.

1. Section Review

1. Define **durable goods.**
2. What were three economic conditions that contributed to the Depression?
3. What measures did Hoover take to fight the Depression? Why did he not do more?
4. Critical Thinking Explain the following statement: When a factory lays off a large part of its work force or shuts down entirely, an entire community can suffer.

2. The First New Deal

Reading Guide

New Term pension

Section Focus **The early years of the New Deal**

1. What actions did Roosevelt and Congress take to fight the Depression?
2. How did the Roosevelts win public support?
3. Who criticized the New Deal, and why?

By February 1933 the banking system had nearly collapsed. Over 5,000 banks had failed since the Crash, and more were failing each day. People began to think it was safer to keep their savings in a mattress than in a bank. Still, Franklin Roosevelt could do nothing until his inauguration.

March 4 was a chilly day. With his wife Eleanor beside him, Roosevelt stood before the Capitol Building. Placing his hand on a 300-year-old family Bible, he took the oath of office. Then in solemn tones he gave his first address as President. Radio networks broadcast his reassuring message across the nation:

"This great nation will endure as it has endured, will revive and will prosper. So first of all, let me assert my firm belief that the only thing we have to fear is fear itself.**"**

The First Hundred Days

To bring about the "New Deal" he had promised, the President and Congress acted swiftly during the first three months. Historians call this time "the Hundred Days." Because the Democrats controlled the presidency and the Senate and the House of Representatives, they were able to set New Deal programs in motion quickly.

Roosevelt's first act was to stop the run on banks. On March 6 he declared a bank holiday, ordering all banks to close. Once the government was sure a bank was sound, it could reopen.

To restore confidence in banks, Roosevelt and Congress created the Federal Deposit Insurance Corporation (FDIC). This agency would inspect banks and insure depositors' accounts. Now, Roosevelt promised, it was safer to "keep your money in a reopened bank than under the mattress."

Helping farmers During the Hundred Days the President and Congress also tackled problems in agriculture and industry. In May Congress passed the Agricultural Adjustment Act. The act created an agency—the Agricultural Adjustment Administration (AAA)—that would encourage farmers to grow less by paying them to farm fewer acres. The program's supporters expected that lower production would increase farm prices.

To help farmers who were struggling to pay their debts, another new agency, the Farm Credit Administration, provided low-cost farm loans. Home owners received similar help through the Home Owners' Loan Corporation.

Helping business and labor To help industry, Congress passed the National Industrial Recovery Act, which created the

National Recovery Administration (NRA). Its goal was to help businesspeople earn reasonable profits while workers earned decent wages.

Promising not to prosecute businesses under antitrust laws, the NRA encouraged them to work together to draw up codes of fair competition. The codes set prices, production quotas, wages, and working conditions. Companies that joined the program displayed a blue eagle with the slogan "We Do Our Part."

FDR thought that if businesspeople were allowed to band together, workers should be, too. The National Industrial Recovery Act guaranteed workers the right to collective bargaining, the process by which unions and employers reach agreement on wages and working conditions. Employers who displayed the blue eagle agreed to minimum hourly wages and a maximum number of hours in the workday.

The National Industrial Recovery Act established another agency, the Public Works Administration (PWA). The PWA provided funds for construction projects—roads, dams, bridges, and warships. It helped businesses put people to work so that they would have money to spend.

Perhaps the most popular program of the first Hundred Days was the Civilian Conservation Corps (CCC). The CCC employed thousands of young men between the ages of 18 and 25. They were stationed in camps across the country, improving public lands by planting trees, clearing trails, and fighting forest fires.

The Tennessee Valley Authority

Most New Deal programs were intended to help the nation recover from the Depression. In May 1933, however, Roosevelt and Congress introduced a measure to help ward off future depressions. They created the Tennessee Valley Authority (TVA) to develop the economic life of an entire region.

The Tennessee Valley suffered from severe flooding. The area's topsoil was thin and its forests overlogged. The people of the valley

The young men of the CCC, like those in this reforestation camp, were known as "Roosevelt's Tree Army." They planted millions of trees from Canada to Texas. The NRA blue eagle was based on an Indian figure, the thunderbird.

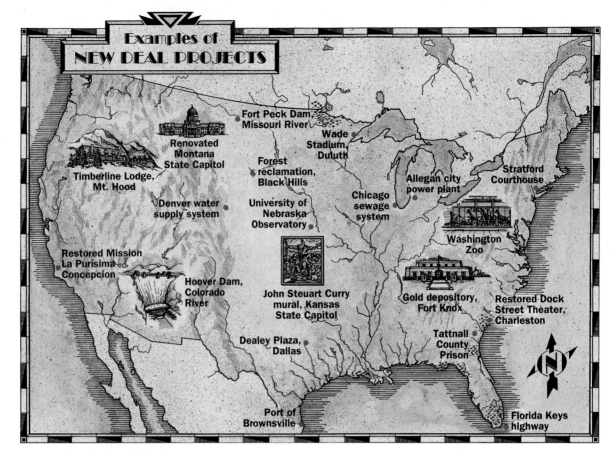

Examples of NEW DEAL PROJECTS

Renovated Montana State Capitol

Timberline Lodge, Mt. Hood

Fort Peck Dam, Missouri River

Wade Stadium, Duluth

Forest reclamation, Black Hills

Allegan city power plant

Stratford Courthouse

Denver water supply system

University of Nebraska Observatory

Chicago sewage system

Restored Mission La Purisima Concepcion

Hoover Dam, Colorado River

Washington Zoo

John Steuart Curry mural, Kansas State Capitol

Gold depository, Fort Knox

Restored Dock Street Theater, Charleston

Dealey Plaza, Dallas

Tattnall County Prison

Port of Brownsville

Florida Keys highway

Reading Maps

Use the information on the map to help you write a statement about the lasting effects of New Deal projects.

had a hard time earning a living. In addition, like most rural areas at that time, in the Tennessee Valley few farms had electricity. Yet the Tennessee and other rivers could be made to supply plenty of waterpower for electricity.

The TVA planned to develop the entire area. Over the next 20 years they improved 5 existing dams and built 20 new ones. The TVA employed thousands of workers. The dams they built provided flood control and a reliable supply of water for irrigation, drinking, and recreation. The TVA also restored the region's soil and its forests. TVA power plants carried electricity to people in seven states.

Roosevelt Reaches Out

To inspire public confidence, Roosevelt explained programs like the TVA over the radio. He wanted to give his talks a personal touch. He imagined that he was speaking to a family in its living room, even though he was broadcasting to millions. Roosevelt called his talks "fireside chats." Listening to the fireside chats, many people grew to trust Roosevelt as they would a friend.

Roosevelt also wanted people to feel that he was strong enough to lead the nation out of the Depression. Polio had paralyzed him from the waist down, but he wore braces that gave the impression that he could stand and walk. The back platform of his train car had a podium with a harness so that he could stand when he gave speeches.

Eleanor Roosevelt Although she was much shier than her husband, Mrs. Roosevelt also learned to demonstrate her strength and caring. She traveled thousands of miles every year, giving speeches, listening to the public, and inspecting conditions in coal mines and prisons and at dams.

Mrs. Roosevelt reached many people through her newspaper column, "My Day," in which she explained issues and also showed the human side of life in the White House. Many praised the First Lady's political role. Others condemned it. "Now we have a pair of Presidents," someone said. That was not true, but Franklin and Eleanor knew that in their own way they were a powerful team.

Critics of the New Deal

Despite the Roosevelts' popularity, not everyone supported the New Deal. Some critics charged that the government had given itself more power than the framers of the Constitution intended.

In Congress Southern Democrats sometimes joined forces with Republicans to block New Deal legislation, with all its agencies and regulations. They drew support from owners of small businesses who thought New Deal programs favored big business. At the same time, wealthy businesspeople and conservative politicians feared that the New Deal would give farmers and labor too much power. They formed the American Liberty League to work against it.

New ways to distribute wealth While some people blamed the government for exercising too much power, other critics

Hands-On *HISTORY*

Holding a fireside chat "My friends, I want to talk for a few minutes with the people of the United States about banking." That is how President Roosevelt began his first "fireside chat" on Sunday, March 12, 1933. In the years that followed, Roosevelt's radio broadcasts went a long way toward calming peoples' fears and winning support for the New Deal.

A fireside chat, 1938

Activity Put yourself in the President's place. Write and present a two-minute chat.

① Choose a New Deal program to talk about—one you have read about in this text or in another source.

② Find out the purpose and main features of the program. Do library research if you need to.

③ Write a script. Explain how the program will help people. Aim for a friendly, reassuring tone.

④ Rehearse your chat, then read it aloud or make an audiotape and play it for the class. Afterward, ask the class what aspect of the chat inspired faith in the future.

**"For gosh sakes, here comes Mrs. Roosevelt!"
exclaims the astonished coal miner in this cartoon.**
Drawing by Robt. Day; © 1933, 1961 The New Yorker Magazine, Inc.

said it did not go far enough. Their schemes attracted many of the desperately poor.

Senator Huey Long of Louisiana accused "Prince Franklin" of going along with the rich and powerful while neglecting the poor. Long gained followers with his "Share Our Wealth" plan. Under Long's plan, government would take surplus money from the wealthy and give everyone else land and an income. Even after an assassin gunned him down in 1935, Long's ideas lingered on.

Francis Townsend, a doctor from California, had another plan. He proposed that all citizens quit working at age 60 and receive a **pension**—retirement income—of $200 a month. To help the economy, people would be required to spend every penny of their pensions. Thousands of Townsend clubs sprang up to promote the plan.

Father Charles Coughlin, a Catholic priest, attracted millions to his weekly radio broadcasts from Detroit. He blamed bankers for the Depression. The government, he said, should take over the banks. People turned away from Coughlin, however, when he began to preach hatred of Jews. The Catholic Church ordered him to stop broadcasting.

Upton Sinclair, author of *The Jungle*, promoted socialism as a cure for the Depression. When he ran for governor of California in 1934, he proposed state-owned farms and factories. Farmers would trade their food for factory goods and vice versa, creating a barter system. Sinclair did not win the election, but nearly a million people voted for him.

Supreme Court Rulings

By the beginning of 1935, the New Deal seemed to be making a difference. Employment and production were up slightly. The *New York Times* said, "No President in so short a time has inspired so much hope."

Then in early 1935 a series of cases challenging New Deal programs began to reach the Supreme Court. In deciding the cases, the Court said that some programs stepped beyond the Constitution.

One case involved the NRA. The Court ruled that the National Industrial Recovery Act gave the executive and legislative branches too much power over the economy. Thus, the Court struck down one of the most important acts of the Hundred Days.

Roosevelt had once advised, "Take a method and try it. If it fails, try another. But above all, try something." It was time, Roosevelt saw, for him to try something new.

2. Section Review

1. Define **pension**.
2. How did Roosevelt restore confidence in banks?
3. Choose one of the following programs and explain how Roosevelt expected it to help the nation out of the Depression: AAA, NRA, PWA, CCC, and TVA.
4. Critical Thinking Why do you think people were attracted to the ideas of Long, Townsend, Coughlin, and Sinclair?

Skill Lab

Skill Tips

- Review the Skill Tips on page 446.
- An opinion that is stated as if it were a proven fact is still an opinion.
- Many historical questions have no "right" answer. Historical interpretations may differ and yet be reasonable.

Thinking Critically

Comparing Historical Interpretations

Soon after Roosevelt took office, a friend told him that if he succeeded in bringing the nation out of the Depression, he would go down in history as the greatest President. If he failed, however, he would be known as the worst. "If I fail," Roosevelt replied, "I shall be the last one."

Question to Investigate

Was the New Deal a success?

Procedure

In the Skill Lab on page 446 you analyzed a historical interpretation. Now you will be comparing two historical interpretations.

1 Summarize the interpretations.
a. How does the writer of **A** view the New Deal? Explain.
b. How do the writers of **B** view the New Deal? Explain.

2 Identify how the writers support their interpretations.
a. What statements of fact, if any, does the writer of **A** offer? What opinions?
b. What statements of fact, if any, do the writers of **B** offer? What opinions?

3 Compare the interpretations.
a. In what ways do **A** and **B** disagree?
b. To investigate whether the New Deal was a success, what are two questions you might ask the writer of **A**? The writers of **B**?
c. Which interpretation do you think makes more sense? Explain.

Sources to Use

A "The New Deal failed to solve the problem of depression, it failed to extend equality and generally countenanced [allowed] racial discrimination and segregation. It failed generally to make business more responsible to the social welfare. . . . The New Deal assisted the middle and upper sectors [classes] of society . . . even at the cost of injuring the lower sectors."

From Barton J. Bernstein, *Towards a New Past: Dissenting Essays in American History* (1968)

B "[Roosevelt] purged American capitalism of some of its worst abuses so that it might be saved from itself. He may even have headed off a more radical swing to the left by what was mistakenly condemned as 'socialism.'. . .

"Roosevelt, like Jefferson, provided reform without a bloody revolution. . . . He was upbraided [scolded] by the left-wing radicals for not going far enough; by the right-wing radicals for going too far. . . . He was in fact Hamiltonian in his espousal [support] of big government, but Jeffersonian in his concern for the 'forgotten man.'"

From Thomas A. Bailey and David M. Kennedy, *The American Pageant* (D. C. Heath, 1991)

3. The Second New Deal

Reading Guide

Section Focus **The last programs of the New Deal**

1. What programs did Congress pass to expand the New Deal?
2. What supporters did Roosevelt win for the Democratic Party?
3. What problems besides economic ills faced the nation in the 1930s?

The quick actions of the President and Congress during the Hundred Days gave Americans hope but did not cure the Depression. New Deal programs still did not reach many who needed help, so Roosevelt vowed to expand them. The Second New Deal—programs that became law after a new Congress met in 1935—included many people who had been left out of the earlier programs.

Broadening the New Deal

In 1935 the President recommended that the government spend more to put the jobless to work on projects of lasting value to the nation. To create the jobs, Congress voted to put more money into public works. Some money went to existing programs such as the CCC, and some to new programs such as the National Youth Administration, which provided jobs for young people.

Congress also created the Works Progress Administration (WPA), which was to employ millions. Many were put to work on construction projects such as schools, libraries, hospitals, roads, sewer systems, and airports.

The WPA gave a boost to culture, as well. It hired musicians to give music lessons and performances. Writers created state guidebooks, artists painted public murals, and actors brought theater to remote towns. WPA workers also collected the oral histories of men and women born into slavery before the Civil War.

Point of View

Should public funds support the arts?

One WPA effort, the Federal Theater Project, ran into opposition. Its director, Hallie Flanagan, hoped that drama could help solve social problems:

"Could we, through the power of the theatre, spotlight the tenements and thus help in the plan to build decent houses for all people? Could we . . . carry music and plays to children in city parks, and art galleries to little towns? Were not happy people at work the greatest bulwark [defense] of democracy?"

Speaking for opponents of the project, Senator Martin Dies objected to using public money for political purposes:

"Do you not also think that since the Federal Theater Project is an agency of the government and that all of our people support it through their tax money, . . . that no play should ever be produced which undertakes to portray the interests of one class [workers] to the disadvantage of another class [the wealthy]?"

Should government support the arts? That issue is as hotly debated today as it was during WPA times.

The Wagner Act In July 1935 Congress passed the National Labor Relations Act. Known as the Wagner Act—after Senator Robert F. Wagner, who introduced it—it strengthened the power of labor unions.

The Wagner Act helped workers by outlawing unfair practices. Employers could no longer refuse to bargain with union representatives or prevent workers from joining unions. The act set up the National Labor Relations Board (NLRB) to oversee union elections and collective bargaining.

Social Security Probably the hardest battle of the Second New Deal was fought over the Social Security Act. Many people opposed such a plan because of its costs to business.

Roosevelt wanted everyone to be included, however. "I see no reason why every child, from the day he is born, shouldn't be a member of the social security system," he told Frances Perkins, Secretary of Labor and the first woman ever appointed to a President's cabinet.

Perkins knew that many people were against such a sweeping bill. In 1935 she drew up the first Social Security Act. The plan was a form of insurance. Employers and workers would pay taxes to create funds to cover unemployment benefits, old-age pensions, programs for the blind, and benefits for children of insured workers who died.

The bill covered only about half the work force. Farm and domestic workers were left out. Despite these limits, however, it gave millions of workers a sense of security.

Influencing the Court

Even as he was expanding the Second New Deal, Roosevelt worried about what the Supreme Court might do. In 1937 he introduced a plan that would let him add as many as six justices to the Court. That way he could create a Court sympathetic to his views.

Link to the Present

Social Security in your life You may think Social Security has no relevance to your life yet. However, you already have a Social Security number (SSN) if you are listed as a dependent on someone else's income-tax return. When you have a job, your employer will deduct a Federal Insurance Contribution Act (FICA) tax from your paycheck, match that amount, and send the money to the government to help pay for Social Security.

During your lifetime, the Internal Revenue Service and Social Security Administration will use your SSN to keep track of you. You will use your SSN when you open a savings account or apply for a credit card. Your SSN may serve as your driver's license number. No matter whether you move, get married, change careers, or change your name, your SSN will never change.

Presidents had changed the number of justices before, but members of Congress were outraged that Roosevelt would so openly try to force his will on another branch of government. Bitter debate followed, and in the end Congress rejected the plan.

Roosevelt Supporters

Roosevelt had said that he wanted "to improve the lot of the men and women whose voices have not always been heard." His determination to broaden the New Deal won him many supporters.

On April 9, 1939, 75,000 people gathered at the Lincoln Memorial to hear Marian Anderson sing.

African Americans and the New Deal The Roosevelts also gained support from African Americans, who left "the party of Lincoln" and flocked to the Democratic Party. Roosevelt was not eager to challenge the powerful white southerners who dominated the Democratic Party in Congress. Yet under pressure from black leaders and from his wife, he moved quietly on behalf of African Americans.

In 1937, for example, Roosevelt appointed the first black federal judge, William Hastie. He also listened to a group of African American advisors, who spoke out against discrimination in New Deal programs.

One of Roosevelt's most influential African American advisors was Mary McLeod Bethune. As director of the Division of Negro Affairs in the National Youth Administration, she distributed funds to schools and training centers for African Americans. "Mrs. Bethune is a great woman," said the President. "She always comes here on behalf of others."

Eleanor Roosevelt set a powerful example in fighting racial prejudice. She made a point of ignoring rules of racial segregation. No African American leader had been invited to the White House during Hoover's term. In contrast, Mrs. Roosevelt arranged for Walter White of the NAACP to meet with President Roosevelt.

In 1939, Mrs. Roosevelt dropped her membership in the Daughters of the American Revolution because that organization refused to allow famed opera singer Marian Anderson to perform in its concert hall in Washington, D.C. Mrs. Roosevelt arranged for Anderson to sing instead at the Lincoln Memorial.

Women and the New Deal The Depression years were hard on working women. With jobs scarce, employers were likely to fire women and hire men in their place. Married women were in the greatest danger. Most states passed laws that barred them from government jobs. When the federal government was ordered not to hire more than one member of a family, it was the wives who usually gave up their jobs.

Throughout the 1930s Eleanor Roosevelt worked to improve opportunities for women. She and Mary Dewson, the head of the women's division of the Democratic Party, pressed hard for the appointment of women such as Frances Perkins to government posts.

When Mrs. Roosevelt learned that the CCC only employed young men, she encouraged her husband to establish the National Youth Administration to help both girls and boys. These efforts paid off in greater support by women for the President and the Democratic Party.

A New Deal for Indians Native Americans were also won over to the Democratic Party by New Deal policies. The poverty that afflicted other rural people hit Indians very hard. To help them fight the Depression, Roosevelt appointed John Collier to head Indian affairs.

Collier had long crusaded for Indian self-determination. In 1934 he championed through Congress the Indian Reorganization Act, which overturned the Dawes Act (page 569). The new law returned reservation lands to ownership by tribes instead of individuals. It gave tribes the right to form corporations and governments. It also guaranteed Indian women the right to vote in tribal elections.

Election of 1936

By 1936 Roosevelt had widespread support. The Democrats happily nominated him and Vice-President John Nance Garner to run again in 1936. Roosevelt vowed to continue the New Deal: "We are waging a great and successful war . . . for the survival of democracy."

The growing power of government and labor under the New Deal led Republicans to attack Roosevelt bitterly. They were worried by his popularity, though. They nominated Alfred M. Landon of Kansas. They hoped that his moderate views would attract New Deal supporters. Meanwhile, followers of Long, Townsend, and Coughlin formed their own party—the Union Party.

Roosevelt won 61 percent of the popular vote—an even greater victory than he had won in 1932. He had the electoral votes of every state except Maine and Vermont.

Dust Bowl

In the midst of hard times, the weather turned exceptionally bad. Floods, windstorms,

 Link to Art

Years of Dust (1936) Ben Shahn created this poster for the Resettlement Administration, later called the Farm Security Administration (FSA). This agency bought especially poor farms and helped the farmers start over on better land. From 1930 to 1946 Shahn worked for several government agencies, including the Federal Arts Project of the WPA. There, his first job was assisting famed Mexican muralist Diego Rivera. Shahn went on to create many murals and posters for the WPA and to photograph rural scenes for the FSA. **Discuss** Posters use art to get a message across. Why are pictures and the artistic arrangement of letters sometimes more effective than ordinary printed material for that purpose?

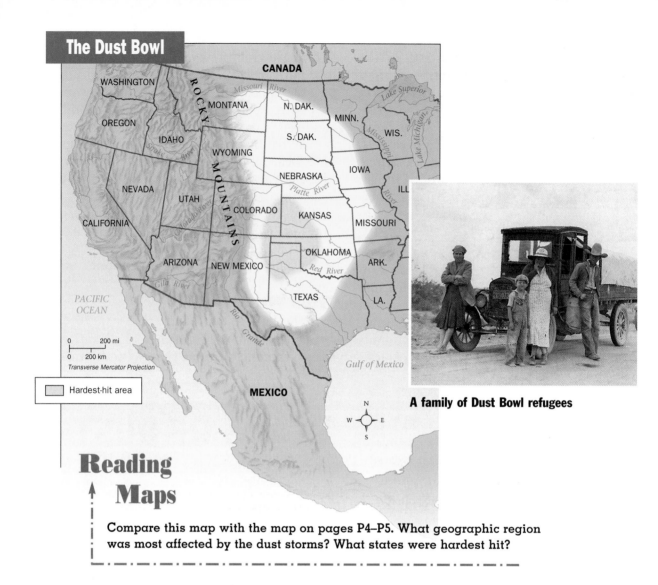

The Dust Bowl

CANADA

WASHINGTON
MONTANA
N. DAK.
MINN.
Lake Superior
OREGON
IDAHO
S. DAK.
WIS.
Lake Michigan
WYOMING
NEBRASKA
IOWA
NEVADA
UTAH
COLORADO
KANSAS
MISSOURI
ILL
CALIFORNIA
ARIZONA
NEW MEXICO
OKLAHOMA
ARK.
TEXAS
LA.
PACIFIC
OCEAN
ROCKY MOUNTAINS
Missouri River
Mississippi River
Platte River
Colorado River
Snake River
Gila River
Red River
Rio Grande

0   200 mi
0   200 km
Transverse Mercator Projection

☐ Hardest-hit area

MEXICO

Gulf of Mexico

N W E S

A family of Dust Bowl refugees

Reading
Maps

Compare this map with the map on pages P4–P5. What geographic region was most affected by the dust storms? What states were hardest hit?

and blizzards destroyed property and lives. Drought added to the toll. Corn withered on the stalk, and grassfires raced across the Great Plains.

Then came the dust. Years of overgrazing and overplowing had killed off the grass that held plains soil. Windstorms carried the dry, dead earth into the sky. One of the first storms struck South Dakota in November 1933. The sky was dark at noon, and people gagged on the dirt.

The drought continued. Without grass and water, cattle died, their lungs full of dust. In May 1934, 12 million pounds of plains soil fell on Chicago. Kansas and Nebraska soil rained down on Boston, New York City, and Washington, D.C., and onto ships hundreds of miles out in the Atlantic.

Throughout the 1930s, the windstorms carried away the hopes of thousands of farmers along with the topsoil necessary for their crops. One Kansas woman described the storms:

"When we opened the door, swirling whirlwinds of soil beat against us unmercifully. The dust seeped into cupboards and closets. It turned everyone's hair gray and stiff. We ground dirt between our teeth.**"**

Farm families piled their belongings onto old trucks, turned their backs on the area they called "the Dust Bowl," and drove off, never to return. Most headed west, especially to California. Many Dust Bowl refugees were taunted with the name "Okies," because so many came from Oklahoma. Without money, they wandered the highways seeking work harvesting crops.

With more farmworkers than jobs in the West and Southwest, competition was keen. One result was that thousands of Mexican citizens, welcomed as farmworkers when the economy boomed in the 1920s, were forced to return to Mexico in the 1930s.

The dust storms could be blamed on drought, but careless farming and ranching practices had played a part. The Dust Bowl tragedy led the federal government to look at farming methods closely. Roosevelt ordered the CCC to plant a belt of trees from Mexico to Canada to break the wind. Congress passed the Taylor Grazing Act in 1934 to regulate grazing on federal lands.

Sit-Down Strikes

During Roosevelt's second term in office, labor continued to gain strength. Protected by the Wagner Act, unions were on the rise.

In 1936 the United Auto Workers demanded that automakers recognize their union. The union was part of a group of industrial unions that were in the process of splitting off from the American Federation of Labor (AFL). The group—the Congress of Industrial Organizations (CIO)—became independent of the AFL in 1938.

When General Motors announced that it would not negotiate with a union, the workers of Chevrolet No. 1 Factory in Flint,

Michigan, decided to act. They sat down at their posts and refused to move until General Motors accepted their union.

Workers in other plants quickly did the same. The autoworkers had invented a new kind of strike—the sit-down strike. As long as they stayed where they were, automakers could not get factories running again.

The strike began late in December and lasted into February. General Motors managers turned off the heat, but the workers stayed put. Friends and families slipped food and clothing past the company guards.

When negotiations stalled, Roosevelt intervened. General Motors finally agreed to recognize the union. Soon, workers in other industries were using the sit-down strike to gain recognition for their unions.

The End of the New Deal

Many thought that the nation was on the road to recovery in 1937. Congress cut back employment programs, and after years of spending more than the government took in, Roosevelt talked of balancing the budget.

Suddenly, the economy took a turn for the worse. Factories shut down once more, and workers returned to unemployment lines.

What had happened? Nobody knew for sure. Some blamed the cuts in employment programs or the costs of the new Social Security program. Roosevelt turned again to relief efforts, and after about a year the economy seemed to improve.

Nevertheless, public confidence in the New Deal began to waver. Some people still believed the government was spending too little. Others, though, heeded Republican arguments that the government should cut spending and lower taxes.

In the congressional election of 1938, Republicans gained 81 seats in the House of Representatives and 8 in the Senate. Republicans used their new power to block further

New Deal measures. Faced with growing opposition, Roosevelt put his energy into supporting existing programs instead of introducing new measures.

By the end of the 1930s, Roosevelt's attention turned to troubles in Europe and Asia. The world was being drawn into another war. No one would ever know if the New Deal had rescued the United States from the Depression, but with the outbreak of World War II, the Depression finally came to an end.

3. Section Review

1. What were the provisions of the first Social Security Act?
2. Why did many African Americans turn to the Democratic Party during the Depression?
3. How had people's actions led to the Dust Bowl? What were some of its effects?
4. Critical Thinking Give two arguments for the Wagner Act and two against it.

Why We Remember

The Depression and New Deal

When Franklin Roosevelt ran for President in the darkest days of the Great Depression, the nation's problems seemed overwhelming. Roosevelt, however, was not overwhelmed. He had been strengthened by his experience with polio. "Once I spent two years lying in bed, trying to move my big toe," he said. "That was the hardest job I ever had to do. After that, anything else was easy." In fact, ending the Depression was not easy, though. As Roosevelt himself admitted in his second inaugural address in 1937, "I see one-third of a nation ill-housed, ill-clad, ill-nourished."

Today we remember the Great Depression not only because of the suffering of that one-third of a nation—and not only because of the Roosevelts' efforts to end that suffering. We remember the Great Depression for another reason as well. It was in these dark years of hunger, homelessness, and human misery that many Americans changed their views of the role of government.

Before the Depression, most Americans probably agreed with Thomas Jefferson that the best government was that which governs least. Franklin Roosevelt, however, put forth a different view of government. In his view, one of the duties of government was "caring for those of its citizens who find themselves . . . unable to obtain even the necessities of mere existence without the aid of others." "That responsibility," Roosevelt asserted, "is recognized by every civilized nation." After the Great Depression, it was also recognized by Americans.

Geography Lab

Pacific Mountains and Valleys

Dust Bowl migrants heading west had little idea of what they would find. What they discovered in the region we call the Pacific Mountains and Valleys were scenes of stunning beauty and great variety. More importantly, they found miles and miles of some of the richest agricultural land on earth. Use the quotation and the photographs on this page to form a mental image of the Pacific Mountains and Valleys.

Cascade Mountains, Washington

Cherry orchard, Oregon

Date palms and bell peppers, California

Cesar Chavez

"When we moved to California, we would work after school. . . . 'Following the crops,' we missed much school. Trying to get enough money to stay alive the following winter, the whole family picking apricots, walnuts, prunes. We were pretty new, we had never been migratory workers."

Developing a Mental Map

Use the maps on pages P4–P5 and R4–R7 to help answer the questions.

1. Which states are partially within the Pacific Mountains and Valleys region? Which state is completely within the region?

2. Name two mountain ranges that lie in the region.

3. How do the photographs confirm what you see on the map on pages R4–R5?

4. Describe one area within the region where you would expect to find a concentration of farming, and tell why.

5. **Hands-On Geography**
Imagine that you are a member of a family that has fled the Dust Bowl. You come upon one of the scenes pictured on this page. Write a poem that describes your reaction to it.

Chapter Survey

Reviewing Vocabulary

Define the following terms.
1. durable goods
2. pension

Reviewing Main Ideas

1. Describe two problems in the economy that contributed to the Great Depression.
2. How did the Depression change Americans' lives?
3. What were the purpose and the methods of each of the following? (a) AAA (b) NRA (c) PWA (d) TVA
4. What criticisms of the New Deal did its opponents offer?
5. Name and describe two programs set up under the Second New Deal.
6. How did the Roosevelts gain the support of each group? (a) women (b) African Americans (c) Indians
7. What is a sit-down strike, how did the first such strike come about, and what were the results?

Thinking Critically

1. **Application** Why do you suppose President Roosevelt thought it so important to inspire hope and confidence in the American people?
2. **Analysis** Imagine that you are the owner of a large company in the 1930s. You claim that Roosevelt has abandoned people like you to help others who are suffering. How do you support the claim?
3. **Why We Remember: Synthesis** In what ways does the New Deal live on in the United States today?

Applying Skills

Comparing historical interpretations
Think of a controversial government program of today. Write brief "historical interpretations" that reflect two different ways the program might be viewed by historians of the future. Exchange interpretations with a classmate. Recalling page 771, write a paragraph in which you do the following:
1. Summarize the two interpretations written by your classmate.
2. Identify how the interpretations are supported.
3. Evaluate the interpretations. Are they thorough? Are they persuasive? Explain.

History Mystery

Answer the History Mystery on page 759. More than 150,000 migrants ended up on the West Coast in just a few years. With so many people seeking work, what problems were these refugees likely to have?

Writing in Your History Journal

1. **Keys to History** (a) The time line on pages 758–759 has nine Keys to History. In your journal, list each key and describe why it is important to know about. (b) Choose three events from the chapter to add to the time line. Write the events and their dates in your journal, and tell why you think each event should be added.
2. **Franklin and Eleanor Roosevelt** Reread the letter that the Chicago boy wrote to the Roosevelts in 1936 (page 763). Imagine that you are either the President or Eleanor Roosevelt. In your journal, write a reply to the boy.
3. **Citizenship** Today, as in the 1930s, Americans disagree about the best role for the First Lady. In your journal, describe what you think the First

Reviewing Geography

↑ **1.** Each letter on the map represents one of the Dust Bowl states. Write the name of each state.

2. Geographic Thinking How people view a place is influenced by their culture. The way people think about a particular environment may differ from one group to another and from one time to another. How might each of the following have described the Great Plains? a Plains Indian of the 1500s, a Spanish explorer of the 1600s, an American explorer of the 1820s, a farmer of the 1880s, a farmer of the 1930s

Lady's role should be, and why. Also tell which First Lady—past or present—has come closest to fulfilling the role as you see it. Explain your answer.

Alternative Assessment

Creating a cause-effect graphic organizer You have been asked to teach a group of younger students about the 1930s. You decide that the best way is to use a graphic organizer. A graphic organizer is made up of symbols such as circles, squares, graphs, and arrows, as well as pictures and words. The elements are arranged to show relationships.

With several classmates, create a graphic organizer showing causes and effects involved in the Great Depression and the New Deal.

❶ Brainstorm events and situations relating to the Great Depression and New Deal. Write each event or situation on a note card as it is mentioned.

❷ Create a "rough draft" of your graphic organizer by arranging the note cards on mural paper, bulletin board, or other surface. Your arrangement should show some or all or the following kinds of cause-effect relationships:

• single cause/single effect
• multiple causes/single effect
• single cause/multiple effects
• chain reaction—one or more causes lead to one or more effects, which in turn cause one or more effects, and so on

❸ Create a "final draft" of your graphic organizer. You might rewrite the note-card items in large, neat print; use lengths of yarn or draw arrows to show relationships; and include artwork.

Your work will be evaluated on the following criteria:
• it presents cause-effect relationships among events and situations of the 1930s thoroughly and accurately
• it is clear and easy to follow
• it has visual appeal

Chapter 28

World War II

Sections

Keys to History

1933
January
Hitler becomes
chancellor
of Germany

1938
November
Crystal Night attack
on Jews in Germany

1933

1938

World

Link

Looking Back

Germany signs Treaty
of Versailles
1919

Lincoln Brigade enters
the Spanish Civil War
1937

HISTORY *Mystery*

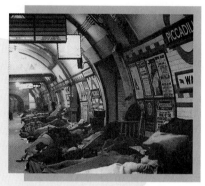

In 1940 and 1941 thousands of people slept in the subways of London. Who were these people and why were they sleeping there instead of in their homes?

1942
February
Japanese American internment begins

General Dwight D. Eisenhower

1944
June
D-Day

1945
August
U.S. drops atomic bombs on Hiroshima and Nagasaki

1945
May
V-E day

1941
December
Pearl Harbor

1941   *1943*   *1945*

Looking Ahead

United States and Soviet Union sign first SALT agreement to control arms race

1972

● **783**

Beginning the Story with

Benjamin O. Davis, Jr.

In 1944, Brigadier General Benjamin O. Davis, Sr., a career soldier who had joined the U.S. Army in 1899, pinned the Distinguished Flying Cross on his son. For both father and son, it was a proud and emotional moment.

Benjamin O. Davis, Jr., had known he wanted to fly since he was 13 years old. That year his father took him to see barnstormers—pilots who thrilled audiences with breathtaking aerial stunts. To Benjamin's surprise, his father bought him a ride. "I cannot explain my father's motives in buying me an airplane ride," Benjamin later wrote. "He was not a frivolous spender, and $5 was a considerable sum in 1926. I can only guess that he was looking far into the future . . . and realized . . . that I would benefit from the experience."

It was a wonderful ambition, but not for an African American at that time. "The harsh reality was," Benjamin soon realized, "that there was no way for a black man to become a professional pilot." His only hope, Benjamin decided, was to follow his father into the army and apply for pilot training. The first step was to win an appointment to the elite United States Military Academy at West Point.

The "Silencing"

Weeks after arriving at West Point in 1932, Benjamin realized that being the only African American at West Point would be a severe test of his character and courage.

❝Certain cadets . . . enforce[d] an old West Point tradition—'silencing.' . . . I was to be silenced solely because cadets did not want blacks at West Point. . . . What they did not realize was that I was stubborn enough to put up with their treatment to reach the goal I had come to attain.❞

Aviation cadets study a map at the Tuskegee Army Air Field training school in Tuskegee, Alabama. In March 1942 the first class of African American pilots completed their training. Benjamin Davis was one of the five graduates.

For the next four years, Davis lived in silence. He bunked alone in a big room designed for two. He ate meals, trained, and went to classes without speaking to another cadet.

In 1936, Davis faced graduation with bittersweet feelings. "I was extremely proud that I had withstood the forces that opposed me so actively . . . and that I would be the first black in the 20th century to graduate from West Point." However, his application to become a pilot was turned down. Disappointed, Davis accepted a position as an officer in the infantry.

The "Experiment"

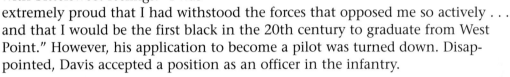

While Davis was beginning his military career, African American leaders were pressuring President Roosevelt to open up opportunities for African Americans in the armed forces. In 1941, with war on the horizon, the army agreed to an "experiment." It set up a flight-training school at Tuskegee Army Air Field (TAAF) in Alabama, with the goal of creating a black flying unit. In the first group of 13 African American volunteers, 5 completed the rigorous training. One was Benjamin Davis.

Even after enough pilots had been trained to form the 99th Fighter Squadron, the Tuskegee airmen were passed over for combat assignments until the day Eleanor Roosevelt visited the base in 1943. Against the advice of her staff, the First Lady took a test flight with one of the black airmen. After this well-publicized vote of confidence, the 99th, under the command of Lieutenant Colonel Benjamin Davis, was ordered into combat in North Africa. "As we said our goodbyes," wrote Davis,

❝we pushed far back and away the ugliness that we had endured. . . . We did not regret leaving TAAF. We knew that there were many decent human beings elsewhere in the world, and we looked forward to associating with them.❞

Hands-On → *HISTORY*

Activity

Benjamin Davis endured the years of "silencing" at West Point because his dream of graduating was so important to him. Think about an important dream of yours. It could involve creating something, winning a competition, or traveling somewhere. Write about this dream and describe some of the hardships or obstacles you might have to overcome to make it come true.

1. Threats to World Peace

Reading Guide

New Terms **arms race, isolationism, dictator, fascism, totalitarian state, appeasement**

Section Focus **How Japanese expansionism and the rise of fascist dictatorships threatened world peace**

1. How did the United States try to maintain world peace?
2. What events in Japan, Italy, and Germany threatened world peace?
3. How did Americans differ in their response to the rise of fascism?

When Benjamin Davis entered West Point in 1932, the horrors of World War I were still fresh in everyone's memory. In spite of Woodrow Wilson's hopes, however, it had not been a "war to end all wars." In fact, no sooner had the peace treaties been signed than an **arms race**—a competition between countries for more and better weapons— began to sow the seeds of future conflict.

Efforts to Keep Peace

President Warren Harding, who followed Wilson, worked to end the arms race. In 1921 he invited delegates from Europe and Japan to the Washington Naval Conference. There they agreed to limit the production of warships. They also agreed not to attack one another's possessions in the Pacific and to respect China's independence.

Another treaty designed to maintain peace was the 1928 Kellogg-Briand Pact. In this treaty 62 nations agreed to stay out of war except in cases of self-defense. Unfortunately, this treaty was impossible to enforce. As one senator said, it was a "worthless, but perfectly harmless treaty."

The United States also tried to stay out of war by adopting a policy of **isolationism**, which means staying out of foreign affairs.

With the onset of the Depression, Americans felt that the government should work on problems at home instead of abroad.

A Good Neighbor

The exception to isolationist policy was Latin America. There the United States had continued to intervene to protect American business interests. President Hoover took a new approach, however, when he announced that the United States wanted to be "a good neighbor." President Roosevelt continued Hoover's Good Neighbor policy. In 1934 he called home the last American troops from Latin American soil.

The Rise of Dictators

The efforts to promote peace failed in Japan, Italy, and Germany. These countries continued to build up armies and weapons, even though all three had taken part in the Washington Naval Conference.

Japan Japan's goal was expansion. An island nation, it needed space for its growing population. It also needed raw materials— coal, oil, rubber—for its booming industries. In 1931 Japan's military leaders, who had taken control of the government, invaded Manchuria in northern China. During the next six years, Japanese armies continued to move through China as well as other parts of the Pacific in order to develop industries.

Italy Even more threatening were events in Europe. Weakened by strikes and riots after World War I, Italy fell under the influence of a dictator named Benito Mussolini. A **dictator** is a person with complete control of a government.

Mussolini organized a government based on fascism. **Fascism** is a political system based on racism and nationalism and ruled by a dictator and a single political party. In 1922 Mussolini seized control of Italy.

Germany In Germany, too, hard times led to fascism. Here the guiding hand belonged to another dictator named Adolf Hitler. Hitler led the National Socialist German Workers' Party—the Nazis—to power by promising Germans that he could rebuild their fallen country. By 1933 the Nazis were the largest party in Germany, and Germany's president made Hitler chancellor.

In 1934, when the president died, Hitler took control. He turned Germany into a **totalitarian state,** a government with total control over the lives of its citizens. Under Hitler, the Nazis controlled schools, newspapers, and radio stations. No one was allowed to criticize the government. Hitler began his reign by building up his armed forces.

Hitler united Germans by telling them that they belonged to a "master race." He played on anti-Semitic feelings by saying that Jews were the Germans' main enemy. Beginning in 1935 Hitler passed laws that stripped Jews of their citizenship, barred them from many types of work, and forbade them from using public facilities. To set them apart, Hitler forced every Jew to wear a yellow Star of David.

Tens of thousands of Jews fled Nazi Germany during this period. In the fall of 1938, though, new German laws made it almost impossible for them to leave. Hitler's troops began rounding up Jews and sending them to concentration camps to work as slave laborers.

On November 9–10, 1938, the Nazis carried out an organized attack on Jews throughout

Nazi storm troopers in Warsaw, Poland, herd a group of terrified Jewish citizens from their homes. Photographs such as this one were later used in court as evidence of Nazi brutality and terrorism.

Hitler Youth, Moravia (1938) In World War II new magazines, such as *Look* and *LIFE*, sent photographers to Europe and the Pacific to document the events of the war. The work of these photographers, who called themselves photojournalists, shaped how Americans viewed the war. Margaret Bourke-White, a talented photojournalist, took some of the war's most memorable pictures. In the photograph at right, taken in Czechoslovakia, she captured German boys training to be Nazi storm troopers. **Discuss** What does this image tell you about Hitler's goals for Germany?

Germany. This tragic event is called Crystal Night for the shattered windows of more than 200 synagogues and 7,000 shops and homes. Nearly a hundred Jews were killed and thousands sent to work camps.

The Axis powers In 1936 Germany and Italy formed an alliance. Mussolini described the ties between their capitals, Rome and Berlin, as the "axis" around which Europe would revolve. The alliance became known as the Axis powers. In September 1940 Japan joined the Axis. The three countries agreed to support each other if the United States attacked any one of them.

Roosevelt and Isolationism

Many Americans were worried by the actions of Japan, Germany, and Italy. However, many were still disillusioned by the results of World War I. As the celebrated hero Alvin York said, "I can't see we did any good. There's as much trouble now as there was then, when we went over there."

It was clear to Roosevelt and to Congress that most Americans did not wish to be involved in Europe or Asia. To ensure that the United States maintained its isolationism, Congress passed a series of neutrality acts. The first act, passed in 1935, banned the sale of weapons to any country engaged in war. Its purpose was to discourage the United States from taking sides in a conflict.

The strength of isolationist feeling presented President Roosevelt with a challenge. He saw another world war coming, yet he feared losing public support if he began to build up the nation's military forces.

The Axis powers did not give Roosevelt much time. By early 1936, Italy had invaded the African nation of Ethiopia, and German armed forces were threatening France.

The Spanish Civil War

Germany and Italy followed these successes by intervening in a civil war that broke out in Spain in 1936. Mussolini and Hitler supported Francisco Franco, a fascist determined to overthrow the democratic government of the Spanish Republic.

Many European leaders realized that the Spanish Civil War was a dress rehearsal for a coming world war, but they did not want to get involved. Finally Russia (renamed the Soviet Union by the Bolsheviks in 1922) sent supplies to the anti-Franco forces. Then 3,000 American volunteers formed the Abraham Lincoln Brigade to help fight Franco. It was a lost cause, however. In 1939 a victorious Franco set up a fascist dictatorship in Spain.

The Third Reich

Meanwhile, Hitler was proceeding with his plan to build a great German empire that he called the Third Reich. One of his goals was to rule over all German-speaking people. In March 1938 he annexed Austria. Then he demanded that Czechoslovakia give him the Sudetenland, home to some 3 million people of German ancestry.

Hoping to avoid war, and willing to believe that Hitler would soon be satisfied, Great Britain and France signed the fateful Munich Agreement in the fall of 1938. The agreement forced the Czech government to surrender the Sudetenland to Germany. In return, Hitler promised to make no more territorial demands on Europe.

Many felt that **appeasement**—giving in to another nation's demands just to keep peace—was cowardly. Rising in Parliament, Winston Churchill, the future British prime minister, declared:

" All is over. Silent, mournful, abandoned, broken Czechoslovakia recedes into the darkness. "

World Link

The Abraham Lincoln Brigade They were writers, teachers, students, farmhands, mechanics, and clerks. They included African Americans, American Indians, and Americans of various European ancestries. They were the men and women volunteers of the Abraham Lincoln Brigade. They all fought in the Spanish Civil War because they believed that isolationism was the wrong response to fascism.

These idealistic Americans bought their own tents, canteens, and mess kits from army surplus stores before they sailed for Europe. The first group arrived in Spain in January 1937. Over the next 21 months, nearly one-third of "the Lincolns" lost their lives fighting for the doomed Republican, or Loyalist, cause. As the surviving Lincolns prepared to leave Spain, a grateful Loyalist leader told them, "You can go proudly. You are history. You are legend."

1. Section Review

1. Define **arms race, isolationism, dictator, fascism, totalitarian state,** and **appeasement.**

2. What are three ways the United States tried to avoid getting involved in the war?

3. How did Hitler gain power and support?

4. Critical Thinking Could the United States have prevented the rise of fascism in Europe? Explain your answer.

2. World War II Begins

Reading Guide

Section Focus **Events that led to the United States entering the war**

1. Why was Germany successful in the early years of the war?
2. How did the United States aid Great Britain?
3. What events led to the bombing of Pearl Harbor?

Churchill's prediction was correct. In the spring of 1939, Hitler's troops took over the entire Czech nation. Then Hitler signed a peace treaty with Joseph Stalin, the Soviet leader. In truth, their treaty was mainly a secret agreement to invade Poland and divide it between them.

On September 1, 1939, Hitler shocked the world by invading Poland. The invasion was such a surprise and so powerful that it was known as a *blitzkrieg*, or lightning war. Realizing at last that the appeasement policy had failed, Great Britain and France declared war on Germany two days later. Within two weeks, the Soviet Union had struck Poland from the east. World War II had begun.

German Triumphs

At first, Germany seemed invincible. By the end of September, with all Polish resistance crushed, Hitler shifted his attention to western Europe.

In April 1940 German armies captured Denmark and Norway. A month later German armored vehicles sliced through the Netherlands and Belgium and swept into France. Within days German troops reached the English Channel, trapping more than 340,000 French, British, and Belgian soldiers in the French port city of Dunkirk.

Although heroic efforts by the British rescued some 338,000 of the stranded soldiers, it was a crushing defeat for the Allies. France surrendered on June 22, 1940, and the German flag fluttered above Paris.

The Battle of Britain

Now Great Britain was fighting Germany alone. In 1940 Hitler launched a series of air attacks in preparation for an invasion. This "blitz" left airfields, ports, and cities in smoldering ruins. Few thought the island nation stood a chance. British prime minister Winston Churchill, though, was confident. Speaking for the British people, he promised:

> **"**We shall fight on the beaches, we shall fight in the fields and in the streets, we shall never surrender.**"**

Indeed, the British spirit never broke. City children were sent to live in the country. By night Londoners used subway stations as air-raid shelters. By day they cleared the wreckage, buried the dead, and tried to carry on. It was, as Churchill rightly said, their "finest hour."

The Royal Air Force was badly outnumbered by the German Luftwaffe, but the British had developed radar, which helped them locate and shoot down German planes. By the spring of 1940, Britain had used up almost all its resources fighting off the German attacks. Despite months of bombing, though, Hitler still had not been able to clear the English Channel for an invasion.

Surveying a bombed building outside London, Winston Churchill shook his fist and shouted, "We shall let them have it back!" Churchill's courage inspired the British people. Hitler had boasted that his troops would take over London within three months, yet by late 1940 Germany had given up its plans to invade Britain.

Aid for Britain

Americans were shocked and outraged by Germany's attacks on England. At this point, wrote one editor, "What the majority of the American people want is to be as unneutral as possible without getting into war."

Roosevelt felt obliged to help England. At his request, in 1939 Congress passed another neutrality act. This act allowed Americans to sell weapons to countries at war. The United States Navy immediately started selling its older planes to Britain.

Roosevelt also knew that the time had come to begin preparing for war. At his urging, Congress voted to expand and modernize the nation's armed forces. In September 1940 Congress passed the first peacetime draft in American history. By October it had voted $17 billion for defense spending. This was equal to American military spending in all of World War I.

In answer to isolationist critics, Roosevelt claimed that aid to Britain and stronger defenses would help keep the United States out of the war. He called on Americans to produce more war goods "to keep war away

Point of View

Should the United States have aided Great Britain?

Defending itself against Germany was crushing Britain. It could no longer afford to buy or make ships and weapons. At his wit's end, Winston Churchill appealed to President Roosevelt "to supply the additional shipping capacity so urgently needed, as well as the crucial weapons of war."

Roosevelt wanted to help. He thought of a way to provide war supplies to Britain without asking for payment. The United States would lend arms and supplies to the British, who would return or replace them after the war. At a press conference in December, 1940 he explained his proposal, which he called "Lend-Lease," in simple, everyday terms:

"Suppose my neighbor's home catches on fire. If he can take my garden hose and connect it up with his hydrant, I may help to put out his fire. Now I don't say to him, 'Neighbor, my garden hose cost me $15.' I don't want $15—I want my garden hose back after the fire is over."

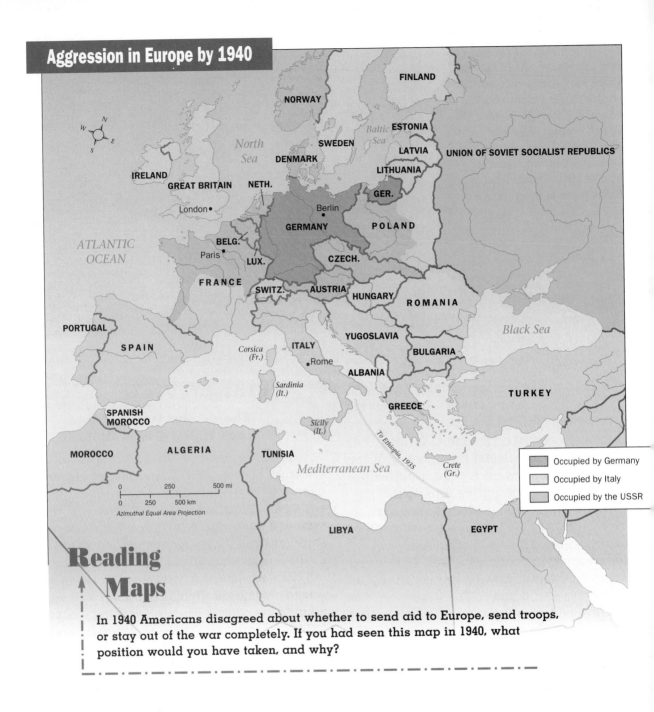

Aggression in Europe by 1940

FINLAND

NORWAY

ESTONIA

Baltic Sea

SWEDEN

LATVIA

North Sea

DENMARK

LITHUANIA

UNION OF SOVIET SOCIALIST REPUBLICS

IRELAND

GREAT BRITAIN

NETH.

GER.

London •

Berlin •

GERMANY

POLAND

ATLANTIC OCEAN

BELG.

Paris •

LUX.

CZECH.

FRANCE

SWITZ.

AUSTRIA

HUNGARY

ROMANIA

Black Sea

PORTUGAL

SPAIN

Corsica (Fr.)

ITALY

• Rome

YUGOSLAVIA

BULGARIA

ALBANIA

Sardinia (It.)

TURKEY

SPANISH MOROCCO

Sicily (It.)

GREECE

To Ethiopia, 1935

Crete (Gr.)

MOROCCO

ALGERIA

TUNISIA

Mediterranean Sea

0   250   500 mi
0   250   500 km
Azimuthal Equal Area Projection

LIBYA

EGYPT

■ Occupied by Germany
■ Occupied by Italy
■ Occupied by the USSR

Reading Maps

In 1940 Americans disagreed about whether to send aid to Europe, send troops, or stay out of the war completely. If you had seen this map in 1940, what position would you have taken, and why?

Isolationists feared that Roosevelt's scheme would drag the United States into the war. If that happened, they argued, we would need those supplies. One senator opposed Lend-Lease with this example: "Lending war equipment is a good deal like lending chewing gum. You don't want it back."

In spite of isolationist opposition, the Lend-Lease bill passed. Soon the United States was sending supplies to Britain.

When Roosevelt ran for an unprecedented third term in 1940, he promised voters, "Your boys are not going to be sent into any foreign wars." He won re-election easily.

The Atlantic Charter

By now, most Americans were preparing themselves mentally for war. This time, when asked his opinion, Alvin York said, "Hitler and Mussolini jes' need a good whuppin', an' it looks like Uncle Sam is gonna have to do it."

In early 1941 military cooperation between Britain and the United States began. The United States Navy sent ships far into the North Atlantic to report to the British on the presence of German U-boats. In April, American troops occupied Greenland and soon replaced British soldiers in Iceland.

In August 1941 Churchill and Roosevelt met to draw up a statement of Allied goals called the Atlantic Charter. They pledged not to seek territory but to support the right of all peoples to choose their own governments and to enjoy the "Four Freedoms"—freedom of speech, freedom of religion, freedom from want, and freedom from fear.

Japan in Southeast Asia

Meanwhile, Japan's leaders were becoming much more aggressive. They seized resource-rich French Indochina and laid plans to conquer the rest of Southeast Asia. To "slow Japan up," Roosevelt declared an embargo on exports to Japan. He also fortified bases in Guam and the Philippines and increased aid to China.

Relations between Japan and the United States became increasingly strained. Japan demanded that the United States cut off aid to China and end the embargo. The United States asked Japan to leave the Axis powers and to withdraw from China and French Indochina. Neither side would give in.

The Japanese made one last offer on November 20. The United States made a counteroffer on November 26. Neither nation agreed to the other's terms. Meanwhile, a Japanese fleet was steaming secretly toward Hawaii.

The battleships *West Virginia* and *Tennessee* were set aflame in the Japanese attack on Pearl Harbor.

Pearl Harbor

President Roosevelt called December 7, 1941, a "day that shall live in infamy." That morning some 360 Japanese bombers filled the sky in a surprise attack on Pearl Harbor, Hawaii. The attack killed 2,403 American military personnel and civilians and sank several American battleships and destroyers. The next day Congress declared that a state of war existed with Japan.

On December 11 Germany and Italy, the other Axis powers, declared war on the United States. What had started in Poland on September 1, 1939, had become a global war.

2. Section Review

1. What were the main reasons for Germany's early military successes?
2. Summarize the arguments for and against Roosevelt's Lend-Lease proposal.
3. Critical Thinking Do you think the United States should have imposed its embargo on Japan? Why or why not?

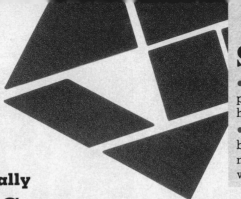

Skill Lab

Skill Tips

• Questions of "why" and "how" pose the greatest challenges to historians.

• Information gaps often occur because witnesses have died, no written records were kept, or written records were lost.

Thinking Critically

Identifying Gaps in Information

On the night of December 7, 1941, a grim President Roosevelt invited congressional leaders to the White House. After hearing about the attack on Pearl Harbor, Senator Tom Connally of Texas exploded. "How did it happen that our warships were caught like tame ducks?" he shouted. "Where were our patrols? They knew these negotiations were going on." The President replied, "I don't know, Tom. I just don't know."

Question to Investigate

Why was the United States unprepared for an attack on Pearl Harbor?

Procedure

Historians often lack complete information. Try identifying gaps in information about events before the Pearl Harbor attack.

1 Identify the information you seek.
a. Why might you want to learn who knew what about the Japanese plans?
b. Tell what else might be useful to learn.

2 Determine what information you have.
a. Make a chart with the headings *What Was Known About Japanese Plans* and *Who Knew*.
b. Fill in the chart with information you know, based on reading **A** through **D**.

3 Identify gaps in the information.
a. List the information you are missing.
b. Name two types of sources you might check to try to find that information.
c. Can the Question to Investigate ever be answered? Explain.

Sources to Use

A In January 1941 Ambassador to Japan Joseph Grew warned: "There is a lot of talk around town to the effect that the Japanese, in case of a break with the United States, are planning to go all out in a surprise mass attack on Pearl Harbor."

B "The island of Oahu, due to its fortifications, its garrison and its physical characteristics, is believed to be the strongest in the world. . . . A major attack . . . is considered impracticable."
Army Chief of Staff George Marshall in a May 1941 memo to President Roosevelt

C On November 27, 1941, the War Department sent a warning to commanders in Hawaii that a Japanese attack was expected within days, probably against the Philippines or another target in Southeast Asia. It did not mention Pearl Harbor.

D Three days before the attack, American military officials picked up a coded radio broadcast to Japanese embassies: "Higashi no kazeme" (East winds, rain). It meant that Japan was going to break diplomatic relations with the United States. Hawaii was not informed.

3. The Early War Effort

Reading Guide

New Term **rationing**

Section Focus **Early struggles and successes on the home front and in the Pacific**

1. How did Americans at home contribute to the war effort?
2. Why did Roosevelt order the internment of Japanese Americans?
3. Why was the Battle of Midway a turning point in the war?

The war affected every American family. In a fireside chat shortly after Pearl Harbor, President Roosevelt put it bluntly:

"We are now in this war. We are all in it—all the way. Every single man, woman, and child is a partner."

Rationing and Producing

To provide American and Allied forces with food, clothing, and war equipment, everyone had an important part to play. One way to conserve resources was by **rationing**—limiting the amount of scarce goods people could buy. Basic foods such as butter, sugar, coffee, and meat were rationed. So were crucial items such as shoes and gasoline. Rationing made life on the home front inconvenient, but most people were glad to help.

The War Production Board To help American industry do its part in the war effort, Roosevelt set up the War Production Board (WPB). The WPB's job was to supervise the changeover from producing goods for peacetime use to producing war materials such as planes, ships, and tanks. The WPB also set high goals for production. Under its guidance, output nearly doubled.

In 1942 alone the WPB directed the spending of $47 billion. Production of airplanes increased from 19,000 a year in 1941 to 95,000 in 1944. Ship tonnage rose from 237,000 in 1939 to 10 million in 1943. The industrialist Henry J. Kaiser, who had never built a ship before, cut the average time it took to build a "Liberty" ship from 355 days in 1941 to 56 days at the end of 1942.

After Mexico declared war on the Axis in 1942, the Mexican government sent 375,000 temporary farm workers to the United States to help grow and harvest crops. Farm production increased by 25 percent.

Workers on the Move

The increase in production meant more jobs—a big change from the Great Depression. By 1943 unemployment had all but disappeared and workers enjoyed real benefits: good wages, paid vacations, extra pay for overtime work, and—in some cases—paid health insurance.

People migrated from rural to urban areas for better jobs. New defense industries, especially in the North and West, attracted thousands of workers. California's population, for example, more than doubled in the 1940s. As men left for the military, more and more women stepped into the jobs they left behind.

Resentment of newcomers This huge migration put great strains on American society. Longtime residents complained that newcomers competed for scarce housing. In many cities the resentment of newcomers—especially those of different races or religious backgrounds—led to racism and violence. In 1943 alone there were more than 200 incidents of racial violence.

Zoot suit riots In Los Angeles, men wearing "zoot suits," a popular Mexican American clothing style, were attacked on the streets. The media blamed the "zoot suit riots" on Mexican Americans. However, Eleanor Roosevelt noted in her newspaper column that the violence was an example of "longstanding discrimination against the Mexicans in the Southwest."

Challenging discrimination In 1941 A. Philip Randolph called for a march on Washington to protest the exclusion of African Americans from defense industries. To head off the march, Roosevelt agreed to issue Executive Order 8802, banning discrimination in defense industries and government jobs. To enforce the order, he set up the Fair Employment Practices Committee (FEPC) to investigate charges of discrimination.

The FEPC—and the growing need for workers—opened many jobs that had previously been closed by racism. By the end of 1944, some 2 million African Americans were working in war plants.

Diversity in the Military

As in World War I, Americans of all backgrounds joined the armed services. Half a million Hispanics served, as did 25,000 American Indians and 900,000 African Americans. In 1940 Congress passed a bill prohibiting discrimination in the draft on the basis of race or color.

Despite this bill, nonwhites still faced racial prejudice in the military. For example, although African Americans enlisted in all branches of the armed forces, most of them, like the pilots who trained and fought with Benjamin Davis, had to serve in all-black units. Most, too, still served in support positions rather than on the battlefield.

Navajo code talkers
One group of American Indians who gained fame in the armed forces were the 420 Navajo marine "code talkers." They helped maintain the security of communications during the war by sending orders in the Navajo language—a "code" that the enemy never broke.

Women in the military
Women were not drafted, but 350,000 volunteered for military service. These women worked mostly as clerks or administrators, but some were map makers, electricians,

Female workers, like these welders, moved into jobs traditionally held by men. By the end of the war, a third of the work force were women.

Hands-On

Creating your own code Specialists on each side of the war tried to "break" (decipher) one another's codes. Often they succeeded. However, the Japanese never broke the code used by the Navajo code talkers in the Pacific.

The Navajo code was so successful because at the time, the language had no written alphabet. Also, a word can have more than one meaning depending on the speaker's tone. The language is so complex and so unlike most European and Asian languages that in the 1940s only 28 non-Navajos understood it.

A Navajo code talker

Activity With four classmates, develop a spoken code to baffle your fellow students.

1 Discuss familiar codes like "pig latin." Consider what makes them work: for example, simple rules that can change any English word into a new word.

2 Once you have an idea for your own code, practice until you can speak it naturally and rapidly.

3 Carry on a conversation in front of the rest of the class. Can anyone break your code?

mechanics, parachute riggers, or welders. As in World War I, women did almost everything but fight.

Japanese Americans

The attack on Pearl Harbor set off a wave of anti-Japanese hysteria. Americans feared that Japanese submarines would blow up military installations, torpedo ships, or shell cities along the West Coast. Some people took this hysteria one step further. They began to distrust their Japanese American neighbors, wondering whether they might be spies working for Japan.

The intense anti-Japanese fears led President Roosevelt to issue Executive Order 9066 in February 1942. The order, which authorized the Secretary of War to remove civilians from military areas, was used as the excuse to remove 110,000 Japanese Americans from their homes in Pacific Coast states.

Many of those forced to move were *nisei*—children born in the United States to Japanese parents. By law they were American citizens. Emotions overruled common sense, though, and nisei as well as foreign-born Japanese were removed to camps in isolated areas. The fears were groundless, however. There was not a single documented case of disloyalty by a Japanese American.

One Japanese American who was forced to leave was Kisaye Sato, who recalled bitterly:

❝We only had 48 hours to get out of our homes. They came in truckloads to buy our things. We had to get rid of our furniture and appliances for whatever the people would pay. They took terrible advantage of us.**❞**

Nevertheless, some 17,600 Japanese Americans showed their loyalty by joining the armed services. Many of them fought in

Japanese Americans arrive at their new home—a relocation camp in Wyoming. Of the 110,000 Americans of Japanese descent forced to relocate, most remained in camps for more than three years.

at airstrips. Despite valiant efforts, American and Filipino soldiers were forced to surrender. Vowing, "I shall return," their commander, General Douglas MacArthur, retreated to Australia.

In the next three months, Japan won victory after victory, advancing into Thailand and Burma on the way toward Australia. Within four months Japan had conquered most of Southeast Asia as well as parts of the Pacific. As the Allies witnessed Japan's string of conquests, they began to feel desperate.

North Africa, Italy, and France with the 442d Regimental Combat Team and the 100th Infantry Battalion. These units, made up entirely of Japanese Americans, won thousands of military awards and medals. Two much-decorated nisei war veterans—Daniel K. Inouye and Spark Matsunaga—were later elected to the United States Senate from the state of Hawaii.

In 1988, 46 years after the internment order, Congress responded to pressure from former internees and their children by passing a bill formally apologizing for the treatment of Japanese American citizens. Each of the estimated 60,000 survivors of the internment camps was to be given $20,000 in recognition of the human rights violations they suffered during World War II.

Japan's Conquests

During the months after Pearl Harbor, Japan seemed as unstoppable as Hitler's forces in Europe. Japanese fighter planes attacked the Philippines, destroying more than half the American planes on the ground

Stopping the Japanese Finally, in early May 1942 American and Australian fleets succeeded in stopping Japan's advance. In the Battle of the Coral Sea, the Allies intercepted the Japanese fleet as it attempted to take more territory.

This battle was fought entirely by carrier-based planes. For the first time there was no ship-to-ship contact—only plane against plane and plane against ship. The Allies prevented Japanese troops from landing at Port Moresby in southern New Guinea and spared Australia from invasion.

The Battle of Midway

In early June 1942 Japan suffered an even worse defeat in the Battle of Midway. The Japanese had planned to take the small Pacific island and use it to launch another attack on nearby Pearl Harbor—which was still the home of the American Pacific Fleet. Learning of the planned attack when code breakers cracked the Japanese naval code, American admirals raced their ships toward Midway Island.

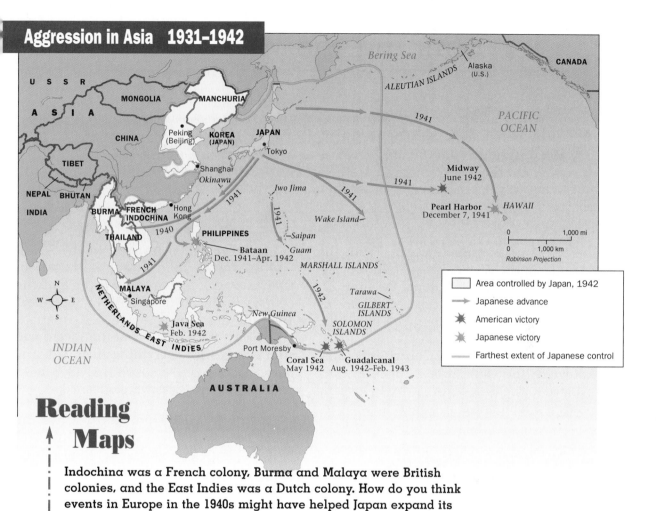

Aggression in Asia 1931–1942

U.S.S.R.

ASIA

MONGOLIA

MANCHURIA

CHINA

Peking (Beijing)

KOREA (JAPAN)

JAPAN

Tokyo

Shanghai

Okinawa

TIBET

NEPAL BHUTAN

INDIA

BURMA FRENCH INDOCHINA

Hong Kong

THAILAND

1940

PHILIPPINES

1941

1941

Iwo Jima

Wake Island

Saipan

Guam

Bataan
Dec. 1941–Apr. 1942

MARSHALL ISLANDS

MALAYA

Singapore

1941

NETHERLANDS EAST INDIES

Java Sea
Feb. 1942

1942

New Guinea

Tarawa

GILBERT ISLANDS

SOLOMON ISLANDS

Port Moresby

Coral Sea
May 1942

Guadalcanal
Aug. 1942–Feb. 1943

INDIAN OCEAN

AUSTRALIA

Bering Sea

ALEUTIAN ISLANDS

Alaska (U.S.)

CANADA

1941

PACIFIC OCEAN

Midway
June 1942

1941

Pearl Harbor
December 7, 1941

HAWAII

0   1,000 mi
0   1,000 km
Robinson Projection

Area controlled by Japan, 1942
→ Japanese advance
✳ American victory
✳ Japanese victory
— Farthest extent of Japanese control

N W E S

Reading Maps

Indochina was a French colony, Burma and Malaya were British colonies, and the East Indies was a Dutch colony. How do you think events in Europe in the 1940s might have helped Japan expand its empire in Asia?

Planes from Japanese carriers attacked the island, but American antiaircraft fire brought many of them down. Arriving just in time, American carriers launched their own planes against the Japanese fleet. Although Japanese fighter planes and ships' guns shot down many of them, American dive-bombers scored direct hits on three of the four carriers, causing heavy losses.

The Battle of Midway was a turning point in the war. After this defeat the Japanese no longer controlled the Pacific. Gradually, the Allied forces began to drive them back to their home islands.

3. Section Review

1. Define **rationing**.
2. Describe at least three ways that the lives of Americans on the home front were changed by the war.
3. Why was it essential that the Allies stop Japan's advance at Midway?
4. **Critical Thinking** If you had been a young nisei man whose family was in an internment camp, would you have volunteered to fight in the war? Why or why not?

4. Winning the War

Reading Guide

Section Focus How the Allies defeated the Axis powers

1. What strategies did the Big Three use to win victory in Europe?
2. Why did the United States drop the atomic bomb on Japan?
3. What was the human cost of World War II?

While American forces clashed with the Japanese in the Pacific, Hitler continued his campaign to conquer Europe. On June 22, 1941, he launched a surprise attack on his ally the Soviet Union. Betrayed by Hitler, Stalin joined the Allied effort.

Stalin, Roosevelt, and Churchill became known as the "Big Three." Together they planned strategies to defeat the Axis. Germany posed a more immediate threat than Japan, so they concentrated on defeating it first.

Early Allied Victories

In the fall of 1942 American and British troops invaded North Africa. Led by the American general Dwight David Eisenhower, their goal was to drive out the German Afrika Korps. Its commander, General Erwin Rommel, was called "the Desert Fox" because of his brilliant desert-warfare tactics.

It was in North Africa that Ben Davis and his pilots from Tuskegee first went into combat. They were to provide air cover on bombing missions. When one of the pilots shot down a German plane—the first aerial victory by an African American pilot—General Eisenhower personally came to the air base to offer his congratulations.

In the spring of 1943, after six months of bitter fighting, the Allies finally forced Rommel's Afrika Korps to surrender. With this defeat, the Axis lost control of Africa as a military gateway to southern Europe.

Stalingrad Meanwhile, in the Soviet Union the German attack had stalled, thanks to a long, brutal winter and the courage of the Soviet people. In September 1942 the Germans had launched an attack on the city of Stalingrad, but the Soviets had struck back with everything they had. The Soviet victory on February 2, 1943, put an end to Germany's eastward advance.

Italy's defeat From North Africa the Allies now mounted a successful invasion of Italy. King Victor Emmanuel III dismissed Mussolini from office, and on September 8, 1943, the new government surrendered. Although the Allies liberated Rome in June 1944, they faced months of fierce fighting before the German forces in Italy finally surrendered in May 1945.

D-Day

In November 1943 the Big Three met at Tehran, Iran, and agreed to an Allied invasion of France. "Operation Overlord" was to be planned and staged in Great Britain.

Although Hitler was expecting an invasion, the Allies succeeded in keeping secret the fact that they would be landing on the beaches of France's Normandy coast (see map, page 801). Despite foul weather, on June 5, 1944, General Eisenhower made the call: "O.K. We'll go." The next day the invasion, known as D-Day, began.

War in Europe and North Africa 1942–1945

Area held by Allies, September 1942
Area gained by Allies by September 1944
Area gained by Allies by May 1945
Area held by Axis by May 1945
Neutral nation
Allied advance
Political boundaries as of 1939

Churchill (left), Roosevelt, Stalin

Reading Maps

To drive the Germans back, Allied forces attacked on three sides. In what areas had the Allies regained control by the end of 1944?

Within a month 1 million troops had stormed ashore. The Germans fought back fiercely, but in late July the Allies broke through German lines. In August another Allied force landed on France's southern coast and advanced northward. On August 25, 1944, the French flag once again waved over Paris.

The election of 1944 While the Allies were driving the Germans out of western Europe, Roosevelt ran for a fourth term. His running mate was Senator Harry S Truman of Missouri. Although Roosevelt's health was failing, he felt it would be a mistake for the nation to change leaders during the war. The Roosevelt-Truman ticket won easily.

Germany Retreats

By September 1944 German forces were retreating on all fronts. As the Allies pressed forward through western Europe, the Soviets launched an attack that pushed the Germans back along an 800-mile (1,287-km) front in eastern Europe. As the war in Europe drew to a close, Allied bombers filled the skies over Germany.

With the bombers flew black guardian angels. In March 1945 alone, African American airmen flew 50 missions. The most notable strike was a 1,600-mile (2,580-km) round-trip bombing run over Berlin in which they destroyed three jets—a type of plane the Germans had just developed. Benjamin Davis's unit received the Distinguished Unit Citation for this spectacular achievement.

When Allied armies closed in on Berlin in late April, Hitler committed suicide. Eight days later, on May 8, 1945, Germany surrendered. May 8 is still known as V-E Day, for Victory in Europe.

Roosevelt's death Franklin Roosevelt did not live to see V-E Day. On April 12, 1945, worn out by ill health and the pressures of the job, he died of a cerebral hemorrhage. The burdens of the presidency now rested on the shoulders of Harry Truman.

Japan Fights On

While the nation mourned the loss of a great leader, the Allies turned their attention to Japan. In successful but bloody assaults, they had already recaptured the South Pacific island clusters of the Solomons, Gilberts, Carolines, and Marianas.

These victories permitted General MacArthur to make good on his vow to return. On October 20, 1944, he waded ashore on the Philippine island of Leyte.

As American forces closed in, Japanese pilots resorted to the desperate tactic of deliberately crashing their planes into American ships. These *kamikaze* ("divine wind") pilots sank 34 Allied ships, but at the frightful cost of 5,000 Japanese lives.

Suicide tactics did not stop the American advance toward Japan, but every inch was bitterly contested. The island of Iwo Jima fell after bloody hand-to-hand fighting that left one-third of the American force either dead or wounded. On April 1, 1945, the Allies landed on Okinawa. More than 100,000 Japanese and 11,000 Americans were killed before the island fell on June 22.

Now all that remained of the Japanese empire was the island nation itself. Because Japan refused to surrender, the Allies faced the prospect of launching the most bloody and costly invasion of the war.

On July 17, 1945, Truman, Churchill, and Stalin met in Potsdam, Germany. From there they issued a strangely worded message. They urged Japan to surrender before August 3 or face "prompt and utter destruction."

The Atomic Bomb

"Prompt and utter destruction" was not an idle threat. Since 1941 American and British scientists had been secretly developing a new weapon—the atomic bomb. Japan let the deadline pass, and three days later a B-29 bomber called the *Enola Gay* dropped the first atomic bomb on the city of Hiroshima. The blast, and the devastating firestorm that followed, killed 66,000, injured another 70,000, and totally destroyed the city.

One woman described the experience:

"I felt I had lost all the bones in my body. . . . I passed out. By the time I woke up, black rain was falling. I thought I was blind, but I got my eyes open, and I saw a beautiful blue sky and a dead city. Nobody is standing up. Nobody is walking around.**"**

Three days later a second atomic bomb was dropped on the city of Nagasaki.

Although later criticized for a decision that brought death to so many innocent civilians, Truman never regretted it. He believed that invading Japan would have meant the loss of many more American lives in the long run. "I regarded the bomb as a military weapon," Truman said, "and never had any doubt that it should be used."

V-J Day On August 15, 1945—V-J Day—Japan surrendered. Joyful Americans took to the streets. Strangers embraced one another. In New York City, a soldier walked up to a group of strangers with a look of shocked disbelief on his face: "I'm alive. I'm alive. The war's over—and I'm alive."

The Human Cost

The most deadly conflict in world history had finally come to an end. Nearly 20 million

On May 7, 1945, American soldiers came upon these starving Holocaust survivors in a Nazi concentration camp in Austria.

Link to the Present

Remembering the Holocaust Each visitor who enters the United States Holocaust Memorial Museum in Washington, D.C., receives an identification card picturing a Holocaust victim. The visitor can use this card to follow the victim's story through a series of computer stations. Visitors can also walk through a railroad car like the ones that brought prisoners to Nazi death camps. They can stand in a barracks like the ones where prisoners slept, and view piles of shoes and other belongings taken from the dead.

The Holocaust Museum, which opened in 1993, is dedicated to keeping alive the memory of the 11 million people—6 million of them Jews—who died in the Holocaust. The museum's message is summed up by the buttons offered for sale to visitors—buttons that say "Remember" and "Never Again."

soldiers and twice as many civilians died. Property losses totaled trillions of dollars. Simple statistics, however, cannot give a real sense of the human cost of the war. Across the globe homes were destroyed and families scattered. Millions were homeless and near starvation.

The Holocaust Only with Germany's defeat were some of the worst horror stories of the war fully revealed. Many of the civilians who died in Europe had been deliberately killed by Hitler in a Nazi extermination policy now known as the Holocaust.

As the Allies marched through Germany and Poland at the end of the war, they came upon Hitler's concentration camps. With horror they realized that more than 11 million people had been murdered by Nazis because they belonged to one of the many groups—including Jews, Gypsies, and the mentally and physically handicapped—that Hitler regarded as inferior to the "master race."

In 1945 and 1946 the Allies held war crimes trials in Nuremberg, Germany. The Nuremberg Trials found thousands of Nazis guilty of war crimes and sentenced 12 Nazi leaders to death.

4. Section Review

1. Describe the major events that led to V-E Day.
2. Give a strong argument for and a strong argument against dropping atomic bombs on Japan.
3. Critical Thinking Why do you think it is important to study the Holocaust? Explain your answer.

Why We Remember

World War II

It was over. After 2,194 days of death and destruction, the most devastating war in history was over. There had never been a conflict like this before. It was fought by more men—some 70 million—using more machines and more destructive weapons over more of the globe than any past war. The cost in human lives was staggering. Nearly 20 million soldiers died on battlefields. More than twice as many civilians lost their lives. The financial costs were just as unimaginable. A trillion dollars had been spent fighting the war worldwide. The amount of property damage was at least twice that figure.

These numbers are reason enough to remember World War II, but there are others equally as important. We remember this war to honor its heroes. Many, like Benjamin Davis, were soldiers who risked their lives in battle. Others were civilians who made huge sacrifices for their countries. All deserve our admiration and gratitude.

We remember this war for its horrors, too. This was the conflict that left us with images of living skeletons in German concentration camps and mushroom clouds rising over Japanese cities. This was the war that showed us that for all our progress in science, technology, and culture, human hate could still create a holocaust. This was the war that gave the world nuclear weapons that would soon be capable of destroying all life on earth.

We remember this war as well for its legacy of hope. For in this terrible conflict, the organized forces of freedom proved stronger than those of fascism. Democracy triumphed over dictatorship. It was far from a total victory, as the coming years would show. Still, the democratic ideals Americans held most dear had survived and, it was hoped, would never be tested in this way again.

Geography Lab

Tracing Events Over Time and Space

After the battle on Iwo Jima, one marine muttered, "I hope to God that we don't have to go on any more of those screwy islands." He had reason to be weary. Beginning in 1942, Allied forces had been following a strategy called "island hopping." They attacked certain Pacific islands held by Japan and then used those islands as bases from which to attack other islands. In all, the Allies launched more than 100 island invasions as they gradually closed in on Japan.

The map shows highlights of the campaigns of General Douglas MacArthur and Admiral Chester Nimitz. Use the map to trace the Allied path to victory in the Pacific.

Using Map Skills

1. Proceeding from Hawaii, where did Nimitz's forces strike first?

2. List in chronological order the battles in which Nimitz's forces took part.

3. Where did Nimitz's and MacArthur's forces first join? What was their joint objective after that?

4. MacArthur left the Philippines in January 1942. How long did it take him to return?

5. **Hands-On Geography**
Imagine that atomic bombs had not been dropped. Trace the map on this page. Add movements and battles that might have taken place after Okinawa. Where and when would the war have ended?

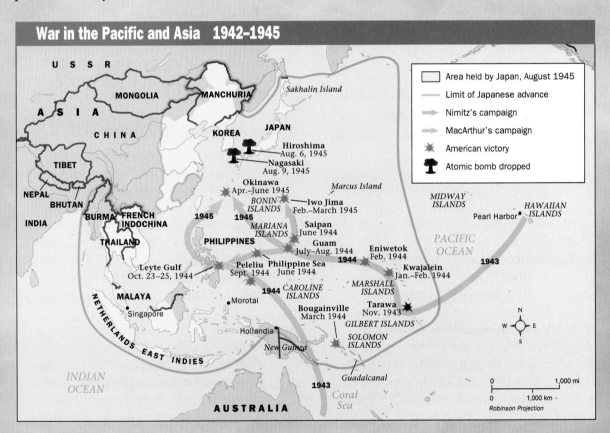

War in the Pacific and Asia   1942–1945

Legend:
- Area held by Japan, August 1945
- Limit of Japanese advance
- Nimitz's campaign
- MacArthur's campaign
- American victory
- Atomic bomb dropped

Chapter Survey

Reviewing Vocabulary

Define the following terms.

1. arms race   **5.** totalitarian state
2. isolationism   **6.** appeasement
3. dictator   **7.** rationing
4. fascism

Reviewing Main Ideas

1. Explain how each country threatened world peace in the 1930s. (a) Japan (b) Italy (c) Germany
2. (a) Why did the United States decide to aid Britain in the war? (b) What forms did the aid and cooperation take?
3. Describe the events that led up to the Japanese attack on Pearl Harbor.
4. How did each group contribute to the war effort? (a) African Americans (b) Native Americans (c) women
5. What was Executive Order 9066, why did Roosevelt issue it, and what result did it have?
6. Summarize how the forces led by the "Big Three" defeated Italy and Germany.
7. What caused Japan to surrender?

Thinking Critically

1. Analysis Both Germany and Japan gobbled up territory as fast as they could. Were their reasons exactly the same, or were they somewhat different? Explain your answer.
2. Synthesis Suppose the Axis, rather than the Allies, had won World War II. In what major ways might the world be different today? Give three possibilities.
3. Why We Remember: Evaluation World War II is sometimes referred to by Americans as "the good war." Why do you suppose that label has stuck? Do you think it is an appropriate label, or not? Explain your answer.

Applying Skills

Identifying gaps in information

Think about an event of World War II, besides the attack on Pearl Harbor, about which you might ask a "how" or "why" question. Write the question. (Example: "How could the Holocaust happen without the entire world knowing?") Then, recalling what you learned in the Skill Lab on page 794, do the following:
1. Describe the types of information you need to answer the question.
2. Summarize the relevant information presented in this textbook.
3. State one gap in that information.
4. Name two types of sources you might consult to try to fill the gap.

History Mystery

The Battle of Britain Answer the History Mystery on page 783. What do the people sleeping in the subways tell you about the war effort in London?

Writing in Your History Journal

1. Keys to History (a) The time line on pages 782–783 has seven Keys to History. In your journal, describe why each one is important to know about. (b) Choose two events on the time line. In your journal, explain how they are related.
2. Benjamin Davis Imagine that you are Benjamin Davis, invited to speak to the West Point graduation class of 1946. In your journal, write the introduction to a speech that he might have given.
3. Citizenship Imagine that you are a Japanese American living in 1942. Write a letter to President Roosevelt urging him to reconsider Executive

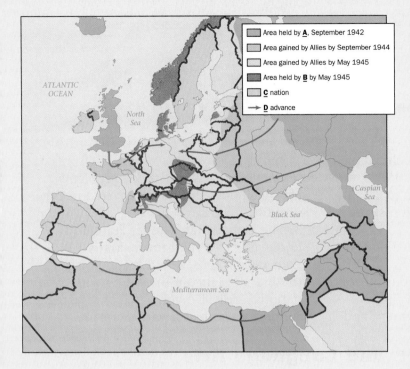

Area held by **A**, September 1942

Area gained by Allies by September 1944

Area gained by Allies by May 1945

Area held by **B** by May 1945

C nation

→ **D** advance

ATLANTIC
OCEAN

North
Sea

Caspian
Sea

Black Sea

Mediterranean Sea

Reviewing Geography

1. Each letter in the map legend stands for a missing word. Write the word.

2. Geographic Thinking
The word "theater" is sometimes used to refer to a major place of action during a war. How do you suppose geography challenged the fighting forces in the three major theaters of World War II: Europe, North Africa, and the Pacific? How do you suppose geography aided the fighting forces in each theater? Consider such things as distance, climate, vegetation, bodies of water, and landforms.

Order 9066. Give as many sound, logical arguments as you can.

Alternative Assessment

Covering the war for radio "This . . . is London." With those words, American correspondent Edward R. Murrow opened his nightly radio broadcast during the blitz. Murrow often spoke from a rooftop as bombs exploded, sirens screamed, and anti-aircraft guns boomed. His broadcasts made the war powerfully real to listeners across the United States.

With a partner, act the roles of correspondents before and during the war.

❶ Choose four events or situations from the chapter to cover: one from each section of the chapter.

❷ Write a brief radio broadcast about each of these events or situations. Include background information you think your listeners may need. Provide colorful details to help your listeners "see" what you are describing.

❸ Plan how to present your four broadcasts. You might take turns speaking in each broadcast, or each cover two "stories." If you plan to include interviews with "eyewitnesses," one of you can be the correspondent while the other acts as the interviewee.

❹ Present your broadcasts to the class.

Your work will be evaluated on the following criteria:

• you report historical events and situations accurately

• your descriptions are lively, specific, and vivid

• your broadcasts capture and hold your audience's imagination

Unit Survey

Making Connections

1. Give one example from each decade to support this statement: Overwhelmed by the rapid changes of the 1920s, 1930s, and 1940s, many Americans reacted to certain ideas and groups of people with distrust and anger.

2. One historian says that United States history runs in cycles, with times of "private interest" (when efforts by businesses and individuals are strong) and times of "public purpose" (when government and the nation as a whole tackle problems). How well does the period covered in this unit fit that idea?

3. The United States under Franklin D. Roosevelt faced hard times. Many historians regard Roosevelt as second only to Abraham Lincoln in dealing with a national crisis. Do you agree or disagree? Support your answer with examples.

Linking History, Art, and Language Arts

A Game About the Home Front

Pitching in for victory was a matter of pride and patriotism during World War II. You have read about rationing and working in war industries. Find out more (and have some fun) by creating a board game about life on the home front.

Project Steps

Work with a partner or a small group.

❶ Do research to learn how ordinary Americans supported the war effort. If possible, interview older relatives. Use the library too. You may discover wartime magazines, cookbooks, or pamphlets about rationing and other topics.

❷ Develop a format and rules for your game. You can use an existing game as a model. Your game must teach or ask questions about the home front.

• You might have "chance" cards like *Bake a birthday cake without sugar—Advance 2 spaces* and *Drive the car when you could have walked—Go back 4 spaces.*

• You might have "trivia question" cards like *Why did some Americans stare at the sky through binoculars?* (acting as volunteer enemy-aircraft spotters) and *What did the Portland (Oregon) Zoo and the Cook County (Illinois) jail yard have in common?* (sites of victory gardens).

❸ Make the game.

• Use markers and poster board to create an attractive game board.

• Make tokens out of materials like clay or paper. Your tokens might look like ration stamps, for example.

• Make game cards by writing questions or information on slips of colored paper.

• Write the rules of the game. Make them thorough but easy to follow.

❹ Play the game with classmates, friends, or family members.

Thinking It Over One wartime saying went, "Use it up, wear it out, make it do, or do without." Is that good advice for peacetime, too? Are modern Americans willing to live by that advice? Explain.

How Do We Know?

The Erminio Viola family. (Joseph is the baby.)

Scholar's Tool Kit
Family Histories

More than a century ago the writer Herman Melville noted, "America has been settled by people of all nations. . . . We are not a nation so much as a world." Melville was right. As you have learned, beginning in Chapter 1 of this book, everyone in America originally came from someplace else. Even Indians, the first Americans, came from else-where thousands of years ago. The stories of where Americans came from are valuable to scholars who use those stories to add flesh to the bare bones of historic events. The stories are one of the building blocks of American history.

Collecting Family Stories

In its simplest form a family history is a list of births, marriages, and deaths, also known as a genealogy. In its most complete form, a family history consists of biographies—life stories—of each person. Many families take great pride in the stories of their ancestors and keep written records or taped interviews with older family members.

In researching history, scholars sometimes interview people about their family histories. Family stories are especially important to scholars studying immigration history, a field of research very popular today. Scholars want to know why immigrants left their homelands and how they adapted to their new homes.

Until recently, scholars assumed that most immigrants stayed in the United States after they got here. Now, however, they are learning

These Viola family documents help tell the family's story. Above are two pages of Maria Incollingo's passport, the cover of which is shown at right. The card above right certified Maria's good health upon leaving Italy.

? Critical Thinking

1. Why do you think that American historians might have overlooked the study of immigrants who returned to their native lands?

that a surprising number of immigrants later chose to return to their native lands. Indeed, many of the returned immigrants had come to earn money and had never intended to stay. Others returned because they were unhappy or discouraged.

The Author's Story

One immigrant who returned to his homeland was Erminio Viola, my grandfather. In the 1890s he came to the United States from the Tyrol region of Austria, leaving his wife and three young children behind. He found a job in a Pennsylvania coal mine, but lost a leg in a mining accident soon after his arrival. Nonetheless, he liked America well enough to send for his family. The family had been in the United States only a short time, however, when Erminio's wife, Louisa, became ill. Having lived in the Dolomite Mountains all their lives, the family thought her illness was due to the change in altitude, so they returned to their village.

? Critical Thinking

2. In what ways did historical events affect the Viola family history?

While in the United States, Erminio and Louisa had had a son, Joseph. After World War I, at age 17, Joseph chose to return to the United States upon completing his apprenticeship as a cabinetmaker.

Although Joseph arrived in New York penniless and unable to speak English, he immediately found a job helping build the New York City subway. When the project was completed, he went to Chicago to help construct that city's elevated train. His boss was Antonio Incollingo, a contractor from Italy. At the time, Italy was suffering through the Great Depression. Benito Mussolini, dictator of Italy, encouraged workers like Antonio to find jobs abroad and send money home to bolster the country's sagging economy.

Antonio's 16-year-old daughter Maria (Mary) came to visit her father in Chicago. She wanted to see the United States before marrying a young man waiting for her at their village near Rome.

Mary immediately fell in love with the new land and did not want to go back. Upon meeting Joseph, who was 11 years older, she asked him to marry her so she could stay in the United States. The marriage took place a few weeks later and lasted until Mary's death more than 50 years later. They had two children: my sister, Mary Lou, and me.

For Joseph and Mary, the United States turned out to be the promised land. They had no regrets about staying, even though their families were in Europe. Joseph never once returned to his Tyrolean village, which is now part of Italy. Mary, however, missed her family very much. Over the years she made several trips to Italy to visit her brother and sisters.

? Critical Thinking

3. If you were to tell your children one important thing about your family, what would it be? Why?

Scholar at Work

Every family has a history. Interview your parents or other family members and record what you learn. Find out if your family has kept any written records, and use them to add to your family history. Then, think of a way to present your family history to the class. You might want to make a poster with your family tree; tell a story of an interesting family member; make a videotape or audiotape of an interview; or bring in old photographs, letters, or other historical documents. Present your history to the class.

Unit *10*

Chapters

Hands-On --------> *HISTORY*

Activity

The Hubble space telescope, launched in 1990, is an astronomical observatory in space. This photo shows astronaut Storey Musgrave (lower right) servicing the telescope. Imagine that you are Christopher Columbus standing on the Hubble telescope. Five hundred years after your explorations, you now have a full view of the earth for the first time. In your journal reflect on how this view might have affected your plans for your voyage.

Hubble space telescope, Johnson Space Center, NASA photo, 1993

Power and Responsibilities

Chapter **29**

The Cold War Era

Keys to History

1945
United Nations
founded

1949
Communists come to
power in China

1948
Marshall Plan
begins

1950–1953
Korean War

1945   *1955*

Looking Back

The Soviet Union
is created
1922

World **Link**

Israel becomes a nation
1948

This small ball of steel, called *Sputnik*, weighed a mere 184 pounds (83 kg). Why did it strike fear into the hearts of Americans?

1965–1973
American troops fight in Vietnam War

1962
Cuban missile crisis

1972
President Nixon visits China

1991
Soviet Union collapses

1965   *1975*   *1991*

Looking Ahead

American and Russian peace-keepers sent to Bosnia
1995

Beginning the Story with

Harry S Truman

On April 12, 1945, Vice-President Harry S Truman received a message to call the White House. "Please come over right away," said a voice choking with emotion. Truman later recalled:

❝ I reached the White House about 5:25 P.M. and was immediately taken in the elevator to the second floor and ushered into Mrs. Roosevelt's study. . . . I knew at once that something unusual had taken place. Mrs. Roosevelt seemed calm in her characteristic, graceful dignity. She stepped forward and placed her arm gently around my shoulder. 'Harry,' she said quietly, 'the President is dead.' For a moment I could not bring myself to speak. . . . 'Is there anything I can do for you?' I asked at last. I shall never forget her deeply understanding reply. 'Is there anything *we* can do for *you*?' she asked. 'For you are the one in trouble now.'**❞**

The Man from Missouri

Born on a Missouri farm in 1884, Truman had not grown up wanting to be President, or even a politician. After serving in World War I, he and his pal Eddie Jacobson opened a men's clothing store in Kansas City, Missouri. In 1922, however, the firm of Truman & Jacobson failed, leaving Truman deeply in debt and with a family to support.

Only then, at the age of 38, did Truman try his luck at politics. When he told a friend he was planning to run for a county office, the response was, "I think you're crazy." Truman replied, "I got to eat." He was elected a county judge in 1926 and won a second term four years later.

In 1934 Truman was chosen by the Kansas City Democratic machine to run for the Senate. However, even his most powerful backer admitted, "I don't feel that Harry Truman has a chance." To almost everyone's surprise,

Truman turned out to be a rousing campaigner and won the election. As he went off to Washington, the man from Missouri described himself modestly as "a humble member of the next Senate, green as grass and ignorant as a fool about practically everything worth knowing."

"Good Luck, Mr. President"

When President Roosevelt decided to run for a fourth term in 1944, his advisors talked about possible candidates for Vice-President. Truman's name came up again and again. His record in the Senate was good. He was acceptable to labor unions. He had a reputation for honesty. One advisor recalled, "Truman was the man who would hurt him [Roosevelt] least."

Truman was not so sure he wanted the job. Roosevelt was in poor health, and many believed he would not live out another term. Asked by a journalist about the possibility of becoming President, Truman replied:

Truman had a reputation for being down-to-earth and energetic. "Being a President is like riding a tiger," he wrote. "I never felt that I could let up for a single moment."

❝ Do you remember your American history well enough to recall what happened to most Vice-Presidents who succeeded to the Presidency? Usually they were ridiculed in office, had their hearts broken, lost any vestige [trace] of respect they had before. I don't want that to happen to me. ❞

When Truman suddenly did have to take office as President, the challenges ahead must have seemed overwhelming. Talking with reporters the day after he was sworn in, Truman said:

❝ Boys, if you ever pray, pray for me now. I don't know whether you fellows ever had a load of hay fall on you, but when they told me yesterday what had happened, I felt like the moon and stars, and all the planets had fallen on me. ❞

One of the reporters called out, "Good luck, Mr. President." Truman turned to him and replied, "I wish you didn't have to call me that."

Hands-On HISTORY

Activity

Imagine that you are Harry Truman after receiving the news that President Roosevelt has died. Write a diary entry expressing your thoughts about the responsibilities of becoming President. Comment on challenges you will face and tell in what ways you think you are suited or unsuited to be President.

1. The Start of the Cold War

Reading Guide

New Terms **Cold War, containment**

Section Focus **The change in American-Soviet relations after World War II**

1. How did the United States contain communism in Europe?
2. Why did the Cold War spread to Asia and the Middle East?
3. What Cold War conflicts arose over Cuba?

During Harry Truman's first months in office, World War II was finally coming to an end. However, the seeds of new conflicts were already planted. The United States and Britain believed the Soviet Union was committed to spreading communism throughout the world. They were determined to prevent that from happening.

The struggle for power between Communist and non-Communist nations came to be called the **Cold War.** Although it was more a war of threats and propaganda than of guns and bullets, the Cold War was to keep the world in a state of fear and hostility from 1945 until 1991.

To tell the whole story of the Cold War, this chapter focuses on events that took place outside of the United States. Chapter 30 tells what was happening at home, including events influenced by the Cold War.

The United Nations

Before his death, President Roosevelt had committed himself to efforts to prevent future wars. At a meeting at Yalta in early 1945 he, Churchill, and Stalin had agreed on the need for a new international body to replace the failed League of Nations.

In April delegates from 50 nations met in San Francisco to draw up a charter for the United Nations (UN). This time, American support was strong. The Senate voted 89 to 2 to approve joining the UN.

The UN has two main parts: the General Assembly and the Security Council. Every member nation sends representatives to the General Assembly. As at a great town meeting, they debate world issues.

The Security Council is responsible for peace-keeping. Each of its five permanent members—the United States, Great Britain, France, China, and the Soviet Union (the seat now held by Russia)—has the right to veto a decision to use UN military force.

The "Iron Curtain"

Cold War tensions cast a shadow over the UN. Stalin soon seized control of Eastern Europe to give the Soviet Union a buffer against attacks in future wars. The nations of Eastern Europe became totalitarian states whose citizens were denied freedom of speech and even freedom to travel.

As the Soviet Union tightened its grip on the nations of Eastern Europe, Churchill warned that "an iron curtain has descended across the continent." For decades that "Iron Curtain" was to divide the democratic nations of "the West" from the Communist nations of "the East."

Containing Communism in Europe

Truman shared Churchill's view that the Soviet Union, having created a Communist empire in Eastern Europe, was eager to expand its power. He saw Soviet threats to Greece and Turkey. Greece was struggling to put down a Communist revolt, and Stalin was demanding land and naval bases from Turkey.

Truman wasted no time. At his urging, in 1947 Congress gave $400 million to Greece and Turkey to help them protect themselves. In what became known as the Truman Doctrine, the President declared that the United States would "support free peoples" to resist Communist takeovers.

Truman's policy of blocking Communist expansion was known as **containment.** To carry out the policy, Congress passed the National Security Act of 1947. The act created the Department of Defense, the National Security Council (NSC) to advise the President, and the Central Intelligence Agency (CIA) to spy on other nations.

To Truman, though, the strongest Cold War weapon was economic aid. He declared:

"The seeds of totalitarian regimes are nurtured by misery and want. They spread and grow in the evil soil of poverty and strife. They reach their full growth when the hope of a people for a better life has died. We must keep that hope alive.**"**

The Marshall Plan It was clear that hope was dying in Western Europe, where the economy had been shattered by the war. Desperate, starving Europeans might be attracted to the false promises of communism, just as their parents had been to fascism and Nazism. In fact, Communist parties were gaining strength in France and Italy.

The United States responded with a bold and generous program announced by Secretary of State George C. Marshall in June 1947.

World Link

The birth of Israel The UN faced its first major challenge in Palestine. Although it was the Jewish homeland in ancient times, Palestine had been home to Arab peoples since the 600s. In 1922 the League of Nations approved placing Palestine under British control. Jewish refugees from Europe poured into Palestine in the 1930s. Many hoped to create an independent Jewish state, an idea the Arab majority opposed. Tensions grew, and eventually Britain asked the UN to step in.

Moved by sympathy for Holocaust victims, the UN voted in 1947 to divide Palestine into Jewish and Arab states. After Jews proclaimed the state of Israel in May 1948, Arab nations sent troops to help the Palestinian Arabs fight the Israelis. The Soviet Union took the Arab side. While supporting Israel, the United States tried to avoid offending the Arab states, which held most of the world's oil reserves. The Arab-Israeli conflict would continue to be tied to the Cold War.

Under the Marshall Plan, Western Europe received $13 billion in American aid from 1948 through 1951. The aid made it possible to rebuild cities, repair railroads, and regain economic prosperity. An outstanding success, the Marshall Plan is credited with saving France and Italy from communism.

The Berlin airlift At the Yalta Conference, the Big Three had agreed to divide Germany into four zones, managed separately by American, British, French, and Soviet

To overcome the Soviet blockade, the Allies flew supplies to West Berlin. During the 318-day airlift, a plane landed every three minutes.

The Soviets, it was believed, would need ten years to develop nuclear weapons. In September 1949, however, Truman received shocking news of a Soviet nuclear test. One nuclear scientist noted:

❝There is only one thing worse than one nation having the atomic bomb—that's two nations having it.❞

What followed was a terrifying arms race. Truman approved plans to build an even more powerful nuclear weapon, the hydrogen bomb, and Congress voted $1 billion to arm NATO.

Fearful of NATO, in 1955 the Soviet Union formed the Warsaw Pact, an alliance of all the Communist countries in Eastern Europe except Yugoslavia. Once again Europe was divided into armed camps ready for war.

Communist Victory in China

Adding to western worries was the Communist takeover of China in 1949. Led by Mao Zedong (mow dzuh-doong), Communist rebels had won a bitter civil war with the ruling Nationalists, who retreated to the island of Formosa (now called Taiwan).

During China's civil war some advisors had urged Truman to give the Nationalists more aid and even to send troops. Truman, though, saw the Nationalist cause as almost hopeless. He preferred to focus on containing communism in Europe. Still, the United States refused to recognize the government of Communist China. With American support, the Nationalists kept China's seat on the UN Security Council.

forces. Germany's capital of Berlin, deep within the Soviet zone, was also divided.

In June 1948 Stalin ordered a blockade of West Berlin, hoping to force out the western allies by cutting off their supplies. They responded with the massive "Berlin airlift." Huge cargo planes flew tons of food, medicine, and other supplies to West Berlin. In May 1949 the Soviets finally gave up the blockade. The West had won a dramatic Cold War victory.

Meanwhile, the three western zones of Germany were merged into the independent West German Federal Republic. The Soviets organized their zone into the East German Democratic Republic. The once powerful German nation had been split in two, with East Germany disappearing behind the Iron Curtain.

NATO In the election of 1948, Truman was returned to office. The next spring the United States helped form the North Atlantic Treaty Organization (NATO), a military alliance to guard against a Soviet attack. NATO counted on the threat of the atomic bomb to keep the Soviets from attacking the West.

ICELAND

ATLANTIC
OCEAN

Warsaw Pact member

Other Communist nation

NATO member

Neutral nation

SWEDEN

FINLAND

NORWAY

UNION OF SOVIET SOCIALIST REPUBLICS

0   250   500 mi
0   250   500 km
Azimuthal Equal Area Projection

Baltic
Sea

North
Sea

DENMARK

REPUBLIC
OF IRELAND

GREAT BRITAIN   NETH.

Berlin

BELG.

EAST
GERMANY   POLAND

N
W   E
S

LUX.   WEST
GERMANY   CZECH.

FRANCE   SWITZ.   AUSTRIA   HUNGARY

Caspian
Sea

PORTUGAL   ROMANIA

SPAIN   Corsica
(Fr.)   ITALY   YUGOSLAVIA   Black Sea

BULGARIA   IRAN

ALBANIA

Sardinia
(It.)   GREECE   TURKEY

SPANISH
MOROCCO   ALGERIA   Sicily
(It.)   Cyprus
(Br.)   IRAQ

MOROCCO   TUNISIA   Crete
(Gr.)   LEBANON

Mediterranean Sea

ISRAEL

Reading Maps

During the Cold War, people spoke of an "iron curtain" dividing Europe into the
East and the West. What nations were on each side of this imaginary curtain?

The Korean War

Meanwhile, to the south of China, trouble was brewing in Korea. Ruled by Japan during World War II, Korea had been divided after the war. Soviet troops occupied North Korea, and American troops occupied South Korea. After setting up governments, the Soviet Union and the United States withdrew their forces.

In June 1950 the North Korean army suddenly invaded South Korea. Truman quickly asked the Security Council to send a UN force to South Korea. The Soviet delegate was not present at the UN debate and so failed to veto the proposal.

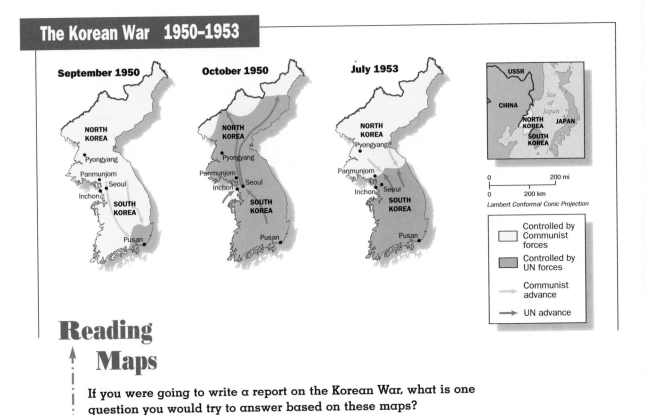

The Korean War 1950–1953

September 1950

October 1950

July 1953

USSR
CHINA
Sea of Japan
NORTH KOREA
JAPAN
SOUTH KOREA

0   200 mi
0   200 km
Lambert Conformal Conic Projection

☐ Controlled by Communist forces

■ Controlled by UN forces

→ Communist advance

→ UN advance

Reading Maps

If you were going to write a report on the Korean War, what is one question you would try to answer based on these maps?

Troops from 16 nations made up the UN force in Korea—with the vast majority of them Americans. The UN commander, General Douglas MacArthur, found himself in a desperate situation as his troops were pushed far to the south. He boldly launched a surprise counterattack by landing at Inchon, deep behind enemy lines. Soon the North's army was in full retreat.

MacArthur pressed on into North Korea. By November UN forces were nearing the Chinese border. Suddenly, what MacArthur called a "bottomless well" of Chinese soldiers swept down to help the North Koreans push the UN forces back into South Korea.

A stunned MacArthur asked to have "thirty to fifty atomic bombs" dropped on military targets in China. Afraid of starting a third world war, Truman refused. When MacArthur criticized him publicly, the President fired the general.

Eventually peace talks ended the war in 1953, leaving Korea still divided. Communist aggression had been stopped, but the war had cost the lives of about 33,000 Americans. The United States had demonstrated that it would stand by its policy of containment.

Foreign Policy Under Eisenhower

Foreign policy took a dramatic turn after Dwight D. Eisenhower was elected President in 1952. While Truman had declared, "*I make foreign policy,*" Eisenhower gave much of that responsibility to his Secretary of State, John Foster Dulles. Dulles wanted to move beyond containment. His goal was to free people from Communist rule.

Dulles declared that the United States would go to "the brink of war" to stop the spread of communism. It would even use nuclear weapons—"massive retaliation"—if necessary. Dulles's critics called his approach "brinkmanship." Dulles also encouraged secret CIA efforts to overthrow governments considered unfriendly to the United States.

Revolution in Hungary Cold War tensions relaxed for awhile when Nikita Khrushchev (nuh-KEE-tuh kroosh-CHAWF) emerged as the Soviet leader after Stalin's death in 1953. Khrushchev proposed "peaceful coexistence" with the West. Western leaders were encouraged when he granted limited self-rule to Poland.

Inspired by events in Poland, rebels in Hungary tried to break free of Soviet control in 1956. As Khrushchev crushed the rebellion with tanks and troops, Dulles's earlier threats proved hollow. The United States was unwilling to go to war over Hungary.

***Sputnik* and the arms race** As Dulles and Eisenhower backed away from threats of massive retaliation, Khrushchev grew bolder. In 1957 the Soviets alarmed the West by launching the first satellite, *Sputnik I.* Americans feared that if the Soviets could send satellites into space, they could also launch intercontinental ballistic missiles (ICBMs) to destroy American cities.

Convinced that the Soviets had surged ahead in the arms race, the United States rushed to build more, and more powerful, nuclear weapons. The threat seemed so real that schoolchildren were taught to duck under their desks in case of a nuclear missile attack. Many families built bomb shelters in their backyards.

The Middle East and Latin America Meanwhile, the Cold War had spread to the Middle East. Both the Soviet Union and the United States sought allies in that oil-rich region. When Iran's leaders acted friendly toward the Soviets, CIA agents helped the Shah of Iran regain control of the government in 1953.

Hungarian rebels, like this woman in Budapest, fought for independence in 1956. Soviet troops and tanks crushed the revolt, killing thousands.

In 1957 Congress approved what became known as the Eisenhower Doctrine—a plan to help Middle Eastern nations resist Communist takeovers. When Lebanon and Jordan asked for aid in 1958, the United States and Britain quickly sent troops.

Eisenhower and Dulles also saw threats in Latin America. In 1954 CIA-backed rebels overthrew Guatemala's pro-Communist government. The United States also sent arms to Honduras and Nicaragua to prevent Communists from coming to power.

Conflict Over Cuba

The threat of communism came closest to home on the island of Cuba. There, in January 1959, a young revolutionary named Fidel Castro forced the military dictator, Fulgencio Batista, to flee the country.

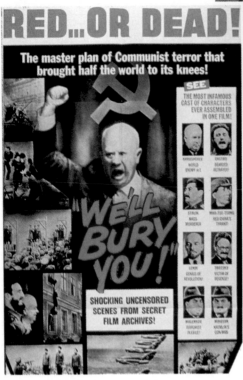

During the 1950s and early 1960s, schools held "duck and cover" drills to prepare for possible Soviet nuclear attacks. Another reflection of Cold War fears is this American film poster, which portrays Communist leaders as villains.

Castro later allied Cuba with the Soviet Union and threatened to spread communism in Latin America. In response, Eisenhower approved a CIA plot to train anti-Castro rebels to invade Cuba and overthrow Castro.

The Bay of Pigs invasion When John F. Kennedy became President in 1961, he approved the CIA's invasion plan. On April 17 nearly 1,500 Cuban rebels landed at Cochinos Bay (the Bay of Pigs), where they hoped to find support among the Cuban people. Instead, most of the invaders were quickly killed or captured.

Within weeks of the Bay of Pigs disaster, Khrushchev tested the new President by demanding that the western powers leave Berlin. Kennedy stood firm, however, and Khrushchev had to back down. The Soviet Union then built a concrete wall to stop people escaping from East to West Berlin. The Berlin Wall became a bitter symbol of the Cold War.

The Cuban missile crisis In October 1962 Kennedy faced still another test—one that brought the world to the brink of nuclear war. Spy planes flying over Cuba had photographed secret Soviet-built nuclear missile sites. Kennedy ordered the navy to blockade weapons shipments to Cuba and demanded that Khrushchev remove the missiles from the island.

As Soviet cargo ships loaded with more missiles approached the American warships, the world held its breath. At the last minute, Khrushchev ordered them to turn back. Over the next few weeks, the Soviets removed their missiles from Cuba, and the United States lifted its blockade. Sobered by how close they had come to war, Khrushchev and Kennedy set up a telephone "hot line" to help avoid future crises.

 1. Section Review

1. Define **Cold War** and **containment**.
2. How did American aid help contain communism in Europe?
3. What Cold War conflicts arose in Asia and the Middle East?
4. What was the Cuban missile crisis?
5. **Critical Thinking** Could the Cold War have been avoided? Explain.

Geography Lab

Reading a Polar Map

In August 1957 the Soviet Union successfully tested the first intercontinental ballistic missile (ICBM). Suddenly, Americans faced the possibility of a long-range nuclear missile attack.

Americans looking for comfort may have found some in maps like the one on pages R2–R3. The Soviet Union looked so very far away. Maps centered on the North Pole, however, gave reason to be concerned.

An American ICBM

The Northern Hemisphere

NATO member

Warsaw Pact member

Lambert Azimuthal Equal Area Projection

Using Map Skills

1. Using the map on pages R2–R3, describe the most direct air route between Moscow and Washington, D.C.

2. Using the polar map on this page, describe the most direct route between Moscow and Washington. Is it the same?

3. Use a globe to measure the actual distance between Moscow and Washington. Which is the most accurate route—the route you chose using the map on pages R2–R3 or the polar map on this page?

4. Would Moscow necessarily be the best place for Soviet missile bases? Explain.

5. **Hands-On Geography** The North American Air Defense System (NORAD) was set up in 1957, with radar stations in Canada, Greenland, and Alaska to detect missiles and aircraft. As a NORAD planner, make a speech in Congress explaining the radar locations.

2. The War in Vietnam

Reading Guide

Section Focus **The causes and effects of American involvement in Vietnam**

1. What led to American intervention in Vietnam?
2. How was the Vietnam War different from other American wars?
3. What were some effects of the Vietnam War?

With the end of the Cuban missile crisis, the nation breathed a sigh of relief. Meanwhile, however, the United States was gradually being drawn into a war in far-off Southeast Asia. When Kennedy took office in 1961, few Americans had heard of the tiny country of Vietnam. Soon, though, it would be a household word.

When informing Kennedy of the conflict brewing in Vietnam, Eisenhower had said, "This is one of the problems I'm leaving you that I'm not happy about. We may have to fight." In fact, the United States did eventually go to war in Vietnam—the longest and most unpopular war in the nation's history.

A Divided Country

The conflict was rooted in a struggle by the Vietnamese to free themselves from French colonial rule after World War I. The leader of that effort, Ho Chi Minh, had asked for American help, but the United States remained loyal to France, its World War I ally. Also, Americans were suspicious of Ho because his followers, called Vietminh, included Communists. Ho soon became a Communist and received Soviet aid.

The Vietminh stepped up their struggle after World War II. Despite millions of dollars in American aid, the French finally gave up in 1954. A peace treaty signed that year in Geneva, Switzerland, divided Vietnam in half. A Communist Vietminh government ruled the North, and a pro-Western government ruled the South.

The treaty did not bring peace, though, for Ho was determined to unify the country. He sent arms to help South Vietnamese guerrillas, called the Viet Cong, to overthrow their new government. The stage was set for a major Cold War conflict.

The "domino theory" Eisenhower was determined to save South Vietnam from communism. In 1954 he compared the situation to playing with dominos:

❝You have a row of dominos set up, and you knock over the first one, and what will happen to the last one is the certainty that it will go over very quickly.❞

American policymakers believed that the fall of South Vietnam would lead to Communist control of all of Southeast Asia. To prevent that from happening, Eisenhower sent more aid and military advisors.

Growing Involvement

Sharing Eisenhower's concern, Kennedy expanded the aid and sent many more military advisors. By the end of 1962, more than 12,000 American advisors were in South Vietnam. Their efforts, however, were hampered by the fact that the corrupt government had little support among the people.

With the tragic assassination of Kennedy in November 1963, Lyndon Johnson became President. When Johnson learned how bad the situation in Vietnam was, he said he felt like a fish that had "grabbed a big juicy worm with a right sharp hook in the middle of it."

Johnson faced a difficult decision: Should he use American force to win the war for South Vietnam or withdraw completely? Unwilling to withdraw, he secretly ordered raids against Communist bases in neighboring Laos. He hesitated, though, to send troops unless he could get support from Congress. That support would come only if American forces were attacked.

The Gulf of Tonkin Resolution On August 2, 1964, an American navy destroyer reported being fired upon by North Vietnamese torpedo boats in the Gulf of Tonkin. Two days later, another attack was reported. Johnson saw his opportunity.

Claiming that the attacks were unprovoked, the President argued that the conflict was no longer a civil war. At his request, on August 5 Congress passed the Gulf of Tonkin Resolution. It gave him the power to enlarge the American role in the fighting. It was not a declaration of war, but it did give the President the power to take any military actions he felt were necessary in Vietnam.

Much later it was revealed that neither of the attacks in the Gulf of Tonkin had been confirmed. The public also learned that the American warships had been there to protect South Vietnamese gunboats that were attacking North Vietnam.

An escalating American role Slowly but surely the United States was drawn deeper into the war. At first it had sent only advisors. Now its planes made massive bombing raids on North Vietnamese factories and military bases. Johnson hoped the raids would break the enemy's will to fight.

Instead, North Vietnam sent Chinese and Soviet weapons to the Viet Cong along a

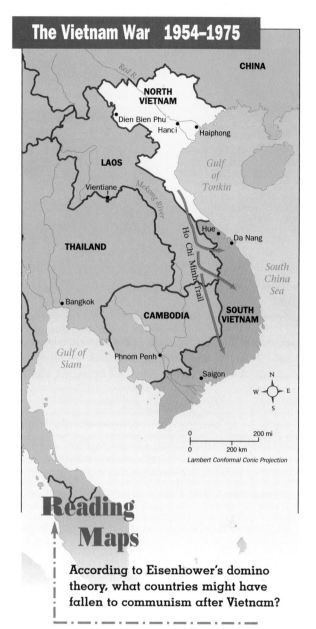

The Vietnam War 1954–1975

Reading Maps

According to Eisenhower's domino theory, what countries might have fallen to communism after Vietnam?

route called the Ho Chi Minh Trail. Troops from the North Vietnamese Army (NVA) soon began pouring south in order to help the Viet Cong.

In response, Johnson decided to use American ground troops. In early 1965, 3,500 marines landed. Within three years the number of American troops had escalated to more than 500,000.

Helicopters played a key role in the war, carrying troops to remote sites for "search and destroy" missions. Despite their high-tech weapons, American forces could not break the Viet Cong's will to fight.

At home, meanwhile, an antiwar movement grew that was stronger than during any previous American war. At first most protests could be heard on college campuses. As the war casualties mounted, however, the movement expanded. Many young men refused to be drafted. Some burned their draft cards, a few went to jail, and thousands fled to Canada and Britain.

Adding to the rising discontent was disgust with the corrupt leaders of the South Vietnamese government. Meanwhile, television coverage was for the first time bringing shocking video images of war into American homes.

Hawks vs. doves Antiwar rallies sometimes drew more than 100,000 protestors. The war divided the American public. Those who wanted the United States to withdraw were called "doves," for the traditional symbol of peace. Those in favor of continuing to fight were called "hawks."

Through 1967 most Americans were still hawks. To withdraw and admit defeat seemed shameful. It would send a signal that the United States no longer stood by its commitment to defend against Communist takeovers. Anyway, since the United States was the world's most powerful nation, most Americans remained confident of victory.

American troops now conducted missions independent of the South Vietnamese Army. Helicopters whisked troops to likely hideaways in the jungle with orders to "search for and destroy" Viet Cong guerrillas, supplies, and bases. As the American role increased, so did North Vietnam's support of the Viet Cong. American casualties rose at an alarming rate. In 1965 there were 2,500 killed, wounded, or missing. A year later the total had risen to more than 10,000.

A Different Kind of War

Both in Vietnam and at home this war was different from any other the United States had fought. It was hard to identify the enemy. The Viet Cong wore no uniforms. They fought at night, often from ambush, then returned to their villages and farmed by day. No matter how much damage American planes and troops did, the Viet Cong kept fighting.

The Tet Offensive

That confidence was shattered on January 30, 1968, the first day of Tet—the Vietnamese New Year. Usually soldiers declared a ceasefire on the eve of Tet. This time, however,

84,000 Viet Cong and NVA soldiers attacked military bases and cities in South Vietnam, including the capital, Saigon.

The "Tet Offensive" came as a complete surprise. Although most of the cities were later recaptured, the damage had been done. American casualties were high and morale plummeted.

The Tet Offensive was the war's turning point. The American public lost faith, having been told too many times that victory was just around the corner. In a poll taken after Tet, approval of Johnson's handling of the war reached a low of 26 percent. In March he announced he would not run for re-election.

The Election of 1968

The war was a major election issue in 1968. The leading candidates for the Democratic nomination were Senators Eugene McCarthy and Robert Kennedy and Vice-President Hubert Humphrey. Both McCarthy and Kennedy were doves, while Humphrey supported Johnson's policies. Kennedy fell victim to an assassin's bullet on June 6. Soon afterward, at a convention in Chicago that was disrupted by antiwar riots, Humphrey won the party's nomination.

The Republicans nominated former Vice-President Richard Nixon. He pledged to end the war and restore "law and order" by cracking down on violent antiwar protests. A third-party candidate, hawkish Alabama governor George Wallace, also ran. Appealing to conservative voters, Nixon won a narrow victory.

"Vietnamizing" the War

Promising "peace with honor," Nixon announced a strategy called "Vietnamization." The United States would build up and equip the South Vietnamese Army so that it could carry on the struggle alone. As Vietnamization took place, American forces would be gradually withdrawn.

Into Cambodia and Laos By the end of 1969 American forces in South Vietnam had been reduced to fewer than 400,000. Their orders were to remain on the defensive unless attacked. Meanwhile, Nixon secretly ordered bombings of Communist bases in Cambodia. When these attacks failed to lead to peace talks, he sent troops into Cambodia and Laos to destroy Viet Cong bases and supply depots.

News of these secret operations leaked out, causing a firestorm of public outrage. The worst incident was at Kent State University in Ohio, where nervous National Guardsmen killed four student protestors.

Demonstrations against the Vietnam War sometimes led to violent confrontations. During this 1967 antiwar rally in Washington, D.C., military police clashed with protestors.

Link to Art

The Vietnam Veterans Memorial (1982) This memorial, which stands in Washington, D.C., is a 500-foot-long (150 m) **V**-shaped wall that rises out of the ground, angles up to a height of 10 feet (3 m), and slopes back into the earth. Carved on its black granite surface are the names of the Americans who were killed or are missing in the Vietnam War. The artist, 21-year-old Maya Lin, described her goal for the memorial: "I wanted something horizontal that took you in, that made you feel safe within the park, yet at the same time reminding you of the dead. So I just imagined opening up the earth." **Discuss** How do you think the memorial reflects the artist's goal?

President Nixon defended his actions by warning that "totalitarianism" would threaten all free nations if the United States acted like a "pitiful, helpless giant."

Like the Presidents before him, Nixon had a tiger by the tail and did not know how to let go. Even as he withdrew troops, he increased the bombing of North Vietnam

and blockaded its coast. Nothing, however, weakened the Communists' will to fight.

The end of the war On December 30, 1972, the United States abruptly halted its air attacks. Two weeks later, Nixon declared that so much progress had been made in secret peace talks that he was ordering an end to

American fighting. On January 27, 1973, representatives of the United States, South Vietnam, North Vietnam, and the Viet Cong signed a peace agreement in Paris.

By the end of March, the last American soldiers had come home, though the situation remained unsettled. When the government of South Vietnam broke its pledge to cooperate with the Viet Cong in organizing elections, the NVA launched a final attack. In April 1975, the South Vietnamese government surrendered, leaving the Communists in control of all of Vietnam.

Costs of the War

The war cost the lives of more than 58,000 Americans. Hundreds of thousands of others suffered permanent physical or mental damage. For many of the survivors, war memories were an unending nightmare. One veteran commented:

“Sometimes I wish I could've just
went ahead and died with my friends.
I used to say, ‘I'm only dreaming.
I'll wake up some day.’”

Another great cost of the war was its effect on the attitude of Americans toward their government. Many people were shaken by the failure of the rich and powerful United States to defeat a poor and tiny nation. Also, the knowledge that government officials had lied about many aspects of the war undermined the public's faith in their leaders.

Vietnam, too, was badly scarred by the war, with as many as 2 million killed, millions wounded, and millions left homeless. Suffering continued as the Communist victors dealt harshly with their former South Vietnamese enemies. Interestingly, though, despite the domino theory, North Vietnam's victory did not result in a Communist takeover of Southeast Asia.

Point of View

What are the lessons of Vietnam?

A junior high school teacher in Oklahoma asked key supporters and opponents of the war: “What should we tell our children about Vietnam?” Here are some responses:

“No American must ever be called upon to sacrifice his life for a cause that is poorly understood, blurred, or deceptively explained.”

Marvin Kalb, television news correspondent

“We were in Vietnam for the same reason we had been in Korea: to stop the spread of communism. . . . The mistake we made was not to allow the military people unlimited authority to win.”

Carl Albert, House Majority Leader, 1962–1971

“The United States should not intervene in other countries with military forces unless that country is a serious threat to our own security.”

J. William Fulbright, U.S. Senator, 1945–1975

One lesson most Americans could agree on was that fighting a war requires the support of the American people. In 1973 Congress passed the War Powers Act, forbidding troops to be sent into combat for more than 90 days without the approval of Congress.

2. Section Review

1. Why did the United States go to war in Vietnam?

2. How did the Vietnam War differ from other American wars?

3. What were the costs of the war?

4. Critical Thinking Was the United States right to fight in Vietnam? Explain.

3. The End of the Cold War

Reading Guide

New Terms détente, strategic arms

Section Focus How the Cold War came to an end

1. How did Richard Nixon improve relations with China and the Soviet Union?
2. What actions did Jimmy Carter and Ronald Reagan take to deal with the Cold War?
3. What led to the collapse of communism in Eastern Europe and the Soviet Union?

Early in his career, President Nixon had carved out a reputation as a fierce foe of communism. As he struggled to end the war in Vietnam, however, he realized that he needed the help of China and the Soviet Union in order to bring North Vietnam to the peace table.

Looking beyond Vietnam, Nixon saw that the United States could not afford to remain bitter enemies with the two most powerful Communist nations. With his chief foreign policy advisor, Henry Kissinger, Nixon began a bold new policy of **détente** (day-TAHNT)—a relaxing of tensions between nations.

Nixon Visits China

Taking the first step in détente, Nixon convinced the UN to accept Communist China as a member:

"We simply cannot afford to leave China forever outside the family of nations. There is no place on this small planet for a billion of its potentially most able people to live in angry isolation.**"**

In 1971 China replaced Taiwan on the Security Council.

Meanwhile, Nixon saw an opportunity in the growing conflict between the Soviet

Union and China over territory and power. He decided to take advantage of this rift by playing off one Communist power against the other.

In February 1972, in a dramatic move, President Nixon traveled to Communist China to meet with its leaders. For more than

In 1972 President Nixon met with China's Premier Chou En-Lai (left) in Beijing. The historic visit paved the way for diplomatic relations with China.

20 years the United States had refused all contact with Communist China. Now, as Nixon said, he had "opened the door for travel, . . . for trade."

The Soviet Union and SALT

Just three months later Nixon made his next move, a visit to the Soviet Union. Soviet leader Leonid Brezhnev (LAY-uh-NEED BREZH-nef), alarmed by Nixon's China visit, agreed to more cooperative relations with the United States.

Most importantly, Nixon and Brezhnev took steps to slow the arms race. They signed the first Strategic Arms Limitation Treaty (SALT I), agreeing to build fewer nuclear missiles. **Strategic arms** are weapons designed to strike at an enemy's military bases and industrial centers. The two leaders also agreed to limit antiballistic missile (ABM) systems—weapons designed to shoot down incoming missiles.

Conflict in the Middle East

Nixon's trips to China and the Soviet Union helped him win re-election in 1972, in a landslide victory over Democratic Senator George McGovern. During his second term, however, détente was threatened by conflict in the Middle East.

On October 6, 1973, Egypt and Syria attacked Israel on the Jewish holy day Yom Kippur. The Yom Kippur War was part of a long-running conflict. Arab nations in the Middle East were determined to destroy Israel and return control of the land to the Palestinians. (See the World Link on the birth of Israel, page 819.) The Israelis were determined to protect their new nation as a homeland for Jews.

When Nixon learned that the Soviets were supplying Egypt and Syria with weapons and

Link to the Present

China's military power Relations with China have thawed since President Nixon's visit. Still, they are far from warm. China's growing military power is one cause of the tension.

China has more than 400 nuclear warheads. Despite international protests, it continues to develop longer-range, more accurate missiles. China has also violated international agreements by selling missiles to other countries.

Selling missiles is a way to make money. In addition, the Chinese may believe that a nuclear threat will help them extend their influence in Asia. For example, China regards Taiwan as its territory and expects official reunification in the near future. In 1996 China carried out missile launches and other military exercises near Taiwan to discourage pro-independence feelings among the island's people.

advisors, he airlifted helicopters, tanks, and other weapons to Israel. The war ended with a UN-arranged cease-fire on October 25.

The oil embargo The United States paid a stiff penalty for supporting Israel. Arab nations halted oil shipments to the United States and its allies, causing a severe energy shortage that winter. Long lines at gas stations showed how much Americans depended on "black gold" from the Middle East. Policymakers now had to balance the nation's commitment to Israel against its need for oil and its fear of Soviet influence in the Middle East.

Carter and Human Rights

The election of Jimmy Carter in 1976 brought a Democratic administration back to the White House. A former governor of Georgia, Carter declared that human rights—rather than rigid opposition to communism—would be the "soul of our foreign policy." He cut off aid to some dictators who abused human rights, even though some were anti-Communist.

Meanwhile, Carter took steps to expand détente. In 1979 he announced that the United States would recognize Communist China, rather than Nationalist Taiwan, as China's rightful government. That same year he and Soviet leader Brezhnev signed a new strategic arms treaty—SALT II.

Later that year, though, détente received a blow when Soviet troops invaded neighboring Afghanistan to put down a rebellion. Carter denounced the invasion, cut off most trade with the Soviet Union, and refused to let the United States take part in the 1980 Olympics in Moscow. His reaction killed SALT II and ended détente.

Reagan and the "Evil Empire"

In the election of 1980, Ronald Reagan won a resounding victory over Carter. A former governor of California, he was known for his tough stance against communism. In a speech he warned that the Soviet Union was an "evil empire" bent on world domination. As you will read in Chapter 31, he stepped up efforts to support anti-Communist leaders, especially in Latin America.

Reagan believed in dealing with the Soviets from a position of strength. During his first three years in office, he got Congress to increase defense spending by 44 percent. He also approved research on a plan to use lasers to destroy incoming missiles.

Changes in the Soviet Union Reagan easily won a second term in 1984. He then softened his anti-Soviet attitude, in part because of changes in the Soviet Union after Mikhail Gorbachev (mih-kIL gōr-bah-CHAWF) became the Soviet leader in 1985.

Gorbachev recognized that the Soviet economy was on the brink of collapse and the people were losing faith in the government. His response was to allow them more freedom of speech and of the press. He also introduced limited free enterprise, allowing private citizens to own businesses.

To succeed in saving the economy, however, Gorbachev knew that he would have to reduce military spending. The arms race and the war in Afghanistan had become costly burdens.

The United States welcomed Gorbachev's new policies. Almost immediately Cold War tensions began to thaw. In December 1987 Reagan and Gorbachev agreed to get rid of all Soviet and American short- and intermediate-range missiles. The Intermediate Nuclear Force (INF) Treaty was the first Cold War agreement to destroy nuclear weapons.

President Reagan met with Soviet leader Mikhail Gorbachev to discuss how to slow the arms race.

Hands-On HISTORY

Planning a Cold War museum With each year, memories of the Cold War fade. You likely remember little about it; your children will have no memory of it.

Activity With a group, plan a museum to give future generations an overview of the Cold War. Each room should illustrate a major theme.

1 Decide on the themes to illustrate, such as The Arms Race, Conflict in Eastern Europe, and War in Vietnam. Choose at least five themes.

2 Briefly describe the items to display in each theme room. You do not have to find or make the items, so you can include almost anything. A model of *Sputnik*, photographs of the Berlin Wall, a diorama of a bomb shelter, and plaques with quotations from President Truman are just a few possibilities.

3 Consider how to arrange the displays. Your arrangement should help visitors understand both the sequence of Cold War events and the cause-effect relationships between events.

4 Draw a floor plan of your museum. Label the theme rooms, and show and label the displays.

The Berlin Wall, 1989

The Fall of the Iron Curtain

Gorbachev's policies encouraged people in Eastern European nations to call for democracy and greater economic opportunity. In 1989 Poland became the first to form a non-Communist government. Others soon followed, as demonstrators took to the streets in Czechoslovakia, Hungary, and East Germany to protest Communist rule.

In November 1989 German students and workers attacked the Berlin Wall with crowbars and sledgehammers. Eleven months after that hated symbol of the Cold War was torn down, East and West Germany were united as a democratic nation. The Iron Curtain was no more.

The collapse of communism in Eastern Europe was soon followed by the stunning breakup of the Soviet Union itself. Nationalistic feelings, long held down by Communist rule, erupted among the diverse peoples of the 15 Soviet republics. Gorbachev's efforts to save the Soviet Union had unleashed a tiger that could no longer be caged.

In August 1991 Communist officials tried to turn back the clock. They arrested Gorbachev, but their attempt to seize the government failed after thousands of angry demonstrators rallied against them.

The attempted takeover sped the breakup of the Soviet Union. By the end of the year all 15 republics had declared independence, leaving what one observer called "the Soviet Disunion." Almost overnight, the totalitarian system that since World War II had challenged the United States for world leadership had collapsed. The Cold War had come to an end.

Truman's prediction In his farewell speech at the end of his second term in January 1953, President Truman had predicted that the West would win the Cold War:

❝As the free world grows stronger, more unified, more attractive to men on both sides of the Iron Curtain—and as the Soviet hopes for easy expansion are blocked—then there will have to come a time of change in the Soviet world. . . . I have a deep and abiding faith in the destiny of free men.❞

Truman's remarkable prediction proved to be correct. His policy of blocking the spread of communism gave communism time to destroy itself.

3. Section Review

1. Define **détente** and **strategic arms.**
2. How did President Nixon pursue his policy of détente?
3. How did the policies of Presidents Carter and Reagan differ?
4. What led to the collapse of communism in Eastern Europe?
5. **Critical Thinking** Do you think the Cold War could ever start again? Explain.

Why We Remember

The Cold War Era

Years after leaving office, Harry Truman sat down at his desk in Independence, Missouri, to write his memoirs. "During the years I was President," he began in his preface, "the one purpose that dominated me in everything I thought and did was to prevent a third world war." Those same words could have been written by each of the Cold War era Presidents.

In 1945 the United States faced a historic choice. Would it retreat into isolationism as it had after World War I? Or would it help create a better world out of the chaos of war? Americans chose to play an active role, helping to protect basic human rights and freedoms around the world.

This was not an easy choice. The Cold War was one of the most frightening times in our history. After World War II, the thought of another global conflict was alarming. Even more terrifying was the knowledge that a war fought with nuclear weapons might mean the end of all life on earth.

No one knew that the Cold War struggle against communism would drag on for more than 40 years. No one knew that it would take Americans into distant conflicts or lead to a costly arms race. Americans did know, however, that they were willing to pay the price to preserve freedom. Victory in the Cold War was victory for freedom-loving people everywhere.

Skill Lab

Using Information

Asking Historical Questions

The Cold War is over. The West won. Yet there is still much controversy over the long conflict between Communist and non-Communist countries. Historians cannot even agree as to which side fired the first "shot."

Question to Investigate

Who started the Cold War?

Procedure

Imagine that you are a historian trying to answer that question. Begin your research by asking historical questions about sources **A** and **B**. Those questions will give you a direction for additional research.

1 State your immediate goal.

2 Identify the information.
a. Read sources **A** and **B** carefully.
b. Make a column for each source. List what each source says or implies about the actions and attitudes of the two sides at the start of the Cold War.

3 Identify questions to ask.
a. Read the Skill Tips for ideas.
b. List four questions for each source.

4 Decide how to get the answers.
a. Write the answers you know.
b. Describe three ways you might get more information.

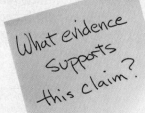
What evidence supports this claim?

Skill Tips

See the Skill Tips on page 477. You might also ask:
- Where did the writer get the information?
- What was the writer's purpose?
- What information is relevant?
- What gaps, if any, are there in the information?

Sources to Use

A "[On April 13, 1945] Truman received [Soviet foreign minister] Molotov in the Oval Office and, as Truman recalled it, chewed him out 'bluntly' for the way the Russians were behaving in Poland. Molotov was stunned. He had never, he told Truman, 'been talked to like that in my life.' 'Carry out your agreements,' Truman responded, 'and you *won't* get talked to like that.'

"That's a good way to talk, if you want to start an argument."

From "A Good Way to Pick a Fight," by Charles L. Mee, Jr., in *American Heritage*, August 1977

B "I told him [Khrushchev] that after World War II we had not been suspicious of Russia. I knew that my husband had hoped we would be able to come to an understanding. 'But then,' I went on, 'we found the Russians did not strictly keep agreements made at Yalta and we became more and more suspicious.'

"'Communism will win in the whole world,' he told me. 'This is scientifically based on the writings of Karl Marx, Engels and Lenin.' He went on to assure me blandly: 'We are against any military attempt to introduce communism or socialism into any country.'"

From Eleanor Roosevelt's description of her 1957 meeting with Khrushchev, in *The Autobiography of Eleanor Roosevelt* (New York: Harper, 1961)

Chapter Survey

Reviewing Vocabulary

Define the following terms.
1. Cold War   3. détente
2. containment   4. strategic arms

Reviewing Main Ideas

1. Give three examples of how the United States contained communism in Europe.
2. Describe Cold War conflicts that arose in each of the following places. (a) China (b) Korea (c) the Middle East
3. How did conflict over Cuba almost lead to nuclear disaster?
4. Summarize the steps by which the United States became more and more involved in the war in Vietnam.
5. Describe two effects of the Vietnam War on the United States and its people.
6. Tell how each of the following Presidents handled relations with the Soviet Union. (a) Richard Nixon (b) Jimmy Carter (c) Ronald Reagan
7. Trace the events that led to the collapse of communism in Eastern Europe and the Soviet Union.

Thinking Critically

1. **Analysis** Why do you think that the United States was willing to intervene in Korea and Vietnam, but did not intervene during the revolt in Hungary?
2. **Evaluation** Do you think that the domino theory was reasonable? Why or why not?
3. **Why We Remember: Synthesis** It is widely agreed that the Cold War ended in victory for the West and for the forces of freedom and democracy. But was the victory a total one? Use what you have learned in this chapter and what you already know about current world events to answer the question.

Applying Skills

Asking historical questions You know that asking questions is useful when studying events of the past, like the Cold War. Asking questions is equally useful when learning about events of today.

Read or listen to two different accounts of a recent event at your school, in your community, or in our nation. Your goal is to compare what the accounts say about the causes of the event. Use what you learned on page 837 to do the following:

1. Summarize the information that each source gives about the causes of the event.
2. List three questions about each source.
3. Write the answers you already know.
4. Name two ways that you might get more information.

History Mystery

Sputnik Answer the History Mystery on page 815. The news of the Soviet launching of *Sputnik* sparked a strong effort to improve science and mathematics education in schools throughout the United States. Why do you think this happened?

Writing in Your History Journal

1. **Keys to History** (a) The time line on pages 814–815 has eight Keys to History. In your journal, describe why each one is important to know about. (b) Decide on a category of additional events for the time line, such as Middle East Events, Growing Involvement in Vietnam, or Defrosting the Cold War. Write the appropriate events and dates in your journal, explaining why you think the events should be added.
2. **Harry Truman** *Although unprepared to be President, Harry Truman rose to the occasion*

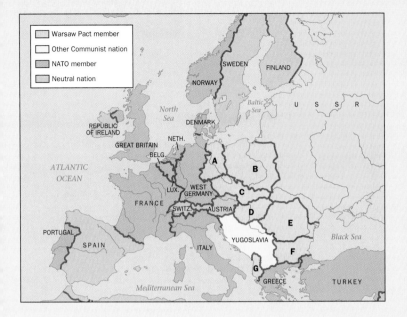

Reviewing Geography

1. Each letter stands for a Warsaw Pact member in Eastern Europe. Write the name of each country.

2. Geographic Thinking Tell how you think location influenced the decision in each of these Cold War situations:
• China's intervention in the Korean War
• The Soviet Union's response to the Hungarian revolt
• U.S. support of the overthrow of Guatemala's government
• The Soviet Union's demand that western powers leave Berlin
• U.S. insistence that Soviet missiles be removed from Cuba

admirably. Do you agree? Explain. Write your responses in your journal.

3. Thinking Historically Suppose you had been a teenager during the Vietnam War. In your journal, tell whether you would have been a hawk or a dove and whether you would have made your feelings known in a public way. Explain why.

Alternative Assessment

Citizenship: Recalling Cold War presidencies Imagine that you and six classmates are Presidents Truman, Eisenhower, Kennedy, Johnson, Nixon, Carter, and Reagan. Prepare individual presentations that answer the following questions. You may include visual aids.

❶ What actions did you take in the Cold War? (Depending on the President, these might include sending troops into battle.)

❷ What was your attitude toward the Soviet Union and communism?

❸ Do you think that your actions helped the West win the Cold War? Explain.

❹ If you had it to do over again, would you do anything differently? Explain.

Your work will be evaluated on the following criteria:
• you present the actions accurately
• you reflect the President's point of view based on what you know about him from reading the chapter
• you make the President seem real

Chapter 30

The Postwar Years at Home

Sections

Keys to History

1950–1954
Senator Joseph McCarthy spreads fear and distrust

1954
Supreme Court rules school segregation unconstitutional
NAACP lawyers celebrate Court's decision

1955
Montgomery bus boycott
Rosa Parks rides an integrated bus

1945

1955

World **Link**

Looking Back

The "Red Scare"
1919

Gandhi wins struggle for India's independence
1947

HISTORY *Mystery*

This young girl lived within 7 blocks of an elementary school. Why did she have to take a bus 21 blocks to another school?

1963
President Kennedy assassinated

1964–1965
Civil rights acts

1965
President Johnson announces Great Society program

Cartoon of President Johnson

1968
Martin Luther King, Jr., assassinated

1974
Watergate scandal leads President Nixon to resign

Marine removes portrait of Nixon

1965

1975

Looking Ahead

First woman appointed to Supreme Court

1981

Beginning the Story with

Martin Luther King, Jr.

Young Martin Luther King, Jr., was confused. "M. L.," as he was called, always played with the two boys who lived across the street from his Atlanta home. When they began school, M. L. went to a different school than his friends. At the end of the first day, when he ran over to their house to compare notes, their mother said they could not play with him anymore. "Why not?" he asked. Her only answer was that "they were white and I was colored." M. L. ran home in tears. He later recalled that his mother

❝tried to explain the divided system of the South—the segregated schools, restaurants, theaters, housing; the white and colored signs on drinking fountains, waiting rooms, lavatories—as a social condition rather than a natural order. Then she said . . . 'You are as good as anyone.'❞

"A Sense of Somebodiness"

Sometimes it was hard for M. L. to feel "as good as anyone." Outside of the close circle of family, friends, and the Ebenezer Baptist Church led by his father, the Reverend Martin Luther King, Sr., it was impossible to ignore the stings of segregation. M. L. would never forget a trip with his father to an Atlanta shoe store. When the two sat down in empty seats at the front of the store, a clerk said politely, "I'll be happy to wait on you if you'll just move to those seats in the rear." Mr. King responded, "We'll either buy shoes sitting here or we won't buy shoes at all." As they walked out, M. L. heard his father mutter, "I don't care how long I have to live with this system, I will never accept it." Nor would his son. King later wrote:

> "My mother taught me that I should feel a sense of somebodiness. On the other hand, I had to go out and face the system, which stared me in the face every day, saying, 'You are less than.' 'You are not equal to.' So this was a real tension within."

"The Best Jitterbug"

Most of the time, M. L. kept this tension hidden. He was a bright child who loved to read. At the age of 8 he had a newspaper route, and by 13 he was the youngest assistant manager of a delivery station for the *Atlanta Journal.*

As a teenager, M. L.'s friends nicknamed him "Tweed" because he spent most of his money on stylish tweed suits. His other street name was "Will Shoot." Whenever he got his hands on the basketball, he was sure to shoot rather than pass. He also loved to dance. According to his brother, he was "the best jitterbug in town."

M. L. could also be just about the best student. He skipped two years of high school, graduating at the age of 15. When he was 14, M. L. entered a statewide speech contest in Dublin, Georgia. Accompanied by his teacher, Mrs. Bradley, M. L. made the trip, delivered his speech, and won first prize. On the way home, though, his joy at winning turned to rage. He later wrote:

Martin Luther King, Jr., became a leader of the struggle against racial injustice. Here, he and his wife, Coretta, lead a march for voting rights.

> "Some white passengers boarded the bus, and the white driver ordered us to give the whites our seats. We didn't move quickly enough to suit him, so he began cursing us. . . . Mrs. Bradley finally urged me up, saying we had to obey the law. And so we stood in the aisle for the 90 miles to Atlanta. . . . It was the angriest I have ever been in my life."

M. L. had grown up with the commandment of Jesus to "love your enemy." On this night, though, it was hard for him to hate the sin but not the sinner. It was easy for him to believe that "the only way we could solve our problem of segregation was an armed revolt." Only after King became a minister would he find a different way to fight injustice.

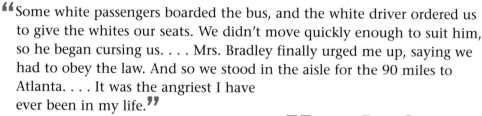

Hands-On
⌐ ➔ HISTORY

Activity

Imagine that you were traveling with Martin Luther King, Jr., on the way home from the speech contest. Create a dialogue between yourself and King about whether you should give up your bus seats.

1. Adjusting to Peace

Reading Guide

New Term **closed shop**

Section Focus **The challenges Americans faced at home after World War II**

1. How did the change from war to peace affect the nation's economy?
2. Why did fear of communism sweep the country?
3. How did prosperity affect Americans in the 1950s?

When World War II ended in 1945, Martin Luther King, Jr., was studying to be a minister at Morehouse College. During the next few years that quiet campus would be flooded with returning war veterans.

For civilians as well as veterans, the first years after the war brought both uncertainty and opportunity. Fears stemming from the Cold War haunted Americans. So did hopes for a better life after a decade and a half of depression and war.

"The Great Boom"

Wartime production had lifted the United States out of the Great Depression. Now the nation rose to new heights of prosperity. "The Great American Boom is on," *Fortune* magazine declared in 1946.

People were eager to use their wartime wages to buy goods they had not been able to get during the war. In addition, the GI Bill, passed in 1944, gave veterans money to spend on businesses, homes, and schooling.

Labor on strike Although industries increased production, there were still shortages of many goods. The prices of scarce items, such as meat, skyrocketed. Workers pressed hard for wage increases to keep pace with rising prices. When employers refused, a wave of strikes swept the nation.

Although President Truman supported labor, he feared that wage increases would lead to even higher prices. In April 1946 he ended a United Mine Workers' strike by seizing the mines. A month later he forced striking railroad workers back to work.

In 1947 Congress passed the Taft-Hartley Act to curb the power of unions. The act banned the **closed shop**—a workplace in which only union members can be hired. It also gave the President the power to delay a strike by declaring a "cooling off" period.

Truman's Second Term

By the presidential election of 1948, the Democratic Party was divided over Truman's policies at home and abroad. Polls predicted a sure win for the Republican candidate, Governor Thomas Dewey of New York. Truman campaigned tirelessly, however, and pulled out a surprise victory.

The Fair Deal In 1949 Truman submitted to Congress his "Fair Deal" plan. His goal was to give all Americans a share in the nation's economic opportunities.

Under Truman, Congress extended the Social Security program to more Americans. It also provided funds for low-income housing. However, southern Democrats joined with Republicans to block many of Truman's proposals, including health insurance.

The Hunt for Communists

There was one thing, though, on which many Americans could agree. They feared that Communists and people sympathetic to communism were trying to overthrow the government.

"Spy fever" gripped the nation, and the hunt for traitors was on. Government workers suspected of disloyalty lost their jobs. Congress searched for Communists in the movie industry. Writers, actors, and directors who refused to answer questions about their political beliefs were "blacklisted." Major studios would not hire them, even when there was no proof of their disloyalty.

When the Soviet Union exploded its first atomic bomb in 1949, many people thought that spies must have given American atomic secrets to the Soviets. In 1953 Julius and Ethel Rosenberg, former members of the Communist Party, were convicted of being atomic spies and put to death.

Joseph McCarthy Senator Joseph R. McCarthy of Wisconsin fanned Americans' fear of communism to gain fame and power. In 1950 he claimed that 205 State Department employees were Communists.

A special committee, led by Senator Millard Tydings of Maryland, investigated and declared the charges a "fraud and a hoax." In response, McCarthy spread false charges that Tydings was pro-Communist. As a result, Tydings lost his 1950 campaign for re-election.

Aware of McCarthy's power to destroy careers, few people were brave enough to oppose him and his scare tactics. In fact, many businesses, schools, and unions joined the hunt for traitors. They required employees to sign "loyalty oaths," and fired them if they refused.

One brave opponent did come forward, however. Senator Margaret Chase Smith of Maine was outraged that people were "afraid to speak their minds lest they be politically smeared as Communists." She declared, "Freedom of speech is not what it used to be in America."

Finally, in 1954 McCarthy went too far. That year 20 million television viewers saw him make false charges against the United States Army. The Senate voted to condemn McCarthy for his conduct. His power gone, McCarthy sank from public view.

President Eisenhower

As the presidential election of 1952 drew near, fear of communism was still strong, and the Korean War was dragging on. Hoping that the voters would welcome a change,

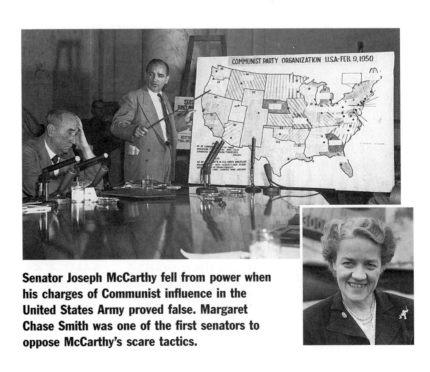

Senator Joseph McCarthy fell from power when his charges of Communist influence in the United States Army proved false. Margaret Chase Smith was one of the first senators to oppose McCarthy's scare tactics.

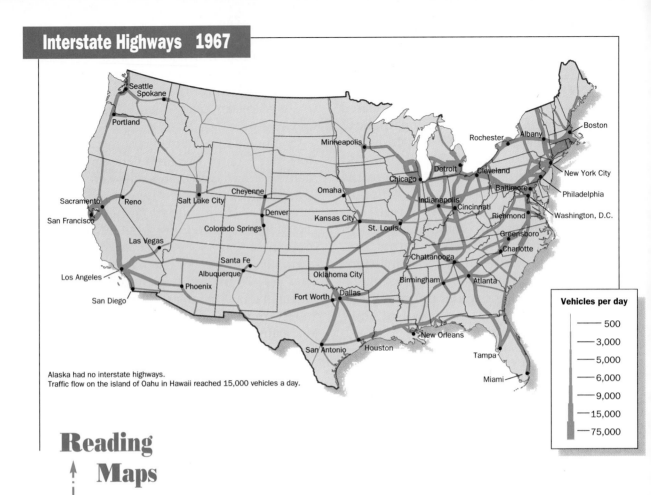

Seattle
Spokane
Portland
Minneapolis
Rochester
Albany
Boston
Detroit
Cleveland
New York City
Sacramento
Reno
Salt Lake City
Cheyenne
Omaha
Chicago
Indianapolis
Baltimore
Philadelphia
San Francisco
Denver
Kansas City
Cincinnati
Richmond
Washington, D.C.
Las Vegas
Colorado Springs
St. Louis
Greensboro
Los Angeles
Santa Fe
Albuquerque
Oklahoma City
Chattanooga
Charlotte
Phoenix
Fort Worth
Dallas
Birmingham
Atlanta
San Diego
San Antonio
Houston
New Orleans
Tampa
Miami

Alaska had no interstate highways.
Traffic flow on the island of Oahu in Hawaii reached 15,000 vehicles a day.

Vehicles per day

— 500
— 3,000
— 5,000
— 6,000
— 9,000
— 15,000
— 75,000

Reading
Maps

In each of the following areas list three cities that are in the center of heavy traffic flow: East Coast, Midwest, West Coast.

---

the Republicans nominated General Dwight ("Ike") Eisenhower.

A war hero, Ike was widely admired. He defeated the Democratic candidate, Adlai E. Stevenson, in 1952 and again in 1956. For the first time since 1933, a Republican occupied the White House.

Eisenhower's goals President Eisenhower believed that the federal government should play a smaller role in the economy. He called for cutting spending, though not for ending programs that helped people. In fact, he increased the number of people who could receive Social Security benefits.

Perhaps Eisenhower's greatest achievement was the Interstate Highway Act of 1956. It provided funds for a vast system of freeways to link all parts of the United States (see map above). The act had far-reaching results. Increasingly, Americans used highways instead of railroads for traveling and for transporting goods.

The Prosperous 1950s

As Europe and Asia struggled to recover from World War II, prosperity continued in the United States. One reason was the many jobs created in industries producing weapons for the Cold War arms race. Another reason was that productivity was increasing. The use of new technology and more efficient machines made workers more productive. Between 1945 and 1960, for example, the time needed to make a car was cut in half.

A third reason for continued prosperity was increasing demand for housing, cars, and consumer goods. Car production soared from 2 million in 1946 to 8 million in 1955. There was also great demand for televisions, which had been developed during the war. Between 1946 and 1960, the number of TV sets soared from 7,000 to 50 million.

With this steady increase in demand for goods came a steep rise in the birth rate, called the "baby boom." Families with four or five children became common. Meanwhile, people were living longer, thanks to advances in medicine such as the discovery of penicillin and a vaccine against polio.

Suburban growth The baby boom created a great demand for better housing. Instead of renting city apartments, families wanted homes of their own in the suburbs. GI loans made buying houses affordable. Cars and good roads made it easy to commute longer distances to work.

During the 1950s the number of Americans living in suburbs grew by 50 percent. Developers met the demand for suburban housing by buying cheap land outside cities. There they built row upon row of mass-produced homes, known as tract houses.

The problem of poverty Unfortunately, some Americans did not share in the prosperity of the 1950s. By 1960 more than one-fifth of the population, including unskilled workers, migrant farmworkers, and the aged, lived in poverty.

Rural areas suffered some of the greatest poverty, but most of the poor were trapped in big-city slums. As families and industries

Link to the Present

Television then and now It is a Sunday evening in 1953, and a family sits down to watch TV. Neighbors who do not yet have TV sets drop by to watch, too. They crowd around the black-and-white screen, which is barely more than a foot (30 cm) wide. At 8 o'clock, there is a choice of three programs.

Today, about 98 percent of American households have at least one TV set. Programs appear in color on screens that may be 4 feet (120 cm) wide or larger. Many families subscribe to cable TV systems or have satellite dishes that allow them to receive 50, 100, 200, or more channels.

moved to the suburbs, cities lost important tax money. City schools and other services declined. Crime rose. More and more, the people who stayed in the cities were those who could not afford to move.

1. Section Review

1. Define **closed shop.**
2. Why did workers strike after the war?
3. Describe at least two ways that the United States changed in the 1950s.
4. Critical Thinking As a senator, would you have voted to condemn McCarthy for his conduct? Why or why not?

Geography Lab

By the 1970s extensive freeway networks connected cities and suburbs.

The Growth of Suburbs

In St. Louis, as in many cities, the suburban boom of the 1950s led to urban "bust." Between 1950 and 1960, the population of St. Louis dropped from 856,800 to 750,000. People were moving to suburbs, which sprouted outside the central city, filling in the spaces between older, once separate communities.

Today the city of St. Louis has about 396,700 people. However, the St. Louis metropolitan area—which includes surrounding communities in Missouri and Illinois—has a population of nearly 2.5 million. Study the map and answer the questions.

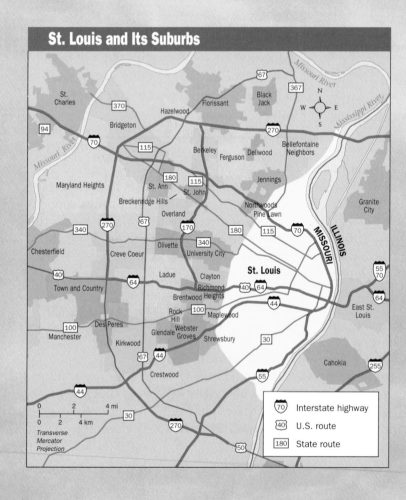

St. Louis and Its Suburbs

70	Interstate highway
40	U.S. route
180	State route

Link to History

1. What makes it possible for people to live in places like Bridgeton and Webster Groves and yet work in downtown St. Louis?

2. You can see that some highways, like Interstate 170, do not go into St. Louis. What inferences about people's jobs and ways of life do you draw from that?

3. Affordable housing was one reason people began moving out of central cities in the 1950s. Name two other reasons that occur to you.

4. **Hands-On Geography** Which suits you better: suburban or city life? Make a collage of pictures and headlines from newspapers and magazines to show why you feel as you do.

2. A Spirit of Change

Reading Guide

New Term civil rights

Section Focus The new domestic goals set by John Kennedy and Lyndon Johnson

1. What "New Frontier" programs did Kennedy propose?
2. How did Johnson pursue his vision of the Great Society?
3. What destroyed Johnson's Great Society plans?

"America is today the strongest, the most influential, and most productive nation in the world." So said President Eisenhower as he prepared to leave office in 1960.

The Presidents who followed Eisenhower faced a two-part challenge. Could they continue to use the nation's strength and wealth to contain communism and protect democracy abroad, and still take care of Americans at home?

The Election of 1960

The presidential election of 1960 focused on that question. The Republicans nominated Vice-President Richard M. Nixon, who promised he would continue Eisenhower's policies.

The Democratic candidate, Senator John F. Kennedy of Massachusetts, faced an uphill battle. Only 43 years old, he was less well known than Nixon. He was also a Catholic, and Americans had never elected a Catholic to the presidency.

This was the first campaign in which television played an important part. In a televised debate, 70 million viewers saw Nixon, weak from a recent illness, looking tired and tense. In contrast, Kennedy, healthy and tanned, looked relaxed and confident. Many historians believe that the debate made the difference, ensuring Kennedy's narrow victory.

Kennedy's "New Frontier"

Filled with idealism and energy, Kennedy immediately set about his goal of "getting the country moving again." He called his program the "New Frontier."

Faced with a recession that had begun in 1960, Kennedy persuaded Congress to pass legislation to create new industries and retrain unemployed workers. He also called for a tax cut to help business.

One of Kennedy's most successful programs still exists—the Peace Corps. Since 1961 thousands of Americans have volunteered for two-year stints in Asia, Africa, and Latin America. They offer their skills as engineers, teachers, and farmers, for example, to help people help themselves.

In 1961 Congress also approved $20 billion for a space program that Kennedy promised would "put a man on the moon" by 1970. The program quickly bore fruit. Within a year, John H. Glenn, Jr., became the first American to orbit the earth.

Poverty Kennedy had less success in attacking problems of poverty and inequality. He had been deeply moved by a book called *The Other America*, by Michael Harrington, who warned: "[The poor] are hungry. . . . They are without adequate housing and education and medical care."

To get at the causes of poverty, Kennedy proposed more federal aid to improve schools and city housing. He also asked for laws providing health insurance for the aged. Congress refused to act. As you will read in Section 3, Congress also refused to pass a bill to enforce African Americans' **civil rights**—the rights guaranteed to all Americans by the Constitution.

Kennedy's Assassination

Looking ahead to a second term, Kennedy hoped to have more success with his programs to fight poverty and protect civil rights. He never got the chance.

In Dallas, Texas, on November 22, 1963, Kennedy and his wife, Jacqueline, were riding in an open car past cheering crowds when rifle shots rang out. The President slumped forward. Struck in the neck and the head, he died quickly.

That day Dallas police arrested a young man named Lee Harvey Oswald and charged him with the President's assassination. Two days later, while police were moving him to another jail, Oswald himself was shot dead by a man named Jack Ruby.

In 1964 an investigation by the Warren Commission, headed by Chief Justice Earl Warren, concluded that Oswald had acted alone. Still, many people were sure that Oswald was part of a group that had planned the assassination. Although the evidence was examined again in the 1970s, the motive for the murder remains a mystery.

Hands-On *HISTORY*

Collecting memories of Kennedy's assassination A woman who was a teenager when John F. Kennedy was assassinated remembers it this way: "I was in English class when the public address system suddenly came on, but it was not the principal talking. It was a radio broadcast, a very confused one. It took us a few minutes to realize what was being said—that President Kennedy had been shot. My teacher started crying. I felt frozen, numb."

This frame from a home movie shows Kennedy being struck by the first bullet.

Activity Interview an adult who remembers the assassination of President Kennedy.

1. Ask the person for permission to do the interview and to share the results with your class.

2. Before the interview, write a list of questions. Plan to ask for personal recollections of the assassination.

3. Conduct the interview. Tape it or make detailed notes. If the person says something you want to hear more about, ask follow-up questions.

4. Report on the interview. Play the tape or quote the questions and answers. Include your observations about the person's reactions.

Americans were stunned by Kennedy's death. They had taken to their hearts their handsome young President, his glamorous wife, and two young children. The nation was plunged into mourning.

Johnson's "Great Society"

Two hours after Kennedy's death, Vice-President Lyndon B. Johnson was sworn in as President. Americans, Johnson later recalled, "were like a bunch of cattle caught in the swamp, . . . circling 'round and 'round." As a Texan who had grown up in cattle country, he knew that

> **"**there is but one way to get the cattle out of the swamp. And that is for the man on the horse to take the lead.**"**

President Johnson was prepared to be that man. He had served in Congress for 23 years. A tireless worker and brilliant political deal maker, he was able to turn Kennedy's vision, as well as his own, into law.

Civil rights Although Johnson was a southerner, he was deeply committed to the cause of civil rights. "I never had any bigotry in me," he explained. "My daddy wouldn't let me. He was a strong anti-Klansman."

As you will read in Section 3, under Johnson's leadership, Congress passed the first significant civil rights laws since Reconstruction. President Johnson also appointed the first black Supreme Court justice—NAACP lawyer Thurgood Marshall—and the first black cabinet member—economist Robert C. Weaver.

The war on poverty Johnson also shared Kennedy's desire to end poverty. As a teacher in Cotulla, Texas, he had known students who were too poor even to bring lunch to school. Early in 1964 Johnson called for a "war on poverty." He told Congress:

First Lady Jacqueline Kennedy, still in her blood-stained clothes, looks on as Lyndon Johnson takes the oath of office aboard Air Force One at the Dallas airport.

> **"**Many Americans live on the outskirts of hope, some because of their poverty and some because of their color, and all too many because of both.**"**

That year Congress passed the Economic Opportunity Act, providing almost $1 billion for antipoverty programs. One program offered job training for unemployed young people in inner cities. Another sent volunteers into cities to teach reading and job skills. A third, the Head Start program, helped preschoolers learn the skills they would need in school.

Johnson hoped that these programs would help Americans to create a "Great Society." This new society, he said, "rests on abundance and liberty for all. It demands an end to poverty and racial injustice."

The 1964 election In the election of 1964 the Republican candidate, Senator Barry Goldwater of Arizona, attacked the Great Society programs as unnecessary and wasteful. He also criticized Johnson for not taking a tougher stand in the Cold War.

Signs (1970) As an art student, Robert Rauschenberg studied photography. Later he began to use collage (kuh-LAHZH), a method of creating a work of art by gluing pictures and other materials onto paper or canvas.

In *Signs,* Rauschenberg made a collage of the 1960s out of newspaper and magazine photographs of memorable people and events of that time. **Discuss** Why might Rauschenberg have chosen these images? What do you think he wants you to think about the 1960s?

The conservative Goldwater did not appeal to all Republicans. Many moderates voted instead for Johnson. On election day, Johnson swept to victory with more than 61 percent of the votes.

Expanding the Great Society Now Johnson pressed successfully for more Great Society legislation. A flood of bills poured through Congress in 1965. The Elementary and Secondary School Act granted more than $1 billion to education. In health care, Congress established the Medicare program for the aged and the Medicaid program to help the needy and the disabled.

Congress also created the Department of Housing and Urban Development (HUD). Headed by Secretary Robert Weaver, HUD made housing available to low-income families and helped local and state governments with urban problems.

The Great Society stalls At the same time that he was building his Great Society, however, President Johnson was pouring money into the war in Vietnam. As the cost of the war skyrocketed, funds for programs at home dried up. "The Great Society has been shot down on the battlefields of Vietnam," said Martin Luther King, Jr., sadly.

As you read in Chapter 29, President Johnson's hopes for re-election in 1968 were shot down as well. Nonetheless, he left a strong legacy. Under his leadership, Congress took its first steps against racial discrimination and the poverty that it had created.

2. Section Review

1. Define **civil rights.**
2. Describe two programs set up as part of President Johnson's war on poverty.
3. How did the Vietnam War affect Johnson's plans for the Great Society?
4. Critical Thinking Do you think that President Kennedy succeeded in leading the nation in a direction different from that of President Eisenhower? Explain.

3. Fighting for Equal Rights

Reading Guide

New Term integration

Section Focus **Struggles to achieve justice and equal rights in the 1950s–1970s**

1. How did African Americans break down legal barriers to equality?
2. How did the African American struggle for equality become a mass movement?
3. What changes did women, Hispanics, and American Indians bring about?

Soon after World War II, when an African American veteran named Medgar Evers tried to vote, he was driven away from his polling place at gunpoint. A Mexican American veteran, Macario García, was refused service in a restaurant.

Before the war, such treatment was common. Now, however, thousands of veterans like Evers and García were no longer willing to accept discrimination. They had fought for democracy around the world, and now they wanted equal rights and opportunities at home.

Taking Court Action

Like many African American veterans, Medgar Evers joined the NAACP. Since its birth in 1909 (see page 662) it had dedicated itself to protecting African Americans' civil rights. The NAACP pressed for laws enforcing those rights, and its lawyers went to court again and again to obtain equal opportunities for black Americans.

However, Jim Crow laws continued to impose segregation in the South. To attack it, the NAACP had to convince the Supreme Court to move away from *Plessy* v. *Ferguson*, which had ruled that segregation laws were constitutional as long as facilities for both races were roughly equal (see pages 540–542).

Brown v. Board of Education In 1952 the Court agreed to review the "separate but equal" rule in the case *Brown* v. *Board of Education*. The case had been filed by Oliver Brown. He had sued the Topeka, Kansas, school board because his 8-year-old daughter, Linda, was forced to go 21 blocks by bus to a black school when there was a white school only 7 blocks from her home.

In court, NAACP lawyer Thurgood Marshall argued that segregated schools could never be equal. The fact of being segregated, he claimed, made children feel inferior no matter how good the school might be. Asked what he meant by *equal*, Marshall replied,

❝Equal means getting the same thing, at the same time, and in the same place.❞

In 1954 Chief Justice Earl Warren delivered the Court's unanimous decision: Segregated schools were unequal and thus unconstitutional. By destroying the legal basis for segregation, this historic decision reopened the road to equality.

Conflict at Little Rock After the *Brown* ruling, many white southern leaders called for resistance to **integration**—the process of ending segregation. In 1957 a federal court ordered the integration of a high school in

Little Rock, Arkansas. Nine black students enrolled, but shouting, spitting white mobs kept them from entering the school.

Finally President Eisenhower sent troops to Little Rock to protect the students. Even so, recalled one of the students, "Every day something more horrible happened."

Bit by bit, though, brave black students, supported by NAACP lawyers, insisted on their right to attend integrated schools and colleges. Lawyers attacked other segregation laws, too. In case after case, the Court struck down segregation in public facilities such as parks and beaches.

Taking Direct Action

While lawyers worked through the courts, black citizens were organizing to take direct action against segregation. This growing civil rights movement made news in 1955 when Rosa Parks was arrested in Montgomery, Alabama, for refusing to give up her seat on a city bus to a white man.

As 15-year-old Elizabeth Eckford tried to enter Little Rock's Central High School, an angry mob screamed, "Get her! Lynch her!" Arkansas National Guardsmen turned her away at the door.

The Montgomery bus boycott The day after Parks's arrest, black citizens of Montgomery called a mass meeting. Led by Martin Luther King, Jr., they voted to boycott all city buses.

The city fought back, jailing many of the boycott leaders. White segregationists turned to violence. They bombed four churches and King's home.

In response, King preached the power of nonviolent resistance. "The only weapon that we have in our hands is the weapon of protest," he said. The peaceful boycott continued until in 1956 the Supreme Court outlawed segregation on local bus lines.

Student sit-ins King's belief in nonviolent protest inspired thousands to challenge discrimination with direct action. Students took a leading role, confronting segregation wherever it occurred.

On February 1, 1960, four black college students sat down at a whites-only Woolworth's lunch counter in Greensboro, North Carolina. When the waitress refused to serve them, they sat there until the store closed. Joined by other students, they returned day after day.

Sit-ins quickly spread through the South. In April student leaders of the movement formed the Student Nonviolent Coordinating Committee (SNCC) to coordinate the sit-in effort.

In the next year, 70,000 people, mostly black, but some white, took part in demonstrations in 100 cities. More than 3,600 were jailed. By the end of 1960, however, lunch counters in Greensboro and many other southern towns were open to African Americans.

Sit-in protestors bravely practiced nonviolent resistance as angry whites shouted abuse and smeared them with catsup, mustard, and sugar.

Freedom Riders A "sit-in on wheels" was equally successful. In May 1961 the Congress of Racial Equality (CORE), founded by James Farmer in 1942, sent a group of black and white "Freedom Riders" to ride interstate buses through the South.

Two buses left Washington, D.C., for New Orleans. They never got there. In Alabama mobs beat the riders and burned one of the buses. New riders arrived and were also attacked. The Freedom Riders won, though. President Kennedy ordered the integration of all buses, trains, and terminals.

Crisis in Birmingham

Nonviolence was met with violence again in Birmingham, Alabama, in April 1963. There King had launched peaceful demonstrations against discrimination in stores, restaurants, and workplaces. Birmingham police chief Eugene "Bull" Connor ordered fire hoses and police dogs turned on the protestors. Televised images of the police attacks helped turn public opinion against segregation.

Gandhi and nonviolence India offered dramatic proof of what nonviolence could achieve. There, Mohandas K. Gandhi used nonviolent resistance to force Britain to grant independence to India.

A lawyer, Gandhi became a leader of the independence movement about 1920. He and his followers refused to buy British goods. They stopped trains by lying down on the tracks. They sat in front of government buildings, forcing officials to climb over them. Gandhi was arrested many times, but India finally won its independence in 1947.

Howard Thurman, an African American teacher and minister, traveled to India in 1935 to learn about Gandhi's philosophy of nonviolence. Thurman later passed the philosophy on to his university students, who included James Farmer and Martin Luther King, Jr.

Point of View

Were the demonstrations in Birmingham necessary?

During the demonstrations Martin Luther King, Jr., was arrested. While he was in jail, a group of white Birmingham ministers criticized the demonstrations as "unwise and untimely." In a letter to the ministers, King defended the need for resistance. He wrote:

❝Injustice must be exposed . . . to the light of human conscience and the air of national opinion before it can be cured.**❞**

As for timeliness, King continued:

> "I have never yet engaged in a direct action movement that was 'well-timed,' according to the timetable of those who have not suffered unduly from the disease of segregation. For years now I have heard the word 'Wait!' . . . This 'wait' has almost always meant 'never.'"

Protestors often face questions about whether and when to take action to call attention to their cause. King's "Letter from Birmingham Jail" has become famous as a defense of nonviolent action and the goals of the civil rights movement.

Enforcing Civil Rights

In June 1963 President Kennedy gave his strong support to the struggle for civil rights. He asked Congress to pass a civil rights bill to provide "the equality of treatment which we would want ourselves."

Police in Birmingham who used fire hoses to break up a civil rights demonstration were fighting "a fire that won't go out."

March on Washington To show their support for Kennedy's civil rights bill, more than 200,000 people took part in a march on Washington, D.C., on August 28. In a famous speech, King captured the idealism of the marchers:

> "I have a dream that one day this nation will rise up and live out the true meaning of its creed . . . 'that all men are created equal.'"

The Civil Rights Act of 1964 After Kennedy's death, Lyndon Johnson pushed the Civil Rights Act of 1964 through Congress. It banned discrimination in public places such as restaurants. It also banned discrimination in hiring on the basis of race, religion, gender, or nationality. It halted federal aid to segregated institutions. This act placed the federal government squarely on the side of the fight for equality.

Voting rights Civil rights leaders knew that the best way to gain and protect the rights of African Americans was through the ballot box. Thus in the summer of 1964 they launched a campaign to register black voters. Hundreds of volunteers, black and white, risked their lives to help.

Early in 1965 King led a march from Selma, Alabama, to Montgomery, the state capital, to demand voting rights. On the way, police attacked the marchers. Shocked by television pictures of "Bloody Sunday," the public demanded that Congress act.

In response, Congress passed the Voting Rights Act of 1965. Where African

Americans had not been able to register, it allowed federal officials to register them. It also banned literacy tests as a voting requirement. The new law, and the Twenty-fourth Amendment banning poll taxes, opened voting booths to black southerners. By 1968, 60 percent were registered, compared with only 20 percent in 1952.

The Movement Splinters

Black southerners rejoiced over the freedoms they were winning for themselves. In northern cities, however, racial discrimination was based on customs rather than on laws that could be challenged in court. Thus there was little improvement in the lives of black northerners, who faced unemployment and decaying housing and schools.

Frustrated, many African Americans in the North turned to Malcolm X. A minister of the Nation of Islam (the Black Muslims), Malcolm X rejected King's call for nonviolence. He told black Americans to fight back. Like Marcus Garvey, he also urged them to start their own businesses, govern their own communities, and take pride in their African heritage.

Bitter disagreements led Malcolm X to quit the Nation of Islam in 1964. A year later three Black Muslims gunned him down.

Malcolm X's ideas lived on, though. They had a powerful influence on a number of young black leaders. One was Stokely Carmichael, who condemned white America as racist and called for "black power."

Most people thought black power meant working together to build black economic and political power. A few, though, took it as a call to armed revolt against white society.

Urban violence Before he died, Malcolm X warned Americans that they were sitting on a "racial powder keg." The keg exploded in August 1965 in Watts, a black neighborhood in Los Angeles. Rumors of

Civil rights marchers of all races and from all parts of the nation took part in the 1963 March on Washington. Martin Luther King, Jr., summed up their hopes in his "I Have a Dream" speech.

police brutality set off a riot that lasted 6 days and claimed 34 lives. During the next three years, almost every major American city was torn by riots.

President Johnson set up the Kerner Commission to investigate the violence. In 1968 the commission reported its findings. One of the basic causes of the riots, it said, was "discrimination in employment and education" and "segregated housing and schools."

King, too, was concerned about the related problems of racism and poverty. In April 1968 he went to Memphis, Tennessee, to support a strike of sanitation workers. While standing on a balcony outside his hotel room, he was shot by a white segregationist.

King's death set off riots in more than 60 cities and an outpouring of grief among Americans of all races.

Gains of the movement Although the struggle for equality and economic opportunity was far from over, the civil rights movement had accomplished a great deal. It had removed the legal basis for segregation. By protecting voting rights it also offered African Americans the keys to political power.

For the first time since Reconstruction, black southerners were elected to political offices. Birmingham, the city where "Bull" Connor had unleashed his police dogs, elected its first black mayor in 1979.

The Women's Movement

Women who took part in the civil rights movement were inspired to take action to gain equality for themselves. In 1960 most working women could find jobs only in low-paying clerical, sales, or food services positions. Even when they did the same jobs as men, they earned less money.

Although the 1964 Civil Rights Act banned job discrimination against women, employment practices were slow to change. "I've suffered more discrimination as a woman," reported Congresswoman Shirley Chisholm, "than as a black."

In 1966 author Betty Friedan helped found the National Organization for Women (NOW). NOW worked with other women's groups to win passage of laws requiring equal pay for equal work.

In 1972 Congress responded by passing the Equal Rights Amendment (ERA) to the Constitution. It would have banned all discrimination on the basis of gender. The ERA failed ratification, though. Opponents argued that it would take away important legal protections for women and make them subject to the draft.

Despite this setback, the women's movement opened new opportunities—in business, government, the armed forces, and sports. By the late 1970s, it was no longer surprising to see women working as coal miners, police officers, doctors, television newscasters, and astronauts.

Hispanics Organize

Since the 1920s Americans of Mexican, Puerto Rican, Cuban, and Central and South American heritage had fought discrimination and encouraged cultural pride through organizations such as the League of United Latin American Citizens (LULAC). The civil rights movement inspired them to new efforts.

For example, in the 1960s Mexican Americans, the largest group of Hispanics, began to organize to demand their rights and fight discrimination. Many Mexican Americans were farmworkers who had none of the rights and protections of factory workers. Their leader, Cesar Chavez, believed that a union was the only way they could win fair treatment from landowners.

In 1962 Chavez, with his wife, Helen, and Dolores Huerta, a teacher, formed the United Farm Workers (UFW) in California. They launched strikes and boycotts to gain better wages and working conditions. Like King, Chavez was committed to a "totally nonviolent struggle for justice." In 1970 the UFW finally won a great victory—the right to bargain for workers in talks with California grape growers.

Meanwhile, in the cities young Mexican Americans launched the *Chicano* (chee-KAH-noh) movement. Their goal was to gain political power, equal opportunities in business and education, and respect for their Mexican heritage. In Miami, with its large Cuban American population, and other cities, Hispanics increasingly won elective office and made their voices heard in schools and the workplace.

Cesar Chavez (above, in sweater) and Dolores Huerta (left) led Mexican and Mexican American farmworkers in the 1965 *huelga*, or strike, against California grape growers.

Indians Seek Recognition

In the 1960s and 1970s American Indians also learned to make the public aware of their need for respect and for better educational and economic opportunities. A central issue was gaining the right to manage their own affairs.

For Indians, World War II had unleashed forces of change that continue to this day. The armed forces and wartime jobs brought Indians off their reservations. After the war Indians continued to move from reservations to urban areas. Still, few Indians could break out of the cycle of discrimination and poverty.

Drawing on the lessons of the civil rights movement, Indian activists found ways to call public attention to their problems. In 1969 a group of Indians took over Alcatraz Island in San Francisco Bay. In 1972 leaders of the American Indian Movement (AIM) took over the offices of the Bureau of Indian Affairs in Washington, D.C. A year later AIM members occupied Wounded Knee, South Dakota.

Self-determination

Indian actions caught the attention of President Nixon, who called for a government policy of self-determination. In 1975 Congress passed the Indian Self-Determination and Energy Act. It was a major step in giving tribes control over the government programs that affected them.

Indians also defended their rights in court. In Alaska, Maine, and Massachusetts they won payment for lands taken by the federal government. They regained old rights to fish and cut timber. Many western tribes also gained control of valuable mineral deposits discovered beneath their lands.

Despite ongoing problems—on reservations and in cities—Indian faith in the future remains strong. In 1990 Cherokee chief Wilma Mankiller predicted that "500 years from now there will still be strong tribal communities . . . where ancient languages, ceremonies, and songs will be heard."

3. Section Review

1. Define **integration**.
2. Explain the reasoning behind the Supreme Court decision in the *Brown* case.
3. Describe two methods that were used for promoting integration in the South. How successful were these methods?
4. Name at least one issue that concerned each group: women, Hispanic Americans, and American Indians.
5. **Critical Thinking** Imagine that Cesar Chavez asked you, as a farmworker, to join his union even though it could cost your job. How would you respond? Why?

4. The Nixon Years

Reading Guide

Section Focus Richard Nixon's presidency and the scandal that ended it

1. What challenges did President Nixon face at home?
2. What events led to the Watergate scandal?
3. Why was the Watergate scandal a serious constitutional crisis?

As he entered the White House in 1969, President Richard Nixon faced a nation deeply divided over the Vietnam War and struggles for equality. In his inaugural address, he called for calm. "We cannot learn from one another until we stop shouting at one another," he said. The government, he promised, "will strive to listen in new ways."

Nixon's Goals

Like Eisenhower, President Nixon thought that the federal government should play a smaller role in the economy. He called for returning power to the states over such matters as education and public health. He also backed away from using federal power to enforce integration. He tried to block renewal of the Voting Rights Act and delay court orders to integrate schools.

In some areas, though, Nixon willingly used federal power. When unemployment rose in 1969, he used federal money to build the economy. To stop soaring inflation in 1971 he placed a 90-day freeze on all wages and prices. To help states pay for social programs, he provided matching federal funds.

Space successes On July 20, 1969, American astronauts Neil A. Armstrong and Edwin E. Aldrin, Jr., landed a spacecraft on the moon. The United States had fulfilled President Kennedy's dream of putting a man on the moon by the end of the decade.

With Nixon's support, the United States took another major leap into space four years later. May 14, 1973, saw the launch of *Skylab,* the first American orbiting space station. Later two more Skylab missions were sent into orbit with researchers photographing the earth and conducting scientific experiments.

Nixon also started a program to develop a space shuttle, a reusable spacecraft that blasted off like a rocket and landed like an airplane. The first space shuttle, *Columbia,* lifted off in 1981.

Environmental Problems

During the 1970s, Americans were becoming more and more concerned about the effects of technology on the environment. Factories and cars were spewing poisons into the air. Industrial wastes, city sewage, and farm pesticides were killing fish and wildlife.

Biologist Rachel Carson had sounded an early warning about the danger of pollution. In her 1962 book *Silent Spring,* Carson declared, "The question is whether any civilization can wage [such] relentless war on life without destroying itself." Her writing helped to spark an environmental movement.

Under pressure from environmentalists, Congress passed a number of laws, such as the Clean Air Act of 1963 and the Water Quality Act of 1965, to fight air pollution and

Skylab

Launched on May 14, 1973, *Skylab* was the United States' first manned orbiting laboratory. Three crews carried out missions on board the space station, gathering information about the earth and its resources, the sun and stars, and the effects of weightlessness on humans. Their findings have been essential in planning future space exploration.

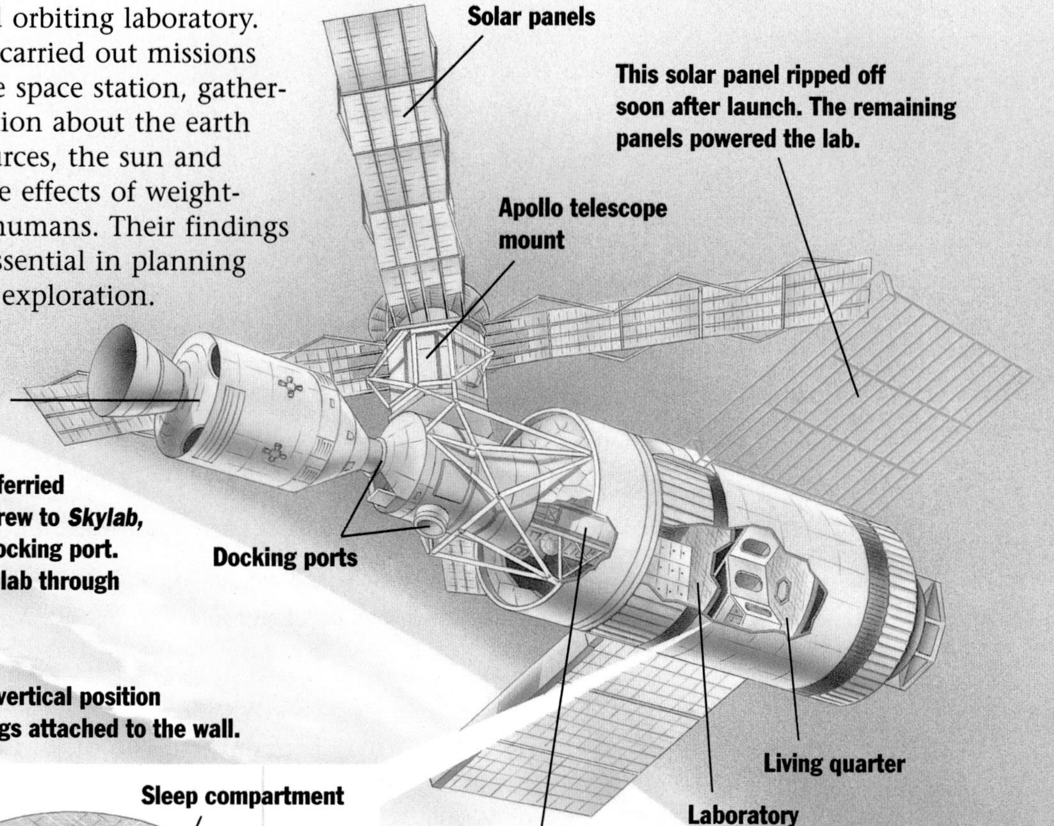

The Apollo telescope mount had special instruments for studying the sun.

Solar panels

This solar panel ripped off soon after launch. The remaining panels powered the lab.

Apollo telescope mount

Apollo spacecraft

An Apollo spacecraft ferried each three-member crew to *Skylab*, and connected to a docking port. The crew entered the lab through the air lock module.

Docking ports

Astronauts slept in a vertical position in special sleeping bags attached to the wall.

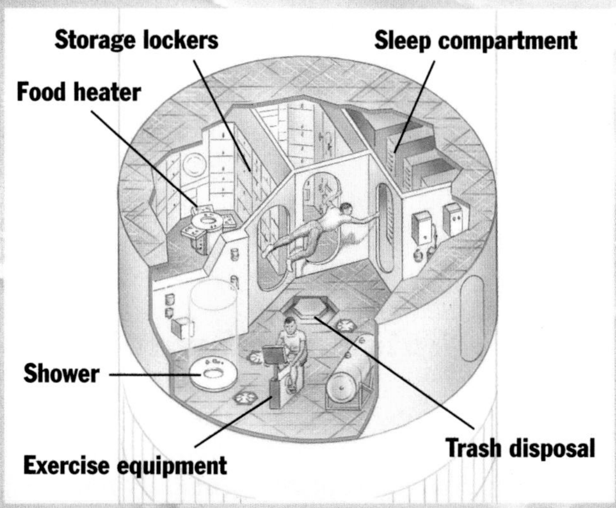

Storage lockers

Food heater

Sleep compartment

Living quarter

Laboratory

Air lock module

Shower

Exercise equipment

Trash disposal

The shower was fully enclosed, and the wastewater was sucked into a storage tank.

Astronauts used exercise equipment to stay in shape and to study whether human fitness is affected by a long stay in space.

The Cuyahoga River in Cleveland, Ohio, was heavily polluted with oil, grease, and debris. Americans learned how dangerous pollution could be when the river caught fire in 1969.

clean up the nation's lakes and rivers. In 1970 President Nixon created the Environmental Protection Agency to carry out federal programs to combat pollution. On the first "Earth Day," April 22, 1970, millions of Americans took part in teach-ins, protests, and cleanup projects to "save the earth."

The Election of 1972

As the 1972 election approached, the Republican Party nominated Nixon for a second term. As you read in Chapter 29, his trips to China and the Soviet Union had sent his popularity soaring.

A curious event occurred early in the election campaign. At 2:00 A.M. on June 17, five burglars were arrested in a Washington, D.C., office complex called Watergate. They had broken into the offices of the Democratic National Committee. They carried cameras and listening devices, or "bugs," for telephones.

Nixon assured the nation that "no one in this administration is involved in this very bizarre incident." By election day it seemed to have been forgotten. Nixon was easily re-elected with 47 million votes to 29 million for the Democrat, George McGovern.

The Watergate Scandal

Early in 1973 the Watergate burglars were tried and convicted. After the trial, one of them charged that high officials had been involved in the break-in. This information led to an investigation by a Senate Committee headed by North Carolina Senator Sam Ervin, Jr.

This cartoon was published after the release of Nixon's tapes of his Watergate conversations. Nixon had promised, "I am not a crook."

Nixon resigns On July 24, 1974, the Supreme Court ruled that the President had to release the tapes of his Watergate conversations. The tapes revealed that Nixon had been involved in the cover-up from the start.

A week later, members of the House Judiciary Committee charged Nixon with blocking the Watergate investigation, misusing his power, and illegally withholding evidence from Congress. They recommended that Nixon be impeached.

It seemed certain that the House would vote for impeachment. Rather than face a trial in the Senate, President Nixon submitted his resignation on August 9, 1974.

As Nixon stepped down, Vice-President Gerald Ford of Michigan assumed office. Ford was the first non-elected President. Nixon's Vice-President, Spiro Agnew, had resigned in 1973 when it became known that he had accepted bribes. With Congress's approval Nixon had then named Ford, the House Republican leader, to replace Agnew.

From May to July 1973, Americans watched the televised Senate hearings with dismay. Witnesses told that the burglars had been hired by the Committee to Reelect the President (CREEP) and that Nixon had tried to "cover up" the Watergate scandal. He had blocked an FBI investigation and approved payments of "hush money" to the burglars.

During the hearings, one witness revealed that many of Nixon's conversations about Watergate had been taped. The committee asked the President for the tapes, and Nixon spent the next year fighting a legal battle to prevent the release of any of the tapes.

Meanwhile the Senate committee uncovered other wrongdoings. CREEP officials had accepted illegal campaign contributions. Nixon had allowed White House employees to use illegal phone taps to stop "leaks" of secret information to the press.

Having resigned rather than face impeachment, Nixon put on a bold face as he boarded a helicopter to leave the White House.

"Our Constitution works" The Watergate scandal taught Americans a painful lesson about the dangers of presidential power. When a 1974 poll asked people how much faith they had in the executive branch of government, 43 percent replied, "Hardly any."

On the other hand, the scandal proved that the Constitution's system of checks and balances is still our best protection against abuses of power. "Our national nightmare is over," President Ford assured Americans, "Our Constitution works."

4. Section Review

1. How did Nixon respond to economic problems?
2. What led Congress to investigate the Watergate burglary?
3. Critical Thinking Describing the Watergate scandal, a political leader said that in the end "the spider got caught in his web." Who was the spider, and what was the web?

Why We Remember

The Postwar Years at Home

The postwar decades were a time of dizzying change in American life. These were the years of the baby boom and the migration of young families from cities to suburbs. This was the time when TV sets arrived in most American living rooms. This was the era when ordinary people became concerned about protecting the environment, a President declared war on poverty, and American astronauts landed on the moon.

Just as important, this was a time when Americans' commitment to the Constitution and their ideals of liberty and equality were tested again and again. The first great test came in the early 1950s, when the accusations of Senator Joseph McCarthy threatened our right to express our beliefs freely. The second great test came in the 1950s and 1960s, when African Americans set out to destroy the terrible injustice of racial discrimination and segregation. Yet another test came in the 1970s, when President Nixon used his power to deceive the public.

The nation and the Constitution survived these challenges. At the same time, Americans were reminded again of a truth that is all too easily forgotten. As Martin Luther King, Jr., reminded us, "Injustice anywhere is a threat to justice everywhere. . . . Whatever affects one directly affects all indirectly."

Skill Lab

Skill Tips

When synthesizing, examine the pieces of information to look for:
- order of importance
- ways to group pieces of information to show similarities and differences, time order, and cause-effect connections

Using Information
Synthesizing Information

As you know, the time spans of Chapters 29 and 30 overlap. Certain names—especially those of Presidents—pop up in both chapters. Suppose you want to show key events during one President's administration. How might you approach the task?

Question to Investigate

What were the key events of one postwar President's administration?

Procedure

When you **synthesize,** you put together information to create a written, oral, or visual product. Here you will create a layout for a group of pictures.

❶ Collect relevant information.
a. Choose one of these Presidents: Truman, Eisenhower, Kennedy, Johnson, or Nixon.
b. Choose six major events from Chapters 29 and 30 having to do with this President.

❷ Identify connections between the pieces of information.
a. For each event, imagine a picture and then write a description and caption for it.
b. Identify the sequence of events and whether each event occurred inside or outside of the country. Decide which two events were most important.

❸ Create a product to show the connections between the pieces of information.
a. Sketch possible layouts for the group of pictures. Try varying the sizes and placement of the pictures.

b. Sketch a final layout that you think would best show highlights of this President's administration. Include captions and descriptions of the pictures. See the partial sample below for President Franklin D. Roosevelt.

Source to Use

> Damaged battleships at Pearl Harbor

> The attack on Pearl Harbor on December 7, 1941, brought the United States into World War II.

> Troops landing in Normandy

> On D-Day, June 6, 1944, Allied troops landed in Normandy to begin freeing France from Nazi rule.

Chapter Survey

Reviewing Vocabulary

Define the following terms.
1. closed shop   3. integration
2. civil rights

Reviewing Main Ideas

1. What happened to people who were suspected of having Communist sympathies after World War II? Give three examples.
2. What were the main causes and effects of American prosperity in the 1950s?
3. (a) In what ways was President Kennedy successful in putting into effect his "New Frontier" plans? (b) In what ways was he unsuccessful?
4. Describe three ways that President Johnson and Congress tried to end poverty.
5. Give an example of how each helped to break down barriers to equality for African Americans. (a) the NAACP (b) students and other ordinary Americans (c) Congress
6. Summarize the gains made by each group as of the mid-1970s. (a) women (b) Hispanics (c) American Indians
7. How did the Watergate burglary lead to the resignation of President Nixon? Describe the chain of events.

Thinking Critically

1. Application Choose two Presidents discussed in this chapter and compare their styles of leadership. Give examples from the text to support your views.
2. Analysis African Americans had been working to gain full citizenship since Reconstruction. Why were they able to accomplish so much in the 1950s and 1960s?
3. Why We Remember: Evaluation Many Americans look back on the 1950s as a wonderful "golden era." They view the 1960s and early 1970s as troubled, unpleasant years. Do you think these views of the United States in the postwar years are realistic, or not? Explain.

Applying Skills

Synthesizing information Apply what you learned on page 865 to create a collage of key events in your life:
1. Collect information. List key events that you remember. Talk to relatives about events that occurred when you were very young. List them.
2. Develop items for your collage. If possible use photographs and artifacts, such as souvenirs and awards, to portray the events you have listed, or write descriptions of the items on index cards. Write captions, too.
3. Arrange the items to show connections. For example, you might group items reresenting events from a particular year or events that relate to a sport or other special interest.

History Mystery

A young girl goes to school Answer the History Mystery on page 841. Segregated schools in many northern and western states as well as in the South were not "separate but equal." States that had segregated school systems spent far more on the education of white students than of black students. How might this situation affect the views of black students? Of white students?

Writing in Your History Journal

1. Keys to History (a) The time line on pages 840–841 has eight Keys to History. In your journal, describe why each one is important to know about. (b) Choose the event from the time line that you think has had the greatest influence on life in the United States today. Explain your choice in your journal.

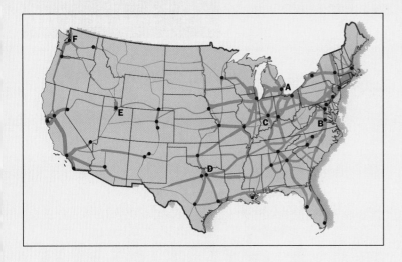

Reviewing Geography

1. Each letter on the map represents a city that lies on the interstate highway system. For each letter, write the name of the city.

2. Geographic Thinking In Chapter 26, you thought about the far-reaching effects of the automobile. Now think about how interstate highways further transformed our way of life. List at least three effects. Consider, for example, effects on the tourist industry.

2. Martin Luther King, Jr. The year is 1963, and a student has written to King expressing anger about the continuing injustices suffered by African Americans. "Nonviolence has had its chance," the teenager writes. "From now on, we have to fight fire with fire." In your journal, write a reply that King might have written.

3. Citizenship Various people you read about in this chapter, from Rosa Parks to Richard Nixon, broke the law and believed they were justified in doing so. When, if ever, is breaking the law justified? Does it matter who is doing the lawbreaking and why they are doing it? Write your responses in your journal.

Alternative Assessment

Writing editorials Imagine that you and a partner are editors of your community's newspaper during the years between 1950 and 1974. Work together to write five editorials, on these topics:

❶ whether Senator McCarthy is doing the right thing in his hunt for Communists

❷ whether President Kennedy's proposed civil rights bill should be enacted

❸ whether President Johnson's efforts to create the Great Society are good policy

❹ whether President Nixon should be impeached

❺ another issue of your choice from the chapter

Your work will be evaluated on the following criteria:
• you provide accurate information to help readers understand the pros and cons of the issue and to support your opinions
• you offer opinions that are realistic for people in your community during the era in question
• you write in a way that is persuasive and to the point

Chapter *31*

New Roles in a Changing World

Sections

Beginning the Story with Jaime Escalante

1. **The Nation After Vietnam and Watergate**
2. **The Post–Cold War Era Begins**
3. **New Challenges and Hopes**

⚷ *Keys to History*

1978
Camp David Accords
Carter, Begin, and Sadat
negotiate a peace

1974
President Ford pardons Nixon
for possible Watergate crimes

1979
Iranian militants seize
American hostages
in Tehran

1970

1980

Looking Back

Watergate scandal
1972–1974

His occupations include nuclear engineering, politics, carpentry, poetry, and peanut farming. Who is he, and why do we remember him?

1981
First woman appointed to Supreme Court
Sandra Day O'Connor

1990
Americans with Disabilities Act

1991
American-led coalition fights Iraq in Persian Gulf War
Oil fields set afire during the war

1993
North American Free Trade Agreement (NAFTA) approved

1990

Present

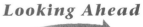

World Link

Democracy triumphs in the Philippines
1986

Looking Ahead

Your generation embraces the opportunities and challenges facing the United States

Beginning the Story with

Jaime Escalante

On May 19, 1982, 18 high-school seniors filed into Room 411 of Garfield High School in a mostly poor and Hispanic area of east Los Angeles. Many had had trouble sleeping the night before. Some had broken down and cried with nervousness as they prepared to take a grueling college examination in calculus. Jaime Escalante (HĪ-mee es-kuh-LAHN-tay), their calculus teacher, paced nervously in a nearby classroom. After three hours, his students finally emerged from Room 411, tired but happy. On seeing their teacher, one student exclaimed, "Kimo! That was a piece of cake."

Escalante's students passed the exam with flying colors. Their joy turned to dismay, however, when 14 of the 18 were accused of cheating because their answers to one question looked suspiciously similar. Escalante was outraged at the accusation. He had known that his drill-like approach to teaching would result in similar student responses to questions. "I stand behind my kids," he said. "I believe in my students."

The Move to California

Growing up in La Paz, Bolivia, Jaime had no idea that he would become a teacher. When he reached his teen years, however, he found that he had a talent for math and science. He decided to become a physics teacher. Soon Jaime earned enough to support his wife and small son.

In 1963 Jaime and his wife left Bolivia for the United States, where they hoped to find more opportunities for their son. Upon arrival in Los Angeles, the Escalantes received a rude shock. Jaime's education in Bolivia did not qualify him to teach in California. He would have to go to college again. This time he would do so in a new language—English.

Jaime found a job mopping the floors at a restaurant while he went back to college. When he finished, he was hired to teach math at Garfield High School. The school's crumbling buildings and graffiti-covered walls depressed

Jaime Escalante works with students at Hiram Johnson High School in Sacramento, California, where he moved after many years of teaching in Los Angeles.

him so much that he planned to quit after his first year. As he came to know his students, however, he became determined to help them succeed by teaching them to believe in themselves. What better way, he thought, than by having them master calculus for the college placement exams?

"We can do it"

When Escalante announced plans to teach a college-level calculus class at Garfield High, few believed he would succeed. Garfield students could not handle college-level math, critics claimed. To start his class, Escalante recruited students from basic math classes much like a coach recruits top athletes for the big league. He enforced strict discipline in his classroom. He also used unusual but effective teaching methods. For example, to help students master difficult mathematical ideas he explained them by using terms from sports and even soap operas.

As the exam approached, Escalante set up after-school cram sessions. Day after day he drilled his students mercilessly. They developed a team spirit and a belief that they could succeed. Imagine, then, how shocked they were by the accusation that they had cheated. When offered a chance to retake the test, 12 of the 14 students decided to do so. As one student explained:

"I want to . . . show Escalante that what he taught me I didn't forget, and that I really appreciate all the time he put in . . . and to prove to . . . ourselves that we can do it again.**"**

They could and they did. On their second try, all 12 students again passed the exam. Jaime Escalante smiled at the results. He had known all along that his students would succeed.

Source: *Escalante: The Best Teacher in America* by Jay Matthews, Harcourt Brace, 1982.

Hands-On *HISTORY*

Activity

Many people did not believe that high-school students in east Los Angeles could succeed in a college-level math class. Jaime Escalante proved them wrong. Imagine that you are Escalante and you have just come home from your first day of teaching the class described above. Write in your diary how you felt standing in front of the class and teaching. What hopes, and what worries, might you have for the students?

1. The Nation After Vietnam and Watergate

Reading Guide

Section Focus **The nation as it recovered from Vietnam and Watergate**

1. How did Presidents Ford and Carter try to restore the confidence of Americans in their government?
2. What were the successes and failures of President Carter's foreign policy?
3. How did President Reagan try to change the role of the federal government?

The Vietnam War and the Watergate affair shook the faith of Americans in their nation's political system and leaders. The three Presidents who followed Nixon—Gerald Ford, Jimmy Carter, and Ronald Reagan—each made his own effort to respond to this "crisis of confidence" and to heal the wounds caused by war and scandal.

Ford: Healing the Wounds

Confidence in the nation's leaders would not be easy to restore, however. A 1975 survey showed that 83 percent of Americans still believed that "the people running this country . . . don't tell us the truth."

President Ford moved quickly in late 1974 to grant former President Nixon "a full, free and absolute pardon" for all crimes that he may have committed as President. Ford's pardon meant that Nixon would never be put on trial. The new President hoped that the pardon would help "heal the wounds" left by the Watergate scandal.

Many Americans disapproved. It was unfair, they argued, to pardon Nixon when his top aides had gone to prison for Watergate-related crimes. The pardon left "a sour smell" in the nation's capital, reported a newspaper.

Point of View

Should President Nixon have been pardoned?

Some called it an act of "compassion" when President Ford pardoned former President Nixon of any possible wrongdoing against the nation. Ford believed that "Richard Nixon and his loved ones . . . [had] suffered enough," and the nation needed to put the Watergate issue to rest. Ford said he was concerned about the "future of this great country. . . . I cannot prolong the bad dreams that continue to reopen [the nation's wounds]."

Harvard law professor Raoul Berger disagreed. The pardoning of Nixon, he argued, would "breed disrespect for the law [and encourage future Presidents] to feel that Presidents are untouchable." Senator Floyd Haskell of Colorado feared that the pardon would only

"confirm what too many Americans already believe: that there is one set of laws for the rich and powerful, another for everyone else."

Some Americans still think it would have been better to seek the truth about Watergate, even if it meant putting Nixon on trial. Others respect Ford for sparing Nixon—and the nation—that painful process.

Carter: Washington Outsider

Distrust of political leaders continued to dominate the thoughts of voters in the 1976 presidential election. The Democrats nominated Jimmy Carter, a nuclear engineer, peanut farmer, and former governor of Georgia. Carter ran as a Washington outsider—someone unconnected to national politics or the Watergate scandal. He won by a narrow margin over Gerald Ford.

Carter's approach to politics seemed like a breath of fresh air. When he traveled, for example, he stayed in the homes of ordinary people. The nation's leaders could not understand people's concerns, he said, if they lived "like royalty here in Washington."

Rising prices and energy problems
As President, Carter convinced Congress to decrease military spending and to lower taxes on businesses and on personal incomes. Inflation, however, had plagued the nation since the late 1960s. Fueled by high oil prices, the prices of goods were soaring. American workers worried as their paychecks bought fewer and fewer goods.

Carter believed that high energy costs were at the root of inflation. If people used less oil, he argued, prices of all goods would drop. In 1977 Carter proposed an energy program that encouraged conservation and use of alternative energy sources, such as solar power. The public, however, failed to support him, and the energy program stalled in Congress.

Then, in January 1979 Muslim revolutionaries in oil-rich Iran overthrew their ruler, the Shah. Soon, Iran's vast flow of oil slowed to a trickle. The entire world now faced an oil shortage. Other oil-producing nations raised their prices.

As they had in 1973, American drivers lined up for hours to buy expensive gasoline. Heating oil costs also rose. In the face of this crisis, Congress finally passed part of Carter's energy program. Americans cut back their use of fuel, too, and the shortage eased.

New Policy Overseas

You read in Chapter 29 that Carter's foreign policy goal was to encourage nations to protect their citizens' human rights. Carter kept this goal in mind as he faced a controversy over the future of the Panama Canal.

By walking in his inaugural parade rather than riding in a limousine, Carter set a new tone for the American presidency on the first day he took office.

New role for an ex-President Since leaving office, Jimmy Carter has devoted his life to causes in which he believes. Helping the poor is one. For example, Carter works as a carpenter with Habitat for Humanity, a group that builds homes for the poor. He has also launched the Atlanta Project, which tries to help neighborhoods solve problems—including crime and unemployment.

Helping bring peace to nations in turmoil is another of Carter's goals. He helped end military rule in Haiti (see page 881) and brought warring parties in both Bosnia and Sudan together for negotiations.

Many people agree with these observations of a newspaper: "Attention to detail. A distaste for politics. Above all, a commitment to doing the right thing. The qualities that hobbled [handicapped] Jimmy Carter in the White House seem to be making him a great ex-President."

Panama Canal Treaty The people of Panama had long resented American control of the Panama Canal. They thought the canal should belong to Panama. Carter agreed. In 1977 he signed a treaty that would return the canal to Panama by 2000. The treaty ran into stiff opposition among Americans. Many did not want the United States to give up control of the canal. Even so, the Senate ratified the treaty in early 1978.

Middle East peace While many Americans opposed the Panama Canal Treaty, most supported Carter's efforts to promote peace in the Middle East. There, the hostility between Israel and the Arab nations around it continued to simmer.

In 1978, in an effort to break the cycle of violence, Carter invited Egypt's Anwar al-Sadat (sah-DAHT) and Israel's Menachem Begin (BAY-gin) to a meeting at Camp David in Maryland. Upon arrival, the two refused to speak to one another. A frustrated Sadat prepared to pack up and return home.

Carter convinced Sadat to stay and steered the two men through days of difficult negotiations. On September 17, 1978, the leaders of Israel and Egypt signed a peace agreement called the Camp David Accords. Weary but triumphant, Carter declared, "This is one of those rare, bright moments of history."

The hostage crisis All too soon, however, Carter faced a new crisis. The Shah, who had fled Iran during the revolution, came to the United States for medical treatment.

For 444 days American hostages were held captive by Iranian revolutionaries who blamed the United States for having supported the former Shah of Iran.

Outraged Iranians demanded that the United States return him to Iran to face trial. Carter refused, and young Iranians stormed the American embassy in Tehran, taking 66 Americans hostage.

Carter first tried to negotiate the release of the hostages. Then he sent military aircraft to rescue them. Both efforts failed. Meanwhile, night after night, Americans watched the blindfolded hostages paraded before television cameras as Iranians chanted, "Death to Carter, death to the Shah."

Carter's handling of the hostage crisis undermined public confidence in his presidency. The tragic events in Iran haunted the President all the way to election day.

The Election of 1980

As the 1980 election approached, the Republicans nominated Ronald Reagan, a former actor who had been governor of California. While Carter talked of the need to make sacrifices and "hard choices," Reagan radiated optimism about the future. "There's nothing the American people cannot do when we try," he declared.

One week before the election, Reagan asked Americans, "Are you better off than you were four years ago?" With inflation climbing and Americans held hostage in Iran, voters answered "No." Reagan won with 51 percent of the vote. Just hours after Carter stepped down as President, Iranian guards freed the American hostages.

The Reagan "Revolution"

In 1981 Ronald Reagan took office, declaring that it was "morning in America." He set forth ideas that some called "revolutionary." Others called them a return to the conservative politics of the 1950s.

In any case, Reagan's style was immensely popular. People enjoyed the smiling, easy-

Ronald Reagan's personal style and political skills re-established the power of the presidency in a way not seen since Lyndon Johnson and Franklin Roosevelt.

going manner of this energetic 69-year-old. They also approved when Reagan made history by appointing Sandra Day O'Connor to the Supreme Court in 1981. She was the first woman to sit on the nation's highest court.

"Government is the problem" Ever since Franklin Roosevelt, Reagan claimed, Americans had depended too much on the federal government. As a result, it had grown too large. Now, Reagan declared, "Government is not the solution to our problem; government *is* the problem." It was time, he said, for Americans to put their faith in American business rather than in the government.

In his effort to shrink the size of government, Reagan pushed for cuts in welfare programs, education, and public transportation. The budgets of government agencies such as the Environmental Protection Agency and Equal Employment Opportunity Commission were slashed. Such actions slowed government efforts to enforce antipollution and antidiscrimination regulations.

Reaganomics Following the tradition of Republicans in the 1920s, Reagan believed that the best way to ensure prosperity was to lower taxes on the wealthy and on businesses. This policy would make more money available to businesses to expand and hire more workers. The benefits of tax cuts would

World Link

Democracy in the Philippines "Today the Filipino people celebrate the triumph of democracy, and the world celebrates with them," said President Reagan in 1986. The world was celebrating the fall of the Filipino dictator Ferdinand Marcos, a one-time friend of the United States.

The end of his rule had been in sight for several years. In 1983 Marcos was suspected of involvement in the killing of Benigno S. Aquino, Jr., his chief critic. The Filipino people grew disgusted with Marcos and forced him to hold elections on February 7, 1986.

Corazon Aquino, widow of the slain leader, ran against Marcos. Despite evidence that Aquino had won, Marcos declared himself the winner. Filipinos took to the streets, forming human barricades against the tanks that Marcos sent to push them back. The last straw came when Reagan withdrew support. Marcos fled to Hawaii, and Aquino became President.

thus "trickle down" from the wealthiest Americans to the poorest. This theory came to be known as "Reaganomics."

In 1981 Congress passed the largest income tax cut in the nation's history. At the same time, prices—including oil prices—were falling. By 1983 a business and construction boom was underway.

The Election of 1984

Reagan's critics claimed that his tax and budget cuts hurt the poor and the elderly as well as the environment. Polls showed, however, that the majority of Americans felt that the President was doing a good job.

In the 1984 election Reagan faced Walter Mondale, who had served as Vice-President under Carter. Mondale chose Geraldine Ferraro as his running mate. She was the first woman to run on the presidential ticket of a major political party.

During his campaign, Mondale warned voters that Reagan's tax cuts were driving the national deficit to its highest levels ever. However, Reagan easily won re-election. As one supporter said, "Reagan is a symbol to a generation happy with itself."

Reagan's Foreign Policy

Foreign policy dominated Reagan's second term. A staunch anti-Communist, the President promised that he would help the United States "stand tall in the world again" by fighting communism abroad. Even though he cut spending on domestic programs, he increased the military budget to record levels.

Grenada When a pro-Communist group took control of the government on the tiny Caribbean island of Grenada in 1983, Reagan ordered American troops to invade and drive them out. Critics at home and abroad denounced American interference in Grenada's affairs. Still, the quick success of the mission there heartened people distressed by American failures in Vietnam.

Nicaragua While the invasion of Grenada went smoothly, Reagan's policy toward Nicaragua hit serious snags. In 1979 rebels—called Sandinistas—in that Central American nation overthrew a brutal dictatorship that had ruled for 43 years. The Sandinista government sought to create an

"C'mon, boys... Somebody had to be driving."

IRAN

CONGRESS

Neither Reagan nor his political advisors wanted to admit responsibility for the arms-for-hostages deal with the government of Iran.

economy that combined elements of both communism and capitalism.

Reagan feared that the Soviet Union was trying to gain a foothold in Central America by supporting the Sandinistas. He urged Congress to give arms to anti-Sandinista rebels known as "contras." Congress opposed arming the contras. Instead, it passed the Boland Amendment, which banned all American aid to the contras.

Civil war in Lebanon Reagan's foreign policy also stumbled in the Middle East. In the 1970s conflict between Christians and Muslims in Lebanon had erupted into civil war. Reagan sent American troops to help as part of a United Nations peace-keeping force. In October 1983 a truck bomb explosion killed 241 American marines. Americans reacted with horror, and Reagan withdrew the remaining troops from Lebanon.

As the conflict dragged on, terrorists sympathetic to Iran kidnapped six Americans and held them hostage. Reagan refused to negotiate for the release of the hostages, declaring, "America will never make concessions to terrorists—to do so would only

invite more terrorism." Behind the scenes, however, his aides were following a different policy.

The Iran-Contra Scandal

In November 1986 Americans learned that Oliver North and other aides to Reagan had been secretly selling weapons to Iran. By doing so, they hoped to gain the release of the hostages in Lebanon. The money from the sales, in turn, was used to buy arms for the contras in Nicaragua. The dealings broke Reagan's ban on negotiating with terrorists and violated the Boland Amendment.

Americans were stunned. Did the President know about the secret dealings? If so, could he be impeached for breaking the law? Reagan denied any knowledge of this illegal use of funds. The Iran-Contra scandal threw a shadow over Reagan's last years as President. Still, he left office in 1989 as one of the nation's most popular Presidents.

1. Section Review

1. Give three reasons why people objected to Ford's pardon of Nixon.
2. How did Carter handle conflicts in Panama, the Middle East, and Iran? What was the result in each case?
3. Critical Thinking If Reagan had looked back to the policies of past Presidents for inspiration, which decade do you think he would have most admired: the 1920s or the 1930s? Give reasons for your choice.

2. The Post–Cold War Era Begins

Reading Guide

New Term **deficit**

Section Focus **Post–Cold War challenges at home and abroad**

1. What were the policies of President Bush both at home and abroad?
2. What were President Clinton's accomplishments and setbacks?

As the 1980s drew to a close, so did the Cold War. You read in Chapter 29 that by 1989 a mostly peaceful "velvet revolution" was sweeping across Eastern Europe, ending decades of Communist rule. The next President faced a new world overseas as well as the legacy of Reagan's presidency at home.

Bush's Presidency

Republicans nominated George Bush, Ronald Reagan's Vice-President, to run for President in 1988. To "stay the course" set by Reagan, Bush promised to take a conservative approach to government. However, he also tried to calm the fears raised by Reagan's cuts in programs such as environmental protection and education. Bush called for more modest cuts in government spending.

Democrats, meanwhile, chose Michael Dukakis, the governor of Massachusetts, to oppose Bush. He promised to increase aid for schools and health care by raising taxes for the wealthy. Bush easily won the election.

As President, George Bush sought ways to make his campaign promises a reality. A Democratic Congress was eager to cooperate in Bush's goal of a "kinder, gentler nation."

To further that goal, Congress passed the Americans with Disabilities Act in 1990. This act was designed to make daily activities—such as entering buildings and crossing streets—possible for disabled Americans. It made it illegal, too, to discriminate against a disabled person who applied for a job.

Next, Congress updated laws protecting the environment. For example, the Clean Air Act of 1990 set tighter standards to control pollution by factories and automobiles. Bush called it "the most significant air pollution legislation in our nation's history."

The AIDS crisis In 1981 a frightening disease—acquired immunodeficiency syndrome (AIDS)—was identified among Americans. It is a disease that destroys the human body's protection against infection. The Ryan White Act was passed in 1990 to help provide services—such as medical care and housing—to the hundreds of thousands of Americans living with AIDS.

Budget problems The greatest challenge facing Bush was the federal deficit. The **deficit** is the amount by which the government's spending is greater than its income. To reduce the deficit, the government must cut spending, raise taxes, or do both.

During Reagan's presidency, government spending—especially on defense—had skyrocketed. Even so, in the 1988 campaign Bush had promised: "Read my lips, no new taxes." In 1990, however, he faced a deficit much larger than expected. That year, Bush broke his "no new taxes" pledge. He struck a bargain with Congress to trim $500 billion from the deficit by cutting spending and raising taxes.

A Post–Cold War President

With the end of Soviet communism, Bush called for a "New World Order." It would, he said, be a world in which nations worked together to prevent small crises from turning into world wars.

The Persian Gulf War The first test of Bush's idea of a New World Order came in the Middle East. In August 1990 the President of Iraq—Saddam Hussein—ordered his army to invade neighboring Kuwait, a small oil-rich nation on the Persian Gulf. Hussein claimed that it belonged to Iraq.

Bush saw the invasion as a threat to peace and to the world's supply of oil—a resource too vital "to be dominated by one so ruthless." When other pressures failed, the United Nations—including Russia—voted to free Kuwait by force. In January 1991 an American-led coalition of 28 nations struck Iraqi forces in Kuwait and Iraq. Six weeks later, the war was over. Bush's popularity soared.

Somalia Bush's New World Order was put to the test again in the African nation of Somalia. A civil war had left up to 2 million Somalis on the brink of starvation. Americans were horrified by TV images of people so thin they resembled skeletons.

In December 1992 Bush sent 28,000 troops to Somalia. Their mission was not to fight a war, but to protect relief workers who were bringing food to the people. The task proved more difficult than anyone had imagined. While the troops did help save many people from starving, they were unable to restore a stable government in Somalia. The American troops finally withdrew in March 1994.

Hands-On HISTORY

Balancing the budget Between October 1, 1994, and September 30, 1995, the federal government took in $1,420 billion. Unfortunately, it spent $1,578 billion. Where did the money go? The table tells you.

Activity Maybe you can succeed where the government has not. Working with two classmates, try to balance the federal budget.

❶ Go through the table and decide which types of spending to cut and by how much. If cuts do not total $158 billion, then decide what taxes you will raise. As you plan your cuts and taxes, consider who will be affected by them and what the results might be.

❷ Be prepared to defend your cuts or taxes. What criticisms might you hear? How will you respond to them?

❸ Present your ideas to your classmates. Can they live with your proposals? If not, what do they suggest?

Federal Spending 1995 (in billions of dollars)	
Social Security	336
Health, education	328
Defense	272
Interest on the debt	232
Welfare, housing	220
Other*	110
Environment, space, science	41
Transportation	39
Total	1,578

*Includes agriculture, energy, foreign affairs, justice, veterans' benefits

Source: *World Book Yearbook 1996*

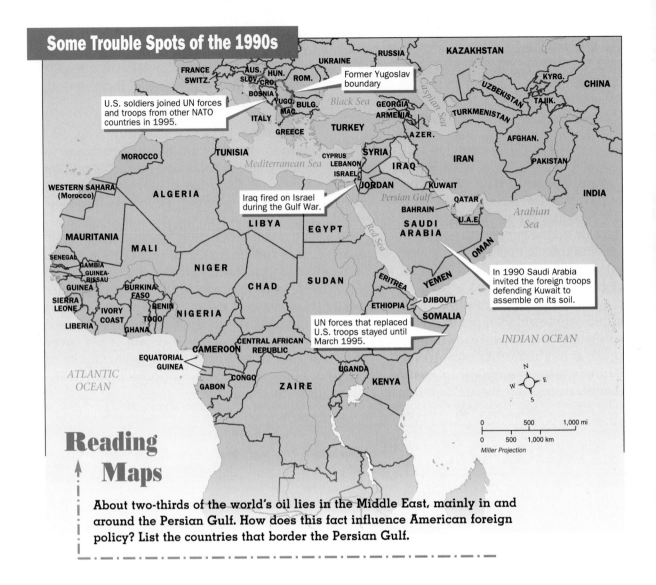

Some Trouble Spots of the 1990s

Former Yugoslav boundary

U.S. soldiers joined UN forces and troops from other NATO countries in 1995.

Iraq fired on Israel during the Gulf War.

In 1990 Saudi Arabia invited the foreign troops defending Kuwait to assemble on its soil.

UN forces that replaced U.S. troops stayed until March 1995.

Miller Projection

Reading Maps

About two-thirds of the world's oil lies in the Middle East, mainly in and around the Persian Gulf. How does this fact influence American foreign policy? List the countries that border the Persian Gulf.

Troubles for Bush

With American successes in Somalia and the Persian Gulf fresh in voters' minds, Bush's re-election in 1992 seemed certain. Problems at home, however, haunted the President.

As you read on page 878, the growing federal deficit plagued the nation. Meanwhile, a banking crisis erupted. Certain banks, called savings and loan associations (S&Ls), had made risky loans. Now they faced collapse. To protect people who had money in the shaky banks, the government paid out $100 billion, further adding to the deficit.

Even worse, by 1991 the nation had fallen into a recession. The number of people without jobs rose sharply. Many Americans now felt the effects of Reagan-era cutbacks in government programs. For example, a shortage of housing for the poor increased the number of homeless Americans. So did the policy of closing large institutions for the mentally ill.

Clinton Takes Over

Public dissatisfaction with President Bush presented Democrats with an opportunity to take the White House for the first time since

1980. They nominated Bill Clinton, the governor of Arkansas, who promised change and talked of putting "people first."

Meanwhile, Ross Perot, a wealthy Texas businessman, entered the race as a third-party candidate. He pushed for a balanced federal budget. With votes split three ways, Clinton was elected President by less than half the voters. He began his presidency promising to create jobs, cut the deficit, and provide health care for all Americans.

Health-care reform Clinton's first priority was health care. In 1992 the United States had spent more on health care than on education and defense combined. Even so, millions of people could not afford medical treatment. To solve the problem, the President appointed a commission led by his wife, Hillary Rodham Clinton, a lawyer.

The commission proposed a complex program that made major changes in the nation's health-care system. Such fierce controversy erupted around the proposal, however, that Congress failed to pass it.

Successful legislation Clinton was more successful at convincing Congress to pass the Family and Medical Leave Act in 1993. This popular law required large businesses to give an employee up to 12 weeks unpaid leave for such urgent situations as an illness or the birth of a child.

Clinton also pushed an anticrime bill through Congress. It provided funds to help states build more jails and hire more police. The act also toughened penalties for some crimes and banned sales of military-style weapons.

Trade agreements As part of his promise to improve trade and create jobs, Clinton got Congress to approve two trade agreements. In 1993 the North American Free Trade Agreement (NAFTA) ended many trade barriers between the United States, Mexico, and Canada.

Critics charged that Americans would lose jobs to lower-paid workers in Mexico. Clinton, though, argued that NAFTA would create jobs by making it easier for Mexicans and Canadians to buy American goods.

In 1994 more than 100 nations ratified a General Agreement on Tariffs and Trade (GATT). It called for lower tariffs and a World Trade Organization to help bring down barriers to trade.

Clinton's Policy Overseas

During the 1992 campaign, Clinton had made clear that he wanted to focus on problems at home. However, events overseas soon demanded his attention.

Haiti One of Clinton's first challenges came in the Caribbean nation of Haiti. Ruled by brutal military dictators for years, Haiti finally held free elections in 1991. Eight months later, the military overthrew the new President, Jean-Bertrand Aristide. To force the military from power and restore Aristide to office, Clinton imposed a blockade of Haiti. He warned the military leaders to leave or face American troops.

As troops prepared to invade, Clinton sent former President Carter to make a final appeal to Haiti's military to give up power. Carter succeeded. The military leaders agreed to step down, and American troops oversaw the return of President Aristide. Restoring democracy in Haiti was a victory for both Clinton and the Haitian people.

Bosnia Clinton's next challenge came in Europe. In 1991 the Communist nation of Yugoslavia had splintered into five republics—including Bosnia, Croatia, and Yugoslavia. Bosnia was home to Serbs, Muslims, and Croats. Having lived side by side in the same villages for centuries, most Bosnians hoped to continue to do so in their young republic.

Before the 1996 election, President Clinton faced a Republican Congress led by his rival, Bob Dole (right), and Newt Gingrich (left).

Above all, Republicans wanted to reduce the deficit by balancing the budget. Early in 1995 they proposed deep cuts in social programs, including school lunches, college loans, and health care for poor and elderly Americans. At the same time, however, they proposed lowering taxes.

Clinton, too, wanted to balance the budget. However, he argued that the Republican plan would hurt the needy, while wealthy Americans benefited from lower taxes. Congress and the President came to a stalemate, both looking for a boost in the 1996 election.

The Election of 1996

Republican hopes that they could unseat Clinton in 1996 were dashed. As the deficit began to shrink and the economy gained strength, voters gave Clinton the credit. He and Vice-President Albert Gore won 31 states to only 19 for Republicans Robert Dole and Jack Kemp.

In spite of Clinton's victory, the Republicans kept majorities in both houses of Congress. Perhaps the public preferred to maintain a balance of power, forcing President and Congress to compromise.

Tragically, however, age-old rivalries, inflamed by Serb leaders greedy for power, unleashed a cruel war. In 1992 Bosnian Serb forces began a brutal policy of "ethnic cleansing"—driving Muslims and Croats out of Bosnia by slaughtering men, women, and children and destroying their farms and towns. European leaders and President Bush backed away from the conflict. Peacemaking efforts by the United Nations failed, too.

In 1995 the tide of war turned against the Serb forces. It was then that they bowed to pressure from Clinton to end the war. Leaders of Bosnia's Muslims, Croats, and Serbs signed a peace agreement in Dayton, Ohio. To enforce it, Clinton sent 20,000 troops to Bosnia.

A Republican Congress

In November 1994 Clinton's presidency suffered a blow when voters elected Republican majorities in both houses of Congress. Confident that their victory meant public approval for drastic change, Republicans pushed to get rid of federal programs and powers—many dating from Franklin Roosevelt's New Deal.

2. Section Review

1. Define **deficit**.
2. How did Bush pursue a New World Order in the Middle East and Somalia?
3. **Critical Thinking** Should the United States get involved in civil wars, such as in Bosnia? Explain your answer.

Geography Lab

The Interior Highlands

Americans thought a great deal about the environment in the early 1990s. One result of their concern was the Arkansas Wild and Scenic Rivers Act of 1992. The law added about 200 miles of streams to the National Wild and Scenic Rivers System, guaranteeing that they will be preserved in their natural state for future generations to enjoy.

Several rivers covered by the act flow through the region known as the Interior Highlands. The crystal-clear waters, abundant fish, and wooded, often rugged banks of these rivers attract thousands of tourists each year. Use the photographs to form an image of the region.

Mountain overlook, Petit Jean State Park, Arkansas. Canoeing on the Buffalo National River, Arkansas (above). Waterfalls near the Buffalo River (right).

Developing a Mental Map

Refer to the maps on pages P4–P5 and R4–R7.

1. What three states are partially covered by the Interior Highlands?

2. What major rivers flow through the region?

3. Judging from the photographs, what is the terrain like in the Interior Highlands? What is the highest elevation range in the region, and where is it located?

4. According to the map on page R8, what kinds of vegetation grow naturally in the region?

5. **Hands-On Geography** Imagine that you are putting together a travel brochure about the Interior Highlands. Using the photos on this page as inspiration, write several paragraphs that will persuade tourists to visit the region. Include the kinds of activities visitors might expect to enjoy.

3. New Challenges and Hopes

Reading Guide

New Term Internet

Section Focus **American society and democracy move into a new century**

1. How is the American population changing?
2. What new challenges do the environment and the economy present?
3. How will democracy fare as the American way of life continues to change?

The United States is a nation that has learned to expect and welcome change. As a new century unfolds, we can be certain that how we live and work will continue to change— sometimes for the better, and sometimes in ways that concern and challenge us.

A Changing Population

In recent years, the American population has become increasingly diverse. It is also older and better educated than at any other time in its history.

Recent immigration The growing diversity of Americans is largely the result of a new wave of immigrants from Asia and Latin America. Like earlier immigrants, these recent arrivals hope to find freedom and opportunity in their new home.

Jaime Escalante was among the 1 million Hispanic immigrants who came to the United States in the 1960s. Just 18 months after his arrival, the 1965 Immigration and Nationality Act opened the doors to more immigrants—including Asians, who had been excluded for decades.

The 1965 law ended policies followed since the 1920s. It doubled the number of immigrants legally admitted—to 290,000 a year. It also set quotas by hemisphere instead of by nation. In 1995 the limit was set at 675,000 immigrants each year.

During the 1980s the nation's Asian population more than doubled. The Hispanic population increased by 53 percent. By the year 2050 almost one-half of the nation is expected to claim Asian, African, Hispanic, or Native American ancestry.

The new diversity affects the nation's schools and neighborhoods. Students in Los Angeles, for example, speak 86 languages. This poses challenges for teachers trying to help students succeed in their new country. Meanwhile, recent immigrants are bringing new life to city neighborhoods that had been losing population since the 1950s.

Changing households As the face of the nation has changed, so has the American household. Perhaps the greatest change has been the increasing number of single-parent households. One in four children born in the 1990s is being raised by a single parent. Meanwhile, people are marrying later and some are choosing not to have children.

An aging nation The nation is also seeing a growing number of people over the age of 55. Improved diets and health care help people live longer. During the 1980s the number of Americans in their eighties doubled. This "graying of America" will increase as the baby-boom generation ages. It will also put greater demands on the Social Security and health-care systems.

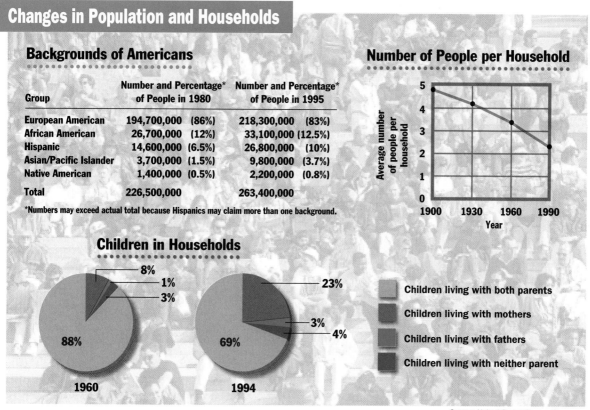

Changes in Population and Households

Backgrounds of Americans

Group	Number and Percentage* of People in 1980		Number and Percentage* of People in 1995	
European American	194,700,000	(86%)	218,300,000	(83%)
African American	26,700,000	(12%)	33,100,000	(12.5%)
Hispanic	14,600,000	(6.5%)	26,800,000	(10%)
Asian/Pacific Islander	3,700,000	(1.5%)	9,800,000	(3.7%)
Native American	1,400,000	(0.5%)	2,200,000	(0.8%)
Total	226,500,000		263,400,000	

*Numbers may exceed actual total because Hispanics may claim more than one background.

Number of People per Household

Average number of people per household / Year

Children in Households

8%
1%
3%
88%
1960

23%
3%
4%
69%
1994

Children living with both parents

Children living with mothers

Children living with fathers

Children living with neither parent

Source: United States Census Bureau

A Changing Environment

In recent decades Americans have been increasingly concerned about the environment. Information about the dangers of toxic substances flowing from smokestacks, car exhausts, and sewer pipes has helped launch a popular environmental movement.

Starting in the 1960s, Congress responded by passing laws to reduce pollution and clean up the nation's water and air. Although pollution remains a problem, environmentalists can point to major improvements in air quality. Lakes and rivers are cleaner, as well. For example, only 20 years after being labeled a "dying sinkhole," Lake Erie is again home to large numbers of fish.

Americans at home and at work are helping to reduce waste by recycling bottles, cans, and paper. In 1995 more than one-fifth of the nation's garbage was made into new products—a rate that doubters had claimed "could not be achieved."

Threats to the atmosphere Meanwhile, other environmental issues have emerged. Some scientists fear that global warming—a rise in the earth's surface temperature—will melt the polar ice caps, raising sea levels and flooding coastal regions. They urge people to cut back on the use of wood, coal, and oil for fuel. However, other scientists say that the danger of global warming is exaggerated.

Destruction of the ozone layer troubles many scientists. The ozone layer—a protective blanket of gases in the atmosphere—screens out harmful rays from the sun. The cause of this destruction is thought to be chlorofluorocarbons—chemicals used in refrigerators, air conditioners, and spray cans. Some people find hope in the swift

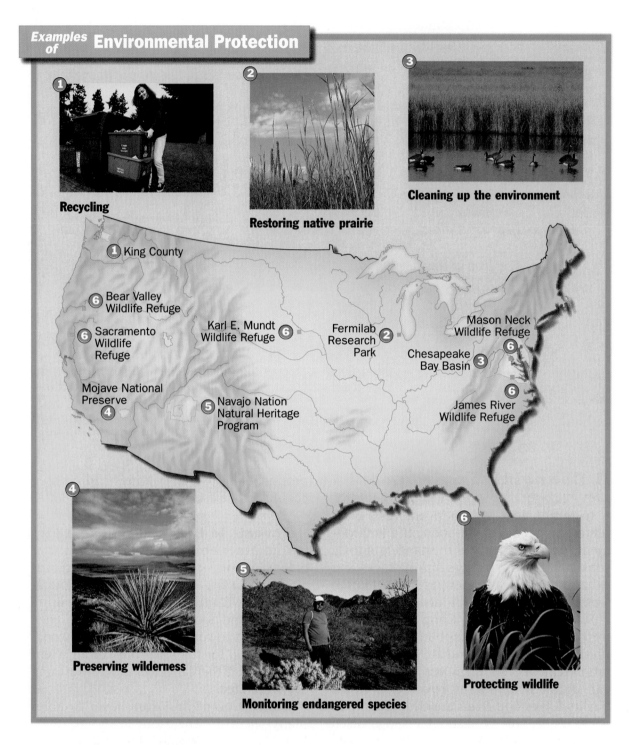

Examples of Environmental Protection

Recycling

Restoring native prairie

Cleaning up the environment

1 King County

6 Bear Valley Wildlife Refuge

6 Sacramento Wildlife Refuge

Karl E. Mundt Wildlife Refuge 6

Fermilab Research Park 2

Mason Neck Wildlife Refuge 6

Chesapeake Bay Basin 3

Mojave National Preserve 4

5 Navajo Nation Natural Heritage Program

James River Wildlife Refuge 6

Preserving wilderness

Monitoring endangered species

Protecting wildlife

Reading Maps

Judging from the examples shown on the map, what are some different kinds of environmental problems that Americans have tried to solve in recent years?

reaction of the world's nations, 93 of which agreed to ban such chemicals by 1996.

A Changing Economy

Since the 1980s new technologies have radically changed people's lives and ways of working. The most striking example is computer technology. Computers were first developed at the end of World War II. Big, bulky, and expensive, the early computers were available only to the military, and to corporations and universities.

Today, improved technology has made computers smaller and less expensive but increasingly powerful. They have become such an essential part of personal and working lives that it is difficult to imagine how people ever lived without them. They are capable of assisting with an amazing range of tasks—from surgery to creating artwork to tracking the earth's climate.

The information revolution The use of computers has created an "information revolution." One CD-ROM can provide as much information as an entire encyclopedia, to say nothing of pictures and sounds.

Through the **Internet**—a web of computer networks linked through telephone lines—people can find information provided by government agencies, libraries, and businesses. The Internet also helps people around the world communicate quickly and at little cost.

Effects on the economy As information flows more easily, the American economy is changing dramatically. Increasingly, jobs are in the service and information industries rather than in manufacturing. At the same time, workers can no longer count on the security of a long-term job.

In earlier times, most Americans expected to spend their whole careers working for one company. In the 1970s, however, many factory jobs disappeared as businesses moved overseas and hired lower-paid workers. New technologies, too, allowed factories to produce more goods with fewer workers. As a result, American factory workers felt less and less secure about their futures.

In the 1980s and 1990s job insecurity spread to other workers, as well. In almost every industry—even in computer-related ones—employers were cutting their work forces in an effort to reduce costs. More confusing still, such job losses occurred in good as well as bad times. Many workers felt betrayed. Dan Skowron, a worker in the Midwest, observed: "My eyes are much more open, now. You can't assume any job will last forever."

The income gap Meanwhile, the income gap between the wealthy and the rest of the population has been growing. The average annual income of the wealthiest 10 percent of American households increased from $68,805 in 1973 to $76,436 in 1993. During the same period, the average income for the lower half of American households decreased from $30,580 to $27,148.

In the 1990s millions of new jobs have been created. People who thrive in this new economy will be educated service and information workers who have the skill to put ideas and information to work to create something of value. Meanwhile, less-educated workers wonder how they will make a living in the new information economy.

The Future of American Democracy

As Americans face major changes in the environment, economy, and technology, they also continue to dream of new opportunities—just as their parents and grandparents did. At the same time, many wonder what effect such changes are having on society. They raise the pressing question: What is the future of American democracy?

Are Americans willing to perform the duties and take the responsibilities necessary for democracy to succeed in a changing world?

Citizens' rights and duties As citizens of the United States, Americans have the right to vote, to have a fair trial, and to express their opinions. These and other rights are based on ideals—freedom, equality, and justice—that Americans share and that are protected by the Constitution.

Americans have certain duties, as well. These duties range from serving on a jury to attending school, paying taxes, and obeying laws.

Citizens' responsibilities Unlike a citizen's duties, a citizen's responsibilities are voluntary. The most basic one is to work for the common good—to contribute to the well-being of society as a whole. This responsibility includes working to make communities, states, and the nation better places for everyone to live.

There are many ways in which individuals can work for the common good. They can vote, hold public office, write letters to elected officials, or attend school board meetings.

They can form or join organizations that seek to solve problems—from protecting the environment to creating new jobs.

Communities in a democracy The tradition of participation in community organizations reaches far back into the nation's history. Thomas Jefferson believed that the willingness of citizens to join together in the task of building a community was at the heart of democracy.

In the 1830s a French writer, Alexis de Tocqueville, noted with approval the number of community organizations he saw while touring the United States. A hundred years later a national women's association concluded:

"Participation is the life of democracy. Without it, democracy dies."

Threats to democracy Since Tocqueville's visit, new technologies—including the automobile, television, and the computer—are changing how Americans interact with one another. Some fear that such technologies, which encourage Americans to lead lives increasingly separate from one another, are a threat to democracy.

A person can now work or watch a movie at home, get money from an automated teller machine, and pick up a meal at a drive-through restaurant—all without talking to anyone else. Is this new way of life replacing an older one in which work and social life involved communicating with strangers as well as with friends?

Many worry, too, that the demands of modern life leave little time for participating in community organizations. Commuting to work, driving children to

People come together in revived public places like Quincy Market in Boston, where they can stroll, shop, eat, and find entertainment.

El Lenguaje Mudo del Alma (The Silent Language of the Soul) (1990) Painting a mural on the outside of a building is a form of community art. Such a mural often becomes a well-loved part of the neighborhood—especially if it reflects the activities or culture of the people who live there. An example is the mural that artists Juana Alicia and Susan Cervantes painted around the entrance to Cesar Chavez School in San Francisco. Neighbors enjoy seeing the images of children using sign language to express their thoughts and feelings. **Discuss** Choose a building in your neighborhood on which you would like to paint a public mural. What would be the purpose of your mural? Describe the scene—including the colors and images—that you would want to depict.

school, shopping in huge malls, and keeping up with friends in far-flung suburbs consumes most hours in a day.

Finally, there is concern that Americans are losing faith in the political system. Public distrust of government, spurred by the painful years of the Vietnam War and the Watergate scandal, remains high. At the same time, the percentage of Americans who vote in elections has been dropping.

New signs of community Despite these signs that people are losing their sense of community, there is also evidence that Americans are making great efforts to come together. For example, public places—such as baseball parks, tree-lined waterfronts, churches, cafés, and health clubs—are growing in popularity.

Today's public places bring together people of different backgrounds and classes. Revived farmers' markets and downtown main streets, as well as malls that include libraries and museums, thrive throughout the nation. A 1996 study revealed that most people would like to live in areas where they can walk to traditional town centers.

Meanwhile, as a *Chicago Tribune* writer observed, Americans continue to feel an "optimism that makes them determined to keep their neighborhood [a good place to live]." Mary Ann Smith helped her Chicago neighborhood clean up a crime-ridden housing complex. Afterward, she concluded:

"We've found [that] every problem is also an opportunity to make people feel powerful.**"**

The confidence that individuals have the power to improve their communities is essential to life in a democracy. Other ways in which people are exercising that power include writing letters to newspapers, calling in to radio talk shows, and participating in chatlines on the Internet.

The renewed yearning for a sense of community in which all people are valued and respected is an important step toward maintaining a democratic society where freedom and opportunity thrive. Indeed, the success of democracy in the United States will always depend upon citizens who are willing to vote, to help out their neighbors, and to respect their fellow citizens.

3. Section Review

1. Define **Internet.**

2. In what ways has the American environment improved in the past 20 years?

3. Critical Thinking To encourage people to participate more in their communities and government, what three changes would you make in American society?

Why We Remember

New Roles in a Changing World

The last decades of the twentieth century have been filled with wonders and worries. For some, the most amazing wonders have been advances in technology and in preserving the environment. Others have been heartened by the end of the Cold War and the spread of democracy. For many, the wonders have been more personal—such as the success of Jaime Escalante's Garfield High students in passing the college placement exam for calculus.

However, our rapidly changing world has brought new worries as well. With a new century dawning, Americans have concerns ranging from AIDS and the income gap to the federal deficit and global warming. As the only remaining superpower, the United States struggles to decide what role to play in the world. Meanwhile, workers seeking a place in the new "information economy" worry that dreams of a better life might be slipping away.

Since all people are "explorers" into a new century, no one knows just what to expect. Still, the past can serve as a guide. History reminds Americans that they live in a nation founded on dreams—dreams of equality, opportunity, freedom, and respect for the rights of the individual. These are dreams that Americans will cherish as they journey into that unknown land that is the future.

Skill Lab

Using Information
Taking Action

Like many people, you may find it frustrating to hear about global environmental problems. After all, what can you do about the ozone layer? Actually, every person can take small steps to help solve environmental problems, especially local ones. As the saying goes, "Think globally, act locally."

Question to Investigate

How can we help solve local environmental problems?

Procedure

In the following steps, you and a group of classmates will deal with an environmental problem in your school or community.

① State your goal.
a. Choose a local environmental problem.
b. State what you want to accomplish.

② Identify resources (what will help you) and obstacles (what you have to overcome).
a. List people to approach for suggestions or other help. List other resources.
b. List problems that may stand in your way.

③ Identify what to do to achieve your goal.
a. List all tasks that need to be done, including those that involve using resources and overcoming obstacles.
b. Assign group members to the tasks.
c. Set a deadline for completing each task.

④ Carry out your plan.
a. Meet regularly to discuss progress.
b. If something does not work, change parts of your plan.

c. Give a presentation to classmates in which you answer the Question to Investigate based on your experience with carrying out your action plan.

Source to Use

Below is a sample of part of an action plan:

Goal
- To make our school a litter-free zone

Resources
- Library (newspaper articles on last year's park cleanup project)
-
-

Obstacles
- Lack of time in school day for project
-
-

Tasks
- Do library research to get more ideas.
- Ask principal's permission to put up anti-litter posters.
-

Chapter Survey

Reviewing Vocabulary

Define the following terms.
1. deficit
2. Internet

Reviewing Main Ideas

1. Why did President Ford pardon former President Nixon?
2. Why did President Carter's image and style of leadership appeal to the American people at the time of his election?
3. (a) How did President Reagan try to shrink the government and boost prosperity? (b) How did he try to improve the image of the United States in the world?
4. Describe two events overseas and how President Bush responded to the challenge that they presented.
5. Give specific examples for each of the following: (a) President Clinton and Congress worked together to solve problems and achieve goals. (b) President Clinton and Congress clashed.
6. Describe one way that each of the following has changed since the 1960s: (a) the American population (b) the environment (c) the economy
7. What concerns do some people have for the future of American democracy?

Thinking Critically

1. **Evaluation** Do you think President Ford did the right thing in pardoning former President Nixon? Explain.
2. **Analysis** What effect did events in the Middle East have on the presidencies of Carter, Reagan, and Bush?
3. **Why We Remember: Synthesis** What do you think is the greatest challenge that Americans face today? Describe what you, as an individual, would want to do to help meet that challenge.

Applying Skills

Taking action We Americans have long been known for our active efforts to improve our nation and ourselves. What change for the better would you like to make in your own life? Maybe you would like to spend more time with friends, improve your grades in school, or increase your skill at playing basketball, singing, or creating computer art. Apply what you learned on page 891 to develop an action plan for making the desired improvement.
1. State your goal.
2. Identify resources that will help you and obstacles to be overcome.
3. Identify what you will do to achieve your goal.
4. Carry out your plan.

History Mystery

Answer the History Mystery on page 869. Which of the former President's occupations would you find most interesting? Which would be most helpful to American society today?

Writing in Your History Journal

1. **Keys to History** (a) The time line on pages 868–869 has seven Keys to History. In your journal, describe why each one is important to know about. (b) Choose a key event and imagine that you are a television reporter assigned to cover it. In your journal, write what you will say in tonight's broadcast. Include background information and predict possible consequences of the event.
2. **Jaime Escalante** Is Jaime Escalante typical of the immigrants who have come to the United States over the past two centuries, or is he markedly different? Explain your response in your journal.

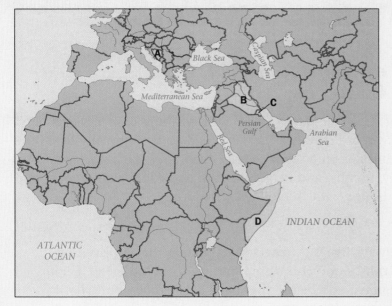

Reviewing Geography

1. Each letter represents a country that was a "hot spot" in the 1980s or 1990s. Write the name of each country.

2. Geographic Thinking Suppose you were asked to update the "hot spots" map to reflect world events today. What additions to and subtractions from the map would you make? Explain. Now try to imagine the world 20 years from now. Where do you think the hottest spot will be? (You can name a continent or other region rather than a country.) Explain.

3. Citizenship The United States is a nation made up of increasingly diverse groups of people. What advantages and disadvantages do you see in this diversity? What beliefs, experiences, or characteristics do you think unify all Americans despite their diversity? Write your responses in your journal.

Alternative Assessment

Acting out political discussions With a partner, prepare and act out discussions between two friends—one a Republican and the other a Democrat—in each of these presidential election years: 1976, 1980, 1988, and 1992. You will act out four 10-minute discussions.

❶ Choose roles. You might make the "characters" more realistic by assigning names and ages, ethnic backgrounds, places of residence, occupations, and so forth. Keep the same roles for all four discussions.

❷ Write scripts for the discussions. In each case, the characters should discuss their positions on current issues as well as the records and qualifications of the two presidential candidates. You might need to do further research on the presidential candidates by looking at magazine or newspaper articles of the times.

❸ Present the discussions to the class.

Your work will be evaluated on the following criteria:
• your scripts accurately present the events and issues of each time period
• you offer opinions in a way that is lively yet clear, logical, and reasonable
• you stay "in character" as a Republican or Democrat of each time period

The House on Mango Street
by Sandra Cisneros

In her novel, *The House on Mango Street,* author Sandra Cisneros tells her story through the eyes of Esperanza Cordero, a young girl growing up in the Latino section of Chicago. In a series of brief chapters, Esperanza vividly describes her family, friends, and neighborhood, and confides her hopes and dreams. The novel begins with the following passage.

We didn't always live on Mango Street. Before that we lived on Loomis on the third floor, and before that we lived on Keeler. Before Keeler it was Paulina, and before that I can't remember. But what I remember most is moving a lot. Each time it seemed there'd be one more of us. By the time we got to Mango Street we were six—Mama, Papa, Carlos, Kiki, my sister Nenny and me.

The house on Mango Street is ours, and we don't have to pay rent to anybody, or share the yard with the people downstairs, or be careful not to make too much noise, and there isn't a landlord banging on the ceiling with a broom. But even so, it's not the house we thought we'd get.

We had to leave the flat on Loomis quick. The water pipes broke and the landlord wouldn't fix them because the house was too old. We had to leave fast. We were using the washroom next door and carrying water over in empty milk gallons. That's why Mama and Papa looked for a house, and that's why we moved into the house on Mango Street, far away, on the other side of town.

They always told us that one day we would move into a house, a real house that would be ours for always so we wouldn't have to move each year. And our house would have running water and pipes that worked. And inside it would have real stairs, not hallway stairs, but stairs inside like the houses on T.V. And we'd have a basement and at least three washrooms so when we took a bath we wouldn't have to tell everybody. Our house would be white with trees around it, a great big yard and grass growing without a fence. This was the house Mama dreamed up in the stories she told us before we went to bed.

But the house on Mango Street is not the way they told it at all. It's small and red with tight steps in front and windows so small you'd think they were holding their breath. Bricks are crumbling in places and the front door is so swollen you have to push hard to get in. There is no front yard, only four little elms the city planted by the curb. Out

Hermanas Juntas Sin Velo (Sisters Together Unveiled) by Nivia Gonzalez

back is a small garage for the car we don't own yet and a small yard that looks smaller between the two buildings on either side There are stairs in our house, but they're ordinary hallway stairs, and the house has only one washroom. Everybody has to share a bedroom—Mama and Papa, Carlos and Kiki, me and Nenny.

Once when we were living on Loomis, a nun from my school passed by and saw me playing out front. The laundromat downstairs had been boarded up because it had been robbed two days before and the owner had painted on the wood YES WE'RE OPEN so as not to lose business.

Where do you live? she asked.

There, I said pointing up to the third floor.

You live there?

There. I had to look to where she pointed—the third floor, the paint peeling, wooden bars Papa had nailed on the windows so we wouldn't fall out. You live there? The way she said it made me feel like nothing. There. I lived there. I nodded.

I knew then I had to have a house. A real house. One I could point to. But this isn't it. The house on Mango Street isn't it. For the time being, Mama says. Temporary, says Papa. But I know how those things go.

A Closer Look

1. How does Esperanza feel about the house she lives in? How did she feel about the flat on Loomis?

2. What does Esperanza hope for?

3. Based on this passage, why do you think Cisneros uses a house as her central image?

Unit Survey

Making Connections

1. What was the main goal of United States foreign policy during the Cold War? How did the United States work toward this goal from the beginning to the end of the Cold War?

2. Give four examples of developments in the United States that were closely linked to international events since World War II. Explain the links.

3. Support the following statement with evidence from the unit: *Television has had a major impact on the course of history since 1950.*

Linking History, Art, and Music

A Fifties, Sixties, or Seventies Party

It may seem odd, but in the 1950s and 1960s, "Roaring Twenties" parties were extremely popular. Female guests dressed like "flappers," male guests tried to look like gangsters, and everyone danced the "Charleston" to loud jazz. Plan your own party centered on one of the following decades that you have read about: the 1950s, 1960s, or 1970s.

Project Steps

Work with a group.

❶ Choose the decade to center your party on. Select a date, time, and place for the party. Make up the guest list.

❷ Decide who in your group will do what in order to get ready for the party. Here is a list of tasks to get you started:

• Make invitations. They should ask guests to wear costumes appropriate to the decade. For example, guests might dress like "hippies" for a Sixties party. To help your guests plan their costumes, draw or photocopy pictures of people from the decade on the invitations.

• Plan and create decorations that relate to the decade. For example, put up authentic posters. Or make posters based on images you find in books about the decade or in magazines from the decade.

• Make arrangements for music. Gather recordings of popular music from the decade. If any group members play instruments, they can perform the decade's hits "live." Also, learn some dances of the decade so you can teach them to your guests.

❸ Carry out the preparations. Ask parents or other adults for ideas on making the party authentic and for help in learning dances. The adults may even have items such as clothing, posters, or recordings that you can borrow. Your library is another source of help.

❹ Have the party—and have fun!

Thinking It Over Someday, your children may attend Nineties parties in which they wear "costumes" like the clothes you wear and dance to "ancient" compact discs of the music you love. People of each generation enjoy this type of "time travel." Why do you think this is so? What do you suppose later generations will think of when they think of the 1990s? Why?

Epilogue

Into the Future

Imagine Waking Up in the Year 2025: A Scenario

It is November 28, 2025: You wake up at 7 A.M. and your biometric bed checks your vital signs. "The old blood pressure is a little high this morning, my friend," the bed warns in a soothing tone. You step into the shower, and the showerhead automatically adjusts from your father-in-law's 6-foot, 4-inch, 240-pound frame to your slimmer body; the spray is rousingly forceful. You listen as the shower room's personal information system reports on the overnight stock activity from Tokyo.

As the shower douses you with antibacterial suds, you ask the information system for a quick personality assessment from the psychotherapeutic expert system you just installed. "Hey, relax! Try to image a sun-drenched beach," you're advised. "You'll be able to handle that marketing presentation much better." You smile, thinking about the fun you had on your last vacation in Hawaii as the shower's heat jets blast you dry. The robotic closet-valet brings out your color-coordinated, temperature-sensitive business suit, and you quickly dress. As you leave your bedroom, you sense the temperature going down behind you and the lights turning off automatically.

You peek into the kids' room to make sure they've transmitted their home-work to school and have gotten dressed for their teleclass, which they "attend" for three hours in your home's media room during what used to be a long Thanksgiving holiday.

You are now ready to face an average workday in the 21st century.

From John Mahaffie and Andy Hines, *The Futurist*, Nov./Dec. 1994. Reproduced with permission from *The Futurist*, published by the World Future Society, 7910 Woodmont Ave., Ste. 450, Bethesda, MD 20814.

The story above is called a scenario. A scenario is an imaginary account of happenings in the future. It is written by futurists—people who try to imagine what the future will be like. Futurists look at information from the past and the present. From that information they make predictions about what might happen in years to come and then draw up a scenario based on their predictions.

Predicting the Future

To make a prediction, a futurist must first detect trends—patterns revealed over time by certain facts. In 1984, for example, 7 million Americans used computers at home. Over 30 million people did so in 1993. To note such an increase is to discover a trend.

To make predictions about the future of education, a futurist might look at—among other things—how many students graduate from high school and how that number has changed over the past 100 years. Having observed a trend, the futurist would try to predict whether more or fewer students will finish high school in the future. Using past and present facts, futurists have made the predictions on these pages.

Robotic hand

City planners

Technology Predictions

● Smart technologies use computer chips to respond to changes in the environment around them. They can adjust a car's temperature or water the garden. With smart technologies, future cars might drive themselves while passengers watch television or take a nap.

● People will rely on information appliances, such as picture phones, computers, and faxes. Americans will increasingly turn to the Internet for information rather than to books and magazines.

Predictions About Education

● Use of information appliances will make individual instruction easier. Classmates will study different topics at the same time. One might watch a CD-ROM on volcanoes while others use computers to work on math problems or to write and illustrate a book.

● Students will learn in a variety of settings, from home to school to a museum. Schoolwork will be telecommunicated—sent by computer—between students and teachers.

Population Predictions

● The population of the United States is expected to rise from 260 million in 1994 to 390 million in 2050.

● By 2010, for the first time, more Americans will be over 55 years of age than under 18 years of age.

● Population will continue to explode in southern and western states. For example, California is expected to shoot up to 41 million people in 2010 from its 1995 population of 32 million.

Predictions About Work

- The number of construction workers will increase. People working in service industries, such as teachers and doctors, will also find more opportunities. There will be 200,000 more lawyers by 2005, and 650,000 more waitresses and waiters.

- Jobs in farming and manufacturing industries, however, will decline in number. New technologies will be one reason behind the decline.

- More people will communicate at work through the Internet and videoconferencing than through face-to-face encounters or by telephone.

Teleconferencing

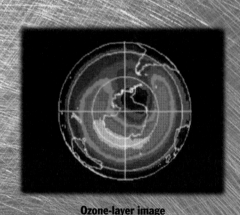

Ozone-layer image

Environmental Predictions

- As many as 50,000 types of plants and animals may die out during the first decades of the 21st century. By the time that century ends, two-thirds of all living species may be lost forever.

- The Amazon rain forest in South America may recover from the destruction that humans have caused. Satellite pictures reveal that new forests are already growing there.

- The "hole" in the ozone layer may begin to shrink in the near future. Such good news would result from the ban on chlorofluorocarbons (see page 885).

Predictions About How We Live

- The world's population will become more urban. In 1900 only 1 in 40 people lived in cities. By 2000 at least 1 in 2 people will live in cities.

- English will be increasingly used as a major language throughout the world.

- Telecommuting will free workers from having to live near their workplaces. With one or both parents working at home, patterns of family life will change.

- Malls will add museums, theaters, and indoor botanical gardens to attract people who are looking for activities outside their homes.

- New forms of travel will be developed. Short-distance trips—from Boston to New York or Los Angeles to San Francisco—will be made easier by trains traveling 200 miles (320 km) an hour or faster.

High-speed train

Creating a Scenario for 2025

Imagine That You Have Been Hired as a Futurist

Your job is to create a scenario—an imaginary setting—of life in 2025. The scenario should present one day in the life of an average 14-year-old American student. She or he will be your main character. Follow the steps below to meet this challenge.

1 First, create the main character of the scenario in your mind. Imagine what one day in her or his life will be like. Think about the technologies that will be available. How will your character interact with people—parents, brothers and sisters, classmates, and teachers, among others? In your scenario describe the main character's life within the home and outside the home. Be sure to explain what schools will be like for young people in 2025.

2 Like any futurist, research your scenario by reviewing the trends of various topics you plan to include in your story. You can trace the changes in work done by Americans, for example, by reviewing information in this text and in other sources. Consider the current state of each topic, such as work, at this time in our history.

3 Present your scenario as a video or as an illustrated story on posterboards. Use both facts and fantasies in creating the script or captions, and in drawing the illustrations for your presentation.

Remember that an effective scenario is a prediction that is based on trends. On what trends will you base your scenario? Be prepared to explain them.

Reference Center

The World: Political

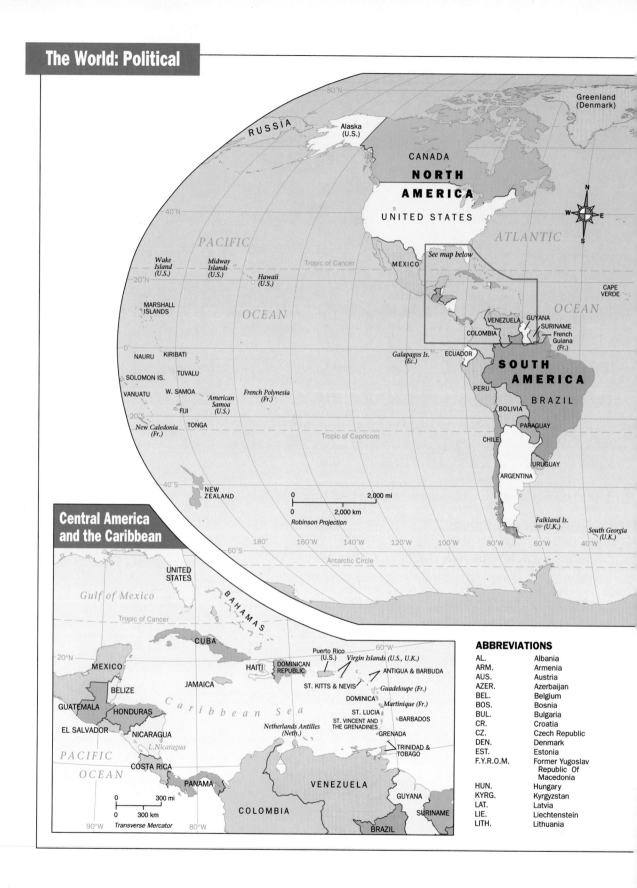

Greenland
(Denmark)

RUSSIA

Alaska
(U.S.)

CANADA

NORTH AMERICA

UNITED STATES

PACIFIC

Tropic of Cancer

MEXICO

See map below

ATLANTIC

CAPE VERDE

OCEAN

Wake Island (U.S.)

Midway Islands (U.S.)

Hawaii (U.S.)

MARSHALL ISLANDS

OCEAN

VENEZUELA   GUYANA
SURINAME
COLOMBIA   French Guiana (Fr.)

NAURU   KIRIBATI

Galapagos Is. (Ec.)   ECUADOR

SOUTH AMERICA

SOLOMON IS.   TUVALU

PERU

VANUATU   W. SAMOA

BRAZIL

American Samoa (U.S.)

French Polynesia (Fr.)

FIJI

BOLIVIA

New Caledonia (Fr.)   TONGA

PARAGUAY

Tropic of Capricorn

CHILE

URUGUAY

NEW ZEALAND

0   2,000 mi

0   2,000 km

Robinson Projection

ARGENTINA

Falkland Is. (U.K.)

South Georgia (U.K.)

180°   160°W   140°W   120°W   100°W   80°W   60°W   40°W

Antarctic Circle

Central America and the Caribbean

UNITED STATES

Gulf of Mexico

BAHAMAS

Tropic of Cancer

CUBA

20°N

MEXICO

HAITI   DOMINICAN REPUBLIC

Puerto Rico (U.S.)   Virgin Islands (U.S., U.K.)

60°W

ANTIGUA & BARBUDA

JAMAICA

BELIZE

Caribbean Sea

ST. KITTS & NEVIS   Guadeloupe (Fr.)

DOMINICA   Martinique (Fr.)

GUATEMALA   HONDURAS

ST. LUCIA   BARBADOS

EL SALVADOR   NICARAGUA

Netherlands Antilles (Neth.)   ST. VINCENT AND THE GRENADINES   GRENADA

L.Nicaragua

PACIFIC

COSTA RICA

TRINIDAD & TOBAGO

OCEAN

PANAMA

VENEZUELA

GUYANA

0   300 mi

0   300 km

Transverse Mercator

COLOMBIA

SURINAME

90°W   80°W

BRAZIL

ABBREVIATIONS

AL.	Albania
ARM.	Armenia
AUS.	Austria
AZER.	Azerbaijan
BEL.	Belgium
BOS.	Bosnia
BUL.	Bulgaria
CR.	Croatia
CZ.	Czech Republic
DEN.	Denmark
EST.	Estonia
F.Y.R.O.M.	Former Yugoslav Republic Of Macedonia
HUN.	Hungary
KYRG.	Kyrgyzstan
LAT.	Latvia
LIE.	Liechtenstein
LITH.	Lithuania

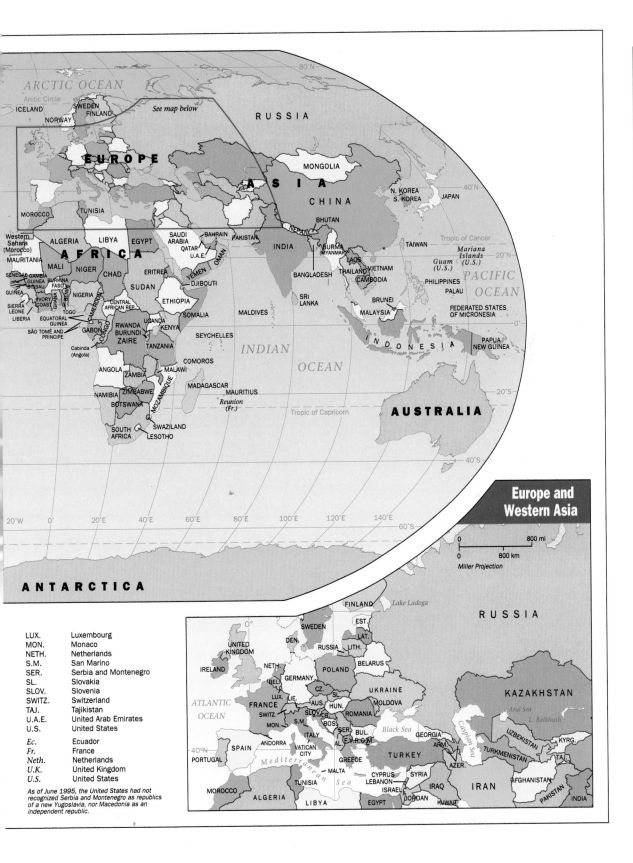

ATLAS

ARCTIC OCEAN
Arctic Circle
ICELAND
NORWAY
SWEDEN
FINLAND
See map below
RUSSIA
EUROPE
ASIA
MONGOLIA
MOROCCO
TUNISIA
AFRICA
CHINA
N. KOREA
S. KOREA
JAPAN
Western
Sahara
(Morocco)
ALGERIA
LIBYA
EGYPT
SAUDI
ARABIA
QATAR
BAHRAIN
PAKISTAN
NEPAL
BHUTAN
Tropic of Cancer
Mariana
Islands
(U.S.)
TAIWAN
20°N
MAURITANIA
U.A.E.
OMAN
INDIA
BURMA
(MYANMAR)
Guam
(U.S.)
PACIFIC
OCEAN
MALI
NIGER
CHAD
ERITREA
YEMEN
LAOS
SENEGAL GAMBIA
GUINEA BURKINA
BISSAU FASO
SUDAN
DJIBOUTI
BANGLADESH
THAILAND
VIETNAM
CAMBODIA
PHILIPPINES
PALAU
GUINEA
NIGERIA
CENTRAL
AFRICAN REP.
ETHIOPIA
SRI
LANKA
BRUNEI
FEDERATED STATES
OF MICRONESIA
SIERRA
LEONE
LIBERIA
IVORY
COAST
TOGO
GHANA
EQUATORIAL
GUINEA
CAMEROON
UGANDA
SOMALIA
MALAYSIA
0°
SÃO TOMÉ AND
PRINCIPE
GABON
CONGO
ZAIRE
RWANDA
BURUNDI
KENYA
MALDIVES
INDONESIA
PAPUA
NEW GUINEA
Cabinda
(Angola)
TANZANIA
SEYCHELLES
INDIAN
COMOROS
ANGOLA
ZAMBIA
MALAWI
MOZAMBIQUE
MADAGASCAR
MAURITIUS
OCEAN
20°S
NAMIBIA
ZIMBABWE
Reunion
(Fr.)
Tropic of Capricorn
AUSTRALIA
BOTSWANA
SWAZILAND
SOUTH
AFRICA
LESOTHO
40°S

60°S

20°W
0°
20°E
40°E
60°E
80°E
100°E
120°E
140°E

ANTARCTICA

Europe and Western Asia

0   800 mi

0   800 km

Miller Projection

LUX.	Luxembourg
MON.	Monaco
NETH.	Netherlands
S.M.	San Marino
SER.	Serbia and Montenegro
SL.	Slovakia
SLOV.	Slovenia
SWITZ.	Switzerland
TAJ.	Tajikistan
U.A.E.	United Arab Emirates
U.S.	United States
Ec.	Ecuador
Fr.	France
Neth.	Netherlands
U.K.	United Kingdom
U.S.	United States

As of June 1995, the United States had not
recognized Serbia and Montenegro as republics
of a new Yugoslavia, nor Macedonia as an
independent republic.

FINLAND
Lake Ladoga
RUSSIA
EST.
SWEDEN
DEN.
LAT.
UNITED
KINGDOM
RUSSIA
LITH.
IRELAND
NETH.
BELARUS
POLAND
BEL.
GERMANY
CZ.
KAZAKHSTAN
LUX.
LIE.
SL.
UKRAINE
Aral Sea
ATLANTIC
FRANCE
AUS.
HUN.
MOLDOVA
L. Balkhash
SWITZ.
SLOV.
ROMANIA
OCEAN
MON.
S.M.
CR.
BOS.
UZBEKISTAN
KYRG.
ANDORRA
ITALY
SER.
BUL.
Black Sea
GEORGIA
Caspian Sea
40°N
SPAIN
VATICAN
CITY
AL.
F.Y.R.O.M.
TURKEY
ARM.
TURKMENISTAN
TAJ.
PORTUGAL
Mediterranean
GREECE
MALTA
AZER.
AFGHANISTAN
PAKISTAN
MOROCCO
TUNISIA
CYPRUS
LEBANON
SYRIA
IRAN
INDIA
Sea
ISRAEL
IRAQ
ALGERIA
LIBYA
EGYPT
JORDAN
KUWAIT

Atlas • **R3**

United States: Physical

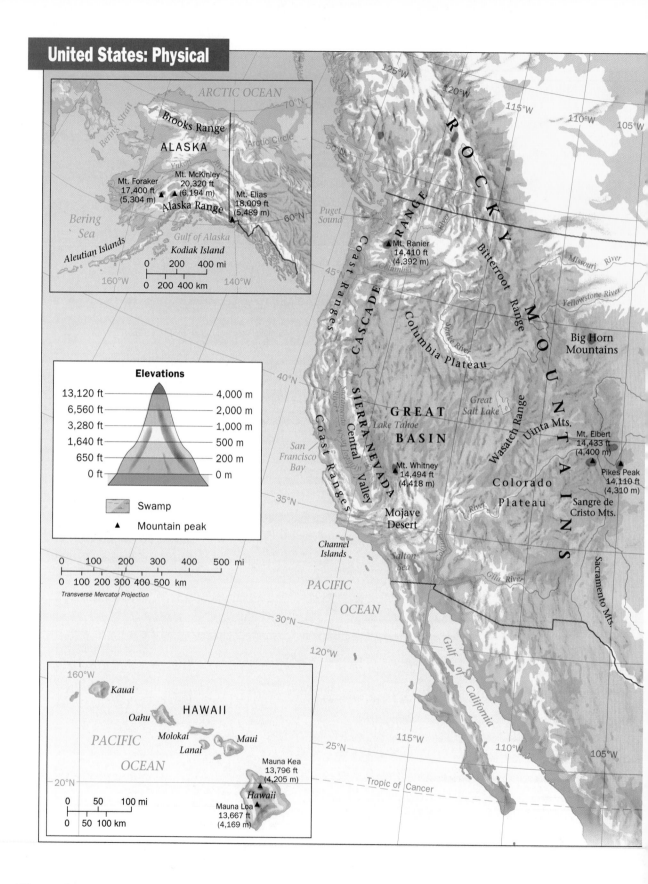

ARCTIC OCEAN

Brooks Range

ALASKA

Bering Strait

Yukon

Mt. Foraker
17,400 ft
(5,304 m)

Mt. McKinley
20,320 ft
(6,194 m)

Mt. Elias
18,009 ft
(5,489 m)

Alaska Range

Bering Sea

Aleutian Islands

Gulf of Alaska

Kodiak Island

Arctic Circle

| 0 | 200 | 400 mi |

| 0 | 200 | 400 km |

Elevations

13,120 ft	4,000 m
6,560 ft	2,000 m
3,280 ft	1,000 m
1,640 ft	500 m
650 ft	200 m
0 ft	0 m

Swamp

▲ Mountain peak

| 0 | 100 | 200 | 300 | 400 | 500 mi |

| 0 | 100 | 200 | 300 | 400 | 500 km |

Transverse Mercator Projection

HAWAII

Kauai

Oahu

Molokai
Lanai

Maui

PACIFIC
OCEAN

Mauna Kea
13,796 ft
(4,205 m)

Hawaii

Mauna Loa
13,667 ft
(4,169 m)

| 0 | 50 | 100 mi |

| 0 | 50 | 100 km |

ROCKY MOUNTAINS

Puget Sound

COAST RANGE

CASCADE RANGE

Bitterroot Range

Mt. Ranier
14,410 ft
(4,392 m)

Columbia

Columbia Plateau

Snake River

Missouri River

Yellowstone River

Big Horn Mountains

Coast Ranges

Sacramento River

SIERRA NEVADA

Central Valley

San Joaquin River

GREAT
BASIN

Lake Tahoe

Great Salt Lake

Wasatch Range

Uinta Mts.

Mt. Elbert
14,433 ft
(4,400 m)

San Francisco Bay

Mt. Whitney
14,494 ft
(4,418 m)

Colorado
Plateau

Pikes Peak
14,110 ft
(4,310 m)

Sangre de
Cristo Mts.

Mojave
Desert

River

Channel Islands

Salton Sea

Gila River

PACIFIC
OCEAN

Gulf of California

Sacramento Mts.

Tropic of Cancer

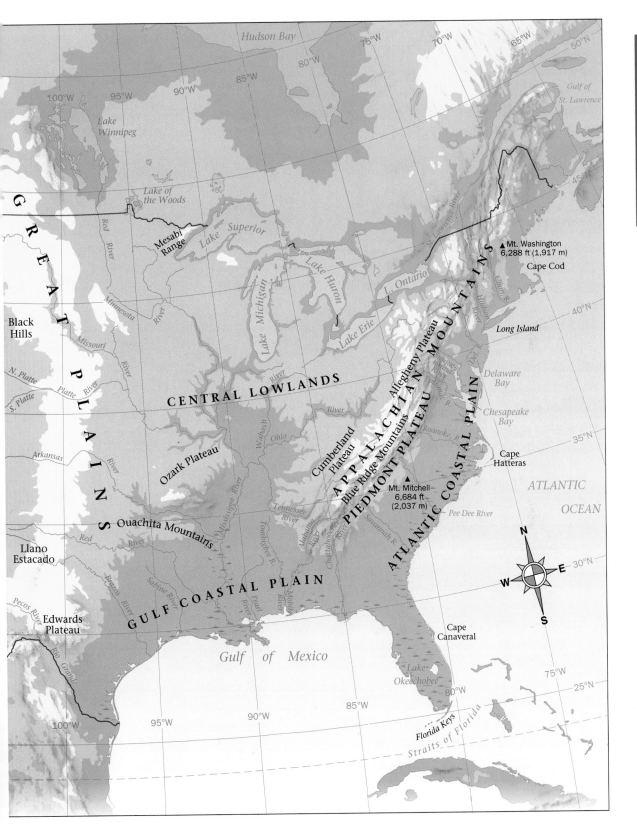

Hudson Bay

50°N

75°W 70°W 65°W

80°W

85°W

90°W *Gulf of*
St. Lawrence

Lake
Winnipeg

95°W

100°W

45°N

Lake of
the Woods

G
R
E
A
T

Red
River

Mesabi
Range

Lake *Superior*

▲ Mt. Washington
6,288 ft (1,917 m)

Cape Cod

Minnesota
River

Lake
Michigan

Lake Huron

L. Ontario

40°N

Long Island

St. Lawrence River

Black
Hills

Missouri

River

Allegheny Plateau

Delaware
Bay

N. Platte

Platte River

S. Platte

P
L
A
I
N
S

CENTRAL LOWLANDS

River

Lake Erie

A P P A L A C H I A N

M
O
U
N
T
A
I
N
S

Hudson R.

Chesapeake
Bay

35°N

Arkansas

River

Ozark Plateau

Cumberland
Plateau

Roanoke R.

Ohio

Wabash

Blue Ridge Mountains

PIEDMONT PLATEAU

Cape
Hatteras

River

Ouachita Mountains

Red

River

Tennessee
River

Mississippi River

▲ Mt. Mitchell
6,684 ft
(2,037 m)

Pee Dee River

Savannah R.

ATLANTIC

OCEAN

Llano
Estacado

Pecos River

Edwards
Plateau

Brazos River

Sabine River

Alabama River

Tombigbee R.

Chattahoochee River

ATLANTIC COASTAL PLAIN

30°N

GULF COASTAL PLAIN

Pearl
River

Mobile R.

N

W E

S

Rio Grande

Gulf *of* *Mexico*

Cape
Canaveral

75°W

Lake
Okeechobee

25°N

100°W

95°W

90°W

85°W

80°W

Florida Keys

Straits of Florida

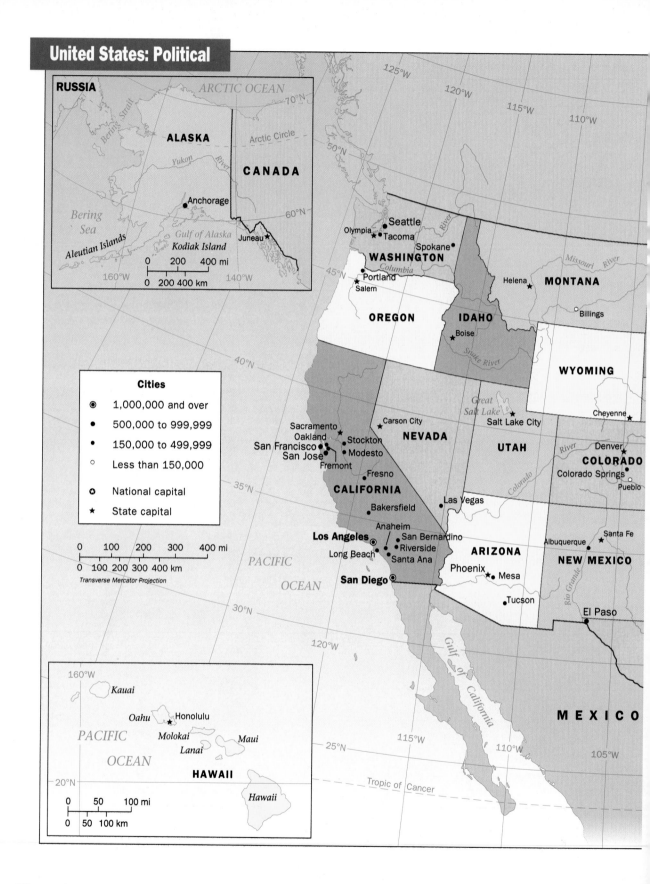

United States: Political

RUSSIA

ARCTIC OCEAN

ALASKA

Arctic Circle

CANADA

Bering Strait

Yukon River

●Anchorage

Bering Sea

Gulf of Alaska

Juneau★

Kodiak Island

Aleutian Islands

0   200   400 mi
0   200 400 km

Cities

◉   1,000,000 and over
●   500,000 to 999,999
•   150,000 to 499,999
○   Less than 150,000

✪   National capital
★   State capital

0   100   200   300   400 mi
0 100 200 300 400 km
Transverse Mercator Projection

Seattle
Olympia●   ●Tacoma
★
Spokane●

WASHINGTON
Columbia River

●Portland
Salem★

OREGON

IDAHO
Boise★

Snake River

Helena★   **MONTANA**

○Billings

WYOMING

Cheyenne★

Carson City★

Great Salt Lake   Salt Lake City★

NEVADA

UTAH

Denver★
COLORADO
Colorado Springs○
Pueblo○

Colorado River

Sacramento★
Oakland● ●Stockton
San Francisco● ●Modesto
San Jose●
Fremont●

●Fresno

CALIFORNIA

●Bakersfield

Anaheim●
Los Angeles◉
San Bernardino●
Long Beach● ●Riverside
Santa Ana●

Las Vegas●

ARIZONA

Phoenix★ ●Mesa

Santa Fe★
Albuquerque●
NEW MEXICO

San Diego◉

●Tucson

Rio Grande

El Paso●

PACIFIC

OCEAN

PACIFIC OCEAN

Gulf of California

MEXICO

160°W
Kauai

Oahu ●Honolulu★
Molokai *Maui*
Lanai
HAWAII

Hawaii

0   50   100 mi
0 50 100 km

70°N
50°N
Arctic Circle
60°N
160°W   140°W
45°N
40°N
35°N
30°N
25°N
Tropic of Cancer
20°N

125°W   120°W   115°W   110°W
120°W   115°W   110°W   105°W

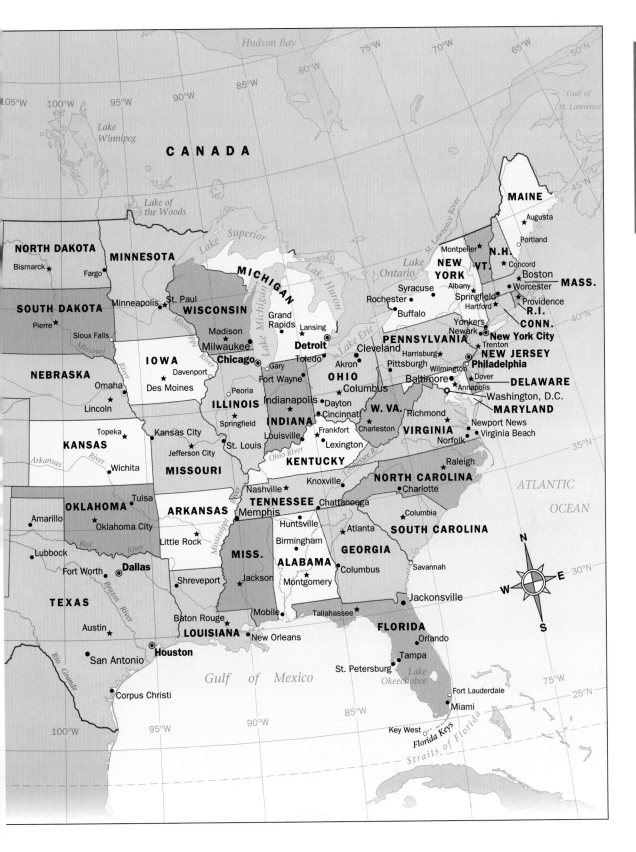

CANADA

Hudson Bay

75°W 70°W 65°W 50°N

Gulf of St. Lawrence

105°W 100°W 95°W 90°W 85°W 80°W

Lake Winnipeg

45°N

Lake of the Woods

MAINE

Augusta

Portland

Lake Superior

NORTH DAKOTA
Bismarck

MINNESOTA
Fargo

Montpelier N.H.
Concord

VT

Lake Huron

MICHIGAN

Lake Ontario

NEW YORK

Boston
Worcester MASS.

SOUTH DAKOTA
Pierre

Minneapolis St. Paul

WISCONSIN

Grand Rapids
Lansing

Syracuse
Albany
Springfield
Hartford

Providence
R.I.

Sioux Falls

Madison

Lake Michigan

Rochester

Buffalo

CONN.
40°N

Missouri River

Mississippi River

Milwaukee

Detroit

Yonkers
Newark New York City

IOWA
Davenport

Chicago
Gary

Toledo

Lake Erie

Cleveland

Harrisburg

PENNSYLVANIA

Pittsburgh

Trenton
NEW JERSEY
Philadelphia

NEBRASKA
Omaha

Des Moines

Peoria

Fort Wayne

OHIO

Columbus

Wilmington
Baltimore

DELAWARE
Dover

Washington, D.C.

Lincoln

ILLINOIS

Indianapolis

Dayton
Cincinnati

W. VA.

Annapolis

MARYLAND

Springfield

INDIANA

Richmond

Topeka
KANSAS

Kansas City

Louisville
Frankfort

Charleston

VIRGINIA

Newport News
Virginia Beach

Jefferson City
St. Louis

Lexington

Norfolk

Arkansas River

Wichita

MISSOURI

Ohio River

KENTUCKY

Tennessee R.

35°N

Knoxville

Raleigh

Nashville

NORTH CAROLINA

OKLAHOMA
Tulsa

ARKANSAS

TENNESSEE

Chattanooga

Charlotte

Amarillo
Oklahoma City

Memphis

Columbia

ATLANTIC

Little Rock

Huntsville

Atlanta

SOUTH CAROLINA

OCEAN

Red River

Lubbock

MISS.

Birmingham

GEORGIA

Fort Worth
Dallas

Shreveport

ALABAMA

Columbus

Savannah

30°N

Brazos River

Jackson

Montgomery

TEXAS

Baton Rouge

Mobile

Tallahassee

Jacksonville

N

Austin

LOUISIANA
New Orleans

FLORIDA

Orlando

W E

Rio Grande

San Antonio
Houston

Tampa

S

Gulf of Mexico

St. Petersburg

Lake Okeechobee

75°W

Corpus Christi

Fort Lauderdale

25°N

Miami

100°W 95°W 90°W 85°W

Key West
Florida Keys

Straits of Florida

Natural Vegetation of the United States

RUSSIA
ALASKA
CANADA

Bering Sea

ARCTIC OCEAN

0 400 mi
0 400 km

CANADA

Hudson Bay

MEXICO

Gulf of Mexico

PACIFIC OCEAN

ATLANTIC OCEAN

Tropic of Cancer

Missouri River
Ohio River
Mississippi
Rio Grande
Gulf of California

Lake Superior
Lake Michigan
Lake Huron
Lake Erie
Ontario

0 200 400 mi
0 200 400 km
Transverse Mercator Projection

HAWAII
PACIFIC OCEAN
0 100 mi
0 100 km

Tropical rain forest
Mainly broad-leaved evergreens

Needleleaf forest
Evergreens, such as spruce and pine

Broadleaf forest
Deciduous trees, such as oak, maple, beech, and hickory; shrubs

Mixed needleleaf and broadleaf forest
Mixed broadleaf, deciduous trees and coniferous evergreens

Grassland
Short and tall prairie grasses

Shrub and short grassland
Grassland with shrubs and trees growing singly or in patches

Desert and desert shrub
Little or no plant life: creosote bush, cactus, sagebrush, chaparral

Tundra
Grasses, low shrubs, moss and lichens; no trees

Natural vegetation is the native plant cover that would probably exist if human beings had not interfered with the existing plants or introduced new plants.

Land Use in the United States

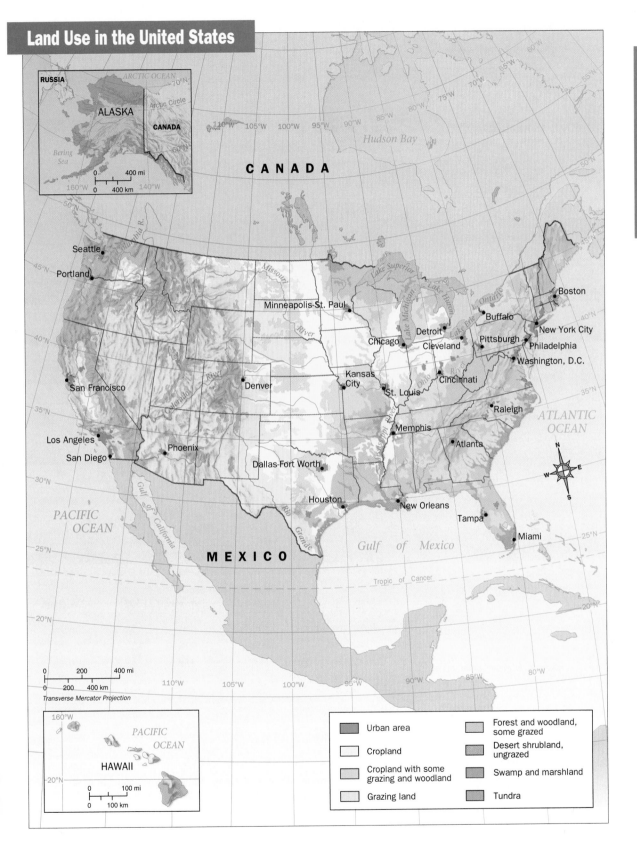

Legend:
- Urban area
- Cropland
- Cropland with some grazing and woodland
- Grazing land
- Forest and woodland, some grazed
- Desert shrubland, ungrazed
- Swamp and marshland
- Tundra

Transverse Mercator Projection

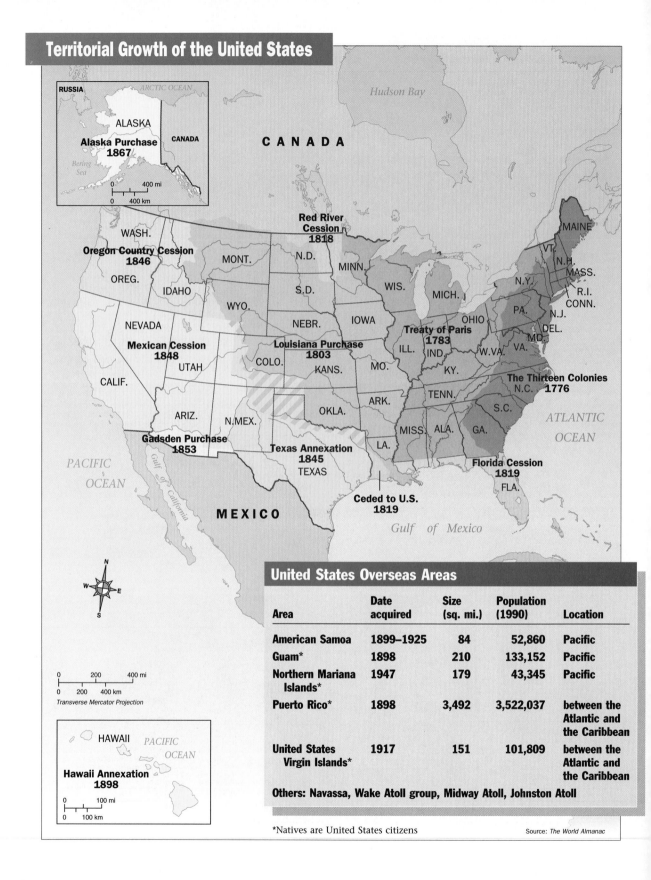

Territorial Growth of the United States

RUSSIA
ARCTIC OCEAN
ALASKA
CANADA
Alaska Purchase 1867
Bering Sea
0 400 mi
0 400 km

CANADA

Hudson Bay

WASH.
Oregon Country Cession 1846
OREG.
MONT.
IDAHO
WYO.
NEVADA
CALIF.
Mexican Cession 1848
UTAH
ARIZ.
N.MEX.
Gadsden Purchase 1853

Red River Cession 1818
N.D.
S.D.
NEBR.
COLO.
KANS.
MINN.
WIS.
IOWA
MICH.
OHIO
IND.
ILL.
MO.
Louisiana Purchase 1803
OKLA.
ARK.
TENN.
KY.
W.VA. VA.
Treaty of Paris 1783
N.Y.
PA.
N.J.
DEL.
MD.
MAINE
VT.
N.H.
MASS.
R.I.
CONN.
The Thirteen Colonies 1776
N.C.
S.C.
GA.
MISS. ALA.
LA.
Texas Annexation 1845
TEXAS
Ceded to U.S. 1819
Florida Cession 1819
FLA.

ATLANTIC OCEAN

PACIFIC OCEAN

Gulf of California

MEXICO

Gulf of Mexico

N
W E
S

0 200 400 mi
0 200 400 km
Transverse Mercator Projection

HAWAII PACIFIC OCEAN
Hawaii Annexation 1898
0 100 mi
0 100 km

United States Overseas Areas

Area	Date acquired	Size (sq. mi.)	Population (1990)	Location
American Samoa	1899–1925	84	52,860	Pacific
Guam*	1898	210	133,152	Pacific
Northern Mariana Islands*	1947	179	43,345	Pacific
Puerto Rico*	1898	3,492	3,522,037	between the Atlantic and the Caribbean
United States Virgin Islands*	1917	151	101,809	between the Atlantic and the Caribbean

Others: Navassa, Wake Atoll group, Midway Atoll, Johnston Atoll

*Natives are United States citizens

Source: *The World Almanac*

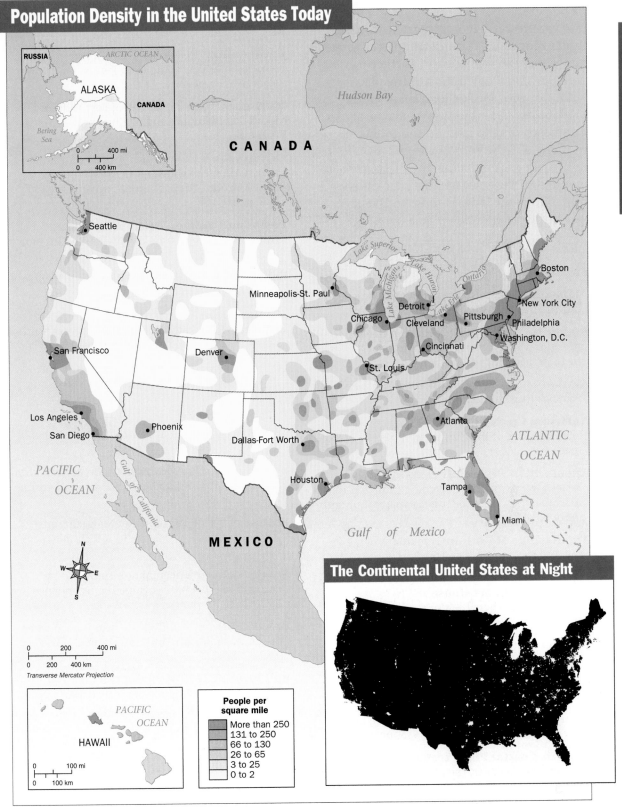

Population Density in the United States Today

RUSSIA

ARCTIC OCEAN

ALASKA

CANADA

Bering Sea

0   400 mi

0   400 km

C A N A D A

Hudson Bay

Seattle

Minneapolis-St. Paul

Lake Superior

Lake Michigan

Lake Huron

L. Ontario

Lake Erie

Boston

Detroit

New York City

Chicago

Cleveland

Pittsburgh

Philadelphia

Washington, D.C.

Cincinnati

San Francisco

Denver

St. Louis

Los Angeles

Phoenix

Atlanta

ATLANTIC OCEAN

San Diego

Dallas-Fort Worth

PACIFIC OCEAN

Gulf of California

Houston

Tampa

Miami

MEXICO

Gulf of Mexico

N W E S

0   200   400 mi

0   200   400 km

Transverse Mercator Projection

PACIFIC OCEAN

HAWAII

0   100 mi

0   100 km

People per square mile

	More than 250
	131 to 250
	66 to 130
	26 to 65
	3 to 25
	0 to 2

The Continental United States at Night

Gazetteer

A gazetteer is a geographical dictionary. It lists geographic features and places where major events have occurred. Each entry includes a brief description of the place.

Entries with specific locations—cities, battlefields, and other sites—have locations given according to latitude and longitude. At the end of the entry is a number that refers to the text page on which the first significant mention of the entry appears. The number that follows the letter *m* refers to the page where the place is shown on a map.

A

Alabama southern state; part of the Confederacy during the Civil War (page 306, *m323*)

Alamo (29°N 98°W) former mission in San Antonio where Texans resisted Mexican troops in 1836 (page 382, *m384*)

Alaska state located in the far northwest of North America (page 331, *mR6*)

Antietam Creek (39°N 78°W) site where Confederate invasion of the North was stopped in 1862 (page 503, *m501*)

Appalachian Highlands elevated region in eastern North America stretching from Canada to Alabama; it includes the Appalachian Mountains (page *mP5*)

Appalachian Mountains mountain range in the Appalachian Highlands region of the eastern United States (page 485, *m155*)

Appomattox Court House (37°N 79°W) Virginia town where Lee's surrender to Grant ended the Civil War in 1865 (page 516, *m513*)

Arizona southwestern state; once part of New Spain and Mexico (page 21, *mR6*)

Arkansas southern state; once part of the Confederacy (page 492, *m323*)

Atlanta (34°N 84°W) capital of Georgia; burned in 1864 by Union forces (page 515, *m513*)

Atlantic Coastal Plain coastal lowlands of the eastern United States; the plain grows wider in the South (page 149, *mR5*)

B

Backcountry in colonial times, a region of low, wooded hills extending from Pennsylvania to Georgia (page 152)

Baltimore (39°N 77°W) site of Fort McHenry; located at the upper end of Chesapeake Bay (page 127, *m135*)

Barbary States four North African states that raided American ships in the early 1800s; states were Morocco, Algiers, Tunis, and Tripoli (page 300, *m301*)

Basins and Ranges region in the western United States consisting of highland basins and mountains (page 399, *mP4*)

Belleau Wood (49°N 3°E) site of an Allied victory that marked a turning point in World War I (page 712, *m712*)

Beringia land bridge that linked Asia and North America during the last Ice Age (page 10, *m11*)

Bering Strait waterway between North America and Asia where a land bridge once existed (page 11, *mR4*)

Berlin (53°N 13°E) city in Germany; split into East and West Berlin after World War II and reunited in 1989 (page 820, *m821*)

Bosnia eastern European nation; broke away from Yugoslavia in 1991; scene of civil war and ethnic violence (page 700, *m702*)

Boston (42°N 71°W) capital of Massachusetts; center of colonial resistance to British rule (page 128, *m131*)

Brazil South American nation colonized by Portugal in the 1500s; it gained independence in 1822 (page 73, *m101*)

Breed's Hill (42°N 71°W) site near Boston where the Battle of Bunker Hill took place in 1775 (page 208)

Bull Run (39°N 77°W) site of two Civil War battles in northern Virginia; also called Manassas (page 498, *m501*)

Bunker Hill, *see* **Breed's Hill**

C

California Far West state gained by the United States from Mexico in 1848 (page 28, *m396*)

California Trail overland route from Wyoming to California, established 1833 (page 386, *m387*)

Canada nation bordering the United States to the north; originally settled by both the French and English (page 209, *m220*)

Canadian Shield lowland region that lies in north central United States and eastern Canada (page 593, *mP5*)

Central Lowlands region of flat to gently rolling land that lies to the west of the Appalachians (page 240, *mP5*)

Chancellorsville (38°N 77°W) town in Virginia; site of Confederate victory in 1863 (page 511, *m513*)

Charleston (33°N 80°W) port city in South Carolina; site of Fort Sumter where the Civil War began (page 134, *m277*)

Chesapeake Bay large bay surrounded by the states of Virginia, Maryland, and Delaware (page 122, *m122*)

Chicago (42°N 87°W) third largest city in the United States; major railroad and shipping center in the 1800s (page 110, *m323*)

China once a large empire in east Asia, now the most populous nation in the world (page 46, *m45*)

Cincinnati (39°N 85°W) major city in Ohio; developed as a port on the Ohio River in the early 1800s (page 411, *m407*)

Coastal Lowlands coastal plain that stretches from Massachusetts to Texas along the Atlantic coast and Gulf of Mexico (page 127, *mP5*)

Colombia South American nation (page 689, *m692*)

Colorado western state located in both the Rocky Mountain and Great Plains regions (page 20, *mR6*)

Colorado River river that flows from the Colorado Rockies to the Gulf of California (page 99, *m295*)

Columbia River explored by Lewis and Clark in 1805, this river separates Oregon and Washington (page 297, *m98*)

Concord (43°N 71°W) village near Boston and early battle site in the American Revolution (page 206)

Connecticut New England state; first settled by the English in 1636 (page 131, *m131*)

Cuba Caribbean island nation directly south of Florida (page 93, *m66*)

Cumberland Gap (37°N 84°W) pass in the Appalachian Mountains by which settlers moved into Tennessee (page *m277*)

Czechoslovakia Eastern European nation created after World War I; split into two separate republics in 1992 (page 789, *m792*)

D

Delaware Atlantic Coastal Plain state; first state to approve the United States Constitution (page 136, *m122*)

Detroit (42°N 83°W) founded as a French fort; now the largest city in Michigan (page 110, *m323*)

District of Columbia, *see* **Washington, D.C.**

E

Egypt Middle Eastern nation (page 833, *m880*)

England southern part of the island of Great Britain (page 52, *m51*)

Erie Canal waterway built in 1825 to link New York City and the Great Lakes (page 325, *m323*)

F

Fallen Timbers (41°N 83°W) battle site at which U.S. troops defeated a force of Ohio Valley Indians in 1794 (page 275, *m277*)

Fall Line edge of the Piedmont Plateau in eastern United States where rivers tumble to the Atlantic Coastal Plain below (page 149)

Florida southern state; explored by Ponce de León in 1513 (page 97, *m323*)

Fort Duquesne (40°N 80°W) French fort built in the early 1750s on the site of present-day Pittsburgh (page 181, *m109*)

Fort Laramie (42°N 104°W) fort located along the Oregon Trail in present-day Wyoming (page 389, *m387*)

Fort McHenry (39°N 76°W) fort in Baltimore harbor; inspired Francis Scott Key's poem that later became "The Star-Spangled Banner" (page 307)

Fort Necessity (40°N 80°W) Pennsylvania fort built by Washington's troops in 1754 (page 181, *m183*)

Fort Sumter (33°N 80°W) fort guarding the harbor of Charleston, South Carolina, where the Civil War broke out (page 483, *m501*)

Fort Ticonderoga (44°N 73°W) British fort on Lake Champlain raided by American troops in 1775 (page 209, *m183*)

France nation in western Europe that first colonized Canada (page 52, *m51*)

Fredericksburg (38°N 77°W) Virginia town; site of Lee's victory over Union troops in 1862 (page 511, *m513*)

G

Georgia southern state; founded by James Oglethorpe in 1732 (page 137, *m135*)

Germany European nation; divided from the end of World War II until 1989 into East and West Germany (page 701, *m702*)

Gettysburg (40°N 77°W) Pennsylvania battle site where Lee was defeated and Lincoln made his Gettysburg Address in 1863 (page 511, *m513*)

Great Basin, *see* **Basins and Ranges**

Great Britain island nation established in 1707 and consisting of England, Wales, and Scotland (page 163)

Great Lakes Lakes Ontario, Erie, Huron, Michigan, and Superior; five large freshwater lakes on the border between the United States and Canada (page 22)

Great Plains region of grasslands east of the Rocky Mountains and west of the Mississippi River (page 656, *mP4*)

Grenada Caribbean island nation; invaded by the United States in 1983 to end threat of Communist influence (page 876, *mR2*)

Gulf of Mexico body of water that lies to the south of the United States (page 22, *m16*)

H

Haiti at one time a French Caribbean colony; gained its independence after an 1801 revolt (page 296, *m330*)

Harlem (41°N 74°W) New York City neighborhood that became the center of African American culture in the 1920s (page 740)

Harpers Ferry (39°N 78°W) West Virginia town where John Brown raided a federal arsenal in 1859 (page 480)

Hartford (42°N 73°W) Connecticut capital where New England Federalists met and demanded an end to the War of 1812 (page 307, *m131*)

Hawaii Pacific Ocean state made up of eight major islands; originally a kingdom established by 1795 (page 275, *mR6*)

Hiroshima (34°N 132°E) city in southern Japan; target of a United States atomic bomb in 1945 (page 802, *m805*)

Hispaniola Caribbean island where Columbus served as governor; now includes nations of Haiti and the Dominican Republic (page 67, *m66*)

Horseshoe Bend (33°N 86°W) Alabama site where Creeks battled Andrew Jackson's troops in 1814 (page 306, *m306*)

Hudson Bay large bay in northern Canada discovered by Henry Hudson in 1610 (page 76, *m77*)

Hudson River largest river in New York state; explored by Henry Hudson for the Dutch in 1609 (page 76, *m122*)

I

Idaho northwestern state; acquired by the United States as part of Oregon Country (page *mR6*)

Illinois state in the Central Lowlands region; originally settled as part of the Northwest Territory (page 23, *m323*)

Independence (39°N 94°W) town in Missouri where the Oregon Trail began (page 386, *m387*)

India Asian nation; goal of European traders in the 1400s and 1500s (page 45, *m45*)

Indiana Central Lowlands state; originally a part of the Northwest Territory (page 275, *m323*)

Interior Highlands hilly region in Missouri, Arkansas, and Oklahoma; also called the Ozark Mountains (page 883, *mP5*)

Iowa Central Lowlands state; originally part of the Louisiana Purchase (page 390, *m323*)

Iran Middle Eastern nation (page 823, *m880*)

Iraq Middle Eastern nation; Iraqi invasion of neighboring Kuwait drew United Nations involvement in 1991 (page 879, *m880*)

Israel Middle Eastern nation; formed in 1948 as a Jewish homeland (page 819, *mR3*)

Italy southern European nation; fought with the Allies in World War I and with the Axis in World War II (page 701, *m702*)

J

Jamestown (37°N 77°W) Virginia site where first English settlement in North America was founded in 1607 (page 122, *m122*)

Japan densely populated industrial nation in East Asia; one of the Axis powers in World War II (page 674, *m683*)

K

Kansas Great Plains state; earlier a territory where proslavery and antislavery forces battled in the 1850s (page 474, *m474*)

Kentucky state in the Central Lowlands and Appalachians; birthplace of Abraham Lincoln (page 278, *m277*)

Korea East Asian nation; divided since World War II into North and South Korea; war there in the 1950s drew United States involvement (page 689, *m683*)

L

Lake Champlain lake situated between Vermont and New York; site of battles during the War of Independence and the War of 1812 (page 218, *m220*)

Lake Erie one of the Great Lakes; scene of battles during the War of 1812 (page 306, *m183*)

L'Anse aux Meadows (51°N 55°W) site of Viking settlement on the Newfoundland coast around A.D. 1010 (page 62)

Lawrence (39°N 95°W) antislavery town in Kansas; set on fire by proslavery residents from Missouri in 1856 (page 475)

Lebanon Middle Eastern nation; civil war there in the 1970s and 80s drew United Nations involvement (page 877, *mR3*)

Lexington (42°N 71°W) village near Boston where the War of Independence began in 1775 (page 206)

Liberia West African nation founded by former American slaves in 1821 and eventually established as a republic (page 440, *mR3*)

Little Bighorn River river in Wyoming and Montana; site of a famous battle between Sioux and Cheyenne Indians and the United States Cavalry (page 549, *m566*)

Louisiana southern state; originally a French and Spanish colony (page 110, *m306*)

Louisiana Purchase land bought by the United States from France in 1803 that stretched from the Mississippi River to the Rocky Mountains (page 294, *m295*)

Lowell (41°N 83°W) Massachusetts city; early site of the Industrial Revolution in the United States (page 320)

M

Maine New England state; originally part of Massachusetts (page 131, *m131*)

Manassas, *see* **Bull Run**

Manhattan (41°N 74°W) island settled by the Dutch as New Amsterdam; now the heart of New York City (page 111)

Maryland Atlantic coastal state; first of the English colonies to tolerate Catholic settlers (page 133, *m135*)

Massachusetts New England state; site of first battles between the Patriots and the British in the War of Independence (page 128, *m131*)

Mexican Cession territory gained by the United States following the War with Mexico in 1848 (page 396, *m396*)

Mexico originally a center of Indian civilizations; now a nation that borders the United States to the south (page 14, *m98*)

Michigan Central Lowlands state; originally part of the Northwest Territory (page 325, *m323*)

Midway Islands (28°N 179°W) Pacific Islands annexed by the United States in 1867; site of a World War II battle (page 674, *m683*)

Minnesota state located in the Central Lowlands and Canadian Shield regions (page 468, *m493*)

Mississippi southern state; part of the Confederacy during the Civil War (page 534, *m323*)

Mississippi River longest river in the United States (page 23, *m98*)

Missouri Central Lowlands state; admitted as a slave state in 1820 (page 334, *m323*)

Missouri River tributary of the Mississippi River and second longest river in the United States (page 296, *m98*)

Monmouth (40°N 74°W) New Jersey town where Patriots battled retreating British troops (page 221, *m220*)

Montana western state; originally part of Oregon Country and the Louisiana Purchase (page *mR6*)

N

Nagasaki (33°N 130°E) city in southern Japan; target of United States atomic bomb in 1945 (page 803, *m805*)

National Road first road built across the Appalachian Mountains (page 322, *m323*)

Nauvoo (41°N 91°W) Illinois town founded by Mormon settlers in the 1840s (page 390, *m387*)

Nebraska Great Plains state; part of the Louisiana Purchase (page 474, *mR7*)

Netherlands European nation; important trading power in the 1600s (page 76, *m77*)

Nevada western state; gained by the United States from Mexico in 1848 (page 399, *mR6*)

New England region in northeastern United States; named by English colonists for their homeland (page 126, *m122*)

New France land that was claimed by France in the 1700s; it stretched from Quebec to Louisiana (page 108, *m135*)

New Hampshire New England state; one of the original 13 states (page 131, *m131*)

New Jersey Atlantic coastal state; first settled by the Dutch and Swedes (page 135, *m135*)

New Mexico southwestern state; settled by the Spanish in 1598 (page 104, *mR6*)

New Netherland Dutch colony along the Hudson River in the 1600s (page 110, *m109*)

New Orleans (30°N 90°W) city founded by the French near the mouth of the Mississippi River (page 110, *m109*)

New Spain northern half of Spain's empire in the Western Hemisphere (page 101, *m98*)

New Sweden colony established by Swedes in Delaware and New Jersey (page 111)

New York Atlantic coastal state; settled by the Dutch in the 1600s (page 135, *m135*)

New York City (41°N 74°W) largest city in the United States; founded by the Dutch as New Amsterdam (page 110, *m135*)

Nicaragua nation in Central America; civil war there in the 1980s drew United States involvement (page 691, *m692*)

North Carolina Atlantic coastal state; one of the original 13 states (page 134, *m135*)

North Dakota northern Great Plains state; location where Lewis and Clark spent their first winter (page 296, *mR7*)

Northwest Territory territory in the early 1800s; bounded by the Ohio River, the Mississippi River, and the Appalachians (page 236, *m235*)

O

Ohio Central Lowlands state; once part of the Northwest Territory (page 275, *m295*)

Ohio River river that flows from Pittsburgh to the Mississippi River (page 181, *m98*)

Ohio Valley region drained by the Ohio River (page 183)

Oklahoma southern Plains state; originally called the Indian Territory (page 362, *mR7*)

Old Northwest, *see* **Northwest Territory**

Oregon Pacific northwest state; first settled in the 1840s (page 394, *m493*)

Oregon Country area in northwest United States; at one time also claimed by Spain, Britain, and Russia (page 328, *m295*)

Oregon Trail 2,000-mile route from Independence, Missouri, to Oregon Country (page 386, *m387*)

Ottoman Empire, *see* **Turkey**

P

Pacific Mountains and Valleys region of the United States that lies along the Pacific coast (page 779, *mP4*)

Panama nation in Central America; crossed by Balboa in 1513 (page 73, *m66*)

Pearl Harbor (21°N 158°W) Japanese bombing of this United States naval base brought the United States into World War II (page 793, *m799*)

Pennsylvania eastern state; founded as a colony by William Penn in 1681 (page 136, *m135*)

Peru South American nation; center of Inca Empire in the 1400s and 1500s (page 96, *m101*)

Petersburg (37°N 77°W) city in Virginia; besieged by Grant's troops for nine months until Lee's troops fled in 1865 (page 515, *m513*)

Philadelphia (40°N 75°W) Pennsylvania city; capital of the United States from 1790 to 1800 (page 136, *m135*)

Philippines East Asian island nation; acquired by the United States in 1898; gained independence in 1946 (page 681, *m683*)

Piedmont Plateau hill country in the southeast United States; it lies upland from the Atlantic Coastal Plain (page 149, *mR5*)

Pittsburgh (40°N 80°W) city in western Pennsylvania where the Ohio River begins (page 185, *m277*)

Plymouth (42°N 71°W) site of first English settlement in Massachusetts in 1620 (page 126, *m122*)

Poland east European nation (page 790, *m792*)

Portugal west European nation; first to begin large-scale overseas exploration in the 1400s (page 52, *m51*)

Potomac River river dividing Maryland and Virginia on which Washington, D.C., is located (page 236, *m513*)

Promontory Point (41°N 112°W) site in Utah at which the transcontinental railroad was completed (page 562, *m562*)

Prophetstown (41°N 90°W) center of Tecumseh's Indian alliance in 1811; located in present-day Indiana (page 303, *m306*)

Puerto Rico Caribbean island and United States commonwealth (page 685, *m66*)

R

Rhode Island New England state; founded as a colony welcoming people of all religions (page 130, *m131*)

Richmond (38°N 77°W) city in Virginia; capital of the Confederacy during most of the Civil War (page 492, *m323*)

Rio Grande river that forms part of the boundary between Mexico and the United States (page 104, *m98*)

Rocky Mountains high mountain range in western North America; reached by Lewis and Clark in 1805 (page 299, *mP4*)

Russia nation that stretches from eastern Europe to Asia (page 331, *m51*)

S

St. Augustine (30°N 81°W) city in Florida founded by the Spanish in 1565; oldest continuous European settlement in the United States (page 104, *m105*)

St. Lawrence River river that connects the Great Lakes and the Atlantic Ocean (page *m77*)

St. Louis (39°N 90°W) Missouri city from which Lewis and Clark set off to explore the West (page 296, *m277*)

San Antonio (29°N 98°W) southern Texas city; site of the Alamo (page 106, *m105*)

San Francisco (38°N 122°W) northern outpost of New Spain; now a major city in California (page 106, *m105*)

San Jacinto River Texan forces defeated a Mexican army along this river resulting in Texan independence (page 384, *m384*)

Santa Fe (36°N 106°W) present-day capital of New Mexico; established by the Spanish in 1609 (page 104, *m105*)

Santa Fe Trail 800-mile-long trail from Independence, Missouri, to Santa Fe, New Mexico (page 379, *m387*)

Saratoga (43°N 74°W) city in New York; site of American victory in 1777 that marked a turning point in the American Revolution (page 218, *m220*)

Serbia Balkan country in southeastern Europe (page 701, *m702*)

Shiloh (35°N 88°W) site of Union victory in Tennessee in 1862 (page 500, *m501*)

Sierra Nevada high mountain range in California and Nevada (page 386, *m295*)

South Carolina southern state; first settled by English from the West Indies (page 134, *m135*)

South Dakota northern Great Plains state; part of the Louisiana Purchase (page *mR7*)

Spain European nation; controlled vast empire in the Americas for 300 years (page 64, *m161*)

Spanish borderlands area of New Spain including present-day northern Mexico and southern United States (page 97, *m105*)

Strait of Magellan (53°S 70°W) waterway at southern tip of South America (page 74)

T

Tennessee southern state; first settled in the 1790s (page 278, *m295*)

Tenochtitlán (19°N 99°W) capital of Aztec empire; now Mexico City (page 16, *m100*)

Texas southern state; part of Mexico until 1836 (page 105, *m323*)

Tippecanoe River river in Indiana where American troops defeated Tecumseh's forces in 1811 (page 304, *m306*)

Trenton (40°N 75°W) capital of New Jersey; site where Washington's army attacked Hessian troops in 1776 (page 216, *m220*)

Turkey Middle Eastern nation; formerly known as the Ottoman Empire (page 701, *m702*)

U

United Kingdom established in 1801 when Ireland was united with Great Britain (page *mR3*)

Utah western state; first settled by Mormons (page 389, *mR6*)

V

Valley Forge (40°N 75°W) winter camp for Washington's troops in Pennsylvania from 1777 to 1778 (page 218, *m220*)

Vermont New England state located in the Appalachian Highlands (page *m235*)

Vicksburg (32°N 91°W) city in Mississippi; site of Union victory in 1863 that secured control of the Mississippi River for the North (page 514, *m501*)

Vietnam nation in Southeast Asia; conflict there drew United States involvement in the 1950s, 1960s, and 1970s (page 826, *m827*)

Vinland (51°N 55°W) site of Viking settlement along the Newfoundland coast (page 62)

Virginia southern state; site of first permanent English colony in North America (page 122, *m122*)

W

Washington state in northwestern United States; once part of Oregon Country (page *mR6*)

Washington, D.C. (39°N 77°W) United States capital; established on banks of the Potomac River in 1800 (page 282, *m306*)

Western Plateaus region of plateaus and mountains in the western United States; it includes the Colorado and Columbia Plateaus (page 24, *mP4*)

West Indies Caribbean islands colonized by European powers in the 1500s and 1600s (page 134, *m161*)

West Virginia Appalachian Highland state; formed by pro-Union residents of Virginia during the Civil War (page 492, *m493*)

Wisconsin Central Lowlands state; originally part of the Northwest Territory (page *m323*)

Wounded Knee Creek site of a clash between Indians and the United States Cavalry; in South Dakota (page 568, *m566*)

Wyoming western state; located in the Rocky Mountain and Great Plains regions (page 299, *mR6*)

Y

Yorktown (37°N 76°W) small Virginia port; site of British surrender to the colonists in 1781 that ended the War of Independence (page 222, *m223*)

The States

Note: Population figures are 1995 estimates.

Alabama
Admitted: 1819
Capital: Montgomery
Population: 4,274,000
Area: 50,750 sq mi
    (131,443 sq km)
"Yellowhammer State"

Colorado
Admitted: 1876
Capital: Denver
Population: 3,710,000
Area: 103,729 sq mi
    (268,658 sq km)
"Centennial State"

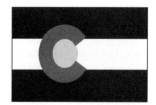

Alaska
Admitted: 1959
Capital: Juneau
Population: 634,000
Area: 570,374 sq mi
    (1,477,269 sq km)
"The Last Frontier"

Connecticut
Admitted: 1788
Capital: Hartford
Population: 3,274,000
Area: 4,845 sq mi
    (12,549 sq km)
"Constitution State"

Arizona
Admitted: 1912
Capital: Phoenix
Population: 4,072,000
Area: 113,642 sq mi
    (294,333 sq km)
"Grand Canyon State"

Delaware
Admitted: 1787
Capital: Dover
Population: 718,000
Area: 1,955 sq mi
    (5,063 sq km)
"First State"

Arkansas
Admitted: 1836
Capital: Little Rock
Population: 2,468,000
Area: 52,075 sq mi
    (134,874 sq km)
"Land of Opportunity"

Florida
Admitted: 1845
Capital: Tallahassee
Population: 14,210,000
Area: 53,997 sq mi
    (139,852 sq km)
"Sunshine State"

California
Admitted: 1850
Capital: Sacramento
Population: 32,398,000
Area: 155,973 sq mi
    (403,970 sq km)
"Golden State"

Georgia
Admitted: 1788
Capital: Atlanta
Population: 7,102,000
Area: 57,919 sq mi
    (150,010 sq km)
"Peach State"

STATES

Hawaii

Admitted: 1959
Capital: Honolulu
Population: 1,221,000
Area: 6,423 sq mi
   (16,636 sq km)
"Aloha State"

Idaho

Admitted: 1890
Capital: Boise
Population: 1,156,000
Area: 82,751 sq mi
   (214,325 sq km)
"Gem State"

Illinois

Admitted: 1818
Capital: Springfield
Population: 11,853,000
Area: 55,593 sq mi
   (143,986 sq km)
"Prairie State"

Indiana

Admitted: 1816
Capital: Indianapolis
Population: 5,820,000
Area: 35,870 sq mi
   (92,903 sq km)
"Hoosier State"

Iowa

Admitted: 1846
Capital: Des Moines
Population: 2,861,000
Area: 55,875 sq mi
   (144,716 sq km)
"Hawkeye State"

Kansas

Admitted: 1861
Capital: Topeka
Population: 2,601,000
Area: 81,823 sq mi
   (211,922 sq km)
"Sunflower State"

Kentucky

Admitted: 1792
Capital: Frankfort
Population: 3,851,000
Area: 39,732 sq mi
   (102,906 sq km)
"Bluegrass State"

Louisiana

Admitted: 1812
Capital: Baton Rouge
Population: 4,359,000
Area: 43,566 sq mi
   (112,836 sq km)
"Pelican State"

Maine

Admitted: 1820
Capital: Augusta
Population: 1,236,000
Area: 30,865 sq mi
   (79,940 sq km)
"Pine Tree State"

Maryland

Admitted: 1788
Capital: Annapolis
Population: 5,078,000
Area: 9,775 sq mi
   (25,317 sq km)
"Old Line State"

Massachusetts

Admitted: 1788
Capital: Boston
Population: 5,976,000
Area: 7,838 sq mi
   (20,300 sq km)
"Bay State"

Michigan

Admitted: 1837
Capital: Lansing
Population: 9,575,000
Area: 56,809 sq mi
   (147,135 sq km)
"Wolverine State"

Minnesota

Admitted: 1858
Capital: St. Paul
Population: 4,619,000
Area: 79,617 sq mi
(206,208 sq km)
"North Star State"

New Hampshire

Admitted: 1788
Capital: Concord
Population: 1,132,000
Area: 8,969 sq mi
(23,230 sq km)
"Granite State"

Mississippi

Admitted: 1817
Capital: Jackson
Population: 2,666,000
Area: 46,914 sq mi
(121,507 sq km)
"Magnolia State"

New Jersey

Admitted: 1787
Capital: Trenton
Population: 7,931,000
Area: 7,419 sq mi
(19,215 sq km)
"Garden State"

Missouri

Admitted: 1821
Capital: Jefferson City
Population: 5,286,000
Area: 68,898 sq mi
(178,446 sq km)
"Show Me State"

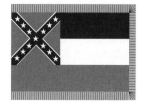

New Mexico

Admitted: 1912
Capital: Santa Fe
Population: 1,676,000
Area: 121,364 sq mi
(314,333 sq km)
"Land of Enchantment"

Montana

Admitted: 1889
Capital: Helena
Population: 862,000
Area: 145,556 sq mi
(376,990 sq km)
"Treasure State"

New York

Admitted: 1788
Capital: Albany
Population: 18,178,000
Area: 47,224 sq mi
(122,310 sq km)
"Empire State"

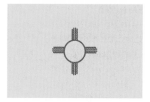

Nebraska

Admitted: 1867
Capital: Lincoln
Population: 1,644,000
Area: 76,878 sq mi
(199,114 sq km)
"Cornhusker State"

North Carolina

Admitted: 1789
Capital: Raleigh
Population: 7,150,000
Area: 48,718 sq mi
(126,180 sq km)
"Tar Heel State"

Nevada

Admitted: 1864
Capital: Carson City
Population: 1,477,000
Area: 109,806 sq mi
(284,398 sq km)
"Sagebrush State"

North Dakota

Admitted: 1889
Capital: Bismarck
Population: 637,000
Area: 68,994 sq mi
(178,694 sq km)
"Flickertail State"

Ohio
Admitted: 1803
Capital: Columbus
Population: 11,203,000
Area: 40,953 sq mi
   (106,068 sq km)
"Buckeye State"

South Dakota
Admitted: 1889
Capital: Pierre
Population: 735,000
Area: 75,896 sq mi
   (196,571 sq km)
"Coyote State"

Oklahoma
Admitted: 1907
Capital: Oklahoma City
Population: 3,271,000
Area: 68,679 sq mi
   (177,879 sq km)
"Sooner State"

Tennessee
Admitted: 1796
Capital: Nashville
Population: 5,228,000
Area: 41,219 sq mi
   (106,757 sq km)
"Volunteer State"

Oregon
Admitted: 1859
Capital: Salem
Population: 3,141,000
Area: 96,002 sq mi
   (248,645 sq km)
"Beaver State"

Texas
Admitted: 1845
Capital: Austin
Population: 18,592,000
Area: 261,914 sq mi
   (678,357 sq km)
"Lone Star State"

Pennsylvania
Admitted: 1787
Capital: Harrisburg
Population: 12,134,000
Area: 44,820 sq mi
   (116,084 sq km)
"Keystone State"

Utah
Admitted: 1896
Capital: Salt Lake City
Population: 1,944,000
Area: 82,168 sq mi
   (212,815 sq km)
"Beehive State"

Rhode Island
Admitted: 1790
Capital: Providence
Population: 1,001,000
Area: 1,045 sq mi
   (2,707 sq km)
"Ocean State"

Vermont
Admitted: 1791
Capital: Montpelier
Population: 579,000
Area: 9,249 sq mi
   (23,955 sq km)
"Green Mountain State"

South Carolina
Admitted: 1788
Capital: Columbia
Population: 3,732,000
Area: 30,111 sq mi
   (77,987 sq km)
"Palmetto State"

Virginia
Admitted: 1788
Capital: Richmond
Population: 6,646,000
Area: 39,598 sq mi
   (102,559 sq km)
"The Old Dominion"

Washington
Admitted: 1889
Capital: Olympia
Population: 5,497,000
Area: 66,581 sq mi
  (172,445 sq km)
"Evergreen State"

Wyoming
Admitted: 1890
Capital: Cheyenne
Population: 487,000
Area: 97,105 sq mi
  (251,502 sq km)
"Equality State"

West Virginia
Admitted: 1863
Capital: Charleston
Population: 1,824,000
Area: 24,087 sq mi
  (62,385 sq km)
"Mountain State"

District of Columbia
Population: 559,000
Area: 61 sq mi
  (158 sq km)

Wisconsin
Admitted: 1848
Capital: Madison
Population: 5,159,000
Area: 54,314 sq mi
  (140,673 sq km)
"Badger State"

The Presidents

1. George Washington (1732–1799)
In office: 1789–1797
no official political party
Elected from: Virginia
Vice-President: John Adams

2. John Adams (1735–1826)
In office: 1797–1801
Federalist Party
Elected from: Massachusetts
Vice-President: Thomas Jefferson

3. Thomas Jefferson (1743–1826)
In office: 1801–1809
Democratic-Republican Party
Elected from: Virginia
Vice-Presidents: Aaron Burr,
    George Clinton

4. James Madison (1751–1836)
In office: 1809–1817
Democratic-Republican Party
Elected from: Virginia
Vice-Presidents: George Clinton,
    Elbridge Gerry

5. James Monroe (1758–1831)
In office: 1817–1825
Democratic-Republican Party
Elected from: Virginia
Vice-President: Daniel D. Tompkins

6. John Quincy Adams (1767–1848)
In office: 1825–1829
Democratic-Republican Party
Elected from: Massachusetts
Vice-President: John C. Calhoun

7. Andrew Jackson (1767–1845)
In office: 1829–1837
Democratic Party
Elected from: Tennessee
Vice-Presidents: John C. Calhoun,
    Martin Van Buren

8. Martin Van Buren (1782–1862)
In office: 1837–1841
Democratic Party
Elected from: New York
Vice-President: Richard M. Johnson

9. William Henry Harrison* (1773–1841)
In office: 1841
Whig Party
Elected from: Ohio
Vice-President: John Tyler

10. John Tyler (1790–1862)
In office: 1841–1845
Whig Party
Elected from: Virginia
Vice-President: none

11. James K. Polk (1795–1849)
In office: 1845–1849
Democratic Party
Elected from: Tennessee
Vice-President: George M. Dallas

12. Zachary Taylor* (1784–1850)
In office: 1849–1850
Whig Party
Elected from: Louisiana
Vice-President: Millard Fillmore

13. Millard Fillmore (1800–1874)
In office: 1850–1853
Whig Party
Elected from: New York
Vice-President: none

14. Franklin Pierce (1804–1869)
In office: 1853–1857
Democratic Party
Elected from: New Hampshire
Vice-President: William Rufus de Vane King

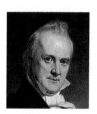

15. James Buchanan (1791–1868)
In office: 1857–1861
Democratic Party
Elected from: Pennsylvania
Vice-President: John C. Breckinridge

16. Abraham Lincoln† (1809–1865)
In office: 1861–1865
Republican Party
Elected from: Illinois
Vice-Presidents: Hannibal Hamlin,
    Andrew Johnson

* Died in office
† Assassinated

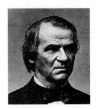

17. Andrew Johnson (1808–1875)
In office: 1865–1869
Democratic Party
Elected from: Tennessee
Vice-President: none

18. Ulysses S. Grant (1822–1885)
In office: 1869–1877
Republican Party
Elected from: Illinois
Vice-Presidents: Schuyler Colfax,
    Henry Wilson

19. Rutherford B. Hayes (1822–1893)
In office: 1877–1881
Republican Party
Elected from: Ohio
Vice-President: William A. Wheeler

20. James Garfield† (1831–1881)
In office: 1881
Republican Party
Elected from: Ohio
Vice-President: Chester A. Arthur

21. Chester A. Arthur (1829–1886)
In office: 1881–1885
Republican Party
Elected from: New York
Vice-President: none

22. Grover Cleveland (1837–1908)
In office: 1885–1889
Democratic Party
Elected from: New York
Vice-President: Thomas Hendricks

23. Benjamin Harrison (1833–1901)
In office: 1889–1893
Republican Party
Elected from: Indiana
Vice-President: Levi P. Morton

24. Grover Cleveland (1837–1908)
In office: 1893–1897
Democratic Party
Elected from: New York
Vice-President: Adlai E. Stevenson

25. William McKinley† (1843–1901)
   In office: 1897–1901
   Republican Party
   Elected from: Ohio
   Vice-Presidents: Garret A. Hobart,
        Theodore Roosevelt

26. Theodore Roosevelt (1858–1919)
   In office: 1901–1909
   Republican Party
   Elected from: New York
   Vice-President: Charles Fairbanks

27. William H. Taft (1857–1930)
   In office: 1909–1913
   Republican Party
   Elected from: Ohio
   Vice-President: James S. Sherman

28. Woodrow Wilson (1856–1924)
   In office: 1913–1921
   Democratic Party
   Elected from: New Jersey
   Vice-President: Thomas R. Marshall

29. Warren G. Harding* (1865–1923)
   In office: 1921–1923
   Republican Party
   Elected from: Ohio
   Vice-President: Calvin Coolidge

30. Calvin Coolidge (1872–1933)
   In office: 1923–1929
   Republican Party
   Elected from: Massachusetts
   Vice-President: Charles G. Dawes

31. Herbert Hoover (1874–1964)
   In office: 1929–1933
   Republican Party
   Elected from: California
   Vice-President: Charles Curtis

32. Franklin D. Roosevelt* (1882–1945)
   In office: 1933–1945
   Democratic Party
   Elected from: New York
   Vice-Presidents: John Garner,
        Henry Wallace, Harry S Truman

* Died in office
† Assassinated

33. Harry S Truman (1884–1972)
In office: 1945–1953
Democratic Party
Elected from: Missouri
Vice-President: Alben Barkley

34. Dwight D. Eisenhower (1890–1969)
In office: 1953–1961
Republican Party
Elected from: New York
Vice-President: Richard M. Nixon

35. John F. Kennedy† (1917–1963)
In office: 1961–1963
Democratic Party
Elected from: Massachusetts
Vice-President: Lyndon B. Johnson

36. Lyndon B. Johnson (1908–1973)
In office: 1963–1969
Democratic Party
Elected from: Texas
Vice-President: Hubert Humphrey

37. Richard M. Nixon‡ (1913–1994)
In office: 1969–1974
Republican Party
Elected from: New York
Vice-Presidents: Spiro Agnew,
    Gerald Ford

38. Gerald R. Ford (b. 1913)
In office: 1974–1977
Republican Party
Elected from: Michigan
Vice-President: Nelson Rockefeller

39. Jimmy Carter (b. 1924)
In office: 1977–1981
Democratic Party
Elected from: Georgia
Vice-President: Walter Mondale

40. Ronald Reagan (b. 1911)
In office: 1981–1989
Republican Party
Elected from: California
Vice-President: George Bush

† Assassinated
‡ Resigned

41. George Bush (b. 1924)
In office: 1989–1993
Republican Party
Elected from: Texas
Vice-President: J. Danforth Quayle

42. Bill Clinton (b. 1946)
In office: 1993–
Democratic Party
Elected from: Arkansas
Vice-President: Albert Gore, Jr.

Key Events in United States History

by 20,000 B.C. Earliest inhabitants spread across North America

7000 B.C. Agriculture begins in the Americas

600 Mound Builders establish the city of Cahokia

1000s Anasazis build cliff dwellings

1300s Aztecs establish their capital, Tenochtitlán

1419 Prince Henry's ships start to explore West African coast

1492 Christopher Columbus reaches the Americas

1497 Search for the Northwest Passage begins

1513 Ponce de León explores Florida

1519 Cortés begins the conquest of Mexico

1519–1522 Magellan's expedition circles the globe

1565 Spain founds St. Augustine in Florida

1570 League of the Iroquois formed

1607 Jamestown founded

1608 Champlain founds Quebec for France

1610 Spanish establish Santa Fe, New Mexico

1619 Virginia House of Burgesses first meets
First Africans brought to Jamestown

1620 Mayflower Compact
Pilgrims land at Plymouth

1630 Puritans found Massachusetts Bay Colony

1644 Roger Williams establishes religious freedom in colony of Rhode Island

1675–1676 King Philip's War

1676 Bacon's Rebellion

1681 Penn plans "holy experiment" in Pennsylvania

1682 La Salle explores the Mississippi for France

1730s The Great Awakening begins

1732 Georgia becomes the last English colony

1754 French and Indian War begins

1763 France gives up claims in North America

1765 Stamp Act

1769 Spanish build first mission in California

1770 Boston Massacre

1773 Boston Tea Party

1774 First Continental Congress

1775 Battles of Lexington and Concord
Second Continental Congress

1776 Declaration of Independence

1781 Articles of Confederation ratified
British surrender at Yorktown

1783 Britain recognizes American independence in Treaty of Paris

1787 Constitutional Convention
Northwest Ordinance

1788 Constitution ratified

1789 George Washington becomes first U.S. President

1791 Bill of Rights ratified

1792 First political parties formed

1793 Eli Whitney invents the cotton gin

1797 John Adams becomes President

1798 Alien and Sedition Acts

Early 1800s Second Great Awakening sweeps the nation

1801 Thomas Jefferson becomes President

1803 *Marbury* v. *Madison*
Louisiana Purchase

1804–1806 Lewis and Clark expedition

1809 James Madison becomes President

1812–1815 War of 1812

1817 James Monroe becomes President

1819 United States acquires Florida

1820 Missouri Compromise

1821 William Becknell blazes the Santa Fe Trail

1823 Monroe Doctrine

1825 John Quincy Adams becomes President
Opening of the Erie Canal

1829 Andrew Jackson becomes President

1830 Indian Removal Act

1831 Nat Turner's Revolt

1832 Nullification Crisis

1833 American Anti-Slavery Society founded

1836 Texans declare independence from Mexico
First families on the Oregon Trail

1837 Martin Van Buren becomes President

1838 The Trail of Tears

**1841 William Henry Harrison becomes President
John Tyler becomes President upon death of Harrison**

1845 James K. Polk becomes President
United States annexes Texas

1846 United States declares war on Mexico

1848 Treaty of Guadalupe Hidalgo
Seneca Falls Convention on women's rights

1849 Zachary Taylor becomes President
California gold rush begins

1850 The Compromise of 1850
Millard Fillmore becomes President upon death of Taylor

1852 Harriet Beecher Stowe publishes *Uncle Tom's Cabin*

1853 Franklin Pierce becomes President
Gadsden Purchase

1854 Kansas-Nebraska Act

1857 James Buchanan becomes President
Dred Scott decision

1859 John Brown's raid on Harpers Ferry

1861 Abraham Lincoln becomes President
Civil War begins

1862 Homestead Act
Battle of Antietam

1863 Emancipation Proclamation
Battles of Gettysburg and Vicksburg

1864 Sherman's forces seize Atlanta

1865 Lee surrenders at Appomattox
Andrew Johnson becomes President upon assassination of Lincoln
Thirteenth Amendment abolishes slavery

1866 National Labor Union organized

1867 Congress passes Reconstruction Act
United States buys Alaska

1868 President Johnson's impeachment and trial
Fourteenth Amendment defines U.S. citizenship

1869 Ulysses S. Grant becomes President

1870 Fifteenth Amendment defines rights of voters

1877 Rutherford B. Hayes becomes President
Reconstruction ends
Great Railroad strike

**1881 James Garfield becomes President
Chester A. Arthur becomes President upon assassination of Garfield**

1882 Standard Oil trust formed
Chinese Exclusion Act
1885 Grover Cleveland becomes President
1886 Haymarket bombing
American Federation of Labor organized
1887 Dawes Act
1889 Benjamin Harrison becomes President
1890 Sherman Antitrust Act
1891 Populist party organized
1892 Homestead Strike
1893 Grover Cleveland becomes President
1894 Pullman Strike
1896 *Plessy* v. *Ferguson*
1897 William McKinley becomes President
1898 Spanish-American War
United States annexes Hawaii
United States acquires Philippines, Puerto Rico,
and Guam
1899 Open Door policy in China
1901 Theodore Roosevelt becomes President upon
assassination of McKinley
Progressive movement begins
1904 Construction of Panama Canal begins
Roosevelt Corollary to Monroe Doctrine
1909 William H. Taft becomes President
NAACP founded
1913 Woodrow Wilson becomes President
Federal Reserve Act
1914 World War I begins
1915 *Lusitania* sunk by German submarine
1916 U.S. troops sent to Mexico
1917 United States enters World War I
1919 United States rejects Treaty of Versailles
"Red Summer" and "Red Scare"
1920 Prohibition begins
Nineteenth Amendment gives women the vote
1921 Warren G. Harding becomes President
First immigration quota law passed
1923 Calvin Coolidge becomes President upon
death of Harding
1929 Herbert Hoover becomes President
Stock market crash
1933 Franklin D. Roosevelt becomes President
Good Neighbor policy proclaimed
New Deal begins
1934 Indian Reorganization Act
1935 Wagner Act and Social Security Act
1938 Congress of Industrial Organizations formed
1939 World War II begins
1941 Japan bombs Pearl Harbor
United States enters World War II
1942 Japanese-American internment
1944 Allies invade France
1945 Yalta Conference
Harry S Truman becomes President upon
death of Roosevelt
Germany surrenders
Atomic bombs dropped on Japan
Japan surrenders
UN charter goes into effect

1946 Philippines becomes independent
1948 Marshall Plan goes into effect
Berlin airlift begins
1949 NATO formed
1950 Korean War begins
1953 Dwight D. Eisenhower becomes President
Armistice in Korea signed
1954 *Brown* v. *Board of Education* decision
Army-McCarthy hearings
1955 Montgomery bus boycott
1956 Suez crisis
1961 John F. Kennedy becomes President
Peace Corps established
Berlin crisis
1962 Cuban missile crisis
1963 March on Washington for civil rights
Nuclear Test Ban Treaty
Lyndon B. Johnson becomes President upon
assassination of Kennedy
1964 Civil Rights Act of 1964
1965 U.S. troop buildup begins in Vietnam
Voting Rights Act of 1965
Immigration quotas based on national origins ended
1966 National Organization for Women founded
1968 Martin Luther King, Jr., and Robert Kennedy
assassinated
1969 Richard M. Nixon becomes President
American astronauts land on moon
1970 U.S. troops invade Cambodia
1971 Twenty-sixth Amendment lowers voting age
to eighteen
1972 President Nixon visits mainland China
Watergate break-in
1973 Cease-fire agreement with North Vietnam
1974 Gerald R. Ford becomes President upon
resignation of Nixon
1975 South Vietnam falls to North Vietnam
1977 Jimmy Carter becomes President
1978 Camp David Accords between Egypt and Israel
1979 Iranian hostage crisis begins
1981 Ronald Reagan becomes President
1983 U.S. troops invade Grenada
1986 Iran-contra scandal
1987 INF Treaty
1989 George Bush becomes President
U.S. troops invade Panama
Communist governments in Eastern Europe fall
1991 Persian Gulf War
Soviet Union collapses
1992 Los Angeles riots
Earth Summit
1993 Bill Clinton becomes President
1995 Republicans take over majority in Congress

Key Events in United States History • **R31**

The Declaration of Independence

*W*hen, in the course of human events, it becomes necessary for one people to dissolve the political bands which have connected them with another, and to assume, among the powers of the earth, the separate and equal station to which the laws of nature and of nature's God entitle them, a decent respect to the opinions of mankind requires that they should declare the causes which impel them to the separation.

We hold these truths to be self-evident, that all men are created equal, that they are endowed by their Creator with certain unalienable rights, that among these are life, liberty, and the pursuit of happiness. That, to secure these rights, governments are instituted among men, deriving their just powers from the consent of the governed. That, whenever any form of government becomes destructive of these ends, it is the right of the people to alter or to abolish it, and to institute new government, laying its foundation on such principles, and organizing its powers in such form, as to them shall seem most likely to effect their safety and happiness.

Prudence, indeed, will dictate that governments long established should not be changed for light and transient causes; and, accordingly, all experience has shown that mankind are more disposed to suffer, while evils are sufferable, than to right themselves by abolishing the forms to which they are accustomed.

But when a long train of abuses and usurpations, pursuing invariably the same object, evinces a design to reduce them under absolute despotism, it is their right, it is their duty, to throw off such government, and to provide new guards for their future security. Such has been the patient sufferance of these colonies; and such is now the necessity which constrains them to alter their former systems of government. The history of the present King of Great Britain is a history of repeated injuries and usurpations, all having in direct object the establishment of an absolute tryanny over these states. To prove this, let facts be submitted to a candid world.

He has refused his assent to laws the most wholesome and necessary for the public good.

He has forbidden his governors to pass laws of immediate and pressing importance, unless suspended in their operation till his assent should be obtained; and when so suspended, he has utterly neglected to attend to them.

He has refused to pass other laws for the accommodation of large districts of people, unless those people would relinquish the right of representation in the legislature; a right inestimable to them and formidable to tyrants only.

He has called together legislative bodies at places unusual, uncomfortable, and distant from the depository of their public records, for the sole purpose of fatiguing them into compliance with his measures.

He has dissolved representative houses repeatedly, for opposing with manly firmness his invasions on the rights of the people.

He has refused for a long time, after such dissolutions, to cause others to be elected; whereby the legislative powers, incapable of annihilation, have returned to the people at large for their exercise; the state remaining in the meantime exposed to all the dangers of invasion from without, and convulsions within.

He has endeavored to prevent the population of these states; for that purpose obstructing the laws for naturalization of foreigners; refusing to pass others to encourage their migrations hither, and raising the conditions of new appropriations of lands.

He has obstructed the administration of justice, by refusing his assent to laws for establishing judiciary powers.

He has made judges dependent on his will alone, for the tenure of their offices, and the amount and payment of their salaries.

He has erected a multitude of new offices, and sent hither swarms of officers to harass our people, and eat out their substance.

He has kept among us, in times of peace, standing armies, without the consent of our legislatures.

He has affected to render the military independent of and superior to the civil power.

He has combined with others to subject us to a jurisdiction foreign to our constitution, and unacknowledged by our laws; giving his assent to their acts of pretended legislation:

For quartering large bodies of armed troops among us;

For protecting them, by a mock trial, from punishment for any murders which they should commit on the inhabitants of these states;

For cutting off our trade with all parts of the world;

For imposing taxes on us without our consent;

For depriving us, in many cases, of the benefits of trial by jury;

For transporting us beyond seas to be tried for pretended offenses;

For abolishing the free system of English laws in a neighboring province, establishing therein an arbitrary government, and enlarging its boundaries, so as to render it at once an example and fit instrument for introducing the same absolute rule into these colonies;

For taking away our charters, abolishing our most valuable laws, and altering fundamentally the forms of our governments;

For suspending our own legislatures, and declaring themselves invested with power to legislate for us in all cases whatsoever.

He has abdicated government here, by declaring us out of his protection, and waging war against us.

He has plundered our seas, ravaged our coasts, burnt our towns, and destroyed the lives of our people.

He is at this time transporting large armies of foreign mercenaries to complete the works of death, desolation, and tyranny already begun with circumstances of cruelty and perfidy scarcely paralleled in the most barbarous ages, and totally unworthy the head of a civilized nation.

He has constrained our fellow citizens, taken captive on the high seas, to bear arms against their country, to become the executioners of their friends and brethren, or to fall themselves by their hands.

He has excited domestic insurrections among us, and has endeavored to bring on the inhabitants of our frontiers, the merciless Indian savages, whose known rule of warfare is an undistinguished destruction of all ages, sexes, and conditions.

In every stage of these oppressions, we have petitioned for redress in the most humble terms. Our repeated petitions have been answered only by repeated injury. A prince, whose character is thus marked by every act which may define a tyrant, is unfit to be the ruler of a free people.

Nor have we been wanting in attentions to our British brethren. We have warned them from time to time of attempts by their legislature to extend an unwarrantable jurisdiction over us. We have reminded them of the circumstances of our emigration and settlement here. We have appealed to their native justice and magnanimity, and we have conjured them by the ties of our common kindred to disavow these usurpations, which would inevitably interrupt our connections and correspondence. They too have been deaf to the voice of justice and of consanguinity. We must, therefore, acquiesce in the necessity, which denounces our separation, and hold them, as we hold the rest of mankind, enemies in war, in peace, friends.

We, therefore, the representatives of the United States of America, in General Congress assembled, appealing to the Supreme Judge of the world for the rectitude of our intentions, do, in the name and by authority of the good people of these colonies, solemnly publish and declare, that these United Colonies are and of right ought to be free and independent states; that they are absolved from all allegiance to the British Crown, and that all political connection between them and the state of Great Britain is and ought to be totally dissolved; and that, as free and independent states, they have full power to levy war, conclude peace, contract alliances, establish commerce, and to do all other acts and things which independent states may of right do. And for the support of this declaration, with a firm reliance on the protection of Divine Providence, we mutually pledge to each other our lives, our fortunes, and our sacred honor.

Constitution
Handbook

he Constitution, which was ratified in 1788, has seven articles, or parts. Since its ratification, 27 amendments have been added to the original document.

The Constitution is organized to serve as a user's manual for government. Long articles and amendments are broken into sections, each covering a single subtopic. Long sections are divided still further into clauses. This arrangement makes it easy to find your way around the Constitution.

Throughout this handbook, the original text of the Constitution appears in the right-hand column. Spelling and punctuation have been modernized where needed. The clauses have been numbered to help you identify them. You will see that some parts of the Constitution have lines drawn through them. These parts have been changed by amendments and are no longer in force.

The Constitution is written in a style of language that is more than 200 years old, making it difficult for people today to understand. To help you grasp its meaning, each section and clause has been rewritten in a simpler, more modern style. These translations appear in the left-hand column of each page, next to each section or clause.

On some pages, information appears below the Constitution text. There are explanations of what the Constitution means or how it works. Diagrams, tables, and photographs present interesting facts and help explain ideas.

Woven into the Constitution are three principles that shape how our government works:

• **Checks and Balances** Each branch of government can limit the powers of the other two.
• **Federalism** Power is divided between the federal government and the states.
• **Flexibility** General principles for running the government will survive the test of time better

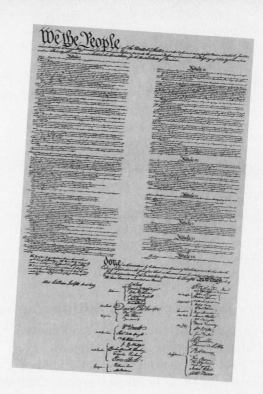

than specific details. If necessary, the Constitution can be changed through amendments.

This handbook is organized to call your attention to these principles. You will see them, for example, in the titles of some explanations.

Guide to the Constitution

The Preamble to the Constitution

The Preamble

The Preamble is the introduction to the Constitution. It lists the six most important purposes of the new government. Those purposes are to:
- unify the states into a strong nation
- create a society based on law and justice
- keep peace among all Americans
- protect the nation from its enemies
- improve the lives of Americans
- ensure that all Americans, now and in the future, live in a free and democratic society

We the people of the United States, in order to form a more perfect Union, establish justice, insure domestic tranquility, provide for the common defense, promote the general welfare, and secure the blessings of liberty to ourselves and our posterity, do ordain and establish this Constitution for the United States of America.

Why the Preamble is Still Important

If your parents or grandparents went to school in the United States, the chances are that by your age they had memorized the Preamble to the Constitution. For generations, American schoolchildren began their study of the Constitution by committing these words to memory. The reason is simple. This one sentence tells us where the power comes from under our Constitution and how it should be used.

Look at first words of the Preamble: "We the people." They tell us that in this country, the power to govern comes from the consent of the governed. The Constitution was "ordained and established" in 1788 only after that consent was given by the people of the United States. It remains in effect today because we still choose to live under this framework of government.

The Preamble also says what the power is to be used for. The first purpose, "to form a more perfect Union," was dear to the hearts of all who had struggled with the very imperfect union created by the Articles of Confederation.

The remaining five purposes are as important today as they were in 1787. We still want to live in a just and law-abiding society. We still want to feel safe in our homes and communities. We still want to be protected from foreign enemies. We still believe that government should help make our lives better. We still treasure the opportunities, rights, and freedoms that are the blessings of liberty. In the pages that follow, you will learn more about the government created by the Constitution and how it serves these purposes.

The Legislative Branch

Section 1. A Two-Part Congress

The legislative branch has the power to make laws. This power is given to both the Senate and the House of Representatives.

Section 2. The House of Representatives

Clause 1. Election of Members
Members of the House are elected every two years by the people of the states. Short terms allow the people to quickly get rid of a representative they don't like.

Clause 2. Qualifications of Representatives
A member of the House must be:
- at least 25 years old
- a U.S. citizen for at least seven years
- a resident of the state from which elected

Article 1.

Section 1.

All legislative powers herein granted shall be vested in a Congress of the United States, which shall consist of a Senate and House of Representatives.

Section 2.

Clause 1. The House of Representatives shall be composed of members chosen every second year by the people of the several states, and the electors in each state shall have the qualifications requisite for electors of the most numerous branch of the state legislature.

Clause 2. No person shall be a representative who shall not have attained to the age of twenty-five years, and been seven years a citizen of the United States, and who shall not, when elected, be an inhabitant of that state in which he shall be chosen.

Why Congress Comes First in the Constitution

The framers of the Constitution put the legislative branch at the center of the national government. Congress alone has the power to make laws. To indicate the importance of this branch, the framers put it first, in Article 1. Nearly half of the original Constitution deals with the organization and powers of Congress.

The structure of Congress is based on the Great Compromise of 1787. It is made up of two chambers: the House of Representatives, which represents the people, and the Senate, which represents the states.

The most important job of Congress is to make laws, the life blood of our political system. Laws do not just tell us what we can and cannot do. They also create government policies, programs, and agencies. Everything from the space agency to the school lunch program begins with a law passed by Congress.

Congress meets in the Capitol building in Washington, D.C.

Clause 3. The Number of Representatives
The number of representatives from each state is based on the state's population. Originally, slaves were counted as three-fifths of a person. When slavery was ended by the Thirteenth Amendment in 1865, the three-fifths rule became meaningless.

A census, or count of the people, must be taken every ten years. The results are used to apportion, or divide, House seats among the states. Each state must have at least one seat, no matter how small its population. Representatives within a state are elected from districts of roughly equal population. A typical House member now represents more than six hundred thousand persons.

Clause 3. Representatives and direct taxes shall be apportioned among the several states which may be included within this Union, according to their respective numbers, ~~which shall be determined by adding to the whole number of free persons, including those bound to service for a term of years, and excluding Indians not taxed, three fifths of all other persons~~.

The actual enumeration shall be made within three years after the first meeting of the Congress of the United States, and within every subsequent term of ten years, in such manner as they shall by law direct. The number of representatives shall not exceed one for every thirty thousand, but each state shall have at least one representative; ~~and until such enumeration shall be made, the state of New Hampshire shall be entitled to choose three, Massachusetts eight, Rhode Island and Providence Plantations one, Connecticut five, New York six, New Jersey four, Pennsylvania eight, Delaware one, Maryland six, Virginia ten, North Carolina five, South Carolina five, and Georgia three~~.

Clause 4. Filling Vacancies
If a House seat becomes vacant between regular elections, the governor of that state can call a special election to fill the seat.

Clause 4. When vacancies happen in the representation from any state, the executive authority thereof shall issue writs of election to fill such vacancies.

Clause 5. Impeachment Power
The Speaker of the House is the leading officer of the House. Only the House can impeach, or bring charges against, federal officials who have done wrong.

Clause 5. The House of Representatives shall choose their speaker and other officers, and shall have the sole power of impeachment.

Seats in the House of Representatives After the 1990 Census

The makeup of the House changed as a result of the census of 1990. Some states, mostly in the West and South, gained seats. The delegation from California, for example, swelled from 45 to 52 members. Other states, including New York, Ohio, Pennsylvania, and Massachusetts, lost seats.

Section 3. The Senate

Clause 1. Elections
The Senate is made up of two Senators from each state. Originally Senators were elected by their state legislatures. Amendment 17, ratified in 1913, calls for the direct election of Senators by the voters of each state.

Clause 2. Terms of Office
Senate terms overlap. Every two years, one-third of the Senators end their terms and must either leave or stand for re-election. As a result, there are always experienced lawmakers in the Senate.

Clause 3. Qualifications of Senators
A member of the Senate must be:
• at least 30 years old
• a U.S. citizen for at least 9 years
• a resident of the state from which elected

Clause 4. President of the Senate
The Vice-President serves as president of the Senate, but votes only in case of a tie.

Clause 5. Election of Officers
The Senate elects officers, including a temporary, or *pro tempore* president. The president pro tem leads the Senate when the Vice-President is absent.

Section 3.

Clause 1. The Senate of the United States shall be composed of two senators from each state, chosen by the legislature thereof, for six years; and each senator shall have one vote.

Clause 2. Immediately after they shall be assembled in consequence of the first election, they shall be divided as equally as may be into three classes. The seats of the senators of the first class shall be vacated at the expiration of the second year, of the second class at the expiration of the fourth year, and of the third class at the expiration of the sixth year, so that one third may be chosen every second year; and if vacancies happen by resignation, or otherwise, during the recess of the legislature of any state, the executive thereof may make temporary appointments until the next meeting of the legislature, which shall then fill such vacancies.

Clause 3. No person shall be a senator who shall not have attained to the age of thirty years, and been nine years a citizen of the United States, and who shall not, when elected, be an inhabitant of that state for which he shall be chosen.

Clause 4. The Vice-President of the United States shall be president of the Senate, but shall have no vote, unless they be equally divided.

Clause 5. The Senate shall choose their other officers and also a president pro tempore, in the absence of the Vice-President, or when he shall exercise the office of President of the United States.

Giving States Equal Representation

The framers saw the Senate as a check on the House of Representatives. With longer terms in office and different interests in mind, Senators would see their role differently than Representatives. If the House passed a bill without fully considering its effects, the Senate might oppose it. When Thomas Jefferson asked George Washington why the delegates had established a Senate, Washington replied by asking, "Why do you pour your coffee into a saucer?" "To cool it," Jefferson answered. Washington replied, "Even so, we pour legislation into the senatorial saucer to cool it."

Article 1: The Legislative Branch

Clause 6. Impeachment Trials
The Senate serves as a jury in impeachment cases. A conviction requires a two-thirds vote of the members present.

Clause 6. The Senate shall have the sole power to try all impeachments. When sitting for that purpose, they shall be on oath or affirmation. When the President of the United States is tried, the Chief Justice shall preside. And no person shall be convicted without the concurrence of two thirds of the members present.

Clause 7. Penalty for Conviction
If an impeached official is convicted of wrongdoing by the Senate, that person is removed from office. The Senate cannot impose any other punishment. The convicted official can, however, be tried in a regular court.

Clause 7. Judgment in cases of impeachment shall not extend further than to removal from office, and disqualification to hold and enjoy any office of honor, trust, or profit under the United States; but the party convicted shall nevertheless be liable and subject to indictment, trial, judgment, and punishment, according to law.

Section 4. Elections and Meetings

Clause 1. Congressional Elections
Each state regulates its own congressional elections, but Congress can change the regulations. In 1872 Congress required that every state hold elections on the same day.

Clause 2. Meetings
Congress must meet once a year. Amendment 20, ratified in 1933, changed the first day of Congress to January 3.

Section 4.

Clause 1. The times, places, and manner of holding elections for senators and representatives shall be prescribed in each state by the legislature thereof; but the Congress may at any time by law make or alter such regulations, ~~except as to the places of choosing senators~~.

Clause 2. The Congress shall assemble at least once in every year, ~~and such meeting shall be on the first Monday in December,~~ unless they shall by law appoint a different day.

Checks and Balances: Impeachment

The framers worked hard to create a system of checks and balances that would keep any one branch of the government from misusing its power. One of the most important of those checks is the power of Congress to impeach and remove officials from office. To impeach means to accuse a government official of serious wrongdoing. Article 2, Section 4 defines such wrongdoings as "treason, bribery, or other high crimes and misdemeanors."

The first two offenses are clear. Treason is aiding the nation's enemies. Bribery involves giving gifts to a public official in exchange for special favors. Just what "high crimes and misdemeanors" means is less clear. The basic idea is that officials can be removed from office if they seriously abuse their power.

The House of Representatives has the power to impeach officials by charging them with such acts. Once impeached, an official is tried by the Senate. If found guilty by a two-thirds vote, the official is then removed from office.

Facing likely impeachment, Richard Nixon resigned from the presidency in 1974.

Section 5. Basics of Organization

Clause 1. Attendance
Each house can judge whether new members have been elected fairly and are qualified. A quorum is the minimum number of members who can act for all. While discussion can go on without a quorum, a quorum is required for voting.

Clause 2. Rules
Each house can:
- set up its own working rules
- punish members who misbehave
- expel a member with a two-thirds vote

Clause 3. Record-keeping
Each house must keep written records of what is done at meetings. Since 1873 the journals of the House and Senate have been published in the *Congressional Record*.

Clause 4. Ending Sessions
Both houses must agree to any adjournment, or ending of a session, for longer than three days.

Section 6. Privileges and Restrictions

Clause 1. Salaries and Privileges
The members of Congress can set their own salaries. When Congress is in session, members cannot be arrested except on certain criminal charges. While working on congressional business, members can write or say anything about anyone.

Clause 2. Employment Restrictions
Members of Congress cannot create new federal jobs or increase the pay for old ones and then leave Congress to take those jobs. Nor can a member of Congress hold a job in one of the other branches of the federal government while serving in Congress.

Section 5.

Clause 1. Each house shall be the judge of the elections, returns, and qualifications of its own members, and a majority of each shall constitute a quorum to do business; but a smaller number may adjourn from day to day, and may be authorized to compel the attendance of absent members, in such manner and under such penalties as each house may provide.

Clause 2. Each house may determine the rules of its proceedings, punish its members for disorderly behavior, and, with the concurrence of two thirds, expel a member.

Clause 3. Each house shall keep a journal of its proceedings and from time to time publish the same, excepting such parts as may in their judgment require secrecy; and the yeas and nays of the members of either house on any question, shall, at the desire of one fifth of those present, be entered on the journal.

Clause 4. Neither house, during the session of Congress, shall, without the consent of the other, adjourn for more than three days, nor to any other place than that in which the two houses shall be sitting.

Section 6.

Clause 1. The senators and representatives shall receive a compensation for their services, to be ascertained by law, and paid out of the Treasury of the United States. They shall in all cases, except treason, felony, and breach of the peace, be privileged from arrest during their attendance at the session of their respective houses, and in going to and returning from the same; and for any speech or debate in either house, they shall not be questioned in any other place.

Clause 2. No senator or representative shall, during the time for which he was elected, be appointed to any civil office under the authority of the United States which shall have been created, or the emoluments whereof shall have been increased, during such time; and no person holding any office under the United States shall be a member of either house during his continuance in office.

Section 7. How Bills Become Laws

Clause 1. Tax Bills

All tax bills must begin in the House. The Senate, however, can thoroughly revise such bills.

Clause 2. Submitting Bills to the President

After Congress passes a bill, it goes to the President. The President can do one of three things at that point:

- Sign the bill, which then becomes law.
- Veto the bill and then return it to Congress with objections. If Congress overrides the President's veto by a two-thirds vote of both houses, the bill becomes law.
- Do nothing. In that case the bill becomes law after 10 days (not counting Sundays), provided Congress is in session. If Congress adjourns within 10 days, the bill dies. This method of killing a bill is called a pocket veto. A President may use it to avoid an open veto of a controversial bill.

Section 7.

Clause 1. All bills for raising revenue shall originate in the House of Representatives; but the Senate may propose or concur with amendments as on other bills.

Clause 2. Every bill which shall have passed the House of Representatives and the Senate shall, before it becomes a law, be presented to the President of the United States. If he approve he shall sign it, but if not he shall return it, with his objections to that house in which it shall have originated, who shall enter the objections at large on their journal and proceed to reconsider it.

If, after such reconsideration, two thirds of that house shall agree to pass the bill, it shall be sent, together with the objections, to the other house, by which it shall likewise be reconsidered, and, if approved by two thirds of that house, it shall become a law. But in all such cases the votes of both houses shall be determined by yeas and nays, and the names of the persons voting for and against the bill shall be entered on the journal of each house respectively.

If any bill shall not be returned by the President within ten days (Sundays excepted) after it shall have been presented to him, the same shall be a law, in like manner as if he had signed it, unless the Congress by their adjournment prevent its return, in which case it shall not be a law.

Checks and Balances: How the Veto Works

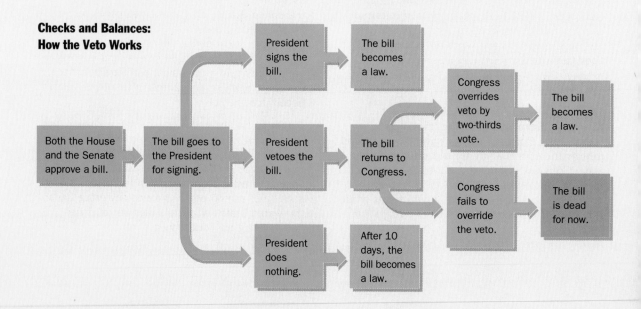

Clause 3. Submitting Other Measures

Any other measures that require agreement by both houses must go to the President for approval. Congress cannot avoid submitting bills to the President by calling them orders or resolutions. When such measures reach the President, they are treated as bills.

Section 8. Powers of Congress

Congress has the power to:

Clause 1. Taxation
- impose and collect taxes and excises (taxes on products, such as cigarettes)
- collect duties (taxes on imported goods)

Clause 2. Borrowing
- borrow money as needed

Clause 3. Regulating Trade
- control trade with foreign nations, with Indian tribes, and between states

Clause 4. Naturalization; Bankruptcy
- decide how foreigners can become citizens, a process called naturalization
- pass bankruptcy laws for the country (laws for those unable to pay their debts)

Clause 5. Coining Money
- coin and print money
- define weights and measures so that they are the same across the country

Clause 6. Punishing Counterfeiting
- punish people who make fake money or government bonds

Clause 7. Providing Postal Service
- set up a postal system

Clause 3. Every order, resolution, or vote to which the concurrence of the Senate and House of Representatives may be necessary (except on a question of adjournment) shall be presented to the President of the United States; and before the same shall take effect, shall be approved by him, or being disapproved by him, shall be repassed by two thirds of the Senate and House of Representatives, according to the rules and limitations prescribed in the case of a bill.

Section 8.

The Congress shall have power:

Clause 1. To lay and collect taxes, duties, imposts, and excises, to pay the debts and provide for the common defense and general welfare of the United States; but all duties, imposts, and excises shall be uniform throughout the United States;

Clause 2. To borrow money on the credit of the United States;

Clause 3. To regulate commerce with foreign nations, and among the several states, and with the Indian tribes;

Clause 4. To establish a uniform rule of naturalization and uniform laws on the subject of bankruptcies throughout the United States;

Clause 5. To coin money, regulate the value thereof, and of foreign coin, and fix the standard of weights and measures;

Clause 6. To provide for the punishment of counterfeiting the securities and current coin of the United States;

Clause 7. To establish post offices and post roads;

Article 1: The Legislative Branch

Clause 8. Encouraging Invention
- grant copyrights to authors and patents to inventors as a way of encouraging progress in science and the arts

Clause 8. To promote the progress of science and useful arts, by securing for limited times to authors and inventors the exclusive right to their respective writings and discoveries;

Clause 9. Establishing Courts
- establish a federal court system

Clause 9. To constitute tribunals inferior to the Supreme Court;

Clause 10. Punishing Crimes at Sea
- punish piracy and other crimes committed on the seas

Clause 10. To define and punish piracies and felonies committed on the high seas and offenses against the law of nations;

Clause 11. Declaring War
- declare war
- authorize private ships to attack and seize enemy ships

Clause 11. To declare war, grant letters of marque and reprisal, and make rules concerning captures on land and water;

Clause 12. Raising an Army
- raise and support an army

Clause 12. To raise and support armies, but no appropriation of money to that use shall be for a longer term than two years;

Clause 13. Maintaining a Navy
- establish and maintain a navy

Clause 13. To provide and maintain a navy;

Clause 14. Regulating the Armed Forces
- make rules to govern the armed forces

Clause 14. To make rules for the government and regulation of the land and naval forces;

Clause 15. Calling Out the Militia
- call out state militia units, now known as the National Guard

Clause 15. To provide for calling forth the militia to execute the laws of the Union, suppress insurrections, and repel invasions;

Clause 16. Regulating the Militia
- organize, arm, and govern the National Guard. The states keep the power to appoint officers of state militias.

Clause 16. To provide for organizing, arming, and disciplining the militia, and for governing such part of them as may be employed in the service of the United States, reserving to the states respectively the appointment of the officers and the authority of training the militia according to the discipline prescribed by Congress;

Checks and Balances: Waging War

The Constitution gives Congress the sole power to declare war, to set up the armed forces, and to fund them. The framers gave these powers to Congress to make sure the nation would enter a war only if it was the will of the people. The President, however, was given the role of commander in chief of the armed forces. Under this authority, several Presidents have ordered American troops into battle without a declaration of war by Congress. In some of these cases, critics have charged that the President was going against the framers' intent.

Clause 17. Controlling Federal Property

- make laws for the District of Columbia and for federal land used for forts, naval bases, national parks, and other purposes. In 1974, Congress gave citizens of Washington D.C. the right to elect their own mayor and city council and run their own affairs. Still, Congress can overrule the council's actions.

Clause 18. The "Elastic Clause"

- make all laws "necessary and proper" to carry out the powers listed above and any other powers of the federal government

Clause 17. To exercise exclusive legislation in all cases whatsoever over such district (not exceeding ten miles square) as may, by cession of particular states and the acceptance of Congress, become the seat of the government of the United States, and to exercise like authority over all places purchased by the consent of the legislature of the state in which the same shall be for the erection of forts, magazines, arsenals, dockyards, and other needful buildings; and

Clause 18. To make all laws which shall be necessary and proper for carrying into execution the foregoing powers and all other powers vested by this Constitution in the government of the United States, or in any department or officer thereof.

Flexibility: The Elastic Clause

The last law-making power given to Congress is known as the "elastic clause" because it gives Congress the flexibility needed to carry out its other powers. For example, Congress has the power to coin and print money. To do so, however, it must pass laws to build mints, buy supplies, and hire workers. None of these powers are listed in the Constitution. Instead, such laws are considered "necessary and proper" under the elastic clause. Over the years the elastic clause has been stretched to allow Congress to do everything from build dams to outlaw some kinds of guns.

Congress has the power to decide how foreigners can become citizens. Here two new citizens attend a naturalization ceremony.

Article 1: The Legislative Branch

Section 9. Limits on Federal Power

Clause 1. Ending the Slave Trade
As part of a compromise between northern states and southern states, Congress was forbidden to end the importing of slaves before 1808.

Clause 2. Suspending Habeas Corpus
The government cannot take away a person's right to a writ of habeas corpus except in times of emergency. This right protects people from being held in jail without evidence.

Clause 3. Unfair Laws
Congress is forbidden from passing any:
- bill of attainder, or law calling for the punishment of a particular person
- ex post facto law, or law that makes an action done legally unlawful afterwards

Clause 4. Taxing Individuals
All taxes levied by Congress directly on land or people must be divided among the states according to their population. This was later changed by the Sixteenth Amendment.

Clause 5. Taxing Exports
Congress may not tax exports, or goods being sent to other countries.

Clause 6. Regulating Trade
Congress cannot favor one state over another in regulating trade and shipping.

Clause 7. Unlawful Spending
The federal government can spend money only when Congress authorizes the spending. This clause is meant to keep government officials or employees from misusing federal funds.

Clause 8. Creating Titles of Nobility
Congress cannot give anyone a title such as duchess or count. Federal officials cannot receive any gift of value from a foreign country. Such gifts are the property of the United States government.

Section 9.

Clause 1. ~~The migration or importation of such persons as any of the states now existing shall think proper to admit shall not be prohibited by Congress prior to the year 1808, but a tax or duty may be imposed on such importation, not exceeding ten dollars for each person.~~

Clause 2. The privilege of the writ of habeas corpus shall not be suspended, unless, when in cases of rebellion or invasion, the public safety may require it.

Clause 3. No bill of attainder or ex post facto law shall be passed.

Clause 4. No capitation or ~~other direct~~ tax shall be laid, unless in proportion to the census or enumeration herein before directed to be taken.

Clause 5. No tax or duty shall be laid on articles exported from any state.

Clause 6. No preference shall be given by any regulation of commerce or revenue to the ports of one state over those of another; nor shall vessels bound to or from one state be obliged to enter, clear, or pay duties in another.

Clause 7. No money shall be drawn from the Treasury but in consequence of appropriations made by law; and a regular statement and account of the receipts and expenditures of all public money shall be published from time to time.

Clause 8. No title of nobility shall be granted by the United States. And no person holding any office of profit or trust under them shall, without the consent of the Congress, accept of any present, emolument, office, or title of any kind whatever from any king, prince, or foreign state.

Section 10. Limits on State Power

Clause 1. Forbidden Actions
The states are not allowed to:
- make treaties with other nations
- coin or print money
- pass bills of attainder, ex post facto laws, or laws excusing citizens from carrying out contracts
- grant titles of nobility

Clause 2. Taxing Trade
A state cannot tax any goods entering or leaving the state. A state can charge a small fee, however, to pay for inspection of the goods.

Clause 3. Foreign Dealings
Without the agreement of Congress, states cannot tax ships that use their ports. Nor can a state prepare for war or wage war unless there is a military emergency.

Section 10.

Clause 1. No state shall enter into any treaty, alliance, or confederation; grant letters of marque and reprisal; coin money; emit bills of credit; make anything but gold and silver coin a tender in payment of debts; pass any bill of attainder, ex post facto law, or law impairing the obligation of contracts, or grant any title of nobility.

Clause 2. No state shall, without the consent of the Congress, lay any imposts or duties on imports or exports, except what may be absolutely necessary for executing its inspection laws; and the net produce of all duties and imposts laid by any state on imports or exports shall be for the use of the Treasury of the United States; and all such laws shall be subject to the revision and control of the Congress.

Clause 3. No state shall, without the consent of Congress, lay any duty of tonnage; keep troops or ships of war in time of peace; enter into any agreement or compact with another state or with a foreign power, or engage in war, unless actually invaded, or in such imminent danger as will not admit of delay.

Limits on State and Federal Power

Concerned that the federal government might become too strong, the framers of the Constitution spelled out the limits on federal power shown on the left. They also made sure to deny to the states the powers shown on the right. Some of these powers were reserved for the federal government alone. Others were denied the federal government as well.

What the Federal Government Cannot Do
- suspend the right to a writ of habeas corpus
- favor one state over another in trade
- spend money without approval by Congress

What No Government Can Do
- pass bills of attainder
- pass ex post facto laws
- grant titles of nobility
- tax exports

What State Governments Cannot Do
- make treaties with other nations
- coin or print money
- make war
- tax ships

The Executive Branch

Section 1. The President and Vice-President

Clause 1. Term of Office

Executive power—power to carry out laws—is granted to the President, chief of the executive branch. The President serves a four-year term, as does the Vice-President.

Clause 2. The Electoral College

The people do not elect the President or Vice-President directly. Instead, both are chosen by a group of electors known as the electoral college. Each state legislature decides how electors are to be chosen in that state. Today electors are chosen by the voters. The number of electors from a state is equal to the number of senators and representatives from that state.

Clause 3. Electing a President

This clause describes the framers' original plan for electing a President and Vice-President. After the election of 1800 showed its weaknesses, the method was changed by the Twelfth Amendment. (See page R62 for more details.)

Vice-Presidents Who Have Taken Over for Presidents

Vice-President	President	Year
John Tyler	William Harrison	1841
Millard Fillmore	Zachary Taylor	1850
Andrew Johnson	Abraham Lincoln	1865
Chester Arthur	James Garfield	1881
Theodore Roosevelt	William McKinley	1901
Calvin Coolidge	Warren Harding	1923
Harry Truman	Franklin Roosevelt	1945
Lyndon Johnson	John Kennedy	1963
Gerald Ford	Richard Nixon	1974

Article 2.

Section 1.

Clause 1. The executive power shall be vested in a President of the United States of America. He shall hold his office during the term of four years, and, together with the Vice-President, chosen for the same term, be elected as follows:

Clause 2. Each state shall appoint, in such manner as the legislature thereof may direct, a number of electors, equal to the whole number of senators and representatives to which the state may be entitled in the Congress: but no senator or representative, or person holding an office of trust or profit under the United States, shall be appointed an elector.

~~Clause 3. The electors shall meet in their respective states and vote by ballot for two persons, of whom one at least shall not be an inhabitant of the same state with themselves. And they shall make a list of all the persons voted for and of the number of votes for each; which list they shall sign and certify, and transmit sealed to the seat of the government of the United States, directed to the president of the Senate. The president of the Senate shall, in the presence of the Senate and House of Representatives, open all the certificates, and the votes shall then be counted. The person having the greatest number of votes shall be the President, if such number be a majority of the whole number of electors appointed; and if there be more than one who have such majority, and have an equal number of votes, then the House of Representatives shall immediately choose by ballot one of them for President; and if no person have a majority, then from the five highest on the list the said house shall in like manner choose the President. But in choosing the President, the votes shall be taken by states, the representation from each state having one vote; a quorum for this purpose shall consist of a member or members from two thirds of the states, and a majority of all the states shall be necessary to a choice. In every case, after the choice of the President, the person having the greatest number of votes of the electors shall be the Vice-President. But if there should remain two or more who have equal votes, the Senate shall choose from them by ballot the Vice-President.~~

Clause 4. Time of Elections

Congress sets the date for choosing electors, as well as the date for their voting. That date must be the same throughout the country.

Today Presidential elections take place every four years on the first Tuesday after the first Monday in November. Electoral votes are cast on the Monday after the second Wednesday in December.

Clause 5. Qualifications

Any American can be President who:
• is at least 35 years old
• is a natural born American citizen
• has lived in the U.S. for 14 years

Clause 6. Presidential Succession

This clause says that Congress can decide who should succeed, or replace, a President if the President dies, resigns, or is removed from office. In 1886 Congress said the line of succession would go from the Vice-President to members of the cabinet. In 1947 Congress changed it to go from the Vice-President to Speaker of the House, then to the president pro tempore of the Senate, and then to the cabinet. Amendment 25, ratified in 1967, prevents a long vacancy in the office of Vice-President. It also sets up procedures in case the President is disabled.

Clause 7. Presidential Salary

The President gets paid like any other federal employee. That salary cannot be raised or lowered during a President's term in office. While in office, the President cannot receive any other salary from the U.S. government or a state government.

Clause 8. The Oath of Office

Before taking office, the President must take an oath promising to carry out the duties of the Presidency and to preserve and protect the Constitution.

Clause 4. The Congress may determine the time of choosing the electors and the day on which they shall give their votes, which day shall be the same throughout the United States.

Clause 5. No person except a natural-born citizen, or a citizen of the United States at the time of the adoption of this Constitution, shall be eligible to the office of President; neither shall any person be eligible to that office who shall not have attained to the age of thirty-five years and been fourteen years a resident within the United States.

Clause 6. In case of the removal of the President from office, or of his death, resignation, or inability to discharge the powers and duties of the said office, the same shall devolve on the Vice-President, and the Congress may by law provide for the case of removal, death, resignation, or inability, both of the President and Vice-President, declaring what officer shall then act as President, and such officer shall act accordingly until the disability be removed or a President shall be elected.

Clause 7. The President shall, at stated times, receive for his services a compensation, which shall neither be increased nor diminished during the period for which he shall have been elected, and he shall not receive within that period any other emolument from the United States or any of them.

Clause 8. Before he enter on the execution of his office, he shall take the following oath or affirmation: "I do solemnly swear (or affirm) that I will faithfully execute the office of President of the United States, and will, to the best of my ability, preserve, protect, and defend the Constitution of the United States."

Article 2: The Executive Branch

Section 2. Presidential Powers

Clause 1. Military and Executive Powers

As head of the executive branch, the President has the power to:

- act as commander in chief of all the armed forces
- manage the federal bureaucracy
- grant a reprieve, or delay of punishment, to a person convicted of a federal crime
- grant a pardon, or excuse from punishment, to someone involved in a federal crime, except in impeachment cases

Clause 2. Treaties and Appointments

The President also has the power to:

- make treaties with foreign nations, with the approval of two-thirds of the Senate
- appoint Supreme Court justices, with the approval of a majority of the Senate
- appoint ambassadors and other important executive branch officials, with the approval of a majority of the Senate

Clause 3. Other Appointments

When the Senate is not in session, the President may make temporary appointments.

Section 2.

Clause 1. The President shall be commander in chief of the army and navy of the United States, and of the militia of the several states when called into actual service of the United States. He may require the opinion, in writing, of the principal officer in each of the executive departments upon any subject relating to the duties of their respective offices. And he shall have power to grant reprieves and pardons for offenses against the United States, except in cases of impeachment.

Clause 2. He shall have power, by and with the advice and consent of the Senate, to make treaties, provided two thirds of the senators present concur; and he shall nominate, and by and with the advice and consent of the Senate, shall appoint ambassadors, other public ministers and consuls, judges of the Supreme Court, and all other officers of the United States whose appointments were not herein otherwise provided for, and which shall be established by law; but the Congress may by law vest the appointment of such inferior officers as they think proper in the President alone, in the courts of law, or in the heads of departments.

Clause 3. The President shall have power to fill up all vacancies that may happen during the recess of the Senate, by granting commissions which shall expire at the end of their next session.

Checks and Balances: The Advice and Consent of the Senate

The framers hoped that the Senate would act as sort of an advisory board for the President on appointments and foreign policy. The Constitution requires that the President submit all treaties and appointments to the Senate for its "advice and consent." This is one of the checks on the President's power.

President George Washington took the idea of seeking advice from the Senate quite seriously. On August 12, 1789, he went to the Senate to discuss a proposed treaty with the Creek Indians. The Senators wasted so much time arguing over details that the President finally left in disgust. This was the last time a President went to the Senate in person for "advice."

Section 3. The President's Duties

This section outlines the President's legislative duties. The President shall:
- Address Congress regularly on the nation's problems and recommend needed laws. This message is called the State of the Union Address.
- Call Congress into special session in times of national emergency.
- Adjourn Congress if needed.

The President shall also:
- Receive ambassadors from other countries. This duty puts the President in charge of the nation's foreign policy.
- Make sure the laws passed by Congress are "faithfully executed," or enforced.

Section 4. Impeachment

The President, Vice-President, and other federal officials including department heads and federal judges can be removed from office by the impeachment process.

Section 3.

He shall from time to time give to the Congress information of the state of the Union, and recommend to their consideration such measures as he shall judge necessary and expedient; he may, on extraordinary occasions, convene both houses, or either of them, and in case of disagreement between them with respect to the time of adjournment, he may adjourn them to such time as he shall think proper; he shall receive ambassadors and other public ministers; he shall take care that the laws be faithfully executed, and shall commission all the officers of the United States.

Section 4.

The President, Vice-President, and all civil officers of the United States shall be removed from office on impeachment for, and conviction of, treason, bribery, or other high crimes and misdemeanors.

The President's Many Roles

Chief of State
Acts as a symbol of the U.S. Performs ceremonial duties

Chief Executive
Appoints officials, runs federal bureaucracy

Chief Legislator
Proposes ideas for bills and urges Congress to support them

Chief Diplomat
Makes foreign policy

Chief of Law Enforcement
Enforces laws, appoints judges, grants pardons

Commander-in-Chief
Controls armed forces; determines military strategy

Chief Citizen
Stands up for the interests of all citizens

Chief of Party
Leads political party, supports party candidates

Article 3: The Judicial Branch

The Judicial Branch

Section 1. Federal Courts

Judicial power is the power to decide legal cases in a court of law. This power is given to the Supreme Court and to lower federal courts established by Congress. A federal judge holds office for life unless impeached and found guilty of illegal acts. The salaries of judges cannot be lowered while they serve. This last protection prevents Congress from pressuring judges by threatening to cut their pay.

Section 2. Jurisdiction

Clause 1. Types of Cases
Jurisdiction is the power of a court to hear certain kinds of cases. The federal courts have jurisdiction over cases dealing with:
• the Constitution
• federal laws
• treaties with Indians or foreign powers
• ships and shipping on the seas
• disputes that involve the U.S. government
• disputes involving two or more states
• disputes between citizens of different states

Article 3.

Section 1.

The judicial power of the United States shall be vested in one Supreme Court, and in such inferior courts as the Congress may from time to time ordain and establish. The judges, both of the Supreme and inferior courts, shall hold their offices during good behavior, and shall, at stated times, receive for their services a compensation which shall not be diminished during their continuance in office.

Section 2.

Clause 1. The judicial power shall extend to all cases, in law and equity, arising under this Constitution, the laws of the United States, and treaties made, or which shall be made, under their authority; to all cases affecting ambassadors, other public ministers and consuls; to all cases of admiralty and maritime jurisdiction; to controversies to which the United States shall be a party; to controversies between two or more states; ~~between a state and citizens of another state;~~ between citizens of different states; between citizens of the same state claiming lands under grants of different states; and between a state, or the citizens thereof, and foreign states, ~~citizens, or subjects~~.

The Federal Courts and Judicial Power

The Constitution places judicial power in the hands of the Supreme Court and any "inferior courts" Congress decides to establish. Judicial power involves the authority to judge:
• **facts**—whether the accused violated the law
• **trials**—whether the case was tried properly
• **laws**—whether the law applied in the case is allowed by the Constitution

In the federal court system that has been set up since the ratification of the Constitution, there are two levels of "inferior" courts. The lowest level, made up of district and special courts, judges facts. The other level, made up of appeals courts, judges the fairness of trials. The Supreme Court is therefore left to judge matters of law, except in certain cases spelled out in the Constitution.

Clause 2. Original and Appeals Cases

The Supreme Court has "original jurisdiction" in cases that involve the states or foreign countries. Such cases go directly to the Supreme Court. All other cases start first in the lower courts. The decisions of these courts may be appealed to the Supreme Court. Nearly all cases heard by the Supreme Court begin in the lower courts.

Clause 2. In all cases affecting ambassadors, other public ministers and consuls, and those in which a state shall be party, the Supreme Court shall have original jurisdiction. In all the other cases before-mentioned, the Supreme Court shall have appellate jurisdiction, both as to law and fact, with such exceptions and under such regulations as the Congress shall make.

Clause 3. Trial by Jury

Anyone accused of a federal crime has a right to a jury trial. The trial is to be held in the state where the crime was committed. The only exception to these rules is impeachment trials.

Clause 3. The trial of all crimes, except in cases of impeachment, shall be by jury; and such trial shall be held in the state where the said crimes shall have been committed; but when not committed within any state, the trial shall be at such place or places as the Congress may by law have directed.

Section 3. Treason

Section 3.

Clause 1. Defining the Crime

Treason is defined as making war against the United States or aiding its enemies. Convicting someone of treason is not easy. At least two witnesses must testify in court that they saw the accused commit an act of treason. Or the accused must confess to the crime in court. Talking or thinking about treason is not a crime.

Clause 1. Treason against the United States shall consist only in levying war against them or in adhering to their enemies, giving them aid and comfort. No person shall be convicted of treason unless on the testimony of two witnesses to the same overt act, or on confession in open court.

Clause 2. Limits of the Punishment

Congress decides how to punish treason. It can only punish the convicted traitor, however. Punishments cannot extend to that person's family.

Clause 2. The Congress shall have power to declare the punishment of treason, but no attainder of treason shall work corruption of blood or forfeiture except during the life of the person attainted.

Checks and Balances: Who Judges the Judges?

The power of the Supreme Court is checked in several ways. First, the other two branches of government decide who gets appointed to the Court. A candidate must first be nominated by the President and then approved by the Senate. Also, if Congress disagrees with the Court's interpretation of the Constitution, it can propose a constitutional amendment relating to the issue in question. If ratified, that amendment can overrule the Court's decision. Finally, Congress can remove a justice from office for wrongdoing.

Supreme Court nominee Ruth Bader Ginsburg answered questions at a Senate confirmation hearing in 1993.

States and Territories

Section 1. Relations Among States

This section outlines the responsibilities of the states to each other in a federal system. Each state must give "full faith and credit" to the laws, official records, and court decisions of another state. This means accepting them as legal. A marriage in one state, for example, is legal in all states.

Section 2. Treatment of Citizens

Clause 1. Equal Privileges
A state cannot discriminate unreasonably against citizens from other states except in special cases. Such cases include residency requirements for voting and higher fees for out-of-state students at state colleges.

Clause 2. Return of Fugitive Criminals
Criminals cannot escape justice by running across state lines. Anyone accused of a crime in one state, who flees to another state and is caught, is to be returned if the government of the state where the crime took place makes such a request.

Clause 3. Return of Runaway Slaves
Runaway slaves could not become free by escaping to another state. They were to be returned to their owners. The Thirteenth Amendment made this clause invalid.

Article 4.

Section 1.

Full faith and credit shall be given in each state to the public acts, records, and judicial proceedings of every other state. And the Congress may by general laws prescribe the manner in which such acts, records, and proceedings shall be proved, and the effect thereof.

Section 2.

Clause 1. The citizens of each state shall be entitled to all privileges and immunities of citizens in the several states.

Clause 2. A person charged in any state with treason, felony or other crime, who shall flee from justice and be found in another state, shall, on demand of the executive authority of the state from which he fled, be delivered up to be removed to the state having jurisdiction of the crime.

~~Clause 3. No person held to service or labor in one state under the laws thereof, escaping into another, shall, in consequence of any law or regulation therein, be discharged from such service or labor, but shall be delivered up on claim of the party to whom such service or labor may be due.~~

Federalism: Cooperation Among the States

Before the Constitution was adopted, the original 13 states behaved almost like independent countries. For the new nation to endure, the states had to give up some of their independence and agree to cooperate, not only with the new federal government, but with one another.

The Constitution spells out only a few ways in which the states must cooperate with one another. Under the principle of federalism, however, the states have worked together for their common good in many ways. Building the nation's railways and interstate highway system, for example, would not have been possible without state cooperation.

Section 3. New States and Territories

Clause 1. Admitting New States

Congress has the power to add new states to the Union. No new states can be formed by dividing up existing states, however, unless both Congress and the states involved agree to the changes.

Clause 2. Governing Territories

Congress has the power to govern federal land and property. This includes federal territory not organized into states and also federal land within states.

Section 4. Protection of the States

The federal government promises that each state will have some form of representative government. It also promises to protect each state from invasion. The federal government also stands ready to send help, when requested, to stop rioting within a state.

Section 3.

Clause 1. New states may be admitted by the Congress into this Union; but no new state shall be formed or erected within the jurisdiction of any other state; nor any state be formed by the junction of two or more states, or parts of states, without the consent of the legislatures of the states concerned as well as of the Congress.

Clause 2. The Congress shall have power to dispose of and make all needful rules and regulations respecting the territory or other property belonging to the United States; and nothing in this Constitution shall be so construed as to prejudice any claims of the United States, or of any particular state.

Section 4.

The United States shall guarantee to every state in this Union a republican form of government, and shall protect each of them against invasion, and, on application of the legislature or of the executive (when the legislature cannot be convened), against domestic violence.

From Territory to State

The framers of the Constitution realized the new nation was likely to continue expanding as Americans settled new lands. They made it possible for territories to become new states and created some basic rules for this process.

Thirty-seven new states have been admitted to the union since the Constitution was ratified. Most gained statehood in the 1800s. The two newest states are Alaska and Hawaii, both admitted in 1959.

The two most recent states to be admitted to the union were Alaska and Hawaii, in 1959.

Article 5: The Amendment Process

Amending the Constitution

Article 5 outlines the process for amending the Constitution. As the diagram below shows, there are two ways to propose an amendment and two ways to ratify it. Congress decides which method of ratification to use.

Article 5.

The Congress, whenever two thirds of both houses shall deem it necessary, shall propose amendments to this Constitution or, on the application of the legislatures of two thirds of the several states, shall call a convention for proposing amendments, which, in either case, shall be valid, to all intents and purposes, as part of this Constitution when ratified by the legislatures of three fourths of the several states, or by conventions in three fourths thereof, as the one or the other mode of ratification may be proposed by the Congress; provided ~~that no amendment which may be made prior to the year 1808 shall in any manner affect the first and fourth clauses in the ninth section of the first article; and~~ that no state, without its consent, shall be deprived of its equal suffrage in the Senate.

Flexibility:
The Amendment Process

The amendment process makes is possible to change the Constitution to meet changing needs and demands. Since 1787, the Constitution has been amended 27 times. Each of these amendments was proposed by a two-thirds vote of both houses of Congress. All but one of these amendments were ratified by three-fourths of the state legislatures.

The exception was the Twenty-first Amendment. For the first time, an amendment was being proposed that would repeal an earlier one—the Eighteenth Amendment. In this case, Congress required ratification by state conventions and set a deadline for ratification of seven years.

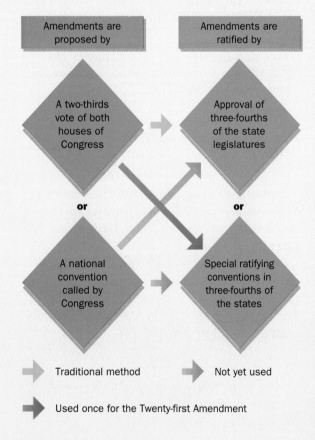

Amendments are proposed by

Amendments are ratified by

A two-thirds vote of both houses of Congress

Approval of three-fourths of the state legislatures

or

or

A national convention called by Congress

Special ratifying conventions in three-fourths of the states

Traditional method   Not yet used

Used once for the Twenty-first Amendment

National Supremacy

Clause 1. Federal Debts
This clause promised that all debts owed by Congress under the Articles of Confederation would be honored by the United States under the Constitution.

Clause 2. The Supreme Law of the Land
The Constitution and federal laws or treaties made under it are the highest laws of the nation. When federal laws conflict with state laws or constitutions, state judges must follow the federal laws.

Clause 3. Government Oaths of Office
All federal and all state officials must promise to support the Constitution. No federal official may be required to meet any religious standards in order to hold office.

Ratification

Nine states had to ratify the Constitution before it could go into effect. By June 21, 1788, the necessary nine states had approved the new framework. The Constitution went into effect on April 30, 1789.

Article 6.

Clause 1. All debts contracted and engagements entered into before the adoption of this Constitution shall be as valid against the United States under this Constitution as under the Confederation.

Clause 2. This Constitution and the laws of the United States which shall be made in pursuance thereof, and all treaties made, or which shall be made, under the authority of the United States, shall be the supreme law of the land; and the judges in every state shall be bound thereby, anything in the Constitution or laws of any state to the contrary notwithstanding.

Clause 3. The senators and representatives before-mentioned, and the members of the several state legislatures, and all executive and judicial officers, both of the United States and of the several states, shall be bound by oath or affirmation to support this Constitution; but no religious test shall ever be required as a qualification to any office or public trust under the United States.

Article 7.

The ratification of the conventions of nine states shall be sufficient for the establishment of this Constitution between the states so ratifying the same.

This 1788 cartoon shows the first nine states that ratified the Constitution as upright pillars supporting a new national government.

The Signers

Done in convention by the unanimous consent of the states present the seventeenth day of September in the year of our Lord one thousand seven hundred and eighty-seven, and of the independence of the United States of America the twelfth. In witness whereof we have hereunto subscribed our names,

George Washington—
President and deputy from Virginia

New Hampshire
John Langdon, Nicholas Gilman

Massachusetts
Nathaniel Gorham, Rufus King

Connecticut
William Samuel Johnson, Roger Sherman

New York
Alexander Hamilton

New Jersey
William Livingston, David Brearley, William Paterson, Jonathan Dayton

Pennsylvania
Benjamin Franklin, Thomas Mifflin, Robert Morris, George Clymer, Thomas FitzSimons, Jared Ingersoll, James Wilson, Gouverneur Morris

Delaware
George Read, Gunning Bedford, Jr., John Dickinson, Richard Bassett, Jacob Broom

Maryland
James McHenry, Dan of St. Thomas Jenifer, Daniel Carroll

Virginia
John Blair, James Madison, Jr.

North Carolina
William Blount, Richard Dobbs Spaight, Hugh Williamson

South Carolina
John Rutledge, Charles Cotesworth Pinckney, Charles Pinckney, Pierce Butler

Georgia
William Few, Abraham Baldwin

Signing the Constitution

On September 17, 1787, the delegates to the constitutional convention met one last time to approve their work. Many were still not satisfied with parts of the document. Knowing this, Benjamin Franklin made this final plea for their support:

"Mr. President

I confess that there are several parts of this Constitution which I do not at present approve, but I am not sure I shall never approve them. . . . I doubt, too, whether any other Convention we can obtain, may be able to make a better Constitution. . . . It therefore astonishes me, Sir, to find this system approaching so near to perfection as it does; and I think it will astonish our enemies.

Thus I consent, Sir, to this Constitution because I expect no better, and because I am not sure that it is not the best. The opinions I have had of its errors, I sacrifice to the public good. . . . I can not help expressing a wish that every member of the Convention who may still have objections to it would, with me . . . put his name to this instrument."

Of the 42 delegates present on that day, only 3 refused to sign the Constitution. Time has shown the wisdom of Franklin's words. The Constitution is not perfect. That it comes "so near to perfection as it does," however, continues to astonish those who study it today.

Amendments to the Constitution

The first ten amendments, called the Bill of Rights, were proposed as a group in 1789 and ratified in 1791. Other amendments were proposed and ratified one at a time. The dates in parentheses are the years of ratification.

Amendment 1 (1791)
Religious and Political Freedoms

Congress cannot establish an official religion or pass laws that limit freedom of worship. It cannot make laws that keep people from speaking or writing what they think. Nor can Congress stop people from holding peaceful meetings or from asking the government to correct a wrong.

Amendment 2 (1791)
The Right to Bear Arms

In order to maintain a state militia for their protection, citizens may own and use guns. Congress has outlawed the possession of certain firearms, however, such as sawed-off shotguns, machine guns, and assault rifles.

Amendment 3 (1791)
Quartering of Soldiers

In peacetime, citizens cannot be forced to provide a place in their homes for soldiers to stay. Even in wartime, this can only be done in a lawful manner.

Amendment 1

Congress shall make no law respecting an establishment of religion or prohibiting the free exercise thereof, or abridging the freedom of speech or of the press, or the right of the people peaceably to assemble and to petition the government for a redress of grievances.

Amendment 2

A well-regulated militia being necessary to the security of a free state, the right of the people to keep and bear arms shall not be infringed.

Amendment 3

No soldier shall, in time of peace, be quartered in any house without the consent of the owner, nor in time of war but in a manner to be prescribed by law.

The Bill of Rights

Amendments 1–10

1. Freedoms of religion, speech, press, assembly, and petition
2. Right to bear arms in a state militia
3. No quartering of soldiers without consent
4. Protection against unreasonable searches
5. Right to due process of law
6. Rights of the accused
7. Right to a jury trial in civil cases
8. Protection against unreasonable fines and cruel punishment
9. Other rights of the people and seizures
10. Powers reserved to the states and to the people

Amendment 4 (1791)
Search and Seizure

People are protected from arrests, searches of their homes, or seizures of their property without good reason. Authorities must get a warrant, or legal document signed by a judge, before making a search or an arrest. To obtain a warrant, they must explain to the judge why it is needed, where the search will take place, and who or what will be seized.

Amendment 5 (1791)
Due Process of Law

This amendment protects people from being abused by the legal system. It says:
- A person cannot be tried in a federal court for a serious crime without a formal indictment, or written accusation, by a grand jury. The grand jury decides whether there is enough evidence to make such an accusation.
- A person found not guilty of a federal crime cannot be tried again for the same offense in a federal court. This protection is known as the double jeopardy rule.
- Accused persons cannot be forced to say anything that might help convict them.
- The government cannot take away a person's life, liberty, or property without following correct legal procedures.
- The government cannot take away a person's property without paying a fair price for it. This power, called eminent domain, allows the government to acquire private property for public uses.

Amendment 4

The right of the people to be secure in their persons, houses, papers, and effects against unreasonable searches and seizures shall not be violated, and no warrants shall issue, but upon probable cause, supported by oath or affirmation, and particularly describing the place to be searched and the persons or things to be seized.

Amendment 5

No person shall be held to answer for a capital or otherwise infamous crime unless on a present-ment or indictment of a grand jury, except in cases arising in the land or naval forces, or in the militia, when in actual service in time of war or public danger; nor shall any person be subject for the same offense to be twice put in jeopardy of life or limb; nor shall be compelled in any criminal case to be a witness against himself, nor be deprived of life, liberty, or property without due process of law; nor shall private property be taken for public use without just compensation.

Your Legal Rights and Protections

Before you are arrested, you are protected from:
- search without a warrant
- arrest without a warrant or sufficient cause (such as being caught in the act of committing a crime)

After your arrest, you have a right to:
- a writ of habeas corpus if held without charges
- remain silent
- consult a lawyer
- be indicted only by grand jury that weighs the evidence against you

(Continued on next page)

Amendment 6 (1791)
Rights of the Accused

Accused people have the right to:
• a prompt, public trial by a local jury
• know the charges against them
• face and question witnesses against them
• call witnesses to speak in their favor
• be represented by a lawyer

Amendment 7 (1791)
Right to a Jury Trial

When disputes involving more than $20 are tried in federal courts, either side can insist on a jury trial. If both sides agree, they can choose not to have a jury. Once a jury reaches a decision, it cannot be overturned simply because a judge disagrees with the jury's findings.

Amendment 8 (1791)
Bails, Fines, and Punishments

Bails, fines, and punishments must not be unreasonably high, cruel, or unusual. Bail is money or property given to the court by an accused person to guarantee that he or she will show up for trial. Usually, the more serious the crime, the higher the bail.

Amendment 6

In all criminal prosecutions, the accused shall enjoy the right to a speedy and public trial by an impartial jury of the state and district wherein the crime shall have been committed, which district shall have been previously ascertained by law, and to be informed of the nature and cause of the accusation; to be confronted with the witnesses against him; to have compulsory process for obtaining witnesses in his favor, and to have the assistance of counsel for his defense.

Amendment 7

In suits at common law, where the value in controversy shall exceed twenty dollars, the right of trial by jury shall be preserved, and no fact tried by a jury shall be otherwise reexamined in any court of the United States than according to the rules of the common law.

Amendment 8

Excessive bail shall not be required, nor excessive fines imposed, nor cruel and unusual punishments inflicted.

After you are indicted, you have a right to:
• know the charges against you
• reasonable bail
• a speedy trial by jury

At your trial, you have the right to:
• question witnesses against you
• call your own witnesses
• refuse to answer questions that might harm your case
• be represented by a lawyer

If you are found innocent, you are protected from:
• being tried again in federal court for the same crime

If you are found guilty, you are protected from:
• excessive fines
• cruel or unusual punishments

Amendment 9 (1791)
Other Rights of the People

The listing of certain rights in the Constitution does not mean that these are the only rights the people have. Nor does it make those other rights less important.

Amendment 10 (1791)
Powers Reserved to the States or the People

The federal government is granted certain powers under the Constitution. All other powers, except those denied to the states, belong to the states or to the people.

Amendment 11 (1795)
Suits Against States

Citizens of other states or foreign countries cannot sue a state in federal court without its consent.

Amendment 12 (1804)
Election of the President

The Twelfth Amendment was passed after both candidates in the election of 1800 received an equal number of electoral votes. This occurred in part because electors voted only for President, leaving the second-place candidate to be Vice-President. (See page 283 for more details.) This amendment calls for electors to cast separate votes for President and Vice-President.

Amendment 9

The enumeration in the Constitution of certain rights shall not be construed to deny or disparage others retained by the people.

Amendment 10

The powers not delegated to the United States by the Constitution, nor prohibited by it to the states, are reserved to the states respectively, or to the people.

Amendment 11

The judicial power of the United States shall not be construed to extend to any suit in law or equity commenced or prosecuted against one of the United States by citizens of another state, or by citizens or subjects of any foreign state.

Amendment 12

The electors shall meet in their respective states and vote by ballot for President and Vice-President, one of whom at least shall not be an inhabitant of the same state with themselves; they shall name in their ballots the person voted for as President, and in distinct ballots the person voted for as Vice-President, and they shall make distinct lists of all persons voted for as President and of all persons voted for as Vice-President and of the number of votes for each, which lists they shall sign and certify and transmit sealed to the seat of government of the United States, directed to the president of the Senate.

The president of the Senate shall, in the presence of the Senate and House of Representatives, open all the certificates and the votes shall then be counted.

If no presidential candidate receives a majority of electoral votes, the House of Representatives chooses a President from the top three candidates. In the House, each state gets one vote.

The person having the greatest number of votes for President shall be the President, if such number be a majority of the whole number of electors appointed; and if no person have such majority, then from the persons having the highest numbers not exceeding three on the list of those voted for as President, the House of Representatives shall choose immediately, by ballot, the President. But in choosing the President the votes shall be taken by states, the representation from each state having one vote; a quorum for this purpose shall consist of a member or members from two thirds of the states, and a majority of all the states shall be necessary to a choice. And if the House of Representatives shall not choose a President whenever the right of choice shall devolve upon them, ~~before the fourth day of March next following,~~ then the Vice-President shall act as President, as in the case of the death or other constitutional disability of the President.

If no candidate for Vice-President receives a majority of electoral votes, the election goes to the Senate. Two-thirds of either the House or Senate must be present when voting for President or Vice-President.

The person having the greatest number of votes as Vice-President shall be the Vice-President, if such number be a majority of the whole number of electors appointed, and if no person have a majority, then from the two highest numbers on the list the Senate shall choose the Vice-President; a quorum for the purpose shall consist of two thirds of the whole number of senators, and a majority of the whole number shall be necessary to a choice. But no person constitutionally ineligible to the office of President shall be eligible to that of Vice-President of the United States.

Electing a President

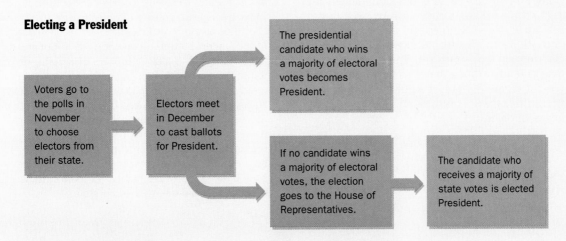

The process outlined in this chart was established by Amendment 12.

Amendment 13 (1865)
Abolition of Slavery

This amendment was the first of three passed shortly after the Civil War. It ended slavery forever in the United States and its territories. No one may be forced to work unless ordered to by a court as punishment for a crime.

Amendment 14 (1868)
Civil Rights in the States

The Fourteenth Amendment was designed to give full citizenship rights to former slaves.

Section 1. Citizenship

All people born or naturalized in this country are citizens of both the United States and the state in which they live. States cannot make laws that keep people from enjoying their rights as citizens. States may not deprive citizens of life, liberty, or property without due process of law. Nor may states deny citizens "equal protection of the laws" by discriminating against any one group.

Section 2. Representation and Voting

This section replaced the old rule, by which slaves were counted as three-fifths of a person in determining a state's representation in the Congress, with a new one. If a state denied the right to vote to some male citizens over age 21—except as punishment for crime or rebellion—those citizens would not be counted in determining representation. The purpose of this new rule was to force states to let former slaves vote. If a state did not, it would lose representation in Congress. This new rule, however, was never enforced.

Amendment 13

Section 1.

Neither slavery nor involuntary servitude, except as a punishment for crime whereof the party shall have been duly convicted, shall exist within the United States or any place subject to their jurisdiction.

Section 2.

Congress shall have power to enforce this article by appropriate legislation.

Amendment 14

Section 1.

All persons born or naturalized in the United States and subject to the jurisdiction thereof are citizens of the United States and of the state wherein they reside. No state shall make or enforce any law which shall abridge the privileges or immunities of citizens of the United States; nor shall any state deprive any person of life, liberty, or property without due process of law; nor deny to any person within its jurisdiction the equal protection of the laws.

Section 2.

Representatives shall be apportioned among the several states according to their respective numbers, counting the whole number of persons in each state, ~~excluding Indians not taxed.~~ But when the right to vote at any election for the choice of electors for President and Vice-President of the United States, representatives in Congress, the executive and judicial officers of a state, or the members of the legislature thereof is denied to any of the ~~male~~ inhabitants of such state, being ~~twenty-one years of age and~~ citizens of the United States, or in any way abridged, except for participation in rebellion or other crime, the basis of representation therein shall be reduced in the proportion which the number of such ~~male~~ citizens shall bear to the whole number of ~~male~~ citizens ~~twenty-one years of age~~ in such state.

Section 3. Punishing Rebel Leaders

Former state and federal officials who had supported the South in the Civil War were barred from voting or holding office again. In 1898, Congress removed this barrier.

Section 4. Legal and Illegal Debts

This section dealt with debts left over from the Civil War. The only legal debt was the federal government's war debt. No government, state or federal, was allowed to pay off rebel war debts. No payment was to be made to slaveholders for the loss of their slaves.

Amendment 15 (1870) Voting Rights

This amendment was intended to protect the voting rights of the freed slaves. It said that neither the United States nor any state can deny citizens the right to vote because of their race or color, or because they were once slaves. Despite this amendment, many states did find ways to keep African Americans from voting. You can read more about this in Chapter 19.

Section 3.

No person shall be a senator or representative in Congress, or elector of President and Vice-President, or hold any office, civil or military, under the United States, or under any state, who, having previously taken an oath as a member of Congress or as an officer of the United States or as a member of any state legislature or as an executive or judicial officer of any state to support the Constitution of the United States, shall have engaged in insurrection or rebellion against the same, or given aid or comfort to the enemies thereof. But Congress may by a vote of two thirds of each house remove such disability.

Section 4.

The validity of the public debt of the United States, authorized by law, including debts incurred for payment of pensions and bounties for services in suppressing insurrection or rebellion, shall not be questioned. But neither the United States nor any state shall assume or pay any debt or obligation incurred in aid of insurrection or rebellion against the United States or any claim for the loss or eman-cipation of any slave; but all such debts, obliga-tions, and claims shall be held illegal and void.

Section 5.

The Congress shall have power to enforce, by appropriate legislation, the provisions of this article.

Amendment 15

Section 1.

The right of citizens of the United States to vote shall not be denied or abridged by the United States or by any state on account of race, color, or previous condition of servitude.

Section 2.

The Congress shall have power to enforce this article by appropriate legislation.

Amendment 16 (1913)
Income Taxes

This amendment was passed to allow Congress to tax the incomes of individuals and businesses. The amendment was needed because Article 1, Section 9, Clause 4 says taxes levied on people must fall equally on the states based on their population. An income tax, however, taxes wealthy states more than poor states of equal population.

Amendment 17 (1913)
Direct Election Of Senators

Section 1. Regular Elections

The Constitution originally called for Senators to be elected by state legislatures. (See Article 1, Section 3, Clause 1.) This amendment gives the voters of each state the power to elect their Senators directly.

Section 2. Special Elections

If a senator dies or resigns before finishing his or her term, the governor must call a special election to fill that senate seat. The state legislature may let the governor appoint a temporary senator until such an election can be held.

Amendment 16

The Congress shall have power to lay and collect taxes on incomes, from whatever source derived, without apportionment among the several states, and without regard to any census or enumeration.

Amendment 17

Section 1.

The Senate of the United States shall be composed of two senators from each state, elected by the people thereof for six years; and each senator shall have one vote. The electors in each state shall have the qualifications requisite for electors of the most numerous branch of the state legislatures.

Section 2.

When vacancies happen in the representation of any state in the Senate, the executive authority of such state shall issue writs of election to fill such vacancies, provided that the legislature of any state may empower the executive thereof to make temporary appointments until the people fill the vacancies by election as the legislature may direct.

Section 3.

This amendment shall not be so construed as to affect the election or term of any senator chosen before it becomes valid as part of the Constitution.

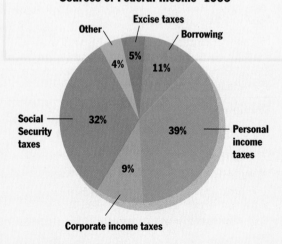

Sources of Federal Income 1995

Other — 4%
Excise taxes — 5%
Borrowing — 11%
Personal income taxes — 39%
Corporate income taxes — 9%
Social Security taxes — 32%

Source: Office of Management and Budget

The Federal Income Tax

The personal income tax is a progressive tax, which means that it taxes people with higher incomes at a higher rate than people with lower incomes. The theory is that the greater tax burden thus falls on the people who have the greatest ability to pay.

Amendment 18 (1919)
Prohibition of Alcohol

This amendment outlawed the making, selling, and transporting of alcoholic beverages in the United States and its territories. It was passed as part of a great reform effort to end the problems caused by the abuse of alcohol. The ban on alcohol, however, proved impossible to enforce. This amendment was repealed in 1933 by the Twenty-first Amendment.

Amendment 19 (1920)
Suffrage for Women

Until the passage of this amendment, most women in the United States were denied suffrage, or the right to vote. The Nineteenth Amendment says that women and men have an equal right to vote in both state and national elections.

Amendment 18

Section 1.

~~After one year from the ratification of this article the manufacture, sale, or transportation of intoxicating liquors within, the importation thereof into, or the exportation thereof from the United States and all territory subject to the jurisdiction thereof for beverage purposes is hereby prohibited.~~

Section 2.

~~The Congress and the several states shall have concurrent power to enforce this article by appropriate legislation.~~

Section 3.

~~This article shall be inoperative unless it shall have been ratified as an amendment to the Constitution by the legislatures of the several states, as provided in the Constitution, within seven years from the date of the submission hereof to the states by the Congress.~~

Amendment 19

Section 1.

The right of citizens of the United States to vote shall not be denied or abridged by the United States or by any state on account of sex.

Section 2.

Congress shall have power to enforce this article by appropriate legislation.

This 1919 cartoon, entitled "Almost Through the Dark Alley," criticizes senators who opposed woman suffrage. Many supporters believed that once the amendment was finally approved by Congress, ratification would follow quickly.

Amendment 20 (1933)
The "Lame-Duck" Amendment

A "lame duck" is someone who remains in office for a time after his or her replacement has been chosen. The outgoing official is considered "lame," or without much power and influence. The main purpose of Amendment 20 was to reduce the amount of time "lame ducks" remained in office after national elections.

Section 1. New Term Dates

In the past, a new President and Vice-President elected in November waited until March 3 to take office. Now their terms begin on January 20. In the past, new members of Congress waited 13 months between election and taking office. Now they are sworn in on January 3, which is just a few weeks after their election.

Section 2. Meetings of Congress

Congress must meet at least once a year, beginning on January 3. Congress may, however, choose a different starting day.

Section 3. Death of a President-elect

If a newly elected President dies before taking office, the Vice-President-elect will become President.

Amendment 20

Section 1.

The terms of the President and Vice-President shall end at noon on the 20th day of January, and the terms of senators and representatives at noon on the 3rd day of January, of the years in which such terms would have ended if this article had not been ratified; and the terms of their successors shall then begin.

Section 2.

The Congress shall assemble at least once in every year, and such meeting shall begin at noon on the 3rd day of January, unless they shall by law appoint a different day.

Section 3.

If, at the time fixed for the beginning of the term of the President, the President-elect shall have died, the Vice-President-elect shall become President. If a President shall not have been chosen before the time fixed for the beginning of his term, or if the President-elect shall have failed to qualify, then the Vice-President-elect shall act as President until a President shall have qualified; and the Congress may by law provide for the case wherein neither a President-elect nor a Vice-President-elect shall have qualified, declaring who shall then act as President, or the manner in which one who is to act shall be selected, and such person shall act accordingly until a President or Vice-President shall have qualified.

Section 4. Death of a Presidential Candidate in a House Election

Amendment 12 says that if no candidate for President wins a majority of votes in the electoral college, the House of Representatives must choose a President from the three leading candidates. If one of those candidate dies before the House votes, Congress can decide how to proceed.

Similarly, Congress can decide how to proceed in case a vice-presidential election goes to the Senate and one of the leading candidates dies before the Senate makes its choice.

Amendment 21 (1933) Repeal of Prohibition

Section 1. Repeal of Amendment 18

Amendment 18, which established a national prohibition of alcohol, is repealed.

Section 2. Protection for "Dry" States

Carrying alcohol into a "dry" state—a state that prohibits alcoholic beverages—is a federal crime.

Section 3. Ratification

Because this was such a controversial amendment, Congress insisted that it be ratified by state conventions elected by the people. This was the only time this system of ratification had been used since the Constitution itself was ratified.

Section 4.

The Congress may by law provide for the case of the death of any of the persons from whom the House of Representatives may choose a President whenever the right of choice shall have devolved upon them, and for the case of the death of any of the persons from whom the Senate may choose a Vice-President whenever the right of choice shall have devolved upon them.

Section 5.

Sections 1 and 2 shall take effect on the 15th day of October following the ratification of this article.

Section 6.

This article shall be inoperative unless it shall have been ratified as an amendment to the Constitution by the legislatures of three fourths of the several states within seven years from the date of its submission.

Amendment 21

Section 1.

The eighteenth article of amendment to the Constitution of the United States is hereby repealed.

Section 2.

The transportation or importation into any state, territory, or possession of the United States for delivery or use therein of intoxicating liquors, in violation of the laws thereof, is hereby prohibited.

Section 3.

This article shall be inoperative unless it shall have been ratified as an amendment to the Constitution by conventions in the several states, as provided in the Constitution, within seven years from the date of submission hereof to the states by the Congress.

Amendment 22 (1951)
Presidential Term Limits

This amendment made the long tradition that Presidents limit their stay in office to two terms part of the Constitution. It says that no person can be elected President more than twice. If a Vice-President or someone else succeeds to the presidency and serves for more than two years, that person is limited to one additional term.

Amendment 22

Section 1.

No person shall be elected to the office of the President more than twice, and no person who has held the office of President or acted as President for more than two years of a term to which some other person was elected President shall be elected to the office of the President more than once. But this article shall not apply to any person holding the office of President when this article was proposed by the Congress, and shall not prevent any person who may be holding the office of President or acting as President during the term within which this article becomes operative from holding the office of President or acting as President during the remainder of such term.

Section 2.

This article shall be inoperative unless it shall have been ratified as an amendment to the Constitution by the legislatures of three fourths of the several states within seven years from the day of its submission to the states by the Congress.

The Presidential Two-Term Tradition

1796
George Washington declines to run for a third term, beginning the two-term tradition.

1808
President Thomas Jefferson follows Washington's example by retiring after two terms.

1880
President Ulysses S. Grant runs for a third term but loses the Republican nomination on the thirty-sixth convention ballot.

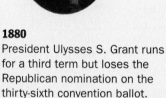

1940
Democrat Franklin Roosevelt wins for a third and then a fourth term. Republicans begin pushing for a two-term amendment, which is ratified in 1951.

1985
After winning a second term, Ronald Reagan says: "I see no reason why the Twenty-second Amendment shouldn't be repealed."

Amendment 23 (1961)
Voting in the District of Columbia

This amendment allowed residents of the District of Columbia to vote in Presidential elections. The District is given the same number of electors it would be entitled to if it were a state. But that number cannot be greater than the number of electors from the state with the smallest population.

At the time this amendment was ratified, more than 781,000 people lived in Washington, D.C. Capital residents paid taxes like all other citizens, but did not have the right to vote in national elections.

Amendment 24 (1964)
Abolition of Poll Taxes

A poll tax is a tax people have to pay in order to vote. For decades, poll taxes were used by some southern states to discourage poor people, especially poor black people, from voting. The Twenty-fourth Amendment says that neither the United States nor any state can require a citizen to pay a poll tax in order to vote in national elections.

Amendment 23

Section 1.

The district constituting the seat of government of the United States shall appoint in such manner as the Congress may direct: A number of electors of President and Vice-President equal to the whole number of senators and representatives in Congress to which the district would be entitled if it were a state, but in no event more than the least populous state; they shall be in addition to those appointed by the states, but they shall be considered, for the purposes of the election of President and Vice-President, to be electors appointed by a state; and they shall meet in the district and perform such duties as provided by the twelfth article of amendment.

Section 2.

The Congress shall have power to enforce this article by appropriate legislation.

Amendment 24

Section 1.

The right of citizens of the United States to vote in any primary or other election for President or Vice-President, for electors for President or Vice-President, or for senator or representative in Congress, shall not be denied or abridged by the United States or any state by reason of failure to pay any poll tax or other tax.

Section 2.

The Congress shall have power to enforce this article by appropriate legislation.

Why Did It Take an Amendment to Outlaw Poll Taxes?

Congress can outlaw many things by passing a bill into law. In the case of poll taxes, however, Congress faced a constitutional barrier. The Constitution gave the states authority over how to hold federal elections. So, if poll taxes were to be forbidden, an amendment specifically outlawing them had to be proposed and ratified.

Amendment 25 (1967)
Presidential Disability and Succession

Section 1. Replacing the President

If the President dies, resigns, or is removed from office, the Vice-President becomes President.

Section 2. Replacing the Vice-President

The President appoints a new Vice-President if that office becomes empty. That appointment must be approved by both houses of Congress.

Section 3. Temporary Replacement with the President's Consent

If the President notifies Congress in writing that he or she is unable to perform official duties, the Vice-President takes over as Acting President. The President may return to office after notifying Congress that he or she is again able to serve.

Section 4. Temporary Replacement Without the President's Consent

If a President is disabled and cannot or will not notify Congress, the Vice-President and a majority of the cabinet (or some other group named by Congress) can send such notice. The Vice-President will then become Acting President.

The Vice-President will step down when the President sends Congress written notice of renewed ability to serve. If the Vice-President and others disagree, they must notify Congress within four days.

Amendment 25

Section 1.

In case of the removal of the President from office or of his death or resignation, the Vice-President shall become President.

Section 2.

Whenever there is a vacancy in the office of the Vice-President, the President shall nominate a Vice-President who shall take office upon confirmation by a majority vote of both houses of Congress.

Section 3.

Whenever the President transmits to the president pro tempore of the Senate and the speaker of the House of Representatives his written declaration that he is unable to discharge the powers and duties of his office, and until he transmits to them a written declaration to the contrary, such powers and duties shall be discharged by the Vice-President as Acting President.

Section 4.

Whenever the Vice-President and a majority of either the principal officers of the executive departments or of such other body as Congress may by law provide, transmit to the president pro tempore of the Senate and the speaker of the House of Representatives their written declaration that the President is unable to discharge the powers and duties of his office, the Vice-President shall immediately assume the powers and duties of the office as Acting President.

Thereafter, when the President transmits to the president pro tempore of the Senate and the speaker of the House of Representatives his written declaration that no inability exists, he shall resume the powers and duties of his office unless the Vice-President and a majority of either the principal officers of the executive department or of such other body as Congress may by law provide, transmit within four days to the president pro tempore of the Senate and the speaker of the House of Representatives their written declaration that the President is unable to discharge the powers and duties of his office.

Congress must meet within 48 hours to discuss whether the President is still disabled. They have 21 days to decide the issue. If two thirds or more of both houses vote that the President is disabled, the Vice-President remains in office as Acting President. If they do not, the President resumes official duties.

Amendment 26 (1971)
Eighteen-Year-Old Vote

Neither the United States nor any state can deny the vote to citizens of age 18 or older because of their age. The effect of this amendment was to lower the voting age in most state elections from 21 to 18.

Amendment 27 (1992)
Congressional Salaries

If members of Congress vote to change their own salaries, that change cannot go into effect until after the next Congressional election. This change gives voters a chance to speak out on pay raises.

Thereupon Congress shall decide the issue, assembling within forty-eight hours for that purpose if not in session. If the Congress, within twenty-one days after receipt of the latter written declaration, or, if Congress is not in session, within twenty-one days after Congress is required to assemble, determines by two-thirds vote of both houses that the President is unable to discharge the powers and duties of his office, the Vice-President shall continue to discharge the same as Acting President; otherwise, the President shall resume the powers and duties of his office.

Amendment 26

Section 1.

The right of citizens of the United States, who are eighteen years of age or older, to vote shall not be denied or abridged by the United States or by any state on account of age.

Section 2.

The Congress shall have power to enforce this article by appropriate legislation.

Amendment 27

No law varying the compensation for the services of the senators and representatives shall take effect until an election of representatives shall have intervened.

The 26th Amendment passed mainly because many people believed that if 18-year-olds were old enough to fight for their country, they were old enough to vote.

Glossary

The Glossary defines terms that are important in the understanding of United States history. The page number at the end of the definition refers to the page in the text on which the term is first defined.

Pronunciation Key

In the text, words that are difficult to pronounce are followed by a respelling in parentheses. The respelling helps the reader pronounce the word. For example, Iroquoian (see page 28) has been respelled as IR-uh-KWOY-uhn. A hyphen separates the syllables. Syllables in large capital letters are stressed the most; syllables in small capital letters are stressed in a weaker tone.

The pronunciation key appears below. Letters used in the respelling of words are listed on the left side of each column. On the right side are commonly used words that show the pronunciation.

Pronounce				
a	as in	hat	*j*	jet
ah		father	*ng*	ring
ar		tar	*o*	frog
ay		say	*ō*	no
ayr		air	*oo*	soon
e, eh		hen	*or*	for
ee		bee	*ow*	plow
eer		deer	*oy*	boy
er		her	*sh*	she
ew		new	*th*	think
g		go	*u, uh*	sun
i, ih		him	*z*	zebra
ī		kite	*zh*	measure

A

abolition putting an end to slavery (page 441)

aliens foreigners who are not yet citizens of the country in which they live (page 281)

allies helpers in times of trouble (page 182)

amendments changes, as in changes to the Constitution (page 248)

anarchism the idea that all forms of government are bad and should be done away with (page 736)

annex to take control of a territory and add it to a country (page 384)

anthropologists scientists who study human beings and how they live in groups (page 1)

anti-Semitism hatred and persecution of Jews (page 616)

appeasement giving in to another nation's demands just to keep peace (page 789)

arbitration using a third party to settle a dispute (page 604)

archaeologists anthropologists who search for clues to how human beings lived in the past (page 1)

armistice a truce (page 713)

arms race a competition between countries for more and better weapons (page 786)

artifacts objects made by human work (page 1)

assembly line a factory system in which the product moves from worker to worker, each of whom performs one task (page 749)

assimilate to be absorbed into the main cultural group (page 619)

B

bias a one-sided or slanted view (page 309)

bicameral a legislature made up of two houses (page 129)

bill of rights a list of the rights and freedoms guaranteed to the people (page 234)

black codes laws passed by white southern politicians after the Civil War that limited the rights and opportunities of African Americans (page 529)

blockade a shutting off of a place by ships or troops to prevent supplies from reaching it (page 185)

bond a piece of paper given in exchange for money with the promise to repay the loan plus interest by a certain date (page 269)

boycott refuse to buy (page 189)

C

cabinet the department heads of the executive branch of government who advise the President and help carry out the nation's laws (page 267)

cape a piece of land sticking out into the sea (page 63)

capital money used to produce goods (page 595)

carpetbaggers northerners, including teachers, ministers, businesspeople, and former Union soldiers, who moved to the South after the Civil War (page 532)

cash crops crops that are raised to be sold for a profit (page 150)

casualties soldiers killed, wounded, captured, or missing (page 500)

caucus a private meeting of political party leaders (page 350)

cede to give up terrritory (page 185)

checks and balances the system by which each branch of government can check, or limit, the power of the other two (page 252)

civilization a society in which a high level of art, technology, and government exists (page 14)

civil rights the rights guaranteed to all Americans by the Constitution (page 850)

civil service the body of government workers who are hired rather than elected (page 648)

claim something that someone says is true (page 423)

closed shop a workplace in which only union members can be hired (page 844)

Cold War the struggle for power between Communist and non-Communist countries (page 818)

collective bargaining the process by which the representatives of a union and a business discuss and reach agreement about wages and working conditions (page 604)

colony settlement made by a group of people in a distant place that remains under the control of their home country (page 53)

communism a system in which property is owned by society as a whole instead of by individuals (page 735)

confederation an alliance of independent states (page 234)

conquistadors conquerors (page 94)

conservation protecting natural resources and using them wisely (page 665)

consolidation combining several companies into one large company (page 591)

constitution plan of government (page 234)

constitutional permitted by the Constitution (page 270)

containment the policy of blocking Communist expansion (page 819)

corporation a type of business that raises money by selling shares of stock to investors (page 595)

corruption when public office is used for illegal purposes (page 535)

credibility believability (page 392)

credit a system in which a buyer takes home a product and then makes monthly payments until it is paid for (page 750)

culture the way of life of a group of people, including arts, beliefs, inventions, traditions, and language (page 13)

customs duties charges on foreign imports (page 188)

D

deficit the amount by which the government's spending is greater than its income (page 878)

depression a long, sharp decline in economic activity (page 238)

détente a relaxing of tensions between nations (page 832)

dictator a person with complete control of a government (page 787)

diplomacy conducting relations with other nations (page 689)

direct primary an election, open to all members of a party, to choose candidates to run for office (page 660)

discrimination unfair treatment of a group of people compared with another group (page 417)

diversity variety (page 25)

dividends part of the profits of a corporation earned by stockholders (page 595)

draft system that requires men to serve in the military (page 508)

due process of law following the legal steps in a court of law (page 248)

durable goods goods meant to last, like machinery and locomotives (page 763)

E

emancipation freeing of slaves (page 440)

embargo to halt trade with one or more other nations (page 302)

ethnic neighborhoods areas where people who share the same languages and culture live (page 617)

evidence information given to support a claim (page 423)

excise tax a tax on the production or sale of a certain product (page 273)

executive branch the branch of government that carries out the laws (page 242)

expansionists people who believe that their country's prosperity depends on enlarging its territory (page 376)

expedition a journey organized for a definite purpose (page 63)

exports goods sent out of one country to sell in another (page 123)

extermination total destruction (page 563)

F

Fall Line the eastern edge of the Piedmont Plateau, where the land drops sharply (page 127)

fascism a political system that appeals to racism and nationalism and is ruled by a dictator and a single political party (page 787)

federalism the division of power between the states and national government (page 251)

feudalism a system of government in western Europe in which a vassal promised to serve a lord in exchange for a grant of land (page 50)

finance to supply the money for something, such as a project (page 63)

financial panic widespread fear caused by a sudden downturn in prices or change in property values (page 332)

flowchart a diagram that uses words and arrows to show steps in a process (page 600)

freedmen former slaves, both women and men, who lived in the South during the Reconstruction period (page 526)

free enterprise the economic system in which businesses are free to compete without government rules (page 592)

G

generalization a broad statement that is meant to sum up the specific characteristics of something (page 337)

glaciers vast slow-moving masses of ice (page 10)

grandfather clause statements in southern voting laws which said that such laws did not apply to anyone whose father or grandfather could have voted before January 1, 1867 (page 540)

guerrillas soldiers who are not part of the regular army and who make hit-and-run attacks (page 222)

H

habeas corpus right that protects people from being held in prison unlawfully (page 492)

historical interpretation a historian's opinion about an event or person (page 446)

homesteaders people who claimed land under the Homestead Act (page 575)

hypothesis a theory to explain an event (page 510)

I

immediate cause something that directly brings about an event (page 285)

immediate effect an effect that occurs right away (page 285)

immigration the movement of people from one country to make their home in another (page 328)

impeach to accuse the President of wrongdoing and bring him to trial (page 531)

imperialism the policy of taking control of governments and resources of other countries in order to build an empire (page 675)

imports products brought in from another country to be sold (page 150)

impressed when someone is forced to serve in another nation's navy (page 276)

inauguration the ceremony that installs a new President (page 266)

income tax tax on money people earn from work or investments (page 509)

indentured servants people who signed a contract agreeing to work a certain number of years without pay for the person who paid their passage to England's American colonies (page 124)

Industrial Revolution the shift of production from hand tools to machines and from homes to factories (page 319)

infectious diseases illnesses that can be passed from one person to another (page 68)

initiative the process by which citizens can propose new laws (page 660)

injunction a court order (page 606)

integration the process of ending segregation (page 853)

Internet a web of computer networks linked through telephone lines (page 887)

interstate commerce business between states (page 592)

invest to use your money to help a business get started or grow, with the hope that you will earn a profit (page 120)

irrigation supplying land with water by use of dams, ditches, and channels (page 19)

isolationism a policy of staying out of foreign affairs (page 786)

isolines lines on maps that mark off areas that are the same in some way (page 413)

J

Jim Crow laws segregation laws passed in the South after Reconstruction (page 540)

joint-stock company a business that raised money by selling shares, called stock, to investors (page 122)

judicial branch a system of courts to interpret the meaning of laws (page 242)

judicial review a court's power to decide whether or not an act of Congress is constitutional (page 293)

L

league a group of people with a common purpose (page 110)

legacy something handed down from past generations (page 71)

legislative branch the branch of government that makes the laws (page 242)

legislature a group of people chosen to make the laws (page 124)

leisure free time (page 629)

libel printing statements that damage a person's good name (page 164)

literacy the ability to read and write (page 148)

long-range cause a cause that may take months or even years to bring about an effect (page 285)

long-range effect an effect that occurs months or even years after the cause (page 285)

loose construction the view that the government has broader powers than the ones listed in the Constitution (page 270)

Loyalists colonists who did not want independence from Great Britain (page 213)

M

martial law rule by the army instead of by the usual government officials (page 492)

mass production using machines to make large quantities of goods faster and cheaper than they could be made by hand (page 320)

memoirs a person's written remembrances of the events of his or her life (page 460)

mercantilism the economic idea that a nation becomes strong by filling its treasury with gold and silver (page 102)

mercenaries soldiers who fight for money for a country other than their own (page 214)

migration movement of people from one region to another (page 10)

militia citizens trained to fight in an emergency (page 163)

minting the government process of printing bills or making coins to use as money (page 237)

minutemen militia volunteers in New England at the beginning of the War of Independence, so called because they were ready to fight on short notice (page 206)

monopoly complete control (page 194)

mudslinging making wild charges and lies about a candidate (page 352)

N

nationalism a strong feeling of pride in one's nation (page 308)

nativism belief that immigrants threaten traditional American culture and institutions (page 421)

nativists people who believe in nativism (page 421)

navigation the science of getting ships from place to place (page 46)

neutral when a nation does not take either side in a conflict (page 273)

nomads people with no permanent home who move in search of food (page 11)

nullify to declare that a certain law will not be enforced (page 282)

O

open range thousands of miles of unfenced grassland used for grazing (page 572)

opinion an expression of a feeling or thought that cannot be proved or disproved (page 210)

oral history historical data in the form of personal recollections or stories passed on by word of mouth (page 341)

P

pacifists people who are against war under any circumstance (page 711)

parallel time lines two or more time lines that cover the same time span but different sets of events (page 31)

Patriots strong supporters of American independence (page 213)

pension retirement income (page 770)

persecution a series of injurious actions—for example, attacking, imprisoning, torturing, or killing—carried out against members of a group for their beliefs (page 108)

plantation a large estate where a single crop that requires a large labor force is grown for profit (page 70)

plateau a large expanse of high, flat land (page 24)

platform a statement of beliefs by a political party (page 476)

point of view the background or position from which a person observes something. Background includes such factors as age, culture, social position, and beliefs (page 249)

political machine the organization of a political party that granted favors in return for votes (page 625)

political parties organized groups of people who have similar ideas about government (page 279)

poll tax a fee enacted by state governments in the South that charged citizens for the right to vote and that successfully prevented black southerners from voting (page 540)

popular sovereignty when voters in a territory were given the right to decide whether to allow slavery or not (page 468)

population density the average number of people in a certain-sized area (page 271)

prairie eastern part of the Great Plains, where the grasses grow tall (page 575)

precipitation moisture from rain and snow (page 413)

prejudice a bad opinion of people based only on such factors as their religion, nationality, or appearance (page 154)

primary source an artifact or record from someone who has experienced the event described (page 193)

proclamation official announcement (page 187)

profiteers people who demand unfair profits for their goods (page 219)

Prohibition the banning of the manufacture, transport, and sale of liquor (page 744)

propaganda the spreading of ideas that help one cause and hurt another (page 706)

proprietary colonies colonies in which the owners, known as proprietors, organized the colonies, controlled the land, and appointed governors (page 133)

protective tariff tax placed on imports to discourage the purchase of foreign goods (page 321)

protectorate a nation protected and controlled by another nation (page 685)

R

racism the belief that one race of people is superior to another (page 156)

radiocarbon dating method of dating the remains of ancient plants, animals, and human beings by measuring the amount of radiocarbon remaining in them (page 2)

ratify to approve, as in to approve a plan of government or an amendment (page 245)

rationing limiting the amount of scarce goods that people can buy (page 795)

rebates refunds of part of shipping costs (page 591)

recall a process for removing an elected official from office before the end of his or her term (page 660)

Reconstruction the task of bringing Confederate states back into the Union (page 529)

referendum the process by which citizens can approve or reject a law passed by a state legislature (page 660)

regulate make rules for (page 592)

relevant information information that applies, relates, or is connected to a particular topic (page 746)

reparations payments for war damages (page 717)

repeal to do away with a law (page 189)

representatives people who are chosen to speak and act in government for their fellow citizens (page 124)

republic a government run by elected representatives of the people (page 234)

reservations areas of land set aside for Indian nations (page 564)

revenue income (page 188)

revival a renewed interest in religion; a stirring up of religious faith (page 155)

royal colony a colony in which the monarch appointed the governor and the council of advisors (page 125)

S

scalawags white southerners who joined the Republican Party during Reconstruction (page 532)

secede to break away from, as in a state breaking away from the United States (page 357)

secondary source an artifact or record made by someone who did not experience the event described (page 193)

sectionalism devotion to the interests of one's own section of the country over those of the nation as a whole (page 334)

sedition actions or speech that might encourage people to rebel against the government (page 281)

segregation the forced separation of races in public places and housing (page 540)

self-determination the right of the people of a certain nation to decide how they want to be governed (page 715)

separation of powers the division of government power into legislative, executive, and judicial branches (page 252)

settlement house a community center that provided services—from English-language classes to hot meals—to the poor (page 626)

sharecropping a system where tenant farmers pay a part of their crop as rent, rather than using cash (page 539)

slave codes laws that tightened owners' control over slaves (page 417)

socialism the belief that government, rather than individuals, should own a nation's major industries (page 607)

social reform the effort to make society better and more fair for everyone (page 433)

sod the thick mat of roots and earth beneath the prairie grasses (page 575)

sovereignty the power of a government to control its affairs (page 357)

speculators people who buy something at a risk, hoping to make money if the price for it rises (page 269)

spheres of influence areas in one nation in which other nations claim exclusive rights to trade and invest (page 687)

spoils system the practice of rewarding political supporters with government jobs (page 356)

stalemate deadlock (page 703)

statement of fact a word, phrase, or sentence that can be either proved or disproved (page 210)

states' rights the theory that states may nullify federal laws (page 282)

statistical table an orderly arrangement of facts in the form of numbers in rows and columns (page 139)

stereotype an oversimplified image of a person, group, or idea (page 369)

stockholders investors who own stock in corporations (page 595)

strait a narrow waterway connecting two larger bodies of water (page 74)

strategic arms weapons designed to strike at an enemy's military bases and industrial centers (page 833)

strict construction the view that government has the power to do only what is written in the Constitution (page 270)

strike employees refuse to work, hoping to force their employer to meet their demands (page 419)

subsistence farming raising just enough food to survive on, with perhaps a little surplus to sell or trade (page 146)

suburbs communities on the outskirts of cities (page 742)

suffrage the right to vote (page 351)

suffragists people who supported the right of women to vote (page 661)

synthesize putting together information to create a written, oral, or visual product (page 865)

T

tariffs taxes on imports (page 267)

temperance moderation in drinking habits (page 437)

tenant farmers people who pay rent for the use of land on which they grow crops (page 539)

tenements apartment houses where large families shared one or two rooms, often without heat or water (page 623)

terrain all the physical features of an area of land (page 100)

Tidewater waterways in the Atlantic Coastal Plain affected by the tide (page 150)

time line a chart that shows when, and in what order, events occurred in the past (page 31)

totalitarian state a government with total control over the lives of its citizens (page 787)

total war war against armies and also against a people's resources and their will to fight (page 514)

trade union group of people who try to improve wages and working conditions in their trade, or craft (page 419)

transcontinental railroad a rail line extending across a continent (page 473)

tribute payment of money or goods made by one people or nation to another for peace or protection or some other agreement (page 16)

trust a form of business combination in which a board of trustees, or managers, controlled the member corporations (page 598)

tyranny the harsh use of power (page 162)

U

urbanization the movement of people into cities (page 622)

utopias perfect societies (page 437)

V

vaudeville a stage show that combined songs, dance, opera, and comedy (page 630)

W

writs of assistance general search warrants (page 188)

Index

The purpose of the Index is to help you quickly locate information on any topic in this book. The Index includes references not only to the text but also to special features, illustrations, and maps. *Italicized* page numbers preceded by an *f, i,* or *m* indicate a feature, an illustration, or a map. **Boldface** page numbers indicate pages on which glossary terms first appear.

A

Abilene, Kansas, 572
abolition, 441. *See also* antislavery movement
Abraham Lincoln Brigade, 789, *f789*
Adams, Abigail, *i264;* advising the President, 280, *i281;* and elections, 279, *f284;* on Jay's Treaty uproar, 276; marriage partnership of, *f264–265,* 272, 280; on unity of states, 268, 282
Adams, John, *i192;* Boston Massacre and, 192; conflicts with Jefferson, 279–280; at Continental Congress, 197, 208; and elections, 279–280, 283, *f284;* as Federalist, 279–280, *f280;* marriage partnership of, *f264–265,* 272, 280; Olive Branch Petition and, 211; presidency of, 279–281, *f282,* 283, 292–293, R24; and protests against British, 191, 192, 195; as Vice-President, 248, 266, 276; and War of Independence, 213
Adams, John Quincy, *i351;* and birth of National Republicans, 352; and elections, *i346,* 350, 352, *m353;* and Panama Congress, *f351;* presidency of, 350–351, R24; as Secretary of State, 328–329, 331, *f331;* and slavery, *f335–336,* 445; and Treaty of Ghent, 307, 328
Adams, Samuel, 191, 192, *i192,* 194, 197

Adams-Onís Treaty, 329, *m330*
Addams, Jane, 626, *f644–645, i644,* 646, 653, 657, 658, 662, *f667,* 684
Adenas, 22
adobe, 20
advertising, 750
AEF. *See* American Expeditionary Force
Afghanistan, 834
AFL. *See* American Federation of Labor
Africa: colonization by freed slaves, 440, 543, 740; cultures, 41–42, *f42, f43, f415;* Europeans dividing up, *f542;* farming developed in, *f13;* piracy and, 300, *i301, m301;* slavery and, *see* slavery; trade, *f37,* 38–41, *m39, i40. See also specific countries and cultures*
African Americans: in American Revolution, 192, 213, *i213,* 214, *f225;* in antislavery movement, 414, 418, *f422,* 440, 442–443; artists, *f454, f481;* black codes, 529–530; civil rights movement, 850, 851, 853–858, *i854–857, f855–856;* after Civil War, 526–529, *i528,* 532, 538; before Civil War, 417–418, *f417;* in Civil War, *f497,* 504, 505, *i505,* 507, 508, 514, *f516, f524–525;* in colonial America, *i142,* 157, 159–160; as cowboys, 573; creating an African American culture, 41–42, 159–160, *f160, f415;* culture in 1920s, *i733,* 740–741; education and, 448, 528–529, *i528,* 530, 539, 543, *i543,* 853–854, *i854;* farmers' alliance of, 652; and Fifteenth Amendment, 533–534, 540; and Fourteenth Amendment, 530, 542; and gold rush, 398; in government, 534, *i535, m540,* 851, 852, 858; as homesteaders, 577–578, *i577;* immigration to Africa of, 440, 543, 740; immigration to Canada of, 328, *f417;* as indentured servants, 157; Jim Crow laws, *i523,* 540–542, *f541, i542,* 853;

Juneteenth, *f529;* and land ownership, 528–529, 531, 539; literature of, 452, *f732–733,* 740, *f756–757;* migration of, 543, 711, *f719,* 740–741; as millionaires, 590; NAACP, 543, 662, 735, 774, 853, 854; New Deal and, 774; racism and, 157, 160, *f166,* 417–418, *f497,* 505–506, 535, 536, *f544,* 796; Progressives and, 662; religion of, 418, 433; Republican Party and, 532, 533, 646, 774; segregation and, 540–543, *f541, i542,* 662, *f842–843,* 853–858; in Seminole War, 363; and social class, 102; in Spanish-American War, 682; in Spanish Civil War, *f789;* tenant farming and, 538–539, *i539;* and Thirteenth Amendment, 527; violence against, 535, 536, *i536, f541,* 662, 734–735, 737–738, *i737,* 853–855, 856–858; voting rights of, 351, *f418,* 529, 530, 531, 532, 533–534, 534, 539–540, 735, 853, 856–857, 860; in War of 1812, 307; and women's movement, *f430, f431,* 450, 662, 858; in work force, 711, *f719,* 796; and World War I, 708, *i708,* 711; and World War II, *f784–785,* 796, 800, 802. *See also* Reconstruction; slavery
Africanus, Leo, 41
After the Dancing Days (Rostkowski), *f722–723*
aging, 770, 850, 852, 884
Agnew, Spiro, 863
Agricultural Adjustment Act (1933), 766
agriculture. *See* farming
Aguinaldo, Emilio, 683, 684, *i684, f686*
AIDS, 878
AIM. *See* American Indian Movement
airplanes, *f704,* 705, 742, 802
air quality, 860, 878, 885
Alabama, 333, 482, *f534,* R19
Alabama (ship), 499
Alamo, *i373,* 382–383, *i382*

Photo Acknowledgments

Front Matter: ii Terry Ashe*; **xxiv** J. L. Atlan/Sygma

P1 David Muench/Tony Stone Images; **P4L** David Muench; **P4R** James Randklev/Tony Stone Images; **P5TL** Larry Lefever/Grant Heilman Photography; **P5TR** Robert Llewellyn; **P5B** Bob Burch/Bruce Coleman Inc.; **P6R** *On the Trail* by Theodore Gentilz. The Witte Museum, San Antonio, Texas; **P6L** California Section, California State Library, Photograph Collection; **P7TL** *Comanche Village, Women Dressing Robes and Drying Meat* by George Catlin 1834–35. National Museum of American Art, Smithsonian Institution. Gift of Mrs. Joseph Harrison, Jr. Photo: Art Resource, NY; **P7C** *Preparation for WAR to Defend Commerce* by William and Thomas Birch. Prints Division, The New York Public Library. Astor, Lenox and Tilden Foundations; **P7B** *A Cotton Plantation on the Mississippi* (detail) by Nathaniel Currier & James Merritt Ives. Library of Congress; **P7TR** *Man Looking at Steel Mills, Homestead, PA.* California Museum of Photography, University of California, Riverside; **P8** Terry Ashe* **1B** Makah Cultural and Research Center, Neah Bay, WA. Photo by Ruth & Louis Kirk; **1T** Cheryl Fenton*; **2T** Makah Cultural and Research Center, Neah Bay, WA. Photo by Ruth & Louis Kirk; **2B** Makah Cultural and Research Center, Neah Bay, WA. Photo by Ruth & Louis Kirk; **3** Cheryl Fenton*

Unit 1: 4–5 Jerry Jacka Photography, 1996

Chapter 1: 6L The Bettmann Archive; **6R** *A Ballgame Player.* Erich Lessing/Art Resource, NY; **7BCL** Peter French/Bruce Coleman Inc.; **7BCR** *God King Quetzalcoatl.* Boltin Picture Library; **7BR** Boltin Picture Library; **7BL** *Nursing Mother Effigy Bottle,* AD 1200–1400. St. Louis Museum of Science and Natural History, Missouri. Photo by Dirk Bakker; **7T** George Gerster/Comstock; **8L** Victor Krantz; **8R** Victor Krantz/National Museum of American History; **12** Tom D. Dillehay; **14** Malcolm S. Kirk/Peter Arnold, Inc.; **15** *Mayan Seacoast Village,* a watercolor copy by Ann Axtell Morris of Mural in Temple of the Warriors, Chichén Itzá, Mexico. 800–1000 A.D. Peabody Museum—Harvard University. Photo by Hillel Burger; **16** *Codice Magliabechiano: Aztec game of "Patolli."* Scala/Art Resource, NY; **17** Kenneth Garett/Woodfin Camp, Inc.; **18** Janis E. Burger/Bruce Coleman Inc.; **19** Mimbres black-on-white bowls. Courtesy of Dennis & Janis Lyon. Jerry Jacka Photography, 1996; **20** Dave Wilhelm/The Stock Market; **21** *Emergence of the Clowns* by Roxanne Swentzell, 1988. The Heard Museum, Phoenix; **22** *Panorama of the Monumental Grandeur of the Mississippi Valley,* 1850. Detail: *Dr. Dickeson Excavating a Mound,* by John J. Egan. The Saint Louis Art Museum. Purchase: Eliza McMillan Fund; **24T** Jack Couffer/Bruce Coleman Inc.; **24C** Rod Planck/Tom Stack & Associates; **24B** Woven Bag. White Dog Cave, Arizona, Basket Maker III, 450–700/750 A.D. Peabody Museum—Harvard University. Photo by Hillel Burger; **31** Cheryl Fenton*

Chapter 2: 34L Michael Holford; **34R** The Bettmann Archive; **35T** Photo from Louise Levathes' *When China Ruled the Seas* (1994); **35BL** The Bettmann Archive; **35BC** *Catalan Atlas* (detail) 1375 by Abraham Cresques. Robert Harding Picture Library; **35BR** *Arte de Navegae* (detail) by Pedro de Medinco, 1545. Rare Book Room & Manuscript Division, New York Public Library; **36** *Henry the Navigator* from 16th c. Portuguese manuscript. Michael Holford; **37** "Cantino" map of the world (detail). Scala/Art Resource, NY; **40** Wolfgang Kaehler; **42L** Werner Forman/Art Resource, NY; **42C** Michael Holford; **42R** Werner Forman/Art Resource, NY; **43** Cheryl Fenton*; **44** B.N. Ms. 2810 (detail). Photo by Bibliothèque Nationale de France, Paris; **46** Ming Dynasty vase (detail). Giraudon/Art Resource, NY; **47** *Tribute Giraffe with Attendant,* 1403–1424 by Shentu (1357–1434). Philadelphia Museum of Art. Given by John Dorrance; **49** Michael Holford; **52** The Bettmann Archive; **53** Werner Forman/Art Resource, NY; **55** Giraudon/Art Resource, NY

Chapter 3: 58R *Capsicum pepper* (detail) by William Blake, 1796. The John Carter Brown Library at Brown University; **58L** *Santa María in Palos de la Frontera.* Robert Frerck/Odyssey/Chicago; **59T** *Mapa Universal de 1507* (detail). Library of Congress, Geography & Maps Division; **59BC** Globe by Martin Behaim. Germanisches National Museum, Nürnberg; **59BR** *The Last Voyage of Henry Hudson* (detail) by John Collier. The Tate Gallery, London/Art Resource, NY; **59BL** Francisco Erize/Bruce Coleman Inc.; **60** *Portrait of Christopher Columbus.* Scala/Art Resource, NY; **61** Jon Levy/Gamma-Liaison; **63TL** Ed Degginger/Bruce Coleman Inc.; **63BL** André Cornellier/Canadian Parks Service; **63R** Canadian Parks Service; **64** *Vasco da Gama* from a Portuguese manuscript, c. 1558. The Pierpont Morgan Library/Art Resource, NY; **67** Adam Woolfitt/Woodfin Camp & Associates; **69** #4051 *Codex Florentino.* Department of Library Services, American Museum of Natural History; **70** Cheryl Fenton*; **72T** *Buffalo Chase with Bows and Lances,* 1832–33 by George Catlin. National Museum of American Art, Washington, D.C./Art Resource, NY; **72B** Coffrin's Old West Gallery; **74** *Portrait of Magellan.* Museo Maritimo, Sevilla. Photo "ARXIU MAS"; **76L** *Eskimo man* by John White, © British Museum; **76R** *Eskimo Woman & Child* by John White, © British Museum; **79** Cheryl Fenton*; **82** © British Museum; **83** Adam Woolfitt/Woodfin Camp & Associates; **85L** Cheryl Fenton*; **85R** Library of Congress; **86L** Cheryl Fenton*; **86–87** Library of Congress

Unit 2: 88–89 © New York State Historical Association, Cooperstown

Chapter 4: 90R The Oakland Museum History Department; **90L** *Map of Florida from "Cosmographic Universelle,"* 1555, by Guillaume Le Testu. Giraudon/Art Resource, NY; **91T** Laurie Platt Winfrey, Inc.; **91BL** Jim Schwabel/Southern Stock; **91BR** Detail from George Catlin's *La Salle Erecting a*

Cross and Taking Possession of the Land, March 25, 1682. Paul Mellon Collection, © Board of Trustees, National Gallery of Art; **91BC** The Bettmann Archive; **92** Ampliaciones y Reproducciones Mas (Arxiu Mas); **93** Ampliaciones y Reproducciones Mas (Arxiu Mas); **94** Laurie Platt Winfrey, Inc.; **95** The Newberry Library; **97** Laurie Platt Winfrey, Inc.; **100** Bibliothèque Nationale de France, Paris; **102** Miguel Cabrera: *Depiction of Racial Mixtures: "1 De español y d India, Mestisa."* Copyright © by The Metropolitan Museum of Art; **103** Carved, painted & gilded ceiling of Santa Clara, Tunja, Columbia. Photo © Wim Swaan; **106** Wendell Metzen/ Southern Stock; **107T** Cheryl Fenton*; **107B** Department of Library Services, American Museum of Natural History. Neg. #329340; **110** The New York Public Library; Astor, Lenox and Tilden Foundations; **112** Laurie Platt Winfrey, Inc., by kind permission of the Marquess of Tavistock, Woburn Abbey

Chapter 5: 116R Culver Pictures; **116L** Colonial Williamsburg Foundation; **117BC** Pie Plate, 1786. Attributed to Johannes Neis, American, Pennsylvania German. Philadelphia Museum of Art. Given by John T. Morris; **117T** The Bettmann Archive; **117BR** The Bettmann Archive; **117BL** American Antiquarian Society, Worcester, MA; **118** *Pocahontas.* Anonymous. English school, after 1616 engraving by Simon van de Passe. National Portrait Gallery, Smithsonian Institution/Art Resource, NY; **119** The Bettmann Archive; **121** *The English Conspirators, including Guy Hawkes.* Anonymous, 17th century. Art Resource, NY; **123** National Park Service, Colonial National Historical Park; **125** Cary Wolinsky/Stock, Boston; **127T** Bob Burch/Bruce Coleman Inc.; **127B** *Baltimore in 1752* by John Moale. Maryland Historical Society, Baltimore; **129** *Hooker and Company Journeying Through the Wilderness from Plymouth to Hartford in 1636* by Frederic Edwin Church. © Wadsworth Atheneum, Hartford; **132** Shelburne Museum, Shelburne, Vermont. Photograph by Ken Burris; **136** Rare Books and Manuscripts Division/The New York Public Library, Astor, Lenox and Tilden Foundations; **137** *The Peaceable Kingdom* by Edward Hicks. Abby Aldrich Rockefeller Folk Art Center, Williamsburg, VA; **139** Cheryl Fenton*

Chapter 6: 142R Embroidery of Harvard Hall. Attributed to Mary Leverett Denison Rogers. The Massachusetts Historical Society; **142L** American Antiquarian Society, Worcester, MA; **143T** Late 19th century handmade 5-string banjo, North Carolina. Aldo Tutino/Art Resource, NY; **143BL** *George Whitefield* by John Wollaston. The National Portrait Gallery, London; **143BR** Rare Books and Manuscripts Division/The New York Public Library, Astor, Lenox and Tilden Foundations; **143BC** Oliver Pelton engraving illustrating *Poor Richard's Almanack.* Franklin Collection, Yale University Library; **144** *Portrait of Benjamin Franklin* by Robert Feke. Harvard University Portrait Collection. Bequest of Dr. John Collins Warren, 1856; **145** Ed Bohon/The Stock Market; **147BL** The

Newberry Library; **147BR** Library of Congress; **147T** Library of Congress; **148** *The School Room* by Jonathan Jennings, 1850s. Private collection; **149** Applique quilt (detail) by Sarah Furman Warner. From the collections of Henry Ford Museum & Greenfield Village. Accession #6341.1; **152** *The Rapalje Children* by John Durand. Collection of The New-York Historical Society, New York City; **153** *Mrs. Hausman killing a hog* (detail) by Lewis Miller. The Historical Society of York County, PA; **157L** From the collection of Gilcrease Museum, Tulsa, Oklahoma; **157R** *Indian Sugar Camp,* drawing by Captain S. Eastman. Collection of The New-York Historical Society, New York City; **158BL** National Maritime Museum, London; **158TL** The British Library; **158R** Collection of The New-York Historical Society, New York City; **159** *Overseer Doing His Duty* by Benjamin Henry Latrobe. Maryland Historical Society, Baltimore; **160** The Research Libraries/The New York Public Library; **163** The Bettmann Archive; **165** *Charleston Harbor* by Bishop Roberts. Colonial Williamsburg Foundation; **167** Cheryl Fenton*; **170** Free Library of Philadelphia; **171** The Bettmann Archive; **173** National Archives; **174** Victor Krantz/National Archives; **175** Cheryl Fenton*

Unit 3: 176–177 Yale University Art Gallery, Trumball Collection

Chapter 7: 178R Colonial Williamsburg Foundation; **178L** Library of Congress, Geography & Map Division. Photo by Breton Littlehales, National Geographic Society; **179BL** *Samuel Adams* (detail), ca. 1772 by John Singleton Copley. Deposited by the City of Boston, Museum of Fine Arts, Boston; **179BC** American Antiquarian Society; **179TL** Culver Pictures; **179TR** The Massachusetts Historical Society; **179BR** Library of Congress; **180** *George Washington in the Uniform of a Colonel in The Virginia Militia* by Charles Willson Peale. Washington/Curtis/Lee Collection, Washington and Lee University, Lexington, VA; **181** Culver Pictures; **184** *A View of the Taking of Quebec,* 1759. Royal Ontario Museum, Toronto; **189R** Massachusetts Historical Society; **189L** Culver Pictures; **190T** Nina Berman/SIPA Press; **190L** Massachusetts Historical Society; **191** Massachusetts Historical Society; **192TL** *Paul Revere* (detail) by John Singleton Copley. Gift of Joseph W., William B., and Edward H. R. Revere. The Museum of Fine Arts, Boston; **192B** *John Adams* by Charles Willson Peale. Independence National Historical Park Collection; **192TR** *Samuel Adams* (detail) by John Singleton Copley. Deposited by the City of Boston/ Museum of Fine Arts, Boston; **193** Cheryl Fenton*; **195** Library of Congress; **196** *The Bostonians Paying the Excise Man.* John Carter Brown Library at Brown University

Chapter 8: 202L Robert Weinreb/Bruce Coleman Inc.; **202R** The Bettmann Archive; **203T** Anne S. K. Brown Military Collection/Brown University Library; **203BR** The National Archives; **203BL** The Bettmann Archive; **203BC** The

Bettmann Archive; **204B** *Pulling Down the Statue of George III at Bowling Green* (detail) by William Walcutt. Lafayette College Art Collection, Easton, Pennsylvania; **204T** The Bettmann Archive; **205** The Bettmann Archive; **206** *The Retreat from Concord.* John Carter Brown Library at Brown University; **208** *The Battle of Bunker Hill* by Howard Pyle. Delaware Art Museum, Howard Pyle Collection; **210** Cheryl Fenton*; **212** Michael Anderson/Folio Inc.; **213** Virginia Historical Society; **214** *Johnson Hall* by E. L. Henry. Collection of the Albany Institute of History and Art; **215** The Bettmann Archive; **217** *Washington Crossing the Delaware* by Emanuel Gottlieb Leutze, 1851. Oil on canvas, 149 x 225 in. (378.5 x 647.7 cm.) The Metropolitan Museum of Art, Gift of John S. Kennedy, 1897; **219** Robert Llewellyn; **220** *The Retreat through the Jerseys* by Howard Pyle. Delaware Art Museum, Howard Pyle Collection; **222** *Marion Crossing the Pedee* (detail) by William T. Ranney, oil on canvas, 1850, Amon Carter Museum, Fort Worth, Texas, #1983.126; **228** West Point Museum; **229** *The Battle of Lexington April 19, 1775.* Plate I by Amos Doolittle. The Connecticut Historical Society, Hartford, Connecticut

Chapter 9: 230R National Archives; **231BC** Independence National Historical Park Collection; **231BR** *Banner of the Society of Pewterers,* 1787. Collection of The New-York Historical Society, New York City; **231T** Independence National Historical Park Collection; **231BL** *Daniel Shays* (detail). National Portrait Gallery/Smithsonian Institution; **232** *James Madison* by Charles Willson Peale. Library of Congress; **233** Reverend Jonathan Fisher, American, 1768–1847, *A North-West Prospect of Nassau Hall with a Front View of the President's House in New Jersey* (detail), 1807. Oil on canvas, 66.6 x 150.8 cm., Princeton University. Presented by alumni headed by A.E. Vondermuhll; **237T** The American Numismatic Society; **237B** Cheryl Fenton*; **238** *Canton Factories,* ca. 1780/Peabody Essex Museum, Salem, Mass.; **239R** The Granger Collection, New York; **239L** Sam Abell, © National Geographic Society; **240** Larry Lefever/Grant Heilman Photography; **242** *2nd Street North of Market* by William Birch. Historical Society of Pennsylvania; **243** The Granger Collection, New York; **244** The Huntington Library, San Marino, California; **247** The Granger Collection, New York; **249** Cheryl Fenton*; **251** Jean Louis Atlan/Sygma; **257B** Cheryl Fenton*; **257T** *Young Omahaw, War Eagle, Little Missouri, and Pawnees* by Charles Bird King. National Museum of American Art/Art Resource, NY; **258B** Cheryl Fenton*; **258L** Lithograph, *Hoowaunneka [Little Elk], Winnebago,* by Charles Bird King, 1841. Peabody Museum, Harvard University. © President and Fellows of Harvard College. Photograph by Hillel Burger; **258R** Painting, *Hoowaunneka [Little Elk], Winnebago,* by Charles Bird King, 1824. Peabody Museum, Harvard University. © President and Fellows of Harvard College. Photograph by Hillel Burger; **259** Cheryl Fenton*

Unit 4: 260–261 Chicago Historical Society

Chapter 10: 262R Collection of The New-York Historical Society, New York City; **262L** *Portrait of George Washington (1732–1799), 1st President of the United States,* by Rembrandt Peale. National Portrait Gallery, Smithsonian Institution/Art Resource, NY; **263BL** The Bettmann Archive; **263BC** Collection of The New-York Historical Society, New York City; **263BR** Library of Congress; **263T** Cheryl Fenton*; **264** *Abigail Adams* by Benjamin Blyth. Massachusetts Historical Society; **265** Bruce M. Wellman/Stock, Boston; **267** The Bettmann Archive; **268** Photri Inc.; **269R** Alex S. MacLean/Landslides, Boston, MA.; **269L** Library of Congress; **271** The Bettmann Archive; **273** Bibliothèque Nationale de France, Paris; **274** *Washington reviewing the Western Army at Fort Cumberland, Maryland* by Kemmelmeyer. The Metropolitan Museum of Art, Gift of Edgar William and Bernice Chrysler Garbisch, 1963. (63.201.2); **275(B inset)** *Little Turtle (Michikinikwa), Chief of Miami tribe,* by Ralph Dille after a painting by Stuart in 1797. Chicago Historical Society; **275T** *King Kamehameha I* (?1758–1819), unknown artist. Bishop Museum, Hawaii; **275(B background)** *Treaty of Fort Greenville* (detail). National Archives; **276** New York State Historical Association, Cooperstown, N.Y.; **278** Collection of The New-York Historical Society, New York City; **280L** *Portrait of Alexander Hamilton,* by John Trumbull, 1806. National Portrait Gallery, Smithsonian Institution/Art Resource, NY; **280R** *Thomas Jefferson* by Rembrandt Peale. Copyrighted by the White House Historical Association; photograph by National Geographic Society; **281R** Larry Downing/Sygma; **281C** J. L. Atlan/Sygma; **281L** *Portrait traditionally said to be that of Abigail Adams,* artist unidentified. New York State Historical Association, Cooperstown, N.Y.; **283** Cheryl Fenton*; **285** Cheryl Fenton*

Chapter 11: 288R Smithsonian Institution, photo #83.3049; **288L** *Portrait of John Marshall* by John B. Martin. Collection of the Supreme Court of the United States; **289BR** Smithsonian Institution, photo #83.7221; **289T** *Battle of New Orleans* (detail). The Hermitage: The Home of Andrew Jackson, Nashville, Tennessee; **289BL** Culver Pictures; **289BC** Collection of The New-York Historical Society, New York City; **290** Field Museum of Natural History (Neg#A93851c), Chicago; **291** *An encampment of Potawatomis at Crooked Creek* by George Winter. Tippecanoe County Historical Association, Lafayette, Indiana. Gift of Mrs. Cable G. Bell; **293TL** *Thomas Jefferson* by Rembrandt Peale. Collection of The New-York Historical Society, New York City; **293TR** Obelisk clock designed by Thomas Jefferson and executed by Louis Chartrot. Private Collection; photo courtesy of Monticello/Thomas Jefferson Memorial Foundation, Inc.; **293B** Monticello/Thomas Jefferson Memorial Foundation, Inc.; **293TC** Sketch of obelisk clock designed by Thomas

Jefferson. College of William and Mary, Earl Gregg Swem Library; **296** The Bettmann Archive; **297L** Oregon Historical Society. Negative number OrHi 38090; **297R** Oregon Historical Society. Negative number OrHi 38091; **298** *Landscape with a Lake* by Washington Allston. Gift of Mrs. Maxim Karolik for the M. and M. Karolik Collection of American Paintings, 1815–1865. Courtesy, Museum of Fine Arts, Boston; **299C** Chase Swift/Westlight; 299B James Randklev/Tony Stone Images; **299T** Larry Lee/Westlight; **301** The Naval Historical Foundation; **302** Prints Division/The New York Public Library. Astor, Lenox and Tilden Foundations; **303** *The Open Door, known as The Prophet, brother of Tecumseh,* by George Catlin. National Museum of American Art, Washington, D.C./Art Resource, NY; **304** The Bettmann Archive; **305** Beverley R. Robinson Collection, United States Naval Academy Museum; **309** Cheryl Fenton*; **312** Independence National Historical Park Collection; **313B** Independence National Historical Park Collection; **313T** Leaf of an evergreen shrub, from William Clark's journal. Missouri Historical Society, St. Louis

Chapter 12: 314L Slater Mill Historic Site, Pawtucket, Rhode Island; **314R** National Museum of American History/ Smithsonian Institution, photo #73-11287; **315BL** *The Clermont on the Hudson.* I. N. Phelps Stokes Collection, Miriam and Ira D. Wallach Division of Arts, Prints and Photographs/The New York Public Library, Astor, Lenox and Tilden Foundations; **315BR** *Portrait of James Monroe* after an oil painting by John Vanderlyn, by James Herring. National Portrait Gallery, Smithsonian Institution/Art Resource, NY; **315T** Library of Congress; **315BC** Library of Congress; **316** Print Collection, Miriam and Ira D. Wallach Division of Art, Prints and Photographs/The New York Public Library, Astor, Lenox and Tilden Foundations; **317** Barfoot/Darton: *Progress of Cotton, No. 5* (detail). Yale University Art Gallery. The Mabel Brady Garvan Collection; **318** The Bettmann Archive; **319** The New York Public Library, Astor, Lenox and Tilden Foundations; **321** *View of Lowell, Massachusetts.* I. N. Phelps Stokes Collection, Miriam and Ira D. Wallach Division of Art, Prints and Photographs/The New York Public Library, Astor, Lenox and Tilden Foundations; **326** Library of Congress; **329** *Panel of the Independence,* detail of center with Father Hidalgo. Mural by Juan O'Gorman. Schalkwijk/Art Resource, NY; **330L** *Portrait of Simón Bolívar,* 1859, by Arturo Michelena. Giraudon/Art Resource, NY; **330R** Culver Pictures; **333** Samuel Finley B. Morse, *The Old House of Representatives,* 1822, oil on canvas, 86 1/2 x 130 3/4 in. (219.71 x 332.11 cm). In the Collection of the Corcoran Gallery of Art. Museum Purchase, Gallery Fund; **335** Joel T. Hart, *Portrait Bust of Henry Clay,* n.d., marble. In the Collection of the Corcoran Gallery of Art. Museum Purchase; **337** Cheryl Fenton*; **341B** Cheryl Fenton*; **341T** Terry Ashe*; **342** Cheryl Fenton*; **343** *Group at Drayton's*

Plantation (Hilton Head, South Carolina) by Henry P. Moore. Moore Collection, New Hampshire Historical Society, Concord

Unit 5: 344–345 Bequest of Sarah Carr Upton, National Museum of American Art, Smithsonian Institution, Washington, D.C./Art Resource, NY

Chapter 13: 346L The Smithsonian Institution, National Numismatic Collection, Washington, D.C.; **346R** *Figurehead of Andrew Jackson,* carved for the frigate "Constitution." Museum of the City of New York, 52.11. Gift of the Seawanhaka Corinthian Yacht Club; **347BL** *Daniel Webster.* Hood Museum of Art, Dartmouth College, Hanover, New Hampshire; Gift of the artists; **347BCL** Stock Montage, Inc.; **347BC** *Endless Trail* by Jerome Tiger. The Philbrook Museum of Art, Tulsa, OK; **347BR** Political History Dept./Smithsonian Institution; **347T** *Chief Vann House.* Courtesy, the Georgia Department of Natural Resources; **348** *Andrew Jackson* (detail), ca. 1812, by Charles Willson Peale. Collections of The Grand Lodge of Pennsylvania on deposit with The Masonic Library and Museum of Pennsylvania; **349** The Bettmann Archive; **351** *Portrait of John Quincy Adams* (detail) by Pieter van Huffel. National Portrait Gallery, Smithsonian Institution, Washington, D.C./Art Resource, NY; **352** *Stump Speaking* (detail) by George Caleb Bingham, 1854. From the Art Collection of The Boatmen's National Bank of St. Louis; **354** The Granger Collection, New York; **355** Illustrations from O. Turner, *Pioneer History of the Holland Land Purchase of Western New York* (1850); **357** Library of Congress; **358** *Webster's Reply to Hayne* by G. P. A. Healy. Courtesy Cultural Affairs, Boston City Hall; **360** *Bull Dance, Mandan O-Kee-Pa Ceremony,* 1832, by George Catlin. National Museum of American Art, gift of Mrs. Joseph Harrison, Jr., Smithsonian Institution, Washington, D.C./Art Resource, NY; **362** *The Trail of Tears* by Robert Lindneux. Woolaroc Museum, Bartlesville, Oklahoma; **363** *Osceola, the Black Drink, a warrior of great distinction* (detail), 1838, by George Catlin. National Museum of American Art, Smithsonian Institution, Washington, D.C./Art Resource, NY; **365** Collection of The New-York Historical Society, New York City; **367L** The Granger Collection, New York; **367R** Stanley King Collection; **369T** Cheryl Fenton*; **369B** The Granger Collection, New York

Chapter 14: 372L The New York Public Library, Rare Book Division, Astor, Lenox & Tilden Foundations; **372R** *Louis— Rocky Mountain Trapper* by Alfred Jacob Miller. Buffalo Bill Historical Center, Cody, WY. Gift of the Coe Foundation; **373T** *Bulls. Feb. 1820* (detail) by Titian Ramsay Peale, American Philosophical Society, Philadelphia; **373C** *Pioneer Women,* 1927 by Bryant Baker. Gift of Bryant Baker, National Museum of American Art, Smithsonian Institution, Washington, D.C./ Art Resource, NY; **373R** National Archives; **373L** US Postal Service; **374R** *Jessie Benton Frémont* by T. Buchanan Read. The Southwest Museum, Los Angeles. Photo #CT 18; **374L**

Portrait of John Charles Frémont, 1856 by Bass Otis. On loan at the National Portrait Gallery, Smithsonian Institution, Washington, D.C./Art Resource, NY; **375** Library of Congress; **377BR** Colorado Historical Society; **377L** *Trapping Beaver* by Alfred Jacob Miller. The Walters Art Gallery, Baltimore; **377TL** *Portrait of Manuel Lisa,* 1818. Missouri Historical Society, St. Louis; **378** *The Trapper's Bride* by Alfred Jacob Miller. Joslyn Art Museum, Omaha, Nebraska (JAM. 1963.612); **381** *East Side Main Plaza, San Antonio, Texas* by William G. M. Samuel. Courtesy of Bexar County and The Witte Museum, San Antonio, Texas; **382L** David Muench; **382R** Collection of the Star of the Republic Museum, Washington, Texas; **385** *Horse Race* (detail), n.d. by Ernest Narjot. Collection of The Oakland Museum of California, gift of Mrs. Leon Bocqueraz, photo by M. Lee Fatherree; **389** *Advice on the Prairie,* 1853 by William Tyler Ranney. Buffalo Bill Historical Center, Cody, WY. Gift of Mrs J. Maxwell Moran; **390** *Handcart Pioneers,* 1900 by C. C. A. Christensen. Museum of Church History and Art, Salt Lake City, Utah; **391** Nevada Historical Society; **392** Cheryl Fenton*; **393** *American Progress* (lithograph) by John Gast. Library of Congress; **396** *Rancho San Miguelito, California,* 1852 by José Rafael. RG 49, Records of the Bureau of Land Management, California Private Land Claims, vol. 1, National Archives; **397** California Section, California State Library, Photograph Collection; **399** David Muench

Chapter 15: 402L *Nat Turner* by William H. Johnson. National Museum of American Art, Washington, D.C. Gift of the Harmon Foundation/Art Resource, NY; **402R** Culver Pictures; **403T** Paul Rezendes/New England Stock Photo; **403BL** National Maritime Museum, London; **403BC** Smithsonian Institution, negative #27979; **403BR** The Bettmann Archive; **404** J.R. Eyerman/Life Magazine, © TIME Inc.; **405** Culver Pictures; **407T** Culver Pictures; **407C** Culver Pictures; **407B** New York Public Library, Astor, Lenox and Tilden Foundations; **411** The Bettmann Archive; **412** *Oakland House and Race Course, Louisville* by Robert Brammer and Augustus A. Von Smith. J. B. Speed Art Museum, Louisville, Kentucky; **413** Rob Crandall/The Image Works; **415** National Museum of American History/Smithsonian Institution, photo #75-2984; **416** Library of Congress; **418L** *Mrs. John Jones (Mary Richardson)* by Aaron E. Darling. Chicago Historical Society (ICHI–18097); **418R** *Mr. John Jones* by Aaron E. Darling. Chicago Historical Society (ICHI–10896); **420** Library of Congress; **423** Cheryl Fenton*; **426** Culver Pictures; **427** *Belair plantation quarter, Plaquemines Parish, Louisiana.* Georges Francois Mugnier (ca. 1857–1938). Gold-chloride print, ca. 1884–1888. Louisiana State Museum, New Orleans

Chapter 16: 428L *The Preacher,* artist unidentified, Abby Aldrich Rockefeller Folk Art Center, Williamsburg, VA; **428R** The New York Public Library, Astor, Lenox and Tilden Foundations; **429T** The Bettmann Archive; **429BL** The Bettmann Archive; **429BC** Culver Pictures; **429BR** Culver Pictures; **430** Sophia Smith Collection, Smith College; **431** Library of Congress; **434** *The Country School* by Winslow Homer. The Saint Louis Art Museum, purchase; **435** Flip Schulke/Black Star; **436** *Dorothea Lynde Dix, 1802–1887.* Daguerreotype. National Portrait Gallery, Smithsonian Institution/Art Resource, NY; **437** Library of Congress; **438L** Jim Schwabel/New England Stock Photo; **438R** *Shakers near Lebanon.* Color lithograph by Currier and Ives. Scala/Art Resource, NY; **439** *Central Park Summer—Looking South,* lithograph by John Bachmann. Museum of the City of New York. The J. Clarence Davies Collection (29.100.1944); **441TL** Moorland-Spingarn Collection, Founder's Library, Howard University, Neg. #146; **441TR** The Historical Society of Pennsylvania; **441B** The Bettmann Archive; **443** From the collection of Madison County Historical Society, Oneida, New York; **445** The Bettmann Archive; **446** Cheryl Fenton*; **447** Daguerreotype of the Emerson School by Southwath and Hawes. The Metropolitan Museum of Art, Gift of I. N. Phelps Stokes, Edward S. Hawes, Alice Mary Hawes, Marion Augusta Hawes, 1937. (37.14.22); **448R** *The Bloomer Costume.* Publisher: Currier and Ives. Museum of the City of New York. The Harry T. Peters Collection; **448L** Culver Pictures; **449L** Library of Congress; **449R** The Bettmann Archive; **450** Cheryl Fenton*; **451B** Hazel Hankin/Stock, Boston; **451T** Library of Congress; **453L** Library of Congress; **453C** By permission of the Trustees of Amherst College; **453BR** Culver Pictures; **453TR** *Herman Melville,* by Eaton. By permission of the Houghton Library, Harvard University; **454** *Landscape with Rainbow* by Robert Duncanson. National Museum of American Art, Washington, D.C./Art Resource, NY; **459** Courtesy Fred Veil; **460** Library of Congress; **461** Cheryl Fenton*

Unit 6: 462–463 Chicago Historical Society

Chapter 17: 464R Department of Special Collections and University Archives, Stanford University Library; **464L** The Bettmann Archive; **465BR** The Museum of the Confederacy, Richmond, Virginia, photo by Katherine Wetzel; **465T** Library of Congress; **465BL** The Bettmann Archive; **465BC** Boston Athenaeum; **466** Meserve-Kunhardt Collection; **467** *The Railsplitter,* 1860. Chicago Historical Society. Gift of Maibelle Heikes Justice; **469** Collection of The New-York Historical Society, New York City; **470** The Granger Collection, New York; **471TL** Collection of The New-York Historical Society, New York City; **471TR** The Bettmann Archive; **471BL** Meserve-Kunhardt Collection; **471BR** Chicago Historical Society; **473R** Schlesinger Library, Radcliffe College; **473** Smithsonian Institution; **475** Kansas State Historical Society, Topeka, Kansas; **476** The Granger Collection, New York; **476T** Cheryl Fenton*; **477B** Cheryl Fenton*; **478** *Dred Scott,* 1881, by Louis Schultze. Missouri Historical Society; **479R** Ira Wyman/Sygma; **479L** *Lincoln-Douglas Debate at*

Charleston, Illinois (detail) by Robert Marshall Root. Henry Horner Lincoln Collection, Illinois State Historical Library; **481** *John Brown Going to His Hanging*, 1942 by Horace Pippin. The Pennsylvania Academy of the Fine Arts, Philadelphia. John Lambert Fund; **485** Robert Llewellyn

Chapter 18: 488L The Bettmann Archive; **488R** Library of Congress; **489T** Private Collection; **489BL** *Forever Free*, 1933 by Sargent Claude Johnson. Wood with lacquer on cloth, 36 x 11 1/2 x 9 1/2 in. San Francisco Museum of Modern Art. Gift of Mrs. E. D. Lederman; **489BC** *First Day of Gettysburg* (detail) by James Walker. The West Point Museum, United States Military Academy, West Point, New York. Photo by Karen Willis; **489BR** Library of Congress; **490** National Archives; **491** The Bettmann Archive; **494T** From *Echoes of Glory: Arms & Equipment of the Union*. Collection of Chris Nelson, photo by Larry Scherer. © 1991 Time-Life Books Inc.; **494BL** From *Echoes of Glory: Arms & Equipment of the Union*. Collection of Chris Nelson, photo by Larry Scherer. © 1991 Time-Life Books Inc.; **494BR** From *Echoes of Glory: Arms & Equipment of the Union*. Collection of Chris Nelson, photo by Larry Scherer. © 1991 Time-Life Books Inc.; **494BC** From *Echoes of Glory: Arms & Equipment of the Union*. Courtesy of The Museum of the Confederacy, Richmond, Virginia, photo by Larry Scherer. © 1991 Time-Life Books Inc.; **494C** The Museum of the Confederacy, Richmond, Virginia. Photo by Katherine Wetzel; **495** Library of Congress; **496** *Sounding Reveille,* 1865 by Winslow Homer. Oil on canvas, 13 1/4 x 19 1/2 in. Private Collection, photo courtesy of Gerald Peters Gallery; **499** *An August Morning with Farragut: The Battle of Mobile Bay, August 5, 1864,* 1883 by William Heysham Overend. Wadsworth Atheneum, Hartford. Gift of the citizens of Hartford by Subscription, May 24, 1886; **502L** Meserve-Kunhardt Collection; **502T** National Archives; **502CR** The Bettmann Archive; **503** Library of Congress; **505** Library of Congress; **507TL** The Granger Collection, New York; **507B** Culver Pictures; **507TR** Eleanor S. Brockenbrough Library/The Museum of the Confederacy, Richmond, Virginia; **508** Library of Congress; **509** National Archives; **510** Cheryl Fenton*; **511** *Stonewall Jackson at the Battle of Winchester, VA.* by L. M. D. Guillaume. R. W. Norton Art Gallery, Shreveport, Louisiana; **512** *First Day of Gettysburg* by James Walker. The West Point Museum, United States Military Academy, West Point, New York. Photo by Karen Willis; **514** Sam Abell, © National Geographic Society; **515** *Surrender at Appomattox* by Tom Lovell. © National Geographic Society; **517** David Muench; **520** Stephen Frisch*; **521** Culver Pictures

Chapter 19: 522L The Bettmann Archive; **522R** Library of Congress; **523BR** *William Edward B. Du Bois* by W. Reiss. The Bettmann Archive; **523T** The Newberry Library; **523BC** Library of Congress; **524** Photographs and Prints Division, Schomburg Center for Research in Black Culture/The New York Public Library, Astor, Lenox and Tilden Foundations; **525** Cook Collection/Valentine Museum, Richmond, Virginia; **527** Culver Pictures; **527** Cook Collection/Valentine Museum, Richmond, Virginia; **530** Culver Pictures; **531** Culver Pictures; **533** David Butow/Black Star; **535** Library of Congress; **536** Rutherford B. Hayes Presidential Center; **537** Cheryl Fenton*; **539** Brown Brothers; **541** *Aspects of Negro Life: From Slavery through Reconstruction* by Aaron Douglas. Photo by Manu Sassoonian. Arts and Artifacts Division. Schomburg Center for Research in Black Culture. The New York Public Library; Astor, Lenox and Tilden Foundations; **542** Elliott Erwitt/Magnum Photos, Inc.; **543** Library of Congress; **545** Old Court House Museum, Vicksburg, MS; **549** James Woodcock/Billings Gazette; **550** NAA/Smithsonian Institution; **551** Scott Rutherford, © National Geographic Society

Unit 7: 552–553 Library of Congress, Geography and Maps Division

Chapter 20: 554L John Deere; **554R** Union Pacific Museum Collection; **555BR** Rod Planck/Tony Stone Images; **555T** John Livzey/Tony Stone Images; **555BL** Negatives/Transparencies #3273(2), courtesy Department of Library Services, American Museum of Natural History; **555BC** Courtesy Frederic Remington Art Museum, Ogdensburg, NY; **556** Photo by Hutchins and Lanney, 1892. NAA/Smithsonian Institution; **557** Smithsonian Institution; **558** *Herd of Bison, Near Lake Jessie* by John Mix Stanley © Smithsonian Books, photo by Ed Castle; **559** National Archives. Photography by PhotoAssist; **561** (inset) José Fuste Raga/The Stock Market; **561** Photo by W. G. Chamberlain, 1860. Denver Public Library, Western History Department; **562** Union Pacific Museum Collection; **565** Oklahoma Historical Society; **567** Library of Congress; **569C** National Museum of the American Indian, Smithsonian Institution; **569R** National Museum of the American Indian, Smithsonian Institution; **569L** Library of Congress; **571** National Archives. Photography by PhotoAssist; **573** The Bancroft Library, University of California, Berkeley; **574** Library of Congress; **575** Corbis-Bettmann; **576** Library of Congress; **577** Solomon D. Butcher Collection, Nebraska State Historical Society; **579** Western History Collections, University of Oklahoma Library; **582** California State Railroad Museum; **583R** Kentucky Historical Society; **583L** California State Railroad Museum

Chapter 21: 584L Corbis-Bettmann; **584R** Library of Congress; **585BC** The George Meany Memorial Archives; **585BL** Brown Brothers; **585BR** Library of Congress; **585T** UPI/Corbis-Bettmann; **586** Culver Pictures; **587** Bethlehem Steel Corporation; **590** Sears, Roebuck and Co.; **591L** Randall Hyman; **591R** Library of Congress; **592** Culver Pictures; **593T** John Elk III/Stock, Boston; **593B** Minnesota Historical Society; **595** Culver Pictures; **598R** Brown Brothers; **598L** The Granger Collection, New York; **600** Cheryl Fenton*; **602L** The

Texas Collection, Baylor University, Waco, Texas; **602TR** Photo by Lewis W. Hine. George Eastman House Collection; **602BR** Brown Brothers; **602C** Photo by Lewis W. Hine. Library of Congress; **604** UPI/Corbis-Bettmann; **605** Library of Congress; **606** *The Ironworkers' Noontime* (1880) by Thomas Pollock Anshutz. The Fine Arts Museums of San Francisco, Gift of Mr. and Mrs. John D. Rockefeller 3rd, 1979.7.4

Chapter 22: 610L Brown Brothers; **610R** Corbis-Bettmann; **611BL** Chuck Pefley/Stock, Boston; **611BC** Phil Degginger/Bruce Coleman Inc.; **611T** Danilo G. Donadoni/Bruce Coleman Inc.; **611BR** *Triangle Fire*, 1911 (detail), by Victor Joseph Gatto. Oil on canvas, 19 × 28 inches. Gift of Mrs. Henry L. Moses, Museum of the City of New York; **612** Culver Pictures; **613** Photograph by Jacob A. Riis. The Jacob A. Riis Collection. Museum of the City of New York; **615** Library of Congress; **617** The Staten Island Historical Society. Photo by E. Alice Austen; **619** RG 85, Records of the Immigration and Naturalization Service, National Archives—Pacific Sierra Region; **620** Jacques Chenet/Woodfin Camp & Associates; **623** Chicago Historical Society, neg. #ICHi-04191; **624** Patricia Layman Bazelon/Lauren Tent, Buffalo, New York; **629R** Culver Pictures; **629L** Susan Lina Ruggles/Third Coast Stock Source; **630** Collection of The New-York Historical Society, New York City; **631** *Central Park, 1901* by Maurice Prendergast. Watercolor on paper. 14 3/8 × 21 5/8 in. (36.5 × 54.9 cm.) Collection of Whitney Museum of American Art. Purchase 32.42. Photograph Copyright © 1996: Whitney Museum of American Art, New York; **637** Library of Congress; **638L** Library of Congress; **638R** Lewis W. Hine Collection, U.S. History, Local History and Genealogy Div., The New York Public Library, Astor, Lenox & Tilden Foundations; **639** Cheryl Fenton*

Unit 8: 640–641 *The Fleet Entering the Golden Gate, May 6, 1908* (Detail) by Henry Reuterdahl, U.S. Naval Academy Museum

Chapter 23: 642R *The Purposes of the Grange* (detail), 1873 lithograph. Library of Congress; **642L** Stanley King Collection; **643BL** The Granger Collection, New York; **643BC** The Granger Collection, New York; **643T** Library of Congress; **643BR** Schomburg Center for Research in Black Culture, The Research Libraries, The New York Public Library; **644** University of Illinois at Chicago, The University Library, Jane Addams Memorial Collection; **645** Brown Brothers; **647** Library of Congress; **648** Bob Daemmrich/Stock, Boston; **649L** Division of Political History/National Museum of American History/Smithsonian Institution; **649R** The Oakland Museum History Department; **649C** Division of Political History/National Museum of American History/Smithsonian Institution; **650B** Culver Pictures; **650T** Cheryl Fenton*; **651** Library of Congress; **653** (portrait) The Kansas City Star Company; **653** (border) The Kansas State Historical Society; **654** S.S. Archives, Shooting Star; **655** Division of Political History/

National Museum of American History/Smithsonian Institution; **656** Grant Heilman/Grant Heilman Photography; **658** Corbis-Bettmann; **659** The Granger Collection, New York; **661L** UPI/Corbis-Bettmann; **661R** Brown Brothers; **662L** Schomburg Center for Research in Black Culture, The Research Library, The New York Public Library; **662R** UPI/Corbis-Bettmann; **664** Culver Pictures; **665** Culver Pictures; **667** Culver Pictures

Chapter 24: 670L National Archives; **670R** Stanley King Collection; **671CL** *The Fleet Entering the Golden Gate, May 6, 1908* (Detail) by Henry Reuterdahl, U.S. Naval Academy Museum; **671T** From *Harper's Pictorial History of the War with Spain*, 1899; **671B** Private Collection; **671CR** Library of Congress; **672** Brown Brothers; **673** Theodore Roosevelt Collection, Harvard College Library; **675** The Granger Collection, New York; **676** Collection of the New-York Historical Society, New York City; **680** Collection of the New-York Historical Society, New York City; **681** Chicago Historical Society; **682** Library of Congress; **684** Charles Phelps Cushing/H. Armstrong Roberts; **686** Cheryl Fenton*; **687** The Granger Collection, New York; **688R** The James A. Michener Collection, Honolulu Academy of the Arts (HAA20,799); **688L** The Metropolitan Museum of Art, Gift of Paul J. Sachs, 1916 (16.2.9); **690L** Library of Congress; **690R** Harvey Lloyd/The Stock Market; **691** The Granger Collection, New York

Chapter 25: 696L Austrian National Tourist Office; **696R** Brown Brothers; **697BL** Library of Congress; **697T** The American Numismatic Society; **697BR** Detail from *The Signing of Peace in the Hall of Mirrors, Versailles, 28th June, 1919* by Sir William Orpen. By courtesy of the Trustees of the Imperial War Museum, London. Photo by Larry Burrows; **697BC** National Archives; **698** Brown Brothers; **699** Culver Pictures; **700** Corbis-Bettmann; **703** Brown Brothers; **707** The West Point Museum Collections, United States Military Academy; **708** UPI/Corbis-Bettmann; **709** Corbis-Bettmann; **710** *The Rope Dancer Accompanies Herself with Her Shadows*, 1916, by Man Ray. Oil on canvas, 52" × 6'1-3/4" (132.1 × 186.4 cm). The Museum of Modern Art, New York. Gift of G. David Thompson. Photograph © 1996 The Museum of Modern Art, New York; **711** Library of Congress; **714B** Library of Congress; **714C** Poster by W. A. Rogers; **714T** Cheryl Fenton*; **718** UPI/Corbis-Bettmann; **722** The West Point Museum Collections, United States Military Academy, photo by Joshua Nefsky*; **723** The Imperial War Museum, London; **725** U.S. Air Force; **726TL** National Archives; **726TR** National Archives; **726B** Cheryl Fenton*; **727** Cheryl Fenton*

Unit 9: 728–729 Copyright The Dorothea Lange Collection, The Oakland Museum of California, The City of Oakland. Gift of Paul S. Taylor

Chapter 26: 730L *Bartolomeo Vanzetti and Nicola Sacco* by Ben Shahn from the Sacco-Vanzetti series of twenty-three paintings (1931–32). Tempera on paper over composition